T0180664

Lecture Notes of the Institute
for Computer Sciences, Social Informatics
and Telecommunications Engineering   238

More information about this series at http://www.springer.com/series/8197

Xiaodong Lin · Ali Ghorbani
Kui Ren · Sencun Zhu
Aiqing Zhang (Eds.)

Security and Privacy in Communication Networks

13th International Conference, SecureComm 2017
Niagara Falls, ON, Canada, October 22–25, 2017
Proceedings

 Springer

Editors
Xiaodong Lin
Wilfrid Laurier University
Waterloo, ON
Canada

Ali Ghorbani
University of New Brunswick
Fredericton, NB
Canada

Kui Ren
University at Buffalo
Buffalo, NY
USA

Sencun Zhu
Pennsylvania State University
Philadelphia, PA
USA

Aiqing Zhang
Anhui Normal University
Wuhu
China

ISSN 1867-8211   ISSN 1867-822X (electronic)
Lecture Notes of the Institute for Computer Sciences, Social Informatics
and Telecommunications Engineering
ISBN 978-3-319-78812-8   ISBN 978-3-319-78813-5 (eBook)
https://doi.org/10.1007/978-3-319-78813-5

Library of Congress Control Number: 2018940136

Printed on acid-free paper

This Springer imprint is published by the registered company Springer International Publishing AG
part of Springer Nature
The registered company address is: Gewerbestrasse 11, 6330 Cham, Switzerland

Preface

The 13th EAI International Conference on Security and Privacy in Communication Networks (SecureComm) was held during October 22–25, 2017, in the beautiful Niagara Falls, Canada. SecureComm is one of the premier conferences in cyber security, which provides an opportunity for researchers, technologists, and industry specialists in cyber security to meet and exchange ideas and information.

We were honored to have hosted keynote speeches by two world renowned cyber security researchers, Dr. Patrick McDaniel, Pennsylvania State University, and Dr. Ninghui Li, Purdue University. Their topics included security and privacy in machine learning, and differential privacy, which are currently hot research topics in cyber security research.

The conference program included technical papers selected through peer reviews by the Program Committee members, invited talks, and special sessions. Out of a total number of 105 submissions, 31 were selected as full papers and 15 as short papers. Besides the main conference, there were two workshops on emerging research topics in the field of security and privacy. The first one, International Workshop on Applications and Techniques in Cyber Security (ATCS), has been affiliated with SecureComm for many years, focusing on all aspects of techniques and applications in cyber security research. In all, 17 papers were accepted and are included in the proceedings. The second one was the First Workshop on Security and Privacy in the Internet of Things (SePrIoT). SePrIoT is intended to reflect the importance of addressing security and privacy in the Internet of Things (IoT). Five papers were accepted and are included in the proceedings. The technical program thus comprised a total of 68 papers.

We would like to thank all of our authors as well as our dedicated organizing team and volunteers for their hard work. SecureComm would not be successful without the dedication and passion of its contributors. Many people worked hard to make SecureComm 2017 a success. We would like to express our gratitude to them. It is also impossible to list here all those individuals whom we are grateful to. But we would like to thank particularly the EAI, especially Prof. Imrich Chlamtac of EAI, for their strong support of this conference. Also, we thank the members of the conference committees and the reviewers for their dedicated and passionate work. In particular, we thank the Program Committee co-chairs, Dr. Kui Ren and Dr. Sencun Zhu, for their great leadership in creating such a wonderful program. We also thank Ms. Dominika Belisová of EAI for her hard work and dedication in taking great care of the conference organization. Without the extremely generous support of EAI, this conference could not have happened. Last but not least, we thank the Steering Committee of SecureComm for having invited us to serve as the general chairs of SecureComm 2017.

We hope you enjoy the proceedings of SECURECOMM 2017 as much as we enjoyed the conference.

March 2018   Xiaodong Lin
                                                                                    Ali Ghorbani

Organization

Steering Committee

Imrich Chlamtac   EAI/Create-Net, Italy
Guofei Gu (Co-chair)   Texas A&M University, USA
Krishna Moorthy   IIT Madras, India
    Sivalingam
Peng Liu   Pennsylvania State University, USA
Z. Morley Mao   University of Michigan, USA
Xiaofeng Wang   Indiana University Bloomington, USA
Vinod Yegneswaran   SRI International, USA

General Co-chairs

Ali Ghorbani   University of New Brunswick, Canada
Xiaodong Lin   Wilfrid Laurier University, Canada

TPC Co-chairs

Kui Ren   SUNY Buffalo, USA
Sencun Zhu   The Pennsylvania State University, USA

Local Chair

Sultan Basudan   University of Ontario Institute of Technology, Canada

Publications Chair

Aiqing Zhang   Anhui Normal University, China

Workshops Co-chairs

Sheng Wen   Deakin University, Australia
Aziz Mohaisen   University of Central Florida, USA

Panels Co-chairs

Wenliang Du   Syracuse University, USA
Anna Squicciarini   Pennsylvania State University, USA

Publicity and Social Media Co-chairs

Rongxing Lu   University of New Brunswick, Canada
Yogachandran   Loughborough University in London, UK
  Rahulamathavan
Hui Zhu   Xidian University, China

Web Chair

Jianbing Ni   University of Waterloo, Canada

Conference Manager

Dominika Belisova   European Alliance for Innovation

Technical Program Committee

Elisa Bertino   Purdue University, USA
Marina Blanton   University at Buffalo,
                                       The State University of New York, USA
Yinzhi Cao   Lehigh University, USA
Neha Chachra   Facebook, USA
Kai Chen   Institute of Information Engineering,
                                       Chinese Academy of Sciences, China
Yu Chen   State University of New York – Binghamton, USA
Sherman Chow   Chinese University of Hong Kong, SAR China
Jun Dai   California State University, Sacramento, USA
Mohan Dhawan   IBM Research, USA
Birhanu Eshete   University of Illinois at Chicago, USA
Earlence Fernandes   University of Michigan, USA
Debin Gao   Singapore Management University, Singapore
Le Guan   Penn State University, USA
Yong Guan   Iowa State University, USA
Heqing Huang   IBM T.J. Watson Research Center, USA
Yier Jin   The University of Central Florida, USA
Murat Kantarcioglu   University of Texas at Dallas, USA
George Kesidis   Penn State University, USA
Qinghua Li   University of Arkansas, USA
Yingjiu Li   Singapore Management University, Singapore
Jingqiang Lin   Institute of Information Engineering,
                                       Chinese Academy of Sciences, China
Zhiqiang Lin   University of Texas at Dallas, USA
Zhe Liu   University of Waterloo, Canada
Yao Liu   University of South Florida, USA
Javier Lopez   University of Malaga, Spain
Rongxing Lu   University of New Brunswick, Canada

Ashraf Matrawy	Carleton University Ottawa, Ontario, Canada
Aziz Mohaisen	University at Buffalo, The State University of New York, USA
Goutam Paul	Indian Statistical Institute, India
Vaibhav Rastogi	University of Wisconsin-Madison, USA
Sankardas Roy	Bowling Green State University, USA
Pierangela Samarati	Università degli Studi di Milano, Italy
Seungwon Shin	Texas A&M University, USA
Jean-Pierre Seifert	Technische Universität Berlin, Germany
Kapil Singh	IBM T.J. Watson Research Center, USA
Anna Squicciarini	The Pennsylvania State University, USA
Martin Strohmeier	University of Oxford, UK
Kun Sun	College of William and Mary, USA
Mahesh Tripunitara	University of Waterloo, Canada
Selcuk Uluagac	Florida International University, USA
Eugene Vasserman	Kansas State University, USA
Cong Wang	City University of Hong Kong, SAR China
Qian Wang	Wuhan University, China
Edgar Weippl	SBA Research, Vienna University of Technology, Austria
Susanne Wetzel	Stevens Institute of Technology, USA
Dinghao Wu	Penn State University, USA
Xinyu Xing	Penn State University, USA
Shouhuai Xu	University of Taxes San Antonio, USA
Mengjun Xie	University of Arkansas at Little Rock, USA
Vinod Yegneswaran	SRI International, USA
Fareed Zaffar	Lahore University of Management Sciences, Pakistan
Kehuan Zhang	Chinese University of Hong Kong, SAR China
Xiao Zhang	Palo Alto Networks, USA
Wensheng Zhang	Iowa State University, USA
Yuan Zhang	Nanjing University, China
Bingsheng Zhang	Lancaster University, UK
Junjie Zhang	Wright State University, USA
Yongbin Zhou	Institute of Information Engineering, Chinese Academy of Sciences, China
Cliff Zou	University of Central Florida, USA
Zhan Qin	UT San Antonio, USA
Fengyuan Xu	Nanjing University, China
Xingliang Yuan	Monash University, Australia
Kuan Zhang	University of Nebraska, Lincoln, USA
Yongzhong He	Beijing Jiaotong University, China

Contents

SecureComm Short Papers

SecureComm Regular Papers

Gray-Box Software Integrity Checking via Side-Channels

Hong Liu and Eugene Y. Vasserman$^{(\boxtimes)}$ iD

Department of Computer Science, Kansas State University,
1701D Platt Street, Manhattan, KS, USA
{hongl,eyv}@ksu.edu

Abstract. Enforcing software integrity is a challenge in embedded systems which cannot employ modern protection mechanisms. In this paper, we explore feasibility of software integrity checking from measuring passive electromagnetic emissions of FPGA-implemented SoCs. We show that clock-cycle-accurate side-channel models can be built by utilizing gray-box analysis and regression techniques. The generality and effectiveness of our methods are shown by three different SoCs, profiled and tested on different chips of the same model. Our technique is non-invasive, and does not interrupt normal execution or change hardware/software configuration of the target device, making it particularly attractive for already-deployed systems.

Keywords: Security · Embedded systems · Side-channel analysis
Software attestation · Soft-core processors · FPGA

1 Introduction

Enforcing software integrity is a fundamental problem in system security: a device runs some software, and a verifier wants to know whether the device runs an unmodified version of the software, or a different piece of code, or original code but in an unintended execution state [13,17,43]. Enforcing software integrity for embedded systems, especially fielded/legacy ones, is extremely difficult. Software-based methods such as hypervisors [41], separation kernels [19], and control flow integrity checking [40,43] detect/prevent tampering by utilizing hardware security features that provide some form of separation such as operation modes and memory protection. Remote attestation [10,23,29], secure boot [16], and watchdog coprocessors [42] rely on trusted hardware and memory access controls to execute attestation code, e.g., to verify memory content and examine signatures appearing on buses. However, many embedded systems do not have such sophisticated capabilities due to hardware cost, high power consumption, and/or the difficulty in updating fielded components. Further, an external verification mechanism may be required no matter which protection method is used, as some security assumptions may weaken with time, and verification of design-time assumptions is needed.

© ICST Institute for Computer Sciences, Social Informatics and Telecommunications Engineering 2018
X. Lin et al. (Eds.): SecureComm 2017, LNICST 238, pp. 3–23, 2018.
https://doi.org/10.1007/978-3-319-78813-5_1

For systems composed of discrete components, sniffing bus traffic between constituent components may suffice to verify that the system acts as expected. For Systems-on-Chips (SoCs), however, internal activities cannot be observed directly, so we utilize "side-channel" emissions to infer them. The idea is to discover the relationships between the internal states of a target device and side-channel information so that when given a new side-channel measurement, it is possible to determine whether the internal state is an expected one or not. Unexpected state may be a sign of incorrect execution or malware. Researchers have tried using external power measurements to detect abnormal behavior at the level of functions or code segments [18,38,45], but attackers can write compact malware (as small as one instruction in size), code-reuse malware, as well as malware that has minimal impact on system-wise side-channel measurements [49]. In such situations, software attestation [9,36,54,62] can be used to detect modification of software down to single instructions. These methods utilize the timing side-channel and do not rely on specialized hardware or sophisticated processors, but do require interruption of normal execution of the target device. In addition, systems must explicitly support software attestation, making retrofitting difficult for legacy and deployed systems.

In this work we explore the possibility of using passive and non-invasive side-channel measurements for software integrity checking on SoCs. Our approach infers internal runtime state of an embedded system at a granularity sufficient to detect compact and side-channel-aware malware, without modifying the target device. This is extremely beneficial since the verifier is external to the device under test and is the only possible effective verifier when all security mechanisms (if any) internal to the device have failed.

Instead of analyzing numerous hardware platforms one by one, we choose field-programmable gate arrays (FPGAs) as the target SoC device. It has unique features compared to other platforms [20], but also poses unique challenges, namely the inability to perform full white-box analysis, as the detailed design and parameters of the base array and the configuration circuits are unknown to developers. The use of IP cores further obscures the electrical characteristics of a device. We therefore work with only partial knowledge, and so term our approach "gray-box" side-channel analysis.

In this work, we make the following contributions:

- We demonstrate the feasibility of using passive electromagnetic (EM) emissions of FPGA-based SoCs for software integrity checking. Our method is scalable, low-cost, and easily applicable to deployed systems.
- We show how to build cycle-accurate models of passive EM radiation of FPGA-based SoCs without access to detailed design specifications and how to efficiency and effectiveness use regression for EM profiling, even for systems with large instruction sets and variable instruction cycles.
- We experimentally validate the generality of our approach on three different FPGA-based SoCs – two based on a soft processor IP core (namely NIOS II), and one on the OpenMSP430 open processor core, and further show that

profiling is robust to manufacturing variations by testing on a different FPGA chip of the same model with the chip for profiling.

- We provide bounds on the (very low) probability that an EM-aware adversary can successfully modify code without being detected.

2 Related Work

Passive side-channel emissions of various embedded systems have long been studied to optimize power usage and perform EMI/EMC analysis [58]. Side-channel models can be built at different levels given different degrees of knowledge on system configurations. At the lowest level, power consumption of FPGAs has been modeled at the transistor level in order to build power-efficient FPGA architectures and power-aware CAD tools [8,25,31,47,50]. Dynamic power consumption is in general modeled as the aggregation of power consumed by each node inside an FPGA whose load and parasitic capacitances are charged and discharged at signal transitions, as well as short-circuit power that occurs in CMOS inverters [8,25,50]. For FPGA-implemented SoCs in which a complex processor is involved, low-level analysis becomes impractical, especially given reliance on detailed design information, so researchers built side-channel models from empirical measurements of real boards. Senn et al. [53] measured system-level power consumption of the NIOS II core and Zipf et al. [63] performed a hybrid functional- and instruction-level power analysis of LEON2, another soft-core processor. However, these estimation models profiled the average side-channel emissions of embedded systems rather than trying to infer system state (which program is running and its runtime state) from side-channel measurements.

In the cryptographic hardware domain, passive side-channel emissions of FPGA-implemented cryptographic routines are used to extract secret materials (e.g., keys) [7,33,34,60]. Such analyses concentrate on a few leakage points of the keys, with cryptographic algorithms often considered to be public (although the implementation details may be unknown), or irrelevant. Secret keys may be exposed regardless of cryptographic algorithms used [11], so the work on cryptographic hardware does not present a comprehensive picture of dynamic side-channel emissions of an entire embedded system.

Work on side-channel analysis of general programs used passive system-wide power measurements to detect anomalous behaviors and/or malware [18,27,28, 38,45,61]. These methods, however, assume malware (code) to be sufficiently long and not written to conceal its side-channel profiles. To use side-channels for rigorous integrity checking, we must consider compact and side-channel-aware malware. Software attestation [9,36,54,62] utilizes the timing side-channel and is capable of detecting malware at such precision. However, the device must support such attestation, and carrying out the process requires interruption of the device execution, a particular drawback for legacy and actively-used systems.

Researchers have tried to build side-channel models of the instruction set for certain smart cards and microcontrollers [22,26,27,46,51,55,56,59], and to build side-channel-based disassemblers by recognizing instruction operations from passive measurements. However, this focused on recognizing instruction operations (e.g., `MOVLW`) instead of the entire instructions including operands (e.g., `MOVLW 0xAA`) and content of operands. In [37], researchers found that passive power measurement of some microcontroller was dominated by a small number of data-dependent relationships, implying that recognizing instruction operations solely from power consumption is unlikely to be reliable.

For integrity checking of the FPGA platforms specifically, previous research on reading SRAM [57] and detection of FPGA trojans [30] shows the fundamental possibility of verifying FPGA configuration logic. The methods however require invasive measurements and specialized equipment, and do not scale well for complex systems. It is not known how to efficiently verify the software of an FPGA-based embedded system in practice.

3   Problem Definition

We define the general software integrity checking problem as follows, shown in Fig. 1. There are two parties: the prover P (a device running the target application software S), and the verifier V (who would like to determine whether P runs S or a modified version S'). V is a trusted entity who knows the initial hardware and software configuration of P. P and V communicate over an explicit channel C and/or a side-channel E. V bases its judgment on evidence that P provides directly through C (e.g., using signatures) or indirectly over E (e.g., by timing or EM radiation).

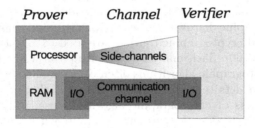

Fig. 1. General software integrity checking problem with explicit communication channels and side-channels

This model can be instantiated in different ways. In a microcontroller-based embedded system, for example, S is naturally the software of the microcontroller, and P is the microcontroller chip and the printed circuit board (PCB). In an FPGA-based embedded system, however, both the hardware and the software are programmable: FPGA configuration logic describes both the embedded system hardware (processor, memory, I/O, etc.) as well as the application software running on the system. Since reconfiguring an FPGA causes considerable difference in observations (such as loss of main clock in EM emissions), it is straightforward to discover tampering with FPGA configuration logic. We focus on detecting tampering with the application software which is modifiable on-the-fly in memory. S is therefore defined as the application software, and P incorporates the PCB, the FPGA chip, and the FPGA configuration logic describing the hardware of the system.

3.1 Threat Model

Attacker. We assume that the attacker is unable to modify or inject faults into the PCB and the FPGA chip of the target embedded system. This is enforceable in practice using physical tamper-resistance or tamper-proof techniques [35]. Moreover, the attacker is not an insider of the FPGA or IP core manufacturers, and cannot tamper the FPGA IC design, IP cores, or the CAD tools, on which we rely to establish the ground truth. We further assume that the attacker is unable to modify the FPGA hardware configuration, i.e., cannot reconfigure the hardware of the FPGA. This can be achieved by authenticating the configuration bit-stream [20], or by removing configuration peripherals before deployment, or by observing the EM emissions as mentioned in last paragraph. However, we assume that the attacker *is* able to modify the application software S, e.g., modifying the RAM of the device through buffer overflows, data-based attacks, etc. We also assume that the attacker is side-channel-aware – actively attempts to evade detection via side-channel emissions by crafting the modified software S' in a fashion that minimizes side-channel deviations from S. Nonetheless, the attacker cannot *invasively* profile the side-channels of the target device.

Verifier. We assume a verifier of very limited capability for applicability of our approach. We assume that the verifier knows the configuration of a target device and is able to profile the side-channel characteristics only on a *different* device of the same model with the target device. The verifier can only perform non-invasive measurements on the target device, which is important for this methodology to be easily applied to deployed devices.

We emphasize that the verifier is completely external to the target device, and *cannot modify the device hardware or software* to change the nature or magnitude of side-channel emissions, so that the verifier has the advantage of invisibility to attackers. The verifier can only passively measure the target device with measurement equipment incurring minimal impact on EMC. For example, the verifier may remove the shielding enclosure for measurements, but may not remove the noise decoupling circuits.

4 Experimental Setup

For a representative legacy and deployed system, we choose a general-purpose development board for the Altera Cyclone III FPGA EP3C5E144C8 as the target device. The FPGA chip is designed for low-cost, small-scale applications. We choose the EM side-channel, which is much more convenient to measure than power consumption. Preliminary test on the chip shows that it is not EM-shielded, which eases our experiment. We implement one SoC on the FPGA at

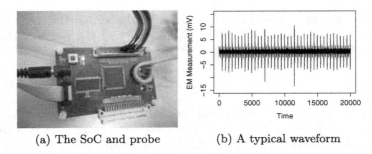

(a) The SoC and probe   (b) A typical waveform

Fig. 2. Experimental setup and an example of a recorded result

a time in the way that the only observable I/O is a parallel peripheral I/O (the memory chip on the development board is not used). Two different chips (i.e., boards) of the same model are used, one for profiling and another for testing.

We find that several positions on the board emit strong EM signals of similar waveform. We have tried both far-field and near-field measurements of EM radiation, and obtained the best result from near-field measurements with a shielded loop probe similar to the EMC probe in [48]. The probe measures the global radiation of the FPGA chip. The resulting setup, with the probe position near one of the power regulators, is shown in Fig. 2a.

The output is amplified by a 20 dB amplifier with bandwidth from 1 kHz to 1 GHz, and then is sampled by a PicoScope 5244B oscilloscope, which has a 200 MHz bandwidth and a maximally 500 MS/s sample rate for each channel. We use the 20 MHz integrated hardware filter of the oscilloscope to avoid aliasing. The processor core clock frequency therefore should be set far lower – we set it to 1 MHz. Our results should be repeatable at higher frequencies using more costly oscilloscopes supporting higher bandwidths. The position and orientation of the probe is then adjusted to gain signals of the maximal signal-to-noise ratio (SNR). Probe location is re-adjusted for each SoC. The resulting SNR of the EM traces, computed by the ratio of the variance of the signal and noise, is around 15 dB. A typical single-captured waveform is shown in Fig. 2b.

We have intentionally used low-cost signal acquisition and analysis equipment in order to show that verification of low-end legacy systems can be accomplished with only modest resources. The most costly component in our experiment setup is the off-the-shelf USB oscilloscope, at about $2,000; putting the total system cost at under $2,100. Combining all components into a single "software integrity measurement device" and manufacturing at scale is likely to further reduce costs.

5   The Test Code and SoC Test Targets

We evaluate our approach on three SoCs, implemented in turn on our FPGA test-bed: a NIOS II-based system capable of running an operating system; a simpler NIOS II-based system with a more constrained resource configuration; and an OpenMSP430-based system that is also operating system-capable.

5.1 System A: NIOS II-Based SoC

Our first experiment is on a NIOS II-based SoC. NIOS II is a general-purpose 32-bit RISC soft processor core from Altera [4]. We chose the NIOS II/e Quartus II 13.1 web edition (the latest edition for the target FPGA). NIOS II/e is designed for simple control logic applications and/or inexpensive systems. It supports over a hundred instruction operations, executed in a variable number of clock cycles, ranging from six to 38. (Our experiments show it is actually seven to 39, contrary to specifications.) The HDL source is not available, and the processor offers only limited configurability. It does not support different operating modes or memory protection, so modern security mechanisms that rely on processor-enforced separation cannot be used.

The NIOS II-based system is composed of the core, 40 kB M9K RAM, a timer, and a 16-bit parallel I/O connected using the Avalon bus. The system can run the FreeRTOS operating system [3] and several application tasks. The entire FPGA-implemented SoC consists of the NIOS II-based system, a small control unit that supplies clock and reset signals to the core, and a phase-locked loop (PLL). Programs are loaded and executed directly in RAM, forming a complete SoC, i.e., with no bus interfaces outside the chip except parallel I/O. We remove the JTAG interface of the processor, as it is unlikely to be present in a deployed device. The 1 MHz clock is obtained by using a PLL core connected to an external 25 MHz clock source. We do not make any effort to enhance the side-channel emissions when generating the system, so the experiment measures the typical EM radiation of a NIOS II-based system.

5.2 System B: Resource-Constrained NIOS II-Based SoC

The second SoC is also NIOS II-based, but simpler, to represent a "bare-bones" system that does not have enough resources to run an operating system. It has only a 16 kB M9K RAM for program and data memory, and an 8-bit parallel I/O. No timers are present. Otherwise is identical to system A.

5.3 OpenMSP430-Based SoC (System C)

The third system is based on OpenMSP430, a 16-bit open-source MSP430 family-compatible processor [5]. It supports 27 core instructions and seven addressing modes. Any valid combination of source and destination addressing modes is possible in an instruction, unlike NIOS II, which uses explicit load and store operations. Instructions of OpenMSP430 can be byte or word operations, whereas NIOS II supports only 32-bit word operations for instructions other than load and store. The number of clock cycles required for an instruction is variable (from one to six), depending both on the instruction type and addressing mode.

The SoC consists of the processor, 32 kB M9K RAM for program memory and 4 kB for data memory, a timer, and a 16-bit parallel I/O. Otherwise configuration is the same for all three systems. Programs are compiled using MSP430-GCC, then binaries are converted to an FPGA RAM initialization file, and loaded and executed directly in RAM, forming a complete SoC.

5.4   Test Code

Ideally, we should exercise all the possible internal states of the target SoCs to build side-channel models (i.e., template analysis). However, this is impractical since our preliminary tests show that the EM radiation depends on instruction operations, operands, and the content of the registers, memories, etc. (see Sect. 8). We can only build side-channel models from a very limited number of programs and data configurations, compared with the entire state space of the system. The validity of the resulting model is tested both by the reasonableness of its form and by the predictive power for side-channel emissions of new programs and data. Our test code is a integration of the FreeRTOS operating system port for each core (except system B) and re-implementation (to fit into available memory) of a part of the CoreMark benchmark suite [1]: integer matrix multiplication, floating-point multiplication, greatest common divisor, quick-sort of vector data, list find, list quick-sort, string hash, and a finite state machine, as well as random assembly code we generate for each core that avoids memory access and bypasses the native compilers: one composed of logic/arithmetic instructions, and one composed of only five types of logic/arithmetic instructions. The program binaries execute in a similar number of clock cycles. We do not model the EM radiation of I/Os, or code that change system-level behaviors, e.g., the timer intervals.

6   Modeling Side-Channels

Our preliminary tests show that EM emissions of different instruction operations largely overlap. Profiling target EM emissions by using general classifiers is therefore difficult [22, 26, 51, 56]. Furthermore, knowing only the instruction operations does not guarantee integrity since an attacker may write malware by varying only the operands and content of registers/memory, while keeping the operations the same. Previous research [37] has shown that the power consumption of a microcontroller can be accurately described as a linear model of a few internal data-dependent activities, e.g., Hamming weight (HW) of instructions and Hamming distance (HD) between operand and result – the contribution of different operations is negligible. We perform a similar experiment using EM measurements (same probe), and find that previous linear model of power consumption still holds for EM radiation. The only difference is the values of regression coefficients and the omission of a near-DC component, which is linear to the HW of instructions in the power model. This strongly suggests that we may be able to build similar regression models for the FPGA-based SoCs.

We assume the EM sample Y_t at time t can be modeled as a function of internal states $\mathbf{x_t} = (x_{1t}, \ldots, x_{pt})$ at t:

$$Y_t = f(\mathbf{x_t}) + N_t$$

where N_t encloses remaining components in the EM radiation including noise and time-dependent components, Y_t and N_t are necessarily random variables. $x_{it}(i = 1, \ldots, p)$ are called the predictor variables and Y_t the response variable.

Since both processors execute instructions in a variable number of clock cycles, depending on operands and bus traffic, we build side-channel models for each clock cycle rather than for each instruction cycle. The sample rate of the oscilloscope is 500 MS/s, meaning at least 500 regression models *can* be built. In practice, however, most information is found at clock rising edges. Y_t is therefore the peak amplitude at rising edges of clock t. A sum of 26 points near the peak gives slightly better results than using the single peak value. We denoise the traces for use in regression by averaging over only 100 EM traces. Selection of the predictor variables still poses a challenge.

Black-box Model-building. Switches of internal signals and voltage differences of neighboring signals are a promising initial choice for $\mathbf{x_t}$, supported by research on power consumption of FPGAs and general circuits [21, 25, 31, 47, 50]. Because the design details of NIOS II are not available, we initially treat the system as a black box and attempt to reason about internal activities directly from the instruction set documents, as in [37]. However, the EM samples correlate poorly with predictions. This is not surprising, as the target SoC systems are much more complex than the PIC microcontroller in previous work. In particular, unlike the PIC chip, there is no dominant power-consuming memory interface. We instead turn to the simulation models of the processor cores.

For system A, register-transfer level (RTL) simulation gives, for example, runtime values of thousands of signals, including 35 bus signals; gate-level post-fit simulation gives runtime values of at least 8259 1-bit internal signals. For system B, and system C, there are over 5800 and 12606 1-bit gate-level signals, respectively. EM radiation must be related with these signals in some form. However, directly estimating $f(\cdot)$ does not work due to the sheer number of signals, and also due to the multicollinearity among the signals (many signals are highly correlated with each other, and thus only one signal in a correlated set may be a useful predictor). Some signals are even identical – a simulation artifact. More variables are identical when considering switches of signals (transitions from 0 to 1 or vice versa). However, removing duplicate variables does not eliminate multicollinearity, showing that more complex correlations exist among the signals and signal switches.

As a first step in selecting representative signals for $\mathbf{x_t}$, we test whether the EM radiation has similar amplitudes when a subset of internal signals stay the same while others vary. If so, we need only to retain the subset of signals for model building. Figure 3a shows pairs of EM measurements (peak amplitudes) when bus signals are identical while other signals vary. The x-axis is one EM measurement, and y-axis is another EM measurement. Figure 3b shows pairs of EM measurements when signal transitions (0-1 and 1-0 are regarded as different transitions) of bus signals are identical. These two figures mean that, *no matter what the form of $f(\cdot)$ is*, the EM radiation is not determined only by the bus signals. This is in contrast with the PIC chip, whose EM radiation is dominated by the Hamming distance of bus signals. Therefore, we must include additional variables in $\mathbf{x_t}$. Because it is impractical to try arbitrary subsets of signals, we have to turn to the gate-level signals, as RTL signals are optimized out in final

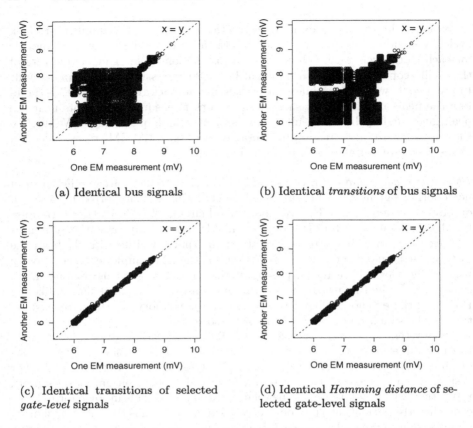

(a) Identical bus signals

(b) Identical *transitions* of bus signals

(c) Identical transitions of selected *gate-level* signals

(d) Identical *Hamming distance* of selected gate-level signals

Fig. 3. Measurements of system A when a subset of internal states are identical

layout of the SoC system. However there are thousands of gate-level signals. To select the most representative ones, we utilize the vendor-provided power estimation tool PowerPlay [6], therefore taking the gray box modeling approach, since PowerPlay encodes partial knowledge of the FPGA design.

PowerPlay is a tool for developers to estimate power consumption of an FPGA system to allow selection of power supply and heat dissipation scheme. Total thermal power estimates are claimed to have ±20% accuracy to silicon. However, since PowerPlay only reports comparatively rough estimates of accumulative power consumption, it cannot be directly used to solve our problem, which requires side-channel models for at least each instruction. PowerPlay can, however, generate a set of signal names for use in a gate-level simulation (which is in turn used for power estimation). It is reasonable to assume that these signals contribute more significantly to power consumption (thus causing more EM radiation). For system A, 1778 (out of 8259) gate-level signals are selected by PowerPlay, a huge reduction in variables requiring post-processing.

We again test whether EM radiation is similar when the 1778 signals are identical while others vary. Figure 3c shows pairs of EM measurements when signal transitions are identical for the 1778 variables, and Fig. 3d shows pairs of EM measurements when the HDs (which do not distinguish between 0-1 and 1-0) are identical. We do not find enough pairs whose absolute values of the 1778 variables are identical. Nevertheless, Fig. 3d already illustrates that it is reasonable to select HD of the 1778 variables as x_t, regardless the real form of $f(\cdot)$ (Note that the set of points in Fig. 3c is a subset of those in Fig. 3d). After modeling is finished, we retry using the original 8259 gate-level signals, and find that indeed modeling with the 1778 signals gives better results. For systems B and C the number of selected signals is 1280 and 2715, respectively.

However, multicollinearity still exists among the selected variables. Since further dividing the selected variables based on SoC structure does not lead to improvement and exhaustive search is computationally impractical, we turn to statistical techniques. There are several which can deal with predictors that have multicollinearity: ridge regression, partial least-square regression (PLS), principal component regression (PCR), and stepwise regression. For the selected variables, we find that all regression techniques produce similarly good regression models in terms of the coefficients of determination R^2, MSE, and F-tests in the model building step. To test validity of the regression techniques, we perform model validation to measure model reasonableness and predictive power.

7   Validation

We perform five-fold cross-validation to test the ability of the regression model in predicting EM radiation. Among the test programs (see Sect. 5.4), half are used for modeling and the other half for testing. One FPGA chip is used for building the EM model and a different FPGA chip of the same model is used for testing the model. This stricter five-fold (compared to the common seven-fold or even ten-fold) validation scheme is used because it is impractical to perform exhaustive exploration and associated physical measurements, so we are forced to use a limited set of programs for side-channel profiling and derive a model which accurately predicts the experimental results from all other possible programs. The goal is to evaluate the validity of using above variable selection approach and regression techniques for side-channel profiling, rather than to obtain a specific "best" model. Since some of the combinations of modeling/testing code may yield better results, cross-validation eliminates this problem by repeating the modeling and testing procedure using different programs for modeling and testing each time. We exhaustively compute all 252 possible combinations. We assume $f(\cdot)$ can be approximated as a first-order linear function for now. Pearson's r and Spearman's ρ are used to evaluate the quality of our models – the larger the correlation, the greater the predictive power. Pearson's r is effective because we observe that slightly moving the probe will only cause the amplitude of EM radiation to change linearly. We still compute Spearman's ρ, which can reveal nonlinear relationships between measurements and models (r and

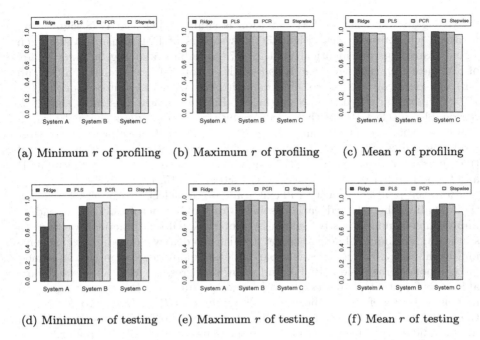

(a) Minimum r of profiling   (b) Maximum r of profiling   (c) Mean r of profiling

(d) Minimum r of testing   (e) Maximum r of testing   (f) Mean r of testing

Fig. 4. Pearson's r for model validation, with the profiling (modeling) results in the top row ((a)–(c)) and the testing (on another chip) results in the bottom row ((d)–(f)); from the darkest bar to the lightest are ridge regression, PLS, PCR, and stepwise regression.

ρ are equivalent when relationships are linear). Pearson's r is shown in Fig. 4. Spearman's ρ results are almost identical, validating our choice, and omitted due to space constraints. In addition, regressing $\mathbf{x_t}$ always has the highest correlation coefficients when $\mathbf{x_t}$ and Y_t are aligned in time (omitted due to space constraints). When profiling and testing using the same FPGA chip, all the r and ρ values are slightly better (omitted due to space constraints), as expected.[1]

The results show that (with few exceptions) linear regression models can predict EM radiation of new programs with satisfactory accuracy, especially for system B. Adding the absolute values of the signals (i.e., Hamming weights) to $\mathbf{x_t}$ does not improve model performance. PLS and PCR outperform other techniques and are stable in all cases (with no unacceptably low-performing outliers $r < 0.80$). PLS and PCR have been used in various domains such as chemistry and biology, where, similar to our situation, one observation is associated with many variables [24,44]. PLS and PCR have nearly identical performance,

---

[1] The parameters of each regression technique are selected to achieve best results for a few pre-selected random modeling/testing combinations and then fixed for all the others. Note that although for a particular combination the best parameter varies, it does not change our conclusions.

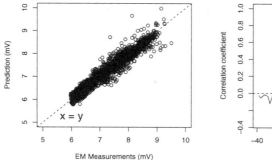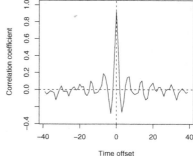

(a) Model prediction (y-axis) versus measurements (x-axis)

(b) Correlation of model prediction and measurement with sliding time window

Fig. 5. Model prediction and measurements for the best PLS model of system A.

which is interesting since unlike PLS, PCR does not take the response Y_t into account when selecting the predictors. Principal component analysis (PCA) has been used in side-channel analysis as a preprocessing step of pattern matching or classification to reduce dimension and to denoise the sampled traces in *time* [12,22]. We instead use PCA to eliminate multicollinearity for regression. Note that there is no noise in the predictors x_t, which are not random variables.

The effectiveness of the regression models is further shown in Fig. 5. The x-axis of Fig. 5a is the actual measurement for a testing program, and the y-axis is the model prediction (of the best PLS model of system A). Although some outliers exist, most measurements and predictions fall along the line of $x = y$. Figure 5b shows the Pearson's r between the actual measurement of a testing program and the model prediction which has an offset in time from the actual measurement. The x-axis of Fig. 5b is the time offset, and the y-axis is r. A sharp peak occurs when the model prediction and real measurement have no time offset, showing the soundness and validity of the model.

Second, we examine the resulting models for the reasonableness of their coefficients. We observe that PLS and PCR result in similar regression coefficients for each system. Several selected signals are clock signals that switch at each clock cycle. These signals do not provide information on internal states, and should only contribute to the constant in the model. Only ridge regression assigns non-zero coefficients to these signals. This is due to the procedure of ridge regression and has caused it to perform worse. PowerPlay reports that the M9K component consumes the majority ($\sim$60%) of the core dynamic power, but only a portion of M9K signals have larger regression coefficients in our resulting models. We have regressed separately with the M9K signals including memory and registers banks, as well as other signals reported in PowerPlay as consuming more power, yet the resulting models are *not* better than original models, especially in cross-validation.

8   Applying Results to Software Integrity Checking

To enforce code integrity, we must guarantee that tampering with the internal states of the system can be detected from side-channel measurements. Given the regression model, we predict EM radiation of new programs by using only gate-level simulation. We can therefore determine whether tampering with the original code will be reflected in the emission or not.

We first consider a conventional attacker, who is unable to analyze the side-channel of the system or unaware of the existence of a side-channel-based integrity checking mechanism. Integrity checking is a hypothetical test of whether a given measurement is from tampered code/data (undesired state) or not. The performance of this integrity mechanism is quantified by (1) the false positive rate (when a normal system state is flagged as tampering), and (2) the false negative rate (when tampering is performed, but is not flagged).

Table 1. False positive rates (%) for a(n) (aligned) single-captured EM trace

Threshold	0.90			0.85		
Number of cycles	7	14	21	7	14	21
System A	14.2	12.9	9.68	8.73	5.92	3.31
System B	13.1	10.3	8.57	8.52	6.14	3.08
System C	16.7	14.7	13.1	9.14	5.53	3.80

Table 2. False negative rates (%) for an aligned single-captured EM trace

Threshold	0.90			0.85		
Number of cycles	7	14	21	7	14	21
System A	20.6	4.65	1.75	30.5	9.83	4.01
System B	5.74	0.99	0.59	10.12	1.98	1.01
System C	0.81	0.18	0.13	1.54	0.22	0.14

Table 3. False negative rates (%) for an arbitrary single-captured EM trace

Threshold	0.90			0.85		
Number of cycles	7	14	21	7	14	21
System A	3.41	0.70	0.24	5.65	1.51	0.56
System B	1.43	0.16	0.09	2.93	0.38	0.16
System C	0.67	0.11	0.10	1.33	0.14	0.10

Recall that the SNR of our experiment is 15 dB. Taking both environmental noise and regression residual into account, we obtain from the best PLS models and EM measurements that for system A, 85.8% of the Pearson's r between

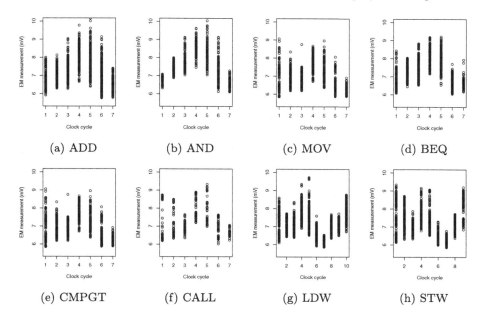

(a) ADD   (b) AND   (c) MOV   (d) BEQ

(e) CMPGT   (f) CALL   (g) LDW   (h) STW

Fig. 6. EM measurements of instructions grouped by operations for system A.

seven-cycle **single-captured** traces (on the testing chip) with the model prediction (from the profiling chip) is greater than 0.90 to execute at most one instruction. We can design the integrity checking mechanism by fixing the threshold 0.90, and then compute the false positive rate of any 7-/14-/21-cycle trace for each system from real measurements. Table 1 lists the false positive rates when the threshold is fixed to 0.90 and 0.85. Seven cycles are chosen because the *actual* number of clock cycles per instruction for NIOS II is from seven to 39. While the actual number of clock cycles per instruction for OpenMSP430 ranges from one to six, we use the same intervals for comparison purpose.

The false negative rate is computed from the percentage of 7-/14-/21-cycle execution traces of different code and/or data on the testing chip, but having r greater than the threshold with the model prediction of executing target code with desired data. Table 2 lists the false negative rates when the EM traces are aligned with starts of execution, applicable to the case in which tampered code/data executes in the same number of clock cycles with the target code. Table 3 lists the false negative rates for arbitrary EM traces that are aligned or misaligned with the original one.

The results show that the probability of random malware evading the integrity checking is very low. Even compact malware (very few instructions) can be detected reliably. Both false positive and false negative rates decrease rapidly as the number of clock cycles increases. When the number of cycles is fixed, there is a tradeoff between false positives and false negatives: a lower threshold will reduce false positives at a cost of higher false negatives. Note that

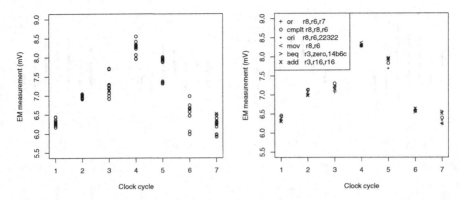

(a) 16 executions of `add r3,r16,r16`   (b) One execution of `add r3,r16,r16` and five different instructions

Fig. 7. EM measurements of `add r3,r16,r16` for system A; red cross indicates the same instance of executing `add r3,r16,r16`. (Color figure online)

the threshold and number of cycles can be computed to achieve desired false positive and false negative rates. Overall, the side-channel-based integrity check is effective to detect a conventional attacker.

Next, we consider a side-channel-aware attacker who actively tries to compute alternative code that has near indistinguishable EM radiation from the original code. To rewrite malware with semantically equivalent code but having similar EM measurements with the normal program, the attacker needs to know the reverse mapping from EM radiation to runtime state including instructions and data. The success rate of preventing the attacker from doing so relies on the hardness to obtain such mapping. We first analyze the side-channel of instructions classified by operations (e.g., `add`, `call`), as done in previous research [14,22,26,51,56]. We find that significant variation exists among instructions of the same operations, and EM measurements of different operations are not discriminatory. Figure 6 shows the EM measurements grouped by operations. Figure 7a shows an example in which even when executing the same instruction (`add r3,r16,r16`), the EM radiation varies significantly. On the other hand, EM measurements of executing different instructions may have nearly the same value. Figure 7b shows an example in which the EM trace of one execution of `add r3,r16,r16` has nearly the same value with those of five different instructions of different operations. This can be quantified by class (i.e., operation) separability by using within-class and between-class scatter matrices:

$$J = \frac{trace(S_m)}{trace(S_w)}, S_m = S_w + S_b$$

$$S_w = \sum_{i=1}^{M} P_i \Sigma_i, S_b = \sum_{i=1}^{M} P_i (\mu_i - \mu_0)(\mu_i - \mu_0)^T$$

where each operation is a class, P_i is the a prior probability of operation i, M is the total number of operations, μ_i is the mean of operation i, Σ_i is the covariance of i, and $\mu_0 = sum_{i=1}^{M} P_i \mu_i$ is the global mean vector. We compute the statistics of 53 common operations. The resulting J is 1.23, very close to one, which means that EM radiation, when grouped by operations, is not well clustered and is nearly indistinguishable from each other. For system C, the number of clock cycles per instruction varies from one to six, and depends on the addressing modes of the source and destination operands. Table 4 shows class separability for different clock cycles. The resulting J is still close to one.

Table 4. Class separability J for system C.

One cycle	3.81	Four cycles	1.71
Two cycles	16.63	Five cycles	1.54
Three cycles	7.51	Six cycles	1.37

As shown in Sect. 6, the EM model is a function of thousands of selected gate-level signal switches. The operations, bus signals, and M9K signals, which can be easily deduced from code, only contribute to a small portion of EM variance. Even if exactly the same instruction is executed, different runtime state of other signals will cause significantly different EM radiation. The attacker has to rewrite malware based on the many thousands gate-level signals which cannot be manipulated arbitrarily, but rather through the programming model of the processor. Furthermore, the gate-level signals are synthesized and optimized results of the processor core, whose relationship with the assembly code is unknown. Without knowing the design of the processor, as in the case of NIOS II, or without the ability to deal with processor complexity, the attacker will have to exhaustively search for alternative malware code that has similar EM radiation. In addition, each combination of operation and operands will result in a different internal state at each clock cycle. As the length of EM measurements increases linearly, the complexity of searching increases exponentially, effectively making the attack impractical. Detailed information on experiment setup, data, two ports of test code, and results are available at [2].

9   Discussion and Future Work

We have quantified the effectiveness and generality of using low-cost acquisition equipment to verify runtime states of three FPGA-based SoCs passively and non-invasively, against both conventional and side-channel-aware attackers. Profiling and testing use different chips (boards) of the same model. We show that by using our variable selection procedure and regression techniques, it is possible to model EM radiation of complex and gray-box processor-core-based SoC systems with high accuracy at clock-cycle granularity. Linear regression has also been used to break cryptographic hardware from side-channel leakage [15,32,39,52]. Note that attacking cryptographic hardware is chiefly concerned with special time points that leak key materials during multiple executions of the same cryptographic routine. In contrast, for integrity checking, we must detect one-time execution of malware from a single measurement and must consider instruction operations, operands, register and memory content.

Since we build side-channel models from simulation results, it can be inferred that directly applying the method for integrity checking requires the system to be deterministic. For example, no context switching should happen when measuring a target program. To what extent our approach can be applied for integrity checking of non-deterministic systems is left for future work.

Acknowledgments. This work was supported in part by NSF grant 1253930.

References

1. CoreMark. http://www.eembc.org/coremark/
2. Experiment Setup and Data. http://cis.ksu.edu/~hongl/fpga/
3. FreeRTOS. http://www.freertos.org/
4. NIOS II Processor Reference Handbook. https://www.altera.com/en_US/pdfs/literature/hb/nios2/n2cpu_nii5v1_01.pdf
5. The OpenMSP430 Project. http://opencores.org/download,openmsp430
6. PowerPlay Early Power Estimator. https://www.altera.com/content/dam/altera-www/global/en_US/pdfs/literature/ug/ug_epe.pdf
7. Aciiçmez, O., Koç, C.K., Seifert, J.-P.: On the power of simple branch prediction analysis. In: ASIACCS (2007)
8. Anderson, J.H., Najm, F.N.: Power estimation techniques for FPGAs. IEEE VLSI **12**(10), 1015–1027 (2004)
9. Armknecht, F., Sadeghi, A.-R., Schulz, S., Wachsmann, C.: A security framework for the analysis and design of software attestation. In: CCS (2013)
10. Asokan, N., Brasser, F., Ibrahim, A., Sadeghi, A.-R., Schunter, M., Tsudik, G., Wachsmann, C.: SEDA: scalable embedded device attestation. In: CCS (2015)
11. Baek, Y.-J., Gratzer, V., Kim, S.-H., Naccache, D.: Extracting unknown keys from unknown algorithms encrypting unknown fixed messages and returning no results. In: Sadeghi, A.R., Naccache, D. (eds.) Towards Hardware-Intrinsic Security: Foundations and Practice, pp. 189–197. Springer, Heidelberg (2010). https://doi.org/10.1007/978-3-642-14452-3_8
12. Batina, L., Hogenboom, J., van Woudenberg, J.G.J.: Getting more from PCA: first results of using principal component analysis for extensive power analysis. In: Dunkelman, O. (ed.) CT-RSA 2012. LNCS, vol. 7178, pp. 383–397. Springer, Heidelberg (2012). https://doi.org/10.1007/978-3-642-27954-6_24
13. Bletsch, T., Jiang, X., Freeh, V.W., Liang, Z.: Jump-oriented programming: a new class of code-reuse attack. In: ASIACCS (2011)
14. Bohy, L., Neve, M., Samyde, D., Quisquater, J.-J.: Principal and independent component analysis for crypto-systems with hardware unmasked units. In: e-Smart (2003)
15. Brier, E., Clavier, C., Olivier, F.: Correlation power analysis with a leakage model. In: Joye, M., Quisquater, J.-J. (eds.) CHES 2004. LNCS, vol. 3156, pp. 16–29. Springer, Heidelberg (2004). https://doi.org/10.1007/978-3-540-28632-5_2

16. Butterworth, J., Kallenberg, C., Kovah, X., Herzog, A.: BIOS chronomancy: fixing the core root of trust for measurement. In: CCS (2013)
17. Checkoway, S., Feldman, A.J., Kantor, B., Halderman, J.A., Felten, E.W., Shacham, H.: Can DREs provide long-lasting security? The case of return-oriented programming and the AVC advantage. In: EVT/WOTE (2009)
18. Clark, S.S., Ransford, B., Rahmati, A., Guineau, S., Sorber, J., Fu, K., Xu, W.: WattsUpDoc: power side channels to nonintrusively discover untargeted malware on embedded medical devices. In: HealthTech (2013)
19. Dam, M., Guanciale, R., Khakpour, N., Nemati, H., Schwarz, O.: Formal verification of information flow security for a simple ARM-based separation kernel. In: CCS (2013)
20. Drimer, S.: Volatile FPGA design security - a survey. http://www.cl.cam.ac.uk/~sd410/papers/fpga_security.pdf
21. Duan, C., Cordero, V., Khatri, S.P.: Efficient on-chip crosstalk avoidance CODEC design. IEEE VLSI **17**(4), 551–560 (2009)
22. Eisenbarth, T., Paar, C., Weghenkel, B.: Building a side channel based disassembler. In: Gavrilova, M.L., Tan, C.J.K., Moreno, E.D. (eds.) Transactions on Computational Science X. LNCS, vol. 6340, pp. 78–99. Springer, Heidelberg (2010). https://doi.org/10.1007/978-3-642-17499-5_4
23. Francillon, A., Nguyen, Q., Rasmussen, K.B., Tsudik, G.: A minimalist approach to remote attestation. In: DATE (2014)
24. Frank, L.E., Friedman, J.H.: A statistical view of some chemometrics regression tools. Technometrics **35**(2), 109–135 (1993)
25. Goeders, J.B., Wilton, S.J.E.: VersaPower: power estimation for diverse FPGA architectures. In: ICFPT (2012)
26. Goldack, M.: Side-channel based reverse engineering for microcontrollers. Master's thesis, Ruhr-Universität Bochum, Germany (2008)
27. Gonzalez, C.R.A.: Power fingerprinting for integrity assessment of embedded systems. Ph.D. thesis, Virginia Polytechnic Institute and State University (2011)
28. Gonzalez, C.R.A., Reed, J.H.: Power fingerprinting in SDR & CR integrity assessment. In: MILCOM (2009)
29. Gu, L., Ding, X., Deng, R.H., Xie, B., Mei, H.: Remote attestation on program execution. In: STC (2008)
30. Jin, Y., Kupp, N., Makris, Y.: Experiences in hardware Trojan design and implementation. In: HOST (2009)
31. Kadric, E., Lakata, D., DeHon, A.: Impact of memory architecture on FPGA energy consumption. In: FPGA (2015)
32. Kasper, M., Schindler, W., Stottinger, M.: A stochastic method for security evaluation of cryptographic FPGA implementations. In: FPT (2010)
33. Kocher, P., Jaffe, J., Jun, B., Rohatgi, P.: Introduction to differential power analysis. J. Cryptogr. Eng. **1**(1), 5–27 (2011)
34. Kocher, P., Jaffe, J., Jun, B.: Differential power analysis. In: Wiener, M. (ed.) CRYPTO 1999. LNCS, vol. 1666, pp. 388–397. Springer, Heidelberg (1999). https://doi.org/10.1007/3-540-48405-1_25
35. Kömmerling, O., Kuhn, M.G.: Design principles for tamper-resistant smartcard processors. In: USENIX Smartcard (1999)
36. Li, Y., McCune, J.M., Perrig, A.: VIPER: verifying the Integrity of PERipherals' firmware. In: CCS (2011)

37. Liu, H., Li, H., Vasserman, E.Y.: Practicality of using side-channel analysis for software integrity checking of embedded systems. In: Thuraisingham, B., Wang, X.F., Yegneswaran, V. (eds.) SecureComm 2015. LNICST, vol. 164, pp. 277–293. Springer, Cham (2015). https://doi.org/10.1007/978-3-319-28865-9_15
38. Liu, Y., Wei, L., Zhou, Z., Zhang, K., Xu, W., Xu, Q.: On code execution tracking via power side-channel. In: CCS (2016)
39. Lomné, V., Prouff, E., Roche, T.: Behind the scene of side channel attacks. In: Sako, K., Sarkar, P. (eds.) ASIACRYPT 2013. LNCS, vol. 8269, pp. 506–525. Springer, Heidelberg (2013). https://doi.org/10.1007/978-3-642-42033-7_26
40. Davi, L., Sadeghi, A.R., Lehmann, D., Monrose, F.: Stitching the gadgets: on the ineffectiveness of coarse-grained control-flow integrity protection. In: SEC (2014)
41. Dam, M., Guanciale, R., Nemati, H.: Machine code verification of a tiny ARM hypervisor. In: TrustED (2013)
42. Mahmood, A., McCluskey, E.: Concurrent error detection using watchdog processors - a survey. Trans. Comput. **37**(2), 160–174 (1988)
43. Mohan, V., Larsen, P., Brunthaler, S., Hamlen, K.W., Franz, M.: Opaque control-flow integrity. In: NDSS (2015)
44. Montgomery, D.C., Peck, E.A., Vining, G.G.: Introduction to Linear Regression Analysis, 5th edn. Wiley, Hoboken (2012)
45. Moreno, C., Fischmeister, S., Hasan, M.A.: Non-intrusive program tracing and debugging of deployed embedded systems through side-channel analysis. In: LCTES (2013)
46. Msgna, M., Markantonakis, K., Naccache, D., Mayes, K.: Verifying software integrity in embedded systems: a side channel approach. In: Prouff, E. (ed.) COSADE 2014. LNCS, vol. 8622, pp. 261–280. Springer, Cham (2014). https://doi.org/10.1007/978-3-319-10175-0_18
47. Muralimanohar, N., Balasubramonian, R., Jouppi, N.P.: CACTI 6.0: A Tool to Model Large Caches (2009)
48. Ott, H.W.: Electromagnetic Compatibility Engineering. Wiley, Hoboken (2009)
49. Perrig, A., van Doorn, L.: Refutation of "On the difficulty of software-based attestation of embedded devices" (2010). http://www.netsec.ethz.ch/publications/papers/perrig-ccs-refutation.pdf
50. Poon, K.K.W., Wilton, S.J.E., Yan, A.: A detailed power model for field-programmable gate arrays. ACM TODAES **10**(2), 279–302 (2005)
51. Quisquater, J.-J., Samyde, D.: Automatic Code Recognition for Smart Cards Using a Kohonen Neural Network (2002)
52. Schindler, W., Lemke, K., Paar, C.: A stochastic model for differential side channel cryptanalysis. In: Rao, J.R., Sunar, B. (eds.) CHES 2005. LNCS, vol. 3659, pp. 30–46. Springer, Heidelberg (2005). https://doi.org/10.1007/11545262_3
53. Senn, L., Senn, E., Samoyeau, C.: Modelling the power and energy consumption of NIOS II softcores on FPGA. In: Cluster Computing Workshops (2012)
54. Seshadri, A., Perrig, A., Doorn, L.V., Khosla, P.: SWATT: SoftWare-based ATTestation for embedded devices. In: IEEE S&P (2004)
55. Strobel, D., Bache, F., Oswald, D., Schellenberg, F., Paar, C.: Scandalee: a side-channel-based disassembler using local electromagnetic emanations. In: DATE (2015)
56. Strobel, D., Oswald, D., Richter, B., Schellenberg, F., Paar, C.: Microcontrollers as (in)security devices for pervasive computing applications. Proc. IEEE **102**(8), 1157–1173 (2014)

57. Sugawara, T., Suzuki, D., Saeki, M., Shiozaki, M., Fujino, T.: On measurable side-channel leaks inside ASIC design primitives. J. Cryptogr. Eng. **4**(1), 59–73 (2014)
58. Tiwari, V., Malik, S., Wolfe, A., Lee, M.T.-C.: Instruction level power analysis and optimization of software. In: VLSI Design (1996)
59. Vermoen, D., Witteman, M., Gaydadjiev, G.N.: Reverse engineering Java card applets using power analysis. In: Sauveron, D., Markantonakis, K., Bilas, A., Quisquater, J.-J. (eds.) WISTP 2007. LNCS, vol. 4462, pp. 138–149. Springer, Heidelberg (2007). https://doi.org/10.1007/978-3-540-72354-7_12
60. Whitnall, C., Oswald, E.: Robust profiling for DPA-style attacks. In: Güneysu, T., Handschuh, H. (eds.) CHES 2015. LNCS, vol. 9293, pp. 3–21. Springer, Heidelberg (2015). https://doi.org/10.1007/978-3-662-48324-4_1
61. Yang, Y., Su, L., Khan, M., Lemay, M., Abdelzaher, T., Han, J.: Power-based diagnosis of node silence in remote high-end sensing systems. ACM Trans. Sens. Netw. **11**(2), 33 (2014)
62. Zhang, F., Wang, H., Leach, K., Stavrou, A.: A framework to secure peripherals at runtime. In: Kutyłowski, M., Vaidya, J. (eds.) ESORICS 2014. LNCS, vol. 8712, pp. 219–238. Springer, Cham (2014). https://doi.org/10.1007/978-3-319-11203-9_13
63. Zipf, P., Hinkelmann, H., Deng, L., Glesner, M., Blume, H., Noll, T.G.: A power estimation model for an FPGA-based softcore processor. In: FPL (2007)

Enhancing Android Security Through App Splitting

Drew Davidson[1]([✉]), Vaibhav Rastogi[2], Mihai Christodorescu[3],
and Somesh Jha[1,2]

[1] Tala Security, 200 Brown Road, Fremont, CA 94539, USA
drew@talasecurity.io
[2] University of Wisconsin-Madison, 1210 W Dayton Street, Madison, WI 53706, USA
{vrastogi,jha}@cs.wisc.edu
[3] Visa Research, 385 Sherman Avenue, Palo Alto, CA 94306, USA
mihai.christodorescu@visa.com

Abstract. The Android operating system provides a rich security model that specifies over 100 distinct permissions. Before performing a sensitive operation, an app must obtain the corresponding permission through a request to the user. Unfortunately, an app is treated as an opaque, monolithic security principal, which is granted or denied permission as a whole. This blunts the effectiveness of the permissions model. Even the recent enhancements in Android do not account for the interactions between multiple permissions or for multiple uses of a single permission for disparate functionality.

We describe app splitting, a technique that partitions a monolithic Android app into a number of collaborating *minion* apps. This technique exposes information flows inside an application to OS-level mediation mechanisms to allow more expressive security and privacy policies. We implement app splitting in a tool called APPSAW. We describe a method for automatically selecting code partitions that isolate permission uses to distinct minion apps, and use existing security mechanisms to mediate the flow of privileged data. Our partitioning strategy based on vertex multicuts ensures that the minion apps are created efficiently. In our experiments, APPSAW was effective at splitting real-world apps, and incurred a low average performance overhead of 3%.

Keywords: Security · Android · Privilege separation · Permissions

1 Introduction

Smartphones have emerged as ubiquitous computing devices accompanied by unique challenges to security and privacy. Through pervasive access, users present troves of personal data to these devices, both by manual interaction and through numerous sensors onboard the device. The misuse of such data can cause significant harm to a user's privacy. Thus, an important goal of a mobile

© ICST Institute for Computer Sciences, Social Informatics and Telecommunications Engineering 2018
X. Lin et al. (Eds.): SecureComm 2017, LNICST 238, pp. 24–44, 2018.
https://doi.org/10.1007/978-3-319-78813-5_2

operating system (OS), such as Android, is to mediate the access that applications (apps) of diverse provenance and trust levels have to this data. A guiding principle in designing mediation mechanisms is the *principle of least privilege* (PLP), which states that a principal, e.g., an app, should be granted no more permissions than necessary to fulfill its intended purpose.

Existing approaches fall short of PLP. Legacy Android versions present the user with a list of all permissions requested by an app at installation time, with no enforceable explanation of purpose, while iOS and recent Android versions present permission requests dynamically while the app runs and when it needs them, in the hope that the UI context hints to the purpose of the permission request. In both cases permissions are granted once and are always available to the app for any purpose, least privilege remains an unachieved goal. Specifically, current mobile OS permission models have two problems:

- **Monolithic apps:** Permissions are granted to an app as a whole: there is no way to approve a permission for one purpose while denying it for another in the same app. A particular case is where application code comes from different sources, e.g., an app including ads and social media integration. A user may want the GPS to be accessible for navigation but not for advertising in a maps app. Previous work has emphasized the importance of isolating these entities in different principals [25].
- **Opaque flows:** Users have no visibility how an app uses its permissions. For instance, permissions cannot help distinguish between a contacts manager app that accesses Internet to show ads and a spyware that leaks contacts to the Internet.

Previous work has attempted to addresses these problems by identifying undesirable information flows through static or dynamic taint analysis [7,12]. Static analysis does not provide any way for users to determine if a flow is actually occurring at runtime. Dynamic taint analysis, on the other hand, has significant runtime overhead. There is also work to rewrite the Android permissions model entirely [14]. However, such approaches require updates to the OS as well as ways developers program apps.

We solve the problems arising due to monolithicity of apps and opaqueness of flows with a technique called *app splitting*. App splitting works by partitioning an app into a number of smaller, collaborating apps called *minions*. Minion apps contain a portion of the original app representing an action that the user can mediate. *Splitting the application into smaller pieces converts sensitive code and data flows from intra-app (invisible to the user and to the OS) to inter-app (visible to the user and the OS for mediation and access-control purposes).* We have implemented APPSAW, which accepts an Android app and a simple, user-defined policy and performs app splitting on the given app. It provides the relevant instrumentation to allow the created minions to communicate with each other via OS-level interprocess communication (IPC) so that they can together provide the functionality provided by the original app while restricting unwanted flows.

Our paper makes the following contributions:

- We formalize app splitting as the problem of finding graph partitions and show how various classes of security policies map to app-splitting strategies. Underlying app splitting is a notion of fine-grained, flow-based permission addressing the entanglement problem.
- We introduce a tool, APPSAW, for performing automatic, optimal app splitting of Android apps based on a specified security policy. APPSAW addresses the monolithic app problem by naturally generalizing the existing work on isolating advertising from the core functionality of an app [25, 26].
- We demonstrate experimentally that APPSAW is practical, supports a variety of app types (from book readers to translation apps to social networking tools), and incurs low overhead: operations that use permissions incur a low overhead of less than 3% and the total runtime of the app does not experience any measurable slowdown.

Given that APPSAW works by retrofitting apps, it does not need support of Android OS developers as well as app developers. It is thus amenable to a range of deployment models. APPSAW comes with a number of scripts that ease the task of using it as well as the apps produced by it. Savvy users could thus develop their own policies and use the tool directly. More practically, however, we envision APPSAW to find a unique spot among other mobile app management (MAM) technologies developed as enterprise solutions [1]. An MAM provider could offer APPSAW as a part of their suite to enterprises, where an IT administrator would be able to use it to enforce custom flow policies on existing apps.

The remainder of the paper is structured as follows. Section 2 discusses the problem and provides an overview of our approach. In Sect. 3 we detail our technique for choosing program points at which to split a portion of an app into a minion. Sections 4 and 5 discuss the technical details of how APPSAW preserves app functionality across minions, allowing minion apps to collaborate. In Sect. 6, we evaluate how applications split with APPSAW perform against their monolithic counterparts. We review related work in Sect. 7. Section 8 discusses limitations. We conclude in Sect. 9 with directions for future work.

2   Overview

In this section, we first motivate the need for fine-grained permission controls with an example. We subsequently present our policies, our approach to implement the policies, the challenges involved, and how our approach can be deployed in practice.

Motivating Example: To illustrate the permission problems identified in Sect. 1, we present a running example app, NetDialer, that demonstrates the challenges users face in the current Android ecosystem. While simple, this app is representative of many similar apps and requires a set of commonly used permissions. NetDialer is an enhanced contact manager app. It allows users to scroll

```
1   // Flow contacts to the phone
2   public void makeCall(){
3     long id = getLong(CONTACT_ID_INDEX);
4     String key = getString(CONTACT_KEY_INDEX);
5     Uri cUri = Contacts.getLookupUri(id, key); // P0
6     number = getNumberFromContact(mContactUri);
7     String action = Intent.ACTION_CALL;
8     Uri asUri = Uri.parse(number);
9     Intent callIntent = new Intent(action, asUri);
10    startActivity(callIntent); // P1
11  }

13  // Flow contacts to the network
14  public void backupContacts(){
15    long id = getLong(CONTACT_ID_INDEX);
16    String key = getString(CONTACT_KEY_INDEX);
17    Uri cUri = Contacts.getLookupUri(id, key) // P2
18    number = getNumberFromContact(mContactUri);
19    Uri numberUri = Uri.parse(number);
20    URL url = new URL(baseURL + numberUri);
21    URLConnection conn;
22    conn = url.openConnection(); // P3
23    conn.connect();
24  }

26  // Pull information from the network
27  public byte[] weatherScreen(){
28    URL url = new URL(urlContactIcon + strurl);
29    Object content = url.getContent(); // P4
30    InputStream is = (InputStream) content
31    byte[] buffer = new byte[8192];
32    ByteArrayOutputStream bkg;
33    int bytesRead;
34    bkg = new ByteArrayOutputStream();
35    while ((bytesRead = is.read(buffer)) != -1) {
36        bkg.write(buffer, 0, bytesRead);
37    }
38    return bkg.toByteArray();
39  }
```

Fig. 1. Snippet of code from NetDialer demonstrating limitations of the Android permission model. The methods that are shown here use an overlapping set of permissions in different ways that are indistinguishable to the user

through the list of contacts maintained by the operating system and place a phone call to a selected contact. The app also allows the user to access auxiliary information from within the app, such as the day's weather forecast.

There are three functions of NetDialer that use permissions, as shown in Fig. 1. These functions illustrate different ways in which the same permissions can be used. The makeCall method uses the READ_CONTACTS permission to collect contact information at program point P_0 which is used to place a phone call using CALL_PHONE permission at P_1. The backupContacts method also uses READ_CONTACTS, at P_2. The data flows to P_3 which uses the INTERNET permission to leak contacts to the network. The weatherScreen method also uses INTERNET to download weather information from the network at P_4, which it returns. The app can execute all three of the above methods by declaring the use of permissions READ_CONTACTS, CALL_PHONE, and INTERNET in its manifest.

Policies: By installing `NetDialer`, the user grants unconditional permission to the app to read from the contact list and send data to the network, as it does in `backupContacts`. Android does not provide any way to determine existence of and control such a flow in the program. Nor can the user completely shut off network access to the app as it would preclude downloading weather information.

Consider a policy in which a user wants to ensure that their contact information is never leaked to the network. Such mediation policies are expressed as a list of instruction pairs $\langle s, t \rangle$, where s is an instruction that is a source of sensitive information and t is a sink instruction, each such pair written as $s \rightsquigarrow t$. The user's policy for `NetDialer` can be expressed as `READ_CONTACTS` $\rightsquigarrow$ `INTERNET`. This policy requires that *every* flow from an instruction that uses `READ_CONTACTS` to one that uses `INTERNET` be mediated.[1]

Approach Overview and Challenges: Since Android uses an app as the fundamental security principal, we implement these policies by partitioning an app into multiple sub-apps or minions that are granted permissions individually. IPC across these minions is mediated according to the policies. In the case of `NetDialer`, APPSAW can isolate each of the program points P_0, P_1, P_2, and P_3 into distinct minions, and replace their invocations with inter-process communication code to retrieve the original behavior of these program points. In the policy example above, since P_2, and P_3 are placed in different minions, the flow between them can be mediated.

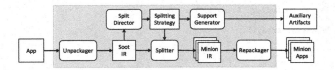

Fig. 2. APPSAW workflow. Rounded components indicate code modules; rectangles indicate artifacts.

APPSAW needs to address two fundamental problems: (1) Given a flow policy, how should the code be split into minions? An important consideration here is to satisfy the policy while keeping the performance impact low. (2) How should the minion apps communicate to collaboratively maintain the functionality of the original app? We address the first challenge by developing formalisms around identifying potential split points using vertex multicuts over the app's control flow graph. For the second challenge we develop a solution rewrites app code to make use of Android IPC to communicate among minions.

The workflow of APPSAW is described in Fig. 2. The input app is first unpackaged with its code converted to the Jimple intermediate representation (IR) using

---

[1] We can specify any permission pair as a policy and APPSAW ensures that any flow between these permissions will cross a minion boundary. It is up to the user to decide if separating these permissions is meaningful.

dexplar [9]. Jimple is a native IR for the Soot framework [27] and is consumed by our Split Director and Splitter modules. The Split Director module converts user policies to a splitting strategy, which identifies at which points the app should be split. The Splitter module partitions the IR into minions, which are packaged back into native Android apps using the Soot dex compiler and Apktool [6] while restraining the permissions requested by these minion apps. In addition, the Support Generator module uses the splitting strategy to provide artifacts, such as rules that allow the OS to mediate communication among minions. In the next three sections we discuss the workings of the three interesting components: the Split Director, the Splitter, and the Support Generator.

3 Splitting Strategies

In this section, we discuss our algorithm for building the splitting strategies described in Sect. 2. First, we formalize the problem in terms of a *labeled control-flow graph (LCFG)* of an application. Let $G = (V, E, L)$ be a LCFG of an A, where V is the set of nodes, $E \subseteq V \times V$ is the set of edges, and $L : V \to \mathcal{P}$ is a function that labels each node with an element (called *permission*) from a set $\mathcal{P}$. We assume that there is a special element $\perp \in \mathcal{P}$ which represents the *null* permission. Intuitively $L(v) = \perp$ means that the statement corresponding to node $v \in V$ does not need any special permissions. Formally, the problem, which we call the *permission separation problem (PSP)* can be defined as follows:

Problem 1. Given a LCFG $G = (V, E, L)$ and a relation $X \subseteq \mathcal{P} \times \mathcal{P}$. The problem is to find a partition $\Pi = \{V_1, V_2, \cdots, V_k\}$ of V, which satisfies the following condition: for all pairs of nodes (v_1, v_2), if $(L(v_1), L(v_2)) \in X$, then v_1 and v_2 are in different sets of the partition Π.

Given a partition $\Pi = \{V_1, V_2, \cdots, V_k\}$, we can create k applications $\{A_1, \cdots, A_k\}$ such that A_i consists of all instructions corresponding to nodes in V_i. We call applications A_i $(1 \leq i \leq k)$ *minions*. A naive algorithm for solving PSP creates a partition as follows: each $v \in V$ such that $L(v) \neq \perp$ is put in its own set and there is a set that consists of all nodes w such that $L(w) = \perp$. We call this naive algorithm *permission isolation splitting*. Of course, our naive algorithm can create a lot of minions. Our goal is to construct as few minions as possible and also minimize data transfer between the minions. Next we present our algorithm to accomplish these goals.

Our Algorithm: Our algorithm works in two stages: (1) We compute a vertex multicut using dominators and post-dominators (defined below). (2) We use the vertex multicut found in step (1) to find a solution to the PSP. The two steps of the algorithm are described below.

(Step 1) An Algorithm for Finding Vertex Multicuts. The *vertex multicut problem (VMP)* is defined below.

Problem 2. We are given a graph $G = (V, E)$, where V is the set of nodes, $E \subseteq V \times V$ is the set of edges and a collection of k pairs of vertices

$H = \{(s_1, t_1), \cdots, (s_k, t_k)\}$. The problem is to remove the minimum number of vertices $V' \subseteq V$ such that in the resulting graph there is no path from s_i to t_i for $1 \leq i \leq k$. In other words, every path from s_i to t_i (for $1 \leq i \leq k$) goes through at least one vertex in V'. This problem is called the *directed graph vertex multicut problem (VMP)*.

Although the problem of computing optimal vertex and edge multicuts is NP-complete, there exist approximation algorithms to solve these problems [3,15]. However, these existing algorithms ignore the structure of the program (i.e., the CFGs resulting from an application have a very special structure). We present an algorithm that exploits the structure of the program and can therefore be used to take into account domain-specific considerations (see the discussion towards the end of this section). Specifically, we present here an algorithm for computing vertex multicuts that is based on the concept of dominators and post-dominators. Recall that dominators and post-dominators are used to find *control dependencies* in programs [19] and there are efficient algorithms to compute dominators and post-dominators [16]. We note that our algorithm is *not* provably polynomial time, but can account for program structure. However, incorporating program structure in other algorithms is an interesting avenue for future research.

Assume that we are given a graph $G = (V, E)$, where V is the set of nodes, $E \subseteq V \times V$ is the set of edges and a collection of k pairs of vertices $H = \{(s_1, t_1), \cdots, (s_k, t_k)\}$. We present an algorithm that demonstrates that an algorithm for finding hitting sets can be used to find a vertex multicut. With each pair (s_i, t_i) we associate a set M_i with the following property: for all $v \in M_i$, every path from s_i to t_i passes through v. The collection of k pairs of vertices $H = \{(s_1, t_1), \cdots, (s_k, t_k)\}$ corresponds to a collection of sets $\mathcal{M} = \{M_1, \cdots, M_k\}$. A *hitting set* Z for $\mathcal{M}$ is a set such that $Z \cap M_i \neq \emptyset$ (for all $1 \leq i \leq k$). Therefore, a hitting set for $\mathcal{M}$ corresponds to a vertex multicut.

The problem now is to associate with a pair of nodes (s, t) a set M such that all vertices in M appear on all paths from s to t. For this, we use the concept of dominators and post-dominators. We assume that the graph $G = (V, E)$ has two distinguished vertices $r \in V$ (called the *start node*) and $e \in V$ (called the *exit node*) such that every vertex in V is reachable from r and e is reachable from every vertex in V.

Dominators and Post-dominators: A vertex v dominates w (denoted as v dom w) iff every path from r to w passes through v. A vertex z post-dominates w (denoted as z pdom w) iff every path from w to e passes through z. The set of dominators and post-dominators of a vertex w are denoted by $\mathrm{DOM}(w)$ and $\mathrm{PDOM}(w)$, respectively.

Proposition 1. Let (s, t) be a pair of vertices and let $M = \mathrm{DOM}(t) \cap \mathrm{PDOM}(s)$. Every path from s to t passes through every vertex in M.

Proof: Consider a path π from s to t. Since s is reachable from the start node $r \in V$, π can be extended to a path from r to t. Similarly, since the exit node e

is reachable from the node $t \in V$, π can be extended to a path from s to e. Let π_f be a path from r to e that is the extension of path π from s to t. Consider a vertex $z \in M$. Let π_f^r be the fragment of π_f from r to t. Since $z \in \text{DOM}(t)$, z lies on the path fragment π_f^r. Similarly, since $z \in \text{PDOM}(s)$, z lies on the path fragment π_f^e of π_f from s to e. This proves that z lies on the path from s to t. Since z was an arbitrary node in M, the result follows. □

Based on the proposition given above we can formulate an algorithm for finding a vertex multicut, which is based on the dominator and post-dominator structure of the control-flow graph (see Fig. 3).

Input: A graph $G = (V, E, r, e)$,
set H of k pairs of vertices $\{(s_1, t_1), \cdots, (s_k, t_k)\}$.
Compute M_i (for $1 \leq i \leq k$) as $\text{DOM}(t_i) \cap \text{PDOM}(s_i)$
Compute hitting set Z for the collection $\{M_1, \cdots, M_k\}$
Output: The hitting set Z.

Fig. 3. Finding vertex multicuts using dominators, post-dominators, and hitting sets.

(Step 2) From Vertex Multicut to Partitions

An algorithm for solving VMP can be used to solve PSP. The description is as follows:

- Assume that we are given an *application* A whose LCFG is $G = (V, E, L)$, where V is the set of nodes, $E \subseteq V \times V$ is the set of edges, and $L : V \rightarrow \mathcal{P}$ is a labeling function. We are also given a relation $X \subseteq \mathcal{P} \times \mathcal{P}$.
- Relation X corresponds to a collection $H(X)$ of pairs of vertices as follows: $(v_1, v_2) \in H(X)$ iff $(L(v_1), L(v_2)) \in X$.
- Now consider the graph $G_1 = (V, E)$ and set $H(X)$. Let $V' \subseteq V$ be a vertex cut for G_1 and $H(X)$. Let G' be the graph obtained from G_1 where outgoing edges from all vertices in V' have been removed. G' induces a partition as shown in Fig. 4. It is not hard to see that the partition $\mathcal{P} = \{V_1, V_2, \cdots, V_k, V_{k+1}\}$ solves the corresponding PSP problem, i.e., for all pairs of nodes (v_1, v_2) such that $(L_A(v_1), L_A(v_2)) \in X$, then v_1 and v_2 are in different sets of the partition $\mathcal{P}$.

Discussion: Our algorithm based on dominators and post-dominators allows a designer to have control over how the split is performed. First, we introduce some notation from [16]. Vertex v is the *immediate dominator* of w (denoted by v i-dom w), if v dominates w and every other dominator of w dominates v. Similarly, vertex v is the *immediate post-dominator* of w (denoted by v i-pdom w), if v post-dominates w and every other post-dominator of w post-dominates v. The relation i-dom and i-pdom form a directed rooted tree. Intuitively, a node "higher" up in the tree corresponding to i-dom represents a statement closer to the entry point of an application (similar intuition can be applied to the tree corresponding to the relation i-pdom). Therefore, if there are two nodes v and w in a set in the collection Z (see Fig. 3) and v is an ancestor of w in the tree

Inputs: A collection $H(X) = \{(s_1, t_1), \cdots, (s_k, t_k)\}$,
a graph G' such that there is no path from s_i to t_i
(for all $1 \le i \le k$).

Consider the sequence $s_1, s_2, \cdots, s_k$ of source vertices and let $G_0 = G'$.
For $1 \le i \le k$,
 define V_i as all vertices reachable from s_i in G_{i-1}.
 To construct G_i, remove all vertices in V_i from G_{i-1}.
Let V_{k+1} be the set $V \setminus \bigcup_{i=1}^{k} V_k$.

Output: $\{V_1, V_2, \cdots, V_{k+1}\}$

Fig. 4. Algorithm for creating partitions from vertex multicuts. Removing a vertex v also means we remove all edges of the form (w, v) and (v, w).

corresponding to i-dom, then v can be preferred over w while constructing the hitting set for Z. Similarly, a designer can specify other conditions. For example, some vertices from the collection Z can be eliminated based on certain conditions before computing the hitting set. Examples of some of these conditions are given below (there are several other domain-specific possibilities).

- Eliminate vertices that correspond to statements in some specific functions (e.g., belonging to a third-party library).
- Eliminate vertices from Z that belong to loops (having the split point in the loop might result in expensive IPC calls because of marshaling and unmarshaling of arguments).

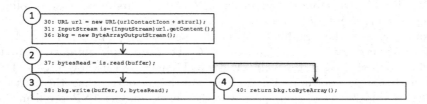

Fig. 5. Control flow graph of the `NetDialer` function `WeatherScreen`.

Figure 5 shows the CFG for the `NetDialer` code of Fig. 1, with line numbers preserved from the original figure. Although simplistic, this example shows the importance of picking good split points: consider the naive solution of including blocks 1 and 2 for a partition: since the variable buffer is live across the boundary from block 2 to 3, making the call to the minion corresponding to the partition will require copying the entire buffer. While this behavior might be acceptable for a single transfer to a minion, but altering the minions in this way causes a transfer on every iteration of the loop that begins on line 32. Thus, the heuristics presented above places blocks 1, 2, and 3 into the minion.

The above example highlights the need to minimize the amount of data that needs to marshaled. This would require us to solve a weighted version of PSP (the PSP version above is unweighted) where the weights on edges correspond to the marshaled data amount and the solution is obtained by minimizing the weights on the multicut. We will investigate this problem in future work.

Split Director Implementation: Our formalism above assumes $L : V \to \mathcal{P}$, so a node is only mapped to a single permission. In practice, a node may require a finite set of permissions. Extending the strategies support this behavior is trivial and our implementation does not have limitations on the labeling function L. Furthermore, L relies on a mapping from Android API to the requisite permissions. We integrate with PScout [8], Stowaway [13], and Flowdroid [7] to use the mapping produced by these tools.

4   Minion App Generation

The previous section dealt with identifying split points in an application. In this section we discuss the actual refactoring of an app into multiple collaborative minion apps. This level of app rewriting is non-trivial to implement, and relies on a number of unique circumstances that are fortunately present for Android apps. In particular, there needs to be an efficient IPC mechanism that allows for objects to be quickly moved from one app to another. We begin with a a background on Android IPC and then discuss the details on minion app generation.

4.1   Android IPC Background

Android apps comprise a number of collaborating components, which may communicate via IPC. Android provides a fast IPC mechanism called *binder*. The binder model uses a client/server architecture where the client (the app core in the case of APPSAW) requests a connection to a service. Upon success, the client is offered an interface to the service through which it can make calls to it as though it were an object in the local process. Th binder API ensures that the proper steps are taken to translate the call into IPC invocations.

One of the ways that binder achieves fast IPC is by allowing custom marshaling and unmarshaling of objects that are passed through IPC. When an object is passed, a process called *Parcelization* invokes the `WriteToParcel` method, which gives developers the opportunity to choose how to pack the object. The class must also provide a static (non-instance) member that implements the Parcelable. Creator interface, which supplies a `createFromParcel` method, that is invokes in the called component to unpack the parcel. Parcelization stands in contrast to Java's Serialization, in which objects implement a marker interface, but are wholly serialized, with the exception of `transient` fields. Although Serialization is still implemented in Android, Parcelization was specifically designed to meet IPC performance requirements that Serialization lacks [24].

4.2   App Splitting Implementation

Our primary concern here is to ensure that executing minion apps preserves the effect of executing the same code in the original, monolithic app. Because the splitting strategies that our tool uses yield regions in which the entry block to the region dominates the exit of the block, and the exit postdominates the entry, there is no need to worry about relocating control flow transfers. However, APP-SAW needs to ensure that data flow that passes through a minion is preserved. While APPSAW could simply instrument an app to copy out all variables that the minion defines, and copy in all variables that the minion uses, doing so would unnecessarily copy data that is not dead. Instead, we perform a simple reaching definition analysis to only copy uses that are live at the beginning minion region and only copy definitions that are live at the end of the minion.

Parceling Objects: Binder IPC provides a means to transfer use and def values across minions but it comes with the additional constraint that objects must be *parcelable*. Unfortunately, it is unlikely that every object that must be transferred to a minion will implement this interface. Thus, APPSAW is faced with a number of challenges:

1. The minion may use or define a non-parcelable user-defined class. In this case, APPSAW has significant power, because it can completely rewrite the definition of the class, adding the requisite `writeToParcel` and `createFromParcel` implementations. A particularly ambitious implementation could even rewrite the class such that it only packs and unpacks the fields used by the minion region, though we leave this as an optimization for future work.
2. The minion may use or define a non-parcelable system-defined class. Here, the previous solution does not apply, because the implementation of the class is not part of the app itself, and therefore cannot be rewritten. A potential solution is to define a parcelable subclass of this class but this fails as the subclass does not have access to the superclass's private fields needed for parcelization or when the class is final.
3. The runtime class of an object may not match its declared class. While the class must be a subclass of the declared type, it may not be an exact match. This is important, because it complicates any attempt to statically insert code to build proxies for the object.

We have developed a solution to the above problem that we call *Parcel Wrappers*. At a high level, a Parcel Wrapper wraps a single object. When the object needs to be transferred to a minion, the Parcel Wrapper uses reflection to decompose the object into its parcelable components. When the component is returned, the Parcel Wrapper uses reflection to get the new values of the object's fields and update it accordingly. Our solution based upon reflection is affected by none of the above problems of private field access (private fields are accessible via reflection) or final classes.

Minion Lifecycle: Android apps operate according to a lifecycle: the system invoke callbacks into the app for events such as creating, starting, pausing, and destroying components. To ensure that the services exposed by minion apps are available to the app as it is launched, APPSAW calls the `bindService` function to binds each minion field at the entry point lifecycle functions of the app. In response to the `bindService` call, the system will invoke the onServiceConnected callback of the app (added by APPSAW, as appropriate), where the service is connected. While this works well for most apps, consider the case in which an entrypoint function itself requires the use of a minion: the onServiceConnected callback cannot be invoked until the app returns from the function, but the function uses minions initialized in onServiceConnected. We resolve this paradox in the following way: For each such callback C that uses a minion, we create a new function C'. The body of C is replaced with code that checks if the service is available, and if so calls C'. If it is not, C raises a global flag f_C indicating that a call to C is necessary, and assigns all arguments of C to newly-added instance fields $args_C$ of the app. When the service is available, onServiceConnected checks f_C, and calls C' with $args_C$.

In effect, this modification of the app results in services being connected before any entrypoint function of the app takes effect. Note that because the C' are all called at entry to onServiceConnected, any user code in onServiceConnected will not run until the entrypoint functions are run. This handles any dependencies in the original body of onServiceConnected to data touched in C.

Discussion: APPSAW generates multiple minion apps from one app. This would unnecessarily clutter the device with apps. Our implementation hides the minion apps from the user interface (e.g., from the launcher screen) but not having the minion apps subscribe to the android.intent.category.LAUNCHER intent, which is necessary for being launched from the UI.

Our app splitting implementation can transfer variables across minion boundaries. However, the case of transfer through persistent resources, such as files, is different. Since Android isolates persistent resources of apps by default, our tool does not automatically support transfer of data in these ways. Adding support for persistent resources is our future work (Table 1).

Table 1. Characteristics of the apps in the Utility Test Suite.

Display name	Package name	Original instruction count	# Permissions
Bible	com.sirma.mobile.bible.android	575472	16
CNN	com.cnn.mobile.android.phone	440211	13
Duolingo	com.duolingo	562020	14
Facebook	com.facebook.katana	272534	17
Job search	com.indeed.android.jobsearch	153580	8
Original borders	com.aviary.feather.plugins.borders-free	54	0
MyFitnessPal	com.myfitnesspal.android	859176	13
Pandora	com.pandora.android	296037	13
Pocket Manga	com.supo.pocket.mangareader	150417	4
Ringtone maker	com.herman.ringtone	135487	9
Zillow	com.zillow.android.zillowmap	788544	16

5   Minion Support Artifacts

The key advantage of app splitting is that opaque, internal functionality of a single app can be exposed to app-centric security mechanisms. However, app splitting increases the complexity of managing the functionality of the app. In addition to the core functionality, APPSAW provides support artifacts both for the purpose of enforcing security as well as improving usability. This section describes the support artifacts produced by APPSAW.

```
 1  <rules>
 2    <activity block="true" log="false">
 3      <component-filter name="com.netdialer.core/" />
 4    </activity>
 5    <broadcast block="true" log="true">
 6      <intent-filter>
 7        <action name="com.netdialer.minion1" />
 8      </intent-filter>
 9    </broadcast>
10  </rules>
```

Fig. 6. A sample Intent Firewall ruleset blocking broadcast intents from the NetDialer core app to a minion.

Install Script: The most immediate drawback of app splitting is that a user needs to manage multiple apps instead of one. To address this concern, the policy generator outputs a script that can be invoked to install minion apps *en masse*. This script can be incorporated into the user flow according to the deployment model: in an MAM offering, the script will be launched directly by the MAM interface.

Table 2. Minion partitioning for the DroidBench programs. For each of the flows detected by the underlying FlowDroid analysis, APPSAW correctly separates the permission into its own minion.

Category	Number of apps	Average number of minions
Aliasing	1	0.0
AndroidSpecific	12	1.25
ArraysAndLists	7	1.57
Callbacks	15	1.47
EmulatorDetection	3	2.33
FieldAndObjectSensitivity	7	2.14
GeneralJava	23	1.65
ImplicitFlows	4	0.0
InterComponentCommunication	18	1.0
Lifecycle	17	1.35
Reflection	4	2.0
Threading	5	1.2

Interaction Graph: APPSAW produces an interaction graph where a node is included for each minion and there is an edge between two minions if a flow may occur between them. This graph allows the user to visualize permission flows and iteratively develop better policies.

Intent Firewall Rules: The goal of APPSAW is to allow OS-level mediation of flows inside the app. We leverage *Intent Firewall*, an integrated feature of the Android framework that mediates intents (and hence binder IPC) based on certain rules. APPSAW generates Intent Firewall rules to enable this mediation across minions at runtime. Figure 6 shows example rules for `NetDialer`, to enforce the policy that the core app may not send any intent to minion1, which corresponds to GPS use (Table 2).

6   Evaluation

This section empirically evaluates the utility, security, and performance of APP-SAW. We ask the following three key questions.

1. *Utility.* Can apps rewritten with APPSAW continue to provide their desired functionality?
2. *Security.* Are apps rewritten with APPSAW prohibited from performing disallowed functionality?
3. *Performance.* Does the rewriting process of APPSAW introduce manageable overhead on apps?

Experimental Highlights: APPSAW preserves the desired functionality of apps while blocking the disallowed functionality in the apps examined. Split apps exhibit an average runtime overhead of 3% over their original variants and use a trivial amount of additional disk space.

6.1   Methodology

We build our experimental setup around three distinct suites of Android apps that evaluate respectively the utility, security, and performance aspects of APP-SAW. This allows us to evaluate APPSAW in depth on a small number of apps and also perform tests in breadth on a larger number of apps. We now describe each of these suites in detail.

Utility Test Suite – Google Play Dynamic Sample: To evaluate utility, we obtained a cross-section of real-world apps, we built a test suite by randomly selecting top apps, each with at least a million downloads, from the Google Play store. To ensure that app splitting did not cause any errors or changes in the functionality of the app, we executed the two app variants (original and split) on the same sequence of user interactions, and then manually inspected the resulting user interface (UI) states. This allowed us to observe any differences in functionality caused by the APPSAW transformation.

Previous work has noted that testing Android apps is challenging [5,28]. Apps are interactive and have significant functionality triggered via GUI. In the absence of a practical, comprehensive app testing approach, one must employ either human-generated or semi-random event sequences. Both of these options have disadvantages. Scalability is a problem for human users, while semi-random input sequences can be shallow in the functionality explored [21]. As the purpose of this test suite is to determine whether the user experiences the same behavior from an app in both its original and split versions, we chose human-generated inputs. This necessarily limited the number of apps in the Utility Test Suite.

We manually interacted with the original apps and recorded all interactions using [30]. We then used this tool to faithfully replay these interactions on the rewritten apps. For each app in the Utility Test Suite we collected two interaction traces, each sufficiently long to perform a logical task in the corresponding app. On average a logical task took 5 s to complete.

Security Test Suite – DroidBench: This consists of 119 applications from DroidBench 2, a testing suite originally developed as part of FlowDroid [7], for the purpose of evaluating static analyses for information-flow tracking. As such, apps in DroidBench are crafted by authors from a variety of institutions to provide challenging data flows. In our experiments, we use the information flows statically reported by FlowDroid as input to AppSaw, with the goal of splitting the DroidBench apps such that all of the FlowDroid-discovered flows are mediated by a cross-minion IPC.

Performance Test Suite – IPC Microbenchmarks: The primary overhead introduced by AppSaw is due to the cost of each IPC call when data is transferred back and worth among minions. While the cumulative cost of AppSaw IPC over the lifetime of an app execution is low enough to be invisible to the user, mostly because apps typically do not cross cut boundaries frequently, this does not give a precise estimate of the overhead. To isolate the overhead, we crafted a number of apps that only create permission-to-permission flows and do nothing else. These apps do not represent the behavior and performance of a useful app, but provide a worst-case analysis and thus an upper bound on the performance impact of app splitting.

The apps forming the Performance Test Suite are fully deterministic, do not depend on user input or any environment settings, and behave as follows.

- *Direct Flow:* In this app, we measure the performance penalty of splitting the most common form of permission leak on Android, a flow of a device-specific identifier (IMEI) to the network. This microbenchmark measures the cost of a single IPC call to a minion. Our measurements are averaged over 12 runs and compare the original app versus the split app.
- *Loop Flow:* Here, we modify the direct flow experiment such that source data is repeatedly queried in a loop. Once the loop is finished, the results of the final query leaked to the network. The purpose of this microbenchmark is to determine if the mechanism can properly identify good candidate regions for including in a single minion: AppSaw should include the entire loop in the

minion and perform a single transfer, rather than performing a per-iteration transfer.

- *Large Flow:* This app tests the overhead of moving a large amount of data into the minion. While a typical app will only include source and the small amount of data that touches it, in this app we ensure that a large, user-defined class is tainted with source data. We measured the overhead of transferring progressively larger classes.

We performed all app rewriting and evaluation on an Intel Core 2 Quad CPU at 3.00 GHz. This machine used the Android emulator configured to emulate an Intel x86 device with 1 GB RAM running Android 4.1.2 with host-GPU acceleration. Our implementation of APPSAW is based on Soot 2.5.0 and consists of 20K lines of new or modified code.

6.2   Experimental Results

Utility Findings: Our experiments with the Utility Test Suite did not show any change in behavior in the split apps compared to their original variants. A number of statistics about each app are shown in Fig. 1.

Security Findings: For each of the 119 apps in DroidBench, APPSAW successfully exposed each flow (as discovered by FlowDroid) to OS-level mediation. As shown in Fig. 1, the number of minions varied between apps, with some apps having no unwanted information flows (and thus no minions in the split version), while others having two or more.

Performance Findings: Our findings are summarized in Table 3. The performance measurements for the *Direct Flow* microbenchmark are shown in Fig. 7. The transfer of IMEI, a small string, across minions is inexpensive and is dominated by the cost of IPC itself, thus incurring only 3% overhead. For the *Loop Flow* microbenchmark, we observed that the loop is rightly placed in a single minion and so the overhead is unsurprisingly similar to that of the *Direct Flow* microbenchmark. Finally, the *Large Flow* microbenchmark showed that the runtime overhead scaled with the size of the data being transferred to the minions, as captured by Fig. 8.

Table 3. Results of the Performance Test Suite. Split apps incur small overhead when transferring low to moderate amounts of data, but can experience slowdowns with larger data transfers.

Microbenchmark	Overhead	Number of permissions	Number of minions	Instructions per minion
Direct flow	3%	2	1	18
Loop flow	3%	2	1	27
Large flow	21%	2	1	12

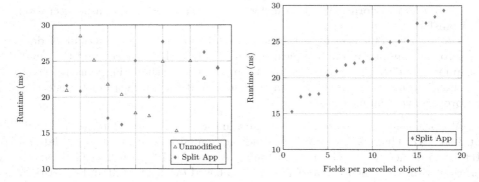

Fig. 7. Runtime measurements of the *Direct Flow* microbenchmark. This scatterplot shows the runtime of minion transfer on 12 runs of the split app compared to the runtime of the same code on 12 runs of the unmodified version of the same app.

Fig. 8. Runtime measurements of the *Large Flow* microbenchmark. The minion-IPC overhead increases with the amount of data transferred.

7 Related Work

Program Partitioning: Several systems exist to partition applications. We note that in general, the Android permissions model allows our system to bootstrap simple policies without the cooperation of the developer which is a benefit of our domain that much previous work did not have available. Chong *et al.* propose a system for splitting web applications [17]. Unlike this work APPSAW does not require the placement of annotations, nor does it require source code, or any effort on the part of the app's developer. However, granting such conditions could potentially improve the performance of APPSAW, though it would require a different threat model. Zheng *et al.* propose a system to partition applications across multiple, mutually distrusting hosts [31]. This scheme also requires annotations to the program source. Program partitioning has also been studied for web apps. Akhawe et al. [4] propose non-invasive techniques to partition real-world web apps but their partitioning is manual. Calzavara et al. [10] detect privilege escalation vulnerabilities in web apps; they do not provide means for privilege separation though. Luo and Rezk [18] automatically partition web mashups to provide greater security. While their work is similar to ours, our work fits cleanly in the domain of Android apps and is backed by different formalisms.

Advertising Isolation: There has been a line of work in isolating advertising from the rest of an application, such as [25,26]. Special-case operation of APPSAW [20,25,26]. The most closely related work to our own is AdSplit, which automatically rewrites an app to use an isolated advertising library [25]. Unlike APPSAW, AdSplit uses Quire [11], which requires modifications to Android itself. APPSAW runs on an unmodified Android device, and thus has no presence on the actual device. Although the approach of APPSAW is similar to AdSplit, the goals of the systems are different and both users may benefit from using both tools in parallel.

Android Rewriting: Aurasium [29] rewrites apps in order to specify policies by hooking system calls, and employing a runtime security monitor. Unlike APP-SAW, Aurasium does not separate apps into multiple pieces, and does not give the user the chance to control permissions in any way.

Android Isolation: Previous work has explored advantages of application level isolation. In particular, Roesner *et al.* developed a modified version of the Android OS, called LayerCake, that allows entities of different trust levels to be embedded into a single app [23]. At a high level, the goal of this work is similar to that of app splitting in that it sharpens the boundaries of security principals. However, the approach taken by Roesner *et al.* differs from our own in that it requires action on the part of the developers to employ new programming practices to comply with a new version of Android. In constrast, our work focuses on enabling existing security mechanisms to work within the current Android security model. Furthermore, the goal of LayerCake is to enable trusted UI components, whereas the goal of our work is to isolate fine-grained functionality of apps.

8 Limitations

APPSAW is effective at splitting apps to expose intra-app flows to OS mediation. However, it has some limitations. Importantly, APPSAW inherits all the limitations of static analysis. It may not work correctly in the presence of reflection, dynamic code loading, and code obfuscation. While lexical obfuscation (renaming identifiers, most Android apps are lexically obfuscated only) is not a problem for APPSAW, commercial Android packers [2] thwart static analysis. However, in the context of enterprise deployment with MAM, it is reasonable for developers to agree on not using such obfuscations in return for the enterprise deploying their apps on a large scale.

Certain Android permissions work on content providers, which are often specified as URL strings. APPSAW will work correctly if our strings analysis can decode these strings (which may not be possible in case of obfuscation). Moreover, since we perform Java-only static analysis, native code is not yet supported. Handling implicit flows efficiently is also an open area of research and we do not currently handle implicit permission flows during splitting. Finally, handling side channel flows is beyond the scope of this work.

9 Conclusion and Future Work

Modern operating systems, such as Android, provide mechanisms for fine-grained control using permissions how apps can use resources. In this paper we used app splitting to extend this control to permission flows. Specifically, we developed app rewriting techniques to split an app into multiple collaborative apps to expose its internal data flows for OS-level mediation. Our evaluation shows that our tool, APPSAW, is practical: it works on real-world apps, fulfills its security purpose, and the rewritten apps have low runtime overhead.

There are several avenues for future for in app splitting and APPSAW. Currently, we replicate all fields of an object when it is passed across minions. We can aggressively optimize this by not replicating fields which have not been initialized or will not be used after transfer. Another level of optimization may be achieved by solving the weighted version of PSP to identify split points with low data transfers. Another avenue is to introduce more fine-grained policies. Currently, our policies are defined in terms of Android permissions, which are known to be coarse-grained [22]. We can in the future introduce syntax and mechanisms for policies that are specified at the finer granularity of API functions. Another direction worth looking at is providing app developers with an SDK to enable easily developing collaborative, split apps that provide permission flow guarantees. By involving the developers we can overcome some of the limitations inherent with retrofitting such as those mentioned in Sect. 8.

References

1. Magic Quadrant for Enterprise Mobility Management Suites. https://www.gartner.com/doc/reprints?id=1-390IMNG&ct=160608&st=sb. Accessed 14 Apr 2015
2. We can still crack you! https://www.blackhat.com/docs/asia-15/materials/asia-15-Park-We-Can-Still-Crack-You-General-Unpacking-Method-For-Android-Packer-No-Root.pdf. Accessed 21 June 2017
3. Agarwal, A., Alon, N., Charikar, M.: Improved approximation for directed cut problems. In: STOC (2007)
4. Akhawe, D., Saxena, P., Song, D.: Privilege separation in HTML5 applications. In: Proceedings of the 21st USENIX Conference on Security Symposium, p. 23. USENIX Association (2012)
5. Amalfitano, D., Fasolino, A.R., Tramontana, P., De Carmine, S., Memon, A.M.: Using GUI ripping for automated testing of android applications. In: Proceedings of the 27th IEEE/ACM International Conference on Automated Software Engineering, ASE 2012, pp. 258–261. ACM, New York (2012). https://doi.org/10.1145/2351676.2351717. ISBN 978-1-4503-1204-2
6. APKTool. Android apktool: a tool for Reengineering Android APK files. code.google.com/p/android-apktool/. Accessed 11 Nov 2015
7. Arzt, S., Rasthofer, S., Fritz, C., Bodden, E. Bartel, A., Klein, J., Traon, Y.L., Octeau, D., McDaniel, P.: FlowDroid: precise context, flow, field, object-sensitive and lifecycle-aware taint analysis for android apps. In: Proceedings of the 35th ACM SIGPLAN Conference on Programming Language Design and Implementation (PLDI). ACM, June 2014
8. Au, K.W.Y., Zhou, Y.F., Huang, Z., Lie, D.: PScout: analyzing the android permission specification. In: Proceedings of the 2012 ACM Conference on Computer and Communications Security, CCS 2012, pp. 217–228. ACM, New York (2012). https://doi.org/10.1145/2382196.2382222. ISBN 978-1-4503-1651-4

9. Bartel, A., Klein, J., Monperrus, M., Le Traon, Y.: Dexpler: converting android dalvik bytecode to jimple for static analysis with soot. In: Proceedings of the International Workshop on the State Of the Art in Java Program Analysis (SOAP 2012) (2012). https://doi.org/10.1145/2259051.2259056. http://hal.archives-ouvertes.fr/hal-00697421/PDF/article.pdf
10. Calzavara, S., Bugliesi, M., Crafa, S., Steffinlongo, E.: Fine-grained detection of privilege escalation attacks on browser extensions. In: Vitek, J. (ed.) ESOP 2015. LNCS, vol. 9032, pp. 510–534. Springer, Heidelberg (2015). https://doi.org/10.1007/978-3-662-46669-8_21
11. Dietz, M., Shekhar, S., Pisetsky, Y., Shu, A., Wallach, D.S.: QUIRE: lightweight provenance for smart phone operating systems. In: 20th USENIX Security Symposium, San Francisco, CA, August 2011
12. Enck, W., Gilbert, P., Chun, B.-G., Cox, L.P., Jung, J., McDaniel, P., Sheth, A.N.: TaintDroid: an information-flow tracking system for realtime privacy monitoring on smartphones. In: Proceedings of the 9th USENIX Conference on Operating Systems Design and Implementation, OSDI 2010, pp. 1–6. USENIX Association, Berkeley (2010). http://dl.acm.org/citation.cfm?id=1924943.1924971
13. Felt, A.P., Chin, E., Hanna, S., Song, D., Wagner, D.: Android permissions demystified. In: Proceedings of the 18th ACM Conference on Computer and Communications Security, CCS 2011, pp. 627–638. ACM, New York (2011). https://doi.org/10.1145/2046707.2046779. ISBN 978-1-4503-0948-6
14. Fragkaki, E., Bauer, L., Jia, L., Swasey, D.: Modeling and enhancing android's permission system. In: Foresti, S., Yung, M., Martinelli, F. (eds.) ESORICS 2012. LNCS, vol. 7459, pp. 1–18. Springer, Heidelberg (2012). https://doi.org/10.1007/978-3-642-33167-1_1
15. Gupta, A.: Improved results for directed multicut. In: SODA (2003)
16. Lengauer, T., Tarjan, R.: A fast algorithm for finding dominators in a flowgraph. ACM TOPLAS 1(1), 121–141 (1997)
17. Livshits, B., Chong, S.: Towards fully automatic placement of security sanitizers and declassifiers. In: Proceedings of the Symposium on Principles of Programming Languages (POPL), January 2013
18. Luo, Z., Rezk, T.: Mashic compiler: mashup sandboxing based on inter-frame communication. In: 2012 IEEE 25th Computer Security Foundations Symposium (CSF), pp. 157–170. IEEE (2012)
19. Muchnick, S.S.: Advanced Compiler Design and Implementation. Academic Press, Cambridge (1997)
20. Pearce, P., Felt, A.P., Nunez, G., Wagner, D.: AdDroid: privilege separation for applications and advertisers in android. In: Proceedings of the 7th ACM Symposium on Information, Computer and Communications Security, ASIACCS 2012, pp. 71–72. ACM, New York (2012). https://doi.org/10.1145/2414456.2414498. ISBN 978-1-4503-1648-4
21. Rafi, D.M., Moses, K.R.K., Petersen, K., Mäntylä, M.: Benefits and limitations of automated software testing: systematic literature review and practitioner survey. In: 7th International Workshop on Automation of Software Test, AST 2012, Zurich, Switzerland, 2–3 June 2012, pp. 36–42 (2012). https://doi.org/10.1109/IWAST.2012.6228988
22. Rasthofer, S., Arzt, S., Bodden, E.: A machine-learning approach for classifying and categorizing android sources and sinks. In: NDSS (2014)

23. Roesner, F., Kohno, T.: Securing embedded user interfaces: android and beyond. In: Proceedings of the 22nd USENIX Conference on Security, SEC 2013, pp. 97–112. USENIX Association, Berkeley (2013). http://dl.acm.org/citation.cfm?id=2534766.2534776. ISBN 978-1-931971-03-4
24. Sayed, S., Hashim, Y., Komatineni, S., MacLean, D.: Pro Android 2. Apress, New York (2010)
25. Shekhar, S., Dietz, M., Wallach, D.S.: AdSplit: separating smartphone advertising from applications. In: Proceedings of the 21st USENIX Conference on Security Symposium, Security 2012, p. 28. USENIX Association, Berkeley (2012). http://dl.acm.org/citation.cfm?id=2362793.2362821
26. Toubiana, V., Narayanan, A., Boneh, D., Nissenbaum, H., Barocas, S.: Adnostic: privacy preserving targeted advertising. In: NDSS (2010)
27. Vallée-Rai, R., Co, P., Gagnon, E., Hendren, L., Lam, P., Sundaresan, V.: Soot-a Java bytecode optimization framework. In: Proceedings of the 1999 Conference of the Centre for Advanced Studies on Collaborative Research, p. 13. IBM Press (1999)
28. Wasserman, A.I.: Software engineering issues for mobile application development. In: Proceedings of the FSE/SDP Workshop on Future of Software Engineering Research, FoSER 2010, pp. 397–400. ACM, New York (2010). https://doi.org/10.1145/1882362.1882443. ISBN 978-1-4503-0427-6
29. Xu, R., Saïdi, H., Anderson, R.: Aurasium: practical policy enforcement for android applications. In: Proceedings of the 21st USENIX Conference on Security Symposium, Security 2012, p. 27. USENIX Association, Berkeley (2012). http://dl.acm.org/citation.cfm?id=2362793.2362820
30. Zadgaonkar, H.: Robotium Automated Testing for Android. Packt Publishing, Birmingham (2013). ISBN 178216801X, 9781782168010
31. Zheng, L., Chong, S., Myers, A.C., Zdancewic, S.: Using replication and partitioning to build secure distributed systems. In: Proceedings of the 2003 IEEE Symposium on Security and Privacy, SP 2003, p. 236. IEEE Computer Society, Washington (2003). http://dl.acm.org/citation.cfm?id=829515.830549. ISBN 0-7695-1940-7

Very Short Intermittent DDoS Attacks in an Unsaturated System

Huasong Shan[1], Qingyang Wang[1(⊠)] [iD], and Qiben Yan[2]

[1] Louisiana State University, Baton Rouge, LA 70803, USA
{hshan1,qwang26}@lsu.edu
[2] University of Nebraska-Lincoln, Lincoln, NE 68588, USA
qyan@cse.unl.edu

Abstract. We present a new class of low-volume application layer DDoS attack–Very Short Intermittent DDoS (VSI-DDoS). Such attack sends intermittent bursts (tens of milliseconds duration) of legitimate HTTP requests to the target website with the goal of degrading the quality of service (QoS) of the system and damaging the long-term business of the service provider. VSI-DDoS attacks can be especially stealthy since they can significantly impair the target system performance while the average usage rate of all the system resources is at a moderate level, making it hard to pinpoint the root-cause of performance degradation. We develop a framework to effectively launch VSI-DDoS attacks, which includes three phases: the profiling phase in which appropriate HTTP requests are selected to launch the attack, the training phase in which a typical Service Level Agreement (e.g., 95th percentile response time <1 s) is used to train the attack parameters, and the attacking phase in which attacking scripts are generated and deployed to distributed bots to launch the actual attack. To evaluate such VSI-DDoS attacks, we conduct extensive experiments using a representative benchmark web application under realistic cloud scaling settings and equipped with some popular state-of-the-art IDS/IPS systems (e.g., Snort), and find that our attacks are able to effectively cause the long-tail latency problem of the benchmark website while escaping the radar of those DDoS defense tools.

Keywords: Long-tail latency · Performance bottleneck
n-tier systems · Pulsating attack · Web attack · DDoS attack

1 Introduction

Distributed Denial-of-Service (DDoS) attacks for Internet services such as social networks and e-commerce are increasing in sophistication and scale. Kaspersky Lab's "DDoS Intelligence Report Q1 2017" [4] reports that the trend of DDoS attacks has been increasing despite numerous DDoS defense mechanisms. One important reason of the increasing popularity of DDoS attacks is due to the ever-evolving new types of DDoS attacks that exploit various newly discovered

© ICST Institute for Computer Sciences, Social Informatics and Telecommunications Engineering 2018
X. Lin et al. (Eds.): SecureComm 2017, LNICST 238, pp. 45–66, 2018.
https://doi.org/10.1007/978-3-319-78813-5_3

network or system vulnerabilities, bypassing the state-of-the-art defense mechanisms [30,38]. The damage that these DDoS attacks cause to enterprise organizations is well-known, and includes both monetary (e.g., $40,000 per hour) and customer trust losses [15]. Therefore, for guarding these Internet services, it is very important to detect, prevent and mitigate various emerging DDoS attacks.

In this work, we present a new low-volume application-layer DDoS attack called Very Short Intermittent DDoS (VSI-DDoS). A VSI-DDoS attacker sends intermittent bursts of carefully chosen legitimate HTTP requests to the target system, with the aim of creating "Unsaturated DoS", where the denial of service can successfully last for short periods of time (i.e., hundreds of milliseconds). VSI-DDoS attacks are not to bring down the system as traditional flooding DDoS attacks do, but rather to degrade the quality of service by causing frequent and sometimes intolerable delays for legitimate users, which will eventually damage the long-term business goal of the target system. For example, given that modern web applications care more about the tail latency than the average latency [12] (e.g., Google requires 99% of its web-search to finish within 0.5 s [13]), a long-tail latency (e.g., 95th percentile response time >1 s) caused by a VSI-DDoS attack can significantly affect the target website's business and reputation.

Compared to previous research on network-layer pulsating DDoS attacks [17, 18,22,23,25,27], VSI-DDoS is a type of application-layer DDoS attacks, with even lower level of traceability and better stealthiness. Unlike the network-layer pulsating attacks which intend to temporarily saturate the bandwidth of network links that connect to the target system, VSI-DDoS attacks aim to create very short saturations of the bottleneck resource (usually in CPU or disk I/O) inside the target system, which we refer to as very short bottlenecks (VSBs) and typically require much less amount of attack traffic to trigger them. Less amount of attack traffic leads to a higher level of stealthiness. In addition, a VSI-DDoS attack adopts legitimate HTTP requests, which can easily penetrate the defense mechanisms adopted by CDNs, network routers or switches in the path to the target system, thereby reducing the detection surface.

To effectively mount VSI-DDoS attacks, we should fully understand the triggering conditions of VSBs inside the target system, and quantify their long-term damages on the overall system performance. We develop a three-phase framework to tackle these challenges, which involves profiling, training, and attacking. Specifically, in the profiling phase we profile all the HTTP requests supported by the target website and select a set of appropriate ones to launch the attack. We find that heavy requests (e.g., the request with long service time consuming more bottleneck resource in the target web system) can achieve significantly better attack efficiency than light requests; only a small burst of heavy requests are needed to trigger VSBs of the target system, reducing the cost of an effective attack. In the training phase we use a typical Service Level Agreement (e.g., 95th percentile response time <1 s) for most e-commerce websites as an evaluation metric to train the key parameters of an effective VSI-DDoS attack, including burst volume, length, and interval. We find that an appropriate combination of these parameters not only achieves high attacking efficiency, but also escapes the radar of the most popular state-of-the-art DDoS defense tools, which further validates the stealthiness of the proposed attack.

In summary, the main two contributions of this work are:

- We present a novel low-volume application-layer VSI-DDoS attack that can broadly threaten a wide range of web applications in a stealthy manner. Unlike the traditional brute-force DoS attacks or pulsating attacks which focus on network bandwidth, VSI-DDoS attacks target the bottleneck resource of the target web system using legitimate HTTP requests, thereby reducing the cost of an effective attack while keeping the attack highly stealthy.
- We develop a three-phase framework via an empirical approach that is able to efficiently launch VSI-DDoS attacks against a target web application. Through a representative web application benchmark under realistic cloud scaling settings and equipped with the most popular state-of-the-art DDoS defense tools, we validate the practicality of our attacking framework.

Through our evaluation of VSI-DDoS attacks under realistic cloud scaling settings and IDS/IPS systems, we confirm that the proposed attacks not only bypass the triggering conditions of the cloud scaling but also invalidate capacity-based threshold monitoring and detection. We further explore two more potential solutions to VSI-DDoS attacks: fine-grained VSBs detection and user behavior model validation, and discuss their strengths and weaknesses in practice.

The remainder of this paper is organized as follows. Section 2 presents the origin and motivation of VSI-DDoS attacks. Section 3 describes the definition of VSI-DDoS attacks, and the design of the VSI-DDoS attack framework. Section 4 evaluates the effectiveness and stealthiness of our attacks. Section 5 discusses some countermeasures and future work. Section 6 presents the related work and Sect. 7 concludes the paper.

2   Background and Motivations

2.1   Origin of VSI-DDoS Attacks

VSI-DDoS attacks originate from the new phenomenon of very short bottlenecks (VSBs), also called transient bottlenecks in recent performance analysis of Internet services deployed in Cloud environments [35,36]. In these previous studies VSBs have been identified as one of the main sources for the puzzling performance anomalies of the cloud-host web applications even though the system is far from saturation. From time to time cloud practitioners have reported that n-tier web applications produce very long response time (VLRT) requests on the order of several seconds, when the system average utilization is only about 50–60%. The VLRT requests themselves do not contain bugs, since the same requests return within tens of milliseconds when no bottleneck exists in the target system. The reason why VSBs can turn these normal short requests into VLRT requests is because VSBs can cause a large number of requests to queue in the system within a very short time. Due to some system level concurrency constrains (e.g., limited threads) of component servers, additional requests that exceed the concurrency limit of any component server will be dropped, causing TCP retransmissions (minimum time-out is 1 s [19]). The requests encountered TCP retransmissions become VLRT requests perceived by the end users.

While most of previous studies focus on VSBs caused by internal system level factors such as Java garbage collection, CPU Dynamic Voltage and Frequency Scaling (DVFS), interference of collocated virtual machines, this newly identified system vulnerability (VSBs) also motivates us to study the hypothetical VSI-DDoS attacks. Our hypothesis is that the external burst of legitimate HTTP requests can cause erratic fluctuation of resource consumption to be injected into the target system and cause VSBs in the weakest node of the whole distributed system, which in turn cause queue overflow and VLRT requests resulting from TCP retransmissions. Such VSI-DDoS attacks can potentially impose significant threats on current cyber infrastructures while remaining stealthy under the radar of state-of-the-art DDoS defense mechanisms and IDS/IPS systems.

2.2   Importance of Tail Latency

In web applications such as e-commerce, rapid responsiveness is vital for service providers' reputation and business. For example, Google requires 99% of its web-search to finish within 0.5 s [13]; Amazon reported that an every 100 ms increase in the web-page load reduces sales by 1% [24]. In practice, the tail latency, instead of the average latency, is of special concern for mission-critical web-facing applications [12–14,20]. In shared infrastructures such as cloud environments, service level agreements (SLAs) are commonly used for specifying desirable response times, typically within one or two seconds [12]. In this case, only requests with response time within the specified threshold have a positive impact to service providers' business, and the requests with long response time (beyond the threshold), not only waste network and system resources, but also cause penalties (negative impact in revenue) to the business of the service provider. In general, 99th, 98th, and 95th percentile response time are representative metrics to measure the performance of web applications [12,26]. In this paper, we also use percentile response time as the evaluation metric to measure the effectiveness of an adversary's VSI-DDoS attacks.

2.3   Measured Long-Tail Latency Caused by VSI-DDoS Attacks

Here, we show the impact of VSI-DDoS attacks through concrete benchmark results. The benefit of benchmark experiments is to have a fully controlled system, which enables a detailed study about how the target system behaves when it is under a VSI-DDoS attack. The design of the VSI-DDoS attack framework and the real production setting evaluation are in Sects. 3 and 4, respectively.

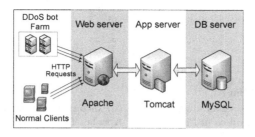

Fig. 1. Experimental sample topology

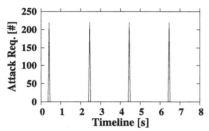

(a) Bursts of attacking HTTP requests in a VSI-DDoS attack during an 8-second time period. We count the # of attacking requests in every 50ms time window.

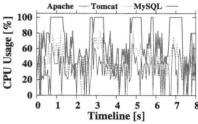

(b) Transient CPU saturations in MySQL coincide with bursts of attacking requests in (a), suggesting that the VSI-DDoS attack creates frequent VSBs in MySQL.

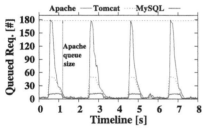

(c) VSBs in MySQL (see (b)) cause requests to queue in MySQL, which in turn push requests to queue in upstream Tomcat and Apache. The horizontal line shows the queue limit in the front-most Apache; once exceeded, new requests are dropped.

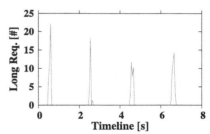

(d) Number of requests (from legitimate users) with response time > 1s during the same 8-second time period. Such long requests are caused by TCP retransmissions once the front-most Apache drops incoming requests (see (c)).

Fig. 2. Measured performance of the benchmark application under a VSI-DDoS attack. Bursts of attacking HTTP requests (a) trigger VSBs in the bottom-most MySQL of the system (b), which cause requests to queue from local to the front-most Apache (c). Queue-overflows occur in Apache, causing TCP retransmissions and long response time requests (d). (Color figure online)

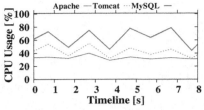
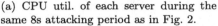

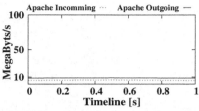

(a) CPU util. of each server during the same 8s attacking period as in Fig. 2.

(b) Incoming/outgoing network traffic of Apache. The bandwidth is 1 Gbps.

Fig. 3. Resource utilization of each server in the system under the VSI-DDoS Attack. Metrics are measured using *vmstat* at every 1 s. (a) and (b) show that both CPU and network bandwidth are not saturated. Utilization of other resources (e.g., memory) are omitted since they are far from saturation.

Benchmark Measurements. We use RUBBoS [6], a representative n-tier web application benchmark modeling the popular news forum website such as *Slashdot*. In Fig. 1, we show the basic configuration for RUBBoS using the typical 3-tier architecture, with 1 Apache web server, 1 Tomcat application Server, and 1 MySQL database server deployed in an academic cloud platform (more details of experimental setup in Sect. 4.1). RUBBoS can emulate the behavior of legitimate users to surf the website. Each user follows a Markov chain model to navigate among different webpages, with averagely 7-s think time between receiving a web page and submitting a new page request. On the other hand, we adopt *Apache Bench* to send intermittent bursts of carefully chosen legitimate HTTP requests; each burst is injected within a very short time window (e.g., 50 ms).

The mechanism of how VSI-DDoS attacks impact the performance of the target n-tier web system can only be seen using fine-grained monitoring. Figure 2 shows such an analysis when the target 3-tier benchmark website serving 3000 legitimate users is under a VSI-DDoS attack. All the metrics in the subfigures are measured at every 50 ms time window. Figure 2a shows that the burst of attacking requests occurs in every 2 s. Each burst contains about 250 legitimate HTTP requests supported by the benchmark website within a 50 ms time window. The bursts of attack requests cause transient CPU saturations of MySQL in Fig. 2b. These transient CPU saturations create VSBs and cause requests to queue in MySQL; MySQL local queue soon fills up (at 0.5 s, 2.5 s, 4.5 s, and 6.5 s), pushing requests to queue in upstream Tomcat and Apache in Fig. 2c. We call this phenomenon as *push-back wave*. Once the queued requests in the frontmost Apache exceed its queue limit (180 in our configuration), new requests from legitimate users will be dropped, leading to TCP retransmissions and very long response time (VLRT) requests as we observed in Fig. 2d.

We also find that the VSBs cannot be observed by our normal system monitoring tools (e.g., *sar, vmstat, top*) with the typical 1-s monitoring granularity. Figure 3a shows that the CPU utilization of each server in the system is not saturated all the time using *vmstat* during the 8-s VSI-DDoS attacking period. Figure 3b shows the outgoing/incoming network traffic of Apache is at very low rate (<10 MBps). We omit the graphs of resource utilization of other resources (e.g., memory, disk I/O) since all of them are far from saturation. Given such monitoring data, it is difficult for system administrators to trace the cause of the performance problem.

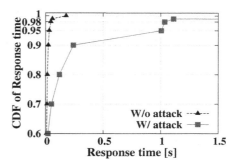

Fig. 4. Percentile response time of the system serving 3000 legitimate users without and with the attack. The 95th percentile response time under attack is >1 s, clearly showing the long-tail latency problem caused by the VSI-DDoS attack. (Color figure online)

To illustrate the negative impact of the VSI-DDoS attack, we compare the percentile response time serving 3000 concurrent legitimate users by the target system under attack and without-attack in Fig. 4. The percentile response time of the system under attack (the red line) uses the same dataset in Fig. 2. This figure shows that all the requests finish within 200 ms without attack (the black line). However, in the attacking scenario, the 95th percentile response time of the target system already exceeds 1 s, clearly showing the long-tail latency problem caused by the VSI-DDoS attack. Such long-tail latency problem is regarded as severe performance issue by most web applications, especially modern e-commerce (e.g., Amazon), as we have introduced in Sect. 2.2.

3   VSI-DDoS Attacks

In this section, we first formally present the adversary's goal of VSI-DDoS attacks and then discuss the key technical challenges of effectively launching VSI-DDoS attacks.

3.1   Goals and Assumptions

In a VSI-DDoS attack scenario the adversary is to create frequent VSBs in the target web system by sending intermittent bursts of legitimate HTTP requests to the target system without being detected. So the goal of VSI-DDoS attacks is not to bring the system down as traditional flooding DDoS attacks do, but rather to degrade the quality of service by causing frequent and sometimes intolerable delays for the legitimate users, which will eventually damage the business of the target system in the long run. Such attacks are stealthy because the target web system is in an "unsaturated state"; the duration of each created VSB is very short (e.g., 50 ms), which can easily escape the detection of normal monitoring tools adopting coarse granularity statistical analysis (e.g., seconds or minutes).

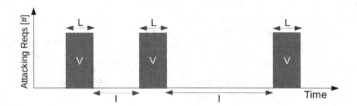

Fig. 5. An illustration of a VSI-DDoS attack, which consists of burst volume V of HTTP requests, burst length L, and burst interval I.

To effectively launch a VSI-DDoS attack, we assume that all the bots under control are coordinated and synchronized so that requests generated by these bots can reach the target web application at the same time or within a very short timeframe. This assumption is reasonable because many previous research efforts already provide solutions, using either centralized [17,33,39] or decentralized methods [23], to coordinate bots to send synchronized traffic and cause network congestion at a specific link. Our focus in this paper is how to create frequent bursts of attacking but legitimate HTTP requests that can effectively trigger VSBs in the target system, causing long-tail latency of the target web system while avoiding being detected. We formally propose VSI-DDoS attacks as follows (Fig. 5):

$$Effect = \mathbb{A}(V, L, I) \tag{1}$$

where,

- *Effect* is the measure of attacking effectiveness; we use percentile response time as a metric to measure the tail latency of the target web system (e.g., 95th percentile response time >1 s). *Effect* is a function of V, L, I.
- V is the number (volume) of attack requests per burst. V should be large enough to temporarily saturate the bottleneck resource in the target system and trigger VSBs. At the same time, V should be small enough to bypass the state-of-the-art threshold-based detection tools [30,38].
- L is the length of each burst. The total requests per burst V will be sent out during the period L. Thus the instant request rate to the target website during a burst period is V/L. L should be short enough to guarantee high instant request rate to trigger VSBs in the target system. Contrarily, too short L will cause large portion of attack requests dropped by the target system due to instant queue overflow (too high V/L), without causing any damage to the target system performance.

- I is the time interval between every two consecutive bursts. I infers the frequency of bursts of HTTP requests to the target system. I should be short enough so that the attacker can generate bursts of HTTP request frequent enough to cause significant performance damage on the target system. On the other hand, too short I makes the attack similar to the traditional flooding DDoS attacks, which can be easily detected.

We note that all the three components need to be carefully coordinated and tuned in order to launch an effective VSI-DDoS attack. To evaluate the effectiveness of such an attack, we measure the tail latency of the target website. We assume that the attack achieves its goal if the measured percentile response time under attack exceeds the predefined threshold, which depends on the SLAs of the target website. Based on this evaluation criteria, we develop an attacking framework which is able to estimate an optimal value of each parameter using an *empirical approach* for an effective VSI-DDoS attack in the following subsection.

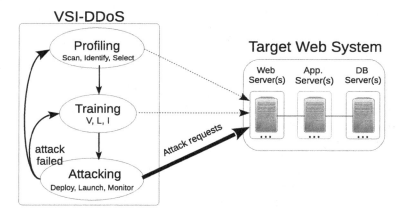

Fig. 6. VSI-DDoS attacks framework

3.2 VSI-DDoS Attack Framework

The proposed VSI-DDoS attack framework contains three phases: profiling, training, and attacking (Fig. 6). The profiling and training phases are to determine the three parameters of a VSI-DDoS attack. The attacking phase generates and deploys attacking scripts to distributed bots and launches the actual attack.

Profiling Phase. This phase selects appropriate types of HTTP requests for attacking in order to create VSBs in the target website with the minimum cost, meaning the least number of attacking requests for each burst. This phase includes the following three steps.

(1) Scanning the supported HTTP requests. To select appropriate HTTP requests, one challenge is to retrieve representative HTTP requests that cover all the transaction types supported by the target website, including both static and GET/POST dynamic requests. Although the requests for static content of a website are easy to retrieve by using some crawling tools (e.g., scrapy), requests for dynamic content are more difficult to get. This is because POST requests are sent out by submitting forms (content is in the body section of a HTTP request), not through the direct URLs. To solve this issue, we adopt a script-based open source web browser *PhantomJS* to retrieve and analyze the form tags inside the HTTP response for every HTTP request. After the attacker provides some initial values for associated input boxes (e.g., user-name and password) inside each form, PhantomJS can submit POST requests automatically. PhantomJS also supports cookies which allows an attacker to conduct consecutive interactions with some websites (e.g., Facebook) which require user login before further website navigation. POST requests are important types of attack requests because they can penetrate Content Delivery Networks (CDN) and attack the original target website. CDNs are widely used by websites nowadays to improve the website performance by caching static content. Since POST requests are dynamic requests which typically require to retrieve/write dynamic information from/to the back-end database, current CDN vendors usually do not support caching responses for POST requests [29]. Thus POST requests are natural candidates to launch effective VSI-DDoS attacks for websites with CDN support.

(2) Identifying *heavy* requests using service time. Once we get enough supported HTTP requests, the next challenge is to decide which requests consume more bottleneck resource (e.g., Database CPU) of the target web system than the others. We term the requests heavily consuming the bottleneck resource as *heavy* requests (e.g., POST requests), meanwhile, those consuming no or little bottleneck resource as *light* requests (e.g., static requests). In this case, *heavy* requests are natural candidates to launch a VSI-DDoS attack because a fewer number of them are needed to trigger VSBs in the target web system than that of light requests. A low number of attacking requests per burst also make the attack stealthy because of the low volume of network traffic. The key question is how do we determine which requests are heavy and which are light?

We use the service time of each type of HTTP requests as a key metric to distinguish the heavy requests from the light ones. Service time of a HTTP request is the time serving the request by the target web system without any queuing delay. Previous research results [35] show that the predominant part of the service time of a request is spent on the bottleneck resource in the system. When the target system is at low utilization[1], service time can be estimated to be the end-to-end response time of a request subtracting the network latency between the client and the target web application. The end-to-end response time of a HTTP request can be easily recorded using *Apache Bench* or *PhantomJS*.

---

[1] Low utilization is to rule out the queueing effect inside the target system.

Lots of tools can be used to measure the network latency (e.g., the *ping* command). We measure the service time of each type of HTTP requests multiple times and employ the average in order to mitigate influence of network latency variation.

(3) Selecting candidate requests. A naive strategy to select candidate attacking requests is always choosing the heaviest type of requests. In this case, the attacker can use the minimum number of requests per burst to create VSBs in the target web system. However, single type of attacking requests in a VSI-DDoS attack has the risk to be identified as abnormal by existing DDoS defense tools using statistical analysis. For example, the defense tool may simply aggregate all the requests sent out from the same IP and identify that some IPs only send one type of HTTP requests, which is highly suspicious. To bypass such statistics-based detection mechanisms [7], an attacker can select a set of top-ranked heavy requests, which can achieve the same attacking goal with slightly increased cost. Some more advanced defense mechanisms use machine-learning based techniques to learn a legitimate user behavior model [32] and infer suspicions requests if the sequence or the transition probability among them significantly deviates from the model (judging based on pre-defined thresholds). In this case the attacker needs to select candidate requests more carefully to make sure that the sequence of HTTP requests sent from a bot is feasible for a legitimate user. We will discuss this in more detail in Sect. 5.

Training Phase. This phase is to train the key parameters $(V, L,$ and $I)$ of an effective VSI-DDoS attack that meets the adversary's goal (e.g., 95th percentile response time >1 s).

(1) Training volume. The technical objective of a VSI-DDoS attack is to create frequent VSBs in the target web system. Thus a key challenge of VSI-DDoS attacks is to determine whether a batch of attacking requests are able to create a VSB in the target system or not. In most cases the attacker has no privilege to monitor the resource utilization of the target system. Thus the attacker cannot depend on internal resource monitoring to determine the occurrence of VSBs. However, we know that the occurrence of a VSB will create temporary request congestion inside the target system; once the queued requests exceed any system-level queue capacity (e.g., thread pool size), new arriving requests will be dropped and TCP retransmissions (minimum time-out is 1 s) will happen, leading to long response time perceived by the end users (see Fig. 2). In this case, long response time caused by queue-overflow and TCP retransmissions can be treated as a signal of the occurrence of VSBs. Given such an idea, a VSI-DDoS attacker can gradually increase the volume of the attacking requests per batch until the observation of requests with abnormally long response time.

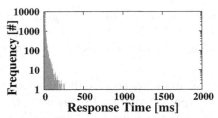
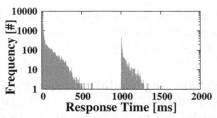

(a) 20 requests per burst case. The low response times of all the requests indicate no TCP retransmission.

(b) 100 requests per burst case. The observed response time over 1s is a signal of the occurrence of TCP retransmissions.

Fig. 7. Training the lower bound of volume for an effective VSI-DDoS attack for our RUBBoS benchmark application. We increase the volume of attacking requests per burst step by step until we observe abnormally long response time of requests sent from legitimate users (see Fig. 7b).

The minimum volume per burst that triggers the long response time requests due to TCP retransmissions is the lower bound V_{min} for the selected attack requests. Figure 7 shows the process of training V_{min} for an effective VSI-DDoS attack for our RUBBoS website, which is serving 3000 legitimate users. When burst volume is only 20, the response time perceived by all legitimate users is lower than 250 ms in Fig. 7a. We increase burst volume step by step (e.g., 10 or 20) until we observe the requests sent from legitimate users experience abnormally long response time in Fig. 7b. The distinct two-

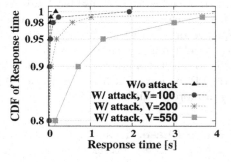

Fig. 8. Impact of volume V per burst. This figure shows the percentile response time of the target system (serving 3000 legitimate clients) gets more damages as the attack volume per burst V increases from 100 to 550 (fixing $L = 50$ ms, $I = 7$ s).

modal response time distribution indicates that 100 reaches the lower bound. In practice we set the volume higher than V_{min} to guarantee the successful triggering of VSBs in the target system and achieve better attack result as shown in Fig. 8. On the other hand, the volume should not be too high otherwise it will trigger the alarm of defense tools (e.g., Snort [7]) deployed in the target web system. We can increase the number of bots and reduce the number of attack requests per bot to bypass the state-of-the-art detection mechanisms.

(2) Training burst length. A good burst length L should maximize the impact of the burst of attacking requests on the requests sent from legitimate users. We observed that the best L should be the service time of the selected attacking requests. A HTTP request that originates from a client arrives at the web server, which distributes it among the application servers, which in turn ask the database to execute the query. Due to the RPC-style synchronous communication between consecutive tiers, the processing threads and other associate soft resources such as database connections of a component server will be occupied until all the activities in the downstream tiers are done. In order to create the most soft resource consumption, the burst of attacking requests should arrive within the service time of the attacking requests. In this case, all the attacking requests will stay in the target system before any of them finishes processing and leaves the system. Once any of soft resources in any tier of the system are exhausted, new requests from legitimate users will be dropped, leading to long response time requests resulting from TCP retransmissions.

Figure 9 shows the impact of the burst length L on the tail latency of our RUBBoS website. We choose the heavy request "ViewStory" as the attacking requests. The service time of such heavy request is about 50 ms. Note that the biggest attacking damage appears when L is 50 ms. Too short L leads to low effectiveness for the attacking burst, since most of the attacking requests will be dropped due to sudden queue-overflow[2], without causing any harm to the requests from legitimate users. On the other hand, too long L (e.g., the $L = 800$ ms case) leads to low instant request rate (V/L), which may not be able to create VSBs in the target system and lead to inferior attacking results.

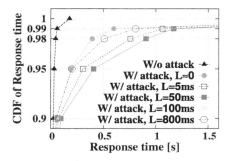

Fig. 9. Impact of the length L per burst. The biggest attacking damage (serving 3000 legitimate clients, and fixing $V = 200$, $I = 7$s) appears when L is 50 ms; the more the burst length deviates from 50 ms, the weaker the damage caused by the VSI-DDoS attack is.

(3) Training interval between bursts. By determining V and L of each burst we can make sure one burst is able to trigger a VSB in the target system. The final goal of a VSI-DDoS attack is to create the long-tail latency problem of the target web system. Too small interval between bursts makes it similar as the traditional flooding DDoS attack, thus can be easily detected. Too large interval creates insufficient number of VSBs in the target web system, thus unable to achieve the adversary's goal. To select a reasonable interval, we start from a relatively large interval and gradually reduce the interval until the measured tail latency meets the adversary's goal. Figure 10 shows such a process of selecting a reasonable interval for our RUBBoS benchmark. To avoid an obvious burst pattern of attacking requests, the interval between consecutive bursts is not necessarily assigned with a fixed value. A VSI-DDoS attacker can design the interval with a random variable following certain statistical distributions, with the mean

---

[2] Short L leads to high instant request rate V/L, OS kernel may not be able to handle packets promptly due to high overhead of interrupt handling [18].

to be similar to a normal user's think time between consecutive requests. Figure 2 in Sect. 2.3 is such an example. The interval between attack bursts follows a normal distribution with the mean of 2 s.

Attacking Phase. This phase is to launch the real VSI-DDoS attack based on the previous profiling and training results of V, L, I for request bursts. Attackers launch the attack by leveraging the resources of multiple hosts, especially Botnet. We note that an attacker should use a probe to continuously monitor the performance of the target website, for example, send a sequence of very light HTTP requests (e.g., html) at regular intervals and check the response time distribution. The profiling and training phase need to redo once the attacking results cannot meet the adversary's goal due to the change of baseline workload or system state (e.g., dataset size change).

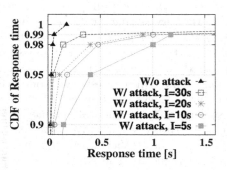

Fig. 10. Impact of the interval I between bursts. This figure shows the percentile response time of the system (serving 3000 legitimate clients) gets more damages as we decreases I from 30 s to 5 s (fixing $V = 200$, $L = 50$ ms).

4 Evaluation

4.1 VSI-DDoS Attacks Under Cloud Scaling

To evaluate the effectiveness of our VSI-DDoS attacks in the real production settings, we deploy RUBBoS in a popular NSF sponsored cloud platform-Cloudlab [5].

Experiment Methodology. In the real production environment, once administrators pinpoint the performance bottleneck of an n-tier system, they can solve the issue by scaling the bottleneck tier. One policy is scaling up (updating the hardware of the bottleneck tier), and the other is scaling out (adding more machines/virtual machines to the bottleneck tier). For example, Amazon Auto Scaling [1] can scale out EC2 instances as the demand of an application increases. We evaluate our attack under both scaling settings. In our experiments, we assume that the bottleneck is MySQL since the bottleneck typically takes place in the database due to the high resource consumption of database operations. To evaluate our attack under the cloud scaling settings, we keep all the software configuration (e.g., queue size, DB connection pool size) the same to rule out their impacts to our evaluation. In the scaling up case, we update the hardware unit (1 CPU core and 1 GB Memory) of MySQL from 1 to 4 Units. In the scaling out case, we increase the number of MySQL VMs from 1 to 4. All the

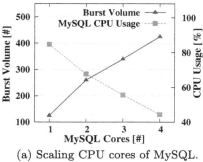
(a) Scaling CPU cores of MySQL.

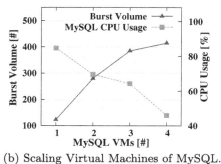
(b) Scaling Virtual Machines of MySQL.

Fig. 11. The required burst volume and the CPU utilization of MySQL in scaling up/out scenarios while achieving our victim goal. Average CPU Usage decreases after scaled, indicating the scaling mitigates the bottleneck. However, we can still get the attacking goal by increasing burst volume.

VMs (Xen-based Emulab virtual nodes) are running CentOS 6.5 on 2.10 GHz Intel Xeon E5-2450 processors. To maximize the impact of our attack, we set the burst length as the service time of attack requests (e.g., 50 ms.), and set the burst interval as 2 s. We conduct the attack experiments for 10 min in each scenario since half of the DDoS attacks last longer than 10 min [31]. Our DDoS bot farm in Fig. 1 consists of 8 machines, one serves as a centralized controller that coordinates and synchronizes the other nodes to launch the attacks.

Results. Figure 11 depicts the required burst volume and the relevant usage of the bottleneck resource at scaling up/out scenarios to achieve our attacking goal. We can see the average CPU utilization of MySQL reduces from high load (>80%) to moderate level (<50%) after the bottleneck tier is scaled, indicating the scaling policies are effective since more CPU cores or VMs can mitigate the impact of the bottleneck resource to the system performance. However, we can still reach our attacking goal by increasing attacking volume per burst even in a large scale scenario, since it requires higher burst volume to trigger VSBs in the system after the capacity of the bottleneck tier increases. On the other hand, increasing the attack requests by each bot obviously increases the risk of detection by the target system, but we can coordinate more synchronized bots to send higher volume per burst to achieve our attacking goal using decentralized synchronization mechanism [23]. As such, we can still keep our attacks under the radar of the state-of-the-art detection mechanism.

Remarks About Cloud Scaling. In real production clouds (e.g., Amazon AWS), the users can customize some triggering conditions to instruct Amazon Auto Scaling [1] to scale out/in instances in response to metrics (such as bandwidth usage or CPU utilization) monitored by Amazon CloudWatch [2]. The monitoring granularity of Amazon CloudWatch for premium users is 1 min [2].

For example, the target system can add more VMs once the average CPU utilization of all the instances exceeds 85% during a 1-min statistical period. From Sampling Theory, our attack is hard to trigger the scaling plans sampling in minutes level, since the VSBs usually occur in milliseconds level (more details about monitoring granularity in Sect. 5). Large-scale web applications typically adopt dynamic scaling strategy for better resource efficiency and load balancing, VSI-DDoS attacks can avoid the triggering conditions of the cloud scaling, thus we expect that the current cloud scaling techniques do not help resolving our attacks.

4.2   VSI-DDoS Attacks Under Defense Tools

To validate the stealthiness of our attacks under the popular defense mechanisms, we deploy some defense tools before the web tier in our RUBBoS environments.

Experiment Methodology. Snort is the most widely deployed network anomaly detection system in the world that is acquired by Cisco Systems on October 7, 2013, and widely used in practice for DDoS defense [7,8]. Snort.AD [9], extended based on Snort, is a threshold and statistics-based network anomaly detection tool, which can analyze the network traffic based on different protocols (UDP, TCP, HTTP, etc.) within a certain period. Here, we take HTTP traffic as a representative metric in Snort.AD to evaluate whether our attacks break through the cordon, since our attacking requests only involve the HTTP packets. In the following experiments, we configure 2000 and 4000 concurrent legitimate users as the baseline for low and high background workload scenarios. We set 95th, 98th and 99th percentile response time (>1 s) as the candidate attacking goals, and call them *95th, 98th, and 99th case* hereinafter. To achieve these different attacking goals, we fix the burst length as the service time of the attacking requests and the burst interval as 2 s, and only tune the burst volume ((250, 150, 100) and (150, 100, 50) for the 95th, 98th and 99th case of 2000 and 4000 baseline, respectively). We conduct the experiments in a 10-min period for each scenario. We modify the code of Snort.AD to trace the number of the HTTP incoming/outgoing packets in a minute interval and the HTTP incoming/outgoing speed in terms of Mega Bytes per second, to evaluate whether they exceed the threshold for these cases with different attacking goals and background workload.

Alert Threshold Setting. How to set the alert threshold is a well-known challenge for administrators [10,11]: a high threshold may not be able to detect anomalies; a low threshold may incur a high number of false positive alarms which an administer tries to avoid in practice. Typically, a widely-adopted setting strategy [10,11] is to set the threshold of each monitoring metric based on the capacity of the target system. Network security company [10] recommends that the company's IT team should conduct the necessary performance tests to determine the capacity, and set the threshold lower than the capacity to prevent resource exhaustion (e.g., define the threshold when reaching 85% bottleneck

Table 1. Measured HTTP traffic in the cases of 95th, 98th and 99th percentile response time (>1 s) as candidate attacking goals. All of measured metrics are less than the predefined thresholds set based on system capacity when the corresponding attacking goal is achieved.

Metrics	Threshold	2000 low load				4000 high load			
		95th	98th	99th	B/L	95th	98th	99th	B/L
In. packets (#/min)	299K	158K	119K	111K	99K	224K	214K	208K	201K
Out. packets (#/min)	349K	171K	134K	127K	116K	259K	249K	241K	233K
In. speed (MB/sec)	9.32	4.68	3.96	3.62	3.11	7.08	6.76	6.45	6.23
Out. speed (MB/sec)	17.83	7.62	6.83	6.48	5.94	12.78	12.46	12.12	11.89

In.: HTTP Incoming, **Out.**: HTTP Outgoing, **B/L**: Baseline

resource utilization of the web system). We also profile the capacity of the target system in our experimental environment under a worst-case scenario (when serving 6000 concurrent users, the bottleneck resource, MySQL CPU utilization, reaches 85%). In our experiments, we take this widely-adopted strategy to define the alert threshold listed in Column 2 of Table 1 to capture our attacks.

Results. Table 1 lists the maximal HTTP incoming/outgoing packets and speed under our attacks for the cases with different attacking goals and background workload. All of the measured traffic metrics are in the moderate level and far from the predefined threshold (based on system capacity) when the corresponding attacking goal is achieved, indicating that our attacks create an "Unsaturated illusion" for Snort. As a result, Snort reports no alert. More importantly, the increased traffic due to our attacks is small compared to the baseline case, especially when the attacking goal is less aggressive (e.g., 99th percentile response time >1 s). For example, an effective VSI-DDoS attack in the 99th case only incurs 10% more traffic when the baseline workload is 2000, and 4% more traffic when the baseline is 4000. This result also suggests that an effective VSI-DDoS attack is easier to achieve as the background traffic increases.

Remarks About Threshold-Based Detection. The fundamental reason that our attack (in *milliseconds* level) can invalidate the traditional threshold-based detection tools (in *seconds or minutes* level) is their coarse monitoring granularity. The coarse monitoring granularity is effective for identifying brute-force DDoS attacks and flash crowds lasting for tens of seconds or minutes [21] (detailed explanation in Sect. 6), but obviously too long to observe any abnormal behaviors triggered by a VSI-DDoS attack lasting for only tens of milliseconds (e.g., the minimum measured rate-interval of the Cisco Adaptive Security Appliance is 1 s [3], the minimum sampling interval of Snort is 1 min [9], the sampling interval of BotSniffer's monitor engine [16] is in seconds level). Indeed, fine-grained monitoring could mitigate the problem, but with the cost of high monitoring overhead and potentially high false positive alarms (falsely block legitimate users), because web application workload is naturally bursty [21]. We will discuss the impact of monitoring granularity in more detail in the following.

5 Discussion of Possible Detection/Defense Mechanisms

Here, we introduce two more candidate countermeasures for VSI-DDoS attacks and discuss their pros and cons in practice.

(1) Fine-Grained VSBs Detection. A natural way to detect a VSI-DDoS attack is to detect the occurrence of VSBs in the target web system, and determine whether they are caused by bursts of malicious HTTP requests. However, detecting VSBs in the target web system is challenging because they usually occur in milliseconds level; from Sampling Theory, these VSBs would not be reliably detectable by normal tools sampling at time intervals from 1 s (e.g., *Snort, BotSniffer* [16], *sar, vmstat, top*) to several minutes (e.g, *CloudWatch*). To reliably detect VSBs and their correlation with a potential VSI-DDoS attack, we need both the system and application level fine-grained monitoring (millisecond level). System-level monitoring is to detect VSBs by collecting the hardware resource utilization of all component servers in the target system using fine-grained monitoring tools (e.g., *collectl*). Application level monitoring is to collect the request processing logs of each component server in the system and analyze the performance metrics such as incoming request rate, queue status, and point-in-time response time in fine granularity. Given the collected fine-grained monitoring data, we apply a timeline correlation analysis to link the observed VSBs in system-level monitoring with the application level performance metrics, as we have illustrated in Sect. 2.3 (see Fig. 2). On the other hand, with "coarse" monitoring granularity (e.g., 1 s), these metrics only show moderate variations or non-saturation (see Fig. 3) over time, which will likely not bring any attention to administrators. Although the fine-grained monitoring approach is conceptually simple, it requires sophisticated fine-grained monitoring tools. [36] shows that VSBs can be caused by the temporary saturation of any system resource that is in the execution path as HTTP requests flow via the system. Specifically, VSBs caused by a VSI-DDoS attack may not necessarily be in hardware resources, but in system soft resources (e.g., database locks, thread pool) that are out of the scope of existing fine-grained monitoring tools (e.g. *collectl*). We observed this phenomenon when we deploy Opentaps, a popular open source ERP/CRM web application, in Amazon EC2 cloud platform. The target Opentaps web application shows a significant long-tail latency problem under a VSI-DDoS attack while *collectl* reports no saturation of any hardware resources. In addition, monitoring overhead is another big concern of the fine-grained monitoring approach. In our RUBBoS experiments, we observe that *collectl* incurs high overhead at sub-second sampling intervals (about 6% CPU utilization overhead at 100 ms interval and 12% at 20 ms).

(2) User Behavior Model Validation. Some advanced defense mechanisms use machine-learning based techniques to learn a normal user behavior model from web server logs. These user behavior models [32,37] are used to differentiate HTTP requests sent by humans from those sent by bots. For example,

Oikonomou and Mirkovic [32] model three aspects of human behaviors such as inter-arrival time of consecutive requests from the same user, choice of content to access, and ability to ignore invisible content. Such user behavior models are indeed effective if a VSI-DDoS attacker chooses single type of requests to attack or a set of heavy requests that have low transition probability among them. However, the attacker can set the interval between consecutive bursts in a VSI-DDoS attack similar to the browsing behavior of a legitimate user (e.g., an average 7-s think time between two webpages). The attacker can also learn a popular sequence of HTTP requests that a legitimate user will likely go through when visiting the target website. Then the same sequence of requests can be selected as the attack requests. Such selection strategy may not be the most cost-efficient one since not all of the selected requests are heavy, but the attacker can still achieve the goal by controlling more bots to launch the attack. Defense mechanisms that adopt user behavior models certainly raise the bar of our attacks, but they do not suffice to detect and defend such attacks.

6 Related Work

DDoS attack and defense mechanisms have been extensively investigated and categorized in survey papers [30,38]. In this section, we review the most relevant work in two aspects: the low-rate network-layer pulsating DDoS attacks and the low-volume application-layer DDoS attacks [28].

Low-Rate Network-Layer Pulsating DDoS Attacks. Many attack mechanisms in this category [17,22,23,25,27] have been proposed, which send bursts of TCP packets to cause packet drops, by exploiting deficiencies in TCP retransmission time-out mechanism known as Shrew attack [25], congestion control response mechanism known as Pulsating attack [23,27], or the transients of the system's adaptation mechanisms known as RoQ attack [17]. These attacks share some similar features with VSI-DDoS attacks, such as the low attacking volume in Shrew and Pulsating attack, and the QoS degradation in RoQ attack. However, our work differs from these work in three aspects: (1) all these attacks are network-layer attacks targeting at network links, while our attacks are at the application-layer, exploiting the bottleneck resource (e.g., CPU, I/O) and the complex resource dependencies (e.g., push-back wave [36]) inside the web system; (2) these attacks usually require a fixed or crafted burst interval to synchronize the Retransmission Timeout (RTO) duration, while our attacks are more flexible in selecting burst volume, length and interval, which allows our attack to be even stealthier; (3) our evaluation metric is based on percentile response time, representing real user experience and provider's service level agreements, which has not been used previously to quantify the attack impact.

Low-Volume Application-Layer DDoS Attacks. One class of low-volume application-layer DDoS attacks specifically related to our attacks are called flash crowds [21], which refer to the scenario when thousands of legitimate users intensively browse an e-commercial website due to a hot event (e.g., Black Friday deals). Previous detection mechanisms are mainly focusing on differentiating traffic from flash crowds created by legitimate users or application-layer DDoS attacks [21,34,37], such as using hidden semi-Markov model [37] and session-level misbehaviors [34] for anomaly detection. VSI-DDoS attacks can be launched with randomized interval and learn from the user behaviors of a legitimate user, which invalidates those user behavior model-based application layer detection mechanisms. More importantly, VSI-DDoS attacks exploit very short bottlenecks (VSBs) as the system vulnerability, VSBs can be much shorter (tens of milliseconds) than the duration of the traditional application-layer flash crowds traffic (tens of seconds or minutes). Thus, the detection mechanisms of identifying DDoS attacks from flash crowds can be defeated by our VSI-DDoS attacks.

7 Conclusions

We presented a new type of low-volume application layer DDoS attack, VSI-DDoS attacks, exploiting a newly discovered system vulnerability (VSBs) of n-tier web applications. Using concrete experimental results we showed that VSI-DDoS attacks can be specially effective and stealthy because they can cause an intolerable long-tail latency issue of the target system while the average usage rate of all the system resources is at a moderate level (Sect. 2.3). We developed a VSI-DDoS attacking framework in which an attacker can systematically profile the target web application and train key attacking parameters for an effective VSI-DDoS attack (Sect. 3). Through a representative web application benchmark under realistic cloud scaling settings and equipped with the most popular state-of-the-art DDoS defense tools, we validated the negative impact and stealthiness of VSI-DDoS attacks, and confirmed the practicality of our attacking framework (Sect. 4). We further explored the pros and cons of two possible countermeasures for our attacks (Sect. 5). VSI-DDoS attack, as a newfound DDoS attack, is an important contribution to complement emerging DDoS attacks.

Acknowledgement. This research has been partially funded by National Science Foundation by CISE's CNS (1566443, 1566388), Louisiana Board of Regents under grant LEQSF (2015-18)-RD-A-11, and gifts, grants, or contracts from Fujitsu. Any opinions, findings, and conclusions or recommendations expressed in this material are those of the author(s) and do not necessarily reflect the views of the National Science Foundation or other funding agencies and companies mentioned above.

References

1. Amazon Auto Scaling. https://aws.amazon.com/documentation/autoscaling
2. Amazon CloudWatch Concepts. http://docs.aws.amazon.com/AmazonCloud Watch/latest/monitoring/cloudwatch_concepts.html
3. ASA Threat Detection Functionality and Configuration. http://www.cisco.com/c/ en/us/support/docs/security/asa-5500-x-series-next-generation-firewalls/113685- asa-threat-detection.html

4. Kaspersky DDoS Intelligence Report for Q1 2017. https://usa.kaspersky.com/about/press-releases/2017_kaspersky-lab-report-on-ddos-attacks-in-q1-2017-the-lull-before-the-storm

5. NSFCloud. https://www.cloudlab.us

6. RUBBoS. http://jmob.ow2.org/rubbos.html

7. Snort. https://www.snort.org/

8. Snort: The World's Most Widely Deployed IPS Technology. http://www.cisco.com/c/en/us/products/collateral/security/brief_c17-733286.html

9. Snort.AD. http://www.anomalydetection.info/?,32

10. Application DDoS Mitigation. Palo Alto Networks, Inc. (2014)

11. Clavister DoS and DDos Protection. Clavister, Inc. (2014)

12. Baset, S.A.: Cloud SLAs: present and future. ACM SIGOPS Oper. Syst. Rev. **46**(2), 57–66 (2012)

13. Curtis, K., Bodík, P., Armbrust, M., Fox, A., Franklin, M., Jordan, M., Patterson, D.: Determining SLO violations at compile time (2010)

14. Dean, J., Barroso, L.A.: The tail at scale. Commun. ACM **56**(2), 74–80 (2013)

15. Fayaz, S.K., Tobioka, Y., Sekar, V., Bailey, M.: Bohatei: flexible and elastic DDoS defense. In: USENIX Security (2015)

16. Gu, G., Zhang, J., Lee, W.: Botsniffer: detecting botnet command and control channels in network traffic. In: NDSS (2008)

17. Guirguis, M., Bestavros, A., Matta, I.: Exploiting the transients of adaptation for RoQ attacks on internet resources. In: IEEE ICNP (2004)

18. Herzberg, A., Shulman, H.: Socket overloading for fun and cache-poisoning. In: ACM ACSAC (2013)

19. IETF: RFC 6298. https://tools.ietf.org/search/rfc6298/

20. Jeon, M., He, Y., Kim, H., Elnikety, S., Rixner, S., Cox, A.L.: TPC: target-driven parallelism combining prediction and correction to reduce tail latency in interactive services. In: ACM ASPLOS (2016)

21. Jung, J., Krishnamurthy, B., Rabinovich, M.: Flash crowds and denial of service attacks: characterization and implications for CDNs and web sites. In: WWW (2002)

22. Kang, M.S., Lee, S.B., Gligor, V.D.: The crossfire attack. In: IEEE S&P (2013)

23. Ke, Y.M., Chen, C.W., Hsiao, H.C., Perrig, A., Sekar, V.: CICADAS: congesting the internet with coordinated and decentralized pulsing attacks. In: AsiaCCS (2016)

24. Kohavi, R., Longbotham, R.: Online experiments: lessons learned. Computer **40**(9) (2007)

25. Kuzmanovic, A., Knightly, E.W.: Low-rate TCP-targeted denial of service attacks: the shrew vs. the mice and elephants. In: ACM SIGCOMM (2003)

26. Li, J., Sharma, N.K., Ports, D.R., Gribble, S.D.: Tales of the tail: hardware, OS, and application-level sources of tail latency. In: ACM SoCC (2014)

27. Luo, X., Chang, R.K.: On a new class of pulsing denial-of-service attacks and the defense. In: NDSS (2005)

28. Mantas, G., Stakhanova, N., Gonzalez, H., Jazi, H.H., Ghorbani, A.A.: Application-layer denial of service attacks: taxonomy and survey. Int. J. Inf. Comput. Secur. **7**(2–4), 216–239 (2015)

29. Mathew, S.: Caching HTTP POST Requests&Responses. http://www.ebaytechblog.com/2012/08/20/caching-http-post-requests-and-responses

30. Mirkovic, J., Reiher, P.: A taxonomy of DDoS attack and DDoS defense mechanisms. ACM SIGCOMM Comput. Commun. Rev. **34**(2), 39–53 (2004)

31. Moore, D., Shannon, C., Brown, D.J., Voelker, G.M., Savage, S.: Inferring internet denial-of-service activity. In: USENIX Security (2001)
32. Oikonomou, G., Mirkovic, J.: Modeling human behavior for defense against flash-crowd attacks. In: IEEE ICC (2009)
33. Ramamurthy, P., Sekar, V., Akella, A., Krishnamurthy, B., Shaikh, A.: Remote profiling of resource constraints of web servers using mini-flash crowds. In: USENIX ATC (2008)
34. Ranjan, S., Swaminathan, R., Uysal, M., Nucci, A., Knightly, E.: DDos-shield: DDos-resilient scheduling to counter application layer attacks. IEEE/ACM Trans. Netw. (TON) 17(1), 26–39 (2009)
35. Wang, Q., Kanemasa, Y., Li, J., Jayasinghe, D., Shimizu, T., Matsubara, M., Kawaba, M., Pu, C.: Detecting transient bottlenecks in n-tier applications through fine-grained analysis. In: ICDCS (2013)
36. Wang, Q., Kanemasa, Y., Li, J., Lai, C., Cho, C., Nomura, Y., Pu, C.: Lightning in the cloud: a study of very short bottlenecks on n-tier web application performance. In: USENIX TRIOS (2014)
37. Xie, Y., Yu, S.Z.: Monitoring the application-layer DDoS attacks for popular websites. IEEE/ACM Trans. Netw. (TON) 17(1), 15–25 (2009)
38. Zargar, S.T., Joshi, J., Tipper, D.: A survey of defense mechanisms against distributed denial of service (DDoS) flooding attacks. IEEE Commun. Surv. Tutor. 15(4), 2046–2069 (2013)
39. Zhang, Y., Mao, Z.M., Wang, J.: Low-rate TCP-targeted dos attack disrupts internet routing. In: NDSS (2007)

Outsourced k-Means Clustering over Encrypted Data Under Multiple Keys in Spark Framework

Hong Rong$^{(\boxtimes)}$, Huimei Wang, Jian Liu, Jialu Hao, and Ming Xian

State Key Laboratory of Complex Electromagnetic Environment
Effects on Electronics and Information System,
National University of Defense Technology, Changsha, China
r.hong_nudt@hotmail.com, freshcdwhm@163.com, ljabc730@gmail.com,
haojialupb@163.com, qwertmingx@sina.com

Abstract. As the quantity of data produced is rapidly rising in recent years, clients lack of computational and storage resources tend to outsource data mining tasks to cloud service providers in order to improve efficiency and save costs. It's also increasing common for clients to perform collaborative mining to maximize profits. However, due to the rise of privacy leakage issues, the data contributed by clients should be encrypted under their own keys. This paper focuses on privacy-preserving k-means clustering over the joint datasets from multiple sources. Unfortunately, existing secure outsourcing protocols are either restricted to a single key setting or quite inefficient because of frequent client-to-server interactions, making it impractical for wide application. To address these issues, we propose a set of secure building blocks and outsourced clustering protocol under Spark framework. Theoretical analysis shows that our scheme protects the confidentiality of the joint database and mining results in the standard threat model with small computation and communication overhead. Experimental results also demonstrate its significant efficiency improvements compared with existing methods.

Keywords: Outsourced k-means clustering · Multiple keys
Cloud environment · Spark framework

1 Introduction

With tremendous amount of data gathered each day, it's increasingly difficult for resource-constrained clients (e.g., mobile devices) to perform computationally intensive task locally. It is a reasonable option to outsource data mining tasks to cloud service provider which provides massive storage and computation power in a cost-efficient way [1]. By leveraging the cloud platforms, a great many giant IT companies have offered machine learning services to facilitate clients to train and deploy their own models, e.g., Amazon Machine Learning [2], Google Cloud Machine Learning Engine [3], IBM Watson [4], etc. Despite these advantages,

© ICST Institute for Computer Sciences, Social Informatics and Telecommunications Engineering 2018
X. Lin et al. (Eds.): SecureComm 2017, LNICST 238, pp. 67–87, 2018.
https://doi.org/10.1007/978-3-319-78813-5_4

privacy issues impede clients from migrating to cloud due to concerns of privacy breach. For example, by collecting medical health records from multiple patients and social networks, hospitals may build more accurate models to improve diagnosis or to predict disease outbreaks [5]. It is, however, crucial to guarantee the security and privacy of e-health records which usually contain a lot of sensitive information, such as personal identity and health condition. A straightforward solution is allowing patients to encrypt the data with their own keys before outsourcing. Whereas it still remains a big challenge for current cloud-based services to perform machine learning operations over encrypted data. Thus, in this paper, we try to solve the above issues by focusing on privacy protection techniques regarding a typical data mining algorithm–k-means clustering [6].

Traditional privacy-preserving clustering schemes cannot be directly adopted to address the privacy issues during outsourcing. Their target is to compute clusters through interactions among participating data holders without revealing respective data to others [7,8], whereas in our case, the data are stored and processed by the cloud rather than clients themselves.

Most existing works on outsourced privacy-preserving clustering require cloud clients to employ the same key data for encryption [9–11]. It is apparent that the single key restriction has some drawbacks: (1) a compromised data owner can easily decrypt others' ciphertexts if they share the identical symmetric or asymmetric keys as methods in [9,10]; (2) without knowing the secret key, owners cannot retrieve their own data downloaded from the cloud if the datasets are encrypted under cloud's public key [11]. To overcome these limitations, data owners should encrypt their datasets with their own keys, which calls for computation over encrypted data under multiple keys. The recent work [12] concerning multi-key scenario is built on geometric transformation to preserve the dot product as KNN scheme [13]. However, this method is weak in security, for all instances may be recovered if the attacker can setup a group of equations with enough linearly independent instances. Furthermore, only one or two cloud servers are adopted in the existing works, the great computing power of distributed cloud environment is not fully exploited to accelerate the outsourcing process.

In this paper, we present a method for Privacy-Preserving Outsourced Clustering under Multiple keys (PPOCM), which enables distributed cloud servers to perform clustering collaboratively over the aggregated datasets encrypted under multiple keys with no privacy leakage. Specifically, the major contributions of this paper are three folds.

- Firstly, we propose a set of privacy-preserving building blocks for basic arithmetic operations. Based on the cryptosystem with double decryption property, our schemes allows to evaluate addition and multiplication over inputs encrypted under different keys. Through these primitives, cloud servers are able to compute Euclidean distances between records and cluster centers.
- Secondly, as the encryptions are probabilistically randomized and incomparable, we propose an efficient method to compare encrypted Euclidean distances

in a privacy-preserving manner. In addition, clients are not required to participate in the comparison operations during k-means outsourcing.

– Thirdly, based on the proposed secure building blocks, we design PPOCM protocol by taking advantage of a big data analytic framework–Spark and distributed cloud resources. Theoretical analysis demonstrates the proposed protocol protects the content of data records, intermediate results as well as the privacy of clustering result in the semi-honest model. Experimental results on real dataset shows that PPOCM is much more efficient than existing methods in terms of computation and communication overhead.

A comparative summary of existing outsourced k-means protocols is presented in Table 1.

Table 1. Comparative summary of existing solutions for outsourced k-means

Protocol	Encryption type	Data privacy protection	Multi-key support	Minimal owner participation	Ciphertext comparison	Big data engine
Lin's [9]	Symmetric	✓	×	✓	×	×
Liu's [10]	Symmetric	✓	×	×	✓	×
Huang's [12]	Symmetric	✓	✓	×	×	×
Rao's [11]	Asymmetric	✓	×	✓	✓	×
Ours	Asymmetric	✓	✓	✓	✓	✓

The rest of the paper is organized as follows. In Sect. 2, we review k-means clustering algorithm and the underlying encryption scheme. The system model, threat model, and design goals are presented in Sect. 3. The design details of our proposed protocol–PPOCM are described in Sect. 4. We also analyze the security of the protocol in Sect. 5. Section 6 shows the theoretical and experimental evaluations. Section 7 discusses related work. Finally, we conclude the paper and outline future work in Sect. 8.

2 Preliminaries

In this section, we briefly introduce the typical k-means clustering algorithm and public key cryptosystem with double decryption mechanism, serving as the basis of our solution.

2.1 k-Means Clustering

Given records $t_1, ..., t_l$, the k-means clustering algorithm partitions them into k disjoint clusters, denoted by $c_1, ..., c_k$. Let μ_i be the centroid value of c_i. Record t_j assigned to c_i has the shortest distance to μ_i compared with its distances to other centroids, where $i \in [1, k]$ and $j \in [1, l]$. Let $V_{l \times k}$ be the matrix defining the membership of records, in which $V_{i,j} \in \{0,1\}$, for $1 \leq i \leq l$, $1 \leq j \leq k$. Note that the ith record belongs to c_j if $V_{i,j} = 1$; otherwise, $V_{i,j} = 0$.

Initial k records are selected randomly as cluster centers $\mu_1, ..., \mu_k$. Then the algorithm executes in an iterative fashion. For t_i, the algorithm computes Euclidean distance between t_i and every centroid μ_j, for $1 \leq j \leq k$, and updates V according to $\arg\min_j ||t_i - \mu_j||^2$, i.e., assigns t_i to the closest cluster c_j. Later, the centroid μ_j is derived by computing the mean values of attributes of records belonging to c_j. With the updated $c_1, ..., c_k$, the clustering algorithm begins next iteration. Finally, the algorithm terminates if the matrix V does not vary any more, or a predefined maximum count of iterations is reached [9].

2.2   Public Key Cryptosystem with Double Decryption

Public key cryptosystem with double decryption mechanism (denoted by PKC-DD) allows an authority to decrypt any ciphertext by using the master secret key without consent of corresponding owner. In this paper, we use the scheme proposed by Youn et al. [14] as our secure primitive, which is more efficient than the scheme in [15] in that Youn's approach applies smaller modulus in cryptographic operations. The major steps are shown in the following.

- **Key Generation** (KeyGen(κ) $\rightarrow N, g, msk, pk, sk$): Given a security parameter k, the master authority chooses two primes p and q ($|p| = |q| = \kappa$), and defines $N = p^2 q$. Then it chooses a random number g in $\mathbb{Z}_N^*$ such that the order of $g_p := g^{p-1} \bmod p^2$ is p. The master secret key $msk := (p, q)$ is known only to the authority. The public parameters are N, g. A cloud user picks a random integer $sk \in \{0, 1, ..., 2^{\kappa-1} - 1\}$ as secret key and computes $pk := g^{sk} \bmod N$ as public key.
- **Encryption** (Enc(pk, m) $\rightarrow C$): The encryption algorithm takes the message $m \in \mathbb{Z}_N$ and pk as inputs, and outputs ciphertext $C = (A, B)$, where $A := g^r \bmod N$, $B := pk^r \cdot m \bmod N$, and r is a random $\kappa - 1$ bit integer.
- **Decryption with user key** (uDec(sk, C) $\rightarrow m$): The decryption algorithm takes ciphertext C and sk as inputs, and outputs the message m by computing $m \leftarrow B/A^{sk} \bmod N$.
- **Decryption with master key** (mDec(msk, pk, C) $\rightarrow m$): Given msk, pk, and C, the authority decrypts C by factorizing N. The secret key of C can be obtained by computing $sk \leftarrow L(pk^{p-1})/L(g_p)$, where function L is defined as $L(x) = \frac{x-1}{p}$. Then, m is recovered by computing $m \leftarrow B/A^{sk} \bmod N$.

By applying the general conversion method in [16], the scheme was claimed to be IND-CCA2 secure under the hardness of solving the p-DH Problem [14]. However, Galindo et al. [17] has constructed an attack by generating invalid public keys and querying for the master decryption, which may lead to factorization of N. To solve this, we adopt a slight modification of the scheme by checking the validity of sk during master decryption proposed in [17]. If $sk \geq 2^{\kappa-1}$, the master entity outputs a rejection message; otherwise, the decryption proceeds as usual.

3   Problem Statement

In this section, we formally describe our system model, threat model and design objectives.

3.1   System Model

In our system model as depicted in Fig. 1, there are three types of entities, i.e., Cloud Users, Computation Service Provider, and Cryptographic Service Provider. Cloud Users consist of Data Owners and Query Clients. Computation Service Provider is composed of one Coordinating Server and a set of Executing Servers; Cryptographic Service Provider comprises a Key Management Server and a set of Assistant Servers.

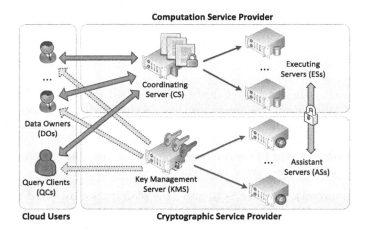

Fig. 1. System model

1. Data Owner (DO): DO is the proprietor of a large dataset. Due to lack of hardware and software resources, DO prefers to outsource his data to the cloud for storage and collaborative data mining. There are DO_1,...,DO_n in the system. DO_i has dataset D_i which contains m attributes and l_i records, for $i \in [1, n]$. The total number of records is $L = \sum_i^n l_i$. Let $t_{j,h}^i$ be the hth attribute value of jth record in D_i for $h \in [1, m]$ and $j \in [1, L]$. We assume DO_i does not collude with the cloud to breach privacy.
2. Query Client (QC): QC is an authorized party requesting k-means clustering tasks over the aggregated datasets. QC should not involve in outsourced computation and is able to decrypt the result with his own secret key.
3. Coordinating Server (CS): CS not only stores and manages combined datasets from multiple DOs, but also deploys cloud computing resources to perform clustering jobs and returns the final calculated clusters to QC.

4. Executing Server (ES): ES is the task node that undertakes the workload assigned by CS. There are $ES_1, ..., ES_\theta$ with massive computing power, making it feasible to implement parallel processing model like Spark paradigm.
5. Key Management Server (KMS): KMS generates and distributes public key parameters of the underlying cryptosystem. It holds the master secret key of PKC-DD, which is used to convert ciphertext's encryption key.
6. Assistant Server (AS): AS holds decryption key generated by KMS. With that key, AS assists ES to execute a series of privacy-preserving building blocks. There are λ ASs, i.e., $AS_1, ..., AS_\lambda$ in the system.

The major workflow of PPOCM is summarized as follows. For $\forall i \in [1, n]$, DO_i generates its own key pair pk_i/sk_i using the parameters produced by KMS, and encrypts D_i with pk_i before outsourcing to CS. With the joint datasets as inputs, the distributed cloud servers are scheduled to perform k-means clustering algorithm in a privacy-preserving manner. The cloud returns QC the encrypted cluster centers under QC's public key after clustering iteration terminates.

3.2 Threat Model

In our threat model, all cloud servers and clients are assumed to be semi-honest, which means that they strictly follow the prescribed protocol but try to infer private information using the messages they receive during the protocol execution. DO, QC, ES, AS and KMS are interested in learning plain data belonging to other parities. Therefore, we introduce an active adversary $\mathcal{A}$ in the threat model. The target of $\mathcal{A}$ is to decrypt the ciphertexts from the challenge DO and challenge QC with the following capabilities:

- $\mathcal{A}$ may compromise all the ESs to guess the plaintexts of received ciphertexts from DOs and ASs during the execution of the protocol.
- $\mathcal{A}$ may compromise all the ASs and KMS to guess the plaintext values of ciphertexts sent from ESs during the protocol interactions.
- $\mathcal{A}$ may compromise one or more DOs and QCs except the challenge DO and the challenge QC to decrypt the ciphertexts belonging to the challenge party.

However, we assume the adversary $\mathcal{A}$ cannot compromise two cloud providers simultaneously; otherwise, $\mathcal{A}$ is able to decrypt any ciphertext stored on CS and ES with secret keys from KMS and AS. In other words, there's no collusion between these two cloud providers, whereas servers from the same provider may collude. We remark that such assumptions are typical in adversary models used in cryptographic protocols (e.g., [11,20]), in that cloud providers are mostly competitors and not willing to disclose business info to others. $\mathcal{A}$ is also assumed to have no prior knowledge about samples for unpublished data.

3.3 Design Objectives

Given the aforementioned system model and threat model, our design should achieve the following objectives:

- **Correctness.** If the cloud users and servers both follow the protocol, the final decrypted result should be the same as in the standard k-means algorithm.
- **Confidentiality.** Nothing regarding the contents of datasets $D_1, ..., D_n$ and cluster centers $\mu_1, ..., \mu_k$ should be revealed to the semi-honest cloud servers.
- **Efficiency.** The most computation should be processed by cloud in a highly efficient way while DOs and QCs are not required to involve in the outsourced clustering.

4 The PPOCM Solution

In this section, we first discuss a set of privacy-preserving building blocks. Then the complete protocol of PPOCM is presented.

Recall that in Sect. 3.1, the semi-honest but non-colluding cloud servers need to cooperate to perform computation over encrypted data under PKC-DD scheme. In the first place, KMS takes a security parameter κ as input, and generates public parameter (N, g) for all parties and master secret key msk for itself by executing $\mathsf{KeyGen}(\kappa)$. After KMS generates a key pair pk_u/sk_u used for ciphertext transformation, pk_u is distributed to cloud ES while sk_u is sent to cloud AS. With N and g, DO_i produces its own public/private key pair pk_i/sk_i and broadcasts pk_i to cloud servers, for $i = 1, ..., n$. Hereafter, let $\mathsf{Enc}_{pk}(\cdot)$ denote the underlying encryption, $\mathsf{uDec}_{sk}(\cdot)$ and $\mathsf{mDec}_{sk}(\cdot)$ denote user-side decryption and master-side decryption, respectively.

4.1 Privacy-Preserving Building Blocks

We present a set of privacy-preserving building blocks in the distributed cloud environment, aiming at solving basic operations on ciphertexts which include secure ciphertext transformation, multiplication, addition, Euclidean distance computation, comparison, etc.

Secure Ciphertext Transformation (SCT) Protocol. Given that CS holds $\mathsf{Enc}_{pk_x}(m)$, and KMS holds (msk, pk_y), the goal of the SCT protocol is to transform encrypted m under public key pk_x into another ciphertext under public key pk_y. During execution of SCT, the plaintext m should not be revealed to KMS or CS, meanwhile the output $\mathsf{Enc}_{pk_y}(m)$ is only known to CS. The complete steps are shown in Algorithm 1.

To start with, CS generates an invertible random number $r \in_R \mathbb{Z}_N$, which denotes r is randomly picked in $\mathbb{Z}_N$. Note that the condition $r < 2^{\kappa-1}$ ensures r is invertible in $\mathbb{Z}_N$ due to $|r| < |p|$. It's obvious that the PKC-DD scheme is multiplicative homomorphic, so we have $\mathsf{Enc}_{pk}(m_1) \times \mathsf{Enc}_{pk}(m_2) \to \mathsf{Enc}_{pk}(m_1 \cdot m_2)$. Then we exploit this to blind m so that KMS does not know m even if it is able to decrypt $\mathsf{Enc}_{pk_x}(r \cdot m)$ via using msk. Hereafter, "$\times$" denotes multiplication operation in the encrypted domain while "$\cdot$" represents multiplication in the plaintext domain. Finally, CS removes the randomness by multiplying the encrypted inverse of r due to $\mathsf{Enc}_{pk_y}(m) = \mathsf{Enc}_{pk_y}(r \cdot m \cdot r^{-1} \bmod N)$.

Algorithm 1. $\mathsf{SCT}(\mathsf{Enc}_{pk_x}(m), pk_y) \rightarrow \mathsf{Enc}_{pk_y}(m)$

Require: CS has $\mathsf{Enc}_{pk_x}(m)$, pk_x, and pk_y; KMS has msk, pk_x, and pk_y.
1: CS:

    a) Generate a random number $r \in_R \mathbb{Z}_N$, which satisfies $r < 2^{\kappa-1}$;
    b) Compute $\mathsf{Enc}_{pk_x}(r \cdot m) \leftarrow \mathsf{Enc}_{pk_x}(m) \times \mathsf{Enc}_{pk_x}(r)$;
    c) Send $\mathsf{Enc}_{pk_x}(r \cdot m)$ to KMS;

2: KMS:

    a) Decrypt $r \cdot m \leftarrow \mathsf{mDec}(msk, pk_x, \mathsf{Enc}_{pk_x}(r \cdot m))$;
    b) Encrypt $\mathsf{Enc}_{pk_y}(r \cdot m) \leftarrow \mathsf{Enc}(pk_y, r \cdot m)$;
    c) Send $\mathsf{Enc}_{pk_y}(r \cdot m)$ to CS;

3: CS:

    a) Compute $\mathsf{Enc}_{pk_y}(m) \leftarrow \mathsf{Enc}_{pk_y}(r \cdot m) \times \mathsf{Enc}_{pk_y}(r^{-1})$;

Secure Addition (SA) Protocol. It takes $\mathsf{Enc}_{pk_u}(m_1)$ and $\mathsf{Enc}_{pk_u}(m_2)$ held by ES and sk_u held by AS as inputs. The output is the encrypted addition of m_1 and m_2, i.e., $\mathsf{Enc}_{pk_u}(m_1 + m_2)$, which is only known to ES. As the encryption scheme is not additively homomorphic, it requires interactions between ES and AS. The major steps are shown in Algorithm 2.

In this protocol, cloud server ES first generates a random number $r \in_R \mathbb{Z}_N$. The ciphertexts of m_1 and m_2 are blinded with r. Using the secret key sk_u, AS is able to decrypt the encrypted randomized inputs $\mathsf{Enc}_{pk_u}(r \cdot m_1)$, $\mathsf{Enc}_{pk_u}(r \cdot m_2)$. AS then computes the sum of two decrypted messages denoted by α, and sends the encryption of α back to ES. Finally, ES obtains $\mathsf{Enc}_{pk_u}(m_1 + m_2)$ by multiplying $\mathsf{Enc}_{pk_u}(\alpha)$ with $\mathsf{Enc}_{pk_u}(r^{-1})$ based on multiplicative homomorphism, since $\mathsf{Enc}_{pk_u}(m_1 + m_2) = \mathsf{Enc}_{pk_u}((m_1 + m_2) \cdot r \cdot r^{-1} \bmod N)$.

Note that m_1 and m_2 are blinded by the same random value, so AS can easily compute the ratio by $m_1/m_2 \leftarrow m_1 r/m_2 r$, which may be used to distinguish inputs. However, our security model is based on the assumption that the adversary has no background knowledge about the raw data distribution, which is common for unpublished data. Hence, the adversary cannot deduce sensitive information about users' data.

Secure Squared Euclidean Distance (SSED) Protocol. For k-means algorithm, we use squared Euclidean distance to measure the distance between the data record and cluster centroid, denoted by $||t_i - \mu_j||^2$. Suppose ES holds the ciphertext of ith data record t_i, and the ciphertext of jth cluster centroid μ_j, while AS holds the secret key sk_u.

Note that μ_j is a vector composed of fractional values which may be rational numbers. However, ring $\mathbb{Z}_N$ supports no rational operation, so a new form of expression is required to represent the cluster center. Let $<s_j, |c_j|>$ denote the new form of cluster center, where s_j and $|c_j|$ represent the sum, the total

---

Algorithm 2. $\mathsf{SA}(\mathsf{Enc}_{pk_u}(m_1), \mathsf{Enc}_{pk_u}(m_2)) \rightarrow \mathsf{Enc}_{pk_u}(m_1 + m_2)$

Require: ES has $\mathsf{Enc}_{pk_u}(m_1)$ and $\mathsf{Enc}_{pk_u}(m_2)$; AS has sk_u.

1: **ES:**

    a) Generate a random number $r \in_R \mathbb{Z}_N$ and $r < 2^{\kappa-1}$;
    b) Compute $\mathsf{Enc}_{pk_u}(r \cdot m_1) \leftarrow m_1' \times \mathsf{Enc}_{pk_u}(r)$;
    c) Compute $\mathsf{Enc}_{pk_u}(r \cdot m_2) \leftarrow m_2' \times \mathsf{Enc}_{pk_u}(r)$;
    d) Send $\mathsf{Enc}_{pk_u}(r \cdot m_1), \mathsf{Enc}_{pk_u}(r \cdot m_2)$ to AS;

2: **AS:**

    a) Decrypt $r \cdot m_1 \leftarrow \mathsf{uDec}(sk_u, \mathsf{Enc}_{pk_u}(r \cdot m_1))$;
    b) Decrypt $r \cdot m_2 \leftarrow \mathsf{uDec}(sk_u, \mathsf{Enc}_{pk_u}(r \cdot m_2))$;
    c) Compute $\alpha \leftarrow r \cdot m_1 + r \cdot m_2$;
    d) Encrypt $\mathsf{Enc}_{pk_u}(\alpha) \leftarrow \mathsf{Enc}(pk_u, \alpha)$;
    e) Send $\mathsf{Enc}_{pk_u}(\alpha)$ to ES;

3: **ES:**

    a) Compute $\mathsf{Enc}_{pk_u}(m_1 + m_2) \leftarrow \mathsf{Enc}_{pk_u}(\alpha) \times \mathsf{Enc}_{pk_u}(r^{-1})$;

---

number of the records belonging to c_j, respectively. It's easily observed that $s_j = \Sigma_{h=1}^{L}(V_{h,j} \cdot t_h)$ and $|c_j| = \Sigma_{h=1}^{L} V_{h,j}$, where $V_{h,j}$ denotes the membership between t_h and c_j. $\Omega_{i,j}$ is defined as the scaled squared distance between t_i and μ_j, which satisfies that $||t_i - \mu_j|| = \frac{\sqrt{\Omega_{i,j}}}{|c_j|}$. So $\Omega_{i,j}$ can be calculated as follows:

$$
\begin{aligned}
\Omega_{i,j} &= (||t_i - \mu_j|| \cdot |c_j|)^2 \\
&= \sum_{h=1}^{m}(|c_j| \cdot t_i[h] - s_j[h])^2,
\end{aligned}
\tag{1}
$$

where $i \in [1, L]$, $j \in [1, k]$, and m is the dimension size. Taking $\mathsf{Enc}_{pk_u}(t_i)$ and $<\mathsf{Enc}_{pk_u}(s_j), |c_j|>$ as inputs, ES and AS jointly execute SSED by invoking SA subprotocol and output $<\mathsf{Enc}_{pk_u}(\Omega_{i,j}), |c_j|>$. We omit the implementation details of SSED since the steps are straightforward. In addition, although the count of data records is directly revealed to cloud server, the numerator of average attribute, i.e., s_j is still encrypted. Thus it's impossible to infer the real centroid value as long as the underlying encryption scheme is semantically secure.

Secure Distance Comparison (SDC) Protocol. Supposing ES holds $<\mathsf{Enc}_{pk_u}(\Omega_{i,a}), |c_a|>$, $<\mathsf{Enc}_{pk_u}(\Omega_{i,b}), |c_b|>$ and AS holds sk_u, where $i \in [1, L]$, $a, b \in [1, k]$, $a \neq b$, the output of SDC is the minimum distance. Since the encryption scheme is probabilistic and does not preserve the order of plaintexts, ES and AS should jointly compute the minimum without revealing $\Omega_{i,a}$ and $\Omega_{i,b}$ to both parties.

Our basic idea is to compute the encrypted difference between the two inputs, based on which AS is able to judge its sign and returns an identifier that indicates the minimum value. It is commonsense that the maximum size of message is normally far smaller than modulus N. Let ε be the maximum size of plaintext. The maximum value is $2^\varepsilon - 1$ and minimum value is $-2^\varepsilon + 1$. After modular computation, the positive difference falls into range $[1, 2^\varepsilon - 1]$ while the negative difference is in the range $[N - 2^\varepsilon + 1, N - 1]$. Normally, if we get a value that is larger than $2^\varepsilon - 1$, then the value can be considered as a negative. The difference between the two squared Euclidean distances can be calculated as follows:

$$\mathsf{Enc}_{pk_u}\left(||t_i - c_a||^2 - ||t_i - c_b||^2\right) = \mathsf{Enc}_{pk_u}\left(\frac{\Omega_{i,a}}{|c_a|^2} - \frac{\Omega_{i,b}}{|c_b|^2}\right)$$
$$\propto \mathsf{Enc}_{pk_u}\left(\Omega_{i,a} \cdot |c_b|^2 - \Omega_{i,b} \cdot |c_a|^2\right). \tag{2}$$

By observation from Eq. (2), it is only required to determine the sign of $\Omega_{i,a} \cdot |c_b|^2 - \Omega_{i,b} \cdot |c_a|^2$, defined as $\delta_{a,b}$. The overall steps are given in Algorithm 3.

As revealing distance difference δ directly to AS may violate privacy, it's necessary to blind δ with random number r, which is selected randomly from a special range. Suppose η is the threshold for sign judgement, which is chosen according to $2^\varepsilon - 1 < \eta < N + 2^\varepsilon - 1$. To preserve the original sign of δ, the blinding factor r should suffice conditions in Eq. (3). They ensure that the scaled positive and negative ranges can still be judged with η. It can be verified that $1 < r < \min\{N - \eta, \lfloor\frac{\eta - \phi N}{2^\varepsilon - 1}\rfloor\}$, where $\phi \in \mathbb{Z}$.

$$\begin{cases} (2^\varepsilon - 1) \cdot r \bmod N < \eta \\ (N - 1) \cdot r \bmod N > \eta \\ (N + 1 - 2^\varepsilon) \cdot r \bmod N > \eta \end{cases} \tag{3}$$

Secure Minimum Among k Distances (SMkD) Protocol. SMkD aims at computing the encrypted minimum value from k encrypted Euclidean distances. Assume that ES holds $d_1, d_2, ..., d_k$, where $d_j = <\mathsf{Enc}_{pk_u}(\Omega_{i,j}), |c_j|>$, $i \in [1, L]$, $j \in [1, k]$, and AS holds the secret key sk_u. The output of SMkD is encryption of the shortest distance among $d_1, d_2, ..., d_k$. Let $d_{\min} = <\mathsf{Enc}_{pk_u}(\Omega_{\min}), |c_{\min}|>$ represent the minimum. To execute SMkD, we compute the minimum by utilizing SDC with two inputs each time in a sequential fashion. The computation complexity of this algorithm is $O(k)$.

4.2   The Proposed PPOCM Protocol

In this subsection, we present our proposed PPOCM protocol for the standard k-means algorithm working in the distributed cloud environment.

The primary goal of PPOCM is to schedule a group of cloud servers to perform clustering task over the joint datasets encrypted under multiple keys, meanwhile no information regarding the content of record attributes should be revealed to the semi-honest servers. In order to improve the performance, we

---

Algorithm 3. $\text{SDC}(\psi_{i,a}, \psi_{i,b}) \rightarrow < \text{Enc}_{pk_u}(\Omega_{\min}), |c_{\min}| >$

Require: ES has encrypted distances $\psi_{i,a}, \psi_{i,b}$; AS has sk_u, where $\psi_{i,a} = < \text{Enc}_{pk_u}(\Omega_{i,a}), |c_a| >$, $\psi_{i,b} = < \text{Enc}_{pk_u}(\Omega_{i,b}), |c_b| >$.

1: ES:

    a) Compute $\text{Enc}_{pk_u}(\Omega'_{i,a}) \leftarrow \text{Enc}_{pk_u}(\Omega_{i,a}) \times \text{Enc}_{pk_u}(|c_b|^2)$;

    b) Compute $\text{Enc}_{pk_u}(\Omega'_{i,b}) \leftarrow \text{Enc}_{pk_u}(\Omega_{i,b}) \times \text{Enc}_{pk_u}(|c_a|^2)$;

    c) Compute $\text{Enc}_{pk_u}(\Omega''_{i,b}) \leftarrow \text{Enc}_{pk_u}(\Omega'_{i,b}) \times \text{Enc}_{pk_u}(-1 \bmod N)$;

2: ES and AS:

    a) Compute $\text{Enc}_{pk_u}(\delta_{a,b}) \leftarrow \text{SA}(\text{Enc}_{pk_u}(\Omega'_{i,a}), \text{Enc}_{pk_u}(\Omega''_{i,b}))$;

3: ES:

    a) Generate a random number $r \in_R \mathbb{Z}_N$ according to Eq. (3);

    b) Compute $\text{Enc}_{pk_u}(\delta'_{a,b}) \leftarrow \text{Enc}_{pk_u}(\delta_{a,b}) \times \text{Enc}_{pk_u}(r)$;

    c) Send $\text{Enc}_{pk_u}(\delta'_{a,b})$ to AS;

4: AS:

    a) Decrypt $\delta'_{a,b} \leftarrow \text{uDec}(sk_u, \text{Enc}_{pk_u}(\delta'_{a,b}))$;

    b) **if** $\delta'_{a,b} > \eta$ **then**

        – Encrypt $sn \leftarrow \text{Enc}_{pk_{ES}}(1)$;

    c) **else**

        – Encrypt $sn \leftarrow \text{Enc}_{pk_{ES}}(r')$, where $r' \in_R \mathbb{Z}_N \wedge r' \neq 1$;

    d) Send sn to ES;

5: ES:

    a) **if** $\text{uDec}(sk_{ES}, sn) == 1$ **then**

        – Compute $\text{Enc}_{pk_u}(\Omega_{\min}) \leftarrow \text{Enc}_{pk_u}(\Omega_{i,a})$, $|c_{\min}| \leftarrow |c_a|$;

    b) **else**

        – Compute $\text{Enc}_{pk_u}(\Omega_{\min}) \leftarrow \text{Enc}_{pk_u}(\Omega_{i,b})$, $|c_{\min}| \leftarrow |c_b|$;

---

leverage a fast engine called Spark for large-scale data processing [21]. Spark uses a data structure called the resilient distributed dataset (RDD) for data parallelism and fault-tolerance, which facilitates iterative algorithms in machine learning. Though it provides a scalable machine learning library MLlib which includes k-means algorithm [22], it does not take privacy protection into consideration and cannot process encrypted data directly. So it's necessary to integrate our proposed building blocks in Sect. 4.1 and the idea of Spark computing framework into designing PPOCM.

The PPOCM protocol is composed of four phases, namely, Data Uploading, Ciphertext Transformation, Clustering Computation, as well as Result Retrieval, the details of which are described in the following.

Data Uploading Phase. To start with, $DO_i (i \in [1, n])$ generates its own public/private key pair, i.e., pk_i/sk_i, by using public parameter N, g [14]. DO_i encrypts D_i with pk_i by calculating $\mathsf{Enc}(pk_i, t_{j,h}^i)$. Recall that $t_{j,h}^i$ means the hth attribute value of jth record t_j^i in D_i for $h \in [1, m]$ and $j \in [1, L]$. Without loss of generality, we assume the sizes of all datasets are equal to be l, so $L = nl$. Let D_i' denote the encrypted D_i. After DO_i uploads the D_i' to CS for $\forall i \in [1, n]$, the server obtains the joint database D', where $D' = \cup_{i=1}^n D_i'$. With D' storing in the cloud, DO_i is able to retrieve its data and decrypt them with its private key sk_i, whereas DO_i cannot decrypt D_j' without sk_i for $i \neq j$.

Ciphertext Transformation Phase. Upon receiving clustering request from QC, CS initiates ciphertext transformation process which aims at converting ciphertexts under pk_i into encryptions under the unified key pk_u, for $i \in [1, n]$. CS first replicates D' into D_r' to ensure DOs' accessibility to their original dataset. Then KMS and CS jointly execute SCT subprotocol. The output of converted dataset (denoted by D_u') is known only to CS while no privacy is revealed to KMS. This phase is essential for two reasons: (1) multiplicative homomorphic operation can be performed by ES independently only under the same key; (2) it no longer requires the key authority (KMS) to decrypt different ciphertexts for non-homomorphic operations during the entire outsourcing period, since KMS may risk broader attack surface and also become the bottleneck for efficiency.

Clustering Computation Phase. With all the converted records $\mathsf{Enc}_{pk_u}(t_{i,j})$ held by CS for $i \in [1, L]$, $j \in [1, m]$, the goal of this phase is to compute the cluster centroids $\mathsf{Enc}_{pk_u}(\mu_1), ..., \mathsf{Enc}_{pk_u}(\mu_k)$ and the membership matrix $V_{L \times k}$ without compromising privacy. The outsourcing process is not only protected by the proposed secure building blocks, but also accelerated by Spark framework. The phase includes four steps, namely, Job Assignment, Map Execution, Reduce Execution, and Update Judgement. The last three steps are performed in an iterative fashion as shown in Fig. 2.

Step 1. Job Assignment. In this step, the CSP assigns various jobs to different computing nodes according to the cloud resource scheduling policy. First, CS selects τ minimum computing units (denoted by MCU) from $\{ES_1, ..., ES_\theta\}$ and $\{AS_1, ..., AS_\lambda\}$ respectively. In other words, MCU = {ES, AS}. Each unit is able to perform cryptographic building blocks independently. We assume that each ES node provides adequate storage space and computation power for its assigned mission. The set $\{MCU_1, ..., MCU_\tau\}$ is divided into two disjoint sets, i.e., Map and Reduce. Without loss of generality, the Map has $MCU_1, ..., MCU_f$ while the Reduce has $MCU_{f+1}, ..., MCU_{f+k+1}$. Then CS divides D_u' into f uniformly distributed partitions $P_1, ..., P_f$, which are sent to their corresponding MCU

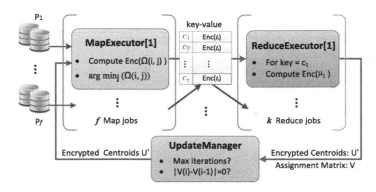

Fig. 2. PPOCM under Spark framework

nodes in Map. In this paper, we assume the k initial clusters are randomly selected from D'_u. Therefore, for $\forall i \in [1, f]$, Mapper[i] knows the vector $U' = <\mu'_1, ..., \mu'_k>$, where $\mu'_j = <\mathsf{Enc}_{pk_u}(s_j), |c_j|>$, for $j \in [1, k]$.

Step 2. Map Execution. As for $1 \leq i \leq f$, given dataset P_i and centroids U' as inputs, Map[i] independently computes encrypted Euclidean distances between data records and centroids, and outputs a key-value table, in which the key is the closest cluster id and the value is the encryption of corresponding record. Suppose P_i has z data records $t'_1, ..., t'_z$, in which $t'_j (j \in [1, z])$ is a m-dimension vector $<\mathsf{Enc}_{pk_u}(t_{j,1}), ..., \mathsf{Enc}_{pk_u}(t_{j,m})>$. The major steps are presented in Algorithm 4.

Algorithm 4. $\mathrm{Map}(P_1, ..., P_f, U') \rightarrow \{T_1, ..., T_f\}$

Require: Mappers have $P_1, ..., P_f$ and centroids U'.

1: $\forall i \in [1, f]$, Mapper[i]:
2: **for** $j = 1$ to z **do**
3:     **for** $h = 1$ to k **do**
4:         Compute $d_h \leftarrow \mathrm{SSED}(t'_j, \mu'_h)$, where $d_h = <\mathsf{Enc}_{pk_u}(\Omega_{j,h}), |c_h|>$;
5:     **end for**
6:     Compute $d_{\min} \leftarrow \mathrm{SMkD}(d_1, d_2, ..., d_k)$, where $d_{\min} = <\mathsf{Enc}_{pk_u}(\Omega_{\min}), |c_{\min}|>$;
7:     Compute $key_j \leftarrow \mathsf{Indexof}(c_{\min})$ and $value_j \leftarrow t'_j$;
8: **end for**
9: Send $T_i = \{<key_1, value_1>, ..., <key_z, value_z>\}$ to Reducer[j], for $j \in [1, k]$;

Step 3. Reduce Execution. Upon receiving the key-value table from Map set, Reducer[i] locates the item where key equals index of c_i, and computes the encryption of updated centroid μ'_i for $i \in [1, k]$. The output is μ'_i as long with an assignment vector $V_{L \times 1}$, in which $V[j] \in \{0, 1\}$ indicates whether j^{th} record belongs to c_i for $j \in [1, L]$. The major steps are presented in Algorithm 5.

Step 4. Update Judgement. CS takes cluster centers $U' = \{\mu'_1, ..., \mu'_k\}$ and assignment matrix $V_{L \times k} = <V_1^T, ..., V_k^T>$ from overall Reducers as inputs. Its

Algorithm 5. Reduce$(T_1, ..., T_f) \rightarrow \{W_1, ..., W_k\}$

Require: Reducers have $T_1, ..., T_f$.
1: $\forall i \in [1, k]$, Reducer$[i]$:
2: Initialize $s_i' \leftarrow \mathsf{Enc}_{pk_u}(0)$, $|c_i| \leftarrow 0$, $V_i \leftarrow \{0, ..., 0\}$;
3: **for** $j = 1$ to f **do**
4:     **for** $h = 1$ to z **do**
5:         **if** $T_j[h].key == i$ **then**
6:             Compute $s_i' \leftarrow \mathsf{SA}(T_{j,h}[w].value, s_i'[w])$, for $1 \leq w \leq m$; $|c_i| \leftarrow |c_i| + 1$;
7:             Compute $V_i[(j-1) \cdot f + h] \leftarrow 1$;
8:         **end if**
9:     **end for**
10: **end for**
11: Send $W_i = \{\mu_i', V_i\}$ to CS, where $\mu_i' = <\mathsf{Enc}_{pk_u}(s_i), |c_i|>$;

target is to determine whether the predefined termination conditions are satisfied. In PPOCM, there are two termination conditions: (1) the maximum iteration $\phi_{\max}$; (2) the matrix V does not vary any more. Therefore, CS not only needs to record the iteration count ϕ during updating clusters each time, but also judges whether the difference $\delta = V_{\phi+1} - V_\phi$ is zero matrix or $\phi \geq \phi_{\max}$. If either termination condition is met, the last phase is activated; otherwise, the cloud moves onto Step 2 to start next iteration, taking U' as inputs.

Result Retrieval Phase. To enable QC to obtain the final clusters, CS and KMS invoke SCT to compute $\{<\mathsf{Enc}_{pk_Q}(s_i), |c_i|>|i = 1, ..., k\}$, which are sent back to QC along with V. After that, QC is able to decrypt the result by his sk_Q. Since s_i and $|c_i|$ are not real center point, QC calculates the final centroids by $\mu_i \leftarrow \frac{s_i}{|c_i|}$, where $i \in [1, k]$. Furthermore, the assignment matrix V is in plain form, which does not require client-side decryption.

5   Security Analysis

We first analyze the security of the privacy-preserving building blocks. Since all parties are semi-honest, security in this model can be proven under "Real-vs.-Ideal" framework [23]: all adversarial behavior in the real world can be simulated by trusted party in the ideal world. We take SDC security proof as an example and the rests can be proved in a similar way.

Since there are two parties i.e., ES and AS, we need to prove SDC is secure not only against semi-honest adversary $\mathcal{A}_{ES}$ corrupting ES, but also against semi-honest adversary $\mathcal{A}_{AS}$ corrupting AS, respectively.

1. **Security Against ES.** The real world view of $\mathcal{A}_{ES}$ in SDC includes input $\{\psi_{i,a}, \psi_{i,b}\}$, a random r, ciphertexts $\{\mathsf{Enc}_{pk_u}(\Omega_{i,a}'), \mathsf{Enc}_{pk_u}(\Omega_{i,b}'), \mathsf{Enc}_{pk_u}(\delta_{a,b}')\}$ and output sn. $\psi_{i,a}$ consists of $\mathsf{Enc}_{pk_u}(\Omega_{i,a})$ and $|c_a|$. From Eq. (1), $|c_a|^2$ is the denominator of $||t_i - \mu_a||^2$, whereas the numerator $\Omega_{i,a}$ is

encrypted under pk_u. Without the decryption key sk_u, $||t_i - \mu_a||^2$ is unknown to $\mathcal{A}_{ES}$. Likewise, $||t_i - \mu_b||^2$ is not revealed to $\mathcal{A}_{ES}$. Note that sn indicates the minimum of inputs, but it cannot be used to infer the actual distances directly. Thus, we can build a simulator $\mathcal{S}_{ES}$ in the ideal world by using encryptions of values randomly distributed in $\mathbb{Z}_N$ and sn is selected from $\{0, 1\}$ randomly. By the semantic security of the PKC-DD scheme, it's computationally difficult for $\mathcal{A}_{ES}$ to distinguish from the real world and the ideal world.

$$\text{Ideal}_{f,\mathcal{S}_{ES}}(\text{Enc}_{pk_u}(\Omega_{i,j})) \stackrel{c}{\approx} \text{Real}_{\text{SDC},\mathcal{A}_{ES}}(\text{Enc}_{pk_u}(\Omega_{i,j})),$$

where $i \in [1, L], j \in [1, k]$, and $\stackrel{c}{\approx}$ means computationally distinguishable.

2. **Security Against AS.** The real world view of $\mathcal{A}_{AS}$ in SDC includes input $\text{Enc}_{pk_u}(\delta'_{a,b})$, blinded message $\delta'_{a,b}$, output sn and randomized $\Omega'_{i,a}, \Omega'_{i,b}$ during SA execution. Note that the blinding factors in SA are randomly distributed in $\mathbb{Z}_N$ and r in SDC is randomly selected in range according to Eq. (3), so we can build a simulator $\mathcal{S}_{AS}$ to simulate the ideal world view of $\mathcal{A}_{AS}$ by using random values in $\mathbb{Z}_N$. Even though $\mathcal{A}_{AS}$ is able to judge the sign of randomized distance, the actual distance and corresponding inputs are still unknown to $\mathcal{A}_{AS}$. Therefore, $\mathcal{A}_{AS}$ is not able to distinguish from the real world and the ideal world.

$$\text{Ideal}_{f,\mathcal{S}_{AS}}(\text{Enc}_{pk_u}(\Omega_{i,j})) \stackrel{c}{\approx} \text{Real}_{\text{SDC},\mathcal{A}_{AS}}(\text{Enc}_{pk_u}(\Omega_{i,j})),$$

where $i \in [1, L], j \in [1, k]$.

The PPOCM protocol includes 4 phases. In the first phase, D_i is encrypted under pk_i for $i \in [1, n]$. In the second phase, SCT subprotocol is invoked to transform ciphertexts. During the clustering phase, SA, SSED, SMkD are invoked as subroutines. At last, the encrypted centroids are converted by SCT. Note that the data held by parties without secret (i.e., CS and ES) key are encrypted while the data held by parties with secret key (i.e., KMS and AS) are randomized. Since the encryption scheme is semantically secure and blinding factors are randomly selected, nothing regarding the data content are revealed to the cloud servers or other owners. Matrix V is known to the server, but it is insufficient to deduce data records using the assignment membership. According to the Composition Theorem [23], the sequential compositions of those phases is secure. In conclusion, PPOCM is secure under the semi-honest model.

6   Performance Analysis

In this section, we analyze the performance of PPOCM protocol from both theoretical and experimental perspectives.

6.1   Theoretical Analysis

Let $\texttt{Exp}$, $\texttt{Mul}$ denote the modular exponentiation and multiplication operations, respectively. Let $|N|$ represent the key size of the double decryption scheme. The encryption of the underlying cryptosystem incurs 2Exp+1Mul. The cost of normal decryption is 1Exp + 1Mul, while that of authority decryption is 2Exp + 2Mul. The encryption and decryption of PKC-DD in [14] are claimed to be 3 times faster than BCP scheme in [15]. We stress that Phase 1 and Phase 2 of PPOCM protocol are executed only once. These overheads are amortized through a number of iterations. As for Clustering Computation Phase, the Map and Reduce steps undertake the most workload, the costs of which in one iteration are given in Table 2. It can be observed that the number of MCU in Map and Reduce sets are closely related to the outsourcing costs, that is, the larger the computing cluster is, the less overheads are exerted on each unit. This is because the Map and Reduce jobs can be parallelized and boosted under Spark.

Table 2. Computational and communication costs of clustering phase

Algorithm	Computational costs	Communication costs (in bits)
Map	$kz(10m + 13)$Exp + $kz(16m + 20)$Mul	$kz(6m + 9)|N|$
Reduce	$8fz$Exp + $11fz$Mul	$6fz|N|$

6.2 Experimental Analysis

The experiments are conducted on our local cluster, in which each server running CentOS6.5 has Intel Xeon E5-2620 @ 2.10 GHz with 12 GB memory. We compare our work with PPODC [11], because the system models are alike, and both protocols are constructed on public key cryptosystem and achieve the same security goals. We implemented all the outsourcing protocols using the Crypto++ 5.6.3 library and Spark framework. The key size $|N|$ is chosen to be 1536-bit, because to achieve the same security level with 1024-bit Paillier encryption used in PPODC and 1024-bit BCP encryption scheme in [20], $|N|$ of PKC-DD should be 500–600 bit more than RSA modulus [24].

To facilitate comparisons, we use KEGG Metabolic Reaction Network dataset [11,25]. The dataset includes 65554 instances and 29 attributes. Before clustering, all records are normalized into integers to prevent impacts of large unit values. Note that the first attribute is excluded from tests, since it is just the identifier of pathway. We assume there are 20 data owners in the system, each dataset of whom is randomly selected from KEGG dataset. They encrypt their data using own keys before outsourcing to the servers. There are three major factors that affect the outsourced clustering performance: (1) the ciphertext transformation scheme; (2) the number of clusters (k); (3) the number of parallelized MCUs (f).

We first evaluate the performance of transforming encrypted datasets under owners' keys into ciphertexts under the unified key. Table 3 shows the ciphertext transformation time for varying size of aggregated datasets (L) in our PPOCM scheme and KeyProd in [20]. It can be seen that the cloud running time grows with increasing value of L. However, our scheme executes about 4 times faster than KeyProd in that our underlying cryptosystem is much more efficient than theirs. Note that [20] aims at privacy-preserving arithmetic operations (i.e., addition and multiplication) rather than k-means algorithm, while PPODC scheme cannot be used to cluster data encrypted under multiple keys.

Table 3. Cloud running time for ciphertexts transformation (in min)

Protocol	$L = 2000$	$L = 4000$	$L = 6000$	$L = 8000$	$L = 10000$
PPOCM	11.6	23.2	35.3	46.5	57.9
KeyProd	43.9	87.9	138.9	175.3	219.4

We then conduct tests on SSED and SMkD to evaluate the performance of the proposed secure building blocks, which utilize SA and SDC as primitives and are frequently invoked during k-means outsourcing. Figure 3(a) shows that the computation cost of both schemes increase with growth of dataset size, but SSED of PPOCM executes much faster. In addition, the increase of dimension size (m) has more impact on PPODC. As shown in Fig. (3)(b), it's observed that with growth of w, the computation time of SMkD in PPODC grows rapidly, where w denotes the bit length of plaintext message. The reason is that every ciphertext should be decomposed into a w-length vector of encrypted bits during execution of SMIN in [11], whereas in contrast, PPOCM's comparison operation is much more efficient by preserving the sign of randomized value.

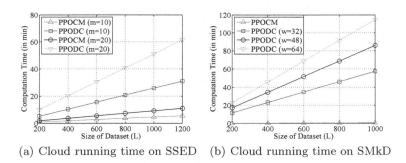

(a) Cloud running time on SSED   (b) Cloud running time on SMkD

Fig. 3. Experiment analysis on SSED and SMkD over samples from the real dataset

Next, we assess the overhead of complete protocols with varying k and m when $L = 2000$ and $f = 4$. PPOCM is compared with the optimized version of PPODC with 4 parallelized server pairs. The results are given in Fig. 4(a) and (b). It can be seen that both the computation time and communication cost grows almost linearly with the count of clusters. It is because more encrypted Euclidean distances need to be calculated and compared with increasing k. Our

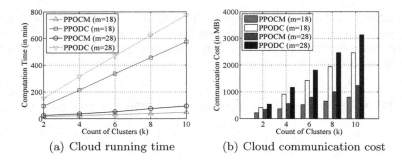

(a) Cloud running time   (b) Cloud communication cost

Fig. 4. Experiment analysis with varying number of clusters (k) over the real dataset

method obviously outperforms PPODC. For instance, when $k = 6$ and $m = 28$, the execution time of PPODC is 469.1 min, whereas that of PPOCM is 51.3 min, almost 10 times faster. The communication cost of PPODC and PPOCM are 1809.1 MB and 796.1 MB, respectively. Furthermore, the growth of dimension size also increases the computational and communication overhead.

Moreover, we evaluate the overhead on cloud servers with varying f when $k = 2$. As shown in Fig. 5(c), the computation time decreases with the growth of f. It can be derived that: (1) the more parallelized MCUs or server-pairs participate in outsourcing, the shorter time it takes both schemes to complete the entire clustering task; (2) with growing size of dataset, it takes PPODC longer time to complete the same amount of work. The reason why PPOCM has better performance should be attributed to the excellent scaling capability of Spark engine and efficient primitiv. Figure 5(d) shows that the communication cost of both schemes remain invariable regardless of f. Though each server pair only handles partial jobs, the total amount of clustering task is fixed. Hence, the mount of transmitted data remain unchanged. In addition, the communication cost of PPOCM accounts for 62.2% of that of parallelized PPODC.

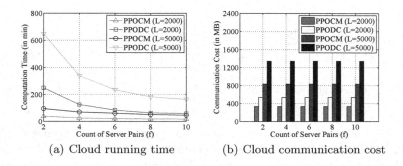

(a) Cloud running time   (b) Cloud communication cost

Fig. 5. Experiment analysis with varying number of parallelized MCUs (f) over the real dataset

7   Related Work

There have been a lot of works on privacy-preserving distributed k-means clustering [7,8]. These works assume clustering task is performed through interactions among different data holders instead of third parties, resulting in different security requirements and design goals compared to our work.

As for outsourced clustering, Lin [9] proposed a privacy-preserving method for kernel k-means based on random linear transformation and perturbation of kernel matrix. But this scheme is neither fit for the standard k-means without kernel function, nor computes the cluster centers. Works in [10,18] leveraged fully homomorphic encryption to perform clustering on a single server and proposed to compare ciphertexts with trapdoor information, while their approach requires data owner's participation in each iteration, which affects the outsourcing performance. PPODC scheme proposed by Rao et al. [11] enables the cloud to perform clustering over the combined encrypted databases from multiple users, which is similar with our scheme. However, their solution does not support database encrypted under multiple keys. Besides, the overhead of secure comparison is too heavy since each inputs have to be decomposed into encrypted bits by calling SBD subroutine. As for arithmetic computation over data encrypted under multiple keys, López et al. [19] studied the FHE under multiple keys. Unfortunately, the efficiency of their scheme suffers from complex key-switching technique and heavy interactions among users. The recent work [20] utilized BCP encryption scheme with double trapdoor decryption [15] to address basic computations under multi-key setting, which yet cannot be used to compare ciphertexts. Besides, none of existing works have utilized big data analytic techniques.

8   Conclusion

In this paper, we proposed an efficient privacy-preserving protocol for outsourced k-means clustering over joint datasets encrypted under multiple data owners' keys. By utilizing double-decryption cryptosystem, we proposed a series of privacy-preserving building blocks to transform ciphertexts and evaluate addition, multiplication, comparison, etc. over encrypted data. Our protocol protects privacy of the combined database under the semi-honest model and requires no cloud client's participation. Another improvement is that the outsourced clustering works under big data processing framework, which significantly boosts the system performance. Experiments on real dataset show that our scheme is more efficient than existing approaches. As future work, we will focus on privacy protection and integrity verification techniques to withstand advanced attacks under malicious model during k-means outsourcing.

References

1. Hajjat, M., Sun, X., Sung, Y.E., Maltz, D., Rao, S., Spripanidkulchai, K., Tawarmalani, M.: Cloudward bound: planning for beneficial migration of enterprise applications to the cloud. In: ACM SIGCOMM, pp. 243–254 (2010)
2. Amazon Machine Learning. https://aws.amazon.com/machine-learning/
3. Cloud Machine Learning Engine. https://cloud.google.com/ml-engine/
4. Do your best work with Watson. https://www.ibm.com/watson/
5. Eubank, S., Guclu, H., Kumar, V.S.A., Marathe, M.V., Srinivasan, A., Toroczkai, Z., Wang, N.: Modeling disease outbreaks in realistic urban social networks. Nature **429**, 180–184 (2004)
6. Jain, A.K., Murty, M.N., Flynn, P.J.: Data clustering: a review. ACM Comput. Surv. **31**, 264–323 (1999)
7. Vaidya, J., Clifton, C.: Privacy-preserving k-means clustering over arbitrarily partitioned data. In: ACM KDD (2003)
8. Jagannathan, G., Gehrke, J., Wright, R.N.: Privacy-preserving distributed k-means clustering over arbitrarily partitioned data. In: KDD, pp. 593–599 (2005)
9. Lin, K.: Privacy-preserving kernel k-means outsourcing with randomized kernels. In: ICDM Workshop, pp. 860–866 (2013)
10. Liu, D., Bertino, E., Yi, X.: Privacy of outsourced k-means clustering. In: ASIA CCS, pp. 123–133 (2014)
11. Rao, F., Samanthula, B.K., Bertino, E., Yi, X., Liu, D.: Privacy-preserving and outsourced multi-user k-means clustering. In: IEEE Conference on Collaboration and Internet Computing, pp. 80–89 (2015)
12. Huang, Y., Lu, Q., Xiong, Y.: Collaborative outsourced data mining for secure cloud computing. J. Netw. **9**(9), 2655–2664 (2014)
13. Wong, W.K., Cheung, D.W., Kao, B., Mamoulis, N.: Secure kNN computation on encrypted database. In: SIGMOD, pp. 139–152 (2009)
14. Youn, T.-Y., Park, Y.-H., Kim, C.H., Lim, J.: An efficient public key cryptosystem with a privacy enhanced double decryption mechanism. In: Preneel, B., Tavares, S. (eds.) SAC 2005. LNCS, vol. 3897, pp. 144–158. Springer, Heidelberg (2006). https://doi.org/10.1007/11693383_10
15. Bresson, E., Catalano, D., Pointcheval, D.: A simple public-key cryptosystem with a double trapdoor decryption mechanism and its applications. In: Laih, C.-S. (ed.) ASIACRYPT 2003. LNCS, vol. 2894, pp. 37–54. Springer, Heidelberg (2003). https://doi.org/10.1007/978-3-540-40061-5_3
16. Kiltz, E., Malone-Lee, J.: A general construction of IND-CCA2 secure public key encryption. In: Paterson, K.G. (ed.) Cryptography and Coding 2003. LNCS, vol. 2898, pp. 152–166. Springer, Heidelberg (2003). https://doi.org/10.1007/978-3-540-40974-8_13
17. Galindo, D., Herranz, J.: On the security of public key cryptosystems with a double decryption mechanism. Inf. Process. Lett. **108**(2008), 279–283 (2008)
18. Liu, X., Jiang, Z.L., Yiu, S.M., et al.: Outsourcing two-party privacy preserving k-means clustering protocol in wireless sensor networks. In: The 11th International Conference on Mobile Ad-Hoc and Sensor Networks, pp. 124–133 (2016)
19. López, A., Tromer, E., Vaikuntanathan, V.: On-the-fly multiparty computation on the cloud via multikey fully homomorphic encryption. In: STOC, pp. 1219–1234 (2012)
20. Peter, A., Tews, E., Katzenbeisser, S.: Efficiently outsourcing multiparty computation under multiple keys. IEEE Trans. Inf. Forensics Secur. **8**(12), 2046–2058 (2013)

21. Ortiz, J.R., Oneto, L., Anguita, D.: Big data analytics in the cloud: spark on hadoop vs MPI/OpenMP on Beowulf. Procedia Comput. Sci. **53**(1), 121–130 (2015)
22. Meng, X., Bradley, J., Yavuz, B., Sparks, E., Venkataraman, S.: MLlib: machine learing in apache spark. J. Mach. Learn. Res. **17**(1), 1235–1241 (2015)
23. Goldreich, O.: The Foundations of Cryptography: Volume 2, Basic Applications. Cambridge University Press, Cambridge (2004)
24. Peralta, R.: Report on Integer Factorization (2001). http://www.ipa.go.jp/security/enc/CRYPTREC/fy15/doc/1025_report.pdf
25. Naeem, M., Asghar, S.: KEGG Metabolic Reaction Network Data Set. The UCI KDD Archive (2011). https://archives.ics.uci.edu/ml/datasets/KEGG+Metabolic+Reaction+Network+(Undirected)

Guilt-by-Association: Detecting Malicious Entities via Graph Mining

Pejman Najafi[(⊠)], Andrey Sapegin, Feng Cheng, and Christoph Meinel

Hasso Plattner Institute (HPI), Prof.-Dr.-Helmert-Straße 2-3,
14482 Potsdam, Germany
{pejman.najafi,andrey.sapegin,feng.cheng,christoph.meinel}@hpi.de

Abstract. In this paper, we tackle the problem of detecting malicious domains and IP addresses using graph inference. In this regard, we mine proxy and DNS logs to construct an undirected graph in which vertices represent domain and IP address nodes, and the edges represent relationships describing an association between those nodes. More specifically, we investigate three main relationships: *subdomainOf*, *referredTo*, and *resolvedTo*. We show that by providing minimal ground truth information, it is possible to estimate the marginal probability of a domain or IP node being malicious based on its association with other malicious nodes. This is achieved by adopting belief propagation, i.e., an efficient and popular inference algorithm used in probabilistic graphical models. We have implemented our system in Apache Spark and evaluated using one day of proxy and DNS logs collected from a global enterprise spanning over 2 *terabytes* of disk space. In this regard, we show that our approach is not only efficient but also capable of achieving high detection rate (96% TPR) with reasonably low false positive rates (8% FPR). Furthermore, it is also capable of fixing errors in the ground truth as well as identifying previously unknown malicious domains and IP addresses. Our proposal can be adopted by enterprises to increase both the quality and the quantity of their threat intelligence and blacklists using only proxy and DNS logs.

Keywords: Belief propagation · Big data analysis for security
Graph inference · Malicious domain and IP detection
Guilt-by-association · Graph mining

1 Introduction

In the case of both targeted threats (e.g., social engineering, spear-phishing, Advanced Persistent Threats, etc.) and mainstream threats (e.g., drive-by download, exploit-kits, malvertising, etc.), there exists an external malicious entity administered by an adversary that successfully reaches the end client (victim). The ability to block these entities from reaching the end client is considered to be an optimum cyber security solution. That's why so many organizations heavily invest in blocking these by deploying various security solutions such as

X. Lin et al. (Eds.): SecureComm 2017, LNICST 238, pp. 88–107, 2018.
https://doi.org/10.1007/978-3-319-78813-5_5

web application firewalls, proxy servers, email and web security appliance, etc. The majority of these solutions try to detect the maliciousness by analyzing the local features of those entities (e.g., URL structure or content of a web page). However, the problem is that the majority of these features are volatile, hence giving an advantage to cybercriminals to evade detection.

Consider Exploit-Kits (EK), e.g., Angler and Neutrino [11,14,29]. At high level internet users are first deceived to visit a previously compromised domain using techniques such as malvertising or malicious iFrames. Next using techniques such as HTTP POST redirection, domain generation algorithm (DGA), and HTTP redirects (302 cushioning) the victims are passed through various gateway pages to finally get to the landing page of the exploit kit. Next the EK tries to identify any potential vulnerabilities within the visitor's browser and plugins. Lastly, upon successful exploitation of a vulnerability, the client browser is silently forced to either download and run a malicious payload (Drive-by downloads) or execute shellcodes.

These tools go above and beyond to make it extremely difficult to detect the malicious entities involved (i.e., domains and IP addresses). For instance, to evade blacklisting exploit-kits use techniques such as domain shadowing [11], fast fluxing domains [10], and domain generation algorithm (DGA). In order to evade static and dynamic analysis of code or content, they use various anti-emulation, anti-sandbox, obfuscation and encoding techniques and dynamically build unique content and code for each request. In this regard, neither the maintenance of blacklists nor dynamic/static analysis of web pages is effective. This is due to the fact that there is no guarantee that next time the same landing page would have any local features shared with the previous observation of the landing page (i.e., different domain name, IP address, content, code, URL structure, etc). However, despite the fact that these tools are capable of mutating the entire local features, it is extremely challenging and sometimes costly to change global features (i.e., attributes shared between different malicious entities), for instance, the authoritative domain responsible for serving fast fluxing domains, the paths leading to two different landing page, or the registrar information.

This observation is not limited to exploit kits. Investigating the correlation between the global features of the previously known indicators of compromise (IOCs) could potentially allow us to better reason about new entities. In this paper, we formulate big data analysis for threat detection as a graph inference problem, with the intuition that malicious entities tend to have homophilic relationships with other malicious entities. More specifically, we focus on the analysis of proxy and DNS logs for the purpose of detecting malicious IP addresses and Domain names based on the relationships observed in those logs and minimal prior knowledge collected from threat intelligence (TI) sources. We achieve this by adopting Loopy Belief Propagation from probabilistic graphical models which allows to propagate the labels from labeled data to unlabeled data using relationships extracted from proxy and DNS logs.

1.1 Contribution and Road Map

The contributions of this paper are as follows:

- Proposal of an alternative approach to proxy and DNS log analysis for the purpose of threat detection using only the information available in those logs. This approach could be used by enterprises to increase both the quality and the quantity of their threat intelligence and blacklists.
- The successful adaptation of belief propagation as a graph based inference algorithm to propagate malicious labels using minimal ground truth to detect other malicious domains and IP addresses.
- Evaluation of the proposed approach on one day of proxy and DNS logs collected from a global enterprise, and demonstrating its capability to correct the inaccuracy in the original ground truth but also detect previously unknown malicious domains and IP addresses.

The rest of this paper is organized as follows. First, we provide some necessary background information while covering the most influential literature. In Sect. 3, we introduce our approach for detecting malicious entities. Section 4 provides an overview of our implementation. Section 5 describes our dataset and the experimental setup. Section 6 focuses on the evaluation and discussion. Section 7 discusses the limitation of our work and the potential directions for the future work, and finally, we conclude this paper in Sect. 8.

2 Background and Related Work

2.1 Proxy and DNS Logs

Nowadays, the majority of organizations, collect and store event logs generated by different components in the organization's premises such as firewalls, operating systems, proxy and DNS servers. Although traditionally the primary usage of these event logs was troubleshooting problems, nowadays they are collected due to mostly regulatory compliances and posthoc analysis. Two most valuable sources of event logs collected by many enterprises are DNS and proxy logs. While grasping the functionalities of proxy and DNS servers are beyond the scope of this paper, we will briefly cover the value of the logged events in the context of security analytics, and we would like to refer the reader to [13,22,23] to learn more about proxy servers and Domain Name System (DNS) respectively.

Due to the fact that web traffic is typically allowed by most of firewalls, HTTP, HTTPS, and DNS traffic is extensively abused by cybercriminals to reach the end users (e.g drive-by download, phishing website, bots communication with command-and-control servers, infrastructure management using fast fluxing [10], etc.), hence leading to the popularity of proxy and DNS log analysis in the security domain.

In this regard, Manners [19] discusses how it is possible to detect malicious entities based on abnormal or rare user agent string. Oprea et al. [25] address the problem of detecting suspicious domains (associated with C & C) using features extractable from proxy logs. These features include domain connectivity (the number of hosts contacting to a domain), the referrer string, the user-agent string, access time correlation (domain visited by the same client within a relatively short time period), and IP space proximity. Ma et al. [16,17] discuss the detection of malicious websites based on lexical and host-based features of their URL (e.g., number of dots) with the intuition that malicious URLs exhibit certain common distinguishing features. Zhang et al. [36] use term frequency/inverse document frequency (TF-IDF) algorithm to tackle malicious URL detection, and Zhao et al. in [37] tackle the same problem using Cost-Sensitive Online Active Learning (CSOAL).

One of the first studies that explore DNS traffic analysis is [31] which proposes the construction of a passive DNS database by aggregating and collecting all unique, and successfully resolved DNS queries. This database is widely referred to as pDNS and is greatly adopted and researched in the security community. In this regard, Bilge et al. [3] introduce EXPOSURE, a system that employs large-scale, passive DNS analysis to detect malicious domains using features such as the number of distinct IP addresses per domain, number of the domains sharing an IP, average TLL, the percentage of numerical characters. In a similar research, Antonakakis et al. [1], propose Notos by focusing on the detection of agile malicious usage of DNS (e.g., fast-flux, disposable domains) using pDNS analysis. Notos distinguish itself by not only analyzing those features used in EXPOSURE, but also harvesting and analyzing complementary information such as the registration, DNS zones, BGP prefixes, and AS information. Later Antonakakis et al. [2] propose another system called Kopise. In contrast to Notos and EXPOSURE which analyze the traffic captured from local recursive DNS servers, Kopis monitor the traffic at the upper level of DNS hierarchy which pose its advantages and disadvantages. Perdisci et al. [27] investigate the detection of malicious flux service networks, and Yadav et al. address the problem of detecting algorithmically generated domain names used in domain and IP fluxes by looking at distribution of alphanumeric characters as well as bigrams of domains that are mapped to the same set of IP-addresses [34].

Our approach is fundamentally different to those mentioned above as those mostly target local features presented in proxy and DNS logs whereas we are interested in global features. We focus on identifying connected malicious entities based on their traces presented in those logs. We shall discuss our approach further in Sect. 3.

2.2 Graph-Based Inference

Inference refers to the process of reasoning about a variable based on a set of observations and evidence related to that variable. In this regard, graphs are ideal for capturing the correlation and dependency among different variables. That is the main reason why graph-based inference has been widely adopted in different research areas to tackle various inference problem with the intuition that neighboring nodes influence each other and this influence can be either homophily (i.e., nearby nodes should have similar labels) or heterophily (i.e., nearby nodes should have different labels).

The most notable and popular graph based inference techniques are *graph-based Semi-Supervised Learning, Random Walk with Restart*, and *Belief Propagation*.

Random Walk with Restarts (RWR) is initially introduced as the underlying algorithm for Google's famous PageRank [4]. At high level, PageRank algorithm uses link information to assign global *importance* scores to all pages on the web (a web page can be considered as important if other important pages point to it). Similarly, TrustRank introduced by [9] adopts PageRank with different random walks to detect web spams by propagating *trust* label rather than importance. Other researchers have also built on top of TrustRank with minor changes introducing Distrust Rank and SybilRank [5,32].

Semi-Supervised Learning (SSL) techniques adopt the inference problem in machine learning to utilize unlabeled data with the intuition that similar data points connected by edges which represent their similarity should have same labels (also known as label propagation). Zhu et al. [38] introduce one of the pioneer works in graph-based SSL. The authors formulate the learning problem in terms of a gaussian random field on a graph in which vertices are labeled and unlabeled data and the edges are weighted similarities between vertices. Understanding the graph-based SSL is beyond the scope of this paper, to learn more, we refer the reader to [39].

Finally, Belief Propagation (BP) originally proposed by Pearl [26] also known as sum-product is one of the most efficient and popular inference algorithm used in probabilistic graphical models such as Bayesian Networks and Markov Random Fields. BP has been successfully applied to various domains such as image restoration [8], error-correcting [21], fraud detection, and malware detection [6].

For the purpose of this research, we have adopted BP due to its scalability and its success in other fields. In this regard, although there are still several important literature to cover for other graph inference techniques, the rest of this paper we will focus only on BP and the most influential literature that have adopted BP for the purpose of threat detection. To better understand the difference between the described graph-based inference techniques we would like to refer the reader to [15] where Koutra et al. compare *graph-based Semi-Supervised Learning, Random Walk with Restart*, and *Belief Propagation*, as this task is also beyond the scope of this paper and perhaps left to our future work.

2.3   Belief Propagation

Marginal probability estimation in graphs is known to be NP-complete, however, belief propagation provides a fast approximate technique to estimate marginal probabilities with time complexity and space complexity linear to the number of edges in a graph.

At the high level, BP infers a node's label from some prior knowledge about that node and other neighboring nodes by iteratively passing messages between all pairs of nodes in the graph. In this regard, in each iteration t every node i

generates its outgoing messages based on its incoming messages from neighbors in iteration $t - 1$. Given that all messages are passed in every iteration, the order of passing can be arbitrary.

Let m_{ij} denote the message sent from i to j which intuitively represents i's opinion about j's likelihood of being in state x_j. This message is a vector of messages for each possible class, i.e., m_{ij} ($x_j = malicious$) and m_{ij} ($x_j = benign$). Mathematical determined as follows:

$$m_{ij}(x_j) \leftarrow \sum_{x_i \in X} \phi(x_i)\, \psi_{ij}(x_i, x_j) \prod_{k \in N(i) \setminus j} m_{ki}(x_i) \tag{1}$$

where $N(i)$ is the set of nodes neighboring node i, and $\psi(x_i, x_j)$ is the *edge potential* which indicates the probability of a node i being in class x_i given that its neighbor j is in class x_j. $\phi(x_i)$ is called the *node potential function* which denotes the prior knowledge about a node, i.e., the prior probability of node i being in each possible class (in our case malicious and benign classes). And x_i represents a state from state space X.

The message passing phase terminates when messages do not change significantly between iterations, i.e., given a similarity threshold, the difference between the message sent from node i to node j at the iteration t and $t - 1$ is less than the threshold, or when the algorithm reaches a predefined maximum number of iteration. At the end, each node will calculate its belief which is an estimated marginal probability, or formally $b_i(x_i)(\approx P(x_i))$ which represented the likelihood of random variable X_i to take value $x_i \in \{x_{mal}, x_{ben}\}$ determined as follows:

$$b_i(x_i) = k\phi(x_i) \prod_{x_j \in N(i)} m_{ji}(x_i) \tag{2}$$

where k is a normalizing constant to ensure the node's beliefs add up to 1 [35].

The original belief propagation algorithm proposed by Pearl [26] was designed to operate on singly connected networks (tree-structured graphical models), and provides an exact inference with all nodes' beliefs converging to the correct marginal in a number of iterations equal to the diameter of the graph (at most the length of the longest path in the graph). Although the presence of loops will cause the messages to circulate indefinitely hence not allowing the convergence to a stable equilibrium, it is possible to apply the algorithm to arbitrary graphical models by ignoring the presence of any potential cycles in the graph. This is typically referred to as loopy belief propagation (LBP) [24]. The convergence of loopy belief propagation is not guaranteed and the results are considered to be approximate, however, in practice, it often arrives at a reasonable approximation to the correct marginal distribution.

We shall later describe how we have adopted and tailored LBP to incorporate our domain knowledge which through the remainder of this paper will be referred to as BP algorithm.

2.4   Threat Detection via Belief Propagation

Malware detection is one of the areas that have successfully adopted BP. In this regard Polonium [6] is one of the first works tackling the problem of malware detection using large-scale graph inference with the intuition that good applications are typically used by many users, whereas, unknown (i.e., potentially malicious) applications tend to only appear on few computers. To test this hypothesis, the authors generated an undirected, unweighted bipartite machine-file graph, with almost 1 billion nodes and 37 billion edges. The graph vertices are of two types: machine and file vertices and the edges indicate the observation of a file on a machine. Polonium was not only evaluated using a prepared validation set but also tested in the-field by Symantec. In this regard according to Symantec's experts, Polonium has significantly lifted the detection rate by 10 absolute percentage points while maintaining 1% false positive rate when compared to other existing methods. This is arguably one of the most successful research adaptation of BP and graph inference in the security domain showing the potentials of this approach.

In a similar research, Tamersoy et al. [30] propose Aesop, a very similar system, that tackles the same problem. In this regard, Aesop utilizes locality sensitive hashing to measure the similarity between files to eventually construct a file to file graph to infer the files' goodness based on belief propagation. while Polonium is more concerned with the observation of malicious files on malicious a machine (i.e., file to machine relationship), Aesop is concerned with the similarity of files (file to file relationship).

Manadhata et al. [18] adopt BP and graph inference to detect malicious domains using enterprise's HTTP proxy logs. This is achieved by running BP on a host-domain graph which captures the enterprise's host connection to external domains. The authors estimate the marginal probability of a domain being malicious based on minimal ground truth. The intuition in this research is that infected hosts are more likely to visit various malicious domains whereas user behavior on benign hosts should result in benign domain access. The authors run BP on a constructed host-domain graph showing their approach capability to classify malicious domains with 95.2% TPR with a 0.68% FPR using 1.45% ground truth (blacklisted and whitelisted entities).

Our approach described in the next section is very similar to the one described by Manadhata et al., however, while Manadhata et al. are interested in machine to domain relationship, we are interested in domain to domain, domain to IP, and IP to IP relationships. More specifically while they mine proxy logs to construct a graph based on the relationship between internal entities and external entities (i.e., connections from client machine to external domains), we mine both proxy and DNS logs to construct a graph based on the relationships between external entities themselves (e.g., domain resolving to an IP address, or domain name referring to another domain name).

Other similar research includes [40] which takes a similar approach to [18] while focusing on DNS logs rather than proxy logs. In his regard, the authors focus on three main relationships extractable from DNS logs: (1) *connectsTo* which indicates enterprise's host connected to a domain, (2) *resolvedTo* (DNS record type A) which indicates a domain resolving to an IPv4 address, and (3) CNAME which indicates a domain being an alias for another domain. [12] investigates the connection between domain, IP and URL. Oprea et al. [25] address early-stage APT detection using BP on host-domain graph extracted from proxy logs. And Rahbarinia et al. [28] propose Segugio to detect new malware-control domains based on DNS traffic analysis with a very similar intuition to [18].

3   Our Approach

3.1   Problem Description

Formally we formulate our inference problem as follows:

Given:

- An undirected graph $G = (V, E)$ where V corresponds to the collection of domain names and IP addresses, and E corresponds to the set of relationships between those domain and IP nodes. V and E are extracted from events in proxy and DNS Logs.
- Binay class labels $X \in \{x_{mal}, x_{ben}\}$ defined over V, where x_{mal} represents malicious label, and $P(x_{mal})$ the probability of belonging to class malicious. Note that $P(x_{mal})$ and $P(x_{ben})$ sums to one.

Find: The marginal probability $P(X_i = x_{mal})$, i.e., the probability of node i belonging to class malicious.

3.2   Graph Construction

The graph $G = (V, E)$ is constructed from events in the proxy and DNS logs.

The set of vertices V consists of two types of nodes: *domain names* and *IP addresses*. Domain names are valid parts of a fully qualified domain name (FQDN) excluding the top-level domain (TLD). For instance, considering x.example.com as a given FQDN, we then take example.com as the second-level domain and x.example.com as the third-level domain. Domain names are extracted from destination URLs in proxy logs, and the query section of A records presented in DNS logs. IP addresses are validated IP version 4 addresses observed in DNS logs (A records), and occasionally in proxy logs (sometimes the URL contains an IP address rather than a FQDN, also some proxy servers log the resolved IP address).

The set of edges E expresses three distinct relationships: *subdomainOf*, *referredTo*, and *resolvedTo*. In this regard, the subDomainOf relationship captures the dependency between different level of a FQDN, e.g., x.example.com is a subDomainOf example.com. This relationship is extracted from any valid FQDN logged in DNS or proxy logs. referredTo captures the connection between two domain/IP nodes if one has referred to the other one. This feature is extracted from the referer field in HTTP request-header logged in proxy logs. And finally, resolvedTo captures the DNS resolution of a domain name to an IPv4 address, which is presented in DNS logs and occasionally in proxy logs. Figure 1 shows the graph constructed from raw events presented in DNS and proxy logs, and illustrates different type of nodes and relationships used in graph G.

Fig. 1. Domain-ip graph constructed from a sample of raw events in DNS and proxy logs showing the association between domain and IP nodes using *subdomainOf*, *referredTo*, and *resolvedTo* relationships

Our Intuition for These Three Relationships is: First, the usage of subdomains is one of the simplest yet effective techniques used by cyber criminals (e.g., DGA and domain shadowing) to evade blacklisting. Intuitively, different levels of a FQDN should belong to the same class. For instance, if x.example.com is listed as a malicious entity by a threat intelligence feed, it is likely that example.com and any other k-level domain under example.com (e.g., y.example.com) is also malicious. Second, the majority of the malware serving networks are composed of a tree-like structure in which the victims are usually redirected through various hops before landing on the main distribution site [20]. Although different victims might land on totally different sites, the redirection paths are usually overlapped. Furthermore, the HTTP referrer is also set while a domain (e.g., a website) is loading its modules from potentially different servers, therefore, indicating association among different domains. In this regard, the HTTP referrer can be used to infer the probability of a node being malicious based on the neighboring malicious nodes that have referred to it or it has referred to. One could also expand the referrer list by implying "referring" based on the correlation among different requests presented in proxy logs (e.g., requests from the same client in a short period of time) And finally, if a domain is listed as a malicious, intuitively we could assume that the resolved IPv4 address of that domain should also be labeled malicious at least for the duration of that resolution and vice versa.

3.3   Adaptation of BP

In this section, we describe our adaptation of BP algorithm described in Sect. 2 while incorporating domain knowledge, ground truth, and relationship weights.

Node Potential: As previously explained the node potential represents the prior knowledge about the state of each node. In this regard, we will assign different node potential to domain and IP nodes based on the ground truth. For example, we assign a prior $P(X_i = x_{mal}) = 0.99$ to the node i, if i is presented in the collected malicious domain/IP list, or assigning $P(X_i = x_{mal}) = P(X_i = x_{ben}) = 0.5$ for the nodes that are neither in the malicious list nor in the benign list (i.e., they are equally likely to be malicious or benign). Note that we avoid assigning a probability of 1 to any nodes to account for possible errors in the ground truth. Table 1 shows the node potentials assigned to each vertex on the graph, based on the prior knowledge (belief).

Table 1. Node potential based on the original state

Node	P (malicious)	P (benign)
Malicious	0.99	0.01
Benign	0.01	0.99
Unknown	0.5	0.5

Edge Potential: We will adjust the edge potential matrices to capture the intuition that neighboring nodes are more likely to have the same state due to a homophilic relationship.

Moreover, due to the fact that our graph consists of three unique edge types (referredTo, resolvedTo, subDomainOf) it is important to introduce a way to incorporate edge weight (importance). For example, two neighboring nodes that are connected via resolvedTo relationship should influence each other more than two nodes that are connected via referredTo. This edge weight is also incorporated in the edge potential. Table 2 shows the adjusted edge potential matrices.

Table 2. Edge potentials matrices

$\psi_{ij}(x_i, x_j)$	$x_j = benign$	$x_j = malicious$
$x_i = benign$	$0.5 + w\epsilon$	$0.5 - w\epsilon$
$x_i = malicious$	$0.5 - w\epsilon$	$0.5 + w\epsilon$

We experimented with different edge potential (adjusting ϵ) and although we noticed changes in final probability distributions, the end results were comparable as long as the weights captured the importance of different relationships. After experimenting with different w and ϵ and we appointed them as follows: $w_{referredTo} = 0.5$, $w_{resolvedTo} = 1.5$, $w_{subdomainOf} = 1.5$, and $\epsilon = 0.1$. It is worth to mention that although the edge weights seem trivial in this research, they will have a much higher impact when adding more edge types, therefore we will investigate them further in our future work.

Message Passing. There are two variants of message updating and passing protocol in BP: *asynchronous* and *synchronous*. At high level, in asynchronous BP, also known as sequential updating scheme, messages are updated and passed one at a time, whereas, in synchronous BP, also known as parallel updating scheme, messages are updated and passed in parallel.

Although BP is computationally efficient, i.e., the running time scales linearly with the number of edges in the graph, it is not sufficient to run it in the asynchronous mode for a graph of billion nodes and edges. Therefore, for large graphs, it is crucial to adopt parallel BP which can utilize multi-core architecture and parallelly execute the message updates and beliefs calculations.

4   Implementation

Due to the scalability requirements, we have implemented the BP algorithm with parallel updating scheme using Apache Spark framework. Apache Spark, the successor to Hadoop MapReduce is one of Apache's open-source projects that has gained so much momentum in both industry and academic due to its power of handling big data analytics. We have not only implemented the BP algorithm in Spark but also the *extract, transform, load* (ETL) modules as well as the graph itself. This design makes it possible to not only scale up (i.e., take advantage of more powerful hardware) but also scale out (i.e., distributing all modules to different machines).

Our implemented system is composed of five modules: (1) *Extraction*, (2) *Transformation*, (3) *Ground Truth Construction* (GTC), (4) *Loading*, and (5) *BP* as shown in Fig. 2. In summary, the extraction module, preprocesses the DNS and proxy logs by extracting, parsing, and validating the fields of interest as described in the previous sections. Then the transformation module converts the extracted values into unique vertices and edges. The ground truth construction (GTC) module is responsible for combining and adjusting the collected list of malicious/benign domain and IPv4 addresses, removing duplicate and the unmatched entities (malicious and benign entities that are in ground truth but not observed in the event logs). This module is also responsible for carefully selecting the validation set. The loading module receives the output of the transformation and GTC modules to construct a property graph and labeling each vertex based on ground truth (malicious, benign, unknown). And finally, BP module converts the constructed graph to Markov Random Field with the provided node and edge potentials, then runs the implemented BP algorithm to compute the beliefs following the procedure described in the previous section. In order to avoid numerical underflow (zeroing-out values), the whole math performed by BP module is carried in the log domain.

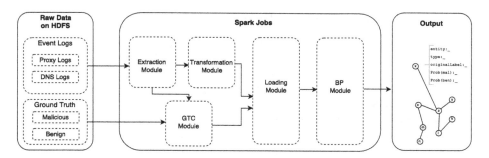

Fig. 2. System architecture diagram

5   Experimental Setup

5.1   Dataset Description

For the purpose of this research, we had access to one-day proxy and DNS logs collected from a large global enterprise. More specifically, 0.74 TB (terabytes) of proxy logs and 1.2 TB of DNS logs containing DNS requests and responses.

There is a total of 0.91B (billion), and 0.35B events in DNS and proxy logs respectively. After running ETL modules on those events we were capable of extracting approximately 1.89M (million) unique vertices and 4.29M unique edges.

5.2   Ground Truth Description

To assign priors to domain and IP vertices, a ground truth set was prepared by collecting a list of known malicious domain and IP addresses from both a commercial threat intelligence platform and various freely available sources including (but not limited) to Google Safe Browsing, AlienVault Open Threat Exchange, malwaredomainlist.com, malwaredomains.com. Similarly, we obtained a list of known benign domains from Cisco Umbrella (top one million most popular domains).

Ultimately, we were capable of collecting approximately 1M (million) unique malicious domains, 1M unique malicious IP addresses, and 1M unique benign domains. Once we checked those against our event logs we had a total of 2.12K (thousand) matched malicious entities and 0.29M (million) matched benign entities. This large gap and bias in the ground truth are due to the fact that it is quite unlikely for the enterprise hosts to be massively infected, i.e., the domains visited by the client were more likely to be benign rather than malicious. Therefore we had to adjust the benign data set to hold a balance between malicious and benign entities.

5.3   Hardware Setup and Runtime

Due to the fact that the entire modules are implemented in Apache Spark, it is possible to run the proposed approach on any configuration of hardware. In this regard, for the purpose of this research, we ran our experiment on a Spark cluster configured with 28-core 2.00 GHz linux machine with 100 GB of RAM.

Although, investigating the efficiency and the performance of the modules is beyond the scope of this research, to get a grasp of its performance, using the dataset and the hardware described above, the Extraction, Transformation, Ground Truth Construction, and Loading Modules all together take almost 50 min. In other words, 50 min to read the raw proxy and DNS logs as well as the collected GT, preprocess them, and write a parquet file containing the prepared unique vertices and unique edges. Then the BP module takes almost 90 min to read that parquet file, construct the Markov network and run 7 iterations of the described BP.

As discussed before, since there is no guarantee of BP convergence, it is important to introduce a convergence threshold. During our experiments, we noticed that 7 to 10 iterations were sufficient to get a reliable estimate. That means after 10 iterations the difference between the messages sent from i to j in iteration t compared to $t - 1$ was negligible. It is worth to mention that the definition of negligible (i.e., convergence threshold) must be proportional to the edge potential matrices. In this regard, trying to spot small convergence threshold while assigning large values to w, or ϵ will produce many unnecessary iterations. In our experiment we set it to 0.01. This is due to the fact that our choice for the edge potential metrics forced a high influence.

It also worth to mention that despite our effort to adopt various techniques and design patterns to increase the performance of our modules, we noticed some idle time in the BP module which we suspect is due to our setup. In this regard our hardware setup with 100 GB of memory seems to be insufficient to hold the whole graph while running the BP and therefore causing SWAPs, IOs, as well as heavy garbage collection. It is possible to greatly improve the above numbers using various techniques suggested by Apache Spark[1] to tune the performance even on the same hardware setup.

6   Results and Discussion

In this section, we describe the evaluation of our approach based on the data set, ground truth and the experimental setup described above.

6.1   Validation

As mentioned before, one the GTC module's tasks is to carefully select a list of samples for the purpose of validation. In this regard, after constructing the ground truth which consists of a balanced number of matched malicious and

---

[1] http://spark.apache.org/docs/latest/tuning.html

benign entities (i.e., domains and IP addresses), the GTC module carefully marks n samples for *validation* and the rest for *training*. Then the BP module uses the training set to set up the priors and assigns an unknown prior to nodes marked for the validation.

This validation set must be chosen carefully as it is quite likely that a node presented in the validation set would have no path to any node presented in the training set therefore not allowing us to properly evaluate our system. This is due to the fact that it is quite rare to find two connected malicious entities both presented in a blacklist or a TI feed (e.g., finding a domain and its resolved IP address both listed in a retrievable list). The majority of these feeds, only list the malicious entities they have observed (e.g., the IP address of the phishing site, or the domain name for a malware hosting domain).

Hence, before taking the samples, we had to calculate the connected components in our GT and choose the validation samples from those. For example, if we take node i as a malicious node for validation, it must have a path to at least another malicious node within the constructed graph. Furthermore, to hold a balance between benign and malicious nodes, we took half of the samples from malicious connected components and the other half from benign connected components.

We present our detection capability as Receiver Operating Characteristic (ROC) plot as shown in Fig. 3. This is achieved by thresholding malicious belief of nodes presented in the validation set. For instance, given a threshold t, and a node i, if i's malicious belief, $P(X_i = x_{mal}) > t$, then we predict i as malicious; else benign. This prediction is then compared to the i's original label to determine this detection as false positive, true positive, false negative, or true negative. After repeating this procedure for all the nodes in the validation set, it is possible to compute FPR and TPR for a given threshold t. And finally, plot the ROC based on different selections of t in the range of $[0,1]$.

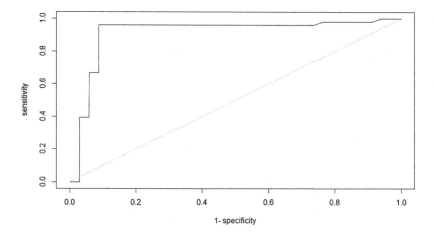

Fig. 3. Receiver Operating Characteristics (ROC) plot

As we can see the area under the ROC curve (AUC) is 91% (the higher the AUC, the better the classification), while we achieve 96% TPR with an 8% FPR.

6.2 Analysis of False Positives and False Negatives

To better understand the classification accuracy and the reason for the high FPR, we investigated the false positives (FPs) and the false negatives (FNs), i.e., benign domains that were wrongly classified as malicious and malicious entities that were wrongly classified as benign. We noticed the following observation when investigating these entities.

The majority of the FNs were entities associated with either cloud-based or online advertising services which introduce a significant challenge to our approach. For instance, we noticed that although some services were marked malicious in our ground truth, after running BP they were classified as benign due to their association with more benign entities. This decision making is reasonable as it does not fully make sense to mark an advertising platform completely malicious due to one malicious ad. Other FNs were malicious IP addresses that our system classified as benign, once investigated, we realized that although they may have been malicious at some point, that was no longer true. This classification can also be explained as these IP addresses were managed by cloud-based services that have reassigned those IP address.

FPs fell into two groups, first, entities that were classified wrongly due to a bad report from a TI source. For example, we noticed that there were some sub-domains that had their top-level domain wrongly blacklisted by Cisco Web Security Appliance[2] and therefore propagated to one of the threat intelligence sources we consumed, causing the subDomainOf relationship to overpower all the other referredTo relationships and eventually be classified as malicious. Second, entities that system correctly identified as malicious despite the fact that they were labeled benign in GT. For instance, we were able to identify 6 entities that had turned malicious just recently and the system was capable of detecting those based the referredTo relationship to other malicious entities.

In summary, the FNs and FPs were mostly the result of bad GT (inaccurate threat intelligence), and the attempt of the system to correct that inaccuracy. This investigation shows that although it is better to validate the crawled and consumed threat intelligence, it is not crucial as such system with more paths could potentially correct the TI inaccuracy.

6.3 Previously Unknown Malicious Entities

We also investigated the ability of our approach to detect new malicious entities (i.e., entities that were not presented in the ground truth). After running the BP, we selected the top 100 entities that were assigned a high probability of belonging to class malicious and did not exist in the GT.

---

[2] https://www.cisco.com/c/en/us/products/security/web-security-appliance/index.html.

Although validating these entities is a challenging task (i.e., how one decides maliciousness), for the purpose of this research we manually validated those entities and concluded maliciousness if we observed a reputable threat intelligence source (e.g., VirusTotal[3], URLVoid[4], AlienVault Open Threat Exchange[5]) reporting on that entity. It is also worth to mention that for this task, we discarded the indicator's time stamp (i.e., the time in which that entity was seen). This is due to the fact that, investigating and validating the maliciousness period, is itself an extremely challenging task.

74% of those entities were, in fact, malicious entities that did not exist in our GT, but have been reported as malicious by several other TI sources. These entities were mostly domains and IP addresses associated with services running on CloudFront[6]. 9% were entities that we could not find any information about. They seem to be either services that were active for a short period of time and detected to be malicious based on their previous association with malicious entities, or the result of DGA. However, we could not validate those intuitions as there was no trace of them on the internet. And the rest were entities that were classified wrongly.

In summary, investigating previously unknown malicious entities showed that our approach was capable of detecting new malicious entities that were not presented in our ground truth. And despite the fact that there were some misclassified entities (FPs), this approach is still extremely effective as blocking these FPs would not have a drastic effect, due to the fact that the main reason for classifying them as malicious, was, not being associated with major benign entities.

7   Future Work

One of the limitations of our work is the experimental setup. In this regard, we only had access to one day of proxy and DNS logs. It could be interesting to investigate how increasing the volume of the event logs will affect the detection. One could expect to have a better detection accuracy, as there will be more paths within the graph.

Next, there was a time gap of 6 months between our ground truth preparation and events collected by the enterprise's servers, i.e., the event logs were already 6 months old by the time we got access to them. This could potentially introduce various errors into our detection capabilities as usually threat intelligence feeds are time sensitive. It would be interesting to evaluate this system on live event logs and based on more accurate ground truth.

The next limitation of this system as in its current status is the fact that a malicious entity (e.g., a malicious domain) is capable of defeating the system by

---

[3] https://www.virustotal.com.
[4] http://www.urlvoid.com.
[5] https://otx.alienvault.com/.
[6] https://aws.amazon.com/cloudfront.

referring to many benign entities. Although it is quite unlikely that this is currently happening, to prevent such scenario, one could adjust the edge potential to only allow propagation in one direction. We plan to investigate this behavior in our future work.

Furthermore, in this paper, we only focused on three main relationships that directly connect domain names and IPv4 addresses. However, one could investigate indirect relationships such as nameServerFor, mailServerFor, aliasFor, with the intuition that cyber criminals tend to reuse infrastructure for their malicious entities. Additionally, it is also possible to take other host-based relationships into consideration (e.g., user agent, IP address, MAC address), thus enabling the propagation of the client machines' reputation to domains and IP addresses (a similar approach to [18, 40]).

In addition, it is also possible to look into enriched relationships such as registrar information, IP ranges, ASN, and BPG in order to construct a larger graph with a higher connectivity. Antonakakis, et al. [1] make use of BGP, AS, and registration features as part of their feature set to detect malicious domains. [25] uses IP space proximity to measure the similarity between domains, [7, 33] investigate features such as name servers, and registrant information to detect malicious domains. In this regard, the investigation of these combined relationships pose an interesting direction for the future work.

Finally, one could combine the global features (i.e., the features that would allow us to either directly or indirectly connect two entities) together with local features, such as, URL structure, port number, request/response length, and etc. This combination of global and local features should, in theory, improve the accuracy.

8   Conclusion

In this paper, we tackled the problem of detecting malicious domains and IP addresses by transforming it into a large-scale graph mining and inference problem. In this regard, we proposed an adaptation of belief propagation to infer maliciousness based on the concept of guilt-by-association using *subdomainOf*, *referredTo*, and *resolvedTo* relationships between IP and domain nodes. We evaluated our approach by running an adaptation of loopy belief propagation on a graph constructed from 2TB of proxy and DNS logs collected from a global enterprise. The results showed that our system attained a TPR of 96% at 8% FPR. While investigating the FP and FN we noticed the mistakes in the GT which was corrected by our system. We also investigated the system's ability to detect previously unknown malicious entities and demonstrated its capability to extend threat intelligence and blacklist by detecting new malicious entities.

References

1. Antonakakis, M., Perdisci, R., Dagon, D., Lee, W., Feamster, N.: Building a dynamic reputation system for DNS. In: USENIX Security Symposium, pp. 273–290 (2010)
2. Antonakakis, M., Perdisci, R., Lee, W., Vasiloglou II, N., Dagon, D.: Detecting malware domains at the upper DNS hierarchy. In: USENIX Security Symposium, vol. 11, pp. 1–16 (2011)
3. Bilge, L., Kirda, E., Kruegel, C., Balduzzi, M.: Exposure: finding malicious domains using passive DNS analysis. In: NDSS (2011)
4. Brin, S., Page, L.: The anatomy of a large-scale hypertextual web search engine. Comput. Netw. ISDN Syst. **30**(1), 107–117 (1998)
5. Cao, Q., Sirivianos, M., Yang, X., Pregueiro, T.: Aiding the detection of fake accounts in large scale social online services. In: Proceedings of the 9th USENIX Conference on Networked Systems Design and Implementation, p. 15. USENIX Association (2012)
6. Chau, D.H.P., Nachenberg, C., Wilhelm, J., Wright, A., Faloutsos, C.: Polonium: tera-scale graph mining and inference for malware detection. In: Proceedings of the 2011 SIAM International Conference on Data Mining, pp. 131–142. SIAM (2011)
7. Felegyhazi, M., Kreibich, C., Paxson, V.: On the potential of proactive domain blacklisting. LEET **10**, 6 (2010)
8. Freeman, W.T., Pasztor, E.C., Carmichael, O.T.: Learning low-level vision. Int. J. Comput. Vis. **40**(1), 25–47 (2000)
9. Gyöngyi, Z., Garcia-Molina, H., Pedersen, J.: Combating web spam with trustrank. In: Proceedings of the Thirtieth International Conference on Very Large Data Bases, vol. 30, pp. 576–587. VLDB Endowment (2004)
10. Holz, T., Gorecki, C., Rieck, K., Freiling, F.C.: Measuring and detecting fast-flux service networks. In: NDSS (2008)
11. Howard, F.: A closer look at the Angler exploit kit (2015). https://news.sophos.com/en-us/2015/07/21/a-closer-look-at-the-angler-exploit-kit/
12. Huang, Y., Greve, P.: Large scale graph mining for web reputation inference. In: 2015 IEEE 25th International Workshop on Machine Learning for Signal Processing (MLSP), pp. 1–6. IEEE (2015)
13. Scarfone, K.A., Hoffman, P.: Guidelines on firewalls and firewall policy (2009). https://www.nist.gov/publications/guidelines-firewalls-and-firewall-policy
14. Kotov, V., Massacci, F.: Anatomy of exploit kits. In: Jürjens, J., Livshits, B., Scandariato, R. (eds.) ESSoS 2013. LNCS, vol. 7781, pp. 181–196. Springer, Heidelberg (2013). https://doi.org/10.1007/978-3-642-36563-8_13
15. Koutra, D., Ke, T.-Y., Kang, U., Chau, D.H.P., Pao, H.-K.K., Faloutsos, C.: Unifying guilt-by-association approaches: theorems and fast algorithms. In: Gunopulos, D., Hofmann, T., Malerba, D., Vazirgiannis, M. (eds.) ECML PKDD 2011. LNCS (LNAI), vol. 6912, pp. 245–260. Springer, Heidelberg (2011). https://doi.org/10.1007/978-3-642-23783-6_16
16. Ma, J., Saul, L.K., Savage, S., Voelker, G.M.: Beyond blacklists: learning to detect malicious web sites from suspicious URLs. In: Proceedings of the 15th ACM SIGKDD International Conference on Knowledge Discovery and Data Mining, pp. 1245–1254. ACM (2009)
17. Ma, J., Saul, L.K., Savage, S., Voelker, G.M.: Identifying suspicious URLs: an application of large-scale online learning. In: Proceedings of the 26th Annual International Conference on Machine Learning, pp. 681–688. ACM (2009)

18. Manadhata, P.K., Yadav, S., Rao, P., Horne, W.: Detecting malicious domains via graph inference. In: Kutyłowski, M., Vaidya, J. (eds.) ESORICS 2014. LNCS, vol. 8712, pp. 1–18. Springer, Cham (2014). https://doi.org/10.1007/978-3-319-11203-9_1

19. Manners, D.: The user agent field: analyzing and detecting the abnormal or malicious in your organization (2011)

20. Mavrommatis, N.P.P., Monrose, M.A.R.F.: All your iframes point to us (2008)

21. McEliece, R.J., MacKay, D.J.C., Cheng, J.F.: Turbo decoding as an instance of pearl's "belief propagation" algorithm. IEEE J. Sel. Areas Commun. **16**(2), 140–152 (1998)

22. Mockapetris, P.: Domain names - concepts and facilities (1987). https://www.ietf.org/rfc/rfc1034.txt

23. Mockapetris, P.: Domain names - implementation and specification (1987). https://www.ietf.org/rfc/rfc1034.txt

24. Murphy, K.P., Weiss, Y., Jordan, M.I.: Loopy belief propagation for approximate inference: an empirical study. In: Proceedings of the Fifteenth Conference on Uncertainty in Artificial Intelligence, pp. 467–475. Morgan Kaufmann Publishers Inc. (1999)

25. Oprea, A., Li, Z., Yen, T.F., Chin, S.H., Alrwais, S.: Detection of early-stage enterprise infection by mining large-scale log data. In: 2015 45th Annual IEEE/IFIP International Conference on Dependable Systems and Networks (DSN), pp. 45–56. IEEE (2015)

26. Pearl, J.: Probabilistic Reasoning in Intelligent Systems: Networks of Plausible Inference. Morgan Kaufmann, Burlington (2014)

27. Perdisci, R., Corona, I., Dagon, D., Lee, W.: Detecting malicious flux service networks through passive analysis of recursive DNS traces. In: Annual Computer Security Applications Conference, ACSAC 2009, pp. 311–320. IEEE (2009)

28. Rahbarinia, B., Perdisci, R., Antonakakis, M.: Segugio: efficient behavior-based tracking of malware-control domains in large ISP networks. In: 2015 45th Annual IEEE/IFIP International Conference on Dependable Systems and Networks (DSN), pp. 403–414. IEEE (2015)

29. Rocha, L.: Neutrino exploit kit analysis and threat indicator (2016)

30. Tamersoy, A., Roundy, K., Chau, D.H.: Guilt by association: large scale malware detection by mining file-relation graphs. In: Proceedings of the 20th ACM SIGKDD International Conference on Knowledge Discovery and Data Mining, pp. 1524–1533. ACM (2014)

31. Weimer, F.: Passive DNS replication. In: First Conference on Computer Security Incident, p. 98 (2005)

32. Wu, B., Goel, V., Davison, B.D.: Propagating trust and distrust to demote web spam. MTW **190** (2006)

33. Xu, W., Sanders, K., Zhang, Y.: We know it before you do: predicting malicious domains. In: Proceedings of the 2014 Virus Bulletin International Conference, pp. 73–77 (2014)

34. Yadav, S., Reddy, A.K.K., Reddy, A.N., Ranjan, S.: Detecting algorithmically generated domain-flux attacks with DNS traffic analysis. IEEE/ACM Trans. Netw. **20**(5), 1663–1677 (2012)

35. Yedidia, J.S., Freeman, W.T., Weiss, Y.: Understanding belief propagation and its generalizations. Exploring Artif. Intell. New Millennium **8**, 236–239 (2003)

36. Zhang, Y., Hong, J.I., Cranor, L.F.: CANTINA: a content-based approach to detecting phishing web sites. In: Proceedings of the 16th International Conference on World Wide Web, pp. 639–648. ACM (2007)

37. Zhao, P., Hoi, S.C.: Cost-sensitive online active learning with application to malicious URL detection. In: Proceedings of the 19th ACM SIGKDD International Conference on Knowledge Discovery and Data Mining, pp. 919–927. ACM (2013)
38. Zhu, X., Ghahramani, Z., Lafferty, J., et al.: Semi-supervised learning using Gaussian fields and harmonic functions. ICML **3**, 912–919 (2003)
39. Zhu, X., Lafferty, J., Rosenfeld, R.: Semi-supervised learning with graphs. Carnegie Mellon University, Language Technologies Institute, School of Computer Science (2005)
40. Zou, F., Zhang, S., Rao, W., Yi, P.: Detecting malware based on DNS graph mining. Int. J. Distrib. Sens. Netw. (2015)

Twisting Lattice and Graph Techniques to Compress Transactional Ledgers

Rémi Géraud$^{(\boxtimes)}$, David Naccache, and Răzvan Roşie

ENS, CNRS, INRIA and PSL Research University, Paris, France
{remi.geraud,david.naccache,razvan.rosie}@ens.fr

Abstract. Keeping track of financial transactions (e.g., in banks and blockchains) means keeping track of an ever-increasing list of exchanges between accounts. In fact, many of these transactions can be safely "forgotten", in the sense that purging a set of them that compensate each other does not impact the network's semantic meaning (e.g., the accounts' balances). We call *nilcatenation* a collection of transactions having no effect on a network's semantics. Such exchanges may be archived and removed, yielding a smaller, but equivalent ledger. Motivated by the computational and analytic benefits obtained from more compact representations of numerical data, we formalize the problem of finding nilcatenations, and propose detection methods based on graph and lattice-reduction techniques. Atop interesting applications of this work (e.g., decoupling of centralized and distributed databases), we also discuss the original idea of a "community-serving proof of work": finding nilcatenations constitutes a proof of useful work, as the periodic removal of nilcatenations reduces the transactional graph's size.

Keywords: Nilcatenation · Subset-sum problem · Lattices · LLL

1 Introduction

Transactional ledgers are a staple of modern technology—whether it is data, value or goods being tracked, concrete implementations require strong consistency guarantees and efficient data structures. Furthermore, it may be useful to perform sanity checks on data, such as in bank ledgers for instance, to ensure that an account's balance is legitimate (i.e., the amount can be explained as an inflow of money, whose source can be tracked). In another setting, namely centralized DBMS, it is typical to undergo high volumes of concurrent queries; auditing data causes extra pressure on the various locking strategies. Moreover, in some blockchains/distributed ledgers, the ledger keeps track over time of *all* individual transactions, and these transactions are *atomic*: they cannot be merged or split. As time passes, the number of transactions grows, and so do the storage requirements.

To give an intuition of the network and storage requirements, the full Bitcoin blockchain claimed (as of June 2017) more than 120 GB [1]. Hopefully, most

© ICST Institute for Computer Sciences, Social Informatics and Telecommunications Engineering 2018
X. Lin et al. (Eds.): SecureComm 2017, LNICST 238, pp. 108–127, 2018.
https://doi.org/10.1007/978-3-319-78813-5_6

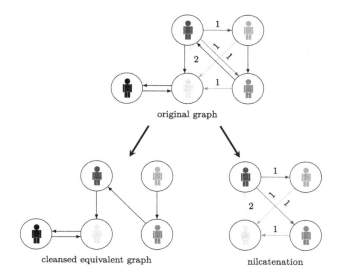

original graph

cleansed equivalent graph   nilcatenation

Fig. 1. Decoupling a transactional multigraph into the cleansed part (left) and the nilcatenation (right).

users do not need to archive the full database, and Bitcoin proposes a form of compressed partial storage.[1] That being said, even with Bitcoin's Merkle-tree-based mechanism, there is considerable stress on the network, in particular when users need to access historic data.

Nevertheless, we think it is important to look for generic solutions beyond this particular case, and these motivational examples highlight the realisation that storage requirements will only grow. This calls for a research into how information can be efficiently stored or cleansed, i.e., *represented*. Such a representation should be *semantically preserving*, at least to the extent that the effect of no transaction is lost in the process.[2] In many cases, some details might become irrelevant (e.g., the precise number of successive transactions between two parties) and it might be possible then to clump some events together into a more compact form. Finding efficient representations of transactional graphs is the main purpose of this work.

The Nilcatenation Problem. Throughout the following sections, we will consider a set of accounts, and the transactions between them represented as labeled edges between nodes in a graph G. More precisely, G is a *multigraph*, as multiple transactions are allowed between users. See Appendix A for precise definitions of these standard notions.

The "nilcatenation problem" (NCP) on G consists in constructing a transaction graph G' which is smaller than G, but provably semantically equivalent.

---

[1] So do a few other cryptocurrencies, such as Ethereum.

[2] Which is very different from "that no transaction is lost in the process".

That the new and old information coincide should be easy to verify, and the shorter ("purged") graph makes duplication and checking easier. Concretely, this consists in identifying a subgraph that can be removed without affecting any account's balance (see Fig. 1). The notion of nilcatenation is generic, in that it applies to any graph labeled with numbers[3], and therefore bears applications in many situations.

Applications. In the context of distributed (anonymous) cryptocurrencies and distributed ledgers, we point out that identifying nilcatenations can be seen as a service to the community, and therefore be rewarded... in coins, just as any other proof of work. In that respect, the perspective of a cryptocurrency allowing users to mine by nilcatenation is not unrealistic, and we discuss it in Sect. 5.

Alternatives. The problem of bookkeeping is certainly not new, and many solutions have been proposed to address storage requirements. In the traditional (centralized) setting, complete archiving is the *de facto* solution.

As we mentioned above, trying to avoid the perpetual duplication of history was an early concern of cryptocurrencies, starting with Bitcoin's Merkle-based fast transaction checking [13]. With this scheme, it is possible to verify that a transaction has been accepted by the network by downloading just the corresponding block headers and the Merkle tree. Nodes that do not maintain a full blockchain, called *simplified payment verification* (SPV) nodes, use Merkle paths to verify transactions without downloading full blocks. Other cryptocurrencies use forgetful mechanisms (e.g. Ethereum and [5,6]). Such approaches prevent auditability, insofar as the origin of old enough transactions is lost.

Related Work. In general, constructing a *useful* proof-of-work (PoW) is a hard problem. One direction, mentioned in [2], is to use the PoW mechanism to solve specific problems having a well-investigated computational complexity (e.g. orthogonal vectors). Some cryptocurrencies, such as Primecoin, propose PoWs challenging the workers to find chains of prime numbers. A different working thread relies on proofs-of-storage, where a prover needs to demonstrate to a verifier that it stores a specific file. Filecoin is a recent, incipient proposal where the miners get rewarded by the amount of data they store. To the best of our knowledge, no prior work attempted to introduce of PoW for finding nilcatenations in a multigraphs, aiming to compress data.

1.1   Contributions

- We introduce and formalise the nilcatenation problem, phrased in terms of weighted multigraphs. We show—via a reduction to the (multi-dimensional) subset-sum problem—that NCP is **NP**-complete (Theorem 1).

---

[3] It may be possible to extend our work to some more general algebraic structures.

- Our main contribution is the introduction of efficient algorithms to find nil-catenations (Sect. 4), which is optimal when the underlying subset-sum problem has a low enough density (Theorem 3). This is expected to be realistic, assuming maximal transactions are in the order of billions of economical units. Our approach is based on a combination of graph-theoretical and lattice reduction techniques, as explained in Sect. 3.3.
- As a complement, we explore the possibility of using NCPs as proofs of work, to be used in cryptocurrency-like settings (Sect. 5). Reward models are presented and the practical precautions needed to correctly fine-tune the resulting incentive are also discussed. We analyse cheating strategies and provide countermeasures. Along the way, we point out several interesting questions raised by the analysis of this problem.

2   Preliminaries

Notations. We will make use of the following standard notations: $[n]$ denotes the set $\{1, \ldots, n\}$. For a set S, we denote by $s \leftarrow_\$ S$ the action of sampling s uniformly at random from S, and by $|S|$ the cardinality of S. PPT stands for a "probabilistic polynomial time". Polynomial-time reductions are written as $\leq_P$. We use standard notations for (multi)graphs, which are detailed in Appendix A.

2.1   The Subset-sum Problem

We recall the well-known definition of the *subset-sum problem* (SSP, [10]):

Definition 1 (Subset-sum Problem). *Given a finite set $A \subset \mathbb{Z}$, and a target value $t \in \mathbb{Z}$, find a subset $S \subseteq A$ such that $\sum_{s \in S} s = t$.*

We denote by the size of the instance the cardinality of A. The SSP is known to be **NP**-complete [9]. The multi-dimensional case considers p "parallel" SSP instances under the constraint that an index-set solution to one problem remains a solution to the other $p - 1$. The *density* of a particular SSP instance of size n is defined [11] as: $d = n/\left(\max_{a \in A} \log a\right)$. While generic SSP instances are hard to solve, low-density instances can be solved efficiently using approximation techniques or lattice reduction [7,11]. We also quickly consider:

Definition 2 (0-target Subset-sum Problem, or 0TSSP). *Given a vector $A \in \mathbb{Z}^n$, find a vector $\epsilon \in \{0,1\}^n$, $\epsilon \neq \mathbf{0}$, such that $\langle A, \epsilon \rangle = 0$, where $\langle \cdot, \cdot \rangle$ denotes the inner product.*

Proposition 1 (SSP $\leq_P$ 0TSSP). *Let $\mathcal{O}$ be a 0TSSP oracle. There exists a PPT algorithm $\mathcal{A}$ that solves an instance of an SSP problem within n calls to $\mathcal{O}$, where n denotes the size of the instance.*

Proof (Intuition). Let an SSP problem be defined by $A = \{a_1, \ldots, a_n\}$ and target sum t. We assume $a_i \neq 0, \forall i \in [n]$ and $t > 0$.[4] If all $a_i > 0$ (or $a_i < 0$), we

---

[4] If $t < 0$, we obtain an equivalent problem by changing the sign for each element a_i and for the target t.

create a new 0TSSP instance of size $n + 1$, $A' = \{a_1, \ldots, a_n, -t\}$, and query $\mathcal{O}$: a solution for A' trivially provides a solution to the original SSP instance (A, t).

When some $a_i < 0$, we set $d \leftarrow \sum_{a_i > 0} a_i$, $e \leftarrow \sum_{a_i < 0} a_i$ and construct n new 0TSSP instances:

$$B_i = \{b_1, \ldots, b_n, -t - i \cdot f\}, \quad t_i'' = 0, \ \forall i \in [n]$$

where $b_i \leftarrow a_i + f$ and $f \leftarrow |d| + |e| + t$. Observe that $b_i > 0, \forall i \in [n]$.

If the original problem has a subset sum t, then one of the new 0TSSP instances will have a solution. On the other hand, if one of these n 0TSSPs has a solution, the original SSP has a solution as well.

Let S be a solution to the i-th 0TSSP B_i, then $\sum_{j \in S} b_j = t + i \cdot f$. Equivalently, $j \cdot f + \sum_{j \in S} a_j = t + i \cdot f$, which is $\sum_{j \in S} a_j = t + (i - j) \cdot f$.

- If $i > j$, then we get that $\sum_{j \in S} a_j > d + e$, which cannot be true.
- If $i < j$, then we get that $\sum_{j \in S} a_j \leq -d - e$, which again cannot be true, since we assumed that all a_i cannot be negative.

Thus, we are only left with the possibility that $i = j$, and thus $\sum_{j \in S} a_j = t$. □

Remark 1. In fact, the polynomial reduction shown in the proof of Proposition 1 shows that SSP is equivalent with its 0 target version, both being **NP**-complete. Indeed, we trivially have 0TSSP $\leq_P$ SSP.

3   Formalising the NCP

3.1   A First Definition

In all that follows, the history of transactions is assumed to form a multigraph $G = (V, E, \phi)$, where the vertices V correspond to accounts, and a labeled edge $e = a \xrightarrow{u} b$ corresponds to a transaction from a to b of amount u, denoted as $\phi(e) = u$.

The *balance* $b(v)$ of an individual account v is given by the difference between incoming transactions and outgoing transactions, i.e., $b(v) = \sum_{e:\bullet \to v} \phi(e) - \sum_{f:v \to \bullet} \phi(f)$, where $(\bullet \to v)$ denotes all incoming edges, i.e. all the elements in E of the form (w, v) for some $w \in V$; similarly $(v \to \bullet)$ denotes all outgoing edges. Let $b(G)$ denote the vector $\{b(v) : v \in V\}$, which we refer to as the graph's *semantics*.

Definition 3 (Nilcatenation Problem, NCP). *Given a weighted multigraph $G = (V, E, \phi)$, find $\widetilde{E} \subseteq E, \widetilde{E} \neq \emptyset$, such that $b(G) = b(G - \widetilde{G})$, where $\widetilde{G} = (V, \widetilde{E}, \phi)$. We call $(\widetilde{G}, G - \widetilde{G})$ the* nilcatenation *of G.*

Remark 2. In other terms, finding a nilcatenation consists in finding edges that can be removed without impacting anyone's balance—i.e., that preserve the graph's semantics. By definition, for every vertex $\tilde{v} \in \widetilde{G}$, we thus have $b(\tilde{v}) = 0$.

3.2 NCP and SSP

Definition 4 (NCP, Alternative Definition). *Let* $G = (V, E, \phi)$ *be a weighted multigraph. Write* $V = \{v_1, ..., v_n\}$, *and represent an edge* $e : v_i \xrightarrow{r} v_j$ *as the vector* $r \cdot e_{ij} \in \mathbb{Z}^n$ *where* e_{ij} *is the vector of* $\mathbb{Z}^n$ *with* 1 *in position* j, -1 *in position* i *and* 0 *in the remaining components. This defines a bijection between* E *and* G*'s adjacency matrix* $\mathbf{E}$. *The matrix* $\mathbf{E}$ *is a list of* m *such vectors* $\mathbf{E} = (e_1, \ldots, e_m)$. *The* nilcatenation problem *consists in finding a non-zero* $\epsilon \in \{0, 1\}^m$ *such that*

$$\sum_{i=1}^{m} \epsilon_i e_i = \langle \mathbf{E}, \epsilon \rangle = 0,$$

where we have extended the notation $\langle \cdot, \cdot \rangle$ *in the obvious way. The* nilcatenation *of* G *is then defined as* $(\widetilde{G}, G - \widetilde{G})$, *where* $\widetilde{G} = (V, \widetilde{E}, \phi)$ *and* $\widetilde{E} = \{e_i \in E, \epsilon_i = 1\}$.

Remark 3. In many cases, we are chiefly interested in the largest ϵ (in terms of Hamming weight), because these result in the largest nilcatenations.

Figure 2 illustrates on a toy example the matrix $\mathbf{E}$ and identifies a nilcatenation.

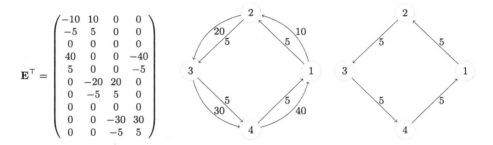

$$\mathbf{E}^\top = \begin{pmatrix} -10 & 10 & 0 & 0 \\ -5 & 5 & 0 & 0 \\ 0 & 0 & 0 & 0 \\ 40 & 0 & 0 & -40 \\ 5 & 0 & 0 & -5 \\ 0 & -20 & 20 & 0 \\ 0 & -5 & 5 & 0 \\ 0 & 0 & 0 & 0 \\ 0 & 0 & -30 & 30 \\ 0 & 0 & -5 & 5 \end{pmatrix}$$

Fig. 2. A simple support example, depicting a multigraph with a nilcatenable subgraph. $\mathbf{E}^\top$ is the transpose of the adjacency matrix introduced in Definition 4, corresponding to the multigraph (middle); the multigraph on right stands for the nilcatenation.

Remark 4. Definition 4 makes clear the parallel between the NCP and the multidimensional version of the SSP (Definition 2). For $n = 2$, the NCP problem consists of a $2 \times m$ matrix with no 0 entries, the goal being to find an index subset for the columns that sum up to the all-zero column. Thus, the NCP and 0TSSP are exactly the same problem when $n = 2$.

In fact, more is true: NCP can be seen as a *multi-dimensional* variant of the subset-sum problem with zero as target, where the entries belong to $\mathbb{Z}^{|V|}$ instead of $\mathbb{Z}$. Note however that NCP is a remarkably *sparse* special case of that multidimensional SSP.

Theorem 1 (NCP $\equiv_P$ 0TSSP)

Proof (Intuition). By the above discussion, a 0TSSP oracle provides a solution to any NCP instance. Vectors of $\mathbb{Z}^{|V|}$ can be described as **integers** using a base $|V|$ encoding. Therefore we have a reduction from 0TSSP to NCP.

Conversely, assume an NCP oracle, then we can construct an NCP instance with all zeros except in two columns (in effect, this is an $n = 2$ instance). Then, by the remark made above, the NCP oracle solves a 0TSSP instance. $\square$

Corollary 1. *NCP is NP-complete.*

Proof. This follows from the fact that SSP is **NP**-complete, then SSP $\equiv_P$ 0TSSP by Proposition 1, and NCP $\equiv_P$ 0TSSP by Theorem 1. $\square$

3.3   Solving a Generic NCP Instance

Following the previous observation, one may be tempted to leverage known SSP solving techniques to tackle the NCP. However, the reduction from NCP to SSP is not very interesting from a computational standpoint: coefficients become very large, of the order of Bb^n, where B is the upper bound of the representation of E, and b is the chosen basis. This encoding can be somewhat improved if we know the bounds $B_i^{\pm}$ for each column, because we can use better representations. However, in practice it becomes quickly prohibitive; even brute-forcing the original NCP is less computationally demanding—the subset-sum problem can be solved exactly (classically) in worst-case time $\mathcal{O}(2^m)$ by brute-forcing all combinations, and even state-of-the-art algorithms only have marginally better complexity, namely $\mathcal{O}(2^{m \cdot 0.291\cdots})$ [3,8].

If we wish to tackle the NCP directly, for $n > 2$, the meet-in-the-middle approaches inherited from subset-sum solvers do not apply, as in that case there is no total order on $\mathbb{Z}^n$. Instead we will leverage the famous LLL lattice reduction algorithm [12]. Given as input an integer d-dimensional lattice basis whose vectors have norm less than B, LLL outputs a reduced basis in time $\mathcal{O}(d^2 n(d + \log B) \log Bf)$ [14], where f stands for the cost of d-bit multiplication.

To see why lattice reduction would solve the problem, first note that E can be represented as an $n \times m$ matrix with rational (or integer) coefficients. It is a sparse matrix, having (at most) two non-zero entries per column, i.e. (at most) $2m$ non-zero entries out of nm. Let I_n be the $n \times n$ identity matrix and let $\mathcal{E} = (I_n|E)$ be the result of concatenating the two blocks: $\mathcal{E}$ is an $n \times (n + m)$ matrix, having at most $n + 2m$ non-zero elements out of $n(n + m)$.

Now if there is a solution to the NCP, then it belongs to the lattice generated by $\mathcal{E}$. In particular this is a short vector: if this is the shortest vector, then LLL[5] will find it with overwhelming probability. The question of solving the NCP from a solution to the shortest-vector problem (SVP) depends on the density, topology and weights' probabilistic distribution of the multigraph. A proof of optimality for some graph families (denoted "hub graphs") is worked out in Sect. 3.4.

---

[5] Or BKZ [17], or one of their variants. We use these algorithms here as SVP oracles.

In practice, however, using this technique directly is impractical. The main reason is that LLL's complexity on a large graph is dominated by m^3, and real-world ledgers handle many transactions, with m being of the order of 10^8 *per day*. Therefore this intuition needs improvements to become practical, as we discuss in Sect. 4.

3.4   Solving NCP Using a Single SVP Oracle Query

The algorithm we propose in Sect. 4 relies on LLL as an SVP-oracle, to find a short vector and solve the given NCP instance. In other terms, we claim that *specific* NCP instances can be solved, with overwhelming probability, using a single query to an SVP-oracle.

We also extend the work of [7,11,15] where similar proofs are laid out for SSP and multi-dimensional SSP (henceforth MDSSP) instances with uniformly sampled entries. As a starting point, we recall the following result:

Theorem 2 (Pan and Zhang [15]). *Given a positive integer A, let a_{ji} where $j \in [n]$, $i \in [m]$ be independently uniformly sampled random integers between 1 and A, $e = (e_1, e_2, \ldots, e_m)$ be an arbitrary non-zero vector in $\{0,1\}^m$ and $s_j = \sum_{i=1}^{m} a_{ji} e_i$, where $j \in [n]$.*

If the density $d < 0.9408\ldots$ then with overwhelming probability the multi-dimensional subset sum problem (MDSSP) defined by a_{ji} and $s_1, \ldots, s_n$ can be solved in polynomial time with a single call to an SVP oracle.

One can attempt to reduce the NCP instance to an MDSSP one; however, the impeding issue is the distribution of a_{ji}, which is not uniform in general, so the above result does not apply directly. However, we may hope to get a useful result, based on the crux point that we are working with sparse subsets of a_{ji} (as defined by the edge multiset E of our multigraph). Here, by a sparse subset, we mean one where at least half of the elements are 0.

We use the following notion: call a "hub multigraph", one that contains a vertex directly connected to all the other nodes (we call this vertex a "hub vertex"). For such graphs, we can prove the following:

Theorem 3 (NCP for Hub Multigraphs). *Given $A \in \mathbb{N}$, let a_{ji} where $j \in [n]$, $i \in [m]$ be a sparse set of independently sampled (not necessary uniform) integers between 0 and A, $e = (e_1, e_2, \ldots, e_m)$ be an arbitrary non-zero vector in $\{-1, 0, 1\}^m$ and $s_j = \sum_{i=1}^{m} a_{ji} e_i = 0$, where $j \in [n]$.*

If the density $d < 0.488\ldots$ and if there exists i such that $\forall j \in [n], a_{ji} \neq 0$, then the MDSSP defined by a_{ji} and $s_1, \ldots, s_n$ can be solved in polynomial time with a single call to an SVP oracle.

Proof. We follow closely the proof of [15], and diverge in the last part of their demonstration, i.e., in obtaining the probability for an SVP-oracle to return an accurate answer, given a uniform, low density instance of the MDSSP.

The multigraph is finite, therefore at a given point in time, the maximum number of arcs connecting one vertex with another one is bounded by M, thus

$\forall i : \deg^+(v_i) \leq M \wedge \deg^-(v_i) \leq M$. Let $m = M \cdot n \cdot (n-1)/2$ and let $\mathbf{e}$ be the solution to the SSP problem.

We begin by defining an appropriate basis for a lattice. The idea is to write the basis as

$$\mathbf{B} = \begin{pmatrix} \mathbf{I_m} | N \cdot \mathbf{E^t} \\ \mathbf{b_{m+1}} \end{pmatrix}$$

where $\mathbf{I_m}$ stands for the identity matrix, $\mathbf{E}$ is the multigraph's adjacency matrix (as described in Definition 4) and $N > \sqrt{(m+1)/4}$. The last component of the basis, namely $\mathbf{b_{m+1}}$, will be a special vector of the form:

$$\mathbf{b_{m+1}} = (\tfrac{1}{2}, \tfrac{1}{2}, \ldots, \tfrac{1}{2}, \tfrac{1}{2}, 0, 0, 0, \ldots, 0, 0)$$

Let L be the lattice generated by $\mathbf{b_1}, \mathbf{b_2}, \ldots, \mathbf{b_{m+1}}$. We can observe that $\mathbf{e} = (e_1 - \tfrac{1}{2}, e_2 - \tfrac{1}{2}, \ldots, e_m - \tfrac{1}{2}, 0, 0, \ldots, 0) \in L$. We define X as the set of vectors different by $\pm\mathbf{e}$ (with a smaller norm) that belong to L:

$$X = \{\mathbf{v} \in L : \|\mathbf{v}\| \leq \|\mathbf{e}\| \text{ and } \mathbf{v} \notin \{\pm\mathbf{e}, \mathbf{0}\}\}$$

Roughly, we want to prove that with overwhelming probability, the problem has a unique solution, which is given by $\pm\mathbf{e}$. We make two remarks and prove the second one:

1. If $X = \emptyset$, then $\pm\mathbf{e}$ are the only short non-zero vectors in L.
2. $X = \emptyset$ with probability exponentially close to 1.

The crux part in the proof is bounding the value of $\Pr[X = \emptyset]$. Let $\mathbf{v} \in X$ such that $\mathbf{v} = \sum_{i=1}^{m+1}(z_i \cdot \mathbf{b_i})$, having $z_i \in \{-1, 0, 1\}$. Since $N > \sqrt{(m+1)/4}$, the last n elements in $\mathbf{v}$ must be 0. Hence, we set up $\mathbf{v}$ as follows:

$$v_i = z_i + \frac{1}{2}z_{m+1}, \text{ for } i \in [m]$$

$$v_{m+1} = \frac{1}{2}z_{m+1},$$

$$v_{m+1+j} = N \cdot \left(\sum_{i=1}^{m} z_i \cdot a_{ji} \right) = 0 \text{ for } j \in [n]$$

By using the previous notations, we now rewrite the condition as:

$$\sum_{i=1}^{m} a_{ji}(v_i - v_{m+1}) = \sum_{i=1}^{m} a_{ji}z_i = 0, \forall j \in [n].$$

Then, following the same technique as in [15], we let

$$D = \left\{ \mathbf{v} \in \mathbb{Z}^{n+1} \middle| \exists(z_1, \ldots, z_{m+1}) \in \mathbb{Z}^{n+1} \text{ s.t. } v_i = z_i + \frac{1}{2}z_{m+1} \wedge v_{m+1} = \frac{1}{2}z_{m+1} \right\}$$

and bound the required probability:

$$\Pr[X \neq \emptyset] \leq \Pr\left[\sum_{i=1}^{m} a_{ji}(v_i - v_{m+1}) = 0 : j \in [n] \wedge \mathbf{v} \notin \{\mathbf{0}, \pm\mathbf{e}\} \right] \times |\{\mathbf{v} \in D \mid \|\mathbf{v}\| \leq \|\mathbf{e}\|\}| \qquad (1)$$

- If z_{m+1} is even, then $\|\mathbf{v}\| = \sqrt{\frac{m+1}{4}}$, implying $|\{\mathbf{v} \in D \mid \|\mathbf{v}\| \leq \|\mathbf{e}\|\}| = 2^m$.
- If z_{m+1} is odd, the cardinality of the second expression in Eq. 1 corresponds to the number of points with integer coordinates in the $m+1$ dimensional ball centered at the origin and having radius $\sqrt{\frac{m+1}{4}}$, which is bounded by $2^{1+(m+1)c}$, where c is a constant described in [11] ($c = 2.047\ldots$).

Thus we get that $|\{\mathbf{v} \in D \mid \|\mathbf{v}\| \leq \|\mathbf{e}\|\}| \leq 2^c$. All that remains is to approximate the first term in Eq. 1.

We now **diverge** from the original proof and investigate what happens if the a_{ji} are not sampled uniformly at random, but rather form a sparse set, following some unknown distribution. This observation is related to the way in which a_{ji} are induced by the multigraph in the blockchain we described. Thus:

$$\Pr\left[\sum_{i=1}^{m} a_{ji}(v_i - v_{m+1}) = 0 : j \in [n] \wedge \mathbf{v} \notin \{\mathbf{0}, \pm\mathbf{e}\}\right] \leq \Pr\left[\sum_{i=1}^{m} a_{ji}z_i = 0 : j \in [n]\right]$$
$$= \prod_{j=1}^{n} \Pr\left[\sum_{i=1}^{m} a_{ji}z_i = 0\right]$$

(2)

We stress that the form of z_i obtained in [15] differ from the form of z_i we use, due to the fact that in our version of the problem, the target sum in the MDSSP is 0. As an observation, the previous probability bound we obtain in Eq. 2 can be equivalently stated: $\Pr[\sum_{i=1}^{m} z_i \cdot a_{ji} = 0] \iff \Pr[\mathbf{z}^t \cdot \mathbf{a_j} = 0]$, where $\mathbf{a_j} = (a_{j1}, \ldots, a_{jm})$.

Let $\mathbf{E^t}$ be the matrix defined by a_{ji} (example given in Fig. 2). The condition $\Pr[\mathbf{z}^t \cdot \mathbf{a_j} = 0]$ states that $\mathbf{z}$ is in the left nullspace of the matrix $\mathbf{E^t}$ (which is sparse, given that the a_{ji} form a sparse set). Because $\mathbf{e}$ is already in the left nullspace ($\mathbf{e}^t \cdot \mathbf{E^t} = \mathbf{0}^t$), the problem to solve becomes now to find the probability that $\mathbf{z}$ exists and that it is shorter than $\mathbf{e}$.

If the matrix $\mathbf{E^t}$ has rank $n - 1$ then the dimension of the left nullspace is 1 (following from the Rank-Nullity theorem); hence $\mathbf{z}$ is an integer multiple of $\mathbf{e}$, thus failing to have a shorter norm than $\pm\mathbf{e}$. Finally, we estimate the probability of $\text{rank}(\mathbf{E^t}) < n - 1$. Observe the form of $\mathbf{E^t}$, as the matrix associated to a random "hub" multigraph ($\exists i$ such that $\forall j, a_{ji} \neq 0$). If there exists a row j for which $a_{ji} \neq 0$, then we can apply elementary matrix operations, such that $\mathbf{E^t}$ will have a sub-matrix of size $n - 1$ which is diagonal.

Hence, we used the hypothesis to prove that $\Pr[\mathbf{z}^T \cdot \mathbf{a_j} = 0] = 0$, which is equivalent to the claim that there is no shorter vector than $\pm\mathbf{e}$ in L, when $L = (\mathbf{I_m}|\mathbf{E}^t)$, with $\mathbf{E}$ being the matrix of a "hub" graph. As shown above, for such graphs, $\Pr[X = \emptyset] = 1$, which completes the proof.   □

4   Faster NCP Solving

While the lattice reduction approach discussed in Sect. 3.3 cannot be efficiently applied directly on a large multigraph to find a solution to the NCP, it can work on small multigraphs. We describe in this section a simple pruning algorithm that reduces the problem size dramatically. This algorithm breaks down the NCP instance into many smaller NCP sub-instances, which can be tackled by LLL. Furthermore, each instance can be dealt with independently, which makes our approach parallelizable. Importantly, nothing is lost in this divide-and-conquer strategy: any solution in the original instance can be found in the pruned instance(s).

In other terms, we first leverage the particular form NCP—namely the graph-related properties—to conservatively reduce problem size. This is possible thanks to the following two observations:

1. We only need to consider strongly connected components. Indeed, if $v, w \in V$ belong to two different strongly connected components of G, then by definition there is no path going from v to w and back. Therefore any amount taken from v cannot be returned, so that the balance of v cannot be conserved. Thus, all the edges of $\widetilde{E}$ are contained in a SCC of G.
2. Let H be a nilcatenation of G. Then H must satisfy a "local flow conservation" property: the flow (Definition 6) through any cut of H is zero; equivalently, the input of each vertex equates the output. Subgraphs failing to satisfy this property are dubbed *obstructions* and can be safely removed.

Definition 5 (First-Order Obstruction). *Let $G = (V, E, \phi)$ be a weighted multigraph. A vertex $v \in V$ is a* first-order obstruction *if the following conditions hold:*

 – *The in-degree and out-degree of v are both equal to 1.*
 – *The weights of the incoming and the outgoing edges are different.*

We may define accordingly "zeroth-order" obstructions, where the minimum of the in- and out-degree of v is zero (but such vertices do not exist in a strongly connected component), and *higher-order* obstructions, where the in- or out-degree of v is larger than 1, still satisfying the local-flow conservation property:

Definition 6 (Local conservation SSP). *Let $v \in V$, let E_I the multiset of v's in-edges, and E_O the multiset of v's out-edges. The* local conservation SSP *is the problem of finding $S_I \subseteq E_I, S_O \subseteq E_O$ such that $\sum_{e \in S_I} \phi(e) = \sum_{f \in S_O} \phi(f)$.*

4.1 Strongly Connected Components

It is straightforward to see that a partition of G into k strongly connected components corresponds to a partition of E into $(k + 1)$ multisets: each strongly connected component (SCC) with its edges, and a remainder of edges that do not belong to SCCs. As explained above, this remainder does not belong to $\widetilde{E}$.

The partition of a graph into strongly connected components can be determined exactly in linear time using for instance Tarjan's algorithm [18]. To each component, we can associate a descriptor (for instance a binary vector defining a subset of E), and either process them in parallel or sequentially, independently.

This corresponds to reordering V so that E is a block diagonal matrix, and working on each block independently.

4.2   The Pruning Algorithm

We can now describe the pruning algorithm (Fig. 3), that leverages the observations of this section.

Data: Multigraph $G = (V, E, \phi)$
Result: Multigraphs $\{G_i = (V_i, E_i, \phi_i)\}$, having no simple obstruction
Function Pruning*(G)*:
    $\{G_1, \ldots, G_\ell\} \leftarrow$ Tarjan(G)
    foreach $G_k = (V_k, E_k, \phi_k)$ **do**
        foreach $v \in V_k$ **do**
            if $\min(d_v^+, d_v^-) = 0$ **then**
             | remove all edges connected to v in E_i
            else if $d_v^+ = d_v^- = 1$ **then**
              denote e_{in} the incoming edge
              denote e_{out} the outgoing edge
              if $\phi_k(e_{in}) \neq \phi_k(e_{out})$ **then**
                | delete e_{in} and e_{out} from E_k
              end
            end
        end
    end
    return $\{G_1, \ldots, G_\ell\}$
end

Fig. 3. The pruning algorithm, used to split components which fail to satisfy the local flow conservation property.

The algorithm works as follows: (1) decomposes the graph into its SCCs; then (2) removes first-order obstructions[6] in each component. Removing obstructions may split a strongly connected component in twain (we can keep track of this using a partition refinement data structure), so we may repeat steps (1) and (2) until convergence, i.e., until no obstruction is found or no new SCC is identified. This gives the obvious recursive algorithm `RecursivePruning`.

Complexity Analysis. The average-time complexity of this algorithm depends a priori on the graph being considered, and in particular on how many SCCs we may expect, how probable it is that an obstruction creates new SCCs, how frequent obstructions are, etc. If we turn our attention to the worst-case behaviour, we can in fact consider a multigraph for which this algorithm would take the most time to run.

Tarjan's algorithm has time complexity $\mathcal{O}(n + m)$, and first-order obstruction removal has time complexity $\mathcal{O}(n)$. Thus the complete pruning's complexity is determined by the number of iterations until convergence. The worst graph would thus have one obstruction, which upon removal splits its SCC in two; each sub-SCC would have one obstruction, which upon removal splits the sub-SCC in two,

---

[6] Higher-order obstructions can also be removed, although there is a trade-off to consider, see Remark 5.

etc. Assuming that this behaviour is maintained all the way down, until only isolated nodes remain, we see that there cannot be more than $\log_2 n$ iterations.

Each iteration creates two NCP instances, each having $n/2$ vertices and around $m/2$ edges. Thus the complete pruning algorithm has worst-case complexity $\mathcal{O}((m + n) \log n)$.[7]

Remark 5. If we now extend the pruning algorithm to also detect higher-order obstructions, say up to a fixed order d, then the obstruction removal step costs $\mathcal{O}(2^d n) = \mathcal{O}(n)$ since 2^d is a constant. Thus the asymptotic worst-case complexity is not impacted. However the constant term might in practice be a limiting factor, especially since higher-order obstructions may be rare. Making this a precise statement requires a model of random multigraphs (see the open questions in Sect. 6). To compensate for the extra cost of detecting them, order-d obstructions should be frequent enough: we *conjecture* in an informal manner that this is not the case, and that there is no gain in going beyond the first order in most practical scenarios.

4.3   Fast NCP Solving

We can now describe in full the fast NCP solving algorithm in Fig. 4. It consists in first using the pruning algorithm of Sect. 4.2, which outputs many small NCP instances, and then solving each instance using an SVP oracle (in practice, a lattice reduction algorithm) as described in Sect. 3.3.

> **Data:** Multigraph $G = (V, E, \phi)$
> **Result:** Nilcatenations $\{\widetilde{G}_i\}$
> **Function** FindNilcatenations(G):
> | $\{G_1, \ldots, G_\ell\} \leftarrow$ RecursivePruning(G)
> | **foreach** $G_k = (V_k, E_k, \phi_k)$ **do**
> | | $\widetilde{E}_k \leftarrow$ SVP$(I|E_k)$
> | | $\widetilde{G}_k \leftarrow (V_k, \widetilde{E}_k, \phi_k)$
> | **end**
> | **return** $\{\widetilde{G}_1, \ldots, \widetilde{G}_\ell\}$
> **end**

Fig. 4. The complete fast NCP solving algorithm.

Remark 6. For completeness, we mention that the algorithm in Fig. 4 is theoretically *guaranteed* to return a result if the density of each problem defined by G_k and used to feed the SVP oracle is small, and G_k defines a hub-graph.

If we are only interested in the largest connected nilcatenation, as will be the case in the following section, then only the largest subgraph needs to be returned.

5   NCP-Solving as a Proof of Work

A proof of work is a computational problem whose solution required (extensive) computation. Such constructions were first introduced to fight against e-mail spam, but they are increasingly popular at the heart of distributed cryptocurrencies, since the inception of the Bitcoin blockchain [13].

---

[7] We ignore the fact that each subproblem can be worked on independently in parallel.

In almost all cases however, computing a proof of work requires operations that, as such, are useless. We think that this waste of energy is unnecessary, and that to a certain extent it is possible to use alternative mechanisms to achieve "community-serving" proofs of work.

The idea in what follows is to recognise as a valid proof of work the result of ledger nilcatenations. As we discussed above, the NCP is hard, and intuitively, larger nilcatenations would require more work to be found. Rewarding nilcatenations would encourage users to look for them and publish them (in the form, maybe, of "nilcatenation blocks", NCB); as a result, all users would benefit from a more compact representation. We stress here that this is **only** a possibility, and that there are implementation details to be accounted for, if this idea is integrated in any existing blockchain.

To give a flavour, we distinguish between **unpermissioned** and **permission-based** blockchains. In the former case, a typical scenario consists of an anonymous user owning multiple public/private key pairs for the transactions in which he/she is involved. Suppose the execution of a transaction involves sending an amount to an address identified through the hash of a fresh public-key; then the addresses (accounts) are not repeated multiple times. In such a case, the multigraph representation of the transactional ledger contains no loops, resulting in trivial, empty nilcatenations. In the latter case—**permission-based** blockchains—the accounts represented via addresses can be reused and therefore a representation of the set of transactions via a multigraph is possible. This enables a PoW implementation based on the NCP problem.

Theorem 4 (Proof of Work). *Let $\mathcal{B} = [\mathcal{B}_1, \ldots, \mathcal{B}_n]$ stand for a transactional blockchain, blocks $\mathcal{B}_i$ being generated by a (deterministic) function $f_n : \mathcal{X}_1 \times \cdots \times \mathcal{X}_n \to \mathcal{X}_{n+1}$ sampled from a family $\{\mathcal{F}_n\}$, for $n \geq 1$. Let $G = (V, E, \phi)$ be the multigraph representation of the transactions and $(\widetilde{G}, G - \widetilde{G})$ a nilcatenation. There exists a blockchain $\mathcal{B}'$ for the multigraph $(G - \widetilde{G}, E - \widetilde{E}, \phi)$ and a blockchain $\mathcal{B}''$ for $(\widetilde{G}, \widetilde{E}, \phi)$, both obtained through $\{\mathcal{F}\}$.*

Proof (Intuition). The proof is straightforward. If the transactional multigraph can be decoupled into its nilcatenation and cleansed multigraph, two ledgers $\mathcal{B}', \mathcal{B}''$ can be generated (through the means of f) for each of these components, and the union of their transactions in $\mathcal{B}', \mathcal{B}''$ can be used to check the validity against $\mathcal{B}$. If the number of transaction in a block is fixed, dummy exchanges with a value of 0 can be artificially added. □

Concretely, an NCB is similar to "standard" blocks, but checked in a different way. Instead of containing only transactions, NCBs also contain a description of the nilcatenation. Users responsible for publishing NCBs get rewarded as a function of the size of their nilcatenations. Users receiving nilcatenation blocks would check them and accept them only if they are valid.[8]

---

[8] Note that NCBs need not be removed from the blockchain.

Cheating Strategies. Before NCBs can be used as a proof of work, however, we must consider cheating strategies and fine-tune the incentives, so that honest computation and quick dissemination are the rational choices for miners. We identify two cheating strategies, dubbed ghost cycles and welding, for which we suggest countermeasures. We then discuss the question of how to reward NCBs.

The following subsections clarify these points; as a summary, to use NCP as a proof of work, one should: (1) require that nilcatenations obey the ghostbusting rules of Sect. 5.1, i.e., belong to a randomly-sampled subgraph of a snapshot of the transaction multigraph; (2) only accept connected nilcatenations as explained in Sect. 5.2; (3) be rewarded linearly in the size of the nilcatenation, as described in Sect. 5.3.

5.1   Ghost Cycles

Ghost Cycle Creation. One attack is the following: a cartel of users may create many transactions with the sole intent to make nilcatenation easier. They may create cycles or cliques of transactions, then reap and share the reward for "finding" this removable set. In fact, they merely need to graft their transactions to an existing, large enough sequence of transactions. Such a strategy could take the following form:

1. Find the longest path of identical transactions that point to the controlled node: write them $v_i \xrightarrow{r} v_{i+1}$, with $i = 0, \ldots, n$ and v_{n+1} being the nodes under adversarial control. Note that r is fixed. Searching for such a cycle can be done by starting from v_{n+1}, and performing a depth-first search on the transaction graph.
2. Compute the expected gain of a nilcatenation-based proof of work that removes $(n + 1)$ transactions: call it G_{n+1}. Such a quantity would be publicly known, and we may assume for simplicity that $G_n > G_m$ whenever $n > m$.
3. If $G_{n+1} > r$, make a new transaction $v_{n+1} \xrightarrow{r} v_0$; then send the nilcatenable cycle $\{v_0, \ldots, v_{n+1}\}$ as a "proof of work".

By using several accounts, artificially-long chains can be created by a user, only to be immediately "found" and removed. We dub these "ghost cycles" (this includes cliques and other structures as well), and this form of cheating is of course highly undesirable.

Ghostbusting. There are two (complementary) ways to combat ghosts. An economical approach, discussed in Sect. 5.3, consists in making ghosts unprofitable. A technical countermeasure, called *ghostbusting* is described in Appendix B, ensures that ghosts cannot be leveraged, except perhaps with negligible probability. The rationale is to ask for miners to solve the NCP on a *randomized* subset of the transaction graph, where it is very unlikely that they have enough accounts to construct ghost cycles.

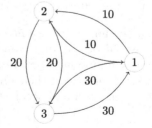

Fig. 5. Concatenation of three independent nilcatenations.

5.2   Welding Nilcatenations

Another interesting question, motivated by the increased number of cryptocurrency miners who parallelize their work, is to measure how much parallel computation helps in solving the NCP. As described previously (see Sect. 4), the pruning algorithm generates many small graphs that can be dealt with independently.

In our scenario, after gathering enough nilcatenations published by peers, a user could assemble them into a single, larger instance and claim the rewards for it. From a theoretical standpoint, a large, disjoint nilcatenation satisfies Definition 4.

However the incentive there would be to produce quickly many small nilcatenations. This is, again, highly undesirable.

As a first countermeasure, users reject disconnected nilcatenations (this is easy to check), i.e., only accept connected ones. This encourages miners to look for larger nilcatenations, and also limits the efficiency of miner pools.

Such an approach does not prevent, in theory, users from joining together partial nilcatenations into a larger one. Consider for instance the graph of Fig. 5, where user 1 finds a nilcatenation 10–10, user 2 finds 20–20, and user 3 finds 30–30. Then they may collude to generate a larger, connected nilcatenation.

However, we *conjecture* that it is a hard problem in general to assemble nilcatenations that are not disjoint into a larger one; or at the very least, that this is as expensive as computing them from scratch. Furthermore, the ghostbusting constraints reduce the possibilities of collusion by preventing adversarially-controlled nodes from participating in the nilcatenation graph.

5.3   Determining the Reward

Using the NCP as a proof of work, we reward users that computed a valid nilcatenation. The exact reward should be finely tuned to provide the correct incentives. Note that this depends on whether or not the cryptocurrency applies transaction fees.

Transaction Fees. If such fees apply, then creating a ghost is a costly operation from an adversarial point of view. The system should set the reward for a nilcatenation with m edges, denoted reward(m), to be lower than or equal to the cost of creating a ghost of size m, which we may assume is $m \cdot c$ where c is the transaction fee. We may settle for reward(m) $= m \cdot c$. Similar techniques may apply where a larger spectrum of transaction fees are available.

Note that using a sub-linear reward function is counter-productive, as it encourages producing many small nilcatenations, rather than a large unique one. Conversely, using a super-linear reward function, while encouraging larger nilcatenations, also makes ghosts profitable above a certain size.

No Transaction Fees. If there are no transaction fees, then the aforementioned method does not apply (since $c = 0$). For cryptocurrencies that do not use transaction fees, ghostbusting (Sect. 5.1) limits the creation of ghost cycles. In such cases, the reward function may be an arbitrary affine function in the size of the nilcatenation.

6   Conclusion and Open Questions

We initiate the problem of nilcatenation, a soon-to-be pressing question for transactional graphs and distributed ledgers of appreciable size. This problem, dubbed NCP, is formalised and shown to be **NP**-complete. We introduce an algorithm, based on a combination of graph and lattice reduction techniques, that finds nilcatenations on a given transactional graph in most practical settings (and approximations thereof in other cases). Since nilcatenations are hard to find, easy to check, and useful, we suggest using them as community-serving proofs of work. We discuss the precautions and incentives of doing so, and discuss how nilcatenation blocks may complement the incentives of cryptocurrencies.

To the best of our knowledge this is the first community-serving proof of work w.r.t. ledger compression to be described and analysed in the literature.

Future Research Directions. As regards future research directions, this work opens many interesting questions in both the theoretical and practical fields:

- What are the graph-theoretic properties of transaction ledgers? Only very few studies address this question [16]. In particular, what would be a realistic "random labeled multigraph" model? Can anything be said about its strongly connected components?
- What is the typical size of an SCC after having run the pruning algorithm?
- How frequent are higher-order obstructions, and what is the most efficient way to detect them?
- Given measurable properties of a transaction ledger (density, degree distribution, etc.), what is the probability that our algorithm returns the optimal result? In other terms, how can the results of Sect. 3.4 be extended to more general settings?
- Are there profitable cheating strategies that work in spite of the proposed countermeasures?

Acknowledgements. The authors want to thank the anonymous reviewers for valuable comments. Roşie was supported by EU Horizon 2020 research and innovation programme under grant agreement No H2020-MSCA-ITN-2014-643161 ECRYPT-NET.

A   Graphs and Multigraphs

We will make use of the following standard definitions: A *graph* $G = (V, E)$ is the data of a finite set V and $E \subseteq V \times V$, called respectively the vertices and edges of G. A sequence of edges $(s_1, t_1), \ldots, (s_n, t_n)$ such that $t_i = s_{i+1}$ for all

$1 \leq i < n$ is called a *directed path* from s_1 to t_n. The *degree* of a vertex $v \in V$ is the number of edges connected to v. The *in-degree* (resp. *out-degree*) of v is the number of edges ending at (resp. starting at) v. In this work we consider an extension of graphs where edges can be repeated and are labeled: A *labeled multigraph* is denoted by $G = (V, E, \phi)$ where now E is a multiset of couples from $V \times V$ (not just a set), and $\phi : E \to \mathbb{Z}$ gives the label associated to each edge[9]. We will use the following notation: If $e = (a, b) \in E$, and $r = \phi(e)$, we represent the edge e by writing $a \xrightarrow{r} b$. The definition of strongly connected components is given below and it naturally extends to multigraphs. In particular, any strongly connected component is connected; the converse does not hold.

Definition 7. *If $G = (V, E)$ is a graph, then a strongly connected component (or SCC) of G is a maximal subgraph of G such that for each two distinct nodes x and y, there exists a directed path from x to y, and a directed path from y to x.*

B   Ghostbusting

A natural idea to fight ghost cycles could be to restrict which part of the transaction graph can be nilcatenated. It could be restricted in "time", or in "space", but straightforward approaches are not satisfactory:

- For instance, if B_t denotes the blockchain at a given time t, we may only consider a threshold time T, and only accept nilcatenations for B_s, where $t - s > T$. However this does not prevent an adversary from creating ghost cycles over a longer period of time.
- Alternatively, observe that since the transaction that "closes the cycle" originates from the cheater, we may require that the nilcatenation doesn't contain this node. This countermeasure is easily bypassed by creating a new account whose sole purpose is to claim the rewards from the associated proof of work.

What the above remarks highlight is the need that nilcatenations are computed on a graph that is *not under the adversary's control*.

Using the procedure described in Fig. 6, we can sample a subgraph SG uniformly in the transaction graph. This procedure relies on the idea that a block on the chain depends on its ancestors, because it carries digests from all the preceding blocks (as per the blockchain mechanism). The principle of ghostbusting is that only nilcatenations among the nodes of SG should be accepted.

Ghostbusting(t, B_t):
1. Let b_t be the block at time t
2. seed $\leftarrow \mathbf{H}(b_t)$
3. $SG \leftarrow$ SubGraphGen(seed)
4. return SG

Fig. 6. The ghostbusting procedure creates a subgraph SG by hashing the defining block b_t. Miners are required to find nilcatenations in SG.

---

[9] We may equivalently replace $\mathbb{Z}$ by $\mathbb{Q}$. Since we know that, in practice, transactions have a finite precision, we may always think of them as integers.

Note that the sampling procedure must be deterministic, so that verifiers can ensure that the nilcatenation indeed belongs to the authorised subgraph, and so that miners all address the same task.

Here we use a pseudorandom function $\mathbf{H}$ for which computing preimages is difficult, i.e. given y it should be hard to find x such that $\mathbf{H}(x) = y$. Most standard cryptographic hash functions are believed to satisfy this property—however we should refrain from specifically using SHA-256 itself, because Bitcoin's proof of work results in blocks whose SHA-256 hash has a large known prefix.

A simple workaround is to use for $\mathbf{H}$ a function different from standard SHA-256, e.g. $\mathbf{H}(x) = \text{SHA-256}(0\|x)$.

The subgraph SG is obtained via $\texttt{SubGraphGen}$ by selecting *nodes* (i.e. accounts, which may be under adversarial control), and all edges between these nodes. To be accepted, a nilcatenation should only contain nodes from this subgraph.

Proposition 2. *Assuming that the adversary has control over k out of n nodes, and that the sampled subgraph contains ℓ nodes, with $k < n/2$, the probability that at least $m \leq \ell$ of these nodes are under adversarial control is*

$$\frac{1}{2k - n} \cdot \frac{k^m}{n^\ell} \left(k^{\ell+1-m} - (n - k)^{\ell+1-m} \right).$$

In the limit that $k \ll n$, this probability is approximately $(k/n)^m$, which does not depend on the choice of ℓ.

Proof. We assume that $\mathbf{H}$ is a random oracle [4]. Thus SG is sampled perfectly uniformly in G. Thus, a given node will have probability k/n to be controlled by an adversary. There are ℓ nodes in SG, hence the probability of choosing at least m adversarial nodes is 0 if $m > \ell$ and $\Pr[C_{\geq m}] = \Pr[C_m] + \Pr[C_{m+1}] + \cdots + \Pr[C_\ell]$ otherwise, where C_p is the event where exactly p chosen nodes are under adversarial control. Since the nodes are picked uniformly at random,

$$\Pr[C_p] = \left(\frac{k}{n}\right)^p \left(1 - \frac{k}{n}\right)^{\ell-p}.$$

Therefore,

$$\Pr[C_{\geq m}] = \Pr[C_m] + \cdots + \Pr[C_\ell] = \sum_{p=m}^{\ell} \left(\frac{k}{n}\right)^p \left(1 - \frac{k}{n}\right)^{\ell-p}$$

$$= \frac{1}{2k - n} \left(k \left(\frac{k^m}{n^m} \left(1 - \frac{k}{n}\right)^{\ell-m} + \frac{k^\ell}{n^\ell} \right) - \frac{k^m}{n^{m-1}} \left(1 - \frac{k}{n}\right)^{\ell-m} \right)$$

$$= \frac{1}{2k - n} \cdot \frac{k^m}{n^\ell} \left(k^{\ell+1-m} - (n - k)^{\ell+1-m} \right)$$

Assuming $k \ll n$, we can use a series expansion in k/n of the above to get:

$$\Pr[C_{\geq m}] = \left(\frac{k}{n}\right)^m \left(1 + \frac{k}{n}(m - \ell + 1) + O((k/n)^2)\right),$$

and in particular the result follows. $\qquad\square$

Hence, the probability that an adversary succeeds in creating a large ghost cycle when the ghostbusting procedure is used gets exponentially small.

As regards how the "seed block" b_t should be chosen, we only require that all miners and verifiers agree on a deterministic procedure to decide whether b_t is acceptable. For simplicity, we suggest to instantiate b_t as the last block in the blockchain.

References

1. Bitcoin's blockchain size (2016). https://blockchain.info/charts/blocks-size
2. Ball, M., Rosen, A., Sabin, M., Vasudevan, P.N.: Proofs of useful work (2017)
3. Becker, A., Coron, J.-S., Joux, A.: Improved generic algorithms for hard knapsacks. In: Paterson, K.G. (ed.) EUROCRYPT 2011. LNCS, vol. 6632, pp. 364–385. Springer, Heidelberg (2011). https://doi.org/10.1007/978-3-642-20465-4_21
4. Bellare, M., Rogaway, P.: Random oracles are practical: a paradigm for designing efficient protocols. In: Proceedings of the 1st ACM Conference on Computer and Communications Security, pp. 62–73. ACM (1993)
5. Bruce, J.D.: Purely P2P crypto-currency with finite mini-blockchain (2013). https://pdfs.semanticscholar.org/3f64/123ce97a0079f8bea66d3f760dbb3e6b40d5.pdf
6. Bruce, J.D.: The mini-blockchain scheme (2014). http://cryptonite.info/
7. Coster, M.J., Joux, A., LaMacchia, B.A., Odlyzko, A.M., Schnorr, C.-P., Stern, J.: Improved low-density subset sum algorithms. Comput. Complex. **2**, 111–128 (1992)
8. Howgrave-Graham, N., Joux, A.: New generic algorithms for hard knapsacks. In: Gilbert, H. (ed.) EUROCRYPT 2010. LNCS, vol. 6110, pp. 235–256. Springer, Heidelberg (2010). https://doi.org/10.1007/978-3-642-13190-5_12
9. Karp, R.M.: Reducibility among combinatorial problems. In: Miller, R.E., Thatcher, J.W., Bohlinger, J.D. (eds.) Complexity of Computer Computations. IRSS, pp. 85–103. Springer, Boston (1972). https://doi.org/10.1007/978-1-4684-2001-2_9
10. Karp, R.M.: Computational complexity of combinatorial and graph-theoretic problems. In: Preparata, F. (ed.) Theoretical Computer Science. CIME, vol. 68, pp. 97–184. Springer, Heidelberg (2011). https://doi.org/10.1007/978-3-642-11120-4_3
11. Lagarias, J.C., Odlyzko, A.M.: Solving low-density subset sum problems. J. ACM (JACM) **32**(1), 229–246 (1985)
12. Lenstra, A.K., Lenstra, H.W., Lovász, L.: Factoring polynomials with rational coefficients. Math. Ann. **261**(4), 515–534 (1982)
13. Nakamoto, S.: Bitcoin: a peer-to-peer electronic cash system (2008)
14. Nguyen, P.Q., Stehlé, D.: An LLL algorithm with quadratic complexity. SIAM J. Comput. **39**(3), 874–903 (2009)
15. Pan, Y., Zhang, F.: Solving low-density multiple subset sum problems with SVP oracle. J. Syst. Sci. Complex. **29**(1), 228–242 (2016)
16. Ron, D., Shamir, A.: Quantitative analysis of the full bitcoin transaction graph. In: Sadeghi, A.-R. (ed.) FC 2013. LNCS, vol. 7859, pp. 6–24. Springer, Heidelberg (2013). https://doi.org/10.1007/978-3-642-39884-1_2
17. Schnorr, C.P.: Block Korkin-Zolotarev bases and successive minima. International Computer Science Institute (1992)
18. Tarjan, R.: Depth-first search and linear graph algorithms. SIAM J. Comput. **1**(2), 146–160 (1972)

Privacy-Preserving Relevance Ranking Scheme and Its Application in Multi-keyword Searchable Encryption

Peisong Shen[1,2], Chi Chen[1,2(✉)], and Xiaojie Zhu[3]

[1] State Key Laboratory of Information Security,
Institute of Information Engineering, CAS, Beijing, China
{shenpeisong,chenchi}@iie.ac.cn
[2] School of Cyber Security, University of Chinese Academy of Sciences,
Beijing, China
[3] University of Oslo, Oslo, Norway
xiaojiez@ifi.uio.no

Abstract. Searchable Symmetric Encryption (SSE) which enables keyword searches on encrypted data, has drawn a lot of research attention in recent years. However, many SSE schemes do not support privacy-preserving relevance ranking which is a necessary feature for users to quickly locate the needed documents in a large number of retrieved documents. In this paper, we proposed two Privacy-Preserving Relevance Ranking (PPRR) schemes based on RSA encryption and ElGamal encryption. The proposed PPRR schemes preserve rank privacy and reduce storage cost at server side. Furthermore, we integrate PPRR with current multi-keyword SSE algorithm to achieve multi-keyword ranked search on encrypted data. Computation complexity, storage complexity and security of composite schemes are verified with an experiment on real-world dataset.

Keywords: Searchable symmetric encryption
Privacy-preserving relevance ranking · Cloud storage

1 Introduction

With wide deployment of cloud storage services, more and more users outsource their data to cloud server. However, a major concern of cloud storage service is privacy of personal data. On one hand, cloud storage service provider (CSSP) may be malicious and trade personal data for profit. On the other hand, CSSP may be compromised by attackers. Worse still, successive data breach events deepen users' concern about data privacy. To protect confidentiality of data, users usually encrypt their data before outsourcing them to cloud server. However, classical cryptographic algorithms disable information retrieval technique. For example, users cannot perform keyword search query on encrypted data to quickly retrieve the documents they want.

In recent years, many Searchable Symmetric Encryption (SSE) schemes [1–6] have been proposed to solve the problem of keyword search on encrypted data. These schemes used symmetric encryption primitives to protect the keywords and files.

© ICST Institute for Computer Sciences, Social Informatics and Telecommunications Engineering 2018
X. Lin et al. (Eds.): SecureComm 2017, LNICST 238, pp. 128–146, 2018.
https://doi.org/10.1007/978-3-319-78813-5_7

Many SSE schemes support retrieving documents containing query keywords from the cloud server. However, returned documents of these schemes are not ranked by their relevance with search query, which poses a big challenge for users to find their documents from large set of search result. This problem motivates researcher's interest in designing SSE schemes supporting relevance ranking.

Wang et al. [7] proposed ranked search symmetric encryption (RSSE) based on Order-Preserving Encryption. However, due to the limitation of OPE, their scheme cannot be extended to multi-keyword search setting. In [14], A fully homomorphic encryption (FHE) method is used to achieve privacy-preserving relevance ranking at server side. However, their scheme was inefficient due to high computation complexity of FHE algorithm.

Cao et al. [8] proposed the first scheme supporting privacy-preserving Multi-Keyword Ranked Search on Encrypted data (MRSE). Based on the innovative work in [8], many practical schemes [9–12] have been proposed to solve the problems such as accuracy, index updates and search efficiency. These creative achievements promote the application of SSE schemes in real-word cloud storage service. However, the storage cost of encrypted indexes of MRSE-based schemes is proportional to the product of dictionary size and file collection size. The size of encrypted indexes will increase quickly with size of the dictionary and file collection.

Besides, many above-mentioned schemes supporting ranked search do not protect rank privacy, i.e. rank order of search result is disclosed to server. A malicious server can correlate same queries based on rank order of search results, then crack the query based on some background knowledge of dataset, such as statistical distribution of document frequency.

In this paper, we propose two Privacy-Preserving Relevance Ranking (PPRR) schemes which has lower storage overhead and protects the rank privacy of search results. The proposed PPRR schemes utilize Term Frequency(TF)-Inverse Document Frequency(IDF) method to capture the relevance between query and documents. The relevance scores are computed in an encrypted manner on the server side. Result ranking is done at client side to protect rank privacy. In order to keep the value of TF and IDF secret, RSA encryption and ElGamal encryption are used. Based on multiplicative homomorphism of both algorithms, relevance scores are computed securely and accurately at the server side. Randomness is introduced into PPRR-2 scheme to confuse distribution of TF and IDF values. Furthermore, we integrate PPRR schemes with current multi-keyword SSE scheme to support multi-keyword ranked search on encrypted data.

The main contribution of this paper is summarized as follows:

(1) Two privacy-preserving relevance ranking algorithms are proposed. Both of PPRR schemes can protect the rank privacy and resist statistical attack in a strong threat model.
(2) We integrate PPRR schemes with a state-of-art multi-keyword SSE scheme. The composite scheme has sublinear search efficiency, low storage overhead and supports dynamic index updates.

2   Related Work

2.1   Searchable Symmetric Encryption

Song et al. [1] proposed the problem of keyword search on encrypted data for the first time. They designed a SSE scheme based on string matching to solve the problem. However, their scheme needs a sequential scan of all encrypted data to find matched documents. Curtmola et al. [2] proposed a formal definition and security notion of searchable symmetric encryption. They also constructed two SSE schemes based on an inverted-index structure. In order to keep keyword privacy and document privacy, symmetric encryption is used to encrypt the indexes. Following their work, some SSE schemes [3, 4] have been proposed to handle index updates. Kamara et al. [3] used a XOR-based private key encryption to modify encrypted pointer when dealing with linked list node addition. File deletion is handled by using a deletion array which marks deleted files. Stefanov et al. [4] designed a dynamic searchable encryption scheme with a novel hierarchical index structure. Their scheme achieves logarithmic search efficiency. However, these SSE schemes mentioned above only support single-keyword search.

Cash et al. [5] proposed the first SSE schemes supporting multi-keyword search and sublinear search efficiency. The main idea of multi-keyword search of the proposed OXT protocol is that the server firstly retrieves documents containing one keyword in query and then decides whether the other keywords of query occurs in these documents or not. To protect data privacy, they devised an oblivious shared computation protocol between client and server based on blinded exponentiation. Furthermore, in [6] they proposed several efficient single-keyword SSE constructions which can be used as components in OXT protocol. Their scheme used a dictionary structure which supports dynamic updates. They also identified the locality issue of search performance of SSE schemes and gave their solutions to fix this issue.

2.2   Searchable Encryption with Relevance Ranking

Wang et al. [7] designed an order-preserving encryption method which ranks search results based on order-preserving-encrypted TF values in single-keyword ranked search setting. Cao et al. [8] first proposed a privacy-preserving Multi-Keyword Ranked Search on Encrypted data (MRSE). Their scheme is based on vector space model, and utilizes the "coordinate matching" to capture the relevance between documents and queries. Secure kNN algorithm is used to encrypt the indexes. However, their scheme needs to sequentially scan all the encrypted document vectors to find search results. Based on MRSE architecture, many enhanced schemes [9–12, 15] have been proposed in recent years. A multi-dimensional tree is used by Sun et al. [9] to improve the search efficiency. Chen et al. [15] designed a hierarchical cluster index to speed up searches on the cloud server. Xia et al. [10] construct a tree-based index structure and propose a "Greedy Depth-first Search" algorithm to provide efficient multi-keyword ranked search. Li et al. [11] proposed an enhanced MRSE scheme supporting logic search query, they also employed classified sub-dictionaries technique to enhance search efficiency.

In order to achieve accurate relevance evaluation at the server side, Shen et al. [14] used fully homomorphic encryption (FHE) to encrypt TF and IDF values of keywords. They also integrate their FHE scheme with OXT protocol to achieve the multi-keyword ranked search semantics. In 2017, Song et al. [12] proposed a privacy-preserved full-text retrieval algorithm over encrypted data. They used hierarchical bloom filters as their encrypted index and proposed the concept of membership entropies of index words to calculate relevance between query and documents on cloud server. Jiang et al. [13] modified Cash's OXT protocol to support top-k search. They precomputed the multiplication of TF and IDF values in index-building phase, then incorporated the result into the index to support relevance score computation on the server side. In order to protect privacy of TF*IDF values and rank order, they utilize the additive homomorphic property of paillier cryptosystem. However, their scheme doesn't support TF/IDF updates well.

3 Problem Specification and Prerequisite

3.1 Notations and Symbols

We list some notations which will be used in the following sections:

F –   File collection

F_j –   the j-th file in file collection or the file with an identifier j

$|F_j|$ –   the number of unique keywords in F_j

w –   keyword

$F(w)$ –   identifiers of files containing keyword w

n –   number of documents in file collection

D –   dictionary composed of all keywords extracted from file collection

m –   number of keywords in dictionary

Q –   query

T_Q –   the trapdoor of query Q

λ –   security parameter

K –   secret key

$TF_{w,j}$ –   the term frequency of keyword w in j-th file

DF_w –   the document frequency of keyword w

IDF_w –   the inverse document frequency of keyword w

I –   encrypted index

R_Q –   the search result of query Q

N_Q –   number of files in the search result of query Q

PRF –   pseudo-random function

a|b –   concatenation of string a and string

3.2 System Model and Searchable Encryption Definition

We design our SSE scheme in system model which is depicted in Fig. 1. Two entities are involved in this scenario: cloud server and data owner. Data owner generates index

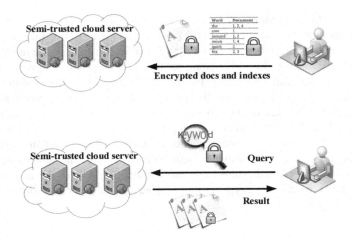

Fig. 1. System model

and encrypt files and index before outsourcing them to the cloud server. To perform a keyword search, the data owner generates the corresponding trapdoor and send it to the cloud server. Once receiving this trapdoor, the cloud server searches index for matched document and calculates relevance score of returning documents. At last, the sorted search results are returned to the data owner. We define searchable encryption as follows:

(1) **Keygen** is a key generation algorithm run by data owner. It takes a security parameter λ, and returns a secret key K.

(2) **Build_Index** is an algorithm run by data owner to generate the encrypted index. It takes a secret key K and file collections F, returns the encrypted index I.

(3) **Trapdoor** is run by data owner to generate a trapdoor for a given query. It takes a secret key K and a query Q, returns trapdoor T_Q.

(4) **Search** is a run by the cloud server in order to find documents containing query keywords. The documents are ranked by their relevance to the query keywords. It takes encrypted index I and trapdoor T_Q, returns the result set of documents.

3.3   Threat Model

In this paper, we suppose cloud server is "semi-trusted" which means the cloud server can dutifully execute the computation and storage operations in daily work. However, it's curious about the file content and index information, so it may try to deduce some information from the encrypted data. In this paper, we adopt the same threat model as [8]. In this model, the server not only knows the content of encrypted index and trapdoors, but also knows some background knowledge about the file collection, such as TF/DF statistical distribution.

3.4 Assessment Criteria

We will evaluate our scheme in three aspects: computation complexity, storage complexity and security.

Computation Complexity: practical multi-keyword SE scheme should achieve logarithmic (sublinear) search efficiency which is essential in real-world scenario.

Storage Complexity: As far as we know, SSE schemes in [5, 6] have the optimal storage overhead $O\left(\sum_{w \in D} DF_w\right)$ which is linear to total number of document-keyword pair.

Security: Security of SSE schemes mainly refers to index privacy and query privacy. Index privacy denotes the privacy of information such as keywords in the document, number of documents, document length and so on. Query privacy refers to privacy of keywords in the search query. If SSE scheme supports TF-IDF based relevance ranking, privacy of TF and IDF should be protected in the construction of SE scheme. Besides, rank privacy should also be considered in threat model.

3.5 TF-IDF Relevance Evaluation Method

In information retrieval community, Term Frequency-Inverse Document Frequency (TF-IDF) method is widely used to calculate the relevance score between a document F_j and a query Q:

$$Score(Q, F_j) = \sum_{w \in Q} TF_{w, F_j} \times IDF_w \tag{1}$$

$$idf = \log \frac{n}{df_w} \tag{2}$$

In detail, TF is abbreviation of Term Frequency which is the number of occurrences of keyword w in document F_j. DF demotes Document Frequency which is the number of documents containing keyword w. IDF is the inverse value of DF.

3.6 Rivest-Shamir-Adlema (RSA) Encryption

RSA encryption is an asymmetric encryption algorithm proposed by Rivest, Shamir and Adlema in 1977. It's widely used in today's information systems and network infrastructure. It can be used for encryption, digital signature method, key distribution and so on. RSA algorithm works as follows:

$$Enc: c = m^{K_{pub}}(mod\,n), Dec: m = c^{K_{pri}}(mod\,n) \tag{3}$$

$$n = p * q, K_{pub} * K_{pri} = 1(mod\,\varphi(n)) \tag{4}$$

In Eq. 4, p and q are big primes. $\varphi(n)$ denotes Euler function. RSA algorithm is homomorphic in multiplication:

$$c_1 * c_2 = m_1^{K_{pub}} * m_2^{K_{pub}} = (m_1 * m_2)^{K_{pub}} (mod\, n) \tag{5}$$

3.7   ElGamal Encryption

ElGamal algorithm is an asymmetric encryption. It works as follows:

$$KeyGen: h = g^d (mod\, p) \tag{6}$$

$$Enc: c_1 = g^r (mod\, p), c_2 = mh^r = (mod\, p) \tag{7}$$

$$Dec: m = c_2 (c_1^d)^{-1} (mod\, p) \tag{8}$$

In above equations, p is a big prime. g denotes a generator of a multiplicative group $Z_p^* = \{1,\ldots,p-1\}$. $0 < d < p-1$ is secret key, h is public key. $m \in Z_p$ is plaintext, (c_1, c_2) is ciphertext. The ElGamal algorithm is homomorphic in modular multiplication:

$$E(m_1) = (g^{r_1}, m_1 h^{r_1})(mod\, p), E(m_2) = (g^{r_2}, m_2 h^{r_2})(mod\, p) \tag{9}$$

$$E(m_1) * E(m_2) = (g^{r_1 + r_2}, m_1 m_2 h^{r_1 + r_2}) = (g^{r_3}, m_1 m_2 h^{r_3}) = E(m_1 * m_2)(mod\, p) \tag{10}$$

4   Privacy-Preserving Relevance Ranking Scheme

4.1   General Idea

In this section, we present the design rationale of privacy-preserving relevance ranking (PPRR) algorithm. Following previous SE schemes supporting relevance ranking, we adopt TF-IDF method to evaluate relevance between query and documents. Our design goal is to construct a privacy-preserving TF-IDF evaluation method in client-server model. As we know, fully homomorphic encryption meets this requirement. However, FHE algorithm is impractical in real-world scenario due to its high computation complexity. Inspired by the fact that a major part of computation complexity is caused by multiplication in TF-IDF algorithm, we calculate the multiplication of TF and IDF values in an encrypted manner at the server-side, leaving the decryption and addition of intermediate results at the client. We choose RSA encryption and ElGamal encryption because of their multiplicative homomorphism.

In our first scheme, TF values are encrypted by RSA while in our second scheme, it is encrypted by the ElGamal. In both schemes, the encrypted TF values are outsourced to cloud server along with the encrypted index. When user submits a search query, IDF values of query keywords are encrypted in the same way as TF values and inserted into

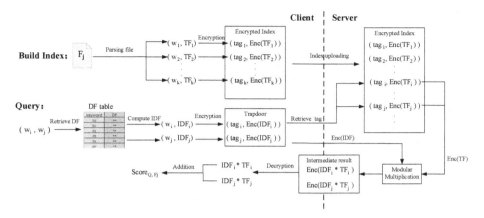

Fig. 2. Illustration of PPRR scheme.

trapdoor. After receiving the trapdoor, the cloud server multiplies encrypted TF with encrypted IDF to get encrypted relevance score for each query keyword. These intermediate results are returned to client. The client decrypts these intermediate scores and sum them up to get the final relevance score. By this way, the result ranking is done by client and rank privacy is protected. In Fig. 2, we demonstrate the architecture and working steps of PPRR scheme.

In PPRR schemes, encrypted TF and IDF are leaked to server. If these values are encrypted deterministically, the distribution of encrypted values remains same as plain values. As a result, a malicious server can deduce plain values based on data collection's statistical knowledge [7, 16]. In order to resist possible statistical attack, the encryption method needs to be a probabilistic one. Because ElGamal encryption is a probabilistic encryption method, PPRR-1 avoids this problem. However, RSA encryption is deterministic. In order to solve this problem, we introduce randomness into PPRR-2 algorithm to protect the privacy of TF/IDF values. In detail, $TF_{w,j}$ is multiplied by a random integer $R[j']$ before encrypted where $j' = j(mod\ T)$ and T is a modular parameter. Therefore, TF values of same keywords in different files are multiplied with different random numbers and TF distribution is confused. In consideration of large size of document collection, we introduce a modular parameter T to restrict the size of random array R. T is a trade-off between storage space and security. Similarly, IDF values of keyword w is multiplied by $R'[w]$ before encrypted where R' is an array which stores a random integer for each keyword in query. R' is reset for each new search request. As a result, query unlinkability is realized and IDF distribution of certain keyword is confused.

4.2 PPRR-1 Description

Detailed description of PPRR-1 scheme is shown in ALGORITHM 1. PPRR-1 uses ElGamal algorithm to encrypt TF values.

ALGORITHM 1.   PPRR-1

Keygen:
>   generate (K_{pub}, K_{pri}) for ElGamal encryption.
>   generate keys K_T for PRF F_p (with range in Z_p^*)

Build_Index:
>   **Inputs**: file collection F, public key K_{pub}
>   Allocate an map I_{TF}
>   **for** each file F_j , **do**
>>   Scan and tokenize F_j
>>   **for** each keyword w in F_j, **do**
>>>   compute $TF_{w,j}$
>>>   set $y = ElGamal\_ENC(TF_{w,j})$
>>>   set $tag = F_P(K_T, \ w \mid j)$
>>>   store $\{tag, y\}$ pair in I_{TF}
>
>   **Outputs**: encrypted index I_{TF}

Trapdoor:
>   **Inputs**: file identifier j, query Q, DF table
>   Allocate an empty array T_Q
>   **for** each keyword w in query Q, **do**
>>   get $DF(w)$ from DF table and calculate IDF value IDF_w
>>   set $z = ElGamal\_ENC(IDF_w)$
>>   set $tag = F_P(K_T, \ w \mid j)$
>>   add pair (tag, z) to the array T_Q
>
>   **Outputs**: trapdoor T_Q

Search:
>   Inputs: encrypted index I_{TF}, trapdoor T_Q
>   Allocate an empty array S_j
>   for each pair in T_Q, do
>>   get value $y = ElGamal\_ENC(TF_{w,j})$ from I_{TF} using tag
>>   compute $EScore_w = y * z$
>>   put $EScore_w$ into the array S_j
>
>   Outputs: array S_j

Post-Processing:
>   **Inputs**: array S_j
>   set $Score_{Q,f} = \sum_w ElGamal\_Dec_{K_{pri}}(EScore_w)$
>   **Outputs**: $Score_{Q,f}$

4.3   PPRR-2 Description

The detailed description of PPRR-2 scheme is shown in ALGORITHM 2 which is based on RSA encryption.

ALGORITHM 2. PPRR-2

Keygen:

  generate modulus n and (K_{pub}, K_{pri}) for RSA encryption.

  generate keys K_T for PRF F_p (with range in Z_p^*)

  initialize an array R and a random integer generator: random()

  for integer $i < T$, **do**

    set $R[i] = $ random(), $R^{-1}[w] = (R[w])^{-1} (mod\ n)$

Build_Index:

  Inputs: file collection F, public key K_{pub}

  Allocate an map I_{TF}

  for each file F_j , **do**

    Scan and tokenize F_j

    for each keyword w in F_j, **do**

      compute $TF_{w,j}$

      set $j' = j\ (mod\ T)$

      set y= $RSA\_ENC(TF_{w,j} * R[j'])$

      set tag = $F_P(K_T,\ w\ |\ j)$

      store $\{tag, y\}$ pair in I_{TF}

  Outputs: encrypted index I_{TF}

Trapdoor:

  Inputs: file identifier j, query Q, DF table

  Allocate an empty array T_Q, R'

  for each keyword w in query Q, **do**

    set $R'[w] = $ random()

    get DF(w) from DF table and compute IDF_w

    set $z = RSA\_ENC(IDF_w * R'[w])$

    set $tag = F_P(K_T,\ w\ |\ j)$

    add pair (tag, z) to the array T_Q

  Outputs: trapdoor T_Q

Search:

  Inputs: encrypted index I_{TF}, trapdoor T_Q

  Allocate an empty array S_j

  for each pair in T_Q, do

    get value y = $RSA\_ENC(TF_{w,j} * R[j'])$ from I_{TF} using tag

    calculate $EScore_w = y * z$

    put $EScore_w$ into the array S_j

  Outputs: array S_j

Post-Processing:

  Inputs: array S_j, array R', array R

  set $Score_{Q,f} = \sum_{w \in Q} RSA\_Dec_{K_{pri}}(EScore_w) * (R'[w])^{-1} * (R[w])^{-1}$

  Outputs: $Score_{Q,f}$

4.4   Index Updates

A practical PPRR scheme should be able to handle index updates in case of document updates. When the file content updates, TF and IDF values needs updates too. TF values are updated in an encrypted manner while IDF values are directly updated at client side. We explain how encrypted TF values are added, deleted or modified:

TF Addition: If a keyword w was added to the document for the first time, we need to generate a pair (tag, y) which stores encrypted TF values of keyword w. then the pair is outsourced to cloud server and inserted into index I_{TF}.

TF Deletion: If all of keyword w was deleted in the document. We need to calculate the tag and send it to cloud server. The server deletes the pair matching tag or uses deletion array I_{TF-D} to mark which TF values have been deleted.

TF Modification: TF modification can be viewed as a combination of TF node deletion and TF node addition.

Because DF values change frequently in case of file updates, we maintain an array which stores DF values for each keyword at the client side. By this way, the trapdoor is generated based on the latest DF values in case of frequent document updates.

4.5   Security Analysis

In PPRR scheme, the cloud server is assumed to be "honest but curious", which means it will execute protocol honestly and try to learn significant information without breaking the protocol. Note that in our security analysis when we say query we mean the encrypted IDF part. Similarly, the ciphertext means the encrypted TF part.

Lemma 1: In PPRR-2, if scalar factors are selected uniformly random for each search query, the query unlinkability is achieved.

Proof Sketch: In the trapdoor generation, each IDF is multiplied by a random number r which is uniformly distributed over range $[0, n]$ where n is modulus of RSA algorithm. So same IDF is encrypted to same ciphertext with possibility of $\frac{1}{n}$ which is negligible. Therefore, lemma 1 is proved.

Lemma 2: If the Elgamal encryption is sematic secure, the adversary has negligible advantage in distinguishing any two ciphertext or queries.

Proof Sketch: Assume there is an adversary that is able to distinguish two ciphertext or queries. Based on the sematic security definition, we can know the encryption algorithm is not sematic secure. However, in our scheme, both TF and IDF are encrypted by Elgamal encryption which is known for semantic secure. Therefore, any two ciphertext or queries are undistinguishable, which is contradict with the assumption. Therefore, lemma 2 is correct.

5 Multi-keyword SSE Scheme Supporting Relevance Ranking

5.1 General Idea

In this section, in order to achieve a practical multi-keyword searchable encryption method supporting relevance ranking, we integrate PPRR algorithms with OXT protocol [5] which is an efficient multi-keyword SSE scheme. The integration is conducted in a keyword search-first, relevance ranking-second manner. A straightforward way of integration is executing OXT protocol firstly and the server returns file identifiers of documents which contains query keywords set. Then the client decrypts the intermediate result and uses it to generate trapdoor of PPRR protocol. The server executes the PPRR search and returns the set of encrypted scores. Finally, the client decrypts these scores and add them up to get the final scores. However, this method needs two round of communication between client and server.

In order to realize the multi-keyword ranked search in one communication round, we move the computation task of tftag from client to server. By this way, the server can retrieve encrypted TF values from I_{TF} with tftag which is computed by himself. In detail, PPRR scheme is changed as follows:

1. Build_Index phase, the client uses PRF function to encrypt the query keyword w. File identifier is encrypted by symmetric encryption in OXT protocol. Then the PRF is applied to both encrypted values to generate the search tag of encrypted TF.
2. In trapdoor phase, client computes PRF-encrypted keywords and put it into trapdoor.
3. In search phase, cloud server computes *tftag* based on PRF-encrypted keyword in trapdoor and Encrypted file identifier in execution result of OXT search.

5.2 OXT-PPRR Scheme Description

In this section, we demonstrate our OXT-PPRR scheme. Because the PPRR-1 and PPRR-2 are integrated in a similar way, we only demonstrate OXT-PPRR-1 scheme in Algorithm 3.

ALGORITHM 3.   OXT-PPRR-1 in one communication round

Keygen:

        generate λ-bit key K_S

        generate keys K_X, K_T, K_I, K_Z for PRF F_p (with range in Z_p^*)

        generate key (K_{pub}, K_{pri}) for ElGamal encryption

Build_Index:

        Inputs: file collection F, keys $K_{pub}, K_S, K_X, K_I, K_Z, K_T$

        Allocate an empty array TF, an empty array T, an empty array I_X

        for each keyword w in D, **do**

                set $K_e = F(K_S, w)$

                set $E_w = F_p(K_T, w)$

                initialize a counter $c = 0$

                for each file F_j containing w, **do**

                        set $xid = F_p(K_I, j)$, $z = F_p(K_Z, w|c)$, $y = xid * z^{-1}$

                        set $e = Enc(K_e, j)$, $stag = F(K_e, c)$

                        add tuple $\{stag, (e, y)\}$ to array T

                        set $xtag = g^{F_p(K_X, w)*xid}$, add $xtag$ to I_X

                        compute $TF_{w,j}$ and set $etf = ElGamal\_ENC(TF_{w,j})$

                        set $tftag = F_p(E_w, e)$

                        store $\{tftag, etf\}$ pair in I_{TF}

                        c ++

        Sort array T in lexical order, and generate: $I_S = T$

        Outputs: outsource encrypted index $I = (I_S, I_X, I_{TF})$ to the cloud server.

Trapdoor:

        Inputs: query Q, DF table, keys K_X, K_I, K_Z, K_S, K_T

        Allocate an empty array T_Q, T_Q'

        Allocate an empty two-dimensional array $xtoken$

        Choose the S-term which has least DF value, suppose it is w_1

        Set $K_e = F(K_S, w_1)$

        for $i = 1, 2, \ldots DF_{w_1}$, **do**

                set $stag_i = F(K_e, i)$, add it to T_Q;

                for $j = 2, \ldots, |Q|$, **do**

                        set $xtoken[i, j] = g^{F_p(K_Z, w_1|i)*F_p(K_X, w_j)}$

                Set $xtoken[i] = \{xtoken[i, 2], xtoken[i, 3] \ldots xtoken[i, n]\}$

        Merge $xtoken$ into T_Q.

        for each keyword w in query Q, **do**

                 get DF(w) from DF table and compute IDF value IDF_w

                set $eidf = ElGamal\_ENC(IDF_w)$

                set $E_w = F_p(K_T, w)$

                add pair $(E_w, eidf)$ to the array A

        add array A to T_Q

        Outputs: trapdoor T_Q

Search:

        Inputs: encrypted index I, trapdoor T_Q

        Allocate an empty array S

for $c = 1, 2, \ldots DF_{W_1}$,**do**

      Retrieve c-th tuple (e, y) from I_S: $(e, y) = Retrieve(I_S, stag_c)$

      initialize counter $= 0$

      for $i = 2, \ldots, n$, **do**

          If $(xtoken[c, i])^y \in I_X$, *counter* $++$

      If *counter* $= n$

          for each pair $(E_w, eidf)$ in A, **do**

              set $tag = F_p(E_w, e)$

              get value $etf = ElGamal\_ENC(TF_{w,j})$ from I_{TF} using

          $tftag$

              set $EScore_w = etf * eidf$

              put $EScore_w$ into S_j

          add $tuple(e, S_j)$ to S

    Outputs: array S

Post-Processing:

    Inputs: array S, K_{pri}

    Allocate an empty array R

    for each $tuple(e, S_j)$ in S, **do**

        set $j = Dec(K_e, e)$

        decrypt values in S_j and add them up:

$$Score_j = \sum_w ElGamal\_Dec_{K_{pri}}(EScore_w)$$

        set $R[j] = Score_j$

    rank the search result R based on scores

    Outputs: search result R

5.3 Computation Complexity

In this section, we analyze the computation complexity of OXT-PPRR scheme. We take OXT-PPRR-1 as example.

Build_Index:

The complexity of Build_Index is $O\left(\sum_{w \in D} DF_w\right)$. For each keyword-file pair, four PRF encryption, two modular multiplication, one ElGamal encryption, one modular exponentiation and one symmetric encryption are needed to encrypt the file identifier and TF value.

Trapdoor:

The query complexity composes of trapdoor complexity, search complexity and post-processing complexity. Trapdoor complexity is $O(|Q| * DF_w) + O(|Q|)$ where $|Q|$ is number of keywords in query Q and DF_w is number of document containing keyword w. Major part of trapdoor complexity is caused by computing OXT trapdoor. It's proportional to DF_w. For each query keyword and file in $F(w)$, two PRF encryption and one modular exponentiation are needed.

Search:
Search phase composes of OXT search and PPRR relevance computation. Complexity of OXT search is $O(|Q| * DF_w)$. For each query keyword and file in $F(w)$, one modular exponentiation and one Bloom Filter retrieval are executed. Complexity of PPRR relevance computation is $O(|Q| * N_Q)$ where N_Q is number of files in the search result of query Q. For each query keyword w and file F_j in search result, one PRF encryption, one modular multiplication and one array retrieval are needed to compute the relevance between keyword w and file F_j.

Post-precessing:
Complexity of post-processing phase is $O(|Q| * N_Q)$. For each query keyword w and file F_j in search result, one symmetric decryption and one ElGamal decryption are needed to get final relevance scores. The time complexity of addition and scores ranking is negligible.

5.4   Storage Complexity

Encrypted index at server-side is comprised of three parts: $I = (I_S, I_X, I_{TF})$. I_S and I_S is inherited from OXT protocol while I_{TF} is generated by PPRR-1. Encrypted index I_{TF} contains encrypted $TF_{w,j}$ for each file F_j containing keyword w. So storage space of encrypted index is $O(\sum_{w \in D} DF_w)$. Because storage complexity of I_S and I_X is also $O(\sum_{w \in D} DF_w)$. Then the overall storage complexity of server in OXT-PPRR-1 scheme is $O(\sum_{w \in D} DF_w)$.

In OXT-PPRR-1, The client stores DF table. So the storage complexity of client is $O(m)$ where m is number of keywords in dictionary D. In OXT-PPRR-2, the client keeps DF table, an array storing T random factors and an array storing $|Q|$ random factors. So the storage cost of client is $O(m + T + |Q|)$.

5.5   Security Analysis

In the integrated scheme, OXT protocol and PPRR protocol are loose-coupled with each other. The majority of composite scheme remains the same as OXT protocol and PPRR protocol except for moving the calculation of search tag of encrypted TF values to the server side. In order to keep privacy of query keyword, we use PRF-encrypted keyword as trapdoor. The cloud server cannot deduce the keyword information from encrypted keyword. As a result, the security of our composite scheme is based on the security of OXT scheme and PPRR scheme.

6   Experiment

Our experiment is implemented in JAVA on a machine equipped with Intel I7-4790 CPU and 16G memory. We choose 5000 documents from 20 newsgroups [17] as our dataset. The dictionary contains 6000 keywords. We compared OXT-PPRR schemes to EDMRS scheme [10] which is a MRSE-based scheme supporting multi-keyword ranked search. In OXT-PPRR-1, we implement ElGamal encryption using Elliptic Curve with 224 bit-length key. In OXT-PPRR-2, we use 1024 bit-length key for RSA.

Storage Space Comparison:
Because $DF_w < n$, $O\left(\sum_{w \in D} DF_w\right) < O(mn)$, the index of OXT-PPRR schemes consume less storage space than EDMRS does. This is verified by our experimental result shown in Fig. 3. We can see that our scheme needs less storage space than EDMRS when dictionary size is 1000 and 2000. Because the index size of EDMRS is proportional to dictionary size, we can infer that OXT-PPRR scheme achieves better storage efficiency than EDMRS when dictionary size is larger than 1000.

Trapdoor Comparison:
Time consumption of OXT-PPRR's trapdoor generation is mainly decided by DF_w, which varies based on query keywords and is uncertain. So we won't make comparison.

Index Build Time Comparison:
Time consumption of three schemes are compared in Fig. 4. Index build time of OXT-PPRR schemes is linear to the size of document collection. Due to high computation overhead of matrix multiplication, EDMRS scheme consumes more time than OXT-PPRR schemes.

Search Time Comparison:
From Table 1, we can see that computation complexity of OXT-PPRR search is linear to least document frequency of all query keywords. Computation complexity of OXT-PPRR post-processing is linear to size of search results. Figure 5 shows search time of three schemes with different collection size. It's worth noting that search time of OXT-PPRR scheme includes duration time of search phase and post-processing phase, while search time of EDMRS scheme only includes duration time of search phase.

Table 1. Comparison between OXT-PPRR and EDMRS. T_{EC_E} denotes encryption time of elliptic curve. T_{EC_D} denotes decryption time of elliptic curve. T_{RSA_E} is encryption time of RSA algorithm. T_{RSA_D} is decryption time of RSA algorithm.

Schemes	OXT-PPRR-1	OXT-PPRR-2	EDMRS[10]
Computation complexity of Build_Index	$O(2 * T_{EC\_E} * \sum_{w \in D} DF_w)$	$O((T_{EC_E} + T_{RSA_E}) * \sum_{w \in D} DF_w)$	$O(m^2 * n)$
Computation complexity of Trapdoor	$O(T_{EC\_E} * |Q| * DF_w)$	$O(T_{EC\_E} * |Q| * DF_w)$	$O(m^2)$
Computation complexity of Search	$O(|Q| * DF_w)$	$O(|Q| * DF_w)$	$O(\theta * m * logn)$
Computation complexity of Post-Processing	$O(T_{EC\_D} * |Q| * N_Q)$	$O(T_{RSA\_D} * |Q| * N_Q)$	
Storage complexity (Server)	$O(\sum_{w \in D} DF_w)$	$O(\sum_{w \in D} DF_w)$	$O(mn)$
Storage complexity (Client)	$O(m)$	$O(m+T+|Q|)$	

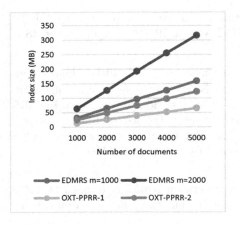

Fig. 3. Index size of three schemes.

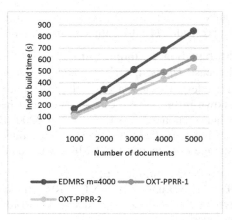

Fig. 4. Index build time

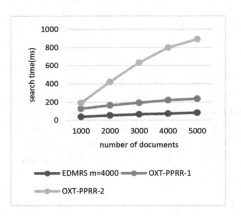

Fig. 5. Search time of three schemes with different size of document collection

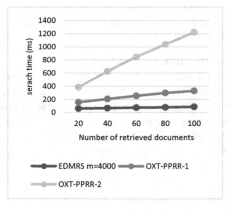

Fig. 6. Search time of three schemes with different size of retrieved documents

Because DF_w and N_Q increase much slower than collection size n, the search time of OXT-PPRR is sublinear to collection size. The tendency of curves in Fig. 5 confirms our judgement. However, due to the fact that RSA decryption and ElGamal decryption is a little time-consuming, OXT-PPRR schemes need more search time than EDMRS does. Besides, Fig. 6 verifies that search time of three schemes are all linear to the size of search results.

7   Conclusion

In this paper, we propose two privacy-preserving relevance ranking (PPRR) algorithms. Both schemes utilize multiplicative homomorphic encryption algorithms to protect TF/IDF and rank relevance scores at client-side in order to protect rank privacy. Besides, randomness is introduced into PPRR-2 to resist possible statistic attack in a strong threat model where attacker may be equipped with TF/IDF distribution knowledge. Furthermore, we incorporate PPRR schemes into Cash's OXT protocol to achieve practical multi-keyword ranked search on encrypted data. Finally, we analyze computation complexity, storage complexity and security of our scheme and experiment result confirms efficiency of our composite scheme.

Acknowledgments. This work was supported by National Science and Technology Major Project (No. 2016ZX05047003).

References

1. Song, D.X.D., Wagner, D., Perrig, A.: Practical techniques for searches on encrypted data. In: Proceedings of S&P, pp. 44–55, Berkeley, CA (2000)
2. Curtmola, R., Garay, J., Kamara, S., Ostrovsky, R.: Searchable symmetric encryption: improved definitions and efficient constructions. In: ACM Conference on Computer and Communications Security (CCS), pp. 79–88, ACM (2006). http://dx.doi.org/10.1145/1180405.1180417
3. Kamara, S., Papamanthou, C., Roeder, T.: Dynamic searchable symmetric encryption. In: ACM Conference on Computer and Communications Security (CCS), pp 965–976. ACM (2012). http://dx.doi.org/10.1145/2382196.2382298
4. Stefanov, E., Papamanthou, C., Shi, E.: Practical dynamic searchable encryption with small leakage. In: NDSS Symposium (2014)
5. Cash, D., Jarecki, S., Jutla, C., Krawczyk, H., Roşu, M.-C., Steiner, M.: Highly-scalable searchable symmetric encryption with support for Boolean queries. In: Canetti, R., Garay, Juan A. (eds.) CRYPTO 2013 Part I. LNCS, vol. 8042, pp. 353–373. Springer, Heidelberg (2013). https://doi.org/10.1007/978-3-642-40041-4_20
6. Cash, D., Jager, J., Jarecki, S., Jutla, C., Krawczyk, H., Rosu, M.C., Steiner, M.: Dynamic searchable encryption in very-large databases: data structures and implementation. NDSS **14**, 23–26 (2014)
7. Wang, C., Cao, N., Li, J., Ren, K., Lou, W.: Secure ranked keyword search over encrypted cloud data. In: International Conference on Distributed Computing Systems (ICDCS), pp. 253–262 (2010). http://dx.doi.org/10.1109/ICDCS.2010.34
8. Cao, N., Wang, C., Li, M., Ren, K., Lou, W.: Privacy-preserving multi-keyword ranked search over encrypted cloud data. In: The 30th IEEE International Conference on Computer Communications, pp. 829–837. IEEE Press, New York (2011)
9. Sun, W., Wang, C., Cao, N., Li, M., Lou, W., Hou, Y.T., Li, H.: Privacy-preserving multi-keyword text search in the cloud supporting similarity-based ranking. In: 8th ACM Symposium on Information, Computer and Communications Security (ASIACCS), pp. 79–88. ACM Press, New York (2013)

10. Xia, Z., Wang, X., Sun, X., Wang, Q.: A secure and dynamic multi-keyword ranked search scheme over encrypted cloud data. IEEE Trans. Parallel Distrib. Syst. **27**, 340–352 (2016). https://doi.org/10.1109/TPDS.2015.2401003

11. Li, H., Yang, Y., Luan, T.H., Liang, X., Zhou, L., Shen, X.: Enabling fine-grained multi-keyword search supporting classified sub-dictionaries over encrypted cloud data. IEEE Trans. Dependable Secur. Comput. **13**, 312–325 (2015). https://doi.org/10.1109/TDSC.2015.2406704

12. Song, W., Wang, B., Wang, Q., Peng, Z., Lou, W., Cui, Y.: A privacy-preserved full-text retrieval algorithm over encrypted data for cloud storage applications. J. Parallel Distrib. Comput. **99**, 14–27 (2017)

13. Jiang, X., Yu, J., Yan, J., Hao, R.: Enabling efficient and verifiable multi-keyword ranked search over encrypted cloud data. Inf. Sci. **403–404**, 23–41 (2017)

14. Shen, P., Chen, C., Tian, X., Tian, J.: A similarity evaluation algorithm and its application in multi-keyword search on encrypted cloud data. In: IEEE Military Communications Conference, pp. 1218–1223. IEEE Press, New York (2015). http://dx.doi.org/10.1109/MILCOM.2015.7357612

15. Chen, C., Zhu, X., Shen, P., Hu, J., Guo, S., Tari, Z., Zomaya, A.Y.: An Efficient privacy-preserving ranked keyword search method. IEEE Trans. Parallel Distrib. Syst. **27**, 951–963 (2016). https://doi.org/10.1109/tpds.2015.2425407

16. Zerr, S., Olmedilla, D., Nejdl, W., Siberski, W.: Zerber+R: top-k retrieval from a confidential index. In: International Conference on Extending Database Technology: Advances Database Technology, pp. 439–449 (2009)

17. NewsGroups dataset. http://qwone.com/~jason/20Newsgroups/

Exploring the Network of Real-World Passwords: Visualization and Estimation

Xiujia Guo[1]([✉]), Zhao Wang[1,2], and Zhong Chen[1,2]

[1] School of Electronics Engineering and Computer Science, Peking University,
Beijing 100871, China
{guoxj,wangzhao,zhongchen}@pku.edu.cn
[2] Key Laboratory of High Confidence Software Technologies, Ministry of Education,
Peking University, Beijing 100871, China

Abstract. The distribution of passwords has been the focus of many researchers when we come to security and privacy issues. In this paper, the spatial structure of empirical password sets is revealed through the visualization of disclosed password sets from the website of hotmail, 12306, phpbb and yahoo. Even though the choices of passwords, in most of the cases, are made independently and privately, on closer scrutiny, we surprisingly found that the networks of passwords sets of large scale individuals have similar topological structure and identical properties, regardless of demographic factors and site usage characteristics. The visualized graph of passwords is considered to be a scale-free network for whose degree distribution the power law is a good candidate fit. Furthermore, on the basis of the network graph of the password set we proposed, the optimal dictionary problem in dictionary-based password cracking is demonstrated to be equivalent in computing complexity to the dominating set problem, which is one of the well-known NP-complete problems in graph theory. Hence the optimal dictionary problem is also NP-complete.

Keywords: Computer security · Visualization · Password sets
Power-law distribution · Scale-free network · NP-complete

1 Introduction

Textual password has been a ubiquitous way to access resources and web services since 1960s and the attempts of password cracking have never stopped ever since. Especially in recent years, the leakage of massive password sets repeatedly reminds us of the urgency of password sets security enhancement. While at the same time, what we can do or what we have done to protect the privacy of users and to assure the security of the system seems plausible but far-fetched. Why? As some researchers pointed out, users remain to be the weakest part of the whole password security system and the answer lies in password itself.

While different password cracking techniques have been adopted in prior works, dictionary based password cracking remains to be the most common way

© ICST Institute for Computer Sciences, Social Informatics and Telecommunications Engineering 2018
X. Lin et al. (Eds.): SecureComm 2017, LNICST 238, pp. 147–166, 2018.
https://doi.org/10.1007/978-3-319-78813-5_8

in numerous attacks nowadays. Conventional dictionary based password cracking techniques, such as the statistical guessing attack, usually start with a preprocessed dictionary and might involve some modification during the guessing process. Related research has been made by MSRA [1]. While due to the variations of original data set and dictionary size, the performance differs from one to the other. Bonneau made the first comparison in [2]. Nevertheless, dictionary based cracking techniques were proved effective and feasible in practice.

Dictionary based password cracking technique was first proposed by Morris and Thompson in their seminal analysis of 3,000 passwords in 1979 [3], and the two approaches, password cracking and semantic evaluation, were widely used ever since, even after Markov and PCFG based password crackers were introduced. Even though dictionary based cracking techniques distinguish themselves with feasible performance in practice and play a role of benchmark in a variety of password cracking implements, the reason why they work well remains unknown.

Meanwhile, even though a great deal of works have been done on password creation policy and password strength meters, the gap between our understanding of the security of one single password and the security of a whole password set was rarely discussed. To prevent a password from being compromised, prior works have focused on two metrics: improving the strength of one single password and blocking out passwords whose usage frequency exceed a particular threshold, which is intuitively reasonable but far from perfect.

For the former approach of assuring security, the first question is the definition of strong passwords, i.e. how to measure the security of a password and how to decide whether a password is strong or weak. Bonneau made a survey of related literature and proposed the concept of guessing entropy, α-guess-work [2]. Common practice is the requirement of the length and the variety of characters in a password, such as having at least 8 characters, one lower case character, one capital letter and one number, etc.

For the latter approach of maintaining a blacklist of popular passwords, it seems to be a game of cat and mouse. For every password that is blocked, the user could always make a way out by performing a minor modification on it, for instance, by adding some characters at the rear, changing one or two digits, switching the first character into upper case, or simply using some other weak password that is not included in the list. The minor modifications not only make the blacklist useless, but also leave a potential threat to the entire system. For the same blacklist, if everyone makes his or her own minor modification based on a group of popular passwords, the results could be different but similar to each other. For example, if we all submit "password" as our password and it was blocked, the possible choices after minor modification might be "password1", "password12", "password123", "p@ssword", "Password", etc. As we will discuss in this study, the leakage of one single vulnerable password could lead the compromise of password one after another, thus creating a chain reaction and endanger numerous accounts.

Our first contribution is the visualization of several empirical password sets including the leakage of 12306 (the official website of China Railway Customer

Service Center), hotmail, phpbb and yahoo[1]. We build networks based on the interconnection of the passwords. To our knowledge, this is the first visualization of large scale password sets in the form of networks. Through the graph of the data, we reveal what the topological structure of a whole password set is like in the complete password space.

The second contribution is the exploration of the spatial structure of the data sets we have. The discussion will shed some light on the distribution of passwords, which has been the concern for many years. Malone and Maher [4] investigated frequency distributions of passwords, they pointed that rather than a theoretically desirable uniform distribution, Zipf model usually provides better predictions than a simple uniform model. Malone et al. claimed that the Zipf's Law is a good candidate for modeling the frequency of users-chosen passwords. While the frequency of passwords only indicates the distribution of identical passwords, in this paper, our results support the claim that the visualized graph of passwords is a scale-free network, because the power law distribution is a good estimation of the degree distribution of a password set's visualized graph. Unlike the frequency of passwords, the degree distribution indicates the density of interconnection within the password set. Furthermore, the intriguing structural characteristics provide a possible explanation of the diminishing returns in cracking curves, which is a phenomenon observed in most attacking results over decades [8].

Our final contribution is the model of statistical guessing attack. Based on the proposed model, we focus on the optimal dictionary problem, which aims at cracking a password set with the minimized size dictionary needed. With the knowledge of password distribution, we manage to map the problem of password cracking to the dominating set problem on the graph we visualized and give a theoretical upper bound of the success rate an attacker could ever possibly achieve. Meanwhile, we also demonstrate that the optimal dictionary problem is equivalent to one of the classic NP-complete problems, the minimum dominating set problem, and the complexity for an attacker to find an optimal dictionary is therefore NP-complete.

2   Visualization of the Empirical Password Sets

2.1   Previous Password Set Analyzing Metrics

Characteristics Description. In most cases, the way of presenting the password sets is a list of the characteristics information of the passwords. For instance, many works on password data sets mentioned the top 10 (or higher) most popular passwords of the data involved. Some of descriptions are linguistic classification, in which passwords are classified into different categories such

---

[1] These data sets were disclosed after a series of serve leakages and were collected subsequently. Each one of the data sets has been mentioned at least once in previous literature. For instance, hotmail in [4], 12306 in [5], phpbb in [6], yahoo in [7]. Details are omitted to conserve space.

as words, places, names, movie lines, email, phone number, home address, etc.
Others may focus on common attributes of passwords, like password frequency,
length, character composition including but not limited to the occurrence number of digits, lower or upper case letters, special characters and so on. Relevant
examples could be found in [9–12] and many others. The major breakthrough
comes with the probabilistic password cracking models, including Markov modeling techniques from natural language processing by Narayanan and Shmatikov
[13] in 2005 and, later in 2009, the Probabilistic Context-Free Grammars model
by Weir et al. [14]. The statistical guessing model is a great leap for password
cracking.

Word Cloud of Password Sets. Word cloud is another option when visualizing words. According to the homepage introduction of Wordle[2], which is an
online word cloud service provider, the word clouds generated from original text
give greater prominence to words that have higher frequency in the source text.
Note that the fonts, layouts and color schemes can be tweaked by the users.

Fig. 1. The word cloud of 12306's top 100 mostly used passwords. (Color figure online)

In [15], Wordle was set up to reveal features in the password set of Rockyou,
such as the mixed numeric and text dates. Figure 1 is a simple word cloud of the
top 100 mostly used passwords in 12306's data set[3].

This method gives more straightforward and obvious information about the
password set than the characteristics descriptions. Through the contrast in size,
the more important password distinguishes themselves from the ones that weight
less. The variations in color also make the visualized data more friendly than a
simple list of numbers. Furthermore, some patterns and features of the data stand
out easily with the help of word cloud. For example, sequences like "123456",
"qwer" (which is a sequence of keys on a standard keyboard), "123" and "woaini"
appear frequently in the given data set.

---

[2] http://www.wordle.net/.

[3] The 12306's data set is one of the data sets used in this paper. Refer to the subsequent
sections for more details about the data sets.

2.2   The Definition of Distance Between Passwords

Since we are trying to figure out the relations between passwords, the first thing is to define the relationship of two passwords. In the literature, there seems to be no general definition of the similarity or dissimilarity between two passwords. Before we make decisions in real life, we usually estimate the pros and cons. Likewise, when we try to compare passwords, we measure the similarity or dissimilarity. Hence, what is the difference of two passwords? How to measure the degree of the dissimilarity? Passwords, as we know, are strings of letters, numbers and special characters. The natural choice is, therefore, the way we measure the similarity or dissimilarity of two strings. In this study, we choose edit distance for the measurement of dissimilarity between passwords.

Edit distance is a way to quantify the dissimilarity of two strings (e.g., words) by counting the minimum number of operations required to transform one string into the other. We use one of the most common and well-known variants called Levenshtein distance, which was named after Levenshtein [16]. Levenshtein distance could also simply be referred to as "edit distance", even though several variants exist [17].

The widespread usage of edit distance is a plus, not to mention the corresponding efficient algorithms for utilization. The computing of the edit distance between passwords is based on an improved version of dynamic programming algorithm, which is commonly credited to Wagner and Fischer [18] and has approximately linear time complexity. The computing efficiency is a non-negligible factor to take into account when processing the data, especially when the quantity of the data accumulates to 6 or higher in order of magnitude.

Moreover, edit distance was chosen for the measurement of dissimilarity between passwords because its definition is in accordance with the standard practice of mangling in dictionary based password guessing. The significance of mangling rules has been highlighted and verified by the famous password cracking tool *John the Ripper* and many experts [2,6,8,11,12,14,19] in the field. The aim of our work is to broaden the knowledge of organization and spatial structure of password sets. As shown in the following sections, the visualization of password networks is based on edit distance between passwords. Thus the networks are in some sense the reflection of connections between passwords when they are under attack.

2.3   The Method of Visualization

The procedure to build the graph of a given data set is as follows:

i   Each unique password is represented by a single node, also known as a vertex, in the graph;

ii   Add an edge between two nodes if the distance $D(i,j)$ between two corresponding passwords is less than a threshold;

iii   Repeat step (ii) until every pair of two passwords in the data set has been compared;

iv   Reorganize the graph and output the layout of the graph.

The threshold of distance between passwords is on the basis of practical metric and the computing capacity available when dictionary based cracking happens. We choose the threshold of 1, 2, 3 in this paper on account of the fact that the computing complexity becomes unacceptable when the edit distance is larger than 3. Note that the computing complexity we are addressing here is not the complexity of computing the edit distance between two passwords, but the computing complexity when an attacker attempt to crack as many accounts as possible within distance less than the threshold. Though the number of nodes is fixed for a given data set, which is equal to the number of unique passwords, the larger threshold means more edges and a graph with higher density.

Meanwhile, for sake of space complexity, we compute the distance between every two passwords and store them in form of adjacent table, instead of adjacent matrix.

2.4   A Simple Example of Our Visualization

To make the procedures of our visualization clear and easy to follow, again, we take the top 100 mostly used passwords of the 12306's data as an example. Table 1 is the source data of the passwords. The password number in the table is usually referred to as the frequency of a password, i.e., the number of the same password occurs in the data set. For instance, there are 392 users of website 12306 use "123456" as their passwords and 165 users choose "123456a".

The adjacent table is taken as input for Gephi (an open-source network analysis and visualization software [20]) and the output is the graph of the network within the distance of 1, 2 and 3 separately. The visualization of 12306's top 100 mostly used passwords is shown in Fig. 2a, b, and c. Figure 2a is the graph of the top 100 mostly used passwords within edit distance 1 in 12306 while Fig. 2b and c are the graphs within distance 2 and 3 separately.

Although a graph within edit distance 3 or 2 is obviously much better connected than a graph within edit distance 1, we stop at distance 3 because of computing complexity. The computing complexity grows exponentially when the

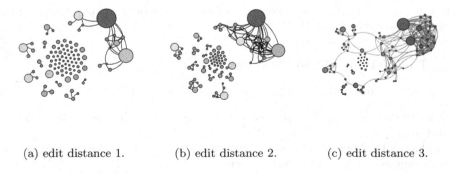

(a) edit distance 1.   (b) edit distance 2.   (c) edit distance 3.

Fig. 2. The graph of 12306's top 100 mostly used passwords within edit distance 1, 2 and 3. (Color figure online)

Table 1. 12306's top 100 mostly used passwords and the corresponding frequency

Password	Password number	Password	Password number
123456	392	a123456	281
123456a	165	5201314	161
111111	157	woaini1314	136
qq123456	98	123123	98
000000	97	1qaz2wsx	93
1q2w3e4r	83	qwe123	80
7758521	76	123qwe	68
a123123	63	woaini520	56
123456aa	55	100200	52
1314520	52	woaini	51
woaini123	50	123321	50
q123456	49	123456789	49
123456789a	48	5211314	48
asd123	48	a123456789	48
z123456	47	asd123456	47
a5201314	45	zhang123	42
aa123456	41	123123a	40
aptx4869	38	1q2w3e4r5t	37
1qazxsw2	37	5201314a	36
1q2w3e	35	aini1314	35
woaini521	34	31415926	34
q1w2e3r4	34	123456qq	34
1234qwer	33	520520	33
a111111	33	110110	29
123456abc	29	111111a	29
7758258	28	w123456	28
abc123	28	159753	26
iloveyou	26	qwer1234	25
a000000	25	123654	24
123qweasd	24	zxc123	24
qq123123	23	123456q	23
abc123456	23	qq5201314	22
12345678	22	000000a	21
456852	21	1314521	20
666666	19	asdasd	19
as123456	19	112233	19
521521	19	zxc123456	19
q1w2e3	18	abcd1234	18
aaa123	18	11111111	17
aaaaaa	17	qazwsx123	17
qaz123	17	123000	17
12qwaszx	17	a123321	17
caonima123	16	asdasd123	16
1123581321	16	110120	16
584520	16	zxcvbnm123	16
753951	16	159357	16
nihao123	16	5845201314	16
wang123	16	love1314	16
s123456	16	147258	16
hao123	15	123456asd	15

distance expands. Actually, it is nearly impossible to reach a full estimation of distance 4, according to our result. It is worth mentioning that we also use the variance of size and color of vertex to deliver a better view. In Gephi, the size of vertex is set to be directly proportional to the frequency of a password. In other words, the size of vertex grows when the frequency of a password increases.

From the example of the top 100 mostly used passwords of the 12306, we expose the evolution of the password network within the distance 1, 2, and 3 and visualize the spatial structure of an empirical password set.

As observed in the graph, some nodes in the network are adjacent to a large number of nodes while some other nodes have only a few edges. In particular, a portion of nodes in the graph are isolated. In other words, they are not connected to anyone.

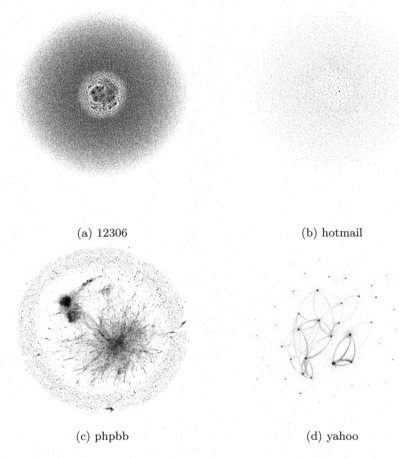

(a) 12306   (b) hotmail

(c) phpbb   (d) yahoo

Fig. 3. The visualized graph of 12306, hotmail, phpbb, yahoo's data sets within edit distance 1.

To further analyze the structure of the graph, we take the community and clustering method to separate the network apart and give a more clear vision of the structure of the data set. The network can be partitioned into different communities, depending on their interconnection. The implementation of community detection in Gephi is based on [21]. Different communities are represented in distinct colors, ranging from dark red to light green. Internal nodes in each community (or group) are linked more closely, which means they have more edges among them, while nodes between the communities contact sparsely. To put it another way, there are less edges between communities. Again, we take the top 100 mostly used passwords of 12306 as the example in Fig. 2c. To our surprise, like the social network of human beings, passwords have their own community and social network. As shown in Fig. 2c, the nodes in different "community" are displayed in different colors.

Figure 3a, b, c, d are the graphs of 12306, hotmail, phpbb and yahoo's password sets within edit distance 1 separately. As shown in the graphs above, the distribution of passwords tends to form communities and clusters. To put it another way, some passwords are closer to other passwords and the whole data set is split into different parts. Table 2 gives the number of nodes and edges in the graph.

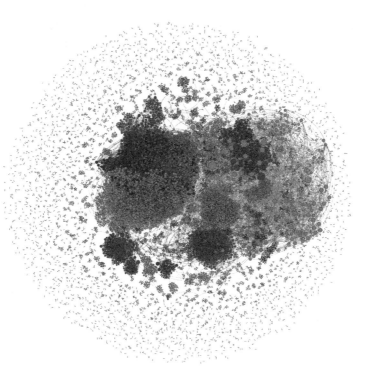

Fig. 4. The visualized graph of 12306's password set within edit distance 3.

To make our observation convincing and solid, we further visualize other data sets avail. Figure 4 is the graph of the full 12306's data set within edit distance 3 after clustering. It is obvious that the drifting isolated nodes is a single community when being analyzed.

Due to a limited number of pages allowed, we only present part of the graphs. Full coverage of graphs on the four data sets ranging from distance 1 to 3 will be available on arXiv[4] with the same paper name and the author's github repository[5].

3   Statistical Analysis on the Visualized Password Networks

The study of networks originates in the ancient graph theory and has become a crucial area in both theoretical research and empirical applications. The electric power grid, the WWW [22] and the pattern of air traffic between airports are early examples of networks in real life. We make friends with others and our friends have friends of their own, so the social network is generated. The boom of social networks in the last decades has made a big step forward in the understanding of social science, as well as the networks of movie actors and scientific collaboration.

Networks are everywhere. As far as we are concerned, the networks that have been studied so far are, to a certain extent, public. The initial motivation of the network is to share or transit information, goods and sorts of data, from one to the other. As the key to access resources or accounts, password, however, is meant to be private in the first place. Unlike the components like people, airports, routers on the Internet that consist of various networks, passwords are chosen independently and are supposed to be personal and private. Unfortunately, it turns out that the passwords generate networks that we have never imagine and that pose inevitable threats for numerous accounts and organizations.

3.1   Statistical Characteristics of the Data

Although not every one of the graphs is displayed in Sect. 2, we conduct a thorough investigation into every result of our visualization. Table 2 is a brief overview of the number of nodes and edges in the graphs of password data sets with the corresponding edit distance ranging from 1 to 3.

As shown in Table 2, the quantity of nodes and edges in the graphs varied from one to the other. For the graph within different distance threshssold, the deviation of the number of edges could be up to 1 or 2 orders of magnitude.

---

[4] https://arxiv.org/.

[5] https://github.com/googlr/.

Table 2. The number of nodes and edges in the graphs of password sets within edit distance 1, 2 and 3.

Password set	Number of nodes	Number of edges within distance 1	Number of edges within distance 2	Number of edges within distance 3
Hotmail	8,930	742	6,107	45,896
12306	117,808	51,299	676,011	5,311,460
Phpbb	184,341	81,220	1,206,322	13,849,678
Yahoo	342,510	144,209	1,477,190	13,691,942

3.2 Hypothesis of the Degree Distribution in the Networks

The distribution with which passwords are chosen has been an intriguing topic for the researchers in the field. The reason is simple: with a sound knowledge of the distribution of human-chosen passwords, we could utilize the statistical techniques to get a better performance in password cracking, like the PCFG or Markov models. In fact, numerous previous works have made such attempts in revealing features and patterns in password creation and distribution. Malone and Maher [4] claimed that Zipf's law is a good candidate to describe the frequency distribution of password choices, which was later endorsed by Wang in [12]. Now that we have obtained the structure of password data sets, the structural characteristics were further explored in the remaining sections.

Given that the structure of the data sets takes the form of a network and our focus is the interconnection of nodes, the degree of nodes, which is the number of nodes adjacent to the node, incorporates more substantial information. The degree distributions of the visualized graphs of the data sets are shown in Fig. 5. On a typical log-log axes, Fig. 5a, b, c and d are from data set of hotmail, 12306, phpbb and yahoo respectively. The plots of degree distribution are generated by R [23], which is a free software environment and comprehensive language for statistical computing and graphics, and ggplot2 [24] package.

To make a solid statistical analysis of the data and reduce the deviation brought in by randomness and skewness of sampling, if not mentioned particularly, we choose the networks of data sets within edit distance 3 as the source input of the analysis. Large data sets are normally preferred in statistics, because natural noise of sampling and insufficiency of sample size are considered the major shortage of smaller data sets which lead to inaccurate analysis.

In any statistical analysis, it is non-trivial to fit a certain distribution to given data and to measure the goodness of the fit as well. Multiple aspects of the data, including the domain-specific characteristics, should be taken into consideration in particular circumstances, otherwise the fitting could be inaccurate.

Conventionally, the standard statistical method for fitting a common distribution consists of three basic steps: visualizing, fitting, and evaluating [25]. The result of visualizing step is in Fig. 5. In subsequent parts of this section, the fitting step is in Sect. 3.3 and the evaluating step is in Sect. 3.4.

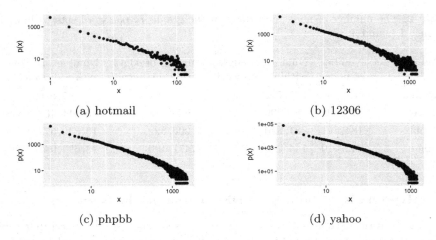

(a) hotmail   (b) 12306

(c) phpbb   (d) yahoo

Fig. 5. The degree distributions of the visualized graphs of the data sets within edit distance 3.

3.3 Fitting to Power Law and Estimating of the Scaling Parameter α

Generally speaking, the first problem, when describing empirical data, is to make a hypothesis of the distribution to which the data may follow. This problem is of such vital significance that it directly determines the accuracy of the fitting and, on the other hand, is sometimes quite tricky. As Alstott et al. pointed out in [25], it is possible that, for the given data set, there is more than one distribution fits well, in which case we for some reason choose one as the hypothesis instead of the other. To make things worse, the distribution that fits the data best might occasionally fall into the alternatives and thus slip out of our scope without being noticed, especially when the one we choose could pass the hypothesis test as well. In consequence, with so many candidate distributions to choose from, it usually requires observations from initial tests and experience to make a decision.

From the plots in Fig. 5, each source of the data could be approximated linearly and has a heavy tail, meaning the tail of the data contains a great deal of probability. On the basis of observations and initial tests, we made the assumption that the degree distribution follows the power law. In this section, we will estimate the parameters of the fitting distribution.

The power law distribution, which is sometimes referred as Pareto distribution, is a probability distribution known for its frequent appearance in natural and man-made phenomenon, as well as its complicated properties. The form of power laws is

$$p(x) \propto x^{-\alpha} \tag{1}$$

Mathematically, α, known as the *exponent* or *scaling parameter*, is a constant parameter of the distribution in Eq. 1.

The fitting is performed with the open-source software package *powerlaw* developed and maintained by Alstott et al. [25], which is a Python implementation of the principled statistical framework proposed by Clauset et al. in [26].

Before fitting, we'd like to go over a few crucial points about the fitting techniques. According to Clauset et al. [26], the approach combines maximum-likelihood fitting methods with goodness-of-fit tests based on the Kolmogorov-Smirnov statistic and likelihood ratios. In practice, power law distribution, in most of the cases, only covers a portion of the data in the tail. In other words, the power law behaviour holds merely on a range of given data and the starting point of the range is referred as x_{min}. When fitting a power-law distributional model to data, the approach[6] estimates alpha for each possible x_{min} and select the value that gives the minimum value of Kolmogorov-Smirnov statistic D as the ultimate estimate [25].

The results of estimation are shown in Table 3. In the second and third column of Table 3, est. alpha is the fitted parameter α and *sigma* is its standard error. Note that this procedure gives estimate of fitted parameters, and the validity of the fit will be covered in the next section.

It is often the case that a line is add to show how close the fit is to the data. While, as Clauset et al. [26] pointed out, the conclusion of such observations is more or less objective and should not be trusted, especially when large scale of fluctuation lies in the tail of empirical data.

3.4   Testing the Power-Law Hypothesis

The goodness of fit of hypothesis distribution must be evaluated before coming to the conclusion that the hypothesis distribution is a good description of the data. As a consequence of fluctuations in sampling, the data collected from a non-power-law process might happen to fit the power law distribution, on the other hand, the data drawn directly from a power law distribution could fail the power law hypothesis test. In the view of Clauset et al. [26], it is recommended that one should prefer large statistical samples to reduce the odds of test failure, as which dwindle with increasing sample size.

When it comes to the techniques of goodness-of-fit tests, there are two options: (1) consider the goodness of fit for each distribution individually, in which case a p-value for the hypothesis is generated by using bootstrapping and the Kolmogorov-Smirnov test, and then check the significance level; (2) compare the candidate hypothesis with alternative distributions by using loglikelihood ratios and identify which one is better. Alstott et al. [25] suggest the latter one, the comparative tests.

Table 4 shows the goodness-of-fit between power law and other widespread heavy-tailed distributions. The list of alternative distributions are the exponential distribution, the lognormal distribution, the lognormal-positive distribution, the stretched exponential (Weibull) distribution and the truncated power law (power law with cut-off) distribution. LR is the loglikelihood ratio between the

---

[6] http://tuvalu.santafe.edu/~aaronc/powerlaws/.

two candidate distributions. This number will be positive if the data is more likely in the first distribution, and negative if the data is more likely in the second distribution. The significance value for the preferred distribution is p.

As usual, the significant level of p is 0.05. From Table 4, the results denoted in **bold** fail ($p < 0.05$) the test and are, therefore, ruled out. From the statistic in the second column, the exponential distribution is not considered to be a proper model. In the third column, there is a fierce competition between the power law distribution and the lognormal distribution. The value of LR is so close to 0 that it is hard to make a trade-off on the sign of LR, which indicates that two distributions are quite close. Or put it in another way, power law is a model that is at least as good as the lognormal model. In the fourth column, the power law model is relatively a better fit than the lognormal-positive model, except a close match for phpbb, in which case power law model is no worse than the lognormal-positive model. In the fifth column of the table, the situation is similar to that of the fourth column and the power law model wins.

Table 3. The estimation result of fitting degree distribution to power law.

Password set	est.alpha	sigma	x_{min}	D
Hotmail-3	1.8532	0.0909	8.0	0.0536
12306-3	1.7573	0.0240	6.0	0.0311
Phpbb-3	2.1541	0.1542	439.0	0.0492
Yahoo-3	2.2636	0.2694	2307.0	0.0343

When it comes to the last column, the truncated power law, also known as power law with a cut-off model stands out except a close match for yahoo. At this point, it seems that we have made the wrong choice of hypothesis. As Alstott et al. noted in [25], those two-parameter distributions, like the truncated power law and the alternative heavy-tailed distributions, have a natural advantage over the power law, which actually has only one degree of freedom for fitting. However, as long as the model describe the data in a sound and solid way, we say it is a good fit. Actually, we could always find a model with enough parameters to describe the data and eventually trap ourselves into overfitting. Moreover, according to the definition, the truncated power law has the power law's scaling behavior over some range but is truncated by an exponentially bounded tail. It does not make sense to claim that the power law model is a worse fit than the truncated power law model when the latter is a nested distribution of the former. By the way, note that when the indicated conclusions contradict each other, we tend to trust the result on larger sample size.

In conclusion, the power law model is a good fit for the degree distribution of the source data. Meanwhile, the scale-free property is that the degree distribution of complex networks is in accordance with the power-law distribution, and a small number of nodes in the network have a large number of edges. So the topological distribution of the password sets could be described as a scale-free network, which is naturally true by definition. Results of other data sets agree with the conclusion we made here.

Until now, the conclusion matches with our common sense that popular passwords are widely used and a great number of users tend to use at least similar passwords. From previous works, we have realized that individuals tend to choose same passwords. In this literature, the networks of passwords reveal the fact that users tend to choose similar passwords in a much higher chance. If considered carefully, it does make sense. Though we are individuals and we choose our passwords independently, if we tend to choose same passwords, the odds that we choose passwords that slightly differ from each other is much higher than that we choose the same passwords. Therefore, the security of one single account and the security of the whole system are no longer isolated and, moreover, are connected for the first time. That is generic mechanism from where the network of our passwords begins.

Table 4. Comparison between power law and alternative distributions.

Data set	Exponential	Lognormal	Lognormal-positive	Stretched exponential	Truncated power law
Hotmail	LR = 97.4145	LR = −0.0020	LR = 2.5885	LR = 0.8370	LR = −0.0859
	p = 0.0045	p = 0.6368	p = 0.2035	p = 0.4253	p = 0.6785
12306	LR = 1315.1101	LR = 0.0089	LR = 30.5096	LR = 7.8778	LR = −1.7073
	p = 5.9110e−11	p = 0.7689	**p = 1.3775e−05**	**p = 0.0199**	p = = 0.0646
Phpbb	LR = 21.9523	LR = -0.0836	LR = -0.0459	LR = −0.0213	LR = −0.1468
	p = 0.0730	p = 0.8064	p = 0.9382	p = 0.9755	p = 0.5880
Yahoo	LR = 10.0664	LR = 0.0004	LR = 0.1109	LR = 0.1378	LR = −0.0089
	p = 0.07295	p = 0.8953	p = 0.7108	p = 0.6878	p = 0.8939

4   The Statistical Guessing Model

4.1   A simple model of password guessing

With the knowledge of the entire targeted password set, it is possible to trace the process of a dictionary based password guessing on the graph and to estimate the maximum success ratio.

To estimate the number of potential maximum successful guesses, the concept of neighborhood is introduced. In graph theory, the **neighborhood** of a vertex v, denoted as $N(v)$, is the set of adjacent vertices of G consisting of all vertices adjacent to v in graph $G(V, E)$. Note that the concept of neighborhood we discuss in this paper is the closed neighborhood, in which v itself is included. There is another version of neighborhood is called open neighborhood when v itself is not included [27].

The concept of neighborhood of one vertex can be naturally extended to a set of vertices V_s, which is the union of all the neighborhoods of the vertices in set V_s, meaning that each of the vertices in the original graph is adjacent to at least one member of V_s. Denoted as $N(V_s)$ and we have

$$N(V_s) = \cup_{i=1}^{|V_s|} N(v_i) \tag{2}$$

in which $|V_s|$ is the number of vertices and v_i is the i-th vertex in V_s.

Given a dictionary of n passwords $Dict = \{p_1, p_2, \ldots, p_{n-1}, p_n\}$. The passwords are arranged in decreasing order of frequency, i.e.

$$f(p_1) > f(p_2) > \cdots > f(p_{n-1}) > f(p_n),$$

where $f(p_i)$ is the frequency of the password p_i in the targeted password set $\mathbf{T}$.

As shown previously, we could build the graph of any specified password data sets. In the corresponding data set, if the attacker guesses one password right, the vertex for which the compromised password stands is covered by the attacker's dictionary. For each vertex that is directly adjacent to the compromised vertex, the attacker could cover them all within affordable time. More details about this one to one mapping mechanism will be stated afterwards in the optimal dictionary problem.

Then for an attacker with dictionary $\mathbf{Dict}$, the maximum set of vertices could be covered in the graph of target $\mathbf{T}$ is the union of passwords that $\mathbf{Dict}$ covered and their neighbors in the graph of $\mathbf{T}$, which is

$$N(Dict) = \cup_{i=1}^{n} N(p_i). \tag{3}$$

Thus the total number of corresponding maximum successful guesses is $\sum_{p \in N(Dict)} f(p)$. The upper bound of the success ratio using dictionary $\mathbf{Dict}$ is the accumulation of the frequency of the node and its neighbors. Of course the attacker can start multiple rounds by searching the closure of the compromised data, but the overall time cost could be intolerable.

4.2   The Optimal Dictionary Problem

In conventional password cracking, the size of dictionary has a significant impact on the success rate of the cracking. The primary reason that attackers prefer large dictionary is straightforward: a larger dictionary means the higher probability of covering more passwords in the targeted set. Meanwhile, due to the efficiency of time and space, all results show diminishing returns as the dictionary size swells [8]. The diminishing guessing curves have been observed in almost every previous attempt to crack as more accounts as possible.

Klein [28] made the first attempt to identify the higher efficient subdictionary. J Bonneau define a success rate α when introducing α-guesswork to evaluate the number of guesses of an attacker [2]. And Mónica and Ribeiro [29] discussed the compression ratio in the implementation of Self-Organizing Maps (SOM) model which preserves the topological position of passwords.

Since we have built a graph of the password set, the search for better subdictionary becomes easier. Our goal is to find a subset of strings to cover as more passwords as possible. Considering we are dealing with this problem on a graph, if we paraphrase the problem a little bit, the goal is to find a subset of nodes that all the other nodes in the graph of the target are adjacent to at least one member of this subset. That is exactly the definition of dominating set in graph theory. Given a graph $G = (V, E)$, a dominating set for a graph G is a subset D of V that every vertex in V is either in D or adjacent to at least one member of D. The number of vertices in a smallest dominating set for G, $\gamma(G)$, is known as the domination number. Refer to [30] for more details of the definition.

To be mathematically precise and concise, we proposed the reductions below to show the equivalence of the optimal dictionary problem of password guessing and the minimum dominating set problem.

For any password set $S = \{p_1, p_2, \ldots, p_n\}$, we can construct the graph $G = (V, E)$ within certain distance threshold through the steps in Sect. 2, which mainly involves in generating the edges and takes polynomial time.

Note that there is a one-to-one mapping between the passwords in S and the nodes in G. Let $\hat{D}$ be an instance of the optimal dictionary of S, meaning that $\hat{D}$ is a minimum subset that is able to recover S. In graph G, the set of nodes which represents the elements of $\hat{D}$ is denoted by D. Now consider the situation in G, we have $V \subseteq N(D)$, in which case D is a dominating set of G.

The next step is to validate that D is a minimum dominating set of G. Assume that D is not a minimum dominating set of G, which indicates that either D is not a dominating set of G or D is a dominating set but not the smallest. In the former situation, at least one node, say p_k, neither belongs to D nor is adjacent to any member of D. Backing to the source data set, the password that p_k represent is neither in $\hat{D}$ nor recoverable by $\hat{D}$, which is contradiction to the our proposition that $\hat{D}$ is a dictionary of S. While in the latter situation that D is not the smallest dominating set, suggesting that at least one node p_t could be removed from D and $D^* = \{D - p_t\}$ serves as a smaller dominating set of G. Then if we remove the password that p_t represent from $\hat{D}$, $\hat{D}^* = \{\hat{D} - p_t\}$, which is smaller than $\hat{D}$ and could also recover S, leads to a contradiction that $\hat{D}$ is not optimal. To summarize, D is a minimum dominating set. Likewise, we can generate an optimal dictionary with a given minimum dominating set of G. As a result, given an instance of the optimal dictionary problem, we can construct an instance of the minimum dominating set problem and vice versa.

The complexity of transformations are polynomial time. In other words, the minimum dominating set problem and the optimal dictionary problem are equivalent in terms of computing complexity. The minimum dominating set problem is a well-known NP-hard problem, which is proved by Garey and Johnson in [31]. Hence the minimum size of the dictionary to cover the targeted password set, i.e. its lower bound, equals $\gamma(G)$. Note that this conclusion also applies to other variants of dictionary based cracking techniques, provided that the corresponding method to build the graph is properly redefined.

5 Conclusion

In this paper, we provide a novel presentation of empirical password sets in the form of networks from scratch. The spatial structure of the password sets is discussed for the first time and is considered to be a scale-free network.

The high density of interconnections between passwords provides a candidate explanation of the diminishing returns observed in previous literature. While many users choose the same password in reality, It went unnoticed that more users tend to choose similar passwords. To make things worse, the difference between those passwords is usually negligible against the computing capacity nowadays and even the strong password could not resist when the chain reaction of leakage started.

Furthermore, at the basis of the network graph of password set we proposed, we give the upper bound of the maximum password attacking success rate based on a certain dictionary. Under the assumption of an attacker who has high performance computing resource, we demonstrate the equivalence of the optimal dictionary problem and the dominating set problem in computing complexity. Therefore the optimal dictionary problem is also NP-complete.

Acknowledgement. The authors would like to thank Ping Wang, Tian Liu, Yongzhi Cao, Wenxin Li, Eric Liang, Kaigui Bian, Haibo Cheng, Ding Wang, Gaopeng Jian, Chen Zhu, Xin Huang, Qiancheng Gu, Hang Li, Jun Yang, Junfeng Zhang, Xuqing Liu, Xiangyu Xu, Xiang Yin, Wenying Teng, Meredith Mante, Justin Edwin Marquez, Alex Wilke and Niall Pereira for helpful conversations and the anonymous reviewers for their insightful comments. This work was sponsored by the National Science Foundation of China under grant No. 61371131.

References

1. Schechter, S., Herley, C., Mitzenmacher, M.: Popularity is everything: a new approach to protecting passwords from statistical-guessing attacks. In: Proceedings of the 5th USENIX Conference on Hot Topics in Security, pp. 1–8. USENIX Association (2010)
2. Bonneau, J.: The science of guessing: analyzing an anonymized corpus of 70 million passwords. In: 2012 IEEE Symposium on Security and Privacy, pp. 538–552. IEEE (2012)
3. Morris, R., Thompson, K.: Password security: a case history. Commun. ACM **22**(11), 594–597 (1979)
4. Malone, D., Maher, K.: Investigating the distribution of password choices. In: Proceedings of the 21st International Conference on World Wide Web, pp. 301–310. ACM (2012)
5. Carnavalet, X.D.C.D., Mannan, M.: A large-scale evaluation of high-impact password strength meters. ACM Trans. Inf. Syst. Secur. (TISSEC) **18**(1), 1 (2015)
6. Weir, M., Aggarwal, S., Collins, M., Stern, H.: Testing metrics for password creation policies by attacking large sets of revealed passwords. In: Proceedings of the 17th ACM Conference on Computer and Communications Security, pp. 162–175. ACM (2010)

7. Das, A., Bonneau, J., Caesar, M., Borisov, N., Wang, X.: The tangled web of password reuse. In: NDSS, vol. 14, pp. 23–26 (2014)
8. Dell'Amico, M., Michiardi, P., Roudier, Y.: Password strength: an empirical analysis. In: INFOCOM, vol. 10, pp. 983–991 (2010)
9. Mazurek, M.L., Komanduri, S., Vidas, T., Bauer, L., Christin, N., Cranor, L.F., Kelley, P.G., Shay, R., Ur, B.: Measuring password guessability for an entire university. In: Proceedings of the 2013 ACM SIGSAC Conference on Computer & Communications Security, pp. 173–186. ACM (2013)
10. Voyiatzis, A.G., Fidas, C.A., Serpanos, D.N., Avouris, N.M.: An empirical study on the web password strength in Greece. In: 2011 15th Panhellenic Conference on Informatics (PCI), pp. 212–216. IEEE (2011)
11. Li, Z., Han, W., Xu, W.: A large-scale empirical analysis of Chinese web passwords. In: USENIX Security Symposium, pp. 559–574 (2014)
12. Wang, D., Cheng, H., Wang, P., Huang, X., Jian, G.: Zipf's law in passwords. IEEE Trans. Inf. Forensics Secur. **12**(11), 2776–2791 (2017)
13. Narayanan, A., Shmatikov, V.: Fast dictionary attacks on passwords using time-space tradeoff. In: Proceedings of the 12th ACM Conference on Computer and Communications Security, pp. 364–372. ACM (2005)
14. Weir, M., Aggarwal, S., De Medeiros, B., Glodek, B.: Password cracking using probabilistic context-free grammars. In: 2009 30th IEEE Symposium on Security and Privacy, pp. 391–405. IEEE (2009)
15. Veras, R., Thorpe, J., Collins, C.: Visualizing semantics in passwords: the role of dates. In: Proceedings of the Ninth International Symposium on Visualization for Cyber Security, pp. 88–95. ACM (2012)
16. Levenshtein, V.I.: Binary codes capable of correcting deletions, insertions and reversals. In: Soviet Physics Doklady, vol. 10, p. 707 (1966)
17. Navarro, G.: A guided tour to approximate string matching. ACM Comput. Surv. (CSUR) **33**(1), 31–88 (2001)
18. Wagner, R.A., Fischer, M.J.: The string-to-string correction problem. J. ACM (JACM) **21**(1), 168–173 (1974)
19. Ur, B., Segreti, S.M., Bauer, L., Christin, N., Cranor, L.F., Komanduri, S., Kurilova, D., Mazurek, M.L., Melicher, W., Shay, R.: Measuring real-world accuracies and biases in modeling password guessability. In: USENIX Security Symposium, pp. 463–481 (2015)
20. Bastian, M., Heymann, S., Jacomy, M.: Gephi: An Open Source Software for Exploring and Manipulating Networks (2009)
21. Blondel, V.D., Guillaume, J.-L., Lambiotte, R., Lefebvre, E.: Fast unfolding of communities in large networks. J. Stat. Mech: Theory Exp. **2008**(10), P10008 (2008)
22. Barabási, A.-L., Albert, R., Jeong, H.: Scale-free characteristics of random networks: the topology of the world-wide web. Phys. A: Stat. Mech. Appl. **281**(1), 69–77 (2000)
23. R Core Team: R: A Language and Environment for Statistical Computing. R Foundation for Statistical Computing, Vienna, Austria (2016)
24. Wickham, H.: ggplot2: Elegant Graphics for Data Analysis. Springer, New York (2009). https://doi.org/10.1007/978-0-387-98141-3
25. Alstott, J., Bullmore, E., Plenz, D.: powerlaw: a python package for analysis of heavy-tailed distributions. PLoS ONE **9**(1), e85777 (2014)
26. Clauset, A., Shalizi, C.R., Newman, M.E.: Power-law distributions in empirical data. SIAM Rev. **51**(4), 661–703 (2009)

27. Hell, P.: Graphs with given neighborhoods i. In: Proc. Colloque, Inter. CNRS, Orsay, pp. 219–223 (1976)
28. Klein, D.V.: Foiling the cracker: a survey of, and improvements to, password security. In: Proceedings of the 2nd USENIX Security Workshop, pp. 5–14 (1990)
29. Mónica, D., Ribeiro, C.: Local password validation using self-organizing maps. In: Kutyłowski, M., Vaidya, J. (eds.) ESORICS 2014. LNCS, vol. 8712, pp. 94–111. Springer, Cham (2014). https://doi.org/10.1007/978-3-319-11203-9_6
30. Hedetniemi, S.T., Laskar, R.C.: Bibliography on domination in graphs and some basic definitions of domination parameters. Discret. Math. **86**(1), 257–277 (1990)
31. Garey, M., Johnson, D.: Computers and Intractability-A Guide to NP-Completeness (1979)

ThiefTrap – An Anti-theft Framework for Android

Sascha Groß$^{(\boxtimes)}$, Abhishek Tiwari, and Christian Hammer

University of Potsdam, Potsdam, Germany
{saschagross,tiwari,chrhammer}@uni-potsdam.de

Abstract. Smartphones store a plenitude of sensitive data. This data together with high values of smartphones make them an attractive target for physical theft. Clearly, the device owner would like to regain the device in such a case. Also, the information should be protected from illegitimate access.

In this paper, we present the first anti-theft solution that effectively handles these issues. Our proposal is based on a novel concept of an anti-theft honeypot account that protects the owner's data while preventing a thief from resetting the device. Thus, a stolen device can be regained by the device owner with high probability, while information leakage to the thief is prevented. We implemented the proposed scheme and evaluated it through an empirical user study with 35 participants. In this study, the owner's data could be protected, recovered, and anti-theft functionality could be performed unnoticed from the thief in all cases.

Keywords: Anti-theft · Data protection · Information hiding
Privacy

1 Introduction

Smartphones play a vital role in everyone's life. Their contribution is significant in every day to day activity. Nowadays, smartphones are used for various activities such as capturing pictures, browsing the internet, and using online banking. However, these great advantages come at a price. If the device gets in the wrong hands, the device owner does not only lose the device but also a great amount of personal data. A thief getting hold of personal data and trying to exploit it may result in fraud or blackmailing. It is of utmost importance to provide some mechanism to protect the theft of smartphone devices and the personal data on them. These device protection mechanisms are called *anti-theft mechanisms*.

At present, the smartphone market ranges from around 50 USD to 1000 USD. Loss or theft of a phone does not only result in financial deprivation but also of the personal data which is stored on the device. According to a study [17], the number of stolen smartphones rose to 3.1 million in 2013. Another study [14] reveals that victims are willing to pay 500 to 1000 USD to regain their personal data including photos and videos.

© ICST Institute for Computer Sciences, Social Informatics and Telecommunications Engineering 2018
X. Lin et al. (Eds.): SecureComm 2017, LNICST 238, pp. 167–184, 2018.
https://doi.org/10.1007/978-3-319-78813-5_9

The Android market share is continuously increasing [13] and it dominates the smartphone market with a share of 86.8%, by the end of Q3 2016. Taking this into the consideration, we targeted the Android platform for the implementation of our approach. At present, there are two possible anti-theft mechanisms:

1. *Anti-theft applications:* Most of the anti-theft applications provide the functionality to lock the phone, erase it or triggering an alarm from remote. Unfortunately, anti-theft applications do not work if they do not have an active network connection e.g., if the SIM card was removed from the device.
2. *Google Device Protection:* Starting from Android version 5.1, Google released a new feature called "Device Protection" [18]. This anti-theft feature makes it impossible for a thief to use a stolen phone after it was factory reset. However, this feature is only available for a small number of devices, which are capable of running Android version 5.1 or greater. More than 45% of the Android phones use a lower Android version [11].

In the majority of these cases, device owners permanently lose their smartphone together with their personal data, which is even worse. As a remedy, we propose a mechanism where a device owner has the option to configure an anti-theft honeypot account, which resembles the owner's regular account except for some modifications. A person that is not the device owner can never distinguish interacting with the anti-theft account or the real account. The anti-theft account hides the personal data of the device owner and performs hidden anti-theft functionality while the thief uses the device. One important feature of this framework is that when the thief performs a factory reset, our approach only gives the illusion that a factory reset is being done, while in reality all of the owner's data is preserved. After a fake factory reset the device hides the owner's account completely but still executes the anti-theft functionality. The thief will then start using the smartphone as a new device, unaware of anti-theft functionality executing in the background. It is likely that after the fake factory reset a thief will establish an internet connection by inserting a SIM card or establishing a WIFI connection. At this point of time the hidden anti-theft functionality can for example send identifying information of the thief to the device owner or start listening for remote commands from the device owner. So the device owner likely will be able to recover the device and the personal data. The key benefit of this approach is that it improves chances of identifying the thief and regaining the stolen phone as well as the personal data.

Our Contributions. In this paper we propose ThiefTrap, an anti-theft framework that uses the Android account feature as a security measure to protect against device thieves. We are the first to use this feature in that we set up a honeypot account simulating the device owner's account. Technically, we provide the following contributions:

1. *ThiefTrap.* We propose ThiefTrap, a novel concept, using a honeypot account for the purpose of theft protection. This concept is the first anti-theft solution that at the same time protects the confidentiality of the owner's user data,

prevents loss of this data and provides the full functionality of every anti-theft solution. An important benefit of the proposed approach compared to existing anti-theft solutions is that a device instrumented with our approach is *indistinguishable* from an ordinary device. Our approach ensures that the device and the personal data on it can be regained with high probability.

2. *Implementation.* We implemented our concept in the latest version of Android (7.1_r1 Nougat) of the Android Open Source Project.

3. *Evaluation.* We evaluated our approach in the form of an empirical user study. Our study with 35 participants, showed that in all cases our approach prevented loss of **owner's personal data** and performed the **required anti-theft functionality**. In the very vast majority of cases the potential thief was completely oblivious to our approach.

2   Background

Android. Android is the world's most popular mobile operating system. Figure 1 depicts the internal structure of Android OS.

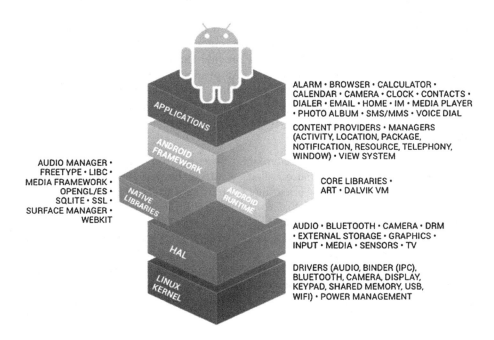

Fig. 1. Android architecture [9]

The Android framework can be best described in the form of different layers. The lowest layer, a customized *Linux Kernel*, is used for drivers and hardware support. The subsequent hardware abstraction layer (HAL) provides a standard interface for exposing the hardware capabilities to the higher-level Android frameworks. HAL implementations are built into shared library modules (.so files).

Android applications are compiled to a specific bytecode format (DEX) designed specially for Android. The Android runtime (ART) provides a Dalvik virtual machine, which is similar to the standard Java virtual machine, but designed and optimized for Android.

The Android framework layer provides many higher-level services in the form of an API to the Application layer. These APIs act as the building blocks to create Android applications. Application developers utilize these APIs in their applications. Most of our changes are implemented in this layer.

The topmost layer, the application layer, provides different applications to be used by end users, such as alarms, browser, calculator etc. Google provides a central store, for developers to publish their applications, called the Google play store. As of December 2016, the Google play store included over 2.5 million apps.

Anti-theft Mechanisms. Anti-theft mechanisms are supposed to prevent device theft or mitigate the damage in case a device gets stolen or is lost. One kind of anti-theft solutions tracks information of the device after it was stolen and provides the information to the device owner. Several anti-theft solutions rely on providing location information and remote administration functionality to the device owner. Some of them also provide the possibility to recover personal data or remotely wipe the device. At present, there are two options for Android owners to protect their device against theft. The first option is to use the Android device theft protection feature (available for devices capable of supporting Android version greater than 5.0). The second option is to use an third party anti-theft application.

- *Android built-in anti-theft mechanisms:* Starting from Android version 5.1, Google released a new feature called "Android Device Protection" [18,26]. This anti-theft feature prevents a thief from using a stolen phone that has been wiped. However, more than 45% of the Android phones use a lower Android version [11]. In addition, this feature will not work without a proper setup. For example, the user needs to log into a Google account on the device. Then, if a device supports this feature, Android Device Protection is enabled as soon as the user enables a locking mechanism. Figure 2 explains the activation of this feature while enabling a device locking mechanism.
  After a factory reset, Android Device Protection requires the user to enter the Google account credentials on which the device was previously configured. This renders the device unusable to the thief even after a factory reset was performed. However, an unlocked bootloader still allows to flash a binary on the device, thus this feature is not available for devices with an unlocked bootloader.
- *Anti-theft Applications:* There is a multitude of third-party anti-theft applications available in the app stores. These applications provide features like locating the device, remotely administrating the device etc.

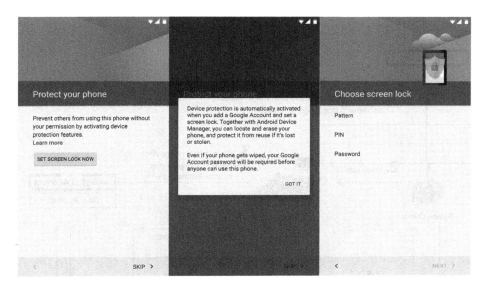

Fig. 2. The Android Device Protection feature [26]

The anti-theft features of these applications heavily rely on a network connection. These applications are mostly not functional if the SIM card was removed from the device. A thief is likely to remove the SIM card from a stolen device and to turn it off, such that the device loses its network connections. Later, in order to reconfigure the device as new, a thief is likely to perform a factory reset, so the anti-theft application is removed from the device, leaving it unprotected. Additionally, the personal data of the device owner is lost unrecoverable.

3   Methodology

When a device is stolen there are two possibilities depending on whether the device is protected by a locking mechanism or not. In case the device is not protected by a locking mechanism, a thief immediately has unlimited access to the device owner's data and may result in abuse of the user data on the device (e.g. credentials) to inflict further harm to the device owner. If the device is locked, it is of no use to the thief as long as the locking mechanism is in place. For this reason it is likely that the thief will factory reset the device, in which case all user data on the device is ultimately lost. Modern smartphones store a lot of valuable private data. Additionally, installed anti-theft applications will be removed from the device so chances are minimal that the device can be retrieved by the device owner. Both of these scenarios are unsatisfying. Therefore, there exists a need for a solution that protects the confidentiality of the user data, while it prevents the device from being factory reset illegitimately. In this work

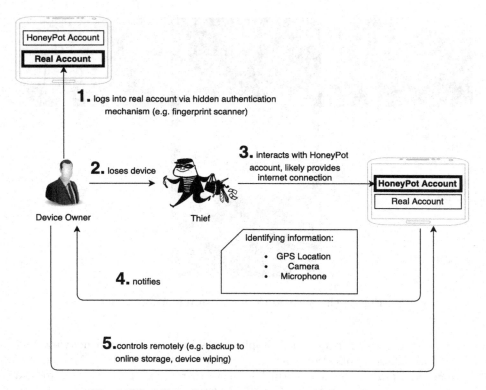

Fig. 3. Workflow of a device instrumented by ThiefTrap

we propose the first approach that can protect the confidentiality of the device owner's user data, while preventing a thief from factory resetting the device and thus removing installed anti-theft applications.

We propose the concept of a honeypot account for theft protection. We leverage the Android guest account feature to implement the honeypot account. Android's multi-account feature was introduced in Android version 4.2. According to statistics provided by Google [12], this feature is supported by 95.8% of devices. The idea of this concept is that it pretends to be the account of the device owner, while it actually is an isolated honeypot account and prevents any access to the user data of the device owner. A thief logging into the device using the home button or power on button, is logged into the honeypot account, which pretends to be the device owner's account. Therefore the honeypot account tricks a thief into believing that he/she is interacting with an unprotected device in an ordinary way, while actually interacting with the honeypot account. The device owner can log into the real account using a hidden mechanism e.g., using fingerprint lock. This mechanism can be configured by the device owner.

Using the proposed concept of a honeypot account, the privacy of the user data is protected. At the same time, in our approach a factory reset initiated from the honeypot account is simulated s.t. the thief believes that the factory reset is being performed, while in reality the owner's data is preserved. After this simulated factory reset, the thief is presented a new account as expected. However, this new account is a customized honeypot account, which runs an anti-theft mechanism in the background hidden from the thief. The great strength of this concept becomes notable when it is combined with existing anti-theft solutions. As the device owner knows that a honeypot account is installed on the phone, he/she will not log into the honeypot account of that device. For this reason it is likely that a user interacting with the honeypot account for some time is not authorised to do so. Therefore, in our approach an anti-theft solution is installed and will be triggered whenever an user interacts with the honeypot account for some time. This anti-theft solution can then for example collect data of the thief and send them to the device owner, who can use them for regaining the device. Figure 3 shows the described workflow.

We would like to stress that there exist numerous ways to implement the concept of an anti-theft honeypot-account on various platforms. We choose to implement our approach on the Android operating system. We use the uncustomized version 7.1_r1 from the Android Open Source Project [10]. At the time of this writing, Android is the most used mobile operating system with over 1.4 billion devices in usage and version 7.1_r1 is the latest version of Android.

3.1   HoneyPot Account, A Simulation of the Owner's Account

The honeypot account is an Android's empty guest account with some modifications. The idea of the honeypot account is to deceive the thief into the belief that he/she is interacting on the real account. Therefore, it is important to provide the illusion of user data in the honeypot account. In principle any concept for simulating user data can be used. In our approach, the applications in the honeypot account are protected by an application called AppLock[1]. AppLock is an ordinary Android application that protects other Android applications by a locking pattern. So, every access to an app is protected by a locking pattern. The thief is under the illusion that there is some data on the device, and it is protected. This step is necessary to convince the thief that the owner's account is being used with some defense mechanism installed. Figure 4 shows the AppLock functionality. This simulates the owner's account, while it frustrates the thief and tricks him/her into performing a factory reset.

It should be mentioned that the mechanism of simulating the owner's user data is independent of the concept of a honeypot anti-theft account. An alternative would be to define some plausible but fake data that is presented whenever applications are opened in the honeypot account.

In the case of a theft, all interactions will inevitably be performed in the honeypot account. In this case, the device should be modified in a way such that it executes anti-theft functionality in the background. It is open to the users and

---

[1] https://play.google.com/store/apps/details?id=com.domobile.applock.

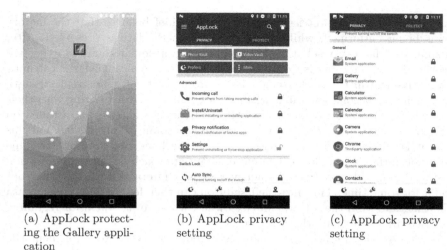

(a) AppLock protecting the Gallery application

(b) AppLock privacy setting

(c) AppLock privacy setting

Fig. 4. AppLock protection

deployers of our techniques to customize the functionality of the anti-theft application. Possible functionalities for an anti-theft application here would be the collection of information of the device and the thief, remote backup functionalities as well as other remote administration functionalities that can be performed hidden from the thief. In our scenario, we implemented the anti-theft application as an Android application that silently tracks and logs the device location.

3.2   Instrumentations

When a device is stolen, chances are high that a factory reset is performed. This is usually done to make the device more usable, and to destroy any evidence of theft. A device can either be factory reset via the Android menu or by pressing a special key combination during the boot procedure. In order to save the owner's data and keep track of the thief, the factory reset is faked in both cases. This means that the device shows a realistic simulation of a factory reset and presents an empty account after the fake factory reset. The thief is in the illusion that all potential tracking mechanisms are removed and the device can now be use in an ordinary manner. Use of the device now inevitably stores the thief's personal information, which will be forwarded by the installed anti-theft application to the device owner.

We implemented the simulation of a factory reset for both mechanisms by instrumenting the Android source code. For preventing the factory reset from the Android settings menu, we instrumented the RecoverySystem[2] and

---

[2] /frameworks/base/core/java/android/os/RecoverySystem.java .

RecoverySystemService[3] classes in such a way that when a user triggers the factory reset, the device shows the default factory reset animation for a realistic amount of time. We instrument the *rebootWipeUserData* function in RecoverySystem.java[2] file. In this function, a call to the *bootCommand* function is made. One of the arguments of the *bootCommand* function, specifies the intent of operation e.g., *–wipe_data* is used to wipe the data partition. Technically, when a factory reset is triggered from the honeypot account, we substitute the argument *–wipe_data* by *–wipe_cache*. This prevents the removal of the user data. Wiping the cache only removes the temporary saved files, e.g., temporary browser files. Thus, it does not affect the device owner in a negative way. Additionally for preventing data loss in case of a factory reset that was triggered during the boot process, we instrumented the recovery system[4].

During the reset, we programmatically remove the AppLock application. We instrument the *setupOrClearBcb* function in the RecoverySystemService.java file to achieve this. Since the honeypot account does not have any data, an empty account is presented to the user, that is functionally equal to a factory reset phone.

When a thief has logged into the honeypot account and potentially "factory reset" the device (which was simulated by our instrumentation), tracking information should be collected and forwarded to the device owner. In our approach, this is done by an anti-theft application. It is obvious that a thief should not notice that an anti-theft application is gathering information or even notice that it is installed. For this reason, in the honeypot account, the used anti-theft application is hidden from the list of installed applications in the settings menu as well as in the Android launcher. In Android there exist places where users can list the installed applications e.g., the Android Launcher and the settings menu in the category "Apps". We have instrumented these[5] such that the installed anti-theft application is hidden from a potential thief, and there are no possible traces of any installed anti-theft application anymore. For example, in the ManageApplications.java[5] file, we instrument the *onRebuildComplete* function such that the anti-theft application is removed from the list of displayed applications.

4   Evaluation

4.1   Evaluation Criteria

For evaluating our approach we determined a set of evaluation criteria that each determines the quality of one central aspect of our approach. We identified the following set of evaluation criteria (EvCrit) that together verify our approach:

---

[3] /frameworks/base/services/core/java/com/android/server/RecoverySystemService. java.

[4] /bootable/recovery/device.cpp, /bootable/recovery/recovery.cpp.

[5] /packages/apps/Launcher2/src/com/android/launcher2/AllAppsList.java,   /packages/apps/Settings/src/com/android/settings/applications/ManageApplications. java.

EvCrit 1 - Simulating Factory Reset. The first advantage of our approach is that it prevents a thief from performing a factory reset on the stolen device. This has two major benefits: First, it prevents the highly valuable personal user data from being deleted. Second, it prevents an installed anti-theft application from being uninstalled. During the evaluation we encouraged the participants to factory reset the device by every way they know. Each time after a participant finished the study, we checked whether any of the device owner's data had been deleted (e.g. by the factory reset).

EvCrit 2 - Successfully Executing the Anti-theft Application. The second advantage of our approach over every other approach is that it enables the device owner to execute an anti-theft application while the device is used by the thief. For each participant we checked whether an installed anti-theft solution was successfully executed while the participant interacted with the device and even after a "fake" factory reset.

EvCrit 3 - Indistinguishability from an Uninstrumented Device. A central property of our approach is that a thief should never notice that he/she is interacting with an instrumented device. More precise: our device should be indistinguishable from a regular stock device. For this reason we checked for both of our instrumentations whether any of them was detected by the participants. This implies the following sub-evaluation criteria:

EvCrit 3a - Hiding the Faking of the Factory Reset. As mentioned, during the study we motivated the participants to perform a factory reset. For every participant that performed the factory reset, we checked whether he/she was convinced that the factory reset was actually performed or experienced any irregularities (hints on the faking of factory reset).

EvCrit 3b - Hiding the Anti-theft Application, Running in the Background. While a potential thief interacts with the device it is crucial that there are no traces of running anti-theft applications. For this reason we motivated the participants to note every protection mechanism installed on the device. We asked them whether the device can be used by a thief after a factory reset (implicitly asking for the presence of an installed anti-theft application) and motivated every participant to note every observed irregularity. As an evaluation for this subcriteria we inspect the number of participants that expressed by any means the presence of an installed anti-theft application.

4.2   Evaluation Procedure

We performed the evaluation in the form of an empirical user study. In this user study we gave each participant a Nexus 6P device that was instrumented by the implementation of ThiefTrap. As in production, our approach would be combined with any authentication mechanism for account switching, we could evaluate our approach on the main account of the device without loss of validity. Additionally, an anti-theft tracking application was installed on the device that continuously tracked the device location. Together with this smartphone, we handed out a questionnaire that asked several questions about the user's opinion of the phone. The participants were given 60 min time to complete the questionnaire.

In total we evaluated the answers of 35 participants. All of the participants were either students or university graduates. The majority of the participants were Master students, while also some PhD students and Bachelor students participated. While the participants studied various disciplines, the biggest group studied computer science or some computer science related studies (12 participants). One of the requirement to participate in the study was to have precise knowledge of the Android OS. We verified this via oral inquiry. The survey participant's knowledge ranged from average to expert.

4.3   Results

For each participant, we performed the described evaluation procedure and evaluated the answers for the mentioned questions. We inspected the device state as additional evaluation results. In the following we will discuss each of the mentioned evaluation criteria:

EvCrit 1 - Simulating Factory Reset. We checked for every participant that performed the factory reset (21 out of 35) that the factory reset did not lead to a loss of any user data. The participants triggered the factory reset via the settings menu from within the operating system, as well as during the boot process via a special key combination. In all inspected cases the deletion of user data had been prevented.

EvCrit 2 - Successfully Executing the Anti-theft Application. To evaluate whether the installed anti-theft application was successfully executed in the background, we implemented an anti-theft tracking application that tracked the location of the device. For every participant we checked whether the anti-theft application was executed and whether it successfully tracked the device during the study. The installed anti-theft application was successfully executed in every case independent of the user interaction. This result proves the robustness of our approach. It should be stressed that our approach is independent from the used anti-theft application. Instead of the used tracking anti-theft application every possible anti-theft application can be silently executed using our approach.

EvCrit 3 - Indistinguishability from an Uninstrumented Device. As described, we enquired for the both places where participants could potentially detect the instrumentation, whether we successfully hide the instrumentation from the users.

EvCrit 3a - Hiding the Faking of the Factory Reset. For evaluating whether we could convince the participants that a factory reset was actually performed (while in reality it is just faked) we asked the following question to the participants: *"Do you think, it is possible for this person [a malicious person e.g. a thief] to completely reset the phone, in order to wipe all the owner's data, e.g. to sell the phone?"*

20 of the participants answered that they were able to perform a regular factory reset and so the device can be used by a thief. 11 participants answered that they were not able to factory reset the device as they did not know how to do it, but persons with more technical knowledge can (or could potentially) reset the device. 3 participants answered that it would not be possible to factory reset the device. When orally asked about their answers after the study, all of the participants answered that they did not know that the possibility of a factory reset exists.

One participant was not convinced of the factory reset. Due to limitations of the used AppLock application, this participant managed to access the apps before the factory reset. Thus he detected the inconsistency after the factory reset and was not convinced of the factory reset. This problem was not caused by our factory reset instrumentation but, by an implementation flaw of the used locking application. We would like to stress that the locking application is not part of our scientific contribution, but a tool we used in order to deceive a thief to believe that he/she is interacting with the real user account of the device owner. This mechanism can be replaced by every other mechanism or application that fulfills this requirement (e.g. simply filling the honeypot account with fake information).

EvCrit 3b - Hiding the Anti-theft Application, Running in the Background. A core feature of our approach is to hide the existence of an installed anti-theft solution. It is necessary that a thief is not aware that an anti-theft application is running on the device (even after triggering the factory reset). For this reason, we directly asked in the questionnaire whether the study participants were able to detect any protection mechanism in the device (*"Do you think that there is a protection mechanism installed to protect the user's data? Please explain."*) In their responses to this question the 33 out of 35 asked participants answered that the only protection mechanism that is used in the device is the locking application. One participant answered that there is no protection mechanism used. Due to the mentioned limitations of the AppLock app, it was possible for one participant to disable the AppLock app, and enter the protected applications. This participant found these applications empty and implied that there is a second protection mechanism present. First, it should be stressed that he did not imply that there is an anti-theft solution running. Second, the mechanism that simulates the owner's account is not part of our contribution and can be substituted by any other mechanism (e.g. another locking application, operating system instrumentations or simply filling the honeypot account with fake data).

Lastly, we provided space in the questionnaire to the participants where they could provide additional comments. We encouraged the participants to note every unusual observation. None of the participants noted that they observed an anti-theft application, tracking application or similar application running in the background.

To summarize the evaluation results, we found every evaluation criteria very satisfactory fulfilled. Evaluation criteria 1 and 2 were fulfilled in every case.

For evaluation criteria 3a just one participant out of 35 did recognized the fake factory reset. For evaluation criteria 3b only one out of 35 participants implied that another protection mechanism is in use while he did not detected the anti-theft application. Both of these cases were caused by an implementation flaw of the used locking application. As mentioned, this locking application is not part of our contribution and can be substituted by any other protection mechanism.

5 Discussion

The proposed concept of an anti-theft honeypot account is novel. It provides a combination of valuable security properties that are not given by any existing approach. These security properties are the maintenance of user data (preventing user data from being deleted), the confidentiality of user data (preventing a thief with physical access to the device from reading out user data) and the accessibility of the device (enabling any remote access mechanism for the owner while the device is physically under the control of the thief). While there exist various anti-theft solutions, none of them can fulfill all of these properties.

An important benefit of the proposed approach compared to existing anti-theft solutions is that *a device instrumented with our approach is indistinguishable from an ordinary device*. A thief can never tell whether he/she has stolen an ordinary device or a device instrumented with the anti-theft honeypot account. Studies [6] have shown that 34 % of Android devices are not protected by a locking mechanism, so there is no way for a thief to determine whether our mechanism is used or not. Also a noticeable proportion of devices are protected by the app locking mechanism that we use to protect user app data initially. So from the existence of a locking app, a thief can never imply the existence of an anti-theft honeypot account. Another aspect that plays a role in this matter is the flexibility of our approach. A locking app is just one mechanism for faking the honeypot account. An alternative for future work is the creation of fake user data. This data will then simulate the user data of the owner, while protecting his privacy. This data can be created either by the deployers of the anti-theft honeypot account, the users or both of them in cooperation.

Device theft is a serious problem with a rapidly growing number of reported cases. Studies [14] reported that in 2013 more than 3 million devices have been stolen. For this reason Google has taken steps to mitigate damage in case of a device theft. The two most important measures to mention here are the Android Device Protection mechanism [8] and anti-theft functionalities within the Android Device Manager [7]. The Android Device Protection mechanism requires that after a factory reset, a user logs into the device with the credentials of his primary Google Account. As a thief can not know these credentials, even after a factory reset, the stolen phone is of no use. The Android Device Manager can be used to track a phone and to remotely wipe. Compared with the combined usage of these two native Android tools, our approach has two advantages: First, it prevents the deletion of user data. Nowadays, a plenitude of valuable user data is stored on modern smartphones. In the vast majority of cases, the user data on such phones is hard to recover or even irreplaceable. In contrast to the mentioned Android tools, our approach can prevent the loss of this data. The second advantage is that any anti-theft application and functionality can be executed while the device is stolen. In contrast, the Android Device Manager just supports tracking and wiping functionalities.

Physical access to a device enables a number of novel attacks, so called hardware based attacks. In the context of Android smartphones prominent examples of these attacks are that by Cannon and Bradford [4] and the work of Ossmann and Osborn [16]. Cannon and Bradford used a so called white card, a special SIM card that authorizes flashing of a custom ROM on a device. Among others, from such a ROM it is possible to read out user data. Also Ossmann and Osborn proposed a hardware based attack with which it is possible to read out user data. By connecting to the Micro USB connector via UART with TTL logic they could connect to an integrated debugger, which enabled them to activate the Android Debugging Bridge functionality and so gain access to the device. Relating to our work it should be mentioned that in principle such hardware attacks might also be possible on devices with our instrumentations in place. Still, it should be stressed that hardware attacks like these require expert knowledge of the used hardware technologies and an existing vulnerability in the smartphone device. It is unlikely that both of these factors apply in the average case of a stolen device and so the impact of hardware based attacks on our proposed approach is negligible.

Another factor that should be discussed in the context of hardware attacks is the confidentiality of user data saved on a SD card in the device. While the AppLocking mechanism protects the confidentiality of user data on the SD card from access within the smartphone, the SD card can also be extracted from the device and read within another device. To protect the confidentiality of user data in this scenario it is necessary to encrypt the content of the SD card. Such an encryption of the SD card is orthogonal to our approach and can be implemented as completion to this approach.

We implemented our changes into the AOSP (Android Open Source Project). Additionally, our changes are portable, generic and thus can be easily integrated with every vendor specific build.

The usability of a device instrumented with our approach may differ from the normal device in terms of logging into the real account. For devices with a fingerprint scanner, the usability is not affected because the login procedure to the real account is equal to an ordinary login. Devices without a fingerprint scanner will require users to enter a pattern in the Honeypot account. This pattern can be configured by users. It is similar to unlocking a device using a pattern or a PIN. Hence, the usability impact is negligible.

Lastly, we would like to stress the flexibility of this approach. The concept of an anti-theft honeypot account can be applied orthogonally to any existing anti-theft mechanism. The honeypot account is responsible for protecting the user data while simultaneously any anti-theft mechanism is implemented. The benefit of the proposed concept is that in contrast to other approaches where a thief will quickly factory reset the device, in this approach it is likely that he/she will even establish an internet connection and so enabling the remote access for the installed anti-theft solution.

6   Related Work

While the idea of a honeypot account for theft protection is novel, there has been extensive research in other theft protection mechanisms in Android. In case of a theft it is likely that a potential thief will remove the SIM card from the device and factory reset it. At the time of this writing, no existing anti-theft mechanism can protect the user's privacy, maintain his data and keep good chances that the device will be found again at the same time.

Dhanu et al. [21] created a software for theft protection. After the theft protection software was installed and configured, it waited for a replacement of the SIM card. Once the SIM card was replaced, it started collecting video material, location information, and sent them via MMS to a phone number previously configured by the device owner.

Also Shetty [20] proposed an anti theft software that was triggered by a replacement of the SIM card. Whenever this event occurred, the software sent a notification SMS to a preconfigured number. From that point of time, it was possible for the device owner to retrieve the current location of the device via a SMS request.

Chouhan et al. [5] created a theft protection software in the form of a web based remote administration tool. Over a web interface the device owner could request the current location of the device. The software also enabled the device owner to record voices of the thief, wipe his/her private data and read the web history from the thief. In addition, the software notified the device owner about replacements of the SIM card.

The work of Al Rassan and Al Sheikh [1] proposed an anti-theft system that was supported by SMS. After being activated by a specially crafted SMS, an application, that was previously installed on the stolen phone could either broadcast its location or lock personal data that was stored on the phone. This data included media and log files, as well as SMS and MMS records.

Kuppusamy et al. [15] proposed a system for theft protection that could also be used as simple remote administration tool. Via SMS messages it was possible to locate the device, erase critical data, trace calls, manage incoming SMS and system access.

Yu et al. [27] proposed a system for remotely wiping stolen phones. This system worked in a way that a device owner could register his/her phone at the emergency call service provider. He could now from any point of time report the phone as stolen to the emergency call service provider. Additionally a background application was installed on the phone. Whenever the SIM card of the phone was removed, the application sent a wipe request to the emergency call service provider. If the device was stolen, the emergency call service provider answers this request with a modified call declined request, after which the phone would be wiped by the application. This scheme had the benefit that it neither requires a WIFI connection, nor an inserted SIM card to trigger the device wiping. However, the personal data and device was lost.

In all of the mentioned work, the thief has initial access to the user data until the anti-theft mechanism is triggered either automatically after a certain event occurs or manually by the device owner. The even more severe limitation of the mentioned approaches is that none of them prevents resetting the device. For this reason in each of this work, after the thief has triggered a factory reset, the anti-theft mechanisms are deleted and there are no chances that the device owner can regain his/her device.

Apart from academic work, there exist commercial solutions for locating and securing a lost or stolen device. Examples for these products are Apple's "Find My Device" [2], Avast's "Free Mobile Security" [3] or Symantec's "Norton Anti-Theft" [24]. These solutions can lock the device, locate it and provide additional functionality for mitigating damage in case of loss or theft. Additionally to the limitations mentioned previously, these solutions suffer from permission restrictions that are imposed by the Android Security Model. These restrictions lead to severe flaws. This insight is supported by the work of Simon and Anderson [22] that have examined various mobile anti-virus solutions for Android. They discovered failures in the implementation of the remote lock and wipe functionalities of these applications. Beside the restrictions imposed by the Android Security Model, they see the reasons for these flaws in certain vendor customizations.

Schneider [19] developed a password manager that uses a similar approach for another domain. This password manager returns fake password information when a wrong master password is used.

Srinivasan and Wu [23] proposed a mechanism that primarily prevented the smartphone from being turned off or being silenced in case of a theft. This approach was implemented by protecting the called functionality with passwords. Additionally, their proposed mechanism could wipe the device after a certain amount of failed password guesses. They rely on a password for preventing the thief accessing sensitive data. This measure is good for protecting the user's privacy but will at the same time trigger the thief to factory reset the device. After the factory reset, the anti theft mechanism will be deleted and there will be no chances for the owner to regain his/her device.

Another approach for protecting the privacy of user data in the case of a device theft was proposed by Tang et al. [25]. In their approach sensitive user data was encrypted and saved in the cloud. Their goal was to minimize the amount of sensitive data that was stored on the phone. The access to this cloud storage could now be restricted by any means, such as access rate limits, complete blocking as soon as the device was reported stolen and logging access. This approach focuses on protecting sensitive data of the user. Unfortunately, it could not help the owner regain his/her device.

7   Conclusion and Future Work

In this work we have proposed ThiefTrap, a novel concept using a honeypot account for the purpose of theft protection. Using this concept it is possible to protect sensitive user data while retaining high chances to regain the device. Our novel approach is the first that can achieve this combination of desired properties. We implemented our approach as modifications on the latest version of the Android operating system, the most used operating system in mobile devices at the time of this writing. Based on this implementation we successfully evaluated our approach in an empirical user study including 35 participants. The results of our study show that for a user it is not possible to distinguish the honeypot account from a regular unlocked device. Additionally we could retrieve information of the participants that in a real world application could be used to regain the device. It should be mentioned that the proposed concept is universal and can be customized on various scenarios and platforms.

While this approach is an important step in the development of anti-theft mechanisms, it can be further extended in the future. Potential extensions include the protection of alternative storages of private user data, such as the SIM card and the device settings. In our approach, these storages were excluded, as the SIM card is rarely used today for storing personal information and the device settings do not contain highly sensitive information. Still, there are some users that would like also to protect these places. A further point of future work is the creation of alternative mechanisms that simulate the owner's account data from within the honeypot account. These mechanisms can include the automatic or semi-automatic generation of fake data.

Acknowledgements. This work was supported by the German Federal Ministry of Education and Research (BMBF) through the project SmartPriv (16KIS0760).

References

1. Al Rassan, I., Al Sheikh, M.A.: Securing application in mobile computing. Int. J. Inf. Electron. Eng. **3**(5), 544 (2013)
2. Apple: Find my iPhone, iPad, iPod touch, or Mac. www.apple.com/support/icloud/find-my-device/
3. Avast: Avast free mobile security, June 2017. http://www.avast.com/en-us/free-mobile-security
4. Cannon, T., Bradford, S.: Into the droid: gaining access to Android user data. In: DefCon Hacking Conference (DefCon 2012), Las Vegas, Nevada, USA (2012)
5. Chouhan, J.G., Singh, N.K., Modi, P.S., Jani, K.A., Joshi, B.N., et al.: Camera and voice control based location services and information security on Android. J. Inf. Secur. **7**(03), 195 (2016)
6. CNBC: CNBC study. http://www.cnbc.com/2014/04/26/most-americans-dont-secure-their-smartphones.html
7. Google: Android device manager, June 2017. https://www.google.com/android/devicemanager

8. Google: Android device protection, June 2017. https://support.google.com/nexus/answer/6172890
9. Google: Android internals, February 2017. https://source.android.com/source/index.html
10. Google: Android open source project, June 2017. https://source.android.com
11. Google: Android OS version usages, January 2017. https://developer.android.com/about/dashboards/index.html
12. Google: Android version usage, 6 July 2017. https://developer.android.com/about/dashboards/index.html
13. IDC: Worldwide smartphone OS market share, November 2016. http://www.idc.com/promo/smartphone-market-share/os;jsessionid=6A0934D1434A49DBFFE74D63DA2C595B
14. Insider, B.: IDG research, May 2014. http://www.businessinsider.com/smartphone-theft-statistics-2014-5?IR=T
15. Kuppusamy, K.S., Senthilraja, R., Aghila, G.: A model for remote access and protection of smartphones using short message service. arXiv preprint arXiv:1203.3431 (2012)
16. Ossmann, M., Osborn, K.: Multiplexed wired attack surfaces. In: BlackHat USA (2013)
17. Reports, C.: Consumer reports, May 2014. http://www.consumerreports.org/cro/news/2014/04/smart-phone-thefts-rose-to-3-1-million-last-year/index.htm
18. Ruddock, D.: Anti-theft. http://www.androidpolice.com/2015/03/12/guide-what-is-android-5-1s-antitheft-device-protection-feature-and-how-do-i-use-it/
19. Schneider, D.M.: iMobileSitter, March 2014. http://www.imobilesitter.com/
20. Shetty, A.: Mobile anti theft system (MATS) (2012)
21. Dhanu, S., Shaikh, A., Barshe, S.: Anti-theft application for Android based devices. Int. J. Adv. Res. Comput. Commun. Eng. (2016)
22. Simon, L., Anderson, R.: Security analysis of consumer-grade anti-theft solutions provided by Android mobile anti-virus apps. In: 4th Mobile Security Technologies Workshop (MoST). Citeseer (2015)
23. Srinivasan, A., Wu, J.: SafeCode – safeguarding security and privacy of user data on stolen iOS devices. In: Xiang, Y., Lopez, J., Kuo, C.-C.J., Zhou, W. (eds.) CSS 2012. LNCS, vol. 7672, pp. 11–20. Springer, Heidelberg (2012). https://doi.org/10.1007/978-3-642-35362-8_2
24. Symantec: Norton mobile security. https://us.norton.com/anti-theft/
25. Tang, Y., Ames, P., Bhamidipati, S., Bijlani, A., Geambasu, R., Sarda, N.: CleanOS: limiting mobile data exposure with idle eviction. In: Presented as part of the 10th USENIX Symposium on Operating Systems Design and Implementation (OSDI 12), pp. 77–91 (2012)
26. Whitwam, R.: Anti-theft (2015). http://www.greenbot.com/article/2904397/everything-you-need-to-know-about-device-protection-in-android-51.html
27. Yu, X., Wang, Z., Sun, K., Zhu, W.T., Gao, N., Jing, J.: Remotely wiping sensitive data on stolen smartphones. In: Proceedings of the 9th ACM Symposium on Information, Computer and Communications Security, pp. 537–542. ACM (2014)

BluePass: A Secure Hand-Free Password Manager

Yue Li[1(✉)], Haining Wang[2], and Kun Sun[3]

[1] College of William and Mary, Williamsburg, VA 23187, USA
yli@cs.wm.edu
[2] University of Delaware, Newark, DE 19716, USA
hnw@udel.edu
[3] George Mason University, Fairfax, VA 22030, USA
ksun3@gmu.edu

Abstract. With the growing number of online accounts a user possesses, managing passwords has been unprecedentedly challenging. Users are prone to sacrifice security for usability, leaving their accounts vulnerable to various attacks. While replacing text-based password with a new universally applicable authentication scheme still seems unlikely in the foreseeable future, password managers have emerged to help users managing their passwords. However, state-of-the-art cloud based password managers are vulnerable to data breach and a master password becomes a single point of failure. To address these security vulnerabilities, we propose BluePass, a password manager that stores the password vault (i.e., the set of all the encrypted site passwords of a user) locally in a mobile device and a decryption key to the vault in the user computer. BluePass partially inherits the security characteristics of 2-Factor authentication by requiring both a mobile device and a master password to retrieve and decrypt the site passwords. BluePass leverages short-range nature of Bluetooth to automatically retrieve site passwords and fill the login fields, providing a hand-free user experience. Thus, BluePass enhances both security and usability. We implement a BluePass prototype in Android and Google Chrome platforms and evaluate its efficacy in terms of security, usability, and overhead.

Keywords: Password manager · Two-factor authentication

1 Introduction

Text-based password still dominates online authentication despite that it has long been plagued by a well-known and long-standing problem: the wide use of weak password. Due to limited human memory, users tend to choose weak passwords [3,5]. However, weak passwords are easy to guess and thus are vulnerable to a variety of attacks [4,19,22,28,32]. Today's increasing number of accounts a user possesses even worsen the problem since the user poorly manage their passwords. For example, on average users may reuse one password for as many

© ICST Institute for Computer Sciences, Social Informatics and Telecommunications Engineering 2018
X. Lin et al. (Eds.): SecureComm 2017, LNICST 238, pp. 185–205, 2018.
https://doi.org/10.1007/978-3-319-78813-5_10

as 3.9 online accounts [11]. As such, instead of impractically expecting users to select a strong password for each account, password managers are developed as built-in or standalone gadgets to help users manage their credentials. A password manager includes a vault that stores all encrypted passwords of a user, and the user only needs to remember one master password, which is used to generate the decryption key to the vault, to access all the passwords in the vault. To support user authentication on different devices, password managers usually synchronize the vaults to their own servers and provide a downloading service to their users. However, a password manager has its own security and usability problem. For example, password managers usually synchronize the local vault to the remote server, which makes data breach possible [2]. Furthermore, to enhance usability, many browser built-in password managers do not necessarily need a master password, which makes it vulnerable to unauthorized use and meanwhile sacrifices portability. Even being used, a master password becomes a single point of failure. Usability issues of a password manager may even lead to reduced security, stemming from incomplete user mental models [7].

For critical online services, users may desire more secure authentication than merely password. Toward this end, two-factor authentication (2FA) is proposed to include another layer of protection to user accounts. Nowadays many leading service providers such as Google and Microsoft, have integrated 2FA into their online systems. However, 2FA suffers from limited adoption due to undesired extra burden on users. It is estimated that in 2015, only around 6.4% of Google users are using 2FA [24]. In order to improve usability, transparent 2FA has been proposed [8,23] by leveraging additional devices (mainly user smartphones) to automatically complete the enhanced authentication procedure without user involvement. However, these approaches are hard to deploy because of imperative modifications at both the web server and the client sides.

In this paper, we propose BluePass, an enhanced password manager that partially inherits the security benefit of 2FA to improve the security and usability of existing password managers. One of the key features of BluePass is to isolate the storage of the password vault from that of the decryption key. Here the password vault is the set of all the encrypted site passwords of a user. Specifically, the password vault is stored locally in a mobile device (e.g., a user's smartphone) and the decryption key is stored in the BluePass server, which can be accessed and downloaded only once to a computer after authentication through a master password. The mobile device communicates with the computer using Bluetooth in a transparent manner. When a user needs to log in a website, the computer will automatically request the site password from the mobile device. The encrypted site password will then be delivered through Bluetooth. Afterwards, the computer is able to decrypt the site password using the local decryption key and auto-fill the web forms for the user. BluePass relies on Bluetooth for communication rather than other channels, because Bluetooth can be both transparent to users and a subtle indicator of co-location of the user mobile device.

BluePass is secure since it does not store password vaults on a server and is not vulnerable to massive password breach. Furthermore, a server data breach is likely to leak both password vaults and hashed master passwords. By cracking the master password table offline, it is almost guaranteed that most master passwords can be craked out, given today's computing power and the weakness of user-selected passwords. Attackers are given direct access to password vaults under such a case, since the vault decryption key is generated from the master password. By contrast, in BluePass, the password vault and its decryption key are stored separately, and decryption key is not generated from master passwords, losing one of them will not practically leak any password.

While BluePass itself uses 2FA, it does not require any modifications on the website servers. Thus, the underlying password framework remains unaltered, i.e., logging into a website still only needs one site password. BluePass is also usable since it demands little effort to configure on the computer and no extra effort from a user to authenticate afterwards.

We implement a BluePass prototype in Android and Google Chrome and evaluate its efficacy in terms of security, overhead, and usability. First, we conduct a comprehensive security analysis to demonstrate that BluePass can defend against various attacks. Then we evaluate the auto-fill time latency of BluePass by recording the time between login forms being detected and the forms being automatically filled. We also run a series of experiments, in which we retrieve passwords under different frequencies, to measure the energy overhead of BluePass. Based on our experimental results, BluePass is energy efficient while automatically filling in the login forms with user-unperceived latency. Afterwards, we conduct a user study including 31 volunteers to examine the usability of BluePass. The results show the test subjects regard BluePass as both secure and usable. Moreover, the majority of testers report that they are willing to use BluePass to manage their passwords.

The remainder of the paper is organized as follows. Section 2 elaborates the system overview and threat model. Section 3 details the system architecture of BluePass and Sect. 4 conducts security analysis on BluePass. Section 5 illustrates the prototype implementation of BluePass. We evaluate BluePass in Sect. 6 and present a user study in Sect. 7. Section 8 discusses BluePass-related issues and its limitation. Section 9 surveys related work and finally, Sect. 10 concludes this paper.

2   System Overview and Threat Model

Before presenting the BluePass system, we first introduce important BluePass notations for clarification purposes.

- *BluePass server:* a server that is mainly responsible for registering users and distributing keys to user computers.
- *Key pair (K_1, K_2):* a pair of RSA keys that are used by the mobile device and the computer to encrypt/decrypt site passwords. K_1 is only stored in the mobile phone while K_2 is stored in the BluePass server for re-distribution. We manage to use only one pair of keys to protect bi-directional communication, and the details can be found in Sect. 8.1.

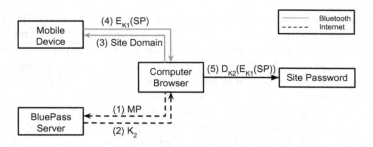

Fig. 1. BluePass authentication.

- *Master password (MP):* a user uses its master password to authenticate itself to the BluePass server and retrieve its own decryption key K_2. A master password is the only password a user needs to remember.
- *Site password (SP):* passwords to access online services, which will be encrypted by K_1 and then stored in the BluePass mobile application.
- *Trusted computer:* a computer that the user trusts, such as the user's personal computer. It stores the decryption key K_2 for a long term.
- *Untrusted computer:* a computer that the user does not trust, such as a library computer. The decryption key K_2 must be retrieved from the BluePass server every time a browser is opened in the untrusted computer. K_2 is only temporarily stored in a browser instance, and is removed when the browser instance is terminated.
- *Client-side (computer/browser) application:* the user installs it on the computer, which is in charge of detecting and auto-filling login forms, communicating with the mobile device, and decrypting the received site passwords.
- *Mobile application:* the user installs the app on its mobile device. The app stores the encrypted site passwords and delivers the encrypted site passwords to the user computer through Bluetooth.

2.1   System Overview

BluePass works on two premises. First, a site password can only be recovered by having both the encrypted site password $E_{K_1}(SP)$ that is only stored in the mobile device and the corresponding decryption key K_2 that is distributed through the BluePass server. Second, the encrypted site password $E_{K_1}(SP)$ can only be retrieved from the mobile device to the user computer through Bluetooth, which requires the proximity of the two devices. The flow chart of BluePass password authentication is shown in Fig. 1.

The working mechanism of BluePass mainly includes three phases, which are detailed as follows.

Phase 1: Registration is a once-in-a-lifecycle operation, in which a user needs to register for the BluePass service. The user installs the BluePass mobile app on its mobile device and uses its master password to log into the BluePass account. The mobile device is then initialized with an empty password vault.

Phase 2: Configuration is to install and configure the user devices. First, a client-side application needs to be installed on the user computer. Then, the user will log into the BluePass server and download the decryption key K_2 into the computer. The user will store the key either for a long term or temporarily, depending on whether the computer is trusted or untrusted. Note that the installation of the client-side application on a computer is also a one-time operation. The retrieval of K_2 from the BluePass server is needed each time opening a browser only when the user is on a untrusted computer.

Phase 3: Authentication is almost transparent to the user. In a trusted device, the user only needs to carry the registered mobile phone and wait for the passwords being automatically filled. In a untrusted device, the user needs to re-enter the master password every time a new browser instance is opened since the key K_2 is deleted when a browser instance is closed.

2.2 Threat Model

Attackers aim at stealing one or (preferably) all site passwords in the password vault. In the design of BluePass, all the site passwords of a user are encrypted and stored in the user's mobile device. We assume that the attacker cannot access the encrypted site passwords in the mobile device and knows the decryption key from the computer at the same time.

All attacks can be classified into two categories: *co-located attacks* and *remote attacks*. A co-located attack can only happen within the Bluetooth communication range of the user mobile device, while a remote attack can be launched from anywhere. In a co-located attack, since the attacker could access the encrypted site passwords through sniffing, we must prevent the decryption key from falling into the hand of the attacker. Therefore, both the BluePass server and the master password cannot be compromised. Moreover, the communications for key distribution must be protected. By contrast, in a remote attack, since the attacker cannot access the mobile device through Bluetooth, either the BluePass server or the master password could be compromised. Also, no secure communication is required for key distribution. As the Bluetooth reachability is very limited (33 feet for class 2 Bluetooth devices), a co-located attack is much more difficult to launch than a remote attack.

3 System Architecture

3.1 Core Functions

As mentioned in Sect. 2.1, BluePass mainly consists of three phases. The first two phases, registration and configuration of BluePass, are mostly one-time effort; however, the third phase, authentication, will be triggered each time a user needs to log in a website. Figure 2 illustrates BluePass architecture and the data flow of these three phases.

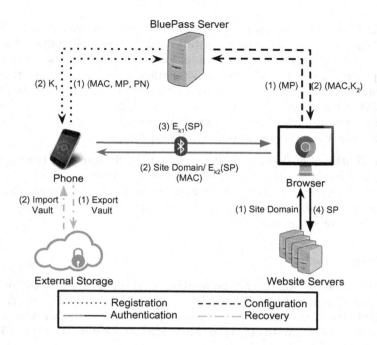

Fig. 2. BluePass architecture

Registration. The black dotted lines in Fig. 2 show the registration process. To register a BluePass service, the user only needs to download a BluePass application to the mobile phone and create a master account on the BluePass server. The creation of the master account is similar to the creation of an account in any website. Upon logging into the master account on the mobile app, the user can choose to bind the mobile device. The binding process should follow a traditional 2FA mechanism. Namely, the user re-authenticate herself with another authentication factor, for example, a sms. Afterward, the device information, specifically, the MAC address of the device Bluetooth, will be uploaded to the BluePass server. The MAC address is used for the client-side application to automatically locate the associated mobile device without user involvement. For a newly associated device, the BluePass Server generates a pair of asymmetric keys (K_1, K_2). It then distributes K_1 to the mobile phone and keeps only K_2 on the server side. We list the database of the BluePass server in Table 1 and that of the mobile device in Table 2 populated with made-up data. The registration should only be done once on the mobile device. After registration, the mobile device is initialized as a password vault. Note that the key pair of (K_1, K_2) is not used as a conventional public-key pair, where the public key is known to all and the private key is kept in secret. Instead, the key pair is used for a two-way communication channel and both of them should be kept in secret.

Table 1. Server side data

Username	Salt	$H(MP + Salt)$	K_2	Device MAC address
Alice	ifu92@fb	$a4f3b3c9e61b838f8cda07\ldots$	$VDSnrzjqFBy9\ldots$	BC:F5:AC:9D:9A:57
Bob	01dm.a<w	$daa4a403bfec911a3ef199\ldots$	$yKhTC3dNAkE\ldots$	BC:F5:AC:9D:9A:58

Table 2. Mobile device data

Domain	Username	K1	$E_{K_1}(Password)$
.yahoo.com/	aliceweb1	$AoGAKooOHMT\ldots$	$Encrypted\_Password_1$
.yahoo.com/	aliceweb2	$VN9SdOeFbo4w\ldots$	$Encrypted\_Password_2$
.google.com/	aliceweb2	$B1FUeDXiqv4j\ldots$	$Encrypted\_Password_3$

After registration, the user has initialize a password vault in its own mobile device and associated the BluePass account with this device.

Configuration. The computer needs to be configured to run BluePass, which is shown in the dashed black lines in Fig. 2. The user installs and runs a client-side application, and then logs into the BluePass server to fetch the Bluetooth MAC address of the mobile device and K_2 generated during the registration. At this point, the user can choose whether the computer is trusted or not. If the computer is trusted, the Bluetooth MAC address and K_2 will be stored in the browser for a long term. Otherwise, they will be deleted after the user closes the current browser instance. Knowing the device Bluetooth MAC address enables the computer to pair with the device automatically by using RFCOMM insecure mode, in which the Bluetooth data is broadcasted and the target MAC address is specified in the data. BluePass does not rely on secure Bluetooth communication. Using RFCOMM insecure mode enhances usability while not degrading security.

Authentication. The authentication phase is the only phase that a user will constantly experience during use of Bluepass. The solid lines in Fig. 2 show the data flow of BluePass authentication process. First, the user directs the browser to a website it wants to login. The BluePass client-side application will examine the Document Object Model (DOM, which is a tree structure representing the webpages) of the returned page and check the existence of a login form. If a login form is present, the application requests the corresponding credentials from the mobile phone using Bluetooth. After receiving the request, the mobile application returns the encrypted credentials. If no related credential exists, BluePass will instead respond with a "NO_PASSWORD" flag. We realize that auto-filling in a non-HTTPS environment is vulnerable to JavaScript injection attacks [26], so we only do auto-filling for websites that are based on HTTPS. For other websites, BluePass will pop up a window for a user's consent before filling the login form. Note that none of the above steps require any user interactions. This fully automated authentication enables users to login a website in a hand-free manner. When there exists more than one account for a specific website, the browser will let the user choose an account to be decrypted and automatically filled in the forms since there is no way to predict which account will be used.

3.2   Account Management

Account management is essential to a password manager. Users should be able to add, edit, or delete the credentials in BluePass. These functions must be correctly designed to guarantee the security of BluePass.

The addition of an online account into BluePass can be done when a user has manually inputted the login credentials into a new website. BluePass adopts a similar approach just as current browser built-in password managers. If the "NO_PASSWORD" flag is sent back, the browser knows that no login credentials are associated to this particular website. If the user manually inputs the credentials, the browser will capture the value in the form before submission and prompt a non-intrusive dialog window, asking whether the user wishes to store the login information into BluePass. Specifically, there are three options: "yes", "not this time", and "never". If "yes" is chosen, the browser will encrypt the credentials using key K_2 and send it to the mobile device (see Fig. 2). The mobile device will decrypt the information using K_1 and encrypt it again using K_1. Mathematically the process is denoted as $E_{K_1}(D_{K_1}(C))$, in which $C = E_{K_2}(SP)$. Then the encrypted credentials are stored in the BluePass database.

The edition of an online account is similar to the addition process. The browser monitors if the user has modified the value in the login form when being submitted. If the password is changed, the browser will prompt a dialog that asks for user permission to update the login credentials in BluePass. Upon user consent, the browser will send the updated values in an encryption and decryption procedure similar to that of adding a new account. Note that the chosen option of "never" should also be recorded in the password vault, which prevents the dialog from prompting repeatedly. In this case, the password vault records the domain name and the username without storing a password. When an empty password is passed back, the application is acknowledged that the user does not wish to store the login credentials. The revocation of the "never" status can be done in the administration page in the mobile applications.

The deletion of login credentials can also be done on the mobile application's administration page. The mobile application shows a list of websites whose site passwords are stored in the mobile phone. The user can choose to delete one of the websites' login credentials. However, the user needs to manually input the website's URL and login credentials. Before the deletion is granted, the user must input the correct master password. This will prevent an attacker from manipulating the user's online accounts.

3.3   Recovery

When using a cloud-based password manager, users can backup their password vaults on the server side. On the contrary, BluePass is de-centralized and stores local copies on mobile devices. Though users usually do not lose their mobile devices quite often, it is essential for BluePass to back up and recover the password vault when the mobile devices are lost, which is illustrated with red lines in Fig. 2.

Users can choose to back up their vaults to an external storage including a portable hard disk, a USB, or a cloud storage. If a user loses the mobile device, it can recover the vault from the external storage. Backing up the vault to a user-owned physical device may require the user to periodically back up and synchronize the password vault to the external storage device. Alternatively, BluePass allows users to synchronize their password vaults to a cloud drive provider. Nowadays many large drive providers, such as Google Drive or Dropbox, have published APIs to facilitate data synchronization. Note such design still ensures the 2FA design of BluePass – an attacker needs to breach both the BluePass Server and the cloud provider server to collect the two necessary pieces of secret.

4 Security Analysis

BluePass is secure in a sense that as long as a user does not lose two factors at the same time, the user's login information is safe. We conduct a security analysis on BluePass to verify the robustness of BluePass against various attack vectors.

4.1 Two-Factor Security

We have introduced that BluePass relies on the premise that two factors need to be possessed to derive a site password. The two factors are user mobile device and a master password. Now we discuss the security of BluePass when one of the factors is compromised.

Master Password. An attacker may be able to compromise the master password of a user, which can be done through different ways such as guessing, phishing, shoulder-surfing, etc. The compromisation of a trusted computer is also equivalent to losing the master password because the only purpose of having the master password is to retrieve K_2 from BluePass server, which can be directly extract K_2 from a trusted computer. In such scenarios, the attacker is able to obtain key K_2. However, if the attacker does not have the password vault of the user, K_2 is merely a meaningless token and the security of BluePass holds. Besides, the user is able to change the master password and re-generate a new key pair.

Mobile Device. If an attacker gains access to the mobile device by either compromising the device or stealing the device, it may be able to access the encrypted password vault and the encryption key K_1. However, without the decryption key K_2, the attacker cannot decrypt the site passwords from the encrypted password vault. Unlike cloud-based password managers, BluePass does not keep master password and the vault on the same storage, thus obtaining K_2 together with the password vault is not practical. Moreover, the mobile phone itself may have its own protection, such as an unlock code or fingerprint verification, and remote data erasal.

4.2   Data Breach and Brute-Force Attacks

A serious threat to a password manager is data breach. Under this scenario, the attacker may be able to mount a brute force attack against the master password of a user. In a normal password manager such as LastPass or 1Password, the loss of a master password also means the loss of an entire password vault, namely, when an attacker successfully mounts a brute force attack against the master password, it can also retrieve all the passwords from the password vault since the key used to encrypt the vault is derived from the master password. Again, BluePass does not centralize the password vault storage. Instead, the password vault of a user is stored locally in its own mobile device. A server data breach would at most leak the user master passwords and then further leak the decryption keys. However, as the password vault of each user is not stored at the BluePass server, a data breach at the BluePass server cannot break BluePass.

On the other hand, assuming that a password vault is lost from a user's mobile device, we believe that brute-force cracking such an encrypted password vault is impractical given the current computing power. We emphasize that the password vault is protected by K_1, which is 2048-bit long randomly generated RSA key. Cracking K_1 is much harder than cracking a master password, which is generated by a human user within limited and predictable password space.

4.3   Broken HTTPS or Bluetooth

If an attacker compromises the HTTPS communication, it will be able to steal the encryption/decryption key pair (K_1, K_2) of a user. However, K_1 and K_2 are only transmitted through the web when a user installs BluePass on its mobile device (K_1) or when the user log on BluePass from a new computer (K_2), which makes the attack strictly time sensitive. Even though, having the key pair does not help the attacker to identify any of the user's site password, unless the attacker can also eavesdrop on the Bluetooth connection (i.e., co-located attack) to capture the encrypted password in transmission. On the other hand, eavesdropping Bluetooth alone does not compromise BluePass either, since the content is encrypted.

To succeed, the attacker needs to compromise both HTTPS and Bluetooth communications to steal site passwords from users. However, such a successful attack is very difficult to launch, due to time (to steal the keys) and location (to eavesdrop the Bluetooth) constraints. Furthermore, a large scale attack is infeasible since Bluetooth signals can only be sniffed within a short range.

5   Implementation

BluePass consists of three major components that cooperate with each other on user authentication, namely, a BluePass server for user registration and key distribution, a BluePass client application on the laptop for detecting and auto-filling the website login forms, and a BluePass app on the mobile phone serving as the password vault and administration console. We build the BluePass client application in a Macbook Air running OS X 10.10.4 and Chrome 46.0.2490.80. We implement the BluePass app on a Nexus 5 running Android version 4.4.2.

5.1   BluePass Server

We implement a BluePass server using Cherrypy [13], a python web framework. We use self-signed certificate in https to protect communication. The key pair (K_1, K_2) is generated using Pycrypto[1] on the server side. Sqlite database is used to store user data (see Table 1 for detail). When registering to the service, we do not use the standard 2FA to verify the phone number since it is not necessary for evaluation and user study. After registration, the user needs to log in BluePass on both mobile application to upload mobile phone Bluetooth MAC address and download K_1 and client-side application to download K_2 and Mobile phone Bluetooth MAC address.

5.2   BluePass Client-Side Application

We build the BluePass client-side application on Chrome platform, which consists of 2 modules: one Chrome application for Bluetooth communication and one Chrome extension for password auto-filling. We use two modules because currently Chrome extension does not support Bluetooth API while Chrome application does. However, only Chrome extensions allow reading and modifying the DOM of web pages, which unavoidably makes us separate client-side application functionality into 2 modules. Chrome application is more like a native application, but it is built on Chrome platform to deliver content in HTML, CSS and Javascript (e.g., Google Doc, Google Drive). It uses the *chrome.Bluetooth* API to connect to the Bluetooth device and then communicate with the smart phone through Bluetooth. The Chrome extension is responsible for detecting the authentication form and automatically fill the form after decrypting the site password from the mobile application.

The communication between the Chrome application and the chrome extension is implemented through Chrome External Messaging[2]. Specifically, this extension specifies the Application ID, which is a unique identifier for the Chrome application. After Chrome extension delivers the data to the application that is binded to the ID and has a pre-added listener, the listener can extract the data. The communication from Chrome application to Chrome extension works similarly.

Our prototype implements the BluePass client on the Chrome platform to simplify the communications among different modules; however, the framework of BluePass can be widely deployed on more platforms as long as both the computer and the mobile device have Bluetooth support and the browser extension

---

[1] https://www.dlitz.net/software/pycrypto/.

[2] https://developer.chrome.com/extensions/messaging.

is able to communicate with local applications on the computer. First, Bluetooth has become a standard device on modern computers and smartphones. Second, communication between browser extensions and native applications has been supported by most modern browsers, including Internet Explorer, Chrome, Firefox, Safari, Opera, etc.

5.3 BluePass Mobile Application

The BluePass mobile application starts a BluePass service, which runs in the background of Android and has a dedicated thread to listen to the incoming Bluetooth connection, which helps transparently authenticate a user to a registered website. The BluePass service inherits from the *Service* class in Android and keeps running until the user explicitly stops the service.

BluePass mobile application has a simple and clear user interface, which shows the status of the background BluePass service, either "running" or "suspended". The user can easily change the service status by clicking "Start BluePass Service" or "Stop BluePass Service" buttons. When the service status is running, the Bluetooth listener starts listening and remains active even the mobile device turns off the screen and goes to sleep. Whenever users would like to stop the service, they just need to open the application and click the "Stop BluePass Service" button.

We use RFCOMM Bluetooth protocol to establish communication between the mobile phone and the computer, since RFCOMM is widely supported and provides public APIs in most modern operating systems. Android supports two modes of RFCOMM connections, *secure mode* and *insecure mode*. The secure mode requires successful pairing before any RFCOMM channel can be established while the insecure mode allows connection without pairing two devices. Secure mode RFCOMM adds another layer of encryption. However, as BluePass communication is secured by (K_1, K_2) so that it does not rely on Bluetooth security. While insecure mode may fit better since it saves a pairing step from the user, Chrome application does not support insecure RFCOMM communication due to security concern. Therefore, we use the secure RFCOMM connection mode. Consequently, in the registration phase, the user also needs to pair the mobile phone and the computer first if they have never been paired before. Note that pairing only needs to be done once in a computer unless the user manually deletes paird devices on the mobile phone or computer.

6 Evaluation

6.1 Comparative Evaluation Framework

We use the comparative authentication scheme evaluation framework [6] to compare BluePass with other related authentication schemes. The results are summarized in Table 3. We can see that BluePass is *physically-effortless* since the entire authentication process is transparent to the user and *Quasi-Nothing-to-Carry* since users still need to carry their mobile phones though they carry

Table 3. BluePass scheme evaluation

Scheme	Memorywise-Effortless	Scalable-for-Users	Nothing-to-Carry	Physically-Effortless	Easy-to-Learn	Efficient-to-Use	Infrequent-Errors	Easy-Recovery-from-Loss	Accessible	Negligible-Cost-per-User	Server-Compatible	Browser-Compatible	Mature	Non-Proprietary	Resilient-to-Physical-Observation	Resilient-to-Targeted-Impersonation	Resilient-to-Throttled-Guessing	Resilient-to-Unthrottled-Guessing	Resilient-to-Internal-Observation	Resilient-to-Leaks-from-Other-Verifiers	Resilient-to-Phishing	Resilient-to-Theft	No-Trusted-Third-Party	Requiring-Explicit-Consent	Unlinkable
	Usability								**Deployability**						**Security**										
Password			●		●	●	○	●	●	●	●	●	●	●		○						●	●	●	●
Firefox (with MP)	○	●	○	○	●	●	●		●	●	●		●	●	○	○					●	●	●	●	●
LastPass	○	●	○	○	●	●	●	○	●	○	●		●		○	○	○	○		○	●	●		●	●
Tapas	●	●	○	○	●	○	●		○	●	●		●	●		○					●	●	●	●	●
BluePass	○	●	○	●	●	●	●	○	●	●	●		●	●	●	○	○	○	○	●	●	●	●	●	●
Sound-Proof		○		●	●	●	○	○	●	●			●		●	○			●	●	●	●	●	●	●

● indicates that the scheme fully carry the characteristic and ○ indicates that the scheme partially carry the characteristic (the Quasi prefix). We take rows 1–3 from [6], row 4 from [20], and row 6 from [23].

them anyway. BluePass is accessible since it does not require the cellphone to have signal or cellular data. BluePass is *Quasi-Resilient-to-Throttled-Guessing* and *Quasi-Resilient-to-Unthrottled-Guessing*. Although BluePass itself does not enhance the security of the underlying password mechanisms, it can help defend throttled and unthrottled guessing by generating long random passwords for users and motivating users to use more secure passwords since they do not need to remember the passwords.

Bonneau et al. [6] points out that the framework does not describe all possible properties of an authentication scheme. Besides these factors, BluePass also keeps a simple and clean user mental model, which is highly suggested since wrong mental models easily make user passwords weaker [7]. Furthermore, BluePass strengthen usability by not requiring users to delete their password traces after use on a untrusted computer as other password manager (e.g., log out master account or delete local password vault).

6.2 Password Auto-Fill Latency

For a usable password manager, the time required to fill the password field should be short. We record the delay between the time that the password input form is detected and the time that the form is automatically filled (denoted as T_{bp}).

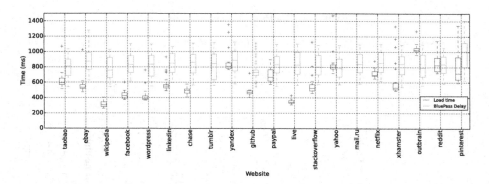

Fig. 3. BluePass latency

Table 4. Delay statistics

	Median	Mean	SD	Skewness
T_{bp}	778.0	814.6	158.3	1.6
T_{load}	599.5	837.6	691.3	2.6
T_{bp} (removed)	775.0	812.5	155.2	1.6
T_{load} (removed)	570.0	631.4	259.8	2.6

Since the delays on different websites may be different due to the specific website design, we choose 20 major providers from Alexa Top 100 website [30]. For each site, we make up a username/password pair and test the pair of credentials for at least 50 times. The password of each site is a randomly generated 16 byte string composed of all 4 characters types (Uppercase character, lower case character, digit, and special character).

Besides the Bluetooth communication latency, we also measure the loading time (denoted as T_{load}) for a website since page rendering (bottleneck to load a page) and Bluetooth communication tasks are running in parallel, indicating that the actual latency a user is experiencing is roughly $T_{bp} - T_{load}$, which is the time difference between BluePass running time and page loading time. T_{load} is measured by injecting a piece of javascript code, which measures the time when all javascripts on the webpage that need to run immediately are being executed subtracting the time that the browser is ready to send the HTTP request.

The results for all 20 sites are shown in Fig. 3. Figure 3 does not show the T_{load} results for two web services, Tumblr and mail.ru, that have much higher T_{load} (averaged 2,700–2,800 ms). Generally the BluePass delay time (T_{bp}) is slightly higher than the page loading time (T_{load}). To illustrate the extent of the time gap, we show statistical analysis in Table 4. In the last two rows, we do not include Tumblr and mail.ru in our analysis since they have significantly higher T_{load} that are not representative for normal cases. With the two sites excluded, the average T_{bp} is 814.6 ms, which is short enough to be acceptable by most users. Furthermore, the actual delay that a user experiences is $T_{bp} - T_{load}$, which is only 181.1 ms in average. The standard deviation for T_{load} is higher than T_{bp}. The loading time T_{load} could be different under various factors, such as network condition, website implementation, etc. Since T_{load} highly depends on the website implementation, heavy javascript use in a site could largely contribute to a high T_{load}.

On contrast, T_{bp} is relatively stable since Bluetooth communication and mobile device computing are almost the same in each login attempt. Since the delay caused by BluePass is bounded by $T_{bp} - T_{load}$, BluePass imposes a very low latency on the password auto-filling process. According to our user study, users can hardly notice the latency.

6.3   Power Consumption

One major concern of BluePass usage is the power consumption overhead on the mobile device, since BluePass requires the mobile device serve as a Bluetooth server that keeps listening to incoming connections. We measure the extra power consumption imposed by BluePass through monitoring the power levels of the mobile device when running BluePass password retrieval process in different frequencies. For comparison, we also record the power level of the device when Bluetooth is turned off (we call it a clean state).

To monitor the current battery level of the mobile device, we register a broadcast receiver in a simple battery monitoring application on the mobile device to listen to battery level changing event, upon which the current battery level and the timestamp are recorded. We tune the login frequency in the browser side (by refreshing a webpage in different frequency) to evaluate different use cases.

Except for the login frequency and BluePass on/off status, we keep all other settings exactly the same, such as installed and running application on the device as well as the network status (e.g., Wifi connection is turned off). We use a Nexus 5 mobile phone for evaluation, which has 2100 mAh battery capacity. As it takes a long time to use up the battery that has been fully charged, we run each experiment for 10 h before charing the phone and running the next experiment. Though the granularity of battery usage broadcasting is in percentage level that may not be highly accurate, it is sufficient to evaluate the power efficiency of BluePass in a 10-h test period.

Figure 4 illustrates the battery level dynamics through time under different experiment setups. "On" means the Bluetooth is turned on and "off" means the Bluetooth is turned off. Other lines represent the Bluepass log-in frequency. A reasonable frequency of login attempted by a normal user should not exceed 100 times a day, which means that the login frequency should lie around 0–10 times per hour. With 10 logins per hour, the power consumption is only 1% more than a clean state. We believe it is an unnoticeable overhead for users, given that almost 90% of users charge their phone more frequently than once per 2 days [27]. Besides, we can see that a significant power overhead is only incurred when the user tries to log in very frequently (17% when trying to log in every 2 s). However, normal users would not try logging in at such a high frequency.

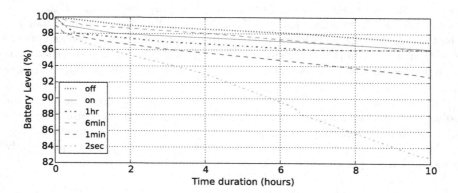

Fig. 4. BluePass power consumption

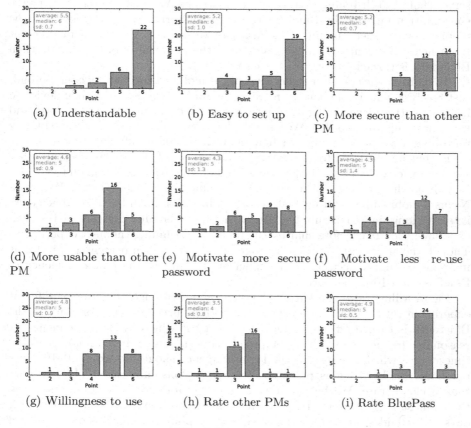

Fig. 5. Survey results

In our experiments, the mobile phone is in a state that does not receive cellular or wifi signal, so the battery drains very slowly. When the mobile phone is in normal daily usage, the battery usage becomes much higher. However, the BluePass power consumption remains the level of 1% of total power with 10 h use.

7   User Study

To verify how real users rate the security and usability of BluePass, we conduct a user study to gather feedback and comments from normal users. Upon approval of IRB of our institution, we recruit 31 volunteers to use and comment on BluePass. The volunteers include 16 males and 15 females. As the study is only in a school scale, most of them age 20–30 years old. Besides, most of them have a bachelor degree. In order to spread our study of different computer expertise, we deliberately recruit volunteers from 10 fields of study.

We ask each of the volunteer to finish a series of tasks. They are (1) register to BluePass server and configure BluePass, (2) create a new account in our self-deployed test site, (3) log in the test site (Migrate password), (4) try using BluePass to log in again (Log in from a primary computer), (5) change the current password and try using BluePass to log in (Change Password), (6) configure BluePass in another computer and log in (Log in from another computer), (7) turn off BluePass and try logging in, and (8) turn on BluePass and try logging in. We also create a test website that has only login and changing password functions for the volunteers to operate on.

After finishing the tasks, the testers take a post-study questionnaire. The questionnaire mainly uses 6-point scale rating where 1 point means strongly disagree and 6 point means strongly agree. The results are shown in Fig. 5. Testers generally think the concept of BluePass is understandable and it is fairly easy to set up. 87% of testers (27 out of 31) agree that BluePass is more usable than any other password manager they have used before.

BluePass motivates the testers to increase password security. More than 70% (22 out of 31) of the testers state they are motivated to choose more secure passwords and less likely to re-use existing passwords, thus making their passwords stronger. However, though the testers report they are motivated to use more secure passwords, we notice that only 4 testers have tried using random passwords generated by BluePass to create/change their passwords, which may result from the fact that users feel "unsafe" to use a non-memorable password.

The majority of testers (94%) expresses willingness to use BluePass to manager their passwords. We also ask the testers to compare BluePass to other favorite password managers they have used, and testers show large preference to BluePass over existing password managers. To summarize, BluePass is generally considered more secure and usable than existing password managers by the testers. Most of them show preference to BluePass and willingness to use it. Thus, it is reasonable to conclude that BluePass does help users secure their passwords.

8 Discussion

8.1 RSA Key Pair

BluePass can use only one RSA key pair (K_1, K_2) to achieve bi-directional communication between the mobile phone and the computer. We must guarantee that the compromise of K_1 will not lead to the compromise of K_2, and vice versa. We know that all public key cryptography algorithms ensure that it is hard to derive the private key from the public key, but not vice versa. For instance, given an ECC private key, it is easy to derive the ECC public key, since $public\_key = private\_key * G$. However, for RSA, in theory, it is hard to derive either e or d from knowing the other one. Therefore, we can use only one pair of RSA keys with careful parameter settings.

There are two minor things to notice in the detailed RSA implementation. First, in practice e is usually chosen a small/fixed number, but this should be avoided. Second, RSA private keys are often stored in their "Chinese Remainder Theorem" form, which includes the two secret numbers often denoted p and q, from which the totient is computed. With totient and the private exponent, the public exponent is quickly computed. Therefore, BluePass cannot use the Chinese Reminder Theorem to speed up the calculation.

8.2 BluePass Limitations

BluePass has several limitations. First, a user has to carry a powered-on mobile phone to make BluePass work; otherwise, BluePass falls back to conventional ways that users remember and input passwords. Second, BluePass cannot work well when the mobile device or the computer does not support Bluetooth communication. In those cases, the hand-free benefit cannot be offered by BluePass. Instead, the users have to use their phones to display their site passwords after inputting their master passwords.

9 Related Work

Password is criticized to be insecure along its survival [17,21,22,31]. It is generally believed that there exists a general trade-off between security and memorability [32].

Whereas numerous evidences show that "easy" passwords are insecure, users generally do not follow advices from security experts and are inclined to choose weak passwords or reuse passwords [1,9,11]. Given a plethora of attack vectors, following security advice that specifically aims to defend against just one or few types of attacks becomes unrealistic for users. Therefore, it is crucial for a website to carefully manage its security policies, even allowing slight security sacrifice [12].

Due to various drawbacks of password authentication, many alternative schemes has been proposed to replace passwords [10,15,16]. However, Bonneau et al. [6] evaluated all mainstream alternative schemes and concludes that none of them is able to replace the dominating status of password authentication.

Facing the dilemma of not being able to replace passwords, many works focus on helping users manage and remember their passwords, which indirectly enhance password strength due to decreased memorability requirement. In consequence, password manager earns its prosperity. Despite ubiquitous "memorize and fetch" type of password managers such as browser built-in password managers or LastPass, researchers also proposed password managers that can enhance password security in addition to usability [14,20,25,29].

Password manager significantly reduce the memory burden on users. However, it has its own usability and security problems [18]. Severe security issues may also be introduced due to the fact that users failed to capture the correct mental model [7]. Silver et al. [26] demonstrated that careless auto-filling policy on non-https websites could make passwords be extracted directly from the web form by an attacker.

10   Conclusion

This paper introduces a hand-free password manager called BluePass for achieving both strong security and high usability. BluePass attains the security level of two-factor authentication by storing password vaults in a mobile device and the decryption key in the user computer separately. Exploiting the automatic bluetooth communication between the mobile device and the computer, BluePass enables a hand-free password retrieval process for users. BluePass also places the decryption keys to remote servers to support password portability while decentralizing the storage of password vaults to prevent a single point of failure. We implement a BluePass prototype on Android and Google Chrome platforms. Through system evaluation, we show that the password retrieval latency a user experiences is less than 200 milliseconds on average, and BluePass only consumes a negligible 1% battery power with 10 h normal use on a mobile device. Through a user study comprising of 31 testers, we demonstrate that BluePass does motivate users to choose stronger passwords and less likely to reuse existing passwords.

References

1. Adams, A., Sasse, M.A.: Users are not the enemy. Commun. ACM **42**(12), 40–46 (1999)
2. Lastpass suffers data breach again (2016). http://www.csoonline.com/article/2936105/data-breach/lastpass-suffers-data-breach-again.html
3. Beautement, A., Sasse, M.A., Wonham, M.: The compliance budget: managing security behaviour in organisations. In: NSPW. ACM (2008)
4. Bonneau, J.: The science of guessing: analyzing an anonymized corpus of 70 million passwords. In: IEEE Security & Privacy (2012)
5. Bonneau, J., Herley, C., van Oorschot, P.C., Stajano, F.: Passwords and the evolution of imperfect authentication. Commun. ACM **58**(7), 78–87 (2015)

6. Bonneau, J., Herley, C., Van Oorschot, P.C., Stajano, F.: The quest to replace passwords: a framework for comparative evaluation of web authentication schemes. In: IEEE Security & Privacy (2012)
7. Chiasson, S., van Oorschot, P.C., Biddle, R.: A usability study and critique of two password managers. In: USENIX Security (2006)
8. Czeskis, A., Dietz, M., Kohno, T., Wallach, D., Balfanz, D.: Strengthening user authentication through opportunistic cryptographic identity assertions. In: ACM CCS (2012)
9. Das, A., Bonneau, J., Caesar, M., Borisov, N., Wang, X.: The tangled web of password reuse. In: NDSS (2014)
10. Davis, D., Monrose, F., Reiter, M.K.: On user choice in graphical password schemes. In: USENIX Security (2004)
11. Florencio, D., Herley, C.: A large-scale study of web password habits. In: ACM WWW (2007)
12. Florêncio, D., Herley, C.: Where do security policies come from? In: SOUPS. ACM (2010)
13. CherryPy - A Minimalist Python Web Framework (2016). http://www.cherrypy.org/
14. Halderman, J.A., Waters, B., Felten, E.W.: A convenient method for securely managing passwords. In: WWW. ACM (2005)
15. Jain, A.K., Ross, A., Pankanti, S.: Biometrics: a tool for information security. IEEE Trans. Inf. Forensics Secur. **1**(2), 125–143 (2006)
16. Jermyn, I., Mayer, A.J., Monrose, F., Reiter, M.K., Rubin, A.D., et al.: The design and analysis of graphical passwords. In: USENIX Security (1999)
17. Li, Y., Wang, H., Sun, K.: A study of personal information in human-chosen passwords and its security implications. In: IEEE INFOCOM (2016)
18. Li, Z., He, W., Akhawe, D., Song, D.: The emperor's new password manager: security analysis of web-based password managers. In: USENIX Security (2014)
19. Malone, D., Maher, K.: Investigating the distribution of password choices. In: ACM WWW (2012)
20. McCarney, D., Barrera, D., Clark, J., Chiasson, S., van Oorschot, P.C.: Tapas: design, implementation, and usability evaluation of a password manager. In: ACSAC. ACM (2012)
21. Morris, R., Thompson, K.: Password security: a case history. Commun. ACM **22**(11), 594–597 (1979)
22. Narayanan, A., Shmatikov, V.: Fast dictionary attacks on passwords using time-space tradeoff. In: ACM CCS (2005)
23. Karapanos, N., Marforio, C., Soriente, C., Capkun, S.: Sound-proof: usable two-factor authentication based on ambient sound. In: Proceedings of USENIX Security (2015)
24. Petsas, T., Tsirantonakis, G., Athanasopoulos, E., Ioannidis, S.: Two-factor authentication: is the world ready?: quantifying 2FA adoption. In: Proceedings of the Eighth European Workshop on System Security, p. 4. ACM (2015)
25. Ross, B., Jackson, C., Miyake, N., Boneh, D., Mitchell, J.C.: Stronger password authentication using browser extensions. In: USENIX Security (2005)
26. Silver, D., Jana, S., Chen, E., Jackson, C., Boneh, D.: Password managers: attacks and defenses. In: USENIX Security (2014)
27. How Often Do You Charge Your Smartphone? (2016). http://lifehacker.com/how-often-do-you-need-to-charge-your-smartphone-1441051270
28. Veras, R., Thorpe, J., Collins, C.: Visualizing semantics in passwords: the role of dates. In: IEEE VizSec (2012)

29. Wang, L., Li, Y., Sun, K.: Amnesia: a bilateral generative password manager. In: 2016 IEEE 36th International Conference on Distributed Computing Systems (ICDCS), pp. 313–322. IEEE (2016)
30. The top 500 sites on the web (2016). http://www.alexa.com/topsites
31. Weir, M., Aggarwal, S., De Medeiros, B., Glodek, B.: Password cracking using probabilistic context-free grammars. In: IEEE Security & Privacy (2009)
32. Yan, J., Blackwell, A., Anderson, R., Grant, A.: Password memorability and security: empirical results. IEEE Secur. Priv. Mag. **2**(5), 25–31 (2004)

Lambda Obfuscation

Pengwei Lan, Pei Wang, Shuai Wang, and Dinghao Wu$^{(\boxtimes)}$

College of Information Sciences and Technology, The Pennsylvania State University,
University Park, PA 16802, USA
{pul139,pxw172,szw175,dwu}@ist.psu.edu

Abstract. With the rise of increasingly advanced reverse engineering technique, especially more scalable symbolic execution tools, software obfuscation faces great challenges. Branch conditions contain important control flow logic of a program. Adversaries can use powerful program analysis tools to collect sensitive program properties and recover a program's internal logic, stealing intellectual properties from the original owner. In this paper, we propose a novel control obfuscation technique that uses lambda calculus to hide the original computation semantics and makes the original program more obscure to understand and reverse engineer. Our obfuscator replaces the conditional instructions with lambda calculus function calls that simulate the same behavior with a more complicated execution model. Our experiment result shows that our obfuscation method can protect sensitive branch conditions from state-of-the-art symbolic execution techniques, with only modest overhead.

Keywords: Software obfuscation · Control flow obfuscation
Reverse engineering · Lambda calculus

1 Introduction

As binary analysis techniques keep advancing, reverse engineering is becoming more effective than ever before. Consequently, malicious parties are able to employ the latest binary analysis techniques to identify exploitable software vulnerabilities for injecting malicious code into legit applications. Binary analysis tools can also get misused to reveal important internal logic of the distributed software copies, potentially leading to intellectual property thefts and therefore severe financial loss to the original developers.

One of the protection techniques that prevents undesired reverse engineering is software obfuscation. Generally, software obfuscation are program transformations that make software more complicated than its original form and difficult for adversaries to understand and analyze, while preserving the program's original semantics [24].

In this paper, we propose a novel obfuscation method, called lambda obfuscation, that utilizes the concept of lambda calculus, a powerful formal computation system widely adopted by the programming language community. The main idea of our approach is to utilize the unique computation model of lambda

© ICST Institute for Computer Sciences, Social Informatics and Telecommunications Engineering 2018
X. Lin et al. (Eds.): SecureComm 2017, LNICST 238, pp. 206–224, 2018.
https://doi.org/10.1007/978-3-319-78813-5_11

calculus, which is vastly different from the widely used imperative programming paradigm, to simulate the security-sensitive parts of the original programs. Instead of imperatively performing computation with data and control step by step, lambda calculus is entirely based on function application and reduction. The concept of control flow becomes insignificant in lambda calculus, and all data structures, including primitive data types like integer, are represented as high-order functions, potentially making conventional information flows implicit. When this highly abstract computation model is implemented and deployed with low-level machine code, a huge semantics gap emerges and imposes great challenges on manual and automated program analysis, therefore hindering reverse engineering.

Being Turing complete and considered as the smallest universal programming language [21], lambda calculus is capable of expressing all kinds of computation patterns available with a typical imperative programming language, e.g., C, Pascal, and Fortran. If the simulated computation is free of side effects, the source-level conversion can be fairly straightforward, yet the resulting program binary after transformation will become much more complicated and obscure.

To demonstrate the feasibility and practicality of lambda obfuscation, we implemented a prototypical lambda obfuscator based on the LLVM compiler infrastructure [13]. The obfuscator transforms qualified branch conditions into lambda calculus terms that simulate their original behavior. In order to return the simulation results, an interpreter that evaluates the lambda calculus is linked to compiled binaries including the procedures and intermediate values for computing the heavily obfuscated results. We comprehensively evaluated our obfuscation technique in four aspects, namely potency, resilience, cost, and stealth. The evaluation result indicates that our method can make the obfuscated programs more obscure and prevent automatic software analyzers from revealing possible execution paths. In particular, we assessed lambda obfuscation's resilience against KLEE, an advanced symbolic execution engine [3] and obtained promising results.

The rest of the paper is organized as follows. We first discuss historical work on control flow obfuscation in Sect. 2. We then briefly introduce the basics of lambda calculus, followed by the design of lambda obfuscation in Sect. 3. The technical details of the implementation are presented in Sect. 4. Section 5 evaluates the performance of our approach. Some research questions are discussed in Sect. 6 and we finally conclude the paper in Sect. 7.

2   Related Work

Software obfuscation techniques can be divided into four major categories, namely layout obfuscation, preventive obfuscation, data obfuscation, and control obfuscation [2]. Arguably as the most popular one, control obfuscation focuses on concealing and complicating control flow information of the program. There has been a large volume of research striving to develop effective control obfuscation techniques from different angles.

One of the classic approaches to achieving control obfuscation is by designing resilient opaque predicates. A predicate is opaque if it evaluates to a predetermined constant regardless of its input, while this invariant is hard to reveal through static analysis [30]. Most opaque predicates are derived from number-theoretic theorems [17], e.g., the quadratic residue lemmas [1]. One of the fundamental drawbacks of employing opaque predicates is that they always evaluate to the same value at run time, thus vulnerable to dynamic analysis. The invariant nature of opaque predicates can result in a likely detection by adversaries through sophisticated program analysis. In order to overcome this disadvantage of invariant opaque predicates, Palsberg et al. [18] introduced dynamic opaque predicates in which a family of correlated predicates whose evaluation results are only invariant in specific execution contexts.

Sharif et al. [22] proposed a conditional code obfuscation technique that leverages the inconvertibility of cryptographic hash functions to protect branch conditions. They used the hash functions to obfuscate the value of variable for which the branch condition can be satisfied. Because of the preimage resistance properties of these cryptographic hash functions, it is not practically feasible for static analyzers to reconstruct the values that satisfy the condition and the control flow logic information is therefore concealed and protected. However, their approach is only applicable to branch conditions evaluated through the equality relation, while it fails to protect conditions that contain inequality relations.

There is a line of research on building obfuscation techniques based on code mobility [7,20,28]. These approaches only deploy partial and incomplete application code on the local machine and retrieve the rest of binary instructions from a remote trusted server. While these obfuscation techniques can reduce attacker's visibility to the software semantics, they also heavily rely on the availability of network communications and remote servers, which limits the application scenarios of their techniques.

Control flow obfuscation can also be implemented by introducing exotic computation gadgets and paradigms. Ma et al. [15] proposed to replace important branch conditions with trained neural networks that simulate the program behavior when the branch conditions are triggered. Their approach can protect program against concolic testing due to the complexity of neural networks. However, it is required to train corresponding neural networks in advanced based on the target branch conditions. Their approach becomes less flexible and tedious to deploy when the number of branch conditions requiring obfuscation increases. Wang et al. [25] introduced another obfuscation framework called translingual obfuscation. They proposed to translate programs written in imperative programming languages, which are relatively easier to reverse engineer, to languages of different paradigms. In particular, they demonstrated the feasibility of obfuscating C programs with Prolog, a logic programming language based on first-order logic resolution. Due to the vastly different execution models of the original and target languages, traditional binary analysis methods have difficulty in countering translingual obfuscation. Another obfuscation method, called Turing obfuscation [27], augmented the concept of translingual obfuscation by transforming C programs into compositions of primitive Turing machines rather than programs written in another language. Our research shares a similar idea with Turing obfuscation, while we adopt lambda calculus as the foundation of obscurity, which is a more heterogeneous computation model.

3 Design

The basic idea of lambda obfuscation is to leverage the unique computation model of lambda calculus for protecting the relatively straightforward imperative computation procedures in common programs. Even though different programming languages adopt different execution models, it is considered relatively easier to reverse engineer imperative languages whose computation schemas align the best with the underlying hardware. Typical imperative languages include C, Fortran, and Pascal. On the contrary, execution models of functional languages, such as lambda calculus, result in greater differences between the source code and compiled binary code, which can increase the difficulty of de-obfuscation. Therefore, we can translate and implement functionalities of a program using different programming languages to mix execution models and conceal sensitive program information. In this paper, our lambda obfuscation technique embeds functional execution model of lambda calculus into C programs that use imperative execution model. It translates the path condition instructions in original compiled binary code into function calls that are implemented using lambda calculus. In this way, we are able to make the execution model of the obfuscated programs more complicated, thus hindering reverse engineering.

3.1 Lambda Calculus Basics

Lambda calculus is a formal system that uses the basic operations of function abstraction and application to describe computation [19]. The basic building blocks of lambda calculus are expressions called lambda terms. There are three types of lambda terms, namely *variable, abstraction, and application*, the syntax of which is defined by the following BNF specifications:

$$\langle expression \rangle ::= \langle variable \rangle \qquad\qquad\qquad \textbf{Variable}$$
$$\mid\ \lambda \langle variable \rangle . \langle expression \rangle \qquad\qquad \textbf{Abstraction}$$
$$\mid\ \langle expression \rangle \langle expression \rangle \qquad\qquad \textbf{Application}$$

A variable in lambda calculus is an arbitrary identifier. An abstraction can be viewed as a notation for defining anonymous functions. For example, lambda term $(\lambda x.e)$ defines an anonymous function whose parameter is the variable x and the function body is another lambda term e. An application term captures the action of applying a function to its arguments. For example, lambda expression $(f\ t)$ means applying function f to an expression t, which is provided as the argument to f. All valid lambda terms can be formed by repeatedly combining the three basic lambda terms. Below are some examples of valid lambda terms:

x	A variable x
$\lambda x.x$	An identity function
$(\lambda x.x)\ y$	Applying identity function to variable y
$\lambda p.\lambda q.p\ q$	A function applying its first argument to the second one

When the λ symbol precedes a variable, it binds all the occurrences of this variable in the abstraction body. A variable is called a *bound variable* if its name is associated with a λ symbol. Other variables in the function body are called *free variables* [11]. For example, in the following expression, variable x is a bound variable while variable y is a free variable.

$$\lambda x.x\ y$$

Reduction. The meaning of lambda calculus is defined by how lambda calculus can be reduced [6]. This reduction process is achieved by substituting all free variables in a way similar to passing the defined parameters into the function body during a function call [23]. The main rule to perform reduction in lambda calculus is called β-reduction, which can be defined as follows:

$$(\lambda x.e_1)\ e_2 \Rightarrow e_1[x \rightarrow e_2]$$

where notation $e_1[x \rightarrow e_2]$ denotes substituting all free occurrences of the variable x with e_2 in e_1. β-reduction captures the essence of function application and can be used to simplify and evaluate lambda terms. During the reduction process, all intermediate function applications are carried out and eliminated. The reduction process stops when β-reduction rule cannot be performed any more. Here are several β-reduction examples.

$$(\lambda x.x)\ y \Rightarrow y$$
$$(\lambda x.x)(\lambda y.y) \Rightarrow \lambda y.y$$
$$(\lambda x.x\ x)(\lambda y.y) \Rightarrow (\lambda y.y)(\lambda y.y) \Rightarrow \lambda y.y$$

3.2 Church Encoding

In lambda calculus, abstracts, or functions, is the only primitive type that is naturally available. Therefore, to perform meaningful computation that resembles what a modern programming language is capable of, it is imperative to find an encoding scheme to express basic data types like integer and operators in lambda calculus. For the purpose of lambda obfuscation, we employ Church encoding to represent natural numbers and operators to implement lambda obfuscation. In this section, we briefly introduce the basics of Church encoding.

Firstly developed by Alonzo Church, Church encoding describes the value of a natural number as the number of times for which a function is applied to an argument. Natural numbers expressed this way are called Church numerals. For example, when encoded as a Church numeral, the natural number 2 is a lambda abstraction that applies its first argument to its second argument twice. The Church numerals can be defined as follows:

$$0 \equiv \lambda f.\lambda x.x$$
$$1 \equiv \lambda f.\lambda x.f\ x$$
$$2 \equiv \lambda f.\lambda x.f\ (f\ x)$$
$$3 \equiv \lambda f.\lambda x.f\ (f\ (f\ x))$$
$$n \equiv \lambda f.\lambda x.f^n\ x$$

As the definition indicates, the Church numeral n can be viewed as a high-order function that takes a input function f and applies it to a value x for n times. Therefore, a successor (SUCC) operator that takes a Church numeral n and returns $n+1$ essentially is appending another application of function f to Church numeral n, which is defined as follows:

$$\text{SUCC} = \lambda n.\lambda f.\lambda x.f\ (n\ f\ x)$$

Within this context, the addition operator can be accordingly defined as a lambda expression. Conceptually, adding m to n is equivalent to adding 1 to n for m times. Therefore, a PLUS operator that adds m to n is identical to applying SUCC operator to n for m times. Therefore, PLUS operator can be defined using SUCC operator as follows:

$$\text{PLUS} = \lambda m.\lambda n.m\ \text{SUCC}\ n$$

The predecessor (PRED) operator that takes a Church numeral n and returns $n-1$ is more complicated to define, but conceptually it is still equivalent to getting the high-order function that applies its argument one less time than Church numeral n. Similarly, subtraction (SUB) operator can be defined based on PRED operator. Other important operators and logical predicates are defined as follows:

$$\text{PRED} = \lambda n.\lambda f.\lambda x.n\ (\lambda g.\lambda h.h\ (g\ f))\ (\lambda u.x)\ (\lambda u.u)$$
$$\text{SUB} = \lambda m.\lambda n.n\ \text{PRED}\ m$$
$$\text{TRUE} = \lambda x.\lambda y.x$$
$$\text{FALSE} = \lambda x.\lambda y.y$$
$$\text{ISZERO} = \lambda n.n\ (\lambda x.\text{FALSE})\ \text{TRUE}$$
$$\text{LEQ} = \lambda m.\lambda n.\text{ISZERO}(\text{SUB}\ m\ n)$$
$$\text{GEQ} = \lambda m.\lambda n.\text{LEQ}\ n\ m$$

Note that the PRED and SUB operators defined above are "truncated", meaning the decrementation stops at 0. This is expected since we have not defined negative integers yet, which it is entirely feasible in lambda calculus. Due to limited space, we do not list the complete definitions of all primitives employed lambda obfuscation. If interested, readers can find the corresponding information in many materials on programing languages and logic[1].

Through implementing the Church encoding of necessary operators, we are able to perform basic arithmetic operations in lambda calculus, including addition, subtraction, multiplication, and division. We can also simulate equality and all kinds of inequality comparisons, e.g., greater than, smaller than. For example, $0 + 1$ is equivalent to perform reduction on the following lambda term in lambda calculus:

$$\text{PLUS } 0 \ 1 \equiv (\lambda m.\lambda n.m \ \text{SUCC } n)(\lambda f.\lambda x.x)(\lambda f.\lambda x.f \ x)$$
$$\equiv (\lambda m.\lambda n.m \ (\lambda n.\lambda f.\lambda x.f \ (n \ f \ x)) \ n)(\lambda f.\lambda x.x)(\lambda f.\lambda x.f \ x)$$

In other words, the Church encoding provides the lambda calculus terms with which we can simulate the computation of path conditions in typical C programs.

From the perspective of program obfuscation, the Church encoding "accidentally" possesses the capability of eliminating explicit control flows. As an example, the ISZERO lambda term simulates a typical branch operation in imperative programming. However, the computation, or more precisely the reduction, of ISZERO does not contain any explicit decision making. Therefore, no logic-significant control flows can be observed, which is one of the major advantages of lambda obfuscation over traditional techniques.

3.3 Data Structures

To implement lambda obfuscation, we need to first design the data structure to represent lambda terms. As introduced earlier, a lambda term can be one of the variable type, abstraction type, and application type. Naturally, we use enum structure to enumerate all three types, namely Tvar, Tlam, and Tapp. Because lambda terms are defined inductively, the data structure we use needs to refer and link to other lambda terms recursively. We define a C struct called term including two main fields, i.e., type and data. The type field stores the type of lambda terms. The data field stores different information based on the type of the lambda term. For a variable, it only stores the identifier, which is a char. For the abstraction structure, it includes a char to store the variable and a term pointer as the function body. An application consists of two term pointers to link the two expressions. Figure 1 presents the SUCC operator and Church numeral 2 using the data structures described above.

The benefit of representing lambda calculus with the term data structure is twofold. Firstly, our data structure, along with the computation model of lambda calculus, makes the execution flow more complicated for analysis tools to reason about. In the imperative execution model, computation is conducted through

---

[1] Our current implementation does not support floating point numbers and arithmetic, but it is feasible and can be added into the implementation with more engineering effort.

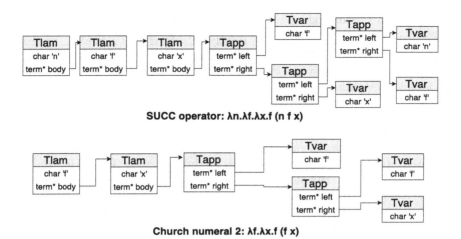

SUCC operator: λn.λf.λx.f (n f x)

Church numeral 2: λf.λx.f (f x)

Fig. 1. SUCC operator and Church numeral 2 in term structure

series of explicit instructions that modify memory states [4]. While in lambda obfuscation, computation is conducted through manipulating **term** objects, such as creating new **term** objects, changing term pointers, modifying variable identifier, and removing existing **term** objects. Thus, it requires analysis tools to trace the modifications of every intermediate steps to understand the internal logic which is not only resource-intensive but also time-consuming. Our data structure and unique execution model and lambda calculus significantly increase the cost and difficulty for binary analysis tools to reveal the internal logic of obfuscated programs. Secondly, the Church encoding, and our implementation of it using **term**, is "unnatural" by itself in the first place. The encoding adopts a significant different approach to encode natural numbers and other data types that are mostly primitive in a traditional imperative computation model. Instead, numbers become a link of **term** objects. As such, there are no more clear indications on what numbers the computation is operating on. This notably increases the cost to trace a value in lambda calculus because it now requires adversaries to trace the whole link of **term** objects to identify the number. Moreover, with Church encoding, every expression can is represented as a function, making data and operation much less distinguishable. In particular, the Church numerals are simply high-order functions that take functions as arguments and return functions as results. From this point, Church numerals are no different than other lambda calculus operators, such as PLUS operator or SUB operator. During the evaluation process, data and operator logic are mixed together. In summary, leveraging this simple data structure we design to represent lambda calculus in our implementation can make the obfuscated programs more obscure for attackers to reverse engineer.

3.4   Lambda Obfuscation

Theoretically, the lambda calculus is mostly as powerful as a modern programming language, due to its Turing completeness. However, obfuscating the entire program is usually against the common software engineering practices due to considerable performance and maintenance cost. Therefore, software developers usually have to manually pick the part of code they consider sensitive and vulnerable as obfuscation candidates.

To demonstrate the value of lambda obfuscation, we particularly pick path conditions as the targets to apply obfuscation to. To be specific, we re-implement the computation of path predicates with lambda calculus. Path conditions, in most software, are the crux of understanding program behavior and computation logic. By focusing on this part, we are able to evaluate lambda obfuscation without domain-specific knowledge about the software we obfuscate.

Branches are usually implemented through comparison. To obfuscate a path condition instruction, we combine the corresponding lambda comparison operator with the compared parameters which are both encoded as lambda terms, forming a lambda expression that represents the path condition computation. At run time, the lambda expression is evaluated to a form that cannot be further reduced. This irreducible lambda term, namely the computation result, will be decoded back to the imperative value it represents. Typically, a boolean value will be returned to guide the execution of following branching instruction. In this way, the branch information gets protected by lambda obfuscation and many potential leakages of sensitive information to adversaries can be prevented.

4   Implementation

We implement lambda obfuscation based on LLVM, a architecture-independent compilation framework supporting flexible program transformations. As shown in Fig. 2, our obfuscation work-flow is divided into three stages. The first step is preprocessing. In this stage, we compile all source code to be obfuscated into the LLVM intermediate representation (IR). The next step is transformation, in which the obfuscator identifies all eligible instructions used for path condition computation and translate these instructions into lambda calculus terms. These instructions will then be replaced by trampolines to a lambda calculus interpreter that accepts the generated lambda calculus terms as input. In the last compilation stage, the obfuscated IR code are compiled to machine code and linked into an executable binary. The lambda calculus interpreter is implemented with 736 lines of C code[2]. We elaborate on the details of each stage below.

4.1   Preprocessing

In LLVM, the majority of program analysis and optimization phases are conducted at the LLVM IR level. In order to leverage the strength of the transformation framework, we compile the source code into LLVM IR code. The compilation

---

[2] For more implementation details, please refer to an extended version of this paper [12].

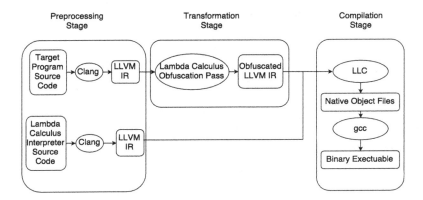

Fig. 2. The work-flow of lambda obfuscation

is conducted without any optimization so the IR code captures the unmodified behavior of the original program. The input source code comprises not only source code of the program to be obfuscated but also the implementation of our lambda calculus interpreter. However, only the LLVM IR code generated from the target program source code will be obfuscated in the transformation stage. Because we select C programs to evaluate the effectiveness of our obfuscator, we use clang as our front-end compiler to generate LLVM IR code during our preprocessing stage.

4.2 Transformation

LLVM provides an easy-to-extend pass-based transformation framework. Users can customize and implement passes at different program level based on their needs and requirements. We implement a function pass that processes each function in a compile unit to identify instructions that are suitable for obfuscation.

Identifying Instruction Candidates. After the preprocessing stage, LLVM IR code generated from the source is fed into another LLVM pass for analysis. Every IR instruction is analyzed to determine whether it meets our obfuscation requirement. In theory, lambda obfuscation is capable of obfuscating all kinds of computation. At this point, our prototype obfuscates path conditions which serve as crucial parts forming the control flows of a program. As for the types of instruction, the pass selects the following six types of instructions that compute different path conditions: equal, not equal, greater than, greater or equal, less than, and less or equal. To allow users to control the strength of obfuscation, the pass picks instruction candidates randomly based on a percentage specified by users.

Transforming Instructions. After identifying the candidates for obfuscation, a translation pass performs lambda transformation for these instructions. Path conditions are replaced by the corresponding lambda calculus function calls to

Source Code

int main() {

...

if (*x + 1 > 1*)

...

Original LLVM IR Code

define i32 @main() #0 {

entry:

...

%0 = load i32, i32* %x, align 4

%add = *add nsw i32 %0, 1*

%cmp = *icmp sgt i32 %add, 1*

br i1 %cmp, label %if.then, label %if.end

...

Obfuscated LLVM IR Code

define i32 @main() #0 {

entry:

...

%0 = load i32, i32* %x, align 4

%add = *call i32 @lambda_add(i32 %0, i32 1)*

%cmp = *call i1 @lamb_callee(i32 38, i32 %add, i32 1)*

br i1 %cmp, label %if.then, label %if.end

...

Fig. 3. LLVM code of a C program before and after obfuscation

lambda calculus interpreter with proper input parameters, including the type of comparison operators and operands. The lambda calculus interpreter simulates the computation of the path condition and returns the result to a register which is send back to the original program as the computed path condition. Figure 3 shows the LLVM IR code of a example C program before and after our obfuscation.

4.3   Compilation

In the final stage, we compile the obfuscated IR code and the IR code of our lambda calculus interpreter into native machine instructions. It is worth noting that since we implemented the lambda calculus interpreter in C, no additional runtime environment is required to execute the obfuscated binary. This implementation decision also increases the stealthy of our obfuscation approach.

5   Evaluation

We evaluate lambda obfuscation in four aspects, i.e., potency, resilience, cost, and stealth, which are firstly proposed by Collberg et al. [5]. Potency measures how complicated and unintelligible the program has become after obfuscation. Resilience indicates how well the obfuscated program can withstand automated reverse engineering. Cost measures how much the software is slowed down as the cost of obfuscation. Stealth describes to what extent the obfuscated program resembles the original program such that the presence of obfuscation is hard to detect.

For the purpose of evaluation, we picked two open source C programs to obfuscate using our lambda obfuscation prototype. The two programs are bzip2, a file compressor, and regexp, a regular expression engine. Both applications contain many integral path conditions therefore enough obfuscation candidates.

In the evaluation, the obfuscation strength is described by a metric called obfuscation level, which is defined as the percentage of obfuscated path conditions with respect to all qualified obfuscation candidates. For example, an application obfuscated at the 20% obfuscation level indicates that the 80% of the original integral path conditions remain unmodified while the rest 20% are transformed into lambda calculus terms. To avoid being biased in the experiments, we randomly select path conditions to obfuscate. In reality, however, the program components to protect are usually identified by developers with care to achieve the highest possible cost-effectiveness.

5.1 Potency

In order to quantify the potency of lambda obfuscation, we first measured three basic software complexity metrics that are derived from call graphs and control flow graphs before and after transformation. The metrics are the number of edges in the call graph, the number of edges in the control flow graph, and the number of basic blocks. With the help of IDA Pro, a disassembler widely used in the industry, we generated call graphs and control graphs from binaries compiled from original and obfuscated LLVM IR code.

In addition to these basic metrics, we also calculated two advanced indicators of software complexity which have long been utilized by the software engineering community, i.e., the cyclomatic number [16] and the knot count [29]. The cyclomatic number is defined as $E - N + 2$ where E is the number of edges and N is the number of vertices in the program's control flow graph. The knot count, on the other hand, is the count of intersections among the control flow paths when all basic blocks in the function are linearly aligned.

Table 1 presents the potency-related statistics of the two evaluated applications before and after obfuscation, at the obfuscation level of 30%. As can be

Table 1. Program metrics before and after obfuscation at obfuscation level 30%

	bzip2	Obfuscated bzip2	regexp	Obfuscated regexp
# of call graph edges	620	1049	144	380
# of basic blocks	2590	2839	392	643
# of CFG edges	3795	4155	562	883
Knot count	3162	3304	482	616
Cyclomatic complexity	1207	1278	172	242

seen through the results, the complexity of both applications has increased by a significant amount after being obfuscated indicating that lambda obfuscation is able to make programs more difficult for attackers to reverse engineer.

5.2 Resilience

For resilience evaluation, we performed concolic testing on an arbitrary C program before and after obfuscation using our approach. Concolic testing is initially a software verification technique combing concrete execution of a program with symbolic execution. Concolic testing aims to cover as many feasible execution paths of a program as possible [10]. However, attackers can use concolic testing to reveal sensitive control flow information of a program and learn about program semantics. By performing concolic testing experiment, we tried to imitate a reverse engineering attack on programs protected by lambda obfuscation. We picked a popular concolic testing tool, KLEE, which is capable of automatically generating test cases and achieving a high coverage of possible execution paths [3]. The program used for testing the matchup between KLEE and lambda obfuscation is the obfuscated binary of a simple C program shown in Fig. 4. We used this extremely simple program to rule out irrelevant factors that can possibly affect the performance of KLEE.

```
1   int test(int a) {
2       int Var = a;
3       if(Var > 16) {
4           Var++;
5       }
6       return Var;
7   }
8
9   int main() {
10      int a;
11      klee_make_symbolic(&a, sizeof(a), "a");
12      return test(a);
13  }
```

Fig. 4. C program to be obfuscated in KLEE experiment

With the experiment, we found that KLEE could successfully finish concolic testing on the unobfuscated binary. To be specific, KLEE succeeded in discovering both paths of the C program and generating test cases for the original program. In contrast, KLEE failed to generate any possible paths for the obfuscated binary. The topmost issue that caused the failure was that there were too many possible states for KLEE to explore and reason such that KLEE kept hitting the maximum memory capacity and eventually stopped without returning any possible paths. This result indicates that lambda obfuscation makes an extremely simple program so complicated that KLEE can no longer reveal any useful control flow information of the protected program.

5.3   Cost

The major source of performance overhead introduced by lambda obfuscation comes from the encoding and decoding translation process and the reduction time of lambda calculus. In order to measure the cost of our technique, we applied obfuscation to bzip2 and regexp at the obfuscation level of 30%. The test input used for the experiments are the original test cases shipped with the source code. Each application was executed 10 times and the average run time is presented with the slowdown.

Table 2. Overhead of lambda obfuscation on bzip2 and regexp

	Interpreter invocations	Average time (original)	Average time (obfuscated)	Overhead
bzip2	375,351	0.0625 s	15.574 s	41.492 μs
regexp	822,873	0.413 s	28.716 s	34.89 μs

Table 2 compares the execution time of both applications before and after obfuscation. We also recorded how many times was our lambda calculus interpreter invoked during each application's runtime and we calculated the average overhead. As Table 2 shown, on average every single call to our lambda calculus API requires 38.19 μs. We believe the cost is moderate and comparable to normal function calls. Besides, we argue that the overhead of our lambda calculus obfuscation is reasonable and can be reduced. Since we chose our path condition instruction candidates totally at random, some of the obfuscated path condition instructions resided in hot spots and these path condition instructions were being intensively called and used during runtime. For example, some of the path condition instructions we obfuscated in bzip2 resided in for loops which eventually accumulated to slowdown the program. In such cases, the overhead introduced by lambda obfuscation is inevitable and forgivable. In practice, users can obfuscate path conditions that are sensitive while less intensively-used to gain the maximum benefit from lambda obfuscation.

5.4   Stealth

To measure how stealthy lambda obfuscation is, we collected the distribution of instructions in the obfuscated sample C programs and compared them with that of the original binary.

Figures 5 and 6 show the instruction distribution of the original and obfuscated programs at obfuscation level of 30%. As we can see from the figures, the distribution of our obfuscated programs is very similar to their original distributions. In this case, we believe that the behavior of the obfuscated programs resembles their original one and it would be very difficult for adversaries to detect the presence of lambda obfuscation through the statistical features of the protected binaries.

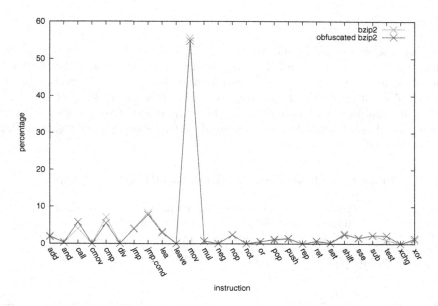

Fig. 5. Instruction distribution of bzip2

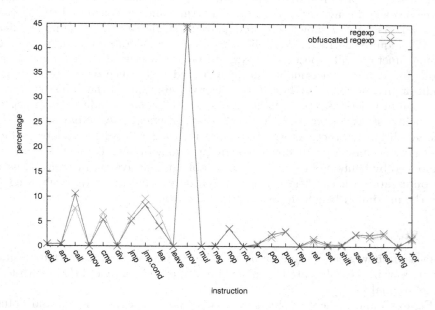

Fig. 6. Instruction distribution of regexp

6   Discussion

6.1   Countering Dynamic Monitoring

Opaque predicates and many other control flow obfuscation methods are inherently vulnerable to dynamic analysis, i.e., attackers monitoring the execution of the obfuscated software and checking control flows at run time. Lambda obfuscation may face similar challenges when only partially applied to protecting branch conditions. Learning from previous work, we find that there are several ways to alleviate this issue. One possible countermeasure is to blur the boundaries between lambda simulation and the original program code, using heuristics like function inlining and jumps across functions [14].

6.2   Potential Extensions

Currently, lambda obfuscation is only applied to the computation of integral path conditions. The limitation of our technique is caused by the fact that Church encoding is only capable of encoding natural number instead of real number. According to Church-Turing thesis, any data types can be encoded using lambda calculus [8]. One way to encode real number is using a Cauchy sequence of rational numbers [9]. After properly encoding real number in lambda calculus, we can extend our approach to obfuscate instructions involving real number.

Lambda calculus can also be extended to obfuscate other instructions besides path condition instructions that we currently focus on. Lambda calculus interpreter is capable of handling multiple arithmetic operations, such as addition, subtraction. Our obfuscator can be applied to any instructions containing such operations. In order to obfuscate these instructions, we can extend our LLVM obfuscator to identify suitable instructions and replace them with corresponding lambda calculus function calls.

Another way to enhance the obfuscating effect is to implement indirect control transferring similar to the obfuscation schema proposed by Ma et al. [15]. Currently, our obfuscator replaces path condition instructions with lambda function calls that return boolean signals to guide following conditional jump instructions. Instead of returning boolean signals, the obfuscator can return instruction addresses and we can modify following conditional jump instructions to be unconditional jump instructions that take instruction addresses. In this way, we can transform conditional logic into unconditional control transfer to make the obfuscated programs even more confusing for attackers to make sense.

We are also envisioning that obfuscating effect can be notably enhanced by "recursively" applying the proposed technique. That means, we first obfuscate the input program with our Lambda obfuscator, and further re-obfuscate the first round product with our technique. As discussed by existing research [26], such recursive process can even be launched for hundreds of iterations, which could largely increase the program complexity to defeat adversary analysis.

6.3   Combining with Other Obfuscation Methods

In this paper, we implement the lambda transformation at LLVM IR level using pass framework. In LLVM, every pass can be considered as an independent optimization of the original program and multiple different passes can be applied if needed. Therefore, lambda calculus is compatible with other obfuscation techniques if they happen at source code level or at LLVM IR level. Lambda calculus obfuscation can serve as an extra obfuscation layer to be applied before compilation of the program with other obfuscation techniques to make the program more obscure and secure. Besides, lambda obfuscator comes with reduction rules to evaluate lambda calculus which means the obfuscated program can run without an extra runtime environment. It can independently encode and decode lambda numerals and perform the whole evaluation process. This independent characteristic makes lambda calculus obfuscation less possible to affect other obfuscation techniques if applied together.

6.4   Obfuscating Complete Branch Predicates

Currently, in the obfuscated program, path condition instructions are replaced with lambda calculus function calls with instruction type and operands as input parameters. In order to further limit adversaries' knowledge to program semantic, we can further obfuscate instruction information. One possible solution is to encode all instruction information using lambda calculus and combine them into one single lambda term. Every instruction can be transformed into a different lambda calculus function which encapsulates the lambda calculus term that represents the instruction type and operands. By calling every instruction-specific function, our lambda calculus evaluator can still simulate the behavior of each obfuscated instruction. In this way, the instruction information is concealed through lambda calculus encoding and less program semantic is leaked to attackers.

7   Conclusion

In this paper, we propose a novel obfuscation technique based on lambda calculus. The behavior of path condition instruction is simulated using lambda calculus while sensitive instruction information is concealed. The complicated execution model of lambda calculus makes the obfuscated programs more obscure for the adversaries to make sense and reverse engineer. We implement a lambda obfuscator that transforms path condition instructions into corresponding lambda calculus function calls. A lambda interpreter is also implemented to evaluate lambda calculus function calls and return boolean signals to guarantee the behavior of original path condition instructions is still preserved. We evaluate our prototypical implementation of lambda obfuscation with respect to potency, resilience, cost and stealthy. The experiment result shows that our obfuscation technique can make the program more obscure with only modest overhead.

Acknowledgment. We thank the anonymous reviewers for their valuable feedback. This research was supported in part by the National Science Foundation (NSF) under grant CNS-1652790, and the Office of Naval Research (ONR) under grants N00014-13-1-0175, N00014-16-1-2265, and N00014-16-1-2912.

References

1. Arboit, G.: A method for watermarking Java programs via opaque predicates. In: Proceedings of the Fifth International Conference on Electronic Commerce Research (ICECR 2002), pp. 102–110 (2002)
2. Balachandran, V., Emmanuel, S.: Potent and stealthy control flow obfuscation by stack based self-modifying code. IEEE Trans. Inf. Forensics Secur. **8**(4), 669–681 (2013)
3. Cadar, C., Dunbar, D., Engler, D.R., et al.: KLEE: unassisted and automatic generation of high-coverage tests for complex systems programs. In: Proceedings of the 8th USENIX Conference on Operating Systems Design and Implementation (OSDI 2008), pp. 209–224 (2008)
4. Chailloux, E., Manoury, P., Pagano, B.: Developing Applications with Objective Caml. O'Reilly France, Paris (2002)
5. Collberg, C., Thomborson, C., Low, D.: Manufacturing cheap, resilient, and stealthy opaque constructs. In: Proceedings of the 25th ACM SIGPLAN-SIGACT Symposium on Principles of Programming Languages (POPL 1998), pp. 184–196 (1998)
6. De Queiroz, R.J.G.B.: A proof-theoretic account of programming and the role of reduction rules. Dialectica **42**(4), 265–282 (1988)
7. Falcarin, P., Di Carlo, S., Cabutto, A., Garazzino, N., Barberis, D.: Exploiting code mobility for dynamic binary obfuscation. In: Proceedings of 2011 World Congress on Internet Security (WorldCIS 2011), pp. 114–120 (2011)
8. Pérez, Á.G.: Operational aspects of full reduction in lambda calculi. Ph.D. thesis, E.T.S. de Ingenieros Informticos (UPM) (2014)
9. Geuvers, H., Niqui, M., Spitters, B., Wiedijk, F.: Constructive analysis, types and exact real numbers. Math. Struct. Comput. Sci. **17**(1), 3–36 (2007)
10. Giantsios, A., Papaspyrou, N., Sagonas, K.: Concolic testing for functional languages. In: Proceedings of the 17th International Symposium on Principles and Practice of Declarative Programming (PPDP 2015), pp. 137–148 (2015)
11. Hudak, P.: Conception, evolution, and application of functional programming languages. ACM Comput. Surv. (CSUR) **21**(3), 359–411 (1989)
12. Lan, P.: Lambda obfuscation. Master's thesis, The Pennsylvania State University (2017)
13. Lattner, C., Adve, V.: LLVM: a compilation framework for lifelong program analysis & transformation. In: Proceedings of the International Symposium on Code Generation and Optimization (CGO 2004), pp. 75–86, March 2004
14. Ma, H., Li, R., Xiaoxu, Y., Jia, C., Gao, D.: Integrated software fingerprinting via neural-network-based control flow obfuscation. IEEE Trans. Inf. Forensics Secur. **11**(10), 2322–2337 (2016)
15. Ma, H., Ma, X., Liu, W., Huang, Z., Gao, D., Jia, C.: Control flow obfuscation using neural network to fight concolic testing. In: Proceedings of 10th International Conference on Security and Privacy in Communication Networks (SECURECOMM 2014), pp. 287–304 (2014)

16. McCabe, T.J.: A complexity measure. IEEE Trans. Softw. Eng. **SE-2**(4), 308–320 (1976)
17. Myles, G., Collberg, C.: Software watermarking via opaque predicates: implementation, analysis, and attacks. Electron. Commer. Res. **6**(2), 155–171 (2006)
18. Palsberg, J., Krishnaswamy, S., Kwon, M., Ma, D., Shao, Q., Zhang, Y.: Experience with software watermarking. In: Proceedings of 16th Annual Computer Security Applications Conference (ACSAC 2000), pp. 308–316 (2000)
19. Pierce, B.C.: Types and Programming Languages. MIT Press, Cambridge (2002)
20. Rauti, S., Laurén, S., Hosseinzadeh, S., Mäkelä, J.-M., Hyrynsalmi, S., Leppänen, V.: Diversification of system calls in linux binaries. In: Yung, M., Zhu, L., Yang, Y. (eds.) INTRUST 2014. LNCS, vol. 9473, pp. 15–35. Springer, Cham (2015). https://doi.org/10.1007/978-3-319-27998-5_2
21. Rojas, R.: A tutorial introduction to the lambda calculus. CoRR, abs/1503.09060 (2015)
22. Sharif, M.I., Lanzi, A., Giffin, J.T., Lee, W.: Impeding malware analysis using conditional code obfuscation. In: Proceedings of the 15th Annual Network and Distributed System Security Symposium (NDSS 2008) (2008)
23. Slonneger, K., Kurtz, B.L.: Formal Syntax and Semantics of Programming Languages. Addison-Wesley Longman Publishing Co., Inc., Boston (1995)
24. Viticchié, A., Regano, L., Torchiano, M., Basile, C., Ceccato, M., Tonella, P., Tiella, R.: Assessment of source code obfuscation techniques. In: Proceedings of 2016 IEEE 16th International Working Conference on Source Code Analysis and Manipulation (SCAM 2016), pp. 11–20, October 2016
25. Wang, P., Wang, S., Ming, J., Jiang, Y., Wu, D.: Translingual obfuscation. In: Proceedings of 2016 IEEE European Symposium on Security and Privacy (EuroS&P 2016), pp. 128–144 (2016)
26. Wang, S., Wang, P., Wu, D.: Composite software diversification. In: Proceedings of the 33rd IEEE International Conference on Software Maintenance and Evolution (ICSME 2017) (2017)
27. Wang, Y., Wang, S., Wang, P., Wu, D.: Turing obfuscation. In: Lin, X., et al. (eds.) SecureComm 2017. LNICST, vol. 238, pp. 225–244. Springer, Heidelberg (2018)
28. Wang, Z., Jia, C., Liu, M., Yu, X.: Branch obfuscation using code mobility and signal. In: Proceedings of 2012 IEEE 36th Annual Computer Software and Applications Conference Workshops (COMPSACW 2012), pp. 553–558 (2012)
29. Woodward, M.R., Hennell, M.A., Hedley, D.: A measure of control flow complexity in program text. IEEE Trans. Softw. Eng. **5**(1), 45–50 (1979)
30. Xu, D., Ming, J., Wu, D.: Generalized dynamic opaque predicates: a new control flow obfuscation method. In: Bishop, M., Nascimento, A.C.A. (eds.) ISC 2016. LNCS, vol. 9866, pp. 323–342. Springer, Cham (2016). https://doi.org/10.1007/978-3-319-45871-7_20

Turing Obfuscation

Yan Wang, Shuai Wang, Pei Wang, and Dinghao Wu$^{(\boxtimes)}$

College of Information Sciences and Technology, The Pennsylvania State University,
University Park, PA 16802, USA
{ybw5084,szw175,pxw172,dwu}@ist.psu.edu

Abstract. Obfuscation is an important technique to protect software from adversary analysis. Control flow obfuscation effectively prevents attackers from understanding the program structure, hence impeding a broad set of reverse engineering efforts. In this paper, we propose a novel control flow obfuscation method which employs Turing machines to simulate the computation of branch conditions. By weaving the original program with Turing machine components, program control flow graph and call graph can become much more complicated. In addition, due to the runtime computation complexity of a Turing machine, program execution flow would be highly obfuscated and become resilient to advanced reverse engineering approaches via symbolic execution and concolic testing.

We have implemented a prototype tool for Turing obfuscation. Comparing with previous work, our control flow obfuscation technique delivers three distinct advantages. (1) Complexity: the complicated structure of a Turing machine makes it difficult for attackers to understand the program control flow. (2) Universality: Turing machines can encode any computation and hence applicable to obfuscate any program component. (3) Resiliency: Turing machine brings in complex execution model, which is shown to withstand automated reverse engineering efforts. Our evaluation obfuscates control flow predicates of two widely-used applications, and the experimental results show that the proposed technique can obfuscate programs in stealth with good performance and robustness.

Keywords: Software security · Control flow obfuscation
Reverse engineering · Turing machine

1 Introduction

Most software exploitation and hijacking attacks start by identifying program vulnerable points (e.g., buffer overflow). To launch attacks directly towards executable files, attackers usually need to first perform reverse engineering activities and recover the control flow structures of the victim programs. Moreover, we also notice that automated software analyzers can leverage advanced symbolic and concolic testing techniques to explore execution paths and hence revealing hidden vulnerabilities in binary code [6,12,20]. Typical concolic engines [5,11] could yield inputs which lead to new execution paths by solving branch conditions as

© ICST Institute for Computer Sciences, Social Informatics and Telecommunications Engineering 2018
X. Lin et al. (Eds.): SecureComm 2017, LNICST 238, pp. 225–244, 2018.
https://doi.org/10.1007/978-3-319-78813-5_12

constraints, and such technique has been proved as very effect in understanding program structures [19].

A lot of software security research has focused on preventing reverse engineering activities on program control structures and execution paths [18,21,26, 27,29]. Control flow obfuscation is one of these cutting-edge techniques to combat both static and dynamic reverse engineering tools. Control flow obfuscation largely changes the program control flow structures, and it has been shown as effective to hide path conditions and complicate the execution flow of a program. By rewriting or adding extra control flow components, the program path conditions become difficult or even impossible to analyze.

In this paper, we propose a novel control flow obfuscation method which leverages Turing machine to compute path conditions. The *Church-Turing thesis* [9] states that the power of Turing machines and λ-calculus is the same as algorithms, or the informal notion of effectively calculable functions. Formally, Turing computable, λ-computable, and general recursive functions are shown to be equivalent, and informally, the thesis states that they all capture the power of algorithms or effectively calculable functions. This means any functional component of software can be re-implemented as or transformed into a Turing machine; the replaced code component and its corresponding semantic equivalent Turing machine is called *Turing Equivalent*.

Our method is to simulate important branch condition statements in a program with semantic equivalent Turing machines. A Turing machine behaves as a state machine which brings in extra control flow transfers and basic blocks to the overall program control flow graph. Moreover, a typical Turing machine leverages transition tables to guide the computation, and such transition table-based execution would introduce complicated execution model and make the program execution much more challenging to analyze. We envision the proposed technique would largely complicate the protected program, and also bring in new challenges for reverse engineering analyzers. In addition, since Turing machine can represent the semantics of any program computation, our method is fundamentally capable of obfuscating any functional component.

To obfuscate a program through the proposed Turing obfuscator, we first translate the original program source code into a compiler intermediate representation. Our Turing machine obfuscator then selects branch condition statements (i.e., branch predicates) for transformation; the transformed statements will invoke its corresponding Turing machine component, which is semantic equivalent to the original branch conditions. After finishing the execution in the Turing machine "black box", the execution flow returns back to the original program point, with a return value to determine the branch selection. Consistent with existing work [8], we evaluate our obfuscator regarding five aspects, namely functionality correctness, potency, resilience, cost, and stealth. Results show that the proposed Turing obfuscator can effectively obfuscate commonly-used software systems with acceptable cost, and impede reverse engineering activities through an advanced symbolic execution analyzer (i.e., KLEE [5]).

The rest of this paper is organized as follows. Section 2 discusses related works on obfuscation, especially control flow obfuscation. Section 3 presents the overall design of Turing machine obfuscator. Obfuscator implementation is discussed in Sect. 4. Section 5 presents the evaluation result of our proposed technique. We further give discussions in Sect. 6, and conclude the paper in Sect. 7.

2   Related Work

In general, reverse engineering techniques can be categorized into static and dynamic approaches. To impede static reverse engineering, researchers essentially focus on hardening disassembling and decompiling process. To combat the dynamic reverse engineering techniques such as concolic testing, sensitive conditional transfer logic is proposed to be hidden from adversaries. Control flow obfuscation has been proved effective in this scenario.

Sharif et al. [21] propose a technique to rewrite certain branch conditions and encrypt code components that are guarded by such conditions. Branch conditions that are dependent on the input are selected and branch condition outputs are transformed with a hash function. Moreover, the code component which is dependent on a transformed condition would be encrypted; the encryption key is derived from the input which satisfies the branch condition. In general, their technique focus on selectively translate branch conditions that are dependent on the input, which could leave many branch conditions unprotected. Also, since the branch condition statement itself is mostly untouched (only the boolean output is hashed), the original branch condition code is still in the obfuscated program, which could be leveraged to reveal the original semantics.

Popov et al. [18] propose to replace unconditional control transfer instructions such as `jmp` and `call` with "signals". Their work is used to impede binary disassembling, the starting point of most reverse engineering tasks. Moreover, dummy control transfers and junk instructions are also inserted after the replaced control transfers. This method is effective in fooling disassemblers in analyzing unconditional transfers but it could become mal-functional when the conditional transfers need to be protected as well. Another related work proposes to protect control flow branches leveraging a remote trusted third party environment [26]. In general, their technique mostly introduces notable network overhead and also relies on trusted network accessibility which may not be feasible in practice.

Ma et al. [15,16] propose to use neural network to replace certain branch condition statements; the propose technique is evaluated to conceal conditional instructions and impede typical reverse engineering analysis such as concolic testing. While the experimental results indicate the effectiveness to certain degree, in general neural network-based approach may not be suitable for security applications. To the best of our knowledge, neural network works like a black box; it lacks a rigorous theoretical foundation to show a correct result can always to generated given an input. In other words, neural networks may yield results which lead to an incorrect branch selection. We also notice some recent work proposing to translate program components implemented in imperial language

(C/C++) into languages of other computation paradigms. It is argued that by mixing languages of different execution model and paradigms, the complexity of software systems grows and reverse engineering becomes more difficult. Wang et al. [23] presents a general framework to translate C statements into a logic statements written in Prolog. Lan et al. [13] proposes to obfuscate program control flow predicates with functional programming language statements.

3   Turing Obfuscation

3.1   Design Overview

In a program, a branch condition statement compares two operands and selects a branch for control transfer based on the comparison result. As aforementioned, Turing machine has been proved to be able to simulate the semantics of any functional component of a program. Hence, any program branch condition statement can be modeled by a Turing machine. Taking advantage of its powerful computation ability as well as execution complexity, we propose to employ Turing machine to obfuscate branch condition statements (the branch condition statement is referred as "branch predicate" later in this paper since its output is usually a boolean value) in a program. A Turing machine obfuscated branch condition statement is shown in Fig. 1. Instead of directly computing a boolean value through a comparison instruction, we feed a Turing machine with the inputs (the value of operands) and let the Turing machine to simulate the comparison semantics.

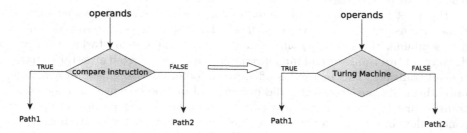

Fig. 1. Obfuscate a branch condition statement through a Turing machine.

3.2   Turing Machine

As shown in Fig. 2, a typical Turing machine consists of four components:

- An infinite-long tape which contains a sequence of cells. Each cell holds a symbol defined in the tape alphabet (the alphabet is introduced shortly). In this work, our proposed Turing machine obfuscator would dynamically allocate new tape cells to construct an infinite tape to store intermediate results.

- A tape head which could perform **read**, **write**, **move left** and **move right** operations over the tape.
- A state register used to record the state of the Turing machine. Turing machine states are finite and defined in the transition table.
- A transition table that consists of all the transition rules defining how a Turing machine transfers from one state to another.

Although simple, a Turing machine model resembles a modern computer in several ways. The head is I/O device. The infinite tape acts like the memory. The transition table defines the functionality of this Turing machine which is comparable to the application code.

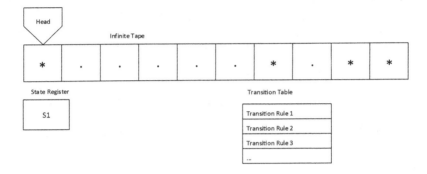

Fig. 2. Turing machine components.

Transition Table. A transition rule could be represented by a five-element tuple (S_c, T_c, S_n, T_n, D) where:

- S_c is the current Turing machine state.
- T_c is the current tape cell symbol read by the head.
- S_n is the new Turing machine state.
- T_n is the symbol head writes to the current tape cell.
- D is the direction towards which the head should move (i.e., "left" or "right").

In general, every five-element tuple represents a transition table rule shown in Fig. 2.

Turing Machine Encoding. Initially, Turing machine is at the "start" (S_0) state and tape records the Turing machine input. Consistent with existing Turing machine simulator project [22], blank symbol is denoted as "*" on the tape, while the length of "·" is used to encode an operand. For instance, integer 5 is represented as five continuous "·" on the tape. Note that a Turing machine could be encoded with various of ways, and our prototype represents only one of them. Turing machine with different encoding strategies operates with totally distinct execution patterns. This also makes Turing machine obfuscation difficult to be analyzed.

In general, our Turing machine tape alphabet includes two symbols, i.e., $\{\cdot, *\}$. The tape in Fig. 2 shows an initial state of a Turing machine. The head of the Turing machine is placed on the leftmost cell. Different operands are separated by a blank symbol "*". Operands encoded on the tape in Fig. 2 are five and one. When Turing machine starts to run, the head reads the current tape cell, combines with the current state register to locate a transition rule in the transition table, and then moves to the next state, accordingly.

Turing Machine Execution. The Turing machine keeps running step by step directed by the transition table until it reaches a `Halt` state. Nevertheless, Turing machine may also keep running forever since the process of solving some problems cannot terminate. In our research, we implement a Turing machine to simulate branch predicates so it should always reach a `Halt` state. When reaching the `Halt` state, the machine stops running and the computation result is shown on the tape. Table 1 shows a transition table example, which guides a Turing machine for the addition (i.e., `add`) operation in our implementation.

Table 1. Transition table of the `add` operation in a Turing machine.

Current state	Current symbol	New state	New symbol	Direction
S_0	*	S_0	*	Right
S_0	.	S_1	.	Right
S_1	*	S_2	.	Right
S_1	.	S_1	.	Right
S_2	*	S_3	*	Left
S_2	.	S_2	.	Right
S_3	*	S_3	*	Left
S_3	.	S_4	*	Left
S_4	*	$Halt$	*	-
S_4	.	S_4	.	Left

Addition Turing Machine. In this section, we elaborate on the design of the addition Turing machine; this machine simulates the semantics of the `add` operation. Other Turing machines (e.g., subtraction and multiplication Turing machines) used in this research are designed in a similar way. Figure 2 presents a sample initial stage of a tape, and the corresponding addition transition rules are shown in Table 1 (this table will be explained shortly). After a sequence of read and write operations based on the transition table, left operand (integer value 5) and right operand (integer value 1) that are separated by a blank symbol "*" are merged into a long series of "." cells on the tape. The length of the output dot cells is 6, which represents the integer value 6 as shown in Fig. 3.

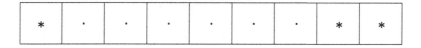

Fig. 3. Execution result of the add Turing machine.

Interpreting a transition table could be difficult for a human being. To represent an understandable description on how the addition transition table works, we summarize the transition table rules in an algorithm description. Algorithm 1 describes the transition table of the addition operation; it states a method to combine two sequences of dot cells on the tape into a longer sequence of cells. Following this algorithm, the isolator cell (i.e., the blank symbol) is written to "." when Turing machine terminates at the "Halt" state.

Algorithm 1. Description of the add transition table.

1: **procedure**
2:    $head \leftarrow$ the blank cell before the left operand starting cell
3:    **while** head != the blank cell after the right operand **do** move right
4:    move left
5:    the last dot cell of the right operand $\leftarrow$ blank symbol
6:    **while** head != the blank cell within these two operands **do** move left
7:    the blank cell $\leftarrow$ dot
8:    **while** head != the blank cell before the left operand **do** move left
9:    **Halt;**

Turing Machine of Other Operations. Besides the aforementioned addition operation, we also implement transition tables of other arithmetic operations. In particular, we construct three more transition tables for subtraction, multiplication and division operations. Their transition tables are relatively more complex than Table 1. Actually in our implementation, we build transition tables of 16, 34 and 80 transition rules for subtraction, multiplication and division Turing machines, respectively. Comparison operations in a branch predicate (e.g., $\leq, \geq, \neq$) is built on the basis of the subtraction Turing machine, and all the arithmetic operations are used to simulate "dependences" of the comparison operations on the IR level (details are given in Sect. 4.3). In sum, we construct 4 transition tables, with overall 140 transition table rules in total.

3.3   Universal Turing Machine

While a Turing machine could perform powerful algorithm simulation, its computation ability is bounded by its initial tape state and embedded transition table. For instance, a Turing machine capable of doing addition operation could only simulate the add operation since other operations would have very different

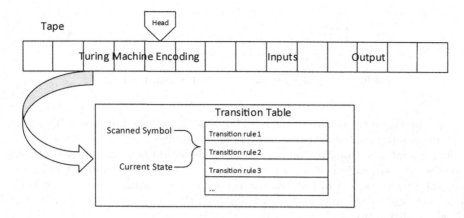

Fig. 4. Universal Turing machine.

transition rules. That means, an `add` Turing machine could not represent the `subtract` operations. Also, since the initial state needs to be encoded on the tape before the computation, a Turing machine encoded with $2 + 3$ could not conduct represent $5 + 6$.

In non-trivial programs, branch predicate could include various arithmetic and comparison operations, and many of these expressions would lead to different Turing machines. Hence, we need a unified translator to represent arbitrary computations. Universal Turing machine is designed to simulate arbitrary computations. As shown in Fig. 4, the typical design of a Universal Turing machine stores all the transition tables and one table is selected each time according to the semantics of the upcoming computation (e.g., add). To maintain the input data, Universal Turing machine dynamically allocates memory cells to initialize one tape before computation. Hence, all the information needed for arbitrary computations exists in the Universal Turing machine.

Universal Turing machine bears the essence of the modern computer which is being programmable. Through storing different transition tables and inputs on the tape, a universal Turing machine can actually perform semantic equivalent computation to represent arbitrary programs; as aforementioned, such Universal Turing Machine and the replaced expression are *Turing Equivalent*. In our Turing machine obfuscator design, all the branch predicates invoke a unified interface towards a Universal Turing machine, where a transition table is selected according to the opcode of the obfuscated instruction, and a tape is constructed to represent the input value.

4   Implementation

Our proposed obfuscator consists several components including a universal Turing machine model and several transformation passes based on the LLVM compiler suite [14]; As shown in Fig. 5, our Turing obfuscator performs a three-phase process to generate the obfuscated output. The first step translates both target program and the universal Turing machine source code into the LLVM intermediate representation (IR). The obfuscator then iterates IR instructions to identify obfuscation candidates (the second phase). After that, we then perform the obfuscation transformation towards all the candidates or a randomly-select portion (the third phase). The instrumented IR code is further compiled into the final obfuscated product. We implement the universal Turing machine model with in total 580 lines of C code and LLVM passes with 341 lines of C++ code.[1] We now elaborate on each phase in details.

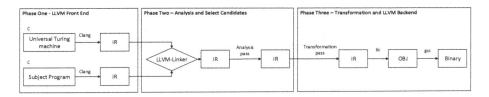

Fig. 5. Workflow of the Turing machine obfuscator.

4.1   Phase One: Translate Source Code to IR

As aforementioned, we first compile the target source program into LLVM IR; the obfuscation transformation is performed on the IR level. Considering a broad set of front end compilers provided by LLVM which can turn programs written by various programming languages into its IR, this IR-based implementation could broaden the application scope of our tool comparing with previous work [15, 16, 26]. Since we employ C programs for the evaluation, Clang (version 5.0) is used as the front end compiler in this paper.

4.2   Phase Two: Collect Transformation Candidate

The LLVM Pass framework is a core module of the LLVM compiler suite to conduct analysis, transformation and optimization during the compile time [14]. In this step, we build a pass within this framework to iterate and analyze every IR instruction in each module of the input program. During the analysis pass, our Turing machine obfuscator locates all the transformation candidates on the IR instruction level.

Locate Candidate Predicates. While the proposed technique is fundamentally capable of obfuscating any program component, the implementation currently focuses on branch predicates since control-flow obfuscation is effective to defeat many reverse engineering activities (Sect. 1). In general, the transformation candidate set includes 10 kinds of branch predicate instructions as: equal,

---

[1] Please refer to an extended version of this paper for more implementation details [25].

not equal, unsigned less than, unsigned greater than, unsigned less or equal, unsigned greater or equal, signed less than, signed greater than, signed less or equal, signed greater or equal.

4.3   Phase Three: Obfuscation Transformation

The second phase provides all the eligible transformation candidates. In this step, We build another transformation pass within the LLVM Pass framework to perform the obfuscation transformation. As shown in Fig. 6, predicate instructions are obfuscated; we rewrite instructions into function calls to the universal Turing machine. The computation of the branch predicate is launched inside the Turing machine, and the computation result is passed to a register which directs the associated path selection. Our technique is able to obfuscate all the branch predicates in a program or only transform a subset of (security sensitive) candidates. Such partial obfuscation is denoted as "obfuscation level", which will be discussed shortly.

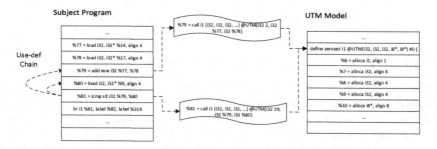

Fig. 6. Obfuscation transformation for an `icmp` instruction. "UTM" standards for universal Turing machine.

For an obfuscated predicate, our current "transform to function call" implementation utilizes a boolean return value to select a branch to transfer. On the other hand, we notice existing work (e.g., [15,16]) leverages a cross-procedure jump at this step; an indirect jump from the black box of the obfuscation component to a selected branch. We present further discussion on both control transfer strategies in Sect. 6.

Operand Type. In general, a branch predicate instruction can have either pointer or numerical data types (i.e., integer or float types). While the proposed technique is generally capable of translating branch predicate of any operand type, considering processing operands of pointer (and float) type would bring in additional complexity, our current prototype is designed to only handle operands of integer type. Actually our tentative study shows that most of the branch predicate instructions would have operands of integer type, hence, our implementation choice is indeed capable of handling most of the real-world cases. On the other hand, we emphasize extending our technique to handle other cases is only a matter of engineering effort. We leave it as one future work to provide such functionalities.

Def-Use Chain Analysis. Since our analysis is performed on IR expressions of the three-address form, one branch predicate in the original program shall be translated into a sequence of IR instructions. Hence, to perform a faithful obfuscation of one branch predicate, we need to first identify a "region" of IR instructions that is translated from one branch predicate.

As shown in Fig. 6, we perform def-use analysis to recover such "region" information. In particular, given a comparison IR instruction (which indicates one branch predicate and the end of the corresponding "region"), we calculate the use-def chains of its two operands, respectively. The identified instructions which provide the "definition" information of these two operands will be included in the "region". After the def-use analysis, we translate arithmetic instructions in the "region" into function calls to the Turing obfuscator.

Obfuscation Level. Obfuscation level is an indicator which weighs how much of a program is transformed by the obfuscation pass. Consistent with previous work [23], the obfuscation level is defined as the ratio between the obfuscated instructions and the total candidates:

$$O = M/N$$

M is the number of instructions transformed by the obfuscation pass. N is the number of all the transformable instructions (i.e., the branch predicate instructions identified in Sect. 4.2).

5   Evaluation

Inspired by previous research [8,15,16], we evaluate our Turing machine obfuscator based on four metrics which are *potency, resilience, stealth* and *cost*, respectively. Potency weighs the complexity of the obfuscated programs, while resilience measures how well an obfuscated program can withstand automated deobfuscation techniques. Stealth is evaluated to show whether the obfuscated programs are distinguishable regarding its origins, and cost is naturally employed to measure the execution overhead of the obfuscation products. In addition, we also evaluate the functionality correctness of the obfuscated binaries.

Two widely-used open source programs are employed in our evaluation: compression tool BZIP2 (version 1.0.6) [1] and regular expression engine REGEXP (version 1.3) [4]. As aforementioned, obfuscation level is an index which stands for the ratio of obfuscated instructions regarding all the candidates. In our experiments, the ratio is set as 50% unless noted otherwise which means half candidates are randomly selected and obfuscated.

5.1 Functionality Correctness

Both programs evaluated in our research (BZIP2 [1] and REGEXP [4]) are shipped with test cases to verify the functionality of the compilation outputs. In particular, the BZIP2 test cases deliver 3 compression samples and 3 decompression samples, while the REGEXP test cases contain 149 samples of various regular expression patterns. We leverage those shipped test cases to verify the functionality correctness of our obfuscated programs. For all the evaluated obfuscation levels (i.e., 30%, 50%, 80% and 100%), we report all the obfuscated programs can pass all the test cases, hence preserving the original semantics after obfuscation.

5.2 Potency

Control flow graph (CFG) and call graph represent the general structure of a program and they are the foundation for most static software analysis. With the help of IDA Pro [2], a well-known commercial binary analysis tool, we recover CFG and call graph information from both original and obfuscated binaries. By traversing those graphs, we calculate the number of basic blocks, number of call graph and control graph edges. We use these information to measure the complexity of a (obfuscated) program, which is aligned with previous research [7]. Analysis results are shown in Table 2. Comparing the original and obfuscated programs, it can be observed that program complexity is increased in terms of each metric.

Table 2. Potency evaluation in terms of program structure-level information.

Program	# of CFG edges	# of basic blocks	# of function
BZIP2	3942	2647	78
obfuscated BZIP2	4195	2828	134
REGEXP	906	619	25
obfuscated REGEXP	1122	773	43

We further quantify the Turing machine obfuscated programs in terms of the cyclomatic number and knot number (these two metrics are introduced in [17, 28]). Cyclomatic metric is defined as

$$Cyclomatic = E - N + 2$$

where E and N represent the number of edges and the number of nodes in a CFG, respectively. Knot number shows the number of edge crossings in a CFG. These two metrics intuitively measure how complicated a program is in terms of logic diversion number. Results in Table 3 shows that knot and cyclomatic number notably increase for both cases after Turing machine obfuscation. Overall, we interpret Tables 2 and 3 as promising results to show programs become much more complicated after obfuscation.

Table 3. Potency evaluation in terms of knot and cyclomatic numbers.

Program	# of cyclomatic	# of knot
BZIP2	1297	5596
obfuscated BZIP2	1369	5720
REGEXP	289	478
obfuscated REGEXP	351	1068

Besides picking 50% as the obfuscation level in this evaluation, we also conduct experiments with obfuscation levels as 30%, 80% and 100%. Figure 7 presents the number of call graph edges with the increase of obfuscation levels. Observation shows that with a higher obfuscation level, the number of call graph edges increases. Naturally, obfuscated programs can become more complicated with the growing of obfuscation levels.

5.3 Resilience

In addition to complicate program structures, a good obfuscation technique should be designed to impede automated deobfuscation tools as well. As aforementioned, symbolic and concolic testing tools are leveraged in automated software analysis to explore the program paths and reveal hidden vulnerabilities. Hence in this evaluation, we adopt a cutting-edge symbolic engine (KLEE [5]) to test the resilience of the obfuscated programs. Ideally program obfuscation brings in new challenges in reasoning path conditions, and hence would impede symbolic tools from finding new paths. In this evaluation, we use KLEE sample code [3] as the test case (the sample code is shown in Fig. 8).

KLEE could detect three paths in the original test case as expected. Actually based on different value of x, this program may traverse branches in which x equals 0, x is less than 0 or x is greater than 0, respectively. In contrast, we report KLEE could only reason **one** path condition for the obfuscated program. Due to limited information released by KLEE, we could not reveal the underlying reason that leads to the failure of the other two path conditions. Nevertheless, since Turing machine obfuscator makes the branch predicates more complicated, we envision that the internal constraint solver employed by KLEE is unable to yield a proper symbolic input which could "drill" into the branches protected by our tool. In sum, we interpret that Turing machine obfuscator can impede automated program analyzers from exploring the program paths.

5.4 Stealth

To evaluate the stealth of the obfuscated programs, existing work [23] propose to compare the instruction distributions of the original and obfuscated programs. If instruction distribution of the obfuscated program is distinguishable from its origin (e.g., `call` or `jmp` instruction proportions are abnormally high), it would

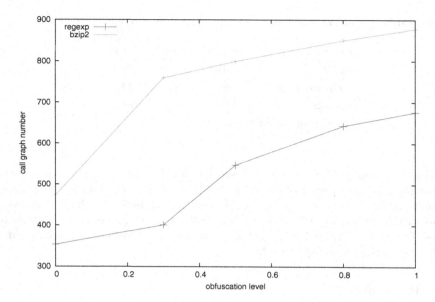

Fig. 7. Number of call graph edges in terms of different obfuscation levels.

```
1        int get_sign(int x) {
2          if (x == 0)
3            return 0;
4
5          if (x < 0)
6            return -1;
7          else
8            return 1;
9        }
10
11       int main() {
12         int a;
13         klee_make_symbolic(&a, sizeof(a), "a");
14         return get_sign(a);
15       }
```

Fig. 8. KLEE sample code used in our evaluation. All the path conditions are obfuscated.

be an indicator that the program is manipulated. In this evaluation, we adopt this metric to measure the stealth of our Turing obfuscator.

Consistent with previous research [23], we put assembly instructions into 27 different categories. Figures 9 and 10 present the instruction distribution of the original and obfuscated programs (BZIP2 and REGEXP). Experimental results indicate that the instruction distribution after obfuscation is very close to the origin distribution. In sum, small instruction distribution variation is a promising result to show the proposed technique would obfuscate programs in a stealthy way.

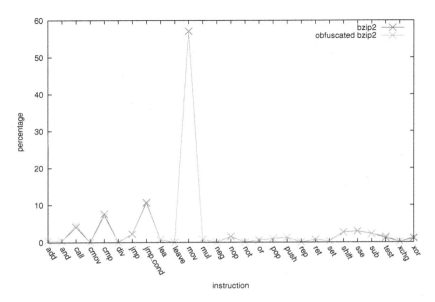

Fig. 9. BZIP2 instruction distribution comparison.

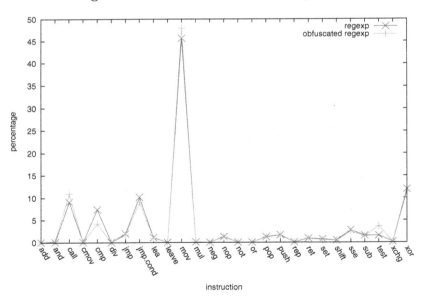

Fig. 10. REGEXP instruction distribution comparison.

5.5   Cost

Performance penalty is another critical factor to evaluate an obfuscation technique. In most obfuscation research work, execution cost is inevitably increased because obfuscation would bring in extra instructions. Measuring the execution time is a convincing way to evaluate the cost.

In our evaluation, both original and obfuscated programs are executed on a server with 2 Intel(R) Xeon(R) E5-2690 2.90 GHz processors and 128 GB system memory. BZIP2 is used to compress three different sample files and regular expression engine REGEXP runs 149 samples provided in its shipped test cases. We run each program three times and calculate the average execution cost.

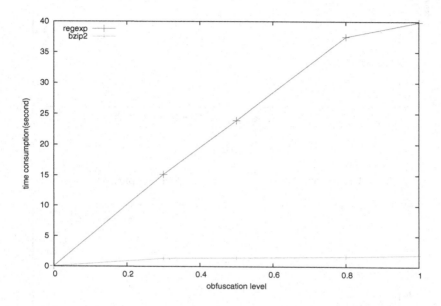

Fig. 11. Execution overhead in terms of different obfuscation levels.

Figure 11 presents the execution overhead results. For both cases, the execution time slowly grows with the increase of the obfuscation levels. As expected, program takes more time to execute when more instructions are obfuscated. Nevertheless, we interpret the overall execution overhead is still confined to a reasonable level. We also notice that there exists a difference between slopes of the two curves. Some further study on the source code shows that REGEXP employs more recursive calls than BZIP2, thus may lead to more invocations of the Turing machine component and contribute to the performance penalty.

6   Discussion

In this section we present the discussion of the proposed Turing machine obfuscation technique.

6.1   Complexity

In general, Turing machine model is a powerful but complex calculator that is capable of solving any algorithm problem. Note that even a simple operation (e.g., "add") may lead to the change of Turing machine states for hundreds of times. Hence, it is hard—if possible at all—for adversaries with manual reverse engineering efforts to follow the calculation logic without understanding the transition table rules and state variables. In addition, automated binary analyzers (e.g., KLEE) can also be impeded due to the runtime complexity of a Turing machine. As shown in our resilience evaluation (Sect. 5.3), the constraint solver of KLEE failed to yield proper inputs to cover two of three execution paths.

To further improve the complexity, a promising direction is to perform "recursive" obfuscation towards the input program. That is, we employ the Turing obfuscator for the first round obfuscation, and further re-apply Turing obfuscator to obfuscate the Turing machine inserted in the first round. Existing work has pointed out that such "recursive" obfuscation approaches can usually improve the program complexity, while may also bring in non-negligible execution overhead [24]. We leave it as one future work to study practical strategies to recursively apply our technique for obfuscation.

6.2   Application Scope

Previous obfuscation work [21] usually targets one or several specific kinds of predicate expressions. Also, most of them performs source code level transformations for specific kind of program languages [23]. Turing obfuscator broadens the application scope to any kind of conditional expression. In addition, it works for programs written in any language as long as they could be transformed into the LLVM IR. Considering a large portion of programming languages have been supported by LLVM, we envision Turning machine obfuscator would serve to harden software implemented with various kinds of programming languages.

6.3   Branch Selection Techniques

As previously presented, our current implementation rewrites path condition instructions to invoke the Turing machine component. While it is mostly impossible for attackers to reason the semantics of the Turing machine code, return value of the obfuscator is indeed observable (since obfuscated branches are rewritten into function calls to the Turing obfuscator). Certain amount of information leakage may become feasible at this point.

We notice that existing work [15,16] proposes a different approach at this step; control flow is directly guided (via `goto`) to the selected branch from their obfuscator. While this approach seems to hide the explicit return value, we argue such technique is not fundamentally more secure since the hidden return value can be inferred by observing the execution flow. Another solution that may be employed to protect the predicate computation result is to use matrix branch logic [10]. Suppose we model a branch predicate with a Turing machine function, the general idea is to further transform Turing machine into a matrix function, and then randomize the matrix branching function. The involved matrix branch logic and randomness shall provide additional security guarantees at this step. Overall, we argue the current implementation is reasonable, and we leave it as one future work to present quantitative analysis of the potential information leakage and countermeasures at this step.

6.4 Execution Overhead

During the Turing machine computation, frequent state change would indicate lots of read and write operations. Also, since tape is infinite in Turing machine model, it needs to allocate enough memory to accommodate complex computations. In general, the complexity of Turing machine may serve as a double-edge sword; it impedes adversaries and potentially increases execution overhead as well. As reported in the cost evaluation (Fig. 11), we observed non-negligible performance penalty for both cases. One countermeasure here is to perform selective obfuscation; users can annotate sensitive program components for obfuscation. Such strategy would improve the overall execution speed without losing the major security guarantees.

7 Conclusion

In this paper, we propose a novel obfuscation technique using Turing machines. We have implemented a research prototype, Turing machine obfuscator, on the LLVM platform and evaluated on open source software with respect to functionality correctness, potency, resilience, stealth, and cost. The results indicate effectiveness and robustness of Turing machine obfuscation. We believe Turing machine obfuscation could be a promising and practical obfuscation tool to impede adversary analysis.

Acknowledgment. We thank the anonymous reviewers for their valuable feedback. This research was supported in part by the National Science Foundation (NSF) under grant CNS-1652790, and the Office of Naval Research (ONR) under grants N00014-13-1-0175, N00014-16-1-2265, and N00014-16-1-2912.

References

1. bzip2 (2017). http://www.bzip.org
2. IDA (2017). https://www.hex-rays.com/products/ida/
3. Klee sample (2017). http://klee.github.io/tutorials/testing-function/
4. slre (2017). https://github.com/cesanta/slre
5. Cadar, C., Dunbar, D., Engler, D.R., et al.: KLEE: unassisted and automatic generation of high-coverage tests for complex systems programs. In: Proceedings of 8th USENIX Conference on Operating Systems Design and Implementation (OSDI 2008), pp. 209–224 (2008)

6. Cadar, C., Ganesh, V., Pawlowski, P.M., Dill, D.L., Engler, D.R.: Exe: automatically generating inputs of death. In: Proceedings of 13th ACM Conference on Computer and Communications Security, CCS 2006 (2006)
7. Chen, H., Yuan, L., Wu, X., Zang, B., Huang, B., Yew, P.-C.: Control flow obfuscation with information flow tracking. In: Proceedings of 42nd Annual IEEE/ACM International Symposium on Microarchitecture (Micro 2009), pp. 391–400 (2009)
8. Collberg, C., Thomborson, C., Low, D.: Manufacturing cheap, resilient, and stealthy opaque constructs. In: Proceedings of 25th ACM SIGPLAN-SIGACT Symposium on Principles of Programming Languages (POPL 1998), pp. 184–196 (1998)
9. Copeland, B.J.: The church-turing thesis. Stanford encyclopedia of philosophy (2002)
10. Garg, S., Gentry, C., Halevi, S., Raykova, M., Sahai, A., Waters, B.: Candidate indistinguishability obfuscation and functional encryption for all circuits. In: Proceedings of 2013 IEEE 54th Annual Symposium on Foundations of Computer Science, FOCS 2013 (2013)
11. Godefroid, P., Levin, M.Y., Molnar, D.: Automated whitebox fuzz testing. In: Proceedings of 15th Annual Network and Distributed System Security Symposium (NDSS 2008) (2008)
12. King, J.C.: Symbolic execution and program testing. Commun. ACM **19**(7), 385–394 (1976)
13. Lan, P., Wang, P., Wang, P., Wu, D.: Lambda obfuscation. In: Proceedings of 13th EAI International Conference on Security and Privacy in Communication Networks (SECURECOMM 2017) (2017)
14. Lattner, C., Adve, V.: LLVM: a compilation framework for lifelong program analysis & transformation. In: Proceedings of International Symposium on Code Generation and Optimization (CGO 2004), pp. 75–86, March 2004
15. Ma, H., Li, R., Yu, X., Jia, C., Gao, D.: Integrated software fingerprinting via neural-network-based control flow obfuscation. IEEE Trans. Inf. Forensics Secur. **11**(10), 2322–2337 (2016)
16. Ma, H., Ma, X., Liu, W., Huang, Z., Gao, D., Jia, C.: Control flow obfuscation using neural network to fight concolic testing. In: Proceedings of 10th International Conference on Security and Privacy in Communication Networks (SECURECOMM 2014), pp. 287–304 (2014)
17. McCabe, T.J.: A complexity measure. IEEE Trans. Softw. Eng. **SE–2**(4), 308–320 (1976)
18. Popov, I.V., Debray, S.K., Andrews, G.R.: Binary obfuscation using signals. In: Proceedings of 16th USENIX Security Symposium on USENIX Security Symposium (USENIX Security 2007) (2007)
19. Sen, K., Agha, G.: CUTE and jCUTE: concolic unit testing and explicit path model-checking tools. In: Proceedings of 18th International Conference on Computer Aided Verification, CAV 2006 (2006)
20. Sen, K., Marinov, D., Agha, G.: Cute: a concolic unit testing engine for C. In: Proceedings of 10th European Software Engineering Conference Held Jointly with 13th ACM SIGSOFT International Symposium on Foundations of Software Engineering (FSE 2013), pp. 263–272 (2005)
21. Sharif, M.I., Lanzi, A., Giffin, J.T., Lee, W.: Impeding malware analysis using conditional code obfuscation. In: Proceedings of 15th Annual Network and Distributed System Security Symposium (NDSS 2008) (2008)
22. SingleTape: Turing machine (2017). http://turingmaschine.klickagent.ch/

23. Wang, P., Wang, S., Ming, J., Jiang, Y., Wu, D.: Translingual obfuscation. In: Proceedings of 2016 IEEE European Symposium on Security and Privacy (EuroS&P 2016), pp. 128–144 (2016)
24. Wang, S., Wang, P., Wu, D.: Composite software diversification. In: Proceedings of 33rd IEEE International Conference on Software Maintenance and Evolution (ICSME 2017) (2017)
25. Wang, Y.: Obfuscation with Turing machine. Master's thesis, The Pennsylvania State University (2017)
26. Wang, Z., Jia, C., Liu, M., Yu, X.: Branch obfuscation using code mobility and signal. In: Proceedings of 2012 IEEE 36th Annual Computer Software and Applications Conference Workshops (COMPSACW 2012), pp. 553–558 (2012)
27. Wang, Z., Ming, J., Jia, C., Gao, D.: Linear obfuscation to combat symbolic execution. In: Proceedings of 16th European Conference on Research in Computer Security, pp. 210–226 (2011)
28. Woodward, M.R., Hennell, M.A., Hedley, D.: A measure of control flow complexity in program text. IEEE Trans. Softw. Eng. **5**(1), 45–50 (1979)
29. Xu, D., Ming, J., Wu, D.: Generalized dynamic opaque predicates: a new control flow obfuscation method. In: Proceedings of 19th Information Security Conference (ISC 2016), pp. 323–342 (2016)

All Your Accounts Are Belong to Us

Vlad Bulakh[1]($\boxtimes$)(iD), Andrew J. Kaizer[1], and Minaxi Gupta[2]

[1] Indiana University, Bloomington, IN 47405, USA
{vbulakh,akaizer}@indiana.edu
[2] Edmodo Inc., San Mateo, CA 94403, USA
minaxi@edmodo.com

Abstract. Over the last several years, there have been a number of high profile and well-publicized data breaches. These breaches led to the theft of personal, financial, and health information from users who are often only notified of such breaches well after they occur and the damage has already been done. Cyber criminals use account cracking tools, which are software programs that help miscreants gain access to users' online accounts, to perform credential stuffing attacks against the credentials exposed by these breaches.

In this paper, we study underground forums where intelligence related to popular account *cracking tools* is exchanged and investigate miscreants' motivations to use such tools to break into accounts. We also study six free and paid cracking tools used to steal user accounts and develop machine learning classifiers capable of detecting network packets generated by them. Organizations maintaining user accounts can utilize our classifiers to identify traffic related to cracking tools and defend against their attacks.

Keywords: Data breach · Underground forum · Credential stuffing
Account cracking · Credential verification · Cracking tools
Sentry MBA · Account Hitman · AIOHNB · Vertex · Classifier
Supervised machine learning · Random Forest

1 Introduction

Over the past several years, there has been an alarming increase in the number of data breaches throughout the world. The victims of these cyber criminals include prominent firms such as the Red Cross [17], Yahoo [21], ClixSense [56], Ubuntu Forums [41], Interpark [44], the Democratic National Committee [39], and Mossack Fonseca [12]. As a result of these breaches, millions of consumers' personal, financial, and medical information has been exposed to cyber criminals, who can use the information for financial, political, and social gains.

One key factor that has led to these breaches is the growing number of malicious tools that miscreants have at their disposal, including malware, credit card skimmers, and online account cracking tools such as Sentry MBA and Account Hitman. In this paper, we gain a better understanding of the online "cracker"

© ICST Institute for Computer Sciences, Social Informatics and Telecommunications Engineering 2018
X. Lin et al. (Eds.): SecureComm 2017, LNICST 238, pp. 245–269, 2018.
https://doi.org/10.1007/978-3-319-78813-5_13

community and investigate defenses against such attacks. In particular, we concentrate our efforts on several popular underground forums specializing in cracking tools, which are computer programs that can be used to gain unauthorized access to other people's online accounts. The forums we analyzed contain configuration files, which are text files with website-specific settings for cracking tools. For example, a Facebook configuration file for the Sentry MBA tool might contain a custom *User-Agent* header field and an HTTPS address of the user login page, which helps the tool avoid being blocked by Facebook by making the traffic appear to be from a legitimate browser user. Configuration files also allow developers and users to keep their software up to date without modifying the source code and recompiling the program, providing an accessible approach for changing targets.

In addition to studying the configuration files exchanged in underground forums, we studied the cracking tools to examine their behaviors and identify defense mechanisms. This included fairly sophisticated cracking tools, including ones that could check the validity of existing/stolen credentials on popular websites such as Gmail, Amazon, eBay, PayPal, Steam, and others. Some tools could also be used to discover username and password combinations through brute force attacks, which use automated means to guess such information through trial and error. Criminals, however, appear to be using them primarily for checking the validity of breached credentials, also known as a *credential stuffing* attack [58].

Detecting these cracking tools then becomes a critical task to mitigate the risk they pose to an organization's users. Although identifying such attacks from the server side is no trivial matter, by analyzing the packets generated by both paid and free cracking tools, we devise a system capable of detecting up to 100% of attacks.

Our contributions in this study are threefold:

1. *Characteristics of underground forums dealing with cracking tools*: We registered on four underground forums – webcracking.com, nethingoez.com, nulled.to and cracking.org – where members discuss cracking tools and exchange information about them, among other illicit discussions related to hacking tutorials or finding serial numbers to popular video games. We then analyzed these forums by scraping information about the number and length of threads and posts, user location, user join date, and user activity. Interestingly, we found that very few people actually ask for help on these forums. Instead, the majority of the posts are non-informative and made only because gaining access to the shared content required posting. Furthermore, judging from the users' browsing and posting habits, we find these forums to be niche places aimed at a fairly narrow, albeit loyal, audience.
2. *Comparison of popular paid and unpaid cracking tools*: We compare and contrast the features and performance of some of the most popular free and paid crackers, including Sentry MBA [1], Account Hitman [30], Vertex [11], AIOHNB [14], vCrack [16], and Multi-Hacker [25]. Surprisingly, we discovered that the free tools contained more features and performed in a similar capacity, indicating that miscreants who pay for crackers may not be deriving any

additional value beyond free tools. We also found both free and paid cracking tools to have a significant number of bugs and glitches, which is surprising considering how mature some of these tools are.

3. *Defending against identity theft*: Finally, we use the knowledge gained from our contributions to develop several machine learning algorithms that companies maintaining user accounts can use to detect when crackers are accessing their websites. Our classifiers rely on the features extracted from the network packets, such as packet size, HTTP version, and HTTP *Connection* and *Accept-Language* header fields, so companies can identify such threats before processing their requests.

2   Analysis of Cracking Forums

Analyzing the users, topics, and posts of these underground forums can provide valuable insight into some of the motivations and trends behind the cracking culture. In particular, we find that forums may share some high level properties – such as bursts of activity and a small core group of posters – but that the config files discussed on each website tended to focus on different targets – e.g. gaming versus file sharing websites. Before continuing with the analysis, a brief discussion of terminology and data collection is necessary to contextualize the problem space.

2.1   Terminology

An **administrator** (also called **admin**) is a forum member who has elevated privileges. Among other things, a typical forum administrator can: edit other members' posts, remove individual messages and complete threads, and issue warnings to and ban misbehaving forum members.

A **configuration file** (also called **config**) is a text file containing website-specific settings for a cracker. For example, an Amazon config file for Sentry MBA might contain a custom *Referer* field and an Amazon-specific timeout. A snippet from a Sentry MBA configuration file for Instagram can be seen below:

```
[Wordlist]
UserIndex=1
PassIndex=2
...
[Settings]
SiteURL=https://instagram.com/accounts/login/ajax/
Timeout=20
RequestMethod=2
Referer=1
...
```

Credential stuffing (also called **credential checking** and **credential verification**) is an attack in which cyber criminals load breached username/password combinations into a cracking tool like Sentry MBA and try to take over other people's online accounts by having the cracking tool check the supplied credentials against the target website.

A **forum** (also called a **message board**) is a website where people can communicate with each other by posting messages. The content of messages can include text, emotions, pictures, and videos.

An **original post** (often abbreviated as **OP**) is the first post in a continuous sequence of postings.

A **post** is a message in a form of text, emotions, pictures, etc. posted on the forum.

A **subforum** is located inside another forum. Subforums are often used to divide a single forum into specific discussion topics. For example, an underground forum might have a cracked programs subforum for cracking tools.

A **topic** (also called **thread**) is a sequence of posts/messages posted in the response to the original post.

A **topic starter** (often abbreviated as **TS**) is the person who posted the first message in a continuous sequence of postings (i.e. original post). A topic starter can also be called **original poster** and abbreviated as **OP**.

2.2   Data Collection and Methodology

The websites studied covered four of the most popular cracking forums: webcracking.com, nethingoez.com, nulled.to, and cracking.org. As of May 2017, all these websites are highly ranked by Alexa, with nulled.to, cracking.org, webcracking.com, and nethingoez.com having global ranks of 25K, 121K, 275K, and 300K, respectively.

We collected complete snapshots of webcracking.com, nulled.to, cracking.org, and nethingoez.com on December 19, 2015, July 8, 2016, September 12, 2016, and August 29, 2016, respectively. The scraping process focused on the subforums dealing with configuration files for the most popular cracking tools, such as Sentry MBA, Account Hitman, AIO Checker, and Vertex. For each snapshot, we collected the threads, posts, and users across all config file subforums. This ensures a *complete* overview of the subforums at that particular point in time.

Data Cleaning

We saw a number of inconsistencies in the collected data, even when that data was from the same underground forum, that could undermine data analysis if not accounted for. For example, the cracking tool field could say "SentryMBA," "Sentry MBA proxyless," "SentryMBA proxylexx," "Sentry," "Sentary MBA," "SMBA," "SenMBA," and "S. MBA," all of which refer to the same cracking tool – Sentry MBA[1]. We also saw a number of incorrect entries and labels. For example, a thread might be located in the Vertex subforum, but have tags corresponding to other cracking tools, e.g. "Account Hitman."

Due to these factors, considerable effort was spent on data sanitization. About 10% of the data we collected had to be cleaned, which involved standardizing the names of the cracking tools (e.g. both "Hitman" and "Acc Hitman"

---

[1] Although it is possible that some of those could be referring to different Sentries, such as the original Sentry [46], which is the predecessor of Sentry MBA [19], a manual analysis of 25 threads revealed that all of them were about Sentry MBA.

became "Account Hitman"), inferring missing information (e.g. determining the cracking tool from the first post in the thread) and ignoring invalid entries. Overall, approximately 2% of all threads and 4% of all posts have been discarded through this process.

2.3   Users

Looking at the number of users who posted at least one message in the config file subforums across all websites, we observe that nulled.to leads with 14,446 unique users and is followed by cracking.org, webcracking.com, and nethingoez.com with 7,500, 2,720, and 1,719 unique users, respectively. This indicates that the degree of popularity for cracking activities varies widely across various underground forums.

Interestingly, we see that all forums have small-to-large gaps between user registration dates that could last from several days to several weeks – except cracking.org which did not show the registration date at the time of data collection. For example, although 721 people created new accounts on nulled.to between April 25–May 5, 2016, with no day having fewer than 24 new registrations, no new accounts were created from May 6–June 23, 2016. Such large gaps could be either due to the websites' doing user registrations in batches or service availability issues.

Additionally, webcracking.com showed a user-supplied location during our data collection period, which, admittedly, could be falsified. Of those users who did specify their location, most came from the United States, followed closely by the United Kingdom, Germany, France, Canada, Italy, Spain, Turkey, India, and Brazil. Notably absent from this list are some of the well-known countries that engage in more insidious forms of consumer-oriented cybercrime, such as Russia or China. A focus on the top countries may indicate a proclivity towards a less tech-savvy, more "script kiddie"-oriented audience.

Also, when we cross-reference user account names across the config file subforums of each underground forum, we see that the overwhelming majority of account names can only be found in one of the four forums, with 3.2% instances of an exact account name match on two different forums, 0.4% matches on three different forums, and only 0.08% matches across all four forums. This implies that either miscreants utilize separate identities on each forum or that they tend to use only one source for their cracking needs.

Furthermore, looking at the average number of active users across all four underground forums, we see that, on a per-hour basis, there are 682 members and 604 guests active on nulled.to, 50 members and 95 guests active on nethingoez.com, and 19 members and 180 guests active on cracking.org. For webcracking.com, we were only able to get the daily statistics, which showed that an average of 271 members and 1,169 guests are active on any given day. Compared to popular, legitimate forums such as reddit.com and 4chan.org, which can have hundreds of thousands of *active* users at any given time with many of them having posted dozens and even hundreds of thousands of messages, these underground forums appear to be niche places aimed at a very narrow audience.

2.4 Threads

When looking at the number of active threads that share and discuss configuration files, cracking.org takes the first place with 3,197 threads – despite having the second-fewest active members at any given hour amongst the four forums. It is followed by nulled.to (833 threads), nethingoez.com (708 threads) and webcracking.com (698 threads), which each have a comparable number of threads. Also, the overall number of threads is disproportionately large compared to the number of websites targeted by the config files. This is due to the fact that once a config-breaking change is made to the target website, some forum users tend to post a new config file thread instead of updating the old one.

The situation is slightly different when we look at the number of views that each thread receives. A typical config file thread on nulled.to gets 1,044 views, while threads created on cracking.org, nethingoez.com, and webcracking.com average 620, 236, and 234 views, respectively. Looking at the number of replies to each configuration file thread, we see that nulled.to leads with 56 replies per thread with nethingoez.com, cracking.org, and webcracking.com taking the second, third, and fourth places with 21, 18, and 10 replies per thread, respectively. More details can be seen in Table 1.

Table 1. Cracking forum threads and posts

	cracking.org	nethingoez.com	nulled.to	webcracking.com
Number of config file threads	3,197	708	833	698
Average number of config file thread views	620.15	235.71	1,044.39	233.90
Average number of config file thread replies	18.24	20.58	55.79	9.50
Number of config file subforum posts per user	8.21	8.86	3.24	2.69
Num. of unique users in config file subforums	7,500	1,719	14,446	2,720

Exploring the number of unique threads created by each topic starter – including website administrators – in the config file subforums, we observe the following: webcracking.com leads with 11.6 threads per user, second place is occupied by cracking.org with 7.2 threads per user, and nethingoez.com and nulled.to are last with 6.6 and 2.1 threads per user, respectively. On the other hand, when it comes to the number of thread creators in the configuration file subforums, cracking.org leads with 446 unique users and is followed by nulled.to, nethingoez.com, and webcracking.com with 390, 107, and 60 unique thread creators, respectively.

Further, we observe a small but extremely active set of users, most of whom are website administrators, on all four web forums. Combined, the config file threads created by those users are as numerous as all config file threads created by 98% of users across all four underground forums. In other words, the vast majority of thread creators in the configuration file subforums tend to create very few threads – between one and 19 – while a few select users are responsible for the creation of dozens and even hundreds of different threads.

Interestingly, the thread posting activity is somewhat similar across all forums in that there are short periods of high activity, such as 10–20 new threads posted in a 24–48 hour period, followed by several weeks of moderate to low activity with only a few config file threads posted per day.

2.5   Posts

When looking at the posting activity on the config file subforums, we see that a typical nethingoez.com user[2] has 8.9 posts/messages under their belt, followed by cracking.org, nulled.to, and webcracking.com users with 8.2, 3.2, and 2.7 posts, respectively (Table 1). In other words, it is safe to say that a typical user downloads between 2.7 and 8.9 config files since one has to post a reply before being able to access the thread attachments such as configuration files, and there is very little incentive for the posters to keep posting in the same config file thread once they have gained access to the attachments except to report an error, which we observed very rarely. If we expand the search to include all messages posted by the config file subforum posters on the four underground forums, we observe that nethingoez.com leads with 272 posts per user, followed by cracking.org (94 posts), nulled.to (71), and webcracking.com (67).

If we look at the individual users who post in the config file subforums, we see 7,500 unique users on cracking.org, 80 of which have more than 100 posts each, and nine have more than 200 posts each. The statistics are even grimmer for the other three forums: out of 1,719 nethingoez.com users, only five have made more than 100 posts, none have made more than 200 posts. None of the 14,446 nulled.to users have more than 100 posts under their belts, and only two out of 2,720 webcracking.com users have made more than 100 posts. Also, if we include all messages posted by the same users and not only those in the config file subforums, we see that only 22 nethingoez.com users, 20 cracking.org users, three webcracking.com users, and two nulled.to users have posted more than 2,000 messages each, with the vast majority of all users having posted fewer than 200 messages. Essentially, this continues to highlight how although a small core are very active, the vast majority of users are generally content to interact infrequently on each website. Our observations coincide with previous studies on the subject [36].

---

[2] In this Section we are looking at the users who posted at least one message in the config file subforums since we are unable to get the data on those who do not post any messages.

2.6 Post Content

When looking at the messages posted by users, we observe that the vast majority of the posts are non-informative and appear to have been made to satisfy web forums' requirements for accessing the content attached to the original posts (OP). Examples of such messages include: "thanks man," "thank for sharing," "thanks bro," "thxxxxxxxxxxxxxx," and "thank for share." We also saw several instances of posters asking for help or reporting a config file that is no longer working due to the recent changes made by Facebook/eBay/etc. However, more often than not, such posts were left un-addressed. This further solidifies our view that most users on these websites are in the "script kiddie" mold of miscreant rather than a more nefarious and skilled hacker.

3 Cracking Tools

All cracking tools that we tested work in a similar manner. First, the user must configure the tool, which typically includes loading the config file (or specifying the parameters manually), selecting the word list to use (which is a text file containing username/password combinations), specifying the keywords for success and failure, loading the proxy list, and selecting the number of threads to use. The tool then sets up the connection by completing the three-way TCP handshake and starts to send HTTP or HTTPS packets to the target website (usually to the login page) with the credentials from the word list. After that, the cracking tool parses the HTML response it receives from the target website and determines whether the credentials are valid or not by looking for success and failure keywords specified earlier.

3.1 Cracking Tool Popularity

Looking at the number of threads dedicated to each cracking tool, we see that Sentry MBA is the most popular one across all forums. This makes sense based on the fact that it is free, relatively stable, has an intuitive graphical user interface, and is one of the oldest crackers in our test, with the first beta version of the original Sentry, the predecessor of Sentry MBA, dating back to April 25, 2003 [45]. Vertex, Account Hitman, and Apex occupy the second, third, and fourth places, interchangeably. Interestingly, all paid cracking tools that we tested – AIOHNB, vCrack, and Multi-Hacker – are orders of magnitude less popular than their free counterparts. One reason for this could be that both AIOHNB and Multi-Hacker do not support config files and, compared to Sentry MBA and Account Hitman, it is considerably more difficult to create a config file for vCrack. In addition, although we were not able to identify cracking tools' names in most of the nulled.to threads, a manual analysis of a 50-thread sample suggests that 98% or more of them are Sentry MBA. More details can be seen in Table 2. Also, due to the underground forums' structure, we had to group several cracking tools, namely EZLeecher, Forum Leecher, ZLeecher, and Fj Leecher, into one supergroup called "Leechers".

Table 2. Cracking tool threads

Cracking tool	cracking.org	nethingoez.com	nulled.to	webcracking.com
Sentry MBA	2,500	579	157	374
Vertex	196	–	–	72
Account Hitman	113	60	–	60
Apex	72	–	–	46
AIO Checker	40	–	–	66
AIOHNB	26	–	–	25
Leechers	16	–	–	27
E.F.R Checker	37	–	–	–
Sparta	31	–	–	–
Other	52	1	1	26
Unknown	114	68	675	2

3.2   Websites Targeted by the Config Files

An analysis of thread titles and attachments across all forums reveals that file sharing and downloading services, such as uploaded.net, 1fichier.com, and real-debrid.com are the most popular targets for the configuration files. Gaming websites and distribution platforms such as leagueoflegends.com, store.steampowered.com, and origin.com take a distant second place. Third place is occupied by adult-oriented websites. More details can be seen on Fig. 1.

When looking at each forum individually, we observe that, contrary to the other three forums, gaming website config files are much more popular on nulled.to than any other category. In contrast, file sharing and adult config file threads are the most pandered about on nethingoez.com and webcracking.com. The gaming website threads are few and far between. Another interesting finding was that fast food restaurants had more config file threads created for them than security software and financial services websites.

At first glance, one might be surprised that shopping and payment/financial services websites such as amazon.com, ebay.com, paypal.com, and wellsfargo.com are not very popular on these forums even though they [arguably] provide the highest return on investment. However, a brief look over several cracking tool discussion subforums would explain such low popularity of config files for payment and financial services websites – apparently, unlike most file sharing and adult sites, large banks and online shopping websites go after the miscreants who use cracking tools against their websites. In fact, a more in-depth search reveals a few posts by people who allegedly served time in jail for trying to brute-force online banking accounts.

Also, it must be noted that although we were able to categorize the majority of websites targeted by the configuration files, approximately 43% of thread titles could not be easily converted to one of the categories. Consequently, such thread

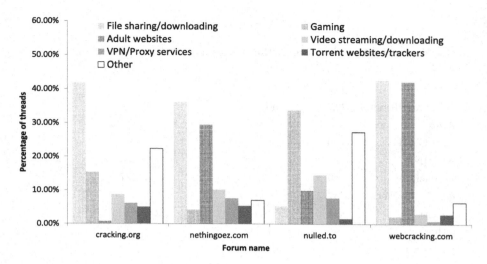

Fig. 1. Websites targeted by the config files

titles had to be omitted. Still, we believe the results reported in this section are representative of the population of websites that crackers target.

3.3 Overview of Cracking Tools' Functionality

To gain a better understanding of cracking software, we created fake accounts on several online social networks and used the most popular free and paid cracking tools to crack them. We chose not to test cracking tools on websites such as bankofamerica.com and ebay.com because, as discussed earlier, there have been several reports in underground forums of banks and large corporations pursuing individuals who tried to brute-force their customers' accounts. The free crackers studied include Sentry MBA, Account Hitman, and Vertex, which are the top three most popular cracking tools. The paid cracking programs were AIOHNB, vCrack, and Multi-Hacker. Similar to other cracking/hacking tools found in underground forums and marketplaces, the crackers we tested are for Microsoft Windows operating systems only. Also, at the beginning of our study, both AIOHNB and vCrack were paid tools. However, starting with version 2.7.0, the former appears to no longer require paid online activation [14] and the latter became open source on April 22, 2016 [16].

Furthermore, although most of the cracking tools we tested have a wide range of features, such as the ability to test proxy servers, check the validity of email accounts, and even optical character recognition (OCR) functionality to bypass CAPTCHAs, we concentrated our efforts on testing their abilities to check credentials.

Our first observation is that neither free nor paid cracking tools are particularly user friendly. One free and one paid cracking tool – Vertex and AIOHNB, respectively – refused to run unless additional files were downloaded (Fig. 2b, c and d). Interestingly enough, initially AIOHNB refused to work claiming that it required additional 'framework' files to operate. The cracker prompted us to install the said files (Fig. 2b), which implies there is a possibility that the miscreant could be downloading malicious files targeting themselves. Once all the required files for Vertex and AIOHNB were installed, we were able to start their graphical interfaces. This is a lot of trouble to go through when another cracking tool could be utilized instead.

Upon launching the cracking programs, we observed that half of them try to listen on a local port or issue HTTP GET requests. For example, Sentry MBA sends TCP packets to dyndns.com on port 80 to determine the external IP address of the machine. Account Hitman, on the other hand, does not send outgoing packets and only attempts to listen on TCP port 13121. Finally, AIOHNB tries to connect to cpc-prod3.canardpc.com on TCP port 80. Vertex, vCrack, and Multi-Hacker neither attempted to listen on a local port nor sent any outgoing packets.

3.4 Issues Encountered

At a glance, both free and paid cracking tools appear to have nice, clean, easy-to-use interfaces. Additionally, they feature a wide array of settings and features ranging from the ability to use regular expressions to extract desired information from brute-forced accounts, such as street addresses and phone numbers, to automatic configuration file downloads directly from the graphical interface.

However, appearances can be deceiving. Upon closer examination, we found advertised features to be broken and others not operating as expected. During our testing, Account Hitman crashed on regular basis, an example of which can be seen on Fig. 2a. Vertex, on the other hand, refused to download updates or configuration files (Fig. 2e). A sleek UI cannot cover up the inability for these tools to function reliably.

In addition, despite being the most polished and widely used of the bunch, Sentry MBA had issues using custom HTTP headers, which require critical updates to circumvent server-based defense mechanisms. Fields such as *Referer*, *Accept-Language*, and *Cookie* could be easily changed via Sentry MBA to match those of any browser. However, using a custom *Accept-Encoding* header field breaks the TCP packet generated by Sentry MBA. Furthermore, we had to restart Sentry MBA several times during testing since it would sometimes refuse to use newly changed settings and would keep resetting itself to the old configuration. In all cases, a restart would solve such problems.

The paid cracking tools were not much better. vCrack for example, refused to work unless the number of threads numbered in the double digits. That is, it would not work with 1, 2, or 3 threads, but would run with 01, 02, and 10 threads. In addition, although vCrack would issue an HTTP GET request once we specified the correct thread number, it would not work as intended and would always claim that it verified the credentials for 0 user accounts even when supplied with valid username and password combinations. Further, although AIOHNB was the most feature-rich paid tool in our test with URL grabbing,

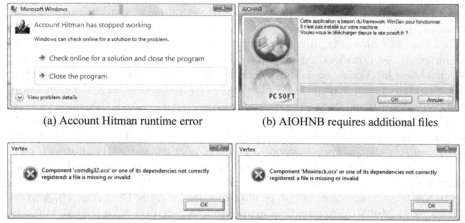

(a) Account Hitman runtime error   (b) AIOHNB requires additional files

(c) Vertex requires comdlg32.ocx   (d) Vertex requires Mswinsck.ocx

(e) Vertex is unable to download config files   (f) Vertex cannot handle HTTPS

Fig. 2. Cracking tool crashes, errors, and notifications

proxy testing, and email checking modules, it had its fair share of issues – such as poor or missing translation, one example of which can be seen on Fig. 2b – even though it required additional files to "run" as described in Sect. 3.3.

Multi-Hacker was also not without its faults. When we tried to crack our Skype account, it claimed that the crack was successful despite the fact that we supplied it with invalid account names. We believe that an outdated Skype module of Multi-Hacker is to blame since Multi-Hacker actually worked on our Facebook and Instagram accounts.

3.5   Feature Comparison

Sentry MBA, Account Hitman, and Vertex all have very similar features, including multithreading support, the ability to use proxies, the ability to use and edit custom configuration files, and the ability to change the *User-Agent* HTTP header field. However, there are quite a few differences between these free cracking tools – some of which we believe to be responsible for that particular cracking tool's popularity (or lack thereof) – that warrants an explanation.

Despite being the most popular and stable of the bunch, Sentry MBA is the only free cracking tool in our test that does not check for updates, whether automatically or via a button click. Although Vertex has the least number of features compared to other free tools, it is the only cracker that supports direct download of configuration files from the underground forum nethingoez.com. Unfortunately, this feature was not working in our test (Fig. 2e), most likely due to the fact that nethingoez.com made several changes to its website during our data collection period.

When looking at the software's ability to create and edit configuration files, we found Sentry MBA's configuration file editor and creator more sophisticated than the one in Vertex, although we felt that it was not as intuitive to use as Account Hitman's.

While testing three crackers against our fake accounts, we noticed that there was virtually no difference in speed between them, and both Sentry MBA and Account Hitman correctly reported the results when supplied with both valid and invalid credentials. Vertex, on the other hand, reported all supplied username/password combinations as valid, despite the fact that half of them were invalid. Furthermore, Vertex refused to work with HTTPS websites (Fig. 2f), which, combined with the previously mentioned issues, make it the most buggy free cracking tool in our test.

Overall, out of free cracking tools, only Sentry MBA and Account Hitman were able to successfully verify credentials to our fake user accounts. They are also somewhat more polished and offer more features than the rest, which explains their popularity. However, it has to be mentioned that a large number of posters in underground forums have had success with Vertex, even though we did not. One possible explanation for this split could be that it needs the access to nethingoez.com in order to function properly. In addition, Vertex had not been updated recently, which, combined with the fact that all but one underground website in our data set had either changed domain names or modified their code during the data collection period, could have resulted in the cracker's failure that we encountered during testing as the program was looking for information that had either been moved or deleted.

Interestingly, we found most paid cracking tools lacking in features compared to their free counterparts. For example, basic functionality such as *User-Agent* selection and pre- and post-login page actions were nowhere to be found in vCrack and Multi-Hacker. Furthermore, although both AIOHNB and Multi-Hacker feature a number of pre-built modules for popular websites like reddit.com and instagram.com, they neither support the external config files nor allow users to make any changes to the built-in modules, which will render the current tool versions useless once the target websites change their login pages. vCrack is the only paid tool in our test that supports the addition of external modules, although the process of creating a new module is much more involved compared to creating a config file for a free cracking tool. In our opinion, one of the very few advantages of the paid cracking tools over their free counterparts is the simplicity of use – one simply has to select the desired module, load the credential list, and click *Start*.

We were also surprised that the paid tools we tested had as many issues as the free cracking tools. Not only that, but vCrack was unable to verify any credentials in our tests, which might explain why the developer has chosen to make it open source.

In addition, it has to be mentioned that we tested all cracking tools on a small set of online social network websites to avoid unpleasant conversations with the authorities. As a result, it is possible that some cracking tools in our test would perform significantly better on websites like ebay.com, bankofamerica.com, and origin.com.

4   Detecting Cracking Tools

The best way to detect cracking tools attempting to access a website is to inspect the packets created by the crackers. Unfortunately, to an administrator or a security specialist who monitors the target website's traffic, the packets generated by the cracking tool would look almost identical to the packets generated by the popular browsers. Another method involves analysis of traffic and behavioral abnormalities, such as a large number of packets being sent from the same IP addresses over a short period of time and disproportionate number of login page requests from the same IP address compared to other web pages. Unfortunately, there are two disadvantages to such approaches. First, a miscreant can easily modify the timeout settings in the cracking tool and, instead of sending a packet every 30 seconds, the tool would wait for several hours in between the requests, which would make it very difficult to detect. Second, even if one could somehow find the pattern in the packet timestamps or user behavior, there would be no way for them to tell whether those requests were generated by a cracking tool or by a browser automator like Selenium.

In this study, we use a modification of the first approach – we capture the packets generated by the cracking tools and use the data from several protocol layers to differentiate between the cracking and legitimate packets. By being more detailed, our methodology focuses on identifying specific differences that can enable operators to flag cracking traffic over legitimate traffic.

4.1   Experimental Setup

A brief analysis of the packets generated by the cracking tools showed very little variation in terms of size and header values between each tool. Furthermore, there were not any noticeable differences when we compared them to the packets generated by several popular Internet browsers. Clearly, a more in-depth analysis was called for.

We started by creating a simple website with an HTML login form which would accept only one value for username and a password. If the supplied credentials are correct, the website would show fake user information, including name, address, and a phone number; otherwise, a short error message would be displayed on the HTML page. We then hosted this website on our own server and made sure that a Wireshark [22] instance was running in the background collecting packets.

We wanted to get both HTTP and HTTPS packet samples, which meant decrypting SSL/TLS data. To achieve this, several modifications had to be made. First, the Apache server had to be forced to use the weakest possible encryption by modifying the *SSLCipherSuite* parameter in the configuration file. Wireshark settings also had to be changed so that it would use the Apache's private RSA key to decrypt all HTTPS traffic.

4.2   Cracking Tool Packet Capture Methodology

All cracking tools were tested on a 64-bit version of Windows Vista SP2. Unfortunately, we were not able to test the three paid tools since all of them come with a pre-defined number of modules for popular websites like Facebook, Twitter, and Instagram, which makes it very difficult (impossible in the cases of Multi-Hacker and AIOHNB) to add a new website module. Using the existing modules would not work since all of them are for pre-defined HTTPS websites only. As a result, we were left with Sentry MBA, Account Hitman, and Vertex for packet generating purposes.

For each cracking tool, we changed the settings in such a way that we would get as many different packets as possible. For example, if a cracking tool worked with SSL, had several pre-defined *User-Agent* fields, and supported both GET and POST HTTP requests, then we would generate the packets for all possible combinations, such as HTTP POST request over an SSL connection with the first pre-defined *User-Agent*, HTTP GET request over a non-secure connection with the second pre-defined *User-Agent* field, and so on.

To get a wide range of packet samples from organic traffic, we used several versions of seven popular browsers and five different computers and virtual machines to simulate traffic of an average Internet user. The operating systems used ranged from Windows XP to Windows 10 to GNU/Linux, while the browsers included Firefox, Opera, Chrome/Chromium, Internet Explorer/Edge, SeaMonkey, K-Meleon, and Midori.

Overall, we captured 39 cracking packets generated by the cracking tools and 39 legitimate packets from the browsers, yielding 78 packets for subsequent analysis.

4.3   Packet Comparison

At first glance, the packets generated by the cracking tools look virtually identical to each other and to the packets created by the browsers. However, a closer examination reveals several differences between the legitimate and cracking packets.

We observe that, on average, the packets created by the cracking tools are 28% smaller than their legitimate counterparts. This difference is mostly due to the smaller HTTP payload in the cracking packets.

Moving down the layers, we see that both Ethernet and IP packet headers generated by the three cracking tools are virtually identical to each other as well as to the legitimate packets (with the exception of the IP length header field, which was explained above), which is what one would expect as developers generally let the networking libraries handle lower level packet creation.

Looking at the TCP header, we see that all packets are very similar with the exception of the source port numbers, options, and window size. Of these, only the last two are of interest to us. The difference in TCP options comes from the fact that, contrary to all cracking tools and browsers running on Windows, all GNU/Linux browsers in our test chose to set TCP option 8 (Timestamp). As for the TCP window size, most cracking tools in our test preferred values of 16,425, 65,040, and 65,700, while the browsers used a variety of different values, ranging from 229 to 65,568.

The most noticeable differences between the packets generated by the cracking tools and the Internet browsers are in the application layer, namely in the HTTP header. The first difference is that, in some instances, Sentry MBA uses HTTP version 1.0 while all browsers and the rest of the cracking tools use version 1.1. Furthermore, we observe that although all browsers in our test set the *Connection* field to *keep-alive*, both Account Hitman and Vertex set it to *close*. In addition, the *Accept-Language* header field varied significantly across the browsers and cracking tools, but it was also completely omitted in all packets generated by Sentry MBA. Also, the *User-Agent* field widely differed not only between legitimate and cracking packets but also between each browser instance. Finally, the HTTP *Pragma* header field was set in all packets generated by Sentry MBA while only two browser instances out of 39 used it.

When looking at the HTTP header fields which were exclusive to either cracking or legitimate packets, we observe that all browsers set the *Accept-Encoding* field while none of the cracking tools did. Further, *Accept-Charset*, *Upgrade-Insecure-Requests*, and *Cache-Control* header fields were set by six, 11, and five browser instances, respectively, while none of the cracking tools used them.

4.4 Classifier Training

Using either *Accept-Encoding* or *User-Agent* features for classifier training would give us a perfect accuracy in most machine learning algorithms since they are either unique to all approaches or provide a perfect split between browsers and cracking tools. However, we will not use them since *Accept-Encoding* and *User-Agent* header fields could be either patched by cracking tool authors or manually edited by advanced users.

Table 3 shows the features that were used to train the classifiers, which denotes that the top three most discriminating features according to both Chi-square and Information Gain tests are *Accept-Language* HTTP field, *Pragma* HTTP field, and packet size. *Accept-Charset* and *Cache-Control* HTTP header fields appear to be the least useful features according to both metrics.

Next, we used the RapidMiner data mining environment [43] to train several supervised machine-learning-based algorithms. For each classification exper-

Table 3. Classifier feature importance

Feature name	Chi-square	Information gain
HTTP Accept-Language	1.00	1.00
HTTP Pragma	0.61	0.62
Packet size	0.50	0.42
HTTP version	0.25	0.29
HTTP Upgrade-Insecure-Requests	0.13	0.15
TCP options	0.10	0.12
HTTP Connection	0.08	0.10
HTTP Accept-Charset	0.02	0.02
HTTP Cache-Control	0.0	0.00

Table 4. Classifier accuracy

Classifier	Accuracy	FP rate	FN rate
Random Forest	100.00%	0.00%	0.00%
J48	100.00%	0.00%	0.00%
PART	100.00%	0.00%	0.00%
CART	100.00%	0.00%	0.00%
Logistic Regression	98.72%	2.56%	0.00%
Neural Network	98.72%	2.56%	0.00%
Naive Bayes	75.64%	48.72%	0.00%

iment, we used a 20-fold cross-validation with stratified sampling. In a 20-fold cross-validation, the sample is divided into 20 parts: 19 parts are used as a training dataset, and the remaining part is used to test the classifier. This process is repeated 20 times, producing 20 results. The results reported subsequently are averages of the 20 runs.

The best performing algorithms were Random Forest, J48, PART, and CART, all of which had perfect accuracies. They are followed by Logistic Regression, Neural Network, and Naive Bayes, with the accuracies of 98.72%, 98.72%, and 75.64%, respectively. More details can be seen in Table 4. Also, although we do not know the exact reasons for such poor performance of the Naive Bayes classifier, one explanation could be that some of the features we used are not independent of each other given the class label, which could result in suboptimal probability estimates and wrong decisions [63].

When using AdaBoost to reduce the bias and improve the classifier accuracy even further, we observe that all classifiers' accuracies stay the same. Furthermore, in most cases the boosting was not possible due to the fact that only one classifier was used.

5   Related Works

There have been a number of studies on underground marketplaces and their economies. In what appears to be one of the first studies of modern cybercrime [35], Mann and Sutton analyzed Internet newsgroups, which are online, forum-like discussion groups where like-minded people can communicate with each other by posting messages. Mann and Sutton concentrated their efforts on two particular newsgroups: one with discussions on hacking encrypted satellite signals and another one on lock picking, safes, and other security devices. During the course of their study, the authors classify newsgroup members into categories, such as *hacker gurus*, *parasites*, *information providers*, and *money makers*. They also investigate the supply of and demand for illicit goods and services, and look into how newsgroup users with different levels of expertise interact with each other. This is in contrast to our study, where we target the subforums of four popular underground forums dedicated to cracking tools used to brute force user accounts and test stolen credentials.

A 2007 measurement study by Franklin et al. [23] focused on underground marketplaces and touched on some topics covered by our work. The authors used publicly posted IRC (Internet Relay Chat) messages to study malicious activities, such as spamming, online credential theft, and the sale of compromised hosts. They also proposed simple, low-cost countermeasures which could be used to disrupt the operations of such marketplaces. Similar studies shortly followed, with works by Cymru [15], Herley and Florêncio [26], and Fallmann et al. [20] concentrating their efforts on studying illegal IRC marketplaces. Unfortunately, not only have IRC chat rooms lost popularity among Internet users since that time, but underground black markets have also evolved from chaotic, difficult-to-control entities where there was little incentive for the miscreants not to scam each other to more orderly and better regulated marketplaces [5]. Further, the majority of these works looked at underground marketplaces as a whole. We focus on several smaller subforums, which allows for an in-depth analysis.

In [65], Zhuge et al. perform a measurement study on the underground economy within the Chinese Web. In the course of their study, the authors concentrate their efforts on underground marketplaces and their participants, which allows them to create a model describing the Chinese underground economy. Several similar and complementary studies followed, including the papers by Motoyama et al. [37], Christin [13], Yip et al. [60–62], Stone-Gross et al. [52], Garg et al. [24], Holt and Lampke [29], McCoy et al. [36], Radianti [42], Allodi et al. [6], Holt [27,28], and Sood and Enbody [51]. Our work is somewhat similar to those studies in that we also study underground marketplaces in the example of Web forums. However, unlike these works, which primarily focus on investigating the structure and organization of the underground forums as well as social interactions among their members, we look into the configuration files for cracking tools and user accounts used to share and download them.

Several studies propose various strategies for fighting cybercrime, ranging from making it more difficult and costly for the miscreants to operate to completely taking down underground communities. In [33], Leontiadis analyzes various types of online criminal networks, including underground forums and marketplaces, from both technical and economical perspectives. Leontiadis' study reveals that online criminal networks tend to have weak links, or *choke points*, which are critically-important components of online criminal networks. The author argues that targeting such components will increase criminal operational costs and reduce online crime. A somewhat similar strategy was proposed by Nadji et al. in [38] where the authors used two graph measures – graph density and eigenvector centrality – to investigate the structure of networks involved in criminal activities. The authors also analyzed different take-down strategies that could be used to shut down sophisticated criminal networks and determined that, in most cases, shutting down a few domain names would remove critical network links, thus, taking the whole criminal network down. Our work is similar to these and other studies [3,34,53,55] in that we also come up with ways to make it more difficult for the miscreants to engage in illegal activities. However, our work differs in that we are not really interested in taking down criminal networks; instead, we analyze the tools used by the criminals and develop machine learning classifiers that could be used by companies to make it more difficult and costly for the miscreants to attack them.

Furthermore, some studies survey existing methods and suggest new strategies for detecting and preventing attacks on computer networks and Web applications. Papers by Sommer and Paxson [50], Lee and Stolfo [32], and others discuss and propose data mining and machine-learning-based approaches for network intrusion detection. Other studies, such as those by Douligeris and Mitrokotsa [18], Kumar and Selvakumar [31], and Bhuyan et al. [9], investigate defense mechanisms against distributed denial of service attacks. Further, some papers, such as the ones by Wang et al. [57] and Abreu [2], propose to use Web pages with dynamically changing content to make it more difficult for the miscreants to perform automated attacks on Web applications. Finally, there are studies that discuss the effectiveness of existing techniques for stopping automated attack tools [40]. Although our study is similar to all these papers in that we investigate automated attacks carried out with the help of computer networks, our work differs in that, in addition to the analysis of underground subforums, we concentrate our efforts on detecting network packets generated by the popular cracking tools, which, to the best of our knowledge, is the first work of its kind.

There are also articles and white papers that talk about credential stuffing attacks and cracking tools like Sentry MBA and suggest defense mechanisms, such as using complex passwords, avoiding password recycling, employing JavaScript anti-bot challenges, monitoring the traffic for specific HTTP *User-Agent* fields, and paying special attention to IP addresses responsible for a large number of failed logins [4, 8, 10, 47, 54, 64]. Our study differs in that, in addition to config file subforum analysis, we go much deeper in our investigations of cracking tools as well as develop classifiers capable of detecting cracking packets.

Finally, there are also a number of short papers and articles, such as an article by Shulman [49] and a paper by Yip et al. [59], which provide a brief background on the operations of underground credential markets and give insights into their economies. In addition, a recent study found that cybercrimes are similar to violent crimes in that they both carry significant indirect and defense costs [7]. This is in contrast to traditional non-violent crimes, like car theft or tax fraud, which usually carry high direct costs, such as the price of a car, and relatively low indirect costs, such as psychological trauma and lost output. Further, Shin et al. [48] studied forum automators, which the miscreants use to spam legitimate forums with unrelated messages promoting their own websites. Shin et al. discovered that forum spam automators are fairly sophisticated and include a number of features – such as the ability to automatically solve CAPTCHAs and use anonymizing proxies – which help miscreants circumvent spam prevention mechanisms and avoid blacklisting. Although not directly related to our work, such articles and papers provide valuable insights into the underground cracking economy, some of which we indirectly use in our study.

6   Discussion

6.1   Data Collection Difficulties

One of the consistent traits encountered throughout this study is the large degree of paranoia that forum operators were operating under. In particular, one of our attempts at collecting data from webcracking.com was upended when our registered user was banned from the forums for "leeching," even though we were not downloading or posting cracking configuration files. We were only browsing. Such actions clearly impact our ability to collect data in a timely and complete manner but also point to a culture of distrust on these communities.

To try to avoid these arbitrary bans, we attempted to utilize a *VIP* membership, where premium content and laxer rule enforcement were supposedly benefits. In order to gain access to the VIP section, a user must send a monthly 'donation,' e.g. of $9.95, to the head administrator of webcracking.com. For this paper, we paid for one month worth of VIP access to determine if our data collection efforts could continue or if we would still be subjected to losing our accounts to bans.

We quickly discovered that the VIP membership was subjected to similar restrictions as the free membership, even though the advertisement promised the lifting of all restrictions. Furthermore, even though we strictly adhered to the specified restrictions, our account was temporarily banned for 10 days for downloading too many configuration files. Once the ban was lifted, we reduced the number of files downloaded to one file per 2–3 days. However, the administrators still permanently banned our account and the associated IP address for downloading too many files without uploading any in return, even though nowhere in the rules did it say that we had to upload any content in addition to paying for the VIP access.

6.2   Classifier Feature Selection

It could be argued that the features we used for classifier training – most of which come from the HTTP header – could be circumvented by the cracking tool authors, rendering our classifiers out-of-date. Although it is true that a developer could modify the packets created by their cracking software to make them virtually indistinguishable from those generated by a modern browser, we find it hard to believe that this thought had not crossed the minds of the cracking tool authors, especially considering that the free cracking tools that we tested were relatively mature with numerous versions released in the past several years. If the developers wanted the HTTP headers in their software's packets to resemble those of the popular browsers, they would have done so already.

6.3   Packet Samples

We also had to create our own config files, which we did without modifying the pre-defined HTTP header fields in any of the cracking tools. As a result, it is possible that the use of some config files for twitter.com, facebook.com, and other popular websites would result in mildly different packets than the ones we used in this study. Additionally, due to the difficultly of decrypting SSL traffic, we were unable to identify the encrypted payloads being sent to certain websites. Based on this shortcoming, we used our own website to get samples of legitimate and cracking packets, which we believe is representative of the packets that would be observed at encrypted websites, although we cannot know with absolutely certainty that this is the case.

6.4 Ethical Issues

In order to gain access to configuration file subforums, we had to post several messages from our underground forum accounts. In addition, for each downloaded configuration file, we were required to post at least one message and/or click on the *thank you* button. We strongly believe that none of these actions had a measurable effect on the underground forum economy.

On the other hand, paying $9.95 for one month worth of VIP access certainly did affect the underground forum economy – it made the cyber criminal(s) running the webcracking.com underground forum $9.95 richer. Furthermore, we violated the terms of use of several legitimate websites by creating fake accounts and carrying out credential stuffing attacks against them. Although these actions might be viewed as unethical, they were paramount to this study. Our actions could be compared to doctors and scientists running experiments on animals – although the lab animals suffer and often die painful deaths, the results of such experiments are used to save and improve human lives, which most consider a fair trade-off. Similarly, although it is unfortunate that we violated the terms of use of several websites and made the cyber criminals $9.95 richer, we feel that the benefits of our work far outweigh any moral or ethical concerns raised by it.

6.5 Future Work

Due to the difficulty and risks of collecting a large sample of cracking tools' packets, we were not able to test our classifiers on the real-world data. To rectify this, in the future we contemplate purchasing a dozen more cracking tools as well as downloading older versions of Sentry MBA, Account Hitman, and Vertex. For legitimate packets, we are considering including mobile browsers' packets as well as adding more flavors of GNU/Linux operating systems to our tests. Finally, we are planning on contacting Twitter, Instagram, and Facebook and asking for access to their decrypted traffic. This should give us a much larger sample of both cracking and legitimate packets, and allow us to test the performance of our machine learning algorithms in the wild, which appear to be very promising in preventing cracking tool based threats.

References

1. Sentry MBA (2016). https://sentry.mba/tool?id=1. Accessed 28 May 2017

2. Abreu, L.P.B.: Morphing Web Pages to Preclude Web Page Tampering Threats (2016)
3. Afroz, S., Garg, V., McCoy, D., Greenstadt, R.: Honor among thieves: a common's analysis of cybercrime economies. In: Proceedings of the eCrime Researchers Summit (eCRS). IEEE (2013)
4. Agarwal, S.: The Half-Day Attack: From Compromise to Cash with Sentry MBA (2016). https://goo.gl/Yb08S9. Accessed 01 June 2017
5. Allodi, L., Corradin, M., Massacci, F.: Then and now: on the maturity of the cybercrime markets (the lesson that black-hat marketeers learned). IEEE Trans. Emerg. Top. Comput. 1, 1 (2015)
6. Allodi, L., Shim, W., Massacci, F.: Quantitative assessment of risk reduction with cybercrime black market monitoring. In: Proceedings of the Security and Privacy Workshops (SPW). IEEE (2013)
7. Anderson, R., et al.: Measuring the cost of cybercrime. In: Böhme, R. (ed.) The Economics of Information Security and Privacy, pp. 265–300. Springer, Heidelberg (2013). https://doi.org/10.1007/978-3-642-39498-0_12
8. Ben-Meir, E.: Sentry MBA: A Tale of the Most Popular Credential Stuffing Attack Tool (2017). https://goo.gl/bFDn1b. Accessed 01 June 2017
9. Bhuyan, M.H., Kashyap, H.J., Bhattacharyya, D.K., Kalita, J.K.: Detecting distributed denial of service attacks: methods, tools and future directions. Comput. J. 57(4), 537–556 (2014)
10. Bleau, H.: Credential Checking Services Soar in Popularity on Dark Web (2016). https://goo.gl/yq3Vxf. Accessed 01 June 2017
11. Buddah: Vertex 1.0.4 (2016). https://goo.gl/yORQUV. Accessed 28 May 2017
12. Burgess, M., Temperton, J.: The security flaws at the heart of the Panama Papers (2016). https://goo.gl/b49RaQ. Accessed 28 Oct 2016
13. Christin, N.: Traveling the Silk Road: a measurement analysis of a large anonymous online marketplace. In: Proceedings of the International Conference on World Wide Web (WWW). ACM (2013)
14. ConfigMasta: AIOHNB tool v 2.7.8 [Full version] (2016). https://goo.gl/PjYLl2. Accessed 28 May 2017
15. Cymru, T.: The underground economy: priceless. Technical report, Login: 31(6) (2006)
16. DavePS: voidproducts (2016). https://goo.gl/GaIKik. Accessed 28 May 2017
17. Davey, M.: Red Cross Blood Service data breach: personal details of 550,000 blood donors leaked (2016). https://goo.gl/ls3ZJM. Accessed 28 Oct 2016
18. Douligeris, C., Mitrokotsa, A.: DDoS attacks and defense mechanisms: classification and state-of-the-art. Comput, Netw. 44(5), 643–666 (2004)
19. Drašar, M.: Behavioral detection of distributed dictionary attacks. Ph.D. thesis, Masaryk University, Brno, Czech Republic (2015)
20. Fallmann, H., Wondracek, G., Platzer, C.: Covertly probing underground economy marketplaces. In: Kreibich, C., Jahnke, M. (eds.) DIMVA 2010. LNCS, vol. 6201, pp. 101–110. Springer, Heidelberg (2010). https://doi.org/10.1007/978-3-642-14215-4_6
21. Fiegerman, S.: Yahoo says 500 million accounts stolen (2016). https://goo.gl/EjJfTt. Accessed 28 Oct 2016
22. Foundation, W.: Wireshark - Go deep (2017). https://www.wireshark.org/. Accessed 20 May 2017
23. Franklin, J., Paxson, V., Perrig, A., Savage, S.: An inquiry into the nature and causes of the wealth of internet miscreants. In: Proceedings of the Conference on Computer and Communications Security (CCS). ACM (2007)

24. Garg, V., Afroz, S., Overdorf, R., Greenstadt, R.: Computer-supported cooperative crime. In: Böhme, R., Okamoto, T. (eds.) FC 2015. LNCS, vol. 8975, pp. 32–43. Springer, Heidelberg (2015). https://doi.org/10.1007/978-3-662-47854-7_3
25. H3God: >> MULTIHACKER << || HACK FB/IG/TWITTER/RED-DIT/SKYPE + MORE ACCOUNTS - 8 HACKERS IN 1 (2016). https://goo.gl/WvRu1Z. Accessed 28 May 2017
26. Herley, C., Florêncio, D.: Nobody sells gold for the price of silver: dishonesty, uncertainty and the underground economy. In: Moore, T., Pym, D., Ioannidis, C. (eds.) Economics of Information Security and Privacy, pp. 33–53. Springer, Boston (2010). https://doi.org/10.1007/978-1-4419-6967-5_3
27. Holt, T.J.: Examining the forces shaping cybercrime markets online. Soc. Sci. Comput. Rev. **31**(2), 165–177 (2013)
28. Holt, T.J.: Exploring the social organisation and structure of stolen data markets. Global Crime **14**(2–3), 155–174 (2013)
29. Holt, T.J., Lampke, E.: Exploring stolen data markets online: products and market forces. Crim. Justice Stud. **23**(1), 33–50 (2010)
30. ImadTheMAD: Introduction: What is Account Hitman? (2011). https://goo.gl/i1dZhj. Accessed 28 May 2017
31. Kumar, P.A.R., Selvakumar, S.: Distributed denial of service attack detection using an ensemble of neural classifier. Comput. Commun. **34**(11), 1328–1341 (2011)
32. Lee, W., Stolfo, S.J.: Data mining approaches for intrusion detection. In: Proceedings of the USENIX Security Symposium (1998)
33. Leontiadis, N.: Structuring disincentives for online criminals. Ph.D. thesis, Carnegie Mellon University Pittsburgh, PA (2014)
34. Li, W., Chen, H.: Identifying top sellers in underground economy using deep learning-based sentiment analysis. In: Proceedings of the Intelligence and Security Informatics Conference (JISIC), pp. 64–67. IEEE (2014)
35. Mann, D., Sutton, M.: NETCRIME more change in the organization of thieving. Br. J. Criminol. **38**(2), 201–229 (1998)
36. McCoy, D., Pitsillidis, A., Jordan, G., Weaver, N., Kreibich, C., Krebs, B., Voelker, G.M., Savage, S., Levchenko, K.: PharmaLeaks: understanding the business of online pharmaceutical affiliate programs. In: Proceedings of the USENIX Security Symposium (2012)
37. Motoyama, M., McCoy, D., Levchenko, K., Savage, S., Voelker, G.M.: An analysis of underground forums. In: Proceedings of the SIGCOMM Internet Measurement Conference (IMC). ACM (2011)
38. Nadji, Y., Antonakakis, M., Perdisci, R., Lee, W.: Connected colors: unveiling the structure of criminal networks. In: Stolfo, S.J., Stavrou, A., Wright, C.V. (eds.) RAID 2013. LNCS, vol. 8145, pp. 390–410. Springer, Heidelberg (2013). https://doi.org/10.1007/978-3-642-41284-4_20
39. Nakashima, E.: Russian government hackers penetrated DNC, stole opposition research on Trump (2016). https://goo.gl/IKkgjt. Accessed 28 Oct 2016
40. Ollmann, G.: Stopping automated attack tools. Whitepaper-NGS software insight security research (2005)
41. Pleasant, R.: Ubuntu Forums data breach exposes 2 million users (2016). https://goo.gl/IZJc0b. Accessed 28 Oct 2016
42. Radianti, J.: A study of a social behavior inside the online black markets. In: Proceedings of the International Conference on Emerging Security Information Systems and Technologies (SECURWARE). IEEE (2010)

43. Ritthoff, O., Klinkenberg, R., Fischer, S., Mierswa, I., Felske, S.: Yale: yet another learning environment. In: Proceedings of the Tagungsband der GI-Workshop-Woche Lernen - Lehren - Wissen - Adaptivitat (LLWA) (2001)
44. Sang-Hun, C.: North Korea Stole Data of Millions of Online Consumers, South Says (2016). https://goo.gl/Ul7dmo. Accessed 28 Oct 2016
45. sentinel.deny.de: Sentry Readme (2003). http://sentinel.deny.de/ReadmeSentry.txt, https://goo.gl/eiTdBL. Accessed 01 June 2017
46. sentinel.deny.de: Sentry (2016). http://sentinel.deny.de/sentry.php, https://goo.gl/Dw2l3k. Accessed 01 June 2017
47. Shadows, D.: Protect Your Customer and Employee Accounts: 7 Ways To Mitigate the Growing Risks of Account Takeovers (2017). https://goo.gl/xrfhaO. Accessed 01 June 2017
48. Shin, Y., Gupta, M., Myers, S.: The nuts and bolts of a forum spam automator. In: Proceedings of the Conference on Large-scale Exploits and Emergent Threats (LEET). USENIX Association (2011)
49. Shulman, A.: The underground credentials market. Comput. Fraud Secur. **2010**(3), 5–8 (2010)
50. Sommer, R., Paxson, V.: Outside the closed world: on using machine learning for network intrusion detection. In: Proceedings of the Symposium on Security and Privacy (SP). IEEE (2010)
51. Sood, A.K., Enbody, R.J.: Crimeware-as-a-service a survey of commoditized crimeware in the underground market. Int. J. Crit. Infrastruct. Prot. **6**(1), 28–38 (2013)
52. Stone-Gross, B., Abman, R., Kemmerer, R.A., Kruegel, C., Steigerwald, D.G., Vigna, G.: The underground economy of fake antivirus software. In: Schneier, B. (ed.) Economics of Information Security and Privacy III, pp. 55–78. Springer, New York (2013). https://doi.org/10.1007/978-1-4614-1981-5_4
53. Stringhini, G., Wang, G., Egele, M., Kruegel, C., Vigna, G., Zheng, H., Zhao, B.Y.: Follow the green: growth and dynamics in twitter follower markets. In: Proceedings of the Internet Measurement Conference (IMC). ACM (2013)
54. Thee, D.: Sentry MBA: A Tale of the Most Widely Used Credential Stuffing Attack Tool (2017). https://goo.gl/n8XY1U. Accessed 01 June 2017
55. Thomas, K., McCoy, D., Grier, C., Kolcz, A., Paxson, V.: Trafficking fraudulent accounts: the role of the underground market in Twitter spam and abuse. In: Proceedings of the Conference on Security (SEC). USENIX Association (2013)
56. Wagner, J.: Reset Those Passwords - Again: Over 6 Million ClixSense Users Compromised by Data Breach (2016). https://goo.gl/YBnkOL. Accessed 28 Oct 2016
57. Wang, X., Kohno, T., Blakley, B.: Polymorphism as a defense for automated attack of websites. In: Boureanu, I., Owesarski, P., Vaudenay, S. (eds.) ACNS 2014. LNCS, vol. 8479, pp. 513–530. Springer, Cham (2014). https://doi.org/10.1007/978-3-319-07536-5_30
58. Williamson, W.: What Happens to Stolen Data After a Breach? (2014). https://goo.gl/0ByDhi. Accessed 30 May 2017
59. Yip, M., Shadbolt, N., Tiropanis, T., Webber, C.: The digital underground economy: a social network approach to understanding cybercrime. In: Digital Futures 2012: The Third Annual Digital Economy All Hands Conference (2012)
60. Yip, M., Shadbolt, N., Webber, C.: Structural analysis of online criminal social networks. In: 2012 IEEE International Conference on Intelligence and Security Informatics (ISI), pp. 60–65. IEEE (2012)
61. Yip, M., Shadbolt, N., Webber, C.: Why forums?: an empirical analysis into the facilitating factors of carding forums. In: Proceedings of the Annual Web Science Conference (WebSci). ACM (2013)

62. Yip, M., Webber, C., Shadbolt, N.: Trust among cybercriminals? Carding forums, uncertainty and implications for policing. J. Polic. Soc. **23**(4), 516–539 (2013)
63. Zaidi, N.A., Cerquides, J., Carman, M.J., Webb, G.I.: Alleviating naive Bayes attribute independence assumption by attribute weighting. J. Mach. Learn. Res. **14**(1), 1947–1988 (2013)
64. Zavodchik, M.: Mitigating "Sentry MBA" - Credentials Stuffing Threat (2017). https://goo.gl/1JT0dQ. Accessed 01 June 2017
65. Zhuge, J., Holz, T., Song, C., Guo, J., Han, X., Zou, W.: Studying malicious websites and the underground economy on the chinese web. In: Johnson, M.E. (ed.) Managing Information Risk and the Economics of Security, pp. 225–244. Springer, Boston (2009). https://doi.org/10.1007/978-0-387-09762-6_11

SDN-Based Kernel Modular
Countermeasure for Intrusion Detection

Tommy Chin[1], Kaiqi Xiong[2($\boxtimes$)], and Mohamed Rahouti[2]

[1] Rochester Institute of Technology, Rochester, USA
tommy.chin@ieee.org
[2] University of South Florida, Tampa, USA
xiongk@usf.edu, mrahouti@mail.usf.edu

Abstract. Software-Defined Networking (SDN) is a core technology. However, Denial of Service (DoS) has been proved a serious attack in SDN environments. A variety of Intrusion Detection and Prevention Systems (IDPS) have been proposed for the detection and mitigation of DoS threats, but they often present significant performance overhead and long mitigation time so as to be impractical. To address these issues, we propose KernelDetect, a lightweight kernel-level intrusion detection and prevention framework. KernelDetect leverages modular string searching and filtering mechanisms with SDN techniques. By considering that the Aho-Corasick and Bloom filter are exact string matching and partial matching techniques respectively, we design KernelDetect to leverage the strengths of both algorithms with SDN. Moreover, we compare KernelDetect with traditional IDPS: SNORT and BRO, using a real-world testbed. Comprehensive experimental studies demonstrate that KernelDetect is an efficient mechanism and performs better than SNORT and BRO in threat detection and mitigation.

Keywords: Aho-Corasick · Bloom filters
Intrusion detection system · Security
Software Defined Networking (SDN)

1 Introduction

Software-Defined Networking (SDN) has played a key role in Science DMZ (demilitarized zone). SDN grants an open-source asset and a great tool for developers and researchers to design and discover new solutions to networking challenges such as end-to-end delay minimization, traffic management, and network attack detection. However, SDN itself is vulnerable to various adverse attacks. Hong et al. [34] identified threats including Denial of Service (DoS) in SDN and examined DoS attacks under the environment of eight different SDN controllers, but there remain grand challenges to detect and mitigate them.

This research considers an environment like Science DMZ where there is a need to high-speed network access to computation and storage for science research. As mentioned before, Hong et al. [34] have presented DoS threats and

© ICST Institute for Computer Sciences, Social Informatics and Telecommunications Engineering 2018
X. Lin et al. (Eds.): SecureComm 2017, LNICST 238, pp. 270–290, 2018.
https://doi.org/10.1007/978-3-319-78813-5_14

proved that the exploitations are serious attacks in an SDN environment. Traditional network approaches to detect and mitigate DoS threats is through the use of Intrusion Detection Systems (IDS) and Intrusion Prevention Systems (IPS), but they present serious concerns including system performance [19], network communication constraints [28], and detection validity [32]. Additionally, IDS detection methods present a critical flaw to identify new or unknown network attacks due to limiting threat signatures and comparison approaches. Recent studies have suggested a variety of threat mitigation and detection solutions including FloodGuard [19], SPHINX [28], and an entropy-based solution [32], but none of them, to the best of our knowledge, has studied a modular kernel-level IDPS approach within SDN environments.

In this paper, we propose KernelDetect, a lightweight modular-based filtering approach inspired by Amann and Sommer [21] and Mekky et al. [18], to detect and mitigate threats within an SDN environment. Specifically, KernelDetect is an independent application-plane network Test Access Point (TAP) approach using Switch Port Analyzer (SPAN) interfaces [20] on SDN switching devices. Moreover, by using a modular approach as a key component, KernelDetect can interchange the technique for string matching in addition to updating its signatures while providing threat mitigation capabilities within a kernel space. As we know, IDS signature methods are to compare a list of given strings or a set of rules with incoming network traffic signatures. In this paper, the proposed KernelDetect provides the ability to dynamically update the rule set in SDN environments in which we can optimize traffic inspection when detecting network threats.

To examine KernelDetect, we utilize Global Environment for Network Innovations (GENI) [27] to conduct our real-world experimental evaluation. Additionally, we comparatively examine KernelDetect to the popular IDS solutions: SNORT [29] and BRO [39] where KernelDetect leverages the Aho-Corasick [26] algorithm and Bloom filter [11] with SDN. To provide hybrid network communications, we utilize D-ITG [33] and iPerf [14] as traffic generation software for normal user data in the SDN experiments. To mix normal user traffic with malicious ones, we implement DoS attacks [32] in our threat detection and mitigation experiments. We further implement KernelDetect in an environment driven by Floodlight [3] using Representational State Transfer (REST) Application Program Interface (API) as our method of communication for KernelDetect to mitigate adverse threats and attacks.

KernelDetect resides on each switching device within an SDN environment and offers management controls using REST API calls. Such controls provide the ability to apply Access Control List (ACL) rules to SDN switches from a controller to mitigate an adverse threat. To be concise, KernelDetect listens to traffic on respective switching devices, and if a threat is detected, then mitigation occurs by informing the controller of the actions needed to thwart the attack. We further comparatively examine KernelDetect over traditional IDPS technologies –SNORT and BRO for the detection and mitigation of DoS attacks in a real-world testbed environment where we test various numbers of packets ranging from 100K to 500K and examine SYN flooding attack with different packet sizes and sampling times. In our extensive experiments, we measure the average load of system resources, inspection time, mitigation time, true positive, false positive, and false negative.

To summarize, we make the following main contributions in this research:

- DoS has been identified as a serious attack in an SDN environment [34]. We present KernelDetect, a lightweight kernel-level IDPS approach to thwarting DoS threats with the ability to interchange string matching detection mechanisms between the Aho-Corasick algorithm [26] and the Bloom filter algorithm.
- Existing IDPS tools such as SNORT and BRO utilize a culmination of user and kernel space due to the necessary user interaction needed to configure both solutions. Contrary to existing conventional studies, KernelDetect is a pure kernel-space solution. Furthermore, the default installations of SNORT and BRO provide many detection rules for their respective systems. The more number of rules we use, the more performance overhead is added. KernelDetect has a much less overhead compared to SNORT and BRO.
- We leverage the common architecture of Science DMZ with SDN technologies to develop KernelDetect. Thus, KernelDetect applies to Science DMZ, and it can enhance data-driven research in academia and national laboratories, and other related applications in industry and government agencies.
- As SNORT [29] and BRO [39] are traditional IDS solutions, we experimentally evaluate KernelDetect against the two well-known kernel-space and user-space detection tools in a real-world testbed, whereas many existing studies are evaluated either through a simulator such as Mininet [4] or in a lab environment whose results are often away from realistic.

The rest of this paper is organized as follows. Section 2 provides the background and challenges of our research problem. Section 3 discusses related work. While Sect. 4 presents threat models and attack vectors, Sect. 5 outlines the architectural design of the proposed solution. In Sect. 6, we give the experimental setup of KernelDetect evaluation with results. Lastly, Sect. 7 concludes our study and gives future work.

2   Research Background and Problem

In this section, we provide a brief background of kernel-space detection techniques and outline our research challenges.

2.1   Kernel-Space Detection Background

Kernel-space detection is a vital catalyst for intrusion detection systems due to its fundamental view of high-performance computing and minimal overhead. The use of deploying such a space/region has limited visibility as a traditional IDS utilizes user and kernel-spaces [28]. Moreover, system applications and services utilize both the regions of computing, but only using one region for such processes is not a common approach. Within SDN, there are numerous IDS solutions, but many utilize a culmination of kernel and user spaces to identify their respective adverse threats. Moreover, SDN switching software such as Open vSwitch (OVS) attaches itself to both user and kernel-spaces and it requires packet data from raw sockets on their respective operating systems to carry appropriate network traffic to the SDN switching service. Using a kernel-space provides capabilities for high-performance and a low overhead but presents a concern due to the instability of a kernel panic, resulting in the following challenges.

2.2   Research Challenges and Assumption

Common approaches to detect and mitigate adverse threats is through the use of an IDPS. One major issue of such a technique is through user-space utilization. Moreover, numerous IDS solutions rely on user-space interfaces to allow administrators to manage and maintain the various services that are implemented to identify and thwart malicious attacks. (1) *Kernel Panic:* The first challenge through the use of a kernel space is when a system is panic. Commonly, when a kernel module or a kernel-space application generates an erroneous issue such as a programming bug or a buffer overflow, a panic occurs such that the operating system is no longer function to provide service to the end user. When such an event occurs, a sequence of recovery mechanisms is executed such as memory dumping and a total system restart. We identify this challenge as a significant area to address as KernelDetect resides purely on a kernel-space. We identify this challenge as a significant area to address as the operation of KernelDetect resides purely in kernel-space and that if KernelDetect malfunctions or generates a programmatic error, a kernel panic would occur. (2) *Root Access and System Vulnerability:* Using kernel-space detection requires a significant level of system access to identify such malicious traffic. This level of access is known as root-access and proposes a serious challenge if the IDPS solution [15] were to be compromised or exploited. Moreover, to both inspect traffic and determine adverse behaviors, elevated access is required on such service to gain a control of raw sockets on an operating system. Using traditional IDS solutions such as BRO and SNORT, service accounts are created to secure the system from exploitation through techniques such as chroot and jailing. These concerns present the second challenge.

For the first challenge, the IDPS solution [16] should be robust from techniques such as a buffer overflow, resilient to obfuscated attacks, and exploitation schemes [24]. Using the operating system's raw socket feature provides the ability to handle and evaluate the large quantity of network traffic in an efficient manner. During a scenario of a DoS [42], excessive packet drops would occur as the system would be unable to handle the quantity properly. Additionally, the overhead and congestion presented from a DoS would create a significant delay as the inspection system would place each packet into a queue for evaluation. Overtime, this queue would significantly increase and may present a concern for a buffer overflow if mishandled incorrectly. The simple solution to prevent an overflow would be to drop packets aggressively to prevent resource exhaustion on the inspection system. One concern for this procedure will be if the network traffic has a level of urgency or priority regarding guarantee delivery [5,10], but this situation would heavily depend on the configuration and design of a network. A more serious concern for the use of kernel space detection is the configuration that the application requires root-level privilege on the IDPS system and presents a concern if the system becomes compromised.

The second challenge of the proposed kernel-space IDPS solutions requires an elevated user or root-access to gain accessibility to a variety of raw socket communication to collect and inspect network traffic [35]. Although such access is necessary for inspection purposes, it raises a potential concern for an emerging threat vector. Moreover, a compromised switching device draws a significant concern as network visibility becomes large such that a threat actor gains a larger attack surface to identify potential targets. One approach to attaining such access is through a vulnerability in the inspection step of our IDPS solution such that a malicious payload may be misinterpreted [1].

In this research, we assume that the implementation of KernelDetect is bugs free on a secure kernel where OVS is also secure.

3   Related Work

A common technique to identify adverse behaviors within network traffic is through the use of string matching techniques. Such identification has been examined using approaches such as Bloom filters [11] and Aho-Corasick [26]. There have been numerous studies to comparatively identify each string matching approach [11,26] for performance evaluation, but these studies lack in the identification of kernel-space detection. Furthermore, there have numerous developments of IDS solutions [6–8,16,19,28,31,36] to deter malicious traffic, but they heavily rely on user-space detection. Examination of IDS solutions in kernel-space detection has been evaluated through research work [17,23] but their approaches do not address traffic dynamics.

In this research, we introduce SDN to address this concern. As SDN has been widely used to improve network management, performance, and usability, FloodGuard [19], SPHINX [28], and FortNOX [31] employed SDN for attack detection and mitigation. Scott-Hayward et al. [35] summarized recent studies on the vulnerabilities of existing approaches in an SDN environment. FortNOX [31] addressed an SDN tunneling attack and solved the rule conflicts of an SDN flow table. Furthermore, Mahout [13] introduced a solution to improve the prevention mechanism for flooding attacks in an OpenFlow environment. SPHINX [28] attempted to detect attacks that contravene learning-based flow graphs and modules by designing a network flow graphs-based prototype. RAID [21] also introduced a control prototype to monitor the network systems passively and to target operational exploitation in a large-scale environment, but the effectiveness of this prototype was assessed only through OpenFlow backed connecting to three hardware switches. Moreover, Wang et al. [32] considered DoS attacks and gave an entropy-based solution to check detection validity. FRESCO [37] suggested a framework to simplify the scheme for the composition of security applications.

TopoGuard [34] considered the security of SDN controllers where TopoGuard attempts to capture attack poison in an SDN environment (i.e. the holistic visibility of a network environment and topology) based on security omission's fixation. Rosemary [38] adopted a practical approach to addressing the issue of control layer resilience through an extension of a NOS design. While their efforts have primarily focused on protecting the data plane of SDN from malicious applications, our proposed solution will have the ability to dynamically update the rule set in SDN environments and optimize traffic inspection when detecting network threats.

Furthermore, existing studies often suggested to combat one type of threats using SDN techniques, e.g., Wang et al. [32]. SDNScanner [40] and AVANT-GUARD [36] introduced solutions to detect and mitigate saturation attacks (data-to-control plane saturation) by altering flow management at a switch level, but their approaches are limited to TCP saturation attacks. Furthermore, they exposed only those flows that complete a TCP handshake based on a SYN proxy implementation.

Moreover, VeriFlow [25] detached a holistic network environment into subclasses that have exactly similar forwarding behaviors exploiting a multidimensional prefix tree so that all forwarding policies and determined policies would be checked in live time whenever a network update occurs. NetPlumber [30] proposes a real-time policy verification tool based on Header Space Analysis (HSA). NICE [16] introduces an approach to detecting network software bugs in OpenFlow applications based on symbolic execution and model checking. While FAST [9] identifies areas in conducting a forensic study on switching devices.

To the best of our knowledge, KernelDetect gives the first kernel-level solution instead of traditional user-space IDPS ones. It is a lightweight kernel-level detection mechanism. Contrary to the existing conventional work, we investigate IDPS on a kernel space that overcomes the implementation difficulty of a kernel space (e.g., SoftFlow [12]). As Snort and Bro are popular tools in this area, we choose them in our comparison study.

Likewise, most existing evaluation techniques deploying SDN for detection and mitigation, for example, TopoGuard [34] prototype evaluation is based on Mininet [4] - a simulator whose results may be practically far from real-world scenarios. Instead, KernelDetect is evaluated on GENI, a real-world testbed.

4   Threat Models and Attack Vectors

This research examines adverse users within an SDN environment where a series of normal traffic will communicate with normal users (or called clients). While SDN is widely used in traffic management, a variety of serious attacks such as DoS [32], LDS [34], and MITM [34] have been found in SDN. That is, the threat model includes the methodologies of launching DoS attacks using research work [32,34]. Although KernelDetect can be used for the detection and mitigation of other emerging network threats, we specifically consider DoS as our attack vector for this paper. To be concise, we will periodically implement our methods of DoS attacks on GENI as described in Sect. 6. Although a threat actor can launch any methods of attacks in a series or simultaneously, we will examine the effects of each threat *individually* for the performance evaluations and detection validity of KernelDetect. Trust needs to be identified in our SDN topology where we outline a variety of weaknesses in our infrastructural design to establish threat detection. To clarify, we assume that all SDN controllers and switching devices are safe from a threat actor, but leave end devices vulnerable to attacks. Mitigation is a critical factor to thwart an attack, and to prevent false positive events carefully; whitelisting will be required.

Whitelisting is a common approach to safeguarding mitigation faults such as disabling the WAN interface at an edge router and a network link to a known trusted computing device. In our threat detection approach, we do not implement any whitelisting for end devices attached to SDN switches as all users can be adverse at some point of time. Moreover, using KernelDetect, we implement detection on each suitable switching device for inspection purposes that will be further described in our experimental evaluation. Inter-switch links, commonly identified as a shared network link between two switching devices, contain a variety of network traffic intent from malicious to a normal user. Moreover, if these links were to be disabled through mitigation techniques, network operations would potentially fail. We inter-switch links to prevent mitigation faults from occurring. Although safeguarding inter-switch links provides reassurance from mitigation faults, a compromised end device has a greater potential to establish a significant threat to an SDN environment.

Lastly, we treat KernelDetect trustworthy even though adverse users can potentially obfuscate, exploit or overfill buffers specific to IDS solutions in addition to our string matching methods, Bloom filter, and the Aho-Corasick algorithm. We will identify an attack method in our experimental evaluation of Sect. 6. Following our evaluation, we have also investigated an IDS solution for other threats. However, we only present our study for DoS in this paper due to the page limit.

5   Design of KernelDetect

This section presents the architectural design of KernelDetect with discussions. We further discuss a threat signature structure for our proposed detection solution.

5.1   KernelDetect Placement and Architecture

The placement of KernelDetect is critical to detection and mitigation timings of an emerging threat. Before we present the architectural design of KernelDetect,

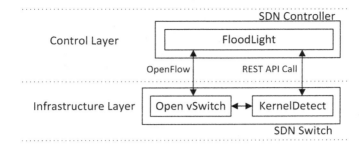

Fig. 1. The placement and functionality of KernelDetect for network traffic flow.

Fig. 1 shows the location and functionality of KernelDetect whose implementation is done in a configuration that operates in tandem with an SDN switching device.

Traffic duplication occurs within KernelDetect as both KernelDetect and OVS utilize raw socket communications in the back-end of the software system. The SDN Controller receives REST API calls from each switch when identifying a threat for mitigation. In this research, we use Floodlight as the controller software due to its REST API features. Figure 2 provides an architectural design of KernelDetect for both traffic inspection and signature matching with decision-making processes.

Let kds be a KernelDetect score, a an administrative-set incremental value for adverse traffic, b a decremental value for trustworthy traffic, and kdt a threshold value to determine whether such traffic should be placed in an inspection through either the Aho-Corasick algorithm or Bloom filter, called *Aho-Corasick inspection* or *Bloom filter inspection*, respectively. M simply denotes the matching scheme for KernelDetect.

When traffic enters an interface on a respective switch, the value is temporarily stored, and the information is forwarded to OVS and KernelDetect for their appropriate purposes of forwarding and inspecting traffic, respectively. During the initial state of KernelDetect, that is, when the service begins, an administrative configuration is examined to verify if a secure mode is enabled. We define the secure mode as a parameter such that if the placement of the switching device is in a critical data region, KernelDetect will enforce a detailed inspection using Aho-Corasick. If the placement does not have severe inspection approaches, then KernelDetect may use Bloom filter for detection. During the inspection process, we identify and examine to see whether the traffic has malicious intent through signature matching. If the intent is considered trustworthy, then we simply forward the traffic and decrease kds by a value of b, and add a when the intent is not trustworthy. Using a threshold condition of comparing kds to kdt, we examine whether future traffic should remain in Aho-Corasick or Bloom filter inspection. If the traffic has a malicious intent, we simply drop the packet from the raw socket and inform the SDN controller using REST API calls to block the adverse threat.

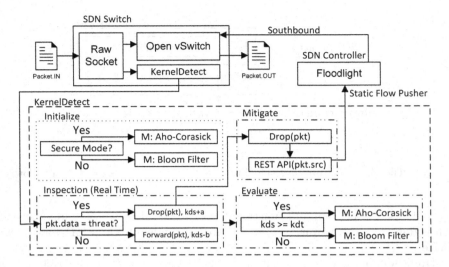

Fig. 2. The architectural design of KernelDetect consisting of four states: "Initialize," the beginning state of the SDN switch operations, "Inspection," a real-time inspection of traffic obtained from the raw socket of the operating system, "Mitigation," a critical step to thwart an attack and to prevent false positive events carefully, and "Evaluation," the examination of incoming traffic through 'Aho-Corasick' or 'Bloom filter' with a global view of the network.

5.2 Threat Signature Structure

Identifying adverse network traffic could be challenging as it depends on IDS signatures and threat identification markings. Particularly, two common approaches are considered to identify traffic threat through string-based matching, and traffic over time where an observation of a pattern of network packets occurs in a given period. As mentioned before, although KernelDetect applies to various attacks, this paper focuses on a DoS attack vector due to the page limit.

DoS: The identification of a DoS attack can be a challenge in an at-scale network. There are multiple methods to create a DoS attack from TCP SYN-flooding to other detailed approaches such as OSI Layer 7-based flooding. Like [32], we can identify a traffic pattern over an interval of time to determine if there is a DoS attack. That is, if the quantity of traffic exceeds a given threshold, KernelDetect considers that a DoS attack occurs, and it raises an alert. This threshold is a fixed value among all the approaches studied in our experiments later. The correlation with signature matching relates towards the frequency of alerts that is, KernelDetect raises an alert when a match occurs. The observation of a threat can originate from one or multiple sources where the attacker may spoof the source address of the DoS. Based on this given knowledge, KernelDetect accounts for such threats.

Signature-based matching may not be the appropriate tool to detect DoS attacks where the adversary can often insert arbitrary data into a packet payload.

This approach renders signature-based detection ineffective. In some cases, DoS attacks may not have any form of data for its payload, such as a low-profile TCP SYN flood attack. However, KernelDetect, considers matching the header information of a network packet rather than its packet payload, which increases the performance of threat detection. Below is the algorithm for KernelDetect where TH and THP are threshold values for time and packet intervals, respectively.

```
P = PACKET_IN
while P do
  TS = TIMESTAMP
  if P.TYPE == ICMP then
    Q{P.SRC_ADDR}++
    if P.SRC_ADDR NOT IN S then
      S{P.SRC_ADDR} = TS
    else
      if TS - S{P.SRC_ADDR} > TH then
        if Q{P.SRC_ADDR} > THP then
          REST API Call to SDN Controller
        else
          S{P.SRC_ADDR} = TS
        end if
      end if
    end if
  end if
end while
```

6 Experimental Evaluation

We have carried out the comprehensive evaluation of KernelDetect by choosing different experimental parameters such as the varying number of packets and threshold time. This section summarizes the evaluation of KernelDetect and presents a part of experimental results. For this purpose, we start with the topology design of our experiments using GENI.

6.1 Experimental Topology Design

To measure the effectiveness of KernelDetect, we utilize GENI [27] for experimental evaluation. GENI is a real-world heterogeneous virtual testbed with networking capabilities including SDN. To evaluate KernelDetect, we construct a topology with the following three constraints: (1) An adverse user attached to a single network link identifying major areas of mitigation. (2) A shared network link used by both a normal user and an attacker. (3) An edge network link that carries both normal and attack traffic. This edge link has limited SDN controller management. Figure 3 gives a visual view of the experimental topology that considers the previous research challenges where the locations of adverse users are

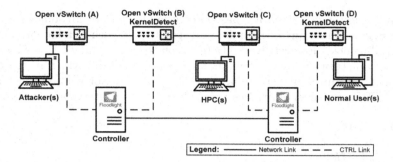

Fig. 3. GENI experimental topology for evaluation where KernelDetect is only implemented in switches B and D as depicted in the diagram. Moreover, CTRL links are the communication medium between each SDN switch and their respective controller. Lastly, our experimental evaluation interchanges KernelDetect-enabled switches with SNORT and BRO for our comprehensive study.

explicitly labeled. For presentation purpose in this paper, we give a relatively simple topology for our evaluation as shown in Fig. 3. However, KernelDetect is applicable to any complex network topology.

Although client nodes may have the potential to be compromised, we do not evaluate this scenario as we do not utilize any white listing techniques to safeguard end-devices from our mitigation approach. Specifically, normal users could have the potential to be prone to mitigation techniques depending on IDS signatures and rule sets.

6.2   Detection Rules in BRO and SNORT

For a detection system to identify adverse traffic, rules are necessary for network traffic evaluation. The following demonstrates the rule to identify a DoS attack for SNORT where an alert is raised once 70 packets are sent within a 10 second interval that is TCP-SYN flagged.

```
alert tcp any any -> $HOME_NET 80(flags:S;
msg:"Possible TCP DoS is Detected !!";
flow: stateless; detection_filter: track by_dist, count 70,
seconds 10; sid 10001;rev:1;)
```

6.3   Traffic Generation Techniques

To mix normal traffic into the grand scheme of our experiments, we utilize iPerf [14]. Although we cannot fully emulate a normal user, we believe that iPerf should provide a fundamental approach to measuring our solution. The main reason for such an approach is that iPerf provides the ability to saturate a network link in addition to real-time network throughput analysis. To be concise, we configure iPerf with the default parameters for operational use.

6.4 Experimental Results

In the evaluation of KernelDetect, we study its inspection time, mitigation time, detection accuracy, and system resource consumption comparatively compared to SNORT and BRO.

Inspection Time. Packet inspection time is critical to the mitigation of threat actors and adverse network traffic. Specifically, as packets arrive at an IDS, the information is placed in a buffer and waits for inspection. This waiting time increases the time needed to mitigate the adverse threat if the packet has malicious intent. To measure such inspection time, we established a near-equal configuration for each IDS solution with the quantities of threat signatures in each respective database for measurement purposes. We establish this approach to examining the effectiveness of each solution to have near mirror-like configurations and to examine the performance of each IDS solution closely.

To measure inspection time, we establish communication between two devices using hping3 where we transmit low packet size with the large quantity of traffic at one nanosecond interval of time, achieving a link saturation. We evaluate three threshold values of 5, 10, and 15 s for detection. In this evaluation, we run all the experiments 10 times and then averge their results. Figure 4 shows the average inspection time for 10-second thresholds. Our experimental results demonstrate that KernelDetect has an overall lowest average inspection time compared to SNORT and BRO.

Table 1. A comparison of the average inspection time in seconds among KernelDetect, SNORT and BRO under various traffic loads of 100K, 200K, and 500K SYN flagged packets using detection thresholds of 5, 10, and 15 s.

Traffic load (K)		100	200	500
Threshold (Sec.)	IDS			
5	KernelDetect	0.0048	0.0047	0.0109
	SNORT	0.0033	0.0186	0.0319
	BRO	2.1264	1.5187	2.3996
10	KernelDetect	0.0106	0.0111	0.0112
	SNORT	0.0128	02686	0.0643
	BRO	2.2656	1.1270	4.3337
15	KernelDetect	0.0067	0.0070	0.0069
	SNORT	0.0067	0.0243	0.0172
	BRO	1.9113	1.3433	2.5786

Table 1 demonstrates that KernelDetect has lower inspection time average comparatively to BRO and SNORT while Table 2 describes a 95% confidence interval statistic. In Table 2, we only compare KernelDetect with SNORT because BRO has much higher inspection time than KernelDetect and SNORT

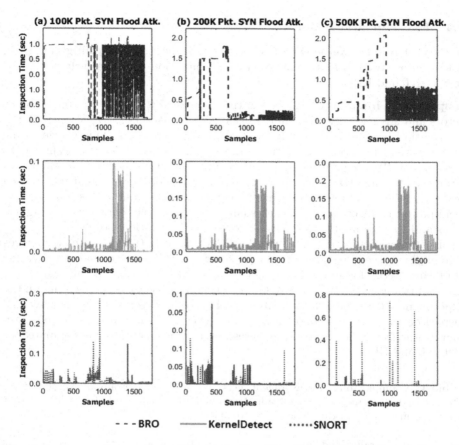

Fig. 4. A comparative analysis of the inspection time for each IDS under 100K, 200K and 500K SYN flagged packet DoS attack using a 10 s threshold signature.

as shown in Table 1 so that it would not be helpful even if we included a 95% confidence interval statistic for BRO in the table. Furthermore, although Ker-nelDetect has some confidence interval overlap with SNORT, it is demonstrated in Table 2 that KernelDetect is still a clear winner in comparison to SNORT under various traffic loads with different signature threshold values regarding inspection time.

Mitigation Time: Mitigation time is the time between an alert raised and the threat stopped. It is key to ensuring the safety and well-being of a network at scale. Although each IDS solution presents its unique attributes to detect an adverse threat, we measure the effectiveness of KernelDetect by studying threat mitigation. To measure the mitigation time, we examine the time between the initiation of each network attack and compared it to the time needed to rectify the threat as expressed in Fig. 5, represented in Table 3 as an average, and described using a 95% confidence interval in Table 4. Table 3 depicts that

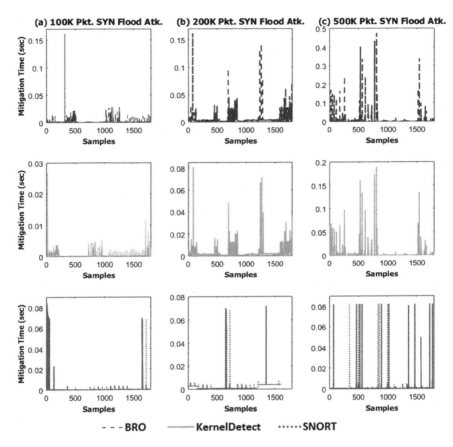

Fig. 5. Threat mitigation time for each IDS under 100K, 200K and 500K SYN flagged packet DoS attack using a 10 s threshold.

Table 2. A 95% confidence interval statistic for inspection time (seconds) between KernelDetect and SNORT where L and U represent their lower and upper bound, respectively.

Traffic load (K)		100			200			500		
Threshold (Sec.)	IDS	Stdev	L	U	Stdev	L	U	Stdev	L	U
5	KernelDetect	0.0142	0.0024	0.0031	0.0025	0.0037	0.0056	0.2009	0.0066	0.0150
	SNORT	0.0229	0.0027	0.0039	0.0624	0.0162	0.0211	0.3644	0.0170	0.0470
10	KernelDetect	0.1711	0.0038	0.0174	0.0183	0.0103	0.0119	0.0186	0.0104	0.0120
	SNORT	0.2309	0.0082	0.0173	0.2217	0.2549	0.2824	0.2566	0.0592	0.0690
15	KernelDetect	0.0522	0.0037	0.0068	0.0602	0.0051	0.0088	0.0654	0.0055	0.0080
	SNORT	0.0558	0.0050	0.0083	0.0984	0.0195	0.0253	0.1205	0.0137	0.0210

Table 3. The average mitigation time in seconds for KernelDetect, SNORT and BRO under various traffic loads of 100K, 200K, and 500K SYN flagged packets using detection thresholds of 5, 10, and 15 s.

Traffic load (K)		100	200	500
Threshold (Sec.)	IDS			
5	KernelDetect	0.0036	0.0074	0.0123
	SNORT	0.0056	0.0012	0.0130
	BRO	0.0060	0.0100	0.0108
10	KernelDetect	0.0060	0.0054	0.0044
	SNORT	0.0055	0.0065	0.0078
	BRO	0.0074	0.0080	0.0118
15	KernelDetect	0.0042	0.0049	0.0086
	SNORT	0.0071	0.0101	0.0200
	BRO	0.0096	0.0635	0.1254

Table 4. A 95% confidence interval measurements for mitigation time (seconds) between KernelDetect and SNORT where L and U represent their lower and upper bound, respectively.

Traffic load (K)		100			200			500		
Threshold (Sec.)	IDS	Stdev	L	U	Stdev	L	U	Stdev	L	U
5	KernelDetect	0.0141	0.0032	0.0040	0.0376	0.0063	0.0087	0.0966	0.0097	0.0149
	SNORT	0.0424	0.0044	0.0067	0.1137	0.0078	0.0167	0.0820	0.0094	0.0166
10	KernelDetect	0.0302	0.0051	0.0068	0.0355	0.0045	0.0063	0.0230	0.0038	0.0050
	SNORT	0.0542	0.0027	0.0037	0.0530	0.0026	0.0037	0.0190	0.0081	0.0093
15	KernelDetect	0.0267	0.0035	0.0060	0.0656	0.0030	0.0067	0.0629	0.0068	0.0104
	SNORT	0.0494	0.0058	0.0085	0.0921	0.0065	0.0137	0.0932	0.0096	0.0240

KernelDetect has a similar mitigation time as SNORT, it is superior to BRO and is still slightly better than SNORT on average. Furthermore, similar to Table 2, we do not include BRO in Table 4 for the same reason. As shown in Table 4, KernelDetect has better performance than SNORT when comparing their confidence intervals. Figure 5 depicts a series of DoS attacks executed in the SDN environment where each solution provided necessary alerting and mitigation procedures. The mitigation technique for each solution utilizes the same function such that when an alarm rose, the message presented will be used to block the respective address. Figure 6 provides the clarity of mitigation time using 10 s threshold, which demonstrates that KernelDetect is the best solution.

True Positive and False Positive. False positive and erroneous threat detection can lead to significant downfalls of network communication. Figure 7 presents the use of Receiver Operating Characteristic (ROC) curve techniques for KernelDetect SNORT and BRO. Notably, the curve demonstrates our detection matching sensitivity for our experimental evaluation where we identify the accuracy of each system. BRO demonstrated to have the poorest accuracy rate

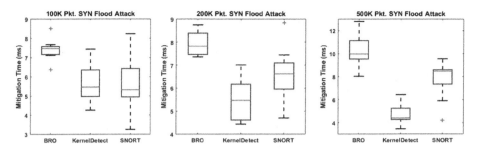

Fig. 6. Threat mitigation for each IDS under 100K, 200K, and 500K SYN flagged packet flood attack using 10 s threshold detection technique and represented as a box plot.

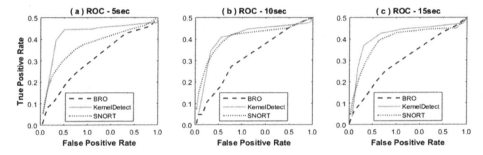

Fig. 7. ROC Curve for threat detection for each IDS under 100K Packets SYN flood attack using various thresholds of 5, 10 and 15 s for threat signatures of a DoS attack.

in comparison to KernelDetect and SNORT where KernelDetect presented the most accurate results based on the analysis of the experimental results.

System Resource Utilization. The performance of an IDS/IPS solution is critical to counter adverse network threats and specifically—threat actors. As traffic flows from one host to another, congestion and computational bottlenecks can occur within a network environment in addition to an IDS solution. Inspection and the level of detail in examining the content of the packet can produce resource strain on a computing device. Figure 8 provides the average system resource utilization for each IDS solution under a variety of network attacks for purposes of evaluating the performance constraint. Samples of system resource utilization are used to measure averaging CPU usage in a kernel space. As shown in experiments, BRO demonstrated a higher-level system resource utilization in comparison to KernelDetect and Snort. Although CPU utilization is critical to examine, memory resource consumption is vital in the operation of an SDN device.

Memory is a critical segment for resource examination as network packets traverse between two devices. The information is stored in a buffer, waiting for inspection and forwarding purposes. In Fig. 9, we express our findings for memory usage under a 100K SYN flagged packet attack.

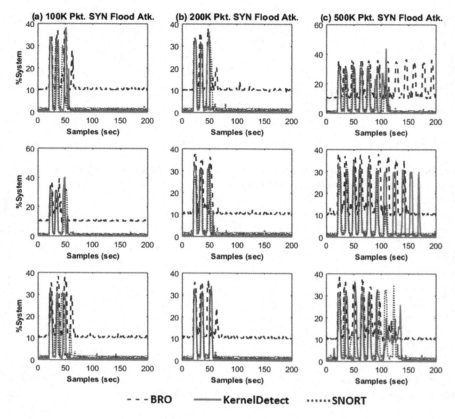

Fig. 8. System usage at 100K, 200K, and 500K packets (Pkt.) loads of SYN flood attack (Atk.)

Memory utilization increases during the events of a DoS attack where KernelDetect is more efficient than SNORT and BRO in the events of a post-DoS scenario. To be concise, once the DoS attack ends, both BRO and SNORT maintain constant memory resource utilization while KernelDetect's usage reduces to the lowest percentage rate.

Discussions. A kernel panic is one serious challenge in the use of kernel-space detection for a security apparatus such as KernelDetect. Moreover, if a kernel panic would occur to an SDN device, practical and operational usage would be lost. Additionally, the library functions that are implemented and imported into the design of KernelDetect may propose a vulnerability that could be haphazardous to the SDN environment. In the design of KernelDetect, this research treats all utilized libraries as trusted modules in the implementation such that the discovery of a serious vulnerability would be well-known and urgent for patching purposes. One configuration that may be sub-optimal for an SDN environment is to implement KernelDetect on an independent computing system

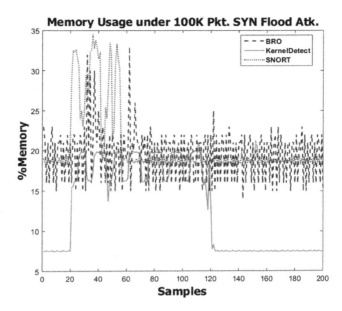

Fig. 9. Memory utilization for each IDS under the scenario of a single attack with 100K SYN flagged packets (Pkt.) using a 10 s threshold detection rate. Additionally, a full-link saturation is achieved during the attack in this evaluation.

that is attached to a port mirroring interface using a SPAN/TAP configuration such that if kernel panic would occur, SDN switching operations would continue to function. Lastly, KernelDetect utilizes raw socket information to read incoming packets. This read procedure could be insufficient for the switching operation such that OVS could process the raw socket information at a faster rate than KernelDetect. We experimented by creating a low packet size full link saturation scenario, but we were unable to emulate the concern. Our belief to such an event would potentially be plausible in a large network throughput interfaces such as 100Gbps. However, our evaluation was limited to only 1 Gbps speeds. Peformance modeling like [41] is helpful to such studies.

7 Conclusions and Future Work

In this paper, we have proposed KernelDetect, a modular countermeasure approach in an SDN environment. It is a new lightweight kernel-level intrusion detection and prevention approach where we have leveraged modular string searching and filtering mechanisms with SDN controller techniques. While KernelDetect is applicable to deal with a variety of adverse network threats, we have specifically explored the events of a DoS attack in an SDN environment.

To combat the above attack, we have considered the Aho-Corasick algorithm that is an exact string matching technique, and Bloom filter that is a partial matching algorithm. In KernelDetect, we have further dynamically leveraged the strengths of the Aho-Corasick algorithm and Bloom filter with SDN controllers. Moreover, we have conducted extensive experiments on GENI, a real-world testbed infrastructure where we have varied the number of network packets ranging from 100K to 500K and launched SYN flooding attacks with different packet sizes and sampling times. We have measured the average load of system resources, inspection time, mitigation time, true positive, false positive, and false negative among 10-run experiments. Section 6 has reported the partial results of our comprehensive experimental evaluation. Through a comparative analysis of KernelDetect with traditional IDS solutions of SNORT and BRO, we have demonstrated that KernelDetect is an effective and efficient solution to detect and mitigate adverse attacks.

We have utilized our inspection approach to detecting network threats within the data plane of an SDN environment. In our future work, we plan to identify the potential areas of threat detection in control plane communications. Moreover, we have stuided DoS attacks in an SDN environment. We plan to examine other adverse threats such as malware where a deep packet inspection is required, and therefore KernelDetect needs to be modified for addressing such threats.

Acknowledgments. We acknowledge National Science Foundation (NSF) to partially sponsor the work under grants #1633978, #1620871, #1620862, and #1636622, and BBN/GPO project #1936 through NSF/CNS grant. We also thank the Florida Center for Cybersecurity for a seed grant. The views and conclusions contained herein are those of the authors and should not be interpreted as necessarily representing the official policies, either expressed or implied of NSF.

References

1. Apache Spam Assassin Public Corpus. https://spamassassin.apache.org/publiccorpus/
2. DDoS attack 2007 dataset, CAIDA, UCSD. http://www.caida.org/data/passive/ddos-20070804dataset.xml
3. Floodlight controller. http://www.projectfloodlight.org/floodlight/
4. Mininet: an instant virtual network on your laptop (or other PC). http://mininet.org
5. Akella, A.V., Xiong, K.: Quality of service (QoS)-guaranteed network resource allocation via software defined networking (SDN). In: DASC 2014. IEEE (2014)
6. Chin, T., et al.: An SDN-supported collaborative approach for DDoS flooding detection and containment. In: MILCOM 2015. IEEE (2015)
7. Chin, T., et al.: Selective packet inspection to detect DoS flooding using software defined networking (SDN). In: ICDCSW 2015. IEEE (2015)
8. Chin, T., Xiong, K.: Dynamic generation containment systems (DGCS): a moving target defense approach. In: CPS Week EITEC 2016. IEEE (2016)
9. Chin, T., Xiong, K.: A forensic methodology for software-defined network switches. Advances in Digital Forensics XIII. IAICT, vol. 511, pp. 97–110. Springer, Cham (2017). https://doi.org/10.1007/978-3-319-67208-3_6
10. Chin, T., Xiong, K., Rahouti, M.: End-to-end delay minimization approaches using software-defined networking. In: RACS 2017. ACM (2017)

11. Dharmapurikar, S., Lockwood, J.W.: Fast and scalable pattern matching for network intrusion detection systems. JSAC **24**, 1781–1792 (2006)
12. Jackson, E.J., et al.: SoftFlow: a middlebox architecture for Open vSwitch. In: USENIX ATC (2016)
13. Curtis, A.R., et al.: Mahout: low-overhead datacenter traffic management using end-host-based elephant detection. In: INFOCOM (2011)
14. Tirumala, A., et al.: iPerf: the TCP/UDP bandwidth measurement tool (2005). http://dast.nlanr.net/Projects
15. Pfaff, B., et al.: The design and implementation of Open vSwitch. In: USENIX Symposium on NSDI (2015)
16. Chung, C.-J., et al.: NICE: network intrusion detection and counter-measure selection in virtual network systems. TDSC **10**, 198–211 (2013)
17. Vasiliadis, G., Antonatos, S., Polychronakis, M., Markatos, E.P., Ioannidis, S.: Gnort: high performance network intrusion detection using graphics processors. In: Lippmann, R., Kirda, E., Trachtenberg, A. (eds.) RAID 2008. LNCS, vol. 5230, pp. 116–134. Springer, Heidelberg (2008). https://doi.org/10.1007/978-3-540-87403-4_7
18. Mekky, H., et al.: Application-aware data plane processing in SDN. In: HotSDN (2014)
19. Wang, H., et al.: FloodGuard: a DoS attack prevention extension in software-defined networks. In: DSN (2015)
20. Ahrenholz, J., et al.: CORE: a real-time network emulator. In: MILCOM (2008)
21. Amann, J., Sommer, R.: Providing dynamic control to passive network security monitoring. In: Bos, H., Monrose, F., Blanc, G. (eds.) RAID 2015. LNCS, vol. 9404, pp. 133–152. Springer, Cham (2015). https://doi.org/10.1007/978-3-319-26362-5_7
22. Ballard, J.R., et al.: Extensible and scalable network monitoring using OpenSAFE. In: INM/WREN (2010)
23. Ko, C., et al.: Detecting and countering system intrusions using software wrappers. In: USENIX Security Symposium (2000)
24. Giotis, K., et al.: Combining OpenFlow and sFlow for an effective and scalable anomaly detection and mitigation mechanism on SDN environments. Comput. Netw. **62**, 122–136 (2014)
25. Khurshid, K., et al.: VeriFlow: verifying network-wide invariants in real time. In: NSDI (2013)
26. Alicherry, M., et al.: High speed pattern matching for network IDS/IPS. In: ICNP (2006)
27. Berman, M., et al.: GENI: a federated testbed for innovative network experiments. Comput. Netw. **61**, 5–23 (2014)
28. Dhawan, M., et al.: SPHINX: detecting security attacks in software-defined networks. In: NDSS (2015)
29. Roesch, M., et al.: SNORT-lightweight intrusion detection for networks. In: USENIX LISA (1999)
30. Kazemian, P., et al.: Real time network policy checking using header space analysis. In: NSDI (2013)
31. Porras, P., et al.: A security enforcement kernel for OpenFlow networks. In: HotSDN (2012)
32. Wang, R., et al.: An entropy-based distributed DDoS detection mechanism in software-defined networking. In: Trustcom/BigDataSE/ISPA (2015)
33. Avallone, S., et al.: D-ITG: distributed internet traffic generator. In: QEST (2004)
34. Hong, S., et al.: Poisoning network visibility in software-defined networks: new attacks and countermeasures. In: NDSS (2015)

35. Scott-Hayward, S., et al.: A survey of security in software defined networks. IEEE Commun. Surv. Tutor. **18**, 623–654 (2016)
36. Shin, S., et al.: AVANT-GUARD: scalable and vigilant switch flow management in software-defined networks. In: CCS (2013)
37. Shin, S., et al.: FRESCO: modular composable security services for software-defined networks. In: NDSS (2013)
38. Shin, S., et al.: Rosemary: a robust, secure, and high-performance network operating system. In CCS (2014)
39. Paxson, V.: BRO: a system for detecting network intruders in real-time. Computer Networks (1999)
40. Shin, S., Gu, G.: Attacking software-defined networks: a first feasibility study. In: HotSDN. ACM (2013)
41. Xiong, K.: Multiple priority customer service guarantees in cluster computing. In: IEEE IPDPS, pp. 1–12 (2009)
42. Xiong, K., Wang, R., Du, W., Ning, P.: Containing bogus packet insertion attacks for broadcast authentication in sensor networks. In: TOSN 2012 (2012)

LinkFlow: Efficient Large-Scale Inter-app Privacy Leakage Detection

Yi He[1], Qi Li[1(✉)], and Kun Sun[2]

[1] Department of Computer Science, Graduate School of Shenzhen,
Tsinghua University, Shenzhen, China
heyi14@mails.tsinghua.edu.cn, qi.li@sz.tsinghua.edu.cn
[2] Department of Information Sciences and Technology, George Mason University,
Fairfax, USA
ksun3@gmu.edu

Abstract. Android enables inter-app collaboration and function reusability by providing flexible Inter-Component Communication (ICC) across apps. Meanwhile, ICC introduces serious privacy leakage problems due to component hijacking, component injection, and application collusion attacks. Taint analysis technique has been adopted to successfully detect potential leakage between two mobile apps. However, it is still a challenge to efficiently perform large-scale leakage detection among a large set of apps, which may communicate through various ICC channels. In this paper, we develop a privacy leakage detection mechanism called LinkFlow to detect privacy leakage through ICC on a large set of apps. LinkFlow first leverages taint analysis technique to enumerate ICC links that may lead to privacy leakage in each individual app. Since most ICC links are normal, this step can dramatically reduce the number of risky ICC links for the next step analysis, where those ICC links are matched among leaky apps. We develop an algorithm to identify privacy leakage by analyzing ICC links and the associated permissions. We implement a LinkFlow prototype and evaluate its effectiveness with more than 4500 apps including 3014 benign apps from five apps marketplaces and 1500 malicious apps from two malware repositories. LinkFlow can successfully capture 6065 privacy leak paths among 530 apps. We also observe that more than 400 benign apps have vulnerabilities of privacy leakage in inter-app communications.

Keywords: Android · Privacy leakage · Large-scale detection

1 Introduction

As an open platform, Android allows users to install apps from the Google Play Store and third-party app marketplaces. Inter-Component Communication (ICC) mechanism enables communication between two components belonging to two different apps, and it allows developers to reuse another app's functionality without reinventing the wheel. However, the easy-to-use ICC can be

© ICST Institute for Computer Sciences, Social Informatics and Telecommunications Engineering 2018
X. Lin et al. (Eds.): SecureComm 2017, LNICST 238, pp. 291–311, 2018.
https://doi.org/10.1007/978-3-319-78813-5_15

misused in application collusion attacks [42] to bypass Android's permission-based security model, which only independently restricts individual apps from accessing sensitive resources. Therefore, malicious app developers may deliberately develop multiple apps that may collude via ICC to achieve permission escalation [19, 24, 27, 31].

Researchers have developed a number of effective mechanisms to detect ICC-based privacy leakage between two apps [20, 21, 23, 26, 29, 32, 34, 34, 38, 38, 41, 44, 46, 49, 50]. However, it is difficult to directly apply those approaches in a large scale detection, since it is very time-consuming to check each pair of apps among the huge number of apps in one app marketplace. For example, according to the existing studies [26, 29, 34, 38, 52], it takes at least 5 min for the-state-of-the-art mechanisms to detect privacy leakage between two apps. Thus, when detecting if there exists privacy leakage among 500 apps, it will take more than 10 thousand hours (about 400 days) to analyze each pair of the 500 apps. Such a long detection delay is not acceptable.

There are two main challenges to efficiently detect the inter-app privacy leakage vulnerabilities among a large set of apps. First, we should be able to precisely resolve ICC APIs in each app and then identify inter-apps data flows through those APIs. Currently *Intent* can use about 40 ICC APIs to exchange information [9]. Moreover, we need to harvest the ICC parameters from the app bytecode and track inter-app data flows by matching ICC channels among different apps. For simplicity, we call those ICC channels as *ICC links*. Second, since there will be a huge number of ICC links among a large set of apps, it is difficult to enumerate all possible ICC links among those apps. Therefore, we should be able to reduce the scale of ICC link analysis without introducing false negative detection results.

In this paper, we propose a large-scale privacy leakage detection mechanism called *LinkFlow* that can efficiently detect privacy leakage through ICC among a large set of apps. Our mechanism is based on one key observation that the most of ICC links among all apps in one app marketplace are benign links. Therefore, instead of detecting leakages in all ICC links, we focus on identifying the ICC links among the app components that may leak information, so we can dramatically reduce the scale of targeted ICC links and significantly decrease the detection delays.

LinkFlow uses static taint analysis to filter out the leaky components that may lead to privacy leakage for each individual app. Next, we propose an efficient ICC match algorithm to quickly mine out all the ICC links among those leaky components. We then separate the flows in the leaky components into two component sets, namely, *OutFlow set* and *InFlow set*, based on its leaky flow and use an ICC matching algorithm to find out ICC links between the two component sets. A privacy leakage vulnerability can be identified if an ICC link really delivers sensitive information. Our mechanism also supports incremental analysis when a new app is submitted to the app market. The analysis results generated by LinkFlow not only identify privacy leakage among the existing apps, but also provide guidelines for app developers to mitigate leakage during app development.

We implement a prototype of LinkFlow and evaluate it with 3014 real-world benign apps and 1500 malicious apps. It successfully identifies 6065 privacy leakage paths among 530 apps. It detects 4622 abnormal data flows among 87 apps, which introduce privacy leakages among their inter-apps data flows. LinkFlow only takes around 5 min to analyze one app against the remaining apps; most time is consumed by the taint analysis and the ICC extraction, which are one-time operations. It takes about 10 s to detect if there exists privacy leakage between an app and the rest 4513 apps, which is efficient in large scale detection.

In summary, this paper makes three folds of contributions.

- We propose a large scale app detection framework to efficiently detect vulnerable inter-app data flows that may lead to privacy leakages.
- We propose an ICC matching algorithm that searches the ICC links and identifies sensitive inter-app data flows in order to detect privacy leakage.
- We implement a LinkFlow prototype and use it to study the privacy leakage in real app stores. The experimental results show that it can finish the detection quickly and effectively identify the vulnerable ICC links among apps.

2 Background

Android apps usually consist of multiple reusable components that can communicate with each other either internally or externally via Inter-Component Communication (ICC) mechanisms. There are four types of components, namely, *Activities, Services, Content Providers,* and *Broadcast Receivers.*

Android provides flexible APIs for components to exchange data or share services through ICC. Components use *Intent* messages or *URI* to describe the corresponding components. *Intent* can be either explicit or implicit [7], where explicit *Intent* requires setting package names and component names of the recipient components in the *Intent* messages and implicit *Intent* needs to define its type by specifying the actions, the categories, and other flags. Using implicit *Intent*, one component that has registered *Intent Filters* to handle one Intent can receive and respond to the *Intent* message.

Android is a permission based operating system and restricts resource accesses by declaring different security level permissions. The protection levels can be one of four levels: *normal, dangerous, signature,* or *signatureOrSystem.* In particular, the later three levels are used to protect resources of apps. Apps declare their permissions in the *Manifest.xml* files with different protection levels, and these permissions are granted forever upon the apps' installation. The usage of ICC also introduces potential privacy leakages that can bypass the permission system [23,34,38,40,41]. For instance, if one component with the permissions to access sensitive data is exported and not protected by *signature* level permission, it may be misused by another component in a privilege escalation attack. Our work focuses on detecting potential ICC privacy leakages among a large number of apps.

3   Threat Model

The component reuse via ICC on Android poses serious security problems against the permission-based security model. Malicious apps may misuse the components in other benign apps to grasp the corresponding permissions, or they can collude to accumulate permissions that will not be granted to a single app.

Component Hijacking. When the exported components of benign apps can be leveraged by malicious apps, sensitive information may be leaked out from the benign apps. For instance, *GoMsg* is a popular app with over a million downloads for sending messages and making phone calls. Its message sending component is exported and can be used by any other apps without permission check. Therefore, malicious apps such as SmsZombie [11] can leverage GoMsg to send premium-SMS. Such component hijacking attacks have been identified in a number of built-in and third-party apps, including Activity Hijacking, Service Hijacking, and Broadcast Theft [23,41].

Component Injection. When benign apps send *Intent* to the corresponding components that have been replaced by components of malicious apps, ICC is manipulated by the malicious apps and ICC information will be leaked to malicious apps [39]. For instance, *One-Password* is a popular password store app, which uses Dropbox SDK to implement the OAuth login function. However, malicious apps can register the same Intent Filter as One-Password to intercept the OAuth access token [14] or return the fake token to One-Password to log in with the attacker's account.

Application Collusion. Since permission model focuses on restricting the access capability of an individual app, it cannot detect application collusion attacks that malicious apps may collude via ICC to achieve permission escalation. For instance, *SoundComber* [47] is a sound-based Trojan that uses sound sensors to record user's keyboard input and other audio data such as phone conversations. Android security protection may deny the installation of apps requesting both sensitive sensors and network permissions. However, SoundComber does not requires the network permission, since it can use ICC to transfer the sensitive data to another colluding app that has the network permission to send the data to a remote server.

In this paper, we focus on developing an efficient approach to detecting inter-app privacy leakage incurred by ICC channels. Privacy leakages incurred by other interfaces (e.g., interfaces defined by Android Interface Definition Language (AIDL)) are not the focus of our paper [20,42].

4   LinkFlow Overview

In this section, we present an overview of LinkFlow architecture that aims to detect privacy leakage across multiple apps on a large scale. It is built upon the following two key observations, which have been correctly verified by our experimental results.

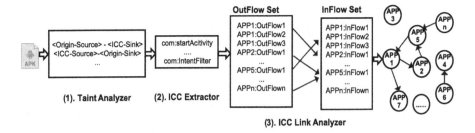

Fig. 1. LinkFlow architecture

Observation 1: *Not all components of an app interact with the other components of the app or other apps, and thus they will not leak privacy.* One component cannot be accessed by any other components (of the app or other apps) if it does not communicate with them via ICC. Therefore, we only need to analyze the code of app components that interact with the other components of the same app or other apps. In other words, we focus on the components that may transfer data out of the app.

Observation 2: *Only a small portion of ICC links are leaky, and the most of ICC links are benign.* Thus, we can identify privacy leakage by analyzing ICC links that deliver sensitive information, which is protected by the permission level at Dangerous, Signature, or SignatureOrSystem.

Figure 1 shows the architecture of LinkFlow, which consists of three major components *Taint Analyzer*, *ICC Extractor*, and *ICC Link Analyzer*. Given a set of apps, these three components run in sequence to identify potential ICC-based leakage among all the apps. First, the taint analyzer performs static taint analysis on each app to identify flow paths that may leak sensitive information. Second, ICC extractor is responsible for extracting and resolving ICC methods and the parameters in ICC links according to flow paths generated by taint analyzer, and generates two sets of components for outgoing flows and incoming flows, respectively. By leveraging the flow paths, ICC extractor significantly reduces the number of ICC links for analysis. Finally, ICC link analyzer matches the ICC links of apps to find out the abnormal data flows that may incur privacy leakages among apps. The first two steps can precisely screen out the leaking components in apps and the ICC APIs used in those components. Based on the reduced ICC links, the third step identifies the leaking ICC links and can generate an ICC link graph to better illustrate the leaking paths.

4.1   Taint Analyzer

The usage of taint analysis is to detect the leaky components that contain ICC-based leaky data flows. A leaky data flow is a path starting from the source API that accesses the sensitive data to the sink API that sends this data out of the application or device. We inspect all leaky flows that send data to ICC APIs (e.g., *Intent.putExtra*) that are called *ICC-Sink* or read data using ICC APIs (e.g., *Intent.getExtra*) that are named *ICC-Source* in this paper.

4.2 ICC Extractor

We use ICC extractor in the second step to extract the parameters of *Intents*, the ICC APIs, the components' *Intent Filters* and other necessary messages. Since it only extracts the ICC APIs that match the flows in ICC-Sink or ICC-Source and analyze the components that may communicate with other apps, it dramatically reduces the number of ICC links under analysis. After this step, we can extract the leaky components and leaky path using ICC APIs in each individual app. We define a tuple $A = \{C, P, F\}$ for each app to record the analysis results, where

- **C** is the set of components in one app. For each component $c \in C$, c contains the ICC extractor's analysis results that are extracted from the Manifest and bytecode. It consists of a set of *Intent Filters*, a set of permissions used in the component, and a set of ICC methods. In addition, it also includes *Intent* messages that are referred as Exit Points.
- **P** is the set of total permissions declared in the app's manifest file.
- **F** is the set of flows resulted from the static taint analysis.

4.3 ICC Link Analyzer

After obtaining the tuple of an app from ICC Extractor, we perform the ICC link analysis to analyze all the necessary data of the leaky components and use a fast ICC matching algorithm to enumerate all ICC links among these apps to identify privacy leakage. In particular, we accurately infer if ICC links really incur privacy leakage by evaluating the corresponding permissions that are mapped from the ICC APIs. After this step, LinkFlow can generate an analysis report to list all the potential privacy leakage among apps, e.g., among all apps in an app marketplace. This report provides guidance to mitigate the vulnerabilities or ban the malicious apps. In particular, it allows app developers to understand what components could be leveraged by other apps and thus help reduce the chances of privacy leakage.

5 LinkFlow Design

In this section, we present the design details of LinkFlow. As shown in Sect. 4, it has three steps to detect privacy leakages.

5.1 Step 1: Taint Analysis for Single App

We leverage static taint analysis to analyze intra-app data flows and trace how the data is created, modified, and consumed. In Android, app actions are triggered by the user events that are handled by specific callback methods. For instance, the *onClick* method is called when the user clicks a button. One app's state is changed by calling the components' lifecycle callback methods such as *onStart* when a component is started or *onResume* when a component is resumed. In order to perform control flow analysis, we need to generate calls for these callbacks that do not have direct calls in the code. LinkFlow generates a dummy main method to be used as the entry-point and creates direct calls for those callback methods. Then LinkFlow uses Spark algorithm [36] to construct a call graph for these methods and perform forward and backward inter-procedural data flow analysis based on the call graph [45].

After discovering all the sensitive intra-app data flows, we can obtain a set of paths recording the sensitive data flows as follows:

$Flows(app) = \{path1: source1 \sim sink1; path2: source2 \sim sink2; ...\}$

Where sources are APIs that return sensitive data of the app or Android system (e.g., reading contacts) and sinks are APIs that transmit sensitive data out of the app (e.g., via an HTTP connection). Since we target at identifying leaky paths that use ICC APIs to obtain and then leak privacy information, we separate ICC API related sources/sinks from the original sources/sinks and name them as ICC-Sources and ICC sinks. For simplicity, we call the sources and sinks excluding ICC sources and ICC sinks as *origin-sources* and *origin-sinks*, respectively.

We focus on two types of leaky paths, origin-source $\sim$ ICC-Sink and ICC-Source $\sim$ origin-sink, since the components with origin-source $\sim$ ICC-Sink paths may suffer component injection attacks and the components with ICC-Source $\sim$ origin-sink paths may suffer component hijacking attacks. When one Intent is sent out of one app via ICC-Sink, this Intent can only be received by the components using the targeted ICC-Source. We summarize the ICC-Sinks and the targeted ICC-Sources in Table 1. Components containing these two types of leaky paths are considered as leaky components. In this way, LinkFlow can find out the leaky components that send sensitive data out the app via ICC APIs or read data in via ICC APIs.

Table 1. ICC-Sinks with targeted ICC-Sources

ICC-Sinks	Targeted ICC-Sources
Context: send*BroadCast(Intent,...)	BroadcastRecevier: onReceive(Intent)
Activity: startActivity*(Intent, ...)	Activity: getIntent()
Context: startService(Intent, ..)	Service: onBind(Intent)
ContentResolver: insert, query, delete, update	(depend on the URI)

5.2   Step 2: ICC Extraction for Single App

Considering a large number of ICC links among apps and most of them are not leaky, we can reduce the ICC link scale by only checking the leaky ICC links among the leaky components and ignoring the normal ICC links, as shown in

Fig. 2. Instead of inspecting all ICC links among all apps, we only need to check the ICC links between two leaky components, since our goal is to find out the leaky ICC links. However, exist ICC leak detection tools such as IccTA [38] and DidFail [34] need to analyze all ICC links to identify the leaky ones, and most of the analysis time is consumed by analyzing the normal ICC links.

After identifying all leaky components, we collect the Intent parameters of the ICC APIs and obtain the Intent Filters of those components. Since inter-component communications via Intent message mechanism are dynamically resolved by Android system, it is difficult for static analysis tools to analyze those links between components. Therefore, to analyze the ICC links among apps, we need to precisely resolve the ICC methods and the Intent messages. There are various ICC APIs and a large number of Intent data handling methods such as *intent.getStringExtra*, *intent.getLongExtra*, etc. We extract the Intent Filters of components from the *Manifest.xml* and the ICC APIs parameters from the bytecode.

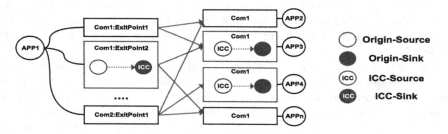

Fig. 2. Only checking the leaky ICC links (red arrow) among the leaky components. (Color figure online)

Now we combine the ICC extraction results with the taint analysis results to obtain the following flow information.

- **Method and Class** with the full method signature in Soot format [35], for instance, *<android.telephony.TelephonyManager: java.lang.String.get DeviceId()>*.
- **Component** where the Flows belong to. We need to find out in which component the source/sink method is called.
- **Category** of the source/sink API. The SuSi [43] project provides a detailed category of the API. As one efficient way to express the behavior of the flows, it is easy for end users to comprehend how the sensitive data is used.
- **Permission** associating with the API. We use the relation map provide by PScout [17] to achieve it.
- **Exit Point.** An Exit Point is an ICC method used to send Intent and communication with other components. When apps start a new context in the *Exit Points* and the Intent messages are passed by the Android OS, the data-flow will discontinue. Therefore, we need to extract all Exit Point methods.

The Component and the Exit Point information are used to identify the ICC-based leaky paths and obtain the Intent messages' parameters and the Intent Filter. The methods, classes, permissions, and categories are used to describe the sources/sinks and identify the privacy leakage due to the misuse of the sensitive API.

5.3   Step 3: ICC Link Analysis for All Apps

The first two steps have extracted detailed flow information for each individual app, and now we can obtain the leaky components, the Intent messages, and the ICC methods of all the apps to perform ICC link analysis.

We define *abnormal data flow* as a leaky ICC link that indicates sensitive data sent out via one ICC-Sink method in App1 and received by one ICC-Source method in App2. We record one abnormal data flow as $A = \{App1: outflow \sim App2: inflow, outflow \in OutFlow, inflow \in InFlow\}$, where InFlow is a set of exported components with an abnormal flow of ICC-Source to origin-sink that reads data from other components and OutFlow is a set of components (may not be exported) with an abnormal flow of origin-source to ICC-Sink that sends data to other components.

We develop an ICC matching algorithm to find out all potential ICC links among the leaky apps and construct an ICC graph where leaky apps are nodes and ICC links are links. The ICC matching algorithm is shown in Algorithm 1. First, we traverse the OutFlow Set and check the ICC APIs and parameters used in the *outFlow* to determine if the Intent is implicit or explicit. For explicit Intent, the receiver components are defined and the destination can be directly obtained from the parameters of Intent. For implicit Intent, there may exist multiple receiver components depending on the apps installed in user's device. To verify if there is an implicit ICC link between an *outFlow* and an *inFlow*, we need to evaluate the ICC-Sink of the *outFlow* and the ICC-Sources of each *inFlow*: (1) if their methods and target component types are matching (as shown in Table 1) and (2) if the Intent Filters of the ICC-Sources can receive the Intent sending by the ICC-Sinks. For instance, to identify the apps that use ICC to link to Contacts Manager, since Contacts Manager's ICC-Sink is *startService*, we need to check the InFlow set to find out the Service Components with the onBind ICC-Source. Because we have extracted the action, categories, and flags of the Intent sent by the ICC-Sink in first two steps, we can check if the Intent Filter of the ICC-Source component can receive the Intent. Our methods can reveal all apps that contain services to handle the Intent sent by Contacts Manager and construct an ICC link graph to save these leaky links and the corresponding apps.

By traversing the ICC link graph, we can obtain the linked apps of each app and then generate a leaky report for each app. The report for an app can tell which apps use ICC to communicate with it and may cause privacy leakage. The report also provides the detailed leaky path, the potential privacy leakages, the potential permission leakages, and the risk level. We can determine the severity of these leaky API by using the categories of these APIs that are summarized

---

Algorithm 1. The ICC Matching Algorithm

Require: InFlowSet, OutFlowSet;
Ensure: LinkedFlowSet: linked ICC flow;
 1: $graph \leftarrow initLinkGraph()$
 2: **for** $inflow \in InFlowSet$ **do**
 3:   $intent \leftarrow inflow.ICCSink.intent$
 4:   **if** $isExplicitIntent(intent)$ **then**
 5:     $app \leftarrow getAppByPackage(intent)$
 6:     $addEdge(graph, app, inflow.app)$
 7:   **else**
 8:     **for** $outflow \in OutFlowSet$ **do**
 9:       $intentFilter \leftarrow outflow.intentFitler$
10:       **if** $intentFilter.canReceive(intent)$ **then**
11:         $addEdge(graph, outflow.app,$
12: $inflow.app)$
13:           $LinkedFlowSet.add(inflow,$
14: $outflow)$
15:       **end if**
16:     **end for**
17:   **end if**
18: **end for**

---

by SuSi [43]. We leverage PScout [17] to map APIs to their corresponding permissions. Then we can confirm if there are permission leaks by checking if the InFlow app contains the permission required by the origin-sink in the OutFlow app. If not, it means the InFlow app can leverage the permissions of the OutFlow app and the privilege escalation happen. In general, the report can help both app developers and users to mitigate the vulnerabilities or ban the malicious apps.

6 LinkFlow Implementation

LinkFlow extends FlowDroid [16] to implement the Taint Analyzer that provides precise taint analysis to efficiently identify all suspicious ICC flows. In particular, it leverages PScout [17] and Susi [43] to generate the required parameters for the taint analysis. Moreover, LinkFlow utilizes ICC Extractor to precisely infer the ICC parameters, e.g., the type of *Intent* values and the parameters of *Intent Filters*. LinkFlow significantly reduces the number of ICC links based on the flow taint analysis results.

6.1 Taint Analyzer

Our Taint Analyzer constructs a call graph for apps and then performs forward data flow analysis to find paths from the source API to the sink. Next, it performs backward dependence analysis to exclude the paths that do not have any dependence on the source APIs.

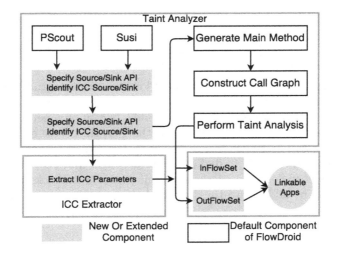

Fig. 3. Implementation of LinkFlow

As shown in Fig. 3, besides leveraging the basic taint analysis functionalities provided by FlowDroid [16], we extend FlowDroid in three First, we extend the source/sink analysis module to identify and analyze sensitive ICC source/sink, which is critical for reducing the complexity of the later ICC analysis. Second, we identify the callbacks of all four types of components and analyze source/sink to find out all non-isolated components that interact with other components. It can reduce the code base to be analyzed. Third, we extend FlowDroid to analyze *Service and BroadCast Receiver*.

Specifying Source/Sink APIs. Since taint paths start from a source API that read or generate private data and end in sink APIs that may leak privacy, we modify the FlowDroid's source/sink manager to analyze two specific types of flows, namely, flows from Origin-source to ICC-Sink and flows from ICC-Source to Origin-Sink. As shown in Fig. 3, we leverage Susi [43] to generate a detailed list of sources/sinks APIs with the API category information, and utilize PScout's [17] to associate APIs with the permissions they require. Thus, LinkFlow can accurately obtain sensitive source/sink APIs and track the data flow of these APIs. Note that, by analyzing two specific flows, we further improve the performance of LinkFlow by reducing the workload of backward flow analysis.

Analyzing ICC Parameters and Excluding Isolate Components. We need to identify components that contain ICC-sink methods may leak data, and thus we need to precisely extract the ICC parameters so as to analyze the Intent receiver components and what data they send. To achieve this goal, we traverse entire app packages by using Soot to analyze the usage of ICC APIs in all components. To reduce the code base under analysis, we need to exclude non-isolated components in LinkFlow. First, during traversing app packages, we also enumerate components that do not have ICC-sink methods. Second we analyze

Intent Filters in the *Manifest.xml* file to find out all public components. These two type components are non-isolated components that need no further analysis. Therefore, we only add these components' lifecycle methods as entry points to the dummyMain methods.

Constructing Call Graph. We extend FlowDroid to construct call paths for all components. In particular, FlowDroid cannot analyze Service and Broadcast Receiver as they use different callback methods. It cannot generate the callback method information in the dummyMain methods so that these methods will not be added to the call graph and cannot be analyzed. Our taint analyzer performs callback resolution analysis to find out the Messenger and Handler used by the Binder interface of Service and the dynamic lifecycle callbacks of Receiver so that they could be added into the dummyMain methods.

6.2   ICC Extractor

The essence of ICC extractor is to precisely extract the ICC parameters. We analyze Intent or URI to obtain detailed ICC parameters since ICC methods use them to set the target components in ICC. The ICC target components can be defined in the two ways, namely, directly set in Intent by using package names or Java.lang.class as the parameters, or set URI by using a permission string.

We can directly obtain ICC parameters by analyzing URI if the ICC methods use URI. For example, an app can use URI.parser("smsto:phone") to call the sending message API, and ContentProvider always uses URI to locate resources. URIs use strings with the special format to describe the resources. In particular, custom URIs are hard-coded in apps' code and system URIs are a limited number of common strings. Therefore, we can extract these URI prefixes via regular expression. In terms of Intent analysis, we need to deal with a serial of Intent related APIs, such as put*Extra, setData*, get*, send*Broadcast*, startActivity* that are capable of reading from, writing to, sending, or receiving Intent.

To extract the parameters, we first perform forward data flow to find the usage of ICC APIs that use Intent to send messages. Then, we do backward intra-procedural data flow analysis to find all callers of Intent. We define a model for Intent to include all the methods of Intent. For each method, we extract the corresponding parameters based on the definitions of Intent methods.

ICC can be explicit and implicit. Explicit ICC methods directly set detailed target components, while implicit ICC methods use IntentFilter to filter the Intent. Explicit ICC can be resolved based on the component setting in the Intent's parameters. For implicit ICC, we set constraints to check if the fields of IntentFilter contain the Intent's parameters.

6.3   ICC Link Analyzer

We implement Algorithm 1 according to the results of ICC Extractor. ICC Link Analyzer constructs an ICC graph and enumerates ICC links that may leak privacy. It generates an ICC link graph and identifies privacy leakage by matching

ICC links in the graph according to the analysis results and the permissions mapped to the ICC APIs. The computed ICC link graph is stored in an *MongoDB* database [8] for privacy leakage query and incremental analysis.

7   Performance Evaluation

We implement a LinkFlow prototype on Ubuntu server 14.04. We perform the experiments on a server with 4 Intel Xeon CPU 2.49 GHZ cores and 14 GB memory. We collect top 1000 popular real world apps from each of five popular apps marketplaces and repositories including Google play [5], APKPure [2], Hiapk [6], Tencent marketplace [12], and F-Droid [4]. We also collect 1500 malware from malware repositories including the MalGenome Project [56] and VirusShare [13]. Then we evaluate if there exists privacy leakage among all those apps. We remove the duplicated apps and the apps that cannot be correctly processed by Flow-Droid, and the final number of benign apps tested by LinkFlow is reduced to 3014. Due to the limitation of FlowDroid [16], we set the flow taint analysis time to five minutes for each app. Our experiments show that when the taint analysis process cannot finish within five minutes, the server has run out of memory and failed to process the app.

We first investigate the privilege escalation problems in ICC links to verify that LinkFlow can identify privacy leakage by analyzing ICC links among a set of apps. Then, we use LinkFlow to analyze real world apps to identify the leaky ICC links among these apps. Finally, we measure the performance of LinkFlow and its scalability on incremental detection.

7.1   Impacts on Privilege Escalation

Android apps tend to be over-privileged especially when they use many SDKs [30]. We study the usages of permissions over 4000 apps and find only 17 components in apps are protected by permissions. Unfortunately, almost all leaky components are not protected by permissions. This means the exported leaky components can be easily exploited by malicious apps. Based on the permissions map computed by PScout [17], we investigate sensitive APIs used by these apps and observe that 1106 permission leaks among 530 apps. On average each leaky app has two permissions that could be exploited by other apps via ICC links. Therefore, to detect permissions that are susceptible to privilege escalation, we can analyze ICC links among apps and find out the exploitation paths in the ICC links.

We also study the privilege escalation problem incurred by app collusion. By analyzing the combined permissions of two linked apps and trace the data flow of their ICC links, we successfully identify 4622 suspicious data flows among those apps. The details of API usage are shown in Table 2. According to the study of Elish et al. [25], the existing dynamic taint analysis mechanisms are unable to detect privacy leakage incurred by app collusion. Based on the ICC link analysis results of all apps, LinkFlow generates a report that lists all potential ICC-based collusion among apps. It can guide app developer to avoid component misuses with leaky ICC links.

7.2   Effectiveness of Privacy Leakage Detection

LinkFlow identifies 417 benign apps with 1723 component leakages. We find 4012 abnormal flows generated by those components. We also find 113 malicious apps with 471 component leakages, and those malicious apps are inclined to use ICC at a higher frequency with 2043 abnormal flows. Those abnormal flows may be triggered by two types of attacks: *component hijacking* and *component injection*. We classify these two types of vulnerabilities based on the types of components in the InFlow and OutFlow sets. As shown in Fig. 4, the leaky paths in OutFlow set mean that these components use the ICC APIs in Table 1 to send sensitive data to other apps and may suffer component injection. The leaky paths in InFlow set means these components may suffer from component hijacking attack via *Intent* spoofing, which leads to privacy leakage.

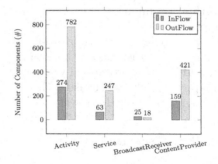

Fig. 4. The number of components included in the InFlow set and OutFlow set

We also study the privacy leakage types. LinkFlow measures the frequency of the sensitivity flows generated by benign apps and malicious apps. The mostly used source category is database information, followed by contact information, network, and location information. Also, we observe three types of sinks in benign apps: *log*, *intent*, and *storage*. In malicious apps, the top sinks are *telephone*, *storage*, *intent*, *log*, and *network*. We examine all these apps to obtain their ICC usages. The top five original sources and sinks methods we collected in the benign apps are shown in Table 2.

We observe that most ICC links are using implicit *Intent* to perform inter-apps communications. Thus, these apps' components may not be safe if they contain abnormal flows. Indeed, the unsafe usage of ICC results in vulnerabilities that can be easily exploited by malware. By performing flow analysis, we find 530 apps with abnormal flows. We verify the exploitability of all those leaky paths by using the ICC matching algorithm and find out all 530 apps have vulnerable

Table 2. The mostly used original sources/sinks

Sources type	Category	Permission	Count
Airpush: onReceive	Message Push	-	1292
ContentResolver: query	SQLite		1097
LocationManager: getLastKnownLocation	Location	ACCESS_LOCATION	861
TelephonyManager: getDeviceId	Indeifier	READ_PHONE_STATE	477
FileInputStream: read	Read File	EXTERNAL_STORAGE	319
Sinks type	Category	Permission	Count
SharedPreferences: putString	Write XML	EXTERNAL_STORAGE	1422
Log:i	Log	-	1035
OutputStream: write	IO	-	531
HttpClient: execute	Network	ACCESS_NETWORK	353
ContentResolver: insert	SQLite	-	254

components. We identify 87 apps that incur privacy leakage through ICC links and 4622 ICC paths among those apps. Typically, the sensitive data is sent to other apps and leaked via log or network.

The number of linkable apps for each app (i.e., the apps that an app can generate data flows with) varies from 20 to 56. On average, each app has three linkable apps. To evaluate the potential impacts of these links, we combine the OutFlow and InFlow sets of each app and map the API to permissions. Then we obtain pairs of linkable flows and linkable permissions that indicate that real flows between the apps and the permissions are enforced on the flows.

We manually confirm the apps incurring privacy leakage. We find that a large number of apps receive Intent messages and leak their data. In particular, most of apps (more than 80% apps) leak their data to logcat, such as Android Guard [1] and Ditty by Zya [3]. These leaky apps leaks device ID, phone numbers, contacts, locations, or SMS Messages. For instance, SMS Popup [10] writes phone numbers and messages to the system log messages that can be directly accessed via ICC.

7.3 Detection Delays of LinkFlow

The delays of flow analysis and ICC analysis are shown in Fig. 5(a). The flow analysis delays increase with the increase of the numbers of sources/sinks numbers, and the ICC analysis delays vary according to the numbers of components. For each app, the total abnormal flows extraction delays are about two minutes. We also evaluate the delays of ICC link analyzer. On average, it takes less than 1 min, which is relatively stable. It is scalable even if the InFlow set and OutFlow sets contain millions of flows. Note that, existing tools such as IccTA [38] cannot work well on a large scale, since they rely on ApkCombiner [37] to combine the bytecode of two apps and then perform ICC analysis. Due to the limitation of FlowDroid, the code size cannot be too large. Also, they can only combine two apps at most. For the current app set with 4514 apps, the analysis time is about

848k hours $\left(\binom{4514}{2}\right)$ * 5 min). In contrast, it takes less than 1 min for the ICC link analysis of LinkFlow to analyze all 4514 apps.

The total analysis delay of LinkFlow on analyzing 4514 apps is about 377 h, including 4514 * 5 min for flow analysis, ICC extractor, and saving to database plus 1 min for ICC link analysis. Our tool supports efficient detection on newly added apps. When a new app is submitted, IccTA needs to run over 377 h to go through the ICC links between the new app and each of the existing apps. This cost is unacceptable as everyday thousands of new apps have been developed and added. In contrast, our taint analysis only needs to run once for each app, so we only need 5 min for taint analysis and ICC extract of the new app plus 20 s for ICC link analysis.

We conduct two experiments to evaluate the scalability of LinkFlow. The first experiment is to evaluate LinkFlow with different number of apps ranging from 500 to 12000. For an app marketplace with millions of apps, there are over ten thousand leaky apps. We randomly select apps from all these 530 leaky apps and repeat 500–12000 times, and obtain different sizes of app sets that contain 500–12000 apps. As shown in Fig. 5(a), on average, LinkFlow takes less than 2 min to detect privacy leakage. Note that, since different apps may have different numbers of non-isolated components, the delays may vary even with the same number of components in the leaky app.

The second experiment is to evaluate the incremental analysis delays. We generate a large set of apps based on the real apps data. The numbers of the newly submitted apps are set to 5, 50, and 100. As shown in Fig. 5(b), when the apps number is over 10k, if we do not use the incremental analysis, the detection delays are about 15 min. However, if we use incremental analysis, it takes less than 1 min. The reason is that we only need to match flows in three flow sets, i.e., matching flow pairs that from new OutFlow set to old InFlow set, from old OutFlow set to new InFlow set, and from new OutFlow set to new InFlow set.

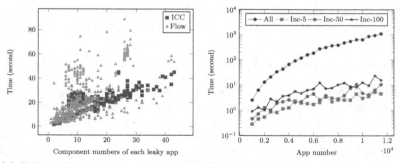

(a) Delays of taint analysis and ICC   (b) Delays of incremental detection
analysis

Fig. 5. The detection delays of LinkFlow.

8 Discussions

ICC Analysis Across Multiple Apps. Though LinkFlow can effectively detect privacy leakage by analyzing leaky ICC links between two apps in a large set of apps, current version cannot detect leakages with leaky ICC links constructed by more than two apps. Fortunately, it can be extended to analyze ICC links among more than two apps, e.g., more than two apps collude to deliver sensitive data. Since we construct the ICC link graph for all apps, we can obtain the privacy leakage chain of multiple apps. Then, we can perform further analysis and check if these apps are colluding. For instance, app A has an ICC link delivering data to app B, while app B has an ICC link to app C, where A does not have direct links with C. LinkFlow can still check whether C can access A's data or permissions by performing taint analysis on app B and detecting if the data from A is delivered to C. To address this issue, we can leverage IccTA [38] together with ApkCombiner [37] in LinkFlow so that LinkFlow can combine bytecode of the three apps (A, B, C) and then analyze the data flows between A and C.

Apps Collusion Detection. LinkFlow can be applied to detect leakage incurred by collusion among multiple apps. However, it can only detect the collusion attacks constructed via ICC. We notice that many *e-book* apps use the same ad lib (com.waps.OffersWebView) to write sensitive data to SD Card and then transfer data to the Internet. These *e-book* apps have been granted with a large set of different permissions, such as installing app, reading SMS, reading location, and reading contacts. It is clear that these permissions are not directly used in their code but in the ad lib they used. LinkFlow cannot detect such app collusion because the leakages in these attack scenarios are not incurred by the ICC channels. Instead, they deliver sensitive data on the server and then steal them there. We consider it as a future work.

Limitation of Taint Analysis. The taint analyzer of LinkFlow is built upon FlowDroid. Due to the limitations of FlowDroid, LinkFlow may fail to analyze some apps. For instance, taint analysis may run out of memory if apps are implemented with huge bytecode or privacy leakage is constructed by native code. Moreover, current LinkFlow design does not address the class name with obfuscating strings, which is an interesting topic for our future work.

9 Related Work

Android Static Analysis. Static analysis has been extensively studied on Android for privacy leakage detection [28,33,39,41,51,54]. ComDroid [23], CHEX [41], and AppSealer [55] applied static analysis approaches to automatically evaluate component hijacking vulnerabilities of apps. FlowDroid [16] and Amandroid [52] provide context sensitive taint analysis to detect privacy leakage on Android. FlowDroid is the-state-of-art analyzer for taint analysis on Android. It is built on Soot [35] and Dexpler [18] to decompile and analyze the bytecode to detect leakage. DidFail [34] and IccTA [38] were built upon FlowDroid to detect privacy leakages of ICC. However, they cannot efficiently analyze a large set of ICC links among a huge number of apps. DroidSafe [29] identifies malicious flows by combining Android runtime analysis and static analysis. Its detection delays are ten times more than FlowDroid. LinkFlow can address this issue by reducing the number of suspicious ICC links before analyzing the leaky ICC flows.

Android Dynamic Analysis. By monitoring the states of the running processes, dynamic analysis can detect privacy leakages missed by static analysis. TaintDroid [26] implemented dynamic taint tracking for Android by modifying the Dalvik virtual machine to track sensitive data. XManDroid [20,21] monitored different communication links between apps in runtime to detect privilege escalation. API call monitoring mechanisms [44,46,50] dynamically monitored the Android system API calls to reconstruct the behavior of apps. FLEXDROID [48] provides an isolation mechanism to enforce in-app privilege separation. Blueseal [32,49] extended the existing permission mechanism by providing runtime flowing permission checking. Afonso et al. [15] performed a large-scale study on the usage of native code and generated native code sandboxing policies to limit malicious behaviors. Dynamic analysis typically is typically time-consuming, so it has the limitation to be applied to large scale leakage detection. In contrast, static taint analysis mechanisms can quickly analyze the codes of a large number of apps, so we leverage static taint analysis in LinkFlow.

Android Permission Analysis. Since Android's permission-based security mechanism cannot prevent privacy leakage from privilege escalation attack [24, 27,31], researchers proposed new mechanisms to solve this problem [22,53]. FlexDroid [22] extended the Android security architecture to enforce privacy protection policies. IntentFuzzer [53] leveraged fuzzy test to generate different *Intent* messages to connect components of Android System apps. It requires modifications of the Android framework to log the actually used permissions of the components. Therefore, it can capture which permissions in these apps may be exploited by other apps. LinkFlow leveraged PScout [17] to statically map ICC APIs to the corresponding permissions. It can accurately verify potential permission leakages by checking if the permissions of the APIs are actually used by the suspicious flows.

10   Conclusion

This paper proposes LinkFlow to provide large-scale privacy leakage detection among Android apps that communicate via Inter-Component Communication (ICC). It addresses the challenge of identifying ICC-based leaky data flow among a large set of apps by only analyzing ICC links among the leaky components. LinkFlow first enumerates all leaky components of apps that may incur privacy leakage and then performs a fast ICC matching algorithm to identify all privacy leakages. We implement a LinkFlow prototype and evaluate our tool over 5000 apps and find out 530 leaky apps. Among these leaky apps, we discover 4622 ICC links among 87 apps that may lead to severe data leakages.

Acknowledgments. The research is partially supported by the National Natural Science Foundation of China under Grant 61572278, the National Key Research and Development Program of China under Grant 2016YFB0800102, and U.S. Office of Naval Research under Grant N00014-16-1-3214 and N00014-16-1-3216.

References

1. Android Guard: http://android.app.qq.com/myapp/detail.htm?apkName=org. androidbeans.guard
2. APKPure. https://apkpure.com/
3. Ditty by Zya. https://play.google.com/store/apps/details?id=com.zya.ditty
4. F-Droid. https://f-droid.org/
5. Google Play. https://play.google.com
6. Hiapk. www.hiapk.com/
7. Intents and intent filters. http://developer.android.com/guide/components/ intents-filters.html
8. MongoDB. https://www.mongodb.org/
9. A part of ICC APIs, the defination of Intent. https://developer.android.com/ reference/android/content/Intent.html
10. SMS Popup. https://play.google.com/store/apps/details?id=net. everythingandroid.smspopup
11. SMSZombie. http://blog.trustgo.com/SMSZombie/
12. Tencent Markletplace. http://sj.qq.com/myapp/
13. VirusShare. https://virusshare.com/
14. Vulnerability of Dropbox SDK. http://www.slideshare.net/ibmsecurity/remote-exploitation-of-the-dropbox-sdk-for-android
15. Afonso, V., Bianchi, A., Fratantonio, Y., Doupé, A., Polino, M., de Geus, P., Kruegel, C., Vigna, G.: Going native: using a large-scale analysis of android apps to create a practical native-code sandboxing policy. In: NDSS (2016)
16. Arzt, S., Rasthofer, S., Fritz, C., Bodden, E., Bartel, A., Klein, J., Le Traon, Y., Octeau, D., McDaniel, P.: Flowdroid: precise context, flow, field, object-sensitive and lifecycle-aware taint analysis for android apps. In: PLDI, vol. 49, no. 6, pp. 259–269 (2014)
17. Au, K.W.Y., Zhou, Y.F., Huang, Z., Lie, D.: PScout: analyzing the android permission specification. In: CCS, pp. 217–228 (2012)
18. Bartel, A., Klein, J., Le Traon, Y., Monperrus, M.: Dexpler: converting android dalvik bytecode to jimple for static analysis with soot. In: SOAP, pp. 27–38 (2012)
19. Bartel, A., Klein, J., Monperrus, M., Le Traon, Y.: Static analysis for extracting permission checks of a large scale framework: the challenges and solutions for analyzing Android. TSE **40**(6), 617–632 (2014)
20. Bugiel, S., Davi, L., Dmitrienko, A., Fischer, T., Sadeghi, A.-R.: Xmandroid: a new android evolution to mitigate privilege escalation attacks. Technische Universität Darmstadt, Technical Report TR-2011-04 (2011)
21. Bugiel, S., Davi, L., Dmitrienko, A., Fischer, T., Sadeghi, A.-R., Shastry, B.: Towards taming privilege-escalation attacks on android. In: NDSS (2012)
22. Bugiel, S., Heuser, S., Sadeghi, A.-R.: Flexible and fine-grained mandatory access control on android for diverse security and privacy policies. In: USENIX Security, pp. 131–146 (2013)
23. Chin, E., Felt, A.P., Greenwood, K., Wagner, D.: Analyzing inter-application communication in Android. In: MobiSys, pp. 239–252 (2011)

24. Davi, L., Dmitrienko, A., Sadeghi, A.-R., Winandy, M.: Privilege escalation attacks on android. In: Burmester, M., Tsudik, G., Magliveras, S., Ilić, I. (eds.) ISC 2010. LNCS, vol. 6531, pp. 346–360. Springer, Heidelberg (2011). https://doi.org/10.1007/978-3-642-18178-8_30

25. Elish, K.O., Yao, D., Ryder, B.G.: On the need of precise inter-app ICC classification for detecting android malware collusions. In: MoST (2015)

26. Enck, W., Gilbert, P., Han, S., Tendulkar, V., Chun, B.-G., Cox, L.P., Jung, J., McDaniel, P., Sheth, A.N.: TaintDroid: an information-flow tracking system for realtime privacy monitoring on smartphones. In: OSDI (2011)

27. Felt, A.P., Wang, H.J., Moshchuk, A., Hanna, S., Chin, E.: Permission redelegation: attacks and defenses. In: USENIX Security, vol. 30 (2011)

28. Fuchs, A.P., Chaudhuri, A., Foster, J.S.: Scandroid: automated security certification of android. Technical report, University of Maryland (2009)

29. Gordon, M.I., Kim, D., Perkins, J.H., Gilham, L., Nguyen, N., Rinard, M.C.: Information flow analysis of android applications in DroidSafe. In: NDSS (2015)

30. Grace, M.C., Zhou, W., Jiang, X., Sadeghi, A.-R.: Unsafe exposure analysis of mobile in-app advertisements. In: WISEC, pp. 101–112 (2012)

31. Grace, M.C., Zhou, Y., Wang, Z., Jiang, X.: Systematic detection of capability leaks in stock android smartphones. In: NDSS (2012)

32. Holavanalli, S., Manuel, D., Nanjundaswamy, V., Rosenberg, B., Shen, F., Ko, S.Y., Ziarek, L.: Flow permissions for android. In: ASE, pp. 652–657 (2013)

33. Kim, J., Yoon, Y., Yi, K., Shin, J., Center, S.: Scandal: static analyzer for detecting privacy leaks in android applications. In: MoST 12 (2012)

34. Klieber, W., Flynn, L., Bhosale, A., Jia, L., Bauer, L.: Android taint flow analysis for app sets. In: SOAP, pp. 1–6 (2014)

35. Lam, P., Bodden, E., Lhoták, O., Hendren, L.: The soot framework for Java program analysis: a retrospective. In: CETUS 2011 (2011)

36. Lhoták, O., Hendren, L.: Scaling Java points-to analysis using SPARK. In: Hedin, G. (ed.) CC 2003. LNCS, vol. 2622, pp. 153–169. Springer, Heidelberg (2003). https://doi.org/10.1007/3-540-36579-6_12

37. Li, L., Bartel, A., Bissyandé, T.F., Klein, J., Traon, Y.L.: ApkCombiner: combining multiple android apps to support inter-app analysis. In: Federrath, H., Gollmann, D. (eds.) SEC 2015. IAICT, vol. 455, pp. 513–527. Springer, Cham (2015). https://doi.org/10.1007/978-3-319-18467-8_34

38. Li, L., Bartel, A., Bissyandé, T.F., Klein, J., Le Traon, Y., Arzt, S., Rasthofer, S., Bodden, E., Octeau, D., McDaniel, P.: IccTA: detecting inter-component privacy leaks in android apps. In: ICSE, pp. 280–291 (2015)

39. Li, L., Bartel, A., Klein, J., Le Traon, Y.: Detecting privacy leaks in android apps. In: ESSoS-DS (2014)

40. Li, L., Bartel, A., Klein, J., Le Traon, Y.: Automatically exploiting potential component leaks in android applications. In: TrustCom, pp. 388–397 (2014)

41. Lu, L., Li, Z., Wu, Z., Lee, W., Jiang, G.: CHEX: statically vetting android apps for component hijacking vulnerabilities. In: CCS, pp. 229–240 (2012)

42. Marforio, C., Ritzdorf, H., Francillon, A., Capkun, S.: Analysis of the communication between colluding applications on modern smartphones. In: ACSAC, pp. 51–60 (2012)

43. Rasthofer, S., Arzt, S., Bodden, E.: A machine-learning approach for classifying and categorizing android sources and sinks. In: NDSS (2014)

44. Reina, A., Fattori, A., Cavallaro, L.: A system call-centric analysis and stimulation technique to automatically reconstruct android malware behaviors. In: EuroSec, April 2013

45. Reps, T., Horwitz, S., Sagiv, M.: Precise interprocedural dataflow analysis via graph reachability. In: POPL, pp. 49–61. ACM (1995)
46. Sakamoto, S., Okuda, K., Nakatsuka, R., Yamauchi, T.: DroidTrack: tracking and visualizing information diffusion for preventing information leakage on android. JISIS **4**(2), 55–69 (2014)
47. Schlegel, R., Zhang, K., Zhou, X.-Y., Intwala, M., Kapadia, A., Wang, X.: Sound-comber: a stealthy and context-aware sound trojan for smartphones. In: NDSS, vol. 11, pp. 17–33 (2011)
48. Seo, J., Kim, D., Cho, D., Kim, T., Shin, I.: FLEXDROID: enforcing in-app privilege separation in android. In: NDSS (2016)
49. Shen, F., Vishnubhotla, N., Todarka, C., Arora, M., Dhandapani, B., Lehner, E.J., Ko, S.Y., Ziarek, L.: Information flows as a permission mechanism. In: ASE, pp. 515–526 (2014)
50. Tam, K., Khan, S.J., Fattori, A., Cavallaro, L.: CopperDroid: automatic reconstruction of android malware behaviors. In: NDSS (2015)
51. Tripp, O., Rubin, J.: A bayesian approach to privacy enforcement in smartphones. In: USENIX Security, pp. 175–190 (2014)
52. Wei, F., Roy, S., Ou, X., et al.: Amandroid: a precise and general inter-component data flow analysis framework for security vetting of android apps. In: CCS, pp. 1329–1341. ACM (2014)
53. Yang, K., Zhuge, J., Wang, Y., Zhou, L., Duan, H.: IntentFuzzer: detecting capability leaks of android applications. In: ASIACCS, pp. 531–536 (2014)
54. Yang, Z., Yang, M.: Leakminer: detect information leakage on android with static taint analysis. In: WCSE, pp. 101–104 (2012)
55. Zhang, M., Yin, H.: AppSealer: automatic generation of vulnerability-specific patches for preventing component hijacking attacks in android applications. In: NDSS (2014)
56. Zhou, Y., Jiang, X.: Dissecting android malware: Characterization and evolution. In: IEEE Symposium on Security and Privacy, pp. 95–109 (2012)

Exposing LTE Security Weaknesses at Protocol Inter-layer, and Inter-radio Interactions

Muhammad Taqi Raza[1(✉)], Fatima Muhammad Anwar[2], and Songwu Lu[1]

[1] Computer Science Department, University of California – Los Angeles,
Los Angeles, USA
{taqi,slu}@cs.ucla.edu
[2] Electrical Engineering Department, University of California – Los Angeles,
Los Angeles, USA
fatimanwar@ucla.edu

Abstract. Despite security shields to protect user communication with both the radio access network and the core infrastructure, 4G LTE is still susceptible to a number of security threats. The vulnerabilities mainly exist due to its protocol's inter-layer communication, and the access technologies (2G/3G) inter-radio interaction. We categorize the uncovered vulnerabilities in three dimensions, i.e., authentication, security association and service availability, and verify these vulnerabilities in operational LTE networks. In order to assess practical impact from these security threats, we convert these threats into active attacks, where an adversary can (a) kick the victim device out of the network, (b) hijack the victim's location, and (c) silently drain the victim's battery power. Moreover, we have shown that the attacker does not need to communicate with the victim device or reside at the device to launch these attacks (i.e., no Trojan or malware is required). We further propose remedies for the identified attacks.

Keywords: LTE security · LTE protocol interactions
LTE interaction with 2G/3G networks

1 Introduction

The fourth-generation (4G) Long Term Evolution (LTE) technology offers wide-area mobile and wireless access to smart-phone and tablet devices. LTE is a complex network technology consisting of multiple subsystems – designed to provide undisrupted connectivity and backward compatibility to legacy 3G/2G networks. The operations of these subsystems are standardized [1]. These standards ensure interoperability between the device and the network. From the security perspective, LTE employs mechanisms to ensure authentication, authorization, access control, and user data confidentiality between the device and the network.

© ICST Institute for Computer Sciences, Social Informatics and Telecommunications Engineering 2018
X. Lin et al. (Eds.): SecureComm 2017, LNICST 238, pp. 312–338, 2018.
https://doi.org/10.1007/978-3-319-78813-5_16

Although both control and data planes in LTE adopt security measures, we have found that security is preserved only for end-to-end user communications. Device operations are carried out by transferring the control-plane packets between different layers of LTE protocols. Similar to the Internet and WiFi designs, LTE protocol layers are functionally independent. Yet these layers communicate with each other to facilitate device operations. Potential loopholes arise when LTE security mechanisms do not guard such inter-layer traffic flows. Certain device control-plane messages may escape authentication and authorization verifications at these layers in the network.

Our study reveals that the LTE network is not secure along the following three dimensions:

1. [**Weak Authentication**] Some messages sent from the LTE network to the device, soon after the device recovers from its idle mode, are executed without any authentication. This gives an adversary a chance to kick the victim out of the network.
2. [**Weak Security Association**] On inter-radio interactions, the target network incorrectly assumes that device has already been authenticated and authorized by the source network. During inter-radio interactions, the adversary can hijack the device location registration procedure and register wrong victim location at the network. The victim device consequently becomes unreachable from the network.
3. [**Lack of Access Control/Non-authorization**] The adversary is authorized to communicate with the victim without having its consent. This vulnerability allows an adversary to drain the victim device's battery by sending periodic control messages.

These security weaknesses arise when (1) different LTE protocol layers communicate with each other, and (2) LTE protocol communicates with its legacy technology, such as WCDMA/3G, and GSM/2G. In the end-to-end protocol interactions, intermediate protocol layers (either at the local device or the remote network) act as forwarding layers. They forward the packets to the layer above or below without inspecting the contents of the forwarded packets. Hence, *packet forwarding blindly facilitates such protocol interactions.*

Furthermore, LTE protocol layers perform atomic network operations to interact with one another. These interactions happen without any integrity check between these layers. This signifies that *the trust among these protocol layers is unconditional.*

We also found that certain control messages are accepted at the network before the device security mechanisms kick in. *LTE network assumes that certain control messages after the device's idle state are legitimate.* These messages specify the device's intent for different types of services, e.g., voice or data service, and set up the network resources accordingly. The device can misuse network resources by generating fake control messages.

Moreover, when the LTE protocol communicates with its legacy technology (such as 3G or 2G), it transfers the user session and security keys to the legacy network. The legacy network does not perform any authentication procedure

Table 1. Summary of findings

Capability	Vulnerabilities	Loophole	Attacks	Root cause	Defense solution
Authentication	Blind execution of messages, non-verification of originator	Authentication bypass	Detach the victim from the network	Network executes message for the device idle mode operation	The device identity should resolve into correct Device-eNodeB-S1AP-ID
Security association	Denial of service, No check on deceptive messages	Network relies on old authentication	Rendering device to be unreachable from the network	Security context mismatch	The device should be re-authenticated after inter-radio switch
Authorization & ACL	Unconditional trust across protocol layers	Strong assumption of secure layers	Draining victims' battery	Device has no authorization process	ACL should be maintained for transitive trust

with the device. Instead, it assumes that the device has already been authenticated at the time of registration with the LTE network. It is possible that the device's native security context gets expired and becomes invalid. This potentially *creates two conflicting security setup views at the device and the legacy network*. Therefore, the device can trick the legacy network by believing that its native security context is valid.

Attacks and Impact. Once we have confirmed the vulnerabilities through analyzing LTE standards, we validate them in operational LTE networks. We thus use the LTE modem diagnostic tool, the non-volatile memory manager, and TeraTerm [2], to capture and analyze traces. After validation, we convert these vulnerabilities into attacks by using our testbed and exploit these weaknesses to compromise the network security. For example, an adversary sends a wireless connection request to the LTE base station and piggybacks the network join request message destined for the LTE core network. Upon receiving the message from the legitimate base station, the core network marks the join request message as being valid and executes it. This procedure can be exploited by an adversary that can make a legitimate wireless connection with the LTE base station but sends unauthorized device messages (e.g., device power-off notification) by impersonating the victim device to the core network. Consequently, the core infrastructure wrongly executes the message (e.g. closes the victim device session).

The potential impacts from such vulnerabilities are quite high. The adversary can kick the victim out of the network, hijack the victim's device location update procedure and register wrong location of the victim at the network, and silently drain the victim's battery. To make things worse, the attacker does not need to interact with the victim device to launch these attacks, (i.e., no Trojan or malware is required). We have summarized our key findings in Table 1.

Prior Studies. Our work differs from existing research efforts that seek to challenge the resilience of LTE security mechanisms under various conditions. Shaik et al. [3] show that a device location can be leaked within $2\,km^2$. They have also demonstrated the Denial of Service (DoS) attack when the LTE device accepts the message from rogue LTE base stations and de-registers from the network. They assume LTE device will send non-integrity *Tracking Area Update Request* message, which is replied by the rogue LTE base station.

Jover [4] present LTE DoS attacks through radio signal jamming and amplification, and subscriber database saturation. In a separate work [5], they argue that attacker can use the LTE System Information Blocks, and Management Information Blocks to craft jamming attacks. Patrick [6] shows that compromising physical radio access network can reveal user traffic sent over unencrypted link between the radio access network and the core. Tu et al. [7] and Huang et al. [8] show that LTE protocol interactions are common and can result in performance issues. They have shown how abnormal LTE protocol interactions can degrade quality of service, e.g., the device does not transition from 3G to 4G after making a circuit-switched voice call, the device registration procedure is delayed because of location update, etc. Contrary to previous studies, our work focuses on LTE security weaknesses arising from standardized specifications; especially at LTE protocol inter-layer and inter-radio communications. Moreover, we demonstrate a different set of attacks not revealed by earlier studies. We have challenged the fundamental security principles of the LTE network and expose the vulnerabilities that lead to active attacks.

Scope. We believe, LTE standard body has well thought all LTE operational scenarios and may not have left any obvious mistakes while defining standards. In this paper, we focus on studying corner cases in LTE operations that may not be commonly observed, but could weaken the LTE security. We limit our scope in studying these cases within the relatively less explored area, i.e., LTE protocol inter-layers, and inter-radio interactions.

2   Background

We provide background on LTE protocol inter-layer interaction[1], and access technologies (4G/3G/2G) inter-radio interactions.

2.1   LTE Protocol Inter-layer Interaction

LTE protocol's functionality is divided across different layers, where each layer is designed to carry out a specific function [9]. Figure 1 shows layered LTE protocol at the mobile device (known as User Agent - UE), LTE base-station (known as evolved NodeB - eNodeB), and LTE core-network entity (known as Mobility Management Entity - MME). The design goal of layered LTE protocol is: (a) to simplify communication design by dividing it into functional layers, and (b) assigning independent tasks to each protocol layer. Although, the layers execute their independent tasks, the successful execution of operations lie in frequent interactions among the protocol layers. Such protocol layer interactions take place within the device, and across the device with the network. For

---

[1] Such interaction can occur within, and across the device and network elements.

example, two procedures known as Hybrid Automatic Repeat Request (HARQ), and Automatic Repeat Request (ARQ) are proposed at Medium Access Control (MAC) layer and Radio Link Control (RLC) layer of LTE protocol stack, respectively [10]. The combination of these two protocol layers (i.e. MAC and RLC) can be viewed as inter-layer protocol interaction. MAC and RLC protocols coordinate back and forth in a feedback channel loop to achieve reliable data transmission, (as shown in Fig. 1).

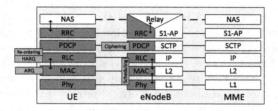

Fig. 1. LTE protocol layering and interaction at device and network side

Another example of LTE protocol inter-layer interaction is shown in Fig. 1, when Radio Resource Control (RRC[2]) layer at UE is communicating with Non-Access Spectrum (NAS[3]) protocol at MME. The RRC layer is responsible for securing radio connection between UE and eNodeB, whereas the NAS ensures secure data connection between UE and MME. Although, RRC and NAS function independently, these two layers coordinate frequently in order to perform certain device/network level operations. One such operation is *device registration procedure (i.e. Attach Request message)* with the network. In this, RRC layer at UE first establishes the radio connection with eNodeB, and then NAS layer at UE registers it with MME. Since NAS operation immediately follows the successful RRC connection, NAS message piggybacks the last successful RRC message [10], to reduce the signaling overhead and, speeds up the device registration procedure [11].

We show that LTE protocol's inter-layer interaction is the culprit of bypassing security setup. For example, LTE core network processes *Attach Request* message, without even authenticating the device. Similarly, *device Power-off, Location Update procedure, device Idle to Connected Mode operation,* and many other messages can be executed without authentication due to inter-layer communication.

In this paper, we show how seemingly innocuous protocol interaction can cause serious security threats to users' activity in the network. We have found that the vulnerabilities arise when different layers (1) accept the messages from each other without inquiring the true identity of the sender and network functions, (2) execute the message without establishing the authenticity of the message, and (3) do not validate the packets that were sent before the authentication was established.

---

[2] The communication between UE and eNodeB is performed by RRC.

[3] The communication between UE and MME is performed by NAS.

2.2   Access Technologies Inter-radio Interaction

Cellular technology evolved from GSM (2G) to WCDMA (3G), and then to LTE (4G). Since LTE coverage is not universal, most cell phones incorporate 2G and 3G systems along with 4G support. This solution of combining WCDMA-GSM-LTE (GWL) has indeed many advantages. First, the device can switch to legacy 2G/3G preferred radio access network in the absence of LTE network coverage. Second, in absence of Voice over LTE (VoLTE) feature, LTE can fallback to 3G/2G voice support over circuit switch (CS).

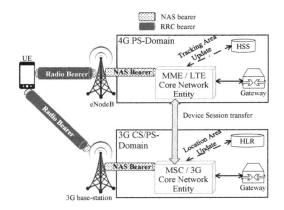

Fig. 2. Inter-radio access technologies (IRAT) interaction

In order to realize preferred network access, GWL radio technologies need to interact with each other via handover procedure, where user session should be seamlessly transferred from one radio technology to the other. Figure 2 depicts an inter-radio communication scenario. At first, the device is connected to LTE network. When handover condition to 3G/2G network arises (such as LTE coverage becomes weaker than 3G signal strength, or LTE system needs to fallback to 3G for CS call), MME transfers user session to 3G core-network function (known as Mobile Switching Center - MSC). This user session also includes the device security vectors on which the device was originally authenticated with the LTE network. The vulnerability arises when target network (3G in this case) skips device authentication procedure, believing that the device native security context is still valid.

When the device successfully completes the handover to 3G, it updates its location at Home Location Register (HLR). This location update procedure is carried out in order to locate the device during its idle period. Since device location update procedure is also part of inter-radio switch, the location update procedure is also exempted from security protection. The attacker tricks the network believing that location update request message is sent by a true originator.

In the next section, we discuss our experimental methodology that discusses vulnerabilities validation in operational LTE network, and converting these vulnerabilities into attack.

3   Experimental Methodology

To validate each vulnerability, we are required to log complete device traces. LTE modem vendors (e.g., Qualcomm or Mediatek) let developers collect LTE protocol traces. Tools such Qualcomm eXtensible Diagnostic Monitor (QXDM) [12] and MobileInsight [13] help to collect LTE protocol traces in operational LTE network. The real challenge is the modification of control message contents for LTE modem. The current modem implementation is hidden and the programmer does not get any interface to inject his commands. Although, AT commands [14] are provided to activate/deactivate the device session with the network, the modem does not allow us to change the contents of these messages (such as security capabilities). We found that LTE modem's functionalities are controlled by non-volatile memory items/NV items. There are around 65535 NV items, holding values from device capabilities to its functioning parameters. In fact, the mobile phone vendors change these NV items to restore phone configurations. Figure 3(left) shows freeware tool that allows us to read/write phone's NV items.

Fig. 3. NV reader/writer tool that modifies non-volatile memory of device (left), service programmer that helps to launch attack from device (center), and our testbed consisting of commodity hardware and open source platform (right) that helps to validate vulnerabilities at the network side

We validated the existence of vulnerabilities by modifying the Non-Volatile Memory of the LTE modem. Then we used Qualcomm's service-programmer tool (QPST Service Programmer) [15], and AT-command tool (TeraTerm) [2] to communicate with the device chipset. For example, we first let the device enter into sleep mode and then issued *"Detach Request (power-off)"* message using AT-command. Section 4 explores this type of attack.

In order to understand how different protocol layers communicate in a feedback loop, we parse the traces and analyse to confirm LTE standard vulnerabilities.

Last, we assess the practical implication of vulnerabilities by converting them into attacks. We launched the attacks either using Qualcomm service programmer [15] or deploying our testbed. The Qualcomm service programmer helps modify device parameters. By changing these parameters, the adversary can impersonate victim device. Since certain messages are accepted without integrity check, the network believes as if it is talking to the actual device. For some other type of attacks, we are required to provide proof of concept model using a testbed. There are a number of 3GPP compliant open source LTE implementations, such as OpenEPC [16], OpenAirInterface [17], and OpenLTE [18]. Our testbed setup includes gateways (Serving-GW and PDN-GW), LTE core-network entity (MME), subscriber information database (HSS), and external network proxy – all implemented in software, as well as an eNodeB. We have used two Android phones (i.e. Samsung S4 (with Qualcomm's LTE modem MDM-9215 chipset), and S5 (with Qualcomm's LTE modem MDM-9635 chipset)) with USIM cards programmed with the appropriate identification name and secret code to connect with the base-station. Figure 3 (right) gives a snapshot of our testbed that consists of commodity hardware devices including two smart-phones, 3G femto-cell, power monitor tool, and a laptop.

The following sections dig deep into the root causes of major exposed vulnerabilities, reveal how these security loopholes arise, and what special attacks can be launched to exploit the LTE protocol's weaknesses.

4 Weak Authentication: Non-authentic Messages Are Accepted

LTE employs power saving mechanisms in which device enters into *RRC Idle state* when it has nothing to send/receive any data (CS or PS). In *RRC Idle state*, the UE releases its radio connection and deactivates the security connection with eNodeB. When UE has some data to send/receive, the UE establishes its radio connection with eNodeB and switches to *RRC Connected state*. After moving to *RRC Connected state*, the device renews its RRC security with eNodeB. However, a threat exists when the UE is able to communicate with the network before activating its radio security procedure. In fact it is allowed by the network to boost device performance by preparing network resources for the UE beforehand.

4.1 Vulnerabilities

When the device enters into connected state, the protocol layers interact to facilitate each other's functions to improve the response time from the network. Issues arise when these protocol functions are used to carry unauthorized traffic.

In the following subsections, we discuss how such protocol interaction can be vulnerable when the security shield is not yet in place.

Blind Forwarding. The logical division of protocols into different layers provide distributed functionality for complex LTE operation. A single protocol cannot perform any functionality without communicating with layers above and below. Such interaction is divided into two different parts where, (1) one layer communicates with the layer immediately above or below, and (2) a layer communicates with another layer which is either significantly far in the protocol stack or located at remote host. In case of (2), the intermediate layers simply relay anonymous packets. For example, a mobile device establishes RRC layer connection with eNodeB while the device forms NAS layer connection with MME through the eNodeB (refer to Fig. 1). The eNodeB relays NAS messages to MME without looking into the message contents [19]. Such an implementation removes security threats between the device and core-network communication, in case the eNodeB is compromised. Hence, message forwarding without any inspection across different layers of protocols is rooted in the design.

Disjoint Identifications. There are a number of different identities used in LTE, grouped based on their function and usage scenarios. For example, IMSI (International Mobile Subscriber Identity) is a permanent subscriber identity used by mobile operators to identify the mobile subscribers. Leakage of such identity can lead to a number of user privacy issues. Therefore, a Temporary Mobile Subscriber Identity (TMSI) is used instead to ensure the privacy of the mobile subscriber. The network provides mapping between IMSI and TMSI to establish on demand network resources for the device.

LTE network further maintains other identities and group them according to their usage in different network functions. Some of these identities are commissioned upon equipment installation, others are provisioned by the operator before or during service operation, and some are created when user accesses the network for its services. Table 2 sums up all LTE identities as per their classification. We find that some of the identities are not mapped with any other identity in their group. That is, these identities do not hold any identity relation and remain disjoint. This introduces the potential threat where one part of user traffic is communicated with its true identity, whereas the rest of communication is allowed to be carried out by fake identity.

Table 2. Classification of LTE identifications

Group	LTE ID name	Usage
UE ID	IMSI, GUTI, S-TMSI, IP address, C-RNTI, eNodeB UE S1AP ID, MME UE S1AP ID, Old UE X2AP ID, UE X2AP ID	UE, eNodeB and MME
Mobile Hardware ID	IMEI	UE and MME
Location ID	TAI, TAC	UE and MME
Session ID	PDN ID (APN), EPS Bearer ID, E-RAB ID, DRAB ID, TEID, LBI	UE and MME

When the device attaches with the network it receives a number of identities. The MME assigns TMSI to UE based on which the UE can be uniquely identified at MME. Similarly, the eNodeB assigns C-RNTI[4] to distinguish the devices within the radio network. The S1AP[5] layer handles the control messages between an eNodeB and an MME. In order to tell which control message is for which UE, an eNodeB allocates an ID (eNodeB UE S1AP ID) to each UE when it sends the message for a UE to an MME. Similarly, in order to tell which control message is for which UE in which eNodeB, the MME allocates an ID (MME UE S1AP ID) to each UE when it sends the first message for a UE to an eNodeB. Both eNodeB UE S1AP ID and MME UE S1AP ID have one to one mapping that distinguishes a UE across MME and eNodeB.

When the eNodeB receives the message, it maps the UE C-RNTI with eNodeB UE S1AP ID and forwards the packet to MME. The S1AP layer of MME receives the message and forwards it to the MME core function. The MME recognizes UE based on IMSI/TMSI and performs the desired action.

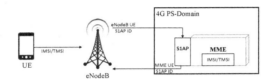

Fig. 4. Different identities are used at various network functions

A potential vulnerability occurs due to the missing mapping between MME UE S1AP ID and IMSI. As shown in Fig. 4, the device generates the NAS message by putting victim's IMSI and sends this to eNodeB. When the eNodeB receives the message from the device, it correctly maps the device C-RNTI and its associated S1AP ID pair, and forwards the message to MME. The MME S1AP layer removes the S1AP header and forwards the actual message to MME core function. The MME core function does not have any mapping between S1AP ID and associated IMSI, therefore, it takes action based on provided IMSI without checking whether the originator of the message is genuine subscriber or not.

Blind Execution of Messages. As stated earlier, when the device switches from idle state to connected state, it is required to establish radio security. Before such security messages exchange take place, certain messages need to be executed first. These messages are (1) type of operation the device has requested (2) the network resources that the device operation may need, etc. Such messages are exchanged between the device and the network, which are executed at both sides in order to establish the type of activity to be performed next.

---

[4] Cell Radio Network Temporary Identifier (C-RNTI) identifies UE over the air.
[5] S1AP facilitates control-plane traffic between eNodeB and MME.

To take an example, NAS *Service Request* message informs MME about the type of service (such as, PS data or CS call etc.) the UE needs imminently. To prepare the resources that the UE requires, eNodeB forwards such request to MME before initiating RRC security procedure[6]. When MME receives the NAS message, it executes the message even if message authentication code included in the message fails the integrity check or cannot be verified (Sect. 4.4.4.3 *Integrity checking of NAS signalling messages* in LTE NAS specification [19]). Such actions help network to quickly prepare network resources for device but comes at the cost of security risks where an attacker can get unauthenticated messages executed at MME. There exists a vulnerability when the attacker makes MME processes non-integrity protected message. For example, the attacker sends a non-integrity protected *Service Request* message to MME and puts victim's TMSI in the message. MME first receives and then processes the NAS *Service Request* message where it finds the message to be non-integrity protected. The MME generates *Service Reject* message by rejecting the request with cause "*UE identity cannot be derived by the network*" and sends this message to victim UE. On receiving *Service Reject* message, victim device enters into deregistered state and initiates the attach procedure. In short, an attacker can exploit those NAS messages which are processed by MME even if these messages are not integrity protected.

4.2   Attacks and Validation

The three vulnerabilities explained above are rooted in the LTE protocol design and can be exploited even when LTE security shields are well in place. We assume that all components function normally without any misconfiguration, malware, or intrusion. We further assume that all other mechanisms in cellular networks and at other mobile clients work properly. Irrespective of such measures, the attacker can still leverage improper operations at network function to launch attacks against victim.

The attacker connects to radio network as a legitimate user. Once the radio connection has been setup, it announces victim's identity in the NAS message and requests radio layer (RRC) to forward it to MME. The MME receives the message from eNodeB and assumes that the message is part of the chain of steps needed for specific device operation. The MME then executes the message and sends back an acknowledgement to the victim.

This threat becomes more powerful when the attacker is able to execute the message on behalf of victim without asking for an acknowledgement.

---

[6] Section 5.3.3 *RRC connection establishment* procedure and Sect. 5.3.4 *Initial security activation* in LTE RRC specification [20]. Note that initial NAS message (such as *Service Request*) is sent as a piggybacked message with *RRCConnectionSetupComplete* message that eNodeB forwards to MME. However, *SecurityModeCommand* message is sent thereafter.

Fig. 5. (a) The victim's identity can be obtained from broadcast paging message (b) Detach message is created by using victim's identity

Detach a Victim from the Network Through Spoofed Message. In this exploit, the attacker can detach any device from the network. This attack is launched when RRC layer at device communicates with the NAS layer at MME. When the device switches from idle state to connected state, it first establishes the RRC connection. The device is allowed to send piggybacked NAS message with the acknowledgement of radio connection setup (i.e. *RRC Setup Complete* message). The attacker takes advantage of this and sends UE *Detach Request* message with an action of *power-off* to MME by putting victim's identity in the message. Once the MME receives the message, it first verifies the integrity of the message by checking message authentication code of the message. Because this message is not originated from legal subscriber, the integrity check fails at MME. However, LTE standard mandates the *Detach Request* message with *power-off* type should be processed by MME even if its integrity check fails or even the message does not include message authentication code (Sects. 4.4.4.3 and 5.5.2.2.2 in [19]). Once the MME receives the message, it takes an action for *power-off* request by releasing victim's network resources. Note that the *device power-off* reason does not trigger acknowledgement from the network to the victim device (Fig. 5.5.2.2.1.1: UE initiated detach procedure in LTE NAS specification [19]) that makes victim device wrongly believe that MME is out of service. The victim device remains out-of-service until victim performs hard-reboot on device or uses airplane mode feature to initiate the device attach procedure.

In order to launch this attack, the adversary needs to expose the victim's identity, which can be obtained from the following procedure.

Exposing Victim's Identity. When the device attaches with the network, it is assigned with TMSI. All the communication between the device and the network is based on TMSI. The TMSI is valid until the UE remains within the reach of serving MME – which typically handles all the devices within a large metropolitan city [21].

The device enters into idle state when it has nothing to send or receive. If a PS data or CS call is destined for the device during idle state, the MME sends *paging-message*[7] to that device. On receiving this *paging message*, the device

---

[7] Paging message is a control beacon sent from LTE network to a device, when packet switched (PS) data, or circuit switched (CS) call is impending at LTE core network. These paging messages are sent when device is in *RRC Idle state*.

enters into connected state and receives the traffic. Since the device has no active connection with the network during idle period, the *paging-messages* are broadcast in nature. All the neighboring devices receive the paging message and discard it if their identity is not listed in the message. Note that the attacker is a legitimate device connected with LTE network which also receives the paging messages destined for other devices. The attacker can simply get the TMSI of the victim out of the paging message.

The attacker can also originate a *paging message* towards the victim device. It should be recalled that whenever the device receives an incoming voice call during idle state, it is paged by the core-network. Therefore, simply calling victim's phone number and then hanging up even before the phone rings, triggers a *paging message*. The attacker gets hold of this paging message (because paging messages are broadcasted within MME tracking area[8]) and maps the victim's TMSI value with its phone number.

We run device traces and get victims identity through *paging message* (as shown in Fig. 5a). Then the adversary generates *Detach request message* (Fig. 5b) piggybacked over RRC (Fig. 6).

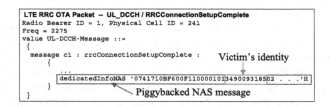

Fig. 6. The RRC layer helps to deliver NAS message when RRC protocol interacts with NAS protocol

To launch this attack, we first register the victim device (Samsung Galaxy S4 smartphone), and the attacker device (Samsung Galaxy S5 smartphone) with our LTE testbed platform. Once both victim device and attacker are registered, the attacker sends *Detach Request message* (i.e. AT + CFUN = 0) in device *RRC idle mode*, as shown in Fig. 7. Note that in this detach request message, attacker can masquerade victim device identity (TMSI). On receiving the detach request message, the MME finds the detach-request type as *Power-off* and immediately releases the associated device connection with Serving GW and PDN GW. We captured wireshark logs (as shown in Fig. 8) that reveal on receiving the detach-request, the UE connection is cleared by MME, serving GW and PDN GW. The associated device is said to be "detached" and "deregistered" from core-network's view.

---

[8] The tracking area is a logical concept of an area where a user can move around without updating the MME. In operational network, one tracking area spans to a number of eNodeBs.

Fig. 7. The device logs showing that the detach procedure is invoked over unsecured channel

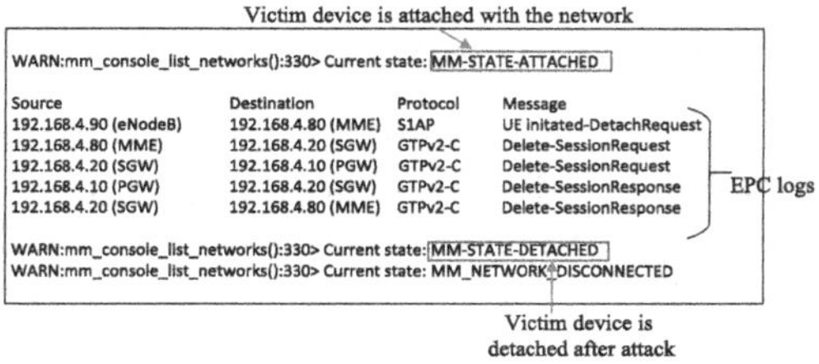

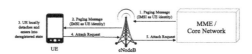

Fig. 8. The victim device is detached from the network on receiving detach request from attacker.

Detach Multiple Victims from the Network Through Broadcast Message. The UE monitors a paging channel during *RRC idle* state to detect its pending notification. The UE can be paged through either of its identities, i.e. TMSI or IMSI. The LTE standard makes distinction between paging messages generated with TMSI and with IMSI. Paging using IMSI is defined as abnormal procedure used for error recovery in the network (Sect. 5.6.2.2.2 *Paging for EPS services through E-UTRAN using IMSI* in LTE NAS specification [19]). The network may initiate paging using IMSI (as shown in Fig. 9) if the TMSI is not available due to a network failure. Upon reception of a paging using IMSI, the UE locally deactivates any bearer context(s), detaches itself locally from LTE network and changes the state to *Network DEREGISTERED*. After performing the local detach, the UE then performs an attach procedure.

Fig. 9. The device detach procedure is invoked over insecure channel

In our attack model, the attacker uses this abnormal condition to its advantage and kicks victim out of the network. Because the paging messages are in plain text and broadcast in nature, these messages cannot be secured. Furthermore, the device executes such messages while it has not maintained any connection with the network (as it has torn down secure connection with the network before entering into idle mode). This fact brings security vulnerability where an attacker can detach the device by simply generating paging messages using IMSI as device identity. The impact of such vulnerability is enormous where an attacker can take down all of the devices connected to one eNodeB [19].

Exposing Victim's IMSI Identity Through Side Channel. The network operator allocates a unique IMSI to each subscriber, and embeds it to customer USIM card. In order to support the subscriber identity confidentiality, the MME allocates TMSI to mobile subscribers, when the mobile device establishes a new connection with MME. Thereafter, TMSI is used as UE identity for all subsequent messages exchange between UE and MME.

Therefore, finding the IMSI of the victim is a challenging task. Although, previous studies [22,23] have used special hardware [24], to expose the IMSI of a device, we discovered a new method to obtain the device IMSI using commodity hardware, i.e. 3G femto-cell.

We discover whenever the 3G femto-cell is brought within the proximity of a UE, this UE detaches from its LTE eNodeB and camps with 3G femto-cell. This is because the UE finds femto-cell signal strength higher than the serving LTE eNodeB and performs handover to femto-cell. We noticed that during this handover messages exchange, the 3G core-network sends an *identity request* message to the device, where UE responds with its IMSI. We observe this behavior because femto-cell and the eNodeB do not have any direct link with each other. As a consequence, the LTE MME does not send device security keys to 3G core-network, and let the 3G network re-authenticate the user. In order to derive the security keys, the 3G core-network needs to expose IMSI of the device and generate challenge/response messages as part of UE authentication procedure.

Note that *identity request/response* message exchange occurs prior to establishment of device security. This makes these message exchange non-encrypted and can be logged at femto-cell. Since the femto-cell is a closed 3G base-station, *we hacked the femto-cell and defeated its in-place hardware and software security mechanisms*[9].

Once we espied victim (connected to operational LTE network carrier) IMSI through side channel, we now require the victim device to perform cell reselection to our testbed eNodeB. LTE defines priority-based cell reselection in which

---

[9] Because femtocells are part of operator network, therefore, operators take both hardware and software security measures to secure it. Therefore, as shown in Fig. 3 (right), we only broke small part of femtocell cover, just to access the debugging pins (JP1, JP2, JP5, JP6, PL2, etc.). We used *screen command* to dump femtocell memory image. Then uncompressed it, reversed the kernel image, and looked for user information in */etc/passwd* file. We then applied brute force technique to decode the password string within 7 days.

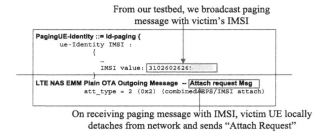

From our testbed, we broadcast paging
message with victim's IMSI

On receiving paging message with IMSI, victim UE locally
detaches from network and sends "Attach Request"

Fig. 10. The network and UE logs show that the paging message with victim's IMSI
can detach the victim device from the network

the device in Idle state periodically monitors its neighboring cells. The priority
based cell reselection ensures that the device always stay connected with higher
priority cell [25]. The operational LTE eNodeB informs its associated devices
about cell priorities through broadcast SIB messages. We sniff SIB4 and SIB5
parameters that define Intra-frequency and Inter-frequency LTE neighboring
cells priorities [20] and configure our testbed eNodeB accordingly. We configure
our eNodeB's cell as of higher cell priorities as compared to operational LTE
eNodeB. This tricks victim device to camp over our testbed eNodeB cell. Once
the victim device is camped with our eNodeB cell, we generate paging message
(where we put UE identity as IMSI) towards the victim device. The victim device
treats forged paging message as if it is coming from legitimate eNodeB. Soon
after sending paging message, we turn-off our configured eNodeB. This is an
important step that makes victim device to camp on operational eNodeB cell
that forwards device attach message to operational MME. It is possible that the
victim device goes through Radio Link Failure (RLF) as it was disconnected
from our testbed eNodeB cell when it initiated the Attach Request message
(after detaching locally). On re-establishing the radio connection (RRCConnec-
tionRestablishment procedure), the victim device re-sends the Attach Request
message (when it does not receive the reply to its first Attach Request message).
We show this in Fig. 10, on receiving the paging message with IMSI, the victim device detaches and sends a new *Attach Request* message to LTE network
operator.

Impact and Limitation. In first variant of UE detach attack, the attacker
can kick victim device out of the network without raising any alarm at victim
device. The victim will observe out-of-network-service symbol until reboot. We
believe that the victim will not reboot his device thinking that his mobile device
will recover from network outage automatically. We must point out that any
implementation that binds the device across all its identities (such as binding of
eNodeB UE S1APID, MME UE S1AP ID, and device IMSI/TMSI) can restrain
the attack. We discuss this in Suggested Remedies Sect. 7.

In our second variant of the attack, we can generate one paging control message, and can potentially take down all the devices connected within the tracking

area (e.g. a shopping mall or an office space etc.). The paging message allows the network to address multiple recipients by putting their identities (IMSI/TMSI) in one paging message body. Such paging message is sent to all eNodeBs defined within one tracking area. This can potentially cause network outage to all the UEs connected to these eNodeBs. The impact of this attack is limited because the device automatically reconnects with the network after detaching. Nevertheless, an attacker can keep generating paging messages with IMSI as UE identity that will keep UE barred from accessing network services.

5   Weak Security Association: Security Handshake is Skipped on Inter-radio Communication

In this section, we disclose weaknesses of inter-radio interactions. Although, each radio access technology (RAT) (e.g. 4G/3G/2G) is secured when working standalone but breaks security mechanisms when these RATs interact with each other. We find that such weaknesses pose serious threats to user privacy and security.

5.1   Vulnerabilities

The handover procedure is initiated when UE's RAT source coverage starts fading and neighboring RAT coverage starts getting better. The Inter-RAT handover is also triggered when the device initiates or receives a circuit switched call. Once the handover decision is made by the source eNodeB, the handover preparation phase is started at the target base station (3G/2G). During this phase, the target network prepares the resources for an incoming connection. Once the target base station is ready to serve the mobile UE's PS/CS functionality, the source eNodeB transfers the device context to the target network. This also includes the transfer of UE security keys, which basically allows the target network and UE to use old security context and avoid lengthy AKA procedure [26]. This security context is transferred once the network can use mapped security context for follow-up communication.

The use of old security session, potentially leads to serious vulnerability, where the unauthenticated messages are accepted by the network, believing that the source device is secure.

Network Accepts Location Area Update (LAU) Request Before Confirming Device Identity. Once a device is in 2G/3G network, it sends the LAU request message to its network. Its possible that the device's temporary identity (TMSI/GUTI) has expired at the network. In this case, the network initiates the identification procedure by sending an *Identity Request* message to the mobile device. Upon receiving the *Identity Request* message, the mobile device sends back an *Identity Response* message containing device identification parameters. Because the device identity was unknown when the network received the original LAU request message, any security context should be considered void.

But we have found that the network accepts the LAU request message after receiving the *Identity Response* and does not ask the device to authenticate itself. The root cause of this issues lies in the way legacy networks treat two procedures. In this case, Identity Request and LAU procedures are treated independently (Sects. 4.7.8 and 4.4.4 of Core Network Protocols specification [27] define Identity and LAU procedures, respectively). As a result, LAU procedure resumes after getting device identity; and do not authenticate the device that has responded the Identity Request message.

There is a potential for an attacker to send masqueraded LAU request message where the network asks the attacker to verify its identity without authenticating it. Figure 11 shows the logs for a device sending LAU request message, and the network does not ask for any authentication.

Fig. 11. Location Area Update procedure is accepted without authenticating the sender

Inter-RAT Switch Can Circumvent Location Update Procedure. LTE to WCDMA handover is a frequent phenomena, where device moves from LTE to WCDMA for CS voice call, and comes back to LTE from WCDMA for PS data access after voice call. We find that on successful handover to LTE network, the device does not perform the LAU procedure - known as Tracking Area Update (TAU) in LTE. This is contrary to the switch from LTE to 3G/2G where the LAU is mandatory.

In fact, this is an accepted operation defined in LTE standard. It is stated that when LTE MME has native security context for the UE and does not receive a TAU request within a certain period of time, after the inter-RAT switch, it "shall *assume*" that UE and MME share a native security context (Sect. 9.2.2 From UTRAN to E-UTRAN in [28]). Furthermore, a separate LTE specification mandates the TAU request procedure as optional when the inter-RAT switch does not induce the device location change (such as user makes a voice call within its tracking area) (Sect. 5.3.3 in [29]). These two statements from two different standards are conflicting, where the device although has changed its tracking area but does not send TAU request, making MME wrongly believe that the device's tracking area has not changed.

5.2 Attacks and Validation

We have shown how an attacker can hijack the LAU request message and can render victim device unreachable from the network. This location hijacking does not raise any alarm at the network, and it believes that the device is not reachable because it is either out of coverage or powered off. On the other hand, the victim device does not make any effort to re-establish the connection with the network, believing that it has correct location registered and currently does not have any data pending from the network to be delivered.

Hijacking Location Update. In this attack, the attacker hijacks the victim location by artificially making the victim device do inter-RAT switch. The attacker ensures that the attack remains unnoticed even when the victim moves back to its original RAT (usually LTE network). Figure 12 shows the steps to launch the attack. First the attacker establishes legitimate radio connection with 3G base station (steps 1 and 2) and artificially induces the inter-RAT switch handover (HO) at victim device, registered with LTE network, (step 3). The attacker can simply do it by dialing a phone call towards the victim device and then hanging it up. Upon receiving the voice call, victim device switches to 3G RAT and sends the LAU request to 3G network (step 4). At the same time, the attacker generates LAU request NAS message by putting victim TMSI and wrong location area code in the message body (step 5) and sends it to 3G base station. The 3G base station will forward this message without looking its content to 3G core-network (step 6). Now 3G core-network has received duplicate LAU messages (but with different location identities) for the same victim device, and updates the device location mentioned in the latter message [30]. When the attacker hangs up the call, victim device again performs the switch back to LTE network. Because the victim device has not moved since it has received the phone call, and its location area code has not changed, it does not need to perform TAU procedure with the LTE network [28]. Therefore, the user context including its location will be propagated to LTE network from 3G/2G network. This will result in an unreachable LTE network (because the LTE system will page the UE at wrong location).

We validated the attack through emulation mode [31]. The device is first attached with LTE core network where device initiates handover to 3G MSC. During LAU procedure, we modify the location area code of the device and

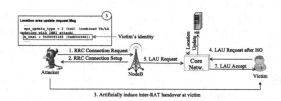

Fig. 12. Location Area Update hijack attack

confirm the device successfully performs handover to 3G (with wrong location area code). On handover from 3G to 4G, the device does not trigger TAU procedure. Afterwards, device initiates the data traffic to confirm 3G to 4G handover was successful.

Impact and Limitation. The attack leaves the victim device in a state in which it can neither receive voice call nor incoming data traffic. The impact of this attack vanishes when both of these conditions are met: (1) the device switches back to LTE from 3G/2G RAT, and (2) the *Periodic TAU* timer has expired at device. The *Periodic TAU* is used to notify the availability of UE to network periodically. The procedure is controlled by UE through *periodic tracking area update* timer, which was sent by the network during device registration procedure. Once *periodic TAU* timer expires, UE establishes the secure network connection and notifies its location, which results in correct UE location to be updated at the network.

However, the timer value is carrier network dependent, which can also be defined as zero (i.e. periodic TAU is deactivated at the device) [26]. In normal operational network, it is defined to be few hours [32].

The second limitation of this attack is related to timing of the attack. The attacker needs to generate a fake LAU request message soon after the victim device has sent out his LAU request message. We believe such timing interval is easy to observe as the attacker can calculate inter-message delay by logging cellular traces prior to launching the attack.

6   Lack of Access Control/Non-authorization

The operators need to deploy servers that keep track of millions of their subscribers, and provide adequate mechanisms for service provisioning, billing, and other services that are available to the subscribers. Once the user is authenticated, the first job of these servers is to identify whether the user is authorized to access certain service or not. In short, the network deploys authorization mechanism even for an authenticated user.

However, LTE standard does not define an authorization procedure at the UE. If the authentication is successful with the network, the device deem all the communication from the network authorized. The authorization measures are also missing for base station (eNodeB). We found that the device subscription and permission control actions are taken only at core-network (MME). When a device fails these checks, it is not allowed to access core-network functions, but this device can still keep its radio connection with eNodeB.

6.1   Vulnerabilities

When the UE is relying on authentication to ensure that the network is authorized to send packets, things change dramatically in the absence of such authentication.

Unconditional Trust Across Protocol Layers. In order to perform an atomic operation, LTE protocol layers need to carry each other messages. There is no defined security mechanism for such inter-layer communication. Thus, the trust model between protocol layers is unconditional.

For example, during *RRC idle state operation*, the UE is *paged* by MME via eNodeB. These *paging messages* contain information which the core-network wants to convey to the device and are used to instruct the device for a particular action. In Fig. 5a, the *paging message* includes the device identity, recognized by MME, and an action to be taken (*cn-domain PS*, i.e. PS data is waiting for the device). Hence, UE blindly authorizes such inter-layer functions to deliver messages. It has been assumed that each link from MME to eNodeB, and from eNodeB to UE is trusted while forwarding the packets to the next link. In this way, the attacker establishes trusted link with eNodeB and injects malicious traffic to the UE and MME.

Permission Control Decisions Are Not Disseminated Across Network. The device authorization procedure is divided into two parts, whether the device is allowed to (1) access particular operator network, and (2) use network services.

When a device powers on, it determines Mobile Network Code (MNC)[10] from USIM and performs cell selection procedure. After appropriate cell selection, the device camps on that cell. Thereafter, UE establishes radio connection with eNodeB. This access control procedure ensures that the device connects to allowed network operator's eNodeB.

If the user is allowed to access network radio resources, it sends NAS control messages to initiate core-network services. On receiving first NAS control message (*Attach Request* message), the HSS authenticates the device and populates device permission control list to MME. In case the device does not have any permission to access the network, the MME refuses the connection request. Since UE and MME communicates over NAS, the eNodeB remains unaware that UE connection has been rejected by MME. As a result, the device radio connection between UE and eNodeB remains alive and the unauthorized device can launch radio attacks. We have found that this vulnerability arises if the MME does not tear down UE connection with eNodeB. In principle, when the UE breaks its connection with MME (such as through *Detach Request* message), the MME propagates UE connection release message to eNodeB (UE Context Release (MME initiated) procedure in S1AP specification [33]). Then the eNodeB releases the device radio connection. But access control verification failure does not trigger UE connection release message from MME to eNodeB. This allows the device to keep only RRC connection even in the absence of NAS connection. It violates the LTE design principle where the device in connected state should keep both connections (RRC and NAS).

---

[10] MNC uniquely identifies a mobile network operator.

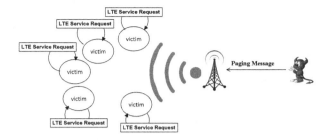

Fig. 13. The paging broadcast message can be used to drain batteries of multiple devices

6.2   Attacks and Validation

This vulnerability is explored through an attacker that can successfully communicate with the device without its consent. Since there is no authorization or access control at UE side, the UE can always be tricked into processing unauthorized packets.

Silently Draining Victims' Battery. In order to save battery power, the mobile device enters *RRC idle state* by switching off its transceiver. In idle state, the device observes Discontinuous Reception (DRX). The DRX duty cycle is divided into DRX active and DRX idle states. On DRX active, the UE listens to the radio channel to receive the control signals from the network. On pending CS call/PS data, the device is instructed (through broadcast *paging messages*) to secure its connection with the network. When the device finds its TMSI in the paging message, it sends the *Service Request*[11] message in plaintext to the network. Thereafter, the security setup procedure starts and device delivers/receives its data.

As shown in Fig. 13, the attacker gets benefit of the fact that device takes action on its paging message. The adversary generates a paging message by addressing multiple victims about their pending CS/PS data. On receiving this message, all addressed victim devices will send *Service Request* message to the network. These devices will stay awake for a configurable amount of period (usually 10 s) [20]. By sending this paging message to these victim periodically, the attacker can never let these victim devices enter into *RRC idle state*. This single *paging message* can drain battery power of multiple mobile devices.

For our validation, we logged LTE packets and ensured the victim UE enters in RRC idle state. The victim UE which is also connected with Monsoon power monitor [34] is placed under good radio coverage (i.e. around −90 dBm). This ensures the device remains in idle state and does not perform any radio measurements for handover procedure.

Once the phone is in idle state, the attacker generates the paging message for the victim. To do so, the attacker dials a voice call to the victim phone, but

---

[11] Service Request establishes UE connection with MME, when uplink/downlink data is to be sent/received at device idle state.

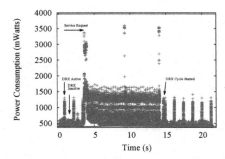

Fig. 14. The energy consumption from idle to connected state transition and then staying in connected state

hangs-up before the phone even rings. We noticed that dialing a call for a couple of seconds, triggers a paging message with *cn-domain CS* (i.e. the device should wake-up to receive CS call).

On receiving the paging message, the victim device enters into *RRC connected mode* and generates *Service Request message* to MME. The MME first authenticates the UE and then establishes the requested core network resources. After few seconds, when MME does not receive any data activity from the victim device, it requests eNodeB to release radio resources for the connected UE. The device enters into idle mode after receiving the *radio connection release* message from eNodeB.

Figure 14 shows power trace for the victim UE under attack. We can see when the device is in idle state, it observes *DRX idle* and *DRX active* states by consuming 500 mW and 1300 mW power values, respectively. But as soon as the phone receives a paging message, it ramps up its radio and sends *Service Request message* that brings the power consumption to as high as 3500 mW. After sending the *Service Request message*, the UE exchanges authentication messages with MME (which is marked by two other high power consumption peaks in Fig. 14) and keeps connected to the radio network. In Fig. 14, we can also see that the overall power consumption in *RRC Connected* state is 3X-4X higher compared to *RRC Idle* state. Therefore, by generating paging broadcast messages, the attacker can silently drain the victim battery power.

We drained victim's device battery by generating paging request messages in an interval of 10 s. Note that, on the expiration of *device inactivity timer* at MME (which is 10 s), the MME releases the device bearers and device switches back to idle state. In this attack, we aim to bypass the victim device's *inactivity timer* by generating paging messages every 10 s.

7   Suggested Remedies

In this section, we suggest some remedies to address the discussed vulnerabilities. Our proposal seeks to mitigate the impact from the attacks, within current LTE standard (i.e. 3GPP standard). We should point out that the device, eNodeB, and core-network entities are 3GPP compliant and any vendor specific implementation, conflicting with the LTE standard, may fail inter-operability between devices and the network functions. Therefore, these vulnerabilities need to be discussed in the 3GPP standard for a permanent solution. Below, we propose some quick fixes for the discussed attacks.

Detach Attack Prevention. Once the operator receives the non-integrity protected "power-off" request message from the device, it should consult its database to resolve device identity (IMSI or TMSI) to eNodeB-S1AP-ID. If the received and look-up eNodeB-S1AP-IDs do not match, the network should discard the "power-off" message.

In order to address device detach using paging message, the device vendor should keep the counter value for "paging using IMSI" request messages. If the counter value exceeds a threshold defined by the vendor, the device should discard any follow-up *paging request messages*. Note that, in this attack, the adversary needs to periodically send "paging using IMSI" request messages to refrain UE from gaining network resources.

Location Update Hijack Attack Prevention. TAU procedure must always be executed whenever the device changes its RAT. We believe this security solution should not impact device performance, because the TAU procedure only generates 2 signaling messages (*TAU Request and TAU Reply* messages). Since the TAU request message is always sent as integrity protected, the attacker cannot generate TAU request message on behalf of victim device.

Moreover, the network must not accept LAU request message for a device whose identity is unknown. In case the network needs to resolve the device identity (by sending *identity request message*), the security setup procedure must be executed before the LAU request message is accepted at the network.

Battery Drain Attack Prevention. The device should keep a mapping between paging request and gaining network resource. That way, no resources are reserved by the network when the adversary is sending fake paging request messages. Therefore, the device can easily count how many fake paging messages it has received. Once the number of fake paging request messages exceed vendor specific counter value, the device should drop subsequent messages.

8   Related Work

Closest to our work are [3, 7]. [7] disclose performance issues on inter-protocol communication in operational LTE network. However, we discover security vulnerabilities that are rooted in LTE standard and do not discuss any performance bottlenecks. [3] discusses privacy attacks in which signalling information is leveraged to infer user privacy information. Moreover, such attacks are only possible if network operator disables integrity and ciphering protection. For LTE DoS attacks, [3] assumes the attacker can change the message contents (such as device capabilities in *Attach Request*) for non-integrity protected *Attach Request* message. In contrast, this paper discloses security weaknesses of common device operations even if all LTE security mechanisms are well in place. [35] studies how to block the CS service caused by the unwanted traffic in the PS domain. [36] shows that current cellular infrastructures exhibit security loopholes (off-path TCP hijacking) due to their NAT/firewall settings. These contributions exploit operational network configuration issues, which can only be local to a specific operator. [37] proposes a denial-of-service attack on cellular networks by consuming the radio resources of control channels via significant spamming SMSs. However, the attack may not be applied to 4G LTE networks, since SMSs can be delivered to 4G LTE users by PS traffic as Whatsapp without 3G↔4G switches. [38] discloses a attack model to drain the battery of mobile phones via low-rate of retrieval of malicious MMS. However, this attack is not valid when the victim device black list the attacker device phone number. Security on mobile devices and their applications focus on permission control [39], inter-application communication [40,41], plagiarizing applications [42] and leaking privacy information [43] by smartphones. Our attack models do not depend on any given mobile data application.

9 Conclusion

In this work, we have uncovered new vulnerabilities in the current LTE security measures. We learn several lessons from our study. The unsecured messages should not be executed unless the device message integrity procedures are in place. The broadcast messages must also be integrity protected. Since all devices are connected to the same core infrastructure, the core-network messages can also be integrity protected using the public-private key pair.

Acknowledgement. We thank anonymous reviewers for their excellent feedback that has helped to improve the paper. This work is also supported in part by NSF grants (CNS-1422835 and 1528122).

References

1. 3GPP Specification series. http://www.3gpp.org/dynareport/36-series.htm/
2. Tera-Term-A Terminal Emulator. http://ttssh2.sourceforge.jp/index.html.en
3. Shaik, A., Borgaonkar, R., Asokan, N., Niemi, V., Seifert, J.-P.: Practical attacks against privacy and availability in 4G/LTE mobile communication systems. In: NDSS (2016)
4. Jover, R.P.: Security attacks against the availability of LTE mobility networks: overview and research directions. In: IEEE WPMC (2013)
5. Jover, R.P.: LTE security, protocol exploits and location tracking experimentation with low-cost software radio. arXiv preprint arXiv:1607.05171 (2016)
6. The Security Vulnerabilities of LTE: Opportunity and Risks for Operators. http://forums.juniper.net/t5/Industry-Solutions-and-Trends/The-Security-Vulnerabilities-of-LTE-Opportunity-and-Risks-for/ba-p/214477/
7. Tu, G.-H., Li, Y., Peng, C., Li, C.-Y., Wang, H., Lu, S.: Control-plane protocol interactions in cellular networks. In: ACM SIGCOMM (2014)

8. Huang, J., Qian, F., Guo, Y., Zhou, Y., Xu, Q., Mao, Z.M., Sen, S., Spatscheck, O.: An in-depth study of LTE: effect of network protocol and application behavior on performance. In: ACM SIGCOMM Computer Communication Review (2013)
9. LTE protocol layer stack. http://www.tutorialspoint.com/lte/lte_protocol_stack_layers.htm/
10. Ahmadi, S.: LTE-Advanced: A Practical Systems Approach to Understanding 3GPP LTE Releases 10 and 11 Radio Access Technologies, 1st edn. Academic Press, Waltham (2013)
11. Stefania Sesia, M.B., Toufik, I.: LTE - The UMTS Long Term Evolution: From Theory to Practice, 2nd edn. Wiley, Hoboken (2011)
12. Qualcomm: QxDM Professional - QUALCOMM eXtensible Diagnostic Monitor. http://www.qualcomm.com/media/documents/tags/qxdm
13. Mobile Insight. http://mobileinsight.net/
14. AT Commands List. http://www.lte.com.tr/uploads/pdfe/1.pdf
15. QPST Service Programming. http://forum.xda-developers.com/showthread.php?t=1180211
16. Open EPC - open source LTE implementation. http://www.openepc.net/
17. OpenAirInterface. http://www.openairinterface.org/
18. Open LTE. http://openlte.sourceforge.net/
19. 3GPP. TS24.301: Non-Access-Stratum (NAS) protocol for Evolved Packet System (EPS); Stage 3, June 2013
20. 3GPP. TS36.331: Radio Resource Control (RRC) (2012)
21. MME Pool Overlap. http://lteuniversity.com/get_trained/expert_opinion1/b/johnmckeague/archive/2012/03/06/mme-pool-overlap.aspx
22. Borgaonkar, R., Udar, S.: Understanding IMSI privacy. In: Vortrag auf der Konferenz Black Hat (2014)
23. Ginzboorg, P., Niemi, V.: Privacy of the long-term identities in cellular networks. In: Proceedings of the 9th EAI International Conference on Mobile Multimedia Communications, pp. 167–175. ICST (Institute for Computer Sciences, Social-Informatics and Telecommunications Engineering) (2016)
24. Strobel, D.: IMSI catcher. Chair for Communication Security, Ruhr-Universität Bochum, p. 14 (2007)
25. 3GPP. TS36.304: User Equipment procedures in idle mode (2013)
26. Securing the Mobile Network. http://www.us.aviatnetworks.com/media/files/Securing_the_Mobile_Network.pdf/
27. 3GPP. TS24.008: Core Network Protocols (2012)
28. 3GPP. TS33.401: 3GPP SAE; Security architecture, September 2013
29. 3GPP. TS23.401: GPRS Enhancements for E-UTRAN Access (2011)
30. 3GPP. TS23.012: Location management procedures (2011)
31. UE Emulation Mode. https://wiki.phantomnet.org/wiki/phantomnet/oepc-protected/openepc-tutorial/
32. LTE Cat-0 Power Saving Mode: What it Could Mean for Cellular IoT. http://www.eleven-x.com/2015/04/29/lte-cat-0s-power-saving-mode-what-it-could-mean-for-cellular-iot/
33. 3GPP. TS36.413:E-UTRAN S1 Application Protocol (S1AP) (2014)
34. MonSoon Power Monitor Tool. https://www.msoon.com/LabEquipment/PowerMonitor/
35. Traynor, P., McDaniel, P., La Porta, T.: On attack causality in internet-connected cellular networks. In: USENIX Security (2007)
36. Qian, Z., Mao, Z.: Off-path TCP sequence number inference attack-how firewall middleboxes reduce security. In: IEEE Security & Privacy (2012)

37. Enck, W., Traynor, P., McDaniel, P., La Porta, T.: Exploiting open functionality in SMS-capable cellular networks. In: ACM CCS (2005)
38. Racic, R., Ma, D., Chen, H.: Exploiting MMS vulnerabilities to stealthily exhaust mobile phone's battery. In: SecureComm 2006 (2006)
39. Barrera, D., Kayacik, H.G., van Oorschot, P.C., Somayaji, A.: A methodology for empirical analysis of permission-based security models and its application to android. In: ACM CCS (2010)
40. Chin, E., Felt, A.P., Greenwood, K., Wagner, D.: Analyzing inter-application communication in android. In: ACM MobiSys (2011)
41. Marforio, C., Ritzdorf, H., Francillon, A., Capkun, S.: Analysis of the communication between colluding applications on modern smartphones. In: ACM ACSAC (2012)
42. Potharaju, R., Newell, A., Nita-Rotaru, C., Zhang, X.: Plagiarizing smartphone applications: attack strategies and defense techniques. In: ACM ESSoS (2012)
43. Schlegel, R., Zhang, K., Zhou, X., Intwala, M., Kapadia, A., Wang, X.: Soundcomber: a stealthy and context-aware sound trojan for smartphones. In: NDSS (2011)

Achieve Efficient and Privacy-Preserving Proximity Detection Scheme for Social Applications

Fengwei Wang[1,4], Hui Zhu[1(✉)], Rongxing Lu[2], Fen Liu[1], Cheng Huang[3], and Hui Li[1]

[1] State Key Laboratory of Integrated Services Networks,
Xidian University, Xi'an, China
zhuhui@xidian.edu.cn
[2] Faculty of Computer Science, University of New Brunswick, Fredericton, Canada
[3] Department of Electrical and Computer Engineering, University of Waterloo,
Waterloo, Canada
[4] Science and Technology on Communication Networks Laboratory,
Shijiazhuang, China

Abstract. This paper proposes an efficient scheme, named CPSS, to perform privacy-preserving proximity detection based on chiphertext of convex polygon spatial search. We consider a scenario where users have to submit their location and search information to the social application server for accessing proximity detection service of location-based social applications (LBSAs). With proximity detection, users can choose any polygon area on the map and search whether their friends are within the select region. Since the location and search information of users are sensitive, submitting these data over plaintext to the social application server raises privacy concerns. Hence, we propose a novel method, with which users can access proximity detection without divulging their search and location information. Specifically, the data of a user is blurred into chiphertext in client, thus no one can obtain the sensitive information except the user herself/himself. We prove that the scheme can defend various security threats and validate our scheme using a real LBS dataset. Also, we show that our proposed CPSS is highly efficient in terms of computation complexity and communication overhead.

Keywords: Location-based social application · Proximity detection
Privacy-preserving · Convex polygon spatial search

1 Introduction

Nowadays, with the flourish of the location-based service (LBS) and social networking, location-based social applications (LBSAs) have attracted considerable interest. These applications enormously benefit people in a variety of contexts ranging from their work to personal life. For example, when a individual is traveling in a strange place, LBSAs can help her/him meet with friends in the

© ICST Institute for Computer Sciences, Social Informatics and Telecommunications Engineering 2018
X. Lin et al. (Eds.): SecureComm 2017, LNICST 238, pp. 339–355, 2018.
https://doi.org/10.1007/978-3-319-78813-5_17

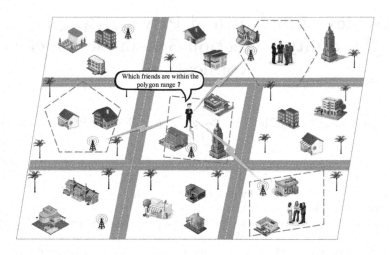

Fig. 1. Conceptual architecture of proximity detection.

surroundings [1–4]. Proximity detection is a high level location based service of LBSAs, which enables a user to choose any range on the map, and search which friends of her/his are within this region, as shown in Fig. 1. Proximity detection with polygon spatial search has been one of the most popular features of LBSAs [5–9].

Although LBSAs benefit people by providing convenient lifestyle, its development still faces severe challenges due to the sensitivity of users' location information [10–16]. For example, users' sensitive information could be analyzed or revealed by LBSAs server easily. Once these sensitive information is obtained by attackers, mobile users may be harmed economically, physically, and legally. Therefore, when users use social applications (such as Wechat, Facebook, Twitter and so on) for location search, their sensitive search and location information cannot be leaked. However, most LBSAs rely on the fact that users submit accurate location over plaintext to the social application server, then the server provides LBS for them. Thus, how to provide accurate LBS search results without divulging users' sensitive information has become a hot spot of LBS research.

Aiming at these above challenges, in this paper, we propose an efficient and privacy-preserving proximity detection scheme for social applications, named CPSS. Specifically, main contributions of this paper are as follows.

- *First*, the proposed CPSS provides a privacy-preserving proximity detection framework for LBSAs. With CPSS, a user can keep her/his search and location information secret from social application servers and other users. Specifically, in our novel CPSS scheme, users' search and their location data are transformed into chipertext with random masking technique in client, thus social application servers cannot obtain any sensitive information of users. Meanwhile, no one but the user knows her/his own sensitive information.

Moreover, based on social applications, users are authenticated when login, therefore, it is impossible for an attacker to disguise a legitimate user to execute a search.

- *Second*, the proposed CPSS provides accurate spatial search service for users. We construct an convex polygon spatial search algorithm based on improving an efficient and privacy-preserving cosine similarity computing protocol [17], named PSS, which can provide high-precision convex polygon spatial search while protecting users' privacy.
- *Third*, CPSS provides proximity detection service in the real environment efficiently. We evaluate the performance of the proposed CPSS in terms of the computation complexity and communication overhead, and deploy CPSS in smart phones and workstation with a real LBS dataset. Extensive experiment results demonstrate that CPSS is highly effective in the real environment.

The rest of this paper is organized as follows: we review the related works in Sect. 2. The efficient and privacy-preserving cosine similarity computing protocol and the strategy of point in convex polygon are reviewed as the preliminaries in Sect. 3. In Sect. 4, we formalize the models, design goal, and propose our privacy-preserving proximity detection scheme with convex polygon spatial search followed the security analysis of the proposed scheme in Sect. 5. Performance evaluation in Sect. 6. Conclusions are discussed in Sect. 7.

2   Related Work

The field of privacy-preserving spatial search has witnessed several different techniques those have been proposed to protect users' privacy ([18–22] and reference therein). In this section, we review some of them resumptively.

K-anonymity [23] is a traditional technique to perform privacy-preserving spatial search. There are few works have been proposed in this direction [18,19, 24]. In 2011, [18] presented a new multidimensional *k-anonymity* algorithm based on mapping and divide-and-conquer strategy. The work in [18] maps the multi-dimensional to single-dimensional and performs much better than *k-anonymity* in privacy protection. In [19], Sharma and Shen et al. utilized the *k-anonmity* mechanism with an entropy factor to check the possible probability of detecting a subscriber in a region by an adversary based on previous traces. In their work, they aimed to maximize the entropy based on a random mobility pattern before generating a new cloaking region. Gedik and Liu et al. [24] proposed a location privacy architecture which use a flexible privacy personalization framework to support location *k-anonymity* for a wide range of mobile clients with context-sensitive privacy requirements. This framework enables each mobile client to specify the minimum level of anonymity. However, *k-anonymity* requires that the anonymous region where the user resides should contain at least other *k*-1 users, if *k* users are in the same location, their location information may also be leaked, and it brings heavy communication overhead to users.

Spatial cloaking technique is widely used to ensure users' privacy through masking the user accurate location into a cloaked spatial regions [20,21,25]. The schemes in [21] proposed to enable mobile users to obtain location-based services without revealing their exact location by designing a spatial cloaking algorithm, which is suitable for mobile peer-to-peer environment. In 2015, [20] proposed a new spatial cloaking technique to hide a user's location with a cloaking of the serving based station. Different from the most existing approaches, the work in [20] selects a properly chosen dummy location from real locations of $eNodeBs$ to minimize side information for an adversary. Wang et al. proposed an in-device spatial cloaking algorithm in [25] to achieve processing data in client. The work in [25] is modified from traditional approaches. However, in general, the schemes using spatial cloaking technique return a list of candidate search answers instead of the exact answer, which brings heavy communication overhead to users.

In order to mitigate the heavy communication overhead involved with the *k-anonmity* and spatial cloaking, homomorphic encryption technique is commonly used to achieve privacy-preserving spatial search. In 2016, [22] proposed a solution for mobile users to preserve their location and query privacy in approximate k nearest neighbor (KNN). The work in [22] is built on the *Paillier* public-key cryptosystem, and can provide both location and query privacy security. In [26], Mu and Bakiras proposed a novel privacy-preserving spatial query approach using *Paillier* and *ElGamal*. In their work, a mobile user is allowed to define an arbitrary convex polygon on the map, and test whether her/his friends are within the polygon. The methods in [27] proposed for secure distance computation over encrypted data, in their work, the underlying security is ensured by the homomorphic encryption scheme which support computation on encrypted data. Thomas et al. using homomorphic encryption proposed a secure point inclusion protocol in [28]. They determined the relationship of a point and the polygon by angles. Nevertheless, most homomorphic encryption schemes require massive resource-consuming computation, which brings heavy computation complexity.

These above-mentioned schemes are not very suitable for mobile devices. Hence, in this paper, we use a new but lightweight technique to construct an efficient and privacy-preserving proximity detection scheme with convex polygon spatial search. Our approach is highly efficient in terms of computation complexity and communication overhead. Most importantly, our scheme doesn't reduce the search accuracy due to the privacy-preserving requirements.

3   Preliminaries

Recently Lu et al. [17] proposed an efficient and privacy-preserving cosine similarity computing protocol and in 1995, Feito et al. [29] proposed the cross product (point in convex polygon strategies). In this section, we review theses as the basis of our scheme.

3.1   Efficient and Privacy-Preserving Cosine Similarity Computing Protocol

Given a vector of P_A, $\mathbf{a} = (a_1, a_2, \ldots, a_n) \in F_q^n$ and a vector of P_B, $\mathbf{b} = (b_1, b_2, \ldots, b_n) \in F_q^n$, we can directly calculate the cosine similarity $\cos(\mathbf{a}, \mathbf{b})$

in an efficient and privacy-preserving way. The main calculation process is as follows.

Step1: (performed by P_A) Given security parameters k_1, k_2, k_3, k_4, choose two large primes α, p such that $|p| = k_1$, $|\alpha| = k_2$, set $a_{n+1} = a_{n+2} = 0$. Choose a large random $s \in \mathbb{Z}_p^*$ and $n + 2$ random numbers $|c_i| = k_3$, $i = 1, 2, \ldots, n + 2$. Then P_A calculates

$$C_i = \begin{cases} s(a_i \cdot \alpha + c_i) \bmod p, & a_i \neq 0; \\ s \cdot c_i \bmod p, & a_i = 0; \end{cases}$$

and $A = \sum_{i=1}^{n} a_i^2$. What's more, P_A should keep $s^{-1} \bmod p$ secret. After these operations, $<\alpha, p, C_1, \ldots C_{n+2}>$ will be sent to P_B.

Step2: (performed by P_B) Set $b_{n+1} = b_{n+2} = 0$, random numbers $|r_i| = k_4$, then calculate

$$D_i = \begin{cases} b_i \cdot \alpha \cdot C_i \bmod p, & b_i \neq 0; \\ r_i \cdot C_i \bmod p, & b_i = 0; \end{cases}$$

$B = \sum_{i=1}^{n} b_i^2$ and $D = \sum_{i=1}^{n+2} D_i \bmod p$. After this P_B sends $<B, D>$ back to P_A.

Step3: (performed by P_A) Compute $E = s^{-1} \cdot D \bmod p$, $\mathbf{a} \cdot \mathbf{b} = \sum_{i=1}^{n} a_i \cdot b_i = \frac{E - (E \bmod \alpha^2)}{\alpha^2}$ and $\cos(\mathbf{a}, \mathbf{b}) = \frac{\mathbf{a} \cdot \mathbf{b}}{\sqrt{A} \cdot \sqrt{B}}$.

During the above calculation, it can be figured that the vectors of P_A and P_B are confidential to each other.

3.2   Cross Products - Point in Convex Polygon Strategies

Given a convex polygon P with n edges and a point p, the vertices $P_1 P_2 \ldots P_n$ are named in anticlockwise direction. Assume that the coordinates of the vertexes and the point are defined as $<(x_1, y_1), (x_2, y_2), \ldots, (x_i, y_i), (x_{i+1}, y_{i+1}), \ldots, (x_n, y_n)>$ and (x_s, y_s), respectively. The point in convex polygon cross product is the protocol to determine whether the point p is within the convex polygon P. We can solve this problem by calculating points orientation [29]. As shown in Fig. 2, the triple points $<P_{i+1}, p, P_i>$ consist of two vertices of the convex polygon and a point p, we defined their orientations as follows.

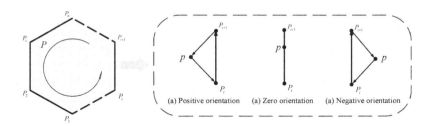

Fig. 2. Orientation of point p and polygon vertex.

- Positive orientation: $<P_{i+1}, p, P_i>$ is a counterclockwise turn.
- Negative orientation: $<P_{i+1}, p, P_i>$ is a clockwise turn.
- Zero orientation: $<P_{i+1}, p, P_i>$ is collinear.

The orientation of the $< P_{i+1}, p, P_i >$ can be computed as follows.

$$S_i = \begin{vmatrix} x_{i+1} & y_{i+1} & 1 \\ x_s & y_s & 1 \\ x_i & y_i & 1 \end{vmatrix} = (x_s \cdot y_i + y_s \cdot x_{i+1} + x_i \cdot y_{i+1}) - (x_s \cdot y_{i+1} + y_s \cdot x_i + x_{i+1} \cdot y_i)$$

Next, for the given convex polygon P and point p, whether the point is within the convex polygon can be determined by the following protocol.

- Let $i \in \{1, 2, \ldots, n\}$, $i' = (i+1) \bmod n$, then compute S_i of the triple points $<P_{i'}, p, P_i>$, where the vertex P_i is visited in an anticlockwise order.
- If all $S_i > 0$, the point p is within the convex polygon P; else, point p is outside the convex polygon P.

4   Models, Design Goal and Proposed CPSS Scheme

4.1   Models and Design Goal

Let us consider that the system model consists of three parts: *Social Application Server* (SS), *Search User* (SU) and *Search User's Friends* (UF), as shown in Fig. 3.

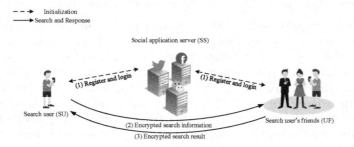

Fig. 3. System model under considered.

- We consider a server of a LBSA as SS, which provides users with various of services including proximity detection. Users registered in SS are allowed to search approximate location of their friends with proximity detection. In our system, SS is responsible for forwarding data among users and protecting the integrity of data.
- A user who wants to execute a search and has already registered in SS is represented by SU. Based on social applications, SU can generate her/his friend list. Then she/he can choose any polygon range on the map, and search which friends of her/his are within the selected region.

- UF present online friends of SU. In the process of polygon spatial search, UF receive blurred search information from SU, then each UF does a hybrid calculation with the blurred search data and her/his own position coordinate to obtain search results, which can only be analyzed by SU with further calculating. Since most calculations are done in client, the computational efficiency of our privacy-preserving scheme should be guaranteed.

Within the system model, let us introduce the threat model and define the following security requirements of the proposed work. In the threat model, we consider that SS is credible-but-greedy, SU and UF are honest-but-curious. Specifically, SS will not be fraudulent, but want to get the sensitive information of users from search requests and result responses. SU and UF will not send false information, nevertheless, both of them want to obtain each other's sensitive information through the blurred data. Meanwhile, attackers may tamper and modify the data, or impersonate a legitimate user to execute a search. Considering above security issues, the following security requirements should be satisfied.

- *Privacy.* On one hand, protecting user's search and location information secret from SS and other users, even if SS can obtain all requests and responses from users, it still cannot identity user's search polygon range and location information accurately. On the other hand, the privacy requirements also include search results, i.e., only the legal SU can decrypt them.
- *Authentication.* Authenticating that an encrypted proximity detection search request is really sent by a legal SU and not modified during the transmission, i.e., if an illegal user forges a search, this malicious operation should be detected. That is, only correct search requests can be received by UF, meanwhile, responses from UF should also be authenticated, so that SU can receive the reliable search results.

Under the aforementioned system model and security requirements, our design goal is to develope an efficient and privacy-preserving proximity detection scheme with accurate search results for social applications. Specifically, the following three objectives should be achieved.

- *Security should be guaranteed.* Once the security of the proposed is not achieved, users' sensitive information (i.e., search and location data) could be disclosed, which may harm users severely. In this way, it is hard for LBSA to step into its flourish. Therefore, achieving the confidentiality and authentication simultaneously is the primary goal of CPSS.
- *Accuracy of polygon search results should be guaranteed.* It is significant that applying the privacy-preserving strategy cannot compromise the accuracy. Therefore, the proposed framework should also provide the same search result as that of the scheme unusing privacy-preserving technique.
- *Low computation complexity and communication overhead should be achieved.* Considering the batteries of mobile devices are very limited today. The proposed scheme should enhance the computational efficiency to reduce the energy consumption in mobile devices. As a result, CPSS should have low overhead in terms of computation and communication.

4.2   Proposed CPSS Scheme

The proposed efficient and privacy-preserving proximity detection scheme mainly consist of two parts: *system initialization* and *privacy-preserving convex polygon spatial search*. Detailed explanation is as follows.

System Initialization. SS first chooses system security parameters p_1, p_2, p_3, p_4, a secure symmetric encryption $E()$, i.e., AES, a secure asymmetric encryption algorithm $E'()$, i.e., ECC and a secure hash function $H()$. Then SS generates its private key sk_{SS} and public key pk_{SS}. SS keeps sk_{SS} secret, and publishes the system parameters $<E(), E'(), H(), p_1, p_2, p_3, p_4, pk_{SS}>$.

When registering in SS, SU sets her/his *password*, and generates private key sk_{SU} and public key pk_{SU}. When logging in, SU is authorized with $<password, SU, pk_{SS}, E'()>$. Meanwhile, a temporary session key k_{SU} is generated through the key negotiation. The authentication scheme of register and login for social applications is sophisticated [30]. After this, SU chooses two large primes such that $|\beta| = p_1$, $|\alpha| = p_2$, a large random number $u \in \mathbb{Z}_p^*$ and random numbers $|v_{in}| = p_3$, where i is the number of polygon edges, $n = 1, 2, \cdots, 6$.

UF represent online friends of SU. For the sake of simplicity, we first consider that only one friend of SU is online, which is represented by UF_j. During the initialization process, UF_j generates a session key k_{UF_j} with SS, and chooses random numbers $|w_i| = p_4$, where i is the number of polygon edges.

Privacy-Preserving Convex Polygon Spatial Search. At the beginning, we design the PSS algorithm for the proposed scheme, which mainly consists of three functions: *SearchGeneration*, *ResultGeneration* and *ResultReading*. The description of the functions is as follows.

- *SearchGeneration*(α, β, u, V, D): The function takes as input two big primes α and β, random number u, an array V with elements v_{in} and vertexes of the search polygon D. It outputs the blurred data of the search polygon, which is presented by Q. Assume that the vertexes of the polygon are $<(x_{q1}, y_{q1}), (x_{q2}, y_{q2}), \ldots, (x_{qm}, y_{qm})>$ in anticlockwise order. Detailed calculations of this function are as follows.

$$Q = Q_1 \parallel Q_2 \parallel \cdots \parallel Q_i \parallel \cdots \parallel Q_m$$
$$Q_i = Q_{i1} \parallel Q_{i2} \parallel Q_{i3} \parallel Q_{i4} \parallel Q_{i5} \parallel Q_{i6}$$
$$Q_{i1} = u(x_{qi} \cdot \alpha + v_{i1}) \bmod \beta$$
$$Q_{i2} = u(y_{qi} \cdot \alpha + v_{i2}) \bmod \beta$$
$$Q_{i3} = u(x_{qi'} \cdot \alpha + v_{i3}) \bmod \beta$$
$$Q_{i4} = u(y_{qi'} \cdot \alpha + v_{i4}) \bmod \beta$$
$$Q_{i5} = u(x_{qi} \cdot y_{qi'} \cdot \alpha + v_{i5}) \bmod \beta$$
$$Q_{i6} = u(x_{qi'} \cdot y_{qi} \cdot \alpha + v_{i6}) \bmod \beta,$$

where $i = 1, 2, ..., m$, $i' = (i + 1) \bmod m$. The process is conducted by SU, after this, the data of the search polygon are blurred into chipertext Q.

- $ResultGeneration(\alpha, \beta, W, Q, C)$: This function is executed by UF_j. It outputs the search result R with the inputs α, β, W, Q and C, where α and β are two big primes, W is an array with elements w_i, Q is the blurred polygon information and C is the location coordinate of UF_j. Assume that the location coordinate of UF_j is $<x_j, y_j>$. Specific computing process is as follows.

$$R = R_1 \parallel R_2 \parallel \cdots \parallel R_i \parallel \cdots \parallel R_m$$
$$R_i = R_{i1} \parallel R_{i2}$$
$$R_{i1} = w_i \cdot \alpha(x_j \cdot Q_{i4} + y_j \cdot Q_{i1} + Q_{i6}) \bmod \beta$$
$$R_{i2} = w_i \cdot \alpha(x_j \cdot Q_{i2} + y_j \cdot Q_{i3} + Q_{i5}) \bmod \beta,$$

where $i = 1, 2, ..., m$. Note that in the operation $R = R_1 \parallel R_2 \parallel \cdots \parallel R_i \parallel \cdots \parallel R_m$, the order of i should be rearranged. After this process, the search result R is generated, which can only be decrypted by legitimate SU.

- $ResultReading(\beta, u, R)$: This function takes as input the big prime β, random number u and search result R. It decrypts R and outputs the judgement J, which shows whether UF_j is with the polygon area. Concretely, the operations are as follows.

$$
\begin{aligned}
J_{i1} &= u^{-1} \cdot R_{i1} \bmod \beta \\
&= u^{-1} \cdot w_i \cdot \alpha(x_j \cdot Q_{i4} + y_j \cdot Q_{i1} + Q_{i6}) \bmod \beta \\
&= u^{-1} \cdot w_i \cdot u[\alpha^2(x_j \cdot y_{qi'} + y_j \cdot x_{qi} + x_{qi'} \cdot y_{qi}) \\
&\quad + \alpha(x_j \cdot v_{i4} + y_j \cdot v_{i1} + v_{i6})] \bmod \beta \\
J_{i1}' &= \frac{J_{i1} - (J_{i1} \bmod \alpha^2)}{\alpha^2} \\
&= w_i(x_j \cdot y_{qi'} + y_j \cdot x_{qi} + x_{qi'} \cdot y_{qi})
\end{aligned}
$$

$$
\begin{aligned}
J_{i2} &= u^{-1} \cdot R_{i2} \bmod \beta \\
&= u^{-1} \cdot w_i \cdot \alpha(x_j \cdot Q_{i2} + y_j \cdot Q_{i3} + Q_{i5}) \bmod \beta \\
&= u^{-1} \cdot w_i \cdot u[\alpha^2(x_j \cdot y_{qi} + y_j \cdot x_{qi'} + x_{qi} \cdot y_{qi'}) \\
&\quad + \alpha(x_j \cdot v_{i2} + y_j \cdot v_{i3} + v_{i5})] \bmod \beta \\
J_{i2}' &= \frac{J_{i2} - (J_{i2} \bmod \alpha^2)}{\alpha^2} \\
&= w_i(x_j \cdot y_{qi} + y_j \cdot x_{qi'} + x_{qi} \cdot y_{qi'})
\end{aligned}
$$

$$
\begin{aligned}
J_i &= J_{i2}' - J_{i1}' \\
&= w_i[(x_j \cdot y_{qi} + y_j \cdot x_{qi'} + x_{qi} \cdot y_{qi'}) \\
&\quad - (x_j \cdot y_{qi'} + y_j \cdot x_{qi} + x_{qi'} \cdot y_{qi})]
\end{aligned}
$$

For $i = 1, 2, ..., m$, if all of the $J_i > 0$, this function outputs that J is *true*, Otherwise, outputs J is *false*.

Algorithm 1. PSS

---

    procedure JUDGE(UF_j)   ▷ Whether UF_j is within the
        for $i = 1$ to $i = m$ **do**   polygon
        SU computes Q;
        UF_j computes R;
        SU computes J_i;
        if $J_i <= 0$ **then**
            return J is $false$;   ▷ UF_j is outside the polygon
        end if
       end for
       return J is $true$;   ▷ UF_j is within the polygon
    end procedure

Correctness of the PSS. As the calculation presented above, PSS should meet constraints $w_i \cdot \alpha^2 (x_j \cdot y_{qi'} + y_j \cdot x_{qi} + x_{qi'} \cdot y_{qi})$, $w_i \cdot \alpha^2 (x_j \cdot y_{qi} + y_j \cdot x_{qi} + x_{qi} \cdot y_{qi'}) < \beta$ and $\alpha(x_j \cdot v_{i2} + y_j \cdot v_{i3} + v_{i5})$, $\alpha(x_j \cdot v_{i2} + y_j \cdot v_{i3} + v_{i5}) < \alpha^2$. Since the values of coordinates are not very big, we can choose applicable security parameters easily (such as $p_1 = 512$, $p_2 = 160$, $p_3 = 75$ and $p_4 = 75$). Note that the expression $J_i = w_i[(x_j \cdot y_{qi} + y_j \cdot x_{qi'} + x_{qi} \cdot y_{qi'}) - (x_j \cdot y_{qi'} + y_j \cdot x_{qi} + x_{qi'} \cdot y_{qi})]$, which is formed by two divisors, one is random w_i, and the other is the cross product of $<P_{i'}, p, P_i>$. Since w_i is a positive number, the sign of the cross product is clear. Then we can find out whether the point is within the polygon through orientations of $<P_{i'}, p, P_i>$, where $i = 1, 2, ..., m$.

Next, based on PSS algorithm, we propose the efficient and privacy-preserving proximity detection scheme with convex polygon spatial search, and illustrate it in Fig. 4. The detailed procedure is described as below.

(1) *Generate the search request*: Based on social applications, SU executes the *system initialization* to generate random numbers α, β, u, V, and chooses vertexes of the search polygon D. Then she/he generates the search data Q by calling $SearchGeneration(\alpha, \beta, u, V, D)$, and creates the message authentication code $MAC_{SU} = E_{k_{SU}}(H(\alpha \parallel \beta \parallel Q \parallel SU \parallel TS))$, where TS is current time to resist the potential replay attack. Finally, SU keeps $u^{-1} \bmod \beta$ secret, and sends $<\alpha \parallel \beta \parallel Q \parallel SU \parallel TS \parallel MAC_{SU}>$ to SS.

(2) *Verify the search request and forward*: SS first checks TS and MAC_{SU} to verify the validity of data, i.e., verify whether $E_{k_{SU}}(H(\alpha \parallel \beta \parallel Q \parallel SU \parallel TS)) = MAC_{SU}$. If it does hold, the packet is valid. Then SS computes $MAC_{SS_q} = E_{k_{UF_j}}(H(\alpha \parallel \beta \parallel Q \parallel SS \parallel TS))$, and sends $< \alpha \parallel \beta \parallel Q \parallel SS \parallel TS \parallel MAC_{SS_q}>$ to UF_j.

(3) *Generate the search response*: UF_j checks the time stamp TS and MAC_{SS_q} to verify the validity of data. Then UF_j executes the *system initialization* to generate random numbers W, and generates the search result R by calling $ResultGeneration(\alpha, \beta, W, Q, C)$, where C is the location of UF_j. Finally, UF_j computes $MAC_{UF_j} = E_{k_{UF_j}}(H(R \parallel UF_j \parallel TS))$, and sends $<R \parallel UF_j \parallel TS \parallel MAC_{UF_j}>$ to SS.

(4) *Verify the search response and forward*: SS first checks TS and MAC_{UF_j} to verify the validity of the packet. Then SS computes $MAC_{SS_a} = E_{k_{SU}}(H(R \parallel SS \parallel TS))$, and returns the search result $<R \parallel SS \parallel TS \parallel MAC_{SS_a}>$ to SU.

(5) *Read the search response*: After receiving $<R \parallel SS \parallel TS \parallel MAC_{SS_a}>$, SU first checks its validity, and determines whether UF_j is within the polygon by calling *ResultReading(β, u, R)*.

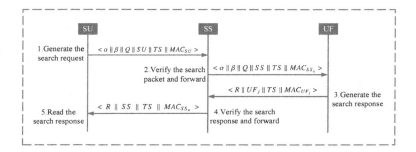

Fig. 4. Proposed CPSS scheme.

5 Security Analysis

Following the security requirements discussed earlier, in this section, we analysis the security of the proposed CPSS. We will focus on how the proposed CPSS can preserve the privacy of users, and the authentication during the search process.

5.1 The User's Sensitive Information is Privacy-Preserving in the Proposed Scheme

In the proposed CPSS, by using random numbers u and v_{in}, the vertexes of the search polygon $<(x_{q1}, y_{q1}), (x_{q2}, y_{q2}), \ldots, (x_{qm}, y_{qm})>$ are encrypted in the form of $Q_1 \parallel Q_2 \parallel \cdots \parallel Q_i \parallel \cdots \parallel Q_m$, where $Q_i = Q_{i1} \parallel Q_{i2} \parallel Q_{i3} \parallel Q_{i4} \parallel Q_{i5} \parallel Q_{i6}$, and $Q_{i1} = u(x_{qi} \cdot \alpha + v_{i1}) \bmod \beta$, $Q_{i2} = u(y_{qi} \cdot \alpha + v_{i2}) \bmod \beta$, $\cdots$, $Q_{i6} = u(x_{qi'} \cdot y_{qi} \cdot \alpha + v_{i6}) \bmod \beta$. Since u and v_{in} are only known by SU, even if SS and other users are curious about the search information, it is impossible for them to obtain the accurate search information. Moreover, the space of search data is increased by random numbers v_{in} to resist the exhaustive attack. Analogously, UF_j computes $R = R_1 \parallel R_2 \parallel \cdots \parallel R_m$ over blurred search data, where $R_i = R_{i1} \parallel R_{i2}$, $R_{i1} = w_i \cdot \alpha(x_j \cdot Q_{i4} + y_j \cdot Q_{i1} + Q_{i6}) \bmod \beta$ and $R_{i2} = w_i \cdot \alpha(x_j \cdot Q_{i2} + y_j \cdot Q_{i3} + Q_{i5}) \bmod \beta$. Since the location coordinate $<x_j, y_j>$ is blurred with random numbers w_i which are only known by UF_j, SS and SU cannot obtain the location coordinate accurately. Moreover, the order of i is rearranged during the operation $R = R_1 \parallel R_2 \parallel \cdots \parallel R_m$, in this way, SU cannot infer the location relationship between UF_j and any edge of the polygon she/he chose on the map. Furthermore, the input values of polygon vertex coordinates are limited with accuracy of two decimal places to guarantee that the distance between two polygon vertexes is at least 1 km, thus SU cannot infer the accurate locations of UF by choosing multiple overlapping polygons or small range polygons on the map. In addition, due to the users' data is all encrypted with random numbers in client, even if attackers can capture users' data, they still cannot achieve available information.

From the above analysis, we can conclude that user's search information and accurate location are secure in the proposed CPSS.

5.2   Authentication is Achieved in the Proposed Scheme

The authentication scheme of register and login for social applications is sophisticated, each registered user generates her/his own private key and its corresponding public key. When the user logs in, mutual authentication and key negotiation will be performed between the user and SS. Therefore, it is impossible for an attacker to disguise a legitimate user to forge a polygon spatial search request. In addition, with the proposed scheme, the message authentication code MAC is computed with the hash function $H()$, and is encrypted with the secure symmetric encryption algorithm $E()$ in each communication between users and SS. Therefore, without knowing the session key k, it is impossible for attackers to modify the data between users and SS. As a result, the search request from the unregistered user and the modified information can be detected in the proposed CPSS.

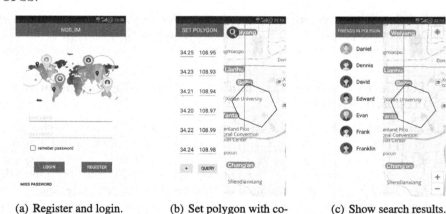

(a) Register and login.   (b) Set polygon with coordinates.   (c) Show search results.

Fig. 5. Implementation of CPSS.

6   Performance Evaluation

In this section, we demonstrate the performance of our scheme in terms of computation complexity and communication overhead of SU and UF by deploying it in the real environment.

6.1   Evaluation Environment

In order to measure the integrated performance, we implement the proposed CPSS in smart phones and workstation. Specifically, smart phones with 2.2 GHz eight-core processor, 3 GB RAM, Android6.0 and a workstation with 2.0 GHz six-core processor, 64 GB RAM, Ubuntu are chosen to evaluate SU, UF and SS, respectively, which are connected through 802.11g WLAN. Based on the proposed scheme, we construct a social application and install it on smart phones to evaluate SU and UF, then, we build SS on the workstation. As shown in Fig. 5, SU can register in SS, search her/his friends, and display result in the smartphone. In order to evaluate CPSS in the real environment, the street map in Xi'an is adopted in our application.

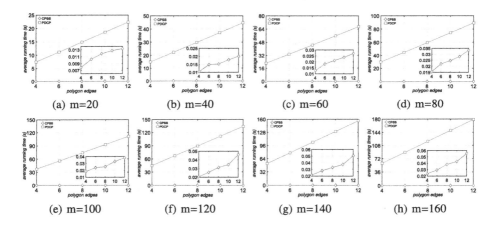

Fig. 6. Average running time of CPSS in SU vs PDCP.

6.2   Computation Complexity

The proposed PSS algorithm requires mathematical operations with random numbers to protect users' sensitive data from social application servers and attackers. Hence let us quantify the mathematical operations required for the proposed algorithm in SU and UF. Specifically, we assume that the number of search polygon vertexes is n, and SU has m online friends. In the process of blurring the search polygon data, it requires $14n$ multiplication operations. When to generate search result, each UF needs to do $8n$ multiplication operations. After receiving the search results from UF, it will cost $4mn$ multiplication operations for SU to read them. Let us define the time complexity for one multiplication as t_{mul}. Therefore, the total computation complexity of SU and UF are $(14n + 4mn) * t_{mul}$ and $8n * t_{mul}$, respectively.

Our PSS algorithm uses lightweight two-party random masking and polynomial aggregation techniques. Different from other time-consumption homomorphic encryption techniques, it can largely reduce the encryption times for mobile terminals while providing accurate proximity detection results. In the following, for the comparison with CPSS, we select an enhanced proximity detection for convex polygons (PDCP) [26], which adopts the same point in convex polygon strategies as CPSS. Denote that the search domain size is measured by l and the time complexity of exponentiation operation is presented by t_{exp}. Therefore, for PCDP, the computation complexities of SU and UF are $(3n + 2m + 3mn + 4l * mn) * t_{exp} + (8n + 4m + 6mn + l * mn) * t_{mul}$ and $(12n + 4l * n + l^2 * n + 9) * t_{mul} + (4n + 4l * n + 9) * t_{exp}$, respectively.

Table 1. Computation complexity of CPSS and PDCP

	CPSS	PDCP
SU	$(14n + 4mn) * t_{mul}$	$(3n + 2m + 3mn + 4l * mn) * t_{exp} + (8n + 4m + 6mn + l * mn) * t_{mul}$
UF	$8n * t_{mul}$	$(12n + 4l * n + l^2 * n + 9) * t_{mul} + (4n + 4l * n + 9) * t_{exp}$

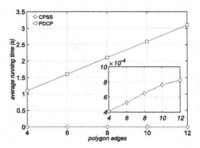

Fig. 7. Average running time of CPSS in UF vs PDCP.

Table 1 presents the computation complexity comparison of CPSS and PDCP. It is obvious that our proposed CPSS can achieve privacy-preserving proximity detection with low computatuon overhead. We test the computation overhead of CPSS and PDCP in SU for various number of SU's friends, and plot the average running time by varying the input number of search polygon edges from 4 to 12 in Fig. 6. It can be obviously seen that with the increase number of polygon edges, the computation overhead of PDCP in SU increase hugely, which is much higher than that of our proposed CPSS. In Fig. 7, we further plot the average running time in UF varying with the increasing number of search polygon edges from 4 to 12, from the figure, it can be clearly seen that the computation overhead in UF of PDCP is much higher than that of our proposed CPSS, and increases extremely, which verify the above analysis of computation complexity. In conclusion, our proposed CPSS can achieve better efficiency in terms of computation overhead in SU and UF.

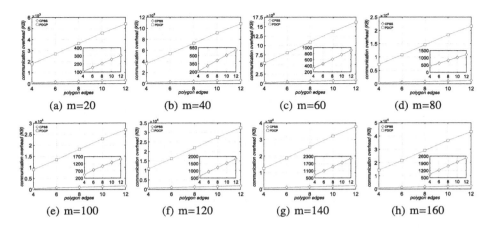

Fig. 8. Communication overhead of CPSS vs PDCP.

6.3 Communication Overhead

In order to test the communication overhead, we record the size of search request packet $<\alpha \parallel \beta \parallel Q \parallel SU \parallel TS \parallel MAC_{SU}>$ and result response packet $<R \parallel UF_j \parallel TS \parallel MAC_{UF_j}>$ with different number of polygon edges and SU's friends, and compare with PDCP in one round. As shown in Fig. 8, with the increase of the polygon edges, the communication overhead of PDCP significantly increases and it is much higher than that of our proposed CPSS scheme when the number of SU's friends does not change. Although the communication overhead of our proposed CPSS scheme also increases when the numbers of polygon edges and SU's friends are large, it is still much lower than that of PDCP. In addition, SU needs to interact with UF twice in CPSS, and nine times in PDCP. In conclusion, our proposed CPSS framework can accomplish better efficiency in terms of communication overhead.

7 Conclusion

In this paper, an efficient and privacy-preserving proximity detection scheme with convex polygon spatial search is proposed, which algorithmically improved the privacy-preserving cosine similarity computing protocol and point in convex polygon strategies to achieve efficiency and privacy-preserving. The proposed scheme is based on randomisation technique and only relies on multiplication and addition. In this scheme, LBSAs users can access proximity detection service without divulging their privacy. It is proved that our scheme is secure in security analysis, and extensive experiments show that it is highly efficient in terms of computation complexity and communication overhead.

Availability

The implementation of the proposed CPSS scheme and relevant information can be downloaded at http://xdzhuhui.com/demo/CPSS.

Acknowledgement. H. Zhu is supported in part by National Natural Science Foundation of China (no. 61672411 and U1401251), National Key Research and Development Program of China (no. 2017YFB0802201), Natural Science Basic Research Plan in Shaanxi Province of China (no. 2016JM6007), Research Foundations for the Central Universities of China (no. JB161507), Research Foundations for Science and Technology on Communication Networks Laboratory (no. KX172600023), and China 111 Project (no. B16037).

R. Lu is supported in part by Natural Sciences and Engineering Research (NSERC) Discovery (no. Rgpin 04009), NBIF Start-Up (Nbif Rif 2017-915012), URF (no. Urf Nf-2017-05), and HMF (no. Hmf 2017 Ys-4).

References

1. Valente, T.W.: Network interventions. Science **337**(6090), 49–53 (2012)
2. Zhu, H., Lu, R., Huang, C., Chen, L., Li, H.: An efficient privacy-preserving location based services query scheme in outsourced cloud. IEEE Trans. Veh. Technol. **65**(9), 7729–7739 (2016)
3. Puttaswamy, K.P., Zhao, B.Y.: Preserving privacy in location-based mobile social applications. In: Proceedings of the Eleventh Workshop on Mobile Computing Systems and Applications, pp. 1–6. ACM (2010)
4. Li, K.A., Sohn, T.Y., Huang, S., Griswold, W.G.: Peopletones: a system for the detection and notification of buddy proximity on mobile phones. In: Proceedings of the 6th International Conference on Mobile Systems, Applications, and Services, pp. 160–173. ACM (2008)
5. Bolic, M., Rostamian, M., Djuric, P.M.: Proximity detection with RFID: a step toward the internet of things. IEEE Pervasive Comput. **14**(2), 70–76 (2015)
6. Huang, C., Lu, R., Zhu, H., Shao, J., Alamer, A., Lin, X.: EPPD: efficient and privacy-preserving proximity testing with differential privacy techniques. In: 2016 IEEE International Conference on Communications (ICC), pp. 1–6. IEEE (2016)
7. Chen, Q., Ye, A., Xu, L.: A privacy-preserving proximity detection method in social network. In: Proceedings of the International Conference on Internet of Things and Cloud Computing. ACM (2016). Article No. 68
8. Šikšnys, L., Thomsen, J.R., Šaltenis, S., Yiu, M.L.: Private and flexible proximity detection in mobile social networks. In: 2010 Eleventh International Conference on Mobile Data Management, pp. 75–84. IEEE (2010)
9. Zhu, H., Liu, F., Li, H.: Efficient and privacy-preserving polygons spatial query framework for location-based services. IEEE Internet Things J. **4**(2), 536–545 (2016)
10. Enserink, M.: Risk of exposure. Science **347**(6221), 498–500 (2015)
11. Li, L., Lu, R., Choo, K.K.R., Datta, A., Shao, J.: Privacy-preserving-outsourced association rule mining on vertically partitioned databases. IEEE Trans. Inf. Forensics Secur. **11**(8), 1847–1861 (2016)
12. Peng, J., Meng, Y., Xue, M., Hei, X., Ross, K.W.: Attacks and defenses in location-based social networks: a heuristic number theory approach. In: 2015 International Symposium on Security and Privacy in Social Networks and Big Data (SocialSec), pp. 64–71. IEEE (2015)

13. Huang, C., Yan, Z., Li, N., Wang, M.: Secure pervasive social communications based on trust in a distributed way. IEEE Access **4**, 9225–9238 (2016)
14. Wang, B., Li, M., Wang, H.: Geometric range search on encrypted spatial data. IEEE Trans. Inf. Forensics Secur. **11**(4), 704–719 (2016)
15. Niu, B., Zhu, X., Li, Q., Chen, J., Li, H.: A novel attack to spatial cloaking schemes in location-based services. Future Gener. Comput. Syst. **49**, 125–132 (2015)
16. Ohno-Machado, L.: To share or not to share: that is not the question. Sci. Transl. Med. **4**(165), 165cm15 (2012)
17. Lu, R., Zhu, H., Liu, X., Liu, J.K., Shao, J.: Toward efficient and privacy-preserving computing in big data era. IEEE Netw. **28**(4), 46–50 (2014)
18. Wang, Q., Xu, C., Sun, M.: Multi-dimensional k-anonymity based on mapping for protecting privacy. J. Softw. **6**(10), 1937–1944 (2011)
19. Sharma, V., Shen, C.C.: Evaluation of an entropy-based k-anonymity model for location based services. In: 2015 International Conference on Computing, Networking and Communications (ICNC), pp. 374–378. IEEE (2015)
20. Firoozjaei, M.D., Yu, J., Kim, H.: Privacy preserving nearest neighbor search based on topologies in cellular networks. In: 2015 IEEE 29th International Conference on Advanced Information Networking and Applications Workshops (WAINA), pp. 146–149. IEEE (2015)
21. Chow, C.Y., Mokbel, M.F., Liu, X.: Spatial cloaking for anonymous location-based services in mobile peer-to-peer environments. GeoInformatica **15**(2), 351–380 (2011)
22. Yi, X., Paulet, R., Bertino, E., Varadharajan, V.: Practical approximate k nearest neighbor queries with location and query privacy. IEEE Trans. Knowl. Data Eng. **28**(6), 1546–1559 (2016)
23. Sweeney, L.: k-Anonymity: a model for protecting privacy. Int. J. Uncertainty Fuzziness Knowl. Based Syst. **10**(05), 557–570 (2002)
24. Gedik, B., Liu, L.: Protecting location privacy with personalized k-anonymity: architecture and algorithms. IEEE Trans. Mobile Comput. **7**(1), 1–18 (2008)
25. Wang, S., Wang, X.S.: In-device spatial cloaking for mobile user privacy assisted by the cloud. In: 2010 Eleventh International Conference on Mobile Data Management, pp. 381–386. IEEE (2010)
26. Mu, B., Bakiras, S.: Private proximity detection for convex polygons. In: Proceedings of the 12th International ACM Workshop on Data Engineering for Wireless and Mobile Acess, pp. 36–43. ACM (2013)
27. Hu, P., Mukherjee, T., Valliappan, A., Radziszowski, S.: Homomorphic proximity computation in geosocial networks. In: 2016 IEEE Conference on Computer Communications Workshops (INFOCOM WKSHPS), pp. 616–621. IEEE (2016)
28. Thomas, T.: Secure two-party protocols for point inclusion problem. Int. J. Netw. Secur. **9**(1), 1–7 (2009)
29. Feito, F., Torres, J.C., Urena, A.: Orientation, simplicity, and inclusion test for planar polygons. Comput. Graph. **19**(4), 595–600 (1995)
30. Zhu, H., Liu, X., Lu, R., Li, H.: Efficient and privacy-preserving online medical pre-diagnosis framework using nonlinear SVM. IEEE J. Biomed. Health Inform. **21**(3), 1 (2016)

Disrupting SDN via the Data Plane: A Low-Rate Flow Table Overflow Attack

Jiahao Cao[1,2], Mingwei Xu[1,2(✉)], Qi Li[1,3], Kun Sun[4], Yuan Yang[1,2], and Jing Zheng[1,3]

[1] Department of Computer Science and Technology, Tsinghua University, Beijing, China
{caojh15,zhengj14}@mails.tsinghua.edu.cn, xumw@tsinghua.edu.cn, qi.li@sz.tsinghua.edu.cn, yyang@csnet1.cs.tsinghua.edu.cn
[2] Tsinghua National Laboratory for Information Science and Technology (TNList), Beijing, China
[3] Graduate School at Shenzhen, Tsinghua University, Beijing, China
[4] Department of Information Sciences and Technology, George Mason University, Fairfax, USA
ksun3@gmu.edu

Abstract. The emerging Software-Defined Networking (SDN) is being adopted by data centers and cloud service providers to enable flexible control. Meanwhile, the current SDN design brings new vulnerabilities. In this paper, we explore a stealthy data plane based attack that uses a *minimum* rate of attack packet to disrupt SDN. To achieve this, we propose the LOFT attack that computes the lower bound of attack rate to overflow flow tables based on the inferred network configurations. Particularly, each attack packet always triggers or maintains consumption of one flow rule. LOFT can ensure the attack effect with various network configurations while reducing the possibility of being captured. We demonstrate its feasibility and effectiveness in a real SDN testbed consisting of commercial hardware switches. The experiment results show that LOFT can incur significant network performance degradation and potential network DoS at an attack rate of only tens of Kbps.

Keywords: Software-Defined Networking · Low-rate attack
Flow table overflow

1 Introduction

By decoupling the control plane and the data plane, Software-Defined Networking (SDN) emerges as a promising network architecture design that provides network with great programmability, flexible control, and agile management. Google data centers [1] and Microsoft Azure cloud platform [2] have deployed SDN to innovate their networks. A large amount of SDN applications have been developed to enable various network functionalities, such as dynamic flow scheduling [3], holistic network monitoring and management [4], and security function deployment in large networks [5].

© ICST Institute for Computer Sciences, Social Informatics and Telecommunications Engineering 2018
X. Lin et al. (Eds.): SecureComm 2017, LNICST 238, pp. 356–376, 2018.
https://doi.org/10.1007/978-3-319-78813-5_18

Unfortunately, the SDN design itself has serious security problems. In particular, the SDN data plane (or SDN switches) is vulnerable to flow table overflow. First, it is "dumb", i.e., for a flow that cannot match any installed flow rules in the switch flow table, the switch will generate packet-in messages to query a logically centralized controller for a new flow rule. Therefore, an attacker may abuse it to send crafted packets to trigger new rule installation. Second, most modern SDN-enabled hardware switches only support a small number of flow rules, e.g., thousands of rules [6–8], which are stored in power-hungry and expensive Ternary Content Addressable Memory (TCAM) to achieve high lookup performance [6,9]. The limited storage space of TCAM may be easily overflowed.

To effectively overflow SDN switches, existing attacks [10–12] normally generate a large number of random packets per second, but they can be easily captured by the existing defenses [10,11,13,14]. Shin and Gu [15] attempted to reduce the number of the required attack packets; however, since they did not systematically consider various configurations of flow rules (e.g., lifetime of flow rules), their attacks can fail in practice. Considering detailed network configurations in SDN, in this paper, we would like to ask:

• *Can we successfully construct a low-rate attack to SDN data plane and keep the flow table overflowed over time by generating a minimal rate of attack packets?*

Our answer is yes, though it is challenging. To decrease the attack packet rate, an attacker should craft packets so that each of them can trigger a new rule installation, which requires the attacker to know precisely what packets will trigger new rule installation. However, the rule installation logic is decided by the separated SDN controller, and the attacker usually has no access to those information. Moreover, flow rules are usually set with timeouts by the controller and will be removed when they expire. The attackers need to understand the timeout settings of the flow rules so as to choose the best attack strategies and decide the minimal attack rate.

To address the above challenges, we present a two-phase low-rate flow table overflow attack called LOFT, which consists of *probing phase* and *attacking phase*. In the probing phase, it aims to accurately infer network configurations of flow rules by generating a small number of probing packets. These network configurations include the match fields along with their bitmasks that indicate what packets will trigger new rule installation and the timeouts that define the lifetime of the rules. The key insight behind inferring configurations is that there exist remarkable forwarding delays for packets that cannot match any existing flow rules in the switches due to the separation of control plane and data plane in SDN. Thus, by measuring round-trip times (RTTs) of customized probing packets, an attacker can accurately infer the settings of the flow rules. In the attacking phase, LOFT generates low-rate attack traffic to overflow flow tables according to the inferred network configurations. It crafts different packets using some specific match fields so that each packet can trigger a new flow rule installation. Meanwhile, based on the timeout configurations, it can compute the minimal packet rate to keep flow tables overflowed over time.

To demonstrate the feasibility and effectiveness of LOFT attack, we conduct experiments in a real SDN testbed that consists of commercial hardware switches. The experimental results show that LOFT can accurately infer flow rule configurations using a small number of probing packets. In particular, by generating less than 10 probing packets per second, it can achieve more than 90% accuracy on probing the detailed timeout settings. During the attacking phase, it can successfully decrease the available maximum throughput from 850 Mbps to 10 Mbps for a new flow, and increase RTT from 0.1 ms to above 1000 ms. Moreover, it incurs a 69% degradation of network throughput at an attack rate of around 50 Kbps. To summarize, we make the following contributions:

- We propose a low-rate flow table overflow attack called LOFT, which can effectively degrade the network performance.
- We develop probing algorithms that can accurately infer network configurations of flow rules and compute the minimal feasible attack rate to successfully launch the LOFT attack.
- We conduct experiments in a real SDN testbed consisting of commercial hardware switches to verify the effectiveness of LOFT attack.

2   Background and Threat Model

2.1   Software-Defined Networking

SDN enables network innovations by decoupling the control plane and the data plane. The control plane contains a logically centralized controller that takes the full control of the network. Various applications can be developed atop the controller to offer complicated network functions, such as traffic engineering. The SDN data plane consists of SDN switches that conduct packets processing and forwarding according to the decisions made by the controller.

Nowadays the leading southbound protocol of SDN is OpenFlow [16]. OpenFlow allows a controller to define various forwarding behaviors of switches by installing related flow rules. There are two approaches to install flow rules, i.e., *proactively* and *reactively*. In proactive approach, flow rules are pre-installed before all the traffic comes. While in reactive approach, flow rules are installed dynamically. When an OpenFlow switch receives a new packet that can not match any installed flow rules, it generates a *packet-in* message to the controller to request a new forwarding rule. The controller may either send *packet-out* messages to the switch for one-time packet processing or send *flow-mod* messages to install flow rules in the switches that are among the calculated routing path.

In OpenFlow, each flow rule mainly consists of (i) match fields to match against incoming packets, (ii) a set of instructions that define how to process the matching packets, (iii) counters to get flow statistics and (iv) timeouts defining lifetime of the rule. Particularly, match fields of a flow rule specify what packets can be handled. According to the OpenFlow Switch Specification 1.3 [9], up to 39 match fields can be added in a rule to provide flexible flow control, such as MAC source/destination address, IPv4 source/destination address, and TCP source/destination port. Each match field in a rule can be exact value, wildcarded (i.e., matching any value) or in some cases with bitmasks. Note that except the default table-miss rule aiming at generating packet-in messages, each rule has at least one match field that conducts exact match with or without bitmasks. Moreover, each flow rule can be set with two types of timeout, namely, *idle timeout* and *hard timeout*. A flow rule will be automatically removed when either the hard timeout has passed or the idle timeout has passed without receiving a packet that matches the flow rule. Both timeouts can be set independently by a controller or applications on the controller.

2.2 Threat Model

In our threat model, the attacker seeks to infer the network configurations and launch LOFT attack to effectively overflow the flow tables of victim switches in a stealthy way. To achieve it, the attacker needs to have (or control) a host that is attached to the victim network and can send packets to other hosts in the network. We do not require that the attacker has any prior knowledge on the network configurations or compromises any switches and controller. Moreover, we assume that the controller adopts *reactive rule installation*, which is widely used in most OpenFlow networks for flexible and dynamic flow control [13,14].

3 Overview of the LOFT Attack

We present an overview of LOFT attack that can efficiently overflow flow tables of switches by generating a minimum number of packets, which can significantly degrade the network performance in a stealthy way. It is based on the key observation that the small-sized flow tables in OpenFlow switches may be easily overflowed by malicious traffic flows and leave no space for normal traffic flows, since the centralized controller treat malicious flows and normal flows equally. This attack can be launched to overflow flow rules of all switches in a network; however, in practice, we only need to overflow flow tables of specific switches, for example, the access switch of a target network server.

LOFT consists of two phases: *the probing phase* and *the attacking phase*, as shown in Fig. 1. The probing phase prepares for the following attacking phase.

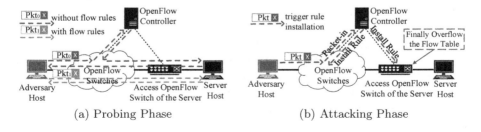

(a) Probing Phase   (b) Attacking Phase

Fig. 1. Two phases of LOFT attack.

In the probing phase, an attacker infers the network configurations of flow rules with a small number of probing packets. The key insight behind our probing schemes is that packets matching no flow rules in SDN switches will experience longer forwarding delays than those matching flow rules. This is because the switches need to query the controller for the forwarding decisions and rule installation. Therefore, by carefully crafting probing packets and analyzing the difference in RTTs between two hosts, the attacker can accurately infer what packets will trigger rule installation and the related timeouts configurations of flow rules. In the attacking phase, according to the inferred results on the network configurations, the attacker crafts the minimum number of attack packets to effectively trigger flow rule installation. Meanwhile, to keep flow tables continuously overflowed over time, the attacker carefully plots the attack strategies and calculates the minimal attack rate according to the timeouts configurations. In the next two sections, we detail the two phases of LOFT attack.

4   The Probing Phase

In this section, we present our probing schemes that aim to infer configurations of flow rules, particularly, the *match fields along with their bitmasks* and *timeouts* that have direct impact on attack strategies in the attack phase.

4.1   Probing Match Fields

In order to accurately infer what fields in a packet header can be used to trigger new rule installation, we generate and craft probing packets with various field values in the packet headers in the network to measure their RTTs. A probing packet can be any packet that can trigger a response packet from a destination. We first send a probing packet to a destination to trigger possible flow rule installation in switches, which ensures that a rule for the packet exists before inferring RTT. Second, we generate a new probing packet that *changes value of one field* of the previous packet to the same destination, and measure the RTT (denoted by RTT_0). Then, we send another probing packet with the same values of header fields and measure the RTT again (denoted by RTT_1). The RTT values of the later two packets meet the following conditions:

$$\begin{cases} RTT_0 \gg RTT_1, & \text{if the changed field triggers rule installation;} \\ RTT_0 \approx RTT_1, & \text{otherwise.} \end{cases}$$

The first equation indicates that the changed field is in the set of the match fields, while the second equation denotes that the changed field is not in the set of the match fields. Based on this, we can enumerate all packet fields and then infer a complete set of match fields used in flow rules. However, there exist two challenges to accurately infer match fields.

Match Fields with Bitmasks Interference. OpenFlow protocol allows some match fields with bitmasks, which can interfere with the probing. For example,

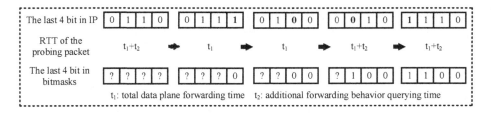

Fig. 2. An example of inferring bitmasks.

suppose that the match field is IP address with a bitmask "255.255.255.0". If we generate a probing packet with IP address "10.0.0.1" and produce another two probing packets with IP address "10.0.0.2". Then, the last two packets will not trigger new flow rule installation. In this case, we infer that IP address is not in the match fields by mistake, since the RTTs of the last two packets are close. To tackle this, we can generate additional probing packets by flipping the values of each bit in turn and reconstruct bitmasks. As shown in Fig. 2, a single bit in the bitmasks can be inferred as 1, if the RTT of the corresponding probing packet is close to the first probing packet. Otherwise, it can be inferred as 0.

Network Jitter Interference. Two RTT values may significantly deviate even if there is no new rule installation because of network jitter. We can apply the *t-test* method [17] to eliminate the impact of network jitters. In t-test, a significance level α is set with a predetermined value, and a p-value p is calculated according to the data, where p indicates the likelihood that the two groups of data share the same distribution. A significant difference between two groups of data is accepted if the calculated p-value p is smaller than α. By changing the values of the same field several times, two groups of RTTs before and after the changes can be obtained. We then can

---

Algorithm 1. Probing Match Fields

Input: dst, F, n, α;
Output: a set of match fields M;
1: $M \leftarrow \emptyset$;
2: **for** *each field* $f \in F$ **do**
3:     $pkt_0 \leftarrow build\_packet(dst, f)$;
4:     **for** $(i = 0 \rightarrow n - 1)$ **do**
5:         $send\_packet(pkt_0)$;
6:         $pkt \leftarrow modify\_field\_val(pkt_0, f)$;
7:         $RTT_0[i] \leftarrow send\_packet(pkt)$;
8:         $RTT_1[i] \leftarrow send\_packet(pkt)$;
9:     **end for**
10:     $p \leftarrow t\_test(RTT_0, RTT_1)$;
11:     $b \leftarrow infer\_bitmask(f)$;
12:     **if** $((p < \alpha)$ or $(b \neq 0))$ **then**
13:         $M.add(\{f, b\})$;
14:     **end if**
15: **end for**

---

evaluate if two groups of RTTs are significant different from each other by calculating their p-value. Thereby, we can accurately infer if there exists new rule installation.

Algorithm 1 shows the pseudo-code of probing match fields. The inputs consist of the IP address of a probing destination dst, a set of fields F to be enumerated, the number of probing packets in a group n, and the significance level of the t-test α. The set of fields F includes typically fields used in flow rules, such as MAC addresses, IP addresses and port number. The significance level α

is set to 0.05, which is a typical value and widely used in t-test. As shown in the algorithm, by conducting several rounds of changing fields, we can infer match fields and the bitmasks (if they exist) used in the network configurations.

4.2 Probing Timeouts

We need to probe timeout values of flow rules so that we can calculate the minimal attack rate to keep flow tables overflowed. A packet will experience remarkable forwarding delay, if the rule matched by the packet is reinstalled by the controller after timeout expiration. Therefore, we can estimate the timeout values by measuring the elapsed time between two remarkable delays.

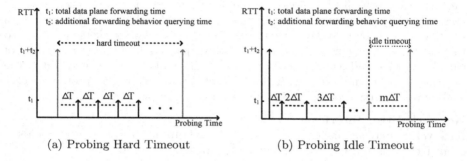

(a) Probing Hard Timeout   (b) Probing Idle Timeout

Fig. 3. Inferring hard and idle timeout values. Note that mutual interference between timeouts is not considered in the figures.

As shown in Fig. 3(a), to infer hard timeout values, we first send a probing packet to trigger initial flow rule installation using the inferred match fields in Algorithm 1. Since there exists a remarkable RTT if a new rule is installed, we can periodically send the probing packets to the network and measure their RTTs. If a remarkable RTT appears again, the hard timeout value can be inferred as the duration since the first probing packet. However, we cannot directly apply the same strategy to probe idle timeout values. The reason is that idle timeout of a flow rule will be reset once a packet matches the rule. Thus, as is shown in Fig. 3(b), we need to generate and send probing packets with increasing time intervals. Once a remarkable RTT occurs again, we can infer that the idle timeout value is equal to the time interval between the two successive probing packets. Here, we need to address the following issues of probing timeout values in practice.

Mutual Interference Between Timeouts. A flow rule may be configured with both hard timeout and idle timeout. In such cases, mutual interference may happen during probing, since a flow rule can be removed because of either hard timeout or idle timeout. Let us take an example. Suppose that the hard timeout of a flow rule is set to 15 s and the idle timeout is set to 10 s. In each round of probing idle timeout, we increase the time interval by 1 s. After 15 s since we start the probing, a remarkable RTT will occur due to hard timeout. While the idle timeout has not taken into effect because it is reset by the probing packets. Thus, we evaluate the idle timeout as 5 s by mistake. Similarly, we may infer a wrong hard timeout value less than the configured value, if the configured idle value is smaller than the interval of two successive packets in probing hard timeout values.

To overcome the problem, we probe hard timeout values first before probing idle timeout values. We note that all timeout values can only be set to an integer and the minimal valid value is 1 s. To eliminate the interference of idle timeout, we send the probing packets in a fixed interval less than 1 s, e.g., 0.5 s. Thereby, idle timeout will always be reset and will not take into effect. Thus, we can accurately infer hard timeout values. Moreover, the inferred hard timeout value is the upper bound of the idle timeout, since an idle timeout value greater than a hard timeout value in a rule is invalid. Therefore, to avoid the hard timeout interference during probing idle timeout, we enumerate all possible idle timeout values from the upper bound in a descending order. Different from the probing shown in Fig. 3(b), we decrease the time interval by 1 s from the upper bound in each round of probing idle timeout. The RTTs of two successive probing packets are close if the probing interval is larger than the idle timeout. They both experience remarkable delays, since flow rules will be removed due to the idle timeout. However, once the RTTs of two successive probing packets exhibit significant deviation, we can know that the idle timeout value is equal to the time interval between the two successive packets.

Probing Duration. It is time-consuming to probe idle timeout, especially when a large hard timeout value is set. The total probing time is calculated as $\sum_{j=t_{idle}}^{t_{hard}} j$, where t_{idle} and t_{hard} are the configured idle timeout value and hard timeout value, respectively. For example, if the hard timeout value is set to 180 s and the idle timeout value is set to 10 s, the total probing time cost is 16,245 s, i.e., around 4.5 h. To effectively reduce the probing duration, we can apply binary search in probing idle timeout, since we can easily infer if an idle timeout value is smaller or larger than a given value by measuring RTTs of probing packet. Note that we also need to eliminate the interference of hard timeout in binary search. We can achieve this by waiting enough time to ensure removal of flow rules before sending packets in a new iteration. Thus, a flow rule will be reinstalled after a probing packet in each iteration. Therefore, the hard timeout will be reset and will not interfere with probing idle timeout in each iteration.

Network Jitter Interference. Network jitter can interfere with probing timeouts. To address this issue, we can simply send a group of packets in parallel in each iteration of probing, and apply t-test mentioned in Sect. 4.1 to determine if there is a significant deviation between two successive groups of RTTs.

The pseudo-code of probing hard timeout values is shown in Algorithm 2. The inputs consist of the IP address of a destination dst, the match fields M inferred by Algorithm 1, n packets which will be concurrently sent, the waiting interval t_{wait}, the maximal execution time of the algorithm t_{max}, and the significance level of the t-test α. Note that t_{wait} must be less than 1 s, which efficiently eliminates the interference of the idle timeout. As shown in Algorithm 2, we generate a group of packets in each iteration to probe the hard timeout value (see steps 4–9). The hard timeout value will be inferred as 0 when the execution time reaches to t_{max}, which indicates the hard timeout is not set in the flow rule (see steps 10–12). The total number of probing packets per second is $\frac{n}{t_{wait}}$. In our experiments, in order to well trade off between probing accuracy and cost, we set n to 5, t_{wait} to 0.5 s, which indicates the algorithm only requires ten packets per second to probe timeout. Moreover, the significance level α is set to 0.05 which is a typical value and widely used in t-test.

Algorithm 2. Hard Timeout Probing

Input: dst, M, n, t_{wait}, t_{max}, α;
Output: hard timeout t_{hard};
1: $pkts[] \leftarrow build\_packets(dst, M, n)$;
2: $t_{start} \leftarrow get\_clock\_time()$;
3: $RTT_0[] \leftarrow send\_packets(pkts, n)$;
4: **repeat**
5:     $sleep(t_{wait})$;
6:     $t_{end} \leftarrow get\_clock\_time()$;
7:     $RTT_1[] \leftarrow send\_packets(pkts, n)$;
8:     $p \leftarrow t\_test(RTT_0, RTT_1)$;
9: **until** $((t_{end} - t_{start} > t_{max})$ or $(p > \alpha))$;
10: **if** $(t_{end} - t_{start} > t_{max})$ **then**
11:     $t_{hard} \leftarrow 0$;
12: **else**
13:     $t_{hard} \leftarrow round(t_{end} - t_{start})$;
14: **end if**

Algorithm 3 shows the pseudo-code of inferring the idle timeout values by applying binary search. The inputs are similar to these used in Algorithm 2, where t_{sup} denotes the upper bound of the algorithm execution time. If the hard timeout value is not equal to zero, t_{sup} is set to t_{hard}. Otherwise, it is set to a value larger than the possible idle timeout value, such as 500 s[1]. We send two groups of packets in each iteration of binary search and measure their RTTs (see steps 3–15). In particular, step 14 aims to ensure that flow rules can be removed after each iteration. Thus, the interference of hard timeout can be eliminated. According to Algorithm 3, we can see that the execution time is equal to $O(t_{sup} \log t_{sup})$ seconds and each iteration of probing only generates $2 * n$ packets. Similar to inferring hard timeout, we set n to 5, which indicates it only generates 10 packets in each iteration.

5   The Attacking Phase

Now we can launch the attack in this phase according to the inferred results in the probing phase. In order to increase the attack effectiveness and keep it stealthy, we generate the minimum number of attack packets that can successfully overflow flow tables. Moreover, we carefully use various attack strategies to overflow flow tables and calculate the minimal attack rates to keep the tables overflowed over time.

---

[1] According to our observation, idle timeout is usually not set to a large value. Normally, 500 s is large enough to serve as the upper bound (see Table 1 in Sect. 5.2).

5.1   Crafting Attack Packets

The key point is to ensure that each attack packet can effectively trigger an unique rule installation in switches. Since we know the match fields along with their bitmasks in the probing phase, we can easily achieve it by carefully changing header field values of each packet. Thereby, the minimal number of packets to overflow flow tables of a switch is equal to the flow table size. Moreover, attack packets do not need to include any real payload. We can generate a packet with 64 B, which is the minimum size of Ethernet packets. Thus, approximate 113 KB traffic can successfully overflow a switch with 1,800 rules. Hence, the volume of the total attack traffic is small. Note that, we can also use multiple match fields with different values in the attack packets to disguise the attack packets as benign packets. For example, if match fields of a flow rule are set with the IP source address, the IP destination address, and the TCP source port, we can change the IP source address in some packets while change the TCP source port in other packets. In addition, we can generate payloads of different sizes in attack packets and then randomize the packet lengths.

5.2   Calculating the Minimal Attack Rate

Now we need to compute the minimal packet rate that can continuously overflow flow tables even after flow rules expire due to hard timeout or idle timeout. Normally, LOFT generates different attack packet rates with respect to different timeout settings. We classify the timeout settings into four categories according to the values of hard timeout and idle timeout. Here, we assume x and y are integers, where $x > y^2$.

(I) $t_{hard} = 0, t_{idle} = 0$: a flow rule will permanently exist in flow tables until the controller actively removes it;

(II) $t_{hard} = x, t_{idle} = 0$: a flow rule will be removed from flow tables after x seconds;

(III) $t_{hard} = 0, t_{idle} = y$: a flow rule will be removed from flow tables if the switch does not receive any packet matching the rule within y seconds;

(VI) $t_{hard} = x, t_{idle} = y$: a flow rule will be removed from flow tables either after x seconds or after y seconds without any received packet.

Algorithm 3. Idle Timeout Probing

Input: dst, M, n, t_{sup}, α;
Output: idle timeout t_{idle};
1: $pkts[] \leftarrow build\_packets(dst, M, n)$;
2: $l \leftarrow 0$, $r \leftarrow t_{sup}$;
3: **while** $(l < r)$ **do**
4:      $RTT_0[] \leftarrow send\_packets(pkts, n)$;
5:      $mid \leftarrow (l + r)/2$;
6:      $sleep(mid)$;
7:      $RTT_1[] \leftarrow send\_packets(pkts, n)$;
8:      $p \leftarrow t\_test(RTT_0, RTT_1)$;
9:      **if** $(p > \alpha)$ **then**
10:         $r \leftarrow mid - 1$;
11:     **else**
12:         $l \leftarrow mid + 1$;
13:     **end if**
14:     $sleep(r)$;
15: **end while**
16: **if** $(t_{idle} \geq t_{sup})$ **then**
17:     $t_{idle} \leftarrow 0$;
18: **else**
19:     $t_{idle} \leftarrow l$;
20: **end if**

---

[2] As we discussed in Sect. 4, SDN does not set hard timeout values larger than idle timeout values.

Among the above four categories, the settings in categories (I) and (II) are rarely used. If the settings in category (I) are applied, a significant amount of resources in the controller are required to actively monitor all flow rules such that flow rules will be removed when there are no matching packets. While the settings in category (II) cannot ensure that flow rules can be removed in time if the network does not generate any packets matching the rules, resulting in the waste of the scarce flow table resources. According to our studies, we find that the settings in category (III) and (IV) are widely used in default settings of different controllers (see Table 1). Thus, in this paper, we focus on developing two attack strategies that use minimal attack rate to overflow flow tables according to the settings in categories (III) and (IV).

Table 1. Default timeout values in different controllers

Controller	Beacon	Floodlight	Maestro	NOX	ONOS	OpenDaylight	POX	Trema
Hard timeout	0	0	180 s	0	0	600 s	30 s	0
Idle timeout	5 s	5 s	30 s	5 s	10 s	300 s	10 s	60 s

Attack Strategy with Settings in Category (III). An attacker needs to fill in the flow table within an idle timeout period, and ensure consumption of entire flow table after the idle timeout expires. To achieve it, the attacker can periodically generate C attack packets, where C is the maximum capacity of the flow table, and evenly distribute them within each idle timeout period (see Fig. 4(a)). Each packet will trigger a new rule installation if there is any available space, and the number of rules in the flow table can gradually increase.

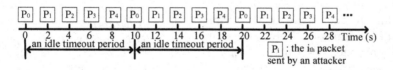

(a) An example to illustrate the attack strategy of category III. Assume that the flow table can support up to 5 rules, and each rule is configured with 0s hard timeout and 10s idle timeout.

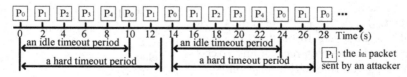

(b) An example to illustrate the attack strategy of category IV. Assume that the flow table can support up to 5 rules, and each rule is configured with 13s hard timeout and 10s idle timeout.

Fig. 4. Examples of different attack strategies.

Meanwhile, if the table is overflowed already, the idle timeout timer of each flow rule can be periodically refreshed within each idle timeout interval, which ensures flow rules are persistently stored in the flow table.

Now we calculate the average rate of sending attack packets within an idle timeout period. Here, C denotes is the maximum capacity of the flow table of a switch, L_i denotes the length of the i_{th} packet within an idle timeout period, and t_{idle} denotes the idle timeout. The average packet rate $\overline{v}$ can be calculated by:

$$\overline{v} = \frac{\sum_{i=0}^{C-1} L_i}{t_{idle}}. \tag{1}$$

Note that, in order to fully consume flow rules, we need to generate at least C packets, each of which triggers a new rule installation. Thus, Eq. (1) gives the minimal attack rate. Any attack rate less than $\overline{v}$ cannot fully consume the table and keep the table full over time because of expiration of flow rules incurred by the idle timeout. According to Eq. (1), we can conclude that the attack rate is small. For example, assuming the flow table capacity is 1,800 flow rules, the idle timeout value is set to 20 s, and the size of each packet is 64B, the minimal attack rate to overflow flow tables is only 46 Kbps. Such low attack rate ensures that no malicious rules will expire and the attack traffic can be effectively concealed in the benign traffic.

Attack Strategy with Setting in Category (IV). Given the settings in category IV, flow rules will be removed when either the hard timeout or the idle timeout expires. Thus, besides sending packets to gradually overflow flow tables within an idle timeout period and periodically refreshing the flow rules, an attacker needs to make a rule reinstalled in time once it is removed due to hard timeout. Since the timeout settings have been known, an attacker can easily achieve it. However, to make the attack have a constant attack rate and easy to be launched, we properly delay the sending time when a rule needs to be reinstalled. As is shown in Fig. 4(b), the rule triggered by p_0 is removed at 13 s due to the hard timeout. We reinstall the rule at 14 s rather than at 13 s so as to keep the time interval between two successive attacking packets equal. In this way, the average attack rate is same with that in category III, which can be calculated by Eq. (1).

We also need to predict the table capacity of the switch to construct the LOFT attack. We develop an online scheme to infer the table size by gradually increasing the number of attack packets and checking if the tables are full. At first, we can construct the attack to occupy n flow rules. After this, we can infer if the flow tables are full by sending some packets to measure the RTT differences. If the RTTs of these packets significantly deviate, it indicates that the flow tables are full since each packet triggers insertion of a new flow rule but none of them have been successfully installed. Otherwise, we can launch another round of probing to occupy n' flow rules. Note that we can not accurately infer the size of flow table since the flow rules used by benign traffic always change. However, in practice, we need not to know the accurate table capacity. We can increase n using a larger number, such as 2,000. By repeating the procedure for several times, we can gradually occupy the flow tables until they are all consumed.

6 Attack Evaluation

6.1 Experiment Setup

Figure 5 shows the topology of our hardware SDN testbed. We use Floodlight [18] OpenFlow controller running in a Intel Xeon Quad-Core CPU E5504 and 12 GB RAM machine. The *Forwarding* application [19] that provides topology discovery and basic forwarding services runs on the controller by default. Two commercial hardware OpenFlow switches, EdgeCore AS4610-54T [20], are deployed in the testbed. Each switch allows 1,800 TCAM-based flow rules and infinite software flow rules[3]. An attacker host controlled by an adversary is attached to one of the switches and generates packets to attack both switches. We implement LOFT attack program in approximate 2,000 lines of C code. Moreover, to simulate real network conditions, we deploy one client host that generates background traffic and one server host that receives the traffic. We use hping3 [21] to generate 200 different benign flows and the rate of a flow is 500 Kbps. Thus, there are total 1,600 flows and 800 Mbps benign traffic in the network.

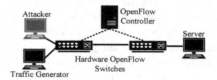

Fig. 5. Hardware SDN testbed.

6.2 Measuring Attack Rate

In this experiment, we measure the attack rate of LOFT and demonstrate that it really generates the minimal rate of attack packets. Note that, in order to accurately measure the attack rate, background traffic is not generated in the experiments. As shown in Eq. (1), the minimal attack rate to overflow the flow table is impacted by the values of idle timeout. Figure 6 shows the theoretical packet rate we computed and real packet rate with respect to different idle timemout values. We can observe that the minimal attack rates are below 100 Kbps, which is consistent with the theoretical values. Moreover, we measure the average packet-in rates at different attack rates before flow table overflow. As is shown in Fig. 7, the packet-in rate is less than 300 Kbps even when the attack rate is 100 Kbps. Note that compared to existing overflow attacks [10–13] that can generate tens

---

[3] The performance is not given by EdgeCore but measured in our experiments.

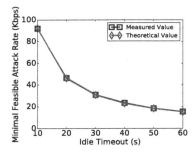

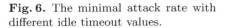

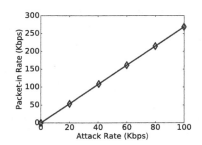

Fig. 6. The minimal attack rate with different idle timeout values.

Fig. 7. Packet-in rate with different attack rate.

of Mbps attack traffic and packet-in traffic, our attack rate is relatively low and does not incur high packet-in rate. These features increase the stealthiness of the attack[4].

6.3 Evaluation of Attack Effectiveness

We conduct our attack experiments in two typical scenarios to demonstrate the effectiveness of LOFT: (I) only idle timeout is set; (II) both hard timeout and idle timeout are set. The idle timeout value is set to 20 s in both two scenarios, and the hard timeout value is set to 200 s in the second scenario. According to Eq. (1), we launch LOFT with the average attack rate at 46 Kbps in both scenarios. Since the attacker does not know the timeouts and match fields of flow rules in advance, they need to probe the configurations before launching the attack. We will evaluate the accuracy of probing in Sect. 6.4.

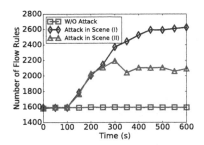

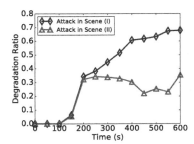

Fig. 8. The number of switch flow rules under LOFT attack.

Fig. 9. Background traffic throughput degradation ratio under LOFT attack.

---

[4] We note that lots of benign traffic will be sent to the controller when the table is overflowed and thus the packet-in rate will significantly increase. However, the attack has successfully caused remarkable damage when it has some obvious features.

Impacts on the Number of Flow Rules. We measure the number of flow rules in the switch that connects to the server with and without the attacks in two scenarios. Figure 8 shows that the number of flow rules is around 1,600 in absence of the attack. When the attack is launched at 100 s in both attack scenarios, the number of flow rules starts to increase. At 600 s, the number of flow rules reaches to 2,610 and 2,090 in scenario (I) and scenario (II), respectively. Since the switch can store up to only 1,800 rules in TCAM, these results demonstrate that our attack can effectively overflow the scarce TCAM resources with low-rate attack traffic. In addition, we can observe that the number of rules continuously increases over time in scenario (I). However, the number of rules in scenario (II) drops at 300 s and tends to convergence after that time. The reason is that hard timeout is configured as 200 s in scenario (II) and the flow rules that are installed by attack flows always expire after the hard timeout. These rules are periodically removed and reinstalled in the switch and the number of them tends to converge.

Impacts on Throughput Degradation. To quantify the impacts of the attack on network throughput, we measure the throughput degradation ratio of the total background traffic in each attack scenario. *The degradation ratio* is the fraction of the traffic decreased by the attack over the total traffic without the attack within a period. Here, for simplicity, we set the period to 50 s. The degradation ratio is shown in Fig. 9. In scenario (I), the ratio continuously increases and reaches to 69% at 600 s. The results demonstrate that the attack can significantly degrade the throughput of the network and have accumulative damage effect on the network over time. In scenario (II), the degradation ratio reaches 36% at 600 s and the throughput degradation is less than that in scenario (I). Moreover, it decreases at 300 s and increases again at 450 s. The reason is that flow rules installed by attack packets will be periodically removed and reinstalled due to hard timeout.

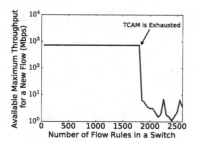

Fig. 10. Maximum throughput of a new flow with different numbers of flow rules.

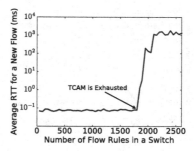

Fig. 11. Average RTT of a new flow with different numbers of flow rules.

Impacts on Maximum Throughput of a New Flow. We use *iperf* [22] to measure the available maximum throughput for a new flow with different flow rules in our attack. As is shown in Fig. 10, the available maximum throughput for a new flow significantly decreases to below 10 Mbps from 850 Mbps when the number of flow rules exceeds 1,800. The reason is that TCAM is overflowed and extra new flow rules are stored in software. Note that storing flow rules in software can not ensure high and stable forwarding performance. These results demonstrate that our attack can significantly degrade the maximum throughput of a new flow when the TCAM is overflowed.

Impacts on Forwarding Delay of a New Flow. We use *ping* to measure the average RTT of a new flow with different numbers of installed rules in our attack. 100 rounds of pings are performed for each different numbers of rules to compute the average RTT. As is shown in Fig. 11, the average RTT of a new flow significantly increases when TCAM is overflowed. We can see that the average RTT reaches to approximate 1,000 ms when the number of rules reaches to 2,100. Compared to forwarding by TCAM, software forwarding introduces remarkable delay. Moreover, the RTT does not tend to increase at the end. The possible reason is that we ignore the ICMP packets that are dropped in calculating the average RTT. Actually, when the number of rules exceeds 2,000, more ICMP packets are dropped along with the increase of the number of flow rules in our measurement. These results demonstrate that our attack can significantly increase forwarding delay of a new flow when the TCAM is overflowed.

6.4   Evaluation of Probing Accuracy

Accuracy of Probing Match Fields. The *Forwarding* application in Floodlight controller conducts fine-grained forwarding. By default, the match fields of it are configured as $\langle src\_mac, dst\_mac, src\_ip, dst\_ip, src\_port, dst\_port \rangle$ without bitmasks. To better evaluate match fields probing accuracy, we configure the match fields as $\langle src\_ip, dst\_ip \rangle$ with different bitmasks. Algorithm 1 are conducted to measure the accuracy of probing match fields. The results are summarized in Tables 2 and 3. As is shown in Table 2, when we change MAC source address, TCP source port or UDP source port in the probed packets headers, both p-values are less than 0.05. However, when we change the IP source address in the packets headers, the p-value increases and reaches 0.92, which is significantly large. Thus, we can easily infer that the IP address field is used in the forwarding rules by evaluating p-value. Table 3 shows the probing accuracy of different bitmasks. The results demonstrate that Algorithm 1 can infer the bitmasks with more than 90% accuracy. The accuracy is enough for an attacker to effectively launch LOFT attack.

Accuracy of Probing Timeout Values. We systematically measure the probing accuracy with different hard timeout and idle timeout settings. 100 rounds of probing are performed for each different setting to compute the average accuracy. Figure 12(a) shows the accuracy rate for various hard timeout values. We observe that hard timeout probing can reach more than 90% accuracy rate with different

Table 2. p-value for each changed packet header field.

Changed header field	p-value
MAC source address	0.01
TCP source port	0.03
UDP source port	0.01
IP source address	0.92

Table 3. Probing accuracy of different bitmasks.

configured bitmasks	Accuracy
255.0.0.0	91%
255.255.0.0	91%
255.255.255.0	92%
255.255.255.255	94%

hard timeout values. Similarly, Fig. 12(b) shows that idle timeout probing can also reach more than 90% accuracy rate with different idle timeout values. Note that the accuracy rate is enough to construct LOFT. We may not be able to infer correct timeout values with one round of probing. However, we can obtain the correct results by performing multiple rounds of probing.

7   Possible Defenses

In this section, we discuss possible countermeasures against the LOFT attack. We can throttle the attack at two phases, i.e., interfering with the probing and dismissing attack packets.

Thwarting Probing. We could interfere with RTT measurement to thwart the probing. An SDN controller can generate artificial jitter during delivery of the very first few packets of flows. For example, the controller does not generate a flow rule for a new flow immediately once it receives packet-in messages. Instead, it deliberately waits for a random delay before sending the packets back to the switches. And it installs the flow rules after receiving several packet-in messages for the new flow. Therefore, an attacker cannot accurately infer whether there are new rules installed or not for probing packets. The potential disadvantage is that the approach also incurs extra forwarding delays for benign packets and requires the controller to process more packet-in messages.

Another approach could possibly adopt dynamic timeout values. According to our investigations, we find that almost all applications atop of the same controllers set flow rules with fixed values. We suggest that the applications set different timeout values once there is a new rule installed or a rule is reinstalled due to rule expiration. Thereby, an attacker could not easily infer the timeout values set by the controller. In this case, overflowing the flow table at low-rate is not likely to succeed due to lacking accurate information of timeout values.

Dismissing Attacks. Significant work exists on taming flow table overflow, which falls in two categories: mitigating normal flow table overflow triggered by many benign flows [23,24], and defending against malicious flow table overflow attacks [10,11,13]. Solutions of the first category assume that there are no overflow attacks. They cannot effectively throttle persistent and malicious flow table

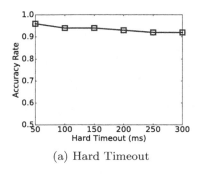

(a) Hard Timeout

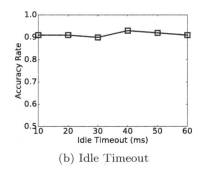

(b) Idle Timeout

Fig. 12. Average timeout probing accuracy. (a) shows the probing accuracy of hard timeout with Algorithm 2; (b) shows the probing accuracy of idle timeout with Algorithm 3.

overflow. Solutions of the second category can effectively resist malicious flow table overflow. However, they are based on the underlying assumption that the attack rate is high. These defenses are not complete in terms of resisting the low-rate overflow attack, as (i) they may not detect the attack until the flow table is overflowed[5], and (ii) they lack the ability to accurately identify low-rate malicious flows so as to throttle them.

In order to specifically defend against the low-rate flow table overflow attack, a possible countermeasure is to monitor and identify flow table consumption patterns generated by the attack and then flush suspicious flow rules in real time. As shown in Fig. 8, under the LOFT attack, we can observe that the number of the installed flow rules continually increase before the table is full, and the increase rate is slow. These features could be used to capture the attack. Once the attack is detected, the SDN controller could actively delete such suspicious flow rules. A suspicious rule could be the rule that is always in the flow table but forwards very few number of packets per second. Besides, since the attack periodically generates packets to refresh the rule, the forwarding rate of a suspicious rule could show an periodicity pattern, which could further help to locate and flush a rule created by the attack packets.

8   Related Work

SDN Probing Techniques. Several SDN probing approaches have been proposed [12,15,25–29]. Shin and Gu [15] present an SDN scanner to infer whether or not a network is using SDN by observing response time of packets. Cui et al. [25] further analyze the feasibility of SDN fingerprint in practical SDN deployments. Achleitner et al. [26] introduce SDNMap to infer the composition of flow

---

[5] The defenses will be enabled only when there are lots of packet-in packets per second. However, our attack does not trigger high-rate packet-in packets before overflowing the flow table.

rules in a network. Klöti et al. [12] identify whether or not there are aggregation flow rules in SDN by timing the TCP setup. Liu et al. [27] build a Markov model of an SDN switch which allows attackers to select the best probes to infer whether a target flow has recently occurred. Sonchack et al. [28] learn host communication patterns, ACL entries and network monitoring settings by injecting lots of timing pings. Leng et al. [29] design an inference attack that can learn the approximate table size of an SDN switch, by estimating the significant changes in response time of requests when flow tables are overflowed. Above work motivates the probing phase of our LOFT attack. However, different from them, we enable probing to accurately infer detailed timeout configurations of flow rules and bitmasks in the match fields, which are essential to quantitatively analyze the minimal attack rate and construct the LOFT attack. Particularly, we can accurately infer the timeout values even if both the idle timeout and the hard timeout are set in a flow rule, which is not addressed in [29].

SDN Data Plane Security. There exist several studies on SDN data plane security [10–12,30]. Antikainen et. al [30] study a wide range of attacks, such as eavesdropping network traffic and man-in-the-middle attacks. They require a strong assumption that an attacker can compromise SDN switches. Prior work [10–12] also studies flow tale overflow threats, which are brute-force and high-rate attacks. They generate many random packets per second and can be easily detected by existing defenses [10,11,13]. Different from them, LOFT is a sophisticated attack that infers SDN network configurations in advance and then efficiently overflows flow tables with low-rate traffic in a stealthy way. LOFT may seem similar to the attack proposed by Shin and Gu [15] that constructs packets according to the probed configurations. However, their attack can fail in practice because it does not consider detailed settings of the flow rules, e.g., lifetime values and bitmasks in the match fields that significantly impacts the effectiveness of the attack. LOFT systematically measures configurations of flow rules and generates packets with minimal feasible attack rate according to the probed configurations such that it ensures the effectiveness of the attack.

SDN Control Plane Security. The security issues of SDN control plane have been widely studied recently. SDN-Rootkits [31] provides rootkit techniques to subvert SDN controllers. SDNShield [32] and SE-Floodlight [33] focus on the application-level security on SDN controllers. These security extensions prevent SDN against malicious or buggy applications. FortNox [34] introduces the dynamic tunneling attacks that violate security policies and provides role-based authorization to defend against those attacks. VeriFlow [35] investigates the correctness of flow rules. AvantGuard [36] and FloodGuard [14] prevent SDN from saturation attacks against the controller. TopoGuard [37] studied SDN topology poisoning attacks. Our paper presents a data plane attack to significantly degrade the network performance with low-rate attack traffic, which is orthogonal to these previous work.

9 Conclusion

In this paper, we design and implement a data plane attack called LOFT that seriously challenges the security of SDN. By accurately inferring the network configurations of flow rules and plotting the attack strategies in advance, LOFT can efficiently overflow the flow tables of switches at minimal feasible attack rate. It can significantly degrade the network performance and incur potential network DoS at an attack rate of only tens of Kbps. Experiments in a real SDN testbed consisting of commercial hardware switches demonstrate the feasibility and effectiveness of the attack.

Acknowledgment. The research is partially supported by the National Natural Science Foundation of China under Grant 61572278 and 61625203, the National Key Research and Development Program of China under Grant 2016YFB0800102 and 2016YFC0901605, and U.S. Office of Naval Research under Grant N00014-16-1-3214 and N00014-16-1-3216.

References

1. Jain, S., et al.: B4: experience with a globally-deployed software defined WAN. In: SIGCOMM. ACM (2013)
2. Microsoft Azure and Software Defined Networking. https://technet.microsoft.com/en-us/windows-server-docs/networking/sdn/azure_and_sdn
3. Jia, S., et al.: Competitive analysis for online scheduling in software-defined optical WAN. In: INFOCOM, pp. 1–9. IEEE (2017)
4. Jang, R.H., et al.: Rflow$^+$: an SDN-based WLAN monitoring and management framework. In: INFOCOM, pp. 1–9. IEEE (2017)
5. Sonchack, J., et al.: Enabling practical software-defined networking security applications with OFX. In: NDSS (2016)
6. Katta, N., et al.: Infinite cacheflow in software-defined networks. In: HotSDN, pp. 175–180. ACM (2014)
7. Cisco Plug-in for OpenFlow Configuration Guide 1.3. http://www.cisco.com/c/en/us/td/docs/switches/datacenter/nexus/openflow/b_openflow_agent_nxos_1_3.pdf
8. IBM Networking OS? 7.4 ISCLI-Industry Standard CLI for the RackSwitch G8264. http://www-01.ibm.com/support/docview.wss?uid=isg3T7000580&aid=1
9. OpenFlow Switch Specification v1.3.4. https://www.opennetworking.org
10. Qian, Y., et al.: Openflow flow table overflow attacks and countermeasures. In: European Conference on Networks and Communications, pp. 205–209. IEEE (2016)
11. Dhawan, M., et al.: SPHINX: detecting security attacks in software-defined networks. In: NDSS (2015)
12. Klöti, R., et al.: OpenFlow: a security analysis. In: ICNP, pp. 1–6. IEEE (2013)
13. Shang, G., et al.: Flooddefender: protecting data and control plane resources under SDN-aimed DoS attacks. In: INFOCOM, pp. 1–9. IEEE (2017)
14. Wang, H., et al.: Floodguard: a DoS attack prevention extension in software-defined networks. In: DSN, pp. 239–250. IEEE (2015)
15. Shin, S., Gu, G.: Attacking software-defined networks: a first feasibility study. In: HotSDN, pp. 165–166. ACM (2013)
16. McKeown, N., et al.: OpenFlow: enabling innovation in campus networks. ACM SIGCOMM Comput. Commun. Rev. **38**(2), 69–74 (2008)

17. Box, J.F.: Guinness, Gosset, Fisher, and small samples. Stat. Sci. **2**, 45–52 (1987)
18. Floodlight SDN Controller. http://www.projectfloodlight.org/floodlight/
19. Floodlight Forwarding Application. https://github.com/floodlight/floodlight/tree/master/src/main/java/net/floodlightcontroller/forwarding
20. AS4610-54T Data Center Switch. http://www.edge-core.com
21. hping3. http://tools.kali.org/information-gathering/hping3
22. iperf. https://iperf.fr/
23. Qiao, S., et al.: Taming the flow table overflow in OpenFlow switch. In: SIGCOMM, pp. 591–592. ACM (2016)
24. Zhu, H., et al.: MDTC: an efficient approach to TCAM-based multidimensional table compression. In: IFIP Networking, 2015, pp. 1–9. IEEE (2015)
25. Cui, H., et al.: On the fingerprinting of software-defined networks. IEEE Trans. Inf. Forensics Secur. **11**(10), 2160–2173 (2016)
26. Achleitner, S., et al.: Adversarial network forensics in software defined networking. In: SIGCOMM SOSR, pp. 1–13. ACM (2017)
27. Liu, S., et al.: Flow reconnaissance via timing attacks on SDN switches. In: ICDCS, pp. 1–11. IEEE (2017)
28. Sonchack, J., et al.: Timing-based reconnaissance and defense in software-defined networks. In: ACSAC, pp. 89–100. ACM (2016)
29. Leng, J., et al.: An inference attack model for flow table capacity and usage: exploiting the vulnerability of flow table overflow in software-defined network. arXiv preprint arXiv:1504.03095 (2015)
30. Antikainen, M., Aura, T., Särelä, M.: Spook in your network: attacking an SDN with a compromised OpenFlow switch. In: Bernsmed, K., Fischer-Hübner, S. (eds.) NordSec 2014. LNCS, vol. 8788, pp. 229–244. Springer, Cham (2014). https://doi.org/10.1007/978-3-319-11599-3_14
31. Röpke, C., Holz, T.: SDN rootkits: subverting network operating systems of software-defined networks. In: Bos, H., Monrose, F., Blanc, G. (eds.) RAID 2015. LNCS, vol. 9404, pp. 339–356. Springer, Cham (2015). https://doi.org/10.1007/978-3-319-26362-5_16
32. Wen, X., et al.: SDNShield: reconciliating configurable application permissions for SDN app markets. In: DSN, pp. 121–132. IEEE (2016)
33. Porras, P.A., et al.: Securing the software defined network control layer. In: NDSS (2015)
34. Porras, P., et al.: A security enforcement kernel for OpenFlow networks. In: HotSDN, pp. 121–126. ACM (2012)
35. Khurshid, A., et al.: Veriflow: verifying network-wide invariants in real time. In: NSDI 2013, pp.15–27 (2013)
36. Shin, S., et al.: Avant-guard: scalable and vigilant switch flow management in software-defined networks. In: CCS, pp. 413–424. ACM (2013)
37. Hong, S., et al.: Poisoning network visibility in software-defined networks: new attacks and countermeasures. In: NDSS (2015)

VCIDS: Collaborative Intrusion Detection of Sensor and Actuator Attacks on Connected Vehicles

Pinyao Guo[1(✉)], Hunmin Kim[2], Le Guan[1], Minghui Zhu[2], and Peng Liu[1]

[1] College of Information Sciences and Technology, Pennsylvania State University,
University Park, PA 16802, USA
{pug132,lug14,pliu}@ist.psu.edu
[2] School of Electrical Engineering and Computer Science,
Pennsylvania State University, University Park, PA 16802, USA
{huk164,muz16}@psu.edu

Abstract. Modern urban vehicles adopt sensing, communication and computing modules into almost every functioning aspect to assist humans in driving. However, the advanced technologies are inherently vulnerable to attacks, exposing vehicles to severe security risks. In this work, we focus on the detection of sensor and actuator attacks that are capable of actively altering vehicle behavior and directly causing damages to human beings and vehicles. We develop a collaborative intrusion detection system where each vehicle leverages sensing data from its onboard sensors and neighboring vehicles to detect sensor and actuator attacks without a centralized authority. The detection utilizes the unique feature that clean data and contaminated data are correlated through the physical dynamics of the vehicle. We demonstrate the effectiveness of the detection system in a scaled autonomous vehicle testbed by launching attacks through various attack channels.

Keywords: Urban vehicular networks · Intrusion detection
Cyber-physical systems

1 Introduction

Modern urban transportation systems are rapidly evolving toward enhanced intelligence and safety. The evolution has been driven by recent developments in wireless communication, mobile computing, sensing, autonomous driving, etc. In particular, vehicle-to-vehicle (V2V) communications [14] are becoming prevalent in modern vehicles. Real-time traffic information is shared between connected vehicles and provided to drivers such that they can gather better awareness and make more informed decisions to increase traffic safety and efficiency. Recently, major technology companies including Google, Uber and Tesla are leading intensive development of autonomous vehicles [19]. Autonomous vehicles integrate wireless communication, in-vehicle sensing and computing into almost every

© ICST Institute for Computer Sciences, Social Informatics and Telecommunications Engineering 2018
X. Lin et al. (Eds.): SecureComm 2017, LNICST 238, pp. 377–396, 2018.
https://doi.org/10.1007/978-3-319-78813-5_19

functioning aspect and provide robust driver-free maneuver in order to handle exhaustive conditions in urban environments.

While the advanced technologies are dedicated to promoting efficiency and safety for vehicles and drivers, they also bring security concerns to the community. Unlike traditional information and communications technology systems such as computers or mobile phones, vehicles are characterized by a strong coupling of the cyberspace where the software runs and the physical world in which they operate. Vulnerabilities rooted from either the cyberspace (e.g., driver backdoor, rootkit) or the physical world (e.g., signal spoofing, wire breakage) could be intentionally exploited by adversaries. Several researchers [15,30,38] conducted jamming, spoofing, and replay attacks on multiple driving guidance sensors including radars, ultrasonic sensors, GPS, etc., on off-the-shelf vehicles. When corrupted sensors are involved in safety-critical decision making, their readings could potentially deceive human drivers or autonomous driving systems and further escalate into disastrous consequences. Furthermore, white-hats recently launched remote hacks into a Jeep Cherokee [21] and multiple models of Tesla [1,2]. The hacks demonstrated the possibility to remotely control vehicular actuators such as steering wheels or gas pedals, which could directly divert vehicles to crashes or severe damages. Given the substantial role security plays in the automotive community, it is imperative to study the attacks before pandemic security problems happen.

In this paper, we focus on the detection of active attacks that are capable of altering vehicle behaviors and directly causing damages to vehicles or drivers. Down to attack consequences, active attacks can be classified into sensor attacks and actuator attacks. *Sensor attacks*, e.g., GPS spoofing, alter authentic sensor readings. *Actuator attacks*, e.g., steering wheel take-over, directly alter control commands to be executed by vehicle wheels. Passive attacks that aim to steal information or break other non-safety aspects are out of our scope.

Table 1. Literature categorization in intrusion detection systems.

Data sources Attack sources	Single host	Network
Cyber attacks	host-based IDSs	mobile ad hoc networks wireless sensor networks
Cyber & physical attacks	control-theoretic approaches	*Our solution*

Intrusion detection has been studied extensively in the past decades. Relevant literature can be partitioned into three categories based on their data audit sources and detection capabilities, as shown in Table 1. Traditional host-based IDSs [18,33,36,39] monitor the system behaviors (e.g. filesystem logs, system calls) of a single host. Network-based approaches [7,17,29,32,37,42] from mobile ad hoc networks and wireless sensor networks incorporate networking traffic in their detection processes. However, both categories are mostly dedicated to the detection of attacks launched within cyberspace. Data corruption attacks launched through physical channels (e.g. sensor spoofing) cannot be detected since no abnormal cyberspace behavior would be triggered and captured. Besides, neither category models the physical mobility of a vehicle, and thus actuator attacks cannot be detected. Control-theoretic approaches [9,12] are proposed to complement existing IDSs. In particular, these approaches leverage the fact that clean and contaminated sensing data and control commands are correlated via physical dynamics of a vehicle. Refer to Sect. 6 for a more comprehensive literature review. A salient limitation of these approaches is that they require one or multiple sensors of a vehicle to be clean. Powerful attackers (as demonstrated in [1,2]) could potentially corrupt all sensors of a vehicle. For instance, an attacker could exploit a backdoor vulnerability in the sensing data processing library and corrupt all sensor readings in a consistent way to avoid the detection.

The goal of this paper is to address the limitation identified in the last paragraph and develop a new IDS for connected vehicles. The key feature of our proposed IDS is the novel integration of V2V communications and control-theoretic approaches. Under the context of connected vehicular networks, V2V communication enables information exchange between nearby vehicles. To our best knowledge, no prior work studies the benefits of V2V communication in intrusion detections of connected vehicles. The paper makes the first attempt to bridge the gap. This paper makes the following contributions:

- We propose a collaborative intrusion detection system, VCIDS, for the detection of sensor and actuator attacks in connected vehicles. The VCIDS fuses local sensing information and that from nearby vehicles to enhance detection capabilities.
- We implement a prototype detection system on a scaled autonomous vehicle testbed and evaluate the system regarding the effectiveness under different attacks launched through multiple attack channels. The results demonstrate detection capabilities under destructive attack cases when all sensors in a vehicle are compromised.

2 Overview

This section presents background information about modern vehicles and vehicle-to-vehicle communication. Then we give an overview of our prior work in intrusion detection for single host and describe its limitation. Finally, we introduce the adversary and defender model considered in the paper.

2.1 Modern Vehicle Platform

A modern vehicle is equipped with a rich set of sensors. In this paper, we only consider the sensors that are related to vehicle motion. Other sensors such as thermometer or tire pressure monitoring sensor are out of our scope. The sensors related to motion fall into two categories according to their functionalities [34]. *Navigation sensors* such as GPS and inertial measurement units (IMU) serve the purposes of localization and motion tracking. *Observation sensors* such as light detection and ranging sensor (LiDAR) and camera perceive the surroundings of the vehicle and provide information for short-term maneuver such as collision avoidance, lane changing, etc. Observation sensors enable the vehicle to recognize surrounding objects such as nearby vehicles or pedestrians, and measure their relative positions [4]. In order to handle massive data volume and provide real-time control, vehicles are equipped with powerful mobile computing devices (e.g., Nvidia Drive PX 2 [3]) for complicated functionalities such as object recognition. The actuators in a vehicle typically include steering, gas pedal, and brake.

In a vehicle control iteration (shown in Fig. 1), the sensors measure the position and orientation of the vehicle and its surrounding environment. Then the sensor readings are fed to the human driver or the controller inside the vehicle[1]. After that, control commands are generated and executed by the actuators in the physical world. Each step from capturing the physical signals (e.g., electromagnetic waves, acoustic waves) to signal digitization, data processing, and sending the data to the controller/human driver is prone to data corruption. Analogously, the execution of the control commands is also prone to corruption.

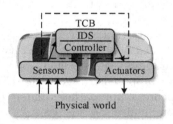

Fig. 1. Vehicle modeling.

2.2   Control Theoretic Approach for Single Host

Modern urban vehicles are cyber-physical systems where the cyberspace (i.e., the computation units) and the physical world in which they operate are strongly coupled. In our prior work [12], we propose a robot intrusion detection system (RIDS) for the detection of sensor and actuator attacks in standalone nonlinear robots. We use a control-theoretic approach and develop a nonlinear unknown input and state estimation (NUISE) algorithm. NUISE exploits the physical dynamics of a single mobile robot and detects attacks by comparing data generated from observed sensor readings and estimates using physical dynamics. In particular, sensor readings can be utilized to estimate new states, and executed control commands can be estimated through state transitions. Therefore, actuator attacks can be detected by comparing planned control commands generated by the controller and executed control commands estimated from sensor readings. With sensor redundancy, sensor attacks can be detected by cross-validating estimated states across the sensors. For the self-containedness of this paper, NUISE algorithm is included in Appendix B.

---

[1] We do not differentiate controller or human driver in the rest of the paper and refer to them as controller.

In our prior study [12], we evaluate the detection performance of an RIDS implementation against different combinations of sensor and actuator attacks launched from different channels including signal interference, sensor spoofing, logic bomb, etc. The results show that false positive rates and false negative rates are all below 1%, and detection delays are within 0.4 s on average. Other than detection, RIDS also identifies attack types and quantifies attack magnitudes.

The RIDS in [12] only considers local information for the detection of attacks. Hence, it requires that there is at least one clean sensor of each robot. However, this assumption may not be valid for urban vehicles. As demonstrated by [1], attackers can successfully achieve access to a vehicle's Controller Area Network (CAN) and take over multiple functionality modules of a vehicle by sending crafted packages.

2.3   Adversary and Defender Models

We consider adversaries that can launch active attacks that can deviate the vehicles from their normal operation. The adversaries can observe real-time vehicle states and have knowledge about vehicle sensing, actuation, and computing systems. They are capable of launching sensor attacks and/or actuator attacks through different channels, including physical damages (e.g., jamming wheels), signal interference (e.g., GPS spoofing), or cyber breaches (e.g., root-kit) on one or multiple vehicles in a vehicular network. Nevertheless, we assume that for each vehicle in a vehicular network, at least one of its neighboring vehicles has at least one clean observation sensor and a clean localization sensor.

Given the adversary model, the defender has no prior knowledge about the targets of attacks nor the types of attacks. In contrast to previous works [9,12] where at least one clean sensor is required to work, the defender does not trust any particular sensors or actuators nor make assumption on the number of corrupted sensors or actuators on a particular vehicle. As shown in Fig. 1, the controller and the intrusion detection system are treated as a trusted computing base (TCB), which could reside in an isolated computing space such as a separated electric control unit, or be protected with hardware isolation technologies such as TrustZone. We assume each vehicle has clean readings at the very beginning of a trip, and attacks are launched during a trip. The V2V communication channel is assumed to be protected and free of attacks. We do not consider attacks on the communication channel.

2.4   Our Approach: Detection with V2V

V2V is a technology that allows nearby vehicles to exchange assorted information for the safety of urban vehicles and the efficiency of urban traffic. There has been considerable study on applying V2V communication for a variety of functionalities such as collision avoidance [13] and traffic control [8]. A vehicular ad hoc network (VANET) is established to connect nearby vehicles in a decentralized and self-organizing manner. Analogous to mobile ad hoc network, when a vehicle joins a swarm of vehicles on road, routings are established between the vehicle and other vehicles in the swarm.

To address the limitation in [12], we leverage the information exchange channel as an extra vector for detection. Specifically, with the state estimates and the observations for neighboring vehicles, a vehicle can generate state estimates for nearby vehicles and broadcast the estimates through V2V communication. Leveraging this information, a vehicle can further validate its own state estimates and make salient decisions for itself and other vehicles. Leveraging information from neighbors, the detection could potentially work even when a vehicle has no clean sensor.

3   System Design

The proposed vehicle intrusion detection system follows a distributed and collaborative design, where each connected vehicle in a formed local network participates in intrusion detection without a central authority. The architecture of VCIDS is illustrated in Fig. 2. Each vehicle consists of an IDS node, which is responsible for detecting intrusion locally and collaboratively with nearby vehicles. The VCIDS structure can be divided into several modules. In the IDS node, the monitor collects sensor readings and control commands of the associated vehicle. Utilizing the physical dynamics of the vehicle, the intra-vehicle IDS generates vehicle state estimates and local sensor and actuator attack detection results. Next, the inter-vehicle IDS collects the results from the intra-vehicle IDS module and data transmitted from nearby vehicles to further confirm and detect attacks globally. The global detection also relies on the physical dynamics of the vehicle. In the meanwhile, a secure V2V module transmits and receives information between the vehicles. Upon receiving results from both IDS modules, the decision maker produces conclusive detection results and state estimates for the vehicle controller.

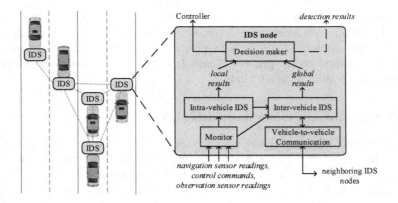

Fig. 2. Vehicle collaborative intrusion detection system architecture.

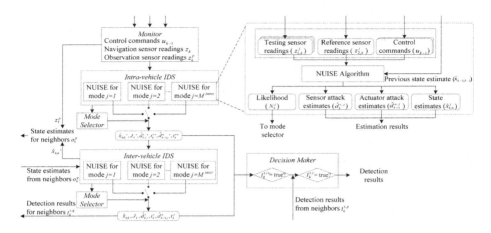

Fig. 3. Vehicle collaborative intrusion detection system schematics.

The VCIDS works iteratively and generates detection results in each control iteration using timely data. Figure 3 shows the schematics of the whole detection system. In the next few subsections, we will first introduce the physical dynamics of the vehicle, and describe how each module works in details.

3.1 Vehicle Physical Dynamics

A vehicle can be modeled as a nonlinear discrete-time dynamic system. Consider current iteration $k - 1$, and let $\mathbf{x}_{k-1}$ be the state at the beginning of the current iteration. The controller generates control commands $\mathbf{u}_{k-1}$ and the actuators execute the control commands in the $(k - 1)$-th iteration. At the beginning of the k-th iteration, the vehicle reaches the new state $\mathbf{x}_k$ and obtains new sensor readings $\mathbf{z}_k$. Considering sensor and actuator attacks, the system model can be described by the following nonlinear equations:

$$\mathbf{x}_k = f(\mathbf{x}_{k-1}, \mathbf{u}_{k-1} + \mathbf{d}_{k-1}^a) + \zeta_{k-1}$$
$$\mathbf{z}_k = h(\mathbf{x}_k) + \mathbf{d}_k^s + \xi_k \tag{1}$$

where actuator attacks and sensor attacks are modeled as corruptions $\mathbf{d}_{k-1}^a$ and $\mathbf{d}_k^s$, respectively. The first equation in (1) is referred to as the *kinematic model*, which describes vehicle state transitions driven by control command execution. The kinematic model specifies the relation between states and control commands based on the actuator properties, e.g., wheelbase (the distance between the front wheels and the real wheels), engine horsepower, etc. When actuator attacks are launched, the executed control commands deviate from the planned control commands. The deviation is denoted by $\mathbf{d}_{k-1}^a$. The second equation in (1) is the *measurement model*, which describes the relations between sensor readings and vehicle states. The measurement model is determined by the vehicle sensor settings, such as sensors types, sensor placement, etc. When sensor attacks are

launched, the obtained sensor readings deviate
from authentic physical values. The deviation is
denoted by $\mathbf{d}_k^s$. Vectors ζ_{k-1} are process noises,
which account for external disturbances in the
kinematic model. Vectors ξ_k are measurement
noises, which account for sensing inaccuracy. We
assume noise vectors are Gaussian with zero
mean and known covariances Q and R, respectively. The kinematic model for a typical rear-
wheel-drive vehicle is presented in Fig. 4. The
states of the vehicle in a 2D plane include the
location and orientation (x, y, θ). The controls
include longitudinal velocity and steering (v, ϕ) . The kinematic model for the
vehicle can be described as:

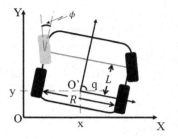

Fig. 4. Kinematic model of a rear-wheel-drive vehicle.

$$x_k = x_{k-1} + T(v_{k-1} + d_{k-1}^v)\cos\theta_{k-1} + \zeta_{k-1}^x$$

$$y_k = y_{k-1} + T(v_{k-1} + d_{k-1}^v)\sin\theta_{k-1} + \zeta_{k-1}^y$$

$$\theta_k = \theta_{k-1} + T\frac{v_{k-1}}{L}\tan(\phi_{k-1} + d_{k-1}^\phi) + \zeta_{k-1}^\theta$$

where $\zeta_{k-1} = [\zeta_{k-1}^x, \zeta_{k-1}^y, \zeta_{k-1}^\theta]^T$ is assumed to be zero mean Gaussian process
noise vector, $\mathbf{d}_{k-1}^a = [d_{k-1}^v, d_{k-1}^\phi]^T$ are the actuator attack vectors, L is the
wheelbase, and T is the control iteration interval. The sensor measurement model
of a vehicle depends on specific sensor types and their configurations. We will
introduce the sensor measurement models of our testbed in Sect. 4.2.

3.2   Monitor

In each control iteration, the monitor gathers three types of real-time local data:
navigation sensor readings $\mathbf{z}_k$, observation sensor readings $\mathbf{z}_k^p$ ($p \in \mathbb{P}_k$, $\mathbb{P}_k$ denotes
the number of nearby vehicles observed at the iteration), and control commands
generated from the controller $\mathbf{u}_{k-1}$ (Algorithm 1 line 3–5).

3.3   Intra-vehicle IDS

The intra-vehicle IDS module uses local data to detect sensor and actuator
attacks, as well as generate state estimates using local data. In particular, the
intra-vehicle IDS applies the *multi-mode estimation algorithm* (Algorithm 2 in
Appendix B) on the local data collected from the monitor (line 6).
    The multi-mode estimation algorithm maintains a set of possible sensor
attack conditions. Each condition is referred to as a *mode*, which represents a
hypothesis that a particular sensor is free of attacks, and the remaining sensors
are potentially corrupted. The clean sensor is referred to as a *reference sensor*,
while the corrupted sensors are referred to as *testing sensors*. Each mode runs a
NUISE algorithm (Algorithm 3 in Appendix B) with the corresponding reference
sensor readings and testing sensor readings in parallel. The mode set is referred

---

Algorithm 1. Vehicle Collaborative Intrusion Detection System (VCIDS)

1: Initialize;
2: **for** $k \leftarrow 1$ to ∞ **do**
3:     Read control commands $\mathbf{u}_{k-1}$;
4:     Read navigation sensor readings $\mathbf{z}_k$;
5:     Read observation sensor readings $\mathbf{z}_k^p, p \in \mathbb{P}_k$;
       ▷ **Intra-vehicle IDS**
6:     Run   Algorithm 2   with $(\mathbf{z}_k, \mathbf{u}_{k-1}, \hat{\mathbf{x}}_{k-1|k-1}, \mathbb{M}^{intra})$ and   generate
       $(\hat{\mathbf{x}}'_{k|k}, J'_k, \hat{\mathbf{d}}^{s'}_{k,t}, t_k^{s'}, \hat{\mathbf{d}}^{a'}_{k-1,t}, t_k^{a'})$;
       ▷ **Inter-vehicle IDS**
7:     Calculate and broadcast state estimates for neighboring vehicles $\mathbf{o}_k^p$ for $p \in \mathbb{P}_k$
       using $\hat{\mathbf{x}}'_{k|k}$ and $\mathbf{z}_k^p$;
8:     Receive state estimates $\mathbf{o}_k^q$ for $q \in \mathbb{Q}_k$ from neighboring vehicles;
9:     Run Algorithm 2 with $([(\mathbf{z}_k^{J'_k})^T, (\mathbf{o}_k^q)^T]^T, \mathbf{u}_{k-1}, \hat{\mathbf{x}}_{k-1|k-1}, \mathbb{M}^{inter})$ and generate
       $(\hat{\mathbf{x}}_{k|k}, J_k, \hat{\mathbf{d}}^s_{k,t}, t_k^s, \hat{\mathbf{d}}^a_{k-1,t}, t_k^a)$;
10:    Broadcast $t_k^{s,q}$ for $q \in \mathbb{Q}_k$;
11:    Receive $t_k^{s,p}$ for $p \in \mathbb{P}_k$;
       ▷ **Decision maker**
12:    **for** each navigation sensor i **do**
13:        **if** $t_k^{s,i'} = true$ or $t_k^{s,i} = true$ **then**
14:            Sensor attack alarm for ith navigation sensor;
15:        **end if**
16:    **end for**
17:    **if** $\exists p \in \mathbb{P}_k$ such that $t^{s,p} = true$ **then**
18:        Sensor attack alarm for observation sensor;
19:    **end if**
20:    **if** $t_k^a = true$ or $t_k^{a'} = true$ **then**
21:        Actuator attack alarm;
22:    **end if**
23:    Return $\hat{\mathbf{x}}_{k|k}$ to the controller;
24: **end for**

---

to as $\mathbb{M}$. NUISE generates new vehicle states, attack sizes, and a likelihood for each mode. Detail descriptions of the NUISE algorithm can be found in our prior work [12].

After the NUISE algorithm finishes, a mode selector selects the most probable mode J'_k with the highest likelihood and uses the state estimates $\hat{\mathbf{x}}'_{k|k}$ from the selected mode as the new vehicle state estimates. After that, we further conduct hypothesis testings on the testing sensors and actuators to confirm and identify the attacks $t_k^{s'}$ and $t_k^{a'}$.

3.4   Inter-vehicle IDS

The inter-vehicle IDS is dedicated to confirming the attacks detected by the intra-vehicle IDS, and identifying a boarder range of attacks. The key data source is the observation sensor readings from nearby vehicles. Once the new state estimates $\hat{\mathbf{x}}'_{k|k}$ is generated, a vehicle can estimate the state of nearby vehicles $\mathbf{o}^p_k$ within the range of its observation sensors (line 7). After that, each vehicle receives the state estimates of itself from nearby vehicles $\mathbf{o}^q_k$ (line 8). Note that the number of observed vehicles $\mathbb{P}_k$ can be different from the number of received state estimates $\mathbb{Q}_k$. Then, the received state estimates $\mathbf{o}^q_k$ are treated as sensor readings from external sources and fed into another round of multi-mode estimation algorithm execution along with the clean sensor readings $\mathbf{z}^{J'_k}_k$ identified by the intra-vehicle IDS (line 9). Finally, the detection results for the received observations $t^{s,q}_k$ are broadcasted, and each vehicle receives the corresponding $t^{s,p}_k$ for decision making, accordingly (line 10–11).

3.5 Decision Maker

The decision maker confirms attacks using the detection results generated by the intra-vehicle IDS and the inter-vehicle IDS (line 12–23). It checks the detection indexes t generated for navigation sensors, observation sensors, and actuators. Each navigation sensor i is detected to be clean only when both detection indexes $t^{s,i'}_k$ and $t^{s,i}_k$ remain negative. An observation sensor can only be declared as clean when global detection results $t^{s,p}_k$ from all nearby vehicles are not positive. Actuator attacks are positive as long as either $t^{a'}_k$ or t^a_k is positive. Under cases when a vehicle is not connected in a vehicular network, the decision maker still works independently with local detection results. However, the detection results only relying on local data cannot make informed decisions under cases when the observation sensor is corrupted, or all navigation sensors are corrupted with consistent attack vectors.

4   Implementation

We build a prototype vehicle collaborative intrusion detection system on an indoor testbed which includes three scaled autonomous vehicles. We elaborate on the testbed as follows.

4.1   Testbed Implementation

Figure 5(a) shows the scaled autonomous vehicle testbed on which we implement the VCIDS prototype. Three vehicles are built based on Tamiya TT02 RC car chassis platform [6]. Each vehicle is mounted with a Nvidia Jetson TK1 (Nvidia Cortex-A15) embedded development board [5] as the mobile computing system. TK1 shares the design architecture of vehicular computing systems such as Nvidia PX2, which has been adopted by several autonomous driving manufacturers such as Tesla and Volvo. Its processor features the ARM Architecture and a GPU integration for visual processing intensive applications. The TK1 runs the Robot Operating System (ROS) [31]. Each sensing and actuation module runs in an isolated ROS node (process) and communicates with each other through

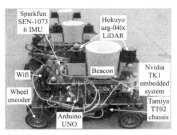

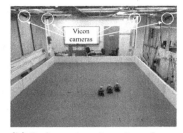

(a) Scaled autonomous vehicle testbed with three vehicles.

(b) Indoor experiment environment with Vicon indoor positioning system.

Fig. 5. Scaled autonomous vehicle testbed and indoor positioning system.

sockets. The V2V communication is built on a local wireless ad hoc network. Each vehicle is equipped with a Wifi dongle and joins the ad hoc network after boot. A ROS module is implemented to broadcast or receive observations and detection results generated by the IDSs of other vehicles in the network.

Each vehicle is equipped with four types of sensors: two wheel encoders, a Vicon indoor positioning system (IPS), an IMU (Sparkfun SEN-10736), and two LiDARs (Hokuyo urg-04lx). Two wheel encoders measure the traveling distances of the two rear wheels in a short period of time. They are built with optical sensors fastened on the rear wheels of each vehicle. The optical sensors detect motion of the wheels and communicate with the TK1 through an Arduino board. IPS is powered by Vicon motion capturing system (see Fig. 5(b)), which tracks the position and orientation of each vehicle. An IMU is mounted at the center of each vehicle and provides inertial navigation data. The wheel encoders, IPS and IMU serve as the navigation sensors of an vehicle. Two LiDARs are placed on the top of each vehicle, where one faces the front of the vehicle and the other faces the rear. Each LiDAR scans laser beams in 240 degrees and receives reflection to obtain distances from surrounding objects. The LiDARs together serve as the observation sensors of a vehicle. After processing, they provide a 360-degree distance information of the surroundings of the vehicle.

4.2   Sensor Measurement Models

At each instant of time, navigation sensor readings include data from three sensors: $\mathbf{z}_k = [\mathbf{z}_{k,I}, \mathbf{z}_{k,W}, \mathbf{z}_{k,M}]^T$, where each vector refers to the sensor readings from IPS, wheel encoders, and IMU, respectively. The observation sensors (LiDARs) provides relative distances and directions $\mathbf{z}_k^p$ of nearby vehicles.

Before sensor readings are transmitted to the controller, data go through a processing phase. Navigation sensor readings are converted into vehicle states, i.e., vehicle position (x, y) and heading θ. We convert the raw sensor readings of the wheel encoders and IMU into vehicle states using the measurement models of each sensor. Details of the data processing can be found in Appendix A.

As observation sensors, the LiDARs generate relative position and orientation $\mathbf{z}_k^p$ for each nearby vehicle p. The raw data from a LiDAR includes points that record the ranges of the nearest object from different angles. In the indoor environment surrounded by walls (shown in Fig. 5(b)), we apply the Hough transformation [10] to filter out the range points for the walls (shown as straight lines). After that, remaining range points are clustered and recognized as nearby vehicles. We associate the recognition results with each vehicle using heuristics.

5   Evaluation

In this section, we evaluate the VCIDS on the scaled autonomous vehicle testbed against various attacks and demonstrate its security capabilities. We intend to answer two research questions for the detection system: (1) What benefits does the VCIDS offer in terms of security capabilities? (2) To what extent does the VCIDS influence the detection performance, i.e., effectiveness and efficiency? We compare the detection results generated by intra-vehicle IDS and that by the complete VCIDS.

The three vehicles in the testbed travel in the indoor environment. For the ease of presentation, we label the three vehicles with fixed numbers. In each experiment, vehicle 1 and vehicle 2 circle around the environment in a predefined two-lane road with an identical preset speed of 6 cm/s as shown in Fig. 6(a). Vehicle 3 stays on the roadside without moving, but all onboard sensors are working. During the mission, the three vehicles communicate through V2V communication and collaboratively detect attacks.

5.1   Attack Scenarios

To demonstrate the effectiveness, we consider the following four attack scenarios where attacks are launched on different targets of the vehicle system. The attack scenarios are conducted independently with each other.

Wheel Encoder Logic Bomb and Wheel Jamming. The attack is launched by replacing the wheel encoder sensor data processing library with a malicious library in vehicle 1. After being triggered at certain instant of time, instead of returning states obtained from motion of the wheel shafts, the malicious library returns the sensor readings with a constant sensor attack vector that shifts the vehicle by -10 cm on the X axis. A plastic stick is placed in the left rear wheel of vehicle 1. The stick adds friction in the wheel and slows down the movement of the wheel (actuator attack).

LiDAR Driver Logic Bomb. Analogous to the wheel encoder sensor logic bomb attack, we add dozens of code in the LiDAR driver program of vehicle 1. After triggering, the customized driver returns fake relative distances and angle measurements of nearby vehicles.

System Hijacking. For advanced attackers, it has been demonstrated that attackers can hijack into the vehicle system and control several components

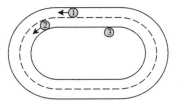

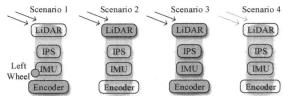

(a) Scaled autonomous vehicle execution in the indoor environment.

(b) Attack scenarios. Scenario 1: Encoder logic bomb and left wheel jamming. Scenario 2: LiDAR driver logic bomb. Scenario 3: System hijacking. Scenario 4: Rogue nodes.

Fig. 6. Experiment setups.

of a vehicle [1,21]. In order to avoid detection, an attacker would modify all sensor readings in a consistent manner. For instance, an attacker would shift all sensor readings on Y axis by $+10$ cm. During the intra-vehicle detection phase, the multi-mode estimation algorithm does not have a clean sensor as the reference sensor. Moreover, since the sensor readings are corrupted consistently, the hypothesis tests would not raise alarm due to the lack of a clean reference. Here, we launch the attack that corrupts all sensor data in vehicle 1 consistently.

Rogue Nodes. Attackers can setup rogue nodes that broadcast fake messages to nearby vehicles in order to cause wrong decision making for the vehicles. For instance, a rogue node can broadcast a phantom vehicle in front of a vehicle and leads to emergency brakes. In this scenario, we assume that a rogue node is set up by the roadside which broadcasts fake observations. The rogue node broadcasts large amount of fake observations of vehicle 1 that contain shifted observations.

5.2 Detection Results

In order to demonstrate the security capabilities of the VCIDS, we compare the detection results generated by the intra-vehicle IDS (i.e., a standalone single host IDS that does not leverage information from neighboring vehicles) and the complete VCIDS. Table 2 shows the detection results against the four attack scenarios we launch in the testbed. We observe that the intra-vehicle IDS can only detect the first attack scenario when a subset of navigation sensors are under attacks. On the contrary, the VCIDS detects all attack scenarios. When the observation sensors are under attacks (Scenario 2), state estimates for nearby vehicles are corrupted. When vehicle 2 and vehicle 3 receive corrupted observations from vehicle 1, their inter-vehicle IDSs raise sensor attack alarms and send the results $t_k^{s,2}$ and $t_k^{s,3}$ back to vehicle 1. When all sensor readings in vehicle 1 are corrupted consistently (Scenario 3), the intra-vehicle IDS of vehicle 1 does not raise any alarm. However, the observations from vehicle 2 (o_k^3) and vehicle 3 (o_k^3) used in the inter-vehicle IDS of vehicle 1 are inconsistent during inter-vehicle IDS execution. Under rogue nodes attack (scenario 4) when fake nodes broadcast erroneous observations, the inter-vehicle IDS raises alarms due to the inconsistencies between observations from other vehicles and the results from intra-vehicle IDS[2].

Table 2. Detection results from intra-vehicle IDS and VCIDS.

Attack scenario	Attack type (channel)	Detected by intra-vehicle IDS	Detected by VCIDS
Wheel encoder logic bomb+wheel jamming	Sensor+actuator (cyber+physical)	Yes	Yes
LiDAR driver logic bomb	Sensor (cyber)	No	Yes
System hijacking	Sensor (cyber)	No	Yes
Rogue nodes	Sensor (cyber)	No	Yes

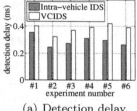
(a) Detection delay.

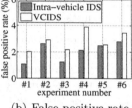
(b) False positive rate.

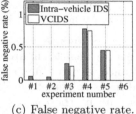
(c) False negative rate.

Fig. 7. Detection performance comparison between results from intra-vehicle IDS and VCIDS against wheel encoder logic bomb & wheel jamming attack.

To investigate the detection performance in terms of detection delay and accuracy, we launch attacks that can be detected by the intra-vehicle IDS and compare the results. A false positive refers to an instant of time that an alarm is raised for a clean sensor, and a false negative refers to an instant of time that alarm is not raised for a corrupted sensor. Figure 7 shows the comparison for detection delays, false positive rates and false negative rates. We notice that detection delays for VCIDS are larger since the VCIDS requires more steps after the intra-vehicle detection. We also notice a slight increases on the false positive rates and a decrease on the false negative rates. All rates are below 4%.

Sensor noises determine the accuracies of state estimates, attack estimates, and decision making. In our approach, sensor noises are modeled with unbound support and propagate along with each calculation step in Algorithms 2 and 3.

---

[2] A detailed explanation on why the NUISE algorithm can determine which mode reflects the authentic values is provided in [12] Sect. 5.2.

The detection system makes decisions under certain level of confidence. Therefore, a vehicle equipped with more accurate sensors could identify attacks with better performance.

6   Related Works

Intrusion Detection for CPSs. Control theory has been utilized to detect sensor attacks for linear cyber-physical systems in recent works [9,22–24]. Several works [11,27,28,40] study both actuator and sensor attacks for linear cyber-physical systems. In contrast, most real world vehicles are modeled as nonlinear systems. In [11,23,24,27], processing and measurement noises rooted in actuators and sensors are not considered or considered with bounded support. In contrast, real world vehicles are subject to stochastic noises with unbounded support. Guo et al. [12] propose NUISE that handles sensor and actuator attack for nonlinear system with unbounded support. However, it requires at least one clean sensor on a single host. Some works study attack-detection on networked systems [20,22,25,26,41]. However, these studies either share the limitations in previously mentioned single host-based solutions or use voting mechanisms in detection making. For instance, Park et al. [25] use Kalman filter to obtain estimates of local agent and use t-tester to leverage inter-observations between neighboring agents to statistically validate estimates. The approach is restricted to linear systems under sensor attacks without actuator attacks. Moreover, the t-testers work under the assumption that majority of the agents are attack-free.

Attacks Targeted on Vehicles. Yan et al. [38] successfully conduct jamming and spoofing attacks on the driving guidance sensors including radars, ultrasonic sensors and forward-looking cameras on a Tesla Model Petit et al. [30] present effective jamming, replay, relay, and spoofing attacks on camera and LiDAR sensors. It has been demonstrated that civilian GPS are vulnerable to spoofing or jamming [15,35]. Several groups demonstrate the possibility to remotely control multiple subsystems in latest off-the-shelf vehicle models such as Tesla [1,2] and Jeep Cherokee [21].

7   Conclusion

The advanced technologies applied in modern vehicles bring both opportunities and security concerns for the community. In this study, we propose a vehicle collaborative intrusion detection system (VCIDS) for the detection of sensor and actuator attacks which target connected vehicles. The detection leverages the physical dynamics of vehicles and utilizes the correlation between clean and contaminated data to estimate attacks. We build a prototype system on a scaled autonomous vehicle testbed and test the system against several types of attacks launched through different attack channels. The results demonstrate that VCIDS can achieve better security capabilities over a single host IDS. Leveraging information from neighboring vehicles, VCIDS works under destructive attack cases even when all the sensors of a vehicle are compromised. VCIDS can promote the resilience of vehicles against attacks. We plan to investigate intrusion response strategies for urban vehicles as our future works.

Acknowledgement. This work was supported by NSF CNS-1505664, ARO W911NF-13-1-0421 (MURI) and ARO W911NF-15-1-0576.

Appendix A Data Processing with Measurement Models

IPS. The IPS sensor directly measures and returns the states of a vehicle.

Wheel encoder. The raw data measured by the wheel encoders are the distances traveled by each wheel (l_L, l_R). In data processing phase, we convert them into vehicle states using previous states $\mathbf{x}_{k-1}$: $x_k = x_{k-1} + (l_L + l_R)\cos\theta_k/2$, $y_k = y_{k-1} + (l_L + l_R)\sin\theta_k/2$, $\theta_k = \theta_{k-1} + (l_R - l_L)/R$, where R is the distance between the left and the right wheel.

IMU. The IMU sensor generates a quaternion $[q_0, q_1, q_2, q_3]^T$, a 3-D acceleration $\mathbf{a}_{k,M}^{local}$, and a 3-D rotational speed $\mathbf{w}_{k,M}^{local}$ on body-fixed coordinate. We first obtain coordinate transformation matrix from body-fixed coordinate to global coordinate [16]:

$$C(q) = \begin{bmatrix} q_0^2 + q_1^2 - q_2^2 - q_3^2 & 2(q_1q_2 - q_0q_3) & 2(q_1q_3 + q_0q_2) \\ 2(q_1q_2 + q_0q_3) & q_0^2 - q_1^2 + q_2^2 - q_3^2 & 2(q_2q_3 - q_0q_1) \\ 2(q_1q_3 - q_0q_2) & 2(q_2q_3 + q_0q_1) & q_0^2 - q_1^2 - q_2^2 + q_3^2 \end{bmatrix}.$$

Acceleration vector and rotation speed on the global coordinate system can be obtained as $C(q)\mathbf{a}_{k,M}^{local}$ and $C(q)\mathbf{w}_{k,M}^{local}$, respectively. Vehicle velocity vector can be updated by: $\mathbf{v}_k = [v_{k,M}^x, v_{k,M}^y, v_{k,M}^z]^T = \mathbf{v}_{k-1} + \mathbf{a}_k^{global}T$. Then the state vector can be calculated by integration as follows: $x_k = x_{k-1} + v_{k,M}^x T + \frac{1}{2}a_{k,M}^x T^2$, $y_k = y_{k-1} + v_{k,M}^y T + \frac{1}{2}a_{k,M}^y T^2$, $\theta_k = \theta_{k-1} + w_{k,M}^z T$.

After the data processing phase for each sensor, sensor readings transmitted to the controller are in the form of vehicle states. For navigation sensors, we have: $\mathbf{z}_{k,i} = \mathbf{x}_k + \mathbf{d}_{k,i}^s + \xi_{k,i}, i = I, W, M$, where $\mathbf{d}_{k,i}^s = [d_{k,i}^{s,x}, d_{k,i}^{s,y}, d_{k,i}^{s,\theta}]^T$, $\xi_{k,i} = [\xi_{k,i}^x, \xi_{k,i}^y, \xi_{k,i}^\theta]^T$ refer to attack vectors and measurement noises for each navigation sensor, respectively.

Appendix B Algorithms

Algorithms 2 and 3[3] are proposed in the Appendix of [12]. We include them here to be self-contained.

---

[3] Notations † and $|\cdot|_+$ refer pseudoinverse and pseudodeterminant, respectively.

Algorithm 2. Multi-mode Estimation Algorithm

Input: Sensor readings $\mathbf{z}_k$; control commands $\mathbf{u}_{k-1}$ from control module; previous state estimates $\hat{\mathbf{x}}_{k-1|k-1}$; mode set $\mathbb{M}$

Output: State estimate; attack vector estimates; mode estimate; confirmed attack indices t_k^s, and t_k^a;

1: Set parameters $w_s, w_a, c_s, c_a, \alpha_s, \alpha_a$;
2: Initialize;
3: **for** mode $j \in \mathbb{M}$ **do**
4:     Run NUISE (Algorithm 3) with input $(\mathbf{u}_{k-1}, \hat{\mathbf{x}}_{k-1|k-1}, \mathbf{z}_{1,k}^j, \mathbf{z}_{2,k}^j, P_{k-1}^x)$ and generate $(\hat{\mathbf{x}}_{k|k}^j, \hat{\mathbf{d}}_k^{s,j}, \hat{\mathbf{d}}_{k-1}^{a,j}, P_k^{x,j}, P_k^{s,j}, P_{k-1}^{a,j}, \mathcal{N}_k^j)$;
5:     $\bar{\mu}_k^j \leftarrow \max\{\mathcal{N}_k^j \mu_{k-1}^j, \epsilon\}$;
6: **end for**
7: **for** mode $j \in \mathbb{M}$ **do**
8:     $\mu_k^j \leftarrow \dfrac{\bar{\mu}_k^j}{\sum_{i=1}^{|\mathbb{M}|} \bar{\mu}_k^i}$;
9: **end for**
10: Sensor mode selection $J_k \leftarrow \operatorname{argmax}_j \mu_k^j$;
11: Obtain estimates and covariance matrices from J_k: $\hat{\mathbf{x}}_{k|k} \leftarrow \hat{\mathbf{x}}_{k|k}^{J_k}$, $\hat{\mathbf{d}}_k^s \leftarrow \hat{\mathbf{d}}_k^{s,J_k}$, $\hat{\mathbf{d}}_{k-1}^a \leftarrow \hat{\mathbf{d}}_{k-1}^{a,J_k}$, $P_k^x \leftarrow P_k^{x,J_k}$;
12: $b_k^s \leftarrow (\hat{\mathbf{d}}_k^{s\,T}(P_k^{s,J_k})^{-1}\hat{\mathbf{d}}_k^s > \chi_{p=|\hat{\mathbf{d}}_k^s|}^2(\alpha_s))$;
13: $b_k^a \leftarrow (\hat{\mathbf{d}}_{k-1}^{a\,T}(P_{k-1}^{a,J_k})^{-1}\hat{\mathbf{d}}_{k-1}^a > \chi_{p=|\hat{\mathbf{d}}_{k-1}^a|}^2(\alpha_a))$;
14: **if** $b_k^s = True$ **and** $\sum_{i=0}^{w_s-1} b_{k-i}^s \geq c_s$ **then**
15:     **for** each testing sensor t in mode J_k **do**
16:         Sensor attack vector estimate for testing sensor t: $\hat{\mathbf{d}}_{k,t}^s = \sum_{i=0}^{w_s-1} \hat{\mathbf{d}}_{k-i,t}^s/w_s$;
17:         **if** $\hat{\mathbf{d}}_{k,t}^{s\,T}(P_{k,t}^{s,J_k})^{-1}\hat{\mathbf{d}}_{k,t}^s \geq \chi_{p=|\hat{\mathbf{d}}_{k,t}^s|}^2$ **then**
18:             $t_k^s = 1$; confirm sensor attack on sensor t;
19:         **end if**
20:     **end for**
21: **end if**
22: **if** $b_k^a = True$ **and** $\sum_{i=0}^{w_a-1} b_{k-i}^a \geq c_a$ **then**
23:     $t_k^a = 1$; confirm actuator attack;
24: **end if**
25:     **return** $\hat{\mathbf{x}}_{k|k}$; based on the confirmations of attacks, find a new mode J_k; sensor attack vector estimates $\hat{\mathbf{d}}_{k,t}^s$ with t_k^s ($t \in \{$testing sensors in mode $J_k\}$); actuator attack vector estimates with t_k^a $\hat{\mathbf{d}}_{k-1,t}^a$ ($t \in \{1, \cdots, n\}$);

Algorithm 3. Nonlinear Unknown Input and State Estimation Algorithm

Input: $\mathbf{u}_{k-1}$, $\hat{\mathbf{x}}_{k-1|k-1}$, $\mathbf{z}_{1,k}^j$, $\mathbf{z}_{2,k}^j$, P_{k-1}^x

Output: $\hat{\mathbf{x}}_{k|k}^j$, $\hat{\mathbf{d}}_k^{s,j}$, $\hat{\mathbf{d}}_{k-1}^{a,j}$, $P_k^{x,j}$, $P_k^{s,j}$, $P_{k-1}^{a,j}$ $\mathcal{N}_k^j$

1: Initialize;
  ▷ **Actuator attack vector $\mathbf{d}_{k-1}^{a,j}$ estimation**
2: $\tilde{P}_{k-1}^j \leftarrow A_{k-1}^j P_{k-1}^x (A_{k-1}^j)^T + Q_{k-1}^j$;
3: $\tilde{R}_{2,k}^{*,j} \leftarrow C_{2,k}^j \tilde{P}_{k-1}^j (C_{2,k}^j)^T + R_{2,k}^j$;
4: $M_{2,k}^j \leftarrow ((G_{k-1}^j)^T (C_{2,k}^j)^T (\tilde{R}_{2,k}^{*,j})^{-1} C_{2,k}^j G_{k-1}^j)^{-1} (G_{k-1}^j)^T (C_{2,k}^j)^T (\tilde{R}_{2,k}^{*,j})^{-1}$;
5: $\hat{\mathbf{d}}_{k-1}^{a,j} \leftarrow M_{2,k}^j (\mathbf{z}_{2,k}^j - C_{2,k}^j f(\hat{\mathbf{x}}_{k-1|k-1}, \mathbf{u}_{k-1}))$;
6: $P_{k-1}^{a,j} \leftarrow M_{2,k}^j \tilde{R}_{2,k}^{*,j} (M_{2,k}^j)^T$;
  ▷ **State prediction**
7: $\hat{\mathbf{x}}_{k|k-1}^j \leftarrow f(\hat{\mathbf{x}}_{k-1|k-1}, \mathbf{u}_{k-1} + \hat{\mathbf{d}}_{k-1}^{a,j})$;
8: $\bar{A}_{k-1}^j \leftarrow (I - G_{k-1}^j M_{2,k}^j C_{2,k}^j) A_{k-1}^j$;
9: $\bar{Q}_{k-1}^j \leftarrow (I - G_{k-1}^j M_{2,k}^j C_{2,k}^j) Q_{k-1}^j (I - G_{k-1}^j M_{2,k}^j C_{2,k}^j)^T + G_{k-1}^j M_{2,k}^j R_{2,k}^j (M_{2,k}^j)^T (G_{k-1}^j)^T$;
10: $P_{k|k-1}^{x,j} \leftarrow \bar{A}_{k-1}^j P_{k-1}^x (\bar{A}_{k-1}^j)^T + \bar{Q}_{k-1}^j$;
  ▷ **State estimation**
11: $\tilde{R}_{2,k}^j \leftarrow C_{2,k}^j P_{k|k-1}^{x,j} (C_{2,k}^j)^T + R_{2,k}^j + C_{2,k}^j G_{k-1}^j M_{2,k}^j R_{2,k}^j + R_{2,k}^j (M_{2,k}^j)^T (G_{k-1}^j)^T (C_{2,k}^j)^T$;
12: $L_k^j \leftarrow (C_{2,k}^j P_{k|k-1}^{x,j} + R_{2,k}^j (M_{2,k}^j)^T (G_{k-1}^j)^T)^T (\tilde{R}_{2,k}^j)^{-1}$;
13: $\hat{\mathbf{x}}_{k|k}^j \leftarrow \hat{\mathbf{x}}_{k|k-1}^j + L_k^j (\mathbf{z}_{2,k}^j - h_2^j(\hat{\mathbf{x}}_{k|k-1}^j))$;
14: $P_k^{x,j} \leftarrow (I - L_k^j C_{2,k}^j) P_{k|k-1}^{x,j} (I - L_k^j C_{2,k}^j)^T + L_k^j R_{2,k}^j (L_k^j)^T - (I - L_k^j C_{2,k}^j) G_{k-1}^j M_{2,k}^j R_{2,k}^j (L_k^j)^T - L_k^j R_{2,k}^j (M_{2,k}^j)^T (G_{k-1}^j)^T (I - L_k^j C_{2,k}^j)^T$;
  ▷ **Sensor attack vector $\mathbf{d}_k^{s,j}$ estimation**
15: $\hat{\mathbf{d}}_k^{s,j} \leftarrow \mathbf{z}_{1,k}^j - h_1^j(\hat{\mathbf{x}}_{k|k}^j)$;
16: $P_k^{s,j} \leftarrow C_{1,k}^j P_k^{x,j} (C_{1,k}^j)^T + R_{1,k}^j$;
  ▷ **Likelihood of the mode**
17: $\nu_k^j \leftarrow \mathbf{z}_{2,k}^j - h_2^j(\hat{\mathbf{x}}_{k|k-1}^j)$;
18: $\bar{P}_{k|k-1}^j \leftarrow C_{2,k}^j P_{k|k-1}^{x,j} (C_{2,k}^j)^T + R_{2,k}^j - C_{2,k}^j G_{k-1}^j M_{2,k}^j R_{2,k}^j - R_{2,k}^j (M_{2,k}^j)^T (G_{k-1}^j)^T (C_{2,k}^j)^T$;
19: $n^j \leftarrow rank(\bar{P}_{k|k-1}^j)$;
20: $\mathcal{N}_k^j \leftarrow \frac{1}{(2\pi)^{n^j/2} |\bar{P}_{k|k-1}^j|_+^{1/2}} \exp(-\frac{(\nu_k^j)^T (\bar{P}_{k|k-1}^j)^\dagger \nu_k^j}{2})$;

References

1. Car Hacking Research: Remote attack Tesla motors. Keen Security Lab of Tencent (2016). http://keenlab.tencent.com/en/2016/09/19/Keen-Security-Lab-of-Tencent-Car-Hacking-Research-Remote-Attack-to-Tesla-Cars/
2. Chinese group hacks a Tesla for the second year in a row (2017). https://www.usatoday.com/story/tech/2017/07/28/chinese-group-hacks-tesla-second-year-row/518430001/

3. Introducing the new NVIDIA DRIVE PX 2 for autocruise driving and HD mapping (2017). http://www.nvidia.com/object/drive-px.html
4. Nvidia driveworks software development kit for self driving cars (2017). https://developer.nvidia.com/driveworks
5. NVIDIA Jetson TK1 (2017). http://www.nvidia.com/object/jetson-tk1-embedded-dev-kit.html
6. RC TT02 Chassis - TT02 Factory Finished (2017). https://www.tamiyausa.com/items/radio-control-kits-30/rc-semi-assembled-chassis-35900/rc-tt02-chassis-57984?product-id=57984
7. Axelsson, S.: The base-rate fallacy and the difficulty of intrusion detection. ACM Trans. Inf. Syst. Secur. (TISSEC) **3**, 186–205 (2000)
8. Bauza, R., Gozalvez, J., Sanchez-Soriano, J.: Road traffic congestion detection through cooperative vehicle-to-vehicle communications. In: 2010 IEEE 35th Conference on Local Computer Networks (LCN) (2010)
9. Bezzo, N., Weimer, J., Pajic, M., Sokolsky, O., Pappas, G.J., Lee, I.: Attack resilient state estimation for autonomous robotic systems. In: IROS (2014)
10. Duda, R.O., Hart, P.E.: Use of the Hough transformation to detect lines and curves in pictures. Commun. ACM **15**, 11–15 (1972)
11. Fawzi, H., Tabuada, P., Diggavi, S.: Secure estimation and control for cyber-physical systems under adversarial attacks. IEEE Trans. Autom. Control **59**, 1454–1467 (2014)
12. Guo, P., Kim, H., Virani, N., Xu, J., Zhu, M., Liu, P.: Exploiting physical dynamics to detect actuator and sensor attacks in mobile robots. arXiv preprint arXiv:1708.01834 (2017)
13. Hafner, M.R., Cunningham, D., Caminiti, L., Del Vecchio, D.: Cooperative collision avoidance at intersections: algorithms and experiments. IEEE Trans. Intell. Transp. Syst. **14**, 1162–1175 (2013)
14. Hartenstein, H., Laberteaux, L.: A tutorial survey on vehicular ad hoc networks. IEEE Commun. Mag. **46**(6) (2008)
15. Humphreys, T.E., Ledvina, B.M., Psiaki, M.L., OHanlon, B.W., Kintner Jr., P.M.: Assessing the spoofing threat: development of a portable GPS civilian spoofer. In: Proceedings of the ION GNSS International Technical Meeting of the Satellite Division (2008)
16. Kuipers, J.B., et al.: Quaternions and Rotation Sequences. Princeton University Press, Princeton (1999)
17. Lee, W., Stolfo, S.J., et al.: Data mining approaches for intrusion detection. In: USENIX Security (1998)
18. Lichodzijewski, P., Zincir-Heywood, A.N., Heywood, M.I.: Host-based intrusion detection using self-organizing maps. In: Proceedings of the 2002 International Joint Conference on Neural Networks, IJCNN 2002 (2002)
19. Litman, T.: Autonomous vehicle implementation predictions. Implications for transport planning (2014). http://www.vtpi.org/avip.pdf
20. Manandhar, K., Cao, X., Hu, F., Liu, Y.: Detection of faults and attacks including false data injection attack in smart grid using Kalman filter. IEEE Trans. Control Netw. Syst. **1**, 370–379 (2014)
21. Miller, C., Valasek, C.: Remote exploitation of an unaltered passenger vehicle. Black Hat, USA (2015)
22. Mo, Y., Garone, E., Casavola, A., Sinopoli, B.: False data injection attacks against state estimation in wireless sensor networks. In: 2010 49th IEEE Conference on Decision and Control (CDC) (2010)

23. Pajic, M., Tabuada, P., Lee, I., Pappas, G.J.: Attack-resilient state estimation in the presence of noise. In: 2015 54th IEEE Conference on Decision and Control (CDC) (2015)
24. Park, J., Ivanov, R., Weimer, J., Pajic, M., Lee, I.: Sensor attack detection in the presence of transient faults. In: ICCPS (2015)
25. Park, P., Khadilkar, H., Balakrishnan, H., Tomlin, C.J.: High confidence networked control for next generation air transportation systems. IEEE Trans. Autom. Control 59, 3357–3372 (2014)
26. Pasqualetti, F., Carli, R., Bullo, F.: Distributed estimation via iterative projections with application to power network monitoring. Automatica 48, 747–758 (2012)
27. Pasqualetti, F., Dorfler, F., Bullo, F.: Attack detection and identification in cyber-physical systems. IEEE Trans. Autom. Control 58, 2715–2729 (2013)
28. Patel, A., Alhussian, H., Pedersen, J.M., Bounabat, B., Júnior, J.C., Katsikas, S.: A nifty collaborative intrusion detection and prevention architecture for smart grid ecosystems. Comput. Secur. 64, 92–109 (2017)
29. Paxson, V.: Bro: a system for detecting network intruders in real-time. Comput. Netw. 31, 2435–2463 (1999)
30. Petit, J., Stottelaar, B., Feiri, M., Kargl, F.: Remote attacks on automated vehicles sensors: experiments on camera and LiDAR. Black Hat, Europe (2015)
31. Quigley, M., Conley, K., Gerkey, B., Faust, J., Foote, T., Leibs, J., Wheeler, R., Ng, A.Y.: ROS: an open-source robot operating system. In: ICRA workshop on open source software (2009)
32. Roesch, M., et al.: Snort: lightweight intrusion detection for networks. In: LISA (1999)
33. Ryan, J., Lin, M.J., Miikkulainen, R.: Intrusion detection with neural networks. In: Advances in Neural Information Processing Systems (1998)
34. Schweber, B.: The autonomous car: a diverse array of sensors drives navigation, driving, and performance (2017). http://www.mouser.com/applications/autonomous-car-sensors-drive-performance/
35. Volpe, J.: Vulnerability assessment of the transportation infrastructure relying on the global positioning system (2001)
36. Warrender, C., Forrest, S., Pearlmutter, B.: Detecting intrusions using system calls: alternative data models. In: Proceedings of the 1999 IEEE Symposium on Security and Privacy (1999)
37. Wu, Y.S., Foo, B., Mei, Y., Bagchi, S.: Collaborative intrusion detection system (CIDS): a framework for accurate and efficient IDS. In: 2003 Proceedings of 19th Annual Computer Security Applications Conference (2003)
38. Yan, C., Xu, W., Liu, J.: Can you trust autonomous vehicles: contactless attacks against sensors of self-driving vehicle. In: 24th DEFCON Hacking Conference (2016)
39. Yeung, D.Y., Ding, Y.: Host-based intrusion detection using dynamic and static behavioral models. Pattern Recognit. 36, 229–243 (2003)
40. Yong, S., Zhu, M., Frazzoli, E.: Resilient state estimation against switching attacks on stochastic cyber-physical systems. In: CDC (2015)
41. Zeng, W., Chow, M.Y.: Resilient distributed control in the presence of misbehaving agents in networked control systems. IEEE Trans. Cybern. 44, 2038–2049 (2014)
42. Zhang, Y., Lee, W.: Intrusion detection in wireless ad-hoc networks. In: Proceedings of the 6th Annual International Conference on Mobile Computing and Networking (2000)

Understanding Adversarial Strategies from Bot Recruitment to Scheduling

Wentao Chang[1], Aziz Mohaisen[2([⊠])], An Wang[1], and Songqing Chen[1]

[1] George Mason University, Fairfax, USA
{wchang7,awang10,sqchen}@gmu.edu
[2] The University of Central Florida, Orlando, USA
mohaisen@ucf.edu

Abstract. Today botnets are still one of the most prevalent and devastating attacking platforms that cyber criminals rely on to launch large scale Internet attacks. Botmasters behind the scenes are becoming more agile and discreet, and some new and sophisticated strategies are adopted to recruit bots and schedule their activities to evade detection more effectively. In this paper, we conduct a measurement study of 23 active botnet families to uncover some new botmaster strategies based on an operational dataset collected over a period of seven months. Our analysis shows that different from the common perception that bots are randomly recruited in a best-effort manner, bots recruitment has strong geographical and organizational locality, offering defenses a direction and priority when attempting to shut down these botnets. Furthermore, our study to measure dynamics of botnet activity reveals that botmasters start to deliberately schedule their bots to hibernate and alternate in attacks so that the detection window becomes smaller and smaller.

Keywords: Distributed denial of service · Botnets
Behavioral analysis

1 Introduction

Botnets are collections of networks of infected machines (aka bots) that are widely used to carry out a variety of malicious activities as instructed by a botmaster. As a result, botnets are notoriously known as one of the primary attack and threat vectors utilized against critical infrastructures and services in activities that include distributed denial of service (DDoS), spam distribution, phishing, scanning and network exploration, among others. Such malicious activities utilize vulnerabilities in existing protocols, and capitalize on their power to disturb large services.

The advent of botnets is often associated with vandalism. However, recent years have witnessed the rise of other uses of botnets, including "hacktivism" [1] and "botnet-as-a-service" [5]. Botnets have been used as a mean of promoting political ends, such as targeting political and ideological opponents, stealing precious data from their networks, or for bringing their networks down. OpIsrael [2],

© ICST Institute for Computer Sciences, Social Informatics and Telecommunications Engineering 2018
X. Lin et al. (Eds.): SecureComm 2017, LNICST 238, pp. 397–417, 2018.
https://doi.org/10.1007/978-3-319-78813-5_20

DarkSeoul [3], and OpUSA [4] are recent prominent examples of hacktivism, where ideas and political beliefs influenced botnet-based cybersecurity events and driven them. The rise of such a direction has facilitated a thriving ecosystem guided by economical profit in what has been coined as botnet-as-a-service [5]. In such a model, botnets are designed to be "rented" easily to underground users, where botmasters are reportedly making large sums of money in underground marketplaces [6].

Understanding botnets through analyses and measurements has been a goal in the research community since their arrival. Such analyses is geared towards understanding attacks, guiding defenses, and helping with bots containment and disinfection by chronologizing their lifecycle. The first and foremost step in the lifecycle of botnets is to recruit and manage a dedicated pool of bots. Such step is done by either recruiting a new group of bots via infection or by renting a network of already infected machines in the botnet-as-a-service marketplace. Once recruited, botmasters utilize their bots (in a given botnet) to launch attacks. Considering them as valuable resources, botmasters want to maximize the return on investment by launching as many attacks as possible without being detected by a defender. To this end, bot scheduling is a critical aspect of botnet management, and further insights into how botmasters schedule their bots could potentially unveil patterns in this ecosystem that could lead to (1) better understanding of botnets, and (2) guide defenses.

In this paper, we advance the state-of-the-art by analyzing the botmasters strategies in recruiting and managing bots based on a large workload collected from more than 300 Internet vantage points across the globe covering 23 most active botnets for a continuous 7 months. Our study reveals several interesting and previously unreported recruitment strategies by botnets in the wild. A highlight of the new sophisticated techniques adopted by modern botmasters includes (c.f. Sect. 5 for implications):

- Our geographical analysis shows that most dedicated bots reside in a small number of countries and organizations. This provides some helpful insights for defenses. For example, pushback models [8–10] of defenses can be guided by this insight in deploying routing-based monitoring closer to the sources of the attack.
- Bots recruitments are not purely random but rather targeted with per-family unique characteristics. Further analysis shows that different botnet families have their unique per-family characteristics (i.e., affinity). This insight can be utilized in postmortem host cleaning. For example, upon taking down a botmaster, cleaning disconnected bots becomes a challenge, and knowing the affinity would guide efforts of disinfection and cleaning.
- Bots are not always active. Instead, they are recruited and used with a clear alternation pattern, and longer periods of hibernation in between. This can effectively minimize the detection window of detection tools and thwart them. This pattern and trend can be utilized to guide defenses: a defense that utilizes the distribution of activity window of bots is more likely to detect an attack earlier than one that uses a fixed (and potentially large) time window.

To the best of our knowledge, *many of the recruitment strategies uncovered in this study are novel and not reported before*, making them interesting in their own right. As we are still unfolding the use of the recruitment strategies, we suggest to leverage such insights to devise new defense and mitigation schemes. While there has been a large body of literature on the problem (e.g., [11–20]; c.f. Sect. 6), all of the prior work draws conclusion on behavior of botnets by analyzing a single botnet (or a limited number of them). To our knowledge, this is the first study that tries to understand recruitment and scheduling patterns by performing a meta-analysis over a large number of botnets and associated behavior.

2   Data and Collection Methodology

Prior work on botnet measurements have mainly focused on their taxonomy and classification by analyzing botnet behavior and common characteristics, including architecture, command and control (C2), communication protocols, and evasion techniques [21,22]. Such efforts have mainly been done via passive measurement or infiltration, and are usually focused on specific botnets. Different from these approaches, our work relies on data provided by the monitoring and attribution unit a DDoS mitigation company, with partnerships of traffic sharing with a large number of major Internet service providers across the globe. The dataset is previously utilized by Wang *et al.* [7] for analyzing trends in DDoS attacks.

2.1   Collection Methodology

The unit constantly monitors Internet attacking traffic to aid the mitigation efforts of its clients, using both active and passive measurement techniques. For active measurements and attribution, malware families used in launching various attacks are reverse engineered, and labeled to a known malware family using best practices. A honeypot is then created to emulate the operation of the reverse-engineered malware sample that belongs to a given botnet and to enumerate all bots across the globe participating in that particular botnet.

As each botnet evolves over time, new generations are marked by their unique (MD5 and SHA-1) hashes. Traces of traffic associated with various botnets are then collected at various anchor points on the Internet, via the cooperation of many ISPs all over the world, and analyzed to attribute and characterize attacks. The collection of traffic is guided by two general principles: (1) that the source of the traffic is an infected host participating in a botnet attack, and (2) the destination of the traffic is a targeted client, as concluded from eavesdropping on C2 of the campaign using a live sample.

2.2   Botnet Families

There are 23 known botnet families in the wild captured in our dataset. Those botnet families are (using their publicly known names assigned by antivirus vendors [7,23]) Aldibot, Armageddon, Asprox , Blackenergy, Colddeath,

Conficker, Darkcomet, Darkshell, Ddoser, Dirtjumper, Gumblar, Illusion, Myloader, Nitol, Optima, Pandora, Redgirl, Storm, Tdss, Torpig, Waledac, Yzf and Zeus. From the dataset multiple botnets are identified for each family, and each botnet is potentially owned by different botmasters. By tracking bots' temporal activities, the monitors of the company generate a log dump every hour. There are 24 hourly reports per day for each botnet family. The set of bots or controllers listed in each report are cumulative over past 24 h. The 24-h time span is counted from time stamp of last known bot activity and time of log dump. The log covers the period from 08/29/2012 to 03/24/2013, a total of 207 days.

2.3 Caveats and Comparisons

While the dataset we use in this paper is comparable in size to other dataset previously used in the literature, it provides a timely insight into the recent state of botnet operations, as opposed to the state of botnets many years ago. Furthermore, the efforts of identifying malware that is used for operating a botnet family provide high fidelity: the techniques involve a combination of dynamic and static analysis utilizing deep understanding and reverse-engineering of the studied families.

We note that some of the hosts infected by the studied malware families may not be included in our data for a few reasons. For example, they may not be included if they do not participate in an attack against a monitored resource, or if they do not contact the C2 server of the studied family. However, we believe that those hosts are of less interest, since they are isolated and do not contribute to the potential attack activity of the botnet. They do not contribute to the recruitment and scheduling aspects studied in this paper, and their disinfection and cleaning is a secondary issue to this study.

3 Bots Recruitment

During about 7 months of our data collection and analysis, over 2 million unique bots across 23 malware families are identified in our dataset. The purpose of our botnet study is to gain insights into active botnets' nature so that security analysts and experts can effectively take down existing botnets by disinfection, or prevent benign hosts from infections for suspicious sources (as previously done in other work; e.g., Stone-Gross et al. [24] and Gu et al. [25]).

One of the primary properties of bots that interests us most is their physical location and how the location shifts in regions across different phases of the botnet's life cycles. We are also interested in whether a certain subset of bots play a more critical role than others in the bots recruitment. Our conjecture is that bots recruitment as a process may not be purely random but rather targeted with per-family unique characteristics, and the geographical distribution analysis confirms our conjecture.

In this section we examine all known bots in our dataset by mapping their IP addresses to a list of countries where they reside, and identifying organizations that such IP addresses belong to. We perform the mapping of the IP addresses using a highly-accurate commercial grade geo-mapping dataset by Digital Envoy (Digital Element services [26]), which provides—besides the country—the individual *city*, and *organization* of each queried IP address.

Addressing NAT Effect. Dynamic IP addresses and NAT constitute a significant portion of the Internet [24,27], preventing a one-to-one mapping between bot and IPs. Addressing NAT is a challenging problem, which falls out of the scope of this work. However, we follow a similar approach to [28] to minimize its impact on our findings. While the NAT effect leads to undercounting bots, such undercounting is corrected by churns, resulting in overcounting, due to DHCP. Thus, in preprocessing, and for each botnet, we aggregate the different bots with unique IP addresses that have distinct patterns into unique bots. For passive IP churn using DHCP at the ISP level, we aggregate the unique IP addresses over shorter hourly time periods to minimize the potential of DHCP churn [28,29]. A recent study [30] shows that the distribution of dynamic IP addresses is not uniform but rather biased towards regions or ISPs. By analyzing IP addresses at the country and organization level, we conclude that the estimated number of bots should be considered as a lower bound, thus minimizing the impact on our recruitment findings.

3.1   Bots Country Preference

Figure 1 shows the heat map of bots' geographical distribution. The darker the color of the country is, the more bots are found to be located in that country. We can see that those two million bots are widely spread all over the world with several harder-hit areas in the darker green regions.

Fig. 1. Geographical distribution of bots (Color figure online)

In Table 1, we list the top 10 countries with most bots. These ten countries together host 66.3% of all bots in our dataset (i.e., 1,512,377 out of 2,280,389). One of the surprising findings in the table is that Israel and Switzerland lead the rank of all countries, with a combined share of 28.0% of bots, despite that they are neither far-flung countries in area nor large countries in population. A reasonable explanation is that our data provider might parterner with major ISPs that have dominant existence in Europe, or during 7-month collection period botnets from aforementioned countries are involved in active campaigns. Drilling down to the per-family bots distribution, some per-family unique characteristics of the country preference are revealed:

Table 1. Top 10 countries with most bots.

Country name	Number of bots
Israel	430,715
Switzerland	207,386
U.S.A	187,483
Vietnam	172,066
Brazil	163,983
India	121,949
China	66,742
Russia	59,158
Thailand	54,135
Argentina	48,760

Bots Preferential Attachment. We notice that for most families their bots are concentrated in a few preferred regions, and those preferred regions tend to vary significantly across different families. In general, the majority of botnet families have tangible bots existence in the top countries we listed in Table 1. Interestingly every family also has their own set of preferred countries. Take the family Optima as an example, we find that the top 5 countries for Optima's 343,524 bots are Israel (21.0%), India (14.5%), United States (12.6%), Switzerland (9.4%), and Brazil (6.1%). The first three countries in the list contain more than 48% of the total bots for Optima, and all these 5 countries can also be found on the top 10 overall list—although in different ordering.

Country Preferential Attachment Unveils Activity Correlations. We observe that for some families bot's geographical preference is somehow preserved at different stages of botnet activities. For example, the activity curve of Optima highlights three sudden spikes dated at 10/18/2012, 10/29/2012 and 11/10/2013, respectively, which could be attributed to 3 active campaigns that were launched around that time frame with a large number of bots participation. Thus, we examine all bots involved in those spike events to expose their preferential attachment. It is evident that 1st and 3rd spike events are correlated, because the overwhelmingly majority of bots in these two spike events originate from Israel, Switzerland, United States, Botswana, and Canada. The high resemblance of bots distribution between the 1st and 3rd spikes implies that they are very likely to be two stages of the same attack. On the contrary, by examining the bots from 2nd spike we find that its bot distribution is significantly different: 37.8% bots (23,499) originate from India and 16.1% (10,027) originate from United States. This can be explained that the second spike is potentially another independent campaign launched by a different botmaster.

Another family shows strong activity correlation is `Dirtjumper`. The top 5 countries of `Dirtjumper`'s 818,452 bots are Israel (37.5%), Switzerland (15.2%), United States (10.5%), Brazil (9.9%), India (4.4%). We find two correlated spike events for this family because they both exhibit the same geographical distribution patterns. The majority of bots in these two spikes originate from Israel, Switzerland and the United States. The other two countries (Brazil and India) in the top 5 list did not contribute much to the spike events.

Local Botnets. The geographical distribution of `Illusion` does not conform to the all bots distribution chart. Pakistan, which has an unnoticeable presence in the overall country ranking of most bots, contributes a dominantly large number of bots to Illusion. This finding strongly suggests that `Illusion` either prefers to or gain privileges to recruit most of its bots from Pakistan. Similarly, bots that belong to `Pandora` show a significantly biased existence in Mexico and Thailand.

Mobility Within Preferred Regions. We explore how bots of each family shift over time. In this analysis we aim to identify whether the newly arrived bots originate from the same country or from different countries. The results show that the majority of bots only shift within their preferred regions. Left y-axis in the Fig. 2 represents the shift rate of `Conficker` within the same country, while

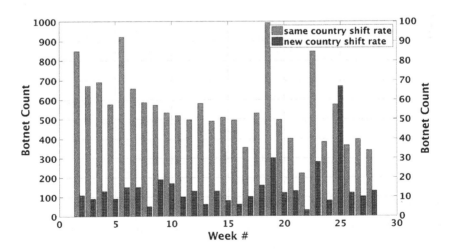

Fig. 2. Bots shift patterns for Conficker

right y-axis represents the shift rate across countries. For `Conficker` the arrival rate of bots from the same country is 20 to 40 times higher than that of bots from a different country. This localized shift pattern can be further validated by our bots alternation analysis in Sect. 4.2. The set of active bots controlled by the same family has a strong location affinity.

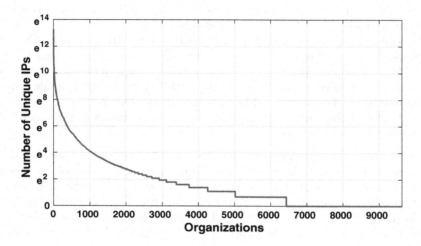

Fig. 3. Number of unique IPs in each organization

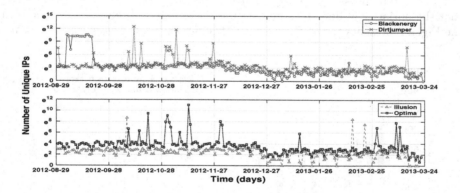

Fig. 4. Activities from top 2 organizations

3.2   Bots Organization Preference

Using the IP mapping dataset, we are also able to identify the organizations that own the IP addresses hosting the infections, which represent the bots we studied in our dataset. Across all botnet families, with 2,280,389 unique IPs in our dataset, we enumerated 9,633 different organizations. We sort the organizations in descending order of the number of associated bots and display them in Fig. 3. The x-axis represents 9,633 organizations, and the y-axis denotes the logarithm number of unique IPs. We learn from the figure that the distribution is heavy-tailed, and that the top 20% of organizations in our study contain more than 90% of all bots. With the impact factor of different organization size considered, we can still draw the conclusion that bots organizational distribution is not purely random, certain organizations become easy targets for bots recruitment or at least are comparably tardy for the mitigation of botnet infection. We list the top 10 organizations with most bots in Table 2. While some of the organizations are service providers, we notice that some of the organizations are businesses that do not provide Internet services to customers–thus highlighting an interesting dimension in such a distribution.

Table 2. Top 10 organizations with most infected hosts

Organization name	Bots
ilan ISP (Israel)	568,200
Switch Swiss Education and Research Network	224,810
Viettel Corporation (Vietnam)	80,872
The Corporation for Financing Promoting Tech. (Vietnam)	79,341
Telebahia (Brazil)	66,154
African Network Information Center (Uganda)	60,403
National Internet Backbone (India)	58,283
Cogent Communications	45,264
Independent Electricity System Operator (Canada)	44,599
China Telecom	37,119

Positive Organization Preference. Similar to the country-level analysis, we explore organizations-preference. The result is shown in Table 3. We find that 14.3% of the bots of `Aldibot` are located in Canada-based organizations, for example, Rogers Cable Communications inc. and Bell Canada. India's "National internet backbone (NIB)" is another favorite organizations for 4 botnet families: `Colddeath, Darkcomet, Darkshell` and `Yzf`. For these 4 families, the number of bots from NIB is in absolute dominance compared to other organizations. We also find that the organization with most bots for `Ddoser` is telecom argentina stet-france telecom s.a., and `Nitol` is found to have a tendency to recruit bots from organization te-as. Similarly the Australia-based organization, Telstra Pty Ltd, owns a large majority of bots for `Torpig`. Organizations with substantial bots existence for `Zeus` are quite a few, and `Zeus` is the botnet family that is discovered from most organizations in our study. The total number of organizations accounted for `Zeus` botnet activity is as high as 5,541—possibly because `Zeus` is a mass-market credential stealing botnet.

Table 3. Organization-level bots preference

Aldibot	Rogers Cable Communications Inc.	1,056
	Bell Canada	675
	Google Inc.	521
	Uninet, S.a. de C.v. (Mexico)	513
	Cox Communications Inc.	429
Blackenergy	ilan ISP (Israel)	179,619
	Viettel Corporation (Vietnam)	62,250
	Switch Swiss Education and Research Network	61,739
	The Corporation for Financing Promoting Technology (Vietnam)	55,337
	Independent Electricity System Operator (Canada)	13,687
Conficker	China Telecom	32,477
	Data Communication Business Group (Taiwan)	27,036
	Telefonica de Argentina	23,013
	TM Net (Malaysia)	21,659
	Telecom Italia	18,975
Dirtjumper	ilan ISP (Israel)	306,144
	Switch Swiss Education and Research Network	124,158
	Telebahia (Brazil)	50,310
	African Network Information Center (Uganda)	27,522
	independent electricity system operator	23,943
Illusion	ilan ISP (Israel)	7,731
	Cyber Internet Services Ltd. (Pakistan)	5,778
	Switch Swiss Education and Research Network	5,564
	African Network Information Center (Uganda)	2,531
	National Internet Backbone (India)	2,076
Nitol	Telecom Egypt	6,539
	National Internet Backbone (India)	2,417
	Tata Teleservices Ltd	533
	China Telecom	319
	China Networks Inter-exchange	304
Optima	ilan ISP (Israel)	71,177
	Switch Swiss Education and Research Network	31,750
	National Internet Backbone (India)	22,003
	African Network Information Center (Uganda)	16,582
	VNPT corp (Vietnam)	7,476
Pandora	Uninet, S.a. de C.v. (Mexico)	1,284
	Cyber Internet Services Ltd. (Pakistan)	1,241
	African Network Information Center (Uganda)	1,041
	National Internet Backbone (India)	991
	San Paulo Research Foundation (Brazil)	522
YZF	National Internet Backbone (India)	2,291
	Nepal Telecommunications Corporation	462
	African Network Information Center (Uganda)	415
	Tata Teleservices Ltd	295
Zeus	Turk Telecommunications	8,833
	Viettel Corporation (Vietnam)	8,663
	Maroc Telecom (Morocco)	7,841
	Cox Communications Inc.	7,142
	The Corporation for Financing Promoting Technology (Vietnam)	6,903

Organization Preferential Attachment Unveils Activity Correlations.
We choose 5 botnet families that were very active during the 7-month data collection period as our analysis candidates. They are `Blackenergy`, `Conficker`, `Dirtjumper`, `Illusion` and `Optima`. After a closer look, we realize that the majority of bots that contribute to 4 of those 5 families come from the top 2 organizations we listed in Table 2, `Conficker` is the only exception due to the multi-variants nature of the family. Bots owned by `Conficker` are widely distributed over 3,522 different organizations and thus it has no clear culprit organizations. To this end, we plot the activity curve of those 4 families considering only bots coming from these 2 organizations. As Fig. 4 shows, the bots from those 2 organizations stay hibernated most of the time during our observation period. The timing of their sudden wake-up coincides with the peak events of the botnet families. This evident behavior strongly suggests the bots from these two organizations are coordinated to perform attacks on purpose. It is very likely bots in these two organizations are zombies, dedicated machines controlled by remote attackers to conduct cyber attacks, which explains the fact that they are infected by multiple instances of botnet families.

4 Bots Scheduling Strategies

In this section, we perform an in-depth study of botnets' dynamics to expose the latest bots scheduling strategies with three aims in mind. First, we closely monitor the bots dynamics in 7-month observation window and conduct a lifespan analysis of all bots in our dataset to understand their involvement in botnet activity. Second, we dive deep into exposing unique activity patterns of short-lived bots, which strongly implies a deliberate action of bots alternation and re-occurrence when scheduling bots. Last but not the least, we find that a substantial number of bots are recruited and reused by more than one botnet families, and we are interested in behind-the-scenes reasons why those bots are favored by botmasters in recruitment and scheduling.

4.1 Bot Lifespan Analysis

The lifespan of a bot is an important indicator of bots' involvement in the botnet activity. To this end, we conduct a weekly pattern analysis for every bot in our dataset to understand their presence and evolvement. Given the confined context of our dataset and the fact that mitigation techniques might have already been in place to take down active bots, it is not far-fetched to speculate that many bots in the dataset are short-lived, and this will be presented as those bots active in week i become dormant in week $i + 1$. Our speculation is confirmed in the analysis result that in general less bots are found with longer lifespan. The number of bots with various lifespan is depicted in Fig. 5 and the short-lived statement is held true for all botnet families in our dataset.

Besides short-lived bots, our analysis reveals a small but steady group of bots that stay active for an extended period of time, in many cases several weeks.

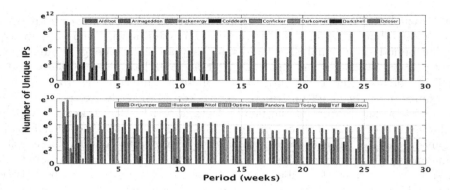

Fig. 5. Bots lifespan analysis

We call them "always-on" bots. For a subset of botnet families we observe, there exist a very small set of "always-on" bots (i.e., single-digit) whose lifespan cover the entire data collection period. One exception is `Conficker`, one of the largest known computer worm infection [13]. The number of "always-on" bots for `Conficker` is approximately 4,400 unique IP addresses, by far the largest among all families we studied. The fact that `Conficker` is a very well-represented botnet with multiple variants in existence, making it difficult to remove from end users' computers as effectively as done for other families.

The role played by bots with a longer lifespan is possibly different from that played by bots with a shorter lifespan. A potential role such bots play include a shadow botmaster (to mitigate failure) and to serve as a dedicated bot. From a defense perspective, it takes precedence to shut down those long-lived bots than others when mitigating large-scale botnet activity. Our bot's lifespan analysis over the large-scale dataset provides a firsthand information of what bots defenders should target to remove in priority. However, the assumption that the consequence of mitigation is the sole reason for many bots' short lifespan is doubtful, because this does not explain the existence of in-negligible amount of long-lived bots, and the number of bots for each family does not always decline linearly as the lifespan increases in Fig. 5. This raises suspicion that those bots might be deliberately hibernated by the botmasters as a countermeasure to thwart detection efforts, thus we will further investigate whether bots hibernation are scheduled purposely and how in following subsections.

4.2   Bots Fast Recruitment and Active Bots Alternation

As shown earlier, the lifespan of most bots is usually short. Thus, to perform large-scale attacks, botmasters need to recruit a large number of bots. In our study, we observe that the majority of bots only appear once in our traces. The fast bots recruitment for `Optima` is depicted in Fig. 6, the dotted vertical line in the figure marks whether corresponding bots from the left y-axis are active or not at the given day, and the curve in the right y-axis represents the

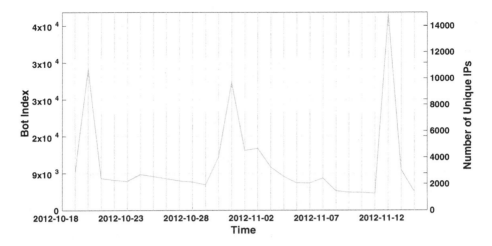

Fig. 6. Fast bot recruitment for Optima

total number of active bots at a given day. Note that the bots from the left y-axis are sorted in the ascending order of their IP addresses. During those 3 peak events tens of thousands of bots suddenly become active and disappear after the completion of a major campaign. Our bots organizational preference analysis in Sect. 3.2 confirms that the abrupt surge of bots is primarily due to a temporary recruitment of bots from other botnets to launch a highly intensive attack—including the borrowing of dedicated bots found at some organizations with vulnerable defenses.

Diving deep into the composition of active bots we find a strong level of bots alternation. We learn from our lifespan analysis that, for all families even in their seemingly stable periods, in which the total number of simultaneously live bots does not change much over one or several weeks, the majority of bots still remain active for less than one week. Analysis results show that the new bots activated by botmasters compensate the loss of old bots. It is unlikely this unnatural harmony of bots alternation is merely due to the effectiveness of bots mitigation, and we believe it is a side effect of countermeasures to defeat defense that botmasters voluntarily utilize, which is to iterate bots from their pool of slave bots to complicate the process of take-down mitigations.

4.3   Bots Re-occurrence Patterns

Excluding a small number of "always-on" bots, majority of bots are only observed once except for a number of bots that consistently reoccur in the 29-week observation window. To understand the root cause of those bots' uncommon behavior, we divide bots into groups by their occurrence count. Note that we count the weekly occurrence for all bots, and if the same bot occurs in two or more consecutive weeks, we only count it as one occurrence. As Fig. 7 shows, a common patten across all families is that the larger the occurrence count is, the less number of bots there are. Another pattern is that a proportional relationship exists across families between bot count per occurrence group and total bot count in their respective family. Given the current data in hand we're still investigating what are the criteria used by botmasters to select bots to occur more than once in their lifecycle.

We also conduct a per-bot re-occurrence analysis to measure their re-occurrence distance. The term "re-occurrence" in this context is used to describe bots that are active in week i, become dormant in week $i + 1$, but are brought back to life in week $i + j$ (where $j > 1$). In this sense, we define j as the re-occurrence distance. Because our observation window is only 7 months rather than years, the chance that the same bot is taken down through disinfection, but becomes re-infected by the same malware, is low. Therefore the impact of false positives is negligible for this analysis. Bots with longer re-occurrence distance could be attributed to either dedicated bots or zombie machines that existing mitigation efforts fail to completely disinfect. As Fig. 8 shows, as the re-occurrence distance increases the number of bots declines near linearly except for 2 families, `Aldibot` and `Dirtjumper`. A closer look at these 2 families in the figure reveals that they both own a relatively large number of bots with long re-occurrence distances compared to others. `Dirtjumper` has over 1000 bots with the re-occurrence distance as high as 18 and 21, while `Aldibot` has a sudden surge at the re-occurrence distance of 16. The re-occurrence pattern associated with both families highlights the lack of response to active hosts in malicious activities, where resources utilized in botnets stay for long time infected—thus reused after a relatively long time.

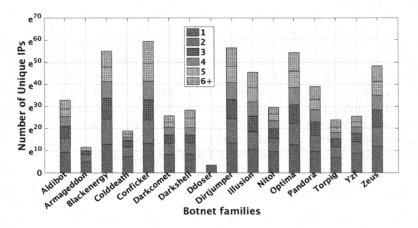

Fig. 7. Number of occurrence for bots

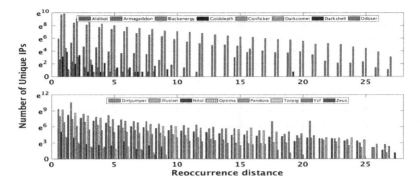

Fig. 8. Bots re-occurrence distance

4.4 Reused Bots Analysis

Another interesting observation we revealed when examining the bots in our dataset is the presence of a large amount of reused bots – the bots belonging to multiple botnet families, which could be due to multiple infections or due to using paid infrastructure (i.e., pay-per-install) [31]. In reality, while one would expect normally a single host to be utilized for a single malicious activity of a certain type, we hypothesize that hosts with multiple infections are often utilized by multiple botnets to perform various types of malicious activities and to participate in many campaigns. This hypothesis, validated through our analysis results below, is of particular interest to the security community for multiple reasons. While the understanding of reuse may shed light on the genealogy of malware and their associations, it most importantly highlights the differential roles that various types of bots play in the cyber underground world, where reusable bots may play much bigger roles in cyber attacks launched via botnets. Host machines that serve as reused bots are more threatening, which means they could be further leveraged to participate in other campaigns. Also, having various infections may highlight those hosts tendency not to disinfect from a compromise over a long period of time (honeypot is an exception). Such nature of reused bots indicates that they are long-living and possibly a good candidate to serve as nodes for botnet C&C channels, or "always-on" piece of the botnet infrastructure. Thus, by correctly identifying those bots, cyber defenders may leverage such information to effectively defend against cyber attacks by guiding efforts of disinfection in a feasible way.

4.4.1 Reused Bots Scheduling Strategies. Among the 2,280,389 unique IPs identified as infected hosts, 320,340 IPs, accounting for roughly 14.0% of total bots, are confirmed to be reused by at least two families during the 7 months. The average reuse ratio across different families varies significantly, where statistics of reuse unveil that some families tend to have a higher reuse ratio of its bots than other families. The number of reused bots and their shift pattern are an important metric to measure the collaboration efforts among different botnet

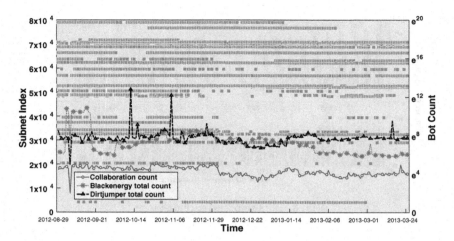

Fig. 9. Reused bots. (An illustration using the case of Blackenergy and Dirtjumper botnet families.)

families. It would be crucial to recognize the correlation between the magnitude of reused bots and the overall activity level of individual families. Thus, in this subsection we inspect the interactions and collaborations via reused bots between two specific families over time.

We choose the `Blackenergy` and `Dirjumper` since they are two of the most active families in our dataset. In our data pre-processing step we aggregate the /24 subnets to group various IP addresses, thus reducing the total number of addresses in our analysis. Figure 9 shows how the activity level of those two families correlates with their collaboration. The x-axis and the left y-axis mark the date and the subnet index, respectively. The right y-axis represents the total number of active subnet in log scale. The dotted horizontal line represents whether the corresponding subnet from left y-axis is reused by both families across time. From the figure it is evident that tens of different subnets are reused by these two families. The three curves represent the number of active bots for `Blackenergy`, `Dirtjumper`, and the reused subnets, respectively. We observe that when there're no spike events, the number of active bots for `Blackenergy` and `Dirtjumper` is in the same order of magnitude, and the number of reused subnets fluctuates roughly in the same pace as that of those two families. Even when the spike events of either families occur, there are no noticeable surges of reused subnet count. These similar behaviors between these two families are less likely to be only coincidental, therefore we infer that the huge number of new bots in spike events is recruited for one-time use of specific campaigns, while reused subnets are treated as backbone of botnet activities. This subtle relationship implies that a master-slave relationship might exist between them.

5 Insights to Botnet Detection and Defense

In previous sections our in-depth analysis of a large botnet dataset expose some new bot recruitment patterns and various sophisticated botnet scheduling strategies. By understanding the trending techniques adopted by bot-masters, security researchers could devise more effective defense mechanisms to detect and mitigate botnet attacks.

Prediction of Bots Origins Based on Their Family. In Sect. 3 county preference study, we learn that many different bot families have their own per-family unique characteristics regarding recruitment preference. For example, some bot families tend to concentrate in a few preferred countries, and some bot families only exist in one or two dedicated countries. These recruitment preference patterns persist during our 7-month data collection period, thus with confidence we could predict participating bots' origins for a campaign launched via certain bot family. This new capability will definitely boost defense to effectively identify attacking traffics from normal ones. For example, when the host machine detects itself under DDoS attacks from bots in `Illusion`, one defense mechanism is to activate a specific firewall rule to block all connections from Pakistan to alleviate the system burden, since we know `Illusion` family exhibits local botnet characteristic. Also, as noted earlier, pushback models, such as the work of Ioannidis and Bellovin [8], Chen *et al.* [9] and Kang and Gligor [10], can benefit from this insight in determining where pushback and filtering (at the Internet-level) are done.

Vulnerable Organizations. Our organization preference analysis shows that bots distribution is not purely random, but rather targeted. Some organizations contain significantly more bots than others, for perhaps having more vulnerable machines, which makes them easy targets for bot recruitments, or for being backbone network service providers. With the list of vulnerable organizations, security researchers can perform a more thorough security audit of host network environment, and even urge third party organizations to improve their security guarantees. This insight can be useful in postmortem host cleaning: upon the take-down of C&C channels, it would be useful to clean hosts. Knowing the affinity of botnets and certain malware families to certain organization would guide such cleaning efforts.

Bots Ordering of Severity. In Sect. 4 we discussed the latest bots scheduling strategies we identified from the dataset. In addition to static attributes such as bots' geographic information, these dynamic attributes of bots increased the complexity of dis-infection efforts. Due to the limited resources and time-sensitive defense requirements to recover from attacks, it calls for a meaningful ordering of bots per their severity. We believe long-lived bots could potentially serve as shadow botmasters (to mitigate failure) or command and control channels for botnets. Thus when mitigating a large-scale botnet activity, it takes precedence to shut down long-lived bots. We also learnt that some short-lived bots are bots shared in a dedicated pool and coordinated by bot-masters to participate in botnet activities.

It is essential to enumerate all short-lived bots in the pool and shut down them all in once, if possible. Those short-lived bots with apparent alternation or re-concurrence patterns will need to be assigned higher level of severity. Reused bots are another important and interesting finding in our study. Different botnets collaborate to some extent to perform malicious actions via reused bots. Taking down one reused bot would mitigate threats from multiple botnets, thus reused bots should be given higher level of severity as well when cyber defenders plan their dis-infection efforts.

6   Related Work

Previous research efforts on botnet measurements have mainly focused on the taxonomy and classification of botnets by analyzing botnet behavior and common characteristics, such as architecture, command and control channels, communication protocols, and evasion techniques. These efforts have mainly been done via infiltration [18], as done by Bacher et al. [32,33] or passive measurement, as done by Abu Rajab et al. [34]. Many early studies looked at the most common IRC-based bots relying on a centralized control, as shown by karasaridis et al. [35] and Barford and Yegneswaran [36]. Later on numerous new botnets began to use http-based C&C channels and leverage the more stable P2P based communication architecture, per Wang et al. [17] and Holz et al. [37], to mitigate failure due to centralization. Other work focused on in-depth case study of individual botnet families, as done by Binsalleeh et al. [19], Andrade and Vlajic [14] and Shin and Gu [38].

Recent work focused on Internet or large scale measurement study of network traffic to develop methods for revealing more properties of botnets, such as their size [29] and activeness [24,38]. In our work, we analyze the bots' static properties and dynamic behaviors from a different angle, focusing on botmaster strategies behind the scenes. By conducting a large-scale measurement study of bots activity from multiple well-known botnet families, we uncover several new bot recruitment and scheduling strategies. To the best of our knowledge, some of our findings, such as bot recruitment preferences and bot resources scheduling, are not reported before. Similar to our study, Chang et al. [39] conducted a measurement study of a commercial dataset to reveal the latest botmasters' strategies. While both works share a common theme of understanding botnets utilized by DDoS attacks, the focus of each work is different. In particular, Chang et al. outlined measurement highlights collectively, focusing on botnet collaboration observations. On the other hand, we study the bot recruitment at both the country and organization levels, and bot scheduling – fast recruitment, bot alternation, bot recurrence – from where we can infer the strategies of botmasters. Furthermore, our work focuses on bot dynamics, which is a topic of independent interest.

Although we utilize the same dataset used by Wang et al. [7], our approach of data analysis is completely different from theirs: the findings and contributions of our work do not share any common ground with theirs. Wang et al. utilized the dataset to understand state-of-the-art of DDoS attacks, while we utilize it to understand the source and tool used for the attacks; botnets. For this purpose they analyzed the geo-distribution of attack sources for many DDoS attacks, the temporal patterns and collaboration trends between botnet families to launch attacks, etc. On the other hand, whereas we focus on a meta-study of various botnets, our goal is to reveal both static attributes and dynamic patterns of all botnets from 23 known families to understand the constantly advancing strategies adopted by botmasters.

7 Conclusion

Botnets today are responsible for most large-scale attacks on the Internet. Thus, it is essential to understand their latest behavioral traits for insight into defenses. In this paper, we have performed a measurement study of bots activity from 23 known botnet families for about 7 months. By conducting a series of in-depth analysis of bots' static properties and dynamic behaviors, we have uncovered that today botmasters have adopted several new strategies to recruit and schedule bots. As we still investigate the potential consequence of those strategies in bots recruitment, we suggest to leverage such insights to devise new defense and mitigation schemes.

Acknowledgment. We appreciate constructive comments from anonymous referees. This work is partially supported by an ARO grant W911NF-15-1-0262, a NIST grant 70NANB16H166, and a NSF grant CNS-1524462.

References

1. Wikipedia: Hacktivism (2014). http://bit.ly/1kM2Vos
2. Wikipedia: Operation Israel (2014). http://bit.ly/1noDUlI
3. Symantec Security Response: Four years of darkseoul cyberattacks against South Korea continue on anniversary of Korean war, June 2013. http://bit.ly/1fbGlFm
4. Bank Info Security: Opusa threatens banks, government, May 2013. http://bit.ly/1kP3Urt
5. McDougall, P.: Microsoft: Kelihos ring sold 'botnet-as-a-service', September 2011. http://ubm.io/MtCSr7
6. Vicario, M.: Four ways cybercriminals profit from botnets, November 2010. http://bit.ly/1e1SIiP
7. Wang, A., Mohaisen, A., Chang, W., Chen, S.: Delving into internet DDoS attacks by botnets. In: IEEE DSN 2015 (2015)
8. Ioannidis, J., Bellovin, S.: Implementing pushback: router-based defense against DDoS attacks (2002)
9. Chen, Y., Kwok, Y., Hwang, K.: MAFIC: adaptive packet dropping for cutting malicious flows to push back DDoS attacks. In: ICDCS 2005 (2005)
10. Kang, M., Gligor, V.D.: Routing bottlenecks in the internet: causes, exploits, and countermeasures. In: Proceedings of ACM SIGSAC 2014 (2014)
11. Wikipedia: Carna botnet (2014). http://bit.ly/1slx1E6

12. Starr, M.: Fridge caught sending spam emails in botnet attack (2014). http://bit. ly/1j5Jac1
13. Thomas, M., Mohaisen, A.: Kindred domains: detecting and clustering botnet domains using DNS traffic. In: Proceedings of WWW 2014 (2014)
14. Andrade, M., Vlajic, N.: Dirt jumper: a key player in today's botnet-for-DDoS market. In: WorldCIS 2012 (2012)
15. Song, L., Jin, Z., Sun, G.: Modeling and analyzing of botnet interactions. Proc. Phys. A **390**(2), 347–358 (2011)
16. Li, Z., Goyal, A., Chen, Y., Paxson, V.: Towards situational awareness of large-scale botnet probing events. IEEE TIFS **6**(1), 175–188 (2011)
17. Wang, P., Sparks, S., Zou, C.: An advanced hybrid peer-to-peer botnet. TDSC (2010)
18. Cho, C., Caballero, J., Grier, C., Paxson, V., Song, D.: Insights from the inside: a view of botnet management from infiltration. LEET (2010)
19. Binsalleeh, H., Ormerod, T., Boukhtouta, A., Sinha, P., Youssef, A., Debbabi, M., Wang, L.: On the analysis of the Zeus botnet crimeware toolkit. In: IEEE PST 2010 (2010)
20. Caballero, J., Poosankam, P., Kreibich, C., Song, D.: Dispatcher: enabling active botnet infiltration using automatic protocol reverse-engineering. In: Proceedings of ACM CCS 2009 (2009)
21. Lee, C.P., Dagon, D., Gu, G., Lee, W.: A taxonomy of botnet structures. In: Proceedings of ACM ACSCA 2007 (2007)
22. Jing, L., Yang, X., Kaveh, G., Hongmei, D.: Botnet: classification, attacks, detection, tracing, and preventive measures. JWCN (2009)
23. Mohaisen, A., Alrawi, O.: AV-Meter: an evaluation of antivirus scans and labels. In: Dietrich, S. (ed.) DIMVA 2014. LNCS, vol. 8550, pp. 112–131. Springer, Cham (2014). https://doi.org/10.1007/978-3-319-08509-8_7
24. Stone-Gross, B., Cova, M., Cavallaro, L., Gilbert, B., Szydlowski, M., Kemmerer, R., Kruegel, C., Vigna, G.: Your botnet is my botnet: analysis of a botnet takeover. In: Proceedings of ACM CCS 2009 (2009)
25. Gu, G., Perdisci, R., Zhang, J., Lee, W., et al.: Botminer: clustering analysis of network traffic for protocol-and structure-independent botnet detection. In: Proceedings of USENIX Security 2008 (2008)
26. Digital Envoy: Digital element services. http://www.digitalenvoy.net/
27. Xie, Y., Yu, F., Achan, K., Panigrahy, R., Hulten, G., Osipkov, I.: Spamming botnets: signatures and characteristics. In: SIGCOMM 2008 (2008)
28. Maertens, M., Asghari, H., van Eeten, M., van Mieghem, P.: A time-dependent SIS-model for long-term computer worm evolution. In: Proceedings of IEEE CNS 2016 (2016)
29. Rajab, M., Zarfoss, J., Monrose, F., Terzis, A.: My botnet is bigger than yours (maybe, better than yours): why size estimates remain challenging. In: Proceedings of USENIX HotBots 2007 (2007)
30. Xie, Y., Yu, F., Achan, K., Gillum, E., Goldszmidt, M., Wobber, T.: How dynamic are IP addresses? In: ACM SIGCOMM CCR 2007 (2007)
31. Caballero, J., Grier, C., Kreibich, C., Paxson, V.: Measuring pay-per-install: the commoditization of malware distribution. In: Proceedings of USENIX Security 2011 (2011)
32. Bacher, P., Holz, T., Kotter, M., Wicherski, G.: Know your enemy: tracking botnets (2005)

33. Baecher, P., Koetter, M., Holz, T., Dornseif, M., Freiling, F.: The nepenthes platform: an efficient approach to collect malware. In: Zamboni, D., Kruegel, C. (eds.) RAID 2006. LNCS, vol. 4219, pp. 165–184. Springer, Heidelberg (2006). https://doi.org/10.1007/11856214_9

34. Abu Rajab, M., Zarfoss, J., Monrose, F., Terzis, A.: A multifaceted approach to understanding the botnet phenomenon. In: IMC 2006 (2006)

35. Karasaridis, A., Rexroad, B., Hoeflin, D.: Wide-scale botnet detection and characterization. In: Proceedings of USENIX HotBots 2007 (2007)

36. Barford, P., Yegneswaran, V.: An inside look at botnets. In: Christodorescu, M., Jha, S., Maughan, D., Song, D., Wang, C. (eds.) Proceedings of Malware Detection. ADIS, vol. 27, pp. 171–191. Springer, Heidelberg (2007). https://doi.org/10.1007/978-0-387-44599-1_8

37. Holz, T., Steiner, M., Dahl, F., Biersack, E., Freiling, F.C.: Measurements and mitigation of peer-to-peer-based botnets: a case study on storm worm. In: USENIX LEET 2008 (2008)

38. Shin, S., Gu, G.: Conficker and beyond: a large-scale empirical study. In: Proceedings of ACM ACSAC 2010 (2010)

39. Chang, W., Mohaisen, A., Wang, A., Chen, S.: Measuring botnets in the wild: some new trends. In: ACM ASIACCS 2015 (2015)

Mending Wall: On the Implementation of Censorship in India

Devashish Gosain[1]([✉]), Anshika Agarwal[1], Sahil Shekhawat[1], H. B. Acharya[2], and Sambuddho Chakravarty[1]

[1] IIIT Delhi, New Delhi, India
{devashishg,ansika1448,sahil13083,sambuddho}@iiitd.ac.in
[2] Rochester Institute of Information Technology, Rochester, NY, USA
acharya@mail.rit.edu

Abstract. This paper presents a study of the Internet infrastructure in India from the point of view of censorship.

First, we show that the current state of affairs – where each ISP implements its own content filters (nominally as per a governmental blacklist) – results in dramatic differences in the censorship experienced by customers. In practice, a well-informed Indian citizen can escape censorship through a judicious choice of service provider.

We then consider the question of whether India might potentially follow the Chinese model and institute a single, government-controlled filter. This would not be difficult, as the Indian Internet is quite centralized already. A few "key" ASes ($\approx$1% of Indian ASes) collectively intercept $\approx$95% of paths to the censored sites we sample in our study, and *also* to all publicly-visible DNS servers. 5,000 routers spanning these key ASes would suffice to carry out IP or DNS filtering for the entire country; $\approx$70% of these routers belong to **only two private ISPs**. If the government is willing to employ more powerful measures, such as an IP Prefix Hijacking attack, *any one* of several key ASes can censor traffic for nearly all Indian users.

Finally, we demonstrate that such federated censorship by India would cause substantial *collateral damage* to non-Indian ASes whose traffic passes through Indian cyberspace (which do not legally come under Indian jurisdiction at all).

Keywords: India · Network monitoring · Anti-censorship

1   Introduction

The current study of Internet censorship is mostly focused on openly censorious countries – China [37,43,52], Iran [34], Pakistan [55], etc. Even world-wide studies of censorship [32] essentially focus on countries well known for their censorship. However, in practice, many other countries still implement some form of censorship, which may even be more insidious because citizens are barely aware of it (for example, Sweden [6] and France [4]). In this paper, we consider the

© ICST Institute for Computer Sciences, Social Informatics and Telecommunications Engineering 2018
X. Lin et al. (Eds.): SecureComm 2017, LNICST 238, pp. 418–437, 2018.
https://doi.org/10.1007/978-3-319-78813-5_21

case of India, a major emerging power with over 450 million Internet users [19] (up from 180 million in 2013, and on track to overtake Europe, which has 520 million users in all). India has been ambivalent about its censorship policy for years [13] (for example, in August 2015, the government ordered 857 target sites blocked, then backtracked in the face of public outcry [24]), but in context of the fact that *legally*[1] the executive branch in India holds unqualified power to block information, it is natural to be concerned about free speech in India. We begin by asking what policy, and what mechanism the Indian government currently employs; how this might change in future; and what unintended effects such censorship might have on foreign traffic transiting Indian ASes.

Our first step was to formally approach the authorities, by filing a *Right to Information* [25] request (RTI), inquiring about the policies and mechanism the government uses to block content. While the policy itself was confidential, the government was willing to share that the responsibility for filtering lies with individual ISPs, and that they could implement any mechanism they choose[2], as long as they *uniformly comply* with the given censorship policy.

In practice, an ad hoc approach to filtering generally leads to inconsistencies and errors [54], especially during updates [48]. Our initial experiments suggest that this is indeed the case; filtering policies are highly inconsistent across ISPs (see Table 1), contrary to the government's expectations as stated in the official response. The current "feudal" approach to policing the Internet in India, *viz.* allowing ISPs to implement their own censorship mechanisms (which, as we show, do not "strictly adhere" to government diktats), results in inconsistent censorship policy enforcement: for *e.g.*, our findings show that users may be able to evade censorship more easily when accessing pornographic sites via Airtel, a large private ISP that screens fewer sites, compared to others such as MTNL.

We next consider the question of how, in future, the government might enforce a unified censorship policy for the whole country. The usual mechanism to enforce a single policy, is to redirect all Internet traffic through a single point of control, where all the traffic can be monitored(this approach has been employed by Iran [34], Venezuela [7], and Saudi Arabia [60]). Even in the case of China, a whole layer of state-controlled ASes must be used to act as a filtering layer that provides Internet connectivity to other ASes [60]. Nearly all the filtering is carried out by two Autonomous Systems - AS 4134 and AS 4812 [62].

Can the government, in future, force all networks to re-route their traffic via a chosen ISP so as to monitor the network? We note that India's Internet infrastructure was grown through a laissez-faire approach (closely correlated with the cellular networking boom), and now consists of ≈900 ASes (over 170 of which are ISPs) [28]; it would require a massive effort to redirect all traffic through this new provider. Quite likely, the amount of disruption caused by such a redirection would make it difficult for a democratic nation to implement by fiat.

---

[1] Information Technology Act of India 2008 (Section 69A).

[2] IP and URL blacklists [38] are common, but ISPs may choose to employ more invasive techniques, such as DNS Injection Attacks [47] or even IP Prefix Hijacking [35,46].

Might the government implement filtering with the existing infrastructure, without necessarily enforcing traffic redirection? For the existing network, is it possible to find a *small set* of "heavy-hitter" ASes (and network elements in these ASes) that can potentially monitor or censor traffic without too much collateral damage? More formally:

- *Is it feasible to filter/monitor India's Internet traffic? If so, how, and where?* Given that India has over 900 ASes,
  1. Are there a small number of key ASes and routers where the government can intercept most Indian traffic to censored sites?
  2. How does the number of censorious ASes required, vary with the censorship technique – *e.g.* IP blacklisting, DNS Injection, IP Prefix Hijacking?
- *How much collateral damage will traffic filtering cause?* Internet censorship by an "upstream" AS can lead to inadvertent traffic filtering for its customers. How much impact can Indian censorship have on traffic that simply transits Indian cyberspace?

To answer the above questions, in this paper, we map the AS-level paths from each Indian AS to the potentially censored websites (our test corpus includes not only the sites publicly announced as being blocked, but also others from public resources such as Herdict [12]). We then construct router-level maps within these ASes, using Rocketfuel [58]. Finally, we identify the "key" ASes and routers, *i.e.* those which appear in an overwhelming majority of paths (and which are, therefore, the logical locations for network filtering).

Our experimental findings reveal that ten ASes cumulatively intercept over 95% of the paths connecting Indian ASes to the sites in our study (i.e. potentially censored sites). Eight of these key ASes, acting together, can poison ≈99% of the network paths leading to DNS resolvers in India (as well as other publicly available services such as GoogleDNS and OpenDNS), thus censoring URL requests. Even more alarming, when we consider another mechanism of censorship - IP Prefix Hijacking - we find five ASes, each of which can individually poison the BGP routes for almost all ASes in the country. Even though the actual number of routers needed for such efforts varies dramatically (from 7 in some ASes, to as high as 1782), overall, a total of less than 5000 routers across all the eight ASes are required for IP or DNS filtering – about 70% of which routers belong to two large private ISPs and any one of five key ASes is enough, if the government resorts to more aggressive measures like IP Prefix Hijack.

Finally, we note that paths that transit Indian ASes but originate outside India form a substantial fraction of the Internet: if India were in fact to adopt a comprehensive censorship scheme in its key ASes, she would censor about 1.15% of *all* Internet paths to the censored sites, worldwide.

Thus, the above findings would indicate that, in fact, ordinary Indian citizens **should** be concerned about censorship, and perhaps start to equip themselves with anti-censorship tools [39].

We begin by discussing the background and related work, in the next section.

2   Background and Related Work

The interaction of the Internet with government policy (especially censorship and privacy issues) is a controversial subject [14,15,30]. Our case study in this paper, India, is a democratic nation, but there is sufficient evidence of Indian censorship [8,21] that anti-censorship research organizations declare India "partly-free" [20]. For example, the Indian government officially demands that organizations (*e.g.* Google Inc., Microsoft *etc.*) censor pages deemed objectionable [9].

At present, the government delegates the censorship of traffic to ISPs, as per ambiguous blacklists[3]. This loose approach to censoring traffic leads to inconsistent filtering across ISPs – some users may be able to evade censorship by virtue of their provider ISP.

The question arises whether the Indian government *can* impose a centralized filter (as seen in *e.g.* Iran). Creating a new AS and redirecting through it would have high costs in network disruption, latency, service quality, and so on. But such a process will not be necessary *if* the current structure of Indian Internet is already well suited for monitoring and censorship.

To determine the set of ASes and routers where adversary may install infrastructure for censoring large fraction of network paths, as they exist today, we generated AS and router-level maps of India. We used such maps to identify such key ASes and routers, and the impact they have.

2.1   Background

Our paper relies heavily on mapping the structure of the Internet, an area of research called *network cartography* [44]. The Internet consists of routers and hosts, but also has some further structure: the routers and hosts belong to Autonomous Systems, which are independent networks (independent in the sense, they themselves choose who to exchange traffic with). Consequently, Internet mapping proceeds at two levels:

1. *AS-level mapping.* For our research, we required Internet maps representing paths connecting IP address of censored site to various ASes. We thus chose Qiu and Gao [56] AS path mapping approach. Their technique uses publicly-available BGP routes (obtained from various Internet Exchange Points across the globe [31])) and the relationships between the ASes [41], and outputs a directed graph of the Internet connecting IP prefixes to all ASes of the world. Other AS-level mapping approaches, such as the CAIDA Ark Project [3] and *iPlane* [53], involve `traceroute` probes from various vantage points to IPs in different ASes. Such approaches rely on `traceroute` and are generally limited by the network locations and availability of the volunteered probing nodes; they may not provide the AS-level path between any two randomly chosen ASes.
2. *Router-level mapping.* An AS is not a black box, but contains hosts and routers. Mahajan *et al.* [58] show how the internal structure of an AS can be

---

[3] Several authors have mentioned how these blacklists vary over time [1,11].

mapped, by a combination of `traceroute` probes, IP alias resolution[4], and reverse DNS lookups.

Powers of the Adversary: Our adversary is a censorious government. The adversary aims to filter Internet traffic, and for this purpose may perform IP filtering, DNS injection/URL Filtering, and IP prefix hijacking attacks. We note that even a government has limitations; for example, it would prefer to implement filtering at a small number of locations, rather than at *every* ISP network in the nation, because of both various political and technical factors (*e.g.* if changing the blacklist implies wide scale router level re-configuration, there will almost certainly be inconsistencies and failures in enforcement).

2.2   Related Research

Much of the study of modern Internet censorship was developed in the context of China [49,61–63], particularly the different censorship techniques employed and the network destinations filtered. For *e.g.*, Winter and Lindskog [61] examine how the Chinese authorities use DPI-capable routers to detect Tor Bridges. Others, such as [33], explored the mechanics of DNS filtering and how China is contributing to collateral damage. A major step forward was made by Verkamp and Gupta [32], who deployed clients in 11 countries (including India) to identify their network censorship activities – IP and URL filtering, keyword filtering and DNS censorship *etc.* Later authors – Nabi [55] in Pakistan, and Halderman *et al.* [34] in Iran – demonstrate different methods of censorship employed by their respective regimes, as well as different forms of content blocked. Such studies of censorship in repressive regimes are often limiting, as they require Internet access from almost all network locations inside the country (Nabi *et al.* were able to get access from only five locations, and Halderman from only one).

We take a different direction with this paper. While we begin by examining instances of network censorship in our target country (India), our main aim is to determine the *potential* for censorship, in case the regime decides to become more censorious. Specifically, how bottlenecked is the Indian Internet? Is it possible for the adversary to place censors in a relatively small set of ASes and routers, and still filter a large fraction of network paths (and thus potentially users)? - if so, this presents a much lower barrier to entry than monitoring in every AS.

The most relevant related work we are aware of, is Singh *et al.*'s study of how Internet censorship correlates to network cartography [59]. The authors show a strong correspondence between the *Freedom House Index* [5] of a nation and its Internet topology, and indeed, claim that a nation's network topology is the best indicator of a countrys level of freedom. Our work makes use of network topology as well: we use it to determine the "key" network locations (ASes and routers) where the adversary (censorious government) would rationally deploy censorship infrastructure, if its aim was to censor all or almost all Internet traffic in the country, and the impact of such measures on network paths originating

---

[4] Different interfaces of the same router, with different IPs, are called IP aliases.

both within and outside the nation (but transiting Indian ASes). We perform this study for various traffic filtering techniques in the following section.

3 Motivation, Problem Description and Methodology

3.1 Preliminary Findings and Motivation

Well-studied censorious countries, such as China, Iran, and Saudi Arabia, tend to have a very clear censorship policy. In contrast, India has a rather ad hoc approach: the government expects all ISPs to (independently) enforce its policies. We find that in practice, traffic filtering is *highly* inconsistent across popular Indian ISPs – the set of blacklisted sites varies by orders of magnitude.

Table 1. Censorship trends in India: some initial results.

ISP	Website categories							
	Escort (150)	Music (100)	Porn (50)	Torrents (30)	Social (20)	Political (20)	Tools (20)	Misc. (150)
Airtel	50, 80, 20	82, 6, 12	1, 49, 0	13, 16, 1	8, 10, 2	2, 15, 3	1, 14, 5	80, 41, 29
Vodafone	24, 87, 39	95, 1, 4	2, 45, 3	16, 11, 3	8, 8, 4	0, 13, 7	4, 11, 5	70, 35, 45
Sify	12, 98, 40	1, 75, 24	1, 48, 1	6, 22, 2	0, 16, 4	0, 15, 5	1, 16, 3	11, 75, 64
NKN	11, 105, 34	57, 33, 10	1, 48, 1	10, 16, 4	4, 12, 4	2, 14, 4	1, 14, 5	65, 56, 29
BSNL	41, 69, 40	68, 12, 20	0, 45, 5	12, 14, 4	7, 10, 3	4, 12, 4	3, 14, 3	88, 27, 35
MTNL	27, 98, 25	81, 2, 17	45, 3, 2	15, 12, 3	9, 8, 3	14, 1, 5	2, 12, 6	73, 23, 54
Siti	23, 99, 28	28, 56, 16	44, 4, 2	14, 13, 3	9, 8, 3	1, 14, 5	1, 12, 7	86, 29, 35
Reliance Jio	0, 123, 27	0, 77, 23	0, 38, 12	2, 26, 2	0, 18, 2	0, 16, 4	0, 15, 5	0, 78, 72

To study such inconsistencies, we selected a list of 540 potentially censored websites, divided into 8 different categories (ranging from escort services, to anti-censorship tools like *Tor* [40]). We then systematically observed the censorship policy in different ISPs, by trying to access our potentially-censored websites through them.

Table 1 summarizes our findings. The rows represent the ISPs, columns correspond to the category of site which being filtered, and each entry is a 3-tuple (c_n, o_n, x_n) representing the number of each type of response – *censored, open,* and *inaccessible*.[5] For example, we probed 150 escort websites through the Airtel network, and observed 50 to be censored, 80 open, and 20 inaccessible.

---

[5] We explain these terms below.

- *Censored:* the ISP intercepted the requests, and responded with an HTML iframe displaying a filtering message (indicating that requested URL had been blocked as per the directions from the Department of Telecommunication).
- *Open:* Websites were accessible without filtering.
- *Inaccessible:* Websites were "down". There was not enough information to determine if the sites were inaccessible due to network or system outages, or requests were deliberately filtered or throttled by the ISP.

We note that the variation of censorship by ISP is quite dramatic: Airtel blocks only 1 out of the 50 pornographic sites probed, whereas MTNL blocks 45.

It is clearly difficult to get hundreds of independent ISPs to correctly comply with censorship orders. The question arises whether, *if* the government decides to enforce a single policy, it is able to do so. So the question arises, *are there a few key bottlenecks in the existing network, where filtering may be carried out?*

3.2   Problem Description

In our research we are particularly interested in finding a small set of key locations (ASes and routers) that intercept a large fraction of network paths. More specifically, our questions are as follows.

- Is it possible for the government to monitor/censor a large fraction of Internet traffic by controlling only a small number of network locations (*viz.* ASes and routers)?
- What fraction of traffic could be filtered, and who would be most affected?
- Would such censorship affect users outside the country as well?

3.3   Evaluation Methodology

Identifying Potential Network locations for IP Filtering: In order to estimate the locations for installing IP filtering infrastructure, we built an AS-level map using paths in the Internet, then focused on Indian ASes and their connections. Our map was built using Gao's algorithm [56], which finds AS-level paths to the home AS of chosen IP prefixes (in our case, censored sites) from every other AS in the Internet. The algorithm uses links from known AS paths in BGP routing tables; we obtained tables from a number of vantage points [31].

Unlike other nations, which have an unambiguous list of blocked sites [55], India has no clear censorship policy. We created a corpus of sites blacklisted by various government decrees (as reported by popular media), and also added the sites reported as blocked in India by the crowd-sourced censorship-reporting sites like Herdict [12]. These included social media sites, political sites, sites related to unfriendly nations, and p2p file-sharing sites. Finally, we added to the list the adult sites popular in India (as per Alexa [2]).

We randomly sampled about 100 sites from this corpus. We then computed the paths between all Indian ASes and these prefixes. The ASes appearing in these paths were sorted by frequency of occurrence; we thus selected the few most frequent ones.

Do these ASes appear in paths to other potentially blocked sites as well? To answer such questions, we re-estimated our paths with another set of about 220 sites, chosen from the corpus. The heavy-hitter ASes for this new set of paths were the same as the ones found before.

Intra-AS Topology Generation: In the second round of experiments, we employed the Rocketfuel algorithm [58] to compute the router-level paths through 10 heavy-hitter ASes (i.e. major Indian ISPs), then identified the routers which occur in a large fraction of paths (i.e. the heavy-hitter routers in heavy-hitter ASes), as follows.

1. Using `planetlab` nodes, we ran `traceroute` probes to three representative IPs in each prefix advertised by the ASes and by their immediate (1-hop) customer ASes.
   `Traceroute` returned router level paths leading to and out of the said ASes.
2. From the `traceroute` trace, we chose the sub-paths consisting of router IPs advertized by the AS under study (*i.e.* router within the ASes, identified from [16]).
3. We resolved the aliases (corresponding to the discovered router IPs) with `Midar` [18] alias resolution tool.
4. Finally, from the discovered `traceroute` paths we selected the minimum number of routers which cumulatively intercept a large fraction of the paths. To do this we chose the following heuristic:
   - If total number of edge routers are less than total number of edge and core routers that intercept a large fraction of the paths (over 90%), then we selected the edge routers alone (as the set of edge routers cover 100% of paths through the AS).
   - Else, we selected the "heavy-hitter" (core plus edge routers), appearing in a very large fraction of the paths (over 90%); not all edge routers may appear as often as others (edge and core routers appearing in the discovered paths).

Identifying Potential Sites for DNS Based Filtering: Another common approach to censorship is to prevent the DNS service from resolving requests. The censor either instructs DNS servers (within its jurisdiction) to filter requests for blacklisted URLs, or installs infrastructure to intercept DNS queries on routers (en-route to DNS servers) and respond with bogus IPs or NXDOMAIN responses – also referred to as *DNS Injection* attack.

Filtering DNS requests, either by simply dropping them, or by responding with bogus responses, could be carried out at the DNS server. However, in a country like India, hosting more than 55000 DNS servers, distributed across different networks, reconfiguring *all* such servers to filter DNS queries for blacklisted sites would not be easy (besides simple disobedience, there would also be misconfiguration bugs, delays, and network downtime). It would be much more practical to identify a few ASes (and routers therein), that intercept all or almost all the network paths connecting DNS servers to all ASes in the country.

To identify key ASes for DNS injection, we began by identifying the DNS resolvers across all Indian prefixes. We probed IP prefixes of every Indian AS for available DNS servers (UDP port 53) using `nmap` [51], and noted whether the response was *open, filtered,* or *closed.* (*Closed* corresponds to ICMP `'destination port unreachable'` message responses from the destination.

Open means the client received a meaningful response. *Filtered* indicates that the client received no response[6].)

Each IP, for which we obtained a *filtered* or *open* response, was sent a request to resolve the IP address of some popular WWW destinations (*e.g.* https://www. google.com). Addresses that allowed resolution were added to our list of publicly available DNS resolvers.

Finally, using Gao's algorithm, we constructed a graph of prefix-to-AS paths connecting the IP prefixes corresponding to DNS resolvers, and all the Indian ASes. To find the ASes which would be most effective at DNS injection, we identified ASes at the intersection of a large number of these paths.

Impact of IP Prefix Hijack Based Censorship: In an IP Prefix Hijacking attack, malicious BGP routers advertise fake AS-level paths[7] in an attempt to poison routes to an IP prefix (see Fig. 1), thus attracting a large volume of traffic [35, 36,42,45,57].

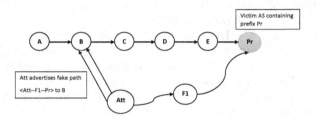

Fig. 1. IP Prefix Hijacking: valid path: $A - B - C - D - E - Pr$. A is the origin AS and Pr the AS with the destination prefix. Attacker *Att* advertises a shorter path $Att - F_1 - Pr$, to AS B. If B chooses this path and directs its traffic to *Att*, the attacker can censor the traffic.

Prefix hijacking is an extremely aggressive attack, and unlikely to be used in practice; but it has been used in the wild (e.g. blocking of YouTube by Pakistani ISPs [23], and also those involving ConEd (US), TTNet (Turkey), Link Telekom (Russia) among others [46]) and remains viable as an orthogonal way of censoring traffic. So for completeness, we have also considered prefix hijacking as a potential tool for censoring the Internet in India.

In general, for a successful prefix hijack attack, the malicious AS either broadcasts a shorter path to the prefix, or claims to own it outright. The attacking AS advertises fake routes for the targeted prefix to all its neighbors. Ballani *et al.* [35] report that receiving ASes accept these advertisements based on the following heuristics:

1. If there exists a customer path towards the target IP and iff the advertisement presents a shorter customer path, then choose it, else reject it.

---

[6] This may be due to unavailability or filtering by firewall(s).

[7] Alternatively, router misconfiguration can also lead to similar situations [54].

2. If there exist a provider path towards the target IP and iff the advertisement presents a shorter provider path, then accept it. For all other cases, the paths are accepted without considering the length.
3. If there exist a peer path towards the target IP and iff the advertisement bears a shorter peer path, accept it. Customer paths are accepted without length considerations while provider paths are ignored.

Estimating the Impact of Prefix Hijack Attack: To study the potential impact IP prefix hijacking, we used the previously constructed AS-level topology and chose an attacker AS with a high *node degree*(i.e. the number of ASes adjacent to the said AS). Inspecting the prefix-to-AS paths, we identified ASes with which the attacker AS had a business relationship, and applied Ballani's heuristics to determine the number of ASes potentially affected by fake advertisements.

Collateral Damage Due to Traffic Censorship: Several non-Indian ASes rely on Indian ASes for Internet connectivity. Censorship activities in Indian ASes may potentially filter the traffic of these non-Indian customers as well [33]. For example, such unintended filtering was reported by Omantel, that peers with the Indian ISP Bharti Airtel [17]. As one of our research objectives, we try to identify ASes outside India that may be affected by Indian censorship. We identify paths which do not originate in India, but pass through or terminate in India. The non-Indian customers on such paths may face unwanted access restrictions.

4   Experimental Results

Continuing from the description of our experiment in the previous section, in this section we present our results. First, we consider router-level filtering, and how many ASes and routers must be selected for effective censorship (in terms of coverage of paths to filtered destinations). Along similar lines, we identify the locations where the adversary could launch a DNS injection attack. We go on to present the results of simulating IP prefix hijack attacks on Indian ASes. Finally, we report the collateral damage to foreign ASes due to IP filtering in India.

4.1   Network Locations for IP (Router-Level) Filtering

As mentioned earlier, we first obtained paths connecting Indian ASes to about 100 potential target sites (chosen from our corpus). Figure 3 represents the number of paths an individual AS intercepts; the horizontal axis of the graph indicates the ASes, ranked according to the number of paths each one intercepts. A small number of Indian ASes appear in the overwhelming majority of these paths; these ASNs and their owner organizations are presented in the Table 2.

The question remains whether the ASes we observe are simply an artifact of the 100 target sites we chose. To check whether this is so, we repeated the experiment with another (non-overlapping) sample of 220 target sites from our

Table 2. AS Ranks, their ASNs and their owners.

Rank	ASN	Owner
1	9498	Bharti Airtel
2	4755	Tata Comm.
3	55410	Vodafone
4	9583	Sify Ltd.
5	9730	Bharti Telesonic
6	9885	NKN Internet
7	55824	NKN Core
8	45820	Tata Teleservices
9	18101	Reliance Comm.
10	10201	Dishnet Wireless

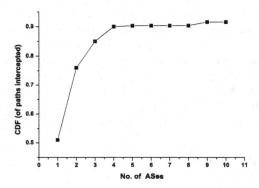

Fig. 2. CDF of Indian paths intercepted by ASes.

corpus. The same 10 ASes covered the vast majority of paths to both sets of target sites, indicating that they are very likely major Indian providers of Internet infrastructure, and cover a majority of paths to *any* target sites.

The cumulative results of *paths intercepted* vs *total number of ASes*, corresponding to both experiments, is presented in Fig. 2. As evident, *we only need 4 ASes to censor over* 90% *of the paths to the censored destinations, and* 10 *ASes for* 95% *of the paths.* Figure 3 represents the number of paths intercepted by each of these ASes individually.

Intra-AS Topology: We now consider the question of which *routers* (in our key ASes) are responsible for carrying the vast majority of Indian Internet traffic. Following Mahajan *et al.*'s approach [58] (as described previously in Subsect. 3.3), we create router-level maps of the key ASes, and identify routers that appear on a large fraction of the paths.

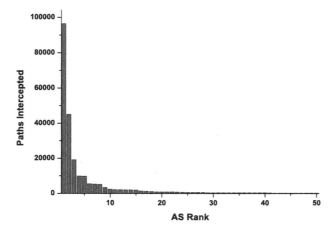

Fig. 3. Paths intercepted by individual ASes vs AS rank (by path freq.) Total 186679 paths from Indian ASes to 211 prefixes (hosting 320 potentially filtered sites).

Figure 4 shows the fraction of paths these routers cumulatively intercept. (For privacy concerns, we refrain from revealing the IP addresses of these routers.)

Table 3 represents the number of edge and core routers that cumulatively appear in over 90% of the `traceroute` paths. The adversary could choose to place filters either at these points - heavy hitter routers of the heavy hitter ASes - or at the edge routers of the ASes, which together see all the traffic that passes through the AS. We find that the total number of edge routers is less than the number of "heavy-hitting" edge and core routers, and conclude that the lowest-

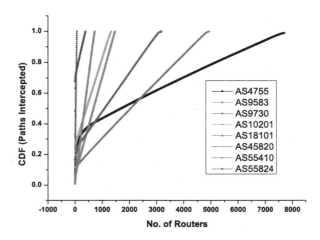

Fig. 4. CDF of `traceroute` paths intercepted by individual routers, sorted by increasing number of paths through each router (for 8 important ASes.)

Table 3. The total number of edge and core routers in 9 ASes that appear in over 90% of the discovered paths. For *eg.,*. AS4755 has a total of 8404 routers (1779 edge + 6229 core). However, the total number of edge routers (1779) is less than the number of heavy hitters (6434).

ASN	# of Edge routers (E)	# of Core routers (C)	# of Heavy hitter routers (H)	# of DR's required min(E, H)
9498	1782	5321	5192	1782
4755	1779	6229	6434	1779
55410	133	594	634	133
9583	484	4458	4275	484
9730	7	63	62	7
55824	66	325	254	66
45820	193	1147	1132	193
18101	462	2724	2677	462
10201	90	1396	1315	90

cost solution for the adversary is to install censorship infrastructure on the (total of 4996) edge routers.

We note that, at present, the number of key routers varies significantly across ASes, from 7 to 1782. In case of the larger ASes, the AS network administrator could likely improve on our figures, by combining our findings with better information about the router-level topology and setting routing policy to pass all traffic through a smaller number of routers. Hence our count of 4996 routers is essentially an upper bound, limited by the policies of the present day.

Collateral Damage: Our graph of paths from censored prefixes to ASes has $186,679$ paths of Indian origin (1.76% of paths). A comparable number - $121,931$ paths of foreign origin (1.15% of paths) - transit through or terminate in an Indian AS. *Censorship by Indian ASes may inadvertently impact a very large number of unintended customers, across Finland, Hong Kong, Singapore, Malaysia, the US, and so on.*

4.2   Censorship Through DNS Filtering

Using our approach for identifying open DNS resolvers, we identified a total of $55,234$ publicly accessible DNS servers from probing all 12.10 million Indian IPs.

After identifying the prefixes corresponding to these each resolver IP, we selected one corresponding to each AS[8] In all, we selected 355 prefixes, representative of 355 unique Indian ASes. Finally, using Gao's algorithm, we estimated the paths from each Indian AS to the (prefixes corresponding to) DNS

---

[8] For multiple prefixes belonging to same AS, we selected one with most resolvers.

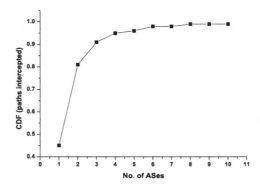

Fig. 5. CDF of DNS paths intercepted by top 10 Ases.

resolvers in India. *Cumulatively, 8 ASes (according to path frequency) can inter-cept* 99.14% *of these paths, and potentially launch DNS based filtering or Injec-tion attacks (see Fig. 5).*

We note that these 8 ASes also appear among the 10 top ASes we identified for IP filtering and IP prefix hijacking. Hence, the same key routers for each of these ASes (as per Table 3) may be selected for installing infrastructure to launch DNS injection (or other DNS level filtering schemes). In all, 4906 routers across the 8 ASes can cumulatively filter DNS traffic for all Indian ASes[9].

4.3   Censorship Through IP Prefix Hijacking

For IP prefix hijacking, we chose to simulate attacks from the ASes with high node degree. Based on our censored-prefix-to-AS topology graph, we identified the top 10 ASes by node degree, and determined the number of ASes potentially vulnerable to attacks from each of these ASes. The results of these simulations are presented in Table 4.

The table shows that a small number of ASes in India can potentially affect traffic from *all* Indian ASes, as well as a considerable number of foreign ones. For example, fake advertisements by *AS4755* can impact a total of 955 ASes (896 Indian and 41 others). To effectively launch an IP prefix hijacking attack, the government needs control over the BGP speakers (which form a small fraction of all the routers of an AS); for ASes such as *AS9730*, with 7 edge and 63 core routers, this number is probably very small.

4.4   Analysis of Results

We observe that a very small number of ASes (less than 10) intercept a large fraction of AS-level paths connecting Indian ASes to our list of potentially cen-sored sites (obtained from public announcements of censored sites in India), and

---

[9] As mentioned in the previous sub-section, this number may be further reduced by routing optimization on the part of the AS network administrator.

Table 4. IP prefix hijack: a single AS (*e.g.* AS9498), is well capable of censoring the traffic of all 896 Indian ASes and few (59) non-Indian ASes through prefix hijack attack.

Owner name	Attacking ASN	Number of affected AS'es	
		Indian	Non-Indian
Bharti Airtel Ltd.	9498	896	59
Tata Comm.	4755	896	41
Reliance Comm. Ltd.	18101	896	41
Vodafone Spacetel Ltd.	55410	896	42
Sify Ltd.	9583	896	58
Bharti Telesonic Ltd.	9730	749	23
Tata Teleservices	45820	560	1
Host Palace	13329	896	45
Dishnet Wireless Ltd.	10201	896	24
Idea Cellular Ltd.	55644	896	37

that this affects a substantial number of foreign users as well. While this result is interesting, there remains the question of whether it applies to censored sites in general, or only the ones in our sample.

Our request to the Indian government, under its own *Right to Information Act* [25], for the complete list of censored sites[10], was refused by the Indian Government Department of Telecommunications and IT, citing confidentiality concerns. Therefore, to cross-validate our results we randomly sampled two sets of target sites from our corpus, and ran our algorithm on each in isolation. The same set of key ASes appeared in both sets.[11]

We believe that DNS filtering is a viable threat. Should the aforementioned ASes filter DNS requests, they would also impact over 99% of the AS-level paths connecting Indian ASes to DNS resolvers both within and outside India (particularly services such as GoogleDNS and OpenDNS). We note in passing that DNS filtering is more powerful than simple IP filtering: even if a censored site were hosted in a Content Distribution Network (CDN), a user would be unable to reach its content on the CDN, as the request would still have the URL of the origin site, and would thus be filtered.

Finally, while IP prefix hijacking is rarely used (owing to its potential to cause major network outages - *e.g.*, the Pakistan Government's blocking of Youtube [23]), there exist five Indian ASes, each of which could censor traffic for all (or nearly all) Indian users by launching an IP prefix hijack attack. Moreover, only a handful of routers in each of these ASes – *viz.* the BGP speaking routers may be sufficient for such attacks.

---

[10] RTI number: DOTEL/R/2017/50126.

[11] We also note that these ASes are, in fact, partners to foreign network providers, and provide connectivity for almost every smaller AS in the country. This is perhaps unsurprising, given the hierarchical nature of the Internet as a whole [41].

5   Limitations and Future Work

5.1   Limitations

Our approach in this paper is to generate AS and router-level maps of India, and identify the key ASes and routers that intercept a large fraction of network paths. This approach is clearly limited to a snapshot of routing at a moment in time, and in fact we intend to see how our results vary over several years in future work. In addition, our AS-level and router-level mapping algorithms have the following limitations.

AS Path Estimation (Gao's Algorithm): *Our path estimation strategy is limited by the quality of publicly-available BGP routes.*

- *Route-collector bias:* It has been argued by Gregori *et al.* that the existing route collectors (like routeviews [27], BGPmon [29], RIPE [26], PCH [22] *etc.*) miss many of the peering relationships between smaller ASes; our map, as it uses Routeviews data, inherits this weakness.
- *Incorrect route advertisements:* In general, BGP routes are known contain artifacts of misconfiguration and bogus advertisements [23,50]. Our estimated paths may also be contaminated with such artifacts.

Router Level Topology Estimation: *The discovered topology may not reveal the actual router-level paths for packets traveling between the IPs of the probed AS and the censored websites.*

- *Router-level path variability:* Router-level maps of an AS are far more variable than AS-level maps: the latter rely on AS peering information (which is based on business relationships, that do not change frequently), while the former change with network conditions. Routing tables themselves are prone to inconsistencies and bogus routes [48,54].
- *Imperfect coverage by Traceroute:* We used a large number of `planetlab` nodes to launch `traceroute` probes[12], but there remains a chance that some routes are simply not covered; further increasing the number of vantage points, i.e. probing hosts, may improve our topology estimation by discovering new paths.
- *Routers filtering `traceroute` probes:* In many cases, routers are configured to not reply to `traceroute` probes with the usual `ICMP TTL Expired` messages, and remain anonymous, thereby reducing the accuracy of our estimated router-level topology.

5.2   Future Work

Our study of Internet censorship in India can be directly extended to other nations; while our case study was done with Indian data, we make use of no

---

[12] The `looking-glass` servers used by the original authors [58] were unavailable at the time of our experiments.

features peculiar to India. We are currently extending our analysis to other countries, and developing metrics for how "centralized" a country is (i.e. how many key ASes it takes to censor traffic in a country), as well as how "central" it is in the global Internet (measured by the extent of collateral damage it can cause). There are several other directions to extend this research, which we will explore next.

First - objectionable content is frequently hosted on social media sites, or other sites with apparently benign URLs. Might the government target search engines and social networking sites as well(as seen in China)? Would this be a full blacklist, or partial?[13] And if so, would our key ASes be different for these target websites?

There is also the question of whether popular anti-censorship and anonymity preserving tools like Tor may be attacked by controlling a few network points. Finally, we also intend to consider the question of policing the cellular data network[14], in our future work.

6   Concluding Remarks

Though the Indian state *declares* that it has a unified Internet censorship policy, the current state of censorship (where the responsibility of network filtering is left to individual ASes) is highly inconsistent. However, our results also show that *if* the Indian government wishes to impose a single policy, the structure of the Indian Internet shows that it would only need to control a small set of locations. (Furthermore, a significant fraction of network paths from foreign customers, which transit India, will be collateral damage for Indian censorship.)

1. Though India has ≈900 ASes, 10 ASes cover ≈95% of AS-level paths; a nationwide censor using IP-filtering functionality would need to control ≈5000 routers – a challenging, but tractable, number. In particular, two private ISP networks control over 70% of those routers (and may optimize the router selection further).
2. DNS based filtering requires only eight of these ASes and impacts >99% of the AS-level paths connecting Indian ASes to the DNS resolvers both within and outside India (for services like GoogleDNS and OpenDNS).
3. Any one of five ASes is capable of disrupting network connectivity for all Indian ASes, through IP prefix hijacking attacks.

India, unlike China, is still ambivalent w.r.t. censorship, but the findings in this paper indicate that ordinary citizens should indeed be concerned (and possibly start to equip themselves with censorship circumvention techniques), as large scale censorship would not be very difficult for the government to implement.

---

[13] Semantics-based filtering is very hard; *e.g.* attempts to block jihadi mouthpiece sites also block sites that monitor jihad as a threat, such as `jihadwatch.org`.

[14] As per reports published in recent years, India has 860 million cellular users [10].

References

1. 830 more websites blocked in India, many torrent links in list. http://indiatoday. intoday.in/technology/story/830-more-websites-blocked-in-india-many-torrent-links-in-list/1/748565.html
2. Alexa - Actionable Analytics for the Web. http://www.alexa.com/
3. Archipelago (ARK) Measurement Infrastructure. http://www.caida.org/projects/ark/
4. Censorship in France. http://www.laquadrature.net/en/french-parliament-approves-net-censorship
5. Censorship in India by Freedom House. https://freedomhouse.org/report-types/freedom-press
6. Censorship in Sweden. https://www.dangerandplay.com/2016/01/29/sweden-caught-censoring-the-internet-1984-style/
7. Censorship in Venezuela: Over 370 internet addresses blocked. https://panampost.com/pedro-garcia/2016/07/20/censorship-in-venezuela-over-370-internet-addresses-blocked/
8. Censorship is India by India Times. http://telecom.economictimes.indiatimes.com/tele-talk/internet-censorship-regulating-india-s-internet/1369
9. Court Cases Regarding Internet Censorship. https://opennet.net/news/india-court-summons-google-facebook-microsoft-executives
10. Government of India Department of Telecom. Telecom Annual report - India, 2012–2013 (2013). goo.gl/H7O13n
11. Govt of India wants 32 URLs, including Dailymotion, Vimeo and Github, banned. http://indianexpress.com/article/technology/social/government-wants-32-urls-including-dailymotion-vimeo-banned-in-india/
12. Herdict: Help Spot Web Blockages. http://herdict.org/
13. India is partly free by freedom house. https://freedomhouse.org/report/freedom-net/2011/india
14. India's supreme court strikes down controversial internet censorship law. https://techcrunch.com/2015/03/23/indias-supreme-court-strikes-down-controversial-internet-censorship-law/
15. The internet censorship saga in India. https://internetdemocracy.in/2012/03/the-internet-censorship-saga-in-india/
16. IP to as mapping, team Cymru. http://www.team-cymru.org/IP-ASN-mapping.html
17. ISP of Oman suffers web filtering by Indian censorship. https://citizenlab.org/2012/07/routing-gone-wild/
18. Midar. http://www.caida.org/tools/measurement/midar/
19. Number of Indian internet users. http://www.internetlivestats.com/internet-users-by-country/
20. ONI report for India. https://opennet.net/research/profiles/india
21. OpenNet Initiative. https://opennet.net/
22. Packet Clearing House, San Francisco, CA, USA. http://www.pch.net
23. Pakistan Hijacks YouTube. https://www.ripe.net/publications/news/industry-developments/youtube-hijacking-a-ripe-ncc-ris-case-study
24. Porn websites blocked in India: Government plans ombudsman for online content. http://gadgets.ndtv.com/internet/news/porn-websites-blocked-in-india-government-plans-ombudsman-for-online-content-723485
25. Right to information, a citizen gateway. http://rti.gov.in/

26. Ripe NCC, Amsterdam, the Netherlands, ripe NCC routing information service. http://www.ripe.net/data-tools/stats/ris/routing-information-service
27. Route views project. http://archive.routeviews.org/
28. Service providers list - telecom regulatory authority of India. http://www.trai.gov.in/Content/ProviderListDisp/3_ProviderListDisp.aspx
29. University of Colorado, Fort Collins, CO, USA, BGPmon. http://bgpmon.netsec.colostate.edu
30. Websites blocked by Indian government. http://sflc.in/wp-content/uploads/2015/12/censorship.-2012-2015.pdf
31. University of Oregon Route Views Project (2000). http://www.routeviews.org/
32. Verkamp, J.P., Gupta, M.: Inferring mechanics of web censorship around the world. Presented as part of the 2nd USENIX Workshop on Free and Open Communications on the Internet. USENIX, Berkeley (2012)
33. Anonymous. The collateral damage of internet censorship by DNS injection. SIG-COMM Comput. Commun. Rev. **42**(3), 21–27 (2012)
34. Aryan, S., Aryan, H., Halderman, J.A.: Internet censorship in Iran: a first look. Presented as part of the 3rd USENIX Workshop on Free and Open Communications on the Internet. USENIX, Berkeley (2013)
35. Ballani, H., Francis, P., Zhang, X.: A study of prefix hijacking and interception in the internet. SIGCOMM Comput. Commun. Rev. **37**(4), 265–276 (2007)
36. Butler, K., Farley, T.R., McDaniel, P., Rexford, J.: A survey of BGP security issues and solutions. Proc. IEEE **98**(1), 100–122 (2010)
37. Crandall, J.R., Zinn, D., Byrd, M., Barr, E.T., East, R.: ConceptDoppler: a weather tracker for internet censorship. In: ACM Conference on Computer and Communications Security, pp. 352–365 (2007)
38. Dalek, J., Haselton, B., Noman, H., Senft, A., Crete-Nishihata, M., Gill, P., Deibert, R.J.: A method for identifying and confirming the use of URL filtering products for censorship. In: Proceedings of the 2013 Conference on Internet Measurement Conference, pp. 23–30. ACM (2013)
39. Dingledine, R., Mathewson, N., Syverson, P.: Tor: the second-generation onion router. In: Proceedings of the 13th USENIX Security Symposium, pp. 303–319, August 2004
40. Dingledine, R., Mathewson, N., Syverson, P.: Tor: the second-generation onion router. Technical report, DTIC Document (2004)
41. Gao, L.: On inferring autonomous system relationships in the internet. IEEE/ACM Trans. Netw. **9**(6), 733–745 (2001)
42. Goldberg, S., Schapira, M., Hummon, P., Rexford, J.: How secure are secure interdomain routing protocols. In: ACM SIGCOMM Computer Communication Review, vol. 40, pp. 87–98. ACM (2010)
43. Guo, S., Feng, G.: Understanding support for internet censorship in China: an elaboration of the theory of reasoned action. J. Chin. Polit. Sci. **17**(1), 33–52 (2012)
44. Haddadi, H., Rio, M., Iannaccone, G., Moore, A., Mortier, R.: Network topologies: inference, modeling, and generation. IEEE Commun. Surv. Tutor. **10**(2), 48–69 (2008)
45. Hu, X., Mao, Z.M.: Accurate real-time identification of IP prefix hijacking. In: IEEE Symposium on Security and Privacy, SP 2007, pp. 3–17. IEEE (2007)
46. Jacquemart, Q.: Towards uncovering BGP hijacking attacks. Ph.D. thesis, Télécom ParisTech, 2015

47. Jones, B., Feamster, N., Paxson, V., Weaver, N., Allman, M.: Detecting DNS root manipulation. In: Karagiannis, T., Dimitropoulos, X. (eds.) PAM 2016. LNCS, vol. 9631, pp. 276–288. Springer, Cham (2016). https://doi.org/10.1007/978-3-319-30505-9_21

48. Le, F., Lee, S., Wong, T., Kim, H.S., Newcomb, D.: Detecting network-wide and router-specific misconfigurations through data mining. IEEE/ACM Trans. Netw. 17(1), 66–79 (2009)

49. Leberknight, C.S., Chiang, M., Poor, H.V., Wong, F.: A taxonomy of internet censorship and anti-censorship. In: Fifth International Conference on Fun with Algorithms (2010)

50. Luckie, M.: Spurious routes in public BGP data. ACM SIGCOMM Comput. Commun. Rev. 44(3), 14–21 (2014)

51. Lyon, G.: Nmap: The Network Mapper - Free Security Scanner. http://insecure.org/fyodor/

52. MacKinnon, R.: Flatter world and thicker walls? Blogs, censorship and civic discourse in China. Public Choice 134(1–2), 31–46 (2008)

53. Madhyastha, H.V., Isdal, T., Piatek, M., Dixon, C., Anderson, T.E., Krishnamurthy, A., Venkataramani, A.: iPlane: an information plane for distributed services. In: Proceedings of 7th USENIX Symposium on Operating Systems Design and Implementation (OSDI), pp. 367–380, November 2006

54. Mahajan, R., Wetherall, D., Anderson, T.: Understanding BGP misconfiguration. In: ACM SIGCOMM Computer Communication Review, vol. 32, pp. 3–16. ACM (2002)

55. Nabi, Z.: The anatomy of web censorship in Pakistan. In: Presented as part of the 3rd USENIX Workshop on Free and Open Communications on the Internet. USENIX, Berkeley (2013)

56. Qiu, J., Gao, L.: As path inference by exploiting known as paths. In: Global Telecommunications Conference, GLOBECOM 2006, pp. 1–5. IEEE (2006)

57. Qiu, J., Gao, L., Ranjan, S., Nucci, A.: Detecting bogus BGP route information: going beyond prefix hijacking. In: Third International Conference on Security and Privacy in Communications Networks and the Workshops, SecureComm 2007, pp. 381–390. IEEE (2007)

58. Rocketfuel: An ISP Topology Mapping Engine. http://www.cs.washington.edu/research/networking/rocketfuel/

59. Singh, R., Koo, H., Miramirkhani, N., Mirhaj, F., Gill, P., Akoglu, L.: The politics of routing: investigating the relationship between as connectivity and internet freedom. In: 6th USENIX Workshop on Free and Open Communications on the Internet (FOCI 2016). USENIX Association (2016)

60. Stevenson, C.: Breaching the great firewall: China's internet censorship and the quest for freedom of expression in a connected world. BC Int. Comp. L. Rev. 30, 531 (2007)

61. Winter, P., Lindskog, S.: How the great firewall of China is blocking tor. In: Proceedings of the USENIX Workshop on Free and Open Communications on the Internet (FOCI 2012), August 2012

62. Xu, X., Mao, Z.M., Halderman, J.A.: Internet censorship in China: where does the filtering occur? In: Spring, N., Riley, G.F. (eds.) PAM 2011. LNCS, vol. 6579, pp. 133–142. Springer, Heidelberg (2011). https://doi.org/10.1007/978-3-642-19260-9_14

63. Zittrain, J., Edelman, B.: Internet filtering in China. IEEE Internet Comput. 7(2), 70–77 (2003)

A Deep Learning Based Online Malicious URL and DNS Detection Scheme

Jianguo Jiang[1], Jiuming Chen[1,2], Kim-Kwang Raymond Choo[3], Chao Liu[1],
Kunying Liu[1], Min Yu[1,2(✉)], and Yongjian Wang[4(✉)]

[1] Institute of Information Engineering, Chinese Academy of Sciences, Beijing, China
[2] School of Cyber Security, University of Chinese Academy of Sciences, Beijing, China
[3] Department of Information Systems and Cyber Security, University of Texas at San Antonio,
San Antonio, TX, USA
[4] Key Laboratory of Information Network Security of Ministry of Public Security,
The Third Research Institute of Ministry of Public Security, Shanghai, China
yumin@iie.ac.cn, wangyongjian@stars.org.cn

Abstract. URL and DNS are two common attack vectors in malicious network activities; thus, detection for malicious URL and DNS is crucial in network security. In this paper, we propose an online detection scheme based on character-level deep neural networks. Specifically, this scheme maps the URL and DNS strings into vector form using some natural language processing methods. The CNN (Convolutional Neural Network) network framework is then designed to automatically extract the malicious features and train the classifying model. Experimental results on real-world URL and DNS datasets show that proposed method outperforms several state-of-art baseline methods, in terms of efficiency and scalability.

Keywords: Network security · Malicious URL detection · Online detection
CNN

1 Introduction

As more of our devices go online, cyber threats seeking to exploit vulnerabilities in people, process and technologies will be increasingly prevalent [1, 2]. For example, the recent WannaCry ransomware virus reportedly infected more than 300,000 devices in at least 150 countries, denying access to data stored on the compromised devices. While there is a wide range of attack vectors, a common tactic used is to lure users to visit malicious websites by clicking on a malicious URL. For example, the number of unique phishing websites detected by the Anti-Phishing Working Group in October 2016, November 2016, and December 2016 is 89232, 118928, and 69533, respectively [3]. As explained in the report, "a single phishing site may be advertised as thousands of customized URLS, all leading to basically the same attack destination".

© ICST Institute for Computer Sciences, Social Informatics and Telecommunications Engineering 2018
X. Lin et al. (Eds.): SecureComm 2017, LNICST 238, pp. 438–448, 2018.
https://doi.org/10.1007/978-3-319-78813-5_22

Therefore, one way of reducing phishing and other cyber attacks is to have the capability to efficiently detect and block malicious URLs, as well as the capability to circumvent efforts used by cyber attackers such as URL obfuscation techniques.

Conventional malicious URL detection methods generally rely on the features extracted based on expert input or using machine learning techniques [4]. Such methods mainly construct massive feature sets, in order to provide a comprehensive coverage. However, in practice, these methods may have high false alarm rate and have a number of limitations, such as the following:

(a) A significant increase in the number of websites and size of network traffic complicate efforts to efficiently and effectively detect malicious URLs (e.g. due to the presence of a large number of new features required for malicious URL detection).
(b) Imbalanced dataset. In comparison with the total volume of online traffic, the number of malicious URLs is relatively small (perhaps analogous to the saying 'finding a needle in the haystack'). Such imbalance (between normal URLs and malicious URLs) can lead to an unstable classification model.
(c) Constant evolution of attack techniques. Attackers often use a wide range of techniques to circumvent or avoid existing detection technologies.

Thus, in this paper, we present an online malicious URL detection scheme by combining deep neural network with natural language processing and threat intelligence. This allows us to automate the extraction of hidden features within the URL strings. Specifically, we design a convolutional neural network (CNN) based deep learning network to train the classification model. In order to map the URL strings into vector, we use the character-level word embedding method to parse the URL inputs to vectors. We then demonstrate the utility of our approach using real-world datasets. The detection scheme combines both deep learning and threat intelligence for malicious URL detection. What's more, the scheme proposed is a general detection scheme for short text detection problem in the security field such as malicious DNS detection.

In the next section, we review related literature. In Sects. 3 and 4, we present our scheme for malicious URL detection and evaluate the scheme, respectively. Finally, in Sect. 5, we conclude the paper and discuss future work.

2 Related Literature

Existing literature on malicious URL detection can be broadly categorized into blacklist based methods, features sets based methods, and machine learning based methods, as well as URL based methods and content based methods.

Webpage content is a rich information source that can be leveraged for detection [5]. Content-based methods are useful for offline detection and analysis but are generally not effective in online detection (e.g. significant latency, as scanning and analyzing page content is computationally intensive).

In this paper, we focus on online detection of malicious URL. Therefore, we will now discuss related literature on URL based methods. URL based detection methods use only the URL structures (e.g. length, domain, name length and number of dots in the URL) for detection. Such methods have been widely used due to its efficiency. These methods usually extract lexical features, either via artificial extraction or automated extraction. They can be divided into two categories, namely: machine learning based detection methods and manually constructed feature sets.

For example, McGrath and Gupta [6] analyzed the differences between normal URLs and phishing URLs to extract features that can be used to construct a classifier for phishing URL detection. Yadav et al. [7] examined more features, such as differences in bi-gram distribution of domain names between normal URLs and malicious ones. These and other related methods require the construction of large feature sets, and the detection outcome relies on the quality of these features. These features are extracted manually by experts and updating these feature sets can be challenging and time consuming. These methods also have a high false positive rate.

To mitigate these two limitations (high false positive rate and difficult to update), researchers have started examining the potential of using machine learning algorithms. In such approaches, the malicious detection problem is viewed as a classification or clustering problem, and machine learning algorithms (e.g. K-means, KNN, decision tree and SVM [8]) are used to train the classify model and extract relevant features. The machine learning based methods firstly construct an annotated URL dataset including both malicious and normal URLs. Then, some machine learning methods are used to train the classification model. Each algorithm has some specific advantages and weakness in malicious URL detection, as summarized in Table 1:

Table 1. Comparative summary of machine learning based detection methods [9, 10].

Model	Speed	Accuracy	Interpretability	Dataset size	Limitation
Bayes	High	Low	Good	Large	Need to assume the data is independent
SVM	Low	High	Pool	Small	Sensitive to data and parameters
Logistic regression	High	High	Good	Large	Maybe non-convergence

In this paper, we use character-level CNN network to automatically extract features hidden within the URL strings, as deep learning based methods have a strong generalization ability. We will present our approach in the next section.

3   Proposed Approach

In this section, we describe our approach to classify URLs and domain names based on CNN (Convolutional Neural Network). DNS content can be viewed as URL content, so we only describe the approach and implementation to classify URL. However, the proposed system can also be used to classify DNS.

CNN network has been widely used in image recognition [11, 12], perhaps due to its ability to directly perform some convolution operations on the original pixel binary data to find hidden features hidden between pixels. This allows one to extract features automatically without the need for manual extraction.

We posit that CNN can also be used in word sequence feature mining with neural language processing, and in our context, both URL and DNS can be viewed as a word sequence. In other words, malicious URL and DNS detection is similar to sentence classification. However, we cannot directly use deep learning methods to detect malicious URLs or DNS without solving the following limitations:

(1) Training time for deep learning model typically ranges from several hours to several days. Thus, it may not be realistic to constantly update the (deep learning) model.
(2) Construction of URL and DNS are more specific compared to other sentence classification scenes. Therefore, the framework for neural network needs to be specifically designed.

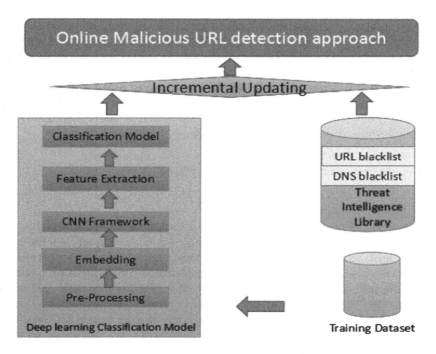

Fig. 1. Proposed online malicious URL detection approach.

In our proposed approach (see Fig. 1) consists of three main components, as follows:

(1) Dataset. The real-world dataset of URLs and DNS can be downloaded (e.g. from collaborating entities, such as APWG) or crawled from some URL or DNS sharing websites – see Sect. 3.1.
(2) Deep learning classification model, which consists of five processes such as pre-processing the input data and training a classification model using deep learning method – see Sect. 3.2.

(3) Incremental update, which allows one to periodically and incrementally update the classification model, based on existing threat intelligence data – see Sect. 3.3.

3.1 Training Dataset

When building the training dataset, we need to define the URL string and its feature, as well as the evaluation method for our approach.

3.1.1 Data Characteristics

The URL string contains three different semantic segments, namely: domain name, directory path and file name. The URL and DNS strings consist of numbers, letters and symbols such as "?", "=", and "&". We define the pattern that could be used to classify the malicious URLs or normal ones as follows:

A URL string is a tuple $p = (h, d, f)$, where h is a URL segment pattern corresponding to the domain name, $d = \{s_1, s_2, \ldots s_n\}$ is a URL sequential patterns corresponding to the directory path, and f is a URL segment pattern represent the file name. For malicious URL strings $p = (h, d, f)$ and normal malicious $p' = (h', d', f')$, if there is a text fragment pattern t' or other patterns t'' such as URL length is covered by p but not covered by p', then we view t' and t'' as features which can be used to classify the URL. We seek to automatically find out these features and use them to build an online detection system.

The following are malicious URL examples:

http://www.aaa.com/1.php?Include=http://www.bbb.com/hehe.php
http://www.sqlinsertion.com/adminlogin.php/**/and/**/1=1.

3.1.2 Model Evaluation

To evaluate the efficiency and accuracy of the detection model, the recalling rate and precision rate are widely used as metrics as they are simple to interpret [10]. We use the number of mislabeled URLs and the precision rate to compare the accuracy between our model and the baseline model. In addition, to evaluate the efficiency of the model, we compare the execution time of one million URLs detection between our model and the baseline model. The indicators we used for model evaluation are defined as follows:

FN (False Negatives) denotes the number of URLs that are normal but classified as malicious, and FP (False Positives) denotes the number of URLs that are malicious but classified as normal. TN (True Negatives) and TP (True Positives) respectively denote the number of URLs which are malicious, normal and are correctly classified.

Mislabeled number: FN + FP
Accuracy rate: TN/FN + TN.

3.2 Character-Level Deep Learning Framework

Using some neural language processing method to map the input URL and DNS string to vector, we design a character-level CNN network to train the classification model (see Fig. 2). The deep learning model is described in Sects. 3.2.1 to 3.2.3.

3.2.1 Pro-processing

Since HTTP and HTTPS protocols are often used, the "http://" and https:// could be safely omitted from the detection. URLs generally consist of numbers, letters and some symbols. In our approach, we filter special symbols such as "_" and "#" which have been deemed to have little effect on the classification results. After pro-processing, the dataset can be more concise to reduce the time and resource requirements in the following steps.

3.2.2 Embedding

We need to map the input sequence URL to vectors as the start of the deep learning framework. We use one-hot which is a famous embedding method in NLP. Our model starts with length L sequence of characters and embeds them into an L * M matrix. Our model views the input URL or DNS string as characters sequence. Then we transform the sequence of characters to a sequence of such m sized vectors with fixed length L. Any character exceeding length L is ignored, and any characters that are not in the alphabet including blank characters are quantized as all-zero vectors.

The alphabet used in all of our models consists of 50 characters, including letters, digits and 14 other special characters. The non-space characters are:

abcdefghijklmnopqrstuvwxyz0123456789
-;!?:@#$^*% = <>

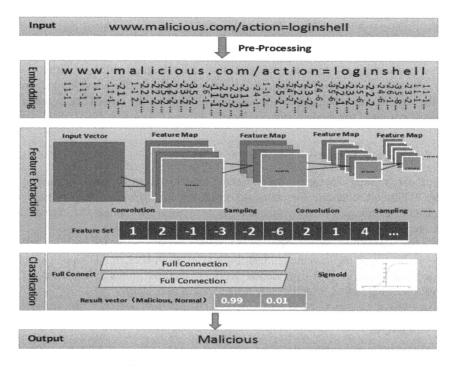

Fig. 2. Deep learning model architecture.

It appears that the value of 256 can capture most of the URL string and considering the balance between accuracy and efficiency of model training, we set the parameter $L = 256$ and $M = 50$ for our experiment described in Sect. 4.

3.2.3   CNN Framework and Classification Model

The system could automated extract features of the lexical features of these URLs using CNN layers after we embed the input strings into 256 * 50 matrix. The CNN framework consists of convolutions layers and pooling layers. The multiple kernel convolutions can learn the local features and the pooling layer such as Sum pooling layer can aggregate the results of the multiple convolutions. We initialize the weights using a Gaussian distribution, and we use layer-wise Batch Norm and Dropout (0.5) between layers to speed up training time and prevent over fitting. Table 2 shows the configurations for convolutions layers and pooling layers. The results are then concatenated together into a 1024 length vector, which represents the feature vector.

Table 2. Convolutional layers used in the experiment.

Layer	Feature map size	Kernel size	Pooling
1	256	5	3
2	256	5	3
3	256	3	N/A
4	256	3	N/A
5	256	3	3

Once we extract the feature vector, we use the full connection layer to classify the URL. We use two full connection layers, followed by the Sigmoid layer with $l = 1024$ units. The full connection layer learns a non-linear kernel given the convolution features, and the sigmoid layer output provides the probability that the input URL is malicious given the output of the final connection layer.

3.3   Incremental Updating

Because the training process for deep learning model is generally time consuming, the model is difficult to update for online detection system. However, to keep pace with advances in techniques used by attackers, it is necessary to update the classification model regularly (similar to patching for software and applications).

We implement the update process using current threat intelligence such as URL and DNS blacklists and the incremental learning model. Both URL and DNS blacklists are updated periodically. The incremental learning method stores information of the previous training model, which can be rolled back if necessary.

3.4   Discussion

We remark that in developing the deep learning model, other options were considered but found to be unsuitable. For example, LSTM has been widely used in text processing and machine translation [13]. However, LSTM requires significantly more time than CNN during the training of the classification model and computing [14]; thus, our choice of CNN.

For the embedding step, we use character-level mapping method instead of word-level mapping method for improved accuracy. Word-level embedding based deep learning model learns the associated features between words. However, in our context, such a model cannot traverse all the words because of the randomly generated URL strings by techniques used by attackers. Generally, the number of different characters in the URL string is less than 300. Thus, character-level feature can cover all the possible features required for effective classification.

4 Evaluations

4.1 Experiment Environment and Baseline

The evaluations were based on the Tensor Flow framework, and the experiment environment and configuration information are as follows.

- Computer Configuration: Ubuntu 16.04, memory 16 GB, CPU i7
- Tensor Flow version: 1.1.0 GPU: GeForce GTX1060, 6 GB Python version: 3.5
- Training Time: 10 h.

We implemented two baseline models. The first baseline model is based on manually extracted features described in [8], which include URL length, number of ".", separators in a URL, and categorical lexical features (e.g. domain name and URL suffix tokens). These features form a very large, but sparse feature vector. To determine the accuracy between character-level embedding based deep learning and word-level embedding based deep learning, we implemented the word-level deep learning framework based on word embedding method.

4.2 Dataset

We built a large URL dataset that consists of more than 7 million URLs. These URLs were obtained from online public datasets or crawled from malicious URL sharing websites. For malicious URLs, we crawled these data from Phish Tank and Virus Total. The normal URLs were mainly downloaded from some public datasets such as Google and DMOZ. The training dataset and the test dataset were randomly assigned according to 9:1; we randomly select ninety percent labeled data for the training dataset, and the other ten percent data as testing dataset. The distribution of the dataset is shown in Table 3.

4.3 Findings

Figure 3 shows the accuracy of the detection models. The x-axis represents three detection models being compared, and the y-axis represents the average number of URLs

Table 3. Distribution of data

URL type	Training dataset (million)	Testing dataset (million)
Malicious URL	0.9	0.1
Normal URL	5.4	0.6
Sum	6.3	0.7

mislabeled for per thousand URLs in the testing dataset. It is clear that our character-level deep learning model outperforms the other baseline approaches. In addition, the deep learning method allows good generalization, which can potentially be used to mitigate techniques used by attackers to avoid detection.

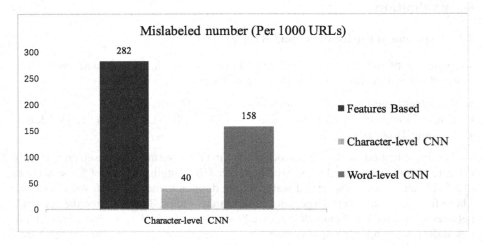

Fig. 3. Accuracy

Figure 4 shows the efficiency of the three detection models being compared. We used two testing datasets which contain 1 thousand URLs and 2 thousand URLs to determine the time required for the classification models. The x-axis represents the detection model with testing dataset, and the y-axis represents the time (in seconds) required for classification. It is clear that our model is as efficient as other baseline models. In addition, our approach allows periodic updates. For example, newly detect malicious URL patterns can be included in the updating model in real-time.

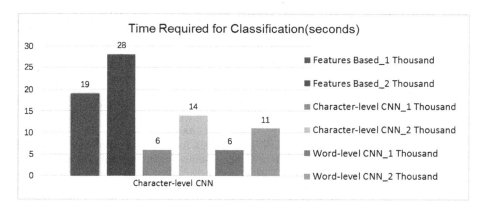

Fig. 4. Efficiency

5   Conclusion

The capability to detect malicious URLs and DNS will be increasingly important in our Internet-connected society, particularly in Internet of Things deployment.

In this paper, we proposed a character-level CNN based malicious URL and DNS detection based on the textual patterns of the URL and DNS. We evaluated our approach using real-world datasets, which demonstrated that our approach is both accurate and efficient. Besides, the scheme proposed is a general detection scheme for short text detection problem and has applications in other contexts.

Future research includes deploying the proposed approach in a real-world environment for further evaluation and fine-tuning, if necessary.

Acknowledgment. This work is supported by National Natural Science Foundation of China (No. 61173008, 61402124), Strategic Pilot Technology Chinese Academy of Sciences (No. XDA06010703) and Key Lab of Information Network Security, Ministry of Public Security (No. C17614).

References

1. Choo, K.-K.R.: A conceptual interdisciplinary plug-and-play cyber security framework. In: Kaur, H., Tao, X. (eds.) ICTs and the Millennium Development Goals, pp. 81–99. Springer, Boston (2014). https://doi.org/10.1007/978-1-4899-7439-6_6
2. Choo, K.-K.R., Grabosky, P.: CyberCrime. In: The Oxford Handbook of Organized Crime. Oxford University Press, Oxford, 24 Oct 2014
3. https://docs.apwg.org/reports/apwg_trends_report_q4_2016.pdf
4. Prokhorenko, V., Choo, K.-K.R., Ashman, H.: Web application protection techniques: a taxonomy. J. Netw. Comput. Appl. **60**, 95–112 (2016)
5. Provos, N., et al.: All your iFRAMEs point to Us. In: Conference on Security Symposium USENIX Association, pp. 1–15 (2008)

6. McGrath, D.K., Gupta, M.: Behind phishing: an examination of phisher modi operandi. In: Usenix Workshop on Large-Scale Exploits and Emergent Threats, 15 April 2008, San Francisco, CA, USA, Proceedings DBLP (2008)
7. Yadav, S., et al.: Detecting algorithmically generated malicious domain names. In: ACM SIGCOMM Conference on Internet Measurement 2010, Melbourne, Australia, November DBLP, pp. 48–61 (2010)
8. Ma, J., et al.: Beyond blacklists: learning to detect malicious web sites from suspicious URLs. In: ACM SIGKDD International Conference on Knowledge Discovery and Data Mining, Paris, France, 28 June – July DBLP, pp. 1245–1254 (2009)
9. Yen, T.F., et al.: Beehive: large-scale log analysis for detecting suspicious activity in enterprise networks. In: Computer Security Applications Conference, pp. 199–208 (2013)
10. Huang, D., Xu, K., Pei, J.: Malicious URL detection by dynamically mining patterns without pre-defined elements. World Wide Web **17**(6), 1375–1394 (2014)
11. Krizhevsky, A., Sutskever, I., Hinton, G.E.: ImageNet classification with deep convolutional neural networks. In: International Conference on Neural Information Processing Systems Curran Associates Inc., pp. 1097–1105 (2012)
12. Ouyang, W., et al.: DeepID-Net: deformable deep convolutional neural networks for object detection. IEEE Trans. Pattern Anal. Mach. Intell. **pp**(99), 1 (2016)
13. Sutskever, I., Vinyals, O., Le, Q.V.: Sequence to sequence learning with neural networks. In: International Conference on Neural Information Processing Systems, pp. 3104–3112. MIT Press (2014)
14. Zhang, X., Zhao, J., Lecun, Y.: Character-level convolutional networks for text classification. In: International Conference on Neural Information Processing Systems, pp. 649–657. MIT Press (2015)

Visual Analysis of Android Malware Behavior Profile Based on $PMCG_{droid}$: A Pruned Lightweight APP Call Graph

Yan Zhang[1,2,3], Gui Peng[1,2,3(✉)], Lu Yang[2,4], Yazhe Wang[1,2],
Minghui Tian[2,4], Jianxing Hu[1,2,3], Liming Wang[2], and Chen Song[2]

[1] State Key Laboratory of Information Security, Beijing, China
[2] Institute of Information Engineering, Chinese Academy of Sciences, Beijing, China
{zhangyan,penggui,wangyazhe,hujianxing,wangliming,songchen}@iie.ac.cn
[3] School of Cyber Security, University of Chinese Academy of Sciences,
Beijing, China
[4] Beijing JiaoTong University, Beijing, China
{13283023,15125043}@bjtu.edu.cn

Abstract. In recent years, there is a sharp increasing in the number of malicious APPs on the Android platform, so how to identify new type of Android malware and its malicious behaviors has been a hot research topic in the security community. This paper presents a visualization framework to help security analysts precisely distinguish malicious profiles of APPs. By labeling target nodes, adding implicit call edges, pruning harmless branches, and a few other operations, we generate a new kind of call graph: $PMCG_{droid}$. This graph not only has a sharp decrease in size comparing to the original APP call graph but also preserves the malicious core of malware well. Based on $PMCG_{droid}$, visual interfaces are designed to assist users in checking the malicious behavior profile of samples with rich user interactive operations. We study real world samples to prove the usability and efficiency of our approach.

Keywords: Android malware analysis · Malware visualization
Machine learning · Assisted manual analysis

1 Introduction

Currently Android malwares are widespread and uncurbed. G DATA security experts have discovered 9 million Android malware samples from 2012 to the first quarter of 2017 [34]. Meanwhile, new instances are gathered daily, and variants of existing families appear quickly too. Although researchers have applied multifarious automatic Android malware analysis techniques [8–13,18] to confront this serious security challenge, manual detection methods are still widely needed, for example, to identify, correct, and disambiguate intermediate results of automatic analysis tools [24], or to understand the malwares and their nature [21].

© ICST Institute for Computer Sciences, Social Informatics and Telecommunications Engineering 2018
X. Lin et al. (Eds.): SecureComm 2017, LNICST 238, pp. 449–468, 2018.
https://doi.org/10.1007/978-3-319-78813-5_23

In consideration of the complexity of Android APP, experts bear a huge burden of work if only manual work used to analyze the samples. Therefore, it is urgent to explore semi-automated visualization analysis approaches to help analysts in reducing heavy workload. Visualization analysis tools take mass of basic trivial analysis works for human and show the machine analytic results in a visual way. Then the security staff can quickly grasp key information under the help of the visual displayed graphs or figures and some interactions, use professional knowledge to deal with something that machine cannot handle, and make precise judgement efficiently.

Since, there are many essential differences between Android applications and traditional personal computer applications. A mass of existing PC application visualization tools [25–31] cannot be directly applied to Android applications [7,33] and the exploitation of visualization for Android application has just started, practical tools are scarce [19,22]. Meanwhile, the existing individual malware visualization analysis methods for PC or for Android platforms rarely concern the visualization of the malicious code logic structure. However, code logic structure usually implies the whole picture of the malicious behaviors. It is worth to be processed and provided to the experts for analysis assistance.

The objective of this paper is providing a malicious code structure and malicious behavior profile visualization analysis method of Android malware. By labeling and appending nodes, adding implicit call edges, pruning harmless branches, and some other operations, we generate a new kind of Android APP call graph: $PMCG_{droid}$. $PMCG_{droid}$ aims to show the targeted risky code distribution and correlations inside an Android APP, helps users to figure out the malicious behaviors set.

We made the following contributions to the visual detection of Android malware in this paper:

(1) Advance a brand new graph $PMCG_{droid}$ which is a pruned lightweight Android APP call graph. Compared to the traditional call graph, $PMCG_{droid}$ not only narrows down the manually inspection scope of a sample but also reserves the core malicious profile effectively.
(2) Design visualization interfaces to display the $PMCG_{droid}$ graph of samples. In the interfaces, not only risky code can be figured out from the graph, but also the complete triggering chain and code logical combinations of such risky points can be revealed visually. Hence the whole malicious behavior profile and structure is clear to the users.
(3) Provide automated methods and user interactivity (implicit edges appending, convergence point analysis and subgraph generations etc.) to help the analysts quickly focus on most suspicious behaviors and explore code details to make accurate judgements.

We use a case study to illustrate the effectiveness and feasibility of our work. Through the analysis of a large number of malicious samples from the real world by using our method, we have a lot of interesting findings, which will be shown in this paper too.

2 $PMCG_{droid}$ Generation

2.1 Target Node Labeling

Our visualization analysis framework focuses on how to visually check the key parts and malicious behavior structure inside the APP's method call graph. Given a call graph of a sample APP, the most important inspection target nodes of it are method nodes that contain risky API calls.

Table 1. Risky APIS and their types

API	Occurrence frequency	Type
java.net.URL.openConnection	25856	Sink
android.telephony.TelephonyManager.getDeviceId	10478	Source
dalvik.system.DexClassLoader	2957	Suspicious
android.telephony.TelephonyManager.getLine1Number	4279	Source
android.telephony.SmsManager.sendTextMessage	4087	Sink
android.location.LocationManager.getLastKnownLocation	3955	Source

The risky APIs we concerned about are from the following 3 sets: (1) The key APIs which are restricted by the Android permission mechanism. (2) The sensitive APIs used by Arp et al. [8] in their machine learning features. (3) A set of malicious behavior most relevant risky APIs identified by us, based on the manual analysis of 300 popular malicious samples.

The number of target APIs directly affects the accuracy and complexity of the experimental results. The more APIs are detected, the more comprehensive the $PMCG_{droid}$ is generated, then the result will be more accurate. However, the cost is to increase the scale and complexity of $PMCG_{droid}$. In order to achieve a balance between the accuracy and complexity, we do a statistics over the public Drebin Android Malware database [39] to study these APIs' occurrence frequency in malware samples. Based on the frequency we identified 130 APIs as the target set finally, to achieve maximum accuracy while reducing the complexity of manual analysis.

Furthermore, according to the threat nature of these dangerous APIs, they are divided into three types: Source, Sink, and Suspicious. "Source" refers to those APIs that can access sensitive information in Android devices, for example, the APIs to read SMS, contact information, GPS Location etc. The APIs that may output sensitive information are "Sink", for example, the APIs to send out information by email, SMS, Bluetooth, network, or write information via SQL database, SharedPreference, file etc. The rest of the APIs are also dangerous and can be classified as "Suspicious". For example, DexClassLoader APIs may be used to execute code which is not installed as part of the application. The Table 1 lists six sample risky APIs and the category to which they belong.

Correspondingly, we label the nodes that contain the source, sink, or suspicious type APIs in their code as API-Source, API-Sink, and API-Suspicious node. Some nodes may contain multiple labels at the same time, because they call different types of APIs in their method code.

Except risky API tagged node, there is another kind of nodes which are worth being concerned about. They are "third-party library" nodes that represent methods from some popular third party libraries imported by APP in programming phase, such as from AdMob [44], umeng [42], google map [43], and so on. The idea behind is to ascertain where the APP's risky behaviors inside come from, the APP itself or some third-party libraries. Currently, the third-party libraries detected by us are mainly advertising libraries. We use the following methods to identify third-party library code nodes. We collect the Software Development Kits of popular third-party libraries, record the key package names, class names, and method names in these libraries. Then the package name, class name and method name of every method node of APPs will be compared with the information recorded above to determine whether the node belongs to some third-party library or not.

2.2   Implicit Edge Generation

Generating an accurate call graph is crucial for static analysis. Special mechanisms for Android programs, such as Inter-Component Communication (ICC), component lifecycle, multithreading, etc., can cause discontinuities in the application method call flow. The existing Android or Java call graph generation tools cannot fill these vacancies. Thus, on the basis of the traditional call graph, we further add the missing method call flow and build a more complete call chain to show the whole picture of malicious behaviors. We call the supplementary edges as implicit edges. There are four kinds of implicit edges considered in $PMCG_{droid}$:

A. ICC Type: Android applications are composed of components. The communication between components utilizes explicit or implicit Intent to perform. Explicit Intent specifies the component to start by name (fully qualified class name), hence it connects the caller to the receiver component directly according to the specified component name; the implicit Intent passes the information of the caller component to those components whose Intent Filter declarations match the implicit Intent's Action, Category, and Data attribute content.

In order to fill the function call edge missing from ICC, we collect information about all the components in APP and their Intent Filter contents, Intent delivery methods and parameters by utilizing the IC3 [2] tool. Then, based on the metadata obtained, we simulated the Android system to match the Intents, both implicit and explicit, discover the call edges between components.

In particular, for the difference of *StartActivityForresult* [13], we add the call edge from the *setResult* of the callee component to the *onActivityResult* of the caller component.

B. Lifecycle Callback Type: Implicit call edges associated with the Activity/Service component lifecycle. Each Activity/Service component in Android has a full lifecycle, which contains different lifecycle callback methods such as *onStart, onResume* etc [45, 46]. The Android framework implicitly calls these methods to convert the component's lifecycle state, such as calling *onStart* to start the component and call *onPause* to pause the component. These lifecycle callback methods are not directly connected in the code, and their calling processes are completely dependent on the Android framework, so the call chains associated with these lifecycle method calls are also missing.

We check the lifecycle transition process of Activity and Service, consider each state transition process as an implicit call edge, add to our $PMCG_{droid}$ graph, so that the code executed in the whole component lifecycle can maintain coherence in our graphs.

In the life cycle of the activity, we currently ignored three kinds of state transition, *onPause*→ *onResume*, *onStop* →*onRestart*, and *onStop* →*onCreate*. In another words, we won't add implicit edges for these three state transitions. Although this ignorance will cause a small part of continuity lose, it helps us reduce many loops.

C. Thread Type: Usually an Android system service creates an auxiliary thread by two ways: Runnable and Handler [38]. In these two mechanisms there also exists the control chain missing phenomenon. For example the *start* method in the Runnable mechanism is used to start a thread, but the thread does not run immediately until the *run* method of the new thread is executed when system recourses are distributed to it. As for Handler mechanism, *sendmessage* method is used to send a message to *handlemessage* for processing, but the call chain from *sendmessage* to *handlemessage* does not exist naturally because the message passed through the framework.

D. Logic Connection Type: This type of implicit call side is primarily related to intent delivery. We find that the intention of the transfer exists in some method pairs, such as broadcast receivers and their registration methods. Broadcast receiver is actually triggered by the broadcast sender via Intent, this relationship is included in ICC Type already. However, broadcast receiver is under the control of broadcast register. The Register decides which broadcast the broadcast receiver should be registered to. There is an intension transmission. In order to complete the malicious behavior call chain, we add the call edge for the method of passing this intention.

2.3   Branch Pruning

The graphical scale of call graph of an Android APP is usually too huge to artificial analysis. We decompile 1000 APP's package files (APK files) whose size distribution range from 27 kilobytes to 32 megabytes, and calculated their method numbers one by one. Our statistics shows every 5 megabytes APK file contains 3702 functions in average. Hence, visually checking the original call graph is a heavy workload. It is necessary to narrow down the node inspection scope and reduce unnecessary detections for security analysts.

As we already discussed in Sect. 2.1, nodes containing risky APIs are considered most relevant to the malicious behaviors, hence we only need to focus on the nodes and edges related to target nodes. Our proposal is to trim all nodes which have no directed path leading to any target risky API nodes. To make this description more precise, we define a Boolean function Dpath to indicate whether there is a directed path existing from one node to another node.

Definition 1. *For any directed graph (N,E), N is the node set while E is edge set, Dpath is a function defined over N, Dpath : $N \times N \rightarrow \{1,0\}$, for $\forall\, n_1, n_2 \in N$:*

$$Dpath(n_1, n_2) = \begin{cases} 1, if\ n_1 = n_2\ or\ \exists\ \{e_1, e_2, \ldots, e_n\} \subset E\ s.t. \\ \quad source(e_1) = n_1,\ target(e_n) = n_2, \\ \quad source(e_{j+1}) = target(e_j)\ for\ j \geq 1; \\ 0, otherwise \end{cases}$$

Here source (e) is the start point of the directed edge e, while target (e) means the targeted node.

We define all the nodes to be removed from as set TN, while all the edges to be cut as set TE:

Definition 2. *Given a directed call graph: $CG = (N_m, E_m)$, TN is the greatest subset of N_m, s.t. for $\forall n_i \in TN$, for $\forall n_j \in N_m$ where $label(n_j) \in \{API - Source, API - Sink, API - Suspicious\}$, $Dpath(n_i, n_j) = 0$.*

Definition 3. *Given a directed call graph: $CG = (N_m, E_m)$ and TN, TE is the greatest subset of E_m, s.t. for $\forall e_j \in TE, \exists n_i \in TN\ s.t.\ target(e_j) = n_i | source(e_j) = n_i$.*

2.4 Convergence Point Discovery

We detect three kinds of Convergence Point (CPoint) to help analysis potential information leak in an APP automatically.

Independent CPoint: such CPoint node directly or indirectly calls an API-source node and an API-sink node concurrently. More strictly speaking, it should be the nearest CPoint for at least one pair of (API-Source, API-Sink). The CPoint may call API-Source to get sensitive info and send out by API-Sink node.

API-Sink Node as CPoint: if one node containing data sending code directly or indirectly calls a API-Source node, it may get the sensitive data first from the API-Source node, then send out by itself.

API-Source Node as CPoint: if one node containing data getting code directly or indirectly calls a API-Sink node, it may send out the sensitive data collected by the get information API of itself.

2.5 Splitting Shadow Node

It is a common phenomenon that nodes may be tagged with a variety of labels. Actually we want to set every kind of node an independent color to assist users' analysis in our visualization tool. So in the last step of generating $PMCG_{droid}$, we introduce the concept of shadow nodes to ensure that each node has only one label. If a node contains N labels, the node is divided into N nodes, by keeping one main node in the original call chains of the method and adding $N - 1$ shadow nodes which have and only have bi-directional edges with the main node. That means, the main node maintains the call relationships with the other nodes in the original call chains, while shadow nodes just represent $N - 1$ labels of the main node.

2.6 $PMCG_{droid}$ Definition

By labeling and appending nodes, adding implicit call edges, pruning harmless branches and shadow node splitting, we generate a new kind of Android APP call graph: $PMCG_{droid}$. The $PMCG_{droid}$ graph is defined by a quintuples = $(N_p, E_p, Label, f_l, f_c)$, where N_p is the set of nodes in the graph and $E_p = \{(n_i, n_j)\}$ is the set of edges/connections between nodes. The adjacency matrix _ij indicates that an explicit or implicit call exists from n_i to n_j (_ij = 1) or that the call is absent (_ij = 0).

In our default $PMCG_{droid}$ version, $Label$ is a string set with five values which is "API-Sink", "API-Source", "API-Suspicious", "third-party library", and "normal", because in the $PMCG_{droid}$, there are five types of nodes, API-Sink, API-Source, API-Suspicious, third-party library, and normal (any nodes that are not tagged to the first four types are normal nodes). $Label$ is used to label the nodes with function f_l. That is to say, f_l maps elements in the set N_p to a value in set $Label$. f_c is a Boolean function defined over Set N_p, it maps every node to Boolean value 0 or 1. It indicates whether a node is a convergence point or not.

3   Visualization

For helping manual analysis, a set of interfaces are built to present the $PMCG_{droid}$.

3.1   Visualization Encode

In order to show the relationship between these nodes in $PMCG_{droid}$, we distinguish the nodes in various colors and sizes, while arrows in different colors and types representing different types of calling. As we can see in Fig. 1(b), we use green circles to represent the third-party libraries and gray circles to represent the normal nodes. Besides, we mark the API-sink and API-source nodes with red and brownish red colors respectively. We use yellow circles to represent API-Suspicious nodes. Black one-way arrows and red one-way arrows stand for explicit call edges and implicit call edges individually, and blue bidirectional arrows represent shadow link nodes. For further pushing convergence points forward, we set them two times the sizes of the normal ones.

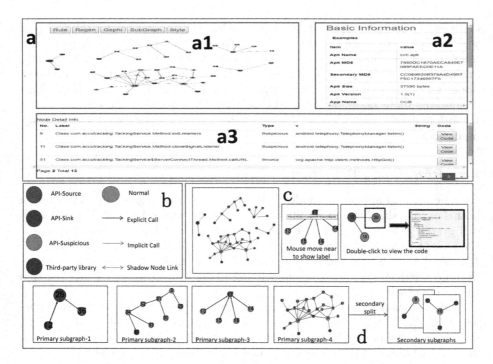

Fig. 1. System interface (a, c and d) and visualization encode (b). Main workspace view (a), including $PMCG_{droid}$ panorama with default force-directed layout (a1), APP basic information (a2) and node detail information overview (a3). The interaction methods of a1 (c) including mouse move, single, and double click. Primary and secondary subgraph view (d).

3.2   Integrated Visualization Interfaces

Based on $PMCG_{droid}$, we develop integrated visualization web interfaces (as Fig. 1 shown) to help users to inspect malicious behaviors from Android APPs.

Users can upload their own APP to check the APP's $PMCG_{droid}$ graph in the interface. The result is presented in the workspace area of the interface as shown in Fig. 1(a1). Figure 1(a3) shows the details of nodes including method name, class name and tag information. Inside the workspace area of Fig. 1(a1), tag details of every node will be shown when the mouse is moved near to it. When double clicking on the node, there would be a message popping up and showing the source code of the node.

In order to help visualization analysis, it is necessary to annotate the key information for each node, so we have defined four kinds of tag information: the first one is correlated to implicit call edge. If the node is a caller correlated to an implicit call edge, the tag of the node shows the method name the node call and corresponding parameters. If the node is a callee correlated to an implicit call edge, the tag shows its own method name and class name. Specially, if the callee is triggered by implicit Intent, its tag also shows the value of the Intent Filter.

The second kind of tag information shows the third-party libraries the node belongs to if it is a third-party library node. Third, for API-Sink, API-Source, and API-Suspicious nodes, their tags show the sink APIs, source APIs and suspicious APIs they call respectively. Finally, for all kinds of nodes, some other information they contains could be risky, such as URL and telephone number, so the last type of tag shows constant string like this.

3.3   Subgraph

Although the scale of $PMCG_{droid}$ has been decreased greatly, when a malware contains numerous risky behaviors, the graph is still too complicated to analysis. Therefore, we further propose a risky behavior slice function to separate the $PMCG_{droid}$ graph into several subgraphs (Fig. 1(d)) for analysts to view.

There are two kinds of subgraphs as Fig. 1(d) shown. The first four graphs are the primary subgraphs of $PMCG_{droid}$. They are independent of each other and there are no edges between them. Analyst can only focus on a single primary subgraph rather than the entire $PMCG_{droid}$.

The graphs on the right side are the secondary subgraphs which only shows the risky paths around one single convergent point. The second subgraph is generated from each CPoint. For each CPoint, find all the API-Sink and API-Source nodes it can reach in the directed graph. The nodes and edges on the path from the CPoint to its reachable API-Sink or API-Source nodes make up a secondary subgraph relevant to this CPoint.

4   Case Study

In this section, we demonstrate the effectiveness and feasibility of our interfaces with a case study. The case study discusses how to reveal the malicious behavior profile of a special malware sample in a public family. Then, we present some other findings based on our large scale analysis.

4.1   Reveal Malware's Malicious Behaviors

We randomly choose a sample from a popular malware family named Fakeinst. Then we found the description about Fakeinst malware family in f-secure website [40]. It says: "Fakeinst malware appear to be installers for other applications; when executed however, the malware send SMS messages to premium-rate numbers or services."

However, we still do not know exactly what malicious behaviors will be triggered by the APP and how. Now we open our visualization interface to see what its real behaviors are. By using our tool to generate the $PMCG_{droid}$, the $PMCG_{droid}$ and nodes' label information are shown in Fig. 2. The $PMCG_{droid}$ is much smaller than the traditional call graph in the lower left corner in size, decreasing by 96.1%. To simplify the introduction, we removed a few nodes which are irrelevant to the malicious behaviors. Based on the Fig. 2, we start the research work.

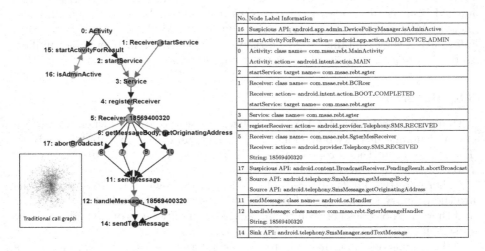

No.	Node Label Information
16	Suspicious API: android.app.admin.DevicePolicyManager.isAdminActive
15	startActivityForResult: action= android.app.action.ADD_DEVICE_ADMIN
0	Activity: class name= com.msae.rebt.MainActivity
	Activity: action= android.intent.action.MAIN
2	startService: target name= com.msae.rebt.sgter
1	Receiver: class name= com.msae.rebt.BCRcer
	Receiver: action= android.intent.action.BOOT_COMPLETED
	startService: target name= com.msae.rebt.sgter
3	Service: class name= com.msae.rebt.sgter
4	registerReceiver: action= android.provider.Telephony.SMS_RECEIVED
5	Receiver: class name= com.msae.rebt.SgterMesReceiver
	Receiver: action= android.provider.Telephony.SMS_RECEIVED
	String: 18569400320
17	Suspicious API: android.content.BroadcastReceiver.PendingResult.abortBroadcast
6	Source API: android.telephony.SmsMessage.getMessageBody
	Source API: android.telephony.SmsMessage.getOriginatingAddress
11	sendMessage: class name= android.os.Handler
12	handleMessage: class name= com.msae.rebt.SgterMessageHandler
	String: 18569400320
14	Sink API: android.telephony.SmsManager.sendTextMessage

Fig. 2. Case 1 (package name: com.message.send, MD5: 4E850BF087512F14A7A EA84909982569)

We start from node 0 which is the entry node of the program. At first, we come to inspect the short call chain $0 \rightarrow 15 \rightarrow 16$. Node 16 calls *android.app.admin. DevicePolicyManager.isAdminActive*. It determines whether the given administration component is currently active in the system. Node 15 calls *startActivity* with the Intent action value *android.app.action.ADD_DEVICE_ADMIN* to register the device manager. By checking the code we confirm that the APP will be registered as a device manager when it starts, which makes it difficult to uninstall the APP.

Next, we investigate the call chains: $0 \rightarrow 2 \rightarrow 3 \rightarrow 4 \rightarrow 5 \rightarrow 10(7/8/9) \rightarrow 11 \rightarrow 12 \rightarrow 14$ and $5 \leftrightarrow 6$, $5 \leftrightarrow 17$. These call chains can be further divided into four stages: stage A: $0 \rightarrow 2$, stage B: $3 \rightarrow 4$, stage C: $5 \rightarrow 10 \rightarrow 11$, $5 \leftrightarrow 6$ and $5 \leftrightarrow 17$, and stage D: $12 \rightarrow 14$. Every two adjacent stages are connected by an implicit call edge.

Stage A starts the service (node 3) in stage B by calling function *start-Service* with an explicit Intent. Stage B registers a broadcast receiver (node 5 in stage C) which monitors *android.provider.Telephony.SMS_RECEIVED*. This allows the APP to directly receive incoming SMS messages. Node 6, 17 are shadow nodes split from node 5. Based on the information of the nodes 6, 17 in the table on the right side of the Fig. 2, it can be seen that on the one hand, it gets the contents of the SMS message and the sender's mobile phone number; on the other hand, the node 5 aborts the current broadcast to prevent any other APPs from receiving the SMS message. Then, the stage C sends the sensitive data to the stage D through the Handler mechanism. Finally, stage D sends the data to the telephone number "18569400320" via function *android.telephony.SmsManager.sendTextMessage*.

Furthermore, by checking the node 5 and 17's code, we find the node 5 also checks whether the received message is from a specific attacker. If the answer is positive, it will call 17 to block this message and do things according to the attacker's indication. This action is remotely controlled by the attacker.

Last but not least, in the upper right corner, node 1 is a broadcast receiver which monitors the phone's boot broadcast *intent.action.BOOT_COMPLETED*. According to the call chain $1 \rightarrow 3$, node 1 also starts the service node 3. So the APP will start the malicious service when phone boots up automatically.

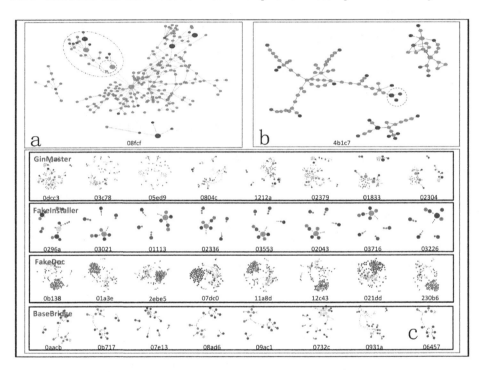

Fig. 3. Other interesting findings. (a) Weak connection structures imply repackage possibilities. (b) It is easy to distinguish which risk is induced by third-party libraries. (c) $PMCG_{droid}$ graphs resemble each other in same family, and differ between different families.

4.2 Other Findings

Besides the abilities above, we analyze a large number of samples in the virus database by using our method, we also find out some interesting phenomenon that could be considered as visual signal tips to help the experts with their analysis.

The first tip is when the connection between two complicated areas is weak and only built by few of nodes and edges, there is a possibility of repackaging. For example, Fig. 3(a) shows the $PMCG_{droid}$ of a confirmed repackaged APP. The malicious methods which are inserted into the original APP mainly concentrate in the red circle. This malicious part connects to the original code only through two nodes. This kind of connection is apparently a "weak" connection. The second one is when a API-Suspicious node and a third-party library node appear in pair, it means that the risk is introduced by third-party library (as Fig. 3(b) shown). And the most interesting one is this: for parts of malware families in Drebin [39] and Malgenome database [37], we found their $PMCG_{droid}$ graphs resemble each other in same family and differ with other families quite a lot. This implies that users may visually compare newly emerged malicious samples with existing samples to simply identify and classify them for these families. For example, in Fig. 3(c), we list four of such kind of families from Drebin database: GinMaster, FakeInstaller, FakeDoc, and BaseBridge. The finding makes us believe that we can further our work to use $PMCG_{droid}$ as an effective visual feature for malware family identification.

5   Evaluation of the Tailored Malicious Profile

In this section, we evaluate the performance of $PMCG_{droid}$ as a malicious profile tailored from the original APK. We conducted two experiments to check its following capabilities comparing to the original call graph: size sharply decreased and malicious core reserved.

Our data set consists of 4910 malware (M-set) and 4979 benign software (N-set). Among them, the M-Set comes from the previously mentioned Drebin Android malware set, while the benign APPs in N-set are collected from Google Play. All applications in N-set were submitted and detected by VirusTotal [41] before April 1, 2017, and no virus was reported by any Antivirus engine in VirusTotal. Based on this dataset, we conduct the following experiments.

5.1   Scale Reduction Experiments

In order to prove that the $PMCG_{droid}$ graph can effectively reduce the size of APP's call graph, we use 173 malware families in M-set, and pick 100 benign APPs from N-set as a benign family. Then we generate call graphs and $PMCG_{droid}$ graphs for all APPs in these families. After that, we do a statistics over the scale of them, calculate the average node and edge difference in number between the two kinds of graphs of each family.

From the Table 2, we can see that for malware, the number of nodes in $PMCG_{droid}$ is reduced by 94.4% from the number of nodes in the traditional call graph on average, and the number of edges decreases by 96.3%. That is to say, the $PMCG_{droid}$ graphs are not bigger than 5.6% of the original call graphs usually. The number of nodes in benign family is down by 92.0% and edges are down by 94% in average. We also show the top 3 and last 3 node and edge number difference of malware families in the Table 2. For example, the family Gasms's difference is (97.0%, 97.9%), while the former number stand for node difference and the later one stand for edge difference.

Among them, the family Gasms achieves the highest node average reduce proportion of 97.0%, while the lowest family CellShark also reached 69.0%. For edges, the highest decreasing proportion reaches 98.0%, the lowest is 75.7%. Hence, $PMCG_{droid}$ graph can greatly reduce the scale of call graph.

5.2   Malicious Core Reservation Experiments

In order to verify that the $PMCG_{droid}$ still retains the core of malicious behavior in the software, we conducted a machine learning experiment. In this experiment, we extract features from $PMCG_{droid}$ graphs to see if they can be used to automatically distinguish between malware and benign applications. The Table 3 shows all the feature sets we extracted, where F1 and F2 represent the total number of nodes and edges in the $PMCG_{droid}$ respectively. F3 represents the diameter of the $PMCG_{droid}$ graph G, that is, the length of the longest call chain.

F4 is a set of features that represent the number of nodes per kind of *Label*. F5 represents the average of the degrees of each label type of node. The degree of the node is defined as the number of other nodes connected to the node. In the directed graph, the degree of the node is divided into indegree and outdegree. Outdegree refers to the number of edges pointing from the node to other nodes, and indegree refers to the number of edges pointing from the other nodes to the node. Correspondingly, F6 and F7 represent the average of outdegree and indegree of each type of node, respectively.

F8 represents the average reversal ripple degree of all nodes. In the directed unweighted graph, the number of all nodes that can be reached in the reverse direction from the node V is called the reversal ripple degree of the node V.

The F9 feature set represents the number of occurrences of the 130 risky APIs we selected in the nodes of the $PMCG_{droid}$ graph. Considering that most of the risky APIs need to apply for specific permissions can we use, we will apply the permissions as a feature set F10.

Table 2. The top/last 3, benign and average difference

	1	2	3		1	2	3	Average
Node top 3	Gasams (97.0%, 97.9%)	Fakeview (96.8%, 97.8%)	Generic (96.6%, 97.7%)	Node last 3	Mobilespy (71.2%, 81.3%)	Flexispy (70.0%, 81.9%)	CellShark (69.0%, 77.5%)	Benign (92.0%, 94%)
Edge top 3	Jifake (95.3%, 98.0%)	Gasms (97.0%, 97.9%)	GlodEagl (95.3%, 97.9%)	Edge last 3	CgFinder (76.4%, 78.8%)	CellShark (69.0%, 77.4%)	FakePlayer (76.2%, 75.7%)	Malware (94.4%, 96.3%)

Based on the feature set of F1-F10, We selected the random forest classification algorithm to classify. In the classification process, we use ten-fold cross-validation to obtain more accurate results. The result of this experiment is shown

Table 3. $PMCG_{droid}$ features and classification results

Features of $PMCG_{droid}$: G = (N_p, E_p, label, f_l, f_c)		
F1: $\lvert N_p \rvert$	F2: $\lvert E_p \rvert$	F3: Diameter(G)
F4: {$\lvert Node_{label} \rvert$}	F5: {AvgDegree($Node_{label}$)}	F6: {AvgOutdegree($Node_{label}$)}
F7: {AvgIndegree($Node_{label}$)}	F8: AvgRRDegree(G)	F9: {OccurenceNum(riskyAPI)}
F10: {AppliedPermission}		
Classification results		
Method (data set)	TPR	FPR
$PMCG_{droid}$ ($PMCG_{droid}$ data)	96.2%	1.1%
Drebin ($PMCG_{droid}$ data)	98.2%	2.6%
Drebin (Drebin data)	94%	1%

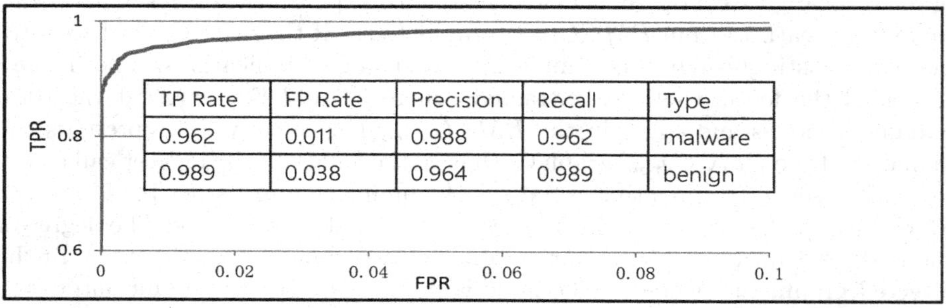

TP Rate	FP Rate	Precision	Recall	Type
0.962	0.011	0.988	0.962	malware
0.989	0.038	0.964	0.989	benign

Fig. 4. ROC curve of $PMCG_{droid}$

in Fig. 4 as ROC curve. It detects 96.2% of the malware samples at a false-positive rate of 1.1%.

We compare the performance of the $PMCG_{droid}$ machine learning approach with related machine learning approaches for Android malware. So far, we know the best way to classify the results is Drebin, which in its own data set achieves TPR 94%, FPR 1% results, significantly outperforms the other approaches. Before it, approaches such as kirin [4], Peng et al. [17] provide a detection rate between 10%–50% at such false-positive rate. Since Drebin did not publish the benign application set it used, we used Drebin's feature extraction method and classification algorithm to classify our data set to compare our results. The experimental results are shown in Table 3. Drebin in our data set, still performed well, achieves TPR 98.2%, FPR 2.6%.

Hence, our classification results are very close to Drebin. Considering that our feature set dimension is only 1571, which is much lower than Drebin, we have reason to believe that though pruned large scale of nodes and edges, $PMCG_{droid}$ still gains a good performance in the automatic distinction between malicious and benign applications. This result confirms its retention of malicious core parts of malware.

6   Related Work

6.1   Android Malware Automatic Analysis

A large body of research has studied methods for analyzing and detecting Android malware. These methods can be roughly categorized into static analysis, dynamic analysis, and machine learning.

Static and dynamic methods intend to identify anomaly behaviors of suspicious samples by checking package code or runtime feature patterns. For example, Zhou et al. [3] extract permissions from APP packages, and then propose a permission-based behavioral footprint scheme to detect new samples of known Android malware families. SCanDroid [11] uses the data flow analysis method for static analysis and detects whether the data flow is consistent with the permissions automatically. AndroidLeaks [12] creates a call graph of an application's code and then perform a reachability analysis to determine if sensitive information may be sent over the network. Droidchecker [36] uses control flow search and stain analysis to automatically analyze possible sensitive data leaks from high permission store to low permission store. They and other static analysis approaches such as [2,23,38] all cannot tell what the whole malicious behavior picture is when they detected an abnormal signal.

Dynamic analysis approaches [5,18,33] monitor the behavior of applications at run-time. They usually suffer from a significant overhead. Among them, only DroidScope [33] is focused on revealing APP's malicious intent and inner workings by collecting detailed native and Dalvik instruction traces, profile API-level activity, and tracking information leakage. However, these data are too fragmental. Users need to use their own imagination to mosaic them into a full picture as shown in their case study.

As for recognizing malware automatically using learning methods, lots of methods have been proposed. Peng et al. [17] apply probabilistic learning methods to the permissions of applications for detecting malware. Puma [6] extracts static features based on permissions' usage, and evaluates the effectiveness of different classifiers, including random trees, random forests, naive Bayesian, and Bayesian networks. Similarly, the methods Crowdroid [16], Droid-Mat [15], MAST [14], Drebin [8], and AMDHunter [50] use features statically extracted from Android applications as there feature vectors. Although the classification effect is getting better and better, most of them cannot help explaining what makes a malware. Only Drebin can infer the risky combination of static properties. But that is still not very clear how the malicious behavior happens for every APP.

Among the existing automated analysis methods, some of the static analysis methods focus on the implicit call study such as [9–11,49,51]. Arzt et al. [9] provide a precise model of Android's lifecycle allows the analysis to properly handle callbacks invoked by the Android framework. Cao et al. [51] have done further research on detecting implicit control flow transitions through the Android framework. Reina et al. [10] dynamically observe interactions between the Android components and the underlying Linux system to reconstruct higher-level behavior. Zhang et al. [49] also contributed to broken links connection when generating call graphs. The detail of these approaches provides lots of references and tools for us in matching the implicit edges. Fuchs et al. [11] provide another tool for reasoning about data flows in Android applications. It focuses on not only the-component but also the inter-APP data flow. We think it is possible for us to try connecting $PMCG_{droid}$ graphs of two APPs together for conspiracy analysis in the future.

Besides, large body of Android data leak research work [12,13,18] help us consider the sources (API-Source type) and sinks (API-Sink type) more comprehensively. For example Enck [18], Beresford et al. [1] only take network sinks of data into considerations. Droidtrack [22] focuses on the message outlet. In SCandal [48], API calls that can transfer data to the network, file or SMS are considered as sinks. Then in our design, we take all the above sinks into considerations and add Bluetooth, email, and multimedia message outlet to make our detections more complete.

6.2   Malware Visualization Work

In 2015, Wagner et al. [24] provide a systematic overview and categorization of malware visualization systems from the perspective of visual analytics. Current individual malware analysis visualizations referred in this paper [25–32,47] are all personal computer platform malware checking methodologies.

What's more, most of the sample features considered in these approaches for building visualization systems, such as the network activity of a malware sample [31], system calls issued over time [27], reversed bytes/byte segments/the repeated bytes sequences of the sample file [25,32], dynamically captured system activities [47], are not logical structure features embedded in the source or decompiled code. Only approaches of Quist, Chan et al. [26,29,30] are a little similar to our approach in constructing structural code profiles. Quist et al. [26,29] monitor and track program execution to construct a directed graph of all the basic blocks of an executable. Chan et al. [30] construct sample minigraph, which is a static control flow graph, to help monitoring and visualizing the dynamic executive path of binary creature. They use their graphs in the reverse engineering process to aid the Run-time debugging of malware, instead of directly helping understanding the malware behaviors.

As for visualizations aiming at supporting the Android malware analysis, the research has just started. Park et al. [20] focused on the checking visual similarity among Android malwares and deciding the degree of similarity. González et al. [21] apply neural projection architectures to analyze malware APPs data and characterize malware families. Both of them aim at analyzing the Android malware family similarity rather than individual malware checking. Androgurad [35] provides a basic generation and view function for Android call graph and control flow graph. However, it does not provide further capability of malware profile detection. Thus, it is more like a data provider rather than a visualization tool. Oscar else [19] proposed a tool to view a list of restricted API functions used at runtime of the application, but they cannot show the full calling chain for that API and the correlation. Base data of [19, 22] is dynamic monitored, which is not as comprehensive and informative as static code since dynamic executions cannot cover all the code paths.

7   Conclusion and Future Work

In this paper, we present a visualization analysis method to help Android security experts to study the structural malicious profiles of APPs. Our method is mainly based on a brand new kind of lightweight APP call graph $PMCG_{droid}$. This graph not only restores the malicious core of malwares for visually checking, but also behaves well in machine learning classification as feature sources. By designing visual interfaces with rich interactions, we show how to assist users in checking the APP's malicious behaviors and their entire triggering paths.

Our current work mainly focuses on sensitive APIs as target objects. In other scenarios, users can set their own targets, for example, code about encryption and decryption (may be used for shelling and shelling-off), advertisements, reflection calls and so on, to meet different security analysis needs or visual needs. Our framework is extensible to meet these requirements just by modifying some labeling rules.

Although we can detect the behavior of developers trying to dynamically load code by detecting related APIs such as "DexClassLoader", our current approach does not work on dynamically loaded code. Meanwhile, though our image similarity results inside same malware family indicate that $PMCG_{droid}$ may be suitable for clustering analysis of malware, we have not done this work yet. We will study them in the future.

In the future, we will further expand the visualization and artificial analysis assistance capability of $PMCG_{droid}$. Also we will study how to visualize the C/C++ code threats inside APPs.

Acknowledgment. We thank the anonymous reviewers for their insightful comments. Our work was supported by the National Key Research and Development Program of China (No. 2017YFB0801900), Key Program of the Chinese Academy of Sciences (No. ZDRW-KT-2016-02, ZDRW-KT-2016-02-6, Y6X0061105), and Youth Innovation Promotion Association of CAS (No. 1105CX0105).

References

1. Beresford, A.R., Rice, A., Skehin, N., Sohan, R.: MockDroid: trading privacy for application functionality on smartphones. In: 12th Workshop on Mobile Computing Systems and Applications, pp. 49–54. ACM (2011)
2. Octeau, D., McDaniel, P., Jha, S., Bartel, A., Bodden, E., Klein, J., Le Traon, Y.: Effective inter-component communication mapping in android with epicc: an essential step towards holistic security analysis. In: 22nd USENIX Security Symposium, pp. 543–558. USENIX (2013)
3. Zhou, Y., Wang, Z., Zhou, W., Jiang, X.: Hey, you, get off of my market: detecting malicious apps in official and alternative android markets. In: NDSS, pp. 50–52. NDSS (2012)

4. Enck, W., Ongtang, M., McDaniel, P.: On lightweight mobile phone application certification. In: 16th ACM Conference on Computer and Communications Security, pp. 235–245. ACM (2009)
5. Sun, M., Wei, T., Lui, J.: Taintart: a practical multi-level information-flow tracking system for android runtime. In: 2016 ACM SIGSAC Conference on Computer and Communications Security, pp. 331–342. ACM (2016)
6. Sanz, B., Santos, I., Laorden, C., Ugarte-Pedrero, X., Bringas, P.G., Álvarez, G.: PUMA: permission usage to detect malware in android. In: Herrero, Á., et al. (eds.) Advances in Intelligent Systems and Computing, vol. 189, pp. 289–298. Springer, Heidelberg (2013). https://doi.org/10.1007/978-3-642-33018-6_30
7. Acar, Y., Backes, M., Bugiel, S., Fahl, S., McDaniel, P., Smith, M.: SoK: lessons learned from android security research for appified software platforms. In: Security and Privacy IEEE, pp. 433–451 (2016)
8. Arp, D., Gascon, H., Rieck, K., Spreitzenbarth, M., Hbner, M.: DREBIN: effective and explainable detection of android malware in your pocket. In: NDSS. NDSS (2014)
9. Arzt, S., Rasthofer, S., Fritz, C., Bodden, E., Bartel, A., Klein, J., Le Traon, Y., Octeau, D., McDaniel, P.: Flowdroid: precise context, flow, field, object-sensitive and lifecycle-aware taint analysis for android apps. In: ACM SIGPLAN Notices, vol. 49, no. 6, pp. 259–269 (2014)
10. Reina, A., Fattori, A., Cavallaro, L.: A system call-centric analysis and stimulation technique to automatically reconstruct android malware behaviors. In: EuroSec, April 2013
11. Fuchs, A.P., Chaudhuri, A., Foster, J.S.: Scandroid: automated security certification of android (2009)
12. Gibler, C., Crussell, J., Erickson, J., Chen, H.: AndroidLeaks: automatically detecting potential privacy leaks in android applications on a large scale. In: Katzenbeisser, S., Weippl, E., Camp, L.J., Volkamer, M., Reiter, M., Zhang, X. (eds.) Trust 2012. LNCS, vol. 7344, pp. 291–307. Springer, Heidelberg (2012). https://doi.org/10.1007/978-3-642-30921-2_17
13. Li, L., Bartel, A., Bissyandé, T.F., Klein, J., Le Traon, Y., Arzt, S., Rasthofer, S., Bodden, E., Octeau, D., McDaniel, P.: IccTA: Detecting inter-component privacy leaks in android apps. In: 37th International Conference on Software Engineering, vol. 1, pp. 280–291. IEEE Press (2015)
14. Chakradeo, S., Reaves, B., Traynor, P., Enck, W.: Mast: triage for market-scale mobile malware analysis. In: The Sixth ACM Conference on Security and Privacy in Wireless and Mobile Networks, pp. 12–24. ACM (2013)
15. Wu, D.-J., Mao, C.-H., Wei, T.-E., Lee, H.-M., Wu, K.-P.: Droidmat: android malware detection through manifest and API calls tracing. In: Information Security IEEE, pp. 62–69. IEEE (2012)
16. Burguera, I., Zurutuza, U., Nadjm-Tehrani, S.: Crowdroid: behavior-based malware detection system for android. In: ACM Workshop on Security and Privacy in Smartphones and Mobile Devices, pp. 15–26. ACM (2011)
17. Peng, H., Gates, C., Sarma, B., Li, N., Qi, Y., Potharaju, R., Nita-Rotaru, C., Molloy, I.: Using probabilistic generative models for ranking risks of android apps. In: 2012 ACM Conference on Computer and Communications Security, pp. 241–252. ACM (2012)
18. Enck, W., Gilbert, P., Han, S., Tendulkar, V., Chun, B.-G., Cox, L.P., Jung, J., McDaniel, P., Sheth, A.N.: TaintDroid: an information-flow tracking system for realtime privacy monitoring on smartphones. ACM Trans. Comput. Syst. (TOCS) **32**(2), 1–29 (2014)

19. Somarriba, O., Zurutuza, U., Uribeetxeberria, R., Delosières, L., Nadjm-Tehrani, S.: Detection and visualization of android malware behavior. J. Electr. Comput. Eng. **2016**, 6 (2016)
20. Park, W., Lee, K.H., Cho, K.S., Ryu, W.: Analyzing and detecting method of android malware via disassembling and visualization. In: International Conference on Information and Communication Technology Convergence, pp. 817–818. IEEE (2014)
21. González, A., Herrero, Á., Corchado, E.: Neural visualization of android malware families. In: Graña, M., López-Guede, J.M., Etxaniz, O., Herrero, Á., Quintián, H., Corchado, E. (eds.) ICEUTE/SOCO/CISIS -2016. AISC, vol. 527, pp. 574–583. Springer, Cham (2017). https://doi.org/10.1007/978-3-319-47364-2_56
22. Sakamoto, S., Okuda, K., Nakatsuka, R., Yamauchi, T.: DroidTrack: tracking and visualizing information diffusion for preventing information leakage on android. J. Internet Serv. Inf. Secur. **4**(2), 55–69 (2014)
23. Grace, M., Zhou, Y., Zhang, Q., Zou, S., Jiang, X.: Riskranker: scalable and accurate zero-day android malware detection. In: The 10th International Conference on Mobile Systems, Applications, and Services, pp. 281–294. ACM (2012)
24. Wagner, M., Fischer, F., Luh, R., Haberson, A., Rind, A., Keim, D.A., Aigner, W.: A survey of visualization systems for malware analysis (2015)
25. Conti, G., Dean, E., Sinda, M., Sangster, B.: Visual reverse engineering of binary and data files. In: Goodall, J.R., Conti, G., Ma, K.-L. (eds.) VizSec 2008. LNCS, vol. 5210, pp. 1–17. Springer, Heidelberg (2008). https://doi.org/10.1007/978-3-540-85933-8_1
26. Quist, D.A., Liebrock, L.M.: Visualizing compiled executables for malware analysis. In: International Workshop on Visualization for Cyber Security, pp. 27–32. IEEE (2009)
27. Trinius, P., Holz, T., Gbel, J., Freiling, F.C.: Visual analysis of malware behavior using treemaps and thread graphs. In: International Workshop on Visualization for Cyber Security, pp. 33–38. IEEE (2009)
28. Grgio, A.R.A., Santos, R.D.C.: Visualization techniques for malware behavior analysis. In: Proceedings of SPIE - The International Society for Optical Engineering, vol. 801905–801905-9 (2011)
29. Quist, D., Liebrock, L.M.: Reversing compiled executables for malware analysis via visualization. Inf. Vis. **10**(10), 117–126 (2011)
30. Chan, L.Y., Chuan, L.L., Ismail, M., Zainal, N.: A static and dynamic visual debugger for malware analysis. In: Communications, pp. 765–769. IEEE (2012)
31. Zhuo, W., Nadjin, Y.: MalwareVis: entity-based visualization of malware network traces. In: The Ninth International Symposium on Visualization for Cyber Security, pp. 41–47. ACM (2012)
32. Donahue, J., Paturi, A., Mukkamala, S.: Visualization techniques for efficient malware detection. In: IEEE International Conference on Intelligence and Security Informatics, pp. 289–291. IEEE (2013)
33. Yan, L.K., Yin, H.: DroidScope: seamlessly reconstructing the OS and Dalvik semantic views for dynamic android malware analysis. In: The 21st USENIX Conference on Security Symposium, p 29. USENIX (2013)
34. G DATA news. https://www.gdata-software.com/news/2017/04/29715-350-new-android-malware-apps-every-hour
35. Androguard. https://github.com/androguard/androguard/
36. Chan, P.P.F., Hui, L.C.K., Yiu, S.-M.: Droidchecker: analyzing android applications for capability leak. In: The Fifth ACM Conference on Security and Privacy in Wireless and Mobile Networks, pp. 125–136. ACM (2012)

37. Android malware genome project. http://www.malgenomeproject.org/
38. Wang, K., Zhang, Y., Liu, P.: Call me back!: attacks on system server and system apps in android through synchronous callback. In: The 2016 ACM SIGSAC Conference on Computer and Communications Security, pp. 92–103. ACM (2016)
39. The Drebin dataset. https://www.sec.cs.tu-bs.de/~danarp/drebin/index.html
40. TROJAN. https://www.f-secure.com/v-descs/trojan_android_fakeinst.shtml
41. VirusTotal. https://www.virustotal.com/
42. Umeng. http://www.umeng.com/
43. Google maps android API. https://developers.google.com/maps/documentation/android-api/
44. AdMob. https://www.google.com/admob/
45. The life cycle of activity. https://developer.android.com/guide/components/activi-ties.html#Lifecycle
46. The life cycle of service. https://developer.android.com/guide/components/service-s.html#Lifecycle
47. Chner, T., Pretschner, A., Ochoa, M.: DAVAST: data-centric system level activity visualization. In: Eleventh Workshop on Visualization for Cyber Security, pp. 25–32. ACM (2014)
48. Kim, J., Yoon, Y., Yi, K., Shin, J.: SCANDAL: Static Analyzer for Detecting Privacy Leaks in Android Applications. Mobile Secur. Technol. Los Alamitos (2012)
49. Zhang, X., Aafer, Y., Ying, K., Du, W.: Hey, you, get off of my image: detecting data residue in android images. In: Askoxylakis, I., Ioannidis, S., Katsikas, S., Meadows, C. (eds.) ESORICS 2016. LNCS, vol. 9878, pp. 401–421. Springer, Cham (2016). https://doi.org/10.1007/978-3-319-45744-4_20
50. Huang, H., Zheng, C., Zeng, J., Zhou, W., Zhu, S., Liu, P., Chari, S., Zhang, C.: Android malware development on public malware scanning platforms: a large-scale data-driven study. In: 2016 IEEE International Conference on Big Data (Big Data), pp. 1090–1099. IEEE (2016)
51. Cao, Y., Fratantonio, Y., Bianchi, A., Egele, M., Kruegel, C., Vigna, G., Chen, Y.: EdgeMiner: automatically detecting implicit control flow transitions through the android framework. In: NDSS. NDSS (2015)

Inferring Implicit Assumptions and Correct Usage of Mobile Payment Protocols

Quanqi Ye[1], Guangdong Bai[2(✉)], Naipeng Dong[1], and Jin Song Dong[1,3]

[1] National University of Singapore, Singapore, Singapore
yequanqi@u.nus.edu, {dcsdn,dcsdjs}@nus.edu.sg
[2] Singapore Institute of Technology, Singapore, Singapore
guangdong.bai@singaporetech.edu.sg
[3] Griffith University, Nathan, Australia

Abstract. Although mobile shopping has risen rapidly as mobile devices become the dominant portal to the Internet, it remains challenging for a developer of mobile shopping Apps to implement a correct and secure payment protocol. This can be partly attributed to the misunderstanding, confusion of responsibility and implicit assumptions among multiple separate participants of the payment protocols, which involve at least users, merchants and third-party cashiers (e.g., PayPal). In addition, the documentation of the payment SDK which is written in informal natural languages is often inaccurate, ambiguous and incomplete, such that the developers might be confused. In this paper, we seek to infer the correct usage and hidden assumptions of the most commonly used mobile payment libraries, i.e., PayPal and Visa Checkout. Our approach starts with building mobile checkout systems strictly following the documents of PayPal SDK and Visa Checkout SDK. Afterwards, we propose an algorithm to automatically generate test cases embedding different attacker models to check the correctness and security of the payment procedure. During the testing, our algorithm analyzes the security violations so as to infer the correct usage of these payment libraries. Using our approach, we have successfully found several non-trivial hidden assumptions and bugs in these two payment libraries.

Keywords: Mobile payment · Payment protocol · Protocol extraction

1 Introduction

Mobile shopping is becoming increasingly popular as it brings great convenience to people and it has become an indispensable part of their daily lives [9]. Numerous merchants start providing mobile shopping Apps as their main portals [12]. Mobile payment, which allows users[1] to pay remotely on their mobile devices, is a critical procedure in mobile shopping. A small vulnerability in the payment

---

[1] User of the merchant App, i.e., customer.

ⓒ ICST Institute for Computer Sciences, Social Informatics and Telecommunications Engineering 2018
X. Lin et al. (Eds.): SecureComm 2017, LNICST 238, pp. 469–488, 2018.
https://doi.org/10.1007/978-3-319-78813-5_24

protocol may cause severe financial lose for users and merchants, as revealed by previous research [14,15,17].

Existing studies on online payment mainly focus on the desktop platform rather than the mobile platform. We highlight that online payment protocols intended for desktop platform cannot be directly applied to mobile platform, due to the disparity of these two platforms, especially w.r.t. security [13]. First, mobile devices have limited computation capability and battery power, and thus it is hard to deploy a malware detection system as powerful as on the desktop. Second, mobile devices are small in screen size, such that particular information on security may be omitted for the sake of usability. For example, the users may not realize that the website they are browsing is not the intended one as the browser often hides the address bar to save space. Third, desktop has deployed well-evolved security mechanisms to control access to security-critical resources, whereas few similar mechanism has been built on mobile platform.

Mobile payment normally involves multiple parties, including at least customers, merchants and third-party cashiers (TPC for short hereafter) such as PayPal. These parties interact with each other following the underlying payment protocol, which is typically designed by the TPC. The problem is that the merchant App[2] developers and the protocol designers are usually different parties. Misunderstanding to certain steps in the protocol, confusion of responsibility and wrong assumptions on the responses from other parties are unavoidable. For example, to facilitate use of the payment protocol, the TPC usually provides App developers with an SDK encapsulating the protocol implementation. This eases the use, but it may exacerbate misunderstanding because the details of the protocol are hidden. Even worse, the documentation of the SDK, which is often written in natural languages, may be inaccurate, ambiguous and incomplete. Consequentially, it is highly likely that the merchant developers fail to correctly implement the payment protocol.

In this paper, we propose a systematic approach to identify the correct usage and the implicit assumptions which the developers of merchant Apps must follow and be aware of to implement a secure payment system. To this end, for each payment SDK, we first build a testbed shopping system which includes both a front-end merchant App embedding the SDK, and a back-end merchant server which processes the payment issued from the App. To minimize the bugs caused by our mis-integration, the testbed system is built by strictly following the official documents and TPC's sample code. By applying protocol extraction techniques [6,20] on the testbed systems, we infer implementation-level payment protocols. These protocols are used to automatically generate test cases for dynamic testing. During the testing, we check whether the payment is secure by observing the integrity of four key elements in a payment, given that the integrity is the key property of a payment protocol [17]. Whenever the integrity is violated, we manually study the test cases and execution traces to learn the cause of the violation. Through the analysis, we are able to infer the correct

---

[2] In this paper, we use *merchant App* to indicate the front-end App running on customer's mobile device and *merchant server* the back-end server.

usage and hidden assumptions to build a secure payment system. By applying our approach on the Android SDKs of two widely-used TPCs, i.e. PayPal and Visa Checkout, we have successfully found several non-trivial usage rules and hidden assumptions. Our approach detects three bugs in these two payment libraries.

We summarize our contributions as follows.

- We extract PayPal and Visa Checkout's mobile payment protocols which can be a reference for other researchers.
- By applying our approach, we have found and reported **three** confirmed bugs in PayPal SDK.
- We summarize **three** rules and **five** implicit assumptions in using PayPal and Visa. These are beneficial to the merchant App developers in building a secure payment system.

2 Background

To ease the understanding, this section briefly introduces the background in mobile payment.

2.1 A General Process of Mobile Payment

Although different TPCs may have different payment protocol implementations, they generally follow a similar process in terms of mobile payment. In this section, we use PayPal payment as an example to introduce such a mobile payment process, as shown in Fig. 1.

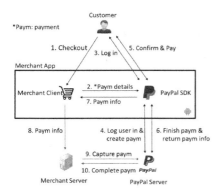

Fig. 1. Correct process to capture payment

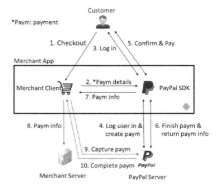

Fig. 2. Dangerous process to capture payment

S1. After ordering, the user clicks on the "Checkout" button to initiate a checkout process (step 1).

S2. The merchant client invokes the PayPal SDK and passes it the payment details (step 2).

S3. PayPal SDK shows a login dialog for the user to login (step 3).

S4. After receiving login credentials, PayPal SDK sends them along with the payment details to PayPal server for verification. After verification, PayPal server creates the payment and sends it back to the PayPal SDK, which then shows the user a button for payment authorization (step 4).

S5. The user confirms the payment details (e.g., amount) and authorizes the payment (step 5).

S6. Upon receiving authorization, PayPal SDK forwards it to PayPal server and the PayPal server sends the payment result back to PayPal SDK (step 6).

S7. The PayPal SDK sends the payment info to the merchant client (step 7).

S8. The merchant client sends (optional) the payment information to its merchant server (step 8).

S9. The merchant server captures the payment with PayPal server using the payment information from merchant App (step 9).

S10. PayPal server replies merchant server with payment completed response (step 10).

2.2 Special Features of PayPal SDK

Despite of the general payment process, each TPC may have special features. In this section, we introduce such special features in PayPal SDK which are relevant to the security of the protocol. PayPal's mobile payment process can be further divided into the following three types, depending on the timing of authorizing the payment and the timing that the merchant captures[3] the payment.

Single Payment. It represents a one-time payment. The single payment can be further divided into three categories.

- Immediate payment, where the user authorizes the payment immediately and the merchant captures the payment immediately.
- Authorization payment, where the user authorizes the payment immediately and the merchant may capture it later.
- Order payment, which is used in the case that the user authorizes the payment in advance when the actual item for sale is not ready yet. Once the item is received by the user, the merchant can capture payment at any time.

Future Payment. It allows the user to authorize the merchant to create and capture payment in the future. In other words, once authorized, the merchant can create and capture payment for multiple times.

Profile Sharing. It is used to share user's profile information in PayPal server to the merchant App. This seems not a payment feature. However, as we show in Sect. 8, this feature actually allows the merchant to capture payment from user's account.

---

[3] *Capture* is a term used in the PayPal documentation, meaning that the merchant completes/cashes the payment.

2.3   An Example of Dangerous Usage

Although the processes of the all three types of single payment in PayPal's Android SDK are the same, there are subtle differences among them. For example, in both authorization payment and order payment, after the user authorizes a payment, the protocol requires the merchant to immediately capture the payment, whereas in the immediate payment, the merchant does not have to do so. Therefore, to guarantee the payment is captured successfully, the following rule must be complied by the merchant.

#1. *For authorization payment and order payment, the merchant server **must** subsequently capture the payment from the **merchant server**[4].*

Following this rule, the merchant server needs to actively perform step 9 and step 10 as shown in Fig. 1 to ensure the authorization or order payment is completed correctly.

A dangerous usage of the protocol example is shown in Fig. 2. In that scenario, the payment capturing request is performed by the App, while it should be done by the merchant server as shown in Fig. 1. The reason is that the environment in which the merchant App resides is out of the control of the merchant, and thus it should be considered as insecure. This is a case that developers without security domain knowledge may not be aware of. If rule #1 is not followed, an attacker could intercept the messages sent from the merchant App to TPC and forges a response from the TPC. Compared to the App side, the merchant server is normally under control of the merchant, and thus performing the payment capturing request on the server side is relatively more secure.

The cause of this security issue is as follows. PayPal may assume that it is the merchant's responsibility to ensure the capturing request is sent from merchant server, while the merchant may assume that the protocol is secure and he/she may not realize it is dangerous to capture payment from merchant App.

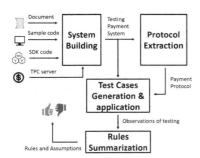

Fig. 3. Method overview

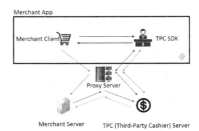

Fig. 4. Testbed mobile checkout system with proxy server

---

[4] We find that this rule also applies for Visa Checkout, in which there is no immediate payment, and the merchant is required to actively capture the payment.

This example demonstrates that, because of such hidden assumptions and confusions of responsibility among participants of the mobile payment protocol, security problems in this scenario are inevitable. This motivates us to identify the hidden assumptions and the correct usage of a payment protocol.

3   Method Overview

In this section, we introduce our overall method. As shown in Fig. 3, our method includes the following steps.

System Building. Taking the documentations from TPC and the sample code (with SDK provided by TPC) as input, we first build the testbed payment systems following the instructions from documents. We mainly need to incorporate two parts - the merchant and the TPC server. For the TPC server, we use the sandbox environment, for example [3], to avoid finance cost to any real merchants during testing. We remark that the sandbox environment is a separate server that provides mirrored functionalities of the live environment that a TPC server uses for real-world applications. All the functionalities needed in this work from live environment can be found in the sandbox environment. Hence, the rules inferred in the sandbox environment are also applicable to the live environment. For the merchant, following the work flow introduced by the official documents, we build both merchant App and merchant server with essential functions needed to accept payment.

Protocol Extraction. In order to understand how the TPC SDKs create a payment and what information is necessary for creating a payment which the SDKs' documents do not cover, we need to perform the protocol extraction to infer the underlying payment protocols. These protocols specify the exact actions of each participant. They are used for generating test cases under different attacker models.

Test-based Rules Summarization. In this step, we infer rules during the dynamic testing. To this end, we propose an algorithm to guide the testing process. The algorithm generates different test cases incorporating various attacker models. It then drives execution of the system by feeding it the generated test cases. The essential idea of the algorithm is to enumerate what an malicious participant can do. When executing each test case, the protocol may either terminate or end normally. In the former case, the attack may have been prevent by the protocol, so we do not further examine it. For the latter case, we check the integrity after the execution finishes. If the integrity is breached, there may be a flaw in the system, and we manually examine it to figure out the cause of the problem and then summarize protocol usage rules or assumptions.

4   System Building

In this section, we introduce the testbed system building. The architecture of the testbed system is shown in Fig. 4. It includes a merchant App including the merchant client and a TPC SDK, a merchant server and a TPC server. We set up two sets of testbed systems integrating respectively PayPal and Visa Checkout SDK.

Merchant App. For each of the merchant Apps, we reuse most of the code from the samples provided by TPC. To simplify the merchant App, we omit the item selection process and provide just two buttons representing two different items with different prices. When one of the buttons is clicked, the user is redirected to TPC SDK to finish the rest of payment protocol. After that, the merchant client[5] receives the payment information returned from TPC SDK and it can either send the information to the merchant server, or perform capture directly depending on the test case. For example, if it is the single payment in PayPal, the merchant client transmits the payment ID back to the merchant server, whereas if it is the future payment, it transmits the authorization code back to the merchant server.

Merchant server. In different test case, the merchant App may send different payment information to the merchant server, which then accordingly perform one or more of the following actions.

For PayPal:

- *Doing nothing.* This action represents that the merchant server does not need to perform any further action. This may happen if the merchant client has captured the payment.
- *Retrieving payment details.* This action represents that the merchant server queries the detailed payment information from the PayPal server, such as amount and capturing status.
- *Verifying payment information.* This action represents that the merchant server validates the payment information retrieved from the PayPal server.
- *Capturing payment.* This action represents that the merchant server captures the payment with PayPal server by providing the payment information received from the merchant client.

For Visa Checkout:

- *Doing nothing.* This action represents the same as in PayPal.
- *Retrieving payment details.* This action represents that after receiving payment ID from merchant client, the merchant server uses it to retrieves the encrypted payment information from Visa server.
- *Decrypting payload.* This action represents that the merchant server decrypts the encrypted payment information returned from Visa server.
- *Updating payment information.* This action represents that the merchant server updates the payment information to the Visa server after validation.

---

[5] The portion of code that is implemented by merchant developers which is representing with a carte label in Fig. 1.

We create a profile for each of the two merchant Apps in the respective TPC servers. The TPC servers generate two unique artifacts for each of the Apps: shared secret and merchant ID (They may be named differently in different TPCs). The shared secret is used to authenticate the merchant and the merchant ID is used to identify the merchant App. In summary, we build two sets of systems which incorporate PayPal SDK and Visa Checkout SDK, respectively. We remark that these testbed systems are representative as we build them based on the official documentations and sample code which can reflect the actual situations where developers are facing as they develop Apps that integrate TPCs.

5   Protocol Extraction

In order to generate test cases for the testbed system, we need to extract the baseline payment protocol from PayPal SDK and Visa Checkout SDK to understand how the payments are created and completed by the protocols. Our approach extracts the protocol from the messages exchanged by the participants during the protocol execution. The messages we take as input include application-layer messages, such as HTTP messages and HTTPS messages. In a nutshell, our extraction approach works as the following steps.

– **Protocol Message Capturing.** During protocol execution, messages are exchanged through the network channels. We capture these messages as traces from our testbed systems for our analysis.
– **Trace Refinement.** The raw traces captured are typically complicated and contain many redundant parameters which are not relevant to our analysis. Therefore, in this step, we remove redundant parameters to get refined traces.
– **Protocol Interpretation.** After trace refinement, we get the baseline payment protocols. However, the concrete semantics of the messages are still unclear for us to understand the precise behaviors of the SDKs. For example, some messages stand for payment creation while some stand for payment update. Therefore, in this step, we aim to identify the semantics of these messages by manual analysis.

5.1   Protocol Message Capturing

To capture the raw protocol messages in the network channels, we need to deploy a proxy server in the network channels intercepting the messages coming in and going out from merchant App. The proxy is not part of our testbed mobile checkout systems, but it facilitates protocol refinement and can simulate the network attacker during the dynamic testing.

Figure 4 shows the testbed mobile checkout system with the proxy deployed. The proxy server is deployed between the merchant App and the two servers (merchant server and TPC server) such that all messages sent out by merchant App can be captured and even changed (for trace refinement). In this

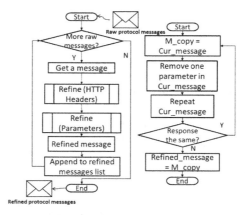

Fig. 5. Trace refinement procedure (The sub-procedure on the right side is the detailed procedure for the "Refine" procedure on the left.)

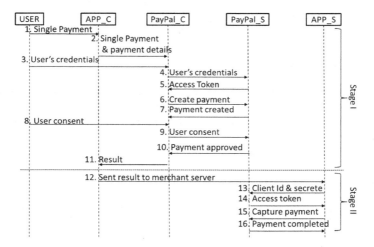

Fig. 6. Single payment protocol (I: The first stage of creating and user consenting the payment. II: The second stage that merchant server verifies or captures the payment.)

work, we only consider the attacks which can control the client-side Apps and communication channels. Therefore, we skip the communication between the merchant server and the TPC server.

After the deployment of the proxy server, once the protocol is executed, all the communications coming in and going out of the mobile device can be recorded by our proxy server. We execute all possible payment methods in PayPal and Visa Checkout such that enough information regarding the protocol can be preserved in the captured traces.

5.2 Trace Refinement

The trace refinement procedure is shown on the left hand side of Fig. 5. The procedure takes the raw protocol messages as input and then outputs the refined traces without redundant parameters. The concrete message refinement procedure is shown on the right hand side of Fig. 5. By using our proxy, we keep replaying every message with one parameter temporarily removed. If the modified message leads to the same response as the original message, the removed parameter is a redundant parameter to the protocol. Hence, we can remove permanently that parameter. We keep doing it until we cannot remove any remaining parameter. The final message therefore is a concise message which excludes all redundant parameters while still produces the same response as the original message.

We iterate the refining procedure on all the raw messages and obtain their refined versions. Eventually, all the messages refined make up the refined trace. In some cases, a replayed message is not accepted when the message carries a parameter that can only be used for once, e.g. timestamp. To address this, we repeat the whole protocol in order to fuzz for the single non-repeatable message.

5.3 Protocol Interpretation

After refining the protocol messages, we then analyze the purpose of each message. Messages sent to different url endpoints with different parameters correspond to invoking different APIs/commands in TPC server to log user in, create or update payment.

We summarize the identified TPC API endpoints from messages of TPC SDKs and messages of the merchant server. We find that different API endpoints serve as different purposes/commands in the protocols.

From the communication trace between PayPal SDK and PayPal server, we observe that different payment methods in single payment use the same set of API endpoints and follow the same sequence when invoking the APIs. We also observe that future payment and profile sharing share the same set of API endpoints and also follow the same sequence. The difference is the intent of the final consent made by future payment and profile sharing. For future Payment, the consent is to authorize the merchant to make payment in the future, whereas profile sharing authorizes the merchant to retrieve personal information from PayPal.

The final outputs of protocol inference are the baseline protocols for different payment methods in PayPal and Visa Checkout. We summarize them as follows. In the protocol, we denote merchant App as APP_C, PayPal SDK as PayPal_C, PayPal server as PayPal_S, the merchant server as APP_S, Visa checkout SDK as Visa_C, Visa server as Visa_S.

- **Single Payment.** As shown in Fig. 6, the first stage of authorization payment and order payment are the same. There is subtle difference at the second stage. In the immediate payment, the merchant server does not have to capture the

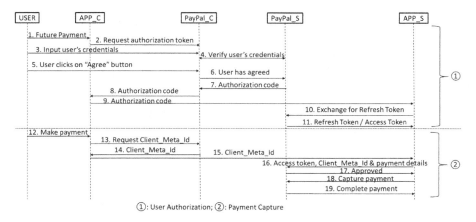

Fig. 7. Future payment protocol

payment. Rather, it only has to verify whether the payment details are correct. To this end, it uses its merchant ID and the shared secret to obtain an access token and makes a direct server-to-server API request to check if the payment details are exactly the same as the one returned from the merchant App.

- **Future Payment.** The procedure of future payment is shown in Fig. 7. We highlight that whenever the refresh token which the merchant obtains using the authorization code is still valid, it can be used by the merchant to create and capture payment. From the official document on PayPal SDK, we know that although the authorization code is short-lived, the refresh token is long-lived and lasts for 10 years [2]. That means that when the refresh token is obtained, the merchant can create and capture the payment within 10 years.
- **Profile Sharing.** The procedure for profile sharing is highly similar to that of future payment. The difference only occurs at the last step. Merchant server makes request to different API endpoints to retrieve user's profile information rather than to create and capture payment as in future payment.
- **Visa Checkout.** As shown in Fig. 8, most steps of Visa Checkout are similar to PayPal's immediate payment. However, in the last two steps (step 9 and step 10), apart from the *callID*, Visa also returns the *encKey* and *encData* which are encrypted data containing the payment details. Merchant needs to first decrypt the *encKey* using the shared secret and then uses the decrypted *encKey* to decrypt the *encData* to get the payment details.

6   System Testing

Based on the extracted protocols, we can generate test cases to dynamically test our testbed systems. During the test case generation, we consider two types of attackers, i.e., the malicious user and the malicious merchant, each of which has specific attack capabilities. Given that the integrity is the predominant property in payment protocols, our dynamic testing mainly targets this property.

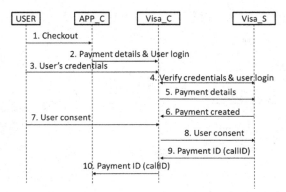

Fig. 8. Visa checkout protocol

6.1   Attacker Models

During the test case generation, we consider the following two attacker models.

Malicious User. The malicious user stands for such a attacker that controls the mobile device where the merchant App is running on. This attacker attempts to shop for free or pays less for the order[6], and the victim of this attacker model is the merchant. We list the capabilities of this attacker as follows.

- To control the network channels of the merchant App such that it can change parameter(s) in protocol messages coming in and going out from the device.
- To record, interrupt and replay the messages sent and received by the merchant App.
- To forge a message to merchant server, merchant App or TPC server.

Malicious Merchant. The malicious merchant stands for such a attacker that controls the merchant App and the merchant server. This attacker attempts to overcharge the user, charge the user without authorization and obtain the profile information of user from the TPC. The victim of this attacker model, thus, is the user. We list the capabilities of this attacker as follows.

- To tamper the total amount in the order or user's authorization.
- To abuse obtained token, e.g., invoke particular APIs out of user's intention.
- To inject malicious code in the merchant client and the embedded TPC SDK.

6.2   Integrity of Payment

A payment consists of the following four elements. (1) the *User* who initiates a payment, (2) the *Order* placed by the user who initiates that payment, (3) the *Payment* made by the user, and (4) the *Merchant* which the order is placed

---

[6] The order contains the items the user has ordered and the prices of the items.

Algorithm 1. Test case generation algorithm

```
 1: procedure TEST CASE GENERATION
 2:     FOR M ∈ attack models
 3:         Bool ENDNORMAL == TRUE
 4:         FOR P ∈ protocols
 5:             FOR step S ∈ P
 6:                 A = M.ChooseActions()
 7:                 R = S.GetActiveRole ()
 8:                 IF R = M.GetRole()
 9:                     A = R.GetProtocolAction()
10:                     A.Perform()
11:                 ELSE A = M.GetRole().GetAction()
12:                     A.Perform()
13:                     IF P.CanProceed()!=TRUE
14:                         ENDNORMAL == FALSE
15:                         BREAK
16:                     ENDIF
17:                 ENDIF
18:             ENDFOR
19:             IF ENDNORMAL == TRUE
20:                 CheckIntegrityOfPayment()
21:             ENDIF
22:         ENDFOR
23: END
```

in and the user should pay. We represent the association of *Payment*, *Order*, *User* and *Merchant* as **POUM**. This association specifies the fact that a user makes a payment for the order to the merchant. Essentially, each transaction can be abstracted as such an association.

To ensure that a payment is conducted in a correct and secure way, the integrity of the **POUM** must be guaranteed. In other words, the integrity of the **POUM** implies that the user has made a payment with correct amount for the intended order to the right merchant. Therefore, after executing the system on each test case, we check the payment's **POUM** from perspective of different parties to ensure that the **POUM** has not been changed by any participant.

6.3 Testing and Evaluation

The algorithm for generating test cases under the above attacker models is shown in Algorithm 1. As shown in the algorithm, during the protocol execution, an honest participant always follows the protocol, while a malicious attacker enumerates the actions it is able to conduct under the capabilities we define in Sect. 6.1. For the malicious user attacker model, we consider user and merchant App as the same role in the protocol execution, given that the mobile device is under the malicious user's control. Therefore, the merchant App in this case should be considered as part of the malicious user. In the malicious merchant attacker model, both merchant server and the merchant App are considered malicious. During the action conducting, the algorithm checks if the protocol can proceed to next step, because the participants may reject the unexpected messages and terminate the protocol. At the end of each protocol execution, we check the integrity of **POUM** to decide whether the test case has revealed a problem of the protocol implementation.

7   Problems Identified and Correct Usages

In this section, we report the identified bugs during system testing and then discuss the correct usages that are summarized from the bugs.

7.1   Identified Bugs

PayPal Android SDK. We find three bugs (shown in Fig. 9) in PayPal payment when we test the system with test cases incorporating the attacker which has compromised the communication channel between the PayPal SDK and PayPal server. This attacker represents several practical system and network attacks. For example, it can be a malicious merchant who incorporates a modified version of SDK to change the parameters; it can be a malicious App which embeds a network proxy (e.g., [8]) and has been installed on the same device as the merchant App; it can be a privileged App which is assigned *root* or *ADB* priviledge [7]; it can be a public WiFi hotspot under attacker's control.

We have reported all the bugs to PayPal who confirmed our findings and stated that the bugs will be fixed in the later version of PayPal Android SDK.

Payment details being Changed. We find that PayPal SDK accesses an API endpoint to create payment and delivers the payment details to the PayPal server. In this step, the attacker modifies the message with different amount and currency. Later, the PayPal SDK displays the payment details to the user and waits for the user to authorize the payment. We observe that when applying the above test case, even after the attacker has changed the payment details in the transmitted messages, the amount displayed to the user remains the one before the attacker changes it. In addition, even the merchant client actively retrieves the payment details by invoking the APIs of the SDK, the returned payment details remain the same as the unchanged one. This implies that even after PayPal's server replies with the changed payment details, PayPal's SDK does NOT update the payment information. This flaw is shown by steps labelled in red in Fig. 9a.

This bug can lead to an attack where a malicious merchant can overcharge an incautious user. For example, a malicious merchant can change the payment amount to a higher number. Since the SDK shows the original payment even after the payment being changed by the merchant App, there is no information for the user to immediately find he/she has been overcharged.

User Credentials being changed. As shown in Fig. 9b, when a user, e.g., Alice, enters her credentials to log into PayPal, the credentials can be changed to Bob's username and Bob's password. In addition, we observe that the Activity in PayPal SDK still shows the username of Alice. This implies that PayPal server never verifies whether the payer in the payment details is the same as the user under authentication.

Although this issue may be less harmful to end users than the previous issue, we highlight that the PayPal server should be responsible to verify the consistency of payer and the authenticated user, and the SDK should in all

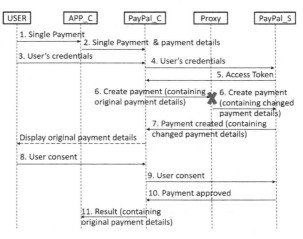

(a) Payment details transmitted being changed.

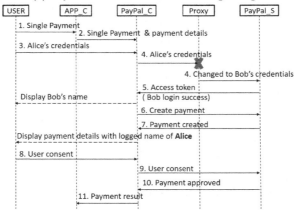

(b) Account credential transmitted being changed.

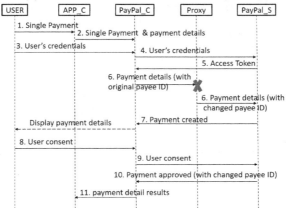

(c) Payee (Merchant) ID transmitted being changed.

Fig. 9. Identified bugs in PayPal SDK.

cases check and verify the payment details returned by the server and displays correct information to the end users.

Payee (Merchant) ID being changed. This bug is shown in Fig. 9c. When a user initiates the login, PayPal SDK accesses to an endpoint with a basic access authentication header using the merchant ID in base64 encoding [11]. The attacker substitutes the merchant ID with another merchant ID under his control. Once the user logs in, the PayPal server returns an OAuth bearer token [10]. This token binds the user to the changed merchant ID, such that the payment is also associated with the changed merchant. Later, once PayPal SDK accesses REST API endpoint to create payment with the token, the payment is paid to the attacker's merchant ID. We remark that unlike the first issue, the payee information is not displayed to the user in this case. Our investigation finds that the payment details returned from PayPal's server to the SDK does not include who the payee (merchant) is. The payee information only appears on the last message from PayPal server, i.e., after the payment is completed.

The above bug can lead to the following scenario. A network attacker might change the parameters when user is making a transaction with merchant. If the user does not check who she is paying to, she might pay to a wrong merchant.

Visa Checkout SDK. We also have done the same testbed building and security analysis on Visa Checkout SDK. We have found that the Visa Checkout SDK follows a very strict step-by-step process. It also does not incorporate as rich functionalities as PayPal, such as the future payment and profile sharing. Therefore, no problem is found from the Visa checkout SDK, and the security problems we have found in PayPal do not exists in Visa Checkout SDK.

7.2 Correct Usage Summarization

In addition to the rule shown in the motivating example, we summarize rule #2 and rule #3 from the three bugs in Fig. 9 introduced in Sect. 7.1.

#2. *A merchant App **should not** assume the payment information returned from PayPal SDK is correct and complete.*

As stated in the first bug (Fig. 9a) and the second bug (Fig. 9b), after receiving payment details which may have been changed by the malicious merchant, PayPal SDK does not accordingly update the information displayed to the user.

#3. *For every payment, the merchant server **must** verify the payment information (**including payer ID, payee ID, amount, currency and freshness of payment**) and the status of the transaction to ensure the correctness of the payment.*

This rule applies for both PayPal and Visa. The messages sent to the merchant server from the merchant App may have been tampered by the malicious users. Therefore, the merchant server should not trust these messages. Instead, it should use the Payment ID received from the merchant client to make a direct API call to the PayPal (or Visa) server to retrieve the detailed payment information.

In particular, the merchant should verify the correctness of payer ID, payee ID, amount, currency and freshness of the payment. In addition, the merchant should not deliver any service or items to the users before the payment is verified. Moreover, since the messages out of the device can be changed by the malicious users, the verification of payment must be performed from merchant server as specified in rule #1.

8   Ambiguity in Documents

In this section, we report the ambiguities between the interpretation of the document and the facts we get from the system implementation.

i. *Future Payment allows the merchant to capture 15% more than the amount in the payment authorized by the user. This **should** be explicitly displayed to users when the users check out with PayPal.*

This ambiguity is observed from a test case with malicious merchant attacker model where the malicious merchant successfully changes the amount to a larger number. Using manual testing, we identify this upper bound of the extra amount (15%) which the merchant can capture. This is not a bug, since we later find this policy in one of PayPal's documents named *Authorization & Capture* [4] which is burred deeply among other documents. It states that the merchant can charge user 15% more with an upper bound of $75. However, since there is no such statement in the document of PayPal Android SDK, this may cause confusion in the responsibility between the merchant App developers and PayPal regarding who should be the party warning user of this policy. An App developer often only focuses on the functionality implementation of the App, but tends to overlook the policy issues. Thus, it is likely that the developers only read the SDK documents, such that they may never notice the policy and let alone to inform the users.

ii. *When a user has authorized the merchant for profile sharing, the merchant becomes able to charge the user through the future payment, even though the user has never authorized the future payment before.*

This is observed in a test case under malicious user attacker model when the malicious user replaces the future payment authorization code with another authorization code he has obtained for profile sharing. To examine the cause, we surprisingly find that the scope of profile sharing includes the permission of future payment. This implies that the merchant can wrap the request for permission of future payment into a request of profile sharing, such that an incautious user who intends to authorize the profile sharing may actually authorize the future payment. In addition, this security-sensitive information on relation of the profile sharing and future payment is not stated clearly in the document of PayPal Android SDK.

iii. *When a user has previously authorized the merchant with future payment, the authorization code of profile sharing to the same merchant from the same user automatically enables the merchant to make future payment without user's authorization, even if the merchant App does not request the future payment access in the profile sharing.*

This is observed in the test case under malicious merchant where he changes the future payment code with profile sharing code that a same user has previously authorized. Contrary to ambiguity **ii.**, if the user has previously authorized the merchant to make future payment, and later the user also consents the merchant to do profile sharing without future payment access in the scope. The authorization code for profile sharing can be used to cerate and capture a payment.

iv. *Although multiple steps are stated necessary by the documents, order payment in single payment can be captured directly without the following steps.*
   − *executing the order,*
   − *and authorizing the order.*

This ambiguity is discovered in a test case under malicious merchant attacker model where the malicious merchant skips the above mentioned steps and captures the payment directly, The PayPal SDK document does not detail the order payment, but only provides a link to a REST API document [1]. In that document, an order payment has to take five steps to complete, starting from the initial step *"Create the order"*, then *"Get customer (user) approval"*, *"Execute the order"*, *"Authorize and order"* and lastly to *"Capture an order"*. However, based on our testing results, the order payment created from the PayPal SDK can be captured directly without the *"Execute"* and *"Authorize"* steps.

v. *Client Metadata ID is not a necessary information for mobile payment protocol of future payment.*

This ambiguity is discovered during the trace refinement. After the client metadata ID is removed from the request sending by SDK to the TPC server, the response from the TPC server does not change. This implies that the client metadata ID is not a necessary information at all. This is contradictory to PayPal SDK's document [2] which clearly states that Client Metadata ID is necessary.

9   Related Work

Our work is related to the following two areas − third party library analysis and flaws detection from integrated applications. In this section, we brief related work in these two areas.

Third party library. In [19], the authors conduct security analysis on the China's mobile payment market. They find security vulnerabilities in different payment libraries and suggest security rules for developers. Different from it, this work aims to use a systematic approach to identify hidden assumptions and ambiguities. In [18], the authors aim to uncover the hidden assumptions for using the SDKs in secure authentication and authorization. In [15], the authors leverage black-box testing with known attack patterns to test the security of multi-party web applications.

Flaws Detection. The other type of related research is detecting flaws in application implementations. In [6], the authors develop a tool to automatically extract and translate the protocol into a formal model. Then vulnerabilities of the protocol can be identified by formally analyzing the extracted model. Similar to this work, a Single Sign-on (SSO) protocol is extracted from network traffic and formally modeled. Through this, security vulnerabilities are identified through formally verifying the formal models [20]. While in Pellegrino et al.'s work [14], the authors use black-box testing to test web applications, aiming at finding logic flaws. [16] uses a static analysis to identify the vulnerabilities in e-commerce web applications. Prior to this, [17] studies Cashier-as-a-Service based web stores and finds that integration of the third-party services might introduce vulnerabilities into the web applications.

10   Conclusion

We propose a systematical approach to identify correct usage and hidden assumptions in mobile payment protocols that developers should be aware of. These identified usage and assumptions urge both the protocol designers and the TPC SDK developers to provide clearer and well-formed documents. More techniques [5] should be used to check, and if possible, to formally verify the security of the payment protocol implementation.

Acknowledgement. We thank all the anonymous reviewers and our shepherd Dr. Xiao Zhang for their invaluable comments and guidance in revising this paper. This research is supported (in part) by the National Research Foundation, Prime Minister's Office, Singapore under its National Cybersecurity R&D Program (Award No. NRF2014NCR-NCR001-30) and administered by the National Cybersecurity R&D Directorate.

References

1. Create and process orders (2016). https://developer.paypal.com/webapps/developer/docs/integration/direct/create-process-order/. Accessed Aug 2016
2. Future payments mobile integration (2016). https://github.com/paypal/PayPal-Android-SDK/blob/master/docs/future_payments_mobile.md. Accessed Aug 2016
3. Paypal sandbox testing guide (2016). https://developer.paypal.com/docs/classic/lifecycle/ug_sandbox/. Accessed Aug 2016

4. Authorization and Capture (2016). https://developer.paypal.com/docs/classic/admin/auth-capture/. Accessed Aug 2016
5. Bai, G., Ye, Q., Wu, Y., Merwe, H., Sun, J., Liu, Y., Dong, J.S., Visser, W.: Towards model checking android applications. IEEE Trans. Software Eng. **PP**, 1 (2017)
6. Bai, G., Lei, J., Meng, G., Venkatraman, S.S., Saxena, P., Sun, J., Liu, Y., Dong, J.S.: Authscan: automatic extraction of web authentication protocols from implementations. In: 20th Annual Network and Distributed System Security Symposium (NDSS) (2013)
7. Bai, G., Sun, J., Wu, J., Ye, Q., Li, L., Dong, J.S., Guo, S.: All your sessions are belong to us: investigating authenticator leakage through backup channels on android. In: 20th International Conference on Engineering of Complex Computer Systems (ICECCS), pp. 60–69. IEEE (2015)
8. ML Communication: Proxydroid (2017). https://play.google.com/store/apps/details?id=org.proxydroid&hl=en. Accessed 7 Aug 2017
9. Denale, R.: U.S. census bureau news-quarterly retail e-commerce sales, 17 May 2016. https://www.census.gov/retail/mrts/www/data/pdf/ec_current.pdf. Accessed Aug 2016
10. Jones, M., Hardt, D.: The OAuth 2.0 authorization framework: Bearer token usage. Technical report (2012)
11. Josefsson, S.: The base16, base32, and base64 data encodings (2006)
12. Meola, A.: The rise of m-commerce: mobile shopping stats and trends, December 2016
13. Oberheide, J., Jahanian, F.: When mobile is harder than fixed (and vice versa): demystifying security challenges in mobile environments. In: Proceedings of the Eleventh Workshop on Mobile Computing Systems and Applications, pp. 43–48. ACM (2010)
14. Pellegrino, G., Balzarotti, D.: Toward black-box detection of logic flaws in web applications. In: 21st Annual Network and Distributed System Security Symposium (NDSS) (2014)
15. Sudhodanan, A., Armando, A., Carbone, R., Compagna, L.: Attack patterns for black-box security testing of multi-party web applications. In: 23rd Annual Network and Distributed System Security Symposium (NDSS) (2016)
16. Sun, F., Xu, L., Su, Z.: Detecting logic vulnerabilities in e-commerce applications. In: 21st Annual Network and Distributed System Security Symposium (NDSS) (2014)
17. Wang, R., Chen, S., Wang, X., Qadeer, S.: How to shop for free online-security analysis of cashier-as-a-service based web stores. In: IEEE Symposium on Security and Privacy, pp. 465–480. IEEE (2011)
18. Wang, R., Zhou, Y., Chen, S., Qadeer, S., Evans, D., Gurevich, Y.: Explicating SDKs: uncovering assumptions underlying secure authentication and authorization. In: Presented as Part of the 22nd USENIX Security Symposium (USENIX Security 13), pp. 399–314 (2013)
19. Yang, W., Zhang, Y., Li, J., Liu, H., Wang, Q., Zhang, Y., Gu, D.: Show me the money! Finding flawed implementations of third-party in-app payment in android apps (2017)
20. Ye, Q., Bai, G., Wang, K., Dong, J.S.: Formal analysis of a single sign-on protocol implementation for android. In: 20th International Conference on Engineering of Complex Computer Systems (ICECCS), pp. 90–99. IEEE (2015)

HSTS Measurement and an Enhanced Stripping Attack Against HTTPS

Xurong Li[1]([⊠]), Chunming Wu[1], Shouling Ji[1,2], Qinchen Gu[3], and Raheem Beyah[3]

[1] Zhejiang University, Hangzhou, China
{lixurong,wuchunming,sji}@zju.edu.cn
[2] Alibaba-Zhejiang University Joint Institute of Frontier Technologies, Hangzhou, China
[3] Georgia Institute of Technology, Atlanta, USA
qgu7@gatech.edu, raheem.beyah@ece.gatech.edu

Abstract. HTTPS has played a significant role in the Internet world. HSTS is deployed to ensure the proper running of HTTPS. To get a good understanding of the deployment of HSTS, we conducted an in-depth measurement of the deployment of HSTS among Alexa top 1 million sites, and investigated bookmarks and navigation panels in different browsers. We found five types of threats, including transmission errors, redirection errors, field setting errors, the auto completion mechanism in bookmarks and the embedded addresses in navigation panels. To demonstrate defects we found, we designed an enhanced HTTPS stripping attack, which was upgraded from the original *sslstrip* attack. Finally, we gave three effective suggestions to eliminate these defects. This paper exposed various risks of HTTPS and HSTS, making it possible to deploy HTTPS and HSTS in a more secure way.

Keywords: HSTS · HTTPS · Stripping attack · Security

1 Introduction

Users value security and privacy more than ever. HTTPS [1], which consists of HTTP [2] and SSL/TLS [3,4] protocols, is created to provide confidentiality and integrity of web browsing. Recently, many companies have taken measures to prompt the deployment of HTTPS. Since 2014, Google has improved rankings of the websites which deploy HTTPS [5]. Furthermore, in Chrome, the websites which do not deploy HTTPS can not even make use of geographic location and the application cache. Eventually they will result in an unsafe symbol in the address bar of the Chrome browser. In the past, obtaining and maintaining of the digital certificates would cost a lot. Therefore small companies or big companies with many domain names might not deploy HTTPS for the cause of expense. Fortunately, Let's Encrypt [6], which is a non-profit organization, provides Domain Validation (DV) certificates for free through a fully automated

© ICST Institute for Computer Sciences, Social Informatics and Telecommunications Engineering 2018
X. Lin et al. (Eds.): SecureComm 2017, LNICST 238, pp. 489–509, 2018.
https://doi.org/10.1007/978-3-319-78813-5_25

process. Apart from Let's Encrypt, several content distribution networks and cloud service providers, including CloudFlare and Amazon, provide free TLS certificates to their customers.

However, there are still many HTTP connections that exist in the Internet. To handle the mix of HTTP and HTTPS connections seamlessly is difficult for browsers due to the stripping attack. HTTPS stripping attacks have raised widespread concerns since Marlinspike put forward *sslstrip* at the blackhat conference in 2009 [7]. Attackers can intercept the communication between the target website and the client, and change all *https* into *http* in the response packets from the website. Even though this attack violates the rule which states TLS/SSL should ensure end to end security, neither the client nor the server can be aware of the attack for the reason that the packets sent from servers are still encrypted.

To defend against the stripping attack, HTTP Strict Transport Security (HSTS) [8] protocol was presented in 2012. It defines a mechanism enabling websites to declare themselves accessible only via secure connections. In consideration of the complexity of protocol and the diversity of communication platforms, we are concerned about whether the HSTS policy has been understood well. In our work, we conducted a comprehensive measurement about the deployment situation of HSTS on both PC and mobile websites. Subsequently, we investigated the bookmarks and navigation panels in browsers. We found five kinds of risks in the deployment on different platforms, which can be ignored easily by users or developers. These risks are categorized in Table 1. According to the risks we found, there is still a great probability of launching a stripping attack. But after our tests, the old *sslstrip* tool failed to attack the current websites. In order to understand the dangers of these risks well, we enhanced the original stripping attack and implemented a new HTTPS stripping attack through adding an script. Finally, we launched the attack in a simulative environment to test various famous sites, including *mail.qq.com*, *www.amazon.com*, *www.baidu.com*, *taobao.com*. The results of stripping attack were all successful based on the defects we found. The major contributions of this paper are as follows:

- We conduct an in-depth measurement of HSTS deployment on both PC websites and mobile websites, and the results show that many problems exist in the deployment, including incorrect setting methods and field setting errors. Particularly, redirection problems in mobile websites pose a risk to HSTS.
- We perform an investigation about bookmarks and navigation panels in different browsers. Through careful observation, we find that defects of the auto completion mechanism in bookmarks and the embedded addresses in navigation panels may lead to a stripping attack.
- We analyze the old *sslstrip* tool, and find it is not suitable for complicated webpages. Besides, we implement an enhanced HTTPS stripping attack.

Based on the defects in browsers and deployment of HSTS, we launch this attack in several simulative scenarios successfully[1].

- We give three kinds of useful suggestions to handle these security threats above.

Table 1. Five kinds of risks found in the measurement

Incorrect setting method	HSTS is set via HTTP
Field setting errors	Many field settings in HSTS headers do not obey the standard
Redirection problems	HSTS is not deployed correctly during redirections
Bookmark in browsers	The auto completion mechanism in bookmarks only provides HTTP
Navigation panels in browsers	The embedded addresses in navigation panels take HTTPS as HTTP

The rest of this paper is organized as follows. Section 2 provides background information about HTTPS and HSTS. Section 3 details the data collection, and introduces the data source. Section 4 gives an in-depth analysis of deployment of HSTS on both PC websites and mobile websites. Section 5 implements an enhanced HTTPS stripping attack, and demonstrates the attack. Section 6 discusses possible mitigations. Section 7 surveys related work. And finally, Sect. 8 concludes our work.

2 Overview of Web Security

HTTPS [1] was created in 2000. It describes how to use TLS to secure HTTP connections over the Internet. In this section, we will give a short introduction to HTTPS and HSTS, and talk about HSTS security and stripping attack.

2.1 HTTPS and Stripping Attack

A few years ago, HTTPS was deployed only in financial or e-commerce payment pages or login pages. However, the situation has changed over time. More and more sites began to deploy HTTPS. One of the reasons is that many studies show that the site owners should provide HTTPS service on all site pages, including whole resource files and thus encryption of part of the sites is proven unsafe [9,10]. Another reason is the emergence of free certificates and TLS accelerator. The cost to maintain HTTPS service was very expensive, which contained the

---

[1] We conducted the experiment in local computers and network, which formed an emulated environment.

cost of applying certificates, the cost of updating certificates, and the performance overhead caused by extra encryption or decryption. Fortunately, these problems have been solved in recent years. Many organizations began to provide free TLS/SSL certificates and websites greatly benefited from HTTPS.

Nonetheless, HTTPS stripping attack poses a risk to HTTPS. When users type a domain name without protocol type (HTTP or HTTPS), the default request type is HTTP rather than HTTPS. Usually, if the server provides HTTPS service, the server will give a 302 redirection after receiving an HTTP request. However, the attacker can intercept the traffic through ARP spoofing and replace all *https* with *http* in the response packet. Thus the browser will still request an HTTP website regardless of the 302 redirection. Again, the attacker can replace all *http* with *https* in the request packet. The attack is shown in Fig. 1. The communication between the attacker and the server is encrypted, but the communication between the attacker and the browser is in plaintext. This attack is called HTTPS stripping attack, which can not be detected by browsers or servers as it follows the HTTP communication protocol.

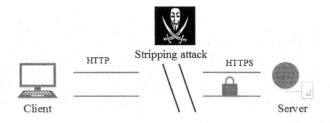

Fig. 1. Stripping attack: the attacker can intercept the traffic, establish an encrypted connection with the server, and communicate with the client via HTTP.

2.2   HSTS Protocol

To avoid the HTTPS stripping attack, HTTP Strict Transport Security (HSTS) policy was created in 2012 [8]. The policy is declared by websites via the Strict-Transport-Security HTTP response header field or by other means, such as user agent configuration. If the server wants to provide HTTPS service all the time, it will send an HSTS header to the browser. According to the information in headers, the browser will remember the domains which want to force to be visited by HTTPS. And when users send an HTTP request next time, the browser automatically converts HTTP to HTTPS in the background. The HSTS policy defines the standard of HSTS headers, and the headers mainly consist of three fields. The first is the *max-age* field, which means the expiration time and it is mandatory. The second is the optional *includeSubdomains* field, which indicates whether the HSTS policy applies to the subdomains of the domain. The last one is the *preload* field and it is also optional. This field indicates whether the domain has been permanently added into the preload list, which is maintained by browser providers. What is essential is that these headers can only be sent by HTTPS requests, hence the attacker can not arbitrarily tamper with the HSTS policy to disable it.

2.3   HSTS Security Consideration

Although HSTS policy can defend against HTTPS stripping attacks to a certain extend, many new security issues still exist. The most common one is the incorrect configuration as many developers do not have a good understanding of the HSTS policy. For instance, if the *max-age* value is set too big or too small, HSTS policy will be reused or invalid. If the *max-age* value is too big, the policy will still work all the time even though the server does not want to provide HTTPS service anymore, which may cause websites unable to be visited. If the *max-age* value is too small, HSTS policy will be invalid in a very short period of time, which can be used to launch MitM attack by attackers. Besides, misuse of *includeSubdomain* and *preload* field will be vulnerable against DoS attacks. If the servers are unaware of being added to preload list and do not provide HTTPS service, the sites will fail to be accessed. In addition, whether the subdomains have properly deployed HSTS, whether each step in the redirection is deployed correctly and whether the web application contains any insecure references to the web application server are all problems concerned. Based on these considerations, we decide to conduct an in-depth measurement about HSTS deployment.

3   Data Collection

We used Python as the programming language in the whole experiment and we rewrote the *urllib2* library so that it could meet our requirements. Not only did we use *urllib2* to send HTTP or HTTPS requests, but also did we record each HSTS information in the event of redirection. First, we surveyed *www* subdomains of top 1 million sites [11] with PC user-agent[2]. The reason we chose this user-agent was that Chrome was the main advocate of HSTS. We sent both HTTP and HTTPS requests for the same domain name and recorded the response packets in each redirection. Then we sent the same requests to 1 million sites, except that mobile user-agent[3] was used instead. We repeated this process for three times to reduce the influence caused by network performance. In total, we sent out 1 million HTTP requests and 1 million HTTPS requests (like *http://www.example, https://www.example*[4]). Finally, we successfully visited 937,430 sites with HTTP requests and 631,833 sites with HTTPS requests, respectively, using PC user-agent. For mobile-agent, the number of successfully accessed sites is 936,268 and 635,041, respectively. Because of several sites which

---

[2] Mozilla/5.0 (Windows NT 10.0; WOW64) AppleWebKit/537.36 (KHTML, like Gecko) Chrome/54.0.2840.59 Safari/537.36.

[3] Mozilla/5.0 (Linux; Android 5.0; SM-G900P Build/LRX21T) AppleWebKit/537.36 (KHTML, like Gecko) Chrome/55.0.2883.95 Mobile Safari/537.36.

[4] Here *example* refers to a domain name.

failed to respond, the number of responses is less than that of requests. As for HTTPS requests, many servers neither provided HTTPS service, nor provided a 302 redirection after receiving an HTTPS request. Based on these facts, many websites could not be visited when we sent an HTTPS request directly. All experiments were conducted in February 2017 and websites may adopt different policies over time.

4   Current Deployment Measurement

There are two ways to deploy HSTS policy. The first one is preload list, which is inserted into the browsers, and the other is dynamic HSTS, which is deployed by HTTP header. Kranch and Bonneau [12] has studied the preload list carefully. Therefore in this paper, we point out several problems about preload list which was not found in their work. What should be emphasized is that our work is completely different from Kranch's. We explain the reason why the maintenance of preload list is risky. Besides, we first conduct the measurement on mobile sites and analyze the redirections problems in detail. Moreover, we list the specific field setting errors and study the deployment in various browsers.

4.1   Preloaded HSTS

If domain has been added into the preload list, the browser will automatically convert HTTP requests for the domain to HTTPS requests in the background. We discovered a few new problems in preload list. The first one was sites added into the preload list do not send HSTS header. Sites with preload list need to set HSTS header as well since not all browsers support preload list. Users would be hijacked easily when they visit these sites on browsers which do not support preload list.

The maintenance of preload list is a hidden risk as well. Google has provided a website [13], which is used to submit domains for inclusion in Chrome's HTTP Strict Transport Security (HSTS) preload list. However, the requirements of submission are very strict and the sites must satisfy all requirements. If a site has been added into preload list before, but later it does not satisfy all requirements anymore, Chrome will delete it from preload list without notification [14]. As a website owner, one will not be visiting the HSTS preload page every week so the site may just be removed from the preload list without warning and the owner may not even notice it until many months later. Moreover, requirements for preload list are always changing. The website's owner has to pay attention to the state of preload list all the time.

Last but not least, sites in preload list have many setting errors and incorrect deployments [14]. For example, many redirections occur when we visit the HTTPS sites, but HSTS is not properly deployed in each event of the redirections. Not all subdomains support HTTPS and many HSTS headers do not contain *preload* or *includeSubdomain* field.

4.2 Alexa Top Million Websites with Dynamic HSTS

We wanted to know if the redirection was different across different platforms, so we conducted the test on both PC and mobile clients. In the rest of the paper, we use PC sites to mean the visit to the websites with PC user-agent, and use mobile sites to mean the visit to the websites with mobile user-agent.

Table 2. Successful responses of 1 million requests

Request type	HTTPS responses	HTTP responses	Total
PC-HTTP	170,883	766,547	937,430
PC-HTTPS	529,555	102,278	631,833
Mobile-HTTP	171,171	765,097	936,268
Mobile-HTTPS	525,724	109,317	635,041

The Overall Data Distribution. The results of all responses summarized in Table 2. As mentioned in Table 2, we got 937,430 PC responses and 936,268 mobile responses through the HTTP requests, and got 631833 PC responses and 635,041 mobile responses through the HTTPS requests. According to the results, we can know that many sites support both HTTP and HTTPS. Most PC sites (81.8%) and mobile sites (81.7%) still supported HTTP. We think the main reason is that many users are still using outdated browsers or systems, which do not support HTTPS well. Hence, website owners would like to remain compatible with these users' web clients and they responded to both HTTP requests and HTTPS requests. As for HTTPS requests, while more than half of the sites supported direct HTTPS access, a number of sites which did not support HTTPS failed to redirect HTTPS requests to HTTP sites. These websites may be vulnerable to DoS attack if the browsers keep sending HTTPS requests. Consequently, we analyzed the deployment of dynamic HSTS based on the results of responses. We counted the HSTS settings according to the HTTP 200 OK headers in Table 3.

Table 3. HSTS header setting

Request type	Sites with HSTS header
PC-HTTP	36,788 (3.9%)
PC-HTTPS	43,301 (6.9%)
Mobile-HTTP	36,643 (3.9%)
Mobile-HTTPS	43,353 (6.8%)

Two years ago, however, Kranch [12] found just 12,593 sites which attempted to send an HSTS header. This may imply an increasing number of sites realized the significance of HSTS and decided to deploy it. We clearly see the results are different for HTTP and HTTPS requests. Further analysis shows that 8296 PC sites deployed HSTS for HTTPS requests but not for HTTP requests. Particularly, when we visited the 8296 PC sites with HTTP requests, we got 8213 HTTP webpages and 83 HTTPS webpages. This is an interesting phenomenon, since the 8213 PC sites may support both HTTP and HTTPS to stay compatible with more users, but the 83 PC sites redirected HTTP requests to HTTPS requests without HSTS header, which may be a threat. Furthermore, we analyzed the distribution of HSTS deployments with Alexa ranking in Table 4.

Table 4. Alexa ranking and sites with HSTS

Request type	Top10	Top100	Top1W	Top10W	Top100W
PC-HTTP	7	30	814	5,607	36,778
PC-HTTPS	8	33	866	6,266	43,301
Mobile-HTTP	8	31	812	5,589	36,643
Mobile-HTTPS	8	31	855	6,242	43,353

From Table 4, we can learn the top websites attached great importance to the deployment of HSTS. More specifically, among the top 10 websites, *www.qq.com*, which is a news site, only supports HTTP requests, and *www.google.co.in* supports HTTPS but does not deploy HSTS. To our surprise, we found that *www.baidu.com* (PC site) took different strategies according to different IPs. When we sent HTTP request to *www.baidu.com* from the US, we received the response without HTTPS deployment, while the response came with HSTS deployment in China.

Incorrect Setting Method. RFC6797 [8] defines that HSTS can not be set via HTTP, thus we counted the invalid settings in Table 5.

Table 5. Invalid HSTS setting via HTTP

Request type	PC-HTTP	PC-HTTPS	Mobile-HTTP	Mobile-HTTPS
Sites of invalid HSTS setting	4,299	533	4,211	566

In order to understand the situation of invalid settings better, we have checked the details of settings. 525 PC sites sent HSTS header for both HTTP requests and HTTPS requests via HTTP, which means they only provided HTTP service but deployed HSTS. Particularly, 8 PC sites sent HTTP pages without HSTS for HTTP requests, and redirected HTTPS requests to HTTP requests of another domain, and that domain would send an HTTP page with HSTS header. For example, for *www.andreicismaru.ro*, we would get normal HTTP page without HSTS header for HTTP request, but also HTTP page with HSTS header from *http://cetin.ro/* after we sent HTTPS request to *www.andreicismaru.ro*. However, if they only provided HTTP service, HSTS policy would be invalid. These sites' owners may have a misconception of the HSTS policy. Namely, HSTS policy does not provide confidentiality of traffic, it just ensures the correct implementation of the HTTPS.

Errors of HSTS Field Settings. In these detected HSTS headers, we found various errors that were contrary to the standard protocol. The protocol points out that *max-age* is a required field but the results showed that both mobile sites and PC sites have several *max-age* setting errors. We took PC websites as an example to avoid duplication.

First, we found errors in headers which were not properly including *max-age*=[5]. For instance, *www.lovdata.no* set the field to *maxage=31,536,000*, which missed the symbol -. *www.mijn-econnect.nl*, *www.xn—-7sbnackuskv0m.xn-p1ai* and *www.bottomline.com* all missed the symbol =.

And *www.chrcitadelle.be* set the field to a single number, like *86,400*.

Then, we checked the headers with *max-age=*. Unfortunately, many formal errors exist and we show them in Table 6. Following this, we found a lot of *max-age* values were not reasonable. If the value is extremely small, HSTS policy will soon expire. To our surprise, 1,484 sites deploy HSTS with *max-age=0*, which means the HSTS policy is invalid. But the big value is not reasonable as well, owing to the fact that sites need to update HSTS policy timely if HTTPS service changes. However, *www.cloudup.com* set the filed to*max-age=100,000,000,000*, and *www.aptopnews.com* set the field to *max-age=9,223,372,036,854,775,807*. Both of them are more than 1,000 years.

Redirection Problems. Usually, lots of redirections exist during our visit to many sites. If HSTS deployment in redirections is incorrect, the final HSTS is equally invalid. We counted the redirection times of the sites where HSTS was deployed in Table 7.

Here we counted every client request until the final visit succeeded. It can be seen from Table 7, most sites who deployed HSTS did not have redirections for HTTPS requests. However, one or more redirections occurred when handling HTTP requests. If the redirections between HTTP and HTTPS did not deal with HSTS deployments well, the attack will be equally easy despite the existence of HSTS. We found that 929 PC sites did not fully deploy HSTS during redirection from HTTP to HTTPS, and the number for mobile sites is 1106. In order to understand the distinction better, we analyzed the detail of redirections. A fact we can not overlook is that many sites provided different domains for mobile requests and PC requests, like *https://m.example* and

---

[5] *max-age=* is the standard format which is defined by RFC document.

Table 6. Examples of *max-age=* errors

max-age=expireTime
%E2%80%9Cmax-age=31536000%E2%80%B3
xa8xb9max-age=31536000xa8xb9xb3xacN
max-age=31536000%E2%80%9D
max-age="157680000"
max-age="10368000"
max-age=<31536000>
max-age=31536eee
max-age=31556926?
xa8xb9max-age=31536000?
x81gmax-age=31536000x81
max-age=
max-age=0.000001

Table 7. Redirection times of sites with HSTS header

Request type	Redirection times			
	0	1	2	≥3
PC-HTTP	7.9%	60.7%	27.0%	4.4%
PC-HTTPS	57.8%	34.6%	6.0 %	1.6%
Mobile-HTTP	7.5%	58.3%	28.7%	5.5%
Mobile-HTTPS	55.6%	35.6%	6.8%	2%

https://www.example. However, many mobile servers just deployed HSTS in the response of *https://m.example* but not *https://www.example*. In the end, if we still send HTTP requests of *www.example*, HSTS policy would not work. We show this process in Fig. 2. Besides, the same situation occurred when the *www* subdomain did not exist.

Specifically, 12 mobile sites did not deploy HSTS in the first response to *https://m.example*. Moreover, 110 sites first gave a response of *http://m.example*, and then redirected to *https://m.example* with HSTS headers. But it was not enough, for the attacker can hijack the request of HTTP. It needs to be emphasized that sites should deploy HSTS in the first response after requesting domain A, if they want to provide a redirection from domain A to domain B.

4.3 Two Ubiquitous Overlooks

Bookmarks in Browsers. Although many sites have already known the significance of HSTS policy, there are still serious problems as described above. In this section, we investigate two kinds of phenomenas that were easily overlooked. Bookmarks in browsers are often used to record a website that users would like to visit later. Sometimes users add the current page being visited to bookmarks, so the scheme attributes will be preserved. However, if users manually type in

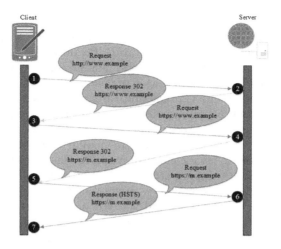

Fig. 2. Mobile sites redirection problem: server gives two redirections without HSTS when handling HTTP request from mobile browser in step ❶~❺, and only deploys HSTS in the response of mobile domain in step ❻~❼.

the URL, they may forget to enter the scheme part. The browsers will add the URL with the HTTP prefix automatically, which means that the browser will send an HTTP request first when the users click the bookmark. In addition, we have learned that mobile devices' bookmarks keep in sync with Safari browser for iOS users. If there are too many redirections before the final visit to the HTTPS site, there will be a threat. We have checked different browsers (Chrome, Firefox, Safari) and found the same threat. Bookmarks did not have a mechanism to check these URLs. Google showed the popular desktop browsers [15] and we checked the bookmarks and navigation panels of these browsers. Opera, Chrome, Edge, and Firefox all support adding URL manually and add the HTTP prefix by default. However, users cannot insert URLs into IE11 and Safari manually. The users can only add the sites which they are visiting in these two browsers.

Navigation Panels in Browsers. Almost all of the browsers' home pages include navigation panels, and websites offer navigation panels services as well. Unfortunately, after our in-depth investigation, we have found that there is an error in the built-in URL of the navigation site. Many sites which only support HTTPS are inserted with HTTP in navigation pages. Users tend to trust the address of navigation panels and click it instead of typing address in address bar. Therefore, browsers will send HTTP requests for these sites even they support HTTPS and it may contain a threat according to the risks mentioned above. In the next section we will introduce an enhanced HTTPS attack based on the risks in these findings.

5   An Enhanced HTTPS Stripping Attack

HSTS allows a web site to opt in to be HTTPS only. For a site with HSTS, a browser will only send HTTPS requests, eliminating the window of insecurity. Apart from this, HSTS maintains a preload list, which is hard coded into browsers and is supported by Chrome and Firefox. However, very few websites have joined the list, and many have chosen to implement dynamical HSTS. The emergence of HSTS can avoid stripping attacks to a great extent, but we have discovered the flaws in the HSTS deployment and browsers. Based on these defects, HTTPS stripping attack can still work. In this section, we will analyze the reason why original stripping attack tool *sslstrip*, which was developed by Marlinspike [7], does not work in new environment. Then, we implement an enhanced HTTPS stripping attack and verify it on famous sites. We only want to prove that HTTPS can be downgraded easily based on the defects.

5.1   Original Sslstrip and Inspiration

Plenty of attacking tools have integrated *sslstrip*, such as *bettercap* [16], *mitmf* [17]. However, through our tests of various websites, we have found that the success rate of *sslstrip* was very low. To learn the reason in detail, we studied the principles of *sslstrip*. After hijacking the traffic, *sslstrip* will search the *https* strings, and replace all *https* with *http* in traffic. Then we analyzed the source code of webpages and found the answer. Old webpages are usually constituted of static text, and the replacement of *https* is simple. However, the web pages have become more complicated over time, and new webpages contain a large number of dynamic elements. Besides, many take new methods to detect stripping attack, like the *location* in srcipts, but *sslstrip* does not have any solution to handle these scripts. Moreover, the time consumption of replacement in *sslstrip* is very large for the reason that *sslstrip* has to wait for all packets and search the target strings. If too much time has been spent on replacement, the connection will fail. After our tests, we found that the users can not visit the most webpages when *sslstrip* works, indicating that the original *sslstrip* is not suitable for the current web pages.

Researchers have pointed out that front-end hijacking is an effective method in the blog [18]. So in this section, we will take a front-end approach to perform stripping attacks according to the ideas mentioned in the blog. The main principle is derived from this blog, but we have improved the method. The differences between our work and the blog are three-folds: First, we handle the *location* field, which can detect the stripping attack. We modify the *location* field in the script and make it invalid. Second, we handle secure cookie. Secure cookie must be deleted from response headers so that we can get plenty of privacy information. Finally, we do a number of tests to verify the effectiveness of the attack. The tests are done on different browsers and famous websites. In our attack, XSS skill is used, but it does not mean that the attacker can inject any content all the time. If we do not downgrade the HTTPS scheme, the following traffic will be encrypted. Actually, we only want to show the possibility of HTTPS being downgraded based on the defects we find. Designing a new attack tool is not our goal.

5.2   Principles of Enhanced Stripping Attack

Precondition of Attack. What needs to be emphasized is that our attack will be invalid if the first request is an HTTPS request. Also, if the domain has been added to the HSTS preload list, our attack will not work. However, based on our previous sections, it is not difficult for us to get HTTP request first. We summarize the reasons below:

- Firstly, the preload list is so short that it can not include all websites and many browsers still did not support preload list.
- Secondly, many sites only support HTTPS service but not HSTS, so the results will be HTTP requests first if the user type the domain name in address bar without scheme.
- Thirdly, if the users have not visited the site, the first request is still the HTTP request due to the fact that HSTS policy has not worked yet.
- Fourthly, many redirection problems occur during HSTS deployment according to our study. Besides, a mix of HTTP and HTTPS connections exists in plenty of websites. Both of them responded to the HTTP request.
- Finally, the records in bookmarks and navigations panels remembered the HTTP request or old domain name.

Therefore, even the sites provided HTTPS service and deployed HSTS policy, it was not very difficult for the attacker to get HTTP request first. Then the attacker must act as a proxy in our attack. It was easy for the attacker to get traffic data by using ARP spoofing or DNS spoofing tools in local area network or WiFi and the attack is carried out in the process of counterfeiting proxy. What should be noted is that our attack is not a perfect attack tool for all webpages. Because our goal is to show the insecurity of incorrect deployment. Hence, our attack mainly focuses on the common web structures.

Detailed Implementation. The whole idea of attack is ingenious to injecting a JavaScript script at the beginning of the traffic. If users do not click the *https* links, the links will not be effective. Therefore, the key is to replace the link at the moment of the click. *DOM-3-Event* is an event capture mechanism, which can be used to capture the global click event. If the clicks fall on the *https* hyperlink, we intercept them and change *https* to *http* and the time cost is very small.

As for form submission, we can listen to the *submit* instead of *click*, and change the *href* to *action*. For frame pages, this is a problem. We only downgrade the main page into HTTP version, but the frame address is still the original, which will cause a cross domain problem for the different protocols. We use *Content Security Policy* to avoid the HTTPS framework page. In the response from our proxy, we added the following HTTP header.

CSP policy

```
Content-Security-Policy: default-src *
data: 'unsafe-inline' 'unsafe-eval';
frame-src http://*
```

'*unsafe-inline*' allows the page to load inline resource, '*unsafe-eval*' allows the page to load dynamic JS code, and *frame-src* specifies the frame's load policy. However, after our test, we found that many websites use script, namely, the *location* attribute of the browser [19], to detect whether the site provides HTTPS protocol. Here we take *mail.qq.com* for example. The *mail.qq.com location* program is showed below.

mail.qq.com location

```
<script>
(function()
{if(location.protocol=="http:"){
document.cookie = "edition=;expires=-1;
path=/;domain=.mail.qq.com";
location.href="https://mail.qq.com";
}
})();
</script>
```

If the protocol of the site has been changed to *http*, the cookie and scheme will be changed back by *location*. Drawing on the idea of the original *sslstrip* attack, we can replace the *http* with *https* in the script in the backend proxy. We only search the *http* in scripts, thus the cost of replacement can be ignored. We first search the *location* in script and then replace the *http* with *https*. Even the protocol scheme is *http*, the jump will not occur. So the whole idea is consisted of two parts. The first one is the XSS script of front end, which listens to events and replaces *https* with *http*. The other is the proxy of back end, which can replace the *http* in *location* field to prevent the script from jumping. To launch the stripping attack successfully, we have to solve two problems, which we summarize as follows:

(1) The problem is how to let the proxy know whether the request is sent by HTTPS or HTTP. The proxy actually is a man in the middle. If it modifies the HTTPS resource, it must restore the HTTPS request to the server, otherwise the attack will be detected by the server.
(2) Many websites redirect HTTP requests to HTTPS websites through 302 redirection and have deployed HSTS. We need to forward the redirection, inject the script and delete the HSTS header.

For the first problem, we use the mark method to distinguish whether the link is replaced. When we replace the HTTPS with HTTP, we can add a mark in the modified URL at the same time. In order to hide the mark, we can choose fraudulent marks, like *utf-8*, *?zh_cn*, *?ssl*. Therefore, when the proxy handles the

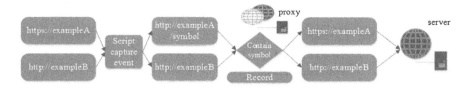

Fig. 3. Proxy mark process: first the XSS script will add a symbol into HTTPS request and HTTPS will be downgraded to HTTP. Then the proxy will change the HTTP request to HTTPS request according to the symbol and forward it to remote server. The HTTP request will be forwarded to the server directly.

URL, it will know how to take measures to forward the requests according to the mark. The proxy also need to record the *https* requests and symbols. The whole processes are described in Fig. 3. For the second problem, we must add a module in proxy to handle it. In that module, we intercept this redirection, obtain the content of redirection with HTTPS request, and finally reply the user with HTTP scheme. The response to the user will include the script and CSP policy we designed. Besides, if we find HSTS header or secure cookie field in responses from server, we delete them in proxy quickly. The redirection problem is handled in Fig. 4.

Fig. 4. Handling redirection: the proxy will forward the http request to remote server in step ❶~❷, and then establish a secure connection with the server in step ❸~❺. Next, the proxy will modify the location and inject the XSS script in the response packet. Finally, the proxy will return an HTTP page with script to the user in step ❻.

5.3   Experiment Results

In this section we demonstrate our attack against several popular websites to verify the defects we found. These websites are shown in Table 8.

Here *mail.qq.com* represents the *qq.com* due to the fact that *www.qq.com* provides HTTP service[6]. And *m.kaskus.co.id* represents mobile sites which did

---

[6] *mail.qq.com* is one of the most popular Chinese e-mail services and provides HTTPS services. Although *mail.qq.com* did not deploy HSTS, it used *location* to detect whether the current protocol is downgraded.

Table 8. Sites to test and relevant security measures

Alexa ranking	Domain	HTTPS	Dynamic HSTS	Preload list
4	www.baidu.com	Y	Y	N
6	www.amazon.com	Y	Y	Y
8	mail.qq.com	Y	N	N
12	www.taobao.com	Y	Y	N
335	m.kaskus.co.id	Y	Y	N

not deploy HSTS in the first response to *https://m.example*. We launched our attack on different scenarios and different browsers[7].

The results of attack are showed in Table 9. Bookmarks and navigation imply default HTTP requests in these mechanisms. Automatic domain means that users typed domain manually and the browser complemented a domain name automatically. These three tests were conducted on Firefox browser, which supports preload list. We show the examples of *www.taobao.com* and *www.amazon.com* in Figs. 5 and 6, which show the hijacked URLs in address bars.

Table 9. The results of new stripping attack

Domain	Scenarios			
	Bookmarks	Navigation	Automatic domain	Other browsers
www.baidu.com	Y	Y	Y	Y
www.amazon.com	N	N	N	Y
mail.qq.com	Y	Y	Y	Y
www.taobao.com	Y	Y	Y	Y
m.kaskus.co.id	Y	Y	Y	Y

According to the results, even the site has deployed HSTS, there is a possibility of being hijacked. As for the websites only provide HTTPS and did not deploy HSTS, the attack will succeed every time when users visit it with HTTP request. These websites which have deployed HSTS but were not in the preload list or did not fully deploy HSTS during the redirection process, will be in danger as well. And the websites in the preload list would be hijacked in the browser that did not support preload list.

---

[7] In this test, other browsers means those which did not support preload list, like UC browser, Sogou browser.

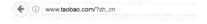

Fig. 5. taobao.com   **Fig. 6.** amazon.com

6   Discussion

To deploy HTTPS and HSTS in a more secure way, we must take measures from both ends.

6.1   Browser/User

Browsers should provide a mechanism which can check the scheme of domain. If the response of the real site is contrary to the check, the browser should give a strict warning and it can prompt the user to manually enter the URL with scheme so as to avoid be hijacked. A preload list is not enough and it is so strict that many websites did not meet the requirements. Many serious problems occur in preload list, so the browsers vendors have to adapt the list to cope with the dynamic change. The list should be accepted by more browsers. Apart from these, active defense should be considered by browsers. Browsers should actively establish a secure bookmark and navigation mechanism. They can not allow users to modify the bookmarks casually, which has security risks. The browsers should check whether the scheme in the bookmark has changed and the navigation in browsers should be updated in time to avoid outdated URL.

As for users, we strongly recommend that users observe the scheme carefully when adding a bookmark. Most of times users should not tend to click the navigation links on unfamous sites, owing to the deceptive attack, particularly financial and other sensitive sites, like online banking, electronic commerce. Users should go to the HTTPS version of the site from users' machine while using a secure network, and then bookmark that page. Besides, always open the site by accessing the bookmark whenever users want to visit that page. At the same time, users should pay attention to the jumps from HTTPS to HTTP or vice versa. It will do great help for users to install the software plugins, like HTTPS Everywhere or ForceTLS, which may reduce the occurrence of stripping attack.

6.2   Server/Website

As for sites owners, first, they should enable SSL site wide and use HTTPS as much as possible. Then the sites should enable HSTS policy and Cert Pinning, but also be careful when dealing with each step of process, i.e., sites should better deploy HSTS in every packet of HTTPS response. In order to let HTTPS and HSTS work better, the sites should enable secure cookies and use mixed content in HTTPS pages as less as possible. Ensure that all cookies are served with the secure attribute, so that user's browsers will only send those cookies back over SSL-protected connections and never disclose them over any non-SSL links. Finally, the sites should use HTTPS everywhere and join the preload list as soon as possible.

7   Related Work

7.1   HTTPS Security

Many researchers studied about HTTPS security in recent years and most focused on TLS/SSL security. Client-end TLS software and non-browser software have defects on implementation and the root causes of these vulnerabilities are badly designed APIs of SSL implementations or negligence [20,21]. Great security threats are present in SSL proxys as well [10,20,22], where proxy can break the end to end security. Another thing that affects SSL security is the certificate. Many studies were dedicated to solve the problems of certificate management, the private key management and certificate validity [23,24]. There are several evaluations of large-scale SSL deployments problems [25,26]. Warnings from browsers are pivotal for users to avoid attacks, so several researchers have investigated the effectiveness of warnings [27,28]. This paper is different from them and we mainly focus on the threat of HTTPS stripping attack.

7.2   HSTS Security

HSTS was born to ensure that HTTPS performs better. However, many flaws exist in deployment of HSTS as well. Researchers have found that even though these protocols are implemented, bad practices prevent them from actually providing the additional security they are expected to provide [29]. They studied the implementations of HSTS in Firefox, Chrome and IE, and found several potential attack scenarios. Kranch and Bonneau [12] have done a measurement about HSTS and HPKP policy. They mainly found errors for sites with HSTS headers and analyzed the security of cookies. Our work is largely distinct from them. We focused on redirection problems and carried on the detailed classification to the setting errors. Besides, we have done the experiments on mobile platforms and have found defects in bookmarks and navigations panels.

7.3   Stripping Attack Studies

Since Marlinspike et al. [7] published the *sslsttrip* attack, researchers have been working on it for years. To overcome *sslstrip* attacks, many schemes have been proposed. ForceHTTPS [30] is a simple browser security mechanism that web sites or users can use to opt in to stricter error processing, but it needs users to install extra plugins. Zhao et al. [31] presented a new defense scheme according to secure cookie as well. However, these defense schemes can only succeed under the specific environment, which can not defend against the attack we implemented perfectly. In our paper, we have strengthened the previous *sslstrip* attack and successfully launched the enhanced stripping attack to various websites in simulated scenarios.

8   Conclusion

In this paper, we have found many sites owner or developers did not understand the HSTS policy well. We have exposed that a lot of top-ranking sites had incorrect deployment and redirection problems. Many websites did deploy HSTS policy, but several redirections occurred when we visited them. Unfortunately, the HSTS is not fully deployed during the redirections, still left the possibility of being attacked. In addition, lots of instructions field setting errors were found by us. Moreover, schemes in bookmarks and navigation are forgotten by users easily. After our investigation, we found that the default HTTP supplementation mode of bookmarks has a security problem and the default address in the navigation is at risk of being downgraded as well. To test the risk of these defects, we designed an enhanced HTTPS stripping attack, which strengthened the previous *sslstrip* attack. The success rate is high based on the pitfalls we found.

In summation, our paper can give some guidance to the sites who want to deploy HSTS correctly. Besides, due to the fact that the defects we found contribute to the stripping attack, our work is able to help users to reduce the risks of being attacked. We hope our research enables HTTPS and HSTS protocol to provide more efficient service and make users' information more safe compared with now.

Acknowledgements. This work was partly supported by the National Key Research and Development Program of China under No. 2016YFB0800102 and 2016YFB0800201, the National High Technology Research and Development Program of China under No. 2015AA015602 and 2015AA016103, the Key Research and Development Program of Zhejiang Province under No. 2017C01064 and 2017C01055, the Fundamental Research Funds for the Central Universities, the NSFC under No. 61772466, the Alibaba-Zhejiang University Joint Research Institute for Frontier Technologies (A.Z.F.T.) under Program No. XT622017000118, and the CCF-Tencent Open Research Fund under No. AGR20160109.

References

1. Rescorla, E.: HTTP over TLS (2000)
2. Berners-Lee, T., Fielding, R., Frystyk, H.: "RFC 1945: hypertext transfer protocol? HTTP/1.0, May 1996." Status: INFORMATIONAL 61 (2005)
3. Freier, A., Karlton, P., Kocher, P.: The secure sockets layer (SSL) protocol version 3.0 (2011)
4. Dierks, T., Rescorla, E.: "RFC 5246: the transport layer security (TLS) protocol." The Internet Engineering Task Force (2008)
5. Google Transparency Report. https://www.google.com/transparencyreport/https/?hl=zh-CN
6. Let's Encrypt. https://letsencrypt.org
7. Moixe, M.: New tricks for defeating SSL in practice. Technical report, BlackHat Conference, USA (2009)

8. Hodges, J., Jackson, C., Barth, A.: "RFC 6797: HTTP strict transport security (HSTS)". IETF (2010). https://tools.ietf.org/html/rfc6797
9. Sivakorn, S., Polakis, I., Keromytis, A.D.: The cracked cookie jar: HTTP cookie hijacking and the exposure of private information. In: 2016 IEEE Symposium on Security and Privacy (SP), pp. 724–742. IEEE Press (2016)
10. Chen, S., et al.: Pretty-bad-proxy: an overlooked adversary in browsers' HTTPS deployments. In: 2009 30th IEEE Symposium on Security and Privacy, pp. 347–359. IEEE Press (2009)
11. Extract DNSSEC support statistics for the top 1 million hosts of the Alexa database. https://github.com/jefmathiot/dnssec-stats
12. Kranch, M., Bonneau, J.: Upgrading HTTPS in mid-air: an empirical study of strict transport security and key pinning. In: NDSS (2015)
13. HSTS Preload List Submission. https://hstspreload.appspot.com
14. Run a daily status scan of the official preload list. http://github.com/chromium/hstspreload.org/issues/35
15. Desktop Browser Market Share. https://www.netmarketshare.com/browser-market-share.aspx?qprid=0qpcustomd=0
16. Bettercap. https://www.bettercap.org
17. Framework for Man-In-The-Middle attacks. https://github.com/byt3bl33d3r/MITMf
18. SSL Frontend hijack. https://www.cnblogs.com/index-html/p/ssl-frontend-hijack.html
19. HTML5. https://www.w3.org/TR/2014/REC-html5-20141028/browsers.html#window
20. de Carnavalet, X.C., Mannan, M.: Killed by proxy: analyzing client-end TLS interception software. In: Network and Distributed System Security Symposium (NDSS 2016), San Diego, CA, USA (2016)
21. Georgiev, M., et al.: The most dangerous code in the world: validating SSL certificates in non-browser software. In: Proceedings of the 2012 ACM Conference on Computer and Communications Security, pp. 38–49. ACM (2012)
22. Soghoian, C., Stamm, S.: Certified lies: detecting and defeating government interception attacks against SSL (short paper). In: Danezis, G. (ed.) FC 2011. LNCS, vol. 7035, pp. 250–259. Springer, Heidelberg (2012). https://doi.org/10.1007/978-3-642-27576-0_20
23. Szalachowski, P., Matsumoto, S., Perrig, A.: PoliCert: secure and flexible TLS certificate management. In: Proceedings of the 2014 ACM SIGSAC Conference on Computer and Communications Security, pp. 406–417. ACM (2014)
24. Cangialosi, F., et al.: Measurement and analysis of private key sharing in the https ecosystem. In: Proceedings of the 2016 ACM SIGSAC Conference on Computer and Communications Security, pp. 628–640. ACM (2016)
25. Bates, A., et al.: Forced perspectives: evaluating an SSL trust enhancement at scale. In: Proceedings of the 2014 Conference on Internet Measurement Conference, pp. 503–510. ACM (2014)
26. Holz, R., et al.: The SSL landscape: a thorough analysis of the x. 509 PKI using active and passive measurements. In: Proceedings of the 2011 ACM SIGCOMM Conference on Internet Measurement Conference, pp. 427–444. ACM (2011)
27. Sunshine, J., et al.: Crying wolf: an empirical study of SSL warning effectiveness. In: USENIX Security Symposium, pp. 399–416 (2009)
28. Akhawe, D., Felt, A.P.: Alice in Warningland: a large-scale field study of browser security warning effectiveness. In: Usenix Security, pp. 257–272 (2013)

29. de los Santos, S., Torrano, C., Rubio, Y., Brezo, F.: Implementation state of HSTS and HPKP in both browsers and servers. In: Foresti, S., Persiano, G. (eds.) CANS 2016. LNCS, vol. 10052, pp. 192–207. Springer, Cham (2016). https://doi.org/10. 1007/978-3-319-48965-0_12

30. Jackson, F., Barth, A.: Protecting high-security web sites from network attacks. In: Proceedings of the 17th International World Wide Web Conference (WWW 2008) (2008)

31. Zhao, S., Yang, W., Wang, D., Qiu, W.: A new scheme with secure cookie against SSLstrip attack. In: Wang, F.L., Lei, J., Gong, Z., Luo, X. (eds.) WISM 2012. LNCS, vol. 7529, pp. 214–221. Springer, Heidelberg (2012). https://doi.org/10. 1007/978-3-642-33469-6_30

Defining and Detecting Environment Discrimination in Android Apps

Yunfeng Hong[1](✉), Yongjian Hu[2], Chun-Ming Lai[1], S. Felix Wu[1],
Iulian Neamtiu[3], Patrick McDaniel[4], Paul Yu[5], Hasan Cam[5],
and Gail-Joon Ahn[6]

[1] University of California, Davis, USA
{yfhong,cmlai,sfwu}@ucdavis.edu
[2] University of California, Riverside, USA
yhu009@cs.ucr.edu
[3] New Jersey Institute of Technology, Newark, USA
iulian.neamtiu@njit.edu
[4] Pennsylvania State University, State College, USA
mcdaniel@cse.psu.edu
[5] U.S. Army Research Laboratory, Maryland, USA
{paul.l.yu.civ,hasan.cam.civ}@mail.mil
[6] Arizona State University, Tempe, USA
Gail-Joon.Ahn@asu.edu

Abstract. Environment discrimination—a program behaving differently on different platforms—is used in many contexts. For example, malware can use environment discrimination to thwart detection attempts: as malware detectors employ automated dynamic analysis while running the potentially malicious program in a virtualized environment, the malware author can make the program virtual environment-aware so the malware turns off the nefarious behavior when it is running in a virtualized environment. Therefore, an approach for detecting environment discrimination can help security researchers and practitioners better understand the behavior of, and consequently counter, malware. In this paper we formally define environment discrimination, and propose an approach based on abstract traces and symbolic execution to detect discrimination in Android apps. Furthermore, our approach discovers what API calls expose the environment information to malware, which is a valuable reference for virtualization developers to improve their products. We also apply our approach to the real malware and third-party-researcher designed benchmark apps. The result shows that the algorithm and framework we proposed achieves 97% accuracy.

Keywords: Android · Malware detection
Environment discrimination

1 Introduction

In the past decade, the smartphone has replaced the PC as the most frequently-used Internet access device [1]. Along with the rising popularity of mobile devices,

© ICST Institute for Computer Sciences, Social Informatics and Telecommunications Engineering 2018
X. Lin et al. (Eds.): SecureComm 2017, LNICST 238, pp. 510–529, 2018.
https://doi.org/10.1007/978-3-319-78813-5_26

malware is also rapidly growing in terms of both quantity and sophistication. For example, reports show that in the first quarter of 2017, 8,400 new malware samples were discovered every day [2], which results in the high demanding of malware detection and analysis. Dynamic analysis is a popular approach for analyzing application behaviors, and is usually deployed on virtual environments for performance and security reasons. However, malware authors are only interested in "real" phones used by actual customers. In contrast to the desktop/server platform, smartphone sandboxes have very limited use on mobile platforms (for both application development and dynamic analysis) because sensors which drive app behavior (such as GPS, camera, microphone) have to be mocked, which complicates development and analysis [3]. Thus, malware authors intentionally develop malware that detects the running environment and adjust malware behavior accordingly, as shown in Fig. 1, when running on virtual environments, "smart" malware hides its suspicious behavior to evade dynamic analysis, and such behavior will be exposed when running on a real device. Some imparities between real devices and virtual machines such as CPU performance and battery consumption are difficult to be eliminated. Furthermore, it is infeasible to enumerate all heuristics that differentiate real devices and virtual machines. Thus, simple mitigation approach such as blacklist filtering is not capable to solve the problem, and a more fundamental and comprehensive approach is required to mitigate environment discrimination in Android applications.

Environment discrimination has been used in many other fields, besides dynamic analysis evasion. For example, some smartphone manufacturers detect when certain benchmarks are running and drive the CPU to maximum power in order to reach an edge in their benchmark ratings [4–6]. In another example from the automotive world, in certain Volkswagen models, the diesel engine controller software detects whether the car is running on a test bench, and changes engine parameters accordingly to subvert emission tests [7].

This paper has three major contributions: First, we formally define environment discrimination by leveraging the concepts of abstract specification and trace assertion [8–10]. Secondly, our work use these abstractions to construct an algorithm that is able to detect both already-known and unknown discriminating behaviors in linear time. Finally, by combining trace assertion with symbolic execution, our algorithm efficiently discovers the set of API calls that trigger environment discrimination: instead of exploring a potentially infinite set of execution paths as a static approach would do, our technique bounds the exploration space to permit efficient analysis: $O(n)$, where n is the size of the trace.

The evaluation result shows that the detection accuracy is 100% when the discrimination is executed during testing, and 97% for all test cases. We also show that the environment discrimination technique is not widely employed in the real malware, but as emulation becomes more and more common over time, we will see more discrimination behaviors in the future.

Note that a program discriminating the environment does not necessarily imply malicious intent. Benign programs can behave differently in different environment as well. For example, Google Maps behaves differently in a virtual

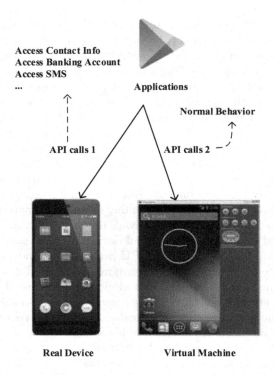

Fig. 1. Example of an application discriminating between virtual machine and real device to evade dynamic analysis.

environment compared to a real device due to lack of GPS in a virtual setting. Accordingly, this paper focuses on detecting environment discrimination, e.g., as employed by malware, but we do not attempt to detect malicious behavior per se.

The rest of this paper is organized as follow: Sect. 2 gives the definition of environment discrimination and the algorithm in theory. The application of definition and algorithm is illustrated in Sect. 3. Section 4 discusses the time complexity and robustness of our algorithm. Sects. 5 and 6 present related work and conclude the paper, respectively.

2   Definition of Environment Discrimination

In this section, we first explain the concept of trace equivalence and trace abstraction, and then discuss the relevance of the two concepts in defining environment discrimination. Finally, we describe symbolic execution against a trace for finding discriminating contributors.

This section proposes the theoretical background of the environment discrimination detection of Android app in Sect. 3. However, readers who do not want to dive into theory may directly jump to Sect. 3 without concern.

2.1 Trace Equivalence

A trace of a program, which is a description of a sequence of calls on functions starting with the program in initial state, consists of *O-functions* and *V-functions* [8]. *V-functions* return values that give information about parts of program, while *O-functions* only change internal data. To begin, we formalize function calls F and traces T.

A function call F consists of its name, parameter list, and return values. Return values are always empty in *O-functions*. Two calls, F_1 and F_2, are equivalent if and only if all three parts are exactly the same (denoted as $F_1 \equiv F_2$; we will describe this check in detail in Sect. 2.2). A trace T is described by the following syntax:

$$
\begin{aligned}
<T> \quad &:: = \{<subtrace>\}.<tailtrace> \\
<subtrace> \quad &:: = \{<O-function>\}.<V-function> \\
<tailtrace> \quad &:: = \{<O-function>\}
\end{aligned}
$$

$\{*\}$ *represents any number of occurrences of* $*$.

F_{ijk} is the kth function call in j^{th} subtrace in i^{th} trace. The definition of the size of trace T is the number of subtraces and tailtrace, denoted as $|T|$. S is a *subtrace*.

A trace T is *legal*, denoted $\lambda(T)$, if the functions in T will not result in a trap. Note that an empty trace is always legal ($\lambda(\_) = true$); and the prefix of any legal trace is always legal, i.e., $\lambda(T.S) = true => \lambda(T) = true$.

If $\lambda(T.X) = true$, and X is a syntactically correct *V-function* call, $V(T.X)$ describes the value returned by X after the execution of T.

Trace specification consists of syntax and semantics. The syntax provides the name, parameter types and return value types of each function. The semantics comprises of three types of assertions: (1) *legality assertions* which describe how to call functions that will not result in a trap; (2) *equivalence assertions* which specify a set of equivalence relations in traces; and (3) *V-function assertions* expressed in terms of values returned by *V-functions*.

We now exemplify these trace concepts by providing Bartussek and Parnas [8] integer stack specification.

Syntax
    $PUSH : <integer> \times <stack> \rightarrow <stack>$
    $POP : P <stack> \rightarrow <stack>$
    $TOP : <stack> \rightarrow <integer>$
    $DEPTH : <stack> \rightarrow <integer>$

Legality
    $\lambda(T) => \lambda(T.PUSH(a))$
    $\lambda(T.TOP) <=> \lambda(T.POP)$

Equivalences
    $T.DEPTH \equiv T$
    $T.PUSH(a).POP \equiv T$

$$\lambda(T.TOP) => T.TOP \equiv T$$

<u>Values</u>
$$\lambda(T) => V(T.PUSH(a).TOP) = a$$
$$\lambda(T) => V(T.PUSH(a).DEPTH) = 1 + V(T.DEPTH)$$
$$V(DEPTH) = 0$$

The "equivalence" in the above specification is a set of assertions defining the semantics of the trace specification, while "trace equivalence" in environment discrimination indicates that the behavior of a program in two environments is not distinguishable from two traces.

Definition 1. *TRACE EQUIVALENCE*

Given 2 traces T_1 and T_2, we claim T_1 is *equivalent* to T_2 (denoted as $T_1 \equiv T_2$) when all the following conditions hold:

(1) Both T_1 and T_2 contain tailtraces or neither one contains a tailtrace.
(2) T_1 and T_2 have the same number of subtraces n.
(3) For each pair of subtraces in T_1 and T_2, we formalize subtrace T_{ij} ($i = 1$ *or* 2, $1 \leq j \leq n$) as:
$$T_{ij} ::= O_{ij1}...O_{ijk}...O_{ijo-1}V_{ij}$$

where o is the length of T_{ij}, and $0 \leq k < o$.
For each pair of subtraces T_{1j} and T_{2j}, where p, q are the lengths of T_{1j} and T_{2j}:
(i) $\lambda(T_{1jp-1}.V_{2j}) = true$
(ii) $\lambda(T_{2jq-1}.V_{1j}) = true$
(iii) $V(T_{1j}) = V(T_{2j})$

Ideally, the legality is ruled by a set of assertions so that all λ expressions above are checked through the pre-defined assertions. However, in practice, it is infeasible to provide a complete set of legality assertions. Thus, we either ignore the legality rules above or enforce the name of *V-function* of subtraces are identical if the legality assertions are not available. Both approaches admit that $\lambda(T_{1jp-1}.V_{2j})$ and $\lambda(T_{2jq-1}.V_{1j})$ are true by default.

We show an example to further illustrate trace equivalence: A stack for integer values S_1 is specified as previously discussed. The other stack S_2 is similar to S_1. The only difference between S_1 and S_2 is the size of each element. Specifically, the size of each element in S_2 is 2 instead of 1:
$$\lambda(T) => V(T.PUSH(a).DEPTH) = 2 + V(T.DEPTH)$$
Assume that a program P, defined next, runs on S_1 and S_2, respectively:

```
1    PUSH (1)
2    PUSH (2)
3    if (TOP == 1)
4       PUSH (3)
5    POP
6    if (DEPTH == 2)
7       PUSH (4)
```

```
8     PUSH (5)
9     TOP
10    DEPTH
11 else
12    PUSH (6)
13    TOP
14    TOP
15 POP
```

We denote the traces generated by the two executions as T_1 and T_2:

$T_1 ::= PUSH(1).PUSH(2).TOP.POP.DEPTH.PUSH(6).TOP.TOP.POP$

$T_2 ::= PUSH(1).PUSH(2).TOP.POP.DEPTH.PUSH(4).PUSH(5)$
$\quad .TOP.DEPTH.POP$

T_1 contains 4 subtraces: $PUSH(1).PUSH(2).TOP$, $POP.DEPTH$, $PUSH(6).TOP$, and TOP along with a tail trace: POP. T_2 also contains 4 subtraces: $PUSH(1).PUSH(2).TOP$, $POP.DEPTH$, $PUSH(4).PUSH(5).TOP$, and $DEPTH$ along with a tail trace: POP. Based on these results, conditions (1) and (2) in Definition 1 hold. T_{11} and T_{21} have the same V-*functions* and return values: 2. However, $V(T_{12}) = 1$ and $V(T_{22}) = 2$ which violates condition (3)(iii). The pairs T_{13} & T_{23} and T_{14} & T_{24} violate condition (3) as well; therefore $T_1 \not\equiv T_2$.

The definition of trace equivalence reveals the equivalent relation of 2 executions from the observation of traces. Note that two equivalent traces are not necessarily identical. For example if we define

$T_3 ::= PUSH(1).POP.DEPTH$

$T_4 ::= DEPTH$

then $T_3 \equiv T_4$ but they are not identical.

2.2   Trace Abstraction and Defining Environment Discrimination

Given two specific traces, Definition 1 is an effective tool for determining execution equality, or semantic similarity. However, finding a proper trace is a challenge. Thus, we propose *trace abstraction* as a procedure for checking $T_1 \equiv T_2$ efficiently. Algorithm 1 (described shortly) lists the steps of trace abstraction. Before introducing the algorithm, the concept of LCCS is introduced.

We first define the *longest common call subsequence* (LCCS), which is similar to the longest common substring (LCS) but replaces characters with function calls. LCCS is defined within the boundary of a subtrace or tail trace (but not the whole trace). To observe discriminating behaviors, we are interested in how a program reacts after a particular return value is obtained.

Parameter lists in function calls will be ignored. Consider how parameters can potentially influence the execution path of a program: given a pair of traces, if a function call returns the same return value regardless of different parameters, the parameter has no effect on the execution path by calling functions. On the other hand, if different parameters cause different return values, we are still able to observe differences by examining return values. Another question worth taking into account is where the different parameters come from. One possible answer is that they are derived from previous different return values. It is interesting to find that even a randomized program can be reduced to this answer because the program always has to call a function to derive the random value. Another possible answer is that the source of different parameters is not captured in the trace, which is not discussed in this paper. Thus, the partial order in a function call abstraction is shown below:

$$ignore\ return\ value \leq ignore\ function\ call$$

The aforementioned partial order indicates that ignoring the function call is more abstract than ignoring the return value.

Algorithm 1 describes the procedure of trace abstraction: the algorithm takes two traces T_1 and T_2 as input and returns a new trace T, which is the abstraction of the input traces. We use the T_1 and T_2 from the previous subsection to illustrate the algorithm.

Algorithm 1. Abstraction for two traces

1: **function** MAIN(T_1,T_2)
2:     $T_{subtrace1}$:=GET SUBTRACE LIST(T_1)
3:     $T_{subtrace2}$:=GET SUBTRACE LIST(T_2)
4:     T:=empty trace
5:     $T_{subtrace}$:=LCSS($T_{subtrace1}$, $T_{subtrace2}$)
6:     i:=0   ▷ i is the index of $T_{subtrace}$
7:     **for** each pair of subtraces S_1, S_2 in $T_{subtrace}$ **do**
8:         $T := T +$ ABSTRACT(S_1, S_2)
9:     **end for**
10:    T_{tail}:=LCCS(T_{1tail},T_{2tail})
11:    $T := T + T_{tail}$
12:    **return** T
13: **end function**
14:
15: **function** ABSTRACT($subtrace_1$, $subtrace_2$)
16:    T_0:=LCCS($subtrace_1$, $subtrace_2$)
17:    $subtrace_1$:=$subtrace_1$-T_0
18:    $subtrace_2$:=$subtrace_2$-T_0
19:    T_1:=LCCS($subtrace_1$, $subtrace_2$)
20:    T:=IN ORDER MERGE(T_0, T_1)
21:    **return** T
22: **end function**

The Algorithm starts with the MAIN() function; lines 2 and 3 cut T_1 and T_2 into subtraces, splitted by *V-functions*. Line 5 finds the Longest Common Subtrace Subsequence (LCSS) by only matching the function name of *V-functions*. In this example, $T_{subtrace}$ will be $\{T_{11}, T_{21}\}$, $\{T_{12}, T_{22}\}$, and $\{T_{13}, T_{23}\}$. Subtraces that are not in $T_{subtrace}$ will not appear in T. The **for** loop on lines 7–9 calls ABSTRACT() for each pair of subtraces in $T_{subtrace}$ and reassembles them into T. Lines 10 and 11 find the LCCS for the tail trace and append T_{tail} to the end of T.

ABSTRACT() finds the minimal abstraction making two subtraces equivalent. T_0 is the LCCS for two traces without ignoring return values or function calls. In our example, when $subtrace_1$ and $subtrace_2$ are T_{13} and T_{23}, $T_0 = PUSH$. Lines 17 and 18 remove the function calls which appeared in T_0. Thus, $subtrace_1 = TOP$ and $subtrace_2 = PUSH.TOP$ after line 17 and 18 are executed. T_1 is the LCCS ignoring return values, $T_1 = TOP$. Line 20 merges T_0 and T_1 in order, ABSTRACT() returns subtrace: $PUSH.TOP$. Similarly ABSTRACT() returns $PUSH.PUSH.TOP$ for $\{T_{11}, T_{21}\}$ and $POP.DEPTH$ for $\{T_{12}, T_{22}\}$. Finally, $T := PUSH.PUSH.TOP.POP.DEPTH.PUSH.TOP.POP$.

Definition 2. *ENVIRONMENT DISCRIMINATION*

If $T_1 \equiv T_2$ under the abstraction of trace T, we say that program P does not discriminate the two environments under the abstraction of trace T. Program P does not discriminate both environments when $T_1 \equiv T_2$ without any abstraction ($T_1 \equiv T_2 \equiv T$).

It is clear that T is not guaranteed to hold its original trace specification; rather it is designed to capture as many common parts in the two executions as possible.

Finally, we claim that minimum abstraction T gives the lower bound of abstraction. Thus, the alias of T is T_{low}. Any abstraction that is finer grained (less abstract) than T_{low} cannot guarantee the equivalence relation between T_1 and T_2. The upper bound of abstraction assuring the correctness of detecting environment discrimination is not ignoring the function calls before p_0, denoted as T_{up}. Any abstraction T' holding $T_{up} \geq T' \geq T_{low}$ is acceptable to detect environment discrimination and its contributor.

2.3 Finding Discrimination Contributors with Symbolic Execution

In order to find relevant/discriminating function calls (i.e., calls that expose environment information leading to programs behaving differently) accurately and efficiently, we propose the use of symbolic execution against traces.

Symbolic execution [11,12] is widely used in software engineering for generating test inputs, e.g., to explore different execution paths. One major limitation of symbolic execution is path explosion. Symbolically executing all program paths cannot scale to large programs because the number of paths grows exponentially with the number of conditional statements encountered: $\Theta(2^n)$, where n is the number of conditional statements encountered. When applying symbolic execution to find the subset of $\{S\}$, our algorithm matches the execution path with the trace to avoid path explosion.

We come back to the example of program P in Sect. 2.1 to illustrate symbolic execution against the trace. In order to find the discrimination contributor, the symbolic executor needs to run against T_1 and T_2, respectively. When the symbolic executor runs against T_1, initially, symbolic $\sigma = \emptyset$, path constraint $PC = true$, and a pointer ptr is pointing to the first function call in trace T_1. Whenever a function call is encountered, the algorithm checks the consistency between the current function call and the function ptr is pointing to in T_1. If they are consistent, ptr moves one function forward and symbolic execution continues. Thus, after line 2 is executed, $ptr \rightarrow TOP$. Every time a V-function is executed, the return values will be marked as a symbolic variable. TOP in line 3 leads to $\sigma = \{TOP_{line3} \rightarrow 2\}$. When if is executed, $PC \rightarrow TOP_{line3} = 1$, which is the constraint of basic block on line 4. $PC' \rightarrow \neg TOP_{line3} = 1$, $ptr \rightarrow POP$. During the execution of line 4, $PUSH$ and POP do not match. Thus, the current branch is not executed in the trace. As a result, PC' will be accepted as PC; ptr stays still, and the rest of the current branch does not need to be executed as well. When line 6 is executed, $PC \rightarrow DEPTH_{line6} = 2 \wedge \neg TOP_{line3} = 1$, which covers the basic block on lines 7–10. When the program symbolically executes to the diverge point of T_1 and T_2 (line 7 and line 12 in our example), $PC_{T_1} \rightarrow DEPTH_{line6} = 2 \wedge \neg TOP_{line3} = 1$. Similarly, $PC_{T_2} \rightarrow \neg DEPTH_{line6} = 2 \wedge \neg TOP_{line3} = 1$ after running symbolic executor against T_2. The discrimination contributors are the variables in the pairs of terms that are exactly reversed in 2 path constraints, which is $DEPTH$ in our example.

The time complexity of the algorithm to detect discriminating behavior and find contributors is $O(n)$, where n is the size of trace.

3   Detecting Environment Discrimination on Android

In this section, our theory is applied to detect environment discrimination on the Android platform. Before illustrating our approach, we introduce a prototype malware: Pi Calculator. To detect its inappropriate behavior, we first find an appropriate abstraction of the trace, and by applying the concept of trace equivalence, the algorithm is able to determine whether an application is behaving differently in two environments. Finally, with the help of symbolic execution, the algorithm finds discrimination contributor.

The procedure of detecting environment discrimination is shown in Fig. 2. The trace collector first collects traces from the emulator ($T_{emulator}$) and the real device (T_{device}), then checks their equivalence under proper abstraction (discussed in detail in Sect. 3.2). If $T_{emulator} \neq T_{device}$, the discrimination contributor is found by performing symbolic execution against $T_{emulator}$ and T_{device}.

3.1   Pi Calculator: An Environment-Discriminating Malware

We have developed a prototype malware, Pi Calculator, that discriminates environments. It is a CPU benchmark application that evaluates CPU single-core performance by recording the time it takes to calculate π to 5,000, 10,000, 15,000, or 20,000 digits (Fig. 3).

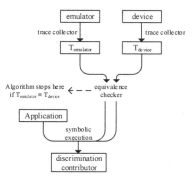

Fig. 2. Overview of our approach.

Fig. 3. Pi Calculator screenshot.

Device performance is reflected in the duration of the calculation (a slower device takes longer to compute π), which is uploaded to a remote database. We compute a *device score* by dividing the number of devices slower than current device by the number of all devices in the database. However, as a malware, Pi Calculator also uploads contact information to the server without informing the user. This application has bypassed the security check provided by one of the major Android markets. Due to privacy concerns, we only upload the first 5 digits of phone numbers (we do not upload the actual contact's name).

Table 1 presents the calculation time on various devices. Note that the CPU performance of the Android emulator is much higher than that of ARM-based real devices. As we mentioned before, dynamic analysis is usually performed on virtual machines. To evade dynamic analysis, Pi Calculator takes advantage of this phenomenon and determines its running environment as a real device if it takes more than 2, 6, 15, 25 s to compute π to 5,000, 10,000, 15,000, and 20,000 digits, respectively. The app will access the contact list and upload all

Table 1. Pi Calculator calculation time. Note that real devices are much slower than the emulator.

Device	5,000 digits		10,000 digits		15,000 digits		20,000 digits	
	Avg (s)	StDev (s)	Avg (s)	StDev (s)	Avg (s)	StDev (s)	Avg (s)	StDev (s)
Emulator (Linux)	1.258	0.020	4.937	0.007	10.044	0.016	17.521	0.023
Mi Note Pro (5.0.2)	2.317	0.058	9.246	0.040	21.193	0.159	39.428	0.235
Google Nexus 6 (5.0.1)	4.304	0.017	18.335	0.022	41.352	0.179	74.398	0.538
Meizu MX3 (5.0.1)	4.970	0.168	19.916	0.480	48.055	1.112	85.559	0.841

information to remote server only when a real device is detected but will not collect contact information when a virtual environment is detected.

The rest of this section explains how our algorithm detects the discrimination behavior employed by Pi Calculator in detail.

3.2 Detecting Environment Discrimination and Contributors

Selecting a proper trace is a key factor that determines the success and efficiency of discrimination detection. Our trace collector collects 3 kinds of function calls: application internal function calls, application calling API, and API internal function calls. Removing API internal calls is important because API internal calls may introduce non-determinism. Application internal call is also removed because it is not our interest. The two generated trace are denoted as T_{device} and $T_{emulator}$.

Instead of applying minimum abstraction T, we abstract T_{device} and $T_{emulator}$ by ignoring all method return values, denoted as T', and then check trace equivalence. Accuracy is guaranteed because $T_{up} \geq T' \geq T_{low}$. Almost all Android API calls have return values. So we regard all API calls in application level as *V-functions*. To apply the definition of environment discrimination, we need to check the definition of trace equivalence (Definition 1): Condition (1) of trace equivalence holds because both traces do not have a tail trace. Condition (2) is determined by whether two traces have the same size. The legality conditions ((i) and (ii)) in condition (3) are always true because there is no *O-function* in the trace. Thus, the trace equivalence check in our case simply reduces to comparing whether two traces call the same functions in order.

Now we consider composing symbolic execution with traces. As shown in Fig. 4, despite different approaches, in order to discriminate, a program first collects information about its environment and determine the environment based on the collected data. Next, the program will behave differently according to the environment, which is the diverge point. We emphasize that information collection and computation are not necessarily in order, and can even be mixed. Thus, we split the trace into two parts. The first part is information collection and computing, and the second part is the divergent part. In this section, we only focus on the first part, that is, $T_{\to p0}$. Specifically, the symbolic executor runs against $T_{device \to p0}$ and $T_{emulator \to p0}$.

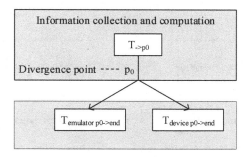

Fig. 4. Relationship between execution and trace.

The following rules describe the process of execution.

· Initially, ptr points to the first call in $T_{device}/T_{emulator}$.
· Whenever symbolic execution encounters an API call, the algorithm checks if the API is the same to the API that the pointer is pointing to in $T_{device}/T_{emulator}$. If not, it indicates this particular branch is not executed in trace, and we mark the PC belonging to that branch as false. If yes, we move the pointer to the next API call and continue executing.
· In T_{device} and $T_{emulator}$, the first pair of API calls after $T_{\rightarrow p0}$ actually are the first pair of API calls in two branches resulting from environment discrimination. Thus, symbolic execution runs until reaching p_0. ($T_{device \rightarrow p0}/T_{emulator \rightarrow p0}$)
· The discrimination contributors are the variables in the pairs of terms that are exactly reversed in $PC_{T_{device \rightarrow p0}}$ and $PC_{T_{emulator \rightarrow p0}}$

We use Pi Calculator as an example to illustrate the procedure of finding discrimination contributor in detail.

In Fig. 5, each box is an API method call. In each call, the first field is the method name, the second field is the method ID, and the third field is the class name the method belongs to; <init> indicates a constructor call. We are not able to locate a unique function call solely by method name because different classes might have methods that have the same method name, so method ID and method declaring class help us recognize a unique method call. During one execution, each method has a unique method ID. However, the same method usually owns a different ID in two executions. We determine a method call in different traces by matching both the method name and method declaring class. For instance, $<init>(0x70c25f20, GetTime.java)$ is called twice in T_{device}, and this constructor is also called in $T_{emulator}$, which is $<init>$ $(0x70ab5c20, GetTime.java)$, although the method ID is different. The algorithm determines that Pi Calculator discriminates the environment by finding a different pair of method calls: $<init>(0x75471a58, ContactsContract.java)$ and $<init>(0x708e92b0, DefaultHttpClient.java)$, which is where p_0 located.

Below is the code segment from Pi Calculator. During the course of symbolic execution against $T_{device \rightarrow p0}$, symbolic state σ and path constraint PC_{device} are

Fig. 5. Two traces generated from Pi Calculator.

maintained. All return values from API call will be marked as symbol. When line 4 and 5 are executed, $\sigma = \{start\_time \rightarrow start\_time_0, end\_time \rightarrow end\_time_0\}$. *start* has not been added to σ until line 7 because it receives a return value from $getCurrentNetworkTime$. At the end of line 12, $\sigma = \{start\_time \rightarrow start\_time_0, end\_time \rightarrow end\_time_0, start \rightarrow start_0, end \rightarrow end_0, result\_text \rightarrow null, time \rightarrow start_0 - end_0\}$, and $PC_{device} = \phi$. Note that symbolic execution does not execute a path that is not reflected in trace. In our example, lines 4 and 5 match the first two method calls in the trace. Similarly, lines 7 and 10 match the third and fifth calls in the trace. Line 9 matches the fourth call but we assign *result_text* as *null* because *setText* does not have a return value. As mentioned before, all API calls are regarded as *V-functions*. Assigning *null* to *setText* does not influence the result. $0x7074c2b0$ is recorded from line 45 that is called from line 13. In line 14, PC_{device} is updated to $PC_{device} = \{end_0 - start_0 > 2000\}$, corresponding to the basic block on line 15. The **if** branch line 19 is satisfied. Line 32, called by line 20, matches $<init>(0x75471a58, ContactsContract.java)$ in T_{device}. The symbolic execution stops because $0x75471a58$ is where p_0 located. $PC_{device} = \{end_0 - start_0 > 2000 \wedge real\_device = true\}$ Similarly, after running symbolic execution against $T_{emulator}$, $PC_{emulator} = \{\neg end_0 - start_0 > 2000 \wedge \neg real\_device = true\}$. Following the rules in Sect. 2.3, discrimination contributors are 2 calls to: **getCurrentNetworkTime()**. Specifically, Pi Calculator determines its running environment by measuring the time it takes to calculate π. If the calculation takes less than 2 s, Pi Calculator regards its environment as an emulator. The execution tree is illustrated in Fig. 6.

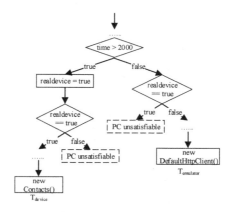

Fig. 6. Execution tree of Pi Calculator.

```
1    public class option extends ActionBarActivity {
2      private void clicked (int digit) {
3      ...
4        GetTime start_time = new GetTime();
5        GetTime end_time = new GetTime();
6        boolean realdevice = false;
7        start = start_time.getCurrentNetworkTime();
8        String pi = my_calculator.get_pi(digit);
9        result_text.setText(pi);
10       end = end_time.getCurrentNetworkTime();
11       time = end - start;
12       if (digit == 5000) {
13         new upload_score_5000().execute();
14         if (time > 2000) {
15           realdevice = true;
16         }
17       }
18       else {...}
19       if (realdevice == true) {
20         readAllContacts();
21       }
22       lower = new grab_lower_score().execute((long)digit, time).get();
23     }
24     private class upload_contacts extends AsyncTask<Contacts, Void, Void> {
25       protected Void doInBackground (...) {
26         HttpClient httpclient = new DefaultHttpClient();
27           ...
28       }
29     }
30     public void readAllContacts() {
31       while (cursor.moveToNext()) {
32         Contacts cur = new Contacts();
33         ...read each contacts info...
34         new upload_contacts().execute(cur);
35       }
36     }
37     private class grab_lower_score  extends AsyncTask<Long, Void, Integer> {
38       protected Void doInBackground (...) {
39         HttpClient httpclient = new DefaultHttpClient();
40           ....
41       }
42     }
43     private class upload_score_5000 extends AsyncTask<Score, Void, Void> {
```

```
44      protected Void doInBackground (...) {
45        HttpClient httpclient = new DefaultHttpClient();
46        ....
47      }
48    }
49  }
```

Note that the key advantage of combining symbolic execution with trace is that this combined analysis shrinks down the time complexity of symbolic execution since we do not execute branches that do not appear in the trace.

4   Evaluation and Discussion

4.1   Practical Malware Evaluation

We apply the framework described in Sect. 3 to 18 real world malware. They come from 10 different apps along with their variants. The result shows that none of the 18 apps discriminates the virtual machine and real device before exposing anomalous behavior, which indicates that the discrimination technique has not been widely applied by the malware developers. Even though discrimination behaviors cannot be found in a while, as emulation becomes more and more common over time, we will see more discrimination behaviors in the future (Table 2).

Table 2. List of practical malware evaluated

App name	Number of variants
DroidKungFu4	3
FakeNetflix	1
Geinimi	1
GGTracker	1
GingerMaster	2
SndApps	2
Tapsnake	2
zHash	2
NickySpy	2
HippoSMS	2

Our detection algorithm is efficient. Checking environment discrimination behavior is in linear time, $O(n)$, where n is the size of trace. The time complexity of detecting discrimination contributors is also $O(n)$, where n is the number of lines of code. The reason is that running symbolic execution against trace matching shrinks down the time complexity of symbolic execution because executer will not execute a path if it cannot be found in trace.

4.2   Benchmark Malware Evaluation

Because environment discrimination is not widely applied in practical malware, we invite the third party researchers who have no knowledge in our algorithm injecting the environment discrimination code into the practical malware, and evaluate the framework against the test bench to perform a blind testing. In particular, the benchmark contains a set of malware injected with environment discrimination code with varieties of heuristics and malware that does not have such behaviors.

Table 3. Benchmark malware set evaluation result

Heuristics	# of apps	Apps discriminate during execution	Detection rate	Contributor detection rate	Accuracy
Property (API) heuristics	5	5	100%	100%	100%
File heuristics	5	5	100%	100%	100%
Component heuristics	5	5	100%	100%	100%
Sophisticated heuristics	5	4	80%	80%	80%
No discrimination	10	0	100%	N/A	100%
Overall	30	19	N/A	N/A	97%

Table 3 lists the evaluation result. 30 apps contained in the benchmark are categorized into 5 categories. The property (API) heuristics take advantage of the API call artifacts such as getDeviceId() and Build.MODEL(). The apps leveraging file and component heuristics check the existance of a specific file or hardware component, respectively. Sophisticated heuristics are more difficult to detect. For example, one app in benchmark tests whether the call log is empty. Another app checks whether the battery is always charging and remaining at 50%, which is the default configuration in most emulators. The last category is a set of apps without any discrimination behaviors for us to evaluate the false positive.

The overall accuracy is 97%, and the only case that fails is an app leveraging the time bomb to discriminate. The time bomb is not exposed during evaluation, thus it is not captured in the trace. Also, even though the false positive is 0%, it is not guaranteed that some discrimination behavior is not intended to differentiate the virtual machine and physical device. For example, false positive may occur when Google Map behaves differently as no GPS signal is found, and virtual machine usually does not provide location information if not configured. However, in this paper, we do not attempt to differentiate the intention of discrimination.

The major limitation of this work is that the detection framework will never be able to detect the discrimination behavior if such behavior is not captured in trace. For instance, our framework failed to detect the time bomb planted in one of the benchmark app because the time bomb was not triggered during the process of trace collection. Even though the time bomb does not directly differentiate the virtual environment from the physical device, malware developers understand the time of malware being tested by security analysts is significantly shorter than the time of the app used by a real user. One potential approach to mitigate this problem is to run static analysis and generate all potential traces. As a trade off, this approach may bring false positive and the runtime can be up to $O(2^n)$, where n is the length of program.

5   Related Work

5.1   Dynamic and Tainting Analysis

Many dynamic analysis tools have been developed to analyze malware. This section cites and introduces the dynamic analysis works often used in either industry or academic. DroidScope [13] is a virtualization-based Android malware analysis platform, which reconstructs the OS-level and Java-level semantics seamlessly and simultaneously. Various analysis tools is also developed on top of DroidScope to collect native and Dalvik instruction traces, profiling API-level activity, and tainting analysis. TaintDroid [14] is an efficient and system-wide dynamic taint tracking and analysis system capable of tracking multiple sources of sensitive data, which leverages different levels of instrumentation to perform the analysis. Even though TaintDroid introduces only 14% overhead, modifying the components of Android exposes TaintDroid to some detection and evasion techniques [15–17]. Andrubis [18] combines static analysis with dynamic analysis on both Dalvik VM and system level, as well as several stimulation techniques to increase code coverage, which is built based on TaintDroid [13] and Droid-Box [19].

Besides the tools introduced above, many other dynamic analysis tools have been developed to analyze malware, most of which extract API calls or system calls [20–24]. Several dynamic analysis tools record traces with in-guest technologies such as Norman Antivirus Sandbox [22] and CSSandbox [20]. Tools such as Ether [23] and HyperDBG [25] are implemented based on hardware-supported virtualization technology. However, for convenience and security reasons, more dynamic analysis tools are deployed on virtual environments. For instance, Google Boucer [26], VMScope [27] and TT-Analyze [21] are based on QEMU [28], which is a popular virtual machine.

5.2   Virtual Machine Evasion

On traditional platforms such as PCs, dynamic analysis systems are usually built based on virtualization. Consequently, PC malware developers design malware that is aware of virtual environments and exhibit benign behavior in such cases [29–31]. However, virtualization has matured in recent years. Many users even migrate physical environments to virtual instances, e.g., as in the Cloud, hence malware that discriminate virtual environments, stand to lose a large number of victim systems.

On the other hand, the application of virtualization on mobile platforms is quite limited. A normal user is very unlikely to run a mobile OS in a virtual environment but dynamic analysis does, as we mentioned before. Recent work has shown that malwares on mobile platforms discriminate running environments to evade dynamic analysis based on virtualization [3,32].

Few efforts have focused on environment discrimination. Morpheus generates heuristics to detect Android emulators and classifies heuristics as file, API, and system property [33]. BareCloud automatically detects evasive malware by using hierarchical similarity-based behavioral profile comparison; profiles are collected by running a malware sample in bare-metal, virtualized, emulated, and hypervisor-based analysis environments [34]. Balzarotti's paper is similar to our project [35], which also collects and compares the trace to find split personalities in malware. However, our work formally defines environment discrimination and employs symbolic execution against trace to find the discrimination contributors, which differentiates from Balzarotti's work.

6   Conclusion

The concept of environment discrimination has been applied in many areas. Dynamic analysis is a convenient and efficient approach to analyze program behavior, but some malware is able to detect the existence of virtual environments and evade detection. Some detection strategy such as evaluating hardware performance is infeasible to block in practice.

In this work, we define environment discrimination and an efficient algorithm to detect and describe such behavior. The time complexity to detect discrimination behavior and discrimination contributor is $O(n)$. The framework we proposed reaches 97% detection accuracy when testing against a malware benchmark developed by the third party researchers. We also examine 18 real world malwares and show that the environment discrimination has not been widely employed by the malware developers.

Acknowledgement. The effort described in this article was partially sponsored by the U.S. Army Research Laboratory Cyber Security Collaborative Research Alliance under Contract Number W911NF-13-2-0045. The views and conclusions contained in this document are those of the authors, and should not be interpreted as representing the official policies, either expressed or implied, of the Army Research Laboratory or the U.S. Government. The U.S. Government is authorized to reproduce and distribute reprints for Government purposes notwithstanding any copyright notation hereon.

References

1. Chaffey, D.: Mobile marketing statistics compilation. http://www.smartinsights. com/mobile-marketing/mobile-marketing-analytics/mobile-marketing-statistics/. Accessed 5 June 2017
2. Christian, L.: 8,400 new android malware samples every day. https://www. gdatasoftware.com/blog/2017/04/29712-8-400-new-android-malware-samples-every-day/. Accessed 25 May 2017
3. Vidas, T., Christin, N.: Evading android runtime analysis via sandbox detection. In: Proceedings of the 9th ACM Symposium on Information, Computer and Communications Security, pp. 447–458. ACM (2014)
4. Shimpi, A.L., Klug, B.: They're (almost) all dirty: the state of cheating in android benchmarks. http://www.anandtech.com/show/7384/state-of-cheating-in-android-benchmarks/. Accessed 19 May 2017
5. Hruska, J.: Samsung goes legit, stops cheating on benchmarks with latest android update. http://www.extremetech.com/computing/177841-samsungs-latest-android-update-no-longer-cheats-on-benchmarks/. Accessed 11 June 2017
6. Mack, E.: HTC admits boosting one M8 benchmarks; makes it a feature. http://www.cnet.com/news/is-the-htc-one-m8-that-good-benchmark-cheating-alleged-again/. Accessed 10 June 2017
7. Hotten, R.: Volkswagen: the scandal explained. http://www.bbc.com/news/business-34324772/. Accessed 4 Jun 2017
8. Bartussek, W., Parnas, D.L.: Using assertions about traces to write abstract specifications for software modules. In: Bracchi, G., Lockemann, P.C. (eds.) ECI 1978. LNCS, vol. 65, pp. 211–236. Springer, Heidelberg (1978). https://doi.org/10.1007/3-540-08934-9_80
9. Guttag, J.V., Horning, J.J.: The algebraic specification of abstract data types. Acta Inform. **10**(1), 27–52 (1978)
10. McLean, J.: A formal method for the abstract specification of software. J. ACM (JACM) **31**(3), 600–627 (1984)
11. James, J.C.: Symbolic execution and program testing. Commun. ACM **19**(7), 385–394 (1976)
12. Clarke, L.A.: A program testing system. In: Proceedings of the 1976 Annual Conference, pp. 488–491. ACM (1976)
13. Yan, L.K., Yin, H.: Droidscope: seamlessly reconstructing the OS and Dalvik semantic views for dynamic Android malware analysis. In: USENIX Security Symposium, pp. 569–584 (2012)
14. Enck, W., Gilbert, P., Han, S., Tendulkar, V., Chun, B.G., Cox, L.P., Jung, J., McDaniel, P., Sheth, A.N.: Taintdroid: an information-flow tracking system for realtime privacy monitoring on smartphones. ACM Trans. Comput. Syst. (TOCS) **32**(2), 5 (2014)
15. Sarwar, G., Mehani, O., Boreli, R., Kaafar, M.A.: On the effectiveness of dynamic taint analysis for protecting against private information leaks on android-based devices. In: SECRYPT, pp. 461–468 (2013)
16. Slowinska, A., Bos, H.: Pointless tainting? Evaluating the practicality of pointer tainting. In: Proceedings of the 4th ACM European Conference on Computer Systems, pp. 61–74. ACM (2009)
17. Cavallaro, L., Saxena, P., Sekar, R.: On the limits of information flow techniques for malware analysis and containment. In: Zamboni, D. (ed.) DIMVA 2008. LNCS, vol. 5137, pp. 143–163. Springer, Heidelberg (2008). https://doi.org/10.1007/978-3-540-70542-0_8

18. Lindorfer, M., Neugschwandtner, M., Weichselbaum, L., Fratantonio, Y., Van Der Veen, V., Platzer, C.: ANDRUBIS -1,000,000 apps later: a view on current android malware behaviors. In: Proceedings of the the 3rd International Workshop on Building Analysis Datasets and Gathering Experience Returns for Security (BADGERS) (2014)
19. Lantz, P., Desnos, A., Yang, K.: Droidbox: Android application sandbox (2012)
20. Willems, C., Holz, T., Freiling, F.: Toward automated dynamic malware analysis using CWSandbox. IEEE Secur. Priv. **2**, 32–39 (2007)
21. Bayer, U., Kruegel, C., Kirda, E.: TTAnalyze: a tool for analyzing malware. (na, 2006)
22. Norman safeground antivirus software. http://www.norman.com/. Accessed 8 June 2017
23. Dinaburg, A., Royal, P., Sharif, M., Lee, W.: Ether: malware analysis via hardware virtualization extensions. In: Proceedings of the 15th ACM Conference on Computer and Communications Security, pp. 51–62. ACM (2008)
24. Rastogi, V., Chen, Y., Enck, W.: Appsplayground: automatic security analysis of smartphone applications. In: Proceedings of the Third ACM Conference on Data and Application Security and Privacy, pp. 209–220. ACM (2013)
25. Fattori, A., Paleari, R., Martignoni, L., Monga, M.: Dynamic and transparent analysis of commodity production systems. In: Proceedings of the IEEE/ACM International Conference on Automated Software Engineering, pp. 417–426. ACM (2010)
26. Hruska J.: Android and security. http://googlemobile.blogspot.it/2012/02/android-and-security.html/. Accessed 11 May 2017
27. Jiang, X., Wang, X.: "Out-of-the-Box" monitoring of VM-based high-interaction honeypots. In: Kruegel, C., Lippmann, R., Clark, A. (eds.) RAID 2007. LNCS, vol. 4637, pp. 198–218. Springer, Heidelberg (2007). https://doi.org/10.1007/978-3-540-74320-0_11
28. Bellard, F.: QEMU, a fast and portable dynamic translator. In: USENIX Annual Technical Conference, FREENIX Track, p. 41 (2005)
29. Fogla, P., Lee, W.: Evading network anomaly detection systems: formal reasoning and practical techniques. In: Proceedings of the 13th ACM Conference on Computer and Communications Security, pp. 59–68. ACM (2006)
30. Lau, B., Svajcer, V.: Measuring virtual machine detection in malware using DSD tracer. J. Comput. Virol. **6**(3), 181–195 (2010)
31. Paleari, R., Martignoni, L., Roglia, G.F., Bruschi, D.: A fistful of red-pills: how to automatically generate procedures to detect CPU emulators. In: Proceedings of the USENIX Workshop on Offensive Technologies (WOOT), vol. 41, p. 86 (2009)
32. Petsas, T., Voyatzis, G., Athanasopoulos, E., Polychronakis, M., Ioannidis, S.: Rage against the virtual machine: hindering dynamic analysis of Android malware. In: Proceedings of the Seventh European Workshop on System Security, p. 5. ACM (2014)
33. Jing, Y., Zhao, Z., Ahn, G.J., Hu, H.: Morpheus: automatically generating heuristics to detect Android emulators. In: Proceedings of the 30th Annual Computer Security Applications Conference, pp. 216–225. ACM (2014)
34. Kirat, D., Vigna, G., Kruegel, C.: Barecloud: bare-metal analysis-based evasive malware detection. In: 23rd USENIX Security Symposium (USENIX Security 2014), pp. 287–301 (2014)
35. Balzarotti, D., Cova, M., Karlberger, C., Kirda, E., Kruegel, C.M., Vigna, G.: Efficient detection of split personalities in malware. In: NDSS (2010)

Query Recovery Attacks on Searchable Encryption Based on Partial Knowledge

Guofeng Wang[1], Chuanyi Liu[2(✉)], Yingfei Dong[3], Hezhong Pan[1], Peiyi Han[1], and Binxing Fang[2]

[1] School of Computer Science, Beijing University of Posts and Telecommunications, Beijing, China
{wangguofeng,hanpeiyi}@bupt.edu.cn
[2] School of Computer and Technology, Harbin Institute of Technology (Shenzhen), Shenzhen, China
cy-liu04@mails.tsinghua.edu.cn
[3] Department of Electrical and Computer Engineering, University of Hawaii, Honolulu, USA
yingfei@hawaii.edu

Abstract. While Searchable Encryption (SE) is often used to support securely outsourcing sensitive data, many existing SE solutions usually expose certain information to facilitate better performance, which often leak sensitive information, e.g., search patterns are leaked due to observable query trapdoors. Several inference attacks have been designed to exploit such leakage, e.g., a query recovery attack can invert opaque query trapdoors to their corresponding keywords. However, most of these existing query recovery attacks assume that *an adversary knows almost all plaintexts* as prior knowledge in order to successfully map query trapdoors to plaintext keywords with a high probability. Such an assumption is usually impractical. In this paper, we propose new query recovery attacks in which an adversary only needs to have *partial knowledge of the original plaintexts*. We further develop a countermeasure to mitigate inference attacks on SE. Our experimental results demonstrate the feasibility and efficacy of our proposed scheme.

Keywords: Searchable encryption · Inference attacks
Query recovery attacks

1 Introduction

Due to security concerns, sensitive data is often encrypted before uploaded to cloud service providers (CSPs). Therefore, Searchable Encryption (SE) has become a critical technique for many secure applications, which allows a user to securely outsource its data to an untrusted cloud server, while maintaining various search functionalities.

Two Common SE Models. Currently, SE schemes mostly explore the trade-offs between query expressiveness, security, and efficiency. Oblivious RAMs

© ICST Institute for Computer Sciences, Social Informatics and Telecommunications Engineering 2018
X. Lin et al. (Eds.): SecureComm 2017, LNICST 238, pp. 530–549, 2018.
https://doi.org/10.1007/978-3-319-78813-5_27

(ORAM) [1] satisfies security and query expressiveness but incurs many interactions for each read and write, which makes it impractical in deployment. Recently, many researchers focus on the *Encrypted-Index SE* model, summarized as follows. A user first encrypts some documents and generates a corresponding searchable index; it then uploads the encrypted documents and the encrypted index to a CSP. To search the documents, the user generates a search *trapdoor* to ask the CSP to search on the encrypted index and return corresponding results. While such a scheme achieves a good balance between security and efficiency, it loses some query expressiveness [2], and it requires modifying current cloud Application Programming Interface (API). In addition, most Encrypted-Index SE schemes leak certain sensitive information to the adversary (i.e., the curious cloud server) for better performance [3]. In the following, we focus on Encrypted-Index SE schemes that leak search patterns and access patterns.

On the other hand, to be compatible with legacy systems, SE schemes such as ShadowCrypt [4] and Mimesis Aegis [5] use the *Appended-Token SE* model, which encrypts each document using a conventional encryption method, and appends a sequence of tokens to the ciphertext. Because a token is deterministically generated by encrypting a corresponding keyword, the search operation for a keyword is conducted in two steps: generate the token of a keyword and request the server to search for the token. Many cloud industry solutions (such as Skyhigh [6], CipherCloud [7]) also advocate this approach. An Appended-Token SE scheme requires no modification on the CSP side. Because such a scheme provides no additional protection of token occurrence patterns, once encrypted documents and tokens are uploaded to a CSP, the count of each indexed keyword, its co-occurrence probabilities with other keywords, and the similarity between documents, can be easily learned by the CSP.

Limitation of Existing Query Recovery Attacks. Islam, Kuzu, and Kantarcioglu (IKK) [8] analyzed the implications of revealing search patterns and access patterns in SE. They showed that user queries can be inferred with a high success rate when an adversary knows all the original documents. Cash, Grubbs, Perry, and Ristenpart (CGPR) [9] proposed a simpler count attack, which outperformed the IKK attack in terms of efficiency and accuracy in the same scenarios. However, for a certain size of keyword vocabulary, both the IKK and CGPR attacks require almost the *complete knowledge* of plaintexts to achieve a good recovery rate of queries. For example, when knowing less than 80% of a document set, both the IKK attack and the CGPR count attack can invert almost no query trapdoors. In this paper, we focus on this issue and emphasize attacks with partial knowledge.

Our Contributions. Normally, an adversary rarely knows the entire document set of a victim, but it usually learns a subset, e.g., some well-circulated emails. Therefore, we focus on this practical case and develop query recovery attacks based on partial knowledge. We have made the following contributions in this paper.

1. *Document identification attack on Appended-Token SE schemes.* To attack an Appended-Token SE scheme, we first establish the mappings between the

known plaintext documents and the encrypted documents of a victim, which called *"document identification attack"*. This attack allows us to apply existing query recovery attack algorithms to invert tokens more accurately.

2. *Extended document identification attack on Encrypted-Index SE schemes.* In an Encrypted-Index SE scheme, before queries are issued, an adversary learns nothing except the sizes of the ciphertexts and the encrypted index. So, the adversary cannot directly perform the proposed document identification attack. However, the adversary can perform this attack in certain situations with some auxiliary information. For example, if the adversary knows widely-circulated emails, the document identification attack can be conducted according to specific protocols and related data items (such as senders and receivers in emails). With a sequence of query results, an inverted index can be built between search trapdoors and returned encrypted documents. Then, the adversary can remove irrelevant encrypted documents from the query results according to the identified encrypted documents, and use query recovery attack algorithms with prior knowledge to obtain query keywords more accurately.

3. *We propose a simple noise addition technique to mitigate the inference attacks.* We minimize information disclosure by spreading search tokens in the Appended-Token SE, to break the statistical relations between keywords and tokens. The proposed model achieves backwards compatibility with legacy systems. Our experimental results show its effectiveness.

The remainder of this paper is organized as follows. We introduce related work in Sect. 2, and present the query recovery attacks with partial knowledge in Sect. 3. We further present our evaluation in Sect. 4. We discuss mitigation methods in Sect. 5, and conclude this paper in Sect. 6.

2   Background and Related Work

In this section, we first introduce SE basics and common SE schemes, and point out their leakage models. We then discuss common inference attacks on SE.

2.1   SE Basics

First, we define terminologies and preliminaries used in this paper. Let n be the total number of documents in a collection $D = (D_1, D_2, ..., D_n)$. We denote the identifier of a document D_i by $ID(D_i)$. Let $D(w)$ be the ordered list consisting of the identifiers of all documents that contain the keyword w in set D. We use m to denote the total number of keywords in a dictionary, and use $W = (w_1, w_2, ..., w_m)$ to denote the set of keywords in a dictionary.

A trapdoor function f takes a keyword w as input, and emits a trapdoor that enables the server to search on the encrypted index while keeping the keyword hidden. A search pattern means the information that given two searches with the same results, we can determine whether the two searches use the same keyword. An access pattern refers to the information that may be leaked in query results. The returned results imply the document IDs containing the query keywords.

2.2   SE Models

In this section, we classify common SE schemes into two models: the Encrypted-Index SE model and the Appended-Token SE model, as shown in Fig. 1.

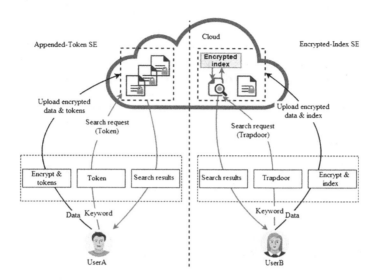

Fig. 1. Architecture for searchable encryption models.

Encrypted-Index SE Model. Curtmola et al. [3] first built an encrypted search mechanism using inverted indexes. For each keyword, it built a linked list of the IDs of the documents containing the keyword, improved the search efficiency to sub-linear time, and enhanced the security of SE. We classify this scheme into the Encrypted-Index SE model. In this scheme, the nodes of every linked list are encrypted with randomly generated keys and scrambled in a random order. A node contains a document identifier, a key used to decrypt the next node, and a pointer to the next encrypted node. Before queries are issued, the server learns nothing except the sizes of the documents and the index. For trapdoors that have been queried, the query results reveal the information about the occurrence counts of the hidden keywords and the co-occurrence patterns of multiple keywords. It can only support exact keyword searches and documents cannot be updated dynamically. Recently, advanced SE functions are further developed based on the above approach, such as multi-keyword SE [12], fuzzy keyword SE [13] and dynamic SE [14]. In summary, the Encrypted-Index SE model improves the search efficiency, but requires modifying current cloud APIs. After all keywords have been queried, the leakage of Encrypted-Index SE degenerates to the same level as the leakage of Appended-Token SE as depicted in the following section.

Appended-Token SE Model. As Fig. 1 shows, this model is compatible with legacy systems: the server can index and search the uploaded tokens. However, the model provides no additional protection of token occurrence patterns and gives the server the exact document-token matrix prior to search.

ShadowCrypt [4] and Mimesis Aegis [5] use this model to support SE in legacy applications. For a given keyword, ShadowCrypt uses a single pseudorandom function to generate a single search token. After that, it sorted the tokens in every document to disturb the correspondence between tokens and keywords. The Mimesis Aegis SE scheme is more secure than ShadowCrypt because it does not reveal a one-to-one correspondence between keywords and tokens. It uses Bloom filter and a family of pseudorandom functions to generate k distinct tokens for each keyword. However, the tokens are deterministically encrypted, that the server can learn the count of each unique indexed keyword and its co-occurrence probabilities with other keywords upon uploading (as in Shadow Nemesis [11]). In addition, the Bloom filter has a small error rate. There may be potential collisions that some tokens may correspond to more than one keyword. Due to the simplicity of the Appended-Token SE, several commercial encryption products from Skyhigh Networks [6], CipherCloud [7], Bitglass [15], and Virtue [16] use this model (or its variants) to support SE in their cloud services.

2.3   Inference Attacks on SE Models

An adversary can use inference attacks to obtain sensitive information against SE schemes based on its leakages and the adversary's prior knowledge.

Adversary's Prior Knowledge. We classify the adversary's prior knowledge into three types. (i) *Distributional document knowledge model:* The adversary has no a priori knowledge of the plaintext messages. In this scenario, an adversary may have the contextual information about the documents, such as whether they are emails or medical documents. (ii) *Full document knowledge model:* All documents are known to the adversary. While it is rare, it may happen sometimes, e.g., a user has a large corpus of emails stored at an email service, and it decides to encrypt all old emails using SE. (iii) *Partial document knowledge model:* As it is unlikely that an adversary knows all documents of a victim, it may only know a subset. In the following, we will focus on the effectiveness of our attacks in this scenario of partial knowledge.

Attack Modes. We classify attacks in two modes. (i) In a *passive attack*, the adversary intercepts communications between a user and a server, to count the frequencies of query keywords or the co-occurrence patterns of multiple keywords in a document set by observing query results. With known plaintext documents, the adversary can map opaque query trapdoors to plaintext keywords. The IKK attack [8] and the Shadow Nemesis attack [11] use co-occurrence matrixes and combination optimization algorithms to perform inference. (ii) In an *active attack*, an adversary proactively sends the client multiple plaintext documents with structured contents; the client will then create an encrypted index based on these documents and upload them to the cloud server. So, the attacker can observe the inserted documents contained in the user's query results to create mappings between the keywords and search trapdoors. CGPR's [9] active attack and ZKP [10] both use this attack mode.

Attack Algorithms. Different attack models are summarized in Table 1. IKK [8] first studied the empirical security of SE and analyzed the implications of revealing search patterns and access patterns. Let q be the number of unique query trapdoors observed. A $q \times q$ trapdoor co-occurrence matrix is built as C_q, where $C_q[i,j]$ represents the number of documents which the i-th trapdoor and the j-th trapdoor both hit. If the server has the prior knowledge of all indexed documents, a $m \times m$ keyword co-occurrence matrix C_m can be constructed, where $C_m[i,j]$ represents the number of documents in which the i-th keyword and the j-th keyword both appear. Then, a simulated annealing algorithm is used to find the best match of C_q to C_m, thus inverting the corresponding query trapdoors. When the information about plaintext is not accurate or only partial plaintext is known, the success rate of IKK query recovery attack is poor.

Table 1. Different attack schemes against SE. EISE represents Encrypted-Index SE, and ATSE represents Appended-Token SE.

Attack schemes	Attack methods	Prior knowledge	Attack SE
IKK [8]	Simulated annealing	Almost all documents	EISE and ATSE
CGPR [9]	Count or file injection	Almost all or partial documents	EISE and ATSE
ZKP [10]	File injection	No or partial documents	EISE and ATSE
Shadow Nemesis [11]	Graph matching	All or auxiliary documents	ATSE

CGPR [9] presented a simpler count attack without using optimization algorithms. It first calculates the number of documents in the query result of a search trapdoor, and then finds a unique keyword appeared in the same number of plaintext documents. If the unique keyword found, the mapping between the trapdoor and the keyword can be directly established. Based on the mappings, given an unknown search trapdoor q with a result length, it first selects the candidate keywords contained in the same number of plaintext documents. Then, to determine whether a keyword w in the candidate keyword set is corresponding to the trapdoor q, for each pair of identified keyword-trapdoor mapping w' and q', it computes the co-occurrence count c_1 of w and w' (the number of documents in which w and w' both appear) in known documents, and the co-occurrence count c_2 of q and q' (the number of documents which both the query q and q' match) in query results. If c_1 is not equal to c_2, then w will be removed from the candidate keyword set. Finally, only one remaining keyword meeting all the conditions can be mapped to the trapdoor q. However, CGPR requires almost the complete knowledge of a victim's documents to achieve a good query recovery rate. When only knowing a portion of the document set (e.g., less than 80%), both IKK and CGPR attacks perform poorly.

The Shadow Nemesis [11] launched inference attacks on the Appended-Token SE model. The attack creates a keyword co-occurrence matrix graph G and a token co-occurrence matrix graph H based on the auxiliary information and target data, respectively. As the Appended-Token SE model leaks the occurrence count of each indexed keyword and its co-occurrence probabilities with other keywords, which is sufficient to convert the attack to the well-known Weighted Graph Matching (WGM) problem. This method did not examine query recovery attacks with partial knowledge.

ZKP [10] used active attacks to infer query trapdoors. An attacker needs to inject known documents to a client, while the client must encrypt the received documents and generate corresponding search indexes. The number of injected documents is dependent on the size of keyword vocabulary. This assumption is often difficult to meet when a client only encrypts and indexes its own sensitive data, as in Virtue [16]. So, we do not investigate the active attack algorithms in the following.

3   Query Recovery Attacks with Partial Knowledge

In this section, we present our query recovery attacks with partial knowledge against two SE models.

3.1   Motivation

Although various attacks on SE have been investigated in different settings, there are still several interesting challenges to be addressed as follows.

(i) *To invert the query with a high accuracy, common query recovery attacks require almost the complete knowledge of a victim's documents, which is unrealistic in normal cases.* For example, an adversary needs to know almost all documents to achieve a high success rate in the CGPR [9] count attack. The IKK [8] attack and the Shadow Nemesis [11] attack consider a more realistic scenario, in which an adversary can collect publicly relevant data based on the distributional knowledge of the victim's documents. However, the adversary must have accurate keyword co-occurrence probabilities and corresponding keywords, which we believe the knowledge can only be obtained by an adversary that has access to all the documents.

(ii) *The recovery rate of queries is poor when an adversary only has partial knowledge of documents.* In this case, as the statistics of partially known documents do not match the statistics of query results on all documents, resulting in a low probability of success. In practice, the adversary usually has partial knowledge about a victim's document set. Therefore, we focus on this issue in our investigation.

3.2 Query Recovery Attacks Against Appended-Token SE Model

Prior to a search, the Appended-Token SE model leaks the count of each unique indexed keyword, its co-occurrence probabilities with other keyword, and the similarity of documents to a cloud server. When having the explicit knowledge of all documents of a victim, the adversary can get a consistent statistical distribution about keywords and tokens. The attacker can invert the underlying tokens to their respective keywords, even when no queries have been issued.

Document Identification Attack. However, if the adversary only has partial knowledge, as the statistics between keywords and tokens do not match well, it is very hard to invert the tokens. To address this issue, we first pre-established the mappings between the known documents and related encrypted documents, which we called *Document Identification Attack*. Then, the server can calculate the count of each token and its token co-occurrence probabilities with other tokens in the identified encrypted documents. Similarly, in the known documents corresponding to the identified encrypted documents, the server can obtain the count of each keyword and its keyword co-occurrence probabilities with other keywords. Finally, the server can build mappings between opaque tokens and plaintext keywords accurately.

Next, we describe our document identification attack algorithm in detail. Let $D = (D_1, D_2, ..., D_n)$ denote a collection of n plaintext documents. A keyword extraction algorithm takes a document D_i as input and outputs a vector W_i, where each component is a character string, namely a keyword w. We assume the keyword extraction algorithm is deterministic and known to the adversary. Let $W = (W_1, ..., W_n)$ be the ordered list of all keyword vectors.

For each known plaintext document D_i, we first choose the unique encrypted document in which the number of tokens is the same as the number of unique keywords in the keyword vector W_i. We name the mapping between the encrypted document and its corresponding plaintext document as a *base mapping*.

If the mapping is not unique, i.e., multiple candidate encrypted documents have the same number of tokens as the number of unique keywords in a plaintext document. We filter the candidate encrypted documents of the plaintext document by comparing the similarity of plaintext documents (i.e., the number of common keywords in two documents) and the similarity of encrypted documents (i.e., the number of common tokens in two encrypted documents) with help of base mappings. Our document identification attack algorithm is shown in Algorithm 1. In line 2, we build the similarity matrix of partial plaintext documents, C_k, where $C_k[i,j]$ represents the number of common keywords in two documents i and j, and the similarity matrix of all encrypted documents, C_t, where $C_t[i,j]$ is computed by counting the number of common tokens in two encrypted documents i and j. A document identification example is shown in Fig. 2, in which *PDoc* means "plaintext document", *EDoc* means "encrypted document". First, because only *PDoc1* has 101 keywords and *EDoc1* has 101 tokens, we have a unique mapping between them. Second, for *PDoc2*, we have two candidate encrypted documents *EDoc2* and *EDoc3*. As *PDoc2* has 25 common keywords with *PDoc1*, we find *EDoc3* has the same number of common tokens with *EDoc1*, while *EDoc2* only has 20 common tokens with *EDoc1*. So, we can determine the mapping between *EDoc3* and *PDoc2*.

Algorithm 1. Document Identification Attack algorithm

---

input : all encrypted document set e, partial plaintext document set p.
output: mapping set between e and p;
1 initialize the base mapping set K;
2 compute the similarity matrix of partial plaintext documents, C_k, and the
   similarity matrix of all encrypted documents, C_t;
3 **while** *size of K is increasing* **do**
4   **for** *each un-mapping plaintext document* $d \in p - K$ **do**
5   set candidate encrypted document set $S = \{s :$ the token count of s is
           equal to the keyword count of d $\}$;
6   **for** $s \in S$ **do**
7   **for** *known base mapping* $(d', s') \in K$ **do**
8   **if** $C_k[d, d'] \neq C_t[s, s']$ **then**
9   remove s from S;
10   **if** *one encrypted document* s *remains in* S **then**
11   add (d, s) to K
12 return the mapping set K;

Based on the document identification algorithm, we can utilize the CGPR count attack to build more mappings between tokens in the identified encrypted documents and keywords in the corresponding plaintext documents, which we called query recovery algorithm, as shown in Algorithm 2.

In the proposed query recovery algorithm, we first build a modified inverted index over the identified known documents. This is an $m \times n$ matrix I, where entry $I_{i,j} = 1$ iff document D_j contains keyword w_i. All other entries are set to zero. The rows are indexed by the keyword set, while the columns are indexed by the document set. In the same way, we build an $m \times n$ matrix I' for the identified encrypted documents, where entry $I'_{i,j} = 1$ iff document D_j contains token t_i. All other entries are set to zero. Based on matrix I and I', we then build a $m \times m$ keyword co-occurrence count matrix K', where $K'[i, j]$ represents the number of documents in which w_i and w_j both appear. Similarly, we build a $m \times m$ token co-occurrence count matrix T', where $T'[i, j]$ represents the number of encrypted documents in which token t_i and token t_j both appear.

3.3   Query Recovery Attacks Against Encrypted-Index SE Model

In the Encrypted-Index SE model, before queries are issued, the attacker learns nothing except the sizes of the documents and indexes. For trapdoors that have been queried, the query results reveal the information about the query keyword occurrence count and the keyword co-occurrence count of the queried keywords.

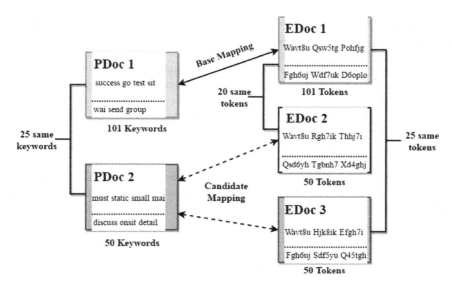

Fig. 2. An example of document identification attack. There are two known plaintext documents and three encrypted documents. As a result, *PDoc1* is mapped to *EDoc1*, *PDoc2* is mapped to *EDoc3*.

Algorithm 2. Query Recovery Attack algorithm

---

    input : Query token set T in identified encrypted documents e', keyword set
              W in identified known plaintext documents p'.
    output: mapping set between T and W;
1 initialize the base mapping set G;
2 compute the token co-occurrence matrix T' for T and the keyword
    co-occurrence matrix K' for W;
3 **while** *size of G is increasing* **do**
4   **for** *each unknown token* $t \in T - G$ **do**
5   build candidate keyword set $S = \{s :$ the occurrence count of s in p' is
          equal to the occurrence count of t in e' $\}$;
6   **for** $s \in S$ **do**
7   **for** *known base mapping* $(t', s') \in G$ **do**
8   **if** $T'[t, t'] \neq K'[s, s']$ **then**
9   remove s from S;
10   **if** *one keyword s remains in S* **then**
11   add (t, s) to G
12 return the mapping set G;

Initially, the attacker (i.e., the cloud server) cannot establish the base mappings between a known subset of plaintext documents and all encrypted documents based on the number of keywords. However, it can establish such mappings in specific scenes with auxiliary information, called *Extended Document Identi-fication Attack*. For example, in the Enron [17] dataset, the public email con-tains auxiliary information, such as senders, receivers, and timestamps. If the attacker knows widely-circulated emails, it can make the association based on specific protocols and related data items. In this way, the attacker can construct the mappings between the identified encrypted documents and the correspond-ing plaintext documents. With the mappings, by counting the trapdoors and the returned results for a period of time, the attacker can build more mappings between trapdoors and corresponding keywords than the one without document identification. In fact, if the adversary intercepts a set of queries Q over a suffi-cient long period, it has a good chance to count most high-frequency keywords.

For queried trapdoors, the attacker can create an inverted index as shown in Fig. 3. The document IDs pointed by dotted arrows means that they are not belong to the constructed mappings of document identification. Then, the attacker performs document pruning to remove the document IDs that do not belong to the constructed document mappings. By this way, the attacker can remove the information that has nothing to do with the known subset of plain-texts. Finally, after performing the document identification and document prun-ing steps, the mappings between trapdoors and keywords can be built accurately using query recovery attack algorithms.

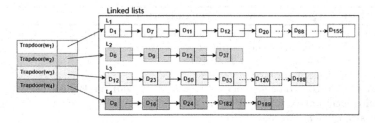

Fig. 3. The inverted index for queried results. D_i stands for document ID, L_i represents a linked list for keyword w_i.

4   Evaluation

We implemented a prototype system and conducted experiments to validate the effectiveness of the proposed document identification attacks: (1) in a single user case and in a multi-user case; (2) the improved success rate of query recovery attack. The configuration of the testing virtual machine includes an Intel 2.5 GHz dual-core with 8 GB memory. For each experiment on the Enron dataset [17], it took less than 5 min to complete, which shows the effectiveness of the proposed attack model.

4.1   Experimental Setup

We used the Enron [17] dataset available online as our test data. We chose emails from the "_sent_mail" folder of 73 employees, resulting in a total of 28,657 messages. There are about 49,835 distinct keywords in the whole dataset.

We extracted keywords from this dataset as follows: An email message is considered as one document. The first few lines of each email usually contain auxiliary information about the email, such as senders, receivers, and timestamps. We strip these lines off in a preprocessing step, because these lines are not part of the original email. The words in each email were first stemmed using the standard Porter stemming algorithm [18]; we remove 200 stop words [19] and duplicate keywords.

Given the set of n documents, the above process produces a set of distinct keywords for each document, resulting in n keyword sets. Assume there are a total of M distinct keywords in all the keyword sets, we then establish a fixed-size keyword vocabulary by taking the most frequent m keywords from these sets.

In our experiments, the adversary only knows a subset of emails. The leaked emails of different users are expected to vary significantly. Therefore, it is hard to adopt a methodology to capture which messages are more likely to be leaked. Without losing the generality, we randomly selected a subset of emails as the known documents for each setting. We present the concrete effect of document identification attack with partial knowledge against the Appended-Token SE model in the following. When attacking the Encrypted-Index SE model, we conduct the Extended Document Identification Attack with auxiliary information.

4.2   Effectiveness of Document Identification Attack

To achieve a high success rate, we first perform document identification attack, which establishes the mappings between the known subset of plaintext documents and the encrypted documents. We show that the attack works well even when just a small fraction of documents are known to the attacker. Note that the result of document identification attack is dependent on the randomly selected subset of known documents; however, we have repeated the experiments in the same setting many times, and the results are consistent.

Document Identification Attack in a Single-User Case. First, we consider the single-user SE scheme, such as in the ShadowCrypt [4] approach, which adds end-to-end encryption to cloud-based applications. It interposed itself between the interface of a legacy application and a user. As different users apply different keys to encrypt data and generate different query tokens, a user can only search for its documents.

Incidentally, an adversary may have partial knowledge about a victim's documents. We randomly selected a user from 73 employees, "allen-p", as the victim. There were 602 emails in its "_sent_mail" folder. While 69% of the emails contain less than 44 distinct keywords, only 8% of emails contain the unique number of keywords (mostly more than 100 keywords). The emails are named with different index numbers. We choose a proportion of the emails as partially known documents.

The experimental results of document identification attack in the single-user case are shown in Fig. 4, with different subsets of known documents. The x-axis represents the percentage of known documents, and the y-axis represents the number of documents that have been identified. The top (green) line with triangle markers represents the number of documents known to the attacker; the middle (red) curve with square markers represents the number of identified documents after the document identification attack; the bottom (blue) line with diamond markers represents the number of documents that have been identified in the base mappings. We can see that only a few documents are identified in the base mappings; with the proposed attack, we can map a large proportion of known documents to their corresponding encrypted documents. On average, we can identify about 81% of known plaintext documents with their encrypted versions. However, the attack is dependent on that at least one document is initially identified in the base mappings. This can be resolved by making an initial guess that maps a document to one in the candidate encrypted document set, and then runs the remainder of the algorithm. If the guess is wrong, the document similarity comparison algorithm detects inconsistency, and we then will try another candidate.

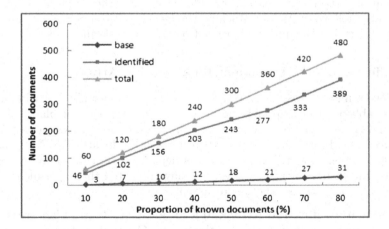

Fig. 4. Document identification results in a single-user case. There are 602 emails in the sent folder of the user. The top (green) line with triangle markers represents the number of documents known to the attacker. The middle (red) curve with square markers represents the number of documents that the attacker can map to specific encrypted documents. (Color figure online)

Document Identification Attack in a Multi-User Case. In a multi-user case, we take the Cloud Access Security Broker (CASB) [20] as the defacto architecture. In a CASB construction, a security control broker sits between cloud applications and a group of customers. Before confidential data is passed into the cloud, the broker intercepts and replaces it with random tokens or encrypted values. Furthermore, several pioneering companies such as Skyhigh Networks [6], CipherCloud [7] and Bitglass [15] have launched their commercial SE products based on CASB.

In this setting, multiple users may share some common documents, and an administrator allows a group of users to generate search tokens. For different users in the same group, the broker may use the same key to generate query tokens. A user query may be performed on the index of documents owned by the group. Initially, an attacker may have partial knowledge about a victim's document set. In the following experiment, assume that the attacker knows the same percentage of User allen-p's documents as in the single-user case, but the encrypted documents include the emails of multiple users. In the extreme setting with 73 users, there are 28,657 emails; 98% of the emails contain less than 252 distinct keywords, and 117 emails contain the unique number of keywords. The experimental results of the base mappings in document identification attack were shown in Fig. 5.

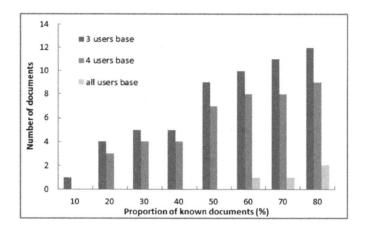

Fig. 5. Base mappings results in a multi-user case. The "3 users base" includes 2825 emails of allen-p, arnold-j and bass-e; the "4 users base" includes 3572 emails of allen-p, arnold-j, bass-e and farmer-d; and the "all users base" includes 28,657 emails of 73 users.

As shown in Fig. 5, in the settings of different proportions of known documents of User allen-p, the bars become shorter as more users are considered. That is, the identified documents in base mappings become fewer as more users are considered. Under the 73-user setting there does not exist a document in the base mappings until the attacker knows 60% of User allen-p's files. From Fig. 6 we can see that, even if the initial base mappings collection contains only one email, the final identified mappings collection can contain as many documents as the document identification result of the single-user case.

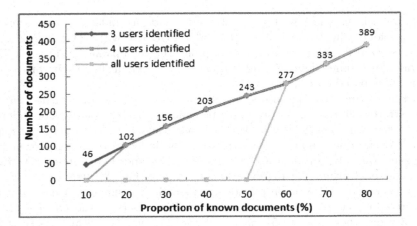

Fig. 6. Results of document identification attack in a multi-user case. Each curve represents the total number of identified documents in different settings.

4.3 Query Recovery Attacks on SE with Partial Knowledge

In this section, we show the experimental results of query recovery attacks after the document identification attack on various SE schemes with partial knowledge. Table 2 shows different numbers of keywords in different identified plaintext documents. In the attack against the Appended-Token SE model that exposing all the search tokens, we select the first 500 most frequent keywords in different identified plaintext documents as the keyword universe, and try to find their corresponding tokens in the identified encrypted documents. In the attack against the Encrypted-Index SE model, based on the selected keyword universe, we randomly selected 150 keywords as the query keyword set. Given the trapdoors of the query keyword set and their query results, we try to find their corresponding keywords in the keyword universe.

Table 2. Identified documents statistics.

Identified documents number	46	102	156	203	243	277	333	389
Keywords number		842	1554	1928	2164	2412	2756	2992	3292

Attack Against the Appended-Token SE Model. After the document identification attack, we use the identified encrypted documents and their corresponding plaintext documents to conduct a query recovery attack against the Appended-Token SE model. As shown in Fig. 7, the x-axis represents the percentage of documents known to the attacker. A "base" point at the bottom represents the number of keywords that have been identified in the base mappings, and the "identified" point at the top represents the total number of identified keywords after applying the keyword co-occurrence comparison algorithm. We use the first 500 most frequent keywords in the identified documents as our keyword universe. When we identify 46 documents of 60 known plaintext documents of User "allen-p", we can invert 44% (220 out of 500) tokens in the identified encrypted documents. When we identify 243 documents of 300 known plaintext documents of the user, we can invert 81% (465 out of 500) tokens. When we identify 389 documents of 480 known plain documents of the user, we can invert all 500 tokens. In contrast, without the proposed document identification attack, the query recovery rates in the settings of different proportional known documents are all close to zero.

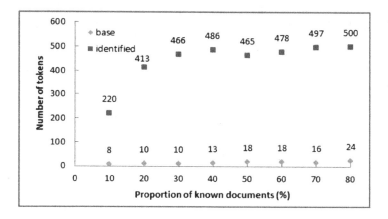

Fig. 7. Invert tokens under the Appended-Token SE model. A "base" point represents the number of tokens uncovered in the base mappings, and an "identified" point represents the number of tokens uncovered when 500 tokens are considered.

Attack Against the Encrypted-Index SE Model. In this setting, if the plaintext content contains timestamps, address or user information, the attacker can also use such auxiliary information to establish the document mappings. For example, in the Enron dataset, the public email contains auxiliary information such as senders, receivers, and timestamps. Since the sender and receiver information cannot be encrypted by the client to use the email service, the server can use this information to build the document identification attack. Using this extended document identification attack with auxiliary information, in a specific application such as email service, we can map any known documents to corresponding encrypted documents. Then, we count the first 500 most frequent keywords in the identified plaintext documents as the keyword universe. We refer $R_q = \{d_1, ..., d_n\}$ as the result sent by the server in response to a query q, such that $d_i = 1$ iff the i-th document contains the keyword corresponding to the query q; and $d_i = 0$ otherwise. For every d_i, if it does not belong to the identified encrypted documents, we set $d_i = 0$ to remove it from the query result. Then, for every query trapdoor, if the returned result contains a unique number of identified encrypted documents, the corresponding keyword has the same occurrence count in the identified known plaintext documents. The server can immediately invert the trapdoor by finding the keyword w such that $count(w) = count(q)$. We can then use a co-occurrence comparison algorithm to build other mappings.

As Fig. 8 shows, we randomly select a subset of 150 keywords from the 500 most frequent keywords in the identified plain documents as query keywords. When we identify 46 documents of known plaintext documents of User "allen-p", we can invert about 48% of the 150 trapdoors. When we identify 243 documents of known plaintext documents of the user, we can invert 93.3% of the 150 trapdoors. Eventually, if we identify 389 documents of known plaintext documents of the user, we can invert all 150 trapdoors. Note that the success rate of query recovery attack is dependent on the randomly selected query keyword set; however, we have repeated the experiments in the same setting many times, and the results are consistent. On the other hand, the success rates of query recovery attack in the settings of different proportions of known documents are all close to zero without the help of our document identification attack, as IKK and CGPR did.

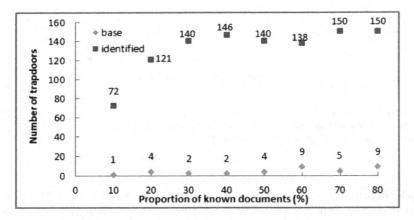

Fig. 8. Invert trapdoors for the Encrypted-Index SE Model. The "base" point represents the number of trapdoors uncovered in the base mappings, and the "identified" point represents the final number of trapdoors uncovered when 150 trapdoors are considered.

5 Mitigation

Inference attacks often use the frequency of keywords and the co-occurrence patterns of multiple keywords to guess the meanings of search trapdoors. So, the protection method needs to disrupt the frequency relationship between keywords and trapdoors. By adding noise to access patterns or search patterns, the observable statistics can be perturbed to a certain extent.

Add Noise to Access Pattern Leakage. To avoid causing an incomplete search result for a keyword, we cannot simply remove items from the search index to add noise to access patterns. An obvious way is padding the number of documents returned for a query. Since we can count the results of queries and filter out irrelevant documents, padding the index using bogus documents does not mitigate our attack effectively. IKK [8] uses the $(a, 0)$-secure index to thwart inference attacks. It aims to make query responses as similar as possible at the expense of increased false positives. Qualitatively, the $(a, 0)$-secure index guarantees that, for each keyword, there are at least other $(a - 1)$ keywords that have exactly the same query results. However, it incurs extra communication costs and the client needs to detect and discard the false positives.

Add Noise to Search Pattern Leakage. To obscure the search patterns, an obvious way is to replace a keyword with multiple trapdoors. Liu et al. [21] proposed a grouping-based construction (GBC) to thwart inference attacks. In this scheme, the query generated by the client is a collection of k trapdoors, which includes one search trapdoor of the real keyword that the client wants to search for, and $(k - 1)$ trapdoors of randomly selected keywords. GBC used "or" search function, which is not supported in some legacy applications.

Our Countermeasure. We outline an approach to add noises in search patterns and access patterns, and which can be applied to existing legacy applications. The basic idea is as follows. Assume we have a collection of documents D to be encrypted, and a set of keywords W to be queried, and set group size to 2. First, we sort the keywords in a descending order referring to keyword frequency. We map the first keyword and the last keyword to the same token T_1, the second keyword and the second-to-the-last keyword to the same token T_2, ..., until mapping the middle of the two to the same token T_i. In this way, the difference of the frequency of every query token is minimized. So, the adversary cannot perform the query recovery attack accurately based on the leakage of search patterns and access patterns. On the other hand, as the query results contain false positives, we need to filter out extra documents using a secondary map before returning it to the user. For space and efficiency, we simply mark the documents that contain at least one keyword of a group using a bitmap to build the secondary map. For most cloud services, a file often has its uploading timestamp as its attribute. So we can use this attribute to filter the extra results. First, in the index building process, we can sort the document set D_g that contain at least one keyword of a group g in a chronological order. For the group g, we build a bitmap in which location $L_i = 01$ if the i-th document of D_g only contains the less frequent keyword, $L_i = 10$ if the i-th document of D_g only contains the more frequent keyword, and $L_i = 11$ if the i-th document of D_g contains the two keywords in the group g. So, when querying a keyword belongs to a group, we can filter extra documents in the returned results based on the timestamps of the encrypted documents and the bitmap of the group.

Efficiency. We conducted experiments on our prototype to validate the efficiency of our countermeasure. We selected User "allen-p" as the victim. There were 602 emails in its "_sent_mail" folder. We count the frequency of every extracted keyword and selected the 500 most frequent keywords as our keyword universe. We group the first and the last one, the second and the second to the last, ..., until the middle of the two as a group. For keywords in each group, we map them to the same token. Then, we perform inference attacks with known documents and encrypted documents that contain query tokens. If the keywords of a group both appear in a document, then the count of tokens appended to the encrypted document is less than the count of keywords in the corresponding plaintext document, so that the document identification attack does not work well. The results show that, even if we know all documents, we can invert almost none of the query tokens. The experimental results show that our protective measures can effectively prevent query recovery attacks.

6   Conclusion

In this paper, we first introduce two searchable encryption models, including the Encrypted-Index searchable encryption model and the Appended-Token searchable encryption model, and related inference attacks. We then present our document identification attack and query recovery attack based on partial knowledge. We show that the attack is effective even when only a small fraction of documents is known to the attacker. We further design and validate a countermeasure to address this issue.

We plan to further investigate related query recovery attacks. Because the mappings in the document identification process can invert some tokens to their respective keywords, the unknown tokens associated with the remaining ciphertext can be guessed based on known tokens, related public documents, and co-occurrence algorithms, in order to invert as many tokens as possible. Moreover, we will design interactive SE constructions hiding access patterns to prevent inference attacks. A simple way is to keep the document identifiers encrypted in the query result of a search trapdoor, and decrypt it on the client side. The disadvantage is that the client has to spend an extra round-trip time to retrieve the documents.

Acknowledgments. This work is supported by the National High Technology Research and Development Program of China (863 Program) under Grant No. 2015AA016001, Production-Study-Research Cooperation Project in Guangdong Province under Grant No. 2016B090921001, Innovation projects in Shandong Province under Grant No. 2014ZZCX03411, and National Natural Science Foundation of China under Grant No. 61370068.

References

1. Goldreich, O., Ostrovsky, R.: Software protection and simulation on oblivious RAMs. J. ACM (JACM) **43**(3), 431–473 (1996)
2. Bsch, C., Hartel, P., Jonker, W., et al.: A survey of provably secure searchable encryption. ACM Comput. Surv. (CSUR) **47**(2), 18 (2015)

3. Curtmola, R., Garay, J., Kamara, S., et al.: Searchable symmetric encryption: improved definitions and efficient constructions. J. Comput. Secur. **19**(5), 895–934 (2011)
4. He, W., Akhawe, D., Jain, S., et al.: Shadowcrypt: encrypted web applications for everyone. In: Proceedings of the 2014 ACM Special Interest Group on Security, Audit and Control, Scottsdale Arizona, USA, pp. 1028–1039 (2014)
5. Lau, B., Chung, S., Song, C., et al.: Mimesis aegis: a mimicry privacy shielda system's approach to data privacy on public cloud. In: Proceedings of the 23rd USENIX Security Symposium, SanDiego California, USA, pp. 33–48 (2014)
6. Skyhigh Networks. https://www.skyhighnetworks.com/
7. CipherCloud. https://www.ciphercloud.com/
8. Islam, M.S., Kuzu, M., Kantarcioglu, M.: Access pattern disclosure on searchable encryption: ramification, attack and mitigation. In: NDSS, vol. 20, p. 12 (2012)
9. Cash, D., Grubbs, P., Perry, J., et al.: Leakage-abuse attacks against searchable encryption. In: Proceedings of the 22nd ACM SIGSAC Conference on Computer and Communications Security, pp. 668–679. ACM (2015)
10. Zhang, Y., Katz, J., Papamanthou, C.: All your queries are belong to us: the power of file-injection attacks on searchable encryption. IACR Cryptology ePrint Archive, 2016:172 (2016)
11. Pouliot, D., Wright, C.V.: The shadow nemesis: inference attacks on efficiently deployable, efficiently searchable encryption. In: Proceedings of the 2016 ACM SIGSAC Conference on Computer and Communications Security, pp. 1341–1352. ACM (2016)
12. Cash, D., Jarecki, S., Jutla, C., Krawczyk, H., Roşu, M.-C., Steiner, M.: Highly-scalable searchable symmetric encryption with support for boolean queries. In: Canetti, R., Garay, J.A. (eds.) CRYPTO 2013. LNCS, vol. 8042, pp. 353–373. Springer, Heidelberg (2013). https://doi.org/10.1007/978-3-642-40041-4_20
13. Li, J., Wang, Q., Wang, C., et al.: Fuzzy keyword search over encrypted data in cloud computing. In: INFOCOM, 2010 Proceedings IEEE, pp. 1–5. IEEE (2010)
14. Kamara, S., Papamanthou, C., Roeder, T.: Dynamic searchable symmetric encryption. In: Proceedings of the 2012 ACM Conference on Computer and Communications Security, pp. 965–976. ACM (2012)
15. Bitglass. http://www.bitglass.com/
16. Virtru. http://www.virtru.com/
17. Enron Email Dataset. www.cs.cmu.edu/~./enron/. Accessed 13 May 2015
18. Porter, M.: An algorithm for suffix striping. Program **14**(3), 130–137 (1980)
19. Common-English-Words. http://www.textfixer.com/tutorials/common-english-words.txt/
20. Gartner Report: How to Evaluate and Operate a Cloud Access Security Broker, 8 December 2015
21. Liu, C., Zhu, L., Wang, M., et al.: Search pattern leakage in searchable encryption: attacks and new construction. Inf. Sci. **265**, 176–188 (2014)

H₂DoS: An Application-Layer DoS Attack Towards HTTP/2 Protocol

Xiang Ling[1(✉)], Chunming Wu[1], Shouling Ji[1,3], and Meng Han[2]

[1] Zhejiang University, Hangzhou, China
{lingxiang,wuchunming,sji}@zju.edu.cn
[2] Kennesaw State University, Kennesaw, GA, USA
menghan@kennesaw.edu
[3] Alibaba-Zhejiang University Joint Institute of Frontier Technologies,
Hangzhou, China

Abstract. HTTP/2, as the latest version of application layer protocol, is experiencing an exponentially increasing adoption by both servers and browsers. Due to the new features introduced by HTTP/2, many security threats emerge in the deployment of HTTP/2. In this paper, we focus on application-layer DoS attacks in HTTP/2 and present a novel H₂DoS attack that exploits multiplexing and flow-control mechanisms of HTTP/2. We first perform a large-scale measurement to investigate the deployment of HTTP/2. Then, based on measurement results, we test H₂DoS under a general experimental setting, where the server-side HTTP/2 implementation is *nginx*. Our comprehensive tests demonstrate both the feasibility and severity of H₂DoS attack. We find that H₂DoS attack results in completely denying requests from legitimate clients and has severe impacts on victim servers. Our work underscores the emerging security threats arise in HTTP/2, which has significant reference value to other researchers and the security development of HTTP/2.

Keywords: Web security · DoS attack · HTTP/2 protocol

1 Introduction

Hypertext Transfer Protocol (HTTP) is a dominant and fundamental application protocol, and it powers the data communication on the Internet. Recently, the latest version of HTTP protocol - HTTP/2 [1] has been standardized and received much attention as it can reduce the load latency of web pages by addressing some performance inhibitors inherent in HTTP/1.1 and HTTPS [8]. HTTP/2 protocol is primarily designed for improving performance by introducing new features, however, which can result in new and potential security threats. Those security threats introduced by HTTP/2 may have damaging effects on the Internet in terms of both end users and web servers, because the current HTTP/2 protocol has been adopted by most major browsers and many websites [8]. This brings up a significant challenge of how to explore new security threats against HTTP/2, and motivates us to begin the research of this paper.

© ICST Institute for Computer Sciences, Social Informatics and Telecommunications Engineering 2018
X. Lin et al. (Eds.): SecureComm 2017, LNICST 238, pp. 550–570, 2018.
https://doi.org/10.1007/978-3-319-78813-5_28

The application-layer Denial-of-Service (DoS) attack is a form of DoS attacks where attackers target at the application-layer of web servers. By exploring characteristics and vulnerabilities of application layer protocols, application-layer DoS attacks aim to exhaust server resources that the application requires to function properly [23]. The application-layer DoS has become one of the most damaging attacks to threat the Internet ecosystem [5] in 2016 and was believed to increasingly escalate in the future. Since the HTTP/2 protocol is a new and significant part of web servers in terms of application layer protocols, HTTP/2 is also supposed to face application-layer DoS attacks. In this paper, we narrow our research scope and focus on application-layer DoS attacks towards the HTTP/2 protocol. We present a novel **H$_2$DoS** attack, which is the first real application-layer DoS attack targeting at HTTP/2-enabled web servers. By exploiting multiplexing and flow-control mechanisms in HTTP/2, the H$_2$DoS attack can completely deny legitimate users from accessing the victim server. Moreover, this attack also inflicts more severe impacts on server resources compared with other application-layer DoS attacks, which can result in severe damages to web servers.

Concretely, to investigate the potential extent of application-layer DoS attacks against HTTP/2 protocol in practice, we first perform a large scale measurement to understand the current deployment and implementation of HTTP/2. We find that 14% of Alexa's top million websites [11] have already begun to support HTTP/2 protocol. Moreover, most of these websites adopt nginx [17] as the server-side implementation, which can be strongly affected by our H$_2$DoS attack. Then, we analyze two new features introduced by HTTP/2: flow-control and multiplexing mechanism, and find that both of them are vulnerable to application-layer DoS attacks. Based on those analyses, we propose the novel H$_2$DoS attack which exploits both flow-control and multiplexing mechanisms. Our proposed H$_2$DoS attack can disrupt or even completely deny legitimate user from accessing the victim web servers. Next, we examine both the feasibility and severity of H$_2$DoS attack in our experiments. Our experimental tests show that victim web servers reply with HTTP 500 (Internal Server Error) code to legitimate users during H$_2$DoS attack. This result indicates that a real denial of service takes place on victim web servers. Even worse, we find that H$_2$DoS attack can massively consume server resources, and compared with other application-layer DoS attacks, it inflicts more severe impacts on the performance of victim servers. Overall, the main contributions of this paper can be summarized as follows:

– We provide a comprehensive security analysis of the HTTP/2 protocol specification, especially focusing on its multiplexing and flow-control mechanisms. According to our analysis, we find that both multiplexing and flow-control mechanisms are vulnerable to application-layer DoS attacks.
– We propose a novel application-layer DoS attack against HTTP/2, H$_2$DoS. H$_2$DoS exploits vulnerable multiplexing and flow-control mechanism of HTTP/2 protocol, and therefore can result in denial of service on victim servers.

– We systematically validate H_2DoS attack (feasibility), and evaluate its impact (severity) by performing extensive experiments, which to the best of our knowledge is first such an attempt.

The rest of this paper is organized as follows. We first review HTTP/2 and application-layer DoS attacks in Sect. 2. Next, in Sect. 3 we briefly describe current deployment and implementation information of HTTP/2 in practice. Section 4 presents the threat model of H_2DoS attack in detail. We examine both the feasibility and severity of H_2DoS attack through extensive experiments in Sect. 5. We also give further discussions on mitigation for H_2DoS attack and summarize the related works in Sects. 6 and 7. Finally, the work is concluded and the future work is addressed in Sect. 8.

2   Background

2.1   Application-Layer DoS Attack

Denial-of-service (DoS) attack is one of the most damaging attacks as it intends to deny legitimate users from accessing network resources and destroy the Internet ecosystem. Originally, DoS attacks basically mean network-layer DoS attacks, which mostly abuse TCP, UDP and ICMP protocols to exhaust network resources of the victim (*e.g.*, bandwidth, sockets, *etc.*) and further deny its services. However, this kind of DoS attacks has been fully studied for years and already been mitigated by many industry solutions. In order to evade such mitigation solutions, DoS attacks have been evolved to sophisticated application-layer DoS attack [22] as their stealthier appearance and lower attack cost than traditional network-layer DoS attacks.

Concretely, application-layer DoS attacks focus on disrupting or even completely denying legitimate users from accessing the victim web server by exhausting its resources, including not only network bandwidth and sockets, but also connections, CPU, memory, I/O bandwidth, *etc.* There are basically two types of application-layer DoS attacks - HTTP DoS and HTTPS DoS attacks, as both of them are based on two dominant protocols that used by the application layer.

1. **HTTP DoS.** HTTP DoS attacks normally exploit seemingly legitimate HTTP GET/POST requests to occupy all available HTTP connections that permitted on the web server. **Slowloris** [6] is one of the most effective HTTP DoS attacks against many popular types of web server softwares like Apache and nginx. If an attacker initiates an HTTP request to open several connections to a server and periodically feeds the server with data before reaching timeout, the HTTP connection would remain to open until the attacker closes it. Ultimately, it easily fulfills the maximum concurrent connections of the web server and takes the server down.
2. **HTTPS DoS.** HTTPS layers HTTP on top of Transport Layer Security (TLS), which encrypts all communication data for end-to-end security and easily evades security managements [13]. Hence, HTTPS DoS can further

challenge many existing web application firewall detection solutions, as most of the solutions do not actually inspect encrypted traffics [10]. In addition to bypassing DoS prevention efforts, as encrypted HTTP attacks add burden of encryption and decryption, HTTPS DoS can exhaust all server resources by leveraging all possible approaches [7], such as encrypted SSL floods, SSL renegotiations and HTTPS floods.

Currently, the application-layer DoS attack increasingly escalates and has become a significantly severe threat for web servers. According to Radware Emergency Response Team's (ERT) annual report [5], 63% of its respondents have experienced application-layer based attacks in 2016, and 43% of experienced an HTTP flood, while 36% experienced an HTTPS flood.

2.2 HTTP/2 Protocol

Overview. HTTP/2 protocol is the latest version of HTTP protocol that dramatically reduces the load latency of web pages by addressing some performance inhibitors inherent in HTTP/1.1 or HTTPS. Shortly after being standardized as RFC 7540 [1] in 2015, HTTP/2 is experiencing an exponential growing industry adoption with both servers and browsers. Originally, HTTP/2 protocol mainly succeeds to SPDY [2], which is an experimental application-layer protocol designed by Google as a replacement for more efficient communication transmission [9]. Basically, HTTP/2 reserves majority of SPDY protocol, except with several changes, such as a new header compression for HTTP/2 - HPACK [3] instead of gzip or deflate used by SPDY.

The primary goal of HTTP/2 is to reduce the web page load latency by providing an optimized communication transmission. HTTP/2 enables fully request and response multiplexing, minimizes transmission overhead with support of flow-control and server push, and replaces with a less redundant header field compression method. Below, we detail three optimized features of HTTP/2 that related to our study and omit the other features.

1. **Frame Unit.** HTTP/2 protocol introduces the frame unit as the basic protocol unit to be exchanged between servers and browsers. There are ten different types of frames used to serve distinct purposes in the establishment and management of HTTP/2 connections or streams. For instance, *WINDOW_UPDATE* is a frame that used for HTTP/2 flow-control mechanisms. But in this paper, we will manipulate it and other frames to create a new application-layer DoS attack against HTTP/2.

2. **Multiplexing.** HTTP/2 initiates only one single TCP connection to one domain and multiples HTTP requests and responses. HTTP/2 can dramatically reduce the load latency of web pages, as the multiplexing feature not only reduces the number of TCP connections but also SSL encryption overhead at both browser and server sides. For the same reason, the multiplexing feature also becomes actually an important amplification factor to enhance the impact of our attack.

3. **Flow-Control.** Flow-control is one of the most distinguish features of HTTP/2, which can be used for both individual streams and the whole connection. The flow-control feature ensures that streams on the same TCP connection do not negatively interface with each other. The flow-control also allows customized algorithms to optimize data transmission between servers and browsers, especially when their resources are limited. This actually poses a severe security threat that an HTTP/2 connection can demand a greater resources to operate than an HTTP/1.1 connection.

The above three features of HTTP/2 protocol enable a significant reduction of page loading time and mitigate some existing security threats [4] to some extent. However, adopting a new protocol can bring new security threats since new features of HTTP/2 extend the new attack surface towards clients or servers. In fact, both multiplexing and flow-control features described above are vulnerable to the application-layer DoS attack, which motivates us to propose our H_2DoS attack. We will discuss those new features and their potential vulnerabilities in more detail in Sect. 4.

3 HTTP/2 Current Deployment

To investigate the potential extent of application-layer DoS attacks against HTTP/2 protocol in practice, a large-scale measurement is performed to investigate the current HTTP/2 deployment and its implementation. To this end, we build a measurement platform to conduct real crawling of the exact domain of all sites provided by Alexa top one million ranking list [11]. In this section, the Application-Layer Protocol Negotiation (ALPN) extension [12] is first employed during TLS handshake to measure how many websites adopt HTTP/2. Then, we extract the HTTP/2 implementation software information within the established HTTP/2 connection. Notice that our statistics results are all based on experiments and observations from January 10th to January 13th in 2017.

3.1 Measurement Setup

Generally, establishing an HTTP connection can be divided into three phrases: TCP handshake, TLS handshake, and application-layer communication. Figure 1 illustrates the process of HTTP/2 connection establishment. To answer the first question that how many websites adopt HTTP/2 protocol, we observe the ALPN extension [12] of TLS handshake within an HTTP/2 connection in step ❸ and ❹ of the Fig. 1. The ALPN extension is used for application-layer protocol negotiation in exchange of *Hello* message: the client provides a list of optional protocols which it supports and the server can respond with a selected protocol that want to use. Therefore in this measurement, if a website negotiates **"h2"** as the selected protocol within ALPN, we consider that the website adopts HTTP/2 protocol in terms of the application layer.

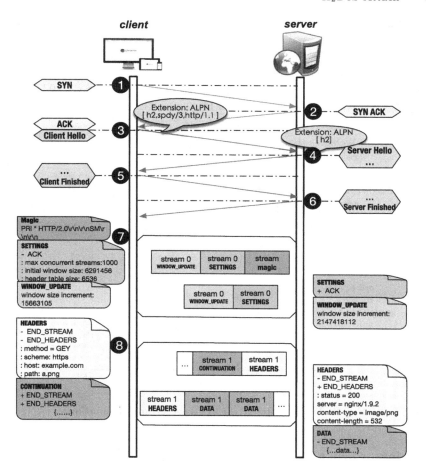

Fig. 1. Establishment process of an HTTP/2 connection: TCP handshake is first completed in step ❶–❸, followed by a TLS handshake in step ❹–❻. Then after step ❼ and ❽, the HTTP/2 connection is finally established.

Another question is how about implementations of websites enabled HTTP/2. Basically, an HTTP/2 connection starts with sending the connection preface, called *Magic* frame and followed by a *SETTING* frame and/or *WINDOW_UPDATE* frame in step ❼, which used for flow-control mechanism in HTTP/2. After that, by sending a *HEADERS* frame, we could receive a *HEADERS* response frame. Normally in *HEADERS* response frame, we find the exact implementation software information of the website through HTTP **"Server"** header field.

Table 1. Summary of protocols deployment of Alexa's top million websites

Protocol	Description	#	%
HTTP/1.x	Websites that not support TLS	465,693	46.57%
HTTPS(pure)	Websites that purely support HTTP/1.1 over TLS	355,025	35.50%
HTTP/2	Websites that support HTTP/2 over TLS	143,471	14.35%
SPDY	Websites that announce support SPDY	25	- - -
Others	Websites that cannot accessible or only support other protocols like QUIC *etc.*	35,786	3.58%

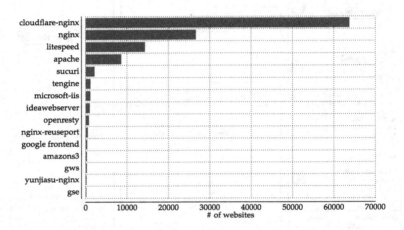

Fig. 2. Top 15 popular HTTP/2 server implementations

3.2   Measurement Result

HTTP/2 Deployment. Table 1 summarizes the current protocols deployment of Alexa top million websites, including HTTP/1.x, pure HTTPS, HTTP/2, SPDY and others. The table shows that there are around 50% websites supporting TLS connection in their web servers, in which 28.78% of websites have already supported HTTP/2 protocol via ALPN extension in TLS handshake. In addition, we also report that 14.35% of websites have supported HTTP/2 in top million websites. It implies that numerous website servers that support HTTP/2 are facing potential security threats including application-layer DoS attacks. We also believe that there will be more websites adopt HTTP/2 along with more security threats, which can leads to severe damage to the Internet.

HTTP/2 Implementation. We record HTTP/2 implementation information among all HTTP/2-enabled websites via HTTP/2 *HEADERS* frame in our measurement platform, in which we observe more than 414 different kinds of server implementations in total. For visibility, Fig. 2 plots top 15 popular server-side implementation softwares powering HTTP/2 websites. In spite that *cloudflare-nginx* and *nginx* are top two that used as implementation softwares of HTTP/2 websites, other variants like *tengine, nginx-reuseport* and *yunjiasu-nginx* also support thousands of HTTP/2 websites. As nginx community is the most prevalent HTTP/2 implementation that adopted by websites on the Internet, we choose the latest nginx stable implementation as the server-side HTTP/2 implementation in latter experiments.

4 Threat Model: H$_2$DoS Attack

In this session, we begin with a comprehensive security analysis of HTTP/2 flow-control mechanism and then present our novel H$_2$DoS attack which exploits multiplexing and flow-control mechanisms of HTTP/2 protocol in details.

4.1 HTTP/2 Flow-Control Mechanism Analysis

Flow-control mechanism is one of the most distinctive features enabled by HTTP/2 protocol that attempts to optimize the traffic transmission between browsers and servers. Generally, there are two types of frame that used for application-level flow-control in HTTP/2 protocol: *WINDOW_UPDATE* and *SETTINGS* frame. In an established HTTP/2 connection, the server and the client exchange configuration parameters including some flow-control parameters in *SETTINGS* frame, then in more fine-grained frame layer, the window size of flow-control can be updated by *WINDOW_UPDATE* frame that applied to a single frame or all frames in the HTTP/2 connection.

SETTINGS Frame. *SETTINGS* frame, which is used to inform the opposite (client or server) of configuration parameters, normally follows *Magic* frame at the start of an established HTTP/2 connection. If the stream identifier (Stream ID) of *SETTINGS* frame is set to be 0×0, It means that *SETTINGS* frame will apply to an entirely HTTP/2 connection instead of a single stream. In HTTP/2 protocol specification [1], there are totally 6 defined configuration parameters, in which 3 of them related to flow-control mechanism in an HTTP/2 connection. Table 2 shows the three flow-control related parameters in *SETTINGS* frame.

WINDOW_UPDATE Frame. The primary goal of *WINDOW_UPDATE* frame is to implement the flow-control mechanism that prevents from exceeding capacity of the receiver in an HTTP/2 connection. *WINDOW_UPDATE* in HTTP/2 protocol specification [1] has two levels of application, one level operates in an individual stream with a specific stream ID, while another level operates in an entire HTTP/2 connection whose stream ID is zero. Basically, HTTP/2 specification requires that receiver of *WINDOW_UPDATE* frame must re-calculate the corresponding window size according to the 31-bit "Window Size Increment" field included in *WINDOW_UPDATE* frame. For instance, if the server-side advertises its initial window size in *SETTINGS* frame to be 16 KB

Table 2. Flow-control parameters in SETTINGS frame

Parameters	SETTINGS_MAX_CONCURRENT_STREAMS	SETTINGS_INITIAL_WINDOW_SIZE	SETTINGS_MAX_FRAME_SIZE
Functionality	Defining the maximum number of concurrent streams that the sender permits receiver to create in this HTTP/2 connection	Defining the initial window size of streams in this HTTP/2 connection	Defining the maximum frame payload size that the sender allows to receive in this HTTP/2 connection
Value	no limit(0–$2^{31} - 1$), but recommended value is ≥ 10	no limit(0–$2^{31} - 1$), initial value is $2^{16} - 1$	range(2^{14}–$2^{24} - 1$), initial value is 2^{14}

and sets "Window Size Increment" 5 KB in *WINDOW_UPDATE* frame, then the window size of server becomes 21 KB. In addition, the window size only applies to *DATA* frame, which means that the flow-control mechanism affected by the window size only constraints *DATA* frame instead of other frames like *HEADERS* frame.

To summarize, both *SETTINGS* and *WINDOW_UPDATE* frame play an important role in HTTP/2 flow-control mechanism by means of altering or updating window size kept by both sides in a stream or connection. Naturally, "Window Size Increment" field in *WINDOW_UPDATE* frame is used to increase window size that receiver can process, while sending new *SETTING* frame with smaller initial window size can cause window size reduces. Even window size can be negative because of receiving *DATA* frame will consume window size, which can make processes in streams stalled in the end.

4.2 H₂DoS Attack Presentation

Conceptually, multiplexing and flow-control are two novel essential mechanisms of HTTP/2 that introduced to improve web performance, however these excellent mechanisms come at an expense that introducing new security threats into servers and clients. In order to understand security threats evolved from HTTP/2, we carry on a comprehensive security analysis of HTTP/2 protocol specification [1] and find that both multiplexing and flow-control mechanisms are vulnerable to application-layer DoS attacks. If exploiting multiplexing and flow-control mechanisms, a DoS attack named **H₂DoS** can be easily launched by one malicious client to attack the victim web server.

The basic idea of H₂DoS attack is natural and straightforward: a massive number of HTTP/2 requests with limited receiving capacity are sent to consume as many resources as possible, or even result in denial-of-service. To this end, H₂DoS attack exploits two following important amplification factors that derived from both multiplexing and flow-control mechanisms.

– One amplification factor is to exploit HTTP/2 multiplexing mechanism since HTTP/2 enables multiplexing vast number of streams over a single TCP connection. Even though the attacker has to initial as many TCP connections

as the victim, in HTTP/2 connection each TCP connection can maintain large amount of streams to amplify malicious HTTP GET requests.
– Another amplification factor is to limit the receive processing window size to a small size, which results in stalling all send processes of victim until the entire response data is transmitted and thus occupying lots of server resources.

Figure 3 presents how a malicious client attack the victim web server by launching application-level H₂DoS attack and its attack proceeds as follows:

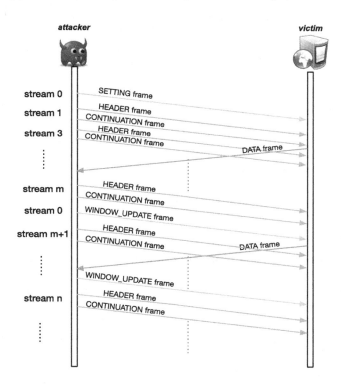

Fig. 3. H₂DoS: HTTP/2 application-level DoS attack presentation

1. Before H₂DoS attack, both TCP handshake and TLS handshake must be completed within a malicious client (called *attacker*) and a web server (called *victim*), followed by a *Magic* frame that initialized for establishing an HTTP/2 connection at first.
2. Then, the *attacker* sends a *SETTINGS* frame in stream 0. It means that the *SETTINGS* frame applies to the entire HTTP/2 connection. Two configuration parameters that mentioned in Table 2 are set up in this attack:
   (a) one parameter is *SETTINGS_MAX_CONCURRENT_STREAM*, which is supposed to set to a big number as it specifies the maximum number of streams created by the victim. And also, more streams in a connection means more threads allocated will be consumed. In fact, the maximum number of streams that the *attacker* can exploit is depend on

the *SETTINGS* frame of *victim*. What attack can do is to acknowledge the biggest *SETTINGS_MAX_CONCURRENT_STREAM* value among all *SETTINGS* frames and open as many streams as it allows.

(b) another parameter is *SETTINGS_INITIAL_WINDOW_SIZE*, which should be set as small as possible that allowed in a specific implementation software of HTTP/2 protocol in order to make the process of HTTP response slower or even make the *victim* stalled.

3. The *attacker* next constructs an HTTP/2 GET request in stream 1, which consists of a *HEADERS* frame and one or more subsequent *CONTINUATION* frames. For the necessity of the subsequent *CONTINUATION* frames, we enable the HTTP/2 GET request with a long header field, only small part of it is sent in *HEADERS* frame and the other is sent in one or more *CONTINUATION* frames.

4. Owing to multiplexing mechanism of HTTP/2, we repeat sending carefully constructed HTTP/2 request streams as above one after the other in odd-numbered stream ID (1, 3, 5, ...).

5. To prevent *victim* web server from rejecting the HTTP/2 request, *attacker* can send *WINDOW_UPDATE* frame in stream 0 periodically with a "Window Size Increment" field, but with a small size.

6. Since above processes are all in one single TCP connection, we can amplify the attack consequence by opening more than one single TCP connection.

In short, to create an effective application-layer DoS attack against HTTP/2, the whole H$_2$DoS attack exploits two amplification factors that derived from vulnerabilities of HTTP/2 in terms of both multiplexing and flow-control mechanisms. As H$_2$DoS attack repeats sending HTTP/2 GET streams to the *victim* infinitely, this attack can instantaneously occupy all available connections of the *victim*. In theory, the starvation of all available connections is the root cause of H$_2$DoS attack. In addition, the H$_2$DoS attack can also consume as much server resources as possible, which further strengthens the effect of DoS attack.

5   Experiments and Results

In this session, we seek to answer two key questions:

– Is H$_2$DoS attack a feasible DoS attack in real attack scenarios?
– Does H$_2$DoS attack have more severe impact on the targeted *victim* compared with other popular application-level DoS attacks? That is, can it become an underlying severe factor of DDoS attack?

The intent of answering above two questions is to demonstrate both the feasibility and severity of it, respectively. To this end, we first present our experiment setup, then observe experiment results from our experiments and analyze the feasibility and severity around them.

5.1 Experimental Setup

Our experiment setup consists of one *victim* web server and two clients: *attacker* and *benign user* as shown in Fig. 4, respectively. Both the *attacker* and *benign user* connect to *victim* server in HTTP/2. The *attacker* is a client that launches H₂DoS attack with malicious attack scripts, while the *benign user* is a normal client that used for testing whether the *victim* is in service. The *victim* is the web server that enabled with an HTTP/2 implementation and can be accessed in HTTP/2 connections. Table 3 summarizes detail configurations of the experiment environment. As mentioned in Sect. 3.2, nginx is the most widely adoption in HTTP/2 implementations, therefore we choose the latest nginx stable version to run on the *victim* server during the experiment execution.

Table 3. Detail configurations of the experiment environment

Configurations	*victim*	*attacker*	*benign user*
Operating system	Ubuntu 16.04.1 LTS	Ubuntu 16.04.1 LTS	Mac OSX 10.11.6
Processor	2 * Intel(R) Core(TM) i5-4590 CPU @3.30 GHz	2 * Intel(R) Core(TM) i5-4590 CPU @3.30 GHz	2.7 GHz Intel Core i5
Memory	4 GB	4 GB	8 GB
HTTP/2 implementation	nginx/1.10.0(stable)	Golang standard http/2 library [16]	Google Chrome 58.0
Others	Built with OpenSSL 1.0.2g TLS SNI support enabled	H₂DoS attack implementation in Go language	Google plug-in for connection checking

Figure 4 illustrates a straightforward process of H₂DoS attack: the *attacker* first launches the malicious attack script towards the *victim* in step ❶, where the malicious attack script implements H₂DoS attack described in Fig. 3 as well as other application-layer DoS attacks introduced in Sect. 2.1 for comparison. In *victim* server, there is a performance monitor program that used to monitor the server performances and record them down. Then during the attack, *benign user* periodically request to access resources of *victim* using normal browser in step ❷. Finally we check what contents that replied in the context of browser request before in step ❸. If we get errors instead of normal contents from received contents in *benign user*, we take it as the Denial-of-Service of *victim* that attacked by H₂DoS attack.

5.2 Experiment Result and Analysis

To answer the above two questions, we analyze in more detail for both the feasibility and severity of H₂DoS attack based on our observed experimental results.

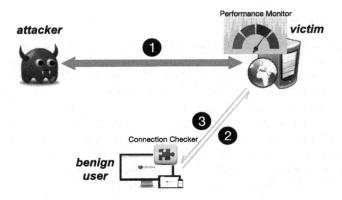

Fig. 4. H$_2$DoS attack experiment setup

Feasibility. We offer evidence of the feasibility of H$_2$DoS attack by checking whether the *victim* web server is always available for a *benign user* during H$_2$DoS attack. The connection checker illustrated in Fig. 4 is a customized browser plug-in that used for application-layer connection checking and recording. Once the H$_2$DoS attack is launched against *victim* web server, we start to observe and record what we receive from the web server in the connection checker. More specifically, if we obtain an entire webpage with HTTP 200 (OK) status code in responses, we consider the *victim* web server is available in service. By contrast, if we obtain any error webpage with HTTP 500 (Internal Server Error) or other 5XX (Server Error) status codes [14], it means that *victim* itself has an error and crashes down, which is a kind of Denial-of-Service atta. Figure 5(a) and (b) visually show the content of *benign user* that received from *victim* web server before and after H$_2$DoS attack, respectively. We observe that the *benign user* receives an entire webpage from the *victim* before H$_2$DoS attack, while after H$_2$DoS attack the *benign user* receives an error webpage with HTTP 500 (Internal Server Error) status code. These observations indicate that H$_2$DoS attack indeed takes effect into the *victim* web server in terms of denial of service attacks.

The root cause of application-layer DoS attack is that H$_2$DoS attack can occupy all available connections of the *victim* server and all streams are possibly stuck on exhausted connection or stream windo. Figure 5(c) further depicts that in our 30-min experiment as long as H$_2$DoS attack starts from *attacker* client to *victim* web server, the HTTP response status code of *benign user* quickly changes from 200 to 500. The 500 status code is used for internal server error when the server suffers from starvation of connections, which prevents the server from replying any request. From what we have observed and analyzed above, the feasibility of H$_2$DoS attack is fully demonstrated in our experiments.

Severity. For severity, we measure the impact of H$_2$DoS attack towards *victim* web server and in what extent it enhances the severity if H$_2$DoS is converted to

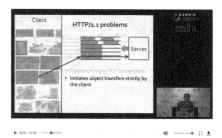

Demo Website to play videos

(a) Content of *benign user* received from the *victim* **before** H₂DoS attack.

500 Internal Server Error

(b) Content of *benign user* received from the *victim* **after** H₂DoS attack.

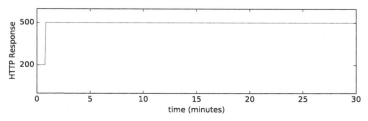

(c) HTTP response status code of *benign user* during H₂DoS attack

Fig. 5. Observations on *benign user* that received from *victim* during H₂DoS attack

Distributed Denial-of-Service (DDoS) attack against *victim*. Application-layer DDoS attack generally consumes less bandwidth and are stealthier in nature compared with other network-based DDoS attacks. Application-layer DDoS attack mainly focuses on disrupting legitimate user services by exhausting the server resources [22] like CPU and memory as much as possible.

Hence in the paper, we choose two key factors: *CPU* and *Memory* to measure the application-layer DoS attack impact. We obtain both *CPU* usage and *Memory* usage of *victim* server with the performance monitor program illustrated in Fig. 4. And the performance monitor is developed based on **psutil** [15], a process and system utilities library in Python. Intuitively, larger *CPU* or *Memory* usage consumption will result in larger probability of denying other benign users as

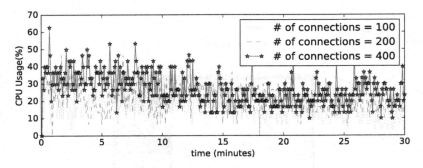

(a) CPU usage on the *victim* web server.

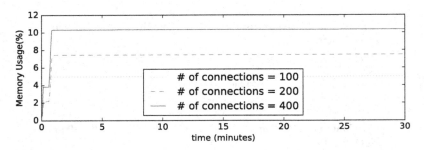

(b) Memory usage on the *victim* web server.

Fig. 6. Observations of resources consumption on *victim* when attacked by H_2DoS with different number of TCP connections.

well as larger attack severity. In this part, we conduct two sets of experiments and analyze the attack impact of H_2DoS attack to confirm the severity intuition.

1. **Severe impact of H_2DoS attack.** In this experiment, we analyze how severe the impact of H_2DoS attack is in terms of *CPU* and *Memory* usage. Once the malicious client *attacker* begins to launch H_2DoS attack against *victim* server, the performance monitor is enabled to monitor both *CPU* and *Memory* usage of *victim* server. Besides, we increase the number of TCP connection within the same H_2DoS attack in our experiment, in order to further observe how the impact of H_2DoS attack behaves in regard to TCP connections.

   Figure 6(a) and (b) illustrate that H_2DoS attack can maliciously consume large volume of CPU and memory on the whole. Specifically, as depicted in Fig. 6(a), the *CPU* usage is very high in the first several minutes and gradually stabilizes later. That is because after several minutes the H_2DoS attack takes effect and the *victim* starts to reply error code instead of real contents, which result in less *CPU* usage later. However, as depicted in Fig. 6(b), the *Memory* usage is nearly unchanged except for the beginning of H_2DoS attack. Furthermore when comparing different number of connections in H_2DoS attack, we observe that the percentage of *CPU* consumption increases with the number of TCP connections in general, while the percentage of *Memory* consumption is amplified by connections all the time in our experiment.

2. **Severe impact of H$_2$DoS attack Versus Others.** As observed above, H$_2$DoS attack has significantly severe impact on *victim* server. But how does H$_2$DoS attack compare with other application-layer DoS attacks is still a challenge question. To evaluate the impact of H$_2$DoS attack comparing with other application-layer DoS attacks, we first fix the number of TCP connections at 400 and examine the *CPU* and *Memory* usage of *victim* server during attack duration in our experiment. Next, we choose **slowloris** [6], **thc-ssl-dos** [7] and our H$_2$DoS attack in regard to application-layer DoS attack based on HTTP/1.1, HTTPS and HTTP/2, respec. Figure 7(b) and (c) show the *CPU* and the *Memory* usage of above three types of application-layer DoS attacks. Specifically, we show our results and evaluations in the following three aspects that related to the impact on *victim*:

- **Connectivity.** Figure 7(a) shows that H$_2$DoS can quickly bring down the *victim* web server and replies with status code of HTTP 500 (Internal Server Error) to the *benign* user. However, at both **slowloris** and **thc-ssl-dos** attack duration, the *victim* server provides service with HTTP 200 status code to the *benign* user all the time. As depicted in Fig. 7(b) and (c), we observe that while both the CPU and Memory usage of *victim* caused by H$_2$DoS attack do not exceed 50% over time in most cases, but H$_2$DoS leads to a real denial-of-service attack. In fact, either CPU and Memory usage is not the exclusive reason for denial-of-service, the main reason is that H$_2$DoS occupies all available connections of the *victim* and denies access to legitimate clients.

- **CPU usage.** As depicted in Fig. 7(b), the H$_2$DoS attack consumes more CPU than other two attacks on average, even though it decreases gradually after around 10 min and becomes less than **slowloris** attack at the end time of attack duration. One possible reason might be that at later time H$_2$DoS attack makes *victim* only reply with HTTP 500 error code and not in the service as H$_2$DoS results in starvation of *victim* connections, while **slowloris** is in the service all the time and maintains the CPU usage.

- **Memory usage.** As depicted in Fig. 7(c), the H$_2$DoS attack depletes around ten times memory more than both **slowloris** and **thc-ssl-dos** attack, because H$_2$DoS can exploit multiplexing mechanism within HTTP/2 to amplify the power of occupying memory resources on the *victim* server.

To summarize, the experiments described above analyze in detail that how the H$_2$DoS attack takes affect on the performance of *victim* web server and demonstrate the feasibility and severity of it in real attack scenarios. From the experiment results, we can conclude that the commercial HTTP/2 implementation nginx can be exploited and severely impacted by H$_2$DoS attack.

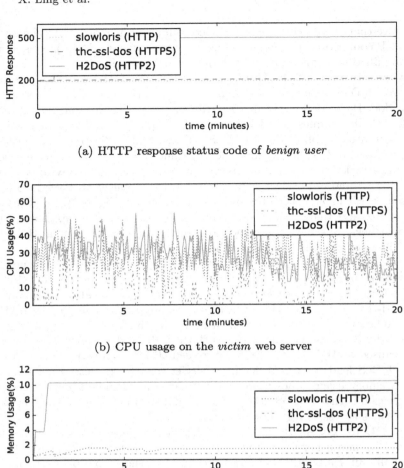

(a) HTTP response status code of *benign user*

(b) CPU usage on the *victim* web server

(c) Memory usage on the *victim* web server

Fig. 7. Observations of HTTP response on *benign user* and resource consumption on *victim* when attacked by different three kinds of application-layer DoS attacks.

6 Discussion

As we have presented, H_2DoS can occupy all available connections of the *victim* and completely deny the legitimate user from accessing the victim web servers. Moreover, H_2DoS attack can also consume more server resources than other application-layer attacks on average in terms of CPU and memory usage. Strictly speaking, this is an implementation and configuration problem of HTTP/2 specification in practice. We have measured that there are many top websites have supported HTTP/2 and therefore the potential impact of the H_2DoS attack is significant. We suggest that websites with such concerns could minimize the impact of H$_2$DoS attack by limiting the rate of requests and total number of connections from the same client. As we believe that the starvation of connections should not be present in any single benign request, we encourage developers of any deployed website that processes HTTP/2 requests should review their rate and total number with this threat in mind.

7   Related Work

Application-Layer DoS Against HTTP/2 Protocol. The understanding and mitigation of security risks of DoS attack have been an active area of research in recent years as DoS is a continuous critical threat on the current Internet ecosystem. Recently, the research community has gradually shifted their research interest from traditional network-layer based DoS attacks to escalating application-layer DoS attacks. There are lots of studies have been done on application-layer DoS attacks [18–23]. Yi and Yu [18] showed that new application-layer-based DDoS attacks can utilize legitimate HTTP requests to overwhelm victim resources and proposed an anomaly detector to detect such attacks on popular websites traffic. Jazi et al. [23] presented several unique features that characterize application-layer attacks and proposed a nonparametric CUSUM detection algorithm to detect them using found characterizes.

However, previous works of application-layer DoS attacks mostly bases on HTTP/1.1 or HTTPS protocol as well as their defense mechanisms for mitigation. To the best of our knowledge, very few studies focus on application-layer DoS attacks against HTTP/2 protocol and its various implementation softwares. We describe these studies as below.

A report of Imperva Defense Center [24] releases four high-profile vulnerabilities in total on new implementations of HTTP/2 from the major vendors. One of the attacks reported is the slow read attack, which exploits a malicious client to read responses very slowly from HTTP/2-enabled servers. Our work contributes further in this regard by broadly exploring the possibilities of a more general DoS against HTTP/2. We exploit both multiplexing and flow-control mechanisms to create such general application-layer DoS attack: H$_2$DoS attack, and also systematically validate its feasibility as well as evaluate the impact of it.

Adi et al. [25] firstly presented that it is possible to launch a DoS attack using apparently legitimate but malicious HTTP/2 flash crowd traffic. The malicious HTTP/2 packets was crafted by exploited the "Window Size Increment" value in *WINDOW_UPDATE* frame to model flooding-based attack against the HTTP/2 victim web server, as well as performed four investigations to observe the effect of resource consumption in the victim web server. Unfortunately, they limited their attacks to *WINDOW_UPDATE* frame and ignored other frames that can also be exploited to further amplify the impact of their attack. Instead, we take all frames into consideration and analyze the novel HTTP/2 flow-control and multiplexing mechanisms in details to construct our H$_2$DoS attack. Moreover, we conduct a systematically experiment instead of four investigation observations to present our attack model and demonstrate its feasibility and severity.

Other Security Threats Against HTTP/2 Protocol. Prior work also has shown others attacks that exploiting new features introduced in HTTP/2. Even before HTTP/2 protocol was standardized, Redelmeier et al. [26] systematically analyzed almost all possible security implications of HTTP/2 and explored a series of potential or known areas of vulnerabilities for HTTP/2, including cross-protocol attacks, intermediary encapsulation attacks and cacheability of pushed resources and so on. (Kate) Pearce and Vincent [29] discussed how we can launch multiplexing attacks over QUIC[1] and within HTTP/2, as well as how to make sense of and defend against H2/QUIC traffic on their network. It also indicated that security tools must keep up with technique updating and people should be aware of. Van Goethem and Vanhoef [28] introduced HEIST techniques and carried out side-channel attacks against SSL/TLS purely in the browser to directly infer the length of the plaintext message. By abusing new features of HTTP/2, they found that the attack remained possible and even further increased the impact of HEIST. Larsen and Villamil [27] introduced threats and vulnerabilities discovered during the course of their research on the HTTP/2 protocol and released first public HTTP/2 fuzzer - **http2fuzz**, which intended to find more security vulnerabilities before HTTP/2 implementations were widely deployed.

8   Conclusion and Future Work

In this paper, we present a novel DoS attack against HTTP/2, H_2DoS, which can result in severe damages to web servers. First, we give the introduction of several new features of HTTP/2 protocol and present how the current HTTP/2 is deployed in practice by performing a large-scale measurement on Alexa top million websites. Second, we analyze the flow-control mechanism and propose the novel H_2DoS application-layer DoS attack, which can disrupt or even completely deny legitimate users from accessing the victim web server. Finally, we conduct a comprehensive study on the feasibility and severity of H_2DoS attack in real attack scenarios. We demonstrate that the malicious client can easily launch H_2DoS attack against web servers which support HTTP/2 protocol and make the service unavailable or massively consume server resources. We also compare our H_2DoS attack with other application-layer DoS attacks, which show H_2DoS attack has more severe impact on the same victim web server.

In future work, we plan to explore more other vulnerabilities and attacks against the HTTP/2 protocol of web security. As new features usually comes unintentionally at the expense of new or unknown security threats, we believe that HTTP/2 with new features also brings a lot of new attack vulnerabilities. Since the proposed H_2DoS attack poses serve threats to HTTP/2, we hope our work will provide insight into those security issues and motivate to study other potential security threats against HTTP/2. Finally, we also plan to open source our H_2DoS attack implementation to further promote the research on web security of HTTP/2 protocol.

---

[1] The QUIC Projects https://www.chromium.org/quic.

Acknowledgments. This work is supported by the National Key Research and Development Program of China under No. 2016YFB0800102 and 2016YFB0800201, the National High Technology Research and Development Program of China under No. 2015AA015602 and 2015AA016103, the Key Research and Development Program of Zhejiang Province under No. 2017C01064 and 2017C01055, the Fundamental Research Funds for the Central Universities, the NSFC under program No. 61772466, the Alibaba-Zhejiang University Joint Research Institute for Frontier Technologies (A.Z.F.T.) under Program No. XT622017000118, and the CCF-Tencent Open Research Fund under No. AGR20160109.

References

1. Mike, B., Roberto, P., Thomson, M: RFC 7540: hypertext transfer protocol version 2 (HTTP/2). Internet Engineering Task Force (IETF), Google Inc. (2015)
2. SPDY: An experimental protocol for a faster web. https://www.chromium.org/spdy/spdy-whitepaper
3. Roberto, P., Ruellan, H.: HPACK: Header Compression for HTTP/2. No. RFC 7541, Internet Engineering Task Force (2015)
4. Thai, D., Juliano, R.: The CRIME attack. In: Ekoparty Security Conference (2012)
5. Radware Emergency Response Team: Global Application & Network Security Report 2016–2017 (2016). https://www.radware.com/ert-report-2016/
6. RSnake, Kinsella, J.: Slowloris HTTP DoS. https://web.archive.org/web/20150426090206/http://ha.ckers.org/slowloris
7. THC-SSL-DOS. http://kalilinuxtutorials.com/thc-ssl-dos/
8. Varvello, M., Schomp, K., Naylor, D., Blackburn, J., Finamore, A., Papagiannaki, K.: Is the web HTTP/2 yet? In: Karagiannis, T., Dimitropoulos, X. (eds.) PAM 2016. LNCS, vol. 9631, pp. 218–232. Springer, Cham (2016). https://doi.org/10.1007/978-3-319-30505-9_17
9. Wang, X.S., Balasubramanian, A., Krishnamurthy, A., Wetherall, D.: How speedy is SPDY? In: 11th USENIX Symposium on Networked Systems Design and Implementation (NSDI), pp. 387–399. Usenix Association (2014)
10. Meyer, C., Schwenk, J.: SoK: lessons learned from SSL/TLS attacks. In: Kim, Y., Lee, H., Perrig, A. (eds.) WISA 2013. LNCS, vol. 8267, pp. 189–209. Springer, Cham (2014). https://doi.org/10.1007/978-3-319-05149-9_12
11. Alexa Top Sites, September 2016. http://www.alexa.com/topsites
12. Friedl, S., Popov, A., Langley, A., Stephan, E.: Transport Layer Security (TLS) Application-Layer Protocol Negotiation Extension, No. RFC 7301, IETF (2014)
13. Dierks, T.: The Transport Layer Security (TLS) Protocol Version 1.2, No. RFC 5246, IETF (2008)
14. David, G., Totty, B.: HTTP: The Definitive Guide. O'Reilly Media, Sebastopol (2002)
15. Rodola, G.: A cross-platform process and system utilities module for Python. https://github.com/giampaolo/psutil
16. Fitzpatrick, B.: Http2 in GoDoc. https://godoc.org/golang.org/x/net/http2
17. NGINX Inc: nginx stable version 1.10.0, October 2016. https://nginx.org/en/linux_packages.html#stable
18. Yi, X., Yu, S.-Z.: Monitoring the application-layer DDoS attacks for popular websites. IEEE/ACM Trans. Netw. (TON) **17**(1), 15–25 (2009)

19. Ranjan, S., Swaminathan, R., Uysal, M., Nucci, A., Knightly, E.: DDoS-shield: DDoS-resilient scheduling to counter application layer attacks. IEEE/ACM Trans. Netw. (TON) **17**, 26–39 (2009)
20. Maci-Fernndez, G., Daz-Verdejo, J.E., Garca-Teodoro, P.: Mathematical model for low-rate DoS attacks against application servers. IEEE Trans. Inf. Forensics Secur. (TIFS) **4**, 519–529 (2009)
21. Durcekova, V., Schwartz, L.: Sophisticated denial of service attacks aimed at application layer. In: IELEKTRO, Nahid Shahmehri (2012)
22. Zargar, S.T., Joshi, J., Tipper, D.: A survey of defense mechanisms against distributed denial of service (DDoS) flooding attacks. IEEE Commun. Surv. Tutor. **15**, 2046–2069 (2013)
23. Jazi, H.H., Gonzalez, H., Stakhanova, N., Ali, A.: Detecting HTTP-based application layer DoS attacks on Web servers in the presence of sampling. Comput. Netw. **121**, 25–36 (2017)
24. Imperva: HTTP/2: In-depth analysis of the top four flaws of the next generation web protocol (2016). https://www.imperva.com/docs/Imperva_HII_HTTP2.pdf
25. Adi, E., Baig, Z.A., Hingston, P., Lam, C.-P.: Distributed denial-of-service attacks against HTTP/2 services. Clust. Comput. **19**, 79–86 (2016)
26. Redelmeier, I.: The Security Implications of HTTP/2.0 (2013). http://www.cs.tufts.edu/comp/116/archive/fall2013/iredelmeier.pdf
27. Larsen, S., Villamil, J.: Attacking HTTP2 implementations. In: 13th PACific SECurity - Applied Security Conferences and Training in Pacific Asia (PacSec) (2015)
28. Van Goethem, T., Vanhoef, M.: HEIST: HTTP encrypted information can be Stolen through TCP-windows, Blackhat, USA (2016)
29. (Kate) Pearce, C., Vincent, C.: HTTP/2 & QUIC - teaching good protocols to do bad things, Blackhat, USA (2016)

Optimizing TLB for Access Pattern Privacy Protection in Data Outsourcing

Yao Liu[1,2](✉), Qingkai Zeng[1,2], and Pinghai Yuan[1,2]

[1] Department of Computer Science and Technology,
Nanjing University, Nanjing 210023, China
yaoliu1985@hotmail.com, zqk@nju.edu.cn
[2] State Key Laboratory for Novel Software Technology,
Nanjing University, Nanjing 210023, China

Abstract. Oblivious RAM (ORAM) is a protocol to hide access pattern to an untrusted storage. ORAM prevents a curious adversary identifying what data address the user is accessing through observing the bits flows between the user and the untrusted storage system. Basically, ORAM protocols store user's data in shuffled form on the untrusted storage and substitute the original access with multiple access to random addresses to cover the real target. Such redundancy introduce significant performance overhead.

Traditional Translation Lookaside Buffer (TLB) exploits temporal locality hide memory latency in DRAM systems. However, the ORAM locality is totally different and thus traditional TLB eviction strategy have a poor performance. In this paper, we propose O-TLB which exploits ORAM temporal locality and optimized TLB eviction strategy to reduce server-side memory I/O operations. Intuitively, exploiting locality for performance may expose this locality which breaks obliviousness. We challenge this intuition by exploiting locality based on server-side ORAM data structures. Unlike previous works, our approach do not sacrifice any provable security. Specifically, previous optimization works leaks access pattern through timing channel and do no fit with adaptive asynchronous obliviousness (AAOB) in a multiple users scenario. While in our method, the timing do not vary with locality of program and O-TLB optimization can be adopted directly keeping AAOB. Our simulation result show that with O-TLB scheme, the underlying ORAM server-side I/O performance is improved by 11%.

Keywords: Data outsource · Access pattern privacy
Oblivious RAM · TLB · Temporal locality

1 Introduction

Outsourcing data to cloud storage become popular for its reliability, low cost and ease of management. Although the service provider can prove that the user's data is encrypted and guarantees integrity, users's access pattern is still exposed. In another word, how users access their data may lead to sensitive information leakage.

© ICST Institute for Computer Sciences, Social Informatics and Telecommunications Engineering 2018
X. Lin et al. (Eds.): SecureComm 2017, LNICST 238, pp. 571–584, 2018.
https://doi.org/10.1007/978-3-319-78813-5_29

Islam et al. [9] proves an attack on searchable encryption scheme by using only access pattern is feasible. For instance, a user stores a sets of encrypted text on the cloud and make queries with various encrypted key words. With continuous observing the addresses touched, the attacker eventually reveals the linkability between different key words and trapdoors. With enough sample queries and a few known queries as prior knowledge, the attacker is capable of recovering a large number of the key words. As a real world example, by observing only access pattern to an encrypted email repository, an attacker can infer up to 80% of the queries.

Access pattern privacy leakage is also found in trusted processor and untrusted memory settings. Shinde et al. [20] show that Intel SGX is vulnerable to page fault side channel. SGX establishes an "enclaved" environment to protect user space process from potentially compromised operating system. Although the underlying OS is not able to hijack control flow of a process inside an enclaved space or extract plain text directly, the OS still manage page fault exceptions. Their experiment indicates, 27% on average and up to 100%, encryption key bits from cryptographic routines in OpenSSL and Libgcrypt can be recovered by only watching the traffic between enclaved process and memory management units.

Oblivious RAM (ORAM) is a cryptographic primitive was proposed by Goldreich and Ostrovsky in their ground breaking work [14] in the aspect of software protection. They claim that access pattern to an external storage may lead to software theft. Their square-root ORAM protocol is the first non-trivial approach to make accesses oblivious. The approach requires only $O(log(1))$ client storage size to keep the protocol flowing but incurs $O((logN)^3)$ bandwidth blowup. Follow-up works [4,6,15,21–24] make efforts to decreasing bandwidth overhead. Part of the works modify on the ORAM protocol itself, as Path ORAM [21] substitutes Goldreich's hierarchical structure with a binary search tree which shrinks the bandwidth blowup to $O(log(N))$ and amortize the reshuffling cost to each ORAM access. SSS-ORAM occupies large amount of server-side storage but has the best performance and [11] is the best solution for limited resources and small block size.

Other works refine the protocol in the aspect of implementation. Treetop caching proposed in [24] moves the hottest part of server-side storage to client for better performance. Fletcher et al. introduced PLB [4] caching most recent accessed blocks of recursive position map which dramatically reduces total number of ORAM accesses with a cost of small extra client storage. As Wang et al. [23] consider a scenario when oblivious program with intense memory accesses reside with a non-oblivious program require relatively low bandwidth. The non-oblivious program cause lots of unnecessary waiting cycles to the oblivious one. They address this problem by filling these waiting cycles with next ORAM cycles. Our work also refines the implementation of ORAM to gain practical improvement.

In this paper, we propose "Oblivious Tree-based Locality" which is completely different from original underlying principle of TLB techniques. We make effort to optimizing TLB eviction strategy by exploiting Oblivious Tree-based Locality from random nature of underling ORAM protocols. However, exploiting data locality for performance and keep this locality hiding from curious server seem contradictory. Intuitively, programs with good locality exhibit better performance than those with poor locality which reveals program's locality to server. We challenge this intuition by speeding up every programs with equal magnitude. In this way, our approach do not sacrifice any provable security of underly ORAM. And we stress that our approach do NOT leak any information through timing channel and do not need any kind of timing channel protection. It is very important since previous optimization leaks programs' locality through timing channel. Enabling ORAM timing channel protection lead to heavy response delay which makes their approaches unpractical. Furthermore, in multiple users setting their approaches break "adaptive asynchronous obliviousness" while ours can be applied without modification.

Our Contributions, in a Nutshell:

1. Traditional TLB eviction strategy is studied in the context of ORAM. We made an observation that directly applies traditional temporal locality to server works poorly.
2. A new concept called Oblivious Tree-based Locality is proposed and we use it to built O-TLB scheme. The implementation of O-TLB is discussed in detail Path ORAM.
3. Security of O-TLB scheme is carefully examined including timing channel and adaptive asynchronous obliviousness. We prove that our scheme achieves the same level of security as underling ORAM protocols.

The rest of the paper is organized as follows: Sect. 2 gives the threaten model and settings. Section 3 provides the background knowledge of general ORAM and Path ORAM in particular. Section 4 studies traditional TLB techniques for ORAM protocols. In Sect. 5, we propose Oblivious Tree-based Locality and O-TLB for Path ORAM and discuss how underlying ORAM can benefit from our scheme. Section 6 security of O-TLB is discussed and compared to related works. Section 7 presents our evaluation methodology. The simulation result is exhibited which proves effectiveness and security of our optimization. Section 8 presents our conclusion (Table 1).

2   Threat Model

In this section, we briefly introduce the two settings and threat model for general ORAM.

2.1   Settings

Client-server setting, which is adopted in this paper, describes a scenario that a trusted client runs a private or public program on encrypted private data stored

Table 1. Notations

N	Total data block number
B	Block size in bit
id	Data block logical identifier
pos	Data block actual position in server
L	Path ORAM tree hight
Z	Path ORAM bucket capacity
l	Level of a specific node

in remote cloud server. Following other ORAM works, we assume the server is honest but curious, which means it correctly evaluate the functions and make no temper with the cipher-text. However, the adversary may continuously observe and take records on the client access opcode (read/write) and target addresses combined with cipher-text to deduct client's sensitive information.

The other setting is trusted processor with an untrusted RAM which is a Trust Computing Base (usually contains processer alone) operates in an untrusted environment for a remote user. The program runs on the TCB can be both private or public but operates on private data. When last-level cache misses, the processor interact with untrusted external memory (e.g. DRAM). The private data is encrypted when going out of TCB boundary but adversary may still tap pins on the memory bus to constantly observe the traffic between TCB and memory.

2.2 Security Definition

Informally, the security definition demands that the server learns nothing about the access pattern. Typical access patterns include:

1. whether an access is a read or write
2. which data unit is accessed and timestamp of last accessed
3. Relative between access like, whether two access refer to the same data
4. overall pattern (sequential, random etc.)

Definition 1 *(ORAM Definition). Let $\overleftarrow{y} = ((op_1, addr_1, data_1), \ldots, (op_M, addr_M, data_M))$ denote a data query sequence of length M ($|\overleftarrow{y}| = M$), where op_i denotes the opcode of the i-th operation (read or write). And $addr_i$ denotes the target address for that operation while $data_i$ denotes the data if the op_i is a write. Let $ORAM(\overleftarrow{y})$ denote the final operation sequence between client and server under an ORAM protocol which is exposed to the adversary. The ORAM protocol guarantees that for any $\overleftarrow{y}$ and $\overleftarrow{y}'$, $ORAM(\overleftarrow{y})$ and $ORAM(\overleftarrow{y}')$ are computationally indistinguishable when $|\overleftarrow{y}| = |\overleftarrow{y}'|$. Also, for any $\overleftarrow{y}$ the data returned to the client from ORAM is consistent with $\overleftarrow{y}$ (functionally equal) with overwhelming probability.*

2.3 Threats Outside of Scope

Timing Channel: Generally speaking, timing channel is not considered in ORAM studies. This is reasonable when timing change, which related to access pattern, is negligible. For example, CPU in client may take few more cycles to access a specific data block locally. This timing change will be overwhelmed by the unstable network delays. However, obvious timing changes closely couple with data locality of program is unacceptable. We will discuss this further in Sect. 6.

Active Adversary: An active adversary can temper with encrypted content breaking integrity of user data or return incorrect evaluation result to client. Many extraordinary works have already addressed this problem which is orthogonal to our work, like MAC (message authentication code) can ensure integrity of user data and correctness of function evaluation. In this paper, we only consider a passive adversary with capability of observing the traffic between server and client.

Total Number of ORAM Accesses: Total number of ORAM accesses normally is not part of access pattern. For AAOB security, it is not entirely true. Further discussion can be found in Sect. 6.

Total Server Side Storage Occupation: The server will definitely know the capacity of ORAM and thus the total ORAM data blocks is not part of access pattern protection.

3 Background

In section, we present necessary background knowledge of Path ORAM since it is representative work. Many related works use Path ORAM as underlying ORAM.

3.1 General ORAM Protocol Introduction

Basically, ORAM substitute an original access with redundant read and write operations. The ORAM is functionally equal to the original access, as user can access their data in ORAM transparently just like normal RAMs. The data is stored in encrypted and shuffled form. Once a data block is accessed by client, it must be re-encrypted with new randomness and relocate to other positions in the server and invalidates the old copy. The operation sequence exposed to server do not varies with client's input. For example, after a ORAM access is completed, whatever client's original access is, the adversary sees only ,say, ten reads and five writes to pure random addresses.

Sequential scan and reshuffling are the most fundamental technique for ORAM. Sequential scan is also referred as trivial ORAM or naive ORAM. To hide real opcode and operand, the access to a specific element from N incurs a complete sequential read and write operation to all N elements, thus, the client have to access 2N (both write and read) data block instead of one. Trivial ORAM are commonly used by ORAM protocol as component when the scale is relatively small. Reshuffling means that once a element is accessed, its real address is exposed to the adversary. It must be relocated somewhere else immediately to prevent the adversary tracing the element. So all ORAM protocols, except trivial ORAM, maintain a lookup table that mapping data block's *id*, which can be seen by client only, to actual position *pos* on the server.

Base of ORAM Randomness: Pseudo-Random Functions (PRFs) are used as the base of ORAM randomness. They provide random numbers for relocating data block and keys for one time encryption. The most important point is that the output of these function do NOT vary with user's input (include write or read, target address, write data) or else the whole protection falls apart. The actual outcomes of our O-TLB optimization for one specific access sequence is wholly decided by output of PRFs and thus have no relationship with user's input.

Evaluation Metric: Usually, using ORAM incurs relatively large overhead. To evaluate the performance of a ORAM protocol, there are two different method.

1. Theoretical Evaluation: Bandwidth blowup and Client Storage are introduced. Basically, bandwidth blowup is how much extra data blocks that the ORAM have to access to hide access pattern. In trivial ORAM, we say the protocol incurs a $O(N)$ asymptotic bandwidth blowup. While the client storage overhead refers to the minimum client space to keep the ORAM running.
2. Practical Evaluation: Some works refining the implementation of ORAM usually do not have an asymptotic improvement. Their optimization is exhibited in a probabilistic manner [4]. Server responding time are used to evaluate these improvement as mention in Sect. 1. Our O-TLB is among this type of work.

3.2   Path ORAM

Path ORAM was introduce by Shi et al. which is adopted by lots of works as underlying ORAM protocol for its extreme simpleness and low bandwidth blowup. Path ORAM departures from Goldreich's square-root ORAM, substitute hierarchical structure with a binary tree for more natural search process. Another highlight is that Path ORAM couples write back with path fetches which amortizes the overhead to every ORAM access. We will presents Path ORAM in two aspect.

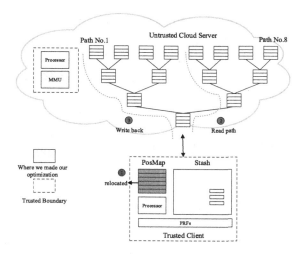

Fig. 1. Path ORAM protocol

Data Organization Protocol: Data Organization Protocol define that how the algorithm organized the data blocks and stored. Path ORAM organize the data blocks as a binary search tree. As figure shows in Fig. 1, Path protocol organizes N blocks to form a complete binary tree with level $L = LogN$. Each node of the tree have Z slots and also called buckets. One bucket is capable to contains up to Z data blocks with a triple of form:

$$\{id||pos||data\}$$

Where id is a private index of a data block revealed only to client, while pos is a leaf identifier specify the "path" on which the block is located, as $data$ is the payload. The term "path" refers to all buckets from leaf node to the root, marked with dash lines in Fig. 1. Finally, Path ORAM maintains a core invariant: If a data block is stored on the server, it must be found on one bucket from the path specified by pos.

Data Block Access Protocol: One complete Path ORAM access consists of tree operations, as indicated in Fig. 1.

1. Relocating: Once the ORAM protocol accepts an access request, the initial step is to get the mapping from id to pos and immediately substitute it with a new random pos'.
2. Read Path: With the mapping, the ORAM load all buckets along the path to stash and decrypt them to find the data block with identifier id. The core invariant guarantees the designated data block can be found.
3. Write Back: The client re-encrypts all blocks with new randomness key and evicts all blocks with pos to current path, greedily fill the buckets from leaf to

root. Remember that the target block is relocated to path tagged with pos', there is a good chance that $pos \neq pos'$. Such that the block stays in stash and waits for another access to pos' to get itself evicted.

Each path have $logN$ buckets and each of them have Z slots such that the protocol roughly have to access $2Zlog(N)$ data blocks to ensure obliviousness. Thus, the asymptotic overhead is $O(logN)$.

4   Traditional TLB on ORAM

In this section, we first review the key points for traditional TLB technique and discuss the problems if applies it to ORAM directly.

Modern Memory Management Unit (MMU) built an abstract layer called virtual memory on top of physical memory for easier allocation, management and security purpose. Before access to a desired physical memory location, MMU need to look up the page table, which is also a regular chunk of the RAM, to translate virtual memory to physical memory. This page table walk is recursive and introduces several extra accesses to the RAM. Since memory access is very fundamental and frequent, the overhead of page translation is significant.

MMU adopt Translation lookaside buffer (TLB) to reduce the delay taken to access a user memory location. The TLB caches a fixed number of the most recent translation result. If a memory location is invoked, the first step is to go though TLB to find whether there is a corresponding entry. If TLB hits, then the expensive page walk operation is skipped. Since the size of TLB is small and fixed, the number of cache entry is very limited. The principle behind the cache is temporal locality. In another word, reasonable TLB hit rate is based on the observation that if a location is invoked then there is a good chance it will be accessed again in short future. This is no longer true if DRAM is substituted by ORAM.

Recall that reshuffle technique, it ensures even several client queries are point to the same block with id, the server will see accesses to random position in the server memory. For traditional TLB in server processor, this is totally against its anticipation. More generally, higher cache hit rate means the actual access pattern is very close to the anticipated access pattern which defines the cache behavior. As such, we make the observation that traditional TLB works poorly for ORAM.

5   Oblivious TLB

In this section, we propose our ORAM locality definitions and use them to make optimizations.

5.1   Oblivious Tree-Based Locality

Based on the observations above we propose **Oblivious Tree-based Locality**:

Target location of tree-base ORAM is purely random and independent. The nodes close to the root have good locality while nodes close to the leaves have poor locality. Equal level nodes have equal locality.

Ongoing Locality is also proposed:

Inside an ORAM access, target eviction path have good locality and will be accessed in short term.

5.2   O-TLB for Path ORAM

As Fig. 1 shows, since each Path ORAM access loads an entire path from root to the leaf, the access possibility for touching each node can be denoted by 2^{-l}. Instead of evict the oldest translation entry, we use a tree level bits to keep track of which level every page belongs to which tree level.

Please recall Path ORAM protocol steps. It loads a whole path, where the corresponding page translation entry is cache with TLB, and the path will be evicted. That means the pages inside the path will be accessed again shortly. We exploit this locality for performance. We maintain a ongoing bit indicate whether the page belong to a unfinished path. When a LoadPath operation is detected, ongoing bit of all TLB entries for this path is set.

When the O-TLB is full and one entry should be evict. O-TLB picks one entry with lowest value (most close to leaf) and check its ongoing bit. If the ongoing bit is cleared, then the entry is evicted. Otherwise, O-TLB picks the second lowest one. Entries with same level bit is chosen randomly, as according to Oblivious Tree-based Locality, this do not hurt performance.

6   Related Works and O-TLB Security Analysis

In this section, related work is presented and explains how O-TLB achieves same security of underlying ORAM.

6.1   Dynamic Super Block Technique

Some works [24,26] exploit ORAM spatial locality for performance. They borrowed the memory prefetch technique from model system. Originally, client data blocks is independent and distribute randomly in the path of ORAM tree storage structure on the server. The key point of their method is that client data blocks exhibiting spatial locality are united to form super block and stored to one path as a whole. As such, once a block, which belongs to a super block, is loaded to the client, other blocks reside in the same super block is loaded as well. If the program do have spatial locality, then it is very likely that next desired data block is already loaded by last ORAM access. A reduction of total ORAM access number surely buys performance gain.

6.2   Access Pattern Leakage from Timing

Although their improvement is significant, we think their optimization is unrealistic. They made a optimization on *client side*, specifically on client data blocks which is extremely tightly coupled with access pattern. The timing should severely varies with locality of program. For example, if the client silent for a period of time, then the adversary may make a good guess that the client is running a program with good locality.

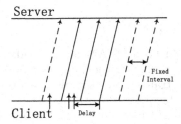

Fig. 2. Periotic timing protection

Although they claim periotic ORAM issue can be mounted to protect timing, we think this incurs too heavy delay as shown in Fig. 2. The idea of periotic ORAM timing protect is simple that one ORAM access is issue in regular interval. If no request is in the queue then a dummy access is issued. The requests for client are no long served in a on-demand way, but they have to wait for next access slot. At present, the research community has turned single client model to multiple. TaoStore [17] describe a multi-client model with proxy as shown in Fig. 3. Concurrency leads to a intense ORAM access requests, where periotic timing protection will incur severe delay. If shorten the interval, lots of resource is wasted when the clients are idle because of dummy ORAM access. If vary interval dynamically, this too leaks locality through timing. On the contrary, our work is a *server side* optimization. This nature ensures O-TLB improves all client program equally. Although, the actual performance gain is decide random number generated by client's PRFs. However underly ORAM must guarantees the output of PRFs do not varies with query parameters. This ensures our optimization have no relationship with access pattern.

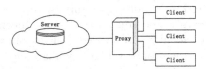

Fig. 3. TaoStore model

6.3   Against Adaptive Asynchronous Obliviousness Security

TaoStore propose Adaptive Asynchronous Obliviousness which is first complete adversary model for multiple-client ORAM model. The relevant key point is once client issue a request or accept query result the adversary is notified. As such, Dynamic Super block optimization will cause the number of request of client differs from the number of proxy request, which immediately leaks the locality. Because proxy may get some desire data blocks from super block to answer clients' request.

While O-TLB only shorten the cost of server PathLoad and Write back process and do not vary the total number of ORAM access. So our optimization do not break AAOB and can be incorporated by multi-client with proxy ORAM model like TaoStore.

7   Evaluation

In this section evaluation settings is given and simulation result is exhibited which proves both efficiency and security.

7.1   Methodology

Graphite [10] is used as the simulator in our experiments. The hardware configurations and ORAM settings are listed in Table 2. We choose a ORAM block size of 1k for simplification, because four 1k blocks form a 4k bucket ($Z = 4$) which equal to regular page size. We use Splash-2 benchmark because programs in the benchmark have different locality to test if our optimization gain varies with programs locality.

Table 2. Processor core configuration

Core	1GHz in order core
L1 Cache	32 KB 4-way
L2 Cache	512 KB 8-way
Cacheline size	64 bytes
TLB	64 entries 4-way

7.2   Metrics

We stress that we do not test overall completion time of programs. We only test how many store and load operations the server memory is saving due to O-TLB hit.

7.3   Result

As Fig. 4 exhibited, the performance gain is around 11% and do not vary with locality of programs.

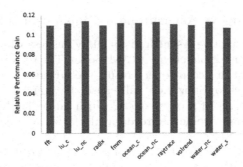

Fig. 4. O-TLB relative performance gain

8   Conclusion

We study and make the observation that traditional TLB works poorly on ORAM. We propose new locality definitions for ORAM and use it to build O-TLB. Related works are presented and compared with O-TLB. We prove O-TLB optimization do not hurt security of underling ORAM in any form, especially timing channel. Furthermore, O-TLB can be easily adopted with multi-client settings and varies of tree-like ORAM protocols. Simulation is made and the result supports our claims.

Acknowledgment. We would like to thank the anonymous reviewers for their constructive and helpful comments.

This work has been partly supported by National NSF of China under Grant No. 61772266, 61572248, 61431008.

References

1. Blass, E.O., Mayberry, T., Noubir, G., Onarlioglu, K.: Toward robust hidden volumes using write-only oblivious RAM. In: Proceedings of the 2014 ACM SIGSAC Conference on Computer and Communications Security, CCS 2014, pp. 203–214. ACM (2014). https://doi.org/10.1145/2660267.2660313
2. Dautrich, J., Stefanov, E., Shi, E.: Burst ORAM: minimizing ORAM response times for bursty access patterns. In: 23rd USENIX Security Symposium (USENIX Security 2014), pp. 749–764. USENIX Association (2014). https://www.usenix.org/conference/usenixsecurity14/technical-sessions/presentation/dautrich
3. Devadas, S., van Dijk, M., Fletcher, C.W., Ren, L., Shi, E., Wichs, D.: Onion ORAM: a constant bandwidth blowup oblivious RAM. In: Kushilevitz, E., Malkin, T. (eds.) TCC 2016. LNCS, vol. 9563, pp. 145–174. Springer, Heidelberg (2016). https://doi.org/10.1007/978-3-662-49099-0_6
4. Fletcher, C.W., Ren, L., Kwon, A., van Dijk, M., Devadas, S.: Freecursive ORAM: [nearly] free recursion and integrity verification for position-based oblivious RAM. In: Proceedings of the Twentieth International Conference on Architectural Support for Programming Languages and Operating Systems, ASPLOS 2015, pp. 103–116. ACM (2015)

5. Fletchery, C.W., Ren, L., Yu, X., Dijk, M.V.: Suppressing the oblivious ram timing channel while making information leakage and program efficiency trade-offs. In: IEEE International Symposium on High PERFORMANCE Computer Architecture, pp. 213–224 (2014)
6. Gentry, C., Goldman, K.A., Halevi, S., Julta, C., Raykova, M., Wichs, D.: Optimizing ORAM and using it efficiently for secure computation. In: De Cristofaro, E., Wright, M. (eds.) PETS 2013. LNCS, vol. 7981, pp. 1–18. Springer, Heidelberg (2013). https://doi.org/10.1007/978-3-642-39077-7_1
7. Goodrich, M.T., Ohrimenko, O., Tamassia, R.: Data-oblivious graph drawing model and algorithms. Computer Science (2012)
8. Gordon, S.D., Liu, F.-H., Shi, E.: Constant-round MPC with fairness and guarantee of output delivery. In: Gennaro, R., Robshaw, M. (eds.) CRYPTO 2015. LNCS, vol. 9216, pp. 63–82. Springer, Heidelberg (2015). https://doi.org/10.1007/978-3-662-48000-7_4
9. Islam, M., Kuzu, M., Kantarcioglu, M.: Access pattern disclosure on searchable encryption: ramification. attack and mitigation. In: Proceedings of NDSS (2012)
10. Kasture, H.: Graphite: a parallel distributed simulator for multicores. In: IEEE International Symposium on High PERFORMANCE Computer Architecture, pp. 1–12 (2010)
11. Kushilevitz, E., Lu, S., Ostrovsky, R.: On the (in)security of hash-based oblivious ram and a new balancing scheme. In: SODA (2012)
12. Liu, C., Hicks, M., Shi, E.: Memory trace oblivious program execution. In: Proceedings of the 2013 IEEE 26th Computer Security Foundations Symposium, CSF 2013, pp. 51–65. IEEE Computer Society. https://doi.org/10.1109/CSF.2013.11
13. Maas, M., Love, E., Stefanov, E., Tiwari, M., Shi, E., Asanovic, K., Kubiatowicz, J., Song, D.: PHANTOM: practical oblivious computation in a secure processor. In: Proceedings of the 2013 ACM SIGSAC Conference on Computer and Communications Security, CCS 2013, pp. 311–324. ACM (2013). https://doi.org/10.1145/2508859.2516692
14. Ostrovsky, R.M.: Software protection and simulation on oblivious rams
15. Ren, L., Fletcher, C., Kwon, A., Stefanov, E., Shi, E., Dijk, M.V., Devadas, S.: Constants count: practical improvements to oblivious RAM. pp. 415–430
16. Ren, L., Yu, X., Fletcher, C.W., Van Dijk, M., Devadas, S.: Design space exploration and optimization of path oblivious ram in secure processors. ACM SIGARCH Comput. Archit. News 41(3), 571–582 (2013)
17. Sahin, C., Zakhary, V., Abbadi, A.E., Lin, H., Tessaro, S.: TaoStore: Overcoming asynchronicity in oblivious data storage, pp. 198–217
18. Shi, E., Chan, T.-H.H., Stefanov, E., Li, M.: Oblivious RAM with $O((\log N)^3)$ worst-case cost. In: Lee, D.H., Wang, X. (eds.) ASIACRYPT 2011. LNCS, vol. 7073, pp. 197–214. Springer, Heidelberg (2011). https://doi.org/10.1007/978-3-642-25385-0_11
19. Shi, E., Stefanov, E., Papamanthou, C.: Practical dynamic proofs of retrievability. In: Proceedings of the 2013 ACM SIGSAC Conference on Computer and Communications Security, CCS 2013, pp. 325–336. ACM. (2013). https://doi.org/10.1145/2508859.2516669
20. Shinde, S., Chua, Z.L., Narayanan, V., Saxena, P.: Preventing page faults from telling your secrets. ACM (2016)
21. Stefanov, E., van Dijk, M., Shi, E., Fletcher, C., Ren, L., Yu, X., Devadas, S.: Path ORAM: an extremely simple oblivious RAM protocol. In: Proceedings of the 2013 ACM SIGSAC Conference on Computer and Communications Security, CCS 2013, pp. 299–310. ACM (2013)

22. Stefanov, E., Shi, E.: ObliviStore: high performance oblivious cloud storage. In: Security and Privacy, pp. 253–267
23. Wang, R., Zhang, Y., Yang, J.: Cooperative path-ORAM for effective memory bandwidth sharing in server setting
24. Wang, X.S., Huang, Y., Chan, T.H.H., Shelat, A., Shi, E.: SCORAM: oblivious RAM for secure computation. In: Proceedings of the 2014 ACM SIGSAC Conference on Computer and Communications Security, CCS 2014, pp. 191–202. ACM (2014)
25. Wang, X.S., Nayak, K., Liu, C., Chan, T.H.H., Shi, E., Stefanov, E., Huang, Y.: Oblivious data structures. In: Proceedings of the 2014 ACM SIGSAC Conference on Computer and Communications Security, CCS 2014, pp. 215–226. ACM (2014)
26. Yu, X., Haider, S.K., Ren, L., Fletcher, C.: PrORAM: dynamic prefetcher for oblivious RAM. In: ACM/IEEE International Symposium on Computer Architecture, pp. 616–628
27. Zahur, S., Wang, X., Raykova, M., Gascon, A., Doerner, J., Evans, D., Katz, J.: Revisiting square-root ORAM: efficient random access in multi-party computation, pp. 218–234

An Efficient Trustzone-Based In-application Isolation Schema for Mobile Authenticators

Yingjun Zhang[1,2(✉)], Yu Qin[1], Dengguo Feng[1], Bo Yang[1], and Weijin Wang[1]

[1] Trusted Computing and Information Assurance Laboratory, Institute of Software, Chinese Academy of Sciences, Beijing, China
zhangyingjun@tca.iscas.ac.cn
[2] University of Chinese Academy of Sciences, Beijing, China

Abstract. Mobile devices have been widely used as convenient authenticators for sensitive transactions and user login. It's a challenge to protect authentication secrets and code from malicious mobile operating systems. Although protecting them using hardware privilege isolation like Trustzone and virtualization is a promising countermeasure, existing approaches either have large TCBs with lots of applications and services installed in the privileged software, or provide only coarse-grained isolation unable to prevent intra-domain attacks, or require excessive intervention from the privileged software. We propose a novel mobile authentication schema called TAuth, which creates isolation execution environments in Trustzone normal world, so the system TCB in the secure world remains small and unchanged regardless of the amount of installed authentication applications. The isolation is also fine-grained which only protects the security-sensitive components of an authentication program, thus could defense not only a malicious OS, but also vulnerability threats inside the same program. Designed closely integrated with the intrinsic property of user authentication, TAuth solves two significant technique challenges, including efficient normal world isolation without excessive intervention into the secure world, and securely using of untrusted external functions from inside the isolated environment. Finally, we implement the prototype system on real TrustZone devices. The evaluation shows that TAuth can prevent both in-application attacks like HeartBleed and kernel-level rootkits. It also shows that TAuth achieves much higher system performance than previous Trustzone normal world isolation solutions.

Keywords: Mobile authentication · Trustzone · Small TCB
In-application isolation

1 Introduction

Mobile devices are increasingly used as authenticators for sensitive transactions and user login. Software authentication tokens free the users from the burdens of carrying multiple hardware tokens at all times. Also, communication ability

© ICST Institute for Computer Sciences, Social Informatics and Telecommunications Engineering 2018
X. Lin et al. (Eds.): SecureComm 2017, LNICST 238, pp. 585–605, 2018.
https://doi.org/10.1007/978-3-319-78813-5_30

with on-board peripherals and sensors allows conveniently enrolling new authentication factors, such as geographical locations and fingerprints. Mobile authenticators achieve both flexibility and low cost, hence are commonly seen as an ideal substitution of dedicated hardware tokens.

However, as modern commodity mobile operating systems are increasingly complex with endless kernel vulnerabilities [1], root attackers could easily intercept peripheral channels or compromise the execution of software tokens to steal authentication secrets, like passwords and private keys. Various attacks to mobile authentication applications (MAPs) have been reported [6,29], indicating the serious security challenges.

Researchers have proposed using Trusted Execution Environment (TEE) to protect sensitive applications against OS compromise. Trustzone [7], the most widely used mobile TEE technology, creates two separated execution partitions on ARM devices, the normal world and the secure world. The trusted applications (TAs) in the secure world enjoy hardware-enforced security capabilities against malware in the normal world OS. Trustzone-based authentication solutions have been proposed [17,23,27,37] and are integrated into mainstream authentication specifications like FIDO [8,28].

However, traditional Trustzone solutions face a major challenge, i.e., the security guarantees will be weakened as the attack surface and TCB size will increase along with the number of TAs and system services installed in the secure world. For example, various kernel-level device drivers are integrated into the secure world to support trusted device I/O, which have enormous code size and much higher bug rate than other kernel components. Since the secure world has a higher privilege, a compromised secure world will compromise the whole mobile device. Recent incidents show that exploiting the secure world's vulnerabilities has become a real threat [22,26,30,31,33]. For security concerns, mobile device vendors usually limit Trustzone resources to their own TAs. This makes it hard for third-party service providers to deploy their specific Trustzone-based MAPs, which poses a substantial barrier to their adoptions.

Unlike traditional Trustzone solutions, another kind of virtualization-based privilege isolation method places the TAs and the untrusted OS in the same privilege domain (a guest VM). Thus the system TCB won't increase along with the number of supported TAs. Such shielding systems [12,15,18] have the potential to resolve the defects faced by previous Trustzone-based authentication solutions. However, hardware virtualization is not commonly supported on mobile platforms and the complex commodity hypervisors are already struggling with their own security problems [4,5]. Also, they only provide coarse-grained isolation at an application level, which won't work well under attacks exploiting vulnerabilities inside a victim TA. For example, the Heart Bleed attack, which exploits a memory disclosure vulnerability in OpenSSL, can cause the victim program to leak critical secrets itself, with no need to directly read its memory.

In this paper, we propose a novel Trustzone-based mobile authentication schema, TAuth, which achieves two key advantages compared with previous solutions. First, it creates isolated execution environments in the normal world for the MAPs. Without concrete applications and system services installed in the secure world, the system TCB remains small and unchanged. Second, the isolation is fine-grained only contains sensitive program components, thus could defense threatens from both the underlying Rich OS[1] and the remaining program components. TAuth aims at addressing the urgent security issues for increasingly popular mobile authentication applications. To achieve these goals, we must solve several challenges.

First, normal world isolation is non-trivial to achieve, given the Rich OS's role in memory management for its applications. Shielding systems leverage hardware MMU virtualization (i.e., the *nested page* mechanism) to achieve exclusive memory access control in their hypervisors. However, the Trustzone normal world, which hosts the Rich OS, has full control over its own resources, including its MMU. Such control would allow the Rich OS to access any normal world memory by manipulating its page tables, including the authentication secrets. Therefore, previous normal world isolation solutions [9, 21] require the secure world to intercept frequent page table updates of the Rich OS, which significantly affects the system performance.

Second, in-program partition may not be easy, as commodity software usually has complex semantics, internal interactions, and lots of cross-component function calls. Existing approaches targeting at Pieces of Application Logic (PAL) [19, 20] require the PAL being self-contained, thus not supporting calling external functions, which are not suitable for real authentication MAPs. For example, they need to call OS services to communicate with I/O peripherals (storage devices, touch screen, sensors..) to obtain initial authentication secrets. However, under the assumption that the Rich OS and other program components are untrusted, how to guarantee the security of these external calls remains a challenge.

TAuth solves all these challenges, based on the intrinsic property of MAPs' authentication procedure. First, through manual source code analysis and automated taint analysis of several popular MAPs (e.g., Google Authenticator), we found that the critical code which controls the authentication secrets only constitutes a tiny fraction of the whole program, and usually follows fixed patterns. Based on these observations, we propose an efficient isolation mechanism by pre-loading these tiny components into a continuous memory region. When the critical part is running, TAuth applies atomicity protection to it, ensuring it's execution won't be unexpectedly interrupted by the untrusted Rich OS. When it is suspended, TAuth temporarily includes its memory into the secure world by dynamically setting the Trustzone controller, thus ensuring its isolation without frequently intercepting the Rich OS's page table updates. Second, according to execution patterns of the critical authentication code, we divide them into three categories: the storage code, the I/O code, the computation code. Then we design a trusted context switch module in the secure world to ensure the securely calling of necessary external functions from these code. Finally, we apply TAuth to Google Authenticator (GA), tiqr and OpenSSL, and use HeartBleed attack, memory disclosure rootkit to demonstrate its effectiveness and security. In summary, we make the following contributions.

---

[1] Rich OS represents the commodity operating systems like Linux, Android in Trustzone normal world.

- A novel Trustzone isolation architecture in the normal world, with both enhanced security guarantees and improved efficiency.
- A fine-grained isolation specially designed for mobile authentication applications, which could defense both in-application and OS-level attacks.
- Thorough evaluations on real authentication software and attack samples, which confirm the security and efficiency of TAuth.

2   Background

2.1   Trustzone

TrustZone is a CPU security extension defined by ARM. It creates two isolated execution domains on ARM platforms: the normal world and the secure world. A new CPU mode called monitor mode is introduced as the only entry point to the secure world. The normal world code needs to call the Secure Monitor Call (*smc*) instruction to enter the secure world. Each world has separated registers and memory and the secure world has a higher privilege with permissions to access all the resources of the normal world, but not vice versa. So it has the potential to control the normal world's behaviors and enjoys the hardware-based protections from attacks that compromise the normal world.

Memory Isolation. Trustzone Address Space Controller (TZASC) partitions continuous physical memory regions into secure or non-secure. Note that the protection strategy defined by TZASC is more privileged than that defined by MMU, i.e., the normal world can't access any secure physical memory even if it maps the region accessible in its page tables. This is essential to realize the normal world isolation without intercepting the frequent page table updates.

I/O Isolation. TrustZone Aware Interrupt Controller (TZIC) partitions device interrupts into secure or non-secure. By configuring TZIC and some related registers, hardware interrupts can be directly handled in the monitor mode, thus enabling flexible routing of interrupts to either world, which is essential to realize dynamic device I/O isolation. By default, TZIC uses Fast Interrupt (FIQ) as secure interrupt and uses Regular Interrupt (IRQ) as non-secure interrupt.

2.2   Mobile Authentication Applications

We explain the aforementioned three types of authentication code using a real-life example, Google Authenticator. The app generates One-Time Password (OTP) tokens using the HMAC-Based (HOTP) and the Time-based (TOTP) OTP generation algorithms. It uses either QR code scanning or manual input to obtain an encoded private key issued by Google and stores it in its database. During the authentication, the key is loaded into memory to calculate a message authentication code (MAC) of a timestamp or a counter to generate OTPs. Then the OTP is displayed to the user to finish the authentication.

As described in this case, the storage code is used to load or store authentication secrets in persistent storage, such as the private key. The I/O code is used

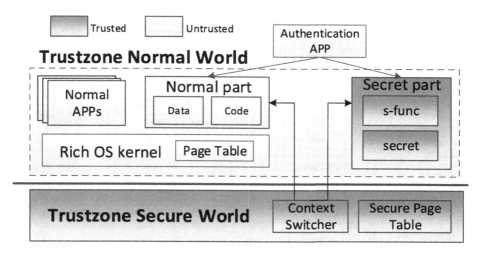

Fig. 1. TAuth architecture.

to import raw I/O secrets, such as the QR code and user inputs via keyboard or touch screen. It is also used to display sensitive information to the users. The computation code is used to make computations on the secrets to generate the authentication response, such as the OTP algorithms.

3   Threat Model and Security Assumptions

TAuth is designed against both malicious operating systems and in-application vulnerability threatens. TAuth completely removes trust of the Rich OS and assumes it can behave in arbitrarily malicious ways to disclose the authentication secrets, including directly accessing the user-level virtual address space, manipulating the page tables, or launching Iago attacks [11] which cause an application to harm itself by manipulating return values of system calls. It can also hijack or manipulate I/O communications of peripherals. We also assume the adversary can exploit in-application vulnerabilities to launch memory over-read attacks like HeartBleed [2], or control flow hijacking attacks like ROP [32], to disclose the authentication secrets in the address space of the same application. We don't consider complex physical attacks like side-channel attacks, which can't be protected by TrustZone. TAuth doesn't guarantee OS availability. A compromised OS can simply shut down or refuse to schedule apps. However, these disruptive behaviors can be easily detected. We assume TAuth is initialized via trusted booting, so that it can verify its own initial state and bootstrap trustworthy execution. Finally, we assume the protected critical code is trusted and wont deliberately send the secrets out. This is usually true for commodity MAPs like GA as the software itself is designed to keep such secrets.

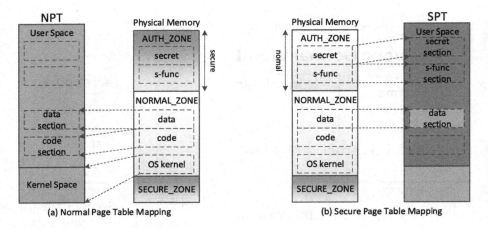

Fig. 2. TAuth memory layout.

4   System Design

4.1   System Overview

Figure 1 shows an overview of the TAuth architecture. In the normal world, the authentication APP is divided into a normal part and several secret parts. Each secret part comprises several authentication secrets and the corresponding critical functions manipulating them. The normal part must call into the secret parts via a trusted context switcher in the secure world. The switcher also allows the secret parts to call necessary external functions. However, TAuth ensures that the secrets can't be accessed by any external entities, including the normal part, other applications and the underlying Rich OS.

4.2   Basic Memory Isolation

This section details how TAuth achieves the efficient normal world isolation.

Physical Memory Layout. By configuring TZASC, TAuth divides the whole physical memory into three separated zones, i.e., NORMAL_ZONE, AUTH_ZONE, SECURE_ZONE. NORMAL_ZONE represents the normal world physical memory holding the Rich OS, the normal APPs and the normal part of MAPs. AUTH_ZONE is used for the secret parts of MAPs. SECURE_ZONE is used for the core components in the secure world. The security states of NOR-MAL_ZONE and SECURE_ZONE are always unchanged while AUTH_ZONE will be dynamically configured into either world to achieve the efficient isola-tion.

Virtual Memory Layout. TAuth maintains separated page tables for each MAP. The normal page table (NPT) is used for the normal part and the Rich OS while a secure page table (SPT) is used for every secret part. The overall

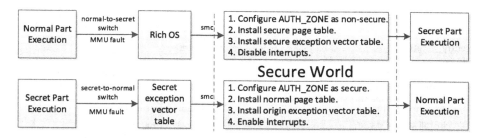

Fig. 3. Context switch actions for efficient isolation.

memory hierarchy is shown in Fig. 2. For data mapping, SPT maps all normal data as well as the secrets, since a secret part may also access normal data besides the secrets. All data pages in SPT are set to non-executable so that they cannot be used to inject malicious code. For code mapping, SPT only maps sensitive functions which can access the authentication secrets. These code pages are verified in the setup phase. In NPT, there isn't any valid mapping of the s-funcs and the secrets. Separated page tables allow TAuth to intercept all cross-part control flows, in a way transparent to the MAPs without modifying their source code. Whenever a cross-part code jump happens, an MMU fault occurs and traps the execution into the kernel mode, where an *smc* instruction is invoked to enter the secure world. Then TAuth performs necessary actions for ensuring the isolation, which is shown in Fig. 3.

Efficient Isolation. When a normal-to-secret switch happens, AUTH_ZONE is configured as non-secure, so that the secret part will run in the normal world. However, TAuth applies atomicity protection to it, ensuring it won't be interrupted unexpectedly. So other untrusted entities are sure to be suspended during its execution, with no chance to access the secret memory. When a secret-to-normal switch happens, TAuth modifies TZASC to include AUTH_ZONE into secure world, so that the untrusted running entity can't access the secret part, even if it is mapped accessible in NPT. So there is no need to intercept the Rich OS's page table updates into the secure world.

Atomicity Protection. In general, the secret part may be unexpectedly suspended in several cases, including hardware interrupts and CPU exceptions. To prevent the secret part from directly switching into the Rich OS, TAuth maintains a secure exception vector table, whose instructions are replaced by *smc*. When a normal-to-secret part-switch happens, TAuth activates the secure vector table to intercept all unexpected events into the secure world. For hardware interrupts, TAuth simply disables unnecessary ones by configuring TZIC, so that the secret part won't be interrupted by them. For CPU exceptions (caused by undefined CPU instructions, MMU faults, etc.), TAuth checks whether it is an MMU fault caused by normal secret-to-normal switch. If it is, TAuth performs a trusted context switch as usual. In other cases, TAuth considers an unexpected fault happens and simply shuts down the secret part, clears the memory contents of AUTH_ZONE.

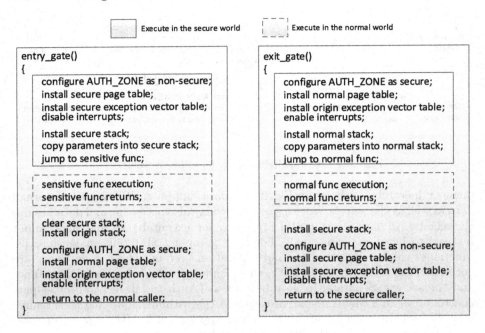

Fig. 4. Secure external function call.

Discussions. Note that both the secure exception vector table and SPT reside in AUTH_ZONE. So they can't be modified by the Rich OS. They can neither be deactivated during a secret part's execution as untrusted entities are all suspended. Malicious OS may try to access the secrets by mapping it into NPT. However, the dynamic isolation mechanism ensures AUTH_ZONE always resides in the secure world when NPT is activated, thus is always inaccessible to the Rich OS. The Rich OS may also refuse to invoke *smc* to deliver a context switch request to the secure world. This only causes unavailability of the secret part, whereas the secrets still only reside in AUTH_ZONE and won't be leaked.

Our efficient isolation requires a continuous physical memory region reserved as AUTH_ZONE, because TZASC only supports security separation for continuous regions. This will clash with the traditional memory allocation mechanism of commodity operating systems like Linux, i.e., the demand paging mechanism, where physical memory pages are dynamically allocated to the processes in greatest need. A large reserved region will significantly affect the utilization efficiency of system memory resources, because most of the region may not be used immediately and can't be used by other processes either. So our solution is not suitable for large commodity software. Fortunately, TAuth leverages the concept of in-application separation and is specially designed for authentication APPs, whose secret part is usually small, thus won't incur great performance overhead to the overall system.

4.3   Securing External Function Call

TAuth divides MAP's program logic into sensitive functions and other code (including application code and OS code). During runtime, functions in the normal part may call sensitive functions, while sensitive functions may also call functions outside of the secret part. As mentioned above, TAuth intercepts every cross-part function call to perform a trusted context switch in the secure world.

Figure 4 shows the whole context switch procedure. When the normal part calls sensitive functions in the secret part, the entry gate code is triggered. TAuth first performs the actions mentioned in Sect. 4.2 to ensure the basic isolation. Then it modifies the statck pointer (the sp register) to point to a secure stack residing in AUTH_ZONE, which is used for the execution of the secret part. If the parameter number is larger than four, which is the maximum number of parameters passed via registers, according to AAPCS (Procedure Call Standard for the ARM Architecture), the remaining parameters should be copied to the secure stack. Then the real sensitive function is called. When the sensitive function returns to the caller in the normal part, an MMU fault occurs as the return address of the normal part is inaccessible in SPT, then TAuth takes over control again. It clears the contents of the secure stack, modifies sp to point to the origin stack, writes the function's return value in it, and finally returns to the caller.

When a sensitive function is executing, it may call functions outside the secret part, including the ones in the normal part, library calls and system calls of the Rich OS. For function calls of the normal part, which won't access the secrets (otherwise they will be added to the secret part), TAuth performs an exit gate code, which simply reverses the procedure of the entry gate. However, calling library functions or system calls faces more challenges, as they may access the secrets. These untrusted functions usually have complex semantics and implementations. System calls even involve the execution of the Rich OS. So it's hard to guarantee their security. Fortunately, TAuth is specially designed for MAPs who have fixed execution patterns, thus having fixed security requirements. We only provide security guarantees for related function calls.

Computation Code. For computation code, library functions for memory operations are needed to perform the authentication algorithms, such as memcpy, strlen. As their implementations are simple and don't rely on the underlying Rich OS, TAuth simply creates a trusted version of these functions and installs them in SPT during a secret part initialization. All these calls will be redirected to the trusted version by TAuth.

Storage Code. For storage code, system functions for file I/O (e.g., *read*, *write*) are needed to load or update persistent authentication secrets, such as private keys, passwords in file or database. TAuth provides privacy protections for these secrets. In particular, it ensures they are encrypted using a secure per-device key and their plaintexts only exist in secure memory of AUTH_ZONE. When the secret part needs to store a secret, TAuth checks whether the external call (e.g., a *write* call) belongs to storage code. If it does, TAuth encrypts the secure buffer containing the authentication secret which is specified in the function parameters, and copies it to the OS's memory page cache, so that external entities can only get the ciphertexts. When loading a secret, the Rich OS first reads the encrypted one into its memory cache, and invokes *smc* to inform TAuth to copy the ciphertext into the secure buffer and decrypt it. Note that a malicious OS may read a wrong secret or directly tamper the secret file, which will cause all authentications unpassed as the secret's integrity has been broken. However, this will be easily detected by the users and won't cause the correct secret being leaked.

I/O Code. For I/O code, system functions for device I/O (e.g., *scanf*, *printf*) are needed to import raw secrets (password from keyboard, fingerprints, GPS locations..), or display sensitive information to the users (OTPs, transaction details). Unlike persistent secrets in files, they can only be obtained from I/O devices or displayed to the users in the form of plaintext. As these secrets are transmitted between the MAPs and I/O devices via untrusted device drivers in the Rich OS, TAuth must intercept all I/O flows passing through the data boundary of the Rich OS with the MAPs and I/O devices.

When receiving an external function call for raw data input (e.g., obtain a password from keyboard via *scanf*), ATuth sets the corresponding keyboard interrupt as secure by configuring TZIC. So when a keystroke occurs, the execution of current CPU will trap into the monitor mode in the secure world, which allows TAuth to get the real keystroke before the Rich OS. Then TAuth sends a read instruction to the keyboard to get the key value, stores it in the secure world, writes a dummy value into the data buffer of the Rich OS's keyboard driver, and jumps to the normal interrupt handler of the driver. After the driver obtains all the dummy inputs, it invokes *smc* to inform TAuth to copy the real values into the secure buffer, and configure keyboard interrupt as normal again.

When receiving an external function call for raw data output (e.g., display an OTP), TAuth changes the buffer address in the function parameter to point to a shared buffer with dummy outputs. When the driver is ready for the display, it invokes *smc* to inform TAuth. Then TAuth sends an write instruction to the display device with the real outputs, and resumes the execution of the device driver to finish this function call.

Note that a malicious OS may serve illegally to display wrong outputs, or simply refuse to deliver the correct *smc* instructions. Similar with handling the storage code, this will cause all authentications unpassed as a wrong password or OTP is being used. However, this will be easily detected by the users and won't cause the correct secret being leaked, as Rich OS can only get dummy values.

Discussions. Our method allows securely calling external functions while still providing privacy protection to the authentication secrets. Particularly, TAuth creates a trusted data path through the complex device drivers to securely loading or exporting the secrets, with no need to reimplement them in the secure world, hence significantly reduce the system TCB size. Although the untrusted Rich OS may serve illegally to break the secret integrity, or simply launch denial-of-service attacks to block all *smc* instructions, these disruptive behaviors can be easily detected and won't cause any secret leakage.

4.4   Lifecycle of a Protected MAP

Program Launch. Before deployed into the TAuth system, an MAP must be divided into a normal part and secret parts, in the form of a configuration file, including the secret parts' start virtual addresses, code size, and per-part code hashvalues. The integrity of the file is protected using the device private key. So neither the file nor the sensitive code can be tampered or forged by attackers. The configuration files are loaded and verified in the secure world during system initialization. When an MAP is launched, the Rich OS first loads all secret parts' code into its memory caches, then informs TAuth to check their integrity using the hashvalues. If the check is passed, TAuth moves the code into AUTH_ZONE and installs the corresponding SPT according to the virtual addresses in the configuration file. Note that it also maps several reserved pages in SPT, which will be used as secure heap and stack later. Therefore, all sensitive code can be correctly loaded into AUTH_ZONE via the Rich OS's untrusted file system code and storage device driver, without reimplementing them in secure world.

Secret Initialization. During a secret part's initialization, it will allocate a secure buffer from stack or heap for loading every authentication secret. For stack allocation, there need no change as the stack pointer (sp register) has pointed to the secure stack. For heap allocation, which needs assistance from the Rich OS via *malloc*, TAuth creates a trusted *secure_malloc* installed in SPT and redirects all *malloc* calls to it to allocate pages from the secure heap. The secrets can be securely loaded via the method described in Sect. 4.3.

Runtime. At runtime, code in the normal and the secret part execute concurrently. TAuth ensures that: (1) all authentication secrets and their copies only exist in SPT mappings, (2) they can only be used during secret parts execution. Any attempts to access the secrets memory from the normal part will cause an MMU page fault and will be considered as malicious by TAuth, who takes further measures like shutting down the secret part, or notifying the user. Note that TAuth provides no protections for authentication responses exported from the secret part, whose security relies on the MAP's protocol design, such as using a secure session key shared with the remote authentication server.

Exit. When the MAP exits, authentication secrets should also be cleared. If the MAP exits normally, TAuth removes the SPT and releases the secure memory. Even if it exits abnormally or the Rich OS refuses to inform TAuth, the secrets still only exist in AUTH_ZONE and thus won't be leaked.

Discussions. Our method relies on the correct partition of the MAP's normal part and secret parts. This assumption is reasonable as mature works exist for automated program partition for privilege separation [10,25,35,36]. MAP providers could leverage these methods to automatically export the configuration file containing a correct and complete closure of all sensitive functions which may access the defined secrets. Moreover, MAPs usually have unified execution patterns and fixed security requirements, making their partition even easier. One of our future work will be integrating automated program partition into TAuth architecture to generate the configuration file at runtime, thus eliminating the extra partition work for MAP providers.

Note that we can also support partition of dynamic libraries, by modifying Rich OS's loader. Then the virtual addresses in the configuration file will be in-application offsets. We do not assume the loader as trusted. Even if it behaves maliciously by refusing to load sensitive functions or loading them to wrong locations, the secrets will still not be disclosed, as TAuth can reject to load the secrets during the integrity checking phase.

5   Security Analysis

TAuth is mainly designed to provide memory, storage, I/O isolation of the authentication secrets. This section discusses several other typical attacks beyond the basic isolation.

Cloning Attacks. Cloning attackers aims to impersonate the victims to perform illegal authentications by copying the persistent secrets to their devices. As TAuth encrypts all secrets using a per-device key, they can only be correctly decrypted on the owner's device. As a common solution, most commodity mobile devices equip with a per-device key in hardware secure storage like eFuse, which can only be accessed in the secure world, making cloning attacks hard to success.

Relay Attacks. A compromised normal part is an ideal man-in-middle attacker, who monitors and relays the messages between the secret part and the authentication server to perform unexpected authentications. Such attacks could be prevented by requiring an explicit physical user consent (e.g., a user's button press) before any authentication actions. TAuth's I/O isolation mechanism ensures the consent can't be tampered, emulated or masked by the normal world. As the hardware interrupt of the physical consent will be first captured in the secure world.

Phishing Attacks. These attacks may display a forged input window to cheat the user to enter his password. Complementary techniques such as a security indicator controlled by the secure world (e.g., an LED light) can be used. Moreover, even if the attacker gets the password, they still can't complete an authentication process as they cannot forge or emulate a physical user consent.

Rollback Attacks. The attacker may rollback the MAP software and the corresponding configuration file to an old version, which still has a valid integrity value signed by the device key. Such attacks could be prevented using a secure counter or clock only accessible to the secure world to track the MAP's states. Moreover, even if the rollback of a vulnerable version is success, program bugs are most likely to exist in the normal part, as the secret part often has small code base and simple logic, especially for MAPs. Exploiting these bugs cannot disclose the authentication secrets due to the TAuth isolation.

Iago Attacks. Iago attack [11] presents a complete example that the malicious Rich OS can cause a protected application to behave abnormally by manipulating the return values of mmap system calls, and can further conduct return-oriented programming (ROP) attacks to disclose its secrets. In TAuth, if there is any system call invocation in the secret part, the return values from the exit gate will be checked to avoid malicious ones. The check strategy is shared with existing solutions against these attacks [18].

ROP Attacks. ROP attacks tamper the program control flow to cause unusual malicious behaviors without modifying the program code, thus could bypass the code integrity verification. First, there is only very small code base in sensitive functions for an attacker to construct ROP gadgets. Second, as the secure stack used by secret parts is isolated, an adversary has no chance to fake a stack to tamper the control flow. Third, TAuth ensures the secret part can only be called through designated function entries, making gadgets in normal part can only be at the function granularity. Even if the attack succeeds in the normal part, the payload still can't disclose the secrets due to the TAuth isolation.

6   Implementation

We develop TAuth prototype system on a Trustzone-enabled development board, Xilinx ZYNQ-7000 AP Soc [34], with a Cortex-A9 dual-core processor, 1 GB external DDR3 RAM and 256 KB on-chip SRAM.

Normal World. We run Linux 2.6.38 as the Rich OS in the normal world, with several modifications. (1) We add a kernel parameter *auth_mem* which indicates the memory region used for MAPs, i.e., the AUTH_ZONE. (2) We change the implementation of the *execve* system call to add an process creation routine specially for MAPs, which informs the secure world to perform the MAP program launching mentioned in Sect. 4.4. (3) We change the implementation of the *fork* system call to add an MAP cloning routine, which informs the secure world to copy the SPT and secure memory to an identical clone. (4) We insert some *smc* instructions in the kernel code to perform necessary communications with the secure world, such as the one in page fault handler for context switch, and the one in the universal file system component for secure I/O.

We implement a prototype trusted I/O path using an UART port on Zynq-7000, which can be configured as secure only or shared by both worlds. We connect a PC to the development board via the UART port, whose keyboard and screen are used as the I/O peripherals. We use Tera Term, a PC terminal tool for serial port debugging on PC to transfer the I/O data between them. *Smc* instructions are inserted into the kernel's UART driver code, which inform TAuth to perform secure I/O transactions for MAP secrets.

Our method requires a little modifications to the kernel code, which may not be feasible for closed source systems. However, TAuth is designed as a system-level security solution for device vendors, who usually maintain their own kernel source code. Also, the modifications contain only about 510 LOC to the kernel, which is pretty light-weight, making TAuth practical to be deployed.

Secure World. We build TAuth in a bare metal secure world retrenched from an open-source secure kernel, Sierra TEE [13], only reserving its boot code. We modify the boot code to divide the physical memory by configuring TZASC. TZASC in our ZYNQ development board is implemented as a secure control register called TZ_DDR_RAM, which can only be accessed in the secure world at 0xF8000430. The register divides the 1 GB external RAM into 16 regions (so each region has 64 MB RAM), using 16 control bits indicating their security status. TAuth reserves the top 128 MB RAM, the top 64 MB of which is configured as secure for SECURE_ZONE. The other 64 MB is for AUTH_ZONE. Our evaluation result proves that the region is enough for the secret parts of most commodity MAPs.

After system initialization, TAuth boots the normal world's Linux kernel. The kernel first loads the MAP configuration files. Then TAuth verifies their signatures using the device private key and moves them into secure world. During runtime, TAuth will only approve the creation of a valid MAP process whose signature has been verified. As the configuration files define all authorized MAPs, device vendors should sign them in a secure offline environment. Though TAuth fills the gap of security and openness for Trustzone, how to make it commercially available to third-party MAP providers concerns business cooperation, which is out of the scope of this paper.

7   Evaluation

7.1   MAP Examples

We use three real-world MAPs to perform our security and performance evaluations: *GA*, *tiqr* and *OpenSSL*.

Google Authenticator. As mentioned in Sect. 2.2, GA generates One-Time-Passwords (OTPs) for Google users as a second authenticator in addition to their username and password to log into Google services or other sites [14]. It uses a secret key provided by Google (scanned or manually entered) to generate a sha1 HMAC using the key and a timestamp or a counter as the authentication OTP. The secret key is stored in the APP's local database, representing the authentication secret in TAuth, and the computation code includes the OTP generation algorithm.

Tiqr. Tiqr is an open-source authentication solution for mobile devices and web applications [3]. It is based on Open Standards from the Open Authentication Initiative (OATH). It performs challenge/response authentication using QR codes. After obtaining the authentication challenge from the QR code, the user needs to enter a pin code to finish the authentication, which represents the secret need to be protected by TAuth.

OpenSSL. We also use OpenSSL as a tested MAP for the convenient of security and performance evaluation, by linking its library into a light-weight embedded web server (Nginx) to establish SSL network connection. We use OpenSSL RSA as the cryptographic scheme. The RSA private key is denoted as BIGNUM data structure, containing the two large prime numbers (p and q), and the key's exponent d. OpenSSL implements its own heap management function *OPENSSL_malloc*. So all *OPENSSL_malloc* calls for BIGNUM are redirected to *secure_malloc* in TAuth.

7.2   Secret Part Size

Since TAuth needs to setup a SPT for each secret part, we calculate how much additional memory is needed for them. First, we use the method introduced in [35] to divide the three MAPs, which combines the use of static taint analysis and dynamic execution track. They have integrated the partition method into their vitalization-based protection architecture and have proved its security. So we believe our partition result is complete and secure, which is proved in our security evaluation. Then we modify the definition of the sensitive functions with different GCC section attribute from *.text*, so that they will be compiled into separated sections. Hence, TAuth could protect them in the page granularity. These MAPs are re-compiled using the arm-linux-gnueabi-gcc cross-compile toolchain to run on our development board.

The memory consumption depends on how many sensitive functions are extracted, and how many secure heap and stack pages are reserved, which is shown in Table 1. The OpenSSL has the biggest secure memory consumption, which is 32 KB (8 pages). The GA and tiqr require less memory as their implementation is simpler than OpenSSL. The consumption is negligible compared with the whole memory, which could hardly affect the system memory utilization efficiency.

7.3   System TCB Size

TAuth code in the secure world mainly consists of the boot code, the context switch code, simple low-level device I/O code, and several function emulation (*memcpy, malloc..*), without any concrete applications, OS services or complex device drivers. As a result, TAuth only has 2200 lines of code. Moreover, the TCB size doesn't increase along with the number of supported MAPs, which is our greatest advantage compared with other Trustzone-based solutions.

Although several library and OS-feature functions are emulated in the secure world, they will only be called in MAPs after being mapped into their SPTs, which all run in the normal world. These code won't increase the system TCB as they will never be executed in the secure world. TAuch could ensure this by only mapping them as non-executable in the secure world.

7.4   Security Evaluation

Memory Disclosure Rootkit. We first evaluate to what extent can TAuth achieve the isolation of authentication secrets against disclosure attackers. So we

Table 1. Secure memory consumption.

MAP	Func num	Func page	Sec heap	Sec stack	Total
OpenSSL	20	5	1	2	8 pages
GA	11	2	1	2	5 pages
tiqr	6	1	1	1	3 pages

write a malicious kernel module, which scans the whole normal world memory and tries to find targeted secrets when running these three MAPs. When running in the origin Linux system, there are several secret values found in the program heaps. But when running in TAuth, no secrets could be found. This proves that our program partition is correct, ensuring that no secret operations reside in the normal part and the secrets will only exist in the secure part.

In-application Vulnerability Exploit. We use the HeartBleed PoC [2] to launch RSA key disclosure attack targeted on the Nginx server with a vulnerable OpenSSL version 1.0.1f. We get private keys after sending 43 HeartBleed requests when running Nginx in origin Linux. However, when running in TAuth, no fragment of private keys is leaked no matter how many HeartBleed requests are sent. The HeartBleed case proves that TAuch could effectively defense attacks exploiting in-application vulnerabilities.

I/O Hijacking. We implement a POC malware acting as a UART logger, who tries to steal the tiqr's pin code entered by the user. It hooks the normal world UART FIQ interrupt handler, and also periodically queries the UART driver buffer to intercept any possible I/O data. When running tiqr in origin Linux, the malware records all the keystrokes. For the TAuth case, the hook code in the FIQ interrupt handler never get executed and only dummy values are obtained from the driver buffer.

7.5   Performance Evaluation

System Overhead. As TAuth is designed specially for MAPs. We first evaluate whether TAuth has performance effects on other system components. We run LMBench, a series of microbenchmarks for OS services to measure the overall system performance overhead. Table 2 shows the results compared with origin Linux. We also list LMBench results of another similar system from its paper, i.e., a Trustzone normal world isolation solution (SecRet [21]). TAuth produces nearly negligible system performance overhead compared with origin Linux, which proves that the performance effect is localized, only affecting the protected MAPs. By contrast, SecRet incurs much higher overhead, as it needs monitor of global system behaviors, including all page table updates and user-kernel mode switches, which are all omitted by the efficient TAuth isolation.

World Switch Times. As the normal part and the secret parts may call each other, we measure the overhead of Trustzone world switches caused by cross-part

Table 2. LMBench Results (in microseconds).

Syscalls	Linux	TAuth	Overhead	SecReT
Null	0.33	0.33	1x	3.9259x
Read	0.42	0.43	1.02x	3.7273x
Write	0.54	0.54	1x	3.7381x
Open/close	6.61	6.69	1.01x	1.6264x
Fork	171.25	173.12	1.01x	1.1819x
Fork+Exec	194.63	201.27	1.03x	1.1791x

Table 3. Trustzone world switch times.

Nginx/req		GA/auth		tiqr/auth	
N→S	S→N	N→S	S→N	N→S	S→N
64	8	18	21	8	19

function calls. We add a counter in the secure world to record world switch times during a MAP's execution. Table 3 shows the total switch times after the Nginx server processed one request, and GA, tiqr performed one user authentication. We also evaluate one world switch time by invoking an empty service running in the secure world, which is about 2 milliseconds (ms). For the Nginx server, the switch cost is about 144 ms per request, which can be negligible compared with a normal user authentication procedure. The cost for GA and tiqr is less.

Application Overhead. We measure the runtime overhead of the three MAPs against running them in origin Linux. We use the standard Apache *ab* benchmark tool to measure the Nginx's overhead. The tool runs on a different client machine connected with the development board over 1 Gbps Ethernet. It sends 5000 requests with 50 concurrent SSL connections, each request asks the server to transfer a 5 KB file. The benchmark result shows that the latency and throughput overhead is 15% and 21%. We also measure the execution time of one user authentication for GA and tiqr, which mainly contain an OTP generation, or a pin code enter. We perform 50 measurements for each case and record the average value. The runtime overhead for GA and tiqr is 10% and 16%.

TAuth introduces a relatively high MAP runtime overhead, which is not less than 10%, mainly due to the extra security operations in the secure world. However, as the whole execution time of one user authentication is usually short, such overhead won't cause obvious degradation for user experience. Moreover, given the high security requirements of MAPs, such performance sacrifice is acceptable. Moreover, such overhead is localized, which won't affect the execution of other system components.

8   Related Work and Conclusion

Trustzone Authentication Solutions. The OBC system (On-board Credentials) [23] is a TEE-based security architecture for protecting critical user virtual credentials, which allows anyone to design and deploy new credential algorithms and secrets. [27] proposes a location-based second-factor authentication solution for modern smartphones using Trustzone. It is designed for the scenario of point of sale transactions to detect fraudulent transactions. TrustOTP [17] proposes a Trustzone-based secure onetime password solution, which achieves various OTP protections against malicious mobile OS. While these works take advantage of TrustZone, they all deploy the concrete MAPs and necessary OS services, drivers in the secure world, which significantly increase the TCB size.

Trustzone Normal World Isolation. Real Trustzone secure world attacks have energized research into moving Trustzone's protection domain to the normal world. TZ-RKP [9] guarantees Rich OS's code integrity relying on a runtime kernel monitor in the secure world. Based on TZ-RKP's kernel protection, SecRet [21] creates an isolated memory region in a normal world process to protect a secure communication key. All these works introduce great performance overhead as they need to intercept frequent global system behaviors, such as page table updates. TrustICE [16] shares a similar isolation method with TAuth while doesn't support securely calling untrusted external functions. Necessary OS services and drivers are still implemented in the secure domain and the TCB size is not effectively reduced. TrustShadow [24] creates zombie processes in the normal world while runs the real code as shadow TAs in the secure world. With only a lightweight runtime module in the secure world kernel, the TCB is effectively reduced but is still threatened by vulnerable shadow TAs.

Virtualization-Based Shielding Systems. Overshadow [12], CHAOS [15] and InkTag [18] use a hypervisor to isolate application memory and CPU state from untrusted OS and still support most OS services. However, they all need frequent encryption and hash operations on the application memory. As virtualization is primarily designed to allow multiple OSs to share the same hardware platform at a heavy cost for performance and code size, these solutions are not practical for resource-constrained mobile devices. Also, they only provide coarsegrained isolation at an application level, which won't work well under attacks exploiting in-application vulnerabilities such as HeartBleed.

Automated Program Partition. Program partition for privilege separation prevents malicious exploitation of applications that run with maximum privilege. Privtrans requires expert knowledge to specify privileged functions and variables [10]. It annotates the source code and partitions source program into only two components: a privileged one and an unprivileged one. [25] develops an approach for automated partitioning of critical Android applications into client code running in Trustzone normal world and critical TEE commands running in the secure world. SeCage [35] combines static taint and dynamic execution analyses to partition C applications w.r.t. sensitive data, and proposes a virtualization-based intra-domain isolation architecture integrating their partition method, which is not suitable for mobile devices.

Conclusion. We propose a novel Trustzone-based mobile authentication security schema called TAuth, which achieves two key advantages compared with previous solutions, i.e., a normal world isolation with a small and unchanged TCB, and fine-grained in-application isolation which defenses threatens from both the underlying Rich OS and in-application vulnerabilities. Designed specially for MAPs, TAuth solves two significant technique challenges, including efficient isolation without excessive intervention into the secure world, and securely using untrusted external functions. We deploy the prototype system on real Trustzone device, and perform thorough evaluations using real commodity MAPs. The evaluation results confirm the security and efficiency of TAuth.

Acknowledgements. Our work was supported in part by grants from the National Natural Science Foundation of China (No. 61602455 and No. 61402455).

References

1. How to root my android device using vroot. http://www.androidxda.com/download-vroot
2. Poc of private key leakage using heartbleed. https://github.com/einaros/heartbleed-tools
3. Tiqr. http://www.rcdevs.com/downloads/download/1/Utils/rcdevs_libs-1.0.15.tgz
4. Vmware: Vulnerability statistics. http://www.cvedetails.com/vendor/252/Vmware.html
5. Xen: Vulnerability statistics. http://www.cvedetails.com/vendor/6276/XEN.html
6. Dmitrienko, A., Liebchen, C., Rossow, C., Sadeghi, A.-R.: On the (in)security of mobile two-factor authentication. In: Christin, N., Safavi-Naini, R. (eds.) FC 2014. LNCS, vol. 8437, pp. 365–383. Springer, Heidelberg (2014). https://doi.org/10.1007/978-3-662-45472-5_24
7. ARM: Building a secure system using TrustZone (2009). http://www.arm.com
8. ARM: Securing the Future of Authentication with ARM TrustZone-based Trusted Execution Environment and Fast Identity Online (FIDO) (2015). https://www.arm.com/files/pdf/TrustZone-and-FIDO-white-paper.pdf
9. Azab, A., Ning, P., Shah, J., Chen, Q., Bhutkar, R.: Hypervision across worlds: real-time kernel protection from the arm trustzone secure world. In: Proceedings of ACM SIGSAC Conference on Computer and Communications Security (CCS 2014) (2014)
10. Brumley, D., Song, D.: Privtrans: automatically partitioning programs for privilege separation. In: Proceedings of the 13th Conference on USENIX Security Symposium (2004)
11. Checkoway, S., Shacham, H.: Iago attacks: why the system call API is a bad untrusted RPC interface. In: The 18th International Conference on Architectural Support for Programming Languages and Operating Systems (ASPLOS 2013) (2013)
12. Chen, X., et al.: Overshadow: a virtualization-based approach to retrofitting protection in commodity operating systems. In: The 13th International Conference on Architectural Support for Programming Languages and Operating Systems (ASPLOS 2008) (2008)

13. Gonzalez, J.: Open Virtulization for Xilinxs ZC-702. https://github.com/javigon/OpenVirtulization
14. Google: Google Authenticator. https://github.com/google/google-authenticator-libpam
15. Chen, H., Zhang, F., Chen, C., Yang, Z., Chen, R., Zang, B., Mao, W.: Tamper-resistant execution in an untrusted operating system using a virtual machine monitor. In: Report FDUPPITR-2007-0801, Parallel Processing Institute, Fudan University, August 2007
16. Sun, H., Sun, K., Wang, Y., Jing, J.: TrustICE: hardware-assisted isolated computing environments on mobile devices. In: International Conference on Dependable Systems and Networks (DSN 2015) (2015)
17. Sun, H., Sun, K., Wang, Y., Jing, J.: TrustOTP: transforming smartphones into secure one-time password tokens. In: Proceedings of the 22th ACM Conference on Computer and Communications Security (CCS 2015) (2015)
18. Hofmann, O., Kim, S., Dunn, A., Lee, M., Witchel, E.: InkTag: secure applications on an untrusted operating system. In: the 18th International Conference on Architectural Support for Programming Languages and Operating Systems (ASPLOS 2013) (2013)
19. Mccune, J.M., Parno, B., Perrig, A., et al.: Flicker: an execution infrastructure for TCB minimization. In: EuroSys (2008)
20. McCune, J.M., Li, Y., Qu, N., et al.: Trustvisor: efficient TCB reduction and attestation. In: Proceedings of the 31st IEEE Symposium on Security and Privacy (2010)
21. Jang, J., et al.: SeCReT: secure channel between rich execution environment and trusted execution environment. In: Proceedings of the Network and Distributed System Security Symposium (NDSS 2015) (2015)
22. Keltner, N.: Here be dragons: vulnerabilities in trustzone (2014). https://atredispartners.blogspot.com/2014/08/here-be-dragons-vulnerabilities-in.html
23. Kostiainen, K., Ekberg, J., Asokan, N., Rantala, A.: On-board credentials with open provisioning. In: Proceedings of the International Symposium on Information, Computer, and Communications Security (2009)
24. Guan, L., Liu, P., Xing, X., et al.: TrustShadow: secure execution of unmodified applications with ARM trustZone. In: Proceedings of the 15th ACM International Conference on Mobile Systems, Applications, and Services (MobiSys 2017) (2017)
25. Rosculete, L., Rosculete, L., Mitra, T., et al.: Automated partitioning of android applications for trusted execution environments. In: Proceedings of the International Conference on Software Engineering (ICSE 2016) (2016)
26. laginimaineb: Bits, please! (2016). https://bits-please.blogspot.com/
27. Marforio, C., et al.: Smartphones as practical and secure location verification tokens for payments. In: Proceedings of the Network and Distributed System Security Symposium (NDSS 2014) (2014)
28. Lindemann, R., Hill, D.B., Tiffany, E.: FIDO UAF Protocol Specification v1.0 (2014). https://fidoalliance.org/specs/fido-uaf-v1.0-ps-20141208/fido-uaf-protocol-v1.0-ps-20141208.html
29. Roland, M.: Applying recent secure element relay attack scenarios to the real world: Google Wallet Relay Attack (2013)
30. Rosenberg, D.: Reflections on trusting trustzone. In: BlackHat USA (2014)
31. Rosenberg, D.: QSEE trustzone kernel integer over flow vulnerability. In: Black Hat Conference (2014)

32. Shacham, H.: The geometry of innocent flesh on the bone: return-into-libc without function calls (on the x86). In: Proceedings of the 14th ACM Conference on Computer and Communications Security (CCS 2007) (2007)

33. Shen, D.: Attacking your trusted core, exploiting trustzone on android. In: Black-Hat USA (2015)

34. Xilinx: Zynq-7000 all programmable SOC ZC702 evaluation kit. http://www.xilinx.com/products/boards-and-kits/EK-Z7-ZC702-G.htm

35. Liu, Y., Zhou, T., Chen, K., et al.: Thwarting memory disclosure with efficient hypervisor-enforced intra-domain isolation. In: Proceedings of the 22th ACM Conference on Computer and Communications Security (CCS 2015) (2015)

36. Wu, Y., Sun, J., Liu, Y., Dong, J.S.: Automatically partition software into least privilege components using dynamic data dependency analysis. In: Proceedings of the 28th International Conference on Automated Software Engineering (ASE 2013) (2013)

37. Zhang, Y., Zhao, S., Qin, Y., et al.: TrustTokenF: a generic security framework for mobile two-factor authentication using trustzone. In: Proceedings of the 14th IEEE International Conference on Trust, Security and Privacy in Computing and Communications (TrustCom 2015) (2015)

A Program Manipulation Middleware and Its Applications on System Security

Ting Chen[1]([⊠])(iD), Yang Xu[2], and Xiaosong Zhang[1]

[1] Center for Cyber Security, University of Electronic Science
and Technology of China, Chengdu 611731, China
chenting19870201@163.com, brokendragon@uestc.edu.cn
[2] School of Mathematic Science, University of Electronic Science
and Technology of China, Chengdu 611731, China
18215522740@163.com

Abstract. A typical program analysis workflow heavily relies on Program Manipulation Software (PMS), incurring a high learning curve and changing to another PMS requires completely recoding. This work designs a middleware, that sits between the applications and the PMS, hides the differences of various PMS, and provides a unified programming interface. Based on the middleware, programmers can develop portable applications without learning the PMS, thereby reducing the learning and programming efforts. The current implementation of the middleware integrates Dyninst (static analysis) and Pin (dynamic analysis). Moreover, we develop five security applications, aiming to prevent systems from stack overflow, heap corruption, memory allocation/deallocation flaws, invocations of dangerous functions, and division-by-zero bugs. Experiments also show that the middleware incurs small space & runtime overhead, and no false positives. Furthermore, the applications developed on the middleware require much less code, negligible runtime overhead, compared with the applications developed directly on Dyninst and Pin.

Keywords: Program manipulation middleware · System security
Unified programming interface · Portable applications

1 Introduction

Program analysis is a fundamental technique for various applications, such as software optimization [23], understanding [13], verification [22], debugging [3], testing [17], and software system protection [20]. When developing a particular application, programmers have to handle the Software Under Analysis (SUA) in a nontrivial way, e.g., translating the machine/source code into an analysis-friendly form, extracting control flows, tracking data flows, parsing symbol information. To alleviate programmers' burden, various Program Manipulation Software (PMS) [4,25,26,31,32] has been proposed to provide programming interfaces. Based on PMS, programmers can handle the SUA by directly invoking the programming interfaces without the need to parse the SUA by hand.

© ICST Institute for Computer Sciences, Social Informatics and Telecommunications Engineering 2018
X. Lin et al. (Eds.): SecureComm 2017, LNICST 238, pp. 606–626, 2018.
https://doi.org/10.1007/978-3-319-78813-5_31

However, the current development mode of program analysis applications has several drawbacks. First, the learning curve of using PMS is high and non-general, because different PMS has different programming interfaces. Second, for the same reason, programmers have to completely recode when their applications are required to change PMS. Different PMS has their own strengths. For example, both Pin [26] and Valgrind [32] are commonly-used dynamic instrumentation tools for offline binary analysis. Pin runs obviously faster than Valgrind [26] but demands application developers to handle machine code/assembly statements. However, Valgrind translates machine code into the VEX Intermediate Representation (IR) which is more analysis-friendly. Hence, the third drawback is that choosing an adequate PMS before developing is tricky because changing to another PMS is difficult.

Although many instrumentation languages have been proposed to simplify program manipulation, they suffer from one or more problems that can limit their effectiveness and utility in practice. These problems include the incapability of languages [19, 29, 34], the restrictions of PMS [8, 9, 15, 19, 27, 28, 34], the limited kinds of insertion points [8, 15, 19, 27, 28, 30], the requirement that applications should be programmed by their proposed languages [8, 15, 18, 19, 30], lack of applications and experiments [27, 28, 33], and the learning efforts to grasp the proposed languages [9, 18].

To overcome the aforementioned drawbacks, this work firstly designs a middleware that integrates different PMS, interacts with underlying PMS, handles the differences of various PMS, and provides an unified programming interface which is independent with PMS. Second, we propose a quick-start programming fashion, allowing programmers to execute arbitrary code feeding with various parameters in specified occasions. Application programmers can benefit from the two innovations. First, programmers can build their applications on the middleware without a deep understanding of the underlying PMS. Specifically, programmers need neither to understand the technical details of PMS nor to learn how to invoke PMS's programming interfaces. Second, applications can change to any other PMS on demand, requiring no modifications to the source code of applications. Consequently, programmers wouldn't feel difficult to choose PMS because porting to another PMS is effortless.

Compared to existing studies, our approach has the following advantages. First, it is designed to be general enough to support the development of various applications. Second, its design puts no restrictions on PMS and the current implementation supports a static PMS, Dyninst, and a dynamic PMS, Pin. Besides, current implementation supports various insertion points that can manipulate the SUA in different granularities. Furthermore, its effectiveness and efficiency are validated by several applications and experiments.

Our work has the following contributions.

1. We design and implement a middleware that provides an unified and easy-to-use programming interface to application developers.
2. On top of the middleware, we implement five applications that intend to protect systems from stack overflow, heap corruption, memory

allocation/deallocation flaws, invocations of dangerous functions, and division-by-zero bugs respectively. For comparison, we also implement those applications directly on top of Pin and Dyninst [5] respectively.

3. We conduct experiments to validate the effectiveness and efficiency of our approach. Results demonstrate that the middleware leads to acceptable space overhead, minimal runtime overhead, and no false positives. Besides, comparisons show that the applications developed on the middleware require much less code and have comparable performance with those developed directly on Dyninst and Pin. Furthermore, the applications are evaluated to be successful in protecting systems from CVE-2004-0597 and CVE-2011-3328.

The remainder of this paper is organized as follows. Section 2 introduces a motivating example. The design & implementation of the middleware are described in Sect. 3. Section 4 presents five applications for system security built on the middleware. Section 5 gives experimental results. We introduce the related work in Sect. 6 and conclude the paper with future work in Sect. 7.

2   Motivating Example

In this section, we use a simple example to illustrate the motivations of our work. The example application is an instruction logger that records the number of executed instructions. Figure 1(a), (b), (c) present the logger's source code built on Pin, Dyninst and our middleware respectively. Figure 1(d) is the related configuration to Fig. 1(c). For the sake of presentation, we omit less important code in Fig. 1(a) and (b), while we show complete code in Fig. 1(c) and (d).

As shown in Fig. 1(a), after initialization (Line 6), the logger registers a callback (Line 7), termed by *Instruction* (Line 3) that will be invoked immediately before a code sequence is executed for the first time. In *Instruction*, an analysis function *docount* (Line 2) is inserted before each instruction (Line 4), ensuring that *docount* will be executed exactly before the execution of each instruction. The *docount* just increases the global variable *icount* by 1, that indicates the number of instructions has been executed so far. Finally, the SUA will be run after invoking *PIN_StartProgram* which is a Pin's API.

The implementation on Dyninst looks more complex (Fig. 1(b)). It firstly opens the SUA (omitted in Line 8) and then creates an integer *intCounter* which can be inserted into the SUA (Line 9). Then the logger enumerates all modules (Line 10) and further all functions of each module (Line 11). The function *rtndeal* is called (Line 12) whenever it finds a function in the SUA. In *rtndeal* (Line 1), the logger enumerates all blocks (Line 2) and further all instructions of each block (Line 3). Afterwards, all insertion points of each instruction are enumerated (Line 4). Then the logger constructs an arithmetic expression *addOne* (Line 5), that has the same effect with the C code *intCounter++*. The constructed expression will be inserted into each insertion point (Line 6). Finally, the modified SUA should be written back to the disk (Line 13).

The implementation on our middleware (Fig. 1(c)) is much simpler, that is a function *TargetCount* increasing a global variable *insnum*. To make the code be

```
1   static UINT incount=0;
2   VOID docount(){icount++;}
3   VOID Instruction(INS ins ,VOID *v){
4     INS_InsertCall(ins ,IPOINT_BEFORE,docount ,IARG_END);}
5   int main(int argc ,char *argv[]){
6     if(PIN_Init(argc ,argv))return Usage();
7     INS_AddInstrumentFunction(Instruction ,0);
8     PIN_StartProgram();
9     return 0;
10  }
```

(a) Instruction logger built on Pin

```
1   void rtndeal(...){
2     for(...)//enumerate blocks
3       for(...)//enumerate instructions
4         for(...){//enumerate insertion points
5           BPatch_arithExpr addOne(BPatch_assign ,*intCounter ,
    BPatch_arithExpr(BPatch_plus ,*intCounter ,BPatch_constExpr(1)));
6           addSpace->insertSnippet(addOne,**point_iter);}}
7   int main(int argc ,char *argv[]){
8     //open the SUA
9     intCounter=addSpace->malloc(*(appImage->findType("int")));
10    for(...)//enumerate modules
11      for(...)//enumerate functions
12        rtndeal(*func_iter ,*module_iter);
13    dynamic_cast<BPatch_binaryEdit*> (addSpace)->writeFile("out");
14    return 0;
15  }
```

(b) Instruction logger built on Dyninst

```
1   int insnum=0;
2   extern "C" void TargetCount(){
3     insnum++;}
```

(c) Instruction logger built on our middleware

```
1   image a.out function all insnstring all before
2   funcalllib TargetCount
```
(d) Configuration of (c)

Fig. 1. The source of an instruction logger

interpreted by the middleware, a configuration (Fig. 1(d)) should be prepared, which is also very simple. It indicates that exactly before each instruction of each function in the SUA *a.out* executes (Line 1), a function *TargetCount* (Fig. 1(c)) should be called (Line 2). The reserved keywords, such as *image, function, all* are self-explanatory. The grammar of configuration will be introduced in Sect. 3. The technical details and differences of various PMS are hidden by the middleware. For example, application developers need not to write code to enumerate all functions in this example.

Several interesting observations can be found from the example. First, the source code of the application on Pin differs greatly from that on Dyninst, indicating that the programmers obeying conventional programming mode have to completely recode when they prepare to change the underlying PMS. Second, programmers have to spend a period grasping the programming interfaces of a particular PMS. Third, based on our middleware, programmers can get start to code much quicker, and develop more concise, PMS-independent as well as PMS-portable applications.

3   Design and Implementation

3.1   Design

Figure 2 shows the high-level architecture of the middleware which sits between the applications and the PMS. The middleware integrates various PMS (PMS 1 to PMS n), that directly interacts with PMS, and provides a PMS-independent programming interface to above applications (App 1 to App m). Applications cannot communicate with PMS directly; instead, they have to delegate the work of program manipulation to the middleware. This work proposes a unified and simple programming mode, so programmers just need to learn how to use the middleware. Programmers need to compile their applications into the form (always binaries) that the chosen PMS can understand, regardless of the source code language used. The middleware works like a virtual machine because it hides the details of the underlying PMS from the upper applications, and it can seamlessly switch from one PMS to another according to the demand of analysts. The middleware is designed to be general-purpose, that should support various applications. We will present several applications that are developed on the agent in Sect. 4.

The architecture takes inputs as the SUA and a configuration which describes where is the code specified by programmers and when the code should be executed. Take Fig. 1(d) as an example, the configuration can be interpreted as "the code is in the function *TargetCount* and the code should be executed exactly before each instruction of each function in the binary *a.out*". The configuration should be provided by application programmers. But as we will show in Sect. 3.2, the grammar is simple and self-explanatory. The outputs of the middleware should be the SUA after process or using the application to analyze the SUA, depending on whether the PMS manipulates the SUA statically or dynamically. Specifically, if a PMS manipulates the SUA when running it, such as Pin, Valgrind, Qemu [4], the code specified by application programmers will be loaded into memory at runtime. On the contrary, if a PMS handles the SUA statically, such as Dyninst, LLVM [25], CIL [31], a modified SUA with the inserted code will be generated. When executing the modified SUA, the inserted code has opportunities to run.

The workflow of the middleware is as follows. First, it loads the SUA and the applications. After that, it parses the configuration to get to know when to execute the code provided by programmers. Third, it interacts with the underlying PMS to insert the specified code into right places, ensuring that the inserted code should be executed at the right time. Finally, it analyzes the SUA or generates a modified SUA depending on the underlying PMS.

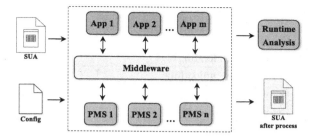

Fig. 2. Architecture

3.2   Implementation

To validate the proposed middleware can integrate various PMS, we choose a representative dynamic PMS, Pin and a representative static PMS, Dyninst. Please note that, although Dyninst is capable of handling programs dynamically, we just take advantage of its static manipulation ability. Few additional efforts are required to extend current implementation to support dynamic instrumentation of Dyninst, because Dyninst exports the same programming interface for both static and dynamic instrumentation abilities.

The versions of the integrated PMS are Pin-2.14-71313 and Dyninst 8.1 respectively. But we believe minor revisions are required in the middleware when porting to other versions, because a PMS usually provides a stable programming interface among different versions. However, Pin and Dyninst differ significantly in programming fashion, as shown in the motivating example (Sect. 2). Therefore, the most coding effort for our implementation is made to handle the differences of Pin and Dyninst. Both Pin and Dyninst are binary manipulation tools, so the SUA and the applications should be given in binary form.

Before starting analysis, the SUA and the applications should be loaded into memory. For Pin, the SUA is specified in the command line, so Pin loads the SUA automatically. On the contrary, programmers need to invoke *BPatch::openBinary* using Dyninst. Pin loading applications is as usual as a normal desktop program loading dynamic libraries, for example, invoking *dlopen*. Differently, to load the applications, Dyninst provides a special API, *BPatch_binaryEdit::loadLibrary*.

The middleware converts the configuration into a special designed structure, *execution bag* that consists of multiple *execution block*s. One execution block provides the code specified by programmers, when the code should be executed, as well as the parameters accepted by the specified code. The specified code should be in form of a function resided in the loaded application. Programmers should give the function names so that the middleware can find function addresses. For Pin, function addresses are found by invoking *dlsym*; while Dyninst-based applications should invoke *BPatch_image::findFunction*. The execution bag puts no restrictions on the number of execution blocks, facilitating application programmers to develop complicated applications.

Table 1. Insertion points supported by the middleware

No.	Granularity	Description
1	Image level	Before image loading
2		Before image unloading
3	Function level	Before function entry
4		Before function exit
5	Instruction level	Before execution of instructions with specified opcode
6		After execution of instructions with specified opcode
7		Before calling a specified function
8		After calling a specified function
9		Before execution of instructions with specified number of operands
10		After execution of instructions with specified number of operands

The middleware provides ten types of insertion points (as shown in Table 1) where programmers can insert their code. We are in process of enriching the insertion points to enable programmers to control the SUA more flexibly. The current implementation allows the inserted code to run when a given image is loading (row 1) or unloading (row 2). Programmers should give the image name in the configuration or 'all' indicating all images should be monitored. When an application chooses to run on Pin, the middleware registers two callbacks, *Imageload* and *Imageunload* respectively by calling *IMG_AddInstrumentFunction* and *IMG_AddUnloadFunction*. The *Imageload* will be invoked whenever an image is loading, while the *Imageunload* will run whenever an image is unloading. When the two callbacks run, they firstly check whether the loading/unloading image is the desired one; if so, the application's code will be invoked. For Dyninst, the middleware firstly enumerates all modules of the SUA and then inserts application's code into the entry points (by invoking *BPatch_module::insertInitCallback*) and the exit points (by invoking *BPatch_module::insertFiniCallback*) of the specified module respectively.

The current implementation of the middleware also allows programmers to run their code before (row 3) or after (row 4) the execution of a specified function. Programmers should give the function name to be monitored or 'all'. When using Pin, the *Imageload* enumerates all functions whenever an image is loading. Then, a function *rtndeal* is used to handle each enumerated function. After that, the *rtndeal* checks whether the handled function is of interest by invoking *RTN_FindByName*. If so, the application's code is inserted into the entry points or exit points by calling *RTN_InsertCall* with the parameter *IPOINT* being *IPOINT_BEFORE* or *IPOINT_AFTER* respectively. The implementation on Dyninst is similar except that it finds the entry points and exit points of each function using Dyninst's APIs *BPatch_function::findPoint(BPatch_entry)* and *BPatch_function::findPoint(BPatch_exit)* respectively.

In instruction level, the middleware allows programmers to handle the SUA more flexibly, as shown in Table 1 that six types of insertion points are supported. Programmers can insert application's code before (row 5) or after (row 6) the instructions with specified opcode. To facilitate programmers, the opcode can be given in string, such as 'add' and 'div'. Moreover, it allows programmers to insert code before (row 7) or after (row 8) calling a specified function. This type of insertion points is useful because function calls are sometimes related to security bugs, e.g., format string vulnerabilities, insecure string functions, memory allocation/deallocation, and taint sources/sinks. Programmers need to give the concerned function name, or simply 'all' indicating all function calls deserve attentions. Furthermore, programmers can specify the operand number, and insert application's code before or after the instructions with the specified operand number (Line 9, 10). The two insertion points can benefit the development of data-flow-related applications (*e.g.* taint analysis) since programmers can handle different instructions with the same operand number in an unified way.

To enable instruction-level program manipulation, the middleware invokes *INS_InsertCall* of Pin. For Dyninst, the *rtndeal* firstly enumerates all blocks of a function and then enumerates all instructions of each block, followed by checking whether the instructions are concerned. If so, the application's code is inserted by invoking *insertSnippet* exported from *BPatch_addressSpace*. To coordinate different PMS, we do not consider implicit operands. Hence, programmers need to handle implicit operands in her own way.

The programming mode is designed to be flexible that programmers can specify a composite insertion point by combing several default ones (one example is shown in Fig. 1(d)). For instance, one can ask the middleware to insert code before each call to *malloc* of a function named *main* in an image *helloworld*, by giving a composite insertion point like '**image** helloworld **function** main **funcall** malloc *before*'.

The middleware is able to handle the parameters specified by application programmers, and send the parameters to application's code. The ability can benefit programmers because the application's code usually needs the information from the SUA, context, and runtime environment, *etc.* The current implementation supports seven kinds of parameters as shown in Table 2. The types of parameters and their usages are easy to understand. We just need to mention that when programmers specify one operand of an instruction as a parameter, both the type (*i.e.*, immediate number, register or address) and the value of the operand will be obtained as two consecutive parameters. We plan to develop a GUI allowing programmers to prepare the configuration by simply choosing and clicking, thereby removing the requirement of learning the grammar of the configuration.

The middleware provides another functionality that may interest programmers when they need to stop the running of the SUA and investigate the runtime context. For example, if a security bug is discovered, programmers always want to know how the bug is triggered. The middleware encapsulates the functionality into a function *dump*, that can be called anywhere in the application. When

Table 2. Types of parameters supported by the middleware

No.	Type	Example	Parameters
1	Constant	Constant 10	Constant value
2	Register	Reg eax	Register's value
3	Disassemble	Dis	Disassemble of the specified instruction
4	String	String abc	String's value
5	Funname	Funname	Function name of specified function
6	Imagename	Imagename	Image name of specified image
7	Operand	Operand 0	Type of operand and the value of the operand

dump is called, the SUA is stopped and the context information including the current instruction, register values, the call stack *etc.* is dumped. Section 5.3 will show that the *dump* function benefits the localization, analysis and debugging of software vulnerabilities.

3.3   Future Extensions for Other PMS

Currently, the middleware supports Pin and Dyninst, while the idea and design are general. We are working to extend our implementation to support more PMS. From the perspective of implementation, we classify the current PMS into several categories. Therefore, we can use similar methods to handle different PMS which belongs to the same category.

The first category is dynamic instrumentation tools, such as Pin, Valgrind, and DynamoRIO [6] that usually provide explicit programming interfaces. Similar to what we have done for Pin, we can take advantage of their APIs, so that we need not care about their internal technical details. The second category is static instrumentation tools, for example, Dyninst and CIL. Fortunately, existing static instrumentation tools also provide rich APIs that facilitate program manipulation. We can extend our implementation to other static instrumentation tools in a similar way with how we deal with Dyninst.

The third category is virtual machines, such as Qemu, Temu [36] and Java Virtual Machine (JVM), which are able to monitor and modify SUA's execution flow. As the current VMs do not often provide explicit APIs, our implementation needs to embed the middleware into the VM which is responsible for inserting application's code into proper places. Alternatively, we can use Virtual Machine Introspection (VMI) [16] to monitor the SUA out of the box. Although the implementation for VMs is more tricky than handling instrumentation tools, the two aforementioned methods have been widely applied in existing VM-based program analysis techniques.

The last category is complier-like program analysis tools, such as GCC and LLVM that conduct analysis statically. In this case, our implementation needs to register the middleware as a plugin (*i.e.*, compiler pass), ensuring that it has chances to manipulate the SUA during the compiling procedure. The compiler-like tools often provide programmer-friendly programming interfaces to develop plugins (for example, KLEE [7] is a symbolic executor which is a plugin of LLVM). Hence, it is technically practical to enhance our implementation with the ability of supporting those compiler-like program analysis tools.

To make our implementation adaptable to various CPU infrastructures (*e.g.*, x86, x64, ARM) and different representations of the SUA (*e.g.* sources, binaries, bytecodes), the introduction of an Intermediate Representation (IR) can benefit programmers a lot. In most cases, there is no need to design a novel IR because existing IRs (*e.g.* VEX used by Valgrind [32], LLVM-IR proposed by LLVM [25], and CIL [31]) could be adequate. Next, what we need to do is translating the SUA into the selected IR. Fortunately, some open-source PMS supports IR translation that could be directly reused by our middleware. For example, Valgrind can convert x86, x64, ARM, PPC, MIPS *etc.* into VEX. LLVM can translate C, C++, Objective-C, Java and so on into LLVM-IR. As another example, McSema [14] and S2E [11] can translate x86 binaries into LLVM-IR.

The current implementation does not modify the program logic of the SUA; instead, it just observes and analyzes. We believe it is not difficult to extend our implementation for program transformation. In most cases, PMS (*e.g.*, Pin, Dyninst, CIL, LLVM) has already provided APIs for program transformation. In the cases that program transformation is not explicitly supported (*e.g.*, VMs), our implementation can achieve this goal by inserting a jump before the code needed to be transformed and then inserting the code after transformation into the jump target.

4   System Security Applications

Various applications can be built upon our middleware, such as instruction tracers, memory operation tracers, code coverage profilers, taint analyzers, concolic executors. This section describes the implementation of five applications that aim to protect software systems from stack overflow, heap corruption, memory allocation/deallocation errors, invocations of dangerous functions and division-by-zero bugs respectively. We only give the full details related to division-by-zero bugs, including the configuration and the inserted code due to page limitation. In the end of the section, we will explain how to implement a taint analyzer and a concolic executor (two of the most compelling and complicated program analysis techniques) based on our middleware. The applications can run on various PMS (Dyninst and Pin of the current implementation) by specifying the PMS through the command line. That's to say, there is no need to modify the applications' source code and the associated configurations.

4.1   Division-by-Zero Bugs

Figure 3 presents the source code as well as related configuration of division-by-zero bugs protector. Please note that the configuration should be written according to a simple grammar as shown in Fig. 3(b), while the source code allows any programming languages that can be compiled into binaries. The configuration informs the middleware that the code in function *TargetDiv* (Line 4) should be executed exactly before *div* (Line 1) and *idiv* (Line 2) in the SUA *a.out*. The first operand of *div* and *idiv* should be passed to *TargetDiv* as a parameter (Line 3). According to Intel instruction manual, the first operand of *div* and *idiv* is the divisor that should be checked in *TargetDiv*.

```
1    extern "C" void TargetDiv(int type,int opVal){
2      bool nonZero=(type==ADDR)? *opVal:opVal;
3      if(!nonZero)dump();}
```

(a) Source of the division-by-zero protector

```
1    image a.out function all insnstring div before
2    image a.out function all insnstring idiv before
3    operand 0
4    funcalllib TargetDiv
```
(b) Configuration

Fig. 3. Source code and configuration of division-by-zero protector

If the programmer specifies an operand parameter, the type and the value of the operand will be passed to the target code. As defined, the first operand of *div* and *idiv* can be an immediate number, a register or an address. If the operand is an address, the value stored will be retrieved. Otherwise, *opVal* itself is the divisor. If the divisor is zero, indicating a division-by-zero bug, the application invokes *dump* to stop the execution of *a.out* and output the vulnerability information.

4.2   Stack Overflow

The stack overflow protector shares the same idea with TRUSS [35], that is similar with StackShield [1]. When calling a function, the return address of the function is stored in a shadow stack. When the function returns, the return address picked from the runtime stack will be compared with the one in the shadow stack. If they do not match, an attack will be detected and the SUA will be terminated. The major difference between TRUSS with our application is that the former is directly built on DynamoRIO, while our application is developed on top of the middleware, thus our protector can port to another PMS easily. StackShield differs a little in idea that it directly restores the return address from the shadow stack without checking.

To record return addresses, the application's code should be executed exactly before the entry points of each function. To compare return addresses, the related code should run before the exit points of each function. The two types of insertion points are supported by the middleware (Table 1 rows 3 and 4). However, during evaluation, we find that the simple store-match method may introduce high false positives due to dynamic loading or compiler optimizations (*e.g.*, *setjmp/longjmp*). As a consequence, modern PMS tries to find all entry points and exit points of a given function, but success is not guaranteed. To reduce false positives, when recording a return address, the protector also records the current stack pointer and the function name (if existed) in the shadow stack. The application will report a stack overflow attack only if the stack pointers and function names match; meanwhile, the return addresses do not match.

4.3 Heap Corruption

The idea to prevent heap corruption is (1) recording the locations and sizes of allocated heaps; (2) monitoring all heap operations; (3) reporting bugs, if any operations override the boundaries of heaps. Our heap corruption protector records the locations and boundaries of heaps by monitoring the invocations of heap allocation and deallocation functions, such as *malloc*, *calloc*, *realloc* and *free*. The protector allows programmers to run specified code before or after calling a given function (Table 1 rows 7 and 8). Whenever the SUA requests for allocating memory, the heap location and size are recorded by the inserted code. After the request, the inserted code checks whether heap allocation is successful. If not, the related record will be removed. Additionally, after the successful deallocation of a heap, the related record will also be deleted.

To monitor heap operations, the protector keeps an eye on the invocations of string and memory functions, such as *strcpy*, *strcat*, *strncpy*, *memcpy* and *memmove*. To detect heap corruption, some parameters of the monitored functions are required to be passed to the inserted code. To do so, the application specifies proper registers as parameters, because function parameters can usually be found in registers or the stack (can be located by the stack register).

4.4 Memory Allocation/Deallocation Errors

The memory allocation/deallocation errors handled in the protector include double free, free a non-heap memory location and free a pointer that points to the middle of a heap and so on (*i.e.*, any memory bugs that deallocate wrong heap locations). The protector firstly records the addresses and boundaries of allocated memory by instrumenting functions like *malloc*, *calloc*, *realloc*. Then it checks memory deallocation to ensure that the freed address is the exact address recorded. Otherwise, the SUA will be stopped and a detailed report will be given.

4.5 Invocation of Dangerous Functions

Detecting the invocations of dangerous functions are similar to the way of detecting the calls of *malloc*. The protector can detect *getpw*, *gets*, *random*, *vfork*, *mktemp*, *mkstemps*, and *mkdtemp*. It is straightforward to enrich the set of dangerous functions by adding a few lines in the configuration, because the application handles various dangerous functions in a unified way as follows.

One kind of functions are dangerous whenever they are invoked. For example, *getpw* is extremely dangerous because it gets user names, passwords and other privacy information from */etc/passwd*. For this kind, the application inserts code before the instructions that call dangerous functions. Whenever a dangerous function of this kind is invoked, the application can stop the attack immediately. The other kind can be considered as dangerous under specific context. For example, *mktemp* becomes dangerous when the file name is too short. To detect this kind of dangerous functions, the application passes the demanded information as parameters to the inserted code.

4.6   Taint Analyzer and Concolic Executor

Taint analysis [12] consists of marking taint sources, tracking taint propagation, and warning if taints enter taint sinks. Taint analysis has wide applications in vulnerability detection, malware analysis, privacy protection *etc.* Programmers are able to develop a taint analyzer based on the middleware via the simple programming mode. Taint sources are usually functions that get data from environment, such as *ReadFile, recv, getenv*. To mark taint sources, the taint analyzer needs to instrument before and after the related functions. To track taint propagation, instruction-level instrumentation is needed that takes responsible for tainting target operands if source operands are tainted. Taint sinks are usually special functions which operate on tainted data, such as *WriteFile, send, system*. Therefore, those sensitive functions should be monitored by function-level instrumentation.

Concolic execution [10] is a variant of traditional symbolic execution [24] that collects path constraints along with concrete execution, and then explores other paths triggered by new test inputs that are solved from negated path constraints. Concolic execution is an iterative procedure that runs the SUA with given inputs, symbolizes inputs, tracks symbol propagation, collects constraints, and then generates new test inputs. Input symbolization is similar with marking taint sources. However, symbolic inputs could be the parameters of given functions, register values, memory values *etc.*, that could be specified as parameters as shown in Table 2. To track symbol propagation, the application also needs instruction-level instrumentation. The instrumented code should interpret instruction semantics, and then compute symbolic expressions of the influenced operands. The application needs to collect constraints when executing symbol-related conditional jumps (*e.g., jz, jnz, ja, jb*). Programmers will feel convenient to handle specific instructions because the middleware allows programmers to specify the concerned instructions by giving the string forms of opcodes, as shown in Table 1 (rows 5 and 6).

5   Experiments

5.1   Research Questions

We attempt to answer the following research questions through experiments.
QA1: Will the SUA modified by the middleware bring about unacceptable

runtime overhead, space overhead and false positives (Sect. 5.2)? **QA2**: Can the application prevent the attacks against real CVE vulnerabilities (Sect. 5.3)? **QA3**: Can the middleware facilitate the localization, analysis and debugging of software defects (Sect. 5.3)? **QA4**: Can the middleware reduce code amount of application development (Sect. 5.4)? **QA5**: Will the middleware lead to obvious runtime overhead (Sect. 5.5)?

All experiments are conducted on a laptop, equipped with a two-core Celeron CPU (1.8 GHz), 2 GB main memory and 64-bit CentOS 7.

5.2   Experiments with Benchmark Programs

We select ten daily-used programs in CentOS arbitrarily as a benchmark set including compilers, compression/decompression software, SSL tools, a multimedia processing library *etc.* As shown in Table 4, the sizes of the SUA range from 7,136 bytes to 772,704 bytes, 385,904 bytes on average (standard deviation is 299,779, indicating significant differences). For convenience, we integrate the five applications into one multi-functional software protector, and demonstrate the experimental results when testing the integrated software protector on Dyninst in Fig. 4.

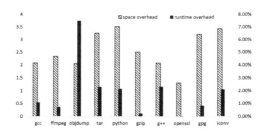

Fig. 4. Experimental results with ten benchmark programs

Figure 4 shows the size expansion of the SUA after processing by the middleware. The space overhead is 2.57x on average, because the software protector is multifunctional that inserts protection code before all entry points and exit points of each function, before all *div* and *idiv* instructions, before and after all memory allocation/deallocation functions, and also before all invocations of dangerous functions. Fortunately, disk space is not as scarce as decades ago, so nowadays it is worthy of trading space for security. Figure 4 also shows that the modified SUA runs slightly slower than the original SUA, 1.92% on average. Furthermore, we find that the runtime overhead has no direct bearing upon the space overhead, because the former depends on how the SUA is executed, while the latter relies on how the SUA is processed. No security problems are reported in those benchmark software, so, there are no false positives.

Hence, we can answer QA1 that *the SUA modified by our middleware incurs acceptable space overhead, minimal runtime overhead, and no false positives.*

5.3   Practical Case Studies

In this section, we will evaluate the effectiveness of the software system security protector against CVE-2004-0597 and CVE-2011-3328. Please note that both the two cases are successfully reproduced on Pin and Dyninst, and we get identical reports regardless of underlying PMS.

CVE-2004-0597. CVE-2004-0597 consists of multiple buffer overflows in *libpng* 1.25 and earlier, allowing remote attackers to execute arbitrary code via malformed PNG images. We examine our protector by testing with one stack overflow vulnerability. The malformed input is shown in Fig. 5(a) that the 48 bytes starting from offset 0x129 are overwritten with 0x41 (*i.e.*, the letter 'A'). The overwritten part is in an *IDAT* truck that contains the actual image data.

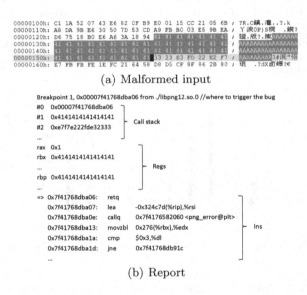

(a) Malformed input

(b) Report

Fig. 5. Test results with CVE-2004-0597

The report (Fig. 5(b)) which is produced by the *dump* function mentioned in Sect. 3.2, consists of four parts. The first part shows the address (0x7f41768dba06) of the instruction that triggers the vulnerability and the buggy executable (*libpng*12.*so*.0). Part 2 presents the call stack. We can see that the call stack is corrupted due to stack overflow. That is, the function address with depth 1 is 0x4141414141414141 (i.e., multiples 'A's) which comes from the malformed input. Besides, the function addresses from depth 2 to the bottom are weird values that should not be function addresses. Part 3 gives register values. We can find that some registers, especial *rbp* that involves control flow transfers are polluted by the input. The final part shows the critical instruction (address and disassemble) as well as some instructions after it. As expected, the critical instruction is *retq*, before which the protector inserts checking code.

CVE-2011-3328. CVE-2011-3328 is a division-by-zero bug located in the *png_handle_cHRM* function of *pngrutil.c* in *libpng* 1.5.4, enabling a denial of service attack via a malformed PNG image containing a *cHRM* chunk. Figure 6(a) shows a malformed input that triggers CVE-2011-3328. Three DWORD variables *y_red*, *y_green* and *y_blue* correspond to offset 0x35, 0x3d and 0x45 respectively in the first *cHRM* chunk. The sum of *y_red*, *y_green* and *y_blue* will be used as a divisor. Hence, we set all of them to be zeros.

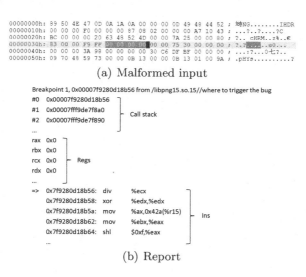

(a) Malformed input

(b) Report

Fig. 6. Test results with CVE-2011-3328

The report is shown in Fig. 6(b) that the instruction which triggers a division-by-zero error locates in 0x7f9280d18b56. The vulnerable binary is *libpng*15.*so*.15. We can see that the attack doesn't subvert the call stack. However, several registers are polluted, especially *rcx* whose lower 32 bits (i.e., *ecx*) are treated as a divisor. As expected, the vulnerable software stops before running the division-by-zero operation, because the protector inserts checking logic before all *div* and *idiv* instructions.

Therefore, we can answer QA2 and QA3 that *(1) the application can prevent software systems from real attacks; (2) the report produced by our middleware can facilitate the localization, analysis and debugging of software defects.*

5.4   Comparison with Dyninst and Pin

This subsection presents the code amount (in lines) of the applications developed on middleware, and those directly developed on Dyninst and Pin respectively, as shown in Table 3. Please note that we implement all five applications directly on Dyninst and Pin respectively for comparison and the code amount is counted by SourceCounter [2]. The figures after '|' indicate times. For example, the code amount of the division-by-zero protector built directly on top of Dyninst is about 30.2 times larger than that developed on our middleware. The last row shows the averages. The observation is that the applications based on our middleware require the fewest code lines, answering Q4 that *our approach can reduce the code amount of applications obviously.* Second, the code amount for Pin-based applications is comparable with that for Dyninst-based applications, indicating that the two PMS encapsulates the manipulations of the SUA in comparable degrees. We have to remind that the metric, code amount cannot reflect the learning curve of various PMS. For example, a well-documented PMS is easier to learn than the PMS with few documents. Besides, code amount can just partially reflect the developing efforts. For example, a line of code invoking a complicated API needs more time to debug and test than a line of assignment.

Table 3. Code amount of the applications (LOC) developed on the middleware, Dyninst, and Pin

Application	Agent	Dyninst	Pin
Division-by-zero	6	181|30.2	130|21.7
Stack overflow	60	169|2.8	174|2.9
Heap corruption	86	279|3.2	272|3.2
Memory allocation/deallocation	41	214|5.2	206|5
Dangerous function	16	133|8.3	159|9.9
Average	**41.8**	**195.2|4.7**	**188.2|4.5**

5.5   Runtime Overhead of the Middleware

Our middleware will lead to runtime overhead for dynamic PMS because it controls dynamic PMS at runtime. Table 4 answers QA5 that *the middleware incurs minimal runtime overhead (i.e., 1.44% on average).* The figures after '|' in the last column indicate the runtime overhead incurred by our middleware, compared to the application directly developed on Pin. Please note that the application tested here is the integrated application which consists of all five functionalities mentioned in Sect. 4.

The overhead incurred by our middleware is negligible, compared to the overhead incurred by the application. The third column gives the time for running each SUA in the environment of Pin (i.e., the SUA is loaded by Pin with an empty application). The figures after '|' in the fourth column present the overhead caused by the application compared to the time consumption shown in the third column, which is 31.11x on average. Hence, the middleware just leads to less than a thousandth of the overhead caused by the application.

Table 4. Runtime overhead incurred by the middleware

SUA	Size (Byte)	Baseline (sec)	Directly on Pin (sec)	On our middleware (sec)
iconv	60320	0.64	5.34|7.37	5.39|0.95%
gpg	749840	2.07	186.73|89.40	186.94|0.11%
openssl	508680	1.24	87.15|69.33	87.74|0.67%
g++	772704	1.15	53.70|45.54	54.99|2.41%
gzip	100744	0.82	6.21|6.54	6.65|7.06%
python	7136	23.40	26.76|14%	26.85|0.34%
tar	345976	1.38	35.28|24.62	36.03|2.11%
objdump	332248	1.34	41.84|30.17	41.89|0.13%
ffmpeg	212800	131.14	141.47|8%	141.96|0.35%
gcc	768592	1.26	49.19|37.96	49.35|0.32%
Average	**385904**	**17.44**	**63.37|31.11**	**63.78|1.44%**

6 Related Work

Substantial studies have been made to reduce the difficulty of manipulating the SUA. However, existing works suffer from a few drawbacks. We just summarize the drawbacks and describe a few of related works due to page limitation.

First, some proposed languages are incapable of supporting complicated applications. To name a few, the capability of Atune-IL [34] is restricted due to the limited expressiveness of *#pragma* annotations. Metric Description Language (MDL) [19] is not general enough for program analysis (MDL is designed for performance measurement) that supports two types of inserted code only. Besides, DiSL [29] is a domain-specific instrumentation language for handling Java program. Several works put restrictions on PMS. Atune-IL [34] can be used by source-level PMS only. MDL [19], Lynx [15], EBT [27,28], and DTrace [8] are designed for dynamic binary instrumentation, while MAQAO Instrumentation Language (MIL) [9] is for static binary instrumentation.

Several studies restrict the types of insertion points [8,15,19,27,28,30]. For example, [30] does not support instruction-level instrumentation, that would be a serious restriction for application development. The types of insertion points supported by DTrace [8] depend on the instrumentation providers (dubbed PMS in this paper). However, we find that the providers integrated into DTrace are single functional, such as function boundary tracing, statically-defined tracing, locking tracing, probably restricting the applications of DTrace. Several works demand programmers write their applications in the proposed languages [8,15,18,19,30]. For instance, to develop on Sprocket Program Rewriting Interface (SPRI) [18], programmers should write the code in the Sprocket-based Assembly Language. As another example, Dtrace [8] requires programmers to develop applications in the proposed D language.

Some proposed languages lack applications and experiments [27,28,33]. Concretely speaking, Reiss and Renieris [33] proposed the requirements of a general dynamic instrumentation language. However, as they admitted, they had not designed a language that meets the requirements. The EBT language might be immature because the related papers [27,28] did not present any practical applications and experimental results based on it, though a motivating example was given. Several works may result in considerable effort for grasping the features of their proposed languages [9,18]. SPRI is a low-level language, so it may not be that easy to use. For example, programmers have to find the addresses where to insert code through static analysis. MIL is a general language that extends the syntax of Lua [21]. Consequently, the programmers who intend to use MIL should be familiar with the rich language features of Lua.

7 Conclusions

This work designs a middleware that hides the differences of PMS and provides an unified programming interface. Based on it, developers can start to develop concise, PMS-independent and PMS-portable applications quickly. Besides, we build five applications on the middleware for protecting system security and conduct extensive experiments on them. Experiments show that the middleware leads to reasonable space overhead, negligible runtime overhead, and no false positives. Then, two practical cases validate that the applications can prevent real attacks. We plan to improve this work in three directions. First, we are working to integrate more PMS (Valgrind, CIL etc.) to give programmers more options. Second, we will enrich the types of insertion points and parameters, allowing programmers to handle the SUA more flexibly. Third, we plan to write more applications on the middleware, so that programmers can develop their applications by reusing our code.

Acknowledgment. This work was supported in part by the National Natural Science Foundation of China, No. 61402080, No. 61572115, No. 61502086, No. 61572109, and China Postdoctoral Science Foundation founded project, No. 2014M562307.

References

1. StackShield: A "stack smashing" technique protection tool for Linux. http://www.angelfire.com/sk/stackshield/
2. SourceCounter, August 2016. http://boomworks.googlecode.com/files/SourceCounter-3.5.33.73.zip
3. Ball, T., Rajamani, S.: The slam project: debugging system software via static analysis. ACM Sigplan Not. **37**(1), 1–3 (2002)
4. Bellard, F.: QEMU, a fast and portable dynamic translator. In: USENIX, pp. 41–46, April 2005
5. Bernat, A.R., Miller, B.P.: Anywhere, any-time binary instrumentation. In: ACM SIGPLAN-SIGSOFT Workshop on Program Analysis For Software Tools, pp. 9–16. ACM, September 2011

6. Bruening, D., Zhao, Q., Amarasinghe, S.: Transparent dynamic instrumentation. ACM Sigplan Not. **47**(7), 133–144 (2012)
7. Cadar, C., Dunbar, D., Engler, D.: KLEE: unassisted and automatic generation of high-coverage tests for complex systems programs. In: OSDI, vol. 8, pp. 209–224 (2008)
8. Cantrill, B., Shapiro, M., Leventhal, A.: Dynamic instrumentation of production systems. In: USENIX, pp. 15–28, June 2004
9. Charif-Rubial, A.S., Barthou, D., Valensi, C., Shende, S., Malony, A., Jalby, W.: MIL: a language to build program analysis tools through static binary instrumentation. In: HiPC, pp. 206–215. IEEE, December 2013
10. Chen, T., Zhang, X., Guo, S., Li, H., Wu, Y.: State of the art: dynamic symbolic execution for automated test generation. Future Gener. Comput. Syst. **29**(7), 1758–1773 (2013)
11. Chipounov, V., Candea, G.: A platform for in-vivo multi-path analysis of software systems. In: ASPLOS, pp. 265–278 (2011)
12. Clause, J., Li, W., Orso, A.: Dytan: a generic dynamic taint analysis framework. In: ISSTA, pp. 196–206. ACM, July 2007
13. Corbi, T.: Program understanding: challenge for the 1990s. IBM Syst. J. **28**(2), 294–306 (1989)
14. Dinaburg, A., Ruef, A.: Mcsema: static translation of x86 instructions to LLVM. In: ReCon, June 2014
15. Farooqui, N., Kerr, A., Eisenhauer, G., Schwan, K., Yalamanchili, S.: Lynx: a dynamic instrumentation system for data-parallel applications on GPGPU architectures. In: ISPASS, pp. 58–67. IEEE, April 2012
16. Garfinkel, T., Rosenblum, M.: A virtual machine introspection based architecture for intrusion detection. In: NDSS, vol. 3, pp. 191–206, February 2003
17. Godefroid, P., de Halleux, P., Nori, A., Rajamani, S., Schulte, W., Tillmann, N., Levin, M.: Automating software testing using program analysis. IEEE Softw. **25**(5), 30–37 (2008)
18. Hiser, J., Nguyen-Tuong, A., Co, M., Rodes, B., Hall, M., Coleman, C., Knight, J., Davidson, J.: A framework for creating binary rewriting tools (short paper). In: EDCC, pp. 142–145. IEEE, May 2014
19. Hollingsworth, J., Niam, O., Miller, B., Xu, Z., Gonçalves, M., Zheng, L.: MDL: a language and compiler for dynamic program instrumentation. In: PACT, pp. 201–212. IEEE, November 1997
20. Huang, Y., Yu, F., Hang, C., Tsai, C., Lee, D., Kuo, S.: Securing web application code by static analysis and runtime protection. In: WWW, vol. 17, pp. 40–52. ACM, May 2004
21. Ierusalimschy, R., Figueiredo, L.D., Filho, W.C.: Lua-an extensible extension language. Softw. Pract. Exper. **26**(6), 635–652 (1996)
22. Ivančić, F., Yang, Z., Ganai, M.K., Gupta, A., Shlyakhter, I., Ashar, P.: F-SOFT: software verification platform. In: Etessami, K., Rajamani, S.K. (eds.) CAV 2005. LNCS, vol. 3576, pp. 301–306. Springer, Heidelberg (2005). https://doi.org/10.1007/11513988_31
23. Kildall, G.A.: A unified approach to global program optimization. In: POPL, pp. 194–206. ACM, October 1973
24. King, J.: Symbolic execution and program testing. Commun. ACM **19**(7), 385–394 (1976)
25. Lattner, C., Adve, V.: LLVM: a compilation framework for lifelong program analysis & transformation. In: CGO, pp. 75–86. IEEE, March 2004

26. Luk, C., Cohn, R., Muth, R., Patil, H., Klauser, A., Lowney, G., Wallace, S., Reddi, V., Hazelwood, K.: Pin: building customized program analysis tools with dynamic instrumentation. ACM Sigplan Not. **40**(6), 190–200 (2005)

27. Makarov, S., Brown, A.D., Goel, A.: An event-based language for dynamic binary translation frameworks. In: PACT, pp. 499–500. ACM, August 2014

28. Makarov, S., Brown, A.D., Goel, A.: PACT: U: an event-based language for dynamic binary translation frameworks (2015). https://src.acm.org/binaries/content/assets/src/2014/sergueimakarov.pdf

29. Marek, L., Villazón, A., Zheng, Y., Ansaloni, D., Binder, W., Qi, Z.: DiSL: a domain-specific language for bytecode instrumentation. In: AOSD, pp. 239–250. ACM, March 2012

30. Mußler, J., Lorenz, D., Wolf, F.: Reducing the overhead of direct application instrumentation using prior static analysis. In: Jeannot, E., Namyst, R., Roman, J. (eds.) Euro-Par 2011. LNCS, vol. 6852, pp. 65–76. Springer, Heidelberg (2011). https://doi.org/10.1007/978-3-642-23400-2_7

31. Necula, G.C., McPeak, S., Rahul, S.P., Weimer, W.: CIL: intermediate language and tools for analysis and transformation of C programs. In: Horspool, R.N. (ed.) CC 2002. LNCS, vol. 2304, pp. 213–228. Springer, Heidelberg (2002). https://doi.org/10.1007/3-540-45937-5_16

32. Nethercote, N., Seward, J.: Valgrind: a framework for heavyweight dynamic binary instrumentation. In: ACM Sigplan Notices, vol. 42, no. 6, pp. 89–10, June 2007

33. Reiss, S., Renieris, M.: Lynx: a dynamic instrumentation system for data-parallel applications on GPGPU architectures. In: WODA ICSE, pp. 41–44, May 2003

34. Schaefer, C.A., Pankratius, V., Tichy, W.F.: Atune-IL: an instrumentation language for auto-tuning parallel applications. In: Sips, H., Epema, D., Lin, H.-X. (eds.) Euro-Par 2009. LNCS, vol. 5704, pp. 9–20. Springer, Heidelberg (2009). https://doi.org/10.1007/978-3-642-03869-3_5

35. Sinnadurai, S., Zhao, Q., fai Wong, W.: Transparent runtime shadow stack: protection against malicious return address modifications (2008)

36. Yin, H., Song, D.: Temu: binary code analysis via whole-system layered annotative execution. Technical report UCB/EECS-2010-3, EECS Department, University of California, Berkeley (2010)

SecureComm Short Papers

Cross-site Input Inference Attacks
on Mobile Web Users

Rui Zhao, Chuan Yue$^{(\boxtimes)}$, and Qi Han

Colorado School of Mines, Golden, CO, USA
{ruizhao,chuanyue,qhan}@mines.edu

Abstract. In this paper, we investigate severe cross-site input inference attacks that may compromise the security of every mobile Web user, and quantify the extent to which they can be effective. We formulate our attacks as a typical multi-class classification problem, and build an inference framework that trains a classifier in the training phase and predicts a user's new inputs in the attacking phase. To make our attacks effective and realistic, we design unique techniques, and address major data quality and data segmentation challenges. We intensively evaluate the effectiveness of our attacks using keystrokes collected from 20 participants. Overall, our attacks are effective, for example, they are about 10.8 times more effective than the random guessing attacks regarding inferring letters. Our results demonstrate that researchers, smartphone vendors, and app developers should pay serious attention to the severe cross-site input inference attacks that can be pervasively performed, and should start to design and deploy effective defense techniques.

Keywords: Mobile · Web · Cross-site input inference · Motion sensor

1 Introduction

Smartphones have been severely targeted by cybercrimes, and their sensors have created many new vulnerabilities for attackers to compromise users' security and privacy. One typical vulnerability is that high-resolution motion sensors, such as accelerometer and gyroscope, could be used as side channels for attackers to infer users' sensitive keyboard tappings on smartphones. Such *input inference attacks* are feasible because motion sensor data are often correlated to the tapping behaviors of users and the positions of keys on a keyboard.

Some researchers have studied the effectiveness of input inference attacks performed by malicious native apps on smartphones, but their threat models and focuses are completely different from ours, and their attacks are not as challenging as ours (Sect. 2). While input inference attacks can be performed by malicious native apps, they can indeed be more **pervasively performed** by malicious webpages to cause even **severer consequences** to *mobile Web users* [8] who interact with webpages through either mobile browsers or WebView components of native apps. On both iOS and Android platforms, JavaScript code

© ICST Institute for Computer Sciences, Social Informatics and Telecommunications Engineering 2018
X. Lin et al. (Eds.): SecureComm 2017, LNICST 238, pp. 629–643, 2018.
https://doi.org/10.1007/978-3-319-78813-5_32

on regular webpages can register to receive device motion events and access motion sensor data. This access does not require a user to explicitly grant any permission, install any software, or perform any configuration, and it can even be performed cross sites to create *a powerful side channel to bypass the fundamental Same Origin Policy* [9] that protects the Web [8].

In this paper, we investigate such severe cross-site input inference attacks and quantify their effectiveness. We formulate our attacks as a typical multi-class classification problem, and build an inference framework that takes the supervised machine learning approach to train a classifier in the training phase for predicting a user's new inputs in the attacking phase. However, two major challenges need to be addressed to make our attacks effective and realistic. The first is on *data quality*, i.e., the quality of the collected motion sensor data for certain keystrokes could be low. The second is on *data segmentation*, i.e., the key down and up events cannot be obtained in the attacking phase to accurately segment motion sensor data for individual keystrokes because cross-site (or origin) collection of key events is prohibited by the Same Origin Policy [9].

To address the data quality challenge, we designed two main techniques: *training data screening* and *fine-grained data filtering*. To address the data segmentation challenge, we designed a *key down timestamp detection and adjustment* technique. To evaluate the effectiveness of our cross-site input inference attacks, we collected keystrokes on 26 letters, 10 digits, and 3 special characters from 20 participants. On average, our attacks achieved 38.83%, 50.79%, and 31.36% inference accuracy (based on F-measure scores) on three charsets *lowercase letters*, *digits together with special characters*, and *all the 39 characters*, respectively. Intuitively, on the letter charset, our attacks are about 10.8 times more effective than the random guessing attacks. Our training data screening technique improved the inference accuracy against all participants by 8.03%, 9.93%, and 7.21% on the three charsets, respectively; our fine-grained data filtering technique improved the inference accuracy against the majority of participants by 1.14%, 1.76%, and 1.27% on the three charsets, respectively. Our key down timestamp detection and adjustment technique achieved 86.32% accuracy on keystroke data segmentation.

2   Threat Model and Related Work

The basic threat model in our attacks is that malicious JavaScript code can collect smartphone motion sensor data and train a machine learning classifier to infer a user's sensitive inputs cross websites, thus bypassing the security protection of Same-Origin Policy [9]. Especially, two types of cross-site input inference attacks, *parent-to-child* and *child-to-parent*, can occur as proposed by Yue [8]. In the *parent-to-child cross-site input inference attacks*, a parent document collects motion sensor data to infer users' sensitive inputs in a child (e.g., *iframe*) document [8]. In the *child-to-parent cross-site input inference attacks*, a child document collects motion sensor data to infer users' sensitive inputs in a parent document [8]. On both iOS and Android platforms, these attacks do not require a user to explicitly grant any permission, install any software, or perform any configuration. Collecting training data is feasible because attackers can trick a user to type specific (i.e., labeled) non-sensitive inputs on their webpages – attackers can collect the motion sensor data as well as the corresponding key down and up events from the same webpages to accurately segment these data.

Some researchers have studied the effectiveness of input inference attacks on smartphones. However, the threat models and focuses of the existing efforts are different from ours, and their attacks are not as challenging as ours. First, they mainly focused on investigating the attacks performed by the native apps [1,2,7], and assumed that malicious apps have been installed on users' smartphones to access the motion sensor data. Second, they mainly focused on investigating the attacks that target at touchscreen lock PINs [1,7], which could be valuable only if they are reused by smartphone owners on online services or if the smartphone itself is stolen. Third, they often used apps' built-in keyboards [1,7] and/or large digit-only keyboards [1,7] to collect motion sensor data and perform experiments, and did not study the attack effectiveness using real alphanumeric keyboards. Fourth, they often collected the key down and up events to accurately segment motion sensor data (i.e., identifying the start and end time) to infer individual keystrokes [1,7]; however, in reality smartphone platforms do not allow the cross-app collection of key events for security reasons.

3 Design of Cross-site Input Inference Attacks

3.1 Overview of the Framework

We formulate our attacks as a typical multi-class classification problem, and build a framework that takes the supervised machine learning approach to train a classifier in the training phase for inferring a user's new inputs in the attacking phase as shown in Fig. 1. The framework consists of six components. The *sensor data segmentation* component segments motion sensor data for individual keystrokes. The *training data screening* component calculates the character-specific quality scores for individual keystrokes and selects the motion sensor data of good-quality keystrokes into the training dataset. The *fine-grained data filtering* component selects user-specific frequency bands with varying lengths for reducing the noise in the motion sensor data. The *feature extraction* component statistically derives both time-domain and frequency-domain features from the filtered motion sensor data. The *model training* component trains a machine learning classifier from the extracted features. The *prediction* component uses the trained classifier to predict new characters tapped by a user.

In the training phase, attackers are capable of using JavaScript code to collect both motion sensor data and *key events* (i.e., key down and up) at the client side on a user's smartphone; these data are then sent to an attacker's server, and further segmented, screened, and filtered for extracting features to train a classifier. By leveraging the corresponding key events for identifying the start and end time, this motion sensor data segmentation for individual keystrokes in the training phase can be accurately performed. By selecting the motion sensor

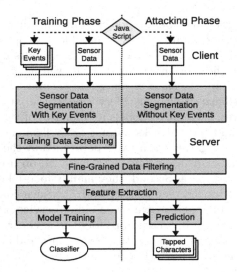

Fig. 1. The framework for cross-site input inference attacks

data of good-quality keystrokes and by further filtering out the noise at a fine granularity, the classifier can be better trained for performing the attacks.

In the attacking phase, attackers are only capable of collecting motion sensor data because cross-site (or cross-origin) collection of key events is prohibited by the Same Origin Policy; the motion sensor data are then sent to the attacker's server, and further segmented and filtered for extracting features to predict the tapped characters using the trained classifier. Due to the lack of key events in the attacking phase, accurate motion sensor data segmentation becomes very challenging and an effective technique must be designed. Character-specific quality scores cannot be calculated in the attacking phase because the tapped characters are unknown and are indeed the targets of the inference attacks. Therefore, our framework currently does not include data screening in the attacking phase.

3.2 Motion Sensor Data Segmentation

Figure 2 illustrates the algorithms used for sensor data segmentation in the two phases. The *Identify-Keystroke-Time Windows* subroutine accepts a sequence of key down timestamps T as the input and returns a sequence of keystroke time windows W as the output. For each key down timestamp T_j, the timestamps $T_j - offset\_start$ and $T_j + offset\_end$ are identified as the start and end of the corresponding keystroke time window, respectively. This time window identification method has been commonly used by researchers in input inference attacks [1, 3, 7]. They often use 100 and 150 ms as the values of *offset_start* and *offset_end*, respectively, based on their observations on the time relationship between motion sensor data and key events; we have the similar observation, and thus used the same offset values in this subroutine.

// $S = (S_{t_1}, S_{t_2}, \cdots, S_{t_n})$: motion sensor data from time t_1 to t_n
// $S_{t_i} = (x_{t_i}, y_{t_i}, z_{t_i}, \alpha_{t_i}, \beta_{t_i}, \gamma_{t_i})$: motion sensor data at time t_i, where $x_{t_i}, y_{t_i}, z_{t_i}$ represent
      acceleration forces on axes x, y, z, and $\alpha_{t_i}, \beta_{t_i}, \gamma_{t_i}$ represent rotation rates on axes z, x, y
// $T = (T_1, T_2, \cdots, T_m)$: a sequence of m key down timestamps
// $W = (W_1, W_2, \cdots, W_m)$: a sequence of m identified time windows,
      where $W_i = (W_i^S, W_i^E)$ represents the start and end time of a window

Segment-SensorData-With-KeyEvents (T) // Used in the training phase
1    $W =$ Identify-Keystroke-TimeWindows (T)
2    $W =$ Adjust-Keystroke-TimeWindows (W)
3   **return** W

Segment-SensorData-Without-KeyEvents (S) // Used in the attacking phase
1    $T =$ Detect-KeyDown-Timestamps (S)
2    $W =$ Identify-Keystroke-TimeWindows (T)
3    $W =$ Adjust-Keystroke-TimeWindows (W)
4   **return** W

Detect-KeyDown-Timestamps (S)
1    $S =$ Filter-Data $(S,$ start_frequency, end_frequency$)$
2    $M^A = M^R = ()$ // Magnitude for acceleration forces and rotation rates
3   **for** t in $t_1 : t_n$
4       $M_t^A = \sqrt{x_t^2 + y_t^2 + z_t^2}; M_t^R = \sqrt{\alpha_t^2 + \beta_t^2 + \gamma_t^2}$
5    $T^A =$ Find-Peak-Timestamps $(M^A); T^R =$ Find-Peak-Timestamps (M^R)
6    $T =$ Merge-Peak-Timestamps (T^A, T^R)
7   **return** T

Identify-Keystroke-TimeWindows (T)
1   **for** j in $1 : m$
2       $W_j^S = T_j - offset\_start; W_j^E = T_j + offset\_end$
3   **return** W

Adjust-Keystroke-TimeWindows (W)
1   **for** j in $1 : m - 1$
2       $overlap = W_j^E - W_{j+1}^S$ // Overlap between two keystrokes
3   **if** $overlap \leq 0$ // No overlap
4   // Do nothing
5   **else if** $overlap > ((W_{j+1}^S + offset\_start) -$
             $(W_j^E - offset\_end)) \times overlap\_threshold$ // Heavy overlap
6   mark W_j and W_{j+1} as heavily overlapped time windows
7   **else** // Slight overlap, split the overlapped region
8          $W_j^E = W_j^E - overlap/2; W_{j+1}^S = W_{j+1}^S + overlap/2$
9   remove the marked heavily overlapped time windows from W
10   **return** W

Fig. 2. Sensor data segmentation algorithms in the two phases

The *Detect-KeyDown-Timestamps* subroutine accepts the motion sensor data S from timestamp t_1 to timestamp t_n as the input, finds their peak values, and returns a sequence of key down timestamps T as the output. The subroutine first applies a band filter from *start_frequency* to *end_frequency* on the sensor data S at line 1. Because the peak values of sensor data are often well captured by their high frequency components, using a filter with a high-pass band (e.g., from 10 Hz to 30 Hz in our case) here can help us accurately detect the key down timestamps. To comprehensively consider acceleration forces and rotation rates along all the three axes, the subroutine computes the Euclidean magnitude values M_t^A (for acceleration forces) and M_t^R (for rotation rates) at line 4 for each timestamp t. At line 5, the peak values in M^A and M^R are identified using a sliding window based on the average keystroke duration observed in the training data, and their timestamps are saved to the sequences, T^A and T^R, respectively. Because T^A and T^R may not always properly align their timestamps, they are further merged at line 6 by including their distinct timestamps and combining their common ones. The merged timestamps are returned for segmenting motion sensor data in the attacking phase.

Many researchers assumed the availability of key events and did not address the data segmentation challenge in the attacking phase; in other words, they only used the Identify-Keystroke-TimeWindows subroutine to perform motion sensor data segmentation in the training and attacking phases [1,3,7]. Cai and Chen used a library of keystroke motion waveform patterns to perform sensor data segmentation in the attacking phase [2]. However, this method requires a library to be pre-built; its accuracy depends on the quality of the library and the applicability of those patterns to different users.

The *Adjust-Keystroke-TimeWindows* subroutine adjusts the identified keystroke time windows in both training and attacking phases because some adjacent time windows may overlap and incur accuracy. For every two adjacent time windows W_j and W_{j+1}, the subroutine calculates the overlap between them at line 2. If they heavily overlap (i.e., the overlap region is greater than a certain percentage threshold, *overlap_threshold*, of the timespan between their corresponding key down events at line 5), the subroutine marks both of them as heavily overlapped time windows at line 6. If they slightly overlap, the subroutine adjusts their boundary to be the middle of the overlapped region at line 8. Finally all the heavily overlapped time windows are discarded at line 9, and the remaining time windows are returned at line 10. This adjustment step was not considered in any existing work; however, we observed in our experiments that about 5% of the identified time windows (either with or without using key events) heavily overlap (with *overlap_threshold* = 80%), and this adjustment can indeed improve the overall inference accuracy (Sect. 4.4) by approximately 1%.

3.3   Training Data Screening

Training data screening is one key technique that we designed to address the data quality challenge in cross-site input inference attacks. It calculates character-specific quality scores for individual keystrokes, and only uses the motion sensor data of good-quality keystrokes to train the classifier. In signal processing, the signal to noise ratio (SNR) is a commonly used quality estimation metric. Calculating SNR requires the characterization of the noise based on either the standard deviation of the random noise or the power spectrum density of the non-random noise. However, motion sensor data in input inference attacks may contain mixed random and non-random noises which are introduced from multiple sources such as human body movements. Therefore, there is no standard way to characterize the noises, and computing SNR in input inference attacks will not be reliable.

We propose a unique motion sensor data quality estimation algorithm *Estimate-Keystroke-Data-Quality* for screening the training data as shown in

Fig. 3. Overall, given m keystrokes of a specific user for a specific key, the algorithm first calculates their mean values of acceleration forces and rotation rates to obtain six averaged waveforms $\bar{c}$ for $c \in \{x, y, z, \alpha, \beta, \gamma\}$ at line 1; it then compares the waveforms of each individual keystroke with the averaged waveforms to calculate a quality score for the keystroke from line 3 to line 7. While it is not reliable to directly compute SNR, averaging m measurements of a signal can ideally improve the SNR in proportion to the $\sqrt{m}$ [4]. This is the reason why our algorithm uses the averaged waveforms as the reference to calculate quality scores. In more details, at line 4, the algorithm computes cross correlation values s_i^c between each individual keystroke K_i and the averaged waveforms $\bar{c}$ for each c to represent their level of similarity. Then at line 5, it computes weights w^c for each c by averaging the cross correlation values of m keystrokes. At line 6 and line 7, it computes a quality score Q_i for each keystroke K_i by adding its weighted cross correlation values on $x, y, z, \alpha, \beta,$ and γ.

Estimate-Keystroke-Data-Quality (K)
// $K = (K_1, K_2, \cdots, K_m)$: m keystrokes of a user for a specific key
// $K_i = ((x_{t_n}^i, y_{t_n}^i, z_{t_n}^i, \alpha_{t_n}^i, \beta_{t_n}^i, \gamma_{t_n}^i), (x_{t_{n+1}}^i, y_{t_{n+1}}^i, z_{t_{n+1}}^i, \alpha_{t_{n+1}}^i, \beta_{t_{n+1}}^i, \gamma_{t_{n+1}}^i), \cdots,$
$\quad (x_{t_{n+j}}^i, y_{t_{n+j}}^i, z_{t_{n+j}}^i, \alpha_{t_{n+j}}^i, \beta_{t_{n+j}}^i, \gamma_{t_{n+j}}^i)$: acceleration forces x, y, z
$\quad$ and rotation rates α, β, γ of the i-th keystroke from time t_n to t_{n+j}
// $Q = (Q_1, Q_2, \cdots, Q_m)$: quality scores for m keystrokes in K
1 $\quad$ calculate each $\bar{c} = (\bar{c}_{t_n}, \bar{c}_{t_{n+1}}, \cdots, \bar{c}_{t_{n+j}})$ for $c \in \{x, y, z, \alpha, \beta, \gamma\}$
$\quad\quad$ where $\bar{c}_{t_k} = $ Mean $(c_{t_k}^1, c_{t_k}^2, \cdots, c_{t_k}^m)$
2 $\quad$ $s = ()$ // Cross-correlation values of m keystrokes for $x, y, z, \alpha, \beta, \gamma$
$\quad\quad$ $w = ()$ // Weights for $x, y, z, \alpha, \beta, \gamma$
3 $\quad$ **for each** K_i in $(K_1, K_2, \cdots, K_m)$
4 $\quad\quad$ calculate each $s_i^c = $ Cross-Correlation $((c_{t_n}^i, c_{t_{n+1}}^i, \cdots, c_{t_{n+j}}^i), \bar{c})$ for $c \in \{x, y, z, \alpha, \beta, \gamma\}$
5 $\quad$ calculate each $w^c = $ Mean $(s_1^c, s_2^c, \cdots, s_m^c)$ for $c \in \{x, y, z, \alpha, \beta, \gamma\}$
6 $\quad$ **for each** K_i in $(K_1, K_2, \cdots, K_m)$
7 $\quad\quad$ $Q_i = s_i^x \times w^x + s_i^y \times w^y + s_i^z \times w^z + s_i^\alpha \times w_i^\alpha + s_i^\beta \times w^\beta + s_i^\gamma \times w^\gamma$
8 $\quad$ **return** Q

Fig. 3. Keystroke data quality estimation algorithm

This algorithm does not rely on any special heuristic or threshold, and it can be executed online efficiently with polynomial time complexity. Using this algorithm, the training data screening component computes quality scores of individual keystrokes of a user for a specific key, and ranks the keystrokes based on their quality scores. Later, only a certain percent of top-quality keystrokes will be selected for further processing and for training a classifier.

3.4 Fine-Grained Data Filtering

Fine-grained data filtering is the other key technique that we designed to address the data quality challenge in cross-site input inference attacks. It selects frequency bands for data filtering at a fine granularity to reduce the noise in the motion sensor data. As shown in Fig. 1, this filtering technique is applied to the screened data in the training phase to identify the most effective filters, which are used to reduce the noise in both the training and attacking phases.

Frequency domain data filtering is a commonly used noise reduction technique. In the context of input inference attacks, researchers applied filters with fixed bands [2], used interpolation-based data smoothing methods [3], or used Discrete Fourier Transformation (DFT) and inverse DFT methods [1]. All these methods essentially discard high-frequency components and are equivalent to using certain fixed-band low-pass filters; however, it is not shown in these studies that a fixed-band low-pass filter is most appropriate and effective.

We propose a fine-grained data filtering technique, in which the frequency bands are selected with varying lengths instead of being fixed, for example, to a low-pass or high-pass band; meanwhile, different frequency bands are selected to effectively attack different users. Specifically, our technique divides the entire frequency band into multiple finer-granularity sub-bands, iterates all the consecutive concatenations of one or multiple sub-bands, and selects the concatenated band that performs the best as the frequency band for a particular user.

One typical band division method is the $\frac{1}{n}$ Octave method [6], which first divides an entire frequency band into two halves, then recursively divides the low frequency half multiple times in the same manner, and finally further equally divides each current sub-band into n new sub-bands. The $\frac{1}{n}$ Octave method favors low frequency components by dividing them into finer-granularity sub-bands, and it is often used in processing audio data that are dominated by low frequency components [6]. We use the $\frac{1}{2}$ Octave method to divide the entire frequency band (i.e., 0 Hz to 30 Hz, which is the mirrored first half of 60 Hz sampling frequency in Google Chrome used for collecting our motion sensor data) into ten sub-bands (four recursive divisions and one final $\frac{1}{2}$ division), but merge the first two low-frequency sub-bands into one due to their small sizes; the second column of Table 1 lists the nine final Octave sub-bands. Alternative division methods exist, for example, a straightforward method is to divide the entire frequency band into sub-bands with an equal size; we also use this method to derive nine equal sub-bands as shown in the third column of Table 1 as a comparison.

Table 1. Nine $\frac{1}{2}$ Octave and nine equal sub-bands

Sub-band index	1/2 Octave sub-bands (Hz)	Equally divided sub-bands (Hz)
1	0–1.88	0–3.33
2	1.88–2.65	3.33–6.67
3	2.65–3.75	6.67–10
4	3.75–5.3	10–13.33
5	5.3–7.5	13.33–16.67
6	7.5–10.61	16.67–20
7	10.61–15	20–23.33
8	15–21.21	23.33–26.67
9	21.21–30	26.67–30

From the nine sub-bands divided using either method, we further derive 45 consecutively concatenated bands from nine length-one concatenations, eight length-two concatenations, and finally to one length-nine concatenation. All these 90 bands together with a commonly used simple (less configuration effort) yet efficient Infinite Impulse Response filter [6] are applied individually and independently to our screened motion sensor data; later, the band for the best-performing classifier is selected as the most effective frequency band for a particular user, and will be used in the attacking phase.

3.5   Feature Extraction and Model Training

As shown in Table 2, we use 30 types of raw and derived motion sensor data of a given keystroke to extract statistical features. Sixteen types of data are singletons, and fourteen are pairs. The 16 singletons include acceleration forces (x, y, z), rotation rates (α, β, γ), the magnitude of acceleration forces (M^A), the magnitude of rotation rates (M^R), and all their first differences (D(x), D(y), D(z), D(α), D(β), D(γ), D(M^A), D(M^R)). The 14 pairs include three pairs of acceleration forces $((x, y), (y, z), (z, x))$, three pairs of rotation rates $((\alpha, \beta), (\beta, \gamma), (\gamma, \alpha))$, one pair of the magnitudes of acceleration forces and rotation rates $((M^A, M^R))$, and seven pairs of their corresponding first differences.

From the 16 singletons, the feature extraction component extracts (from both time and frequency domains) nine types of statistical features: maximum value, minimum value, mean value, variance, standard derivation, root mean square (RMS), skewness, kurtosis, and area under curve (AUC); as a result, $16 \times 2 \times 9 = 288$ features are extracted from the 16 singletons. Given the motion sensor data of a keystroke in the time domain, the maximum and minimum values are the peak and valley values; the mean value is the averaged amplitude; the variance, standard deviation, and RMS measure the deviations on amplitude; the skewness measures the symmetry of the motion sensor data; the kurtosis measures whether the motion sensor data are heavily or lightly tailed in comparison to a normal distribution; the AUC measures the power of the motion sensor data. In the frequency domain, all these nine features statistically measure the distribution of frequency components of the motion sensor data. From the 14 pairs, the component extracts their 14 cross correlation values in the time domain. Therefore, in total, $288 + 14 = 302$ statistical features are extracted from the motion sensor data of a keystroke, and are used in training and prediction.

In the model training, we experimented with a variety of machine learning algorithms using Weka [10], and observed that using the default Sequential Minimal Optimization (SMO) [5] for training a Support Vector Machine (SVM) classifier (with default parameters and the default linear kernel) outperforms all the other algorithms (with their default configurations) in inference accuracy. We only present the evaluation results of using SMO for SVM in the next section.

Table 2. Extracted statistical features

Data (16 singletons and 14 pairs)		Domain	Extracted features	Number of features
x	$D(x)$	Time	Max, Min,	$2 \times 2 \times 9 = 36$
y	$D(y)$	&	Mean,	$2 \times 2 \times 9 = 36$
z	$D(z)$	Frequency	Variance,	$2 \times 2 \times 9 = 36$
α	$D(\alpha)$		Standard deviation,	$2 \times 2 \times 9 = 36$
β	$D(\beta)$		Root mean square, Skewness,	$2 \times 2 \times 9 = 36$
γ	$D(\gamma)$		Kurtosis,	$2 \times 2 \times 9 = 36$
M^A	$D(M^A)$		Area under curve	$2 \times 2 \times 9 = 36$
M^R	$D(M^R)$			$2 \times 2 \times 9 = 36$
(x, y)	$(D(x), D(y))$	Time	Cross correlation	$2 \times 1 \times 1 = 2$
(y, z)	$(D(y), D(z))$			$2 \times 1 \times 1 = 2$
(z, x)	$(D(z), D(x))$			$2 \times 1 \times 1 = 2$
(α, β)	$(D(\alpha), D(\beta))$			$2 \times 1 \times 1 = 2$
(β, γ)	$(D(\beta), D(\gamma))$			$2 \times 1 \times 1 = 2$
(γ, α)	$(D(\gamma), D(\alpha))$			$2 \times 1 \times 1 = 2$
(M^A, M^R)	$(D(M^A), D(M^R))$			$2 \times 1 \times 1 = 2$

*$D()$ is the first differences of a sequence, e.g., $D(x) = (x_2 - x_1, x_3 - x_2, \cdots, x_n - x_{n-1})$.

4 Evaluation

4.1 Data Collection

Participants: With the IRB approval from our university, we recruited 20 adults for data collection. We asked all the participants to use their own or our provided Android smartphones, and use the Google Chrome Web browser with the default Google Keyboard to perform input tasks. In the recruitment process, potential participants were administered the informed consent.

Websites Setup: We created two websites: one of them (i.e., the "malicious" website) uses JavaScript code to perform cross-site motion sensor data collection from the other website (i.e., the "victim" website). From the "victim" website that we own, we were also able to collect the key events for segmenting the motion sensor data, and the tapped characters for labeling the corresponding individual keystrokes. The "victim" website contains four webpages. Each webpage displays a different letter pangram and a different digit pangram, and asks our participants to type the two pangrams in two input fields, respectively. As shown in Table 3, each letter pangram is a sentence using every letter of the alphabet exactly once so that a participant does not need to type a longer sentence in each input field. Each digit pangram contains ten unique digits, and three special characters at the left, middle, and right parts of the keyboard.

Procedure and Dataset: We asked every participant to perform four tasks by visiting the four webpages and typing the displayed pangrams in each session. We asked each participant to complete a total number of 26 sessions in two weeks,

Table 3. Pangrams used in the study

Webpage	Letter pangrams	Digit pangrams
1	cwm fjord bank glyphs vext quiz	@83294&60571)
2	squdgy fez blank jimp crwth vox	&56920)71438@
3	tv quiz drag nymphs blew jfk cox	)45372&80916@
4	q kelt vug dwarf combs jynx phiz	@28513)97604&

but allowed them to do so at any places; therefore, we were able to collect a relatively large amount of data from participants in their real daily environments without any restriction. Overall, we collected $4 \times 26 = 104$ keystroke samples for each of the 39 characters (lower-case letters, digits, and three special characters) from each individual participant. Due to the error correction in typing, our participants indeed contributed 17,571 additional keystroke samples in their sessions. As a result, the total number of keystroke samples in our final dataset is $104 \times 39 \times 20 + 17,571 = 98,691$.

4.2   Accuracy Metrics and Evaluation Methodology

To evaluate the accuracy of a trained multi-class classifier, we first count the *true positive* (TP), *false positive* (FP), *true negative* (TN), and *false negative* (FN) numbers. For a given class (e.g., letter "a"), a true positive is an instance correctly predicted as belonging to that class (e.g., letter "a" is correctly predicted as "a"), a false positive is an instance incorrectly predicted as belonging to that class (e.g., letter "b" is incorrectly predicted as "a"), a true negative is an instance correctly predicted as not belonging to that class (e.g., letter "b" is correctly predicted not as "a"), a false negative is an instance incorrectly predicted as not belonging to that class (e.g., letter "a" is incorrectly predicted not as "a"). We further calculate *false positive rate* (FPR), *precision, recall* (i.e., true positive rate, or TPR), and *F-measure* accuracy metrics for each class, and average their corresponding values across classes as the accuracy for the multi-class classifier. The F-measure metric is the harmonic mean of precision and recall; thus, we mainly present and analyze the results based on this metric.

In the evaluation, our classifier is trained and assessed using the 10-fold cross validation, and we run the cross validation for 5 rounds and present their averaged results. We evaluate the inference accuracy explicitly on all the three charsets: the letter charset (i.e., 26 lower-case letters), the digit charset (i.e., 10 digits together with 3 special characters), and the mixed charset (i.e., all the 39 characters). This is because in real scenarios, an attacker may know the type information of an input regarding if it is a letter or digit, and can directly use a classifier specific to the inference of either letters or digits.

4.3 Overall Accuracy with Training Data Screening

We evaluate the overall accuracy of our inference attacks with the focus on quantifying the extent to which our training data screening technique can improve the accuracy. We use the keystroke data quality estimation algorithm (Fig. 3) to rank the keystrokes of a given participant for each specific key, and select a certain percent of top-quality keystrokes for training a classifier and performing the 10-fold cross validation. Specifically, we choose 10 percentage values from 0.1 (i.e., 10%), 0.2 (i.e., 20%), ..., to 1.0 (i.e., 100%). In particular, the 100% value means that all the keystrokes will be used in training, and the corresponding inference accuracy serves as the baseline in our accuracy comparison. Given a specific percentage value and a specific charset, we ensure that the sample sizes are roughly equal for different characters to avoid training a classifier using unbalanced data. Eventually, the percentage value that yields the highest inference accuracy will be selected for each participant as the best percentage value for screening the training data. In this percentage value selection process, fine-grained data filtering is turned off to avoid circular dependency.

Figures 4(a), (b), and (c) illustrate the overall inference accuracy for the 20 participants on the three charsets, respectively. In each subfigure, we compare the inference accuracy (i.e., F-measure) for each participant between that from the baseline (i.e., 100%) and that from his or her best percentage value. Regarding the inference accuracy from the baseline, the F-measure scores for the 20 participants vary from 12.97% to 58.14% with the average at 30.12% for the letter charset, from 21.21% to 66.91% with the average at 39.71% for the digit charset, and from 9.17% to 46.97% with the average at 23.45% for the mixed charset. By using training data screening with the best percentage values, the F-measure scores for the 20 participants are improved (upon those of the baseline) from 3.41% to 20.45% with the average at 8.03% for the letter charset, from 1.96% to 18.75% with the average at 9.93% for the digit charset, and from 2.8% to 16.96% with the average at 7.21% for the mixed charset. The inference accuracy is improved for all the 20 participants, demonstrating that our training data screening technique is indeed effective.

Two additional observations from Fig. 4 are worth mentioning. One is that for almost all the participants, the corresponding inference accuracy on the digit charset is higher than that on the letter charset, which is further higher than that on the mixed charset. For example, for participant P12, the inference accuracy on the digit, letter, and mixed charsets is 49.13%, 38.63%, and 31.29%, respectively. The other observation is that the relative inference accuracy differences among the participants are highly consistent across the three charsets. For example, the inference accuracy for participant P7 is the lowest among all the participants across the three charsets, while that for participant P17 is always the highest.

4.4 Overall Accuracy with Fine-Grained Data Filtering

Our fine-grained data filtering technique (Sect. 3.4) improves the inference accuracy for the majority of the participants; meanwhile, the $\frac{1}{2}$ Octave method performs better on the digit charset, while equally dividing the entire frequency band

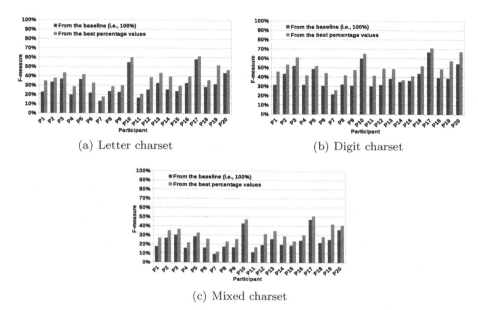

(a) Letter charset

(b) Digit charset

(c) Mixed charset

Fig. 4. Overall accuracy on letter, digit, and mixed charsets

performs better on the mixed charset. With this further improvement, our input inference attacks overall (1) achieve 2.45%, 39.74%, 38.77%, and 38.83% regarding FPR, precision, recall (TPR), and F-measure, respectively, on the letter charset, (2) achieve 4.1%, 51.45%, 50.75%, and 50.79% regarding the four metrics, respectively, on the digit charset, and (3) achieve 1.81%, 32.04%, 31.42%, and 31.36% regarding the four metrics, respectively, on the mixed charset. Note that *a smaller training dataset can still achieve good inference accuracy.* For example, using 41 keystroke samples for each character in 10-fold cross validation (thus less than 37 samples for training) can still give us a 33% F-measure score for the letter charset.

4.5 Further Overall Accuracy Comparison and Analysis

Because our trained classifier (using SMO for SVM) is a probabilistic classifier that predicts the probabilities over a set of classes, we further consider the top-n predicted results and define the *hit probability* as the probability that the ground truth is among them. This hit probability corresponds to the probability of hitting the ground truth in at most n tries of the top-n results. Figure 5 illustrates the hit probability curves from one try to four tries, for our input inference attacks denoted by the solid lines and for the random guessing attacks denoted by the dashed lines. The hit probability increases with the increase of the number of tries. For example, it increases from 41.5% in one try to 79.52% in four tries for our input inference attacks on the letter charset. Note that these numbers are averaged over all the predictions across the participants. Our input inference attacks are much more effective than the random guessing attacks. For example, on the letter charset, our attacks are about 10.8 times and 5.2 times more effective than the random guessing attacks (i.e., guessing a letter from 26 possibilities) in one try and four tries, respectively.

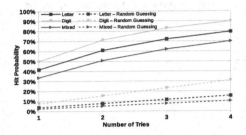
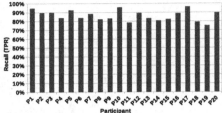

Fig. 5. Hit probability in one to four tries for three charsets

Fig. 6. Overall data segmentation accuracy

4.6   Accuracy of Sensor Data Segmentation Without Key Events

In this subsection, we evaluate the accuracy of the *Detect-KeyDown-Timestamps* subroutine by comparing its detection results with the collected ground-truth key down timestamps. This accuracy determines the accuracy of the *Segment-SensorData-Without-KeyEvents* algorithm shown in Fig. 2.

For the purpose of this evaluation, we need to define a new set of accuracy metrics. If a time window (identified by the *Identify-Keystroke-TimeWindows* subroutine in Fig. 2) for a detected key down timestamp contains any ground-truth key down timestamp, a true positive (TP) is counted; otherwise, a false positive (FP) is counted. If a ground-truth key down timestamp is not in any of those identified time windows, a false negative (FN) is counted. However, we are not able to count true negatives because they are simply not definable.

Because Google Chrome on Android does not report the key down and up events of special keys (e.g., caps lock key, keyboard switching key, and enter key) to the JavaScript code on regular webpages, we do not have the ground-truth to exclude the keystrokes for special keys, and our false positive numbers are unavoidably over-counted in this evaluation. Therefore, to represent the accuracy of the key down timestamp detection, it is more reasonable for us to use the recall (TPR) scores instead of the precision or F-measure scores (which are affected by the over-counted false positives).

Figure 6 illustrates that the recall scores are above 80% for the majority of the participants, demonstrating that our *Segment-SensorData-Without-KeyEvents* algorithm is indeed effective in segmenting sensor data for true keystrokes. In real attacks without key events, the overall input inference accuracy depends on the data segmentation accuracy, and thus could be slightly reduced.

5   Conclusion

We investigated severe cross-site input inference attacks that may compromise the security of every mobile Web user, and quantified the extent to which they can be effective. We formulated our attacks as a typical multi-class classification problem, and built an inference framework that trains a classifier in the training phase and predicts a user's new inputs in the attacking phase. We addressed the data quality and data segmentation challenges in our attacks by designing and experimenting with three unique techniques: training data screening, fine-grained data filtering, and key down timestamp detection and adjustment. We intensively evaluated our attacks and found they are effective. Our results demonstrate that researchers, smartphone vendors, and app developers should pay serious attention to the severe cross-site input inference attacks that can be pervasively performed, and should start to design and deploy effective defense techniques.

Acknowledgment. This research was supported in part by the NSF grant DGE-1619841.

References

1. Aviv, A.J., Sapp, B., Blaze, M., Smith, J.M.: Practicality of accelerometer side channels on smartphones. In: Proceedings of the Annual Computer Security Applications Conference (ACSAC), pp. 41–50 (2012)
2. Cai, L., Chen, H.: On the practicality of motion based keystroke inference attack. In: Katzenbeisser, S., Weippl, E., Camp, L.J., Volkamer, M., Reiter, M., Zhang, X. (eds.) Trust 2012. LNCS, vol. 7344, pp. 273–290. Springer, Heidelberg (2012). https://doi.org/10.1007/978-3-642-30921-2_16
3. Miluzzo, E., Varshavsky, A., Balakrishnan, S., Choudhury, R.R.: TapPrints: your finger taps have fingerprints. In: Proceedings of the International Conference on Mobile Systems, Applications, and Services, pp. 323–336 (2012)
4. Orfanidis, S.J.: Introduction to Signal Processing. Prentice-Hall Inc., Englewood Cliffs (1995)
5. Platt, J.: Sequential minimal optimization: a fast algorithm for training support vector machines. Technical report (1998)
6. Smith, S.W.: The scientist and engineer's guide to digital signal processing (1997)
7. Xu, Z., Bai, K., Zhu, S.: TapLogger: inferring user inputs on smartphone touchscreens using on-board motion sensors. In: Proceedings of the ACM Conference on Security and Privacy in Wireless and Mobile Networks, pp. 113–124 (2012)
8. Yue, C.: Sensor-based mobile web fingerprinting and cross-site input inference attacks. In: Proceedings of the IEEE Workshop on Mobile Security Technologies (2016)
9. Same Origin Policy. https://www.w3.org/Security/wiki/Same_Origin_Policy
10. Weka 3: Data Mining Software in Java. http://www.cs.waikato.ac.nz/ml/weka/

BKI: Towards Accountable and Decentralized Public-Key Infrastructure with Blockchain

Zhiguo Wan[1(✉)], Zhangshuang Guan[1], Feng Zhuo[1], and Hequn Xian[2]

[1] School of Computer Science and Technology, Shandong University,
Jinan, Shandong, China
wanzhiguo@sdu.edu.cn, gzs_1994@163.com, 2906719340@qq.com
[2] College of Computer Science and Technology, Qingdao University,
Qingdao, Shandong, China
xianhq@126.com

Abstract. Traditional PKIs face a well-known vulnerability that caused by compromised Certificate Authorities (CA) issuing bogus certificates. Several solutions like AKI and ARPKI have been proposed to address this vulnerability. However, they require complex interactions and synchronization among related entities, and their security has not been validated with wide deployment. We propose an accountable, flexible and efficient decentralized PKI to achieve the same goal using the blockchain technology of Bitcoin, which has been proven to be secure and reliable. The proposed scheme, called BKI, realizes certificate issuance, update and revocation with transactions on a special blockchain that is managed by multiple trusted maintainers. BKI achieves accountability and is easy to check certificate validity, and it is also more secure than centralized PKIs. Moreover, the certificate status update interval of BKI is in seconds, significantly reducing the vulnerability window. In addition, BKI is more flexible than AKI and ARPKI in that the number of required CAs to issue certificates is tunable for different applications. We analyze BKI's security and performance, and present details on implementation of BKI. Experiments using Ethereum show that certificate issuance/update/revocation cost 2.38 ms/2.39 ms/1.59 ms respectively.

Keywords: Blockchain · PKI · Security

1 Introduction

Public key infrastructure (PKI) plays a critical role for network security, e.g. SSL/TLS for secure web communication, public key crypto-based security protocols. The security of the PKI is of paramount importance to applications relying on it. However, traditional PKIs suffer from a well-known vulnerability in case

Z. Wan—This work was supported by the National Natural Science Foundation of China under Grant 61370027.

© ICST Institute for Computer Sciences, Social Informatics and Telecommunications Engineering 2018
X. Lin et al. (Eds.): SecureComm 2017, LNICST 238, pp. 644–658, 2018.
https://doi.org/10.1007/978-3-319-78813-5_33

of compromised or malicious CAs. That is, a compromised or malicious CA may issue a certificate for some domain, which can use it to launch impersonation or Man-in-the-Middle attacks.

Many attacks have demonstrated the serious vulnerability of traditional PKIs. Recently, fraudulent certificates have been issued for domains of Google.com, Yahoo.com, mozilla.org from well-known CAs [1]. Such bogus certificates may have been used by the adversary to eavesdrop communication. This vulnerability is because current PKIs lack mechanisms to detect and prevent CA misbehavior.

To counter against this problem, different approaches have been proposed recently to make certificate issuance transparent and accountable. Among them, the public log-based schemes have been the most effective approach to achieve this goal. Recent advanced proposals, AKI [1], ARPKI [2], EICT [3] and DTKI [4], all follow this methodology. Schemes including ARPKI and DTKI even have formal proofs to ensure their security. Although these solutions have solved the vulnerability of traditional PKIs to some extent, they have several drawbacks for their complex operations and interactions. To prevent misbehavior, CAs and other entities (e.g. log servers) need to monitor each other's activities, incurring too much communication cost for the PKI system.

We turn to Bitcoin [5] for a better solution for this problem. Bitcoin has proved itself an overwhelming success over other alternatives as a digital cryptocurrency. The underlying blockchain technology of Bitcoin has gained tremendous attention, and it has been used in many different fields, ranging from decentralized storage, crowd funding, equity trading to notary services.

Observing the similarity between the PKIs with a public log as in AKI and ARPKI and the Bitcoin system, we take advantage of the blockchain technology to design a full-fledged decentralized PKI, referred to as **BKI**. In our design, the certificate issuance for one's public key is realized by creating a transaction. Since for each transaction to be valid, it must be signed by the senders. This is similar for CAs to certify a public key by generating signatures over the public key along with other related data.

To reduce trust on a single CA as AKI, a user can request certificates from multiple CAs and combine the certificates together to obtain his final certificate. The user needs to choose at least k CAs he trusts to certify his public key, where k is the minimum number of CAs needed for generating a valid certificate and it can be set as a system-wide parameter. With the blockchain technology, this can be implemented with a transaction which has multiple CAs as the senders and the certificate applicant as the receiver. The first advantage is BKI has a smaller certificate status update interval, which is determined by the block generation speed. For blockchain like Ethereum [6,7], a block is generated every 12 s, which is much smaller than the update interval in AKI or ARPKI. Secondly, BKI has a special Merkle Patricia Tree used for certificate status checking. This makes BKI more efficient than AKI and ARPKI in terms of certificate storage cost and verification cost. Thirdly, system parameters in BKI like the number of required CAs to issue a certificate are tunable according to different security requirements.

Contributions. In this paper we propose a novel solution for the vulnerability of PKIs based on the blockchain technology of Bitcoin [5] to deliver an accountable and efficient decentralized PKI. Our proposal, called BKI, takes advantage of the blockchain technology to implement a decentralized certificate log, on which it gracefully achieves certificate issuance, revocation and update. Main contributions of our work include:

- We propose BKI, an accountable and decentralized PKI built from the blockchain technology of Bitcoin to conquer the vulnerability of traditional PKIs. BKI achieves short certificate status update interval of tens of seconds, as compared to 1 h update interval in AKI/ARPKI, significantly reducing the vulnerability window and improving security. In addition, BKI is flexible in that system parameters like the number of CAs to issue a certificate are tunable.
- A detailed comparison between AKI and BKI is provided to highlight the advantages of our proposal. We also give a detailed discussion and a thorough analysis of BKI on its security, efficiency and flexibility.
- A prototype of BKI is implemented using Ethereum blockchain for performance evaluation. Experiments show that certificate issuance/update/revocation cost 2.38 ms/2.39 ms/1.59 ms respectively.

Organization. The rest of the paper is organized as follows. Background knowledge about log-centric PKIs and blockchain are presented in next section. Then We define the problem to be solved in this paper in Sect. 3. After that, we describe BKI in detail in Sect. 4, followed by discussion and analysis on security, efficiency and availability of BKI. Details on the implementation of the prototype of BKI are described in Sect. 6, and we also evaluate its performance there. Finally, concluding remarks are given in the end.

2   Background

Quite a few schemes have been proposed to deal with the vulnerability in current PKIs. Readers are referred to [2] for a comprehensive review of these works, which are categorized into client-centric, CA-centric, and domain-centric approaches. However, there is a special group of schemes built on the certificate log idea, which should be categorized as the log-centric approach. Here we review the schemes from the log-centric approach since they are very close to our proposal.

Log-centric PKIs. Certificate transparency (CT) [8] employs the Merkle hash tree structure to build an append-only log to record all registered certificates. After registering one's certificate with the log server, each domain is given a non-repudiable audit proof that its certificate is on the append-only log. This audit proof and the certificate are both provided to the client for validation. However, CT is only designed to make certificate issuance transparent, and it does not has revocation function. Hence it cannot detect or prevent registration of bogus certificates generated by compromised CAs. To amend this problem, Revocation Transparency (RT) [9] was proposed to implement certificate revocation.

Enhanced Issuance and Revocation Transparency (EICT) [3] combines the idea of CT and RT to achieve a more efficient transparent PKI. Although EICT can detect bogus certificates issued by compromised CAs, it cannot prevent them from happening as it lacks monitoring mechanisms. DTKI [4] further extends EICT by using multiple logs and maintainers, and web users collectively monitor the logs to detect misbehavior. Although the public logs are monitored by web users, it is still possible that some fraudulent certificates escape monitoring and stay on the logs for quite some time. Sovereign Keys (SK) [10] uses a timeline server to maintain an append-only and read-only certificate log, and that log is mirrored to avoid performance bottleneck. However, SK cannot prevent attacks due to compromised sovereign keys. Meanwhile, the mirrors is assumed to be trusted, which is a strong assumption.

Accountable Key Infrastructure (AKI) [1] intends to solve the single point of failure of CAs with public certificate logs. The log is organized using a lexicographic Merkle tree, such that certificate revocation can be done efficiently. Meanwhile, CAs and other entities monitor each other frequently to detect and prevent misbehavior. Attack Resilient PKI (ARPKI) [2] enhances AKI with stronger security guarantees and formal treatment. Using a system model similar to AKI, ARPKI specifies more details about log synchronization, validation and monitoring.

Bitcoin and Blockchain. Bitcoin [5] is a completely decentralized digital currency without relying on any trusted party. All participants of the Bitcoin system are connected by Internet and form a P2P network. They follow a suite of protocols to maintain coin generation, coin transmission, transaction verification and data synchronization etc. More importantly, the underlying technology of Bitcoin, called blockchain technology, has been a very useful tool in many areas, like decentralized storage, crowd funding, equity trading, notary services etc. This work is also an example of application of the blockchain technology in a new area (Fig. 1).

Blockchain. The blockchain is the core data structure of Bitcoin, containing all coin generation and transaction information. As its name implies, it is a chain of blocks, starting from the very first block with ID number 0 to the latest block. This chain of blocks serves as the decentralized ledger and it is maintained by peers of the Bitcoin P2P network. Each block is chained to the previous block by containing a hash of the previous block, and it also contains some transactions in its header.

A blockchain can be permissionless like Bitcoin or Ethereum [6,7], or can be permissioned like Hyperledger [11], which is maintained by privileged parties. Permissionless blockchains can use consensus mechanisms like Proof of Work (PoW), Proof of Stake (PoS) [12,13] and Delegated Proof of Stake (DPoS) [14], while permissioned blockchains can use Practical Byzantine Fault Tolerance (PBFT) [15], which is more scalable and efficient.

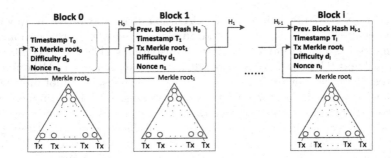

Fig. 1. Blockchain of Bitcoin: a block header contains a hash of its previous block header, a time stamp, a Merkle root computed from all transactions in this block, the current difficulty, a nonce which is the proof of work.

Transaction. A transaction is defined as follows:

$$\mathcal{TX} = \{TX\_ID, TX\_ID_{old}; Input : S_1, S_2, \ldots, S_k;$$
$$Output : PK_{R_1}, PK_{R_2}, \ldots, PK_{R_k}\},$$

where TX_ID is the identity of this transaction, TX_ID_{old} is the preceding transaction from which the Bitcoins are from, S_i is the sender of the transaction, R_i is the receiver and PK_{R_i} is R_i's public key. Each transaction references a previous transaction from which it spends Bitcoins to new destinations. Our certificate transaction has at most one preceding transaction, and it extends the Bitcoin transaction with two fields: domain name and expiry time. All senders must sign the transaction so as to be verified successfully by others.

3   Problem Definition

We attempt to tackle the vulnerability of single point of failure in traditional PKIs using the blockchain technology. The new PKI should be able to effectively detect misbehavior of compromised CAs and thereby prevent further damages. It should also be simple and efficient in certificate maintenance. More importantly, it must be highly secure since it is the basis for PKC-based security protocols. In this section, we first describe the system model, assumptions and the adversary model of our PKI system. Then the design goals of our proposed PKI are presented.

System Model. In BKI there are four types of participants: CAs, blockchain log maintainers (BLMs), certificate owners and clients. Figure 2 illustrates the system architecture of BKI and their interactions in certificate management.

- **Certificate Authorities.** CAs are responsible for identity verification and certificates issuance for users. Similar to ARPKI and DTKI, CAs are not fully trusted and compromised CAs may generate fraudulent certificates to impersonate users.

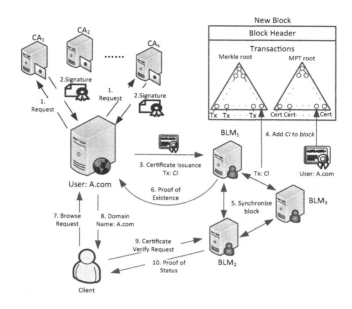

Fig. 2. BKI system architecture and certificate management

- **Blockchain-based Log Maintainers (BLMs).** Blockchain-based log maintainers (BLMs) are responsible for maintaining the blockchain, and each transaction in the blockchain-based log is a certificate transaction. Just like the Bitcoin blockchain, our blockchain-based log is also an append-only log, and the log is synchronized among BLMs to ensure it is up to date.
- **Certificate Owners.** Certificate owners can be of any type user of the PKI, e.g. domain owners or PGP users. They are also referred to as the users of the PKI. They need to provide their credentials to the CAs to obtain signatures for their public keys. Once the user certificate is added into the blockchain-based log, the user can use it to construct secure connections.
- **Clients.** Clients are those who need to verify validity of certificates. For example, a browser that needs to verify a SSL certificate when it visit a SSL-secured web site is a client of BKI.

Adversary Model. We assume that the adversary has full control over the communication channels between infrastructure entities of the PKI and users, i.e. the adversary can eavesdrop, modify and inject any message in the system. Furthermore, it can compromise and control some infrastructure entities, e.g. CAs or log maintainers. But the number of CAs compromised by the adversary is limited to a threshold k. However, the adversary is assumed to have limited computation resources and cannot break the cryptosystem used in our proposal. For the same reason, the adversary cannot produce proofs of work with extraordinary speed, and thus cannot generate new blocks as many as possible.

Design Goals. Our proposed scheme aims to achieve the following design goals:

- **Resilience.** The security of the new PKI should not rely on a single entity, and any entity is not completely trusted unconditionally. In the case of any entity being compromised, the new PKI should be able to detect its misbehavior immediately, and henceforth prevent any attacks, e.g. damages due to fraudulent certificate issued by compromised CAs.
- **Accountability.** All certificate operations are public and accountable, and everyone (users and certificate authorities) can check the blockchain to monitor certificate issuance, update and revocation.
- **Efficiency.** Communication efficiency is of importance for delay-sensitive applications such as web browsing. Hence it is important to reduce communication delay for operations including certificate verification.
- **Flexibility.** CA selection and security parameters should be flexible in the new PKI, so that the user can choose what they trust and prefer in certificate management.

4   BKI: The Blockchain-Based Decentralized PKI

In this section, we first give an overview of the proposed scheme, which helps readers to understand the underlying design principles. Then we describe our BKI in detail.

4.1   The Design of BKI

BKI consists of the following algorithms: initialization, certificate issuance, certificate verification, certificate update, and certificate revocation.

Initialization. In the initialization phase, each CA generates its own public key and private key pair (PK_{CA}, SK_{CA}), and publishes its public key on its website (or other secure places) such that every user can verify its pubic key. Blockchain log maintainers form a peer-to-peer network to maintain a blockchain which contains transactions about certificates, just like the Bitcoin system.

Similar to the peer-to-peer network of the Bitcoin system, the P2P network in our BKI has a specific communication protocol to exchange data on transactions, blocks and the blockchain. It enables BLMs, CAs and users to verify transactions, construct blocks and synchronize the blockchain with each other. The blockchain in BKI is open to everyone, so that anyone can monitor the activities of BLMs and any misbehavior will be detected at once.

Certificate Issuance. Certificate issuance is implemented by signing a transaction for a certificate requester, and this type of transaction is referred to as *certificate issuing (CI)* transaction. Specifically, a user u first generates his own public key and private key pair (PK_u, SK_u), and then request a certificate by asking k CAs to sign a transaction containing the public key PK_u for him. k can be system-wide parameter or a number chosen by u. A larger k means better security, so it is required that $k \geq 3$ for security.

An *unsigned CI* transaction is defined as follows:

$$\mathcal{CI} = \{TX\_ID, NULL, DN, ET; Input : CA_1, CA_2, \ldots, CA_k;$$
$$Output : PK_u\} \ or \ \{PK_{CA_1}, PK_{CA_2}, \ldots, PK_{CA_k}\}_k^t\}, \tag{1}$$

where CA_i is the identity of a CA, PK_u is the public key of user u, DN is the domain name and ET is the expiry time. DN and ET are not allowed to be modified in any case. TX_ID_{old} is set to $NULL$ as it is the first transaction. For this transaction to be valid in a blockchain, all senders must sign the transaction. The actual effect is that all CAs sign user u's public key with their private keys, meaning that the user's public key is certified by these CAs. To this end, u needs to approach each CA with his credential and each CA should check the credential before signing the transaction. This can be done with a secure out-of-band channel. The outputs include public keys, domain name and expired time of user u and t CAs. It is demanded that either user u or any t out of the k CAs can "spend" the output of this transaction. When the certificate needs to be revoked, any t of the k CAs can do it since they are in the output of the CI transaction.

The certificate issuing process proceeds as follows:

– **Step 1.** User u selects k CAs as his certificate issuing authorities. Then u creates an unsigned version of the CI transaction of (1), and sends it to each of the k CAs along with his credential *cre* for certification using an out-of-band channel.

$$\mathcal{CI}, cre \tag{2}$$

– **Step 2.** Upon receiving the request from u, CA_i verifies u's credential, signs the transaction with its private key, and then returns the signed transaction to u.

$$Sig_{CA_i}(\mathcal{CI}) \tag{3}$$

– **Step 3.** After collecting all k signed transactions, u can merge $Sig_{CA_i}(\mathcal{CI}), i = 1, 2, \ldots, k$ into a final CI transaction as showed below:

$$\mathcal{CI}, \{Sig_{CA_i}(\mathcal{CI})\}_{i=1}^k. \tag{4}$$

Then u publishes the CI transaction to the P2P network for verification.

– **Step 4.** If $\mathcal{CI}$ is verified successfully, BLM will check whether the domain name is registered in the blockchain, and update the state of MPT by checking new transactions in this new block only when the domain name is not occupied, then $\mathcal{CI}$ will be added into a new candidate block waiting for confirmation by some consensus algorithm.

- **Step 5.** Then the block containing the *CI* transaction will be appended into the blockchain after successful consensus, and the block will be synchronized throughout the P2P network. Subsequently, everyone can check the blockchain and verify the *CI* transaction of u.
- **Step 6.** Finally, the BLM contacted by the user sends a response back to the user. If the domain name is not occupied, this response will include the header of the block containing CI and a proof-of-existence of CI in the block. The proof-of-existence consists of the hash values on the Merkle tree which can prove that CI is on the Merkle tree. Otherwise, user will receive an error message.

Certificate Verification. This step utilize MPT [16] combines the advantages of Patricia tree and Merkle tree. It can not only perform efficient keyword query like Patricia tree, but also implement efficient verification of data at leaf nodes like Merkle tree. Ethereum's MPT uses the public keys of accounts as keys and treat balances as values at leaf nodes, while we use $\mathsf{SHA256}(DomainName)$ as keys, and treat the public keys and the expiration time as values at leaf nodes.

After a user, e.g. a domain owner, gets his certificate issued by BKI, the certificate issuance is also recorded on the blockchain maintained by BLMs. If a client intends to establish a secure connection with the domain server, then he needs to ensure that: (1) the certificate is indeed recorded on the blockchain; (2) the certificate has not been revoked. To this end, he follows the procedure below:

- **Step 7 and 8.** The client sends a request to the certificate owner, who will respond with the domain name of the domain owner. But whether this domain is valid or has been revoked is unknown, so the client needs to contact BLMs to verify this.
- **Step 9 and 10.** The client contacts BLMs to verify that a certificate corresponding to the domain name is on the blockchain and has not been revoked. On receiving the request, any BLM can check the MPT on whether a certificate corresponding to the domain name is on the MPT, and whether the certificate is revoked or not. Finally, the BLM returns a proof-of-status of the domain certificate to the client. The proof-of-status consists of the domain's certificate along with the hash values on the MPT which can prove that the certificate is on the MPT.

Certificate Update. The user can update his certificate whenever he feels necessary, without requesting help from any CA. This is achieved by the user generating a certificate update (*CU*) transaction, which "spends" the output of his *CI* transaction to his new public key. In order for the CAs to revoke the updated certificate, the output of the newly generated *CU* transaction should contain the same k CAs as the user's *CI* transaction.

Suppose user u has the following CI transaction:

$$CI = \{TX\_ID, NULL, DN, ET; Input: CA_1, CA_2, \ldots, CA_k;$$
$$Output: PK_u \ or \ \{PK_{CA_1}, PK_{CA_2}, \ldots, PK_{CA_k}\}_k^t\}$$

Then the CU transaction is as follows:

$$CU = \quad \{TX\_ID', TX\_ID, DN, ET; Input: u;$$
$$Output: PK'_u \ or \ \{PK_{CA_1}, PK_{CA_2}, \ldots, PK_{CA_k}\}_k^t\}$$

The transaction CU references the transaction ID, i.e. TX_ID, of the transaction CI, indicating it updates the public key PK_u in CI to PK'_u. Note that there is only one sender u in the input of CU. The output must contain the same CAs as those in CI, so that the same CAs can collaborate to revoke CU. Furthermore, user u can continue to update his public key by creating a new CU transaction in the same way.

Whenever the user's public key is updated, his old pubic key is invalidated and can not be used anymore. All the user's public keys and their update ordering are recorded in the blockchain. Anyone can check the blockchain to obtain one's latest public key.

Certificate Revocation. Certificate revocation is necessary when a user's private key is compromised. In this case, an adversary may use the user's private key for malicious purposes, or update the user's public key to a new one so that the user's old public key certificate is invalidated. Thus, the user should seek the help of CAs to revoke the old public key certificate.

At least t CAs from the output of the CI or CU transaction should collaborate to accomplish the revocation task. Suppose the t CAs that decide to revoke the user's old public key are $CA_{i_1}, CA_{i_2}, \ldots, CA_{i_t}$, where $i_1, i_2, \ldots, i_t \in \{1, 2, \ldots, m\}$. They generate the following certificate revocation (CR) transaction to revoke the user's certificate in CI:

$$CR = \{TX\_ID'', TX\_ID, DN, ET; Input: CA_{i_1}, CA_{i_2}, \ldots, CA_{i_t}; Output: NULL\}$$

5 Discussion and Analysis

In this section, we first compared BKI with ARPKI and AKI, and then analyze its security.

5.1 Comparison with ARPKI and AKI

There are some similarities between BKI and AKI (also ARPKI). Both BKI and AKI are based on a synchronized certificate log to manage certificate; both utilize multiple CAs to reduce trust on a single CA and remove single point of failure in CAs; Both employs multiple signatures to generate certificates for users. However, there are a number of differences in design making BKI more preferable.

Certificate Management. Merkle hash trees (forming a chain) are used by AKI and ARPKI to manage certificates, while certificate operations are recorded as transactions on blockchain in BKI. AKI relies on the Merkle tree to add new certificate, remove certificate and produce proof of absence of a certificate. In BKI, the Merkle hash tree is only used to obtain the Merkle root of transactions in a block, and Merkle hash trees from different blocks are independent from each other.

Another difference between BKI and AKI is that revoked certificates are removed from the latest Merkle hash tree in AKI, while revocation is realized as a revocation transaction in BKI. In order to make certificate verification more efficient, BKI employs Merkle Patricia Tree (MPT) to record the latest status of certificates. Therefore, it is more efficient to check certificate validity in BKI. Moreover, a complete life cycle of a certificate can be easily obtained from the blockchain in BKI.

Trustworthy Timestamping. BKI also inherits one additional advantage of the blockchain technology, trustworthy timestamping. Each block is generated by the consensus algorithm in fixed intervals, thus all transactions in that block are timestamped accordingly. These timestamps are trustworthy and can be used to prove when a certificate is issued, updated or revoked. The Merkle hash tree update interval in AKI is about one hour, while the block generation interval can be seconds in BKI, i.e. the timestaming precision can be seconds in BKI.

Flexibility. BKI is more flexible than AKI and ARPKI in that parameters can be chosen by certificate owners. The least number of CAs required for certificate issuance is variable for different applications in BKI. The number needs to be higher for sensitive applications like online banking, and it can be smaller for online forums. The least number of CAs required for certificate update can also be chosen differently for different applications.

5.2 Security Analysis

Due to space limit, we provide here an informal discussion on security of our proposed scheme from the following aspects. Rigorous formal treatment of BKI is left as our future work.

Compromise of CAs. We assume that a user must obtain k signatures from k different CAs of the n CAs in the system. Suppose the adversary can compromise a CA with probability p. Then the number of compromised CAs X follows binomial distribution $B(n, p)$. Then the probability of $X \geq k$ is as follows:

$$P(X \geq k) = \sum_{m=k}^{n} C_n^m p^m (1-p)^{n-m}$$

The relationship between P and n, k is showed in Fig. 3. We can see that, for any n, one can choose an appropriate k such that the $P(X \geq k)$ can be as small as possible. Actually, the probability of that a CA is compromised is far less than 0.05 in real life. So the security of BKI is guaranteed in the case of comprised CAs when we choose multiple CAs to manage certificates.

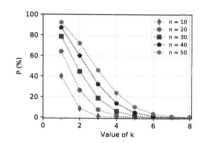

Fig. 3. The probability of forging a valid certificate by compromising at least k CAs for CA compromise probability $p = 0.05$.

Compromise of BLMs. The consensus algorithms used by BLMs in BKI have significant impact on security of BKI. Accordingly, the adversary can take different attack strategy against different consensus algorithms. For the Proof of Work (PoW), the adversary can launch "51%" attack only if he has more than 50% computation power of the whole system. For Practical Byzantine Fault Tolerance (PBFT), the adversary needs to compromise more than $(N-1)/3$ BLMs among all N BLMs. And when BKI uses Proof of Stake (PoS) or Delegated PoS (DPoS), the adversary can launch the "51%" attack, which requires more than 50% resources of the system or controlling more than 50% delegators. Compared with the attacks against CAs, these attacks may incur big cost, resulting less economic incentives for the adversary. So the adversaries may mainly aim at attacking CAs instead of BLMs.

Vulnerability Window. Vulnerability window is determined by the certificate status update interval (i.e. ILS update interval in AKI or ARPKI). When the certificate private key is leaked or the adversary succeeds in forging the certificate with the help of enough compromised CAs, the system should revoke the bogus certificate as soon as possible to reduce losses during revocation The vulnerability window in BKI is determined by block generation frequency, which can be only 10 min with Bitcoin or 12 s with Ethereum. From this perspective, BKI is more secure than AKI or ARPKI in that certificate status can be updated in seconds.

6   Implementation and Performance Evaluation

In this section, we describe our implementation of BKI and evaluate its performance. We implement our proposal using Ethereum, an open-source blockchain

Table 1. Average processing time(in ms) for certificate operations ($k = 3, t = 2$).

Time	Issue	Update	Revoke
TotalTime	2.385	2.387	2.386
SignTime	0.752	0.753	0.753
VerifyTime	1.633	1.633	1.633

Table 2. Average processing time(in ms) for certificate operations with different threshold.

Threshold	Issue	Update	Revoke
$k = 3, t = 2$	2.385	2.387	1.593
$k = 5, t = 3$	3.997	4.006	2.391
$k = 7, t = 4$	5.766	5.766	3.190
$k = 9, t = 5$	7.413	7.408	3.990
$k = 10, t = 8$	8.007	8.003	6.386

system that extends Bitcoin blockchain with smart contract functionality, which enables a simple and convenient implementation of BKI.

Implementation. BKI is implemented on Ethereum as a smart contract using a special javascript-like language called Solidity. A user initiates the smart contract to register with CAs, while CAs interact with the smart contract by sending certificate issuance, update and revocation transactions.

Our implementation supports multiple CAs (CA_1, CA_2, ..., CA_n) that provide certificate services to users. Each CA or user is represented by an address associated with a public/private key pair. With the smart contract implementation, a CA can generates a certificate issuance, update or revocation transaction that interacts with the smart contract. Note that each transaction is signed by its originator, so the user's certificate is issued, updated or revoked if enough transactions are received by the smart contract.

Preliminary Experiment Results. We evaluate the performance of our proposed scheme based on our implementation. Extensive experiments are conducted on a laptop with Intel Core i5-4200U 1.60GHz*4 and 4GB RAM running 64bit Ubuntu 16.04. In each experiment, a user request his certificate from a given number of CAs, which generate appropriate transactions for the user. The time for certificate issuance, update and revocation is measured for evaluation, while transmission time is not considered. We run the experiments for 100,000 times and average measurements are presented in the following two tables.

In Table 1, the average processing time shows the time for CAs to issue/update/revoke a public key certificate for $k = 3$ and $t = 2$. k and t ($t < k$) denote the threshold operated certificate, and k is used for *Issue* and *Update*, and t is used for *Revoke*. TotalTime denotes the average time spent on signatures and verifications. SignTime denotes the average time spent on signatures, and VerifyTime denotes the average time spent on verification. *Issue*, *Update*, and *Revoke* are the certificate operations k (or t) CAs execute. From the table, we can see that a certificate operation (issue/update/revoke) requires around 2ms.

We provide results for the different value of k and t and give measurements as the average over 100,000 runs. And we present the result in Table 2. The average processing time shows the time for CAs to issue/update/revoke a public key certificate for different k and t. As k and t increase, the time cost also increases accordingly, approximately linear to k.

Figure 4 shows the total time cost for certificates issued, updated or revoked with different value of k and t for the different number of users. The abscissa represents the number of users, and the ordinate represents the total time required for the corresponding number of certificate operations. For given k and t, as the number of users grows, the total time required for certificate operation is growing linearly.

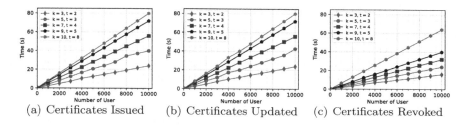

(a) Certificates Issued   (b) Certificates Updated   (c) Certificates Revoked

Fig. 4. The total time that CAs operate certificates.

7   Conclusion

We have proposed BKI, a PKI built from the blockchain technology of Bitcoin to address the vulnerability of traditional PKIs. We have provided in-depth discussion and analysis on security and performance issues of BKI. A prototype of BKI has been implemented on Ethereum blockchain, and comprehensive experiments have been conducted to evaluate its performance. It has showed that certificate operations can be accomplished in about 2 ms. We plan to work out a formal security proof for our proposed scheme as the future work.

References

1. Kim, T.H.J., Huang, L.S., Perring, A., Jackson, C., Gligor, V.: Accountable key infrastructure (AKI): a proposal for a public-key validation infrastructure. In: Proceedings of the International World Wide Web Conference, pp. 679–690. ACM (2013)
2. Basin, D., Cremers, C., Kim, T.H.J., Perrig, A., Sasse, R., Szalachowski, P.: ARPKI: Attack resilient public-key infrastructure. In: Proceedings of ACM CCS 2014, pp. 382–393. ACM (2014)
3. Ryan, M.D.: Enhanced certificate transparency and end-to-end encrypted mail. In: Proceedings of NDSS (2014)
4. Yu, J., Cheval, V., Ryan, M.: DTKI: a new formalized PKI with no trusted parties (2014). http://arxiv.org/abs/1408.1023

5. Nakamoto, S.: Bitcoin: a peer-to-peer electronic cash system (2008). http://bitcoin. org/bitcoin.pdf
6. Wood, G.: Ethereum: a secure decentralised generalised transaction ledger (2014). http://gavwood.com/Paper.pdf
7. Buterin, V.: Ethereum white paper: a next generation smart contract and decentralized application platform (2013). https://github.com/ethereum/wiki/wiki/ White-Paper
8. Laurie, B., Langley, A., Kasper, E.: Certificate transparency. IETF RFC 6962 (2013)
9. Laurie, B., Kasper, E.: Revocation transparency. Google Research, September 2012
10. Eckersley, P.: Sovereign key cryptography for internet domains (2011). https://git. eff.org/?p=sovereign-keys.git
11. Androulaki, E., Cachin, C., Christidis, K., Murthy, C., Nguyen, B., Vukolić, M.: Hyperledger fabric proposals: next consensus architecture proposal (2016)
12. King, S., Nadal, S.: PPCoin: Peer-to-peer crypto-currency with proof-of-stake (2012). http://peerco.in/assets/paper/peercoin-paper.pdf
13. Buterin, V.: Slasher: a punitive proof-of-stake algorithm (2014). https://blog. ethereum.org/2014/01/15/slasher-a-punitive-proof-of-stake-algorithm
14. Larimer, D.: Delegated proof-of-stake (DPOS). Bitshare whitepaper (2014)
15. Castro, M., Liskov, B.: Practical byzantine fault tolerance. In: OSDI. **99**, pp. 173– 186 (1999)
16. Work2Heat: understanding the ethereum trie (2014). https://easythereentropy. wordpress.com/2014/06/04/understanding-the-ethereum-trie/

FRProtector: Defeating Control Flow Hijacking Through Function-Level Randomization and Transfer Protection

Jianming Fu[1,2,3], Rui Jin[1,2]([✉]), and Yan Lin[4]

[1] Computer School, Wuhan University, Wuhan, China
jmfu@whu.edu.cn, r-jin@foxmail.com
[2] State Key Laboratory of Aerospace Information Security and Trusted Computing
of the Ministry of Education, Wuhan, China
[3] State Key Laboratory of Software Engineering, Wuhan University, Wuhan, China
[4] School of Information Systems, Singapore Management University, Singapore,
Singapore
yanlin.2016@phdis.smu.edu.sg

Abstract. Return-oriented programming (ROP) and jump-oriented programming (JOP) are two most common control-flow hijacking attacks. Existing defenses, such as address space layout randomization (ASLR) and control flow integrity (CFI) either are bypassed by information leakage or result in high runtime overhead. In this paper, we propose *FRProtector*, an effective way to mitigate these two control-flow hijacking attacks. *FRProtector* shuffles the functions of a given program and ensures each function is executed from the entry block by comparing the unique label for it at *ret* and indirect *jmp*. The unique label is generated by XORing the stack frame with return address instead of with a random value and it is saved in a register rather than on the stack. We implement *FRProtector* on LLVM 3.9 and perform extensive experiments to show *FRProtector* only adds on average 2% runtime overhead and 2.2% space overhead on SPEC CPU2006 benchmark programs. Our security analysis on RIPE benchmark confirms that *FRProtector* is effective in defending control-flow hijacking attacks.

Keywords: Control flow hijacking · Control flow protection
Function-level randomization · Code reuse attack

1 Introduction

Control-flow hijacking [1] is one of the most common attack method today, which modifies the target of control flow transfer instruction (e.g., indirect jump, function return instruction) to the code carefully crafted by the attacker. The traditional control-flow hijacking [1], code injection attack, redirects the control flow to the code snippet (shellcode) which is injected by the attacker through memory corruption vulnerabilities. This attack has been defeated by data execution prevention (DEP) [2]. Today, attackers are widely using code reuse attacks

© ICST Institute for Computer Sciences, Social Informatics and Telecommunications Engineering 2018
X. Lin et al. (Eds.): SecureComm 2017, LNICST 238, pp. 659–672, 2018.
https://doi.org/10.1007/978-3-319-78813-5_34

(CRA) [3,4], which re-construct code snippets (gadgets) that already exists in code segments to achieve the malicious purpose.

To counter control-flow hijacking, several hardening techniques have been widely adopted, including stack guard (GS) [5], address space layout randomization (ASLR) [6] and control flow integrity (CFI) [7–11]. Stack guard inserts an unpredictable number between return address and local variables. This unpredictable number is obtained by XORing a random value with the stack frame value. ASLR increases the entropy of the process by randomizing the base address of the memory segment. CFI constructs the control flow graph (CFG) of the program statically and forces the program to comply with the rules of the CFG. It marks the valid targets of indirect control flow transfers with unique labels. Before each transfer instruction of the program, CFI checks whether the label of the destination address is the same as expected.

However, the first two can be bypassed by BlindROP [12] or information disclosure [13], and the last one usually brings expensive runtime overhead. Moreover, having an accuracy static analysis is known to be hard. In this paper, we present *FRProtector*, a more effective way to counter control-flow hijacking. The purpose of *FRProtector* is to make it hard for attackers to guess the expected code location and to ensure each function is executed from the entry block. *FRProtector* first reorders the locations of functions. But this function-level randomization is a mitigating method that can not provide deterministic defense. Sometimes, it can be bypassed by well-structured information disclosure. In order to obtain better security, for each function, a unique label is generated by XORing the stack frame pointer with the return address. Then, *FRProtector* adds runtime checks into the program to check whether the label generated at the ret and indirect jump instruction is the same one.

FRProtector is similar to GS in some respects, but it achieves better security. First, *FRProtector* can effectively detect attacks that do not leverage stack buffer overflow to overwrite the return address as it uses return address to generate the label, while GS cannot defend this kind of attack. In addition, *FRProtector* stores the label in the register rather than storing it onto the stack, which increases the difficulty for the attacker to obtain it. Finally, *FRProtector* also checks the label before indirect jump instructions to defend control-flow hijacking attacks that modify the registers used in indirect jump instructions.

Although the idea sounds simple, the key to a successful defense that can gain acceptance by developers is a low runtime overhead in the resulting binary executable. To achieve this goal, we have implemented *FRProtector* on LLVM 3.9. The extensive experiments show that *FRProtector* results in a small runtime overhead of 2% and space overhead of 2.2% on average. *FRProtector* is effective as it prevents all attacks that overwrite the return address in the RIPE benchmark [14].

In summary, this paper makes the following contributions:

1. We propose *FRProtector*, an effective control-flow hijacking defense that reorders the locations of functions and ensures a function is executed from

the entry block by comparing the unique label for it at ret and indirect jump instruction.

2. We perform extensive experiments to show *FRProtector* results in low runtime and space overhead.

3. We compare *FRProtector* with CFI and GS. *FRProtector* achieves similar security compared to CFI. While comparing with GS, *FRProtector* provides better security.

The paper is organized as follows. Section 2 introduces the background of control-flow hijacking attack and the thread model. Section 3 presents the *FRProtector*. Section 4 describes the implementation of our solution on LLVM. We demonstrate the efficiency of *FRProtector* with extensive performance evaluations and present the security analysis in Sect. 5. Section 6 compares *FRProtector* with CFI and Stack Guard. Related work and conclusion are presented in Sects. 7 and 8.

2   Background

In this section, we start with a brief summary of control-flow hijacking and then define our threat model.

2.1   Control Flow Hijacking

Control flow hijacking is a kind of memory corruption attack. The attacker redirects the program's code pointer to the location of the shellcode or gadgets. Shellcode is used for the code injection attack, while gadgets for CRA.

Code Injection Attack. The attacker can inject malicious code into the memory, and then redirect the control flow to the memory address of malicious code through memory vulnerabilities. For example, an attacker controls the area near the overflow area through a stack overflow vulnerability, and injects malicious code into this area, then modifies the return address to the first instruction of the malicious code. Now, it can be defeated by Data Execution Prevention (DEP).

Code Reuse Attack. Code Reuse Attacks (CRA) use code in the program or libraries to construct code snippets (called gadgets), each of which has a specific feature (e.g., writing a specified value to a fixed register). A gadget is a small sequence of binary code that ends in an indirect instruction. By chaining different functional gadgets, an attacker can construct a code execution sequence that implements the same functionality as malicious code. For example, by constructing the appropriate parameters, the return-into-libc attack, a kind of CRA, redirects the control flow to the standard libraries to call a library function. At this stage the most popular code reuse attacks are Return-Oriented Programming (ROP) [3] and Jump-Oriented Programming (JOP) [4].

ROP is an exploit technique that has evolved from stack-based buffer overflows. In ROP exploits, gadgets end in ret instructions. By carefully crafting a sequence of addresses on the software stack, an attacker can manipulate the ret instruction to jump to arbitrary addresses that corresponding to the beginning of gadgets. ROP has proved to be Turing complete. JOP is similar as ROP, excepting that JOP uses the indirect jump instructions to modify the program's control flow.

To complete the CRA, one of the challenges is to identify the exact address of each gadget in the memory space. ASLR makes the attacker harder to get these accurate addresses by randomizing the base address of the target program. But information disclosure [13] or brute force can assist the attacker to find the accurate address. For instance, Just-In-Time Code Reuse [15] uses memory disclosure to bypass ASLR, and Blind-ROP [12] uses brute force.

2.2   Threat Model

The proposed defense, *FRProtector*, is aimed to protect a vulnerable application against control-flow hijacking attacks, including ROP and JOP attacks. The left of Fig. 1 shows an example of ROP attack. Function 1 has the input instruction, and the attacker uses it to push the payload into the stack. Function 2 has an overflow vulnerability, in which the attacker can modify the return address to the payload. So, if Function 1 is called before Function 2, the attacker will hijack the control flow successfully. An example of modifying the stack frame to construct CRA is shown in the right of Fig. 1. Function 3 is similar to Function 1. Function 4 has a vulnerability which modifies the register of stack frame to the payload. So, when Function 4 is called, the control flow will be transferred to the address where the payload pointing to.

It seems that Stack Guard (GS) can counter both attacks mentioned above. But if the attacker just overwrites the return address without the overflow vulnerability, GS cannot defend it. Moreover, such as $func5$ in Fig. 1, attackers can modify the registers that are used in indirect jump instructions to point to the location where the control flow will be transferred to. It is out of the range that GS can protect. These four kinds of exploitations need to be considered. We can divide them into three categories.

- The return address is redirected to the gadget address. It can be achieved by stack buffer overflow or by modifying the return address directly.
- The stack frame is modified to the address where the payload (gadgets chain) located in.
- The register used in the indirect jump instruction is modified to the gadget address.

On the other hand, we assume attackers cannot modify the code segment, because the corresponding pages are marked read-executable and not writable. This assumption ensures the integrity of the original program code instrumented at compile time. Meanwhile, the attacker cannot examine the memory dump of the running process and is unaware of how exactly the code is randomized. Our assumptions are consistent with prior work in this area.

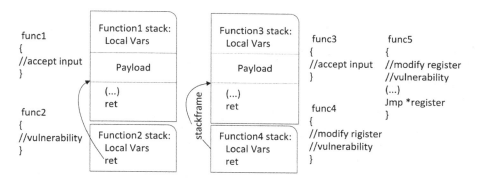

Fig. 1. Control-flow hijacking

3   FRProtector Design

To show how *FRProtector* achieves its objects in defending against control-flow hijacking attacks, we present our design of *FRProtector*, an effective way to detect the anomaly of control flow. In this section, we will begin with the design overview, and then present its detailed design.

3.1   Design Overview

We design *FRProtector* to support multiple security mechanisms to defend against control-flow hijacking attacks. The first one is function-level randomization. Under this mechanism, *FRProtector* reorders the locations of functions to increase the entropy of the program code segment in memory. *FRProtector* also supports control flow transfer protection. Randomization is a mitigating method which can be bypassed by some well-structured information disclosure, so we provide control flow transfer protection for deterministic defense. Under such mechanism, *FRProtector* marks each function with a unique label generated by XORing the stack frame pointer with the return address. Before the control flow transfer instruction (*ret* and indirect *jmp*) is executed, the program calculates the unique label with the same method, and then checking whether the two label is same. The overhead is lower if we compare the return address and the stack frame respectively. But taking into account the information disclosure, if the attacker gets the value of stored return address or stack frame in the register, then he can carefully build comparison labels to bypass the defense. But with the XOR method, it is very challenging that an attacker needs to change the value of the stack frame and the return address at the same time to meet the label which is calculated in the beginning of the function.

3.2   Function-Level Randomization

Today, most of the operating systems use ASLR to increase the difficulty of attackers to guess the layout of memory space. ASLR changes the base address of the memory segment, making it difficult for an attacker to write the exploits directly with the results of static analysis. However, with the information disclosure, the attacker can bypass the ASLR through a memory address leakage. Function-level randomization achieves a more fine-grained code space layout randomization granularity, making the attacker to get the entire memory layout from memory leakage difficult. Thus, it mitigates the possibility of constructing a CRA with the slightest disclosure of information and static analysis.

Function-level randomization is mainly to reorder the location of functions. In an executable file, the code is stored in the code segment. When executing the file, the entire contents of a segment are stored in the (virtual) memory space. With ASLR, the offset of the code segment is different for every execution, but the relative locations of functions in memory do not change at all. With the function-level randomization, the relative orders of the functions will be disrupted, and function-level randomization may add some irrelevant instructions between functions such as NOP, which makes the entropy of the program to be further increased. Figure 2 shows an example of function layout in memory after function-level randomization. Therefore, with the help of function-level randomization, the gadget location obtained in the static analysis is no longer applicable. Attackers need to use other means (such as a lot of information disclosure) to get the gadgets.

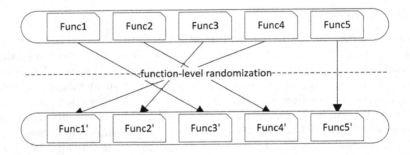

Fig. 2. Function-level randomization

There is a trade-off between security and performance when choosing at what time to do function randomization – reordering functions at loading time gives better security in that every execution of the program results in a different process memory image, but also adds more runtime overhead and bigger memory usage. *FRProtector* chooses to shuffle functions at compile time as we do not only depend on function randomization to defend against control-flow hijacking attack.

3.3   Protection of Control Flow Transfer

Now researchers mainly use CFI to prevent control flow hijacking. But CFI has been cautious about the problem of identification inaccuracy, compatibility and overhead. *FRProtector* does not need to construct the CFG of a given program and it does not involve the correlation between functions, so that there is no compatibility problem between protected function and unprotected function.

In order to protect the control flow, *FRProtector* uses two mechanisms. First, in many cases, the attacker will hijack the control flow by modifying the return address, so the first mechanism is to detect whether the return address is changed. On the other hand, since the attacker may use other methods to hijack the control flow such as modifying the destination of indirect jump, *FRProtector* detects whether a function's internal execution flow is from the starting point of the function to the control flow transfer instruction.

Internal Control Flow Validation. As we know, a function consists of many basic blocks. There is a control flow transfer instruction at the end of each basic block. A function is executed from the entry block, and then the control flow is transferred to other basic blocks or functions. The mechanism for the internal control flow validation is to detect whether the control flow of the function is performed from the entry block. Therefore, we insert a random value that uniquely identifies the function at the entry block of the function, and check whether the re-calculated random value at *ret* and indirect *jmp* equals to the random value we inserted.

The random value is generated by XORing the stack frame pointer with the value of the return address rather than with a random value that is implemented in Stack Canaries [5]. This is because the control flow between functions is affected by the return address, and the return address can be used as a factor to see if the control flow is hijacked by modifying the return address.

Figure 3 shows the example that how function's internal control flow is protected. First, when Function 2 is called, *FRProtector* gets the value of the stack frame pointer and moves it into the register, and then XORs it with the value of the return address at the entry block of Function 2. Then it fetches and stores the value of the return address in another register and XORs it with the value of the stack frame before *ret*. Finally, *FRProtector* verifies whether the two register value are consistent. If true, the control flow will execute the *ret*, else the check_fail function will be executed. The detection point of this mechanism is before *ret* and indirect *jmp*, so it can detect both ROP and JOP.

4   Implementation

We have implemented *FRProtector* on top of the LLVM 3.9.1 compiler infrastructure [16]. *FRProtector* works on unmodified programs and supports Linux in 32-bit modes.

4.1   Function-Level Randomization

We implement the function-level randomization for *FRProtector* as an LLVM pass. The LLVM pass operates on the LLVM Intermediate Representation (IR),

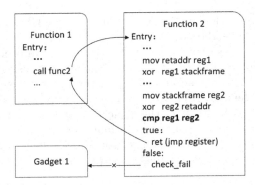

Fig. 3. Function's internal control flow detection

which is a low-level strongly-typed language-independent program representation. Although if we disrupt the location of the basic block the IR layer, the binary program will not change with the back-end compiler optimization. But the disruption of the location of the function will not be affected.

The function *CloneFunction* provided by LLVM can copy the information of a function into another function. Therefore, we randomize the order of the functions by copying them into other functions, deleting the original ones and then re-creating the new ones. We use a replacement algorithm to reorder the functions. For every function, a random number is created to decide the function that exchanges to.

This kind of randomization mechanism can be used to cloud environment. Multi-version of the randomization can make the applications have different memory layouts between offline version and the server side version. Therefore, it is harder for attackers to guess the addresses of gadgets.

4.2   Control Flow Transfer Protection

For control flow transfer protection, we use functions *llvm.returnaddress* and *llvm.frameaddress* to get the return address and the value of the stack frame pointer respectively. When using llvm.address instructions twice in ONE basic block, llvm's back-end always reuses the first address value that the llvm.address has generated instead of getting the value from the stack twice. So in the implementation of this mechanism, we make a constant true transfer after retrieving the value generated by XORing the return address with the stack frame.

For example, the verify_password function has an unrestricted *strcpy* function, which can cause a buffer overflow to hijack control flow of the program. This function with *FRProtector* shown in Fig. 4 adds a check operation to see whether the XOR value is consistent with the value calculated at the beginning of the function before the return instruction. As the buffer overflow can modify the return address, so with our check at the end of the basic block the process will find errors and jump to *exit()* to quit execution for avoiding further losses.

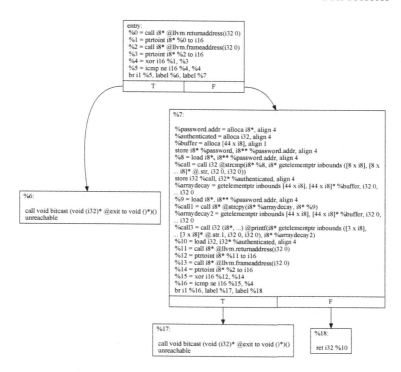

Fig. 4. verify_password function with FRProtector

5   Evaluation

In this section, we perform a number of experiments to demonstrate the effectiveness and efficiency of *FRProtector*. We experimentally show that *FRProtector* can effectively prevent all attacks that overwrite the return address in the RIPE benchmark. We evaluate the efficiency of *FRProtector* on SPEC CPU2006, and find average runtime overhead and space overhead are about 2% and 2.2% respectively.

All experiments were performed on a desktop computer with i7-4770 CPU running the x86 version of Ubuntu 16.04.

5.1   Effectiveness on the RIPE Benchmark

Runtime Intrusion Prevention Evaluator (RIPE) [14] is a benchmark test that detects all buffer overflow attacks. The goals of these attacks are to create files, Returntolibc and ROP. We find that there are 10 attacks which overwrites the ret instruction can be successfully launched with ASLR. When we use *FRProtector*, we find that all these 10 attacks are not available. So, we can effectively prevent the attack which overwrites the return address.

According to the design of *FRProtector*, the ret and indirect jump are both protected. So, if the attacker hopes to modify the destination address of the ret or indirect jump instruction in the middle of a function, *FRProtector* can detect it successfully.

5.2 Efficiency on SPEC CPU2006 Benchmarks

In this section, we evaluate the space overhead and the runtime overhead of StackGuard (*GS*) and *FRProtector*. We report numbers on SPEC CPU2006 benchmarks written in C and C++.

Space Overhead. Figure 5(a) shows the space overhead of our experiments with the benchmark programs. As shown, *GS* and *FRProtector* have nearly the same space overhead for most programs, it's for two reasons. First, both *GS* and *FRProtector* only insert several (about 4) instructions in a function, so the variation of the program is hairlike. Second, *FRProtector* protects more function than *GS*, but *GS* needs a function to create the random number. So, wane and wax, the space required is similar. The average space overhead of *FRProtector* is about 2.2%. For most programs, the space overhead experienced by *FRProtector* can be ignored. But some programs, such as *astar* and *omnetpp*, the space overhead is more than 6%. There are two reasons. First, we add instructions in every function, so the number of functions is an important factor. On the other hand, the checking instruction is inserted before every ret and indirect jump instruction, so the number of the transfer instructions also affects the space overhead.

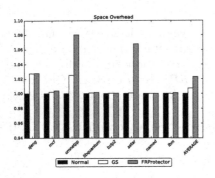

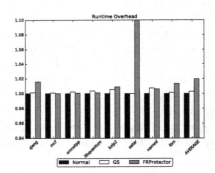

(a) Space overhead of *FRProtector*   (b) Runtime performance of *FRProtector*

Fig. 5.

Runtime Overhead. The runtime overhead of *FRProtector* is shown in Fig. 5(b). Results show that the average runtime overhead is about 2%. In [17], we know that the average performance overhead should be less than 5% when the new method hopes to be used in industry. So, *FRProtector* could be adapted to industry requirements. *Astar* experiences much higher runtime overhead than other programs. We find this is due to the large number of short basic blocks it has makes the number of checking instructions increase. Meanwhile, the two registers *FRProtector* used to save the XOR value may reduce the number of registers available in a function. However, in the 64-bit program, the number of registers is increased, so the runtime overhead may be reduced.

Compared with *GS*, the runtime and space overhead of *FRProtector* only increased by about 1%. But with the disassembly file of the program, we find that *GS* protects less functions than *FRProtector*. It's due to *GS* is designed to protect functions that may have a stack vulnerability, while *FRProtector* hopes to check every function. *FRProtector* is less expensive than *GS* when adding protection to the same number of functions as *FRProtector* doesn't need to generate a random number and adds the similar number of instructions.

6   Discussion

In this section, we first compare *FRProtector* with CFI and Stack Guard, and then discuss the compatibility and limitations of *FRProtector*.

6.1   Comparison with CFI

FRProtector can be seen as one CFI method by enforcing policies for indirect *jmp* and *ret* instructions. For indirect *jmp*, *FRProtector* ensures the target of indirect jumps can be the entry of any functions by validating the control flow of a function must start from the entry block. The coarse-grained CFI has the same policy too. For *ret*, *FRProtector* ensures it must return to the corresponding caller by checking whether the target of a *ret* is overwritten. Therefore, *FRProtector* can achieve similar security compared with existing CFI approaches. Moreover, *FRProtector* does not need to analyze the source code or binary of a given program statically to compute the CFG.

6.2   Comparison with Stack Guard

Both *FRProtector* and stack guard (GS) introduce a random number. However, the role and the generation of the random number are different. Stack guard get the value by XORing a random number with the stack pointer, then the value is put between the return address and local variables in stack to detect whether the local variables' overflow overwrites the return address. The random number in *FRProtector* is the value generated by XORing the return address and the stack frame, then storing it in the register only. It can detect any attacks which change the return address, not just overflow. In addition, *FRProtector* also checks whether a function is executed from the entry basic block. GS just protects functions that may have buffer overflow vulnerabilities, while the protection is provided to all functions by default by *FRProtector*. *FRProtector* stores the label in the register to increase the difficulty for the attacker to find it instead of storing it onto the stack. Finally, *FRProtector* also checks the label before indirect jump instructions to defend control-flow hijacking attacks that modify the registers used in indirect jump instructions.

6.3 Compatibility and Limitations

FRProtector is written on the IR layer of LLVM, and has nothing to do with source code. So it is source-level compatibility. It means that the problems caused by binary level protection such as function pointer errors do not occur in *FRProtector*. Since the function is the base unit for *FRProtector* in which *FRProtector* only checks whether the control flow is transferred from the first block, so it can be compatible with legacy libraries, functions and programs that do not enforce *FRProtector*.

The main limitation of *FRProtector* is it cannot defend against the control-flow hijacking that does not use the return or indirect jump instructions. For example, Counterfeit Object-Oriented Programming (COOP) [18] and Call Oriented Programming (COP) [19,20] use virtual functions and function calls respectively to achieve control flow hijacking. We leave it our future work – a more complete mechanism to defend against control flow hijacking.

7 Related Work

7.1 Function-Level Randomization

We implement function-level randomization in LLVM to mitigate the information disclosure and change the function's address for randomizing the return address. There are several techniques which have implemented function-level randomization. Marlin [21] is a bash shell that can randomize the target executable before launching it. It shuffles the functions in the executable code. Bin_FR [22] randomizes the binary directly, which adds random padding between functions and randomizes the order of functions. The advantage of Bin_FR is that it does not rely on the source code.

7.2 Compiler Techniques Counter Control Flow Hijacking

Lots of compiler techniques have been published to defend control-flow hijacking, especially to defend ROP. StackGuard [5] is an oldest method to prevent buffer overflow attacks by inserting a canary (random number) between the return address and local variables. G-free [23] is a compiler-based approach against ROP which uses the return address or indirect call/jump. Return-less [24] is a technique that aims to defend return-oriented rootkits (RORs). It replaces the return address in a stack frame into a return index and disallows a ROP to use it. It also proposes register allocation and peephole optimization to prevent legitimate instructions that happen to contain return opcode from being misused.

The stack pivot is an essential component in most ROP by modifying a stack pointer to point to the payload. PBlocker [25] is a technique which asserts the sanity of stack pointer whenever the stack pointer is modified to denial of stack pivot. But the stack pivot check can be bypassed by an attack mentioned in [26].

8   Conclusion

In this paper, we present *FRProtector*, a novel defense against control-flow hijacking. *FRProtector* implements the function-level randomization to increase the difficulty of the attacker to guess the code layout and also to change the return address of functions. On the other hand, *FRProtector* implements the control flow transfer protection by checking whether the address of transfer instruction has been modified, which can effectively protect the control flow of the program. *FRProtector* has implemented in LLVM. We evaluate *FRProtector* on SPEC CPU2006 and show that the average runtime overhead is 2% and the space overhead is 2.2% on average.

Acknowledgment. Supported by the National Natural Science Foundation of China (61373168, U1636107), and Doctoral Fund of Ministry of Education of China (20120141110002).

References

1. Heelan, S.: Automatic Generation of Control Flow Hijacking Exploits for Software Vulnerabilities (2009)
2. Andersen, S., Abella, V.: Data execution prevention. changes to functionality in microsoft windows XP service pack 2, part 3: memory protection technologies (2004)
3. Shacham, H.: The geometry of innocent flesh on the bone: return-into-libc without function calls (on the x86). In: ACM Conference on Computer and Communications Security, CCS 2007, Alexandria, Virginia, USA, pp. 552–561, October 2007
4. Bletsch, T., Jiang, X., Freeh, V.W., Liang, Z.: Jump-oriented programming: a new class of code-reuse attack. In: ACM Symposium on Information, Computer and Communications Security, pp. 30–40 (2011)
5. Cowan, C., Pu, C., Maier, D., Hintony, H., Walpole, J., Bakke, P., Beattie, S., Grier, A., Wagle, P., Zhang, Q.: StackGuard: automatic adaptive detection and prevention of buffer-overflow attacks. In: Conference on Usenix Security Symposium, p. 5 (1998)
6. PaX Team: Pax address space layout randomization (ASLR) (2003)
7. Abadi, M., Budiu, M., Erlingsson, Ú., Ligatti, J.: Control-flow integrity. In: ACM Conference on Computer and Communications Security, pp. 340–353 (2005)
8. Abadi, M., Budiu, M., Erlingsson, Ú., Ligatti, J.: Control-flow integrity principles, implementations, and applications. ACM Trans. Inf. Syst. Secur. (TISSEC) **13**(1), 4 (2009)
9. Zhang, M., Sekar, R.: Control flow integrity for cots binaries. In: Usenix Security, vol. 13 (2013)

10. Zhang, C., Wei, T., Chen, Z., Duan, L., Szekeres, L., McCamant, S., Song, D., Zou, W.: Practical control flow integrity and randomization for binary executables. In: 2013 IEEE Symposium on Security and Privacy (SP), pp. 559–573. IEEE (2013)

11. Mohan, V., Larsen, P., Brunthaler, S., Hamlen, K.W., Franz, M.: Opaque control-flow integrity. In: NDSS Symposium (2015)

12. Bittau, A., Belay, A., Mashtizadeh, A., Mazieres, D.: Hacking blind. In: IEEE Symposium on Security and Privacy, pp. 227–242 (2014)

13. Strackx, R., Younan, Y., Philippaerts, P., Piessens, F., Lachmund, S., Walter, T.: Breaking the memory secrecy assumption. In: European Workshop on System Security, Eurosec 2009, Nuremburg, Germany, pp. 1–8, March 2009

14. Wilander, J., Nikiforakis, N., Younan, Y., Kamkar, M., Joosen, W.: RIPE: runtime intrusion prevention evaluator. In: Twenty-Seventh Computer Security Applications Conference, ACSAC 2011, Orlando, Fl, USA, 5–9 December, pp. 41–50 (2011)

15. Snow, K.Z., Monrose, F., Davi, L., Dmitrienko, A.: Just-in-time code reuse: on the effectiveness of fine-grained address space layout randomization. In: Security and Privacy, pp. 574–588 (2013)

16. The LLVM compiler infrastructure. http://llvm.org/

17. Szekeres, L., Payer, M., Wei, T., Song, D.: SoK: eternal war in memory. In: IEEE Symposium on Security and Privacy, pp. 48–62 (2013)

18. Damm, C.H., Hansen, K.M., Thomsen, M.: Tool support for cooperative object-oriented design: gesture based modelling on an electronic whiteboard. In: Proceedings of the SIGCHI Conference on Human Factors in Computing Systems, pp. 518–525. ACM (2000)

19. Göktas, E., Athanasopoulos, E., Bos, H., Portokalidis, G.: Out of control: overcoming control-flow integrity. In: IEEE Symposium on Security and Privacy, pp. 575–589 (2014)

20. Sadeghi, A., Niksefat, S., Rostamipour, M.: Pure-call oriented programming (PCOP) chaining the gadgets using call instructions. J. Comput. Virol. Hacking Technol. 14, 1–18 (2017)

21. Gupta, A., Habibi, J., Kirkpatrick, M.S., Bertino, E.: Marlin: mitigating code reuse attacks using code randomization. IEEE Trans. Dependable Secur. Comput. 12(3), 1 (2015)

22. Fu, J., Zhang, X., Lin, Y.: Code reuse attack mitigation based on function randomization without symbol table. In: Trustcom, pp. 394–401 (2016)

23. Onarlioglu, K., Bilge, L., Lanzi, A., Balzarotti, D., Kirda, E.: G-free: defeating return-oriented programming through gadget-less binaries. In: Computer Security Applications Conference, pp. 49–58 (2010)

24. Li, J., Wang, Z., Jiang, X., Grace, M., Bahram, S.: Defeating return-oriented rootkits with "return-less" kernels, pp. 195–208 (2010)

25. Prakash, A., Yin, H.: Defeating ROP through denial of stack pivot. In: Computer Security Applications Conference, pp. 111–120 (2015)

26. Yan, F., Huang, F., Zhao, L., Peng, H., Wang, Q.: Baseline is fragile: on the effectiveness of stack pivot defense. In: IEEE International Conference on Parallel and Distributed Systems, pp. 406–413 (2016)

VaultIME: Regaining User Control for Password Managers Through Auto-Correction

Le Guan[1]([✉])(iD), Sadegh Farhang[1], Yu Pu[1], Pinyao Guo[1], Jens Grossklags[2], and Peng Liu[1]

[1] Pennsylvania State University, State College, PA, USA
{lug14,farhang,yxp134,pug132,pliu}@ist.psu.edu
[2] Technical University of Munich, Munich, Germany
jens.grossklags@in.tum.de

Abstract. Users are often educated to follow different forms of advice from security experts. For example, using a password manager is considered an effective way to maintain a unique and strong password for every important website. However, user surveys reveal that most users are not willing to adopt this tool. They feel uncomfortable or even threatened, when they grant password managers the privilege to automate access to their digital accounts. Likewise, they are worried that individuals close to them may be able to access important websites by using the password manager stealthily.

We propose VaultIME to nudge more users towards the adoption of password managers by offering them a tangible benefit with minimal interference with their current usage practices. Instead of "auto-filling" password fields, we propose a new mechanism to "auto-correct" passwords in the presence of minor typos. VaultIME innovates by integrating the functionality of a password manager into an input method editor. Specifically, running as an app on mobile phones, VaultIME remembers user passwords on a per-app basis, and corrects mistyped passwords within a typo-tolerant set. We show that VaultIME achieves high levels of usability *and* security. With respect to usability, VaultIME is able to correct as many as 47.8% of password typos in a real-world password typing dataset. Regarding security, simulated attacks reveal that the security loss brought by VaultIME against a brute-force attacker is at most 0.43%.

Keywords: Password manager · Auto-correction · IME
Usable security

1 Introduction

To keep their digital accounts safe, Internet users are advised to adopt strong passwords that are hard to crack and guess [14]. However, long and random pass-

---

L. Guan—The authors' full manuscript can be found at http://guanleustc.github.io/research/vaultime.

© ICST Institute for Computer Sciences, Social Informatics and Telecommunications Engineering 2018
X. Lin et al. (Eds.): SecureComm 2017, LNICST 238, pp. 673–686, 2018.
https://doi.org/10.1007/978-3-319-78813-5_35

words are also difficult for users to remember [11]. Further, the sizable number of online accounts users need to manage has introduced an additional burden [5]. Using a *password manager* (e.g., 1password, lastpass and keepassdroid), which saves user credentials into a database, is a highly recommended approach by security experts. Contents in the credential database are encrypted for data protection, where the encryption/decryption key is generated from a master password only known to the user [5].

Unfortunately, adoption of password managers is behind expectations despite the benefits apparent to security experts: (1) enhancing convenience by "auto-filling" password fields on behalf of the user [14], and (2) improving security by allowing for long and complex passwords. In addition, a password manager would reduce the perceived need for insecure practices such as storing passwords in clear-text as a memory help etc. Nevertheless, surveys indicate adoption figures as low as 6% [2] and at most as high as 21% [4], which leave a lot to be desired. Further, since password manager adopters are generally more security-savvy [4], this leaves behind those users who would most benefit from the technology.

Prior survey research has shown a split between the perceptions of adopters of password managers and those that hesitate [4]. While adopters echo the security benefits lauded by experts, 78% of non-adopters perceive "some" or "a lot" of individual risk from using a password manager [4]. Some factors for hesitation are quite reasonable, and hard to address. For example, some people simply do not trust providers of password managers [19], and software vulnerabilities may lead to exposure of all user passwords to hackers [6].

Other impeding factors are more amendable to solution approaches. Specifically, the threat of a lost phone or merely unmonitored access to the phone may be perceived quite disconcerting if high value data and important services such as social networking and online banking are left more vulnerable due to the stored credentials in a password manager. In fact, otherwise trusted individuals such as family members are often the cause of such invasions [18]. According to a Javelin Research study, in 2014, there were 550,000 reports of identity theft caused by someone the victim knew [7]. Taking advantage of the bond of trust, individuals are able to more easily access family members' digital accounts and use the stolen identities to gain financial benefits [7,12,18]. Further, trust is especially impeded when the provider stores the password file on the cloud [19], rather than on the user's machine. In addition, empirical work shows that people prefer a high *degree of control* when completing form-fields with personal information over having the same done by auto-fill [10]; we anticipate that a similar finding could be made in the highly related context of passwords.

With our work, we want to provide a stepping stone to nudge people towards adopting a password manager by providing an easy-to-understand benefit, while limiting interference with their habituated usage practices. Further, we target adoption hesitation due to the aforementioned reasons by allowing for a higher degree of control by the user.

Concretely, we propose a mechanism to *auto-correct* passwords in the presence of minor typo errors by utilizing a client-side password vault. While the user is still required to input a "near correct" password to activate the auto-correction feature, the approach allows users to apply longer and less trivial passwords. At the same time, user frustration can be substantially reduced by a tangible reduction of failed attempts. In this sense, our solution provides a potentially sensible middle-ground for the adoption of password managers by leaving full control over authentication in the hands of the user, and reducing the threat of stolen data when a mobile device is lost or individuals with access to the device betray the trust of the user.

While the first systematic work of password auto-correction appears in [3], it is implemented on the server-side with the purpose of increasing the password acceptance rate. The authors found that almost 10% of failed login attempts are caused by simple, easily correctable typos that should otherwise be accepted. Following this observation, the authors proposed an auto-correction framework that can be integrated into existing password-based authentication systems on the server-side. In particular, a set of correctors[1] are first defined, and a received password is adjusted by each of the correctors to generate a set of candidate passwords. The login attempt is granted provided that at least one of the candidate passwords results in a password hash value that matches the one stored on the authentication server. When it comes to the security of the typo-tolerant authentication scheme, the authors show that it does not downgrade the security of user passwords by offering a formal proof of a free correction theorem.

Different from previous server-side auto-correction, we aim to provide added convenience of password typing on the client-side to further enhance user control. We propose VaultIME, a mobile-centric password manager granting users control of password input. VaultIME integrates the functionality of a password manager into an *Input Method Editor (IME)*, which is an app that displays a software keyboard and enables users to enter text. In particular, VaultIME remembers a user password on a per-app basis. If a password input interface is detected, the auto-correction feature is activated, which replaces a mistyped password (within an acceptable set) with the correct one.

The design goals of the new password manager are as follows. First, to mean-ingfully reduce user frustration, the auto-correction mechanism should cover a wide range of mistypes. Second, our mechanism should not downgrade pass-word security even if an attacker has access to the phone and could perform a brute-force attack to stored passwords. To achieve the first goal, we conducted a mobile-centric password typing analysis. Based on it, we developed a new set of password correctors, which differ from the previous work [3] and cover 26.3% more typos. To achieve the second goal, we designed VaultIME to be compatible with the free auto-correction theory of [3], which states that with a certain fil-ter policy, auto-correction introduces *zero* security loss. To measure the security loss, we ran simulation attacks to our auto-correction scheme. In the worst case, we show that the security loss is 0.43%, assuming that a brute-force attacker has 10 tries. When configured with the filter complying with the free auto-correction theory, VaultIME introduces *zero* security loss as expected. We have developed

---

[1] For example, switching caps status, removing the last character, etc.

a proof-of-concept prototype of VaultIME. With reasonable optimization, the prototype results in no user-perceivable delay when auto-correcting passwords. However, interface features could be added to increase awareness of the benefits of auto-correction.

Contributions. Our work provides the following key contributions:

1. We propose a design for password managers addressing user concerns substantiated in related work. Without losing control to the login process, our design ameliorates users' concerns for using password manager in a "too open" way and maintains users' habituated login process.
2. To cover a maximum range of typos, while maintaining tight control over security, we analyze the nature of typos on a mobile platform in a systematic way. Based on the analysis results, we develop a new set of correctors, and run simulation attacks to measure the security loss introduced by VaultIME.
3. We implement a prototype of VaultIME as a normal Android IME app. Therefore, VaultIME can be instantly deployed on existing mobile platforms.

2   Background

This section explains the concept and design of the input method framework in the Android mobile OS as well as password managers.

Input Method Editor. Since API level 3.0, Android, the most popular mobile operating system, provides an extensible input-method framework. By extending the `InputMethodService` class, developers are able to implement a customized soft keyboard for better experience and capabilities. Besides, extending the `KeyboardView` class allows for the rendering of a personalized keyboard layout. These classes are packaged together to compose an *Input Method Editor (IME)* which provides user control to enable users to enter text.

When a user inputs text for an app, the default IME pops up. The framework allows an IME to completely control user input, including reading current input, and making arbitrary modifications. These functions are supported by operating on an `InputConnection` class. In particular, method `getTextBeforeCursor` and `getTextAfterCursor` can be invoked to read input before and after the current cursor, while an app ultimately receives an input string determined by the `commitText` methods.

Password Managers. Memorizing passwords has become a significant challenge for users. Although difficult to crack by attackers, strong passwords that are sufficiently long and random are also hard for users to remember [11].

Using a password manager is one of the most recommended approaches that can free users from the duty of memorizing lots of complex passwords. Mainly developed as a plug-in for web browsers, or as stand-alone web/smartphone applications, password managers save user credentials into a database, and later automatically auto-complete requests for the credentials on behalf of users [14].

In order to ensure security of the credential database, a user controls access to the password manager database via a master password. Specifically, contents in a credential database are typically encrypted for data protection, where the encryption/decryption key is generated from a master password [5].

3   Server Side Typo-Tolerant Checking Scheme

To allow for a direct comparison, our work follows the formalization of a password authentication system proposed in [3], and also applies the same model for evaluating security loss in the presence of a brute-force attacker. To begin with, we review some of the important concepts and notations.

3.1   System Model

Checking Passwords. Two phases are involved in a password authentication process. In the registration phase, a user registers his password, e.g., w, with the server, and the server stores another string, s, derived from a hash function mixing a random salt value and w. In the checking phase, a user submits a password, $\tilde{w}$, to the authentication server, and the server verifies the request by calculating on $\tilde{w}$ and the stored value s. The request is granted only if it returns true. In an *exact checker* (ExChk), the checker returns true only if the typed password $\tilde{w}$ is exactly equal to w, i.e., $\tilde{w} = w$.

Typo-tolerant Scheme. Contrary to an exact checker ExChk, a typo-tolerant scheme runs a *relaxed checker*, which may return a true value for multiple strings other than w. When a user submits $\tilde{w}$, the authentication algorithm, instead of only examining $\tilde{w}$, examines a set of strings neighboring $\tilde{w}$. This set is represented by a ball of $\tilde{w}$ denoted by $B(\tilde{w})$. If any element in the ball passes the exact checker ExChk, $\tilde{w}$ is accepted. Formally, the ball is derived by applying a set of correctors (or transformation functions) $\mathbf{C} = \{f_0, f_1, .., f_c\}$ to $\tilde{w}$.

Brute-force Attacker and Security Loss. Before formalizing a brute-force attacker, we first model the password distribution and typo distribution. The theoretical analysis of security loss introduced by a brute-force attacker against a relaxed checker assumes an attacker with exact knowledge of these distributions.

We associate a distribution p to a set of all possible passwords. Therefore, $p(w)$ is the probability that a user selects a string w as a password. A user with password w may type a password $\tilde{w}$ upon authentication. The probability of this event is represented by $\tau_w(\tilde{w})$. If $w \neq \tilde{w}$, a typo occurred. Furthermore, we say $\tilde{w}$ is a neighbor of w if $\tau_w(\tilde{w}) > 0$.

Let $\{w_1, w_2, w_3, ...\}$ be a non-increasing sequence of passwords ordered by their probabilities. $\lambda_q = \sum_{i=1}^{q} p(w_i)$ is called the q-success rate. The success rate of an attacker $\mathbf{A}$ trying to guess a user's password is denoted by

Att(checker,$\mathbf{A}$,q), in which checker is the checking algorithm, and q represents the maximum number of tries attacker $\mathbf{A}$ can make. For an exact checker, it is obvious that Att(ExChk,$\mathbf{A}$,q) $\leq \lambda_q$. To achieve λ_q, a brute-force attacker must choose the password with the highest probability in each round.

Regarding a relaxed checker, we define an *optimal attacker* to be able to achieve the maximum password guessing probability. Formally, the probability that an optimal attacker successfully guesses a password in q time is denoted by $\lambda_q^{fuzzy} = \max_{\mathbf{A}} \text{Att}(\text{Chk},\mathbf{A},q)$. Similar to the case of an exact checker, where the attacker chooses the passwords with the highest probabilities, an optimal attacker against a relaxed checker tries to guess a password $\tilde{w}$, so that the corresponding ball $B(\tilde{w})$ has the highest aggregate probability in each round. The construction of such an optimal attacker is NP-hard. However, in [3], the authors proposed a greedy algorithm to realize this attacker in practice. As a result, the security loss caused by such a greedy attacker against a relaxed checker can be calculated by $\Delta_q^{greedy} = \lambda_q^{greedy} - \lambda_q$.

3.2 Secure Typo-Tolerant Checker

The naïve relaxed checker downgrades the security of an authentication system in the presence of an optimal attacker, i.e., $\Delta_q > 0$. However, there exists an optimal relaxed checker, OpChk, that avoids causing security degradation (*free corrections*), i.e., $\Delta_q = 0$ [3]. When a user submits a string $\tilde{w}$ as password, the relaxed checker creates a set of candidate passwords based on a set of correctors $\mathbf{C}$, and thereby a candidate set $\hat{B}(\tilde{w}) = \{w'|w' = f_i(\tilde{w}), p(w')\tau_{w'}(\tilde{w}) > 0, f_i \in \mathbf{C}\}$. To guarantee security, the optimal checker OpChk further rules out some of the candidate passwords by solving an optimization problem with a brute-force algorithm. OpChk maximizes the password acceptance rate without losing security. For the detailed explanation of the algorithm see [3, Sect. V.D].

3.3 Limitations of Server-Side Password Auto-Correction

Previous work is invaluable as it provides a theoretical basis for a secure typo-tolerant authentication scheme, in contradiction to the common belief that accepting more than the one correct password would significantly degrade security. However, as shown in the paper, the proposed scheme cannot handle proximity typos, which, however, are the most prevalent form of all typos (21.8%). Their occurrence is even more pronounced for mobile clients (29.6%). Proximity typos occur when a user accidentally hits a key adjacent to the intended one (e.g., hitting an 'a' instead of an 's'). The reason for this limitation is that correcting a proximity typo necessitates the coverage of a larger space of possible passwords, and running the hash-based authentication algorithm for each possible password requires considerable computational resources. For enterprises, this requires more infrastructure investments to enhance computing capability. For customers, the introduced latency can be unacceptable.

Drawing on the specific situational context of the mobile environment and ecosystem, we design VaultIME to overcome innate limitations of the previous work, and enable VaultIME to cover more typos. Specifically, implemented as a password manager on smartphones, VaultIME is aware of the correct password. Therefore, checking a candidate password is as simple as performing a string matching, as opposed to the complex hash calculations needed by previous work. Since computationally intensive hash computation is avoided, covering proximity typos becomes possible.

4   Empirical Study of Typos on Mobile Devices

Prior studies have shown that strong passwords are difficult to type [8,9,16]. For example, users could easily mistype a character by slipping to an adjacent position on the keyboard, or they may forget to switch off the caps lock status. These human problems are further exacerbated on mobile devices. In particular, the cramped, and less tactile virtual keypad, which is widely used on today's mobile phones, has a negative influence on error-free typing [13,15]. As a result, it has been reported that the error rate is 8% higher for text typed on virtual keypads than for physical keyboards [13].

To understand the most frequent types of typos on mobile devices, we need to analyze a sizable number of real-world password-typing observations. For this purpose, we work on publicly available password-typing datasets from the previous work [3], and particularly focus on the data collected on touchscreen mobile devices.[2] In this section, we first briefly introduce these datasets. Then, we present our analysis results. Our results uncover several new findings, which guide us in designing new mobile-centric auto-correction schemes.

4.1   Password-Typing Dataset on Touchscreens

In [3], the authors carried out two experiments on the Amazon Mechanical Turk (MTurk) platform to collect typo records during the entering of passwords. One experiment collected data from either PC or mobile platforms, while the other only collected data from mobile devices with touchscreens. In collecting the latter dataset, human-intelligence tasks (HITs) were assigned to participants over the web, where each participant was required to type 10–14 passwords in an HTML password input box within 300 s. The participants could only use touchscreen mobile devices. The results were later verified by the user-agent field in the HTTP header of the workers' browsers. The passwords were sourced from the RockYou password leak [17], one of the largest leaked password databases. In total, 24,000 password-typing records were collected by 1,987 HITs.

4.2   Understanding Typos on Mobile Devices

In this section, we explain our findings by analyzing the dataset mentioned above. We first list top typos and their corresponding correctors in Table 1. A corrector

---

[2] The dataset collected on touchscreen devices can be downloaded from https://www.cs.cornell.edu/~rahul/data/mturk15-touchonly.json.bz2.

Table 1. Top typos and their corresponding correctors.

Typo explanation	Typo	Corrector
Proximity errors, i.e., hitting an adjacent key regardless of the intended keyboard status[a], e.g., typing an 'a' as an 'S'	prox[b]	n/a
Proximity errors with correct status, i.e., hitting an adjacent key in the same keyboard status with the intended one, e.g., typing an 'a' as an 's'	prox-rs	rep-prox-rs
All letters are flipped	swc-all[b]	swc-all
First letter is flipped	swc-first[b]	swc-first
An extra character is added to end	ins-last[b]	rm-last
An extra character is added to front	ins-first[b]	rm-first
Forget pressing shift for symbol at the end	n2s-last[b]	n2s-last
Miss a character at an arbitrary location	rm-any	ins-any
Insert an extra character at an arbitrary location	ins-any	rm-any
An arbitrary letter is flipped	swc-any	swc-any

a: The keyboard statuses are "normal", "capitalized", and "symbolized" in the AOSP keyboard.
b: The definition of the typo is also used in [3].

Table 2. Top typos that occur in the mobile dataset and general dataset.

Environment	Typo percentages						
Any	prox	swc-all	ins-last	swc-first	ins-first	n2s-last	others
	21.8	10.9	4.6	4.5	1.3	0.2	56.6
Mobile	prox-rs	rm-any	ins-any	swc-all	swc-any	ins-last	others
	21.4	20.4	10.8	8.0	7.6	1.2	32.6

1. The "Any" row covers the results drawn directly from [3]. The dataset is collected from participants with PC or mobile devices.
2. The "Mobile" row covers the results obtained from mobile devices only.
3. The sum of all items in the mobile environment is greater than 1. This is because our definitions of typos are not exclusive. For example, ins-last is a special case of ins-any.

is the reverse operation of the corresponding typo. It returns a set of passwords that could potentially contain the intended one. For example, corrector rm-last removes the last character in the received password, which effectively corrects typo ins-last. While the definitions of many correctors can be found in work [3], the newly introduced ones are quite self-explanatory. For example, rep-prox-rs means for each character, replace it with each of the adjacent ones in the correct keyboard status.

In Table 2, we show top typos that occur in both the mobile and general datasets. Let us first have a look at the "any" row drawn directly from previous work [3]. Their solution can handle all typos except for prox and others, resulting in a coverage rate of 21.5%. However, prox alone contributes 21.8% of all typos, which the previous solution does not address. We have discussed the reason why previous work cannot handle proximity errors in Sect. 3.3.

We independently conducted a typo distribution analysis on the mobile dataset, the results of which are shown in the "Mobile" row in Table 2. Our study differs from the previous work as we are more concerned with specifics in the mobile environment. We differentiate between a virtual keyboard and a physical one, and pay more attention to the respective influences on typing.

We explain our new findings in the following. First, we find that PC users frequently make proximity typos with incorrect keyboard status, such as typing 'a' as 'S'. This can be explained by the combined effect of finger slipping and unnoticed caps status. However, mobile users seldom make such mistakes. The reason is that a virtual keyboard typically reflects the keyboard status directly on the display of each key, which a user is likely to notice. Therefore, we define a new mobile-centric proximity error, i.e., prox-rs. The difference to the general prox is that prox-rs only considers proximity errors with correct caps and symbol status.[3] Therefore, typing 'a' as 'S' or '@' is not considered as a proximity error in our analysis[4].

Apart from proximity errors, we found that mobile users frequently miss (20.4%) or insert (10.8%) a character at arbitrary locations. In addition, they may also ignore capitalization, either completely (8.0%) or only for a single letter (7.6%). Compared with the "any" environment, where the users frequently *add* an additional character, mobile users are more likely to *miss* a character. Indeed, unintentional extra key-strokes can happen due to inertia in high-speed input on physical keyboards. Among these typos, we found that correcting a missing character is challenging, i.e., a huge number of password candidates would need to be examined. This number is roughly estimated as the number of all possible characters (over 100) multiplied by the length of a password. Therefore, we do not consider this kind of typo in this work. It is also interesting to mention that both of swc-all and swc-any contribute substantially to mobile typos. While the previous work only handles swc-all, we argue that people are equally likely to flip only one letter, which has already been validated by our experiments. In the next section, we show how we auto-correct these typos. In total, our correctors can handle as many as 47.8% of the typos, which is the union of typos of type prox-rs, ins-any, swc-all, and swc-any.

5   Password Auto-Correction for Mobile

VaultIME implements a password auto-correction scheme on the mobile client side. Instead of letting the authentication algorithm on the server judge whether

---

[3] In the default AOSP keyboard layout, there are three statuses ("normal", "capitalized", and "symbolized"), which map the letter 'a' to 'a', 'A', and '@' respectively.

[4] As a result, the results of the previous work exhibit a higher proportion of proximity error (29.6%) than measured with prox-rs (21.4%) on the same raw data.

a password should be accepted or not, VaultIME directly auto-corrects the passwords on the mobile client's side if only minor typos occur. To achieve this, VaultIME, as a special IME, stores the correct password for users on a per-app basis, and runs a password checker as defined in Sect. 3. Before a typed password is fed to the corresponding app, the checker checks the received input. If the checker returns true, the stored correct password is forwarded to the app, otherwise, the received input is forwarded as is.

More specifically, after the user is done with password input, the checker in IME first checks the received password $\tilde{w}$. If it matches with the correct password, w, recorded in the password vault, the IME leaves the password as is and returns. Otherwise, a ball $B(\tilde{w})$ of candidate passwords is derived from a predefined transformation function set $\mathbf{C} = \{f_1, ..., f_c\}$, where f_i is a corrector defined in Sect. 4. Then, w is compared with each element in the ball. If a match is found, $\tilde{w}$ is replaced by w; otherwise, $\tilde{w}$ is left as is.

This section first defines the used transformation function sets. Then, we present how these functions influence the ball size under different checking policies. A checking policy is a filter applied to the candidate ball obtained by the naïve relaxed checker. A stricter filter leads to a reduced ball size, but retains more security of the password. Our results show that the optimal checker, OpChk, does not reduce the ball size significantly. Since OpChk has been proven to lose zero security of a password, our system can achieve both high security and high usability. Finally, we also run simulation experiments to demonstrate that our scheme is secure against a greedy attacker.

5.1   Transformation Function Sets

A transformation function is also called a corrector, which is the reverse operation of a typo, and can be used to recover the correct password. We have listed top-rated mobile correctors in Table 2. Based on their capabilities (i.e., coverage of typos) to correct typos, we define four transformation function sets. They are $\mathcal{C}_{top1} = \{rep\text{-}prox\text{-}rs\}$, $\mathcal{C}_{top2} = \mathcal{C}_{top1} \cup \{rm\text{-}any\}$, $\mathcal{C}_{top3} = \mathcal{C}_{top2} \cup \{swc\text{-}all\}$, and $\mathcal{C}_{top4} = \mathcal{C}_{top3} \cup \{swc\text{-}any\}$, respectively.

5.2   Ball Size Estimation

In [3], three checking policies are discussed. In Chk-All, the algorithm tries all the derived passwords in the ball $B(\tilde{w})$. In Chk-wBL, the ball is filtered by a predefined blacklist that is comprised of a set of frequently used passwords. In Chk-AOp, based on empirical distri-

Table 3. Average ball size for all RockYou passwords over different checker policies and transformation function sets.

	$\mathcal{C}_{top1}$	$\mathcal{C}_{top2}$	$\mathcal{C}_{top3}$	$\mathcal{C}_{top4}$
Chk-All	59.25	69.61	70.54	79.16
Chk-wBL	59.24	69.60	70.53	79.14
Chk-AOp	53.80	58.77	57.87	64.06

butions of passwords and typos (p, τ), a brute-force algorithm is executed to filter the ball. The algorithm maximizes the password acceptance rate without losing security against a greedy attacker who knows both the distribution (p, τ) and the algorithm of the checker.

To understand the effect of policies applied to the ball, we run a simulation to calculate the averaged ball size after filtering. As shown in Table 3, the ball size decreases when policies are applied (Chk-All can be viewed as an all-pass policy), and increases as more transformation functions are added to the set $\mathbf{C}$. Each increase is a reflection of the added corrector. From $\mathcal{C}_{top1}$ to $\mathcal{C}_{top2}$, we observe an increment of around 10, indicating that rm-any produces 10 password candidates, which conforms to the length of a password. From $\mathcal{C}_{top2}$ to $\mathcal{C}_{top3}$, only one new password is produced. This is expected because swc-all is a one-to-one mapping. Lastly, swc-any produces less than 9 new passwords as there are around 9 letters in a password on average.

Statistically, all the checkers in Table 3 significantly increase the number of candidate passwords to be checked. On the one hand, this indicates that our checkers could achieve a high auto-correction rate, because more passwords are examined in each query. On the other hand, security could be degraded because an attacker gains more information about the real password in each query. Interestingly, from Chk-All to Chk-AOp, we do not observe an abrupt shrinkage of the ball size. Since Chk-AOp leaks no more information about the real password than an unmodified exact checker leaks to an optimal brute-force attacker, this proves that our checker can achieve both a high auto-correction rate and a low security loss. In the next section, we show results from our simulation experiments. We emulate a greedy attacker who has complete knowledge about the implementation details of the used typo-tolerant checker.

5.3   Security Evaluation

We begin by clarifying the threats we consider in this work. Then, we show the measured security losses under a set of simulated attacks.

Threats in Scope. We consider an attacker who has physical access to an unlocked victim phone. This is particularly likely to happen considering an in-house betrayer. However, we do not consider a fully compromised mobile OS. In a compromised mobile OS, the attacker may retrieve user's credential data (including all keystrokes) remotely.

We consider a brute-force attacker who is given q chances to query the authentication system. Such an attacker has been formalized in Sect. 3.1. Specifically, the attacker follows the greedy algorithm mentioned in Sect. 3.1, and the security loss can be represented by $\Delta_q^{greedy} = \lambda_q^{greedy} - \lambda_q$.

Results. In Fig. 1, we show the security loss of each checker for different query numbers. We set the upper bound of q to 10, because it is a reasonable upper bound for queries given observations in practice before a device is locked. Mobile devices often enforce a long waiting time if consecutive failed login attempts are detected.

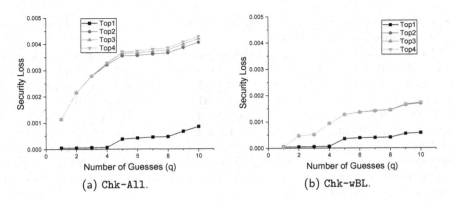

Fig. 1. Security loss measured for different checkers and query numbers. Note that the security loss for Chk-AOp is zero, so we omit it for the sake of fine typography.

It is obvious that the security loss increases with q. However, Chk-AOp remains zero throughout our experiments, because it is an optimal checker that suffers no security loss in theory. For Chk-All and Chk-wBL shown in the figure, there is a clear gap between the transformation function set $\mathcal{C}_{top1}$ and others. This indicates that the security loss caused by applying rep-prox-rs alone can be quite limited – as low as 0.085% ($\lambda_q^{greedy} = 0.02937$ and $\lambda_q 0.02852$) in the worst case when $q = 10$ using checker Chk-All. This can be explained by the fact that a proximity typo often leads to low probability passwords, which do not increase the overall aggregate probability of the attacker's ball. For example, when checking the password 'password', rep-prox-rs will derive a huge ball containing candidate passwords such as 'oassword' and 'psssword', which are rarely used by humans. On the other hand, applying swc-all will obtain 'PASSWORD', which is also a frequently used password. In the worst case, the security loss is 0.427% ($\lambda_q^{greedy} = 0.03279$ and $\lambda_q = 0.02852$) when $q = 10$ and using checker Chk-All under the transformation function set $\mathcal{C}_{top4}$.

6   Implementation

We have implemented a proof-of-concept prototype of VaultIME for the Android OS. A user is able to customize the transformation function set ranging from $\mathcal{C}_{top1}$ to $\mathcal{C}_{top4}$, and the checking algorithms among Chk-All, Chk-wBL, and Chk-AOp.

The prototype uses the standard QWERTY US keyboard layout. It automatically detects the attribute of the current TextView, and inserts an "AuCo" key in the bottom right of the keyboard for the YPE_TEXT_VARIATION_PASSWORD and YPE_TEXT_VARIATION_VISIBLE_PASSWORD input types. VaultIME records a new password entry when the "AuCo" key is pressed. We use the package name of a login app and the account information as the key to index the password. Once a correct password has been recorded, subsequent login attempts will go through the typo-tolerant checker to auto-correct possible typos. As with traditional password vaults, the file storing passwords is encrypted by a secure master key [1]. The master key is randomly generated, and managed by the Android KeyStore provider.

7 Future Work

In the future, we plan to conduct user studies to investigate the usability of the VaultIME app as well as adoption intentions in detail. Specifically, by empirically evaluating how users interact with our system, we aim to deliver a more usable and secure user experience for mobile phone users. Moreover, we are interested to learn to which degree users prefer our method to the traditional auto-fill password manager, whether users feel less threatened, have less frustration, and whether the correction process fits users' habituated login process.

In evaluating the security loss imposed by VaultIME, we mainly focus on a brute-force attacker who attempts to maximize the possibility coverage in each guessing. However, given that some personal data is publicly available (e.g., user name, birthday, etc.), particularly to family members or close friends, a targeted guessing attack could be more efficient [20]. Building an attack model which incorporates personal information into the on-line guessing and designing a new free auto-correction schema specific to this model constitutes an interesting research topic.

8 Conclusion

In this paper, we present VaultIME, a new password auto-correction scheme for mobile platforms. Our work ameliorates concerns of password manager users that they lack control over the use of their credentials. We achieve this by requiring the user to type a "near correct" password, which is automatically replaced with the correct one.

In designing the auto-correction policies, we conduct a mobile-centric password typo analysis, and are able to categorize the observed typos occurring while using virtual keyboards. Based on these empirical observations, we are able to develop a customized set of password correctors, which can cover as much as 47.8% of the detected password typos on mobile systems. This substantial coverage is made possible through a client-side implementation of our password-correction scheme as an app which allows for the treatment of the most common typographical errors, i.e., proximity typos. Moreover, the proposed auto-correction scheme is secure against a brute-force attacker under the formal model proposed in [3]. Our experimental results reveal that in the worst case, our scheme causes a security loss of 0.43%, indicating our auto-correction scheme has a high level of security robustness.

Acknowledgments. We would like to thank the anonymous reviewers for their insightful comments that helped to improve our paper. This work was supported by

NSF CNS-1422594, ARO W911NF-13-1-0421 (MURI), and the German Institute for Trust and Safety on the Internet (DIVSI).

References

1. AgileBits, Inc. 1password security. https://support.1password.com/1password-security/
2. Butler, R., Butler, M.: The password practices applied by South African online consumers: perception versus reality. S. Afr. J. Inf. Manag. **17**(1), 1–11 (2015)
3. Chatterjee, R., Athalye, A., Akhawe, D., Juels, A., Ristenpart, T.: pASSWORD tYPOS and how to correct them securely. In: IEEE Security and Privacy (S&P) (2016)
4. Fagan, M., Khan, M.: Why do they do what they do?: A study of what motivates users to (not) follow computer security advice. In: SOUPS 2016 (2016)
5. Gasti, P., Rasmussen, K.B.: On the security of password manager database formats. In: Foresti, S., Yung, M., Martinelli, F. (eds.) ESORICS 2012. LNCS, vol. 7459, pp. 770–787. Springer, Heidelberg (2012). https://doi.org/10.1007/978-3-642-33167-1_44
6. Gott, A.: Important security updates for our users (2017). https://blog.lastpass.com/2017/03/important-security-updates-for-our-users.html/
7. Grant, K.: Identity theft victims: you might know the culprit (2015). http://www.cnbc.com/2015/07/21/identity-theft-victims-may-know-the-culprit.html
8. Keith, M., Shao, B., Steinbart, P.: The usability of passphrases for authentication: an empirical field study. Int. J. Hum.-Comput. Stud. **65**(1), 17–28 (2007)
9. Keith, M., Shao, B., Steinbart, P.: A behavioral analysis of passphrase design and effectiveness. J. Assoc. Inf. Syst. **10**(2), 63–89 (2009)
10. Knijnenburg, B., Kobsa, A., Jin, H.: Counteracting the negative effect of form auto-completion on the privacy calculus. In: ICIS 2013 (2013)
11. Komanduri, S., Shay, R., Kelley, P., Mazurek, M., Bauer, L., Christin, N., Cranor, L., Egelman, S.: Of passwords and people: measuring the effect of password-composition policies. In: ACM CHI 2011 (2011)
12. Kossman, S.: Familiar fraud: when family and friends steal your identity (2014). http://www.creditcards.com/credit-card-news/familiar_fraud-damage-1282.php
13. Lee, S., Zhai, S.: The performance of touch screen soft buttons. In: CHI 2009 (2009)
14. Li, Z., He, W., Akhawe, D., Song, D.: The emperor's new password manager: security analysis of web-based password managers. In: USENIX Security 2014 (2014)
15. Park, Y., Han, S., Park, J., Cho, Y.: Touch key design for target selection on a mobile phone. In: MobileHCI 2008 (2008)
16. Shay, R., Komanduri, S., Durity, A., Huh, P., Mazurek, M., Segreti, S., Ur, B., Bauer, L., Christin, N., Cranor, L.: Can long passwords be secure and usable? In: ACM CHI 2014 (2014)
17. Siegler, M.: One of the 32 million with a RockYou account? You may want to change all your passwords. Like now. TechCrunch (2009). http://techcrunch.com/2009/12/14/rockyou-hacked
18. Stroup, J.: Who Commits Identity Theft? (2016). https://www.thebalance.com/who-commits-identity-theft-1947637
19. Tabini, M.: Review: lastpass takes your passwords to the cloud (2013). http://www.macworld.com/article/2032046/review-lastpass-takes-your-passwords-to-the-cloud.html
20. Wang, D., Zhang, Z., Wang, P., Yan, J., Huang, X.: Targeted online password guessing: an underestimated threat. In: ACM CCS 2016 (2016)

TOPHAT: Topology-Based Host-Level Attribution for Multi-stage Attacks in Enterprise Systems Using Software Defined Networks

Subramaniyam Kannan[1]([✉]), Paul Wood[1], Larry Deatrick[2], Patricia Beane[2], Somali Chaterji[1], and Saurabh Bagchi[1]

[1] Purdue University, West Lafayette, USA
{kannan5,pwood,schaterji,sbagchi}@purdue.edu
[2] Northrop Grumman, Falls Church, USA
{larry.deatrick,Patricia.Beane}@ngc.com

Abstract. Multi-layer distributed systems, such as those found in corporate systems, are often the target of multi-stage attacks. Such attacks utilize multiple victim machines, in a series, to compromise a target asset deep inside the corporate network. Under such attacks, it is difficult to identify the upstream attacker's identity from a downstream victim machine because of the mixing of multiple network flows. This is known as the attribution problem in security domains. We present TOPHAT, a system that solves such attribution problems for multi-stage attacks. It does this by using moving target defense, *i.e.*, shuffling the assignment of clients to server replicas, which is achieved through software defined networking. As alerts are generated, TOPHAT maintains state about the level of risk for each network flow and progressively isolates the malicious flows. Using a simulation, we show that TOPHAT can identify single and multiple attackers in a variety of systems with different numbers of servers, layers, and clients.

Keywords: Multi-stage attacks · Attack attribution
Software defined network · Moving target defense

1 Introduction

Multi-stage attacks (MSA) have plagued distributed system administrators for decades. In these attacks, multiple computers are used simultaneously to breach a particular target, and attackers often rely on a series of privilege escalation attacks to circumvent access controls protecting assets. One of the most challenging aspects of MSA comes as an attribution, mixing, or traceability problem [4]. Defenders wish to know what particular network traffic resulted in a privilege escalation, to prevent it in the future, but from a network perspective, the traffic output at each stage is not associated with any particular input. Consequently, defenders cannot distinguish legitimate from malicious network traffic,

© ICST Institute for Computer Sciences, Social Informatics and Telecommunications Engineering 2018
X. Lin et al. (Eds.): SecureComm 2017, LNICST 238, pp. 687–703, 2018.
https://doi.org/10.1007/978-3-319-78813-5_36

and identifying or disrupting vulnerabilities remains a daunting task. In this paper we present TOPHAT (TOPology-based Host-level ATtribution), a technique for identifying malicious users and their network traffic.

Multi-stage attacks operate on top of distributed systems where each distributed layer has different access privileges to sensitive business assets. An attacker must penetrate multiple layers to access some protected information, a *crown jewel*. As the attacker progresses, she generates some intrusion alerts due to some traffic with a malicious signature passing through intrusion detection systems (IDS). These alerts, while useful for finding single stage attacks, are less useful in the MSA because the {source, destination} pairs are both machines inside of the distributed system, instead of an external attributable source (as would be the case for an Internet-facing web server, for example). Consequently, there is no obvious relationship between alerts deep in the distributed system and the outsider, and this problem is referred to as the attribution, traceback or un-mixing problem [3,20]. In this context, an attributable alert is one which identifies an external source directly, and an unattributable alert is one which identifies no source or identifies an internal or intermediate source, which cannot actually be the attacker.

Existing solutions [1,2,5,14–16,19] to the attribution problem have a few common shortfalls that TOPHAT addresses. First, solutions such as [1,14,16] rely on attack graphs to perform alert inferencing, where existing relationships between alerts are known via expert system knowledge. For example, an expert would claim that a port scanning alert deep in the distributed system follows from a wrong password alert in the Internet-facing layers. In practice, such relationships are complex, numerous, and difficult to derive. Furthermore, it is challenging to keep such information updated because systems are dynamic with new vulnerabilities being discovered, new digital assets being brought online, and new users being added. TOPHAT solves this issue without relying on attack graphs, thus providing a more general, robust, and adaptive solution to solving the attribution problem. Second, solutions such as [2,5,15,19] rely on causal links between stages or layers of the MSA. For example, inside the system, it is known that input I_1 causes output O_1, and these relationships are logged and analyzed so that network traffic can be effectively tagged and tracked in the system. This approach relies on application support, however, to provide the causal links. TOPHAT does not rely on such information from the underlying application and can identify attackers without this causality link.

TOPHAT is a network-based solution to the attribution problem. We represent incident flows from external clients to alert sources in a directed acyclic graph, where each node in the graph models the mixing property of intermediate servers and softwares. Some of these flows are malicious, and they generate one or more alerts at various nodes, and at various depths, on its path. For each alert, we generate and track partial attribution for all clients that can reach the alerted node as a stateful metric called *risk factor*, or equivalently, *risk value*. TOPHAT, taking into consideration current risk for each network flow, adjusts the servers that the flow will pass through, using a process called *shuffling* [10]. Through the shuffling process, TOPHAT isolates the suspect flows and keeps adjusting the risk factor. With a sufficient number of shuffles, the risk factor of the malicious flows exceeds a user-set threshold, i.e., the cumulative partial attributions for an attacker reaches a level of complete attribution, and the attacker is identified.[1]

In TOPHAT, we utilize detection techniques that resemble moving target defenses (MTD) [8], through our shuffling algorithms. Using software defined networks (SDN) [12], TOPHAT is able to manipulate or re-route the network flows to desired nodes that in turn helps in identifying the attacker in the distributed system. Using SDN-based load balancers [18], entering flows from external clients are mapped to any replica of an entry-level server in the distributed system. Then, whenever an alert is generated, by an IDS placed at a replica of any server in the system, some risk is attributed to all flows that are passing through that server replica. Using two different approaches corresponding to two different variants of TOPHAT, it tracks this risk and assigns clients so that the malicious flows have progressively increasing risk factor. Finally, those with risk values above a user-settable threshold can be isolated, blocked, or studied in a honey-pot.

Using this approach, TOPHAT is able to identify a single attacker in a system of 1000 clients and 3 servers at the entry layer in 6 shuffles, requiring 1000 seconds whenever the attacker repeats the attack for approximately every 150 seconds. In the same system with 4 attackers, all of the attackers are identified in 27 shuffles. We also show that the same system with 10 attackers, the shuffling mechanism requires the attacker to repeat their exploits over 1000 times before gaining access to the crown jewel, thus significantly increasing the attacker's efforts under TOPHAT. Finally, we demonstrate how TOPHAT impacts the legitimate clients, showing that after 3–4 shuffles a majority of clients can retain continuous connectivity while the attacker is still identified.

The main contributions that we present in this paper are:

1. TOPHAT can attribute multi-stage attacks on a distributed system to a single external source, without relying on attack graphs or modifying the server softwares.
2. The MTD-style defense significantly increases attacker's effort, and can support identification of multiple simultaneous attackers.
3. TOPHAT can support high availability for legitimate clients while still identifying attackers in the system.

2   Background and Assumptions

2.1   System Model

TOPHAT is designed to protect a distributed system where servers exist at multiple layers in a distributed system as shown in Fig. 1. Each layer has multiple

---

[1] *Terminology clarification*: In this paper, we will use the term "attacker" synonymously with "attacking flow" or "malicious flow".

instances of one specific kind of server for load balancing and is connected to the next layer by an open flow switch and managed by a SDN Controller [6]. As a running example, we consider a web-based e-Commerce system operated by a publicly traded company. External clients access a web front end instance (layer 1) that connects to a database back end to store orders, interact with inventory, and otherwise manage transactions. In layer 3, a corporate reporting server analyzes the database to create sales reports, track hot products, and manage inventory at a macro level. It interfaces with the database layer and stores reports on layer 4, the corporate file servers. Inside of the corporate file server is an upcoming earnings statement for the next quarter (the *crown jewel*), and its early release would allow for insider trading since the company's performance, relative to projections, can have a significant impact on stock prices. The attacker(s) wish to ex-filtrate the earnings report.

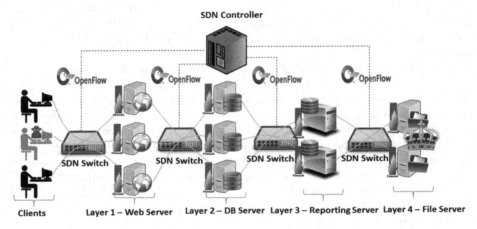

Fig. 1. A sample distributed system that can be protected by TopHat.

2.2   Network Structure

At its core, TopHat relies on intrusion detection systems to provide the alerts that drive its identification techniques. In this paper we make a simplifying assumption that each server instance has an IDS to remove resource management constraints.

Legitimate Client Model: We define a legitimate client as a system user that has no malicious intent and is using the target application for its designed purpose. The client connects to the application by sending a request to the outward facing service IP address. Further details on this process are described in Sect. 4.4.

Attacker Model: The attacker begins as a normal client and starts exploring for vulnerabilities in the outward facing layer 1. Once an exploit is found in layer 1, the attacker stages an attack on layer 2 by leveraging elevated access privileges that she has gained at the outer layer 1. If an ongoing attack is flagged by an IDS at any layer then TOPHAT is activated. If the attack is undetected by any of the IDS, then it may proceed to the next layer, until reaching the *crown jewel*. TOPHAT works by making a few assumptions about the nature of the multi-stage attackers:

- **Persistent Attacks (PA)** if a server is reset, or the attacker connects to a new server, then the attack must be repeated.
- **Strong Alerts (SA)** the attacker will generate at least one strong alert during a MSA for which TOPHAT responds. The strong alert is known to be part of an attack with high certainty (*e.g.*, brute force attacks, known exploit signatures, or other high priority[2] alerts).

3   Solution Overview

TOPHAT utilizes software defined networks (SDN) and intrusion detection systems (IDS) to monitor and attribute alerts to specific attackers. At its core, TOPHAT sits along side a SDN controller such as an OpenDaylight [13] where it can observe the network flows and make decisions about changes to the network. The algorithm chooses which clients will be connected to which outward-facing servers, and which downstream servers are connected to which upstream servers in the distributed application. TOPHAT's algorithm operates by maintaining a risk factor for each connected client and then modifying that risk factor whenever alerts are generated. As more alerts are generated, the attacker's stateful *risk factor* is increased until she can be discriminated from the other connected clients. Whenever an alert is generated, the risk is increased for all the flows that are passing through the alerting service. The clients are then shuffled based on their risk so that over time, the attacker ends up with the maximum risk. The risk factor is initialized to zero for all clients and this monotonically increases with alerts in the system, till the attacker is identified and isolated. Then the risk factors of all the clients that are found to be legitimate in retrospect are reduced (Risk Rebalancing as explained in Sect. 4.3). We classify our protocol as an instantiation of Moving Target Defense (MTD), though it is somewhat different from the traditional notion of MTD. Here we are moving the clients and the assignment of flows to servers, while in traditional MTD, the protected system is "moved", *i.e.* reconfigured [7].

3.1   TopHat's Intuition

Several challenges exist in protecting a distributed system that has the structure shown in Fig. 1. First, alerts generated at any layer $(i + 1)$ look as if they are coming from layer i, not from an external attacker. This argues against the

---

[2] http://manual-snort-org.s3-website-us-east-1.amazonaws.com/node31.html# Snort_Default_Classifications in Snort, rules are tagged with priority where "high" priority correlates with strong in our solution.

simple solution of blocking flows from a particular source because that would create a service interruption—if a server in layer $(i+1)$ blocks a server in layer i, then the application stops working for all the clients connected to that particular server in layer i. TOPHAT overcomes this limitation by attributing an attack to all clients that are connected to the alerting server in layer i and then stopping the ongoing attack using the MTD approach. When an alert event happens, *all* of the clients are disconnected from the servers in layer 1 (for purposes of randomization), assigned to new servers, and the alerting server is refreshed to a clean state and restarted. TOPHAT then constantly tracks the attack history of each client with the help of the *risk factor* as we describe in detail in Sect. 4, so that the attacker is identified due to multiple alerts, which in turn is due to the persistence of the attack (as assumed in our attack model). The persistent attack property fundamentally allows TOPHAT to converge given a sufficient number of alerts.

3.2 Legitimate Client Impacts

The SDN-based shuffling in TOPHAT can have some negative impacts on legitimate client connections. First, whenever a shuffle involves a client, the client's connection is reset. This overhead cannot be avoided since the attackers and legitimate clients share the same network flow paths—a connection reset that disrupts an attacker's flow also disrupts the legitimate client's flow. Its impact can be mitigated, however, with state management approaches [17]. Second, when a server is being reset and restarted (to clear the infected status), the clients assigned to that server cannot function. This case can be minimized by using fast restart hardware or by keeping hot spares for the server instances.

4   Detailed Design of TopHat

TOPHAT probabilistically identifies attackers in the system by repeatedly attributing alerts to suspect sets until the likelihood of a client being the attacker is sufficiently large to certify identification. In the case of multiple attackers, this process is repeated so that multiple identification events occur until all of the attackers are exhausted.

Alert Group Attribution: In TOPHAT, there always exists a mapping between a server in any particular layer and the clients that, through any possible path, have access to that server. For example, if clients 1–5 are assigned to server S1 in layer L1, and S1/L1 is connected to S2/L2, then an alert sourced from S2/L2 will be attributed to *all* the clients 1–5. The relationship of how any given flow passes through the servers at the different layers is itself controlled by the SDN controller and thus this relationship is always known to our algorithm. Now we define a term *client group*. Consider that an alerting server has flows $F_1, F_2, ..., F_{N_G}$ going through it. By tracing each flow back to layer 1 servers, we can map each flow F_i to the client generating that flow C_i. The clients $C_1, C_2, ..., C_{N_G}$ form the client group here. Each such client has its stateful parameter, *risk factor*, increased by $\frac{1}{N_G}$, where N_G is the number of clients in that particular group. In the earlier example, each client would have its risk increased by $1/5$.

Likelihood of a Client Being the Attacker: We define the likelihood as follows:

$$P(C_i = A) = \frac{R(C_i)}{\sum R(C_j) \; \forall \; R(C_j) \geq R(C_i)} \tag{1}$$

where C_i is client i, $C_i = A$ is the indicator that C_i is an attacker, $R(C_i)$ is the risk factor of client i, and $\forall \; R(C_j) \geq R(C_i)$ implies that client j has a risk factor at least as large as client i, and $i = j$ is allowed. When a client has the highest risk factor of any client, then this probability value becomes 1. The control and convergence of TOPHAT is discussed in detail in Sect. 4.1 in [9].

4.1 Uniform Assignment Algorithm ("Uniform")

The uniform assignment algorithm is responsible for assigning arriving client flows to different servers at layer 1. There are N_S assignment pools available, where N_S is the number of servers in layer 1. For each client i, an assignment is made: $A : C_i \rightarrow [1, N_S]$ such that the imbalance in risk between any two servers is minimized. At the beginning of the operation of the system, each client will have the same risk factor and so this will be a uniform random assignment. However, in subsequent mappings (which happen after an alert arrives at TOPHAT) the risk factors will be different and the mapping A will be a weighted random assignment, using the risk factors as the weights. The goal is to balance the aggregate risk at any of the servers in level 1. The assignment process proceeds as follows:

1. A client seeks an assignment, either when it is connecting to the protected system for the first time, or in response to a disconnection forced by TOPHAT.
2. The client is given the assignment to $[1, N_S]$ according to the assignment function A.
3. When a new alert is received, the assignments between clients and servers are reset, and all clients return to step 1 and re-assigned to new servers.

This algorithm effectively assigns clients such that there is a uniform aggregate risk assigned to any particular server. Each attribution event reduces the set of ties ($N_T = |\forall \; R(C_j) \geq R(C_i)|$) to $\frac{N_T}{N_{AS}}$, where N_{AS} is the number of servers in the alert layer. For example, if there are 100 clients and 4 alert groups and every client has a risk of 1, then by Eq. 1, $P(C_i = A) = \frac{1}{100} \; \forall \; i$. After an attribution event, given uniform assignment (each server having balanced risk of 25, thus 25 clients per server), then the likelihood for those 25 becomes $\frac{1.04}{1.04 \times 25}$ because the 25 clients that were attributed with risk have an additional 0.04 added. The size of the set $|R(C_j) \geq R(C_i)|$ is now $\frac{100}{4} = 25$, following the reduction.

4.2 Low-Risk Isolation Algorithm ("LRA")

This variant of the algorithm shelters low risk clients into a *safe zone*, defined as a set of servers in layer 1 such that clients which are assigned to this set are not shuffled around by TOPHAT. These clients do not suffer from any disconnections, and their risk factors do not change. Each alert/attribution event tells TOPHAT something about who may be the attacker, but it can also indicate who is *not* an attacker. In the uniform case, the legitimate clients are mixed in with the attackers, and this causes them to rise in risk, whenever they share a server with the malicious clients. It also dilutes the attribution power of a single attack since N_G remains near-constant. The LRA variant avoids this issue by placing some portion of the clients with the lowest risk into a safe zone:

1. Clients are assigned as in the uniform risk case, except for clients that exist in a safe set S_S, initialized as empty.
2. After an attribution event a portion of the clients, $I_R, I_R \in (0, 1)$, is moved from the active set S_A to the safe set S_S. The $|S_A| \cdot I_R$ clients with the lowest risk are moved to S_S.
3. The assignment of the safe clients S_S is fixed to a particular server, and then the clients in the active set S_A are redistributed among the remaining $N_S - N_{safe}$ servers using the uniform risk approach. N_{safe} is the number of servers used for the safe zone.
4. In the event an alert is generated from any of the S_S clients, then the entire set of clients is moved back to the S_A set.

Much less risk is assigned to the legitimate clients in the system using LRA with a single attacker. Additionally, uninterrupted connection paths to the protected application are provided, decreasing the probability of failed transactions. The convergence condition for both of the algorithms are explained in detail in Sects. 4.2 and 4.3 in [9].

4.3 Risk Rebalancing Approach ("RRB")

Once one of the attackers is identified by using any one of the above described algorithms, the risk factor of the remaining clients are updated using *Risk Rebalancing* (RRB) technique in order to speed up identification of the remaining attackers. Each alert attribution is stored in the SDN controller that contains the list of clients and the amount of risk factor attributed to each client due to that particular alert. Whenever an attacker is identified, the list of alerts is searched, and the set of alerts that involved the attacker are collected. The accumulated risk for each client due to each alert in that list is removed because of the insight that the alert is attributable to the now discovered attacker and not the other clients. Thus, legitimate clients have their risk lowered leading to faster identification of the other attackers.

4.4 End-to-End Workflow

We detail the end-to-end workflow of TOPHAT in the context of the SDN-based system:

1. **Initial:** The SDN switch at ingress node forwards each new client's request to the SDN controller as the flow table will be initially empty. TOPHAT, which is installed as an application over the SDN controller, stores the associated risk and the server allocated at each layer for all the clients.

2. **Server Assignment:** TOPHAT assigns each client to a particular server at layer 1 as described in Sects. 4.1 and 4.2. Then the corresponding flow rules are installed at the SDN switch in layer 1 and subsequent layers. The initial risk factor of all the clients are set to 0. (T_S: Time for server assignment).

3. **Connection Establishment:** Each client establishes a connection with the servers at layer 1 using TCP 3-way handshake. At this point, all the clients except the attackers can access the servers in subsequent layers using their respective access privilege. (T_C: Time to establish connection).

4. **Attacker Exploration:** In order to get access to the subsequent layers, the attackers have to explore the layer 1 server for vulnerabilities and then exploit a vulnerability. Let T_x denote the time to exploit a server at a particular layer. T_x varies across different layers and across different attackers.

5. **Alert Generation:** The attacker continues to compromise the servers at subsequent layers until an IDS detects a malicious action (e.g., port scan, known CVE, etc.) or alert correlation from multiple IDS alerts generates a strong alert. Let T_A be the time to generate a strong alert.

6. **Connection Termination:** The strong alert is sent to the SDN controller, which initiates the shuffling by disconnecting the clients from the servers in layer 1 (except those in the safe set for LRA) and reassigning them.

7. **Risk Updation:** The risk factor of the clients are updated according to either the Uniform or the LRA scheme. Let T_{RA} be the time to update risk values.

8. **Attacker Identification:** After the risk updation, the probability of each client is calculated using Eq. (1). The clients with a probability $P(C_i = A) \geq \tau$ (τ: user settable threshold) are identified as attackers and isolated.

9. **Risk Rebalance:** After the attacker is identified, TOPHAT rebalances the risk factor of all the remaining clients (Sect. 4.3).

10. **Server Reset:** TOPHAT instructs the SDN controller to reset all the active servers in the network by broadcasting a control message which ensures that the attackers need to exploit it again, in order to re-initiate the MSA. (T_R: Time to reset a server).

11. **Connection Re-establishment:** All the clients including the attackers will re-initiate connections to the servers in layer 1 and the steps repeat.

4.5   Multiple Attackers

Multiple simultaneous attackers can be handled by TOPHAT, without any modification. We model multiple attackers as each having independent, random times to exploit (T_X), where a successful exploit results in an alert being generated. If one attacker is more aggressive (smaller T_X), then alerts will be generated due to this attacker and this attacker will be identified by TOPHAT before moving on to the next attacker. This essentially makes the process of identifying multiple attackers sequential. If on the other hand, there are multiple attackers with similar T_X values, then it will be a matter of chance which attacker gets identified first. But the risk factor of the other attackers will be retained in TOPHAT, thereby helping in the convergence time for the subsequent attackers.

False Positives and Mitigation: It is possible for TOPHAT to generate false positives with multiple attackers present that have similar T_X. For example, if there are four clients C1-C4, of which C2 and C4 are malicious and two servers S1 and S2. In the first round, C1 and C2 are assigned to S1 and C3 and C4 to S2. C2 alerts resulting in reshuffling. In the next round, C1 and C4 happen to be assigned to S1 and C2 and C3 to S2. Now C4 alerts and as a result, the legitimate client C1 is falsely flagged. This is a relatively rare occurrence and we show the false positive rate in Experiment 3 (it is below 5% even in the most pathological case).

5   Experimentation

5.1   Model System

The SDN Network used for evaluation is described in the Fig. 2. All the experiments are evaluated using the default values given in Tables 1 and 2 unless otherwise specified. As shown in Fig. 2, for the sake of simplicity we consider that each server in layer i has a stove piped connection or one-one connection (represented by different colors) to any server in layer $i+1$ in order to avoid mixing of network flows at later stages. The experiment 4 shows the convergence for non-stove piped case. In LRA approach, the server 3 is considered to be safe server and the clients in active set S_A are shuffled between the server 1 and server 2.

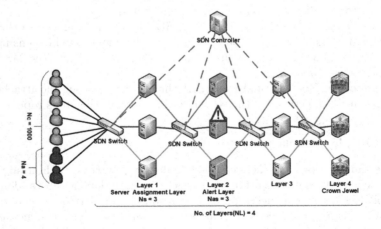

Fig. 2. SDN model system considered for the evaluation.

Table 1. Default network and time parameter values.

Notation	Meaning	Default value
N_C	No. of clients	1000
N_A	No. of attackers	4
N_S	No. of servers at layer 1	3
N_L	No. of layers	4
L_{alert}	Strong alert layer number	2
I_R	Ratio of clients moved from active set to safe set	0.25
T_S	Server allocation time	1 ms
T_C	Connection establishment time	30 ms
T_A	Alert generation time	1 ms
T_{RA}	Risk assignment + attacker identification time	1 ms
T_R	Server reset time	45 s [11]
T_X	Attacker exploit time	Normal distribution

Table 2. Default attacker exploit time T_X for 4 attackers.

Attacker no.	T_X at layer 1		T_X at layer 2	
	Mean (s)	Variance (s)	Mean (s)	Variance (s)
1	20	5	30	5
2	40	5	60	5
3	10	2	15	2
4	80	5	80	5

Simulation Environment: Along with TOPHAT, the SDN environment is modeled using the network and time parameters in C++[3]. Each event in the SDN environment is represented by a corresponding time component as described in Sect. 4.4. The clients are assigned to the available servers using uniform random distribution and the attacker's exploit time is modeled based on normal distribution as in Table 2. For each attacker, the exploit time varies by mean across each layer and varies by variance across different iterations or shuffles. For some experiments, where multiple simulations can be aggregated, we take the median of 20 runs to provide data smoothness with respect to the random attack times.

Evaluation Parameters: For simplification, we assume all the clients send requests to the servers at layer 1 at the same time. All the experiments described below are evaluated using the following parameters:

1. **Experiment Time:** The time at which particular event like server assignment or alert generation happens.

---

[3] https://github.rcac.purdue.edu/DependableComputingSystemsLab/TopHat.

2. **Convergence Time:** The time at which single attacker or all the attackers are found.
3. **Probability of Attacker found** (P_A)**:** The probability of client being identified correctly as an attacker given by Eq. 1.
4. **Percentage of Failed Transactions (PFT):** The number of client disruptions during the time of attacker identification. It is a function of time given by

$$PFT(t) = \frac{No.\ of\ Failed\ Transactions}{Total\ No.\ of\ Transactions} \qquad (2)$$

where we model client transactions as continuous time event for simplicity. We aggregate PFT across clients and all time to compute a **cumulative PFT** for the purpose of comparing per-simulation metrics. Note that the PFT is per-client, and not all clients are disrupted simultaneously during a shuffle event in TOPHAT.

5.2   Experiment 1: Convergence over Time

The experiment 1 demonstrate TOPHAT's operation in the time domain for both single and multiple attackers. During each attack, the two primary metrics (PFT and P_A) are collected based on the experiment time at which an alert is generated. Default values are used for all parameters except N_A. Figure 3 shows the results from our simulation and the results are explained in the next sections.

Convergence: In case of single attacker, the convergence is given directly by P_A and for two attacker's case, it is given by average probability. At each alert generation, the probability is updated, and the value for the attacker increases as shown in the figures. The uniform algorithm converges more quickly in both cases primarily because it has 3 servers to use for risk attribution while LRA reserves a server for the safe pool and uses only 2 servers for risk attribution. The step function increases as the number of ties are broken, and the attacker is repeatedly involved in high-risk attribution events.

In the case of multiple attackers, one attacker has a faster exploit time than the other. Since shuffles occur on the fast attacker's alert, the slow attacker is statistically unlikely to ever generate an alert until the fast attacker has been disrupted. This causes a time-domain crowding of alerts early in the simulation until the first attacker is identified, and then the alerts become more spaced out as opposed to an independent case where the alerts would be interleaved. Upon close inspection, one of the LRA's potential weaknesses can be seen in that it is using more shuffles to identify the attacker in the two attacker case. Furthermore, because the slow attacker has low risk, she can be placed in the safe zone, and it is more likely that a slow attacker can generate an alert inside of the safe area–something that does not happen in this experiment, but will in a later experiment.

PFT: The PFT shows how clients are impacted through time. In all cases, the width of the PFT bar represents the reset time for cleaning impacted servers

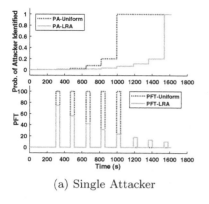

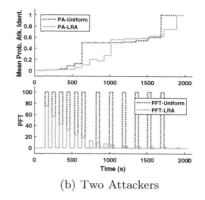

(a) Single Attacker   (b) Two Attackers

Fig. 3. The convergence of TOPHAT is shown for the single attacker and two attacker cases with both the uniform and low-risk assignment (LRA) algorithms.

in the system T_R. For the uniform algorithm, all clients are re-assigned and all servers on the attack path are cleaned, resulting in outages for all of the clients, hence the peak is always at 100. In the LRA case, only those clients remaining in the active set are impacted for each attack. This results in a decaying PFT over time as the low risk clients are assigned to the safe server at the rate I_R. Consequently, system operators have a choice between faster convergence and attacker identification (the Uniform variant) or slower convergence with better client access (the LRA variant).

For multiple attackers, in the Uniform case the PFT follows the single attacker profile, but it is repeated for the second attacker with a higher width due to T_X. For the LRA case, since less shuffling servers are available, it takes more alerts to converge and thus more shuffles, and more period of high PFT. The impact of all the parameters on the convergence time and PFT is explained in detail in Sect. 5.3 in [9].

5.3   Experiment 2: Attacker Effort

In this experiment, we demonstrate how TOPHAT, by utilizing MTD, is able to increase the total attack effort that must be expended to compromise the protected system. We measure attacker effort as the number of times a server must be compromised, at any layer, by any attacker. This includes the effort spent exploiting servers that have been reset. We also measure the number of shuffles or alerts generated in the system, and this metric covers the number of trials an attacker has at penetrating a system for which the exploit is not known.

Figure 4 shows the effort in these two metrics. In Fig. 4a, the total exploits goes up with the number of attackers. This process is not linear, however, because many attackers will be reset even when they do not generate an alert themselves due to the moving target nature of TOPHAT. Each attacker may penetrate layer 1 and be shuffled before making an attempt on layer 2, for example. Consequently,

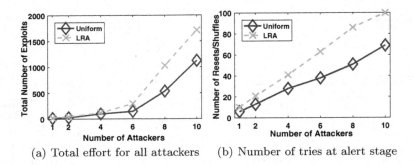

(a) Total effort for all attackers   (b) Number of tries at alert stage

Fig. 4. Attacker efforts until identified

TOPHAT is able to make it much more difficult to attack the system when multiple attackers are present, even if the attacker identification takes some time. In Fig. 4b, the total number of resets are shown. This scales roughly linearly with the number of attackers because there is a lower limit to this number until the attackers can be found, as described in Sect. 4.1. of note here, however, is that there are a limited number of exploit attempts allowed at layer 2 before the attackers are identified and a layer 1 patch can be created. These 5–100 alerts will attribute the attacker, and upstream compromises (at layer 1) can be patched as a result, a key benefit of TOPHAT.

5.4 Experiment 3: Effect of Risk Re-balancing

For this experiment, we evaluate the impact of the risk re-balancing (RRB) technique (Sect. 4.3) on the convergence time and the false positives. We stress the system by having multiple attackers with the same distribution for T_X. Without RRB, when an attacker is identified, the risk for *all* other clients is reset to zero. With RRB, when an attacker is identified, only the legitimate clients that had been mixed in with the identified attacker have their risk reduced, not reset to zero.

Figure 5a shows the impact of RRB on both the Uniform and the LRA algorithms. In both cases, the use of the RRB speeds up convergence as expected. The number of false positives is higher for LRA. This is because the placement of many clients in the safe zone and subsequent alerts from that zone can degrade the process of identification of the attackers. TOPHAT is still able to provide low false positive rates (less than 0.5%) for small numbers of attackers relative to the total number of clients (10), even in this challenging scenario of similarly aggressive attackers.

5.5 Experiment 4: Effect of Number of Server Replicas

For this experiment, we use a system with 5 layers having [5, 4, 3, 2, 2] replicas in the layers, starting from layer 1. The inter-layer connections are uniformly

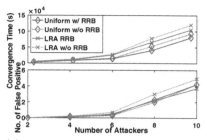
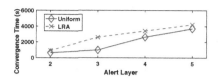

(a) Impact of maintaining state (w/ RRB) on convergence and false positive rates.

(b) As the alert becomes deeper in the system, it requires more shuffles and thus increases the time to converge.

Fig. 5. Experiments 3 (left) and 4 (right)

balanced as much as possible. We evaluate the impact of alert depth on the risk attribution. Figure 5b shows the impact of the alert layer on the convergence speed of both algorithms. The number of replicas decreases as one goes further inside the system. This is not uncommon because the number of requests that touch servers deep inside the enterprise typically decrease. We expect that alerts deep in the system will provide less discriminating information about the attackers because the shuffling can occur with coarser granularity, thus lumping more number of clients (legitimate with a few attacking) together on the same server. In the case of LRA, the safe zone is on a single stove-piped layer while the other shuffling servers are all connected into the multi-layer system. As the layer deepens, it is similar to reducing N_S because the size of the alert group increases and the number of groups N_G decreases. Therefore there is a logarithmic increase in the convergence time as the depth of the alert layer increases.

6   Conclusion

In this paper, we presented TOPHAT, a solution to the problem of attributing an alert to an attacker in a multi-layered system. The problem is challenging due to the mixing of multiple flows at servers inside the periphery of the system. TOPHAT utilizes moving target defense techniques, namely shuffling, implemented on top of a software defined network infrastructure. We provided two algorithms for shuffling, one that focuses on convergence speed and another that focuses on improving client connectivity during attacks. Further, we show that TOPHAT increases the attackers effort by requiring multiple re-exploiting of the target systems. We evaluate TOPHAT using the metrics of time to detect and isolate the attackers and the impact on the legitimate clients in the system. Using our system, network administrators can begin to attribute alerts and attacks, to external flows so that they may be blocked or studied for further defense improvement.

References

1. Alserhani, F., Akhlaq, M., Awan, I.U., Cullen, A.J., Mirchandani, P.: MARS: multi-stage attack recognition system. In: 2010 24th IEEE International Conference on Advanced Information Networking and Applications (AINA), pp. 753–759. IEEE (2010)
2. Baba, T., Matsuda, S.: Tracing network attacks to their sources. IEEE Internet Comput. 6(2), 20–26 (2002)
3. Clark, D.D., Landau, S.: The problem isn't attribution: it's multi-stage attacks. In: Proceedings of the Re-architecting the Internet Workshop, p. 11. ACM (2010)
4. Clark, D.D., Landau, S.: Untangling attribution. Harv. Nat. Secur. J. 2, 323 (2011)
5. Dawkins, J., Hale, J.: A systematic approach to multi-stage network attack analysis. In: Proceedings of Second IEEE International Information Assurance Workshop, pp. 48–56. IEEE (2004)
6. Feamster, N., Rexford, J., Zegura, E.: The road to SDN: an intellectual history of programmable networks. ACM SIGCOMM Comput. Commun. Rev. 44(2), 87–98 (2014)
7. Jafarian, J.H., Al-Shaer, E., Duan, Q.: Openflow random host mutation: transparent moving target defense using software defined networking. In: Proceedings of the First Workshop on Hot Topics in Software Defined Networks, pp. 127–132. ACM (2012)
8. Kampanakis, P., Perros, H., Beyene, T.: SDN-based solutions for moving target defense network protection. In: 2014 IEEE 15th International Symposium on A World of Wireless, Mobile and Multimedia Networks (WoWMoM), pp. 1–6. IEEE (2014)
9. Kannan, S., Wood, P., Deatrick, L., Beane, P., Chaterji, S., Bagchi, S.: TopHat: topology-based host-level attribution for multi-stage attacks in enterprise systems using software defined networks. Technical report, CERIAS Tech Report TR 2017-4 (2017). https://www.cerias.purdue.edu/apps/reports_and_papers/
10. MacFarland, D.C., Shue, C.A.: The SDN shuffle: creating a moving-target defense using host-based software-defined networking. In: Proceedings of the Second ACM Workshop on Moving Target Defense, pp. 37–41. ACM (2015)
11. Mao, M., Humphrey, M.: A performance study on the VM startup time in the cloud. In: 2012 IEEE 5th International Conference on Cloud Computing (CLOUD), pp. 423–430. IEEE (2012)
12. McKeown, N.: Software-defined networking. INFOCOM Keynote Talk 17(2), 30–32 (2009)
13. Medved, J., Varga, J., Tkacik, A., Gray, K.: OpenDaylight: towards a model-driven SDN controller architecture. In: 2014 IEEE 15th International Symposium on A World of Wireless, Mobile and Multimedia Networks (WoWMoM), pp. 1–6. IEEE (2014)
14. Modelo-Howard, G., Sweval, J., Bagchi, S.: Secure configuration of intrusion detection sensors for changing enterprise systems. In: Rajarajan, M., Piper, F., Wang, H., Kesidis, G. (eds.) SecureComm 2011. LNICST, vol. 96, pp. 39–58. Springer, Heidelberg (2012). https://doi.org/10.1007/978-3-642-31909-9_3
15. Savage, S., Wetherall, D., Karlin, A., Anderson, T.: Practical network support for IP traceback. In: ACM SIGCOMM Computer Communication Review, vol. 30, no. 4, pp. 295–306. ACM (2000)
16. Strayer, W.T., Jones, C.E., Schwartz, B.I., Mikkelson, J., Livadas, C.: Architecture for multi-stage network attack traceback. In: The IEEE Conference on Local Computer Networks 30th Anniversary, pp. 8–pp. IEEE (2005)

17. Sultan, F., Srinivasan, K., Iyer, D., Iftode, L.: Migratory TCP: connection migration for service continuity in the internet. In: Proceedings of 22nd International Conference on Distributed Computing Systems, pp. 469–470. IEEE (2002)
18. Wang, R., Butnariu, D., Rexford, J., et al.: Openflow-based server load balancing gone wild. Hot-ICE **11**, 12 (2011)
19. Xu, Z., Wu, Z., Li, Z., Jee, K., Rhee, J., Xiao, X., Xu, F., Wang, H., Jiang, G.: High fidelity data reduction for big data security dependency analyses. In: Proceedings of the 2016 ACM SIGSAC Conference on Computer and Communications Security, pp. 504–516. ACM (2016)
20. Zhu, Y., Bettati, R.: Unmixing mix traffic. In: Danezis, G., Martin, D. (eds.) PET 2005. LNCS, vol. 3856, pp. 110–127. Springer, Heidelberg (2006). https://doi.org/10.1007/11767831_8

JSForce: A Forced Execution Engine for Malicious JavaScript Detection

Xunchao Hu[1(✉)], Yao Cheng[1], Yue Duan[2], Andrew Henderson[1], and Heng Yin[2]

[1] Department of EECS, Syracuse University, Syracuse, USA
{xhu31,ycheng}@syr.edu, hendersa@icculus.org
[2] Department of Computer Science and Engineering, University of California, Riverside, Riverside, USA
yduan005@ucr.edu, heng@cs.ucr.edu

Abstract. The drastic increase of JavaScript exploitation attacks has led to a strong interest in developing techniques to analyze malicious JavaScript. Existing analysis techniques fall into two general categories: static analysis and dynamic analysis. Static analysis tends to produce inaccurate results (both false positive and false negative) and is vulnerable to a wide series of obfuscation techniques. Thus, dynamic analysis is constantly gaining popularity for exposing the typical features of malicious JavaScript. However, existing dynamic analysis techniques possess limitations such as limited code coverage and incomplete environment setup, leaving a broad attack surface for evading the detection. To overcome these limitations, we present the design and implementation of a novel JavaScript forced execution engine named JSForce which drives an arbitrary JavaScript snippet to execute along different paths without any input or environment setup. We evaluate JSForce using 220,587 HTML and 23,509 PDF real-world samples. Experimental results show that by adopting our forced execution engine, the malicious JavaScript detection rate can be substantially boosted by 206.29% using same detection policy without any noticeable false positive increase.

Keywords: Malicious Javascript · Forced execution

1 Introduction

Malicious JavaScript has become an important attack vector for software exploitation attacks. According to a recent report from Symantec [3], there are millions of victims attacked by malicious JavaScript on the Internet each day. A number of techniques [7–9,12–14,18] have been proposed to detect malicious JavaScript code. Due to the dynamic features of the JavaScript language, static analysis [9,10] can be easily evaded using obfuscation techniques [24]. Consequently, researchers rely upon dynamic analysis [8,11,14] to expose the typical

---

A full version of this paper can be found at https://arxiv.org/abs/1701.07860.

© ICST Institute for Computer Sciences, Social Informatics and Telecommunications Engineering 2018
X. Lin et al. (Eds.): SecureComm 2017, LNICST 238, pp. 704–720, 2018.
https://doi.org/10.1007/978-3-319-78813-5_37

features of malicious JavaScript. More specifically, these approaches rely on visiting websites or opening PDF files with a full-fledged or emulated browser/PDF reader and then monitoring the different features (e.g., heap health [18].) for detection.

However, the typical JavaScript malware is designed to execute within a particular environment, since they aim to exploit specific vulnerabilities, as opposed to benign JavaScript, which will run in a more environment-independent fashion. Fingerprinting techniques [22] are widely adopted by JavaScript malware to examine the runtime environment. A dynamic analysis system may fail to observe some malicious behaviors if the runtime environment is not configured as expected. Such configuration is quite challenging because of the numerous possible runtime environment settings. Hence, existing dynamic analysis systems usually share the limitations of limited code coverage and incomplete runtime environment setup, which leave attackers with a broad attack surface to evade the analysis.

To solve those limitations, we propose JSForce, a forced execution engine for JavaScript, which drives an arbitrary JavaScript snippet to execute along different paths without any input or environment setup. While increasing code coverage, JSForce can tolerate invalid object accesses while introducing no runtime errors during execution. This overcomes the limitations of current JavaScript dynamic analysis techniques. Note that, as an amplifier technique, JSForce does not rely on any predefined profile information or full-fledged hosting programs like browsers or PDF viewers, and it can examine partial JavaScript snippets collected during an attack. As demonstrated in Sect. 4, JSForce can be leveraged to improve the detection rate of other dynamic analysis systems without modification of their detection policies. While the high-level concept of forced execution has been introduced in binary code analysis (X-Force [17]), we face unique challenges in realizing this concept in JavaScript analysis, given that JavaScript and native code are very different languages by nature.

We implement JSForce on top of the V8 JavaScript engine [5] and evaluate the effectiveness, and runtime performance of JSForce with 220,587 HTML files and 23,509 PDF samples. Our experimental results demonstrate that adopting JSForce can greatly improve the JavaScript analysis results by 206.29% without any noticeable increase in false positives and with reasonable performance overhead.

Our main contributions are summarized as follows:

(1) We propose JavaScript forced execution technique that forces a JavaScript snippet to execute along different paths while requiring no inputs or any environment setup, to overcome the current limitations of existing JavaScript dynamic analysis techniques: limited code coverage and incomplete runtime environment setup.
(2) To enable forced execution of JavaScript, we develop a type inference model to detect and properly recover from exceptions. We have also developed path exploration algorithms for malicious JavaScript code analysis.

(3) We implement the technique with a prototype system, named `JSForce`, and evaluate its effectiveness, and runtime performance. Experimental results show that by adopting `JSForce`, the malicious JavaScript detection rate is substantially increased by 206.29% while still using the same detection policy. This increase comes without any noticeable increase in false positives and with runtime performance that is very suitable for large-scale analysis.

2   Related Work and Overview

Malicious JavaScript Code. Malicious JavaScript code is typically obfuscated and will attempt to fingerprint the version of the victim's software (browser, PDF reader, etc.), identify vulnerabilities within that software or the plugins that software uses, and then launch one or more exploits. Figure 1 shows a listing of JavaScript code used for a drive-by-download attack against the Internet Explorer browser. Line 1 employs precise fingerprinting to deliver only selected exploits that are most likely to attack the browser. Lines 5–7 contain evasive code to bypass emulation-based detection systems. More precisely, the code attempts to load a non-existant ActiveX control, named `UMOQS4dD` (line 6). When executed within a regular browser, this operation fails, triggering the execution of the `catch` block that contains the exploitation code (lines 7–14).

```
1  if (( navigator . appName . indexOf ("
     Microsoft Inte" + "rnet Explorer"
     ) == 1) && ( navigator . userAgent .
     indexOf("Windows N" + "T 5.1") ==
     1) && ( navigator . userAgent .
     indexOf("MSI" + "E 8.0") == 1))
     {
2  att = btt + 1;
3  }
4  if ( att == 0) {
5  try {
6  new ActiveXObject ("UMOQS4dD");
7  } catch (e) {
8  var tlMoOul8 = '\x25' + 'u9' + '\
     x30' + '\x39' + YYGRl6;
9  tlMoOul8 += tlMoOul8 ;
10 var CBmH8 = "%u";
11 var vBYG0 = unescape ;
12 var EuhV2 = "BODY";
13 . . .
14 }
15 }
16 setTimeout ("redir ()", 3000);
```

Types:
$$\tau ::= \Sigma_{i \in T, T \subseteq \{\bot, u, b, s, n, o\}} \varphi_i$$
Rows:
$$\varrho ::= str{:}\tau, \varrho$$
$$\quad | \quad \varrho_\tau$$
Type environments:
$$\Gamma ::= \Gamma(x : \tau)$$
$$\quad | \quad \varnothing$$
Type summands
and indices:
$$\varphi_\bot ::= \text{Undef}$$
$$\varphi_u ::= \text{Null}$$
$$\varphi_b ::= \text{Bool}(\xi_b)$$
$$\xi_b ::= false \mid true \mid \top$$
$$\varphi_s ::= \text{String}(\xi_s)$$
$$\xi_s ::= str \mid \top$$
$$\varphi_n ::= \text{Number}(\xi_n)$$
$$\xi_n ::= num \mid \top$$
$$\varphi_f ::= \text{Function}(this : \tau; \varrho \to \tau)$$
$$\varphi_o ::= \text{Obj}(\Sigma_{i \in T, T \subseteq \{b, s, n, f, \bot\}} \varphi_i)(\varrho)$$
$$\varphi_{fo} ::= \text{FObj}$$
$$\varphi_{ff} ::= \text{FFun}$$

Fig. 1. The Malicious JavaScript sample   **Fig. 2.** Syntax of JavaScript types

However, an emulation-based detection system must emulate the ActiveX API by simulating the loading and presence of any ActiveX control. In these systems, the loading of the ActiveX control will not raise this exception. As a result, the execution of the exploit never occurs and no malicious activity is observed. Instead, the victim is redirected to a benign page (line 16) if the fingerprinting or evasion stage fails. Attackers can also abuse the function `setTimeout` to create a time bomb [6] to evade detection. Detection systems can not afford to wait for long periods of time during the analysis of each sample in an attempt to capture randomly triggered exploits.

Challenges and Existing Techniques. Static analysis is a powerful technique that explores all paths of execution. But, one particular issue that plagues static analysis of malicious JavaScript is that not all of the code can be statically observed. For example, static analysis cannot observe malicious code hidden within `eval` strings, which are frequently exploited by attackers to obfuscate their code. Therefore, current detection approaches [8,11,14] rely upon dynamic analysis to expose features typically seen within malicious JavaScript. More specifically, these approaches rely upon visiting websites or opening PDF files with an instrumented browser or PDF reader, and then monitoring different features (`eval` strings [11], heap health [18], etc.) for detection.

However, dynamic analysis techniques suffer from two fundamental limitations. The first limitation is limited code coverage. This becomes a much more severe limitation within the context of analyzing malicious JavaScript. Attackers frequently employ the *cloaking* [23] technique, which works by fingerprinting the victim's web browser and only revealing the malicious content when the victim is using a specific version of the browser with a vulnerable plugin. Cloaking makes dynamic analysis much harder because the sample must be run within every combination of web browser and plugin to ensure complete code coverage. The widely-used event callback feature of JavaScript also makes it challenging for dynamic analysis to automatically trigger code. For example, attackers can load the attack code only when a specific mouse click event is captured, and automatically determining and generating such a trigger event is difficult.

The second limitation is the complexity of the JavaScript runtime environment. JavaScript is used within many applications, and it can call the functionality of any plugin extensions supported by these applications. For dynamic analysis, any pre-defined browser setup handles a known set of browsers and plugins. Thus, there is no guarantee that this setup will detect vulnerabilities only present in less popular plugins. While it is possible to deploy a cluster of machines running many different operating systems, browser applications, and browser plugins, the exponential growth of possible combinations rapidly causes scalability issues and makes this approach infeasible.

Rozzle [13] attempts to address this code coverage problem by exploring environment-related paths within a single execution. For instance, because `att` in Fig. 1 depends upon the environment-related API's output, Rozzle will execute lines 5–15 and reveal the malicious behaviors hidden in lines 8–14 by executing both the `try` and `catch` blocks. But, it requires a predefined environment-related profile for path exploration. Construction of a complete profile is a challenging task because of the numerous different browsers and plugins, especially for newer proposed fingerprinting techniques [15,16,22]. These new techniques do not rely upon any specific APIs. For instance, the JavaScript engine fingerprinting technique [16] relies upon JavaScript conformance tests such as the Sputnik [4] test suite to determine a specific browser and major version number. There are no specific APIs used for the fingerprinting. Thus, Rozzle cannot include it within the predefined profile and explore the environment-related paths. Rozzle also introduces runtime errors into the analysis engine, which may stop the analysis before any malicious code is executed. In contrast, JSForce does not rely upon predefined profile for path exploration and handles runtime errors using the forced execution model presented in Sect. 3.1. By overcoming those limitations of Rozzle, JSForce achieves greater code coverage.

Revolver [12] employs a machine learning-based detection algorithm to identify evasive JavaScript malware. However, it requires that the malicious sample is present within a known sample set so that its evasive version can be determined based upon the classification difference. By design, it can not be used for 0-day malware detection.

Symbolic execution has also been applied to the task of exposing malware [6]. This technique, while improving code coverage over dynamic analysis, suffers from scalability challenges and is, in many ways, unnecessarily precise [13]. Within the context of JavaScript analysis, symbolic execution becomes more challenging [19]. JavaScript applications accept many different kinds of input, and those inputs are structured as strings. For example, a typical application might take user input from form fields, messages from a server via `XMLHttpRequest`, and data from code running concurrently within other browser windows. It is extremely difficult for a symbolic string solver [21] to effectively supply values for all of these different kinds of inputs and reason about how those inputs are parsed and validated. The rapidly evolving JavaScript language and its host programs (browsers, PDF readers, etc.) make the modeling of the JavaScript API tedious work. Furthermore, the dynamic features (such as the `eval` function) of JavaScript make symbolic execution infeasible for many analysis efforts.

Overview. JSForce, our proposed forced-execution engine for JavaScript, is an enhancement technology designed to better expose the behaviors of malicious JavaScript at runtime. Different detection policies can be applied to examine malicious JavaScript. While the forced execution concept is first introduced for binary code analysis (X-Force [17]), we face unique challenges, such as type inference and invalid object access recovery, in enabling the forced execution concept for JavaScript.

We now illustrate how the forced execution of JavaScript code works. Consider the snippet shown in Fig. 1. JSForce forces the execution through the different code paths of the snippet. So, the exploitation code within the `catch` block (lines 7–14) will be executed, no matter how the ActiveX API is simulated by the emulation-based analysis system. Moreover, JSForce will immediately invoke the callback function passed to setTimeout to trigger the time bomb malware.

JSForce's path exploration forces line 2 to be executed, regardless of the result of the fingerprinting statement (line 1). Since btt is not defined within the code snippet under analysis, which is a common scenario because collected JavaScript code may be incomplete due to multi-stages of the attack, the execution of line 2 raises a ReferenceError exception when running within a normal JavaScript engine. When the exception is captured, JSForce creates a FakedObject named btt, which is fed to the JavaScript engine to recover from the invalid object access. However, the type of btt is unknown at the time of FakedObject's creation. JSForce infers the type based upon how the FakedObject is used. For example, if this FakedObject is added to an integer, JSForce will then change its type from FakedObject to Integer. We call this *faked object retyping*.

3 JavaScript Forced Execution

This section explains the basics of how a single forced execution proceeds. The goal is to have a non-crashable execution. We first present the JavaScript language semantics and then focus on how to detect and recover from invalid object accesses. We then discuss how path exploration occurs during forced execution.

3.1 Forced Execution Semantics

The JavaScript Language. JavaScript is a high-level, dynamic, untyped, and interpreted programming language. At runtime, the JavaScript engine dynamically interprets Java-Script code to (1) load/allocate objects, (2) determine the types of objects, and (3) execute the corresponding semantics. Given an arbitrary JavaScript snippet, execution may fail because of undefined/uninitialized objects or incorrect object types. For instance, the execution of line 2 in Fig. 1 raises a ReferenceError exception because btt is not defined. To tolerate that, forced execution must handle such failures.

The basic idea behind forced execution is that, whenever a reference error is discovered, a FakedObject is created and returned as the pointer of the property. During the execution of the program, the expected type of the FakedObject is indicated by the involved operation. For instance, adding a number object to a FakedObject indicates that the FakedObject's type is number. When the type of a FakedObject can be determined, we update it to the corresponding type.

Potentially, we could assign FakedObject with the type Object and reuse the dynamic typing rules of the JavaScript engine to coerce the FakedObject to an expected type. Nevertheless, the dynamic typing rules of the JavaScript engine are designed to maintain the correctness of JavaScript semantics and do not suffice to meet our analysis goal of achieving maximized execution.

This can be attributed to two reasons. First, while the JavaScript engine can cast the `FakedObject:Object` to proper primitive values, it cannot cast the `FakedObject:Object` to proper object types. For instance, when a `FakedObject` with the type `Object` is used as a function object, the JavaScript engine will raise the `TypeError` exception according to ECMA specification [1]. Second, the casting of `FakedObject` to primitive values by the JavaScript engine can lead to unnecessary loss of precision. To understand why, consider the following loop:

```
1 c = a/2;
2 for( i= c; i <10000; i++)
3   memory[i] = nop + nop + shellcode;
```

Since a is not defined, a `FakedObject` will be created. With the built-in typing rule of the JavaScript engine, c will be assigned the value NaN. The loop condition $i<10000$ will always evaluate to false. Thus, the loop body, which contains the heap spray code, will never be executed. Although the path exploration of JSForce will guarantee that the loop body will be executed once, without executing the loop 10,000 times, it will likely be missed by heap spray detection tools because of the small chunk of memory allocated on the heap.

Therefore, to overcome the above two issues, JSForce introduces two new types, FObj and FFun, to the JavaScript type system. The JavaScript type system defined in [20] is extended to support these two new types. Figure 2 summarizes the new syntax of these JavaScript types. Type FObj is for `FakedObject`. At the moment `FakedObject` is created, we assign type FObj as the temporary type of `FakedObject`. It can be subtyped to any types within the JavaScript type system. When `FakedObject` is used as a function object, `FakedObject` is casted to `FakedFunction` with type FFun. The `FakedFunction` with type FFun can take arbitrary input and always returns `FakedObject:FObj`. Following JSForce's dynamic typing rules, a in the above loop sample will be typed to Number because it is used as a dividend. c is then assigned to Number and the loop body is executed repeatedly until the loop condition i < 10000 is evaluated to false. By introducing these two new types and their typing rules, JSForce solves the two issues mentioned in the above paragraph. In the following paragraphs, we detail the JavaScript forced execution model.

Reference Error Recovery. To avoid `ReferenceError` exceptions, we introduce the `FakedObject` and recover the error by creating the `FakedObject` whenever necessary. There are two cases that lead to reference errors. The first case (ER_1) is a failed object lookup. Every field access or prototype access triggers a dynamic lookup using the field or prototype's name as the key. If no object is found, the lookup fails. Such failures happen when the running environment is incomplete or some portion of the JavaScript code is missing. For example, a browser plugin referenced by the JavaScript is not installed, or only a portion of the JavaScript code is captured during the attack (Fig. 4).

To handle this error, JSForce intercepts the lookup process and a `FakedObject` named as the lookup key is created whenever a failed lookup is captured. The corresponding parent object's property is also updated to the

```
1 var  a  =  null ;
2 var  b  =  c  +  1;
3 var  d  =  a . length ;
4 var  func  =  null ;
5 a  =  "Hello  World";
6 var  e  =  new  abc ();
7 if  (b  <  5)  {
8      func  =  function (x)
       {
9          return  x
10     };
11 }
12 d  =  func (6);
13 var  f  =  Math . abs (d);
14 array [5]  =  f ;
```

Fig. 3. JavaScript sample

Statement	Action	Rule
1: var a = null;	$a \leftarrow FakedObject$	ER_2
2: var b = c + 1;	$c \leftarrow FakedObject$	ER_1
	$c \leftarrow RanNumber$	R_BINOPE RATOR1
3: var d = a.length;	$a.length \leftarrow FakedObject$	ER_1
4: var func = null;	$func \leftarrow FakedObject$	ER_2
5: a = "Hello World";	$a \leftarrow "HelloWorld"$	R_ASSIGN
6: var e = new abc();	$abc \leftarrow FakedObject$	ER_1
	$abc \leftarrow fakedFunction$	R_NEW
7: if(b <5)	NO ACTION	NONE
12: d = func(6)	$func \leftarrow fakedFunction$	R_CALL1
	$d \leftarrow FakedObject$	R_ASSIGN
13: var f = Math.abs(d)	$d \leftarrow RanNumber$	R_CALL2
14: array[5] = f;	$array \leftarrow FakedObject$	ER_1
	$array \leftarrow arrayObject$	R_INDEX1
	$array[5] \leftarrow f$	R_ASSIGN

Fig. 4. Forced execution of sample in Fig. 3

FakedObject. Line 2 in Fig. 3 presents such an example. The JavaScript engine searches the current code scope for the definition of c, which is not defined. JSForce returns the FakedObject as the temporary value of c so that the execution can continue.

The second case (ER_2) occurs when the object is initialized to the value null or undefined, but later has its properties accessed. JSForce modifies the initialization process to replace the null to a FakedObject if an object is initialized as value null or undefined. For example, the variable a defined on line 1 in Fig. 3 is assigned the value FakedObject instead of null under the forced execution engine. The variable a may later be updated to another value during execution, but this does not sabotage the execution of JavaScript code.

Faked Object Retyping. When a FakedObject is used within an expression, it must be retyped to the expected type. Otherwise, incorrect typing raises a TypeError exception and stops the execution. JSForce infers the expected type of FakedObject by how the FakedObject is used. Figure 5 summarizes the dynamic typing rules introduced by JSForce. The rules are divided into the following five categories:

(1) *R-ASSIGN.* This rule deals with assignment statements. When a FakedObject e_0 is assigned to a new value e_1, e_0 is updated to the new value $e1$ with the type τ. The JavaScript engine handles this naturally, so no interference is required. For example, variable a in Fig. 3 is assigned FakedObject at line 1 by JSForce. At line 4, the variable a is retyped as a string object.

R-CALL1

R-ASSIGN

$$\frac{\Gamma \vdash_{ths} e_0 : \varphi_{fo} \qquad \Gamma \vdash e_1 : \tau}{\Gamma \vdash_{ref} e_0 = e_1 : \tau}$$

$$\frac{\tau_0 \trianglerighteq Obj(Function(this : \tau'; [0] : \tau_1, ..., [n{-}1] : \tau_n, \varrho \to \tau))(\varrho') \qquad \Gamma \vdash_{ref} e_0 : \varphi_{fo}/\tau}{\vdash_{upd} e_0 : \varphi_{fo}, \varrho'@\tau \hookleftarrow \varphi_{ff}, \Gamma \vdash_{ref} e_0(e_1, ..., e_n) : \varphi_{fo}/\bot}$$

R-CALL2

$$\frac{\tau_0 \trianglerighteq Obj(Function(this : \tau'; [0] : \tau_1, ..., [n{-}1] : \tau_n, \varrho \to \tau))(\varrho') \qquad \Gamma \vdash_{ref} e_0 : \tau_0/\tau'}{\Gamma \vdash e_1 : \tau_1 \quad ...\Gamma \vdash e_{(i-1)} : \tau_{(i-1)} \quad \Gamma \vdash e_i : \varphi_{fo} \quad \Gamma \vdash e_{(i+1)} : \tau_{(i+1)} \quad ... \quad \Gamma \vdash e_n : \tau_n}$$
$$\frac{}{\vdash_{upd} e_i : \varphi_{fo}@\tau \hookleftarrow \tau_i, \Gamma \vdash_{ref} e_0(e_1, ..., e_n) : \tau/\bot}$$

R-NEW

$$\frac{\tau_0 \trianglerighteq Obj(Function(this : \tau'; [0] : \tau_1, ..., [n{-}1] : \tau_n, \varrho \to \tau))(\varrho') \qquad \Gamma \vdash_{ref} e_0 : \varphi_{fo}/\tau}{\vdash_{upd} e_0 : \varphi_{fo}, \varrho'@\tau \hookleftarrow \varphi_{ff}, \Gamma \vdash_{ref} new\ e_0(e_1, ..., e_n) : \varphi_{fo}/\bot}$$

R-BINOPERATOR1

$$\frac{\Gamma \vdash e_1 : \varphi_{fo} \qquad \Gamma \vdash e_2 : \tau' \qquad \neg(e_2\ is\ \varphi_{fo})}{\vdash_{upd} e_1 : \varphi_{fo}@\tau \hookleftarrow \tau', \Gamma \vdash e_1\ op\ e_2 : \tau'}$$

R-BINOPERATOR2

$$\frac{\Gamma \vdash e_1 : \varphi_{fo} \qquad \Gamma \vdash e_2 : \varphi_{fo}}{\vdash_{upd} e_1 : \varphi_{fo}@\tau \hookleftarrow \varphi_n, \vdash_{upd} e_2 : \varphi_{fo}@\tau \hookleftarrow \varphi_n, \Gamma \vdash e_1\ op\ e_2 : \tau}$$

R-INDEX1   **R_UNARYOPERATOR**

$$\frac{\Gamma \vdash e_1 : \varphi_{fo} \quad \tau_1 \trianglerighteq Obj(\varphi_1)(\varrho_1) \quad \Gamma \vdash e_2 : \varphi_n}{\vdash_{upd} e_1 : \varphi_{fo}@\tau \hookleftarrow \tau_1, \Gamma \vdash_{ths} e_1[e_2] : \varphi_{fo}} \qquad \frac{\Gamma \vdash e_1 : \varphi_{fo}}{\vdash_{upd} e_2 : \varphi_{fo}@\tau \hookleftarrow \varphi_n, \Gamma \vdash op\ e_1 : \tau}$$

R-INDEX2

$$\frac{\Gamma \vdash e_1 : \tau_1 \quad \tau_1 \trianglerighteq Obj(\varphi_1)(\varrho_1) \quad \Gamma \vdash e_2 : \varphi_{fo} \quad \vdash_{upd} \varrho_1@\varphi_n \mapsto \tau'}{\vdash_{upd} e_2 : \varphi_{fo}@\tau \hookleftarrow \varphi_n, \Gamma \vdash_{ths} e_1[e_2] : \tau'}$$

Fig. 5. Typing rules

(2) *R-CALL1* and *R-NEW*. These two rules describe the typing rule for the scenario when a FakedObject:FObj is used as a function call or by the new expression. Function calls and the new expression both expect their first operand to evaluate to a function. So, JSForce updates the FakedObject:FObj to FakedFunction:FFun for this situation. The FakedFunction is a special function object which is configured to accept arbitrary parameters. The return value of the function is set to a FakedObject:FObj so that it can be retyped whenever necessary.

(3) *R-CALL2*. This rule describes the case where the callee is a known function, but a FakedObject:FObj is passed as a function parameter. JSForce types the FakedObject:FObj to the required type of the callee's arguments. The JavaScript language has many standard built-in libraries such as Math and Date. When a FakedObject:FObj is used by the standard library function, we update the type based upon the specification of the library function [1]. Currently, JSForce implements retyping for several common libraries (e.g., Math, Number, Date).

(4) *R-BINOPERATOR1/2* and *R-UNARYOPERATOR*. These three rules describe how to update the type if the FakedObject:FObj is involved in an

expression with an operator. JSForce updates the `FakedObject:FObj`'s type based upon the semantics of the operator. For unary operators, it is straightforward to determine the type from the operator's semantics. For instance, the postfix operator indicates the type as `number`. For binary operators, the typing becomes more complicated. If both operands are `FakedObject:FObj` and the operator does not reveal the type of the operands, JSForce types them to `number`. This is because the `number` type can be converted to most types naturally by the JavaScript engine. For example, the `number` type in JavaScript can be converted to the `string` type, but it may fail to convert a `string` to a `number`. Later during execution, if the types can be determined, JSForce will update the type to the correct type. If only one of the two operands is `FakedObject:FObj`, JSForce determines the type based upon the other operand's type and the operator's semantics.

(5) *R-INDEX1* and *R-INDEX2*. These two rules describe how to update the type when there are indexing operations. A `FakedObject:FObj` is updated to an $ArrayObject : \phi_o$ whenever a key is used as an array index to access elements of the `FakedObject`. JSForce creates an $ArrayObject$ and initializes the elements to `FakedObject:FObj`. The length of the $ArrayObject$ is set to $2*CurrentIndex$. If an Out-Of-Boundary access is found, JSForce doubles the length of $ArrayObject$. If the array index is `FakedObject`, JSForce types it to `number` and initializes it as 0, which avoids Out-Of-Boundary exceptions. If both the index object and base object are `FakedObject:FObj`, the R-INDEX2 rule is first applied to update the index object to `number`, then the R-INDEX1 rule is applied to update the base object to $ArrayObject$.

Example. Figure 4 presents a forced execution of the sample shown in Fig. 3. In the execution, the branch in lines 8–11 is not taken. At line 1, JSForce assigns a `FakedObject:Fobj` to a, instead of `null`. This is because at line 3 the access to property `length` raises an exception if a is `null`. At line 2, we can see a `FakedObject:FObj` is first assigned to c. Once c is added to 1, JSForce updates the value of c to a random number. Lines 6 and 7 show that if a `FakedObject:FObj` is used in the function call or `new` expression, JSForce updates it to `FakedFunction:FFun`. The return value of the faked function is still configured to `FakedObject:FObj`, so that at line 13, d is updated to hold a random number.

JSForce also automatically recovers from other exceptions by intercepting those exceptions to eliminate the exception condition. For example, JSForce will update a divisor to a non-zero value if a division-by-zero exception is raised.

3.2 Path Exploration in JSForce

One important feature of JSForce is the capability of exploring different execution paths of a given JavaScript snippet to expose its behavior and acquire complete analysis results. In this subsection, we explain the path exploration algorithm and strategies.

Algorithm 1. Path Exploration Algorithm

Definitions: *switches* - the set of switched predicates in a forced execution, denoted by a sequence of predicate offsets in the source file(SrcName:offset). For example, $t.js$: $15 \cdot t.js : 83 \cdot t.js : 100$ means the branch in source file $t.js$ with the offset 15, 83, 100 is switched. EX, WL - a set of forced executions, each denoted by a sequence of switched predicates. $preds : \overline{Predicate \times boolean}$ - the sequence of executed predicates.

```
Input: The tested JS
Output: FULL_EX
 1: FULL_EX ← ∅
 2: SRC ← {JS}
 3: while SRC do
 4:     WL ← {∅}
 5:     EX ← ∅
 6:     js ← SRC.pop()
 7:     while WL do
 8:         switches ← WL.pop()
 9:         EX ← EX ∪ switches
10:         (preds, newJS) ← EXECUTE-
    CODE(js, switches)
11:         SRC ← SRC ∪ newJS
12:         t ← len(switches)
13:         preds ← remove the first t elements
    in preds
14:         for all (p, b) ∈ preds do
15:             if !covered(p, ¬b) then
16:                 WL ← WL ∪ switches · (p, b)
17:             end if
18:         end for
19:     end while
20:     FULL_EX ← FULL_EX ∪ {EX : js}
21: end while
22: procedure EXECUTECODE(JS, switches)
23:     preds ← switches
24:     CBQ ← ∅
25:     newJS ← ∅
26:     for all stmt ∈ JS do
27:         if isNoneEvalFunctionCallStmt(stmt)
    then
28:             if CalleeTakesStrings(stmt) then
29:                 newJS    ←    newJS    ∪
    GetJSFromString(stmt)
30:             end if
31:             if    CalleeRegisterCallback(stmt)
    then
32:                 CBQ ← CBQ∪ ExtractCBFunc(stmt)
33:             end if
34:         else if isBranchStmt(stmt) then
35:             if GetSwitch(stmt) ∈ switches then
36:                 Execute according to switches
37:             else
38:                 preds ← preds·GetPredicate(stmt)
39:             end if
40:         end if
41:     end for
42:     for all cb ∈ CBQ do
43:         (preds', newJS') ← EXECUTE-
    CODE(cb, ∅)
44:         newJS ← newJS ∪ newJS'
45:         preds ← preds · preds'
46:     end for
    return (preds, newJS)
47: end procedure
```

In practice, attackers constantly adopt the dynamic features of JavaScript to evade detection. This results in incomplete path exploration under two circumstances. The first is when strings are dynamically generated. For instance, `document.write` is often abused to inject dynamically decoded malicious JavaScript code into the page at runtime. The second is when event callbacks are used. As discussed in Sect. 2, attackers can abuse event callbacks to stop the execution of malicious code. JSForce solves this by employing specific path exploration strategies. Within the execution, if faked functions take strings as input, JSForce examines the strings and executes the code if they contain JavaScript. This strategy is only applied on faked functions since original functions (`eval`) can handle the strings as defined. JSForce also detects the callback registration function and invokes the callback function immediately after the current execution terminates.

JSForce treats `try-catch` statements as `if-else` statements, ie., it executes each `try` block and `catch` block separately. Ternary operators are also treated as `if-else` statements: both values are evaluated.

There are several different path exploration algorithms: linear search, quadratic search, and exponential search [17]. The goal of path exploration in JSForce is to maximize the code coverage to improve the detection rate of mali-

Table 1. Effectiveness results.

Table 2. Num of path exploration during analysis.

Sample set	Total	Without JSForce	With JSForce	Improvement
Old HTML	66,325	193	357	84.9%
New HTML	106,018	2,250	20,649	817.3%
HTML total	**172,995**	**2,443**	**21,006**	**759.8%**
Old PDF	22,081	6,306	6,475	2.7%
New PDF	1,428	32	170	431.2%
PDF total	**23,509**	**6,338**	**6,645**	**4.8%**

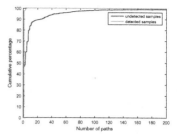

cious payload with an acceptable performance overhead. Quadratic and exponential searches are too expensive, so JSForce employs the linear search only.

Algorithm 1 describes the path exploration algorithm, which generates a pool of forced executions that achieve maximized code coverage. The complexity is $O(n)$, where n is the number of JavaScript statements. n may change at runtime because JavaScript code can be dynamically generated. Initially, JSForce executes the program without switching any predicates since switches is initialized as $\emptyset$ (line 8) for the first time. JSForce executes the program according to the switches at line 10 and returns preds and dynamically generated code newJS. In lines 12–17, we determine if it would be of interest to further switch more predicate instances. Lines 11–13 compute the sequence of predicate instances eligible for switching. Note that it cannot be a predicate before the last switched predicate specified in switches. Switching such a predicate may change the control flow such that the specification in switches becomes invalid. Specifically, line 16 switches the predicate if the other branch has not been covered. In each new forced execution, we essentially switch one more predicate.

The procedure ExecuteCode (lines 22–47) describes the execution process. It collects dynamically generated JavaScript code (lines 28–30) and the executed predicates (lines 34–38). The new generated JavaScript code, newJS, will be executed after the path exploration of the current js finishes. The registered callback functions (lines 31–33) are also queued and invoked after the current execution finishes (lines 42–46). As an example, recall the callback function redir() used in line 16 of Fig. 1. Instead of waiting for the timeout, JSForce will trigger the redir() function immediately after the current execution finishes.

4   Evaluation

JSForce is implemented by extending the V8 JavaScript engine [5] on the X86-64 platform. It is comprised of approximately 4,600 lines of C/C++ and 1,500 lines of Python. In this section, we present details on the evaluation of effectiveness and runtime performance of JSForce using a large number of real-world samples.

4.1 Dataset and Experiment Setup

Dataset. The dataset used for our evaluation consists of two sets: a malicious sample set and a benign sample set. For the malicious set, we collected a sample set with 172,995 HTML files and 23,509 PDF files from various databases. For the benign sample set, we crawled the Alexa top 100 websites [2] and collected 47,592 HTML files.

Experiment Setup. For JavaScript code analysis, we leverage the jsunpack [11] tool. Jsunpack is a widely used malicious JavaScript code analysis tool that utilizes the SpiderMonkey JavaScript engine for code execution. For the sake of our evaluation, we replaced the SpiderMonkey from jsunpack with JSForce and relied upon the detection policies in jsunpack for malicious code detection. We conducted our experiments on a test machine equipped with Intel(R) Xeon(R) E5-2650 CPU (20M Cache, 2 GHz) and 128 GB of physical memory. The operating system was Ubuntu 12.04.3 (64 bit).

4.2 Effectiveness

For the evaluation of effectiveness, we would like to demonstrate that JSForce can indeed help the malicious JavaScript code analysis by performing efficient forced execution. In order to achieve that, we utilize our malicious HTML and PDF sample sets and run the sample sets against jsunpack both with or without JSForce for the evaluation. In the interest of showing how useful our faked object retyping is, we also conduct another experiment that disables the retyping and only keeps the reference error recovery component and path exploration component.

Experimental Results. Table 1 illustrates the experimental results for effectiveness. It demonstrates that JSForce could greatly improve the detection rate for JavaScript analysis. We can see detection rate improvements of 759.84% and 4.84% for HTML and PDF samples, respectively, when using JSForce-extended jsunpack instead of the original version for analysis. And all the samples detected by original jsunpack are also flagged by JSForce-extended jsunpack. We further break down the numbers into old and new sample sets and perceive that the extended version could perform much better than original jsunpack in analyzing new samples. For new HTML samples, jsunpack with JSForce is able to detect 817.3% more samples while for old samples, the number is 84.97%. Similar results are also observed for PDF samples. After manual inspection, we confirmed that this is because many of the old samples have been analyzed for quite sometime and jsunpack already has the signatures stored in its database, leaving only a small margin for JSForce to improve upon. For the faked object retyping evaluation, we reran the test using 106,018 new HTML malicious samples with retyping component disabled. The result shows that only 8,677 samples can be detected by JSForce in contrast to 20,649 with retyping enabled. This result reveals the usefulness of our faked object retyping component during analysis. Nevertheless, through our experiments, we are able to draw the conclusion that JSForce is quite effective for boosting the effectiveness of JavaScript analysis.

Number of Paths Explored. Potentially, there may be a large number of paths that exist inside of a single JavaScript program. The effectiveness and efficiency of JSForce are closely related to the number of paths explored during analysis. Hence, we would like to show some statistics on the number of paths that JSForce explored during analysis.

The result depicted in Table 2 shows that JSForce is able to detect the maliciousness of samples with a limited number of path explorations. An interesting observation is that over 96% of the samples were detected by exploring only a single path. Even though most of the analysis for detected samples can be finished by exploring just one path, the path exploration of JSForce is still essential. Note that 98% of the samples missed by the default jsunpack, but detected by the JSForce-extended version, explore at least two paths. So, the analysis could still receive an enormous benefit from JSForce in terms of path exploration. As for any undetected samples, JSForce will explore the entire code space during analysis, which requires a larger amount of path exploration and longer analysis runtime.

4.3   Runtime Performance

In this section, we evaluate the runtime performance of JSForce by using our malicious and benign datasets with a comparison between the original jsunpack and the JSForce-extended version.

Runtime for Detected Samples. In this section, we compare the runtime performance using the HTML and PDF samples that can be detected by jsunpack both with and without JSForce. The reason why we chose this sample set is that we wished to observe whether the JSForce-extended version can achieve efficiency comparable to the original jsunpack when using a detectable malicious sample. The results are displayed in Figs. 6 and 7. The results conclude that JSForce-extended version has better runtime performance than jsunpack for over 90.9% of HTML and 83.6% of PDF samples. This conclusion is quite surprising as the JSForce-extended version tends to explore multiple paths while jsunpack only probes for one.

In theory, jsunpack should have better runtime performance. However, after investigation, we found that many of the JavaScript samples require specific system configurations (such as specific browser kernel version) to run. As a result, when jsunpack performs analysis, it will run the JavaScript programs under multiple settings. This results in multiple executions, which take additional time to complete. In contrast, the JSForce-extended version handled this issue with forced execution, resulting in better runtime performance in practice.

Runtime for Undetected Samples. Figures 8 and 9 show the runtime performance of JSForce for undetected samples. We empirically set the time limit to be 300

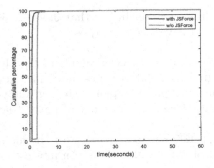
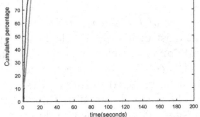

Fig. 6. Runtime for detected HTML.   **Fig. 7.** Runtime for detected PDF.

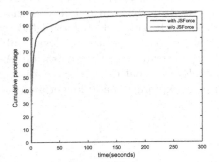
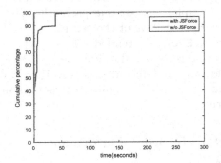

Fig. 8. Runtime for undetected HTML.   **Fig. 9.** Runtime for undetected PDF.

s in consequence of the fact that experiment shows almost all (99.6%) HTML and PDF samples can be analyzed within 300 s. As demonstrated in the figures, the average analysis runtime for HTML and PDF samples are 12.02 and 8.15 s, while the analysis for a majority (80%) of HTML samples and PDF samples are finished within 8.54 and 7.4 s, respectively. When compared with the original jsunpack, the JSForce-extended version achieves an average runtime of 16.08 s and 7.97 s for undetected HTML and PDF samples while jsunpack finishes execution in 1.13 s and 1.37 s, correspondingly. Our conclusion from these experiments are that the performance overhead of JSForce is quite reasonable and can certainly meet the requirements of large scale JavaScript analysis.

5   Conclusion

In this paper, we presented the design and implementation of a novel JavaScript forced execution engine named JSForce which enables non crashable execution model while ensuring complete code coverage. We evaluated JSForce using a large number of HTML and PDF samples. Experimental results showed that by adopting JSForce, the malicious JavaScript detection rate can be greatly improved without any noticeable false positive increase and the runtime overhead was generally neglectable.

Acknowledgments. We would like to thank anonymous reviewers for their feedback. This research was supported in part by National Science Foundation Grant #1664315, and DARPA Grant #FA8750-16-C-0044. Any opinions, findings, and conclusions in this paper are those of the authors and do not necessarily reflect the views of the funding agencies.

References

1. http://www.ecmascript.org/
2. http://www.alexa.com/topsites
3. 2015 symantec internet security threat report. https://goo.gl/UIPdR8
4. Sputnik. https://code.google.com/p/sputniktests/
5. V8 javascript engine. https://developers.google.com/v8/
6. Brumley, D., Hartwig, C., Liang, Z., Newsome, J., Song, D., Yin, H.: Automatically identifying trigger-based behavior in malware. In: Lee, W., Wang, C., Dagon, D. (eds.) Botnet Detection. ADIS, vol. 36, pp. 65–88. Springer, Heidelberg (2008). https://doi.org/10.1007/978-0-387-68768-1_4
7. Cao, Y., Pan, X., Chen, Y., Zhuge, J.: JShield: towards real-time and vulnerability-based detection of polluted drive-by download attacks. In: Proceedings of Annual Computer Security Applications Conference (ACSAC) (2014)
8. Cova, M., Kruegel, C., Vigna, G.: Detection and analysis of drive-by-download attacks and malicious javascript code. In: Proceedings of the 19th International Conference on World Wide Web (2010)
9. Curtsinger, C., Livshits, B., Zorn, B.G., Seifert, C.: Fast and precise in-browser javascript malware detection. In: USENIX Security Symposium, Zozzle (2011)
10. Feinstein, B., Peck, D., SecureWorks, I.: Caffeine monkey: automated collection, detection and analysis of malicious javascript. In: Black Hat USA (2007)
11. Hartstein, B.: Jsunpack: an automatic javascript unpacker. In: ShmooCon Convention (2009)
12. Kapravelos, A., Shoshitaishvili, Y., Cova, M., Kruegel, C., Vigna, G.: Revolver: an automated approach to the detection of evasive web-based malware. In: USENIX Security, pp. 637–652. Citeseer (2013)
13. Kolbitsch, C., Livshits, B., Zorn, B., Seifert, C.: Rozzle: de-cloaking internet malware. In: 2012 IEEE Symposium on Security and Privacy (SP) (2012)
14. Lu, G., Debray, S.: Automatic simplification of obfuscated javascript code: a semantics-based approach. In: Proceedings of the 2012 IEEE Sixth International Conference on Software Security and Reliability (2012)
15. Mowery, K., Bogenreif, D., Yilek, S., Shacham, H.: Fingerprinting information in javascript implementations. In: Proceedings of W2SP, vol. 2 (2011)
16. Mulazzani, M., Reschl, P., Huber, M., Leithner, M., Schrittwieser, S., Weippl, E., Wien, F.: Fast and reliable browser identification with javascript engine fingerprinting. In: Web 2.0 Workshop on Security and Privacy (W2SP), vol. 5 (2013)
17. Peng, F., Deng, Z., Zhang, X., Xu, D., Lin, Z., Su, Z.: X-force: force-executing binary programs for security applications. In: Proceedings of the 2014 USENIX Security Symposium, San Diego, CA, August 2014 (2014)
18. Ratanaworabhan, P., Livshits, B., Zorn, B.: Nozzle: a defense against heap-spraying code injection attacks. In: Proceedings of the USENIX Security Symposium (2009)
19. Saxena, P., Akhawe, D., Hanna, S., Mao, F., McCamant, S., Song, D.: A symbolic execution framework for javascript. In: 2010 IEEE Symposium on Security and Privacy (SP) (2010)

20. Thiemann, P.: Towards a type system for analyzing javascript programs. In: Sagiv, M. (ed.) ESOP 2005. LNCS, vol. 3444, pp. 408–422. Springer, Heidelberg (2005). https://doi.org/10.1007/978-3-540-31987-0_28
21. Trinh, M.-T., Chu, D.-H., Jaffar, J.: S3: a symbolic string solver for vulnerability detection in web applications. In: Proceedings of the 2014 ACM SIGSAC Conference on Computer and Communications Security, pp. 1232–1243. ACM (2014)
22. Upathilake, R., Li, Y., Matrawy, A.: A classification of web browser fingerprinting techniques. In: 2015 7th International Conference on New Technologies, Mobility and Security (NTMS). IEEE (2015)
23. Wang, D.Y., Savage, S., Voelker, G.M.: Cloak and dagger: dynamics of web search cloaking. In: Proceedings of the 18th ACM Conference on Computer and Communications Security, pp. 477–490. ACM (2011)
24. Xu, W., Zhang, F., Zhu, S.: The power of obfuscation techniques in malicious javascript code: a measurement study. In: 2012 7th International Conference on Malicious and Unwanted Software (MALWARE), pp. 9–16. IEEE (2012)

ROPOB: Obfuscating Binary Code via Return Oriented Programming

Dongliang Mu[1]([⊠]), Jia Guo[1], Wenbiao Ding[1], Zhilong Wang[1], Bing Mao[1], and Lei Shi[2]

[1] State Key Laboratory for Novel Software Technology,
Department of Computer Science and Technology, Nanjing University,
Nanjing, China
mudongliangabcd@163.com, njuguojia@163.com, wbdingzx@163.com,
njuwangzhilong@163.com, maobing@nju.edu.cn
[2] Zhengzhou University, Henan, China
shilei@zzu.edu.cn

Abstract. Software reverse engineering has been widely employed for software reuse, serving malicious purposes, such as software plagiarism and malware camouflage. To raise the bar for adversaries to perform reverse engineering, plenty of work has been proposed to introduce obfuscation into the to-be-protected software. However, existing obfuscation methods are either inefficient or hard to be deployed. In this paper, we propose an obfuscation scheme for binaries based on *Return Oriented Programming* (ROP), which aims to serve as an efficient and deployable anti-reverse-engineering approach. Our basic idea is to transform direct control flow to indirect control flow. The strength of our scheme derives from the fact that static analysis is typically insufficient to pinpoint target address of indirect control flow. We implement a tool, ROPOB, to achieve obfuscation in Commercial-off-the-Shelf (COTS) binaries, and test ROPOB with programs in SPEC2006. The results show that ROPOB can successfully transform all identified direct control flow, without causing execution errors. The overhead is acceptable: the average performance overhead is less than 10% when obfuscation coverage is over 90%.

Keywords: Obfuscation · Return-oriented programming
Reverse engineering

1 Introduction

Along with the booming development of software market, illegal reuses of software with malicious purposes, such as *software plagiarism* and *malware camouflage*, bring a lot of negative influence. Software plagiarism happens when the adversaries develop and release software with components "stolen" from programs owned or licensed under others' names. Malware camouflage refers to cases where the adversaries repackage released software to embed malicious payloads, and then publish the resulted in "malware" with the name of the original

© ICST Institute for Computer Sciences, Social Informatics and Telecommunications Engineering 2018
X. Lin et al. (Eds.): SecureComm 2017, LNICST 238, pp. 721–737, 2018.
https://doi.org/10.1007/978-3-319-78813-5_38

software. These intentional torts are causing billions of dollars worth of damage to the software market every year [1].

Commercial softwares always appeal to adversaries for malicious reuse. As most of them are released in the form of binaries, adversaries can analyse the binaries to extract their working logic to reuse them. The analysing process is commonly termed as *software reverse engineering.* A major line of effort on preventing software from being reverse engineered is to introduce *obfuscation* into software. Basically, obfuscation deliberately transforms readable codes into obfuscated codes that are difficult for humans or tools to understand, aiming to conceal the original logics of the software.

Plenty of techniques have been proposed to achieve software obfuscation in different phases of reverse engineering. Linn and Debray propose to obfuscate executable code to disrupt static disassembly [2], which is often the first step of binary reverse engineering. Igor et al. propose to keep control flow under cover by signal handlers [3]. However, leveraging signal mechanisms to handle control flow introduces significant overhead (typically higher than 21%). and it is not thread-safe. Chen et al. leverage the characteristic - information tracking support of Itanium processor, to obfuscate control flow with exception handling [4]. This mechanism is more efficient but can only be deployed when the required processors are available.

Before we introduce our approach, we first briefly explain the concept of ROP. ROP is a type of advanced code-reuse attack proposed by Hovav Shacham in [5]. A ROP attack hijacks the control flow to a sequence of code pieces (or "gadgets") that end with a return instruction. The ROP attack will pre-set the return address for the return instruction in each gadget on the stack, to make sure these gadgets are executed sequentially.

RopSteg [6] is proposed for code protection that attempts to hide selected instruction sequence by executing their "unintended matches" located elsewhere. And instruction snippet that they can hide is much smaller than the whole program.

In this paper, we propose a new ROP-based approach to perform software obfuscation. The core idea of our approach is to take advantage of ROP to obfuscate control flow in basic block granularity as follows. First, we disassemble a to-be-protected ELF file and divide executable code into basic blocks. Then, do some instrumentation on basic blocks to convert them into gadgets. We transform all identified direct control flow and hide them by ret instruction. Finally, add all those gadgets and designed payload into original file and leverage binary rewrite to produce obfuscated file. Note that the designed payload will be used for control flow transfers and will be stored in a newly added payload section. As we use ROP payload and gadgets to complete control flow transfer, static reverse engineering methods can not find the real control flow, even though they can disassemble software correctly. And it is a lightweight method to do obfuscation with ROP. As ROP works only in user space, does not involve signal handler or other kernel space, the whole process of control flow transfer is quicker than signal methods theoretically. And ROP method can be thread-safe.

Our contributions are as follows:

- We propose a novel ROP based approach to achieve control flow obfuscation. Our experiment proves that this method is effective and practical against static reverse engineering analysis.
- Our obfuscation approach is efficient and widely deployable.
- We develop a tool ROPOB to implement our approach. Experiment results show that ROPOB can correctly transform all identified direct control flow. The average overhead introduced by our obfuscation is less than 10% when obfuscation coverage is above 90%.

The remainder of this paper is organized as follows. In Sect. 2, we explain the overview of our approach. Section 3 details our design of ROPOB. Then we present the evaluation of our approach in Sect. 4. Section 5 summarizes related work and Sect. 6 discusses some issues. Section 7 concludes this paper with future work.

2 Overview

Our goal is to convert ELF (Executable and Linkable Format) files to ROP-obfuscated ones, whose control flow information has been concealed, so that static de-obfuscation methods will fail to construct the control flow graph (CFG). The obfuscated files are semantically equal to the original ones. In this section we will give an overview of our method.

We consider a model, in which the defender develops a commercial software, prepares to obfuscate and release its binary version, and the adversary aims to reverse engineer the binary for malicious reuse. The following assumptions should be satisfied in this model:

- The un-obfuscated binary file is in ELF file format (with or without symbol information);
- The obfuscated binary file is supposed to run on unmodified Linux systems;
- The adversary only employs static reverse engineering tools, such as IDA Pro [7], to analyse the obfuscated binary file.

Our approach takes a to-be-protected ELF file as input and outputs the obfuscated version. The workflow of our approach is shown as Fig. 1(a), which consists of four major steps:

- Disassemble the text section of an ELF file and divide executable code into basic blocks;
- Do some instrumentation on basic blocks to convert them into gadgets, which are ended with *ret* instruction;
- Write all those gadgets and designed payload into an assembler file and assemble it into a new ELF file. Note that the designed payload is a list of start address of gadgets. Its function is to guide the execution of all the gadgets.
- Copy text and payload section of new ELF file into original ELF file to produce our obfuscated file;

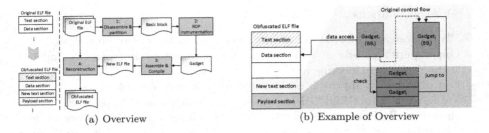

(a) Overview   (b) Example of Overview

Fig. 1. Workflow of our approach

When the above steps are finished, we wipe out the original text section from the resulting ELF file. Otherwise the adversary can still recover the control flow information from this section. Note that all sections copied to the obfuscated ELF, including the new text section and the payload section, do not overlap with any previous sections. Notably, we maintain the data section to be intact, which will be directly reused by the obfuscated code section. Therefore, we essentially maintain the data integrity.

In summary, all our work is in user space and does not involve kernel space. Furthermore, our method can invalidate all static de-obfuscation techniques, because there is no control flow information in static analysis. Meanwhile, it can increase the difficulty for dynamic de-obfuscation methods. Because there is no function call in our obfuscated files, it is hard to extract high level semantics, even when attackers find an execution path dynamically.

The workflow of our approach is straightforward. However, there are multiple challenges to be tackled in the workflow, which are summarized as follows:

- Basic blocks can't be partitioned thoroughly. Therefore, some indirect control flow may jump into the body of basic block (or gadget), rather than the entrance. That will fail payload entrance check (used for gadget location when ROP runs).
- Indirect control flow can't be analysed statically. It is necessary to make indirect control flow jump to destination correctly. We design a control flow map table to solve this problem.
- We must keep data access correct, with control flow obfuscated. We design a reconstruction framework to reuse the whole data sections of original programs.

Figure 1(b) depicts an instance of our design. The dotted line in this figure represents there is a control flow path from BB_i to BB_j in the original file (BB means basic block). After basic blocks (BB) are transformed to gadgets ($Gadget$), we maintain the control flow path from BB_i to BB_j through designed payload. Before $Gadget_i$ executes ret, we push the address of $Gadget_j$ onto the stack. Therefore, we can direct the control flow to $Gadget_j$.

3   Design and Implementation

We design our method as a tool, called ROPOB, which takes an ordinary ELF file as input and generates an ROP-obfuscated ELF file with the same semantic as output. This tool has a basic reconstruction framework, which supports instrumentation works on the input ELF file. Apart from this framework, there are other challenges needed to be resolved in ROPOB, such as basic block partition and control flow integrity. We will present all technical details in this section.

3.1   Reconstruction Framework

Our goal is to transform an original ELF file to a ROP-obfuscated one, keeping the semantics equal. We design a framework to reconstruct an ELF file, and to support any assembly-level instrumentation, including our ROP-obfuscation work. This framework mainly analyzes the assembly code, which is obtained from disassembling the original ELF file, and then recompiles it into a new ELF file. Our reconstruction framework is shown in Fig. 2.

Fig. 2. Reconstruction framework

Generally speaking, the text section of original ELF file starts from address 0x8048xxx. In our reconstruction framework, we extract the text section from the original ELF file, disassemble the text section and divide the text section into basic blocks. Meanwhile the control flow information between basic blocks are collected. Thus, we can apply any assembly-level instrumentation work on those basic blocks, such as our ROP obfuscation instrumentation. Then we use the rewritten basic blocks and previously collected control flow information to write an assembly file. After recompiling the assembly file, we can get an intermediate ELF file, whose text section is lowered down to address 0x7000000. The reason for changing base of text section to 0x7000000 is that we will copy the text section into the original ELF file as new text section. As we do some instrumentation works, the scale of text section in intermediate file is larger than that of the original one. So if we set the base address of text section in intermediate file the same as that of the original one, some data sections of the original file will be destroyed, which is not expected. We integrate new text section and some new data sections into original file by *objcopy* tool after recompilation in order to reuse all data sections from the original file. The last step of our framework is to modify the program header table to include new text section and data sections, whose addresses are all above 0x7000000. For some security reasons, we need to wipe out the original text section in case of control flow information leak. By means of this framework, we can maintain the same semantics between the original file and the ROP-obfuscated file.

3.2   Basic Block Partition

It is common sense that control flow information exists in relationship between basic blocks. A basic block is a straight-line code sequence, with no branches in except to the entry and no branches out except at the exit. The rules we use to divide basic blocks are as follows:

- A control flow related instructions, like a *jmp/jcc/call/ret* instruction, indicates an exit of a basic block. The target operand of a direct *jmp/jcc/call* instruction is an entrance of a basic block.
- We ignore the target operand of indirect *jmp/jcc/call* instructions.
- The next instruction of a *jmp/jcc/call/ret* instruction is an entrance of a basic block.

We do not deal with the target operand of indirect *jmp/jcc/call* instructions (control flow related instruction, CFRI for short), because the target operand is unknown in static method. Although it is possible to explore some information through some data sections, such as finding a jump table in rodata section, it is hard to locate the boundary of a jump table. However, some basic blocks cannot divided correctly, for example, an entrance of a jump table is not found. To deal with this problem, we design a control flow mapping table, which will be discussed in next subsection.

3.3   Control Flow Mapping Table

The control flow information of direct CFRI is obvious. However, we can't work out control flow information of indirect CFRI, whose target operand is often determined by some data sections during the runtime. As we have mentioned, we reuse all data sections from original file, and the target addresses computed by original indirect CFRIs are the same as those calculated by indirect CFRIs in new text section of ROP-obfuscated file. Under the circumstances, if we make no change to the target address calculated by indirect CFRI in new text section, control flow will be guided into wiped text section which will crash the program. So, we will redirect such addresses and design a control flow mapping table to solve this problem. Figure 3 illustrates the principle of control flow mapping table.

There is a basic block (BB_1) of bzip2 presented in Fig. 3. After instrumentation, we get $Gadget_1$. 0x804cac4 and 0x7007dff are entrance addresses. The

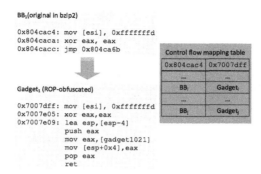

Fig. 3. Control flow mapping table

control flow mapping table is in the right side of Fig. 3. If the target of an indirect CFRI is entrance of BB_1, we will calculate the target address first and check control flow mapping table to locate the correct target address 0x7007dff in $Gadget_1$.

It is tricky to solve the problem presented in Sect. 3.2 by means of control flow mapping table in Fig. 3. Just thinking that if our basic block partition misses a basic block, whose entrance is 0x804caca in BB_1 and an indirect CFRI jumps to 0x804caca, we can't find any table entry to match 0x804caca. But the offset between 0x804caca and 0x804cac4 equals that between 0x7007e05 and 0x7007dff, with the acknowledgement that we only apply instrumentation at the end of basic block, rather than in the middle. Therefore we can locate 0x7007e05 correctly.

3.4   ROP Instrumentation

Our goal is to use ROP technique to hide control flow information, so that static method can't analyze the control flow information. Control flow from one basic block to another is completed by *ret* instruction and ROP payload. The payload is a list of entries of all generated gadgets, converted from original basic blocks. We design different instrumentation policy for different control flow cases.

- **Case 1:** For each basic block ended with non-CFRI (maybe *mov* or *add* instruction), we push the start address of next gadget onto the stack. Note that the next gadget is transformed from the basic block next to it and its address is stored in the payload;
- **Case 2:** For each basic block ended with direct CFRI, there is only one target address of *call/jmp*. If the direct CFRI is *call/jmp*, we push the start address of next gadget onto the stack like Case 1. But the next gadget is transformed from the basic block starting from the target address. Figure 3 shows a simple example about direct *jmp* (Note that [*gadget*1021] stores the start address of next gadget). The difference between *call* and *jmp* is that for *call* instruction, return address is pushed onto the stack at first. If the direct

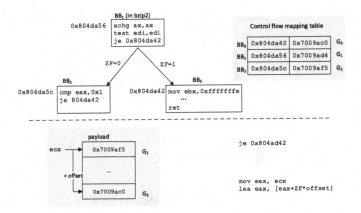

Fig. 4. Jcc transformation

CFRI is *jcc* with two target addresses, we provide two paths at the end of gadgets and deal with each path like direct *jmp* instructions, or we can use characteristic of ROP to transform two paths into one unified form. We will discuss this transformation later in this subsection;

– **Case 3:** For each basic block ended with indirect CFRI, we take advantages of control flow mapping table to relocate the target address. Then the remaining work is like Case 2;

– **Case 4:** For each basic block ended with *ret* instruction, nothing is to be done. The return address has been pushed in the stack previously;

Figure 4 tells how we transform jcc instruction into a unified form. There is a branch from BB_1 to two destinations: BB_2 and BB_3 in program bzip2. If condition is met at instruction 'je 0x804da42' ($ZF = 1$), control flow goes to BB_3. Otherwise, control flow goes to BB_2. Accordingly, there are gadgets, G_2 and G_3, in payload. The difference of start address between G_2 and G_3 in payload is offset, a parameter shown in Fig. 4. Then we can get the condition flag and use it to compute the proper target address. For example, we use register eax to store address of G_2 in payload, and then we calculate the target address with the help of flag and offset. The flag is the conditional judgment bit in *eflags*. We ensure that if condition is satisfied, *eax* points to G_3 in payload. Otherwise, register *eax* points to G_2 in payload.

3.5 Special Case of Data Access

In ROPOB, we reuse all data sections from original file. The major data accesses are absolute addressing, with addresses in data sections directly. However, there are special cases - access data with relative addressing. Since we have dropped the new text section to a low address space - 0x7000000, it is a mistake to access data relative to instructions in new text section. This problem is addressed in

Oxymoron [8]. Here we hold the same viewpoint as Oxymoron, where the authors believe this is not a general case and can be located statically.

4 Evaluation

We tested our method on fourteen programs in SPEC2006, and succeed to obfuscate those programs and evaluate our method in three aspects, including control flow concealing, program size and program execution speed. Our experiments are performed on CentOS 6.6 x86, with 2G memory and kernel version - 2.6.32.

4.1 Control Flow Concealing

There is no standard for obfuscation strength. But in the aspect of concealing control flow, we work out two metrics to measure obfuscation degree of our method. They are CFG-level stealth and instruction-level stealth. We measure those two metrics on all the fourteen programs in SPEC2006.

CFG-Level Stealth. We choose CFG fragmentation to measure it. Our method hides paths between basic blocks, so an original big CFG is cut into small pieces. We use the ratio of independent CFG (a function is an independent CFG) to measure the degree of fragmentation (DF).

$$DF = ObCFG/OrCFG$$

$ObCFG$ represents the number of independent CFG in obfuscated program. $OrCFG$ is the number of independent CFG in original program. The bigger DF is, the more difficult can the reverse engineering analysis dig out control flow information statically. The result is shown in Table 1. The average DF is 22.79 (from 8.32 to 63.66).

Instruction-Level Stealth. Direct CFRIs are major leakage points of control flow information. The direct CFRIs between basic blocks must be replaced to hide control flow information. We check whether direct CFRIs exist in original and obfuscated programs and analyze those existing cases. The columns jmp_{dec}, $call_{dec}$, jcc_{dec} in Table 2 represent the decrease degree of CFRIs, which is calculated by the following formula.

$$DecCFRI = \frac{OrC(CFRI) - ObC(CFRI)}{OrC(CFRI)}$$

$OrC(CFRI)$ represents the number of direct CFRIs in original program and $ObC(CFRI)$ is the count of direct CFRIs in obfuscated program.

It is obvious to find that there are almost no direct jmp instructions in our obfuscated programs. While direct call and jcc instructions are still there, these cases don't leak any control flow information. Because direct call instructions in

Table 1. CFG fragmentation

Programs	Original	Obfuscated	DF
astar	97	1367	14.09
bzip2	81	1942	23.98
gobmk	2535	32453	12.80
h264ref	531	14166	26.68
hmmer	501	11451	22.86
lbm	28	233	8.32
libquantum	108	1509	13.97
mcf	33	451	13.67
milc	244	3962	16.24
namd	105	6684	63.66
perlbench	1723	53973	31.33
sjeng	143	4904	34.29
soplex	900	15575	17.31
sphinx3	335	6670	19.91

obfuscated programs all call the same one function, which is used for indirect control flow redirection. And direct jcc instructions inherit from original programs but the targets of jcc are inside basic blocks in obfuscated programs rather than outside basic blocks. So control flow information remains under cover through our method. The average $DecCFRI$ of jmp is 96.85% and that of call is 94.80%. The $DecCFRI$ of jcc is negative. Because including inherited jcc instructions, there are other jcc cases in our inserted functions. If we do not take inherited jcc instructions into account to measure $DecCFRI$, the $DecCFRI$ of jcc will be modified as

$$DecCFRI = \frac{2 * OrC(jcc) - ObC(jcc)}{OrC(jcc)}.$$

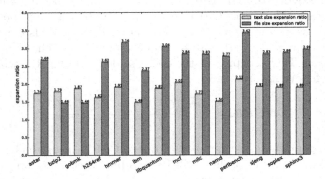

Fig. 5. Size expansion ratio

Table 2. CFRI Decrease. jmp_{or}, $call_{or}$, jcc_{or} represents the number of $CFRI$ in original file; jmp_{ob}, $call_{ob}$, jcc_{ob} represents the number of $CFRI$ in obfuscated file.

Programs	Original			Obfuscated			$DecCFRI$			
	jmp_{or}	$call_{or}$	jcc_{or}	jmp_{ob}	$call_{ob}$	jcc_{ob}	jmp_{dec}	$call_{dec}$	jcc_{dec}	jcc_real
astar	174	400	587	11	9	595	93.71%	97.74%	−1.36%	98.64%
bzip2	356	338	1058	8	30	1065	97.73%	91.10%	−0.67%	99.33%
gobmk	4475	9112	13076	17	66	13085	99.63%	99.27%	−0.07%	99.93%
h264ref	2575	2729	7346	43	373	7354	98.33%	86.32%	−0.11%	99.89%
hmmer	1697	3542	5075	47	41	5082	97.26%	98.85%	−0.13%	99.87%
lbm	26	73	83	4	8	90	84.64%	89.06%	−8.42%	91.58%
libquantum	252	452	592	3	8	599	98.84%	98.25%	−1.16%	98.84%
mcf	64	89	230	3	8	238	95.34%	90.98%	−3.47%	96.53%
milc	528	1543	1367	19	17	1374	96.38%	98.90%	−0.52%	99.48%
namd	1110	1129	4206	14	23	4213	98.72%	98.00%	−0.16%	99.84%
perlbench	10167	13869	25777	25	221	25789	99.75%	98.40%	−0.05%	99.95%
sjeng	940	1102	2504	8	24	2511	99.16%	97.85%	−0.28%	99.72%
soplex	2881	4210	6011	31	719	6018	98.92%	82.92%	−0.12%	99.88%
sphinx3	850	2502	2629	21	12	2637	97.50%	99.52%	−0.31%	99.79%

The real $DecCFRI$ of jcc instructions is listed in the last column of Table 2. The average $DecCFRI$ of jcc instructions is 98.80%.

4.2 Size Measurement

The scales of programs expand in different degrees after being obfuscated by our method. We measure size of text section and size of ELF file in original and obfuscated program respectively. Figure 5 describes the expansion ratio of text section and file size. The mean expansion ratio of text section is 1.81 (from 1.48 to 2.12), and the mean expansion ratio of file size is 2.66 (from 1.46 to 3.42). There are several factors leading to size expansion. Our instrumentation work increases the size of text section. Additionally, we integrate some data sections, such as payload and mapping table, into our obfuscated program, which certainly increases the file size.

4.3 Overhead

As we translate direct CFRIs into indirect ones, memory accessing time will increase and CPU pipe-line will be affected and slow down. Theoretically, our method will increase overhead of programs. We apply our method to those fourteen programs with 100% obfuscation coverage. The overhead is unacceptable and is shown in Fig. 6. There are twelve programs' overhead beyond 200%, with the highest of 1194.74% (libquantum). The average overhead in Fig. 6 is 524.87% (from 15.8% to 1194.74%). To cut down overhead, we adopt an optimization policy of decreasing the obfuscation coverage.

Under our optimization policy, we gain acceptable (overhead,coverage) pairs. We test our obfuscated programs under four coverage standards (95%, 90%, 85%,

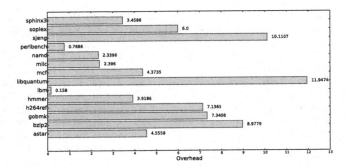

Fig. 6. Overhead with 100% obfuscation coverage

0%). Our optimization policy works on nine programs, depicted in Fig. 7(a). The mean overhead of 95% obfuscation coverage is 20.31% (2.0%–69.54%). That is a great progress, comparing to 100% obfuscation coverage in Fig. 6. When obfuscation coverage is decreased to 90%, the mean overhead is 7.86% (0.91%–31.45%). And for each program, the overhead is cut down to 10% or less, except mcf, whose overhead is 31.45%. As obfuscation coverage comes to 85%, all the nine programs' overhead are below 8.49%, and some programs' overhead approximate to 0%.

Other five programs' overhead is not shown in Fig. 7(a), as their overhead is still very high (mean overhead is up to 110.41%, in arrange from 61.9% to 244.61%) even when obfuscation coverage is 0%. These five programs' overhead are shown in Fig. 7(b). We analyze these five programs deeply, and find that they execute indirect CFRIs frequently. Our method utilizes a function to redirect indirect control flow during the runtime. That is time-consuming. No matter how low our obfuscation coverage is, the overhead is still high.

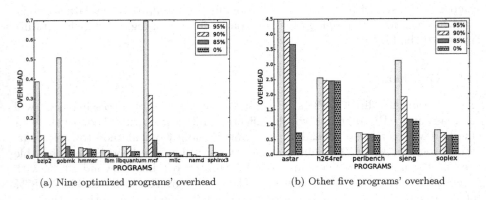

(a) Nine optimized programs' overhead   (b) Other five programs' overhead

Fig. 7. Overhead with four kinds of obfuscation coverage

5   Related Works

ROP, proposed by Hovav Shacham to enhance return-into-libc attack, is a code-reuse technique [5]. Its execution unit is gadget, a piece of instruction snippet ended with *ret* instruction. ROP uses payload on stack and *ret* instruction to organise its control flow. This code-reuse technique is developed by researchers in many ways. Jiang find gadgets ended with *jmp* instructions can also be used for code-reuse attacks [9]. Q is an automatic method to construct ROP payload to bypass ASLR defense [10]. Printable ROP, whose payload is all printable ASCII bytes, is another branch of ROP attacks [11]. Although defenses against ROP vary too much, such as ASLR , new attack methods can still utilize ROP to launch attacks, such as JIT ROP [12], side channel ROP [13,14]. Not only on traditional PC platform, but also on mobile devices, ROP is an effective way to attack [15–17].

Binary obfuscation focuses on fighting against reverse engineering analysis. Cohen is the first to present binary obfuscation. He changes the layout of instructions to prevent disassembling [18]. Later Igor finds another way to fool disassembler by inserting junk bytes to replace useless instructions [3]. This way is based on an assumption of disassembly algorithms, which treats CFRIs and their targets as hints of instructions' beginning. Nevertheless, Igor does more than that. They utilize signal handling mechanism to conceal control flow information. Their method is effective for obfuscation. However, overhead of their method is unacceptable even their obfuscation coverage is 90%.

Control flow obfuscation aims to protect programs' semantics from being analysed. One way is to hide control flow information like Igor and Chen [4]. Chen takes advantages of characters of Itanium processors, which support information flow tracking. Their method resolves the problem of high overhead but it is not in common use on x86. Another way is to make CFG complicated, so that reverse engineering can't reconstruct high-level program structure. Xin et al. attaches many useless or semantics-equal paths to CFG [19] and fakes a different CFG. Thus some analysis methods based on birthmark or pattern matching fail to dig out real semantics of programs. Control flow flattening also changes the whole CFG of a program [20]. They obfuscate C++ source code to a large loop, and use switch statements to judge which case to be executed in each iteration. Yet their work is based on source code.

ROPSTEG [6], also leverages ROP to perform binary obfuscation, but is different. First, ROPSTEG aims to make use of *unintended instructions* to hide sensitive instructions, while our approach takes advantage of ROP payload and gadgets to hide direct control flow in the form of indirect control flow. And chaining payloads by gadget and *ret* instruction is the core idea of ROP, other than unintended instructions. Consequently, major control flow information can still be recovered from binary obfuscated by ROPSTEG, which, however, is completely hidden by our approach. Second, applicability and obfuscation strengthen of ROPSTEG are restricted by certain properties of the to-be-protected binary, such as the available unintended instructions. To the contrary, our approach has no requirements on the binaries.

Virtualization based methods are also effective for obfuscation. [21–25] mentioned, it is possible to use emulated instruction sets to rewrite programs. Programs' representation is neither IA32 instructions nor ARM instructions and becomes difficult to analyze.

On the opposite side, software reverse engineering is to analyse programs and dig out useful information [26–30]. It can be classified into two kinds, static method and dynamic method. Static reverse analysis often start with disassembling and translate binary code into high level programs. IDA and Hex-Ray are practical business de-compiler tools [31]. Phoenix [32] is another state-of-art decompiler, which uses semantics-preserving structural analysis, and it can reconstruct high-level control flow structure. But all those static methods do not work on control flow obfuscation programs. Dynamic method can find some control flow paths through execution. TOP reconstructs control flow structures dynamically [33]. However, path coverage is the main limitation of dynamic method, since execution can't find out all paths in CFG.

6   Discussion and Limitation

Since gadgets itself is helpful for ROP attacks, it is dangerous to transform basic blocks of original programs into gadgets. We prevent reuse of generated gadgets in two aspects. On one hand, our instrumentation design is unfriendly to ROP attacks, because our generated gadgets all do the same thing, reading data from memory addresses. On the other hand, we can implement load-time basic block level ASLR just like binary stirring [34], as our generated gadgets are independent from each other. Here, we discuss the potential limitations of ROPOB:

- **Dynamic analysis.** As discussed in Sect. 1, ROPOB does not hide control flow information from dynamic analysis as the operand of indirect jmp instruction will be shown when executing. We have an idea to defend from dynamic analysis and show it in Future Work.
- **Payload hiding.** As shown in Sect. 3, ROPOB puts payload into one data section named ".payload". As this section is in the binary, it may raise suspicion in static method.
- **Compatible with ROP Defense.** Since ROPOB makes use of ROP to obfuscate control flow information, our work should be compatible with ROP defense schemes. Although ROPOB does not make use of "unintended instructions" in ROPSTEG [6], there are also CFI security policies which ROPOB violates.

7   Conclusion and Future Work

In this paper, we design and implement ROPOB, a ROP-based binary obfuscation scheme that obfuscates the control flow of programs by chaining basic blocks as ROP gadgets. We show that ROPOB can protect programs against static analysis, effectively and practically.

Here we show our work in future in the aspect of reuse or replace gadgets. Control flow graphs of functions in original program are independent. If we can reuse gadgets in our obfuscated programs, or replace the gadgets with gadgets in the libraries just like ROP attacks, the independence of CFGs will be broken, and code of each function will interweave together. That will make function extraction difficult. Thus, we need to analyse functionality of each gadget and automatically construct ROP payload to replace functionality-equal gadgets [10].

Acknowledgments. We thank the anonymous reviewers for their helpful feedback. This work was supported by Chinese National Natural Science Foundation 61272078.

References

1. Alliance, B.S.: Global software privacy. http://globalstudy.bsa.org/2010/index.html
2. Linn, C., Debray, S.: Obfuscation of executable code to improve resistance to static disassembly. In: 10th ACM Conference on Computer and Communications Security, pp. 290–299. ACM, October 2003
3. Debray, S.K., Popov, I.V., Andrews, G.R.: Binary obfuscation using signals. In: USENIX Security. USENIX, August 2007
4. Chen, H., et al.: Control flow obfuscation with information flow tracking. In: Proceedings of 42nd Annual IEEE/ACM International Symposium on Microarchitecture, pp. 391–400. ACM (2009)
5. Shacham, H.: The geometry of innocent flesh on the bone: return-into-libc without function calls (on the x86). In: Proceedings of the 14th ACM Conference on Computer and Communications Security, pp. 552–561. ACM (2007)
6. Lu, K., Xiong, S., Gao, D.: Ropsteg: program steganography with return oriented programming. In: Proceedings of 4th ACM Conference on Data and Application Security and Privacy (CODASPY), pp. 265–272. ACM (2014)
7. The IDA Pro disassembler and debugger. http://www.hex-rays.com/idapro/
8. Backes, M., Nürnberger, S.: Oxymoron: making fine-grained memory randomization practical by allowing code sharing. In: Proceedings of 23rd Usenix Security Symposium, pp. 433–447 (2014)
9. Bletsch, T., Jiang, X., Freeh, V.W., Liang, Z.: Jump-oriented programming: a new class of code-reuse attack. In: Proceedings of 6th ACM Symposium on Information, Computer and Communications Security, pp. 30–40. ACM (2011)
10. Schwartz, E.J., Avgerinos, T., Brumley, D.: Q: exploit hardening made easy. In: USENIX Security Symposium (2011)
11. Lu, K., Zou, D., Wen, W., Gao, D.: Packed, printable, and polymorphic return-oriented programming. In: Sommer, R., Balzarotti, D., Maier, G. (eds.) RAID 2011. LNCS, vol. 6961, pp. 101–120. Springer, Heidelberg (2011). https://doi.org/10.1007/978-3-642-23644-0_6
12. Snow, K.Z., Monrose, F., Davi, L., Dmitrienko, A., Liebchen, C., Sadeghi, A.-R.: Just-in-time code reuse: on the effectiveness of fine-grained address space layout randomization. In: 2013 IEEE Symposium on Security and Privacy (SP), pp. 574–588. IEEE (2013)

13. Seibert, J., Okkhravi, H., Söderström, E.: Information leaks without memory disclosures: remote side channel attacks on diversified code. In: Proceedings of 2014 ACM SIGSAC Conference on Computer and Communications Security, pp. 54–65. ACM (2014)
14. Bittau, A., Belay, A., Mashtizadeh, A., Mazieres, D., Boneh, D.: Hacking blind. In: 2014 IEEE Symposium on Security and Privacy (SP), pp. 227–242. IEEE (2014)
15. Wang, T., Lu, K., Lu, L., Chung, S., Lee, W.: Jekyll on iOS: when benign apps become evil. In: Usenix Security, vol. 13 (2013)
16. Davi, L., Dmitrienko, A., Sadeghi, A.-R., Winandy, M.: Privilege escalation attacks on android. In: Burmester, M., Tsudik, G., Magliveras, S., Ilić, I. (eds.) ISC 2010. LNCS, vol. 6531, pp. 346–360. Springer, Heidelberg (2011). https://doi.org/10.1007/978-3-642-18178-8_30
17. Lee, B., Lu, L., Wang, T., Kim, T., Lee, W.: From Zygote to Morula: fortifying weakened ASLR on android. In: 2014 IEEE Symposium on Security and Privacy (SP), pp. 424–439. IEEE (2014)
18. Cohen, F.B.: Operating system protection through program evolution. Comput. Secur. **12**(6), 565–584 (1993)
19. Xin, Z., Chen, H., Wang, X., Liu, P., Zhu, S., Mao, B., Xie, L.: Replacement attacks on behavior based software birthmark. In: Lai, X., Zhou, J., Li, H. (eds.) ISC 2011. LNCS, vol. 7001, pp. 1–16. Springer, Heidelberg (2011). https://doi.org/10.1007/978-3-642-24861-0_1
20. László, T., Kiss, Á.: Obfuscating C++ programs via control flow flattening. Annales Universitatis Scientarum Budapestinensis de Rolando Eötvös Nominatae, Sectio Computatorica **30**, 3–19 (2009)
21. Sharif, M., Lanzi, A., Giffin, J., Lee, W.: Automatic reverse engineering of malware emulators. In: 2009 30th IEEE Symposium on Security and Privacy, pp. 94–109. IEEE (2009)
22. Wang, C.: A security architecture for survivability mechanisms. Ph.D. dissertation, University of Virginia (2001)
23. Oreans Technologies: Code virtualizer: total obfuscation against reverse engineering. http://www.oreans.com/codevirtualizer.php
24. Oreans Technologies: Themida: advanced windows software protection system. http://www.oreans.com/themida.php
25. VMProtect-Software: VMProtect - new-generation software protection. http://www.vmprotecct.ru/
26. Christodorescu, M., Jha, S., Seshia, S.A., Song, D., Bryant, R.E.: Semantics-aware malware detection. In: 2005 IEEE Symposium on Security and Privacy, pp. 32–46. IEEE (2005)
27. Kruegel, C., Kirda, E., Mutz, D., Robertson, W., Vigna, G.: Polymorphic worm detection using structural information of executables. In: Valdes, A., Zamboni, D. (eds.) RAID 2005. LNCS, vol. 3858, pp. 207–226. Springer, Heidelberg (2006). https://doi.org/10.1007/11663812_11
28. Lakhotia, A., Kumar, E.U., Venable, M.: A method for detecting obfuscated calls in malicious binaries. IEEE Trans. Softw. Eng. **31**(11), 955–968 (2005)
29. Singh, P.K., Moinuddin, M., Lakhotia, A.: Using static analysis and verification for analyzing virus and worm programs. In: Proceedings of 2nd European Conference on Information Warfare and Security, pp. 281–292 (2003)
30. Xu, Z., Miller, B.P., Reps, T.: Safety checking of machine code. In: ACM SIGPLAN Notices, vol. 35, pp. 70–82. ACM (2000)
31. Guilfanov, I.: Decompilers and beyond. Black Hat USA (2008)

32. Schwartz, E.J., Lee, J., Woo, M., Brumley, D.: Native x86 decompilation using semantics-preserving structural analysis and iterative control-flow structuring. In: Proceedings of USENIX Security Symposium, p. 16 (2013)
33. Zeng, J., Fu, Y., Miller, K.A., Lin, Z., Zhang, X., Xu, D.: Obfuscation resilient binary code reuse through trace-oriented programming. In: Proceedings of 2013 ACM SIGSAC Conference on Computer & Communications Security, pp. 487–498. ACM (2013)
34. Wartell, R., Mohan, V., Hamlen, K.W., Lin, Z.: Binary stirring: self-randomizing instruction addresses of legacy x86 binary code. In: Proceedings of 2012 ACM Conference on Computer and Communications Security, pp. 157–168. ACM (2012)

DiffGuard: Obscuring Sensitive Information in Canary Based Protections

Jun Zhu(✉), Weiping Zhou, Zhilong Wang, Dongliang Mu, and Bing Mao

State Key Laboratory for Novel Software Technology, Department of Computer
Science and Technology, Nanjing University, Nanjing, China
junzhu0406@gmail.com, zhouweipingcs@163.com, njuwangzhilong@163.com,
mudongliangabcd@163.com, maobing@nju.edu.cn

Abstract. Memory Corruption attacks have monopolized the headlines
in the security research community for the past two decades. NX/XD,
ASLR, and canary-based protections have been introduced to defend
effectively against memory corruption attacks. Most of these techniques
rely on keeping secret in some key information needed by the attackers to
build the exploit. Unfortunately, due to the inherent limitations of these
defenses, it is relatively difficult to restrain trained attackers to find those
secrets and create effective exploits. Through an information disclosure
vulnerability, attackers could leak stack data of the runtime process and
scan out canary word without crashing the program. We present Diff-
Guard, a modification of the canary based protections which eliminates
stack sweep attacks against the canary and proposes a more robust countermeasures against the byte-by-byte discovery of stack canaries in forking programs. We have implemented a compiler-based DiffGuard which
consists of a plugin for the GCC and a PIC dynamic shared library that
gets linked with the running application via LD PRELOAD. DiffGuard
incurs an average runtime overhead of 3.2%, meanwhile, ensures application correctness and seamless integration with third-party software.

Keywords: Information leak · Brute-force attacks
Canary-based protection · Canary re-randomization

1 Introduction

Buffer overflows, sensitive data exposure and related memory corruption vulnerabilities constitute an important class of security vulnerabilities. According
to the CNNVD Situation Report in 2016 [1], there exists a notable increase in
vulnerability number, from 5128 in 2011 to 8336 in 2016. Buffer overflows remain
the most frequently encountered [2], which brings a huge threat to network and
information security. Over the last years, several techniques have been developed
to prevent adversaries from abusing them. Stack canaries [3–5], Address Space
Layout Randomization [6] and non-executable stack (NX/XD) [7] are widely
deployed due to the low overhead,simplicity and effectiveness. However, none of

© ICST Institute for Computer Sciences, Social Informatics and Telecommunications Engineering 2018
X. Lin et al. (Eds.): SecureComm 2017, LNICST 238, pp. 738–751, 2018.
https://doi.org/10.1007/978-3-319-78813-5_39

these techniques has fully eliminated stack smashing attacks and several attack vectors are still effective under all these protections [8–11].

Stack buffer overflows are often used as a stepping stone in modern, multistage exploits like Return-Oriented Programming (ROP) [15]. For instance, Blind ROP (BROP) [13] attack requires only a stack-based memory corruption vulnerability and a service that restarts after a crash to automatically construct a ROP payload. Security researchers believe that only the forked networking servers are prone to brute force attacks, based on the fact that in forking application, all the children processes inherit/share the same memory layout from the parent process. The attacker can try in bounded time all the possible values of canary (for SSP) and memory layouts (for ASLR) until the correct ones are found. There exists a dangerous form of SSP vulnerability, called byte-for-byte, which allows the attacker to try each byte of the canary independently and to find the value of the canary with a little number of attempts. There exists some techniques effectively armoring protections against brute-force attacks on forking program, but they could not guarantees the correctness of child process [14]. The different function frames of the process share the same canary word stored in TLS, which greatly weaken the security of process data. Through CVE-2012-3569 VMware OVF Tool format string vulnerability [12], we successfully leaked the runtime stack data and scanned out the canary without crashing the program.

The severity and plethora of these exploits underline the redesign of canary-based protections. To address the aforementioned issue, we present a modification of the SSP technique, called DiffGuard (Different function frames with different canaries), which consist of assigning different canaries for different function frames and setting a number of new canary words for each child process when the fork() system call is invoked. Specifically, through a lightweight, per-frame randomizing mechanism, our design smashes the consistency issue of traditional canary based protections and enables the runtime update of the canary values in all protected function frames of the running thread, so that newly-forked processes get a number of fresh canaries, different from the canaries of their parent process. Contrary to previous work [14,15], our approach makes the canary of different frames independent of each other in both non-forking and forking programs and guarantees correctness while preventing brute force attacks against stack canary protection on forking programs. DiffGuard provides protection based on source code, which is a compiler-level version of tool, implemented as a GCC plugin, incurs just 3.2% runtime overhead over native execution, and is fully compatible with third-party libraries that are protected with the default canary mechanism.

In summary, the main contributions of this work are the following:

1. We present DiffGuard, a robust solution for obscuring sensitive information(canary word) in Canary based Protections.
2. The SSP byte-by-byte attack in forking applications is no longer applicable to the DiffGuard.

3. We have evaluated the effectiveness of the recently proposed solution [14, 15] to the problem of identical canary stored in each function frames, and demonstrate how DyffGuard overcomes its design limitations.
4. We have implemented a compiler-level DiffGuard, demonstrating the practicality of our approach, which incurs a runtime overhead of 3.2% and shows that it can be easily adopted by popular compiler toolchains to further address security issues arising from the process creation mechanism of modern OSes.

The rest of the paper is organized as follows. We provide a background on the existing defenses and review their weaknesses with respect to canary based protections in Sect. 2. We detail the design of DiffGuard in Sect. 3. We describe the implementation details in Sect. 4. We evaluate our system in Sect. 5, and we cover some related work in Sect. 6, and conclude in Sect. 7.

2   Background

In this section, we first introduce simply the stack smashing attack and canary-based protection. Then we briefly describe the existing work and propose a stack scan algorithm based on the limitations of existing works bypassing canary based protections.

2.1   Canary-based Protection and Brute-force Attacks

The general principle of stack smashing attack is to change the control flow to execute attacker-supplied code. Stack smashing relies on the fact that most C compilers store the saved return address on the same stack used for local variables. The common form of buffer overflow exploitation is to attack buffers allocated on the stack. A well-accepted countermeasure against stack smashing attacks is the Canary-based Stacking Smashing Protection. The basic idea is to place a canary right after the return address in stack frame to detect buffer overflows.

Processes created with fork() are a duplicate of the calling process. Both, father and child have the same canary value. On a forked server, where the service is attended by children of the server process, an attacker can build **brute force attacks** by guessing the value of the canary as many times as needed.

Bit-by-bit Attack: The frame-canary word is overwritten on each trial. If the guessed word is not correct then the child process detects the error and aborts. As consequence, the attacker does not receive a reply, which is interpreted as an incorrect guess. The guessed value is discarded, and attacker proceeds with another value until all the possible values are guessed.

Byte-by-byte Attack: The basic idea in leaking canaries with byte-by-byte attack is to overflow a single byte, overwriting a single byte of the canary with value x. If x was correct, the server does not crash. The algorithm is repeated for all possible 256 byte values until it is found (128 tries on average). The attack continues for the next byte until all 8 canary bytes (on 64-bit) are leaked.

Table 1 shows the complexity of using bit-by-bit versus byte-by-byte attacks. Most canary implementations set to zero one of the canary bytes (the most significant in x86) for preventing the buffer overflow attacks when the overflow is performed by a string copy functions. For this reason, the number of bytes needed to guess is three (for 32-bit systems) or seven bytes (64-bits systems). Statistically, the bit-by-bit attack is described as a "**sampling without replacement**" and since all the values has the same probability $(\frac{1}{c})$ it is modelled by the uniform distribution with a support range of $[1, c]$ and a mean of $\frac{c+1}{2}$ [14]. With the standard SSP, bit-by-bit attack needs at most 2^{24} trails to break the system (and 2^{23} in average) in 32-bit systems. On a byte-by-byte attack, the process of finding each byte is modelled as a uniform distribution whose mean is $256/2$ and the support range is $[1, 256]$, the attacker needs at most 768 trails to break the system (and 384 in average) in 32-bit systems. The average requests in 64-bit systems is calculated as above. With this figures, the standard canary technique provides a weak protection for this kind of bugs.

2.2   Previous Works

The basic idea of preventing brute force attacks focuses on re-randomizing the reference-canary of the child right after the **fork()**. RAF-SSP'renew canary at fork strategy consist in renew the value of the reference-canary of the child process right after it is created (forked). The new value is also a random value and every child process have a different reference-canary. However, this partial update will result in an abort if execution reaches the frames inherited from the parent process, as the canary cookies in these frames still hold their old values [15]. RAF-SSP assumes that a child process never reuses inherited frames legitimately. DynaGuard use per-thread bookkeeping mechanism to guarantee program correctness. At a high level, DynaGuard operates as follows: after a fork system call, and right before any instruction has executed in the child process, DynaGuard must update the canaries in both the TLS and all inherited stack frames in the child process.

2.3   Threats

Rather than a detailed explanation on how to bypass the SSP, we will present only the weaknesses of the existing canary based protections that enables the possibility of an attack. Basically, there are three ways to bypass the canary:

1. Overwriting the target data (return address, function pointer, etc.) without needing to overwrite the frame canary.
2. Overwrite the frame-canary with the correct value.
3. Disclosure runtime memory data.

With a view of situation 1, since GCC v4.6.3, local variables are reordered so that buffers are located first (higher addresses) and below them the function pointers and the saved registers. Based on this fact, directly overwriting the target data could not achieve the goal. We had discussed situation 2 in Sect. 2.1 and introduced existing works which prevent brute force attacks against canary based protections in Sect. 2.2. So we will focus on the memory data disclosure against the canary value.

The different function frame shared the same canary stored in TLS, which greatly weakened the randomness of canary. Through an information disclosure vulnerability, attackers could leak stack data of the runtime process and scan out canary word without crashing the program. We proposed a scanning algorithm to find out canary. The input is runtime-stack data which have been leaked by program vulnerability(format string, dangling pointer, etc.) and platform information. The output is the most possible canary words. The intuition here is that all the function frames of the runtime-stack stored the same canary words, this consistency allows us to find canary from the disclosure data. In this algorithm, we set the size of the sliding window to memory address width (e.g., 4 bytes for a 32-bit operating system). The scan of the runtime stack data starts from the top of the stack indicated by the value of stack pointer ESP plus an offset equal to the memory address width (e.g., ESP + 4 for a 32-bit operating system). We add repeated words which frequency of occurrence is more than three times in the candidate tag. In order to find out canary from the candidate collection, We made the following three rules to determine:

1. Terminator value: most canary implementations set the last byte of canary to the terminator value. the value is composed of different string terminators (CR, LF, NULL and −1).
2. Randomization: canary is a random value generated by reading the device /dev/random. Such as 0xAAA0, 0xABA0, 0xAAB0(A and B represent hexadecimal numbers) could be directly removed.
3. Function prologue: The prologue of each function is fixed. In GCC version's canary based protections, canary is usually stored in the position of EBP + 8. Through this relative offset, we can further screen out the possible canary.

Through the above rules, We can screen out the canary value. Considering XOR canaries implemented in Windows, the canary is generated by $canary_t \otimes EBP_f$, $canary_t$ is the original canary value stored in TLS and EBP_f is the base address of the function frame. Since the upper 2 or 3 bytes are fixed, our scanning algorithm is still working.

Table 1. Comparison of different canary based protections

Protextion	Brute force attack	Correctness	Consistency
StackGuard	F	T	F
RAF-SSP	T	F	F
DynaGuard	T	T	F

As shown in Table 1, due to the same canary in both parent and child process, StackGuard [3] is specially prone to brute force attacks in forking applications.

RAF-SSP could prevent brute force attacks against SSP, but could not guarantee correctness of the program. Althrough RAF-SSP and DynaGuard ensure that parent process has a different canary value with the child process, but the different frames still store the same canary in a process. These three protections can not solve the problem of consistency. In the following sections, we discuss how DiffGuard solves the problems discussed above while preserving application correctness and preventing brute force attack against canary based defenses.

3   Design

At a high level, DiffGuard operates as follows: (1) for non-forking program, DiffGuard assigns a separate canary to each stack frame in the process. (2) for forking program, after a fork system call, and right before any instruction executed in the child process, DiffGuard must update canaries inherited from the parent process. Once the canaries have been updated, it can resume the execution of the child. This runtime update renders byte-by-byte brute-force attacks infeasible, since every function frame of forked process has a fresh canary.

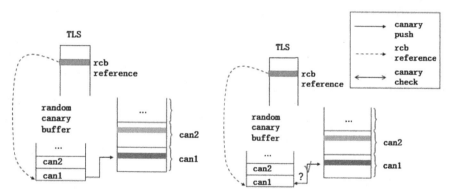

(a) the canaries stored in random canary buffer(RCB) are pushed on the stack.

(b) Epilogue check for function can1 succeeds.

Fig. 1. The design of DiffGuard allows for a complete independence of all canaries in the process.

To the best of our knowledge, current canary protections do not provide multiple different canaries for different function frames in the process. Therefore, DiffGuard's design should allow each running process to generate, access and modify all of its stack canaries at runtime. To achieve this goal, DiffGuard performs a per-thread runtime randomization of all the canaries that will be pushed in the stack during execution, using a lightweight buffer allocated dynamically upon each thread's creation (this buffer is stored in the heap). Figures 1 and 2 illustrate this scheme in more detail.

DiffGuard's random canary buffer (RCB, Fig. 1a) holds all the canaries of the runtime process. When a function is called, DiffGuard takes a canary word from the RCB and pushes it on the function frame. As the function execution is finished, DiffGuard detects the change of the canary word before the function returns (Fig. 1b). To ensure DiffGuard could prevent brute force attacks against canary based protections, we refresh the contents of the RCB. When a child process is forked, the RCB of the parent process is copied to the child process (Fig. 2a). Before execution starts in the child context, DiffGuard modifies all the canary values of the RCB excepted the canaries inherited stack frames in child process (can3). Likewise, whenever a canary-protected frame is pushed onto the stack, the canary is token from the RCB and, once a canary-protected function returns, the respective RCB index is diminished (Fig. 2b). The aforementioned design allows DiffGuard to successfully provide multiple different canaries for different function frames in the process and to modify the canary values for newly-created processes (child process). Specially, it allows for a seamless integration with third-party software and libraries that only support the existing stack protection mechanisms. In addition, the proposed architecture allows for the effective handling of stack unwinding, irrespectively of whether the latter occurs in the context of an exception, due to a signal, or setjmp/longjmp: as the canary saved in the function frame corresponds to the one in the RCB, We can determine the position of the canary in the RCB. Thus, DiffGuard can hook any stack unwinding operation and modify the RCB index accordingly. In this manner, application correctness is preserved. Apart from ensuring correctness, the proposed design has the added benefit of not breaking compatibility with legacy software or current canary protections. Compilers only need to add this bookkeeping mechanism on top of their current stack canary implementations, without altering the well-established conventions on the format of the canary check or a function's prologue and epilogue.

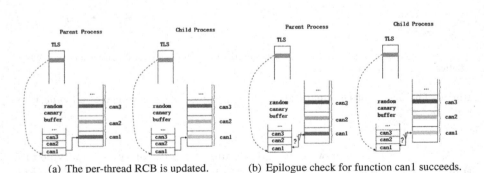

(a) The per-thread RCB is updated.   (b) Epilogue check for function can1 succeeds.

Fig. 2. The design of DiffGuard modifies all the canary values of the RCB excepted the canaries inherited stack frames in child process.

4   Implementation

The compiler-based DiffGuard consists of a plugin for the GNU Compiler Collection (GCC) and a position independent (PIC) dynamic shared library that gets linked with the running application via LD_PRELOAD. Combined, they consist of more than 2500 lines of C++ code. Several requirements must be accomplished to implementing DiffGuard at the compiler level, while maintaining compatibility with third-party software at the same time:

1. DiffGuard must instrument all the canary push/pop events and perform its randomization on a per-thread basis;
2. DiffGuard must hook each fork system call and update the canaries in the child process' RCB as described in Sect. 3;
3. DiffGuard must intercept all calls related to stack unwinding and ensure that the RCB index gets updated accordingly.

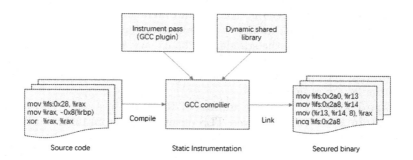

Fig. 3. Overview of system architecture.

The first requirement is handled by DiffGuard's GCC plugin. All other requirements are handled by DiffGuard's dynamic shared library (runtime), which ensures the proper management of the RCB for every thread.

The overview of DiffGuard architecture is shown in Fig. 3. To generate a binary secured against information disclosure vulnerabilities and brute force attacks, developers should compile the source code of the target program with DiffGuard. Given the source code, DiffGuard first identifies instructions that push/pop canary events and then inserts a call to the routine (a static instrumentation in Sect. 4.1). At runtime, with the help of instrumented instructions, DiffGuard initializes a number of random canaries which are stored in RCB for the function frame being created. On every fork system call, DiffGuard updates the per-thread RCB (a runtime library in Sect. 4.2). Later in this section, we describe each component of DiffGuard (the static instrumentation and the runtime library), and explain how we maintain RCB.

4.1   Static Instrumentation

The static instrumentation of DiffGuard is performed at the GCC IR [17] level, registered as an RTL optimization pass and loaded by GCC right after the var-track pass. The first reason for placing DiffGuard late in the RTL optimization pipeline is to ensure that most of the important optimizations have already been performed, and, as a result, DiffGuard's instrumentation is never added to irrelevant code. In addition, in this manner, we ensure that all injected instructions, which performs the necessary randomization, will remain at their proper locations and will not be optimized by later passes.

The DiffGuard GCC plugin must modify the canary setup and check inside each canary-protected frame, to prevent the DiffGuard-protected application from using the standard libc canaries. This is necessary to allow the modification of the canary at runtime without affecting any checks in libraries that are not complied with DiffGuard. The canary initialization that occurs during the creation of threads and processes is exactly the same in DiffGuard and in glibc, with the only difference being that the DiffGuard canaries are stored at RCB and the reference to the RCB is stored at a different location in the TLS area. Therefore, the entropy of canaries is not affected, but now the TLS holds two different types of canaries: the standard glibc canary and the DiffGuard canary. Upon a fork, all DiffGuard canaries excepted the canaries inherited stack frames in child process get updated without affecting any checks in modules or libraries that use the legacy glibc canaries.

DiffGuard stores the starting address of RCB, its total size, and its index, in the TLS. In x86-64, the reserved TLS offsets range from 0x2a0 to 0x2b8. In particular, %fs:0x2a0 holds the base address of RCB, %fs:0x2a8 keeps the current index in the RCB (i.e.,how many function frames are created), and finally, %fs:0x2b8 stores the reference to the DiffGuard canary which belongs to the function frame that is currently executing.

Figure 4 shows the canary push/pop instructions inserted by the DiffGuard GCC plugin. Right after the function prologue, before the canary gets pushed to the stack, the reference to the starting address of RCB must be read. Initially, DiffGuard retrieves the address of the RCB from the TLS (1) and the index of the next element to be written (3). Next, it reads canary from RCB (4) and increments the buffer index (5). Finally, the canary is fetched from the RCB and saved onto the stack. For this purpose, if no registers are free, DiffGuard needs to spill two registers for its push/pop canary events ((1),(6)). Likewise, the canary check in the function epilogue is modified to check against the DiffGuard canary instead of the glibc canary (7) and decrease the index in RCB (8).

4.2   Runtime Library

The runtime library of DiffGuard maintains the RCB setup and update, as well as the hooking of fork system calls and stack unwinding routines. The library (PIC module) implementing that runtime is loaded via the LD_PRELOAD mechanism into the address space of the runtime application.

Original	DiffGuard	
;function prologue	push %rbp	
push %rbp	mov %rsp, %rbp	
mov %rsp, %rbp	sub $0x40, %rsp	
sub $0x40, %rsp	push %r13	(1)
;canary stack placement	push %r14	
mov %fs:0x28, %rax	mov %fs:0x2a0, %r13	(2)
mov %rax, -0x8(%rbp)	mov %fs:0x2a8, %r14	(3)
xor %rax, %rax	mov (%r13, %r14, 8), %rax	(4)
	incq %fs:0x2a8	(5)
	pop %r14	(6)
	pop %r13	
	mov %rax, -0x8(%rbp)	
	xor %rax, %rax	
...	...	
;canary check	mov -0x8(%rbp), %rcx	
mov -0x8(%rbp), %rcx	xor (%fs:0x2b8), %rcx	(7)
xor %fs:0x28, %rcx	decq %fs:0x2a8	(8)
je <exit>	je <exit>	
callq <__stack_chk_fail@plt>	callq <__stack_chk_fail@plt>	

Fig. 4. Assembly excerpt for a binary compiled with -fstack-protector, with and without DiffGuard. The canary randomizing code added by the DiffGuard plugin is shown on the right (highlighted).

The RCB is allocated in the heap for each thread of the running program. In order to allocate the RCB before the main thread starts executing, we register-in the DiffGuard runtime-a constructor routine to be called before the main function of the application. This routine performs the RCB allocation, generates a number of random words by reading the device /dev/random and places them in the RCB. Finally, it sets the reference, size and index of RCB in the main thread' s TLS. For all other threads that get created, DiffGuard hooks the pthread_create call and sets the respective TLS entries prior to calling the start_routine of each thread. Finally, a routine to free the allocated RCB for each thread that finishes execution is registered via the pthread_cleanup_push(/pop) mechanism.

To ensure that the canaries in RCB of each thread are sufficient to use, DiffGuard marks the final page in the RCB as write-only and registers a signal handler for the SIGSEGV signal. Inside the signal handler, DiffGuard detects whether the fault is due to DiffGuard's instrumentation (i.e., when DiffGuard tries to read a canary out the boundary of the RCB) and allocates additional memory for the RCB if necessary.

As there may be multiple running threads, and the exception handler may execute in the context of a different thread than the one that generated the SIGSEGV, DiffGuard maintains a hashmap of all the running threads and their TLS entries. Inside the signal handler, DiffGuard iterates through all the threads in the hashmap and examines whether the memory location that caused the fault falls within an allocated RCB.

Lastly, in order to ensure that the RCB' index will correspond to active frame, DiffGuard checks for any stack unwinding and revises the index of RCB. This is based on the simple observation that, as the canary saved in the function frame corresponds to the one in the RCB, We can determine the position of the canary in the RCB. DiffGuard hooks the following calls that result in stack unwinding: __cxxabiv1::__cxa_end_catch and (sig)longjmp. In the cases of siglongjmp and longjmp, the new value of the stack pointer is retrieved from the contents of the __jmpbuf entry of the jump buffer that is passed to the calls, and we adjust the RCB index according to the canary in the stack frame pointed to by ESP.

Once all the components for ensuring the correctness of the canary randomizing are in place, DiffGuard provides different canaries for different function frames in the process. Meanwhile, DiffGuard registers a hook for the fork system call. Once fork is executed, in the context of the child process, and before fork returns, DiffGuard updates the canaries stored in child process' RCB except for the canaries of the function frames inherited from the parent process.

5   Evaluation

In this section we evaluate the performance overhead of DiffGuard and its effectiveness in protecting against byte-by-byte canary brute-force attacks. For our measurements we use the SPEC CPU2006 benchmark suite [18], as well as a series of popular (open-source) server applications. Overall, our GCC-based implementation of DiffGuard incurs an overhead ranging from 0.454% to 11.746%, with an average of 3.2%.

5.1   Effectiveness

We evaluate the effectiveness of DiffGuard from the following two aspects:

1. The identity of each function frame: DiffGuard ensure that each stack frame has its own canary. In order to verify the independence of canary in different stack frames, we instrument the SPEC CPU2006 benchmark suite, the purpose is to create a scan routine which is responsible for disclosing runtime stack data. Through stack sweeping algorithm introduced in Sect. 2, we confirmed that DiffGuard defends against the canaries disclosure attacks perfectly. In the contray, the existing canary based protections are prone to canaries disclosure attacks, and we have more than 90% probability to find canary when the number of function frames on runtime stack is greater than 10.
2. Preventing brute force attacks against canary based protections: We confirmed that DiffGuard defends against a set of publicly-available exploits [13,19] targeting the Nginx web server, which rely on brute-forcing stack canaries using the technique outlined in Sect. 2.

To verify that DiffGuard does not affect software correctness, we evaluated it over the SPEC CPU2006 benchmark suite, and also applied it to a variety of popular forking applications, such as the Apache and Nginx web servers, and the MySQL database servers. We observed no incompatibilities or any altered program functionality. As a final step of our correctness evaluation, we manually stress-tested DiffGuard over a series of scenarios that included combinations of multi-threaded and forking programs that executed setjmp/longjmp and triggered exceptions. In all cases we verified that DiffGuard successfully randomized the stack canaries (RCB) for all newly-created processes without causing any unexcepted behavior.

5.2   Performance

To obtain an estimate of DiffGuard's overhead on CPU intensive applications, we utilized the SPEC CPU2006 benchmark suite. The applications were compiled with the -fstack-protector option enabled. All experiments were performed on a virtual machine running Debian GNU/Linux v8, equipped with two 3.50 GHz four-core CPUs and 8 GB of R. Figure 5 summarizes the performance overhead of our GCC-based implementation of DiffGuard. All binaries were compiled with the DiffGuard plugin and had the -fno-omitframe-pointer compiler option asserted. DiffGuard incurs an average slowdown of 3.2% on the SPEC CPU2006 benchmarks. In all cases, the overhead of the GCC implementation of DiffGuard is below 11.74% for the SPEC CPU2006 benchmarks.

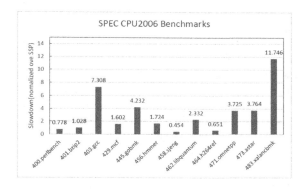

Fig. 5. The runtime overhead of DiffGuard (normalized over native execution).

6   Related Work

Canary-based stack protections were popularized by StackGuard [3]. Subsequently, ProPolice [20] introduced a series of GCC patches for StackGuard, which, among others, reordered the local variables in the stack, placing buffers after (local) pointers and function arguments in the stack frame. ProPolice was subsequently integrated in GCC, by RedHat, as the Stack Smashing Protector (SSP). As modern stack protectors follow a design similar to that of SSP, DiffGuard's architecture can be (easily) adopted by popular compilers due to its low performance overhead. With respect to preventing canary brute-force attacks, RAF-SSP [14] and DynaGuard [15], similarly to DiffGuard, aim to refresh stack-based canaries in networking servers. However, upon a fork system call, RAF SSP only updates the canary in the TLS area, ignoring the frames inherited by the parent process. This design fails to guarantee program correctness. DynaGuard use per-thread bookkeeping mechanism to guarantee program correctness, but the function frames of per-thread shared the identical canary word. This kind of identity makes it possible to be leaked.

A series of mechanisms have been proposed to protect the integrity of return addresses. RAD [21] is implemented as a compiler patch and creates a safe area where a copy of the return address is stored. Similar defenses have been implemented at the micro-architectural level [22], using binary rewriting [22], or by utilizing a shadow stack [23]. Apart from the fact that the previous mechanisms do not tackle the same problem as DiffGuard, they have not gained traction, mainly due to compatibility and performance issues (e.g., such mechanisms nullify several micro-architectural optimizations, like return address prediction) [25]. On the contrary, DiffGuard enhances a mechanism that has already seen wide adoption, without breaking accepted conventions around the format of the function prologue and epilogue, or the stack layout.

7   Conclusion

In this paper, we address a limitation of the current canary based protection mechanisms, which allows for brute-forcing the canary, byte-by-byte, in forking applications and stack-sweeping the canary, via information disclosure in non-forking applications. We resolve this issue by providing different canaries for different frames and proposing the dynamic update of the canaries in forked processes upon their creation. We present a design that utilizes a per-process, in-memory data structure to update the stack canaries at runtime, and we prototype the proposed architecture in DiffGuard, which is a compiler-based tool operating at the source code level. We evaluate that DiffGuard incurs an average overhead of 3.2% and can be easily integrated to modern compiler toolchains.

Acknowledgments. We would like to thank Theofilos Petsios et al. for their open source implementation of DynaGuard which helps ours quickly getting start of out work. When we have trouble in using SPEC CPU2006, Theofilos Petsios give us some advice. This work was supported in part by grants from the Chinese National Natural Science Foundation (61272078).

References

1. China National Vulnerability Database of Information Security(CNNVD)[Z/OL]. http://www.cnnvd.org.cn/
2. van der Veen, V., dutt-Sharma, N., Cavallaro, L., Bos, H.: Memory errors: the past, the present, and the future. In: Balzarotti, D., Stolfo, S.J., Cova, M. (eds.) RAID 2012. LNCS, vol. 7462, pp. 86–106. Springer, Heidelberg (2012). https://doi.org/10.1007/978-3-642-33338-5_5
3. Cowan, C., Pu, C., Maier, D., Hintony, H., Walpole, J., Bakke, P., Beattie, S., Grier, A., Wagle, P., Zhang, Q.: StackGuard: automatic adaptive detection and prevention of buffer overflow attacks

4. Etoh, H.: GCC extension for protecting applications from stack-smashing attacks
5. Microsoft.GS (Buffer Security Check) (2002). https://msdn.microsoft.com/en-us/library/8dbf701c.aspx
6. PaX Team: Address Space Layout Randomization (2003). https://pax.grsecurity.net/docs/aslr.txt
7. PaX Team: Non-executable pages design & implementation (2003). https://pax.grsecurity.net/docs/noexec.txt
8. Bulba and Kil3r: Bypassing stackguard and stackshield. Phrack, 56 (2002)
9. Richarte, G.: Four different tricks to bypass stackshield and stackguard protection, World Wide Web, 1 (2002)
10. Shacham, H., et al.: On the effectiveness of address-space randomization. In: Proceedings of the 11th ACM Conference on Computer and Communications Security. ACM (2004)
11. Buchanan, E., et al.: When good instructions go bad: generalizing return-oriented programming to RISC. In: Proceedings of the 15th ACM Conference on Computer and Communications Security. ACM (2008)
12. CVE-2012-3569.   http://cve.mitre.org/cgi-bin/cvename.cgi?name=CVE-2012-3569
13. Bittau, A., Belay, A., Mashtizadeh, A., Mazieres, D., Boneh, D.: Hacking blind. In: 2014 IEEE Symposium on Security and Privacy, pp. 227–242 (2014)
14. Marco-Gisbert, H., Ripoll, I.: Preventing brute force attacks against stack canary protection on networking servers. In: 12th IEEE International Symposium on Network Computing and Applications (NCA), pp. 243–250, August 2013
15. Petsios, T., Kemerlis, V.P., Polychronakis, M., Keromytis, A.D.: Dynaguard: armoring canary-based protections against brute-force attacks. In: Proceedings of the 31st Annual Computer Security Applications Conference, ACSAC 2015, pp. 351–360. ACM, New York (2015)
16. Bryant, R., David Richard, O.H., David Richard, O.H.: Computer Systems: A Programmer's Perspective, vol. 2. Prentice Hall, Upper Saddle River (2003)
17. Stallman, R.M.: The GCC Developer Community: GNU Compiler Collection Internals (2017). https://gcc.gnu.org/onlinedocs/gccint/
18. Henning, J.L.: SPEC CPU2006 benchmark descriptions. ACM SIGARCH Comput. Archit. News 34(4), 1–17 (2006)
19. Metasploit. Nginx HTTP Server 1.3.9-1.4.0 - Chuncked Encoding Stack Buffer Overflow (2013). http://www.exploit-db.com/exploits/25775/
20. Etoh, H.: GCC extension for protecting applications from stack-smashing attacks (2005). http://goo.gl/Tioc4C
21. Chiueh, T.-C., Hsu, F.-H.: RAD: a compile-time solution to buffer overflow attacks. In: Proceedings of ICDCS, pp. 409–417 (2001)
22. Park, Y.-J., Lee, G.: Repairing return address stack for buffer overflow protection. In: Proceedings of CF, pp. 335–342 (2004)
23. Corliss, M.L., Lewis, E.C., Roth, A.: Using DISE to protect return addresses from attack. ACM SIGARCH Comput. Archit. News 33(1), 65–72 (2005)
24. Sinnadurai, S., Zhao, Q., fai Wong, W.: Transparent runtime shadow stack: protection against malicious return address modifications (2008). http://citeseerx.ist.psu.edu/viewdoc/summary?doi=10.1.1.120.5702
25. Dang, T.H., Maniatis, P., Wagner, D.: The performance cost of shadow stacks and stack canaries. In: Proceedings of ASIACCS, pp. 555–566 (2015)

A Sudoku Matrix-Based Method of Pitch Period Steganography in Low-Rate Speech Coding

Zhongliang Yang[1,2]([✉]) [ID], Xueshun Peng[1,2], and Yongfeng Huang[1,2]

[1] Department of Electronic Engineering, Tsinghua University,
Beijing 100084, China
yangzl15@mails.tsinghua.edu.cn
[2] Tsinghua National Laboratory of Information Science and Technology,
Beijing 10084, China

Abstract. Using low-rate compressed speech coding for large-capacity steganography is always a big challenge due to its low redundant information. To overcome this challenge, we propose a method of embedding and extracting steganography in low-rate speech coding using three-dimensional Sudoku matrix. Analysis shows that this method can enhance the concealment of steganographic information and improve the steganography capacity of low-rate speech coding. The experimental results showed that using the current typical low speech coding standard G.723.1 achieved a steganographic capacity of 200 bit/s and a reduction of less than 10% in the sensory evaluation value of the speech quality of the coded speech.

Keywords: Information hiding · Low bit-rate speech codec
Pitch period · Sudoku matrix

1   Introduction

Low-rate speech coding is widely used in mobile communications, voice over IP (VoIP) and some instant messaging tools, and has become the main data traffic on the Internet. Due to its wide range of applications, dynamic generation and interactive transmission, low-rate speech coding is a good carrier for information concealment [1–3]. In recent years, there have been many studies exploring steganography methods for low-rate speech coding. For example, Yuan et al. [4] proposed a quantization index-modulated steganography based on the multidimensional vector concealment space, Huang et al. [5] proposed an information concealment method by replacing certain bits of mute frames, and Zhou et al. [6] proposed an extended Least Significant Bit (LSB) method based on hidden states.

However, current steganography methods are limited by low embedding capacity and poor concealment. Additionally, it is often difficult to apply these

© ICST Institute for Computer Sciences, Social Informatics and Telecommunications Engineering 2018
X. Lin et al. (Eds.): SecureComm 2017, LNICST 238, pp. 752–762, 2018.
https://doi.org/10.1007/978-3-319-78813-5_40

algorithms in practice due to their low steganographic capacity. Therefore, improving the concealment of steganography and increasing the steganographic capacity pose a main challenge in low-rate speech coding steganography.

There have been efforts to utilize Sudoku matrices to enhance concealment under the conditions of large hidden capacity for image steganography [7,8]. These approaches allow good concealment with high hidden capacity. However, there have been no reports of low-rate speech coding strategies based on the use of Sudoku matrices to achieve information steganography.

In this paper, we describe a steganographic method based on three-dimensional Sudoku matrices by analyzing the characteristics of low-rate speech coding. The most popular G.723.1 coding was used to verify this method. The results show that the steganography method proposed in this paper can achieve a steganographic capacity of 200 bps and provides better concealment performance in the G.723.1 carrier than other methods.

2 Related Work

2.1 Steganography Methods for Low-Rate Speech Coding

Low-rate speech coding efficiently compresses speech to decrease the redundant information of the encoded bitstream. Performing steganography using low-rate speech coding is a challenging task. In [9], the Least Significant Bit (LSB) method was used according to the anti-noise of the G.729. A coding strategy was proposed in [10], but using the LSB method in the pitch period of the low-rate speech G.723.1 encoder results in significant speech distortion. In [11], the authors found that in the LSB-embedding algorithm, better speech quality can be obtained by adjusting the perceptual weighting filter parameter values. There are also methods that seek to quantify the index modulation, or Quantization Index Modulation (QIM). For example, the basic concept of the method described in [12] is to group the quantized codebooks and then to search the quantized codebook packets according to the concealment information. This method is suitable for digital audio signals with vectorization and allows small quantization error but has low hidden capacity. In [13], the QIM information concealment method was proposed for pitch period prediction of low rate speech G.723.1. This method has a maximum embedding capacity of 4 bits per frame and small hidden capacity. In [14], a more secure algorithm was proposed based on the QIM algorithm that uses a key to control the inversion state of each subtree in the QIM algorithm to improve security. In [15], matrix coding is introduced into information steganography, which reduces the amount of bit modification. Additional details about current approaches in speech steganography are summarized and described in [16].

The Sudoku matrix has been widely used in steganography, encryption authentication, digital watermarking and other fields. The number of matrices satisfying the properties of the soliton matrix is very large, nearly 5.525×10^{27}. The application of the Sudoku matrix in information steganography will greatly improve its security [7,8]. The hidden capacity of a steganographic method based on the Sudoku matrix can be varied according to the changes of the Sudoku matrix size. Additionally, the quantization noise is small and the anti-detection ability is relatively strong. Image steganography based on Sudoku matrix is of growing interest, many kinds of Sudoku matrices and their variants have been tested in information steganography research [17,18]. There are also steganographic variants of 3D chaotic maps [19]. Overall, image steganography methods that utilize a Sudoku matrix can improve image quality and enhance the hidden capacity. However, there are no reported methods for low-rate speech coding that utilizes Sudoku matrices for information steganography.

The main idea of this study was to exploit the advantages of the Sudoku matrix for low-rate speech quantization coding with high concealment capacity.

2.2   Analysis of the Pitch Period in Low Rate Speech Coding

The pitch period is the periodicity of the vocal cord vibration that occurs when sending out voiced sound, a very important parameter for speech signal processing. However, it is difficult to predict and detect the pitch period. Existing methods of pitch detection have limitations and it is hard to predict the exact value by signal processing. The main difficulties of pitch detection are as follows:

(1) The change of speech signal is very complex and the pitch periodicity is not completely periodic.
(2) The resonant peak of the sound channel sometimes affects the harmonic structure of the excitation signal, making it difficult to extract the complete information about the vibration of the vocal cords.

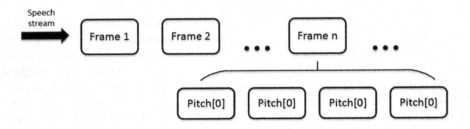

Fig. 1. The pitch period of low-rate speech sub-frame coding.

Since the existing pitch period detection technique is unable to obtain the true value of the true pitch period, modification will be tolerable if a slight modification of the predicted pitch period value is made to embed the secret information. This will not have a serious impact on the restoration of voice quality, suggesting that taking the pitch period as a hidden information embedded point is feasible. In addition, in low-rate speech signal coding, the pitch period is a common coding parameter, making it a reasonable approach. The low-rate speech signal coding must be processed by frames, such as with the G.723.1

encoder, where each speech frame consists of four subframes and each subframe has its own pitch period, as shown in Fig. 1. As the predicted values of the pitch period are sequential numbers, it is obvious that the influence of the pitch period on the quality of speech recovery is monotonically continuous. Thus, the physical modification is positively correlated to the logical variation.

3   Methodology

3.1   The Overall Framework for Low-Rate Speech Coding Steganography

Pitch period prediction is one component of low-rate speech coding. In the prediction process, by using a Sudoku matrix, steganography can be achieved by replacing the optimal pitch period value with the adjacent second best index value. To better introduce the principle, we next describe G.723.1 coding examples to illustrate the basic principles of steganography as follows.

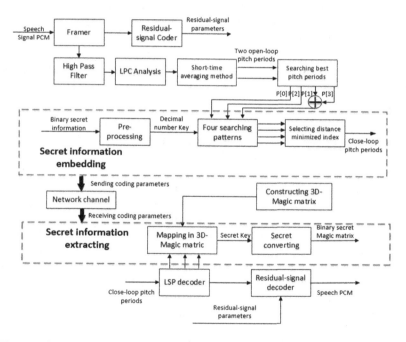

Fig. 2. The overall framework of steganography based on G.723.1 encoding.

The G.723.1 coding process is shown in Fig. 2. The speech signal PCM is divided into frames, and then high-pass filtered and LPC -filtered to obtain the residual signal. The pitch period of the open-loop is then estimated by the short-time averaging method, and then the fourth best closed-loop pitch period is obtained by searching for close-loop pitch periods. The sum of the second and fourth closed-loop pitch periods, the first closed-loop pitch period and the third closed-loop pitch period form a three-dimensional numeric space. The three-dimensional numeric space composed of the pitch period values and the three-dimensional Sudoku matrices have a certain mapping relationship. There is secret information of the four search patterns near the coordinate of the best index value. By selecting the secret information of the search pattern with the smallest distance between values and then changing the three best index values to the coordinate values of the secret information value, the quantization error can be reduced and the concealment ability can be enhanced. In this way, the final transmitted signal is the modified closed-loop pitch period information. The overall scheme of low-rate speech steganography is shown in the portion of Fig. 2 within the dashed line.

As shown in Fig. 2, the most critical component is how to construct a three-dimensional Sudoku matrix for low-rate speech coding steganography and how to design embedding and extraction algorithms using the matrix for steganography. Previous paper [20] focused on the generation of circulated motions of the three-dimensional Sudoku matrix. In this paper, we directly apply this three-dimensional Sudoku matrix to design a steganography method for hidden pitch features in low-rate speech coding.

3.2 Steganography Embedding Algorithm Based on Sudoku Matrix Steganography

In the G.723.1 encoding process, the 3D Sudoku matrix is first initialized using the circulated motion construction method of the 3D Sudoku matrix. Since the size of the 3D Sudoku matrix using this method is $8 \times 8 \times 8$, the range of the pitch period is 18–142, the bit allocation is 7 bits and the space size is 128. The $8 \times 8 \times 8$ Sudoku matrix is then expanded in a periodic manner, to fill the entire three-dimensional numeric space (0–127). Then, the pitch period values of the four sub-frames output by the pitch predictor are combined to form three temporary coefficients in combination, assigned as $index_x, index_y$ and $index_z$. These values are then mapped to a three-dimensional Sudoku matrix, searching for the smallest index value in the four patterns as the final pitch period value.

Let the original $8 \times 8 \times 8$ matrix be represented by the coordinate function, $g = Magic(x, y, z)$, where x, y and z represent the three coordinate values of the 3D Sudoku matrix and $x, y, z \in [0, 7]$, and g denotes the values of 3D Sudoku matrix, $g \in [0, 63]$. The coordinate function after the periodic expansion is represented by $q = Magic\_Expand(x', y', z')$, where $x', y', z' \in [0, 255], q \in [0, 63]$. The function obtained after the periodic expansion is shown in Eq. 1:

$$q = Magic\_Expand(x', y', z') = Magic(x, y, z), \begin{cases} x = x' \mod 8 \\ y = y' \mod 8 \\ z = z' \mod 8 \end{cases} \quad (1)$$

During pitch period detection, it is necessary to search for the index value of the optimal pitch period and then perform the index value replacement based on the 3D Sudoku matrix. Therefore, when performing steganographic embedding for each frame of speech, the following algorithm is performed.

Step 1: Two pitch estimates are calculated for each frame, one for the first two subframes and one for the remaining two subframes. The open-loop pitch period estimation L_{OL} is calculated using perceptually weighted speech $f[n]$. A cross-correlation judgment criterion $C_{OL}(j)$ maximization method is used to determine the pitch period, and the resulting open-loop pitch periods are $L_{OL}[0]$ and $L_{OL}[1]$, according to the following expression:

$$C_{OL}(j) = \frac{(\sum_{n=0}^{199} f[n] \times f[n-j])^2}{\sum_{n=0}^{199} f[n-j] \times f[n-j]}, 18 \leqslant j \leqslant 142. \tag{2}$$

Step 2: For sub-frames 0 and 2, the closed-loop pitch lag is selected from the appropriate open-loop pitch hysteresis in the range ± 1 and encoded with 7 bits (the final transmitted data is a closed-loop pitch period). For subframes 1 and 3, the closed loop pitch lag is differentially encoded using 2 bits (the final transmitted data is the differential coded data) and may differ by only -1, 0, $+1$, or $+2$ from the previous subframe lag. The quantized and decoded pitch lag values are referred to as L_i from this point on, where

$$\begin{cases} L_0 \in \{L_{OL}[0]-1, L_{OL}[0], L_{OL}[0]+1\}, 18 \leqslant L_0 \leqslant 142, \\ L_1 \in \{L_0-1, L_0, L_0+1, L_0+2\}, \\ L_2 \in \{L_{OL}[1]-1, L_{OL}[1], L_{OL}[1]+1\}, 18 \leqslant L_2 \leqslant 142, \\ L_3 \in \{L_2-1, L_2, L_2+1, L_2+2\}. \end{cases} \tag{3}$$

Step 3: The values of the four closed-loop pitch periods are combined and the coefficients of output are $index_x$, $index_y$ and $index_z$. The formula is as follows:

$$\begin{cases} index_x = L_0 - 18 \\ index_y = L_2 - 18 \\ index_z = L_1 - L_0 + L_3 - L_2 + 2 \end{cases} \tag{4}$$

The difference ranges of $L_1 - L_0 + 1$ and $L_3 - L_2 + 1$ are both 0–3, the addition of the two can expand the range of $index_z$ to expand the scope of the following search patterns. Based on the above analysis, we then need to map these values into the 3D Sudoku matrix and perform the following embedding operation.

Step 4: Preprocess the binary secret information stream and convert it into decimal key. Convert six consecutive binary numbers to decimal numbers Key. $Key \in [0, 63]$.

Step 5: Search for the Key values in the 3D Sudoku matrix function $Magic\_Expand(x, y, z)$ according to the following four patterns. Each of the search patterns includes a matrix search range, where the matrix range contains 0-63 non-repeating numbers, and the so-called search is to find the Key value in these element numbers. Obtain the four coordinates of the Key value $(index_x, index_y, index_z)$, $1 \leqslant i \leqslant 4$. Search for the Key value by looking up the index table for optimization, which is not described in detail here due to space limitations.

$$\begin{cases} x = index_x \\ index_y - 3 \leqslant y \leqslant index_y + 4 \\ index_z - 3 \leqslant z \leqslant index_z + 4 \end{cases} \quad (5)$$

$$\begin{cases} index_x - 3 \leqslant x \leqslant index_x + 4 \\ y = index_y \\ index_z - 3 \leqslant z \leqslant index_z + 4 \end{cases} \quad (6)$$

$$\begin{cases} index_x - 3 \leqslant x \leqslant index_x + 4 \\ index_y - 3 \leqslant y \leqslant index_y + 4 \\ z = index_z \end{cases} \quad (7)$$

$$\begin{cases} \lfloor index_x/4 \rfloor \times 4 \leqslant x \leqslant \lfloor index_x/4 \rfloor \times 4 + 3 \\ \lfloor index_y/4 \rfloor \times 4 \leqslant y \leqslant \lfloor index_y/4 \rfloor \times 4 + 3 \\ \lfloor index_z/4 \rfloor \times 4 \leqslant z \leqslant \lfloor index_z/4 \rfloor \times 4 + 3 \end{cases} \quad (8)$$

Step 6: Compare the Euclidean distance between the four coordinates and the original coordinates. Since the smaller the Euclidean distance, the smaller the quantization error, the coordinates with the smallest Euclidean distance are selected as the best pitch period after the information concealment. The index coordinates of the final Sudoku matrix are $(bestindex_x, bestindex_y, bestindex_z)$. The information embedding is completed.

$$(bestindex_x, bestindex_y, bestindex_z)$$
$$= \arg\min_{i=1-4}[(index_x - indexi_x)^2) + (index_y - indexi_y)^2) + (index_z - indexi_z)^2]$$

3.3 Steganography Extraction Algorithm Based on Sudoku Matrix Steganography

Extracting secret information is relatively simple compared to encoding embedded secret information. Here, the $8 \times 8 \times 8$ Sukodu matrix is periodically expanded to become a three-dimensional Sudoku matrix of $128 \times 128 \times 128$. When the pitch period values of the four subframes are decoded, the four pitch period index values are extracted, and the sum of the pitch period values of subframes 1 and 3 and subframes 0 and 2 are converted to three-dimensional coordinates. Then, the coordinates are mapped in the three-dimensional Sudoku matrix named Key. The value is the secret information that is then converted into a binary data stream. The detailed secret information extraction algorithm is as follows.

Step 1: Extract the pitch period value of four sub-frames and assign them to $L_0, L_1, L_2,$ and L_3.
Step 2: Perform the following operations on the four pitch period values, assigned to $(bestindex_x, bestindex_y, bestindex_z)$.

$$\begin{cases} bestindex_x = L_0 - 18 \\ bestindex_y = L_2 - 18 \\ bestindex_z = L_1 - L_0 + L_3 - L_2 + 2 \end{cases} \quad (9)$$

Step 3: Build and initialize the three-dimensional Sudoku matrix. The receiver shares the sender's three-dimensional Sudoku matrix. This three-dimensional Sudoku matrix is written as $Magic\_Expand(x, y, z)$.

Step 4: Locate the coordinate points into the three-dimensional Sudoku matrix, obtain the secret information as Key as shown in formula 6, and then the decoding is completed.

$$Key = Magic\_Expand(bestindex_x, bestindex_y, bestindex_z) \tag{10}$$

4 Results and Analysis

4.1 Concealment Capacity Analysis

To perform the information concealment method based on the 3D Sudoku matrix for the G.723.1 speech coded stream, the range of pitch period of each frame was set to $[0, 63]$, implying that 6 bits can be hidden in every frame. The length of each G.723.1 frame is 30 ms, so the concealment capacity of the concealment algorithm based on the three-dimensional Sudoku matrix is 6 bit/0.03 s = 200 bit/s in the pitch period. The modification method of the lowest two significant bits of the method in [10] has 3 sub-vectors for each frame and each sub-vector can hide 2 bits. Therefore, each frame can hide $3 \times 2\,bit = 6\,bit$. The overall concealment capacity of this method is 6 bit/0.03 s = 200 bit/s. In the QIM information concealment algorithm based on pitch period proposed in [13], the codebook division method is odd-even division. Each subframe can hide 1 bit hence, each frame can hide $4 \times 1\,bit = 4\,bit$. So, the overall concealment capacity of proposed method is 4 bit/0.03 s = 133.3 bit/s. The above concealment capacity analysis shows that the concealment capacity of this model based on three-dimensional Sudoku matrix proposed is equal to that of a previously reported method [10] and 1.5 times better than the method described in [13].

4.2 Concealment Analysis

The concealment of speech carrier steganography can be evaluated by the quality of speech. There are two evaluation methods of speech quality, i.e., subjective and objective. The most popular method of subjective speech quality evaluation is Perceptual Evaluation of Speech Quality (PESQ) and the most popular method of objective speech quality evaluation is the signal-to-noise ratio (SNR).

Subjective Speech Quality. Multiple speech clips of different speakers were selected to form the speech sample dataset. Speech clips from 4 categories were used, i.e., English male voice (EM), English female voice (EW), Chinese male voice (CM) and Chinese female voice (CW). Each category contains 10 long samples of 10 ms. Each voice clip is of 8 kHz sampling rate, in 16bit quantized PCM format. The subjective sampling speech evaluation method uses speech quality perception to evaluate the PESQ. The values of this test range from 0 to 5, and the higher the value, the better the voice quality.

Table 1. PESQ values and loss ratios for different hidden algorithms

Scheme	CM		CW		EM		EW		Average
	PESQ	Loss	PESQ	Loss	PESQ	Loss	PESQ	Loss	
Standard scheme	3.74	-	3.43	-	3.81	-	3.67	-	-
Paper [10] scheme	2.40	36.00%	2.51	26.84%	2.92	23.39%	2.33	36.33%	30.7%
Paper [13] scheme	3.69	1.41%	3.34	2.38%	3.79	0.52%	3.60	1.98%	1.57%
Proposed scheme	3.39	9.84%	3.15	8.04%	3.66	4.01%	3.29	10.03%	7.98%

Table 1 shows the comparison of PESQ values for information concealment
for the method of [10], the method of [13] and our method. The influence of
the steganography method on the PESQ of speech is less than that of [10],
which indicates that proposed steganography method is better than the method
presented in [10]. The influence of method [13] on the PESQ of speech is smaller
than that of proposed method, but both values are small. Additionally, the
hidden capacity of our method is 1.5 times that of [13]. The average deterioration
rate of PESQ was 9.84%, 8.04%, 4.01%, and 10.03%, respectively. The overall
mean rate of deterioration was 7.98%, which was within an acceptable range.
Thus, the algorithm meets the requirements of good concealment.

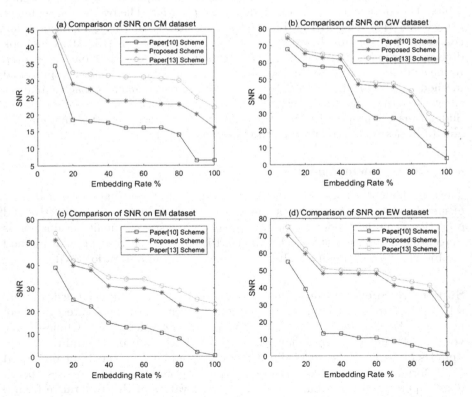

Fig. 3. Comparison of SNR values of three kinds of steganography methods.

Objective Speech Quality. The objective speech quality evaluation method uses the SNR and the test results are shown in Fig. 3. By comparing the SNRs of the three steganography methods for different sample sets, we can see that in general, the higher the embedding rate of the secret information, the lower the SNR value is and the higher the quantization noise. For the different sample sets, the SNR of the steganography method in this paper was larger than that in [10] for equal concealment capacity, indicating that the quantization noise of our method is smaller than that of [10]. The SNR of proposed steganography method was slightly smaller than the SNR of [13], but it should take into consider that the concealment capacity of proposed method was 1.5 times that of [13].

5   Conclusions

The use of a Sudoku matrix was first introduced for using in a speech-carrier-based information concealment algorithm. In order to satisfy the specific distribution characteristic of the speech coding coefficients, the two-dimensional Sudoku matrix was extended to a three-dimensional Sudoku matrix to further enhance the speech concealment capacity with maintenance of good perceptual speech concealment.

The G.723.1 speech coding protocol was chosen as the basic method of information concealment. When the pitch period was estimated, the best index was mapped by using $8 \times 8 \times 8$ Sudoku matrices. Using this method, the secret information was successfully embedded with an embedding capacity of $200 \, bit/s$. Finally, a large number of speech samples were used to test and evaluate the proposed method and compare it to other methods found in the literature. The speech quality loss was evaluated based on the subjective speech quality perception criterion and the quantization error was evaluated by an objective SNR method. Results show that the proposed method can provide considerable concealment capacity with better imperceptibility.

Acknowledgements. This research is supported by the National Natural Science Foundation of China (No. U1536115, No. U1536113 and No. U1636113).

References

1. Janicki, A.: Novel method of hiding information in IP telephony using pitch approximation. In: 2015 10th International Conference on Availability, Reliability and Security (ARES). IEEE (2015)
2. Mazurczyk, W., Szaga, P., Szczypiorski, K.: Using transcoding for hidden communication in IP telephony. Multimed. Tools App. **70**(3), 2139–2165 (2014)
3. Yang, Z., Huang, Y.F., Tao, H.Z., Yang, W.X.: Protocol of steganography in streaming media on VoIP network based on variable length coding. In: National Conference on Information Technology and Computer Science (CITCS 2012), Lanzhou, China (2012)
4. Yuan, J., Huang, Y.F., Li, X.: A quantitation method to the imperceptibility of hiding-vector in multi-dimensional hiding space. Chin. J. Electron. 4(22), 826–832 (2013)

5. Huang, Y.F., Tang, S.Y., Yuan, J.: Steganography in inactive frames of VoIP streams encoded by source codec. IEEE Trans. Inf. Forensics Secur. **6**(2), 296–306 (2011)
6. Zhou, K., Liu, J., Tian, H., Li, C.: State-based steganography in low bit rate speech. In: Proceedings of 20th ACM Multimedia Conference (ACM-MM2012), Nara, Japan, 29 Oct–2 Nov 2012, pp. 1109–1112 (2012)
7. Chang, C.C., Chou, Y.C., Kieu, T.D.: An information hiding scheme using sudoku. In: Proceedings of 3rd International Conference on Innovative Computing Information and Control (ICICIC), Dalian, China, p. 17, June 2008
8. Chang, C.C., Chen, Y.H., Wang, Z.H., Li, M.C.: A data embedding scheme based on a magic matrix and wet paper codes. In: Proceedings of 2009 International Conference on Computational Intelligence and Natural Computing (CINC), Wuhan, China, pp. 303–306, June 2009
9. Liu, L.H., Li, M.Y., Liang, Y.: Perceptually transparent information hiding in G.729 bitstream. In: Proceedings of IEEE International Conference on Intelligent Information Hiding and Multimedia Signal Processing (IIHMSP 2008), Harbin, China, pp. 406–409 (2008)
10. You, P., Ji, X., Lu, P.: Performance analysis of using G.723.1's high-rate codes to hiding information in packed communication system. Comput. Sci. **35**(5), 194–197 (2008)
11. Malhotra, N.A., Tahilramani, N.: Steganography approach of weighted speech analysis with and without vector quantization using variation in weight factor. Int. J. Curr. Eng. Technol. **4**(3), 1334–1336 (2014)
12. Chen, B., Wornell, G.W.: Quantization Index modulation: a class of provably good methods for digital watermarking and information embedding. IEEE Trans. Inf. Theory **47**(4), 1423–1443 (2001)
13. Huang, Y.F., Liu, J., Tang, S.Y., Sen, B.: Steganography integration into a low-bit rate speech codec. IEEE Trans. Inf. Forensics Secur. **7**(6), 1865–1875 (2012)
14. Tian, H., Liu, J., Li, S.: Improving security of quantization-index-modulation steganography in low bit-rate speech streams. Multimed. Syst. **20**(2), 143–154 (2014)
15. Zhi, J., Hai, J., Dou, Z.: An approach of steganography in G.729 bitstream based on matrix coding and interleaving. Chin. J. Electron. **24**(1), 57–165 (2015)
16. Bilal, I., Kumar, R., Roj, M.S., Mishra, P.K.: Recent advancement in audio steganography. In: International Conference on Parallel Distributed and Grid Computing, vol. 11, pp. 1945–1953. IEEE (2015)
17. Sarada, P., BalaSwamy, C.: Improving image data hiding capacity scheme using sudoku puzzle in color images. Int. J. Eng. Res. App. (IJERA) **2**(3), 2741–2744 (2012)
18. Maji, A.K., Pal, R.K., Roy, S.: A novel steganographic scheme using sudoku. In: Proceedings of IEEE International Conference on Electrical Information and Communication Technology (EICT), Khulna, pp. 1–6, February 2014
19. Valandar, M.Y., Ayubi, P., Barani, M.J.: High secure digital image steganography based on 3D chaotic map. In: Information and Knowledge Technology. IEEE (2015)
20. Peng, X.S., Huang, Y.F., Li, F.F.: A steganography scheme in a low-bit rate speech codec based on 3D-sudoku matrix. In: 2016 8th IEEE International Conference on Communication Software and Networks (ICCSN 2016), Beijing (2016)

A Framework for Formal Analysis of Privacy on SSO Protocols

Kailong Wang[1], Guangdong Bai[2(✉)], Naipeng Dong[1], and Jin Song Dong[1,3]

[1] National University of Singapore, Singapore, Singapore
{dcswaka,dcsdn,dcsdjs}@nus.edu.sg
[2] Singapore Institute of Technology, Singapore, Singapore
guangdong.bai@singaporetech.edu.sg
[3] Griffith University, Nathan, Australia

Abstract. Single Sign-on (SSO) protocols, which allow a website to authenticate its users via accounts registered with another website, are forming the basis of user identity management in contemporary websites. Given the critical role they are playing in safeguarding the privacy-sensitive web services and user data, SSO protocols deserve a rigorous formal verification. In this work, we provide a framework facilitating formal modeling of SSO protocols and analysis of their privacy property. Our framework incorporates a formal model of the web infrastructure (e.g., network and browsers), a set of attacker models (e.g., malicious IDP) and a formalization of the privacy property with respect to SSO protocols. Our analysis has identified a new type of attack that allows malicious participants to learn which websites the victim users have logged in to.

Keywords: Single Sign-on · Privacy · Formal verification framework

1 Introduction

Single Sign-on (SSO) protocols, which allow users to log in to a website, i.e., the relying party (RP), using the accounts registered with another website, i.e., the identity provider (IDP), are becoming the cornerstone of user identity management in contemporary websites. These protocols serve as the safeguard of various privacy-sensitive web services. Nonetheless, they have been continually found vulnerable and insecure by previous research [1–6].

Given the critical role that SSO protocols are playing, they deserve a rigorous security assessment, and formal verification ideally, before they are implemented and deployed for practical use. However, the challenge on formally verifying SSO protocols is at least twofold. First, formal verification requires an accurate formal model of the underlying web infrastructure which SSO protocols rely upon. The web infrastructure is complicated as it involves the server-side infrastructure (e.g., web servers and SSO SDKs), the client-side infrastructure (e.g., web browsers) and various communication channels. In addition, SSO protocols often rely on new techniques and features (e.g., HTML5's `postMessage`) to fulfill its

© ICST Institute for Computer Sciences, Social Informatics and Telecommunications Engineering 2018
X. Lin et al. (Eds.): SecureComm 2017, LNICST 238, pp. 763–777, 2018.
https://doi.org/10.1007/978-3-319-78813-5_41

advanced functions (e.g., cross-domain communication on the client side). These features increase the complexity of the SSO protocols. For example, misusing `postMessage` or client-side storage may lead to credential leakage [1,7].

The second challenge is regarding the comprehensiveness of the attacker behaviors and the targeted properties. Since SSO protocols rely on web clients, web servers and various communication channels, they are naturally exposed to a large attack surface. As a result, the behaviors of malicious participants (e.g., malicious IDPs) have to be formalized when analyzing the SSO protocols. As for the properties, the *privacy* property – whether an attacker is able to track which RP a user has logged in to, is becoming a public concern [3]. However, existing studies have mainly focused on the authentication property [4,5,8].

In this work, we propose a framework for analyzing the privacy property of SSO protocols. Our framework consists of a formal model of the web infrastructure, three types of attacker models and a formal definition of the privacy property of SSO protocols. We abstract the whole infrastructure into three parts which are essential in SSO, including the *web browser*, the *network* and the *web server*. Our attack models contain three types of malicious IDP – the Honest-But-Curious IDP Server which infers the user's login information based on his own knowledge, the Malicious IDP Server which is capable of sending fake information to requesters and the Malicious IDP Client which is an IDP's client-side web page capable of invoking browser APIs (for example, to request the browser to open a new window). In our framework, we use the *applied pi calculus* [9] as our modeling language, given that it can be automatically verified using the state-of-the-art verifier ProVerif [10]. The privacy property is thus formalized as the observational equivalence [11].

We apply our framework to analyze a novel privacy-respecting protocol named SPRESSO [12]. This protocol is representative and is suitable to test our framework, because modeling it covers most of the web techniques, including end-to-end communication between web servers and the browser, HTML5's cross-domain communication, AJAX and so on. We have found that SPRESSO suffers from a privacy flaw which allows a malicious IDP to abuse two key pairs to learn which users have logged in to a particular RP.

2   A Verification Framework for SSO

In this section, we present our verification framework for formally analyzing SSO protocols. First, we introduce the used modeling language. Next, we explain our web infrastructure model, followed by the three attacker models. Finally, we present our formalization of the privacy property of SSO protocols.

2.1   The Modeling Language

We use a variant of the applied pi calculus [9] for modeling protocols, attackers and the privacy property. This calculus assumes an infinite set of names which are used for modeling communication channels and atomic data, an infinite set

$P, Q :=$	plain process	$A, B :=$	extended process
0	null process	P	plain process
$P \mid Q$	parallel composition	$A \mid B$	parallel
$!P$	replication	**new** $x;\ A$	variable restriction
new $n;\ P$	name restriction	**new** $n;\ A$	name restriction
in$(u,\ x);\ P$	message input	$\{M/x\}$	active substitution
out$(u,\ M);\ P$	message output		
if $M =_E N$ **then** P **else** Q	conditional		
let $x = M$ **in** P **else** Q	term evaluation		

Fig. 1. Applied Pi syntax

of variables, and a signature Σ consisting of finite number of symbols (with arity) which are used for modeling cryptographic primitives. Terms are defined as names, variables as well as function symbols applied to terms. A system is modeled as a plain process, whose syntax is defined in Fig. 1. The reasoning on the models in the applied pi calculus is with respect to the built-in Dolev-Yao attacker model [13] who can block, obtain, tamper and/or insert messages over public channels. A process is closed if all variables are either bound by restriction or input, or defined by an active substitution.

Null process 0 does nothing. Process $P \mid Q$ models two processes P and Q running in parallel. Process $!P$ models infinite number of process P running in parallel, capturing unbounded number of sessions. Name restriction **new** $n;\ P$ binds the name n in process P, capturing both fresh random numbers and private names and channels. Message input **in**$(u,\ x);\ P$ describes that the process reads a message from channel u and binds the received message to x in process P. Message output **out**$(u,\ M);\ P$ describes that the process sends a message M on channel u and runs P afterwards. The conditional evaluation **if** $M =_E N$ **then** P **else** Q runs P when equation $M =_E N$ is true under equational theory E otherwise runs Q. If Q is null, this process can be reduced to **if** $M =_E N$ **then** P. The term evaluation **let** $x = M$ **in** P **else** Q bounds x to M and takes process branch P, otherwise, Q is taken. If Q is null, the term evaluation can be simplified to **let** $x = M$ **in** P. We denote **new** $n_1; \cdots ;$ **new** n_m by **new** $\tilde{n}$. The extended process $\{M/x\}$ indicates the substitution of variable x with term M. An evaluation context is an extended process with a hole which is not in a scope of a replication, a conditional, an input, or an output.

2.2 Web Infrastructure Model

Figure 2 shows our abstraction of the web infrastructure. In the abstraction, the web infrastructure consists of three components: the *web browsers*, the *network* and the *web servers*. It represents a common scenario where users use the browsers to download documents and communicate with the web servers via the network.

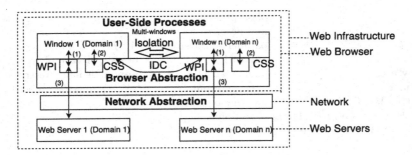

Fig. 2. Web infrastructure abstraction

Web Browser Model. The web browser model has a list of *windows/iframes* (denoted by *window* 1, ..., *window* n in Fig. 2) which are containers for the client-side documents of the websites. In addition, the model includes the *webpage parser/interpreter* (denoted by *WPI*), the *client-side storage* (denoted by *CSS*), the *inter-domain communication* (denoted by *IDC*) and the *isolation*. They are important features for analyzing the privacy property of SSO protocols.

WPI parses and interprets the programs downloaded from the web servers. The WPI includes complex functions which may not be relevant to the SSO protocols, such as page rendering. Therefore, our framework only models the part that processes the SSO-relevant commands, as shown in the following model. These commands include open windows OW (line k_1–k_2), get the parent window parentOf (line k_3), establish http(s) connections http(s)Connect (line k_4–k_5), send http(s) messages http(s)Send (line k_6–k_7) and receive http(s) messages http(s)Receive (line k_8–k_9). Note that terms w_1 and w_2 denote window names, terms $e_1, \cdots, e_m$ denote participants interacting with each other, such as windows and web servers, and terms $msg_1, \cdots, msg_l$ denote messages. Name priv denotes the private channel to call the browser commands, and name priv′ denotes the private channel to send and receive the http(s) messages through the *network* which is defined later.

$$
\begin{aligned}
WPI := \ &(\mathbf{in}(\mathrm{priv}, (= \mathrm{OW}, w_1)); \mathbf{let}\ w_2 = \mathsf{Child}(w_1)\ \mathbf{in} &&k_1\\
&\mathbf{out}(\mathrm{priv}, (\mathrm{OW}, w_1, w_2)); &&k_2\\
&!\mathbf{in}(\mathrm{priv}, (= \mathrm{parentOf}, = w_2)); \mathbf{out}(\mathrm{priv}, (\mathrm{parentOf}, w_2, w_1)))| &&k_3\\
&(\mathbf{in}(\mathrm{priv}, (= \mathrm{http(s)Connect}, e_1, e_2)); &&k_4\\
&\mathbf{out}(\mathrm{priv'}, (\mathrm{http(s)Connect}, e_1, e_2)))| &&k_5\\
&(\mathbf{in}(\mathrm{priv}, (= \mathrm{http(s)Send}, msg_1, e_3, e_4)); &&k_6\\
&\mathbf{out}(\mathrm{priv'}, (\mathrm{http(s)Send}, msg_1, e_3, e_4)))| &&k_7\\
&(\mathbf{in}(\mathrm{priv'}, (= \mathrm{http(s)Receive}, msg_2, e_5, e_6)); &&k_8\\
&\mathbf{out}(\mathrm{priv}, (\mathrm{http(s)Receive}, msg_2, e_5, e_6))). &&k_9
\end{aligned}
$$

CSS includes both short-term storage (i.e., cookies and SessionStorage) and long-term (i.e., LocalStorage) storage that can only be accessed by the client-side web page of the same URL domain. In particular, we explicitly model Local-Storage because it may store data relevant to the privacy property. For example, compromising the LocalStorage may disclose the user's login status at a certain RP [3]. As shown in the following model, the LocalStorage is modeled as a process LS where LSS denotes the command of storing messages and LSR denotes that of retrieving messages. We do not explicitly model the short-term storage since it can be recorded in the local variables.

$$LS := \mathbf{in}(\mathbf{priv}, (= \mathtt{LSS}, (index, msg))); !\mathbf{out}(\mathbf{priv}, (\mathtt{LSR}, (index, msg))).$$

IDC is mostly achieved by an API called `postMessage` in HTML5. It is extensively used in the SSO protocols since the involved participants (at least RP and IDP) which have to communicate with each other are typically from different domains. As shown in the following model, the `postMessage` is modeled as a process PM where PMS and PMR denote sending and receiving messages respectively. The sender and the receiver window identities (i.e. w_1 and w_2) are required to indicate the two endpoints of the `postMessage`.

$$PM := \mathbf{in}(\mathbf{priv}, (= \mathtt{PMS}, w_1, w_2, msg)); \mathbf{out}(\mathbf{priv}, (\mathtt{PMR}, w_2, msg)).$$

Isolation among domains is a security feature (the *same origin policy*) provided by the web browsers. This feature ensures the domains at the client side are isolated such that scripts from one domain cannot access data belonging to other domains. Since we model the windows as individual and parallel processes, the documents received by a window cannot be accessed by others. In addition, cross-domain messaging between different windows is via private channels, restraining messages only to the intended processes according to the protocol. Thus, isolation property is implicitly retained in our web browser model.

Network Model. The network model covers both http and https channels which are the basis for data transmission in the SSO protocols. The network model in our framework is shown below. The terms $e_1, \cdots, e_m$ denote communicating participants, while the terms $Msg_1, \cdots, Msg_l$ denote exchanged messages.

$$
\begin{array}{lll}
HTTPconnect & := \mathbf{in}(\mathrm{priv}', (= \mathtt{httpConnect}, e_1, e_2)); \mathbf{out}(\mathtt{c}, (e_1, e_2)). & l_1 \\
HTTPsend & := \mathbf{in}(\mathrm{priv}', (= \mathtt{httpSend}, Msg_1, e_3, e_4)); \mathbf{out}(\mathtt{c}, Msg_1, e_3, e_4). & l_2 \\
HTTPreceive & := \mathbf{in}(\mathtt{c}, (Msg_2, e_5, e_6)); \mathbf{out}(\mathrm{priv}', (\mathtt{httpReceive}, Msg_2, e_5, e_6)). & l_3 \\
HTTPSconnect & := \mathbf{in}(\mathrm{priv}', (= \mathtt{httpsConnect}, e_7, e_8)); & l_4 \\
& \quad \mathbf{let}\ k = \mathsf{httpskey}(e_7, e_8)\ \mathbf{in}\ \mathbf{out}(\mathtt{c}, (e_7, e_8)). & l_5 \\
HTTPSsend & := \mathbf{in}(\mathrm{priv}', (= \mathtt{httpsSend}, Msg_3, e_9, e_{10})); \mathbf{new\ nonce}; & l_6 \\
& \quad \mathbf{let}\ key = \mathsf{httpskey}(e_9, e_{10})\ \mathbf{in} & l_7 \\
& \quad \mathbf{out}(\mathtt{c}, \mathsf{enc}((\mathbf{nonce}, Msg_3), key), e_9, e_{10}). & l_8 \\
HTTPSreceive & := \mathbf{in}(\mathtt{c}, (EncMsg, e_{11}, e_{12})); \mathbf{let}\ key = \mathsf{httpskey}(e_{11}, e_{12})\ \mathbf{in} & l_9 \\
& \quad \mathbf{let}\ (Nonce, Msg_4) = \mathsf{dec}(EncMsg, key)\ \mathbf{in} & l_{10} \\
& \quad \mathbf{out}(\mathrm{priv}', (\mathtt{httpsReceive}, Msg_4, e_{11}, e_{12})). & l_{11}
\end{array}
$$

The *http channels* are not encrypted. Hence, we simply model the http messages to be sent and received on the public channel c (line l_1–l_3). The *https channels* include two parts: *session key establishment* which sets up a session key between the two communicating participants using handshake protocols (line l_4–l_5), and *message exchange* which uses the established session key to protect the messages. In particular, the message is encrypted when it is sent out (line l_6–l_8) and decrypted when it is received (line l_9–l_{11}).

Web Servers. Web servers are the server-side SSO participants such as the RPs and IDPs. Their behaviors need to be manually modeled according to the protocol specifications.

Table 1. Interfaces: infrastructure inputs

Interfaces	Functionality
$\mathbf{out}(\mathrm{priv}, (\mathtt{OW}, w_1))$	Open window request from window w_1
$\mathbf{in}(\mathrm{priv}, (= \mathtt{OW}, w_1, w_2))$	Return created child window w_2 of w_1
$\mathbf{out}(\mathrm{priv}, (\mathtt{parentOf}, w_1))$	Request parent window of window w_1
$\mathbf{in}(\mathrm{priv}, (= \mathtt{parentOf}, = w_1, w_2))$	Return parent window w_2 of window w_1
$\mathbf{out}(\mathrm{priv}, (\mathtt{PMS}, w_1, w_2, msg)$	Send $\mathtt{postMessage}$ from w_1 to w_2
$\mathbf{in}(\mathrm{priv}, (= \mathtt{PMR}, = w_1, msg)$	Receive $\mathtt{postMessage}$ intended for w_1
$\mathbf{out}(\mathrm{priv}, (\mathtt{LSS}, (index, msg)))$	Store message msg to LocalStorage
$\mathbf{in}(\mathrm{priv}, (= \mathtt{LSR}, (= index, msg)))$	Retrieve message msg from LocalStorage
$\mathbf{out}(\mathrm{priv}, (\mathtt{http(s)Connect}, e_1, e_2))$	Request http(s) connection over e_1 and e_2
$\mathbf{in}(\mathtt{c}, (e_1, e_2)$	Establish http(s) connection over e_1 and e_2
$\mathbf{out}(\mathrm{priv}, (\mathtt{http(s)Send}, msg, e_1, e_2)$	Send http(s) message msg from e_1 to e_2
$\mathbf{in}(\mathrm{priv}, (= \mathtt{http(s)Receive}, msg, e_1, e_2))$	Receive http(s) message msg from e_1 by e_2

In summary, we provide the interfaces listed in Table 1 to facilitate modeling of the SSO protocols using our web infrastructure. Each interface includes an

out message representing the command from a client-side process to the web infrastructure and an **in** message representing the response from the web infrastructure to the client-side process. Overall, the web infrastructure is defined as a process where all the above processes run in parallel, $WebInfra = WPI \mid LS \mid PM \mid HTTPconnect \mid HTTPsend \mid HTTPreceive \mid HTTPSconnect \mid HTTPSsend \mid HTTPSreceive$.

2.3   Attacker Models

In the SSO protocols, the privacy property is violated if the attacker learns which RPs the users have logged in to. Therefore, we mainly consider the malicious IDP since the privacy property would be trivially violated if either the user or the RP is malicious. According to the attacker's capabilities, we define three attacker models namely the *Honest-But-Curious IDP Server*, the *Malicious IDP Server* and the *Malicious IDP Client*.

Honest-But-Curious IDP Server tries to break the user's privacy based on its own knowledge. It records messages generated and received by itself and tries to derive the user's login information from those recorded messages. This attacker can be simulated in the applied pi calculus by sending the built-in Dolev-Yao attacker all the messages of base type (i.e., not of channel type) generated and received by the IDP, such that the existing reasoning techniques can be reused to check whether the privacy property is satisfied or not.

Malicious IDP Server can forge messages based on its knowledge and send them out upon requests in place of the authentic messages from the IDP server.

Malicious IDP Client mainly follows the behavior of an honest IDP's client-side web page but contains a malicious iframe. The malicious iframe has the capability of invoking the web infrastructure interfaces. Take the BrowserID, which is a well-known SSO protocol, as an example. It suffers from the attack that when a user logs in, a malicious window can be triggered to inform the attacker the RP the user has logged in to [2].

2.4   Formalization of SSO Privacy Property

We use the observational equivalence relation defined in the applied pi calculus [9] to formalize the privacy property. Intuitively, two processes are observationally equivalent if the Dolve-Yao attacker cannot distinguish the two processes. In order to further explain our formalization, we define the generalized evaluation context of SSO processes in the applied pi calculus as follows.

Definition 1 (Evaluation Context of General SSO Processes). *We define an evaluation context D as the following SSO process with a hole ([_]).*

$D :=$ **new** $\tilde{n}$;

$\quad C(account, rp)\sigma_{11} \mid C(account, rp)\sigma_{12} \mid \cdots \mid [\_] \mid \cdots \mid C(account, rp)\sigma_{nm} \mid$

$\quad !RP_1 \mid \cdots \mid !RP_m \mid !IDP \mid !WebInfra,$

- $\tilde{n}$ indicates private channel names and data in this process.
- Process $C(account, rp)$ models the client-side login process including the behaviors of the client-side RP, the client-side IDP, etc., together with the user's behaviors (e.g., input the password). The *account* and the *rp* are two free variables denoting the user account and the RP domain which are instantiated by $\texttt{Account}_i$ and $\texttt{RPname}_j$ respectively using the substitution σ_{ij} where $\sigma_{ij} = \{\texttt{Account}_i/account, \texttt{RPname}_j/rp\}$. There are totally n accounts and m RP domains, therefore σ is a set $\sigma = \{\sigma_{11}, \cdots, \sigma_{nm}\}$. The $RP_1, \cdots, RP_m$ and the IDP are honest RPs and IDP. Any sub-process can be null except $WebInfra$.
- The hole [_] can be filled with a process $C(account, rp)\sigma_{ij} \mid C(account, rp)\sigma_{lk}$ with $\sigma_{ij}, \sigma_{lk} \in \sigma$.

With the evaluation context, we formally define privacy property as follows.

Definition 2 (SSO Protocol Privacy). *An SSO protocol preserves user's privacy if the following observational equivalence query is true*

$$D[C\{\texttt{Account}_1/account, \texttt{RPname}_1/rp\} | C\{\texttt{Account}_2/account, \texttt{RPname}_2/rp\}] \approx$$
$$D[C\{\texttt{Account}_1/account, \texttt{RPname}_2/rp\} | C\{\texttt{Account}_2/account, \texttt{RPname}_1/rp\}]$$

for accounts $\texttt{Account}_1$ *and* $\texttt{Account}_2$ *and RPs* $\texttt{RPname}_1$ *and* $\texttt{RPname}_2$.

In this definition, $\texttt{Account}_1$ and $\texttt{Account}_2$ represent two user accounts, and $\texttt{RPname}_1$ and $\texttt{RPname}_2$ represent two RP domains. Intuitively, the definition indicates that an SSO protocol respects user's privacy when $\texttt{Account}_1$ logs in to $\texttt{RPname}_1$ and $\texttt{Account}_2$ logs in to $\texttt{RPname}_2$ cannot be differentiated from (i.e., observationally equivalent to) $\texttt{Account}_1$ logs in to $\texttt{RPname}_2$ and $\texttt{Account}_2$ logs in to $\texttt{RPname}_1$. Note that two account and two RPs are required in order to define privacy, given that if there is only one account or RP, the malicious IDP can trivially know who is logging in to the RP based on the RP-IDP or user-IDP communication.

3   Case Study

In this section, we use SPRESSO [12] as a case study to illustrate how to apply our framework to analyze an SSO protocol. The general process of the SPRESSO protocol is shown in Fig. 3. Following this process, the SPRESSO protocol is modeled, as shown in Figs. 4, 5 and 6.

Figure 4 shows the overall model of the SPRESSO protocol. The client-side process is modeled as $C(\texttt{Account}, \texttt{RPname})$ where $\texttt{Account}$ and $\texttt{RPname}$ are

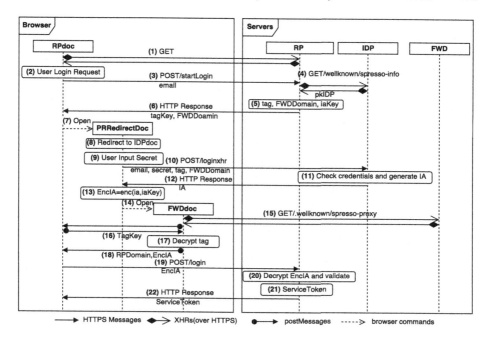

Fig. 3. SPRESSO protocol flow chart [12]

$SPRESSO\_proc :=$

s_1	**new** skidp; **let** $pkidp$ = pk(skidp) **in**
s_2	**new** IDPname; **new** RPname; **new** Account;
s_3	(!**out**(c, IDPname) |!**out**(c, RPname) | C(Account, RPname) |
s_4	!IDP_proc(IDPname) |!RP_proc(RPname) |! $WebInfra$)

Fig. 4. SPRESSO protocol

instantiations for the free variables *account* and *rp* in the process $C(account, rp)$. The process $C(\texttt{Account}, \texttt{RPname})$ is comprised of subprocesses namely the $RPdoc\_proc$, the $IDPdoc\_proc$ and the $FWDdoc\_proc$, which represent the behaviors of the client-side web pages (i.e., the RPdoc, the IDPdoc and the FWDdoc) of the corresponding web servers. The IDP and the RP servers are modeled in the $IDP\_proc(\texttt{IDPname})$ and the $RP\_proc(\texttt{RPname})$. In the rest of this section, we detail the modeling of the client-side process and the server-side processes.

$C(account,\ rp) :=$

q_1 **in**$(c, IDPname)$;

q_2 **let** $email = (account, IDPname)$ **in**

q_3 **let** $RPname_1 = rp$ **in**

q_4 **new** root; **out**$(\text{priv}, (\text{OW}, \text{root}))$;

q_5 **in**$(\text{priv}, (= \text{root}, rpdoc))$;

q_6 $RPdoc\_proc \mid IDPdoc\_proc \mid FWDdoc\_proc$

$RPdoc\_proc$ $:=$

q_7 **out**$(\text{priv}, (\text{httpsConnect}, rpdoc, RPname_1))$;

q_8 **out**$(\text{priv}, (\text{httpsSend}, email, rpdoc, RPname_1))$;

q_9 **in**$(\text{priv}, (= \text{httpsReceive}, (tagkey, fwdomain,$
           $logsesstoken), = rpdoc, = RPname_1))$;

q_{10} **out**$(\text{priv}, (\text{OW}, rpdoc))$; **in**$(\text{priv}, (= rpdoc, rddoc))$;

q_{11} **out**$(\text{priv}_{rd}, (logsesstoken, rddoc))$;

q_{12} **in**$(\text{priv}, (= \text{PMR}, fwdoc, = rpdoc, = \text{ready}))$;

q_{13} **out**$(\text{priv}, (\text{PMS}, fwdoc, rpdoc, tagkey))$;

q_{14} **in**$(\text{priv}, (= \text{PMR}, = fwdoc, = rpdoc, (EncIA,$
           $= \text{getrpdomain}(RPname_1))))$;

q_{15} **out**$(\text{priv}, (\text{httpsSend}, (EncIA, logsesstoken), rpdoc, RPname_1))$;

q_{16} **in**$(\text{priv}, (= \text{httpsReceive}, = \text{success}, rpdoc, RPname_1))$.

$IDPdoc\_proc$ $:=$

q_{17} **in**$(\text{priv}_{rd}, (logsesstoken_1, rddoc_1))$;

q_{18} **out**$(\text{priv}, (\text{httpsConnect}, rddoc_1, RPname_1))$;

q_{19} **out**$(\text{priv}, (\text{httpsSend}, logsesstoken_1, rddoc_1, RPname_1))$;

q_{20} **in**$(\text{priv}, (= \text{httpsReceive}, (= rddoc_1, tag, fwdomain1,$
           $= email, iakey), = rddoc_1, = RPname_1))$;

q_{21} **new** idpdoc; **out**$(\text{priv}, (\text{httpsConnect}, \text{idpdoc}, IDPname))$;

q_{22} **let** $password = \text{getpss}(email)$ **in**

q_{23} **out**$(\text{priv}, (\text{httpsSend}, (email, password, fwdomain_1, tag),$
           $\text{idpdoc}, IDPname))$;

q_{24} **in**$(\text{priv}, (= \text{httpsReceive}, ia, = \text{idpdoc}, = IDPname))$;

q_{25} **let** $EncIA = \text{enc}(ia, iakey)$ **in**

q_{26} **out**$(\text{priv}, (\text{OW}, rddoc_1))$;

q_{27} **in**$(\text{priv}, (= rddoc_1, fwdoc_1))$;

q_{28} $(\textbf{out}(\text{priv}_{fw}, (EncIA, tag, fwdoc_1)))$.

$FWDdoc\_proc$ $:=$

q_{29} **in**$(\text{priv}_{fw}, (EncIA_1, tag_1, fwdoc_2))$;

q_{30} **out**$(\text{priv}, (\text{parentOf}, fwdoc_2))$;

q_{31} **in**$(\text{priv}, (= \text{parentOf}, rddoc_2, = fwdoc_2)$;

q_{32} **out**$(\text{priv}, (\text{parentOf}, rddoc_2))$;

q_{33} **in**$(\text{priv}, (= \text{parentOf}, rpdoc_1, = rddoc_2)$;

q_{34} **out**$(\text{priv}, (\text{PMS}, fwdoc_2, rpdoc_1, \text{ready}))$;

q_{35} **in**$(\text{priv}, (= \text{PMR}, = fwdoc_2, = rpdoc_1, tagkey_1))$;

q_{36} **let** $(RPdomain_1, nonce_4) = \text{dec}(tag_1, tagkey_1)$ **in**

q_{37} **out**$(\text{priv}, (\text{PMS}, fwdoc_2, rpdoc_1, (EncIA_1, RPdomain_1)))$.

Fig. 5. The client-side process

3.1   Client-Side Process

The model of the client-side process of the SPRESSO protocol is shown in Fig. 5.

RPdoc_proc models the RP login page, i.e., the RPdoc in Fig. 3. We assume the user has an account (*account*) from the IDP (*IDPname*) (line q_1–q_2 in Fig. 5)[1]. If the user wants to log in to the RP (*RPname$_1$*) (line q_3), he opens the RP's login page, i.e. the RPdoc, by sending the OW command to our framework (line q_4–q_5). The RPdoc sends a login request and establishes an https connection with the RP server by sending the httpsConnect command to our framework in ((1,2), line q_7). Then the RPdoc sends the email address to the RP server by sending the httpsSend command to our framework ((2,3), line q_8) and receives the response by waiting for the message marked by the httpsReceive command from our framework ((6), line q_9). Next, the RPdoc opens the window RPRedirectDoc (line q_{10}) and passes the *loginsesstoken* and the RPRedirectDoc identity *rddoc* via a private channel priv$_{rd}$ ((7), line q_{11}). Then the RPdoc receives the ready from its grandchild window FWDdoc via postMessage by waiting for the message marked by the PMR command from our framework (line q_{12}), and replies the received *tagKey* back via postMessage by sending the PMS command ((16), line q_{13}). Then, the RPdoc delivers the encrypted identity assertion (*EncIA*) from the FWDdoc ((18), line q_{14}) to the RP server by https ((19), line q_{15}). Then the RPdoc waits for the successful login notification ((22), line q_{16}).

IDPdoc_proc models the IDP login page, i.e., the IDPdoc in Fig. 3. The previously created window RPRedirectDoc redirects itself to the IDPdoc ((8), line q_{17}–q_{20}). This step is to avoid the identity leak of the RP to the IDP due to the referrer header set by the browser. Since our browser model does not include the referrer header, we can simply continue the IDPdoc process right after the RPRedirectdoc process (line q_{21}–q_{28}). The IDPdoc extracts the IDP domain from the received email address and establishes an https connection with the IDP server ((8), line q_{21}). The user sends his credentials (i.e., email address and password) to IDP server ((9, 10), line q_{22}–q_{23}). Next, the IDPdoc receives the identity assertion *ia* ((12), line q_{24}) and generates an encrypted identity assertion (*EncIA*) with *iakey* ((13), line q_{25}). Finally, the IDPdoc opens a new window FWDdoc (line q_{26}–q_{27}), and passes the *EncIA*, the *tag* and the FWDdoc identity *fwdoc$_1$* to the FWDdoc ((14), line q_{28}).

FWDdoc_proc models the FWDdoc in Fig. 3. The FWDdoc is a proxy within the browser to transfer information between windows, hiding the identity of the RP from the IDP. The FWDdoc first receives the encrypted identity assertion (*EncIA$_1$*), the tag (*tag$_1$*) and the FWDdoc identity (*fwdoc$_2$*) from its parent IDPdoc (line q_{29}). Then he identifies its grandfather window *rpdoc$_1$* by sending the parentOf command to our framework (line q_{30}–q_{33}). Next the FWDdoc sends the ready to its grandfather window *rpdoc$_1$* and receives the *tagkey$_1$* via

---

[1] For simple reference to the same information in different figures, we use the following format ((k), line x_j) to represent the step k in Fig. 3, line x_j in Fig. 5 (when x_j is a q_j) or Fig. 6 (when x_j is a p_j).

postMessage (line q_{34}–q_{35}). Finally, the FWDdoc decrypts the tag with the $tagkey_1$ to extract the $RPDomain_1$ (line q_{36}) and sends the $EncIA$ back to the RPdoc specified by the $RPDomain_1$ ((17,18), line q_{37}).

3.2 Server-Side Processes

*RP_proc(*RPname*)* models the RP server in Fig. 6. The RP establishes an https connection with the RPdoc upon the request (line p_1) and receives an email address ((3), line p_2). The RP extracts the IDP domain name from the received email address and requests the public key from the corresponding IDP ((4), line p_3–p_4). Next, the RP generates the following session sensitive values: a nonce ($nonce_3$), a symmetric key to encrypt the identity assertion ($iaKey_1$), a key to

---

$RP\_$ $\mathbf{proc(}RPname_2\mathbf{)} :=$
p_1 $\mathbf{in}(c, (rpdoc_2, RPname_2));$
p_2 $\mathbf{in}(priv, (= \mathtt{httpsReceive}, (account_2, IDPname_2), = rpdoc_2, = RPname_2));$
p_3 $\mathbf{out}(priv, (\mathtt{httpsConnect}, RPname_2, IDPname_2));$
p_4 $\mathbf{in}(priv, (= \mathtt{httpsReceive}, pkidp, = RPname_2, = IDPname_2));$
p_5 $\mathbf{new}\ nonce_3;\ \mathbf{new}\ iakey_1;\ \mathbf{new}\ tagkey_2;\ \mathbf{new}\ logsesstoken_2;$
p_6 $\mathbf{new}\ fwdomain_2;$
p_7 $\mathbf{let}\ RPdomain_2 = getrpdomain(RPname_2)\ \mathbf{in}$
p_8 $\mathbf{let}\ tag_2 = enc((RPdomain_2, nonce_3), tagkey_2)\ \mathbf{in}$
p_9 $\mathbf{out}(priv, (\mathtt{httpsSend}, (tagkey_2, fwdomain_2, logsesstoken_2),$
        $rpdoc_2, RPname_2));$
p_{10} $\mathbf{in}(c, (rddoc_2, = RPname_2));$
p_{11} $\mathbf{in}(priv, (= \mathtt{httpsReceive}, = logsesstoken_2, = rddoc_2, = RPname_2));$
p_{12} $\mathbf{out}(priv, (\mathtt{httpsSend}, (rddoc_2, tag_2, fwdomain_2,$
        $(account_2, IDPname_2), iakey_1), rddoc_2, RPname_2));$
p_{13} $\mathbf{in}(priv, (= \mathtt{httpsReceive}, (EncIA_2, = logsesstoken_2),$
        $= rpdoc_2, = RPname_2));$
p_{14} $\mathbf{let}\ ia_2 = dec(EncIA_2, iakey_1)\ \mathbf{in}$
p_{15} $\mathbf{let}\ (= tag_2, = (account_2, IDPname_2), = fwdomain_2) = getmsg(ia_2, pkidp)\ \mathbf{in}$
p_{16} $(\mathbf{out}(priv, (\mathtt{httpsSend}, \mathtt{success}, rpdoc_2, RPname_2)))$
p_{17} $\mathbf{else}(\mathbf{out}(priv, (\mathtt{httpsSend}, \mathtt{retry}, rpdoc_2, RPname_2))).$

$IDP\_$ $\mathbf{proc(}IDPname_3\mathbf{)} :=$
p_{18} $\mathbf{in}(c, (RPname_3, = IDPname_3));$
p_{19} $\mathbf{out}(priv, (\mathtt{httpsSend}, pkidp, RPnanme_3, IDPname_3));$
p_{20} $\mathbf{in}(c, (idpdoc_1, = IDPname_3));$
p_{21} $\mathbf{in}(priv, (= \mathtt{httpsReceive}, (email_2, password_1,$
        $fwdomain_3, tag_3), = idpdoc_1, = IDPname_3));$
p_{22} $\mathbf{if}\ password_1 = getpss(email_2)\ \mathbf{then}$
p_{23} $\mathbf{let}\ ia_3 = sign((tag_3, email_2, fwdomain_3), skidp)\ \mathbf{in}$
p_{24} $\mathbf{out}(priv, (\mathtt{httpsSend}, ia_3, idpdoc_1, IDPname_3)).$

Fig. 6. The server-side processes

encrypt the tag ($\mathtt{tagKey_2}$) and a login session token ($\mathtt{logsesstoken_2}$) (line p_5) and chooses a forward domain ($\mathtt{fwdomain_2}$) (line p_6). The RP generates the tag (tag_2) by encrypting the $\mathtt{nonce_3}$ and its domain name $RPdomain_2$ using the $\mathtt{tagKey_2}$ ((5), (line p_7–p_8)). The $\mathtt{tagKey_2}$, the $\mathtt{fwdomain_2}$ and the $\mathtt{logsesstoken_2}$ are sent to the RPdoc ((6), line p_9). Then the RP receives the $\mathtt{logsesstoken_2}$ from the RPRedirectDoc (line p_{11}). Finally, the RP receives the encrypted indentity assertion ($EncIA_2$) together with the $\mathtt{logsesstoken_2}$ from the RPdoc (line p_{13}), after which it extracts the identity assertion (ia_2) (line p_{14}) and checks the signature of the IDP as well as the signed messages ((20), line p_{15}). Upon successful checks, the RP sends the $\mathtt{success}$ to the RPdoc. Otherwise, the $\mathtt{retry}$ is sent ((21), line p_{16}–p_{17}).

IDP_proc($\mathtt{IDPname}$***)*** models the IDP server in Fig. 6. The IDP establishes an https connection with the RP upon the request and passes its public key ((4), line p_{18}-p_{19}). Next, the IDP establishes an https connection with the IDPdoc upon the request and receives the email address ($email_2$), the password ($password_1$), the forward domain ($fwdomain_3$) and the tag (tag_3) from the IDPdoc ((10), line p_{20}-p_{21}). The IDP checks the validity of the password associated with the email address (line p_{22}). Once succeeds, the IDP generates an identity assertion (ia_3) by signing the tag_3, the $email_2$ and the $fwdomain_3$ with its private key (line p_{23}), and sends the identity assertion to the IDPdoc ((13,14), line p_{24}).

3.3   Verification Results

We transform the IDP_proc into the honest-but-curious attacker and query the privacy property in ProVerif. Next we add the malicious IDP client to the $SPRESSO\_proc$ and query the privacy property. The verification results show that SPRESSO preserves the privacy property against the above two attacker models. Finally, we transform the IDP_proc into the malicious IDP server and query privacy. The verification result shows that SPRESSO does not preserve privacy property against the malicious IDP server. By analyzing the trace generated by ProVerif, we summary the following attack.

A Logic Flaw in SPRESSO. When a victim user uses his/her account $\mathtt{Account}$ which is registered from a malicious IDP to log in to an RP, the RP server requests a public key from the malicious IDP server. At this step, for a particular RP $\mathtt{RP_i}$, if the malicious IDP wants to learn its login users, the IDP can issue a fake public key $\mathtt{pkIDP_i}$ to it ((4) in Fig. 3); for other RPs, the IDP issues the normal public key $\mathtt{pkIDP}$. Later in identity assertion ($\mathtt{IA}$) generation, the IDP always uses the private key corresponding to $\mathtt{pkIDP}$ ((11) in Fig. 3). As a result, a failure is caused when $\mathtt{RP_i}$ verifies the $\mathtt{IA}$ using the public key $\mathtt{pkIDP_i}$ it fetched previously ((20) in Fig. 3). This implies that the user is successfully logged in to the IDP, but actually fails to log in to the RP. We assume that the user will log in again upon receiving a login failure notification, which is common in reality. Upon receiving the second log in request ((10) in Fig. 3), the malicious

IDP knows the identity of the user who wants to log in to RP_i. This sabotages the declared privacy property of SPRESSO.

4   Related Work

SSO Privacy Property has drawn little attention until recently. Not much work has been done on the SSO privacy checking and verification. BrowserID developed by Mozilla is claimed to preserve the SSO privacy that prevents IDPs from learning which RP a user is trying to log in to. Fett et al. [2,3] have analyzed the privacy property of BrowserID manually by trace indistinguishability with a comprehensive protocol model and have found an attack. In our work, we have discovered a new privacy attack which is not considered in their analysis.

Web Infrastructure Modeling is also a relatively new research area with few models incorporating crucial web mechanisms. Previous work associated with SSO web security analysis [5,8,14,15] only considers a very limited web model. TrustFound [16,17] has proposed a model for network attacker. Akhawe et al. [18] have built a general model of the web and have verified the model using an automatic verification tool Alloy. Bansal et al. [19,20] have proposed a more comprehensive web infrastructure model WebSpi in the applied pi calculus and have analyzed the authentication property of OAuth2.0 using WebSpi. Fett et al. [2,3,12] have built and applied a complex and complete web infrastructure model that closely follows the published standards and specifications for the web. Compared to this work, our web infrastructure model is compact and specific to SSO protocols, which can successfully run on ProVerif.

5   Conclusion

In this paper, we present a formal framework consisting of a web infrastructure formal model, three attacker models, and the formalization of the privacy property. We have analyzed SPRESSO using our framework and have detected a previously-unknown flaw which allows a malicious IDP to use an incorrect public key to differentiate the users which log in to a particular RP.

Acknowledgment. This research is supported by the National Research Foundation, Singapore (No. NRF2015NCR-NCR003-003).

References

1. Wang, R., Chen, S., Wang, X.: Signing me onto your accounts through Facebook and Google: a traffic-guided security study of commercially deployed single-sign-on web services. In: IEEE S&P (2012)
2. Fett, D., Küsters, R., Schmitz, G.: An expressive model for the web infrastructure: definition and application to the BrowserID SSO system. In: IEEE S&P (2014)

3. Fett, D., Küsters, R., Schmitz, G.: Analyzing the BrowserID SSO system with primary identity providers using an expressive model of the web. In: ESORICS, pp. 43–65 (2015)
4. Bai, G., Lei, J., Meng, G., Venkatraman, S.S., Saxena, P., Sun, J., Liu, Y., Dong, J.S.: AuthScan: automatic extraction of web authentication protocols from implementations. In: NDSS (2013)
5. Sun, S.-T., Hawkey, K., Beznosov, K.: Systematically breaking and fixing openid security: formal analysis, semi-automated empirical evaluation, and practical countermeasures. Comput. Secur. **31**, 465–483 (2012)
6. Ye, Q., Bai, G., Wang, K., Dong, J.S.: Formal analysis of a single sign-on protocol implementation for android. In: ICECCS, pp. 90–99 (2015)
7. Hanna, S., Shinz, E.C.R., Akhawe, D., Boehmz, A., Saxena, P., Song, D.: The emperor's new API: on the (in)secure usage of new client side primitives. In: W2SP (2010)
8. Armando, A., Carbone, R., Compagna, L., Cuellar, J., Tobarra, L.: Formal analysis of SAML 2.0 web browser single sign-on: breaking the SAML-based single sign-on for Google apps. In: Workshop on Formal Methods in Security Engineering (2008)
9. Abadi, M., Fournet, C.: Mobile values, new names, and secure communication. In: POPL, pp. 104–115 (2001)
10. Blanchet, B.: An efficient cryptographic protocol verifier based on prolog rules. In: CSFW, pp. 82–96 (2001)
11. Delaune, S., Kremer, S., Ryan, M.: Verifying privacy-type properties of electronic voting protocols. J. Comput. Secur. **17**, 435–487 (2009)
12. Fett, D., Küsters, R., Schmitz, G.: SPRESSO: a secure, privacy-respecting single sign-on system for the web. In: CCS, pp. 1358–1369 (2015)
13. Dolev, D., Yao, A.C.C.: On the security of public key protocols. IEEE Trans. Inf. Theory **29**, 198–207 (1983)
14. Jackson, D.: In: Tools and Algorithms for the Construction and Analysis of Systems: 8th International Conference, TACAS, p. 20 (2002)
15. Kerschbaum, F.: Simple cross-site attack prevention. In: Workshop on Security and Privacy in Communications Networks, pp. 464–472 (2007)
16. Bai, G., Hao, J., Wu, J., Liu, Y., Liang, Z., Martin, A.: Trustfound: towards a formal foundation for model checking trusted computing platforms. In: FM, pp. 110–126 (2014)
17. Hao, J., Liu, Y., Cai, W., Bai, G., Sun, J.: vTRUST: a formal modeling and verification framework for virtualization systems. In: ICFEM, pp. 329–346 (2013)
18. Akhawe, D., Barth, A., Lam, P.E., Mitchell, J., Song, D.: Towards a formal foundation of web security. In: CSF, pp. 290–304 (2010)
19. Bansal, C., Bhargavan, K., Delignat-Lavaud, A., Maffei, S.: Keys to the cloud: formal analysis and concrete attacks on encrypted web storage. In: POST, pp. 126–146 (2013)
20. Bansal, C., Bhargavan, K., Maffeis, S.: Discovering concrete attacks on website authorization by formal analysis. In: CSF, pp. 247–262 (2012)

A Hypervisor Level Provenance System to Reconstruct Attack Story Caused by Kernel Malware

Chonghua Wang[1,4], Shiqing Ma[2], Xiangyu Zhang[2], Junghwan Rhee[3],
Xiaochun Yun[1], and Zhiyu Hao[1(✉)]

[1] Institute of Information Engineering, Chinese Academy of Sciences, Beijing, China
haozhiyu@iie.ac.cn
[2] Purdue University, West Lafayette, USA
[3] NEC Laboratories America, Princeton, USA
[4] School of Cyber Security, Chinese Academy of Sciences, Beijing, China

Abstract. Provenance of system subjects (e.g., processes) and objects (e.g., files) are very useful for many forensics tasks. In our analysis and comparison of existing Linux provenance tracing systems, we found that most systems assume the Linux kernel to be in the trust base, making these systems vulnerable to kernel level malware. To address this problem, we present HProve, a hypervisor level provenance tracing system to reconstruct kernel malware attack story. It monitors the execution of kernel functions and sensitive objects, and correlates the system subjects and objects to form the causality dependencies for the attacks. We evaluated our prototype on 12 real world kernel malware samples, and the results show that it can correctly identify the provenance behaviors of the kernel malware.

Keywords: Provenance tracing · Kernel malware
Forensic investigation

1 Introduction

Nowadays, enterprises are suffering from rapidly increasing serious attack threats, especially Advanced Persistent Threat (APT). Compared to traditional attacks, APT attacks are stealthier and more sophisticated by employing multi-step intrusive attacks. This kind of attacks would impose disastrous impacts on the systems if the associated attack vector aims at kernel [1]. Detecting such attacks is an urgent matter in enterprise environments, but is far from enough. In addition to detecting the existence of the attacks, deep investigation should be performed to find out where the attacks are, how the attacks are derived, and when they are introduced. For instance, a kernel mode attack can modify kernel objects or entities, which is potentially more dangerous. Acquiring such details about how the kernel objects and entities are manipulated is crucial to understand the attack for forensic investigations.

© ICST Institute for Computer Sciences, Social Informatics and Telecommunications Engineering 2018
X. Lin et al. (Eds.): SecureComm 2017, LNICST 238, pp. 778–792, 2018.
https://doi.org/10.1007/978-3-319-78813-5_42

Provenance tracing [4,12,16–18,25] is an efficient approach to address these challenges since it can associate these events together to find the causality dependencies among them. The provenance records provide the holistic view of the whole system, thus can be well suited to system forensics. Even though the system is subverted by malware, provenance points out the possibility to restore the victim system to a good state in confidence. For a provenance system, the provenance information should be complete and faithful to provide the holistic view of the events occurred in the system for forensic applications. If the investigator fails to foresee the need for a particular kind of provenance information to be captured, then it would be difficult to rebuild the complete causality dependencies. Whereas an untrusted kind of provenance information could infer an innocent source.

State-of-the-Art: Lots of existing works employ audit logging to record events (e.g., memory reads and writes, process reading a file, messages being sent or received, etc.) during system execution and then correlate these events for building the causality dependencies during investigation [4,12,16–18,25]. These systems assume the Linux kernel to be in the trusted computing base (TCB), making these systems vulnerable to kernel malware. If an intruder employs a kernel malware to compromise the kernel, it is trivial to cheat or even undermine the audit logging, thus leading to inaccurate provenance results. However this assumption does not hold in practical settings in the examples of kernel malware.

Our Approach: The key to solve the above problem is to backtrack an untrusted kernel using an external monitor. Thus, we choose to employ virtualization techniques to exclude the kernel from our TCB to keep the provenance information secure and complete. In specific, we present a hypervisor level provenance tracing system, HProve, to address the above problems and complement existing provenance systems. On one hand, HProve ports the logging module to the hypervisor to keep the log recorded trustworthy, especially for kernel malware. On the other hand, in order to obtain complete provenance information, HProve employs lightweight record and replay techniques to record the whole execution of system and replay the system meanwhile instrumenting hypervisor for provenance. For efficiency, execution traces recorded do not include the state of emulated hardware devices focusing on the provenance tracing process rather than replaying a generic VM. HProve is able to replay and analyze a trace without having access to the VM image that was used for recording. Meanwhile to reduce runtime overhead, the instrumentation code is inserted into the hypervisor only when necessary during replay. After obtaining the execution traces, the backtracking technique is applied to the kernel APIs to find out the caller-callee chain using *function call convention*. HProve achieves this by our *provenance tap points uncovering* technique. In summary, we make the following contributions:

- We present HProve, a hypervisor level provenance tracing system that can replay kernel level malware attack to acquire accurate provenance details.
- To provide valuable insights about how kernel malware impacts on the kernel internals, we devise a novel approach to backtrack the kernel for acquiring

caller-callee chain of kernel functions reversely and correlate malware behaviors with tampered kernel objects to explore the causality dependencies.
- We have built a proof-of-concept prototype of HProve to demonstrate the feasibility of our approach. We have conducted extensive experiments with a variety of representative malware samples collected in the wild, and demonstrated that our system could correctly build the causality dependencies within the victim system.

2 Motivation

Kernel malware is considered as one of the most stealthy threats in computer security field and becomes a major challenge for security research communities [3,5,23] since it has the equal privilege as the kernel and often higher privileges than most security tools. We collect a variety of kernel malware samples and manually analyzed them. In summary, there are several categories that kernel malware falls into: system service hijack-

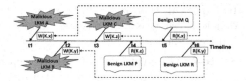

Fig. 1. An abstract diagram to illustrate a scenario that needs kernel malware attack provenance. W denotes *write* operation, R denotes *read* operation and K.x denotes kernel object x. The end that the dash line points to is the source of the data read by benign LKMs.

ing (e.g., hooking *system call table* entries and replacing *system call table*), dynamic kernel object hooking (KOH, e.g., VFS hooking) and DKOM [20,23]. Recently lots of work were proposed to tackle this attack: kernel rootkit detection [10,19,24], kernel rootkit prevention [14,20,21] and kernel rootkit profiling [11,15,22,26]. However, detection is done after the victim system has been attacked, but the malware behaviors may have been missed. Prevention is adapted to detection systems, which is mainly to enforce kernel integrity, whereas it lacks the understanding of what had happened in the past. Profiling is capable of producing malware traces, such as hooking behavior, target kernel objects, user-level impact and injected code [26], whereas it fails to obtain the connections among these traces. These systems do not meet the goal of comprehensively revealing the causality dependencies among kernel malware behaviors and impacts on the victim system. For this goal, we need to solve three key challenges: *(1)* What kernel functions, kernel APIs and system calls have been called by malware?, *(2)* What kind of kernel objects (e.g., pointer fields and data values, etc.) have been accessed or damaged by malware?, *(3)* How to connect kernel malware behaviors and impacts on the victim system?

Scenario. Suppose a user wants to install a kernel driver and downloads a loadable kernel module (LKM) without being aware that it is malicious. The malicious LKM subverts important kernel objects (e.g., $K.x$, $K.y$ and $K.z$ as shown in Fig. 1) to hide itself and transfers confidential information. The system investigator inspects the victim system and starts scanning and monitoring work as usual. But nothing has been detected for some days which may raise questions to the administrator. Also the user may download more than one malicious LKM which manipulates multiple kinds of kernel objects. What the system investigator needs to know is which LKM tampered with what kind of kernel objects. He has to design some investigation techniques to detect dependences among LKMs, files, kernel objects and memory accesses or even instructions and build causality dependencies through

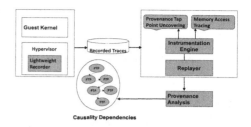

Fig. 2. System overview of HProve. PTP in the causality dependences denotes *provenance tap points* defined in next section.

causal analysis of the historical events. Figure 1 shows that three different kernel malware issue malicious activities (e.g., hide processes, hide files and directories, etc.) by tampering with kernel objects (e.g., x, y, z, etc.) at different time t1, t2 and t3 respectively. At time t4, t5 and t6, the benign LKMs begin to read the tampered objects as usual. How the investigator knows where the kernel objects read by the benign LKMs come from? Have they been modified by the malicious LKM A or B or C? All these questions can be answered by kernel malware provenance (Fig. 2).

3 System Overview

3.1 Scope, Assumptions and Threat Model

In this paper, we do not differentiate the terms of kernel malware and kernel rootkit. Both of them represent the kernel-mode components of malicious behaviors. They may issue malicious activities in different ways, but the essence is the same: they need to tamper with kernel objects. Regarding the scope of different categories of kernel malware and to focus on the provenance problem itself for kernel malware, system call hooking is our initial implementation decision for a prototype and our approach can be extended with other approaches which handle DKOM and VFS hijacking. Once the detection of DKOM and VFS hijacking is included [27], our method can perform provenance tracing from there.

We assume we can acquire the knowledge of kernel APIs, e.g., the kernel object allocation functions (e.g., *kmalloc/kfree, vmalloc/vfree, kmem_cache_alloc/kmem_cache_free*, etc.) so that we can instrument and track the creations and deletions of the kernel objects, and the kernel APIs as well as the function arguments. In addition, we assume that we can get knowledge of the *system call table* and the corresponding entries so that we can locate them in memory and reveal each access on them. Meanwhile, we assume the *function call conventions* is not variable so that we can infer the caller of kernel APIs accurately. As HProve is implemented on Linux, these assumptions are reasonable and practical.

We define a threat against HProve as any way of compromising the fidelity or completeness of the provenance information collected. HProve guarantees that even though the kernel is compromised by the adversaries, we can track the tampered objects and further conduct provenance tracing. The hypervisor level attack is out of scope of HProve, and we can employ hypervisor integrity checking techniques such as [21] to ensure the intactness of the hypervisor before conducting provenance tracing.

3.2   Overview

HProve is designed to comprehensively reveal the causality dependences among kernel malware behaviors and impacts on the victim system. It is capable of obtaining a deep insight on what kind of behaviors kernel malware may conduct. HProve ports the logging module to the hypervisor to keep the log recorded trustworthy, especially for kernel malware. In order to obtain complete provenance information, HProve employs lightweight record and replay techniques to record the whole execution of system and replay the system meanwhile instrumenting hypervisor for provenance. In particular, the kernel functions being tracked include those being executed by the kernel from loading the kernel malware to allocating memory for them. With the captured execution traces, the backtracking technique is applied to the kernel functions to find out the caller-callee chain using *function call convention* in runtime. Meanwhile, HProve records memory accesses to sensitive kernel objects (e.g, *system call table*, etc.) that kernel malware may tamper with. HProve correlates these events happened within the kernel to reconstruct the attack story. For efficiency, execution traces recorded do not include the state of emulated hardware devices focusing on the provenance tracing process rather than replaying a generic VM. HProve is able to replay and analyze a trace without having access to the VM image. Meanwhile to reduce runtime overhead, the instrumentation code is inserted into the hypervisor only when necessary during replay.

4   Design and Implementation

In this section, we first present several definitions used in our approach. Then we describe the design and implementation of HProve in details.

4.1   Definitions

Provenance Tap Points. We define a *provenance tap point*, an execution point [7] in the kernel at which we wish to capture a set of function callers. It is defined as a four-tuple: (*call_site, func_entry, func_arg, func_ret_val*), where *func_entry* is the kernel function whose caller to be tracked, *func_arg* refers to the argument of the function, *func_ret_val* is the return value of the function and *call_site* denotes the caller of the function_entry.

Memory Access Trace. *Memory Access Trace* is used to connect the kernel events and function calls within the kernel, where each access *m* is formatted as a four-tuple: *m = (addr, data, type, program_counter)*. *Addr* is the address of memory being accessed. *Data* is the amount of data written or read. *Type* is the type of the memory access (either a read or a write). *Program_counter* is the address of the instruction invoking the access.

4.2   Recording Non-deterministic Events

HProve leverages Panda [6], built atop on QEMU to record the non-deterministic events. Panda extends the original recording process of the QEMU and the recorded information can be replayed deterministically for the entire execution at any later time. Since the execution traces recorded do not include the state of emulated hardware devices, it does not support the execution of device code during replay. Fortunately, this feature satisfies our requirements. Eliminating the execution traces of device code helps to reduce the logging overhead significantly.

4.3   Instrumentation During Replay

QEMU Translation Block. The guest code is split into "translation blocks" (corresponds to a list of instructions terminated by a branch instruction). QEMU then translates them into an intermediate language using TCG (Tiny Code Generator), which provides the APIs to insert additional code. This intermediate translated block is converted into a corresponding basic block of binary code that can be directly executed on the host. Figure 3 shows how the guest code is transformed into translation blocks.

Instrumentation Before/After Execution.   HProve instruments analysis code during replay to obtain the *Provenance Tap Point* and *Memory Access Trace*. As seen in the dashed translation block shown in Fig. 3, analysis code can be instrumented before or after the execution of each translation block by the instrumentation engine. We take LKM kernel malware as an example for describing our techniques. At the conceptual level, HProve works as follows.

First, it conducts off-line analysis of the typical execution route of kernel malware and reveals the common characteristics of them. We found that before loading a LKM malware, it is inserted into the kernel using utilities such as *insmod* or *modprobe*. Then the kernel initializes the LKM through system calls, calls *load_module* function to load the LKM, and allocates memory space for it. We set the *insmod* or *modprobe* operation as the start point and the allocating memory operation as the end point of the work done by kernel for all the LKMs. We define the timeline between the start point and the end point as *Top-Half*, and the timeline after the end point is defined as *Bottom-Half*. The analysis of the events ocurrs during *Top-Half* and *Bottom-Half* is completed by *Provenance Tap Point Uncovering* and *Memory Access Tracing* respectively.

Uncovering Provenance Tap Points.
No matter what kind of objects will
the kernel malware manipulate, its
execution file should be allocated into
the memory. Since HProve records
whole execution of the running kernel, it instruments analysis code into
the recorded traces to track the kernel
allocation/deallocation related func-

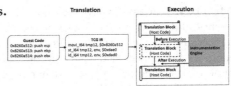

Fig. 3. Illustration on how our instrumentation engine works during replay

tions (e.g., *kmalloc/kfree, vmalloc/vfree*). Whenever these kinds of alloca-
tion/deallocation events occur at runtime, HProve replays the execution for capturing the allocated address range and location of the code that calls the memory allocation function. HProve determines the *call_site, func_entry, func_arg,
func_ ret_val* for *Provenance Tap Point* in the replay phase. HProve instruments
provenance code before (after) the execution of each basic block during replay
as depicted in Fig. 3. Take an allocation function (e.g.,*vmalloc*) as a *func_entry*,
the address of objects being allocated can be determined by the *func_arg*, and
the size of object can be determined by *func_ret_val*.

Take a deallocation function (e.g., *vfree*) as a *fuc_entry*, the address of objects
being deallocated can be determined by the *func_arg*. *Call_site* determines which
function calls the *func_entry*. Each item of the *Provenance Tap Point* can be captured by analyzing *function call conventions* within the hypervisor. To capture
the *call_site*, HProve uses the return address of the call to *func_entry*. In the
instruction stream, the return address is the address of the instruction after the
CALL instruction. *Func_arg* and *func_ret_val* can be captured through the stack
or registers. Integers up to 32-bits as well as 32-bit pointers are delivered via
the *EAX* register. *Func_arg* is delivered through the *EBP* with corresponding
offsets. *Func_arg* and *func_ret_val* are only available when *func_entry* returns to
the call_site. In order to capture *func_arg* and *func_ret_val* at the correct time,
HProve uses a shadow stack to store these values. Specifically, HProve checks if
it ends with a *CALL* instruction after each basic block executes during replay.
If so, the return address is pushed into a shadow stack. Correspondingly, before
execution of each basic block, HProve checks whether it matches a return address
on the shadow stack; If so, we know that the current function has returned, thus
HProve pops it from the shadow stack and captures the return value from the
EAX register as well as the function arguments from *EBP* with corresponding
offsets. Then HProve reads the value from the registers and memory addresses
using the introspection technique [8]. The obtained values of *provenance tap
points* will be stored in the form of (*calle_site, func_entry func_arg,func_ret_val*).

Memory Access Tracing. After malware being allocated into the memory, it
is able to start carrying out malicious activities. These events occur in the phase
of *Bottom-Half*. Typically, LKM malware would try some tricks (e.g., bypass
CR0 protection and search for *System.map* file) to get the entry address of

system call table, and manipulate the relative *system call entries* for different purposes. SYSTEM keeps track of the changes of these entries, obtains the allocated memory region of the *system call table* and records memory access of the memory region. Fortunately, there are a few hundreds of entries in the *system call table* (e.g., 350 and 312 entries in Linux 3.2 kernel for 32-bit and 64-bit respectively), thus only a few hundreds of memory addresses are to be tracked by HProve.

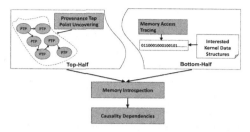

Fig. 4. Building causality dependencies among kernel malware behaviors and impacts on the victim system. PTP denotes *provenance tap point*

Note that the writes to system call table entries make the relative system call service routine points to the malicious function in kernel malware, which are considered as suspicious. Specifically, if there is a write, HProve records the *PC* that initiates the *write* operation. The retrieved values of *memory access traces* will be stored in the form of $m = (addr, data, type, program\_counter)$.

4.4 Causality Dependencies

To build causality dependencies, HProve uncovers the connections among the events occurr in the *Top-Half* and *Bottom-Half*. When the allocation function allocates memory for LKM malware, HProve acquires the address range that is being allocated by interpreting the *func_arg*. Then HProve gets a address range that is being allocated for the LKM malware. Once the *PC* is captured during *Memory Access Tracing*, HProve checks whether the *pc* locates within one of the address range that has been allocated for malware. If so, HProve correlates the writes on *system call entries* with the *func_entry* that execute the allocation. Then HProve determines the *call_site* of the *func_entry* that executes the allocation by the *Provenance Tap Point Uncovering* technique. Through backtracking successively, HProve acquires the complete *call_site* to determine the original malware source that initials the write operation on *system call entries* (Fig. 4).

5 Evaluation

In this section we present the effectiveness of using HProve to build causality dependencies among kernel malware behaviors and impacts on the system. Then we evaluate HProve's efficiency to show that our approach does not incur significant overheads. In our experiments, the host machine is an Intel Core i5 desktop running Ubuntu 12.04. We use Linux kernels as the guest VM. To validate our experiments results with the ground truth, we have collected 12 kernel malware samples that contain a mix of malicious capabilities found in the wild, including 10 system services hijacking malware (e.g., *kbeast*, *xinqyiquan*, etc.), 1 DOH malware (e.g., adore-ng-.0.56), and 1 DKOM malware (e.g., hp rootkit).

5.1   Effectiveness

To evaluate the effectiveness of our system, we should obtain *provenance tap points* and *memory access traces* of the targeted kernel objects accurately with HProve. In the experiment setup, HProve loads 12 kernel malware samples and 6 benign LKMs into the guest kernel. Once all of these modules are loaded into the kernel, HProve starts recording whole execution of the guest kernel with the lightweight recorder. Then the recorded traces are instrumented with provenance code during its replay to obtain *provenance tap points*, and *memory access traces*. After that provenance information is retrieved to build the causal dependencies.

Provenance Tap Points. The utilities that insert LKMs encapsulate *sys_init _module* which performs initialization and calls the *load_module* function. This function is responsible for loading the LKM from the user space to the kernel space. First, it calls the *copy_and_check* function which calls the *vmalloc* function to allocate temporary memory for copying the LKM file into the memory region. Second, the *load_module* function calls *layout_and_allocate* to allocate the final memory for a specific section of the LKM (e.g., *core space*, *.init.text*, etc). The remaining caller-callee relationship chain is shown as below:

$$layout\_and\_allocate \longrightarrow move\_module \longrightarrow module\_alloc\_update\_bounds$$
$$\longrightarrow module\_alloc \longrightarrow \_\_vmalloc\_node\_range.$$

After initialization, allocation and relocation are finished, and the LKM can execute as expected. With this prior knowledge, HProve treats these functions as the *function_entry* of one of the *provenance tap points*. Take *__vmalloc_node_range* as an example, it is used for allocating specific pages in physical memory for LKMs. We can infer other items of *provenance tap points* (e.g., *call_site*, *function_argument*, *function_return_value*) with *provenance tap point uncovering* and memory introspection techniques [8]. Specifically, once we have inferred *module_alloc_update_bounds*, HProve acquires the allocation information of LKMs including the address range from the *provenance tap point*. The address range is critical for HProve to link the causality dependency between *Top-Half* and *Bottom-Half* as discussed in Sect. 4.4. In our experiments, HProve uncovers *provenance tap points* for all kernel malware samples. The address range allocated for each malware sample is shown in Table 1. Since DKOM type malware are loaded into kernel in terms of */dev/kmem*, we do not list it in the table.

Memory Access Traces. Before building the complete causality dependencies, the memory region which the LKMs belong to needs to be identified. HProve achieves this by recording the memory access to the system call table for the running malware. We then build the *Memory Access Trace* tuple for each system call entry manipulated by each kernel malware. In the tuple, PC is critical field to determine which LKM is manipulating the relative system call entry. As discussed above, HProve acquires various memory regions that are allocated for the LKMs loaded into the kernel. If PC follows in one of the memory

Table 1. Allocated start address range for each kernel malware

Address range	Kbeast	Xingyiquan	Suterusu	Knark	Enyelkm	Synapsys	Rial	Kis	Kbdv3	Adore-0.42	Adore-ng0.56
Start address	0xf86-73000	0xf86-82000	0xf86-85000	0xf86-83000	0xf86-75000	0xf86-77000	0xf86-71000	0xf86-89000	0xf86-68000	0xf86-79000	0xf86-64000
Size/ bytes	215	308	276	413	356	218	196	525	298	418	382

regions, then the two events are correlated. A table for the *Memory Access Trace* tuples is constructed for each kernel malware sample. Table 2 shows one of the results obtained by HProve. As we can see, in the second row, _NR_open entry is located at *0xc1541234* and has been written by *PC 0xf867445f*. HProve refers to the result of Table 1 and determines that this *PC* and other *PCs* in Table 2 belong to the memory region allocated for *Kbeast*.

After correlating *memory access traces* with *provenance tap points*, HProve is able to identify which malware manipulates which kind of kernel objects. Table 3 shows the system call entries that are manipulated by kernel malware samples of system services hijacking we collect. For instance, *Kbeast* tampered with _NR_open, _NR_read, _NR_write, _NR_rmdir, _NR_unlink, etc. We also analyze the source code of all the malware samples for the validation purposes, and it turned out that the entries discovered by our provenance tracing method correctly matched the malware behaviors in the source code.

5.2 Efficiency

We conduct several experiments to evaluate the efficiency of HProve. In the first experiment setup, we insert all the LKM samples, including the malicious and benign ones into the guest kernel and start HProve. Once the kernel begins to load these samples, HProve records the execution once, and then replays it multiple times for different provenance requirements. In the following experiments, we insert one malware sample into the kernel at a time and repeat 10 times. For each case, we report the recording time, the size of a record, the size of a memory trace, and the replay time in Table 4. The second column of Table 4 presents the recording time of the sample's execution. The third column shows the size of impact traces that are recorded by the lightweight recorder of HProve. The forth column lists the size of memory access traces of the system call entries. The fifth and sixth columns present the replay time for *Provenance Tap Points Uncovering* and *Memory Access Tracing* respectively.

As we can see, a record size in the table is at most 30 MB for the evaluated LKM samples, which is acceptable for these samples executing millions of instructions. Since there are only a few hundreds of memory addresses to be tracked, the size of memory traces is at most 17 KB. The duration of replaying *Memory Access Tracing* for all LKM samples is 113 min and the average duration of replaying *Memory Access Tracing* for each malware sample is 32.2 min. Replaying for uncovering *Provenance Tap Points* took 62 min for all LKM samples and 11.8 min for each malware sample in average.

Table 2. One of *memory access trace* table obtained by HProve.

Data	Addr	Type	PC
_NR_open	0xc1541234	W	0xf867445f
_NR_read	0xc154122c	W	0xf86743b4
_NR_write	0xc1541230	W	0xf86743c9
_NR_rmdir	0xc15412c0	W	0xf867411
_NR_unlink	0xc1541248	W	0xf86743f9
_NR_rename	0xc15412b8	W	0xf8674447
_NR_kill	0xc15412b4	W	0xf8674477
_NR_getdents64	0xc1541590	W	0xf86743e1
_NR_unlinkat	0xc15416d4	W	0xf867442c
_NR_delete_module	0xc1541424	W	0xf86743d4

Table 3. Manipulated system call entries. '√' denotes that the entry has been manipulated.

System call entry	Kbeast	Xingyiquan	Suterusu	Knark	Enyelkm	Synapsys	Rial	Kis	Kbdv3	Adore-0.42
_NR_open	√	√				√	√	√		√
_NR_read	√		√	√			√			
_NR_write	√		√			√				√
_NR_rmdir	√	√						√		
_NR_mkdir								√		
_NR_unlink	√	√						√		
_NR_chdir		√						√		
_NR_kill	√	√		√	√	√				√
_NR_fork		√				√		√		√
_NR_ioctl		√								
_NR_close										√
_NR_clone		√				√	√	√		√
_NR_exit								√		
_NR_execve		√								
_NR_rename	√	√						√		
_NR_utime									√	
_NR_unlinkat	√									
_NR_socketcall								√		
_NR_getdents			√			√	√	√		
_NR_gentdents64	√			√	√					
_NR_getuid						√				
_NR_getuid32									√	
_NR_gettimeofday										
_NR_quiry_module						√	√			
_NR_init_module								√		
_NR_delete_module	√									
_NR_stat								√		
_NR_lstat								√		

6   Discussion

HProve employs Panda [6] to record the whole execution of system, it shares the overhead with Panda for keeping track of instructions and the program counter at the instruction level. On average, for every 1 min of recorded execution, the replay takes 30 min It so far is not easy to port it to real systems even though the replay phase could be done off-line. We consider to use introspection technique with hardware virtualization instead of record-and-replay (e.g., PANDA) to keep track of a series of kernel functions (e.g., *kmalloc*, *vmalloc*, *load_module*, etc.). However, Jain et al. [9] had shown that there are non-trivial challenges associated with introspection because of the *strong semantic gap problem* without trusting the kernel. Regarding the scope of different categories of kernel malware and to focus on the provenance problem itself for kernel malware, system call hooking is our initial implementation decision for a prototype. HProve can not deal with all the types of kernel malware (e.g., DKOM and VFS hijacking). The system will fail if an object that are not being tracked is modified (e.g., the malware creates new kernel objects with altered semantics). We have tested a type of DKOM and VFS hijacking malware (e.g., *hp rootkit, adore-ng-0.56*) that can elude our system. But our approach can be easily extended with other approaches which handle DKOM and VFS hijacking. Once the detection of DKOM and VFS hijacking is included [2,27], our method can perform provenance tracing from there. Other than *system call table*, we can keep track of other sensitive kernel objects that DKOM or VFS hijacking malware may manipulate. We leave the above limitations of HProve to our future work.

Table 4. Evaluation for space and time for provenance

Sample	Recording time	Record size	Memory traces size	Replaying time	
				Provenance tap points	Memory access tracing
Kbeast	1.2 min	26 MB	11 KB	13 min	50 min
Xingyiquan	0.8 min	17 MB	7 KB	12 min	33 min
Suterusu	0.2 min	4 MB	2 KB	10 min	10 min
Knark	1.1 min	24 MB	10 KB	13 min	45 min
Enyelkm	0.3 min	6 MB	3 KB	10 min	12 min
Synapsys	1.1 min	25 MB	12 KB	14 min	51 min
Rial	0.4 min	9 MB	3 KB	11 min	13 min
Kis	1.5 min	30 MB	17 KB	14 min	78 min
Kbdv3	0.3 min	5 MB	2 KB	10 min	9 min
Adore-0.42	0.6 min	14 MB	5 KB	11 min	21 min
All LKMs	11 min	148 MB	80 KB	62 min	113 min

7   Related Work

Kernel Malware: Many researchers have studied the behaviors of kernel malware and proposed lots of effective approaches to detect their existence. Hook-Finder [15] identifies all the impacts made by the malicious code and keeps track of the impacts flowing across the system to identify the hooking behavior of a rootkit in the kernel execution. HookMap [24] employs a more elaborate method to identify all potential hook in the execution path of kernel code that could be utilized by the kernel level malware. K-Tracer [11] discovers information about rootkit capabilities through its data manipulation behavior to help defend against rootkit as well as user-level malware that gets help from them. PoKeR [22] is a kernel rootkit profiler that generates multi-aspect kernel rootkit profiles (e.g.,hooking behavior, targeted kernel objects, user-level impacts and injected code) during rootkit execution. Rkprofiler [26] is also a kernel malware profiler that can track both pointer-based and function-based object propagation, while PoKeR only tracks the pointer-based object propagation. To complement these work, our work analyzes the behavior of kernel malware reversely (from bottom to top and from impact to cause) which is orthogonal to theirs.

Provenance Tracing: Provenance tracing provides the ability to describe the history of a data object, including the conditions that led to its creation and the actions that delivere it to its present state. Hi-Fi [18] leverages Linux Security Module to collect a complete provenance record from early kernel initialization through system shutdown. It maintains the fidelity of provenance collection under any user space compromise. BEEP [12] instruments an application binary at the instructions and use the Linux audit system to capture the system calls triggered by the application for investigating which application brings the malware into the system for provenance. LogGC [13] employs the garbage collection method to prune some system objects such as temporary files that have a short life-span and have little impact on the dependency analysis to save space. ProTracer [16] proposes to combine both logging and unit level tainting techniques, aiming at reducing log volume to achieve cost-effective provenance tracing. Bates et al. [4] proposes Linux Provenance Module, a generalized framework for the development of automated, whole-system provenance collection on the Linux. However, these systems rely on the safety of provenance collector (e.g., Linux audit system, Linux Security Module). In the events of kernel malware, the adversary is able to compromise the provenance collector or even the kernel, which makes the provenance results untrusted. Our contribution is to complement these techniques by porting the provenance collector as well as the analysis module into the hypervisor for the resistance to kernel level malware.

8   Conclusion

We develop HProve, a hypervisor level provenance tracing system that can backtrack the causality dependencies among impacts on a victim system and kernel malware behaviors. It is capable of understanding the kernel APIs triggered and the objects manipulated by kernel malware. HProve is a new system that provides the capability of replaying kernel malware attack story for provenance tracing. Such hypervisor level technique is needed in current cloud computing environment. Due to the limitations of HProve discussed in Sect. 4, more efficient designs for kernel malware provenance are still highly needed.

Acknowledgement. We would like to thank the anonymous reviewers for their insightful comments that greatly helped improve this paper. This work is a part of the project supported by Beijing Municipal Science Technology Commission (Z161100002616032), Beijing Natural Science Foundation (4172069) and a joint Ph.D program funded by Chinese Academy of Sciences.

References

1. Unmasking kernel exploits. https://www.lastline.com/labsblog/unmasking-kernel-exploits/
2. Aristide, F., Andrea, L., Davide, B., Engin, K.: Hypervisor-based malware protection with AccessMiner. Comput. Secur. **52**, 33–50 (2015)
3. Bahram, S., Jiang, X., Wang, Z., Grace, M., Li, J., Srinivasan, D., Rhee, J., Xu, D.: DKSM: subverting virtual machine introspection for fun and profit. In: SRDS, pp. 82–91 (2010)
4. Bates, A., Tian, D., Butler, K., Moyer, T.: Trustworthy whole-system provenance for the Linux kernel. In: USENIX Security, pp. 319–334 (2015)
5. Carbone, M., Cui, W., Lu, L., Lee, W., Peinado, M., Jiang, X.: Mapping kernel objects to enable systematic integrity checking. In: CCS, pp. 555–565 (2009)
6. Dolan-Gavitt, B., Hodosh, J., Hulin, P., Leek, T., Whelan, R.: Repeatable reverse engineering with panda. In: Proceedings of 5th Program Protection and Reverse Engineering Workshop, pp. 4:1–4:11 (2015)
7. Dolan-Gavitt, B., Leek, T., Hodosh, J., Lee, W.: Tappan zee (north) bridge: mining memory accesses for introspection. In: CCS, pp. 839–850 (2013)
8. Garfinkel, T., Rosenblum, M.: A virtual machine introspection based architecture for intrusion detection. In: NDSS, pp. 191–206 (2003)
9. Jain, B., Baig, M.B., Zhang, D., Porter, D.E., Sion, R.: SoK: introspections on trust and the semantic gap. In: Proceedings of 35th IEEE S&P, pp. 605–620 (2014)
10. Jiang, X., Wang, X., Xu, D.: Stealthy malware detection through VMM-based out-of-the-box semantic view reconstruction. In: CCS, pp. 128–138 (2007)
11. Lanzi, A., Sharif, M., Lee, W.: K-tracer: a system for extracting kernel malware behavior. In: NDSS (2009)
12. Lee, K., Zhang, X., Xu, D.: High accuracy attack provenance via binary-based execution partition. In: NDSS (2013)
13. Lee, K., Zhang, X., Xu, D.: LogGC: garbage collecting audit log. In: CCS, pp. 1005–1016 (2013)
14. Li, J., Wang, Z., Jiang, X., Grace, M., Bahram, S.: Defeating return-oriented rootkits with "return-less" kernels. In: EuroSys, pp. 195–208 (2010)
15. Liangnd, Z., Yin, H., Song, D.: HookFinder: identifying and understanding malware hooking behaviors. In: NDSS, pp. 41–57 (2008)
16. Ma, S., Zhang, X., Xu, D.: ProTracer: towards practical provenance tracing by alternating between logging and tainting. In: NDSS (2016)

17. Pei, K., Gu, Z., Saltaformaggio, B., Ma, S., Wang, F., Zhang, Z., Si, L., Zhang, X., Xu, D.: HERCULE: attack story reconstruction via community discovery on correlated log graph. In: ACSAC, pp. 583–595 (2016)
18. Pohly, D., McLaughlin, S., McDaniel, P., Butler, K.: Hi-Fi: collecting high-fidelity whole-system provenance. In: ACSAC, pp. 259–268 (2012)
19. Rhee, J., Xu, D., Riley, R., Jiang, X.: Kernel malware analysis with un-tampered and temporal views of dynamic kernel memory. In: RAID, pp. 178–197 (2010)
20. Rhee, J., Riley, R., Xu, D., Jiang, X.: Defeating dynamic data kernel rootkit attacks via VMM-based guest-transparent monitoring. In: 2009 International Conference on Availability, Reliability and Security, pp. 74–81 (2009)
21. Riley, R., Jiang, X., Xu, D.: Guest-transparent prevention of kernel rootkits with VMM-based memory shadowing. In: RAID, pp. 1–20 (2008)
22. Riley, R., Jiang, X., Xu, D.: Multi-aspect profiling of kernel rootkit behavior. In: EuroSys, pp. 47–60 (2009)
23. Rudd, E., Rozsa, A., Gunther, M., Boult, T.: A survey of stealth malware: attacks, mitigation measures, and steps toward autonomous open world solutions. IEEE Commun. Surv. Tutor. **PP**(99), 1–28 (2016)
24. Wang, Z., Jiang, X., Cui, W., Wang, X.: Countering persistent kernel rootkits through systematic hook discovery. In: RAID, pp. 21–38 (2008)
25. Xu, Z., Wu, Z., Li, Z., Jee, K., Rhee, J., Xiao, X., Xu, F., Wang, H., Jiang, G.: High fidelity data reduction for big data security dependency analyses. In: CCS, pp. 504–516 (2016)
26. Xuan, C., Copeland, J., Beyah, R.: Toward revealing kernel malware behavior in virtual execution environments. In: RAID, pp. 304–325 (2009)
27. Zeng, J., Fu, Y., Lin, Z.: Automatic uncovering of tap points from kernel executions. In: RAID, pp. 49–70 (2016)

An On-Demand Defense Scheme Against DNS Cache Poisoning Attacks

Zheng Wang[1(✉)], Shui Yu[2], and Scott Rose[1]

[1] National Institute of Standards and Technology, Gaithersburg, MD 20899, USA
zhengwang98@gmail.com, scott.rose@nist.gov
[2] School of Information Technology, Deakin University, Burwood,
VIC 3125, Australia
syu@deakin.edu.au

Abstract. The threats of caching poisoning attacks largely stimulate the deployment of DNSSEC. Being a strong but demanding cryptographical defense, DNSSEC has its universal adoption predicted to go through a lengthy transition. Thus the DNSSEC practitioners call for a secure yet lightweight solution to speed up DNSSEC deployment while offering an acceptable DNSSEC-like defense. This paper proposes a new On-Demand Defense (ODD) scheme against cache poisoning attacks, still using but lightly using DNSSEC. In the solution, DNS operates in DNSSEC-oblivious mode unless a potential attack is detected and triggers a switch to DNSSEC-aware mode. The modeling checking results demonstrate that only a small DNSSEC query load is needed by the ODD scheme to ensure a small enough cache poisoning success rate.

Keywords: DNS Security Extensions · DNS cache poisoning
Model checking · Query load · Success rate

1 Introduction

The Domain Name System (DNS) is todayąŕs largest name resolution system in use. As a critical component in networking infrastructure, the DNS is becoming an increasingly lucrative target for adversaries. However, the early design of DNS did not pay sufficient attention to its security in 1980s. One major progress on securing DNS is DNS Security Extensions (DNSSEC) [1,2] as a set of core specifications agreed by IETF in 2005. DNSSEC provides security capabilities by digitally signing DNS data using public-key cryptography.

DNSSEC deployment was essentially motivated as a response to the Kaminsky vulnerability [3] which allows attackers to inject bogus DNS responses with a considerable success rate. While DNSSEC convincingly secures the DNS from the Kaminsky attacks, the concerns over DNSSEC overheads have posed big obstacles to its adoption. The impacts of DNSSEC on DNS performance are multi-facet:

© ICST Institute for Computer Sciences, Social Informatics and Telecommunications Engineering 2018
X. Lin et al. (Eds.): SecureComm 2017, LNICST 238, pp. 793–807, 2018.
https://doi.org/10.1007/978-3-319-78813-5_43

- The number of queries required by DNSSEC-aware resolution is amplified [4].
- The average packet size generated by DNSSEC is enlarged [6].
- The query processing cost at both authoritative servers and recursive servers is increased by DNSSEC [5, 7].

Hence DNSSEC deployment commonly means heavy investments, great efforts, and stability risks for DNS operators and DNS service providers. Such concerns may best explain the fact that the universal DNSSEC adoption is still very far from completion despite of the prominent demands for DNS security.

One promising way of promoting DNSSEC deployment is to limit DNSSEC overheads in order to make DNSSEC more affordable for DNS operators and DNS service providers. Perhaps the most obvious way to cut DNSSEC costs is to limit DNSSEC transactions between authoritative servers and recursive servers. That is, minimizing DNSSEC-enabled queries issued from recursive servers and processed by authoritative servers. Admittedly, the tradeoff between DNSSEC usage and security capability always stands. Nevertheless, an efficient use of DNSSEC, hopefully, mitigates DNS servers loads while offering an acceptable DNSSEC-like defense.

The defense proposed in this paper, namely ODD (On-Demand Defense), basically secures recursive resolvers against any off-path cache poisoning attacks. It still uses but lightly uses DNSSEC in a bid to lower its DNSSEC overheads. ODD makes full use of the detection capability of recursive resolvers to take up DNSSEC whenever needed. The rest of this paper is organized as follows. Related work is presented in Sect. 2. The ODD scheme is elaborated in Sect. 3. In Sect. 4, we present the performance analysis of the ODD scheme. Section 5 evaluates the ODD scheme through model checking. Finally, Sect. 6 concludes the paper.

2   Related Work

Before or in parallel with the DNSSEC rollout, there have been some proposals attempting to address the DNS cache poisoning risks in a light-weight way. As a non-DNSSEC solution to the DNS security, Fan et al. [8] proposed preventions embedded in security proxies. But their deployment costs are fairly high because security proxies need to be deployed at both authoritative servers and recursive resolvers to support packing and unpacking of all DNS packets with security label. Schomp et al. [9] proposed to remove shared DNS resolvers entirely and leave recursive resolution to the clients. That radical change fails to account for the complexity of DNS clients, the intranet attacks, and the overwhelming pressure on the DNS service providers. Sun et al. [10] proposed DepenDNS as a countermeasure which query multiple resolvers concurrently to verify a trustworthy answer. The reliability and availability of history response data used by DepenDNS is a great concern. Besides, the performance concern about DepenDNS is when the queries are multiplied, their processing overheads will also be multiplied. An extension to DNSSEC was proposed in [15], making the trust islands verifiable through extended chain of trust. Nevertheless, the overheads of DNSSEC are not lessened by the extension.

Shulman and Waidner [11] performed a critical study of the prominent defense mechanisms against poisoning attacks by off-path adversaries, concluding that existing easy-to-deploy defenses are not so reliable and thus transition to DNSSEC deserves the efforts. The capability of the DNS cache poisoning attacks was studied in [12,13], which are helpful to better understand our proposed defense.

3   The ODD Defense

To "condense" DNSSEC as best as possible while retaining its security capability against cache poisoning attacks, we propose that DNSSEC can coalesce with attack detection to lower its overheads.

3.1   Attack Detection

Off-path cache poisoning attacks are characterized by massive guessing attempts. Cache poisoning is where the attacker manages to inject bogus data into a recursive resolver's cache with carefully crafted and timed DNS packets. A cache poisoned resolver will response with its wrongfully accepted and cached data, redirecting its clients to the bogus and possibly malicious sites. For the sake of being accepted by the target resolver, bogus responses have to guess the transaction ID, port number, and source address of their genuine counterparts.

For one DNS question, an unmatched response satisfies:

(a) It matches the DNS question (or precisely the triple $< qname, qtype, qclass >$) of the outstanding queri(es). Note that attackers may exploit multiple outstanding queries for the same question to significantly increase the success rate of caching poisoning. This is referred to as "birthday attack". In that case, more than one outstanding queries may share one question.

(b) If (a) holds, it mismatches at least one item among transaction ID, port number, and source address of the outstanding queri(es).

A number of unmatched responses with wrong guessing are expected to be found by the target resolver before one bogus response may accidentally succeed. So we propose that presence and accumulating of unmatched responses can be treated as indicator of possible cache poisoning attacks. As a means of attack detection, the recursive resolver counts the incoming unmatched responses for each outstanding DNS question. When the count amounts to a threshold of defense (ToD), the attack traffic is identified and the attack response is triggered.

The appropriate setting of ToD should consider: on one hand, a too large value will result in a non-negligible increase of cache poisoning success rate ahead of any defense in place. e.g., the number of forgery responses is in the order of ten thousands to ensure a 50% chance of compromise in most cases of DNS

```
 1: BogusCount ← 0;
 2: SEND THE REQUEST;
 3: while BogusCount < ToD do
 4:    if time out then
 5:       RETURN(TIME_OUT);        % The name resolution times out
 6:    LISTEN TO THE RESPONSE;
 7:    if the response is bogus then
 8:       BogusCount ← BogusCount + 1;
 9:    else
10:       RETURN(THE RESPONSE);       % The authentic response received
11: SEND THE DNSSEC REQUEST;
12: while not time out do
13:    LISTEN TO THE RESPONSE;
14:    if the response is validated then
15:       RETURN(THE RESPONSE);       % The validating response received
16: RETURN(TIME_OUT);        % The name resolution times out
```

Fig. 1. The responding process of the DNSSEC-aware mode.

operations [12,13]; on the other hand, a too small value will too readily trigger the defense. Problem of false positive stands here when non-malicious or negligent users may unintentionally create a small amount of malformed responses which are identified as unmatched responses. Another exploit of a small threshold is that adversaries may deliberately feed a few unmatched responses on the target resolver in a bid to overload it with excessive defenses.

3.2 DNSSEC-Oblivious Mode

The DNSSEC-oblivious mode lets recursive resolver refrained from sending out DNSSEC-enabled requests nor validating responses unless explicitly required by the client (which sets the DO bit). More than the simple DNSSEC-oblivious DNS, a resolver in the DNSSEC-oblivious mode should perform attack detection and switch to the DNSSEC-aware mode once caching poisoning attack is detected. Therefore the costs of the DNSSEC-oblivious mode are comparable to the simple DNSSEC-oblivious DNS. As long as no caching poisoning attack is detected, the DNSSEC-oblivious mode continues as a normalcy.

3.3 DNSSEC-Aware Mode

The DNSSEC-aware mode uses DNSSEC transactions to authenticate suspicious responses to any potentially targeted DNS question. The responding process of DNSSEC-aware mode is illustrated in Fig. 1. When the count of unmatched bogus responses reaches ToD, the recursive resolver should immediately initiate a separate DNSSEC request for that targeted DNS question. If validated, the response, which is called "validating response" hereinafter, is taken as the trustworthy authority for that question. Thus all valid responses arriving prior to the validating response are hold on rather than accepted. Note that the hold-on responses may include the genuine response and one or more bogus responses which look like genuine because they totally matches the outstanding question.

3.4   Integration of the Two Modes

We present in detail how the two modes are integrated to defend against cache poisoning attacks. In particular, our example in Fig. 2 shows the defense procedure under the most mighty version of Kaminsky class attacks:

① The attacker client sends the target resolver a query for the IP address of "asq50pn.foo.com" below the target domain "foo.com". The domain "asq50pn.foo.com" is delicately crafted with random characters so that it is likely to miss the resolver's cache to trigger an outstanding query.

②a The forgery authoritative server tries to send cache poisoning attempts to the target resolver guessing the transaction ID, etc. of the genius response. Each unmatched response may, e.g., guess a wrong transaction ID, and intends to inject the IP address of the forgery authoritative server, say "Y.Y.Y.Y".

②b Roughly in parallel with (2a), the target resolver in the DNSSEC-oblivious mode sends a request to the real authoritative name server for "asq50pn.foo.com".

③a When the attack detection count the unmatched responses to ToD, the target resolver switches to the DNSSEC-aware mode and sends a DNSSEC request for "asq50pn.foo.com".

③b Perhaps at the same time as (3a), the genuine response arrives at the target resolver informing the IP address of the real authoritative server, say "X.X.X.X". However, as the DNSSEC-aware mode is already turned on, the response is hold on rather than simply accepted.

③c The target resolver may still persistently be fed with cache poisoning responses in the DNSSEC-aware mode. And the continuous response guessing efforts do have a chance of being holding on.

④ When the validating response is obtained by the target resolver, the relevant records in the validating response are subject to DNSSEC validation using the verified public key. That DNSSEC validation may render further DNSSEC transactions such as step (5) and (6) because some signatures (RRSIG records) over the interested data may be absent from the original validating response.

⑤ The target resolver initiates a new DNSSEC transaction to validate the IP address of the authoritative server ("ns.foo.com").

⑥ The new validating response contains a RRSIG record over the A type (IP address) record of "ns.foo.com". By then, the validating response can be validated.

⑦ By checking the hold-on list against the validating response, the IP address of "ns.foo.com", namely "X.X.X.X", is identified as genuine and "Y.Y.Y.Y" as bogus. The validated record can thus be used by the target resolver in the final answer as well as in the cache.

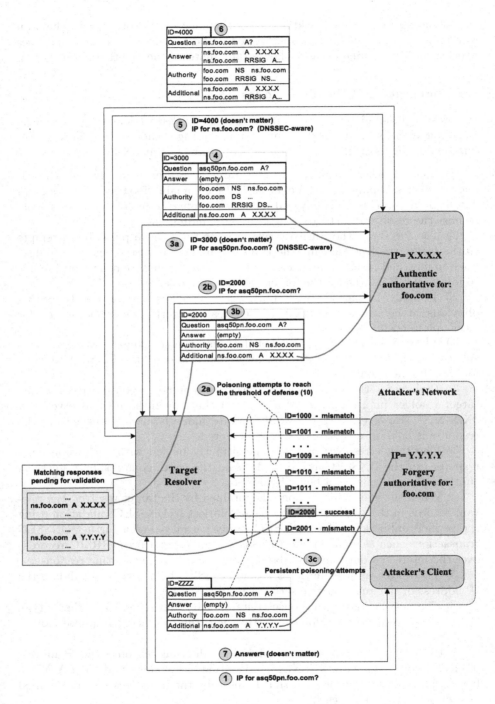

Fig. 2. An example of the integration of the two modes.

3.5   Caching and Proactive Updating of Validating Response

(a) Caching of Validating Response

To overcome the short-lived protection, we propose that recursive resolver should retain validating responses in cache for a long-lived defense rather than just use them once.

The signed records contained in the validating responses and validated by the recursive resolver should be regarded as more trustworthy than the unsigned records in the valid but unsigned responses. Similar to conventional DNS caching, those validating records should be cached by the recursive resolver for a period of TTL (Time-To-Live). Hence the recursive resolver can first search its cache for any relevant validating records before it has to solicit the authoritative servers. Nevertheless, the caching of validating responses differs from conventional DNS caching in the following:

- The validating records are given a priority over the unsigned records, and thus they are stored in a priority cache other than a normal cache. Here "priority" means: a record in the priority cache can overwrite its unsigned counterpart in the normal cache if any conflict exists between them; in turn, a record in the priority cache cannot be overwritten by any unsigned record in a more recent unsigned response; any record in the priority cache can only be replaced by a more recent validating response.
- The records in the priority cache are basically used for validating unsigned responses. When an unsigned response arrives with any record conflicting with the priority cache, the recursive resolver should not accept the response. Instead it waits for its possible successor consistent with the priority cache until timeout.

(b) Proactive Updating of Validating Response

The problem of cache consistency arises if simply respecting the priority of validating records in cache. Consider a more recent unsigned response containing up-to-date records R_u, and the virtually outdated validating records R_v in cache, which conflict with R_u, would deny R_u because R_v are more trustworthy.

For the sake of maintaining strong priority cache consistency, the recursive resolver should seek to proactive update validating response in case of cache inconsistency. The hold-on mechanism specified in DNSSEC-aware mode is slightly changed for caching of validating response. That is, the responses inconsistent with the priority cache are temporally hold on rather than discarded. Because the inconsistent responses may include the genuine response due to cache inconsistency, they are reserved for further validation. To still obtain up-to-date validating records in cache when timeout (indicating the possibility of cache inconsistency), the resolver should acquire a fresh validating response. The new validating response will have two usages: validating the hold-on responses and then returning the validated response if any; updating the corresponding validating records in cache. The responding process for aggressive use of validating response is detailed in Fig. 3.

```
1: BogusCount ← 0;
2: SEND THE REQUEST;
3: while BogusCount < ToD do
4:    if time out then
5:        RETURN(TIME_OUT);        % The name resolution times out
6:    LISTEN TO THE RESPONSE;
7:    if the response is bogus then
8:        BogusCount ← BogusCount + 1;
9:    else if the response is NOT consistent with ValidCache then
10:        break;        % Update the possibly outdated valid cache
11:    else
12:        RETURN(THE RESPONSE);        % The authentic response received
13: SEND THE DNSSEC REQUEST;
14: while not time out do
15:    LISTEN TO THE RESPONSE;
16:    if the response is validated then
17:        ValidResponse ← the response;
18:        USE ValidResponse TO UPDATE ValidCache;
19:        RETURN(THE RESPONSE);        % The validating response received
20: RETURN(TIME_OUT);        % The name resolution times out
```

Fig. 3. The responding process of the DNSSEC-aware mode with caching and proactive updating of validating response.

4   Performance Analysis

4.1   Overheads of DNSSEC Transactions

ODD never initiates DNSSEC transactions unless possible cache poisoning attack is detected at the target resolver. Thus for a vast majority of recursive resolvers which are not constantly targeted by cache poisoning adversaries, ODD is lightweight in terms of name resolution cost at both recursive resolvers and authoritative servers in comparison with the existing DNSSEC deployment strategy.

Consider the worst case of cache poisoning attack. That is, the attacker continuously sends caching poisoning responses at a high rate towards the target resolver. A DNSSEC transaction is generated by the target resolver if and only if:

- The validated records expire from cache so that an immediate flurry of caching poisoning responses triggers the switch to DNSSEC-aware mode.
- No validated response is found until timeout because of the updated authoritative record.

To investigate the event of DNSSEC transactions, we first discuss the events of TTL expiration and the events of authoritative record updating separately. Without loss of generality, we assume the TTL of any validated record follows a probability distribution function. If the target record is heavily requested, the times between successive events (queries) can be approximated by the value of TTL at the instances of events. Let the TTLs or the successive inter-event times are independently and identically distributed. Then we have

Assumption 1. *There is a renewal process in operation for TTL-expiration-triggered DNSSEC transactions.*

Assume that the successive times between the updates of authoritative records are independently and identically distributed. Then we have

Assumption 2. *There is a renewal process in operation for authoritative-update-triggered DNSSEC transactions.*

The process of DNSSEC transactions initiated by ODD is obtained by superposing the two renewal processes assumed above. However, we can prove the following theorem.

Theorem 1. *The two renewal processes are NOT independent of each other.*

Proof: No matter how long the validating record's TTL elapses, every authoritative-update-triggered DNSSEC transaction should be initiated immediately after the instance of authoritative update (given the intense enough cache poisoning attempts). So the renewal process of authoritative-update-triggered DNSSEC transactions is independent of that of TTL-expiration-triggered DNSSEC transactions. Nevertheless, the renewal process of TTL-expiration-triggered DNSSEC transactions is dependent of that of authoritative-update-triggered DNSSEC transactions. For example, if there is no authoritative update between two successive TTL-expiration-triggered DNSSEC transactions, the inter-even time between the two DNSSEC transactions is roughly TTL; but if there is one authoritative update between them, the residual TTL is renewed to a full TTL at the instance of authoritative update, and so their inter-even time is prolonged to be a full TTL plus a residual TTL; further, if there is more than one authoritative update between them, the residual TTL is renewed more than one time and their inter-even time becomes a full TTL plus more than one residual TTL. ☐

Given Theorem 1, the process of DNSSEC transactions initiated by ODD cannot be considered to be formed by superposing the two individual renewal processes. Instead, we describe the process of DNSSEC transactions using the codes in Fig. 4.

4.2   Cache Poisoning Success Rate

In Kaminsky cache poisoning attacks, an attacker can balance between the number of outstanding requests and the number of bogus response attempts at will to achieve maximum efficiency [12]. Because the number of effective bogus response attempts is limited by ODD, the attacker often exploits duplicate requests in a bid to increase the probability of successful compromise. However, the number of outstanding requests are bounded by two aspects in practice:

```
 1:  % The present time is initialized at an instance of update-triggered query
 2:  t ← 0;        % The time is initialized as zero
 3:  T ← TTL;       % The residual TTL is a TTL after an update-triggered query
 4:  while True do
 5:     if T = 0 then
 6:        SEND A REQUEST;       % Initiate a TTL-triggered query
 7:        T ← TTL;
 8:     else if an authoritative update occurs at t then
 9:        SEND A REQUEST;       % Initiate an update-triggered query
10:        T ← TTL;
11:     t ← ELAPSE(t);       % Time elapses
12:     T ← T − (ELAPSE(T) − T);   % The residual TTL decreases as time elapses
```

Fig. 4. The process of DNSSEC query event by ODD.

- The maximum number of outstanding requests is set as a default configuration in some widely used authoritative server implementations. Authoritative servers thereby discard excessive outstanding requests surpassing the configured limit, say L_a. So any efforts of producing more than L_a outstanding requests will prove fruitless [13].
- The window allowed to persistently elicit outstanding requests is bounded by the response time T_r perceived by the target resolver. Let the average query sending rate of attacker be R. The window can be converted to the number of outstanding requests roughly as T_r/R. In summary, the maximum number of outstanding requests D is the minimum of the two limits, namely $D = min\{L_a, T_r/R\}$.

Within one round of ODD validation, there are at most ToD-1 bogus response attempts left for effective cache poisoning. Letting H =ToD-1, we can express the cumulative probability of cache poisoning failure in all attempts up to and including the H th attempt as

$$P_D(H) = P(the\ 1st\ attempt\ misses,\ the\ 2nd\ attempt$$
$$misses,\ ...,\ the\ H\ th\ attempt\ misses\ |\ D \qquad (1)$$
$$identical\ outstanding\ queries)$$

Suppose the number distinct IDs available I, the number of ports used P, and the number of authoritative servers for a domain N. If $H \ll (I + P) * N$, $P_D(H)$ can be written as

$$P_D(H) = (1 - D/((I + P) * N))^H \qquad (2)$$

The worst case of ODD validation is when no relevant validating record is available at cache and thus a DNSSEC transaction is initiated for it. And then the validating record fetched is cached for it TTL to protect from any further cache poisoning attempts. Being the minimum window of opportunity for H attempts, the interval can be approximated by two response times, one for the proceeding non-DNSSEC response and the other for the following validating response, plus the TTL of validating record. So we have

$$T_H = 2 * T_r + TTL \tag{3}$$

where T_H denotes the minimum window of opportunity for H attempts and TTL denotes the TTL of validating record. That is, one round of ODD validation takes at least two response times plus one TTL to obtain a success rate of $1 - P_D(H)$. The success rate of cache poisoning within i rounds of cache poisoning attempt is $1 - P_D(H)^i$.

As illustrated in Fig. 4, the duration of defense by validating record in cache may be further prolonged to more than TTL. That extension to the window of opportunity occurs if authoritative update is identified by the resolver to refresh the validating record in cache before its TTL expires. In such case, the continuous elapse of TTL is interrupted by any authoritative update which renews the residual TTL to a full TTL. Therefore the effects of window extension are better pronounced for more frequent authoritative update, which provides a better chance of repeated TTL renewals.

Table 1. Parameters and their settings.

Parameter	Setting
Number distinct IDs available (I)	65536
Number of ports used (less than 1024 are unavailable) (P)	64000
Number of authoritative servers for a domain (N)	2.5
Response time (T_r)	0.02 s
Number of identical outstanding queries (D)	20
Query sending rate from resolver to authoritative server	100 qps
Query responding rate from authoritative server to resolver	100 qps
Query sending rate from attacker to resolver (R)	1000 qps
ToD	3
Bogus responding rate from attacker to resolver	100
Minimum window of opportunity for H attempts (T_H)	10 h

5   Model Checking Results

Probabilistic model checking is one of the most commonly used formal verification technique for the modeling and analysis of stochastic systems. We model Kaminsky cache poisoning attack as a continuous-time Markov chain (CTMC) using PRISM [14]. In modeling the attack, we assume that the queries originated from the attacker look up a random generated domain such that they will never hit the target resolver's cache. We also assume that the IP addresses of the target domain's authoritative servers are always in the cache of the target resolver.

5.1 Results of Query Load

To investigate the combined effects of TTL expiration and authoritative update on the inter-time of DNSSEC queries, we generate a sequence of authoritative update events following a probabilistic distribution while setting the TTLs in the DNSSEC responses as constant and probabilistic values respectively. The inter-time of authoritative updates follows exponential distribution. We use Monte Carlo method to estimate the mean of inter-times of DNSSEC queries. In each experiment, 100,000 times of authoritative updates are generated from an exponential distribution. A number of TTLs, taking either constant values or probabilistic values, are also produced to cover the same time span at the instances when the predecessor TTL expires or authoritative update takes place.

Figure 5 illustrates how DNSSEC query intervals change with authoritative update intervals. We can see that a very small authoritative update interval has almost the same DNSSEC query interval because TTL expiration rarely happens. But for a larger authoritative update interval, the effect of TTL expiration is better pronounced because a TTL has more chance of being smaller than an authoritative update interval thus more chance of expiration. Random TTLs, though have the same mean as constant TTLs, tend to cause a slightly larger DNSSEC query intervals and thereby a smaller DNSSEC query load on authoritative servers. The ratio of TTL-expiration-triggered queries is illustrated in Fig. 6. We can see that the ratio of TTL-expiration-triggered queries grows as the mean of update intervals increases. But authoritative update tends to pronounce more than TTL expiration on triggering DNSSEC queries even if they share the same mean interval. As shown in Fig. 7, when both update interval and TTL take a mean of 1000s, TTL-expiration-triggered DNSSEC queries only account for about 36% of the total. That can be explained by the fact that the event of authoritative update is independent of and never superseded by the event of TTL expiration while the arrival of TTL expiration may be interrupted and renewed by authoritative updates.

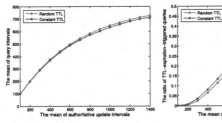 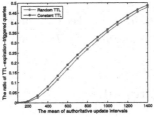 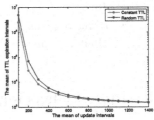

Fig. 5. DNSSEC query intervals vs authoritative update intervals.

Fig. 6. Ratio of TTL-triggered queries vs authoritative update intervals.

Fig. 7. TTL expiration intervals vs authoritative update intervals.

It is obvious that DNSSEC query interval will be larger if authoritative update and TTL expiration are independent. So in order to examine the lower bound of DNSSEC query interval or the upper bound of DNSSEC query rate, we assume that authoritative update and TTL expiration are independent. Then the mean DNSSEC query interval can be written as

$$I_{overall} = \frac{I_{update} * I_{ttl}}{I_{update} + I_{ttl}} \tag{4}$$

where I_{update} and I_{ttl} represent authoritative update interval and TTL respectively. As illustrated in Figs. 5 and 6, we conclude that the maximum DNSSEC query rate of ODD under intense cache poisoning attempts is of the same order as the minimum of authoritative update rate and the reciprocal of TTL.

5.2   Results of Cache Poisoning Success Rate

We configure the default values in Table 1 for the parameters in the model checking unless their values are otherwise defined.

First, we illustrate the time needed for a 50% success rate under different minimum window of opportunity in Fig. 8 (ToD=3). We can see that the time cost of cache poisoning roughly grows linearly with minimum window of opportunity. For a minimum window of opportunity above 10 h, the time required for a 50% success rate amounts to no less than 2 years. This is because the longer are the validating records available in cache to defend against cache poisoning attacks, the longer does an attacker have to wait to embark the next round of cache poisoning attempts (if the current round fails). As the TTLs of many authoritative records are set in the order of days or even weeks, it is very hard in practice to compromise them through cache poisoning attacks. Figure 8 also shows creating more identical outstanding queries may dramatically decrease the difficulty of cache poisoning. Thus in the defense, the resolver should not allow excessive identical outstanding queries in order to prevent an unacceptable success rate of cache poisoning.

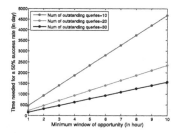

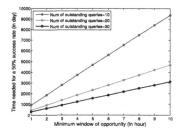

Fig. 8. Time needed for a 50% success rate vs minimum window of opportunity (ToD = 3).

Fig. 9. Time needed for a 50% success rate vs minimum window of opportunity (ToD = 2).

Second, we investigate the impacts of ToD on the success rate. In Fig. 9, the time needed for a 50% success rate is shown when the ToD is lowered to 2. We can see that limiting ToD helps significantly to suppress the success rate of cache poisoning. Since ToD defines the maximum number of forgery responses (ToD-1) allowed without defense, a larger ToD means more chance of guessing attempts thus a larger success rate. To ensure the efficacy of ODD, ToD should be set as a sound small value.

Third, we study how the cache poisoning success rate evolves over time. In Fig. 10, we can see that the success rate over time grows like a stair-step shape. In the curve, each step virtually represents a cache poisoning attempt in time and an accumulation of ToD-1 forgery responses in success rate. And the width of each stair-step is dominated by minimum window of opportunity. When ToD is three in Fig. 10, there are two forgery responses aggregated in a round of cache poisoning attempts to increase the overall success rate.

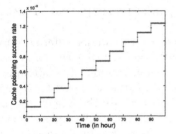

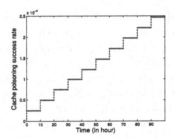

Fig. 10. Cache poisoning success rate vs time (ToD = 3).

Fig. 11. Cache poisoning success rate vs time (ToD = 5).

Fourth, how the setting of ToD impacts the cache poisoning success rate is studied. As illustrated in Fig. 11, the increase of ToD from 3 to 5 will lessen the defense of ODD against cache poisoning attacks. While the width of each stair-step stays the same as Fig. 10, the jump of each stair-step in the success rate is doubled. So the overall success rate grows much faster than Fig. 10. This shows again that a large ToD may undermine the defense capability of ODD.

6   Conclusions

DNSSEC deployment suffers from its significant costs which slow its progress. To speed up DNSSEC adoption, a lightweight DNSSEC solution was proposed. The proposed ODD defense greatly lowers the DNSSEC overheads while reserving the DNSSEC defense capability against cache poisoning attacks. Because of its efficiency and efficacy, ODD can serve as an interim mechanism for speeding DNSSEC adoption over a long-term transition to DNSSEC.

References

1. Arends, R., Austein, R., Larson, M., Massey, D., Rose, S.: Resource records for the DNS security extensions. In: RFC 4034, March 2005
2. Arends, R., Austein, R., Larson, M., Massey, D., Rose, S.: Protocol modifications for the DNS security extensions. In: RFC 4035, March 2005
3. Kaminsky, D.: It's the end of the cache as we know it. In: BlackHat (2008)
4. Huston, G., Michaelson, G.: Measuring DNSSEC performance (2013). http://www.potaroo.net/ispcol/2013-05/dnssec-performance.pdf
5. Migault, D., Girard, C., Laurent, M.: A performance view on DNSSEC migration. In: Proceedings of the International Conference on Network and Service Management (CNSM 2010), pp. 469–474 (2010)
6. Ager, B., Dreger, H., Feldmann, A.: Predicting the DNSSEC overhead using DNS traces. In: Proceedings of the Conference on Information Sciences and Systems (CISS 2006), pp. 1484–1489 (2006)
7. Lian, W., Rescorla, E., Shacham, H., Savage, S.: Measuring the practical impact of DNSSEC deployment. In: Proceedings of the USENIX SEC 2013, pp. 573–588 (2013)
8. Fan, L., Wang, Y., Cheng, X., Li, J.: Prevent DNS cache poisoning using security proxy. In: Proceedings of theInternational Conference on Parallel and Distributed Computing, Applications and Technologies (PDCAT 2011), pp. 387–393 (2011)
9. Schomp, K., Allman, M., Rabinovich, M.: DNS resolvers considered harmful. In: Proceedings of the ACM HotNets 2014, pp. 16–22 (2014)
10. Sun, H.-M., Chang, W.-H., Chang, S.-Y., Lin, Y.-H.: DependDNS: dependable mechanism against DNS cache poisoning. In: Garay, J.A., Miyaji, A., Otsuka, A. (eds.) CANS 2009. LNCS, vol. 5888, pp. 174–188. Springer, Heidelberg (2009). https://doi.org/10.1007/978-3-642-10433-6_12
11. Shulman, H., Waidner, M.: Towards forensic analysis of attacks with DNSSEC. In: Proceedings of the IEEE Security and Privacy Workshops (SPW 2014), pp. 69–76 (2014)
12. Wang, Z.: POSTER: on the capability of DNS cache poisoning attacks. In: Proceedings of the ACM CCS 2014, pp. 1523–1525 (2014)
13. Wang, Z.: A revisit of DNS Kaminsky cache poisoning attacks. In: Proceedings of the IEEE GLOBECOM 2015, pp. 1–6 (2015)
14. Kwiatkowska, M., Norman, G., Parker, D.: PRISM 4.0: verification of probabilistic real-time systems. In: Gopalakrishnan, G., Qadeer, S. (eds.) CAV 2011. LNCS, vol. 6806, pp. 585–591. Springer, Heidelberg (2011). https://doi.org/10.1007/978-3-642-22110-1_47
15. Wang, Z., Rose, S., Huang, J.: Securing DNS-based CDN request routing. IEEE COMSOC MMTC Commun. - Front. **12**(2), 45–49 (2017)

MPOPE: Multi-provider Order-Preserving Encryption for Cloud Data Privacy

Jinwen Liang[1], Zheng Qin[1]([✉]), Sheng Xiao[1], Jixin Zhang[1], Hui Yin[1], and Keqin Li[1,2]

[1] College of Computer Science and Electronic Engineering,
Hunan University, Changsha, Hunan, China
{jimmieleung,zqin,xiaosheng,zhangjixin}@hnu.edu.cn, yhui@ccsu.edu.cn
[2] Department of Computer Science, State University of New York,
New Paltz, NY, USA
lik@newpaltz.edu

Abstract. Order-preserving encryption (OPE) has been proposed as a privacy-preserving query method for cloud computing. Existing researches of OPE diverge into two groups. One group focuses on single data provider scenarios and achieves strong security notion such as indistinguishability under ordered chosen plaintext attack (IND-OCPA). Another group of research designs multi-provider schemes and provides weaker security guarantees than those of single provider schemes. In this paper, we propose a novel security notion for multi-provider scenario, indistinguishability under multi-provider ordered chosen plaintext attack (IND-MPOPCA), which guarantees equivalent security level as IND-OCPA while hiding the frequency of plaintexts and enabling multi-provider data submissions and queries. We develop a multi-provider randomized order technique to construct our MPOPE scheme to achieve the IND-MPOPCA security notion. We also conduct extensive experiments to prove the practicality and efficiency of our proposed scheme.

Keywords: Order-preserving encryption · Multiple data provider
Cloud security

1 Introduction

The flexibility of storing data on a cloud and making queries anywhere in the Internet is attractive. While the risk of data privacy breach severely weakens the desire of uploading data to the cloud [1]. With such a contention, a common solution is to encrypt data before uploading to the cloud. However, it becomes complicated to query the encrypted data, and even more difficult to hide the queries from being understood by the semi-trusted cloud.

Various methods had been proposed for privacy-preserving cloud queries, such as keyword query, fuzzy query, range query, etc. [2]. Among these categories of privacy-preserving query methods, range query gains the most research efforts because it is arguably the most promising direction to provide practically efficient and accurate solution for the privacy-preserving query problem [3–6].

© ICST Institute for Computer Sciences, Social Informatics and Telecommunications Engineering 2018
X. Lin et al. (Eds.): SecureComm 2017, LNICST 238, pp. 808–822, 2018.
https://doi.org/10.1007/978-3-319-78813-5_44

Order-preserving encryption (OPE) is the main technique used in range query schemes. The plaintext and ciphertext are kept in the same order under some value-mapping function [7,8]. Although a significant amount of work on OPE has been proposed, most of these works focus on the single data provider scenario, such as [3–6,9]. Since collecting and storing a large amount of data provided by multiple data providers is a common work-flow for many cloud storage applications, these single data provider schemes are not widely applicable. Single data provider scheme are more of theoretic attempts to push the security notions to the limit, such as indistinguishability under ordered chosen plaintext attack (IND-OCPA).

On the other side, multiple data provider schemes (or abbreviated as multi-provider schemes or multi-user schemes), such as [10,11], focus on the practicality and achieve weaker security notions than IND-OCPA, which had been implemented in many single-provider order-preserving encryption schemes, such as [3–5]. Also, a common foe to the multi-provider schemes is frequency analysis attack. As a comparison, the security feature of frequency hiding had been implemented in Kerschbaum's single-provider scheme [5] but not in any of existing multi-provider scheme.

Therefore, it is desirable to design a multi-provider scheme that achieves security notion as strong as IND-OCPA in the single-provider schemes and ensure such a scheme also stands against frequency analysis attacks.

In this paper, we propose *multi-provider randomized order* technique for increasing the security of multi-provider order-preserving encryption. We propose a new security notion for multi-provider order-preserving encryption. We also develop a novel multi-provider order-preserving encryption scheme under this security notion.

We summarize our contributions as follows.

- We propose a stronger security notion for multi-provider order-preserving encryption than IND-OCPA: *indistinguishability under multi-provider ordered chosen plaintext attack* (IND-MPOCPA).
- We develop a novel multi-provider order-preserving encryption scheme under IND-MPOCPA by implementing the *multi-provider randomized order*.
- We provide theoretical analyses and experimental evaluation for our scheme.

2   Definitions

2.1   Definitions for Our Scheme

We provide Table 1 to summarize notations and their definitions for our scheme. Our (stateful) multi-provider order-preserving encryption (MPOPE) can be defined below:

- MPOPE.$KeyGen(N) \to T$: initialize the secret state T.
- MPOPE.$Enc(T, DETcipher_k, DP_k, n_k) \to T', C$: Compute an OPE ciphertext set C after encrypted n_k DETcipher, and update the state T to T'.
- MPOPE.$Dec(T, c_i) \to DETcipher$: Find the corresponding DETcipher for the OPE ciphertext c_i based on state T.

Table 1. Summary of notations and definitions

Notation	Definition
S	The cloud server
K	The number of data providers
DP_k	The k th data provider, k = 1, 2, ..., K
n_k	The number of plaintexts provided by data provider DP_k
P_k	The plaintext set with n_k values provided by DP_k
$p_{k,i}$	A plaintext provided by data provider DP_k, i = 1, 2, ..., n_k
D	The plaintext domain, namely, $\forall p_{k,i} \in [1, D]$
DET	A deterministic encryption scheme, which satisfies DET = (DET.$KeyGen$, DET.Enc, DET.Dec)
sk_k	The DET symmetric key generated by DP_k
$DETcipher_k$	The corresponding DET ciphertext set of P_k encrypted by DP_k, i.e., $DETcipher_k = \{DETcipher_{k,1}, DETcipher_{k,2}, ..., DETcipher_{k,n_k}\}$
$DETcipher_{k,i}$	The corresponding DET ciphertext of $p_{k,i}$
HOM	A homomorphic encryption scheme, which satisfies HOM = (HOM.$KeyGen$, HOM.Enc, HOM.Dec)
PK	The public key of HOM published to each data provider
SK	The secret key of HOM generated by S
MPOPE	Our (stateful) multi-provider order-preserving encryption
T	The secret state of MPOPE
N	The number of distinct ciphertexts
C	The OPE ciphertext set with N values
$c_{k,i}$	An OPE cipher provided by DP_k, i = 1, 2, ..., N
M	The ciphertext domain of our order-preserving encryption scheme, namely, $\forall c_{k,i} \in [0, M]$

2.2 Model

System Model. Our system model involves multiple data providers (multi-provider) and a semi-trusted cloud. As is shown in Fig. 1, multiple data providers outsource their data to the cloud server in the encrypted form, which still enables comparison operation.

Threat Model. In our threat model, an honest-but-curious adversary will follow our protocol honestly but try to analyze and extract information about data. Both the cloud server and the data providers are considered as honest-but-curious adversary.

We consider about three types of attacks:

1. Type 1: Ordered Chosen Plaintext Attack. The cloud server try to extract relation between plaintexts and ciphertexts by asking the challenger to encrypt plaintext sequences [12].
2. Type 2: Frequency analysis. The cloud server try to confirm some plaintexts by observing the distribution of ciphertexts [5].

3. Type 3: Analysis between data providers. A data provider try to detect whether other providers encrypted the same data by observing the cipher-texts.

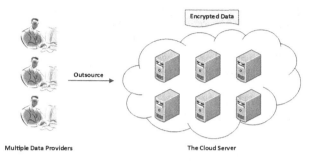

Fig. 1. Our system model

2.3 Security Definition

In order to resist those three types of attacks in our threat model, we propose a novel security notion for multi-provider order-preserving encryption: *indistinguishability under multi-provider ordered chosen plaintext attack* (IND-MPOCPA). Previous IND-OCPA security notion for order-preserving encryption is secure against Type 1 attack [8]. However, it has not considered about both Type 2 and Type 3 attacks. We define a multi-provider randomized order to enhance the ideal-security notion and resist both two attacks.

Definition 1 *(Multi-provider randomized order).* Let the plaintexts provided by different data providers are integrated into a sequence $W = \{w_{*,1}, w_{*,2}, \ldots, w_{*,n}\}$ with n not necessarily distinct plaintexts, where $*$ denotes any data provider. A multi-provider randomized order $\Pi = \{\pi_{*,1}, \pi_{*,2}, \ldots, \pi_{*,n}\}$ of W which satisfies that $\forall i \in [1, n], \pi_{*,i} \in [1, n]$ and $\forall i, j \in [1, n], i \neq j \Rightarrow \pi_{*,i} \neq \pi_{*,j}$, holds that

$$\forall i, j \, . \, w_{*,i} < w_{*,j} \Rightarrow \pi_{*,i} < \pi_{*,j}$$

and

$$\forall i, j \, . \, \pi_{*,i} < \pi_{*,j} \Rightarrow w_{*,i} \leq w_{*,j}$$

Our multi-provider randomized order is a permutation of the order of not necessarily distinct plaintexts uploaded by different data providers. Namely, the multi-provider randomized order not only preserve the order of distinct plaintexts but also randomize the order of identical plaintexts provided by different data providers. Therefore, the multi-provider randomized order can perfectly resist Type 2 and Type 3 attack.

Our IND-MPOCPA security game involves an adversary, a challenger, and K data providers. The adversary generates two n value sequences $W^0 = \{w^0_{*,1}, w^0_{*,2}, \ldots, w^0_{*,n}\}$ and $W^1 = \{w^1_{*,1}, w^1_{*,2}, \ldots, w^1_{*,n}\}$, which have the same order relation (namely, $\forall i, j \in [1, n], w^0_{*,i} < w^0_{*,j} \Leftrightarrow w^1_{*,i} < w^1_{*,j}$). Therefore, those two sequences have at least one common multi-provider randomized order.

IND-MPOCPA Security Game.

(1) The adversary sends W^0 and W^1 to the challenger.
(2) The challenger chooses a random bit $b \in \{0, 1\}$.
(3) The challenger and the set of providers engage in n rounds. At round i:
   (a) The challenger sends $w_{k,i}^b$ to DP_k, where k denotes any provider who provides the i-th plaintext and is defined by the adversary.
   (b) DP_k returns $c_{k,i} = \text{MPOPE}.Enc(w_{k,i}^b)$ to the challenger.
(4) The challenger returns the corresponding OPE ciphertext sequence $C = \{c_{*,1}, c_{*,2}, \ldots, c_{*,n}\}$ to the adversary, where $*$ denotes any provider from the provider set $DP_1, DP_2, \ldots, DP_k, \ldots, DP_K$.
(5) The adversary outputs b', its guess for b.

We say that the adversary wins the game if his guess is correct, i.e., $b' = b$. Let $win_{\mathcal{A}}$ be the random probability that indicates the success of the adversary wins the above game. We define the indistinguishability under a multi-provider ordered chosen plaintext attack (IND-MPOCPA) notion below:

Definition 2 *(IND-MPOCPA: indistinguishability under multi-provider ordered chosen plaintext attack).* A multi-provider order-preserving encryption scheme is IND-MPOCPA secure if for all p.p.t. adversaries, $Pr[win_{\mathcal{A}}] \leq \frac{1}{2}$.

Since the multi-provider randomized order only leaks the order of data and permutates the order of identical plaintexts provided by different data providers randomly, our IND-MPOCPA is secure against Type 1, Type 2, and Type 3 attack. Since the IND-OCPA security notion can only resist Type 1 attack, IND-MPOCPA security is strictly stronger than IND-OCPA security. Therefore, our IND-MPOCPA security notion is an enhancement of IND-OCPA security notion for multi-provider order-preserving encryption.

3 Our Scheme

We propose a secret state, which implements the multi-provider randomized order technique, to achieve this goal. Later, we construct a novel multi-provider order-preserving encryption scheme based on the secret state.

Our comparing protocol is the key technique to implement the multi-provider randomized order technique. The goal of our comparing protocol is: (1) to compare values from multiple data providers secretly, (2) to randomize the comparison result of two identical plaintexts provided by different data providers, and (3) to achieve IND-CPA security notion.

Our comparing protocol is a secure three-party computation protocol. We utilize Paillier cryptosystem [13] to construct it. We use E() and D() to denote HOM.$Enc()$ and HOM.$Dec()$ respectively. We provide our comparing protocol in Algorithm 1.

In Algorithm 1, DP_i uses b_i to randomize the compare result R. We show the relation between b_i and R in Table 2. Since DP_i chooses b_i randomly, the compare result R of two identical data is randomized. In our three-party comparing protocol, DP_i uses r_i and r_i' to randomized the ciphertext of $(-1)^{b_i} \cdot (p_{i,x} - p_{j,y})$, DP_j uses b_j, r_j, r_j' to re-randomize the result. Therefore, S cannot recover $(-1)^{b_i} \cdot (p_{i,x} - p_{j,y})$ by decrypting $v_{2,3}$.

Algorithm 1. Comparing Protocol

Input: DP_i, DP_j, S, $DETcipher_{i,x}$, $DETcipher_{j,y}$.

Output: A compare result R

initialization: The cloud server runs $HOM.KeyGen()$. Data provider DP_i and DP_j decrypt $DETcipher_{i,x}$ and $DETcipher_{j,y}$ and obtain the corresponding plaintexts $p_{i,x}$ and $p_{j,y}$ respectively.

1: DP_i computes $E(p_{i,x})$.

2: DP_j computes $E(-p_{j,y})$, and sends it to DP_i.

3: DP_i computes a vector $V = (v_{1,1}, v_{1,2}, v_{1,3})$ and sends it to DP_j. Firstly, he flips a random coin $b_i \in \{0, 1\}$. Secondly, he randomly chooses two large random numbers r_i and r_i', which satisfy $r_i > r_i'$. Then he calculates:

$$v_{1,1} = E(1)$$
$$v_{1,2} = E(0)$$
$$v_{1,3} = (E(p_{i,x}) \cdot E(-p_{j,y}))^{(-1)^{b_i} \cdot r_i} \cdot E(-r_i')$$
$$= E(r_i \cdot (-1)^{b_i} \cdot (p_{i,x} - p_{j,y}) - r_i')$$

Finally, he sends V to DP_j.

4: DP_j re-randomized the vector $V = (v_{2,1}, v_{2,2}, v_{2,3})$ and sends it to S. Firstly, he flips a random coin $b_j \in \{0, 1\}$. Secondly, he randomly selects two large numbers r_j and r_j' which satisfy $r_j > r_j'$. Then he calculates:

$$v_{2,1} = v_{1,1+b_j} \cdot E(0)$$
$$v_{2,2} = v_{1,2-b_j} \cdot E(0)$$
$$v_{2,3} = v_{1,3}^{(-1)^{b_j} \cdot r_j} \cdot E((-1)^{1+b_j} \cdot r_j')$$
$$= E((-1)^{b_j} \cdot (r_j \cdot v_{1,3} - r_j'))$$

Finally, he sends V to S.

5: S decrypts the vector V. If $D(v_{2,3}) < 0$, then the cloud server sends $D(v_{2,1})$ to DP_i. Else, the cloud server sends $D(v_{2,2})$ to DP_i.

6: DP_i calculates $R = D(v_{2,k})$ xor b_i, where $k = 1$ or 2.

We proceed as our secret state construction. Our secret state refers to an AVL tree T with a set of nodes $\{t\}$, which should be shared to the cloud server and multiple data providers. We show and explain the data structure of our AVL tree in Table 3. Then we provide a protocol to initialize and refresh the state of our scheme in Algorithm 2.

Table 2. A description of Algorithm 1

Case					
$p_{i,x} < p_{j,y}$		$p_{i,x} = p_{j,y}$		$p_{i,x} > p_{j,y}$	
b_i	R	b_i	R	b_i	R
0	1	0	1	0	0
1	1	1	0	1	0

Table 3. Parameters and explanation for tree node structure

Parameters	Explanations
Int *providerid*	A data provider, for example, DP_k
ElementType *DETcipher*	A DET ciphertext encrypted by *providerid*
ElementType *OPEcipher*	The OPE ciphertexts
AVLNode **left*	A pointer point to the left child
AVLNode **right*	A pointer point to the right child

Algorithm 2. Refreshing the secret state REFRESH

Input: An AVL tree T with nodes $\{t\}$, DP_k, $DETcipher_k$, S.
Output: An AVL tree T' with nodes $\{t\} \bigcup \{DETcipher_k\}$.
Initialization: Create an empty AVL tree.

1: **for** $i = 0$ to n_k **do**
2: 　**if** $DETcipher_{k,i}$ was not in the set $\{t\}$. **then**
3: 　　DP_k asks the server for the root node of the AVL tree.
4: 　　S returns a node r to DP_k.
5: 　　**if** The node r was provided by DP_k. **then**
6: 　　　DP_k decrypts both $r.DETcipher$ and $DETcipher_{k,i}$, and compare the corresponding plaintexts p_r with $p_{k,i}$.
7: 　　**else if** The node t was not provided by DP_k. **then**
8: 　　　DP_k invokes the comparing protocol (Algorithm 1) to compare $p_{k,i}$ with p_r secretly.
9: 　　**end if**
10: 　　If $p_{k,i} < p_r$, DP_k asks S for the left child node; If $p_{k,i} > p_r$, DP_k asks S for the right child node.
11: 　　**if** S does not arrive at an empty spot in the AVL tree. **then**
12: 　　　S returns the next node based on DP_k's information, and goes back to step 4.
13: 　　**end if**
14: 　　S inserts the new node into the AVL tree and balances the AVL tree.
15: 　**end if**
16: **end for**
17: The algorithm outputs a new AVL tree T'.

In Algorithm 2, we initialize and refresh the secret state by constructing an AVL tree. Each node in our AVL tree is arranged based on the order of the plaintext value. The AVL tree is constructed and stored on the cloud server. Multiple data providers help the cloud server to find the location for his plaintexts in the tree as well as to construct the AVL tree by using the DET ciphertexts.

We provide Algorithm 3 to produce OPE ciphertexts by utilizing the secret state. We initialize the lower and the upper bounders Min and Max in Algorithm 3 to be -1 and M respectively. Each node's $OPEcipher$ is the mean value of Min and Max, and is generated by recursion. Note that the update algorithm is run on the cloud server S. We provide our multi-provider order-preserving encryption scheme in Algorithms 4 and 5.

Algorithm 3. Update UPDATE

Input: S, AVLNode $*t$, Min, Max.
State: The AVLTree T of nodes $\{t\}$.
1: **if** $T \neq NULL$ **then**
2:     $t.OPEcipher = \lceil \frac{Max+Min}{2} \rceil$
3:     $Update(t.left, Min, t.OPEcipher)$
4:     $Update(t.right, t.OPEcipher, Max)$
5: **end if**

Algorithm 4. MPOPE Encryption ENCRYPTION

Input: DP_k, S, n_k, $DETcipher_k$.
State: The AVL tree T of nodes $\{t\}$.
1: DP_k invokes Algorithm 2 to refresh the secret state.
2: S invokes Algorithm 3 to update the OPE ciphertexts.

Algorithm 5. MPOPE Decryption DECRYPTION

Input: $OPEcipher$.
Output: $DETcipher$.
State: The AVL tree T of nodes $\{t\}$.
1: Search $OPEcipher$ on the AVL tree.
2: **if** $t.OPEcipher = OPEcipher$ **then**
3:     **return** $t.DETcipher$
4: **end if**

We provide an example to describe our scheme in Fig. 2. In Fig. 2, DP_A, DP_B, and DP_C provide plaintexts $\{15, 19, 81\}$, $\{3, 1, 14\}$, and $\{91, 15, 15\}$ respectively. Later those three data providers use DET encryption scheme to encrypt their data respectively. Then each data provider helps the cloud server to construct the secret state (the AVL tree) by invoking the REFRESH Algorithm (Algorithm 2). Note that DP_C only insert $\{91, 15\}$ in the secret state because repeated plaintext 15 only insert once. In the secret state, we can find that identical plaintexts 15 provided by DP_A and DP_C have different position in

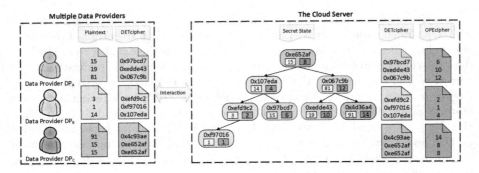

Fig. 2. Overview of our MPOPE scheme. Our MPOPE scheme involves 3 steps: Firstly, each data provider uses DET encryption to encrypt their data. Secondly, data providers help the cloud server to construct the secret state, which only involves the DET ciphertexts. Thirdly, the cloud server generates the OPE ciphertexts by using the secret state. Note that the left rectangles in the node of secret state denotes the plaintext provided by data providers, but there are not stored in the cloud server.

the AVL tree because our comparing protocol randomize the compare result of 15 provided by different data provider. After constructing the secret state, the cloud server invokes the UPDATE Algorithm (Algorithm 3) to generate the OPE ciphertexts. Finally, we can find that the corresponding ciphertexts of plaintexts $\{15, 19, 81, 3, 1, 14, 91, 15, 15\}$ are $\{6, 10, 12, 2, 1, 4, 14, 8, 8\}$.

4 Theoretical Analysis and Discussion

4.1 Security Analysis

Security Proof. We assume that DET encryptions are computationally indistinguishable from random values. Recall our security notion defined in Sect. 2.3. We provide the security goal of our scheme in Theorem 1.

Theorem 1. Our multi-provider order-preserving encryption scheme is secure against multi-provider ordered chosen plaintext attack. Namely, our scheme is IND-MPOCPA secure.

Proof. Due to space constraints, we provide a formalized proof in our extended paper, and we provide intuition here.

We prove Theorem 1 by induction. Consider that when no value was encrypted, then our scheme starts with the same initial state which is independent of the bit b. Then we assume that it holds for i encryptions. In the $(i + 1)$-th encryption, we assume that $c_{*,i+1}$ was produced by DP_k and hence $c_{*,i+1}$ is $c_{DP_k,i+1}$. We have three possibilities.

The first one is $w^b_{DP_k,j} = w^b_{DP_k,i+1}$ and $j < i + 1$. The secret state of both sequences will not change, and the OPE cipher of $w^b_{DP_k,i+1}$ will equal to $w^b_{DP_k,j}$. Since $c_{DP_k,j}$ is independent of b, $c_{DP_k,i+1}$ is independent of b.

The second is $w^b_{DP_k,i+1} = w^b_{DP_t,j}$, and $j < i+1$. Then the secret state will be refreshed, and the result of refreshment is depended on a random coin b_k. Since b_k is randomly chosen by DP_k and is independent of b, $c_{DP_k,i+1}$ is independent of b.

The last is that plaintext $w^b_{DP_k,i+1}$ has not been encrypted. DP_k interacts with the cloud server and refreshes the secret state. Since W^0 and W^1 have the same order relation, the secret state of both plaintexts are the same. Therefore, $c_{DP_k,i+1}$ is independent of b.

Therefore, our encryption algorithm produces the same OPE ciphertext sequence in both cases, and hence our scheme is IND-MPOCPA secure. $\square$

4.2   Theoretical Performance Analysis

We analyze the time complexity of our scheme.

Key Generation. In our scheme, the secret state plays a role as the key of our encryption scheme. Hence, the complexity of our key generation algorithm is the complexity of the initiation of secret state, which requires $\mathcal{O}(1)$.

Encryption. The encryption involves Algorithms 2 and 3. Algorithm 2 requires to refresh distinct plaintexts. Kerschbaum and Schroepfer [4] investigated the expected number of distinct plaintexts, and we restate it in Theorem 2.

Theorem 2. Let D be the number of distinct plaintexts in the plaintext domain. For a uniformly chosen plaintext sequence of size n with S distinct plaintexts, the expected number of distinct plaintexts is

$$E[S] = D(1 - (\frac{D-1}{D})^n) \tag{1}$$

Let N be the total number of values in the secret state. We conclude the expected value of N in Lemma 1 by using the Eq. 1.

Lemma 1. The expected number of N is

$$E[N] = \sum_{k=1}^{K} D(1 - (\frac{D-1}{D})^{n_k}) \tag{2}$$

Since the secret state is an AVL tree, which has logarithmic height, the time complexity of Algorithm 2 is $\mathcal{O}(\log N)$. The update Algorithm (Algorithm 3) is a pre-order traversal of the AVL tree, and hence the time complexity of it is $\mathcal{O}(N \log N)$. Since Algorithm 2 requires 8 times modular exponentiation computation per comparison, each secret state refreshment requires $\log N$ times complex computation, which requires more time than the operation of OPE ciphertext update. Hence, our encryption requires $\mathcal{O}(\log N)$ complex computation.

Decryption. The decryption algorithm is to find the corresponding DET ciphertext of an OPE ciphertext in the AVL tree and decrypt the DET ciphertext.

Assume that there are N values in the AVL tree, the time complexity of the decryption algorithm is $\mathcal{O}(\log N)$.

Hence, the time complexity of our key generation algorithm, encryption algorithm, and decryption algorithm are $\mathcal{O}(1)$, $\mathcal{O}(\log N)$, and $\mathcal{O}(\log N)$ respectively.

4.3   Ciphertext Domain

The ciphertexts of our scheme are generated by the secret state with N values. Let H be the height of an AVL tree, then $M = 2^H$. Foster [14] has investigated the relation between N and H, and we restate his work in Theorem 3.

Theorem 3. N and H satisfy the following inequality:

$$H < \frac{3}{2}\log_2(N+1) - 1 \tag{3}$$

Then, we can conclude that:

Lemma 2. In order to store N values in an AVL tree, the minimum height of the tree is $H_{min} = \lceil \frac{3}{2}\log_2(N+1) - 1 \rceil$.

Lemma 2 shows that the minimum bit length of a ciphertext is H_{min}. Hence, for N plaintext values, the ciphertext space M should not less than $2^{H_{min}}$. For simplicity, We define that $M = 2^{\lceil H_{min} \rceil}$.

5   Experiments

We evaluate the efficiency and the statistical security of our scheme (**MPOPE**). We use **DOPE** and **FHOPE** to denote the scheme in [4] and the scheme in [5] respectively. The result of our experiments answer the following questions:

- How is the MPOPE encrypting time affected by the number of data providers and the number of plaintexts?
- How does the encryption time of MPOPE compare with DOPE and FHOPE?
- How does the statistical security of MPOPE compare with DOPE and FHOPE?

We implement our experiments in Java 1.6. Our experiments are carried out on a 64-Bit workstation with an Intel Xeon E-1226 CPU with 3.30 GHz and 32 GB RAM. We set D and M to be 16000 and 2^{25} respectively. In our experiments, each data provider encrypts the same number of plaintexts. We set the key length of Paillier cryptosystem to be 1024 bits.

5.1   The Encrypting Time of Our Scheme

We evaluate the average encrypting time when 2, 4, 8, 16, 32 data providers encrypt 4000, 16000, 64000 total plaintexts in Fig. 3a. Figure 3a depicts that when the number of providers grows, the average encrypting time grows slightly. We also measure the average encrypting time when 2, 8, 32 data providers encrypt 4000, 8000, 16000, 32000, 64000 total possibly identical plaintexts in Fig. 3. Figure 3b depicts that the average encrypting time firstly increases and then decreases when the total number of plaintexts increases.

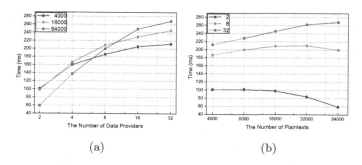

(a)   (b)

Fig. 3. (a) and (b) depict the encrypting time of MPOPE affected by the number of data provider and the number of plaintext respectively.

5.2 A Comparison to Previous OPE Schemes

We extend DOPE and FHOPE to the multi-provider environment by using our comparing protocol. We use the AVL tree as the state of those schemes to improve the efficiency of insertion and searching.

We compare the average encrypting time of MPOPE with DOPE and FHOPE. We evaluate the average encrypting time of those three schemes when 1, 2, 8, 32 data providers encrypt 4000, 8000, 16000, 32000, 64000 possible repeated plaintexts in Fig. 4a, b, c, and d respectively.

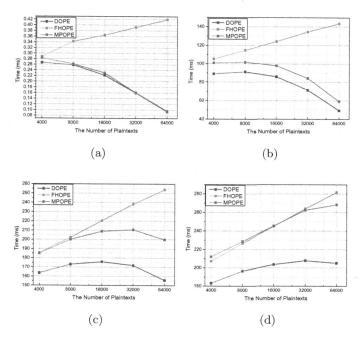

(a)   (b)

(c)   (d)

Fig. 4. (a)–(d) depict a comparison of encrypting time between MPOPE, DOPE, and FHOPE in 1, 2, 8, 32 data provider environment respectively.

Overall, those figures depict that the time overhead of MPOPE is lower than FHOPE but higher than DOPE. Therefore, the efficiency of MPOPE is better than FHOPE but worse than DOPE.

5.3 Statistical Security

We measure the effectiveness of statistical attack for our scheme by estimating the Pearson correlation coefficient between plaintexts and ciphertexts. The smaller the correlation, the more secure against statistical cryptanalysis.

We make 300 experiments to evaluate the Pearson correlation coefficient for 4000, 8000, 16000, 32000, 64000 plaintext-ciphertext pairs. We compute the 90% confidence intervals as error bars. We compare the Pearson correlation coefficient of the plaintext-ciphertexts pairs generated by MPOPE to DOPE and FHOPE. The compare results in 1, 2, 8, 32 data provider environment are depicted in Fig. 5a, b, c, and d respectively. Overall, we find that the confidence intervals of the correlation coefficient for each different cases clearly overlap. Hence, we can conclude that MPOPE is no weaker than DOPE and FHOPE under the statistical attack.

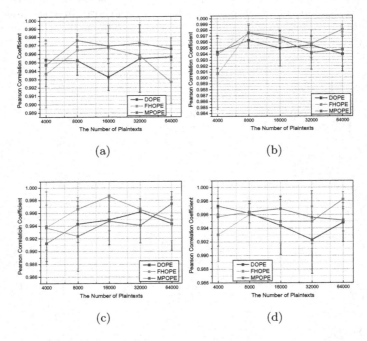

Fig. 5. (a)–(d) describe a comparison of Pearson correlation coefficient of the plaintext-ciphertexts pairs generated by MPOPE, DOPE, and FHOPE in 1, 2, 8, 32 data provider environment respectively.

6   Conclusions

We propose the IND-MPOCPA security notion for multi-provider order-preserving encryption. Moreover, we construct MPOPE which captures IND-MPOCPA. In summary, our scheme is a new option for order-preserving encryption in the cloud, which provides strong security guarantee with operation efficiency for cloud applications with multiple data providers.

Acknowledgement. This work is partially supported by the National Science Foundation of China under Grant No. 61472131, 61300218, 61472132, 61300217; Science and Technology Key Projects of Hunan Province (2015TP1004, 2015SK2087, 2015JC1001, 2016JC2012).

References

1. Zhang, Y., Chunxiang, X., Liang, X., Li, H., Yi, M., Zhang, X.: Efficient public verification of data integrity for cloud storage systems from indistinguishability obfuscation. IEEE Trans. Inf. Forensics Secur. **12**(3), 676–688 (2017)
2. Li, J., Wang, Q., Wang, C., Cao, N., Ren, K., Lou, W.: Fuzzy keyword search over encrypted data in cloud computing. In: 29th IEEE International Conference on Computer Communications, Joint Conference of the IEEE Computer and Communications Societies, INFOCOM 2010, 15–19 March 2010, San Diego, CA, USA, pp. 441–445. IEEE (2010)
3. Popa, R.A., Li, F.H., Zeldovich, N.: An ideal-security protocol for order-preserving encoding. In: 2013 IEEE Symposium on Security and Privacy, SP 2013, Berkeley, CA, USA, 19–22 May 2013, pp. 463–477. IEEE Computer Society (2013)
4. Kerschbaum, F., Schroepfer, A.: Optimal average-complexity ideal-security order-preserving encryption. In: Proceedings of the 2014 ACM SIGSAC Conference on Computer and Communications Security, CCS 2014, pp. 275–286. ACM, New York (2014)
5. Kerschbaum, F.: Frequency-hiding order-preserving encryption. In: Proceedings of the 22nd ACM SIGSAC Conference on Computer and Communications Security, CCS 2015, pp. 656–667. ACM, New York (2015)
6. Roche, D.S., Apon, D., Choi, S.G., Yerukhimovich, A.: Pope: partial order preserving encoding. In: Proceedings of the 2016 ACM SIGSAC Conference on Computer and Communications Security, CCS 2016, pp. 1131–1142. ACM, New York (2016)
7. Agrawal, R., Kiernan, J., Srikant, R., Xu, Y.: Order preserving encryption for numeric data. In: Proceedings of the 2004 ACM SIGMOD International Conference on Management of Data, SIGMOD 2004, pp. 563–574. ACM, New York (2004)
8. Boldyreva, A., Chenette, N., Lee, Y., O'Neill, A.: Order-preserving symmetric encryption. In: Joux, A. (ed.) EUROCRYPT 2009. LNCS, vol. 5479, pp. 224–241. Springer, Heidelberg (2009). https://doi.org/10.1007/978-3-642-01001-9_13
9. Lewi, K., Wu, D.J.: Order-revealing encryption: new constructions, applications, and lower bounds. In: Proceedings of the 2016 ACM SIGSAC Conference on Computer and Communications Security, CCS 2016, pp. 1167–1178. ACM, New York (2016)
10. Xiao, L., Yen, I.-L., Huynh, D.T.: Extending order preserving encryption for multi-user systems. IACR Cryptology ePrint Archive, 2012:192 (2012)

11. Yao, X., Lin, Y., Liu, Q., Long, S.: Efficient and privacy-preserving search in multi-source personal health record clouds. In: 2015 IEEE Symposium on Computers and Communication, ISCC 2015, Larnaca, Cyprus, 6–9 July 2015, pp. 803–808. IEEE Computer Society (2015)
12. Boldyreva, A., Chenette, N., O'Neill, A.: Order-preserving encryption revisited: improved security analysis and alternative solutions. In: Rogaway, P. (ed.) CRYPTO 2011. LNCS, vol. 6841, pp. 578–595. Springer, Heidelberg (2011). https://doi.org/10.1007/978-3-642-22792-9_33
13. Paillier, P.: Public-key cryptosystems based on composite degree residuosity classes. In: Stern, J. (ed.) EUROCRYPT 1999. LNCS, vol. 1592, pp. 223–238. Springer, Heidelberg (1999). https://doi.org/10.1007/3-540-48910-X_16
14. Foster, C.C.: Information retrieval: information storage and retrieval using AVL trees. In: Proceedings of the 1965 20th National Conference, ACM 1965, pp. 192–205. ACM, New York (1965)

SLIM: Secure and Lightweight Identity Management in VANETs with Minimum Infrastructure Reliance

Jian Kang[2], Yousef Elmehdwi[1], and Dan Lin[2(✉)]

[1] Department of Mathematics and Computer Science,
Emory University, Atlanta, USA
yousef.Elmehdwi@emory.edu
[2] Department of Computer Science, Missouri University of Science
and Technology, Rolla, USA
{jkb7c,lindan}@mst.edu

Abstract. Vehicular Ad-hoc Networks (VANETs) show a promising future of automobile technology as it enables vehicles to dynamically form networks for vehicle-to-vehicle (V2V) communication. For vehicles to securely and privately communicate with each other in VANETs, various privacy-preserving authentication protocols have been proposed. Most of the existing approaches assume the existence of Road-Side Units (RSUs) to serve as the trusted party during the authentication. However, building RSUs is costly and may not be able to capture the speed of the deployment of the VANETs in the near future. Aiming at minimizing the reliance on the infrastructure support, we propose a Secure and Lightweight Identity Management (SLIM) mechanism for vehicle-to-vehicle communications. Our approach is built upon self-organized groups of vehicles which take turns to serve as captain authentication unit to provide temporary local identities for member vehicles. While ensuring the vehicles' identities are verifiable to each other, we also prevent any vehicle in VANETs including the captain authentication unit from seeing the true identities of other vehicles. The proposed authentication protocols leverage the public key infrastructure in a way that the key generation workload is distributed over time and hence achieve authentication efficiency during the V2V communication. Compared to the previous related work, the proposed SLIM mechanism is more secure in that it can defend more types of attacks in VANETs, and is more efficient in that it requires much shorter response time for identity verification between vehicles.

Keywords: VANETs · Privacy · Authentication · Lightweight
Vehicle-to-vehicle communication

1 Introduction

Vehicular Ad-hoc Networks (VANETs) are being touted as the crux of the future of automobile technology. In VANETs, vehicles can leverage onboard

© ICST Institute for Computer Sciences, Social Informatics and Telecommunications Engineering 2018
X. Lin et al. (Eds.): SecureComm 2017, LNICST 238, pp. 823–837, 2018.
https://doi.org/10.1007/978-3-319-78813-5_45

computing and communication devices to form dynamic networks for vehicle-to-vehicle communication. This technology would foster a variety of new and interesting applications such as obtaining real-time road safety and traffic information from peer vehicles, and sharing files among neighboring vehicles similar to that in Internet. Almost all the major automobile manufacturers have invested heavily on research regarding VANETs. Current prototypes like NOW (Network on Wheel) [2] and SeVeCom [16] have already provided workable testing-models for real-world use.

Since many VANET applications are based on vehicle-to-vehicle (V2V) communication, it is critical to ensure the integrity and authenticity of the messages exchanged by vehicles. Meanwhile, it is also important to preserve the privacy of the vehicle owners during the communication. This is not only because people may not feel comfortable to disclose their true identities to strangers, but also because a series of attacks (such as impersonation) may be easily launched when true identities are disclosed. In order to achieve secure and private V2V communication, various privacy preserving authentication protocols have been proposed [6,9,23]. Most of the existing approaches assume the existence of Road-Side Units (RSUs) to serve as the trusted party during the authentication. However, building RSUs is costly and may not be able to capture the speed of the deployment of the VANETs in the near future.

Aiming at minimizing the reliance on the infrastructure support, we propose a Secure and Lightweight Identity Management (SLIM) mechanism for V2V communications. Specifically, the SLIM scheme has an initial registration phase where the vehicles only need to contact a central authority once the first time they log on VANETs to obtain a global identity. This global identity is tied to the vehicle's identification number (VIN) without explicitly revealing this information. Then as vehicles move around, they self-organize into groups of similar interest or destinations using our previously proposed moving-zone forming protocols [11]. Inside each moving zone, vehicles take turns to serve as the captain authentication unit (CAU) who will be in charge of generating a temporary local identity for each member vehicle to communicate with peers. The local identities are computed from the vehicle's global identity, and do not reveal the true identity of vehicles to the CAU or peer vehicles. Moreover, the SLIM mechanism also support traceability in that the true identity of a malicious vehicle can be recovered through the collaboration between other peer vehicles and the central authority. We have implemented our approach and compared the performance with the most related V2V-based authentication approach [22]. The experimental results show that the SLIM is much faster during the V2V authentication.

The proposed SLIM mechanism has the public key infrastructure as the building block similar to many existing works. However, compared to the existing works, the SLIM has three major advantages:

1. The SLIM mechanism does not rely on infrastructure support during V2V communication.

2. The SLIM mechanism is more secure than other V2V-based authentications such as [22] in that the SLIM can defend more types of attacks as discussed in Sect. 5.
3. The SLIM mechanism is more efficient for V2V authentication by distributing the authentication workload such as the key generation over time.

The rest of the paper is organized as follows. Section 2 reviews related works on privacy-preserving vehicle authentication. Section 3 introduces the threat model, design goals and notations. Section 4 presents the details of the proposed SLIM scheme. Section 5 discusses the reaction of the SLIM scheme to various attacks in VANETs. Section 6 reports the experimental results. Finally, Sect. 7 concludes the paper.

2   Related Work

There have been lots of efforts in developing privacy-preserving authentication protocols in VANETs, which can be roughly classified into two main categories based on the fundamental techniques: (i) pseudonym-based and (ii) group-based approaches. An early work on pseudonym-based authentication protocol is by Raya and Hubaux [19]. They allow vehicles to randomly select a private key from a huge pool of certificates issued by the authority and use this private key to verify the vehicle's identity. However, the vehicles may need to check a long list of revoked certificates when verifying a received signed-message, which could be very time consuming. Raya et al. in [20] proposed efficient revocation schemes. However, these schemes do not preserve the location privacy [12] and are subject to a movement tracking attack. Later, more works [10,21,23,30] have been proposed to further improve the key revocation efficiency when using pseudonyms. Rajput et al. proposed a hierarchical privacy preserving pseudonym-based authentication protocol [18] that the primary pseudonyms were issued by a central authority, and the secondary pseudonyms were issued by RSUs. Yet another recent work called RAU (Randomized AUthentication) by Jiang et al. [8] proposed to use two cloud servers to generate any number of pseudonyms for vehicles.

The group-based protocols [5,14,26] may look more similar to our proposed scheme in the sense that they also group vehicles before authentication. Many group-based protocols leverage the group signature scheme, ring signature or blind signature [24,28,29]. Under the group signature scheme, vehicles can only verify that the messages are from a valid group member but do not know who is the actual sender. In our proposed SLIM scheme, message receivers know the anonymous ID of the sender vehicles and vehicles are also traceable in the case of dispute. More recently, Whyte et al. [27] presents a security credential management system for V2V communication by implementing a Public-Key Infrastructure (PKI) with additional new features. It issues digital certificates to vehicles to establish trust among them. Hasrouny et al. [7] also proposed a group-based V2V authentication and communication solution. They assume the mutual authentication were done by RSUs and decentralize their system via group leaders to make the system more efficient. Want et al. [25] proposed a two-factor lightweight privacy-preserving authentication scheme which employs the decentralized certificate authority (CA) and biological-password-based authentication. Their protocol depends on the RSUs which are responsible for message forwarding and key updating.

Most existing privacy preserving authentication schemes such as those discussed in the above, all heavily rely on some sort of infrastructure such as RSUs. However, RSUs would be expensive to deploy and are not expected to be widely available anytime soon. Very few works provide privacy preserving authentication based on pure V2V communication. One representative work could be the PAIM scheme proposed by Squicciarini et al. [22]. Since our work will be compared with PAIM, we provide more detailed review of this system as follows. The PAIM protocol dynamically constructs groups via pure vehicle-to-vehicle communication, and leverages Pedersen commitment and secret sharing scheme to achieve anonymously authentication of vehicles. The biggest drawback of the Pedersen commitment scheme is that it is malleable. A commitment scheme is non-malleable [1,3,4] if one cannot transform the commitment of another person's secret into one of a related secret. Unfortunately, this property is not achieved by Pedersen commitment scheme [17] because it is only designated to hide the secret. Compared to PAIM, the SLIM scheme also has the concepts of global identities and local identities. However, the protocols to generate the global and local identities are totally different, which makes the proposed SLIM scheme more secure and more efficient during the V2V authentication.

3   Threat Model and Design Goals

3.1   Threat Model

Our proposed SLIM scheme aims to defend the following attacks in VANETs as some are also pointed out in [13]:

- **Eavesdropping Attack:** The attacker can eavesdrop on any communication in the VANET.
- **Impersonate Attack:** Attackers may pretend to be another vehicle in the network to fool the others.
- **Movement Tracking:** An adversary who constantly eavesdrops messages exchanged in VANETs and therefore tracks other vehicles' travel routes.
- **Message Replay Attack:** Replay the valid messages to disturb the traffic.
- **Man-In-The-Middle Attack:** Attackers may relay and alter the messages during the transmission between two vehicles who believe they are communicating with each other directly.
- **Denial of Service (DoS) Attack:** The attacker may send a large amount of junk messages to prevent legitimate users from accessing other vehicles' computing and communication resources.

3.2   Design Goals

Our proposed SLIM aims to achieve the following design goals:

- **Data Origin Authentication and Integrity:** Every exchanged message should be unaltered during the delivery and can be authenticated by the receiver. Authentication and integrity of the messages must be verified [15].
- **Anonymous User Authentication:** The process of authenticating the vehicle should not reveal the vehicle's real identity to other peer vehicles.
- **Vehicle Traceability:** In case there is any dispute, the authority should be able to reveal the real identity of the suspect vehicle.
- **Message Unlinkability:** Observers can not link messages observed in different groups to the same vehicle so that observers cannot track other vehicles.

We list the description of the notations used throughout this paper in Table 1.

Table 1. Notations and definitions

Notation	Definition
v_i	Vehicle i
ID_i	Vehicle's identity encrypted by DMV_{pubkey}
CAU^j	Captain authentication unit of zone j
GIT_i	Global identity token for vehicle i
LIT_i^j	Local identity token for vehicle i for a specific zone j
$\{...\}_{key}$	Encryption using key
$Sign(...)_{key}$	Generate signature using key
$key_{i,k}$	Session key between two vehicles v_i and v_k
R_i	Role of vehicles i (government car, emergence car, etc.)
r_i	Nonce generated randomly by CAU^j for vehicle v_i

4   Secure and Lightweight Identity Management Scheme

In this section, we present the details of the proposed Secure and Lightweight Identity Management (SLIM) scheme in VANETs. The SLIM scheme is built upon moving zones self-organized by vehicles using the zone forming protocols in [11]. Each self-organized moving zone is formed by a group of vehicles with similar movement patterns or social interest. These moving zones are dynamic and will change as vehicles move. Each zone has a captain vehicle which helps pass messages among member vehicles. In SLIM, we assign the captain vehicle a new task to serve as the authentication unit and name it captain authentication unit (CAU) similar to [22]. The SLIM scheme ensures that the vehicles' identities are verifiable to each other while preventing any vehicle in the VANET including the CAU from seeing the true identities of other vehicles.

Procedure 1. Registration

Each Vehicle v_i executes the following steps

   Generate global key pair $Gpubkey_i$ and $Gprikey_i$

   Encrypt $ID_i = \{Identity_i, VIN\}_{DMV_{pubkey}}$

   Generate signature $rs_i = Sign(ID_i, Gpubkey_i)_{Gprikey_i}$

   $v_i \xrightarrow{\{ID_i || Gpubkey_i || rs_i\}_{IDMC_{pubkey}}} IDMC$

IDMC executes the following steps

   Decrypt using $IDMC_{prikey}$

   Verify signature rs_i using $Gpubkey_i$

   Verify v_i's identity ID_i with DMV

   IF v_i's identity is verified

      Generate a random number r_i

      Generate signature $s_i = Sign(r_i, R_i, Gpubkey_i)_{IDMC_{prikey}}$

      Generate $GIT_i = \langle r_i, R_i, Gpubkey_i, s_i \rangle$

      $IDMC \xrightarrow{\{GIT_i\}_{Gpubkey_i}} v_i$

   ELSE Reject Request

Each Vehicle v_i executes the following steps

   Verify signature s_i using $IDMC_{pubkey}$ and obtain GIT_i

---

The SLIM scheme is composed of three phases: *Registration*, *Inner-zone Authentication* and *Peer-to-Peer Communication*. During the registration phase, a vehicle will contact Identity Management Center (IDMC) to be verified and then obtain a global identity that does not reveal the vehicle's real identity. During the authentication phase, vehicles will send its global identity to the CAU to obtain a local identity. This local identity is later used for communication among vehicles in the same moving zone. In what follows, we elaborate the detailed algorithms for generating the global and local identities.

4.1   Registration

Procedure 1 presents the registration phase of our proposed scheme. This phase is executed only once for each new vehicle joining the VANET. The first time that a vehicle v_i logs onto the VANET, it will communicate with the IDMC to obtain a global identity token GIT. Specifically, before logging onto the VANET, v_i need to generate a pair of global keys $Gpubkey_i$ and $Gprikey_i$, encrypt its ID_i using DMV_{pubkey} and generates a digital signature rs_i. The first time that v_i enters the VANET, it sends a encrypted registration request to IDMC.

   When receives the registration request, the IDMC decrypts it and verifies v_i's signature rs_i to make sure that the message is sent by v_i who owns $Gprikey_i$. Then the IDMC verifies the received encrypted identity information ID_i with DMV (Department of Motor Vehicles). Since the verification message can only be decrypted by DMV, the IDMC will only know whether v_i has a valid identity but don't know what this true identity is. In this way, the vehicles' privacy is

---

Procedure 2. Joining Existence Zone j

Each Vehicle v_i executes the following steps
    Generate local key pair $Lpubkey_i^j$ and $Lprikey_i^j$
    Generate signature $vs_i = Sign(GIT_i, Lpubkey_i^j)_{Gprikey_i^j}$

$$v_i \xrightarrow{\{GIT_i || Lprikey_i^j || vs_i\}_{CAU_{pubkey}^j}} CAU^j$$

CAU^j executes the following steps
    Decrypt using CAU_{prikey}^j
    Verify IDMC's signature on GIT_i
    Verify signature vs_i using $Gpubkey_i^j$
    IF verified
        Generate timestamp T_c
        Generate signature $cs_i = Sign(R_i, T_c, Lpubkey_i^j)_{CAU_{prikey}^j}$
        Generate $LIT_i^j = \langle R_i, r_i, Lpubkey_i^j, cs_i \rangle$

$$CAU^j \xrightarrow{\{LIT_i^j\}_{Lpubkey_i^j}} v_i$$

    ELSE Reject Request
Each Vehicle v_i executes the following steps
    Verify timestamp T_c and signature cs_i using CAU_{pubkey}
    Obtain LIT_i^j

---

also protected against the IDMC. Only if the validation result is true, for v_i, the IDMC generates a global identity token GIT_i. Upon receiving the GIT_i, v_i decrypts and verifies it to ensure that the GIT_i was issued by the IDMC and has not been altered. At this point, v_i has a global identity token that does not reveal any sensitive information about its actual identity.

4.2 Inner-Zone Authentication

After vehicle v_i obtains the global identity token, it can use this token to be authenticated in any moving zone that it belongs to during the movement. Specifically, when v_i joins a new moving zone Z_j, it will contact the captain authentication unit CAU^j to obtain a local identity token LIT_i^j. This local identity LIT_i^j will only be used within this zone. When v_i moves to another zone, it will need to seek another local identity so that it would not be easily tracked by observers. Procedure 2 illustrates how the local identity tokens are issued.

In Procedure 2, vehicle v_i first randomly generates a pair of local keys $Lpubkey_i^j$ and $Lprikey_i^j$ during any free time before v_i wants to enter a new zone so that the generation procedure would not affect the authentication time. Then, v_i computes a digital signature vs_i and sends a join request to CAU_j.

When receives the join request, the CAU^j decrypts it using its private key, extracts v_i's global identity token GIT_i and verifies IDMC's signature s_i in GIT_i

---

Procedure 3. Peer-to-Peer Communication (v_i, v_k) within Zone j

Vehicle v_i executes the following steps

$$v_i \xrightarrow{LIT_i^j} v_k$$

Vehicle v_k executes the following steps

Verify CAU^j's signature on LIT_i^j

IF Verified

Generate session key $key_{i,k}$

Generate signature $ts_k = Sign(LIT_k^j,\ key_{i,k})_{Lprikey_k^j}$

$$v_k \xrightarrow{\{LIT_k^j,\ key_{i,k},\ ts_k\}_{Lpubkey_i^j}} v_i$$

ELSE Reject Request

Vehicle v_i executes the following steps

Decrypt using $Lprikey_i^j$ and extract LIT_k^j

Verify CAU^j's signature on LIT_k^j

IF Verified

v_i and v_k authenticate each other and both share the session key $key_{i,k}$

ELSE Reject Request

---

to validate this global identity. The CAU^j also verifies v_i's signature vs_i to ensure that this GIT_i belongs to v_i. Only if the verification results are true, the CAU^j generates a randomized number r_i, issues a local identity LIT_i^j and sends this local identity to v_i.

Once receives the response from CAU^j, vehicle v_i will extract and verify the authenticity and integrity of this response. At this point, v_i has obtained a local identity token LIT_i^j until it leaves current moving zone.

4.3   Peer-to-Peer Communications

After vehicle v_i obtains the local identity LIT_i^j, it is now ready to securely communicate with any other vehicles in the same zone. As illustrated in Procedure 3, in particular, when v_i intends to establish a fresh session communication channel with another vehicle (say v_k), the first step is to generate a session key between them. For this, v_i first send a session request along with its local identity LIT_i^j to v_k. When receives this request, v_k first verify the validity of v_i's local identity by checking the CAU^j signature in LIT_i^j and generate a random session key $key_{i,k}$ and a signature ts_k. Then, encrypts the following message using v_i's local public key so that attackers can neither eavesdrop or modify it: $\{LIT_k^j, key_{i,k}, ts_k\}$. After that, sends it to v_i. Once receives this response, v_i will decrypt the message and verify the identity of v_k in the same way that v_k just did.

After the above peer-to-peer authentication, v_i and v_k are able to communicate securely by encrypting the messages using the session key in the following form: $\{LIT_{v_i}^j, msg\}_{key_{i,k}}$. It is worth noting that as long as v_i and v_k stay communicating with each other, the peer-to-peer authentication between these two vehicles just need to conducted once. If more security is desired, the two vehicles can change the session keys over time.

To sum up, the SLIM scheme involves one-time communication between the IDMC and the vehicle, and vehicles can have different local identities in different moving zones for privacy preserving.

5   Security Analysis

In this section, we analyze the reactions of our proposed SLIM scheme to common attacks in the VANETs.

Eavesdropping Attack: With our SLIM scheme in place, any outside attacker cannot obtain any sensitive identity information of vehicles by eavesdropping the VANETs. When sending the registration request to IDMC, the vehicle's identity information was encrypted by DMV_{pubkey}, and the whole request was encrypted by $IDMC_{pubkey}$ too. It is impossible for any attacker to decrypt the registration message because they do not have the required private keys. For the same reason, outside attackers cannot eavesdrop any valuable private information during the peer-to-peer authentication and communication.

Considering inside attackers, the IDMC can only verify v_i's identity with DMV without knowing any detail personal information because only DMV can extract the private information from ID_i. Moreover, the $CAUs$ cannot eavesdrop their member vehicles' communication either. This is because CAUs do not know the session keys established between member vehicles.

Impersonation Attack: In SLIM, a vehicle v_i cannot be impersonated because no other vehicles knows v_i's $Gprikey_i$ or $Lprikey_i$. Thus, it is impossible for other vehicles to generate v_i's signature or decrypt the messages received by v_i. More specifically, during the peer-to-peer communication, suppose that an attacker knows v_i's LIT_i and plans to impersonate v_i. When the attacker sends this local identity to another vehicle v_k in the same moving zone, v_k will generate a session key encrypted using vehicle v_i's $Lpubkey_i$ and send it back to the attacker. Since the attacker does not possess vehicle v_i's local private key, it would not be able to decrypt the message received from v_k and hence cannot pretend to be v_i.

Movement Tracking: As previously mentioned, any outside attacker cannot see sensitive ID information by eavesdropping the network that is using the SLIM scheme. Thus, outsiders would not be able to find out the traveling routes of vehicles. Considering the insider attacks, we separate the cases of CAU and member vehicles. Any member vehicle only knows the local identities of vehicles in the same zone that communicates with it, but does not know the global identity of these vehicles. Thus, member vehicles may only be able to track the vehicles who are communicating with it within the same zone, but will not be able to keep tracking the same vehicle which has moved to another zone. Note that member vehicles even do not know if they are communicating with the same vehicle that they have met in the past since the same vehicle will use a different local identity in a different zone.

As for CAUs who know the global identities of its member vehicles, the CAU may be able to track the same vehicle whenever the vehicle enters its moving zone. However, this risk can be mitigated by a proper CAU election which forbids a vehicle to serve as a CAU continuously and frequently. This can be achieved since member vehicles know the CAU's global identity and they can verify if the same vehicle wants to serve CAU again when they move along together from one zone to another. On the other hand, a normal CAU may not want to serve as CAU frequently either since in that way it exposes its global identities for a long time for others to track.

Message Replay Attack: In our system, if an attacker replays a registration or inner-zone authentication request sent by vehicle v_i, it would not be able to decrypt the response messages from IDMC or CAU without knowing the private keys obtained by v_i. Also, if an attacker replays a message sent by v_i to v_j, it would not be able to know the content of the response sent back by v_j since the attacker does not know the session key used by v_i and v_j. As a result, the attacker would not be able to continue meaningful conversation with v_j further.

Man-In-The-Middle Attack: All the messages in our SLIM scheme are either signed or encrypted, which prevents attackers to modify or reuse. Specifically, the global identity GIT_i cannot be modified by other vehicles because it's signed by the IDMC. Vehicle v_i's inner-zone authentication request can only be verified by $Gpubkey_i$ which is included in GIT_i. Thus, any other entity cannot modify this request and regenerate the signature without knowing v_i's $Gprikey_i$. Also, attackers cannot put itself into the communication between vehicles. When v_i communicates with the IDMC, its message is encrypted using the IDMC's public key and hence only the IDMC can open it. When the IDMC responds to v_i, the message is encrypted using v_i's public key and hence only v_i can open the message. The case with the CAU is similar.

During the peer-to-peer communication, when v_k received the local identity LIT_i^j from v_i, a possible attack that it may conduct is to pass this local identity to another v_l and try to play a middle role in this communication. However, the v_l's response will be encrypted by $Lpubkey_i^j$. Since v_k does not know the local private key of v_i, v_k would not be able to decrypt the message sent back by v_l and obtain the session key inside the message. Also, v_k cannot generate new response to v_l since v_k is not able to produce v_i's signature.

Denial of Service (DoS) Attack: In the SLIM system, outside attackers' messages can be filtered because they do not have valid identity tokens. When they try to replay the registration or inner-zone authentication request, the IDMC or CAUs can reject those messages because the $Gpubkey$ or $Lpubkey$ have been used in the previous requests. The inside attackers also will eventually be caught as they have been authenticated and will leave all these malicious behavior in records.

6   Performance Study

We now move to evaluate SLIM's efficiency in the authentication process. We compare its performance with the most related V2V-based authentication scheme – PAIM [22]. The implementations are conducted using a machine equipped with an Intel Core i7 at 2.6 GHz with 16 GB of RAM running UNIX system. Each procedure in the program has been run 1000 times and the mean values are reported in milliseconds.

The network simulation was conducted using the Network Simulator NS-3 (version 3.26) and vehicular mobility simulator SUMO (version 0.23.0). Vehicles' movements along with the main roads of three real maps: Manhattan (4.5 km × 5.5 km), Chicago (6 km × 7 km) and Los Angeles (5 km × 4.5 km). Vehicles' speed ranging from 30 to 60 miles/h. In NS-3, the maximum transmission range is set to 100 m, the network delay is 10 ms, and the wireless transmission rate is 6 Mbps. Unless noted, otherwise we use the Manhattan map and set the number of vehicles to 800. The simulation was run for 15 s to insert all vehicles, then begin registration phase. After 60 s, at random time, each vehicle become group manager respectively, select up to 10 vehicles over a range of 80 m and start Inner-Zone Authentication. The simulation time is 120 s.

6.1   Registration Phase Performance

In the first round of experiments, we measure the average time needed for a vehicle to register at the IDMC using the SLIM and the PAIM scheme respectively. As shown in Fig. 1(a), the average registration time per vehicle under SLIM is about 40 ms, which was faster than PAIM's 80 ms. This could be attributed to the efficient protocol of SLIM which does not need extra rounds to establish a session key between the IDMC and the vehicle. Note that the vehicles' private/public key pairs in SLIM scheme can be generated during the vehicle's free time and hence would not affect any authentication performance.

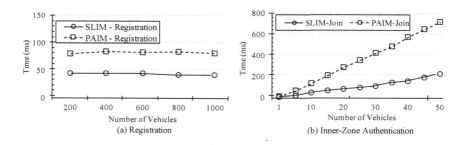

Fig. 1. Time performance

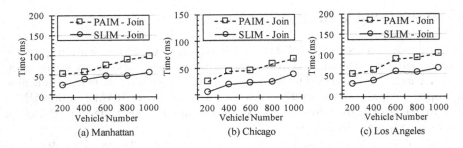

Fig. 2. Time performance during inner-zone authentication on three maps

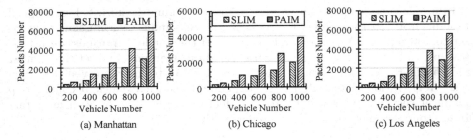

Fig. 3. Communication cost during inner-zone authentication

6.2 Inner-Zone Authentication Phase Performance

Next, we measure the performance of the inner-zone authentication for both the SLIM and the PAIM schemes. Figure 1(b) shows the total inner-zone authentication time at the CAU side when the number of vehicles in its zone varies from 1 to 50. Observe that SLIM is clearly faster than the PAIM. With the increase of the number of vehicles in the zone, the performance gap between the two approaches widened. Specifically, when there are 50 vehicles, our proposed SLIM scheme is more than 3 times faster than PAIM. In Fig. 2, with the increasing of the number of vehicles, the time raises due to more packets, larger network delay and heavier workload, and our SLIM protocol is obviously performs better than PAIM. This is because the SLIM scheme requires much fewer rounds of message exchanges to generate a local identity for a vehicle as shown in Fig. 3.

6.3 Peer-to-Peer Communication Performance

Finally, we compare the efficiency of the two approaches in terms of peer-to-peer communication. Figure 4 presents the time performance of these two protocols on three maps. In SLIM scheme, the time taken for two vehicles to mutually validate each other's local identity is only 3.5 ms excluding network delay. However, in PAIM, since two vehicles need to conduct the zero-knowledge proof which could take as long as 13.6 ms, it is clearly much slower than the SLIM scheme.

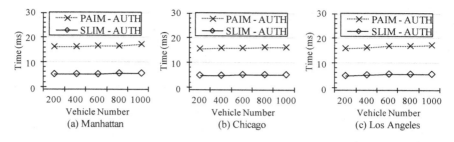

Fig. 4. Communication cost during peer-to-peer communication

7 Conclusion

In this paper, we proposed a lightweight privacy preserving vehicular authentication protocol SLIM, which alleviates the reliance on infrastructure support. The SLIM scheme leverages the PKI in an efficient way to create anonymous global identity and then local identities for vehicles to preserve their privacy when communicating with other vehicles. The SLIM is not only robust against various types of attacks but also very efficient as compared to the state-of-the-art.

Acknowledgement. This work is partially supported by National Science Foundation under the project DGE-1433659.

References

1. Di Crescenzo, G., Katz, J., Ostrovsky, R., Smith, A.: Efficient and non-interactive non-malleable commitment. In: Pfitzmann, B. (ed.) EUROCRYPT 2001. LNCS, vol. 2045, pp. 40–59. Springer, Heidelberg (2001). https://doi.org/10.1007/3-540-44987-6_4
2. Festag, A., Noecker, G., Strassberger, M., Lübke, A., Bochow, B., Torrent-Moreno, M., Schnaufer, S., Eigner, R., Catrinescu, C., Kunisch, J.: Now-network on wheels: project objectives, technology and achievements. In: Proceedings of 6th International Workshop on Intelligent Transportations (WIT), Hamburg, Germany (2008)
3. Fischlin, M., Fischlin, R.: Efficient non-malleable commitment schemes. In: Bellare, M. (ed.) CRYPTO 2000. LNCS, vol. 1880, pp. 413–431. Springer, Heidelberg (2000). https://doi.org/10.1007/3-540-44598-6_26
4. Fischlin, M., Fischlin, R.: Efficient non-malleable commitment schemes. J. Cryptol. **24**(1), 203–244 (2011)
5. Hao, Y., Yu, C., Zhou, C., Song, W.: A distributed key management framework with cooperative message authentication in VANETs. IEEE J. Sel. Areas Commun. **29**(3), 616–629 (2011)
6. Harsch, C., Festag, A., Papadimitratos, P.: Secure position-based routing for VANETs. In: Vehicular Technology Conference, pp. 26–30. IEEE (2007)
7. Hasrouny, H., Bassil, C., Samhat, A.E., Laouiti, A.: Group-based authentication in V2V communications. In: Digital Information and Communication Technology and its Applications (DICTAP), pp. 173–177. IEEE (2015)

8. Jiang, W., Lin, D., Li, F., Bertino, E.: No one can track you: randomized authentication in vehicular ad-hoc networks. In: IEEE International Conference on Pervasive Computing and Communications (PerCom). IEEE (2017)

9. Jung, C.D., Sur, C., Park, Y., Rhee, K.-H.: A robust conditional privacy-preserving authentication protocol in VANET. In: Schmidt, A.U., Lian, S. (eds.) MobiSec 2009. LNICST, vol. 17, pp. 35–45. Springer, Heidelberg (2009). https://doi.org/10.1007/978-3-642-04434-2_4

10. Li, J., Lu, H., Guizani, M.: ACPN: a novel authentication framework with conditional privacy-preservation and non-repudiation for VANETs. IEEE Trans. Parallel Distrib. Syst. **26**(4), 938–948 (2015)

11. Lin, D., Kang, J., Squicciarini, A., Wu, Y., Gurung, S., Tonguz, O.: MoZo: a moving zone based routing protocol using pure V2V communication in VANETs. IEEE Trans. Mob. Comput. **PP**(99), 1 (2016)

12. Lin, D., Bertino, E., Cheng, R., Prabhakar, S.: Location privacy in moving-object environments. Trans. Data Priv. **2**(1), 21–46 (2009)

13. Lin, X., Sun, X., Ho, P.H., Shen, X.: GSIS: a secure and privacy-preserving protocol for vehicular communications. IEEE Trans. Veh. Technol. **56**(6), 3442–3456 (2007)

14. Lu, R., Lin, X., Zhu, H., Ho, P.H., Shen, X.: ECPP: efficient conditional privacy preservation protocol for secure vehicular communications. In: Proceedings of IEEE Conference on Computer Communications, pp. 1229–1237 (2008)

15. Mohanty, S., Jena, D., Panigrahy, S.: A Secure RSU-Aided Aggregation and Batch-Verification Scheme for Vehicular Networks (2012)

16. Papadimitratos, P., Hubaux, J.: Report on the "secure vehicular communications: results and challenges ahead" workshop. IEEE Commun. Mag. **12**(2), 53–64 (2008)

17. Pedersen, T.P.: Non-interactive and information-theoretic secure verifiable secret sharing. In: Feigenbaum, J. (ed.) CRYPTO 1991. LNCS, vol. 576, pp. 129–140. Springer, Heidelberg (1992). https://doi.org/10.1007/3-540-46766-1_9

18. Rajput, U., Abbas, F., Oh, H.: A hierarchical privacy preserving pseudonymous authentication protocol for VANET. IEEE Access **4**, 7770–7784 (2016)

19. Raya, M., Hubaux, J.P.: Securing vehicular ad hoc networks. J. Comput. Secur. **15**, 39–68 (2007)

20. Raya, M., Jungels, D., Papadimitratos, P., Aad, I., Hubaux, J.P.: Certificate revocation in vehicular networks. Laboratory for Computer Communications and Applications (LCA) School of Computer and Communication Sciences, EPFL (2006)

21. Shim, K.A.: CPAS: an efficient conditional privacy-preserving authentication scheme for vehicular sensor networks. IEEE Trans. Veh. Technol. **61**, 1874–1883 (2012)

22. Squicciarini, A., Lin, D., Mancarella, A.: PAIM: peer-based automobile identity management in vehicular ad-hoc network. In: 2011 IEEE 35th Annual Computer Software and Applications Conference (COMPSAC), pp. 263–272. IEEE (2011)

23. Sun, J., Zhang, C., Zhang, Y., Fang, Y.: An identity-based security system for user privacy in vehicular ad hoc networks. IEEE Trans. Parallel Distrib. Syst. **21**(9), 1227–1239 (2010)

24. Tan, Z.: A lightweight conditional privacy-preserving authentication and access control scheme for pervasive computing environments. J. Netw. Comput. Appl. **35**(6), 1839–1846 (2012)

25. Wang, F., Xu, Y., Zhang, H., Zhang, Y., Zhu, L.: 2FLIP: a two-factor lightweight privacy-preserving authentication scheme for VANET. IEEE Trans. Veh. Technol. **65**(2), 896–911 (2016)

26. Wang, Y., Zhong, H., Xu, Y., Cui, J.: ECPB: efficient conditional privacy-preserving authentication scheme supporting batch verification for VANETs. IJ Netw. Secur. **18**(2), 374–382 (2016)
27. Whyte, W., Weimerskirch, A., Kumar, V., Hehn, T.: A security credential management system for V2V communications. In: 2013 IEEE Vehicular Networking Conference (VNC), pp. 1–8. IEEE (2013)
28. Yeh, L., Chen, Y., Huang, J.: PAACP: a portable privacy-preserving authentication and access control protocol in vehicular ad hoc networks. Comput. Commun. **34**(3), 447–456 (2011)
29. Zeng, S., Huang, Y., Liu, X.: Privacy-preserving communication for VANETs with conditionally anonymous ring signature. Int. J. Netw. Secur. **17**(2), 135–141 (2015)
30. Zhang, C., Ho, P.H., Tapolcai, J.: On batch verification with group testing for vehicular communications. Wirel. Netw. **17**(8), 1851–1865 (2011)

A-Tor: Accountable Anonymity in Tor

Quanwei Cai[1,3], Jonathan Lutes[2], Jingqiang Lin[1,3,4], and Bo Luo[2(✉)]

[1] State Key Laboratory of Information Security,
Institute of Information Engineering, Chinese Academy of Sciences,
Beijing 100093, China
[2] Department of Electrical Engineering and Computer Science,
The University of Kansas, Lawrence, KS 66045, USA
[3] Data Assurance and Communications Security Research Center,
Chinese Academy of Sciences, Beijing 100093, China
[4] School of Cyber Security, University of Chinese Academy of Sciences,
Beijing 100049, China

Abstract. Tor is the most popular anonymous communication system. In Tor, each user chooses onion routers (ORs) to construct a circuit to relay the traffic. The final OR of the circuit, called exit node, forwards regular traffic for the Tor user to the destination. As a result, the exit nodes are often accused of the anonymous users' illegal activities. In this paper, we propose an extension for Tor, called A-Tor, to provide accountable anonymity. A-Tor protects the exit nodes with verifiable evidences that the illegal or malicious packets are originated from the certain users but not the exit nodes. An A-Tor user firstly constructs a Tor circuit to apply for an anonymous certificate. Then, a second Tor circuit is constructed to access the destination server as in Tor, and the anonymous certificate is presented as a credential to the exit node; otherwise, the exit node refuses to forward his/her packets. A-Tor provides anonymity with the same level of assurance as Tor, and cooperative ORs are able to trace the anonymous A-Tor user (when illegal or malicious packets are detected in the future). Moreover, non-repudiation is achieved in the revocation of anonymity; that is, during the application of anonymous certificates and the subsequent anonymous communications through Tor circuits, a chain of evidences are generated by the A-Tor user and the ORs, and these evidences cannot be forged by collusive ORs. The performance overhead introduced by the A-Tor extension is also evaluated.

Keywords: Tor · Accountability · Revocable anonymity

1 Introduction

Tor is the most popular anonymous communication system in the Internet [11]. Anonymity is critical for personal privacy, but the Internet does not provide anonymity by default. So several anonymity networks such as Tor [10], Mixminion [8], Mix-master [19], and PipeNet [4,7], are designed and implemented to

© ICST Institute for Computer Sciences, Social Informatics and Telecommunications Engineering 2018
X. Lin et al. (Eds.): SecureComm 2017, LNICST 238, pp. 838–851, 2018.
https://doi.org/10.1007/978-3-319-78813-5_46

unlink a communication party from his/her network activities. Tor balances anonymity, usability and efficiency well, and is deployed all over the world. Currently there are more than 2,000,000 Tor users, and the peak number is nearly 6,000,000 in 2013 [23].

A Tor user chooses a sequence of onion routers (ORs) to construct a circuit, and each OR in the circuit only knows its predecessor and successor. Encrypted packets sent by the user are wrapped by a symmetric key at each OR, and the final OR (or the *exit node*) forwards plaintexts IP packet to the destination server. Network packets from the destination server are iteratively encrypted by each OR and relayed to the next node, and the Tor user finally decrypts the packets with all symmetric keys.

Due to its excellent anonymity and general availability, Tor is misused to launch network attacks. As a result, the exit nodes are often accused of the anonymous Tor users' illegal network activities by law enforcement agencies. For example, Rapid7 revealed a botnet called SkyNet, which adopts Tor for the command-and-control communications [2]. Austrian seized computers from the owner running a Tor exit node because cyber crimes were committed through this exit node, and announced that it is illegal to run Tor exit nodes [3]. Moreover, the insufficient protection and possible liability burden of Tor exit nodes discourage volunteer ORs to be exit nodes; then, if there are only a very limited number of exit nodes, it becomes easier to associate an anonymous Tor user with his/her network packets by traffic analysis [10,21].

With the original anonymity functionality of Tor, it is extremely difficult for the exit nodes to prove that the IP traffic is originated from other nodes; otherwise, the anonymity will be degraded somehow. Some extensions for Tor are proposed to protect the exit nodes, by enforcing exit policies [10,22] or appending specific packet headers [10]. These extensions offer options for exit nodes and ORs, but such packet headers are not verifiable and cannot disclose the Tor user's identity such as its IP address. Trusted third parties are introduced [6,15] to escrow the Tor user's identity before the anonymous communications and revoke the anonymity when necessary; however, the extra trust on the third party degrades the anonymity of Tor, because a single compromised party is able to reveal the user's identity. A reputation system is designed for exit nodes to rank the anonymous Tor user's activities [12], and the users with low reputation will be marked. This scheme depends on the intrusion-detection capability of exit nodes, and brings a significant overhead to the exit node.

In this paper, we propose *A-Tor*, *accountable anonymity* in Tor, which protects exit nodes with *verifiable evidences* to revoke the anonymity of Tor users. A-Tor designs a two-phase protocol. In the first phase (called the *anon-cert* phase), an A-Tor user firstly constructs a Tor circuit to apply for an anonymous certificate from the last OR (called the *certification node* in this paper). A chain of evidences is generated by the user and the ORs during the application, and these evidences will be used to trace the A-Tor user based on the anonymous certificate. Then, in the second phase (called the *anon-comm* phase), a second Tor circuit is constructed to access the destination server, and this certificate is presented as a credential to the exit node; otherwise, the exit node refuses to forward his/her IP packets to the destination. The forwarded packets are signed by the anonymous user, and verified by the exit node using the anonymous certificate before sent to the destination server.

In summary, A-Tor achieves accountable (or revocable) anonymity with the following properties:

- It is built on top of Tor, and the anonymity of Tor is not degraded. In the anon-cert phase, the anonymous certificate is generated through a Tor circuit, with the same level of assurance as Tor. The anonymous certificate is visible only to the A-Tor user, the certification node and the exit node. In the anon-comm phase, the certificate is presented as an anonymous credential to the exit node, and no any other identity information is transmitted on the second Tor circuit. The anonymity would be broken, only if (a) the ORs of the anon-comm Tor circuit, or (b) the ORs of the anon-cert Tor circuit and the exit node of the anon-comm Tor circuit, collude to link the A-Tor user to his/her network activities.
- Non-repudiation is achieved in the revocation of anonymity. In the application of anonymous certificates, a chain of evidences are generated by the A-Tor user and the ORs, and each evidence is signed by the generator and sent to in the next node of the anon-cert Tor circuit. During the anonymous communication, the network packets to the destination server are signed and verified by the exit node using the anonymous certificate. Therefore, these evidences are also verifiable to law enforcement agencies, and could not be forged by malicious ORs cooperatively against an innocent user.
- A-Tor is an extension of Tor, and interoperable with the existing Tor ORs. No additional component is needed in A-Tor, compared with Tor. A-Tor extension functions are implemented by Tor ORs, and transparent to the destination servers. An anonymous user may enable the A-Tor extension or use the original version of Tor, to construct the anonymous communication circuits. Then, the exit node chooses to forward or reject the packets, according to its own policy.

2   Background and Related Work

Various schemes are proposed to protect the exit nodes in Tor. [10,22] provide mechanisms for exit nodes to limit the relayed traffic. That is, each node may specify its exit policy to describe the addresses and ports that it will connect to; the exit node uses port restrictions for certain services (e.g., HTTP, SSH and FTP). However, it does not provide a complete protection for exit nodes, as most of the abuse cases are based on the protocols widely supported. [10] allows an OR to add specific information in the header of the forwarded messages, to indicate that the traffic is originated from some users of the anonymity service. However, the auditor cannot distinguish whether the traffic was truly originated from an anonymized user, or from a malicious exit node which added fake header attributes to its own messages. A reputation system is built based on the activities of anonymous users, and the exit node may reject an anonymous user based on its history [12].

Different accountable anonymity schemes in Tor have been proposed by introducing trusted third parties. [6] requires a trusted party to generate a blind signature as the ticket for the anonymous user to access the anonymity services, and the user's anonymity is revoked with the ticket and the trusted party. The ticket plays the similar role as the anonymous certificate in A-Tor, but the trusted party is able to reveal the user's identity [6] while the certification node in our scheme cannot without the cooperation of ORs in the anon-cert circuit. The directory server is utilized as the verifier of message transmitted from anonymous Tor users [15]. A Tor user divides its IP address into multiple shares, and the directory server signs a ticket for the shares and the hash value of messages to be transmitted. Then, the IP address shares are distributed to Tor ORs, and the signed ticket is presented as a credential to relay the messages. The IP address shares are collected to revoke the user's anonymity when necessary. These two schemes degrade the anonymity of Tor, as the trusted party or the directory server may collude with the exit node to break the users' anonymity.

Different mechanisms are also proposed to incentivize ORs to relay Tor traffic. When a well-behaving OR, acts as a Tor user to construct a circuit, the traffic of this circuit will be relayed with higher priority [20]. BRAIDS [14] motivates anonymous users to relay Tor traffic by introducing generic tickets for service accounting. The ticket is generated using blind signatures, which ensures the ticket signers do not know the ORs chosen by the user. These schemes work compatibly with A-Tor.

Anonymous blacklisting schemes [17,18,24,25] are proposed to prevent future abusive anonymous access. These schemes are classified into two classes: one [17, 25] depends on trusted third parties to provide tokens for users to access the service providers (i.e., destination servers), while in the other schemes [18,24], each user presents the proof that it is not blacklisted. However, the identities of abusive users are not revealed in these schemes.

There are also revocable anonymity schemes, not designed for Tor. In [9], each user registers with the trusted authority and a chosen registration node, to link its unique identifier to an identification pseudonym, and the identification pseudonym to another pseudonym for anonymous services. The two pseudonyms are verifiably encrypted using the public key of Judge, who identifies the initiator of the malicious traffic, based on the information from the exit node of the anonymity network, the register node and the trusted authority. THEMIS [26] relies a trusted key generator to achieve accountable anonymity and non-frameability based on proxy re-encryption. The trusted key generator who does not know the user's identifier, distributes an anonymous certificate and the corresponding index to the user and the identity database, respectively. The cooptation between the trusted key generator and the identity database will combine the anonymous certificate with the user's identity.

In [16], each user firstly connects to a group of servers (called anonymisers) to obtain an encrypted identity, and applies for an anonymous certificate signed by blind signature algorithms to bind the encrypted identity to a key pair that is used in anonymous communications. When necessary, a threshold atomic proxy re-encryption is triggered at the chosen anonymisers to transfer the user's identity encrypted using the auditor's public key. Compared with [16], A-Tor also utilizes anonymous certificates to support accountable anonymity; but A-Tor seamlessly integrates the application of anonymous certificates into Tor so that the anonymity is evaluated explicitly.

To protect Tor gainst abuse by botnets, one possible medium-term response is to deanonymize the command and control (C&C) server [13]. The Tor Project attempts to discover the entry nodes of the C&C server, by repeatedly changing their availability (e.g. by rotating identity keys), and eventually learn the IP address of the C&C server. However, it will pose significant organizational and engineering challenges [13], while A-Tor finds the malicious Tor user with fewer overhead as described in Sect. 4.3.

3   Overview of A-Tor

3.1   Threat Model and Design Goal

A-Tor follows the same assumptions as Tor [10]. A great number of ORs run over the Internet, each of which maintains a key pair by itself. The public key of an OR is published in directory servers, and then known by all users and other ORs. A correct OR follows the protocol strictly and compromised ORs behave arbitrarily. We assume that the ORs of a Tor circuit are not compromised simultaneously; so a user will increase the number of ORs in a circuit, to enhance the assurance level of anonymity.

A-Tor attempts to prevent attackers from linking a pair of communication parties (i.e., an A-Tor user and the destination server) or from linking multiple communications to or from a single user as Tor does, while provides verifiable evidences to link (the packets of) a specified communication to an anonymous user when enough ORs cooperate. The anonymity of an A-Tor user is compromised only if a certain number of ORs are compromised to link his/her activities, and this number is specified by each user according to his/her own security concern. These evidences are stored on multiple ORs for the period of time specified in data retention laws, and presented together to reveal the user's identity of a specified communication when a law enforcement agency requires the ORs to do. Moreover, malicious ORs could not collude to forge a complete chain of evidences against an innocent user.

Finally, because A-Tor attempts to provide verifiable and unforgeable evidences to reveal the user identity, we assume that each A-Tor user has an identity credential (e.g., a non-anonymous X.509 certificate to certify his/her IP address or other alternative identity), which is verifiable to the ORs. More discussions about this credential are included in Sect. 6.

3.2 Basic Idea

The basic idea of A-Tor is, (a) in the anon-cert phase, an A-Tor user constructs a Tor circuit to apply for an anonymous certificate from the last OR (or the certification node), and (b) in the anon-comm phase, the anonymous certificate is presented as a credential to the exit node of the second Tor circuit.

In the anon-cert phase, the A-Tor user constructs the anon-cert Tor circuit. Then, the user sends the credential of his/her identity to the first OR of the anon-cert Tor circuit (called the *registration node*). After verifying the credential, the OR signs an anonymous-certificate request, encrypts the message by the public key of the next OR of the circuit, and sends it. Then, after decrypting the message and verifying the signature, the receiver OR signs, encrypts and sends it to the next OR, until the anonymous-certificate request is transmitted to the certification node. Finally, the certification node signs the anonymous certificate, and it is relayed to the A-Tor user. The certificate is encrypted iteratively by each OR as regular Tor packets. Note that the A-Tor's identity is not included in either the anonymous-certificate request or the certificate. The signed request messages are stored on the receiver ORs as verifiable evidences to reveal the A-Tor user's identity in the future.

Next, after constructing the anon-comm circuit as Tor, the A-Tor user sends the anonymous certificate to the exit node, and the exit node verifies that the certificate is signed by another OR. Then, each relayed packet is signed by the A-Tor user, and the exit node verifies the signature using the anonymous certificate before forwarding it to the destination server. These signatures are stored on the exit node as verifiable evidences. The anonymous certificate and the signatures are invisible to other ORs of the anon-comm Tor circuit. Signing every packet one by one is expensive, and optimizations are discussed in Sect. 6.

No additional component is needed in A-Tor, compared with Tor. Each OR of A-Tor is first an OR of Tor, and the A-Tor functions are extended on the ORs of the anon-cert Tor circuit and the exit node. Anonymous-certificate request messages and signed network packets are transmitted by extended commands in the Tor circuit [10].

4 The A-Tor Protocol

This section describes the A-Tor protocol in details, including the steps to apply for anonymous certificates, to perform anonymous communications, and to link the anonymous communication to the A-Tor user.

These notations are used in this paper:

- ID_i^{OR}, PK_i, SK_i: the identity, the public key and the private key of OR_i.
- PK_u, SK_u: an ephemeral key pair generated by the user.
- ID_i^c: the connection identity between the user and OR_i in the Tor circuit.
- $Enc_K[e]$, $Dec_K[e]$: encrypt and decrypt message e by key K.
- $Sign_K[e]$: sign message e by key K.

4.1   Anonymous Certificate

As shown in Fig. 1, the A-Tor user constructs the anon-cert Tor circuit consisting of m ORs, denoted as OR_i and $1 \leq i \leq m$. OR_1 is the registration node, and OR_m is the certification node. After the circuit is constructed, the user shares a secure connection with OR_i, which is identified as ID_i^c. The detailed steps to construct a Tor circuit is described in [10].

Then, the user generates an ephemeral key pair (PK_u, SK_u), constructs an anonymous certificate request $ACertReq_{m+1} = Sign_{SK_u}[PK_u, T_s, T_e]$, and computes $ACertReq_i = ID_i^{OR} \| Enc_{PK_i}[ID_i^c, ACertReq_{i+1}]$ iteratively, where (T_s, T_e) is the period of validity and $1 \leq i \leq m$. The certificate requests are also encrypted like the layers of an onion. Next, the user sends $ACertReq_1 \| cred$ to OR_1, where $cred$ is a credential of his/her identity.

Upon receiving $ACertReq_1 \| cred$, OR_1 verifies $cred$ and decrypts it to obtain $ACertReq_2$. Then, it sends $Sign_{SK_1}[ACertReq_2]$ to OR_2. Upon receiving $Sign_{SK_{i-1}}[ACertReq_i]$, OR_i verifies the signature and decrypts it to obtain $ACertReq_{i+1}$, until OR_m obtains $ACertReq_{m+1}$. At the same time, OR_i stores $Sign_{SK_{i-1}}[ACertReq_i]$ as a verifiable evidence.

OR_m signs the certificate $ACert_{u,m} = Sign_{SK_m}(PK_u, ID_m^{OR}, T_s, T_e)$. This anonymous certificate is relayed back to the user through the Tor circuit, encrypted iteratively by ORs.

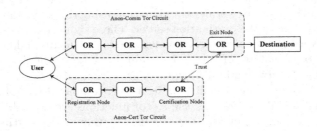

Fig. 1. The A-Tor protocol.

4.2   Anonymous Communication

The steps to perform anonymous communication in A-Tor is almost the same as those in Tor, except that the relayed network packets are signed by the A-Tor user and verified by the exit node.

As shown in Fig. 1, an A-Tor user constructs a Tor circuit consisting of n ORs, denoted as OR_j and $1 \leq j \leq n$. OR_n is the exit node, and no OR is in the anon-cert Tor circuit and the anon-comm Tor circuit at the same time. After the Tor circuit is constructed and before any packet to the destination is sent, the A-Tor user sends $ACert_{u,m}$ to the exit node through the circuit. The exit node verifies that the certificate is signed by another OR, and in its period of validity, and replies with an acknowledgement. Otherwise, it rejects to forward any packet.

Then, the user begins to send packets through the Tor circuit. It signs every packet using SK_u and transmits the signed packet to the exit node. The exit node forwards a packet (without the signature) to the destination server, only if it is sent along with a valid signature. The Tor circuit shall be closed before the anonymous certificate expires. The certificate and signatures are stored by the exit node as verifiable evidences in the future.

4.3   Accountable Anonymity

If the traffic forwarded by the exit node is detected to be illegal or malicious, an auditor who is authorized by law enforcement agencies, performs the following steps to reveal the user's identity.

The auditor brings the illegal or malicious packets to the exit node, and the exit node will present the corresponding certificate $ACert_{u,m}$ and signatures. After verifying the certificate and signatures, the auditor requires OR_m to present $Sign_{SK_{m-1}}[ACertReq_m]$. Otherwise, if the certificate or any signature is invalid, the exit node is liable for these illegal or malicious packets.

OR_m decrypts $ACertReq_{m+1}$ from $ACertReq_m$, and the auditor checks whether the anonymous-certificate request message $ACertReq_{m+1}$ matches the certificate $ACert_{u,m}$ or not; if they match, the auditor verifies the signature by OR_{m-1} and then requires OR_{m-1} to present $Sign_{SK_{m-2}}[ACertReq_{m-1}]$.

The auditor finds out the ORs one by one in the anon-cert Tor circuit and finally the registration node presents $ACertReq_1 || cred$. The user's identity is revealed in $cred$ verifiably. In the above steps, if any OR cannot present a valid certificate request message, the OR is liable for these illegal or malicious packets.

5   Security Analysis and Performance Evaluation

This section analyzes the accountable anonymity of A-Tor. We first evaluate the assurance level of anonymity, the verifiable evidences to reveal the A-Tor user's identity, and the performance overhead of A-Tor. Finally, some optimizations and extended discussions are presented.

5.1   Anonymity

A-Tor provides anonymity with the same level of assurance as Tor. Firstly, in the anon-comm phase, all steps of A-Tor are the same as those of Tor, except that an anonymous certificate is transmitted to the exit node. Because there is no identity in the anonymous certificate and no OR of the anon-comm Tor circuit is involved in the steps to apply for anonymous certificates, attackers cannot obtain more information than a Tor circuit to break the anonymity. Secondly, no (anonymous) communication with destination servers is performed in the anon-cert phase, so attackers cannot obtain any information by only compromising the ORs of the anon-cert Tor circuit.

Next, let's consider the scenario that some ORs of two Tor circuits were compromised, and assume that the certification node runs independently of the exit node. Because the certificate requests are also encrypted like the layers of an onion, only when all ORs of the anon-cert Tor circuit collude, they reveal the user's identity and link it to the anonymous certificate; and only the exit node is able to link the anonymous certificate to the network activities. So, only if all ORs of the anon-cert Tor circuit and the exit node of the anon-comm circuit are compromised, they are able to collude to link the A-Tor user to his/her activities.

Compared with Tor, there are two sequences of ORs that are able to link the communication to an A-Tor user: one is composed of the ORs in the anon-comm Tor circuit, and the other is the ORs of the anon-cert Tor circuit and the exit node. Therefore, $m = n - 1$ is reasonable (provided that the certification node runs independently of the exit node), and two sequences establish equal difficulties for attackers to break the anonymity. Moreover, in the second sequence, each OR only knows its predecessor and successor as that in the first sequence, except that the certification node does not know its successor (i.e., the exit node). Note that the anonymous certificate is transmitted as ciphertext always to the exit node through two Tor circuits.

As for other passive attacks, active attacks and directory attacks, A-Tor provides the same protections as Tor [10]. A-Tor constructs two Tor circuits to generate verifiable evidences for accountable anonymity, and the accountable anonymous communications are wrapped as regular Tor packets.

A-Tor does not introduce additional traffic patterns, compared other application protocols on top of Tor. Passive attackers cannot distinguish an A-Tor user from Tor users, because the additional anon-cert phase works over regular Tor circuits. Active attacks do not have more attack opportunities, because the ORs in A-Tor do not have more security assumptions than Tor. Each OR holds its key pair, and only know its predecessor and successor in the two Tor circuits. Finally, directory servers maintain the same information as those in Tor.

5.2   Verifiable Evidences

The verifiable evidences are composed of: (a) the certificate and signatures stored on the exit node, and (b) the certificate requests stored on the ORs of the anon-cert Tor circuit. Section 4.3 shows that, the A-Tor user's identity will be revealed, if the auditor follows the evidences to find out the ORs one by one.

Next, we will show that, (a) nobody can forge such a chain of evidences, unless the A-Tor user and ORs involved in the accountable-anonymous communications, and (b) the ORs cannot misguide the auditor to innocent ORs or users, either intentionally or unintentionally.

As all evidences are signed messages, nobody can forge these evidences unless a private key was compromised. In particular, in the trace path to reveal the A-Tor user's identity, the exit node is located by the IP address of packets. Then, the signatures of forwarded packets and the anonymous certificate are signed by the A-Tor user and the certification node, respectively. The anonymous-certificate requests are signed by the ORs one by one in the anon-cert Tor circuit, and $ACertReq_1$ is sent along with $cred$, which is also verifiable and unforgeable.

When OR_i decrypts $ACertReq_{i+1}$ from $ACertReq_i$, a malicious OR might present an unrelated anonymous-certificate request signed by OR_k, but intentionally output $ACertReq_{i+1}$. Note that, the private key of OR_i shall not be disclosed to the auditor, so the decryption is performed by OR_i itself. Then, the auditor will mistakenly require OR_k instead to present valid certificate request messages, and OR_k will be liable for the illegal or malicious packets for it is unable to do so. Therefore, the public-key encryption algorithm shall be deterministic but not probabilistic, and the auditor needs to check whether the plaintext (i.e., $ACertReq_{i+1}$) and the ciphertext (i.e., $ACertReq_i$) match or not. If a probabilistic public-key encryption algorithm such as RSA or ECIES, is adopted, $ACertReq_i$ is revised to $ID_i^{OR}||Enc_{K_i}[ID_i^c, ACertReq_{i+1}]||H(K_i)||Enc_{PK_i}[K_i]$ and signed by OR_{i-1}, where $H()$ is a one-way hash function and K_i is a one-time session key of symmetric encryption algorithms. Therefore, when O_i outputs K_i, the auditor firstly checks whether K_i and $H(K_i)$ match or not and then decrypts $ACertReq_{i+1}$ by itself.

5.3 Performance Evaluation

We evaluated the performance overhead introduced by the A-Tor extension, by measuring the average processing time for the circuit establishment and the network packet relay. The same as the lastest version of Tor [1], we adopt ECC-Curve25519 [5] and SHA-256 for key negotiation. In details, we use the implementation of Curve25519 and Ed25519 in Tor for key negotiation and signature generation. For symmetric encryption and hash function, we adopt AES-128 and SHA-256 in OpenSSL v1.01f. The process in each node is implemented using C++. The numbers of ORs in the anon-cert Tor circuit and the anon-comm Tor circuit satisfy the equation $m = n - 1$. All experiments ran with one user. These nodes were deployed on the identical workstations with an Intel i7-3770 (3.4 GHz) CPU and 12 GB of memory. The operating systems of all the nodes are CentOS v6.6. We measured the average processing time by constructing a Tor circuit and sending a cell 100 times.

To construct a circuit, a Tor user negotiates a symmetric key with each OR in the circuit. The A-Tor user needs to construct two Tor circuits. The anon-comm Tor circuit is constructed as the original Tor circuit. The anon-cert Tor circuit construction includes the following processes: the A-Tor user negotiates the symmetric key with each OR, constructs the anonymous-certificate request and binds its credential (in our experiments, a signature of the transmitted message using its long-term private key); the registration node checks the user's credential and generates the signature of the transmitted messages; the other OR except the certification node verifies the received signature and generates a new one for its transmitted message; and the certification node constructs the anonymous certificate after verifying the received signatures. In our implementation, as described in Sect. 5.2, ID_i^c and $ACertReq_i$ are encrypted using the symmetric key shared with each OR, and the digest of the symmetric key is

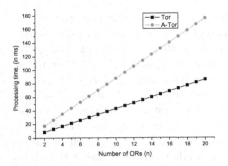

Fig. 2. Circuit establishment.

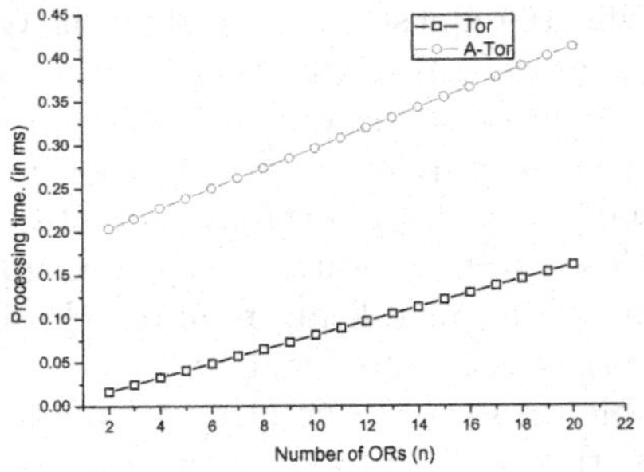

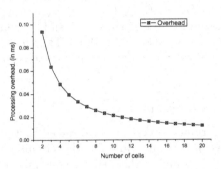

Fig. 3. Anonymous cell processing.

Fig. 4. Anonymous cell processing (accumulatively signed).

included in *ACertReq*. From Fig. 2, we find that when $n \leq 20$, the time to construct the two Tor circuits (the anon-cert circuit and the anon-comm circuit) is about 2.049 times of the one to construct the original Tor circuit.

After establishing the circuits, the user begins to send the network packets to destination servers. In Tor, the traffic is split into cells of 512 bytes, while the size of A-Tor cell is at most 498 bytes. In addition to AES encryption/decryption, each A-Tor cell involves two extra processes: the user generates the signature (64 bytes) of the cell, and the exit node verifies the signature. From Fig. 3, we find that the ratio of anonymous cell processing in A-Tor to that in Tor decreases with the number of ORs, from 12.207 ($n = 2$) to 2.555 ($n = 20$). The primary overhead is caused by the signature generation (0.05521 ms) and verification (0.13239 ms).

We adopt the optimization described in Sect. 6.1 to reduce the overhead of anonymous cell processing in A-Tor. That is, instead of generating and verifying the signature for each cell, we accumulatively compute the digest of these cells, generate and verify the signature of these digests. From Fig. 4, it is found that, the average overhead of A-Tor reduces with the number of cells for accumulative digests, and is reduced to 0.01254 ms when the number of cells is 20, which is modest compared to the processing time (0.01674 ms) for one cell in original Tor when the number of ORs is 2.

6   Extended Discussion

6.1   Signing and Verification in the Anonymous Communication

It is very expensive to sign and verify each packet one by one in the anonymous communication. The following optimizations of coarse-grained evidences are designed to reduce the overheads. Firstly, the A-Tor user may only sign a description file on his/her visit to the destination server. The description includes, for example, the destination server, the port, the duration, and the accessed web pages, but not any specific packets.

Or, after verifying the certificate, the exit node randomly sends some packet-signing commands through the Tor circuit to the A-Tor user during the anonymous communication. The A-Tor user signs the next packet, once it receives a signing request from the exit node. A portion of signed packets in the attack traffic shall be enough to play as verifiable evidences, and the frequency of signing requests is determined by the exit node.

Another optimized mode is as follows. The A-Tor keeps sending packets and the exit node forwards these packets while accumulatively computing the digest of these packets, until a threshold of sent-but-unsigned packets is triggered and the exit node sends a sign-all-packet command. Then, the A-Tor user signs all sent-but-unsigned packet as a whole, and sends the signature to the exit node. Next, unsign packets are forwarded again. The maximum count (or length) of sent-but-unsigned packets also depends on the policy of exit nodes.

6.2   Credential of the User's Identity

In Sect. 4.1, we assume that the A-Tor user has an identity credential verifiable to the registration node. A typical example is an non-anonymous X.509 certificate, and the A-Tor user signs the anonymous-certificate request as the verifiable credential. Or, the registration node cooperate with ISPs to verify the A-Tor user's identity.

Because A-Tor attempts to provide unforgeable evidences to reveal the user identity but the default identity in the Internet (i.e., IP address) can be forged, an extra trusted identity shall be presented to the registration node.

6.3   Key Revocation of ORs

The key pair (PK_i, SK_i) of OR_i might be revoked due to security incidents. The revoked key pair may be needed for the auditor to reveal the malicious user's identity. Therefore, the directory server should record the revoked public key and the corresponding period of validity correctly, while each OR maintains the corresponding private key. The storage period should be no less than the one specified in data retention laws.

An OR in the anon-certificate Tor circuit or the exit node, should check the validity of public keys when receiving certificate requests and anonymous certificates, and reject any message signed using a revoked key pair; otherwise, it will be accused instead of the OR whose key pair has been revoked at the directory server.

7 Conclusion

In this paper, we propose A-Tor, an extension of Tor, protecting the exit nodes in Tor by verifiable evidences. An A-Tor user firstly applies for an anonymous certificate through a Tor circuit, and the anonymous certificate is used as credentials in another Tor circuit for the next anonymous communications to destination servers. A-Tor provides anonymity with the same level of assurance as Tor, and cooperative ORs are able to trace the anonymous user (when illegal or malicious packets are detected in the future). The Tor circuit of anonymous certificates does not cut down the attack difficulties to break the anonymity, and the same number of ORs shall be compromised as in Tor before the attacker links an A-Tor user to his/her network activities. A chain of verifiable evidences are generated during the application of anonymous certificates and the anonymous communications, and non-repudiation is achieved.

Acknowledgments. Q. Cai, and J. Lin were partially supported by National 973 Program of China under Award No. 2014CB 340603. B. Luo was partially supported in part by US National Science Foundation under NSF CNS-1422206, NSF DGE-15655701.

References

1. Tor project. https://github.com/torproject/tor
2. Skynet, a Tor-powered botnet straight from Reddit (2012). https://community. rapid7.com/community/infosec/blog/2012/12/06/skynet-a-tor-powered-botnet-straight-from-reddit
3. Austrian Tor exit node operator found guilty as an accomplice because someone used his node to commit a crime (2014). https://www.techdirt.com/articles/20140701/18013327753/tor-nodes-declared-illegal-austria.shtml
4. Back, A., Möller, U., Stiglic, A.: Traffic analysis attacks and trade-offs in anonymity providing systems. In: 4th International Workshop on Information Hiding (IH), pp. 245–257 (2001)
5. Bernstein, D.J.: Curve25519: new Diffie-Hellman speed records. In: Yung, M., Dodis, Y., Kiayias, A., Malkin, T. (eds.) PKC 2006. LNCS, vol. 3958, pp. 207–228. Springer, Heidelberg (2006). https://doi.org/10.1007/11745853_14
6. Claessens, J., Diaz, C., Goemans, C., Dumortier, J., Preneel, B., Vandewalle, J.: Revocable anonymous access to the Internet? Internet Res. **13**(4), 242–258 (2003)
7. Dai, W.: PipeNet 1.1. Technical report, Usenet Post (1996)
8. Danezis, G., Dingledine, R., Mathewson, N.: Mixminion: design of a type III anonymous remailer protocol. In: 24th IEEE Symposium on Security and Privacy (S&P), pp. 2–15 (2003)
9. Díaz, C., Preneel, B.: Accountable anonymous communication. In: Petković, M., Jonker, W. (eds.) Security, Privacy, and Trust in Modern Data Management, pp. 239–253. Springer, Heidelberg (2007). https://doi.org/10.1007/978-3-540-69861-6_16

10. Dingledine, R., Mathewson, N., Syverson, P.: Tor: the second-generation onion router. In: 13th Usenix Security Symposium, pp. 303–320 (2004)
11. Elahi, T., Danezis, G., Goldberg, I.: PrivEx: private collection of traffic statistics for anonymous communication networks. In: 21st ACM Conference on Computer and Communications Security (CCS), pp. 1068–1079 (2014)
12. Groš, S., Salkić, M., Šipka, I.: Protecting Tor exit nodes from abuse. In: 33rd International Convention MIPRO, pp. 1246–1249 (2010)
13. Hopper, N.: Protecting Tor from botnet abuse in the long term (2013). https://research.torproject.org/techreports/botnet-tr-2013-11-20.pdf
14. Jansen, R., Hopper, N., Kim, Y.: Recruiting new Tor relays with BRAIDS. In: Proceedings of the 17th ACM Conference on Computer and Communications Security (CCS), pp. 319–328 (2010)
15. Kane, A.M.: A revocable anonymity in Tor. Technical report, IACR Cryptology ePrint Archive (2015)
16. Köpsell, S., Wendolsky, R., Federrath, H.: Revocable anonymity. In: Müller, G. (ed.) ETRICS 2006. LNCS, vol. 3995, pp. 206–220. Springer, Heidelberg (2006). https://doi.org/10.1007/11766155_15
17. Lofgren, P., Hopper, N.: BNymble: more anonymous blacklisting at almost no cost (a short paper). In: Danezis, G. (ed.) FC 2011. LNCS, vol. 7035, pp. 268–275. Springer, Heidelberg (2012). https://doi.org/10.1007/978-3-642-27576-0_22
18. Lofgren, P., Hopper, N.: FAUST: efficient, TTP-free abuse prevention by anonymous whitelisting. In: ACM Workshop on Privacy in the Electronic Society, pp. 125–130 (2011)
19. Möller, U., Cottrell, L., Palfrader, P., Sassaman, L.: Mixmaster Protocol - Version 2. IETF Internet-Draft (2004)
20. "Johnny" Ngan, T.-W., Dingledine, R., Wallach, D.S.: Building incentives into Tor. In: Sion, R. (ed.) FC 2010. LNCS, vol. 6052, pp. 238–256. Springer, Heidelberg (2010). https://doi.org/10.1007/978-3-642-14577-3_19
21. Serjantov, A., Sewell, P.: Passive attack analysis for connection-based anonymity systems. In: Snekkenes, E., Gollmann, D. (eds.) ESORICS 2003. LNCS, vol. 2808, pp. 116–131. Springer, Heidelberg (2003). https://doi.org/10.1007/978-3-540-39650-5_7
22. Syverson, P., Reed, M., Goldschlag, D.: Onion routing access configurations. In: DARPA Information Survivability Conference and Exposition (DISCEX), vol. 1, pp. 34–40 (2000)
23. The Tor Project: Tor metrics (2017). https://metrics.torproject.org/
24. Tsang, P.P., Au, M.H., Kapadia, A., Smith, S.W.: PEREA: towards practical TTP-free revocation in anonymous authentication. In: Proceedings of ACM Conference on Computer and Communications Security (CCS), pp. 333–344 (2008)
25. Tsang, P.P., Kapadia, A., Cornelius, C., Smith, S.W.: Nymble: blocking misbehaving users in anonymizing networks. IEEE Trans. Dependable Secure Comput. 8(2), 256–269 (2011)
26. Xu, G., Aguilera, L., Guan, Y.: Accountable anonymity: a proxy re-encryption based anonymous communication system. In: 18th IEEE International Conference on Parallel and Distributed Systems (ICPADS), pp. 109–116 (2012)

Author Index